Ita

a travel survival kit

Helen Gillman
John Gillman

Italy – a travel survival kit

1st edition

Published by

Lonely Planet Publications
Head Office: PO Box 617, Hawthorn, Vic 3122, Australia
Branches: 155 Filbert St, Suite 251, Oakland, CA 94607, USA
10 Barley Mow Passage, Chiswick, London W4 4PH, UK
71 bis rue du Cardinal Lemoine, 75005 Paris, France

Printed by

Colorcraft Ltd, Hong Kong

Photographs by

Stefano Cavedoni (including pp 117, 585 & 639) (SC)
Sonia Berto (SB)
Greg Elms (GE)
Helen Gillman (HG)
John Gillman (including pp 179, 339 & 487) (JG)
Guy Iacono (GI)
Andrius Lipsys (AL)
Azienda di Promozione Turistica (APT)
Comitato Assistenza Italiani (COASIT)
Ente Provinciale per il Turismo (EPT)

Front cover: Leaning Tower of Pisa (Paul Steel)
Back cover: Colosseum (EPT)

Published

September 1993

Although the authors and publisher have tried to make the information as accurate as possible, they accept no responsibility for any loss, injury or inconvenience sustained by any person using this book.

National Library of Australia Cataloguing in Publication Data

Gillman, John, 1964-
Italy : a travel survival kit.

Includes index.
ISBN 0 86442 195 8.

1. Italy – Guidebooks. I. Gillman, Helen. II. Title. (Series : Lonely Planet travel survival kit).

914.504929

Helen Gillman

Helen worked as a journalist and newspaper editor in Melbourne, Australia, for 12 years, including three years as the editorial manager of 10 suburban newspapers. Trying to manage journalists is not easy, so Helen 'retired' in 1990, at the age of 31, and went to live in Italy. She continues to work on a freelance basis as an editor and writer, and has decided that her new incarnation as a Lonely Planet travel writer is far preferable to sitting behind a desk in a newspaper office. While researching and writing this book, Helen took a few days off to marry her Italian boyfriend, Stefano, in a medieval palace in Bologna. Their baby girl, Virginia, was conceived in Apulia, caused morning sickness in Trentino-Alto Adige and slowed down the writing process somewhat. She was born a short time after the manuscript was completed.

John Gillman

Helen's brother John travelled through Italy with his wife Mini Goss for 10 months before hotfooting it back to Melbourne to await the arrival of their baby, Dexter, who was born shortly after. In honour of the city of his conception, Dex was to have been called Roma, had he been a she. As a journalist in Melbourne, John, aged 28, worked for the *Sunday Herald* for two years and then Telecom Australia before setting off to Italy for Lonely Planet. Despite the hard work and occasional setbacks, John has decided that being a travel writer is far more interesting than what he did before.

From the Authors

Numerous organisations, friends and relatives contributed to the planning and research of this travel survival kit. We would like to thank Dr Vincenti Mareri and Signora Gigliola Lantini at ENIT in Rome for their invaluable support and assistance. The directors and staff of the following tourist organisations also gave valuable assistance: the Südtirol/Alto Adige Ufficio Provinciale per il Turismo; APT del Trentino; Ente Sardo Industrie Turistiche; Assessorato al Turismo, Regione Puglia; Assessorato al Turismo, Regione Calabria; Calabria Turismo; Dipartimento Turismo, Regione Toscana; Azienda Regionale per la Promozione Turistica, Regione Autonoma Friuli-Venezia Giulia; Assessorato del Turismo, Regione Valle d'Aosta; Assessorato Regionale al Turismo, Regione Lombardia; Assessorato Regionale al Turismo, Regione Piemonte; Servizio Promozione Turistica, Regione Liguria; Ufficio Promozione Turistica, Regione dell'Umbria; Dipartimento Regionale Turismo Servizio Promozione, Regione Veneto; Azienda Autonoma di Turismo, Siracusa; AAST, Taormina; AAST, Isole Eolie; Azienda Autonoma Provinciale per l'Incremento Turistico, Trapani; Azienda Autonoma Provinciale per l'Incremento

Turistico, Enna; APT Bologna e Provincia; APT Firenze; APT del Comasco; APT di Venezia; APT d'Assisi; APT di Milano; and Dawn Caputo at the CIT travel office in Melbourne.

We would also like to thank the foreign press office of Alitalia in Rome for its assistance.

Preparing this book was certainly a family effort, though Virginia and Dexter probably hampered, more than helped, proceedings. A big thanks to Stefano, who assisted with the research and took the photographs for Apulia, Trentino-Alto Adige, Sicily, Sardinia, Lazio and Rome. His company through the south of Italy and into the Alps, combined with his extensive knowledge of Italy and his desire to explore rather than always follow the beaten track, made the trip an experience, not just work.

Mini deserves top billing in this book. Everywhere John went, she went too. Even suffering from morning sickness in the horrendous Tuscan heat, Mini was there when travelling became a challenge and the end seemed years away. Not even the Vespa-riding bandits in Naples who ripped the Ray Bans from her face while she was crossing at an intersection deterred her enthusiasm.

Thanks also to our parents, who did a lot of footslogging in Rome, Turin, Liguria, Venice and other places to check hotels and restaurants, and who provided useful suggestions for the book based on their own travel experiences during eight months in Italy. Their support was, as always, invaluable.

As deadlines and Virginia's birth loomed closer, it was necessary to call on the help of friends to complete the manuscript. Helen Grimaux put in an enormous effort to research and write the History section, and Carolyn O'Donnell researched and wrote most of the Arts section with help from Virginia Maxwell.

Thanks to Virginia Maxwell and Peter Handsaker for their company in Tuscany and the Veneto, and their fearless efforts at searching out the best eateries in Florence and Venice. Also to Ian Goss and Brigitte Saker for managing John and Mini's Australian finances and their dog, Arnold.

From the Publisher

This book was edited at the Lonely Planet headquarters in Melbourne, Australia, by Rob van Driesum and Kristin Odijk, with help from Simone Calderwood. LP's phrasebook editor, Sally Steward, wrote the Language section, Adrienne Costanzo did the proofreading and Sharon Wertheim produced the index. The maps were drawn by Richard Stewart, with help from Paul Clifton, Chris Klep, Louise Keppie, Sandra Smythe and Michelle Stamp; Pacific Camtech and Ralph Roob supplied additional maps. Richard Stewart also designed the book, with help from Chris Lee Ack, and produced some of the illustrations. Other illustrators were Ann Jeffree, Rosemary Keevins, Chris Klep, Michelle Stamp and Tamsin Wilson (Tamsin produced many illustrations, including the main title page). Margaret Jung designed the cover. Thanks to Sue Mitra for logistical support, and to Dan Levin for keeping the computers humming in tune.

Warning & Request

Things change – prices go up, schedules change, good places go bad and bad places go bankrupt – nothing stays the same. So if you find things better or worse, recently opened or long since closed, please write and tell us and help make the next edition better. Your letters will be used to help update future editions and, where possible, important changes will also be included in a Stop Press section in reprints.

We greatly appreciate all information that is sent to us by travellers. Back at Lonely Planet we employ a hard-working readers' letters team to sort through the many letters we receive. The best ones will be rewarded with a free copy of the next edition or another Lonely Planet guide if you prefer. We give away lots of books, but, unfortunately, not every letter/postcard receives one.

Contents

INTRODUCTION **9**

FACTS ABOUT THE COUNTRY **12**

History 12
Geography 30
Climate 32
Flora & Fauna.......................... 33
Government 35
Economy 36
Population & People................. 37
Education 38
Art 38
Culture 48
Religion................................... 50
The Mafia................................ 50
Language................................. 52

FACTS FOR THE VISITOR **57**

Visas & Embassies 57
Documents................................ 59
Customs 60
Money...................................... 60
When to Go 64
What to Bring 64
Tourist Offices 65
Useful Organisations 66
Business Hours 67
Holidays................................... 67
Cultural Events 68
Post & Telecommunications 70
Time 72
Electricity................................ 72
Laundry.................................... 72
Weights & Measures................. 73
Books 73
Maps 74
Media....................................... 74
TV & Radio 75
Film & Photography 75
Health...................................... 75
Women Travellers..................... 81
Special Needs........................... 81
Dangers & Annoyances 82
Work.. 84
Activities................................. 85
Highlights................................ 87
Accommodation....................... 89
Food 92
Drinks...................................... 97
Entertainment.......................... 98
Things to Buy.......................... 99

GETTING THERE & AWAY **101**

Air... 101
Land... 105
Sea... 109
Tours 109

GETTING AROUND **110**

Air... 110
Bus... 110
Train.. 111
Taxi 112
Car & Motorbike 112
Bicycle 114
Hitching 114
Boat... 115
Local Transport....................... 115
Tours.. 115

ROME **119**

Orientation............................... 120
Information............................... 121
Things to See & Do 127
Organised Tours....................... 145
Places to Stay.......................... 146
Places to Eat 153
Entertainment.......................... 160
Things to Buy 161
Getting There & Away............. 162
Getting Around 164
Lazio **166**
Ostia Antica 167
Tivoli....................................... 169
Etruscan Sites.......................... 169
Civitavecchia 173
Viterbo.................................... 173
Around Viterbo 176
The Lakes................................ 177

NORTHERN ITALY **181**

Liguria................................... **181**
Genoa....................................... 181
Around Genoa 189
Riviera di Levante 189
Riviera di Ponente 197
Piedmont **203**
Turin.. 205
Around Turin 211
The Susa Valley 212
Southern Piedmont 213
Eastern Piedmont..................... 213
Northern Piedmont 215
Valle d'Aosta **216**
Aosta.. 216
Around Aosta........................... 221
Pila.. 221
Courmayeur 222
Valtournenche 224
Gran Paradiso 225
Monte Rosa 226
Lombardy **227**
Milan.. 227
Pavia.. 244
Mantua 246
Cremona 249
Brescia..................................... 251
Bergamo.................................. 253

Around Bergamo 257	Stelvio National Park.......... 274	Around Vicenza 322
Valtellina.................... 257	San Martino di Castrozza 274	Belluno......................... 322
The Lakes District........... 257	The Sella Group.................. 275	Verona.......................... 323
Lake Como 258	Cortina d' Ampezzo 278	**Friuli-Venezia Giulia 327**
Lake Maggiore 260	Bolzano......................... 279	Trieste.......................... 328
Lake Garda 261	Merano......................... 281	Around Trieste 333
Other Lakes 264	**The Veneto 282**	Gorizia......................... 333
Trentino-Alto Adige......... 265	Venice......................... 283	Aquileia........................ 333
Trekking in the Dolomites...... 266	The Brenta Riviera 313	Lignano Sabbiadoro............ 334
Skiing in the Dolomites 269	Padua.......................... 313	Udine........................... 334
Trento......................... 269	Around Padua 317	Cividale del Friuli 337
The Brenta Group.............. 272	Treviso 318	Carnia.......................... 337
Val di Non..................... 274	Vicenza 319	

CENTRAL ITALY 341

Emilia-Romagna.............. 341	San Gimignano 421	**The Marches 462**
Bologna........................ 341	Collè di Val d'Elsa.............. 423	Ancona......................... 464
Modena........................ 349	San Galgano Abbey 424	Frasassi Caves................. 466
Reggio Emilia................. 353	Volterra........................ 424	Urbino......................... 467
Around Reggio Emilia 354	Arezzo......................... 426	Pesaro......................... 469
Parma.......................... 354	Sansepolcro.................... 428	Fano........................... 471
Around Parma 358	Cortona........................ 429	Senigallia...................... 471
Piacenza....................... 358	Montepulciano................. 430	Macerata....................... 472
Ferrara......................... 360	Etruscan Sites.................. 431	Ascoli Piceno 472
The Po Delta 363	Elba........................... 432	Monti Sibillini 474
Ravenna....................... 364	Argentario Peninsula 433	**Abruzzo 475**
Rimini......................... 368	**Umbria 434**	L'Aquila....................... 475
San Marino 371	Perugia........................ 436	Gran Sasso d'Italia............ 479
Tuscany 371	Lake Trasimene................ 442	Sulmona 479
Florence....................... 373	Deruta......................... 443	Around Sulmona 480
Around Florence............... 398	Todi........................... 444	Abruzzo National Park 481
Prato.......................... 399	Assisi.......................... 444	Pescara........................ 481
Pistoia......................... 402	Spello......................... 449	**Molise 483**
Lucca 404	Gubbio......................... 449	Campobasso 484
The Garfagnana 407	Around Gubbio 451	Around Campobasso 484
Massa & Carrara............... 407	Spoleto........................ 452	Isernia......................... 484
Pisa........................... 408	Orvieto........................ 456	Around Isernia 484
Livorno 413	Around Orvieto 459	Termoli........................ 486
Siena 415	Terni.......................... 459	
Chianti 421	The Valnerina.................. 461	

SOUTHERN ITALY 489

Campania...................... 489	Troia.......................... 538	Castellaneta.................... 565
Naples......................... 490	Manfredonia................... 538	**Basilicata...................... 565**
Around Naples................. 506	Gargano Promontory 538	Matera......................... 565
The Bay of Naples.............. 508	The Tremiti Islands 543	Aliano......................... 569
South of Naples................ 515	Trani.......................... 544	Metaponto...................... 569
The Amalfi Coast 523	Around Trani 545	**Calabria 570**
Salerno........................ 529	Bari........................... 546	Catanzaro...................... 570
Paestum........................ 532	The Trulli Area................. 552	The Ionian Coast 574
Around Paestum 533	Brindisi 554	Cosenza........................ 575
The Cilento Coast 534	Lecce 557	The Sila Massif 577
Apulia......................... 534	Galatina....................... 561	Reggio di Calabria 578
Foggia......................... 536	Otranto 561	The Aspromonte Massif........ 582
Lucera......................... 537	Taranto 562	The Tyrrhenian Coast.......... 582

SICILY 587

Getting There & Away 588
Getting Around 590
Palermo **590**
Around Palermo 598
Aeolian Islands **600**
Lipari 601
Vulcano 604
Salina 605
Panarea 606
Stromboli 607
Filicudi & Alicudi 609

The East Coast **609**
Messina 609
Taormina 612
Around Taormina 615
Catania 615
Mt Etna 618
South-East Sicily **620**
Syracuse 620
Noto 624
Around Noto 625
Ragusa 625

Central Sicily **627**
Enna 627
Piazza Armerina 628
Agrigento 629
North-West Sicily **633**
Marsala 633
Selinunte 634
Trapani 634
Erice 637
Segesta 637
Golfo di Castellammare 637

SARDINIA 641

Getting There & Away 641
Getting Around 643
Cagliari **643**
Around Cagliari 647
Southern Sardinia **648**
Sant'antioco & San Pietro
Islands 648
Iglesias 649
Around Iglesias 649

Western Sardinia **650**
The Costa Verde 650
Oristano 650
Around Oristano 652
Northern Sardinia **654**
Alghero 654
Around Alghero 655
Sassari 656
Porto Torres 658

Stintino 659
Santa Teresa Gallura 659
Palau & La Maddalena 660
Costa Smeralda 661
Olbia 661
Golfo Aranci 664
Eastern Sardinia **664**
Nuoro Province 664
Central Sardinia **667**

GLOSSARY 668

INDEX 671

Maps 671   Text 671

Map Legend

BOUNDARIES

—— · —— · —— ....International Boundary
—— · —— · —— ....Internal Boundary
+++++++++++ ....National Park or Reserve
— — — — — — ....The Equator
· · · · · · · · · · · · · · · · ....The Tropics

SYMBOLS

◉ NATIONAL ....National Capital
● PROVINCIAL........Provincial or State Capital
● Major ....Major Town
● Minor ....Minor Town
■ ....Places to Stay
▼ ....Places to Eat
⊠ ....Post Office
✈ ....Airport
i ....Tourist Information
⊜ ....Bus Station or Terminal
P ....Parking
66 ....Highway Route Number
⚲✝🛉✝ ......Mosque, Church, Cathedral
∴ ....Temple or Ruin
✚ ....Hospital
※ ....Lookout
⚑ ....Camping Area
⌂ ....Hut or Chalet
▲ ....Mountain or Hill
Ⓜ ....Metro Station
+——■—+ ....Railway Station
═══ ....Road Bridge
+++++ ....Railway Bridge
⇒ ⇐ ....Road Tunnel
→) (← ....Railway Tunnel
⌣⌣⌣ ....Escarpment or Cliff
‿ ....Pass
лллл ....Ancient or Historic Wall

ROUTES

——— ....Major Road or Highway
– – – – – – .... Unsealed Major Road
——— ....Sealed Road
– – – – – – ..... Unsealed Road or Track
═══ .... City Street
+++++++++++ ....Railway
●——◉——● ....Subway
· · · · · · · · · · · · ....Walking Track
– – – – – – ....Ferry Route
+|+|+|+|+|+ .... Cable Car or Chair Lift

HYDROGRAPHIC FEATURES

.....................River or Creek
– – – – ....Intermittent Stream
⬭ ⬭ ....Lake, Intermittent Lake
...........................Coast Line
⟜ ....Spring
≈|| ....Waterfall
⊥⊥ ⊥⊥ ⊥⊥ ....Swamp

.... Salt Lake or Reef

...................................Glacier

OTHER FEATURES

Park, Garden or National Park

.... Built Up Area

... Market or Pedestrian Mall

.... Plaza or Town Square

...........................Cemetery

Note: not all symbols displayed above appear in this book

Introduction

Since the days of the Grand Tour, travellers to Italy have speculated on the 'fatal spell' of the country. This special charm has been attributed to the flair of its people, the art, the history, even the air. What is it that makes Italy so seductive? The Italian writer, Luigi Barzini, had this to say on the question:

It made and still makes unwanted people feel wanted, unimportant people feel important and purposeless people believe that the real way to live intelligently is to have no earnest purpose in life.

This land of vibrant, expressive people has given the world pasta and pizza, Michelangelo and da Vinci, Dante and Machiavelli, Catholicism and a vast array of saints and martyrs, Verdi and Pavarotti, Fellini and Sophia Loren, not to mention the Mafia, a remarkable sense of style and *la dolce vita*. In Italy you can visit Roman ruins, study the art of the Renaissance, stay in tiny medieval hill towns, go mountaineering in the Alps and Apennines, feel romantic in Venice, participate in traditional festivals and see more beautiful churches than you imagined could exist in one country. Some people come simply to enjoy the food and wine.

Do your research before coming to Italy, but arrive with an open mind and you will find yourself agreeing with Henry James, who wrote on his arrival in Rome: 'At last, for the first time, I live.'

Facts about the Country

HISTORY

Italy's strategic position in the Mediterranean made it a target for colonisers and invaders, whose comings and goings over thousands of years have left a people with a diverse ethnic background. But it also gave the Romans, and later the Christian Church, an excellent base from which to expand their respective empires. Italy's history is thus a patchwork of powerful empires and foreign domination, and from the fall of the Roman Empire until the formation of the Kingdom of Italy in 1861, the country was never a unified entity.

Prehistoric Italy

The Italian peninsula has supported human life for thousands of years. Extensive archaeological finds show that Palaeolithic Neanderthals lived in Italy during the last Ice age, more than 20,000 years ago. By around 5000 BC, Neolithic, or New Stone Age, humans were no longer exclusively nomadic hunters and had started to establish farms across the peninsula. At the start of the Bronze Age, around 2000 BC, Italy had been settled by several Italic tribes, which continued to develop their more sophisticated, although still primitive, cultures until their

Etruscan necropolis near Orvieto

eventual absorption into the Roman Republic. These tribes included the Ligurians, the Veneti, the Apulians, the Siculi, the Latins and the eastern Italics.

The Etruscans

Historians differ on the exact origins of the Etruscan people and when they arrived in the Italian peninsula, although it is widely agreed that they migrated from the Aegeo-Asian area around the end of the 8th century BC. Another school of thought has them arriving in Italy in the 12th century BC and some modern scholars argue that there is enough evidence to support this theory.

What is beyond doubt is that the Etruscans established a flourishing civilisation between the Arno and Tiber valleys, with other important settlements in Campania, Lazio (Latium) and the Po Valley. The earliest evidence of the Etruscan people was the Villanovan culture (around the 9th and 8th centuries BC) in the north of the peninsula, centred around present-day Bologna and characterised by the practice of cremating the dead and burying the ashes in urns.

From the 8th to the 6th centuries BC, Etruscan culture was at its height. The nation was based on large city-states, among them Caere (Cerveteri), Tarquinii (Tarquinia), Veii (Veio), Volsinii (believed to be either Bolsena or Orvieto), Felsina (Bologna), Perusia (Perugia), Volaterrae (Volterra), Faesulae (Fiesole) and Arretium (Arezzo). Etruscans were predominantly navigators and traders, competing for markets in the Mediterranean against the Phoenicians and Greeks.

A good deal of what is known about the Etruscan culture has been learned from the archaeological evidence of their tombs and religious sanctuaries. Their belief in life after death necessitated the burial of the dead with everything they might need in the afterlife, such as food and drink, clothing, ornaments and weapons. Painted tombs depicting scenes of everyday life, notably those discovered at Tarquinia, near Rome, provide an important document of how the Etruscans

dressed, ate and lived, as well as other cultural practices.

The long period of Etruscan decline began in the 5th century BC, when they began to lose control of their trade routes to the more powerful Greeks. By the 4th century BC, they had lost their northern territories to Gallic invaders and their settlements in Campania to the Samnites, confining Etruria to its original territories in central Italy. While Etruscan civilisation continued to flourish during this period, its development was by then greatly determined by its relationship with the growing power of Rome.

Rome had long been profoundly influenced by Etruscan culture and was in fact ruled by Etruscan kings, known as the Tarquins, for at least a century until 509 BC, when the Roman Republic was established. The Etruscan and Roman civilisations coexisted relatively peacefully until the defeat of the great Etruscan city of Veii and its incor-

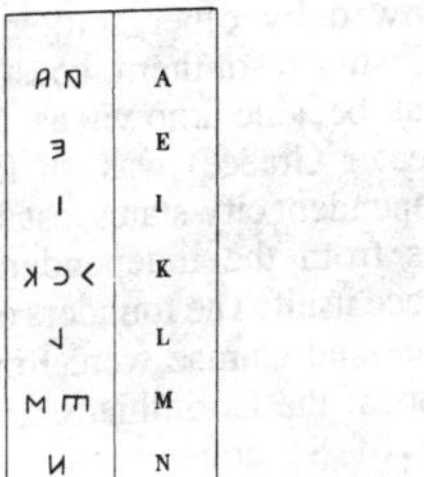

A Ꭴ	A
Ǝ	E
I	I
ꓘ Ɔ ᐸ	K
↲	L
M �177	M
И	N
↑	P
◁ ٩	R
ξ	S
↑ Y	T
V ꓘ ⊐	V
⊙ ◈	Th
B	F
⅄	Z
⊟	H

Etruscan alphabet

poration into the territory of Rome in 396 BC. During the ensuing century, Etruscan cities were either defeated or entered into peaceful alliance with an increasingly powerful Rome, although they maintained a fair degree of autonomy until 90 BC, when the Etruscans (as well as all the Italic peoples of the peninsula) were granted Roman citizenship. Thus absorbed into what was to become the Roman Empire, the separate Etruscan culture and language rapidly disappeared. Scholars of the day attached little importance to the need to preserve the Etruscan language, and few translations into Latin were made. No Etruscan literature survived and the only remaining samples of the written language are related to religious and funerary customs.

Greek Colonisation

The first Greek settlements in Italy were established in the early 8th century BC – first on the island of Ischia in the Bay of Naples, followed by other settlements along the peninsula's southern coast and in Sicily. What became known as Magna Graecia (Greater Greece) was, in fact, a group of independent city-states, established by colonists from the independent city-states of Greece itself. The founders of the colonies at Ischia and Cumae were from the island of Euboea; the Corinthians founded the great city of Syracuse; and exiled Spartans founded the wealthy city of Taranto.

The civilisation of Magna Graecia spanned about six centuries, and the ruins of magnificent Doric temples in Italy's south (at Paestum) and in Sicily (Agrigento, Selinunte and Segesta), and other monuments such as the Greek Theatre at Syracuse, stand as testament to its splendour. Syracuse became so powerful that Athens considered it enough of a threat to launch an attack on the city. In one of the great maritime battles in history, Syracuse managed to destroy the Athenian fleet in 413 BC. By the end of the 3rd century BC, Magna Graecia had succumbed to the might of the advancing Roman Republic, though not before playing a major role in introducing Hellenic culture to Rome.

The Expansion of Rome

The traditional date for the founding of Rome by Romulus is 753 BC, but the story of modern Italy begins with the founding of the first Roman Republic in 509 BC. It is a complex, fascinating saga of a quest to create an intellectual and economic national entity from a fiercely independent, and primarily regionally focused, family and community-oriented people.

History tells us that when Rome chose its first Republic, the foundations of democracy were laid. It introduced a basic principle of political philosophy which still inspires Italian society today – that of the sovereign rights of people. In modern Rome the initials SPQR are stamped on public property to this day, testimony to the phrase governing the first Senate, *Senatus Populusque Romanus*, the Senate & People of Rome.

More realistically though, if history is to offer more than a string of popular stories, the Latin aristocracy which overthrew their last Etruscan king, Tarquinius Superbus, and created the first Republic, did so only in order to establish their individual territorial claims.

Inadvertently, their concept for sharing the new-found power set the stage for centuries of physical and intellectual struggle, as the 'common people' strove to exploit the concept of democracy and to secure sovereignty for themselves, their families and their communities. In practice, the first Senate never allowed people any real power, dominated as it was by a coalition made up of the old upper class and a new breed of rich Republicans drawn mainly from Roman nobility. The combination of the old imperialism and the new democracy ensured that the political and cultural unification of Italy that occurred over the next six centuries was based less on any real sense of togetherness among the peoples of the peninsula than a controlled programme of colonisation inscribed into the Roman constitution.

In the 4th century BC about 40 different

languages were spoken in Italy and there were also several written languages. In addition to Latin, two languages were particularly widespread. The Umbrians, a separate, civilised people, left the world the *Eugubian Tables* written in Umbrian in about 200 BC, which are said to contain the largest body of religious ritual to have survived pre-Christian Europe. The other significant linguistic tradition to have survived is Oscan, spoken widely throughout the south – in Campania, Apulia and Calabria – and which has been found inscribed on coins dating back to the 3rd and 4th centuries BC and was still employed as graffiti on the walls of Pompeii in 79 AD. Almost all these languages gave way to Latin in the course of two or three centuries as the language of the Romans triumphed, first across Italy and then as the language of literate Europeans, although Greek was still spoken in Naples and the south until the 6th century AD.

The Punic Wars

The use of Latin became widespread as a result of the expansion of Rome, an expansion strongly influenced by Rome's long wars with Carthage, called the Punic Wars, the first of which started in 264 BC and raged for 24 years.

In 264 BC Carthage was much more powerful than Rome. Originally one of several Phoenician trading posts located at the narrow point of the Mediterranean opposite Sicily, Carthage had built up an empire which extended to Morocco and included western Sicily, Corsica, Sardinia and even parts of Spain. But the Roman destruction of Carthaginian civilisation was to be total, with little remaining knowledge of her culture and no known literature surviving.

During the Punic Wars, the Romans were called upon for the first time to fight a war across the sea against the greatest naval power of the age. The Greek historian, Polybius, claimed that the Romans had no idea even of how to construct a large warship until a Carthaginian vessel was grounded and taken by the Romans, who were then able to construct a replica.

Carthage was fighting on all fronts. Internally, there was much jealousy of the officers abroad who were accumulating great spoils of war, although these same officers were faced daily with the problem of controlling mercenary troops, added to which there was the ever-present possibility of insurrection in Carthage's own hinterland, Libya. In less than a century, after two further periods of intense warfare (the Second Punic War, 218-211 BC, and the Third Punic War, 153-146 BC), the annihilation of Carthage was complete.

The First Punic War was fought over control of Sicily and the great city of Syracuse. Between the first two wars Carthage extended her empire to Spain and it was with Spanish wealth and Spanish mercenaries that

Roman coins

Hannibal launched his famous offensive, employing elephants to cross the Alps and attack Rome.

Between the First and Second Punic Wars, Rome was also confronted with an invasion by the Gauls, whose territory at the time included the fertile agricultural lands of the Po Valley in what is now northern Italy. Soon after the beginning of the 1st century BC, the Romans had wrested the Po Valley from the Gauls and had driven them from the Ligurian coastline and the Alps, consolidating for the first time in history the frontiers of Italy as we know it now.

In 171 BC, before the Third Punic War, Perseus, the son of Philip V of Macedon, confronted Rome with a Greek army in a three-year war. The Romans defeated the incursion, destroyed the Macedonian monarchy which had once belonged to Alexander the Great, and turned it into four republics.

From Republic to Empire

Until 146 BC, the history of the Roman Republic was one of external warfare but relative peace at home. The constitution, with its government of two Consuls and its Senate representing the ruling class, worked efficiently. Rome had extended its control throughout Italy, although the complete unification with the inclusion of the north only finally occurred after the founding of the Roman Empire by Augustus in 27 BC.

Roads and aqueducts were built to link the new estates of the Roman Republic. New cities were founded across the nation. The Via Appia had been started as early as 312 BC, when Rome was linked to Capua, and the road was extended to Brindisi in 244 BC. The Via Flaminia was built northwards over the Apennines to Fano in 220 BC and was subsequently extended to Rimini. The Via Aurelia hugged the west coast, eventually reaching Genoa, and is still in full use as state road No 1, the ss1.

As well as the great wealth gained from the conquest of the Carthaginian and Hellenic worlds, Italian society found itself changed by another spoil of war, the long-term effects of which were to prove less than beneficial to the Republic.

To achieve the visions of its rulers and satisfy its lifestyle, Rome needed slave labour. In its last years, the Roman Republic supported around two million slaves, about 35% of the population, all of whom were completely dependent on their masters for their existence.

The influx of slave labour ensured the growth of large estates for the select few at the expense of the many small freeholdings that had characterised pre-Punic-War

Marble statue of a Roman Senator, 1st century BC

society. The demise of smaller holdings created an agrarian disaster which brought social disruption and human misery. With power in Rome securely in the hands of successful militia commanders, the Social War of 83 BC was to be recognised as the last attempt by the free people of the peninsula to press their claims on Rome. The affairs of state were to be decided more and more by the select few.

Another, more bloody, social war was fought from 73 to 71 BC. In an attempt to secure freedom for his fellows and as a protest against the inhumanity of the ever-popular gladiatorial games, a slave named Spartacus escaped from a school for gladiators at Capua and built up a force of some 70,000 runaway slaves and others on Mt Vesuvius. After initially repelling the Roman forces sent to suppress the uprising, Spartacus was killed and some 6000 of his followers were crucified, lining the Via Appia from Capua to Rome.

By then Rome's military greats – Gnaeus Pompeius (Pompey), Crassus (who was one of the wealthiest men in Rome), Julius Caesar, Mark Antony and Octavian – controlled the Senate and, in 60 BC, Pompey, with Caesar and Crassus, formed an unconstitutional triumvirate, effectively ending any semblance of government 'for and by the people'.

In 52 BC, Pompey finally took the title of sole Consul and dictator, with the full support of Caesar, who, having secured command of the legions in Gaul, declared southern Britain part of Rome after two raids on the island Celts, in 55 and 54 BC. Caesar's flagrant disregard for the authority of the Senate, which had ordered him to disband his legions and return to Rome, gained him enormous popularity, particularly among his troops.

Following the murder of Pompey in Egypt in 48 BC, Caesar returned to Rome and was made Consul and dictator. His brief four-year reign was marked by feverish activity both in Italy and throughout the territories under Roman control. He instigated land reforms which limited the holdings of single individuals, and framed a uniform system of local government which extended throughout Italy and the outer provinces, notably at Corinth and Carthage. Most significantly, he introduced the Julian calendar, which was to be used throughout Europe for many centuries.

But Caesar continued to treat the political establishment of Rome with scant respect. He increased the number of Senators to 900, effectively undermining and dissipating the Senate's power and, when he was murdered on 15 March 44 BC at the foot of Pompey's statue in the Senate house, it was said that among his murderers were more of his friends than his enemies.

Caesar's dictatorship paved the way for further domination by Rome's military imperialists, starting with Mark Antony (Consul for the year 44 BC before he became embroiled in power struggles and eventually met his demise with Cleopatra in Egypt in 30 BC) and followed by Gaius Octavianus, adopted by Caesar as his son and heir. Gaius became Rome's first emperor in 27 BC, adopting the title of Augustus, the Grand One.

Augustus ruled for 45 years, a period of great advancement in engineering, architecture, administration and military arts as well as literature. This period of relative calm was more due to the Romans' desire for peace after so many years of internal and external strife than any acceptance within the empire of Roman imperialism.

Julius Caesar

The twelve planet gods

The Augustan age enabled the blossoming of Latin literature, the foundations of which had been laid down by great writers and philosophers such as Cicero (106-43 BC) and the early humorous dramatists, Plautus (c 254-184 BC) and Terence (c 195-159 BC). Virgil and the two great poets of the Augustan era, Horace (65-8 BC) and Ovid (43 BC-c 17 AD), had enormous influence on European thought and literature well beyond the boundaries of the Italian peninsula. Augustus claimed that he had found Rome a city of brick and left her a city of marble.

The Rise of Christianity

The succession of Augustus by his stepson Tiberius (14-37 AD) heralded an era which was to eventually break the back of Roman imperialism, not because of any decline of military might but because the common people of Europe became touched by the message of a religious teacher from Nazareth. The doctrine of the young man Jesus inspired a revolution no army could quell, even though its influence on the culture of medieval Europe was used to create a papal establishment often far more cruel and perverted than that of the Roman emperors.

Despite the fledgling Christian movement, the Roman Empire continued to grow and flourish, with significant cultural expansion under emperors such as Claudius, who introduced major reforms to ministerial government, created a modern system of sanitation, shops and public baths, and built aqueducts on the massive Porta Maggiore and an artificial harbour at Ostia at the mouth of the Tiber, which remain today.

The extravagant and undoubtedly deranged Emperor Nero (ruled 54-68 AD) is best known for the burning of Rome and his persecution of the Christians, who were forced to conduct their ceremonies in underground catacombs.

After a short period of instability, Vespasian, the son of a civil servant from the Italian provinces and the first of the Flavian dynasty, carried out some of the most ambitious building projects of the empire, with the vast Colosseum witnessing his regime's mass slaughter of men, women and animals. His son, the popular Titus, succeeded him as emperor (78-81 AD) and is remembered in Roman architecture by the triumphal Arch of Titus, dated 81 AD, which is located where the Via Sacra enters the Roman Forum, the form of which was to exert considerable influence on the architecture of the Renaissance.

Roman headdress

Emperor Hadrian (117-138 AD) was responsible for two of Rome's most famous landmarks, the Pantheon and the Castel Sant'Angelo, having designed them himself in conjunction with the great Roman architect Appollonius.

A terrible plague swept Europe during the 2nd century and, combined with the ideological invasion of Eastern religions and increasing pressure from Teutonic tribes on the Rhine and Danube frontiers, Rome began to lose its grip.

With the Edict of Milan in 313 AD, Emperor Constantine gave official recognition to Christianity, prompting the successors of St Peter, Bishop of Rome, to claim this city as the headquarters of the Christian movement. Formal recognition also sparked off a widespread building programme of cathedrals and churches throughout the land.

Division of the Empire

The empire remained beset by civil wars as the once all-conquering Roman legions shifted their support from one would-be emperor to another. Tribes along the empire's borders took advantage of the power vacuum by grabbing ever-larger chunks of territory, and there was little Rome could do about it. Cutting his losses, and recognising the growing importance of the wealthy eastern regions of the empire, Emperor Constantine moved his capital city from Rome to Byzantium, a city on the northern shore of the Bosporus, which he renamed Constantinople (present-day Istanbul).

The demise of Rome continued when the ruling brothers Valentian and Valens divided the empire into a western and eastern half in 364, a division that was formalised after the death of Emperor Theodosius I in 395. Theodosius' son Honorius moved the capital of the Western Roman Empire to Ravenna.

Separated from its Roman roots, the Eastern Roman Empire embraced Hellenistic (Greek-Egyptian) culture and developed into the mighty Byzantine Empire, the most powerful Mediterranean state throughout the Middle Ages. It would remain in existence until the capture of Constantinople by the Turks in 1453.

The Early Middle Ages (400-600)

The population decline throughout the 2nd and 3rd centuries continued with a dramatic decline in 4th century caused by plague, famine and war.

The arrival of the Vandals in North Africa cut off Rome's corn supplies, while the western Teutonic tribe of Visigoths consolidated their control of much of the northern Mediterranean coast and northern Italy, bringing new blood to the northern regions. In 452, Attila the Hun, leader of a tribe from the central Asian steppes, invaded and, it is said, caused the people of Aquileia and Grado to found a city of refuge called Venice.

This city was to become a great trading and seafaring city and the birthplace, in 1254, of one of Italy's most well known adventurers, Marco Polo. But Italians of the early Middle Ages were not in any position to purvey the exotic realms of the Orient, and it would be several centuries before Marco

A Goth (left) and Swabian, just two of the different invaders

Polo introduced them to the noodle, which became the basis of their national cuisine.

In 476, the year traditionally recognised as the end of the Roman Empire, the last Western Roman emperor, Romulus Augustulus, was deposed by a mutinous Germanic captain of mercenaries called Odovacar (476-493), whose reign the 19th century Italian nationalist writer Cesare Balbo described in his work *Storia d'Italia* as 'a war of Italian independence against the German peoples, which has lasted for 1357 years and is not finished'.

Gothic rule in Italy reached its zenith with the Ostrogothic emperor Theodoric (493-526). The greatest of the Ostrogothic rulers, Theodoric had spent several years as a hostage in Constantinople where he acquired great respect for Roman culture. When the eastern emperor Zeno put him in charge of Italy, Theodoric, ruling from Ravenna, brought peace and prosperity to the area.

After Theodoric's death, the Eastern Roman emperor Justinian (527-565) and his wife, Theodora, reconquered Italy and laid the groundwork for the Byzantine era, of which early examples can be found in the mosaic portraits of Justinian and Theodora in the church of San Vitale at Ravenna, and in Rome, where the finest remaining examples are the mosaics in the Church of SS Cosma e Damiano. Though the Justinian

reconquest was soon rolled back by the Lombards, Byzantine emperors and empresses managed to hold on to parts of Italy until the 11th century.

During the middle years of the 5th century, Pope Leo I 'the Great' (440-461), known as the founder of Catholicism, had ensured the temporal power of the papacy by persuading Attila not to attack Rome. Using a document known as the *Donation of Constantine*, which 1000 years later was exposed as a forgery, Leo I secured the Western Roman Empire for the fledgling Catholic Church.

In 590, Pope Gregory I, son of a rich Roman family, returned from his self-imposed exile in a monastery, having given all his wealth to the poor. He set the pattern of Church administration which was to guide Catholic services and rituals throughout history. He oversaw the Christianisation of Britain, improved conditions for slaves, provided free bread in Rome and repaired Italy's extensive network of aqueducts, as well as leaving an enormous volume of writing on which much future Catholic dogma has been based.

Lombard Italy & the Papal States (600-800)

Even before Gregory became pope, the Lombard invasion of Italy had begun. The Lombards were a Swabian people who appear to have originally inhabited the lower basin of the Elbe; but as so often happened to conquerors of the Italian peninsula, they were soon incorporated into the local culture. Their language did not last long after their arrival, and their culture too was almost completely integrated, particularly with regard to property. Their more communal concept of land and property tenure was soon overthrown by the Romans' regard for private property, either absolute or leased, and the Lombards, who mainly settled around Milan, Pavia and Brescia, soon became city dwellers, building many churches and public baths which still grace these cities.

In an effort to unseat the Lombards, the pope invited the Franks to invade Italy, which they did in 754 and 756 under the

Theodoric's mausoleum in Ravenna

command of their king Pepin, disenfranchising the Lombards and establishing the Papal States which were to survive until 1870. Using the *Donation of Constantine* as his precedent, Pepin issued the *Donation of Pepin* in 756, which gave land that was still nominally under the Byzantine Empire to Pope Stephen II and proclaimed the pope heir of the Roman emperors. The bond between the papacy and the Byzantine Empire was thus forever broken, and political power in what had been the Western Roman Empire shifted north of the Alps, where it would remain for more than 1000 years.

When the Frankish king Charlemagne visited Rome in 774, he confirmed the *Donation of Pepin* and reinstated the imperial practice of crowning his son 'King of Italy'. After the early death of his son, Charlemagne himself was crowned Emperor of Rome on Christmas Day 800 by Pope Leo II in St Peter's Basilica.

After Charlemagne's death, his Carolingian heirs became absentee kings until Louis II, who became emperor in 850 and who settled there for the 25 years of his reign. The special ties between Rome and what used to be the eastern parts of Charlemagne's empire were evidenced by the founding of the Holy Roman Empire by the Saxon king Otto I in 962, who took the title Holy Roman Emperor. This title was to remain the privilege of Germanic emperors until 1806.

Meanwhile the Muslim Arabs had invaded Sicily and in 831 took Palermo as their capital, while Syracuse, an important city since the first Greek settlements, fell to them also in 878. Cotton, sugar cane, oranges and lemons were introduced in the south, taxes there were lower, and the Sicilians lived relatively peacefully under their Arab lords for more than two centuries. Hundreds of mosques were built and the elegant, unique Arabian architecture survived even after Sicily was returned to the papal fold.

Amalfi, which had secured independence from Naples in the 840s, soon became a major trading republic in the western Mediterranean, and, with her sister republics of Gaeta and Naples along with Salerno, which was still a Lombard principality, became a centre of great cosmopolitan civilisation and learning. In the 11th century, Salerno was famous for its medical school, and it now claims to house the oldest university with a continuous existence in Europe. It was not a university in the true sense of the word, however, and the University of Bologna is more strictly entitled to this claim.

While the south prospered under Arab rule, the rest of Italy was not so calm. Following the death of Louis II in 875, warfare broke out in earnest between local Italian rulers who were divided in their support of Frankish and Germanic claimants, all absentee landlords, to the imperial title and throne. Italy became the battleground of Europe as rival factions fought for ascendancy and refugees flooded safe cities from the devastated countryside.

In the early 11th century the Normans began arriving, first as mercenaries in southern Italy where they fought against the Arabs, but changing allegiances as profit dictated. Fanatically Christian, the Norman knights spearheaded the powerful movement of papal reform instigated by Hildebrand (c 1020-85), who was to become Pope Gregory VII in 1073.

The Norman & Holy Roman Eras

Hildebrand's campaign to bring the world under the rule of one loving God was, in reality, a struggle for power between the Church and the state represented by foreign emperors, which provided a rallying cry for parties in Italy. Both the Frankish and Germanic claimants were distracted, temporarily, by the summons of Christendom to recapture the Holy Land from the Muslims – the First Crusade, a tragic disaster, moved primarily from what is today Germany and France. Although the crusades do not feature greatly in Italian history, they were to lead to the eventual demise of the Sicilian association with the Arab world.

The Muslims of Sicily were displaced by Normans when Roger II was crowned king of Sicily in 1130. The Normans brought with them a fine appreciation of majestic spaces characterised by Romanesque architecture. Blended with the Oriental legacy of arabesque decoration, southern Italy still supports a unique cultural and architectural synthesis of two faiths, which to this day have difficulty living in harmony together. The Church of San Giovanni degli Eremiti at Palermo might equally pass as a mosque or a Greek or Norman basilica. Mosaics such as those in the Cathedral of Monreale (just outside of Palermo) combine the vitality and expression of Oriental influences with all the glory of Byzantine architecture.

Norman rule in the south gave way to Germanic claims when Holy Roman Emperor Henry VI invaded in 1194, declaring himself king. His heir, Frederick II, was a half-Norman southerner, even though he was patron of the Germanic order of Teutonic Knights. Frederick II, an enlightened ruler who became known as Stupor Mundi (Wonder of the World), patronised the Italian vernacular, gave freedom of worship to Muslims and Jews, and earned a place in Italian history as one of her earliest poets. In 1224, Frederick founded the University of Naples and was a near contemporary of a man whose philosophy of fundamentalist Christian communism flourished under the new era of religious tolerance – St Francis of Assisi, whose movement of mendicant friars stressed God's love of man rather than man's fear of God.

City-States & Communes

Between the 12th and 14th centuries, government in Italy evolved into a new kind of political institution – the city-states or city-republics, whose political organisation became known as the commune (comune).

In the north and centre of Italy, administration from the commune produced a new middle class, headed by a great many lawyers who replaced the rule of the bishops. Although many were from landowning and noble families, there were a significant number of more humble, though literate, officials.

In the south however, Charles of Anjou, who had defeated and beheaded Conradin, Frederick's 16-year-old grandson and heir, ousted Germanic rule. French dominion under Charles brought heavy taxes, particularly on rich landowners, who did not accept such measures graciously. Although always a hated foreigner, Charles supported muchneeded road repairs, reformed the coinage, imposed standard weights and measures, improved the equipment of ports and opened silver mines.

Despite his grip on papal power and his subsequent conquests of Jerusalem and Constantinople, the reign of Charles of Anjou was to become infamous throughout Italy for a popular uprising, sparked off by the assault of a Sicilian woman by a French soldier in Palermo. A crowd gathered, killing the soldier, and a widespread massacre of the French ensued as communities throughout Sicily rose against their warlords. Known as the Sicilian Vespers, the events of this time led to the citizens of Palermo declaring an independent republic and endorsing Peter of Aragon as king, effectively separating themselves from the Neapolitan mainland and bringing themselves under Spanish rule.

The latter decades of the 13th century were marked by decreasing economic vitality as Europeans battled an invasion far more deadly than a mere army. The Black Death, as it came to be known, was commonly called the plague or, in Italy, la peste, and combined with famine and deprivation from years of war to cause the death of over half the population of many major cities.

Meanwhile, in north and central Italy, the growing importance of communes dissipated rule by the bishops, with the centre of law reform being the University of Bologna. The legal debate of this time and the ensuing changes to Italian society, together with the dawning of a new era of powerful literary and artistic expression, were to form the basis of the humanist culture of the 13th and 14th centuries which was to usher in the Renaissance.

Humanism

The artist whose works signify the breakthrough from the Byzantine or Gothic style to the first light of the Renaissance was Giotto (see the Arts section later in this chapter). In literature, Averroes, an Arabic philosopher born in Cordova in southern Spain, resurrected the influence of Aristotle's doctrine that immortality was gained through individual efforts towards universal reason. This emphasis on the autonomy of human reason, based on the groundwork laid by the classic philosophers instead of the ideas of the current Church hierarchy, was a revolutionary new philosophical position that became known as humanism.

Translated into Latin, Averroes became a strong influence on another interpreter of Aristotelian thought, St Thomas Aquinas, who was educated at Monte Cassino by the Benedictines and at the University of Bologna, before joining the Dominicans in 1243. Aquinas bridged the gap between the existence of God and Aristotle's respect for the validity of reason with his *Summa Theologica*. This had the beneficial effect that Italian Christianity never lost its grip on the real world, or its respect for good works.

The new era saw independent artisans flourish, and their guilds became influential in the power structure of the cities, particularly in Florence, which retained the trappings of the new republicanism until 1434, when the Medici family brought back a comparatively mild despotism.

The Florentine houses of Peruzzi and Bardi were the business moguls of Europe, minting some 400,000 units of their currency, the florence or florin, each year. Florentine prosperity was based on the wool trade, and on finance and commerce in general. Craft and trade guilds became increasingly powerful in the affairs of the city.

The Arte della Lana (the wool guild) of Florence employed a workforce of more than 5000, but these workers were not citizens and could not take part in the elections of the republic. In 1378, the poorest workers, the wool-carters or *ciompi*, revolted against their city fathers, taking power in the city-state for

at least six weeks during which time they created new guilds which could represent them.

But Europe's first working-class uprising was short-lived as Florence had a power struggle within its higher ranks which took precedence. This struggle was connected with the conflict between the pope and the Holy Roman emperor, which formed the focal point of Italian politics in the late Middle Ages, and Italian political thought split into two camps – Guelph (support of the pope) and Ghibelline (support of the emperor).

While the first decades of the 14th century were years of economic and cultural growth in Italy, not all cities shared the relatively liberal and less religiously dominated calm of Florence. By contrast, Milan, like many of the Italian communes, was still strictly dominated by single families, or *signori*. The Della Torre family, which represented the popular party of the city-state, came into dire conflict with the Visconti family, which represented the Ghibelline nobility. Ottone Visconti had been made Archbishop of Milan in 1262, and his nephew, Matteo, was made imperial vicar by Henry VII. He subsequently destroyed the power of the Della Torre, extending Milanese control over Pavia and Cremona, and later Genoa and Bologna. Giangaleazzo Visconti (1351-1402) would turn Milan from a city-state into a strong European entity, and although the Viscontis were unappreciated as dictators by the Milanese, Milan managed to resist French attempts at invasion.

The 'Babylonian Captivity'

Meanwhile, the Church was going through a crisis of its own. The papacy's ongoing crusades against the Eastern infidels during the 13th century had turned into campaigns against European heretics in the 14th, campaigns in Italy were thinly disguised grabs for wealth and prosperity by claimants from Italian ruling families and the related nobility of the rest of Europe.

Pope Boniface VIII (1294-1303) came from Italian nobility and his emphasis was obviously directed at ensuring his family's continuing wealth and power. His papal bull of 1302, *Unam Sanctum*, claimed papal supremacy in worldly and spiritual affairs – claims of temporal might which achieved its ends by identifying and eliminating heretics, particularly those speaking out against its fearful imperialism.

When the French pope John XXII (1316-34) chose to base the papacy in Avignon, the Church of Rome, and indeed Rome in general, suddenly lost its main *raison d'être*. Goats and cows grazed on the Capitoline Hill and in the Forum, and residential support for the city's many churches and cathedrals disappeared. The Italian ruling families challenged the papacy's ongoing claim to be temporal rulers of Rome, a claim it attempted to enforce by way of agents.

There were to be seven popes in Avignon from 1305 to 1377, a period that became known as the 'Babylonian Captivity', a phrase coined by the Roman poet laureate Petrarch to castigate the evils of the French papal court. Eventually the popes in Avignon found themselves unable to secure their papal holdings via agents, and nominated the lords of the Italian ruling families as their vicars, restoring the imperial pact once more.

When Pope Gregory XI took the papal headquarters back to Rome in 1377 he found a ruined and almost deserted city. Gregory made the Vatican his papal base because it was fortified and had the formidable Castel Sant'Angelo nearby. When Gregory died one year after returning to Rome, Roman cardinals tried to ensure their continuing power by electing as pope the unpopular and often bizarre Urban VI, sparking off a renegade movement of cardinals, mainly French, who, a few months later, elected a second pope, Clement VII, who set up his claim back in Avignon. So began the Great Schism, and the papacy was not to be reconciled with Rome until 1417.

The Renaissance

Fifteenth century Italians could no longer accept the imperialist papal domination of earlier times. A remarkable treatise by the

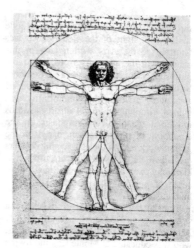

Leonardo da Vinci's study of proportions

humanist Lorenzo Valla (1407-57) debunked the *Donation of Constantine*, which purported to make the western empire of Constantine a gift to the papacy ad infinitum, as a forgery. Serious study of the Greek classics and the writings of others, such as Hebrew and Arabic scholars, pervaded the literary works of the later 15th century and highlighted the place of the individual in the universe.

The 15th and early 16th centuries showed unparalleled creativity and visionary accomplishments in all aspects of political, cultural and social life. The Medici family of Florence patronised one of the most remarkable explosions of artistic and literary achievements in recorded history. See the Arts section later in this chapter for more information about this period.

This phenomenal creativity was disrupted by the preaching of Savonarola, a Dominican monk who had an extremely negative effect on humanist thinking and who allied himself with the French King Charles VIII to overthrow the Medici family in 1494. Savonarola created the Grand Council of Florence, an assembly of some 3000 members whose duty it was to elect the executive body of nine men, the Signoria. Savonarola persuaded the Florentines to burn many works of art that he claimed were inspired by pagan thinking, until the Florentines took matters into their own hands, trying and hanging Savonarola, and burning his corpse in the Piazza della Signoria.

The Medici family, briefly reinstated, could not regain their positive influence on the Florentines who eventually rejected them, setting up a second democratic republic in 1527. In 1530 this republic was in turn overthrown when Emperor Charles V, who had sacked Rome in 1527, brought back the Medicis, whose rule over Florence for the next 210 years was, more typically, an unhappy oligarchy.

One public official of the Florentine republic was Niccolò Machiavelli (1469-1527), whose short handbook, *The Prince*, outlined somewhat cynically the prerequisite skills for securing and retaining power. Machiavelli advocated the banishment of all foreign rule in Italy and urged the people to employ all their native wit and cunning to achieve this end. He also wrote a history of Florence, in Italian rather than Latin, although his efforts were less original than those of his contemporary and friend, Francesco Guicciardini (1483-1532).

The Counter-Reformation

Not all Italian states experienced the great social blossoming we know as the Renaissance. In the south, continuing quarrels over rulership and landholdings by the Visconti family, in league with Alfonso V of Aragon against the house of Angevin, ensured repression of the liberty and freethinking which had inspired a new sense of creativity and productivity in other parts of the country.

The early years of the 16th century saw Italy once more become the battleground for competing interests, both foreign and domestic. The north suffered a steep economic decline as a result of the fighting and population loss from migration to the relative calm of the south.

The broad-minded curiosity of the Renaissance gave way to the puritanical intolerance of the Counter-Reformation, the Church campaign against the Reformation, a collective term for the movement that aimed to reform the Church and led to the rise of Protestantism in its many forms. The transition was epitomised by the reign of Pope Paul III (1534-49), who promoted the building of the classically elegant Farnese Palace but who also, in 1540, allowed the establishment of Ignatius Loyola's order of the Jesuits and the organisation in 1542 of the Holy Office. This was the final (and ruthless) court of appeal in heresy trials which began to gather momentum with the increased activities of the Inquisition (1232-1820), the judicial arm of the church whose aim was to discover and suppress heresy.

Pope Paul III's fanatical opposition to Protestantism and his purging of clerical abuse, as he saw it, resulted in a widespread campaign of torture and fear. In 1559, the Church published the *Index Librorum Prohibitorum*, the Index of Prohibited Books, and the Roman Church's new determination to regain papal supremacy over the Christian churches set the stage for what was to become a dark era of persecution for intellectuals and free thinkers.

Two great Italian intellectuals who were to feel the brunt of the Counter-Reformation were Giordano Bruno (1548-1600) and Galileo Galilei (1564-1642). A Dominican monk, Bruno was forced to flee Italy for Calvinist Geneva, from where he travelled extensively throughout Europe before being arrested by the Inquisition in Venice in 1592. In 1870, the Kingdom of Italy erected a statue of him in Rome's Campo de' Fiori, where he had been burnt at the stake.

An advocate of Aristotelian science, Galileo was forced by the Church to renounce his approval of the Copernican astronomical system, which held that the earth moved round the sun rather than the other way round. But where Bruno had rejected the Catholic Church, Galileo never deviated from the faith which rejected him.

However, the latter years of the 16th century were not all counterproductive. Pope Gregory XIII (1572-85) replaced the Julian calendar with the Gregorian in 1582, fixing the start of the year on 1 January and adjusting the system of leap years to align the normal, 365-day year with the seasons. The city of Rome was greatly embellished by the architectural and sculptural achievements of Giovanni Bernini (1598-1680).

Despite these exceptions, Italy was to lose her position as the matriarch of European cultural expression. Epidemics and wars, particularly the War of the Spanish Succession (1701-14), tossed the nation from Spanish domination during the 17th century to Austrian occupation, which began with the conquest of Naples in 1707.

The Enlightenment

The Italy of the 18th century, although mainly ruled from abroad, was set to become part of an era which broke down many of the national barriers of Europe, a development which was as much due to the extent of intermarriage of its monarchies as to new trading laws necessitated by bad harvests in many areas of the continent. The papacy became less influential in this era known as the Enlightenment, especially after the expulsion of the Jesuits from Portugal, France and Spain.

The 18th century Enlightenment swept away the dark days of the Counter-Reformation, producing great thinkers and writers such as Cesare Beccaria (1738-94), whose masterpiece *Of Crimes & Punishments* attacked torture and capital punishment as barbarism, and advocated reform of the criminal code, a proposal taken up by Grand Duke Leopold of Tuscany, who abolished the death sentence.

New economic ideas advocating the liberalisation of trade laws were put forward by the influential writer Pietro Verri (1728-97) who, with his brother Alessandro, introduced reforms in schools and universities as well as in the government administration of Lombardy. Alessandro Volta (1745-1827), after whom the volt is named, invented the electric battery when he was professor of natural philosophy at Bologna.

Napoleon

Italy had been the source of many enlightened political ideas, but the concept of national sovereignty had not been one of them. But when the 27-year-old, Corsican-born French general Napoleon Bonaparte invaded Italy in 1796 and declared himself, quite unofficially, its dictator, a nationalist movement began in earnest. Inspired by the ideas of another Frenchman, Jean-Jacques Rousseau, the French leftist Jacobin movement gained significant support in Italy when, before the end of his first year of occupation, Napoleon used Italy as the base for his expedition into Egypt.

The Jacobin movement established a republic in Rome, setting off a resurgence of debate about Italy as a nation and the sovereign rights of its people, dubbed the Risorgimento, or Revival, by Italian dramatist Vittorio Alferi (1749-1803). But the mainly middle-class movement found itself unable to bring about social reforms quickly enough for the peasants, particularly the very poor of Naples. A peasant army sacked Naples, littering its streets with dead Jacobins.

Although having declared himself First Consul of Italy in 1799, Napoleon acceded to the calls of Italian deputies in the north to proclaim an Italian Republic and, for the first time in history, the political entity known as Italy came into being, albeit with Napoleon as its first, self-elected president.

When in 1804 Napoleon made himself Emperor of France, he established the Kingdom of Italy and elected himself its first king, inviting Pope Pius VII to officially crown him in Paris. Pius delayed his visit, reluctant to give his endorsement to the power brokers of the French Revolution, which had greatly curtailed the importance of the Catholic church; nor was he keen on endorsing the marriage of Napoleon to the divorcee Josephine. When the pope finally arrived several days late, Napoleon was 'not amused'. As the pope raised the emperor's crown to his head, Napoleon took it and crowned himself, a reaction which outraged the Italians and greatly enhanced the popularity of the pope as a consequence.

Unification

Napoleon's demise at Waterloo in 1815 heralded a new era of peace for the Italians. Their rulers were reinstated with the absolute powers they so enjoyed, although their actual power was counteracted by the rapid growth of secret societies made up in the main of disaffected middle-class intellectuals.

In the south, the republican Carbonari pushed hard and often ruthlessly to ensure a valid constitution, leading a revolutionary uprising in Naples in 1820. Another leading revolutionary figure of these secret societies was Filippo Buonarroti, who strove for independence from Austria and the establishment of a communist society devoid of private-property interests.

But these movements were quelled as others before them by Europe's noble families. Using what was known as the Congress System, a series of conferences through which the major European powers strove to maintain the status quo after Napoleon's defeat, Europe's rulers consistently voted to suppress any threats to their claims to the lands of the Italian peninsula. Only as the broader European movement for national identity strengthened during the middle and latter years of 19th century was Italy able to gain any support for her own sovereignty.

One of Italy's key proponents of nationhood and political freedom was a Genoan called Giuseppe Mazzini (1805-1872). Having quit the Carbonari movement in 1830, Mazzini founded Young Italy, a society of young men whose aims were the liberation of Italy from foreign and domestic tyranny and its unification under a republican form of government. The means to be used were education and, where necessary, revolt by guerrilla bands.

Exiled from his homeland for his former activities with the Carbonari, Mazzini was responsible for organising a number of abortive uprisings throughout Italy during the 1830s and 1840s which left dead many of the young men who had flocked to join his Young Italy movement. Twice sentenced to death, Mazzini was to live out his days in England, from where he wrote many articles and solicited as much support as he could from influential allies to raise the consciousness of Europeans about the 'Italian question'.

In 1848, there were revolutions in almost every major city and town of Europe. In their newspaper, *Il Risorgimento*, one of several publications to have sprung up as the Italian nationalist movement gained ground among Italians of all classes, Cesare Balbo, a nationalist writer, and Count Camillo Benso di Cavour of Turin pressed for a constitution. In 1848, they published their *Statuto*, advocating a two-chamber parliament with the upper chamber to be appointed by the crown and the lower chamber to be elected with voting restricted to educated taxpayers. In 1861, the *Statuto* was to become the constitutional basis of the Kingdom of Italy, but not before almost two more decades of warring between the European princes and

Count Camillo Benso di Cavour

their subjects had left a great many more Italians dead.

Returning to Italy in 1848 from his famous exploits in South America, where he is still remembered as a founding hero of Uruguay, Giuseppe Garibaldi (1807-82) was to become the hero Italians needed to lead them towards a unified Italy. Garibaldi's personal magnetism, signified by his respect for people rich and poor, drew more average Italians into fighting for their nationhood than ever before. The armies of common people that arose under Garibaldi over the ensuing years were solely concerned with the creation of a united Italy.

Despite significant personal animosity, Garibaldi and Cavour were to find themselves fighting side by side, each in their chosen arena, to break the stranglehold of foreign domination. The brilliant diplomacy of Cavour, coupled with the independent efforts of Garibaldi and his 'people power', finally caught the attention of the wider European communities, particularly the British, who were to become staunch supporters of a free and united Italy.

When the sympathetic Piedmontese monarch, King Carlo Alberto, granted a constitution based on the *Statuto* in March 1848, Cavour stood for election. In 1850 he was given three ministries – navy, commerce and finance – in the government headed by Massimo d'Azeglio. When Cavour's centre-left faction joined forces with the centre-right, headed by Urbano Rattazzi, behind d'Azeglio's back, the prime minister resigned and Cavour was asked by the king to take the top government post. As prime minister, Cavour focused on forging an alliance with the French emperor Napoleon III, in a move destined to overthrow Austrian domination of Piedmont.

Meanwhile the unification movement was literally on the move, as Garibaldi led his Expedition of One Thousand, taking Sicily and Naples in 1860. The Kingdom of Italy was declared on 17 March 1861 and Victor Emmanuel II, the king of Sardinia-Piedmont from 1849, was proclaimed king. But Italy was still not completely united: Venice remained in the hands of the Austrians and Rome was held by France.

Cavour was to die within six months of achieving the first parliament of the Kingdom of Italy. He had been betrayed by his French allies when Napoleon III signed the armistice of Villafranca, ending the Franco-Austrian war (fought in Italy, largely by Italians). Venice was wrested from the Austrians in 1866 and it wasn't until the Franco-Prussian War of 1870 that Napoleon III's hold over Italy was to be broken. Needing all available troops, he withdrew his occupation of Rome, leaving the way clear for the Italian army, led by Garibaldi, to breach the walls at Porta Pia and reinstate the Italian capital, which Napoleon III had moved to Florence.

The only resistance to Garibaldi's push on Rome came from the papal soldiers of Pope Pius IX who had refused to recognise the Kingdom of Italy, and who was to find himself stripped of his remaining temporal powers as well as his palace, the Quirinale.

Victor Emmanuel II

Giuseppe Garibaldi

Garibaldi on an election poster,
as an upside-down Stalin

The papacy regained some of its autonomy in the 1920s when the Fascist dictator Mussolini restored the independent papal state, but in the interim, the papacy forbade Catholics to participate in the elections of their government.

As the 20th century dawned, the economic crisis of Europe was reflected in Italian politics by constant fluctuations as socialist democrats and right-wing imperialists gained and lost the populace. When, in the general elections of 1894, Pope Pius X formally gave Catholics the right to vote (although many had already been doing just that), there was a widespread backlash against socialism. Giovanni Giolitti, one of Italy's longest serving prime ministers (heading five governments between 1892 and 1921), managed to bridge the extremes and was able to embark on parliamentary reforms which gave the vote to all literate men from the age of 21 and all illiterate men who had completed military service or were aged 30 or over. But while male suffrage had been achieved, Italian women were still denied the right to vote until after WW II.

Fascism

When war broke out in Europe in July 1914, Italy, unable and unwilling to align herself, chose to remain neutral rather than become caught between old enemies. But caught she became when senior politicians allied themselves with the British, Russians and French, while the papacy spoke out against the 'atheist' French in favour of Catholic Austria.

In October 1914, the editor of the Socialist newspaper *Avanti!* also came out strongly in favour of alignment with the Allied forces. For his views, young Benito Mussolini was forced to resign. He started his own newspaper in November, the *Popolo d'Italia*, a propaganda publication financed by French, British and Russian interests.

In 1919 he founded the Fascist Party, with its hallmarks of the black shirt and Roman salute. These emblems were to become the symbols of violent oppression and national disease for the next 23 years. In 1921, the party won 35 of the 135 seats in parliament, and in October 1922, after being asked by the king to form a government, Mussolini started his dominance of Italy. With an army of 40,000 Fascist militia, he began the famous March on Rome to 'free the nation from the Socialists'.

In April 1924, following a campaign marked by violence and intimidation, his party won the national elections and Mussolini created the world's first Fascist regime. By 1925 the term 'totalitarianism' had entered the language. By the end of 1925 Mussolini had become head of state, expelled opposition parties from parliament, gained control of the press and trade unions and had reduced the voting public by two-thirds. In 1929, Mussolini and Pope Pius XI signed the Lateran Pact, whereby Catholicism was declared the sole religion of Italy and the Vatican was recognised as an independent state. In return, the papacy finally acknowledged the united Kingdom of Italy.

In the 1920s, Mussolini embarked on an aggressive foreign policy, leading to skirmishes with Greece over the island of Corfu and to military expeditions against nationalist forces in the Italian colony of Libya. In 1935, Italy sought a new colonial conquest by invading Abyssinia (present-day Ethiopia) from the Italian base in Eritrea, only capturing Addis Ababa after seven months. The act was condemned as aggression by the League of Nations which imposed limited sanctions on Italy.

Fearful of international isolation, Mussolini formed the Rome-Berlin Axis with Hitler in 1936 which was soon joined by Japan, and Italy entered WW II as an ally of Germany in June 1941. After a series of military disasters and the invasion by the Allies in 1943, Mussolini surrendered Italy to the Allies and went into hiding. He was shot, along with his mistress, by partisans in April 1945, and hung upside down from the roof of a petrol station in Milan's Piazzale Loreto.

The Republic

In 1946, following a referendum, the constitutional monarchy was abolished and the republic established. In the decades since WW II, the national government has consistently been dominated by the Christian Democrats, generally in coalition with other parties, excluding the Communists. From 1983 to 1986 the Socialists held government, with Bettino Craxi serving as prime minister.

Italy was a founding member of the European Economic Community in 1957. The country was seriously disrupted by terrorism in the 1970s, following the appearance of neo-Fascist terrorists and the fanatically left-wing Red Brigades. The latter were blamed for the kidnapping and assassination of the Christian Democrat prime minister, Aldo Moro, in 1978, although recent revelations may yet shift responsibility to the Mafia. Moro was on the verge of achieving a historic breakthrough which would have brought the Communists into national government, but the plan was shelved.

The country enjoyed significant economic growth in the 1980s, a period known as *Il Sorpasso*, during which the country became one of the world's leading economic powers. However, the 1990s have heralded a new period of crisis for the country, both economically and politically. High unemployment and inflation rates, combined with a huge national debt and an extremely unstable lira, led the government to introduce draconian measures to revive the economy.

Meanwhile, the very foundations of Italian politics have been shaken by a national bribery scandal variously known as *tangentopoli* ('kickback cities') and *mani pulite* ('clean hands'). This has seen an increasing number of public officials, company executives and leading politicians either arrested or notified that they are under investigation for corruption. See the Government section later in this chapter for more details.

The early 1990s also saw the Italian government take on the Mafia. Prompted by the 1992 assassinations of anti-Mafia judges Giovanni Falcone and Paolo Borsellino, the government sent troops to Sicily and, using the testimonies of *pentiti* (repentant mafiosi turned informers), made several important arrests – most notably of the Sicilian godfather, Salvatore 'Toto' Riina.

GEOGRAPHY

Italy's boot shape makes it one of the most recognisable countries in the world, with the island of Sicily appearing somewhat like a football at the toe of the boot and Sardinia situated in the middle of the Tyrrhenian Sea to the west of the mainland.

The country is bounded by four seas, all part of the Mediterranean Sea. The Adriatic Sea separates Italy from Slovenia, Croatia and Montenegro; the Ionian Sea laps the southern coasts of Apulia, Basilicata and Calabria; and to the west of the country are the Ligurian and Tyrrhenian seas. Coastal areas vary from the cliffs of Liguria and Calabria to the generally level Adriatic coast.

More than 75% of Italy is mountainous, with the Alps stretching from the Gulf of Genoa to the Adriatic Sea north of Trieste and dividing the peninsula from France, Switzerland, Austria and Slovenia. The highest Alpine peak is the Mont Blanc on the border with France, known in Italy as Monte Bianco, standing at 4807 metres, while the highest mountain in the Italian Alps is the Monte Rosa (4634 metres) on the Swiss border. The Alps are divided into three main groups – western, central and eastern – and undoubtedly are at their most spectacular in the Dolomites (Dolomiti) in the eastern Alps in Trentino-Alto Adige and the Veneto. There are more than 1000 glaciers in the Alps, remnants of the last Ice age, which are in a constant state of retreat. The best known in the Italian Alps is the Marmolada glacier on the border of Trentino and the Veneto, a popular spot for summer skiers.

The Apennines (Appennini) form a backbone extending for 1220 km from Liguria, near Genoa, to the tip of Calabria and into Sicily. The highest peak in the Apennines is the Corno Grande (2914 metres) in the Gran Sasso d'Italia group in Abruzzo. Another interesting group of mountains, the Apuan Alps (Alpi Apuane), is found in north-western Tuscany and forms part of the sub-Apennines. These mountains are composed almost entirely of marble and, since Roman times, have been mined almost continuously. Michelangelo selected his blocks of perfect white marble at Carrara in the Apuan Alps.

Lowlands, or plains, make up less than a quarter of Italy's total land area. The largest plain is the Po Valley, bounded by the Alps, the Apennines and the Adriatic Sea. The plain is heavily populated and industrialised, and through it runs Italy's largest river, the Po, and its tributaries, the Reno, Adige, Piave and Tagliamento rivers. Other, smaller plains include the Tavogliere di Puglia and the Pianura Campana around Mt Vesuvius.

Italy has three active volcanoes: Stromboli (in the Aeolian Islands), Vesuvius (near Naples) and Etna (Sicily). Stromboli and Etna are among the world's most active volcanoes, while Vesuvius has not erupted since 1944 – a source of concern for scientists, who estimate that it should erupt every 30 years. Etna's most recent major eruption occurred in 1992, when a trail of lava on its eastern flank threatened to engulf the town of Zafferana Etnea. The lava flow stopped before it reached the town, but not before it had destroyed orchards and a house. Related volcanic activity produces thermal and mud springs, notably at Viterbo in Lazio and in the Aeolian Islands. The Phlegraean Fields near Naples are an area of intense volcanic activity, including hot springs, gas emissions and steam jets.

Central and southern Italy, including Sicily, are also subject to sometimes devastating earthquakes. Messina and Reggio di Calabria were devastated in 1908 by an earthquake which had its epicentre in the sea off the coast of Sicily. In November 1980 an earthquake south-east of Naples destroyed several villages and killed more than 3000 people.

Italy is a dramatically beautiful country, but since Etruscan times humans have left their mark on the environment. Pollution problems caused by industrial and urban waste exist throughout Italy, with air pollution proving a problem in the more industrialised north of the country and in the major cities such as Rome, Milan and Naples, where car emissions poison the atmosphere with carbon monoxide and lead. The seas, and therefore many beaches, are fouled to some extent, particularly on the Ligurian Coast, in the northern Adriatic (where there is an algae problem resulting from industrial pollution) and near major cities such as Rome and Naples. However, it is possible to find a clean beach, particularly in Sardinia. Litter-conscious visitors to Italy will be astounded by the extraordinary Italian habit of discarding and dumping rubbish when and where they like.

The Italian government's record on ecological and environmental issues is not good. The Ministry for the Environment was created relatively recently, in 1981, and many environmental laws are not adequately enforced. The Italian consciousness of environmental issues is growing slowly and several environmental organisations exist, such as the Lega Ambiente (Environment League), the World Wide Fund for Nature (WWF) and the Lega Italiana Protezione Uccelli (LIPU, the Italian Bird Protection League).

CLIMATE

Situated in the temperate zone and jutting deep into the Mediterranean, Italy is regarded by many tourists as a land of sunny, mild weather. The country's climate is, however, quite variable, because of the length of the peninsula and the fact that it is largely mountainous. In the Alps temperatures are lower and winters are long and severe. Generally the weather is warm from July to September, although rainfall can be

high in September. While the first snowfall is usually in November, light snow sometimes falls in mid-September and the first heavy falls can occur in early October.

The Alps shield northern Lombardy and the Lakes area, including Milan, from the extremes of the northern European winter and Liguria enjoys a mild Mediterranean climate similar to southern Italy because it is protected by both the Alps and the Apennines.

Winters are severe and summers very hot in the Po Valley. Venice can be hot and humid in summer and, although not extremely cold in winter, it can be unpleasant as the sea level rises and *acqua alta* (literally, 'high water') inundates the city.

Farther south, at Florence, which is encircled by hills, the weather can be extreme, but as you travel farther towards the tip of the boot, temperatures and weather conditions become milder.

Rome, for instance, has an average temperature in the mid-20s (Celsius) in July/August, although the impact of the sirocco, a hot, humid wind blowing from Africa, can produce stiflingly hot weather in August, with temperatures in the high 30s for days on end. Winters are moderate and snow

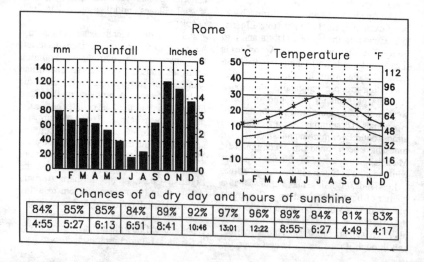

Rome

Rainfall — Temperature

Chances of a dry day and hours of sunshine

84%	85%	85%	84%	89%	92%	97%	96%	89%	84%	81%	83%
4:55	5:27	6:13	6:51	8:41	10:46	13:01	12:22	8:55	6:27	4:49	4:17

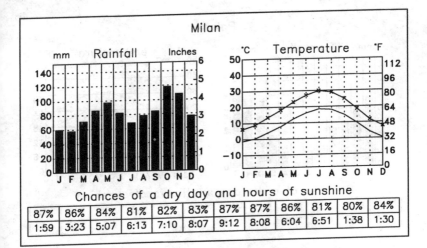

Milan

Chances of a dry day and hours of sunshine

87%	86%	84%	81%	82%	83%	87%	87%	86%	81%	80%	84%
1:59	3:23	5:07	6:13	7:10	8:07	9:12	8:08	6:04	6:51	1:38	1:30

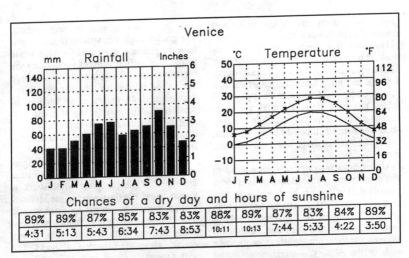

Venice

Chances of a dry day and hours of sunshine

89%	89%	87%	85%	83%	83%	88%	89%	87%	83%	84%	89%
4:31	5:13	5:43	6:34	7:43	8:53	10:11	10:13	7:44	5:33	4:22	3:50

is very rare in Rome, although winter clothing (or at least a heavy overcoat) is still a requirement.

The south, Sicily and Sardinia have a mild Mediterranean climate, with long, hot and dry summers, and moderate winters with an average temperature around 10°C. These regions are also affected by the sirocco in summer.

FLORA & FAUNA

The long presence of humans on the Italian peninsula has had a significant impact on the environment, resulting in widespread destruction of original forests and vegetation and their replacement with crops and orchards. Aesthetically the result is not displeasing – much of the beauty of Tuscany, for instance, lies in the interaction of olive

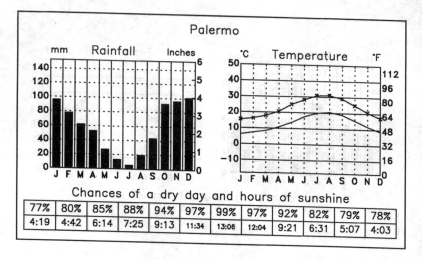

Palermo

	J	F	M	A	M	J	J	A	S	O	N	D
Chances of a dry day	77%	80%	85%	88%	94%	97%	99%	97%	92%	82%	79%	78%
Hours of sunshine	4:19	4:42	6:14	7:25	9:13	11:34	13:06	12:04	9:21	6:31	5:07	4:03

groves with vineyards, fallow fields and stands of cypress and pine.

However, this alteration of the environment, combined with the Italians' passion for hunting (la caccia), has led to many native animals and birds becoming either extinct, rare or endangered. Hunters are a powerful lobby group in Italy, although the most recent referendum on whether hunting should be banned attracted a large 'yes' vote. Supporters of hunting, however, won the day.

Under laws progressively introduced in this century, many animals and birds are now protected. The brown bear, which is protected in several national parks, and the lynx are now extremely rare and found only in isolated parts of the Alps and Apennines. Wolves and foxes are slightly more common and, in the Alps, you might come across marmots, chamois and deer. Among the native animals in Sardinia are wild boar, the mouflon sheep, fallow deer and a variety of wild cat. Commonly available maps in national parks in the Alps and Apennines detail the local wildlife and indicate areas where they might be found.

Hunters continue to denude the countryside of birds. However, enough remain to make bird-watching an interesting pastime. The golden eagle can still be found, if you have the patience, in parts of the Alps, while a colony of griffon vultures survives on the western coast of Sardinia near Bosa. A large variety of falcons and hawks are found throughout Italy, as are many varieties of small birds. The irony is that it is easier to spot the colourful smaller birds in city parks – among the few refuges they have from the Italian hunter – than in the countryside.

Italy is home to remarkably little dangerous fauna. It has only one poisonous snake, the viper. While the great white shark is known to exist in the waters of the Mediterranean, particularly in the southern waters, attacks are extremely rare. Italians will generally respond with a blank stare if you enquire about the presence of sharks. The seas around southern Italy and Sicily are home instead to large numbers of blue-fin tuna and swordfish. The Egadi Islands, off the southern coast of Sicily, are famous for their annual tonnara or mattanza, the bloody netting and killing of tuna which occurs between April and July.

There are numerous national parks in Italy. The largest and most important include the Gran Paradiso in Valle d'Aosta, the

Stelvio National Park straddling Lombardy and Trentino-Alto Adige, and the Abruzzo National Park.

GOVERNMENT

Italy is a parliamentary republic, headed by a president, who appoints the prime minister. The parliament consists of two houses – a senate and a chamber of deputies – both with equal legislative power. Following a referendum in 1946, the republic replaced the former constitutional monarchy and operates on the basis of a constitution which came into force on 1 January 1948.

The seat of national government is in Rome, an increasingly sore point for the new force in Italian politics, the Northern League (Lega Nord). The president resides in the Quirinal Palace, the chamber of deputies sits in the Palazzo Montecitorio and the senate in the Palazzo Madama, near Piazza Navona.

Members of parliament are elected by what is probably the purest system of proportional representation in the world – which was the intent of the country's intensely democratic constitution. Italians are conscientious voters, with an average 88% turnout at the frequent elections where voters are often confronted with numerous separate party lists, some containing the names of up to 50 candidates. Another disadvantage of proportional representation is the plethora of small political parties which gain representation in parliament, and sometimes in government.

A strong 'yes' vote in a 1993 referendum heralded a change to this electoral system, whereby three-quarters of the Senate will be elected on the basis of who receives the most votes in their district, rather than by the proportional system. Eighty per cent of voters supported the change and it is likely that the lower house, the Chamber of Deputies, will eventually be forced to follow suit.

A solid majority also voted 'yes' on a second important question in the referendum (which posed a total of eight questions to voters), signalling the end to the practice of handing out government campaign funds to parties that win at least 5% of the vote in national elections.

While some 16 parties were represented in parliament following the 1992 elections, the five major parties are the Christian Democrats (Democrazia Cristiana), the Socialist Party (Partito Socialista Italiano), the Republican Party (Partito Repubblicano Italiano), the Northern League (Lega Nord) and the former Communist Party, now called the Democratic Party of the Left (Partito Democratico della Sinistra, PDS).

The right-of-centre Christian Democrats (DC) have consistently dominated government at the national level since the formation of the republic, although Italy's electoral system has generally forced them to form unstable coalition governments. Since the declaration of the republic in 1946 there have been 52 governments, with an average lifespan of one year. For many years the DC formed coalitions with other right-wing parties, but in 1963 they were forced to share power for the first time with the Socialist Party (PSI). In 1983 the PSI leader, Bettino Craxi, became the second non-DC prime minister (after the Republican Giovanni Spadolini). Craxi's term as prime minister lasted for four years until his resignation in 1987.

Political Scandals

The heritage of consistent one-party domination is a system which Italians call *partitocrazia* (partyocracy), which operates on the basis of *lottizzazione*, by which the major parties divide control of the country's public bodies and utilities. The resulting patronage system means that government jobs and other positions of power and influence are handed out virtually as political favours, and that no government service is excluded from potential manipulation.

The *tangenti*, kickbacks or bribes to government officials and politicians, are another unfortunate offshoot of the system. These can range from payments by companies wanting to secure government building contracts to payments by individuals wanting to speed up bureaucracy.

In February 1992 the tangentopoli scandal started in Milan with the arrest of a PSI functionary on charges of accepting a L7 million bribe from businesspeople in exchange for public-work contracts. Led by Milanese magistrate Antonio di Pietro, dubbed a 'reluctant hero', investigations eventually implicated about 2500 politicians, public officials and businesspeople at the highest levels. Charges ranged from bribery, making illicit political payments, and receiving kickbacks, to blatant thievery. It is ironic that few ordinary Italians were surprised that many of their politicians, at all levels of government, were entrenched in a system whereby they demanded secret payments, or bribes, as a matter of course.

The former Socialist leader, Bettino Craxi, was forced to resign as party secretary after he was served with five notifications that he was under investigation for corruption. In early 1993, the seven-times former prime minister and Italy's leading postwar politician, Giulio Andreotti, became the investigation's most spectacular 'catch' when he was accused of having illegal connections with the Sicilian Mafia.

When the scandal first broke, voters took the opportunity at general elections in April 1992 to express their discontent with the way the country was being run, resulting in a major shake-up in the balance of power. The DC remained the dominant party, but their share of the vote dropped by just under 5%. A significant feature of the elections was the success of the Northern League, an alliance of regionalist right-wing groups which won about 7% of the vote nationwide and more than 20% in Lombardy, making it the fourth-largest party in parliament. The League's political platform has two fundamental pillars: reaction against corruption in government and against the use of taxes paid by the richer north to support the poorer south. Later in the year, the League's leader, Umberto Bossi, was calling for the division of Italy into three federal states – north, central and south – with greater autonomy from Rome.

Following the election shake-up, parliament elected Christian Democrat Oscar Scalfaro, a man noted for his personal integrity, as president of the republic. PSI deputy leader Giuliano Amato was later appointed prime minister. His government, which had a parliamentary majority of only 16 and did not contain any important members of the DC, introduced massive cuts in public spending which led to paralysing strikes. It also initiated a series of new measures to control the Mafia following the assassinations of Judge Falcone and his colleague, Judge Paolo Borsellino, in separate car-bomb explosions in Palermo.

However, as the tangentopoli scandal gathered pace in 1993 and several ministers of the Amato government resigned after being advised that they were under investigation for corruption, the prime minister himself resigned in April. The president moved quickly to appoint the governor of the Bank of Italy, Carlo Ciampi, as the new prime minister. Ciampi's government was expected to act in a transitionary capacity, pending national elections to be held later in the year.

The Regions

For administrative purposes Italy is divided into 20 regions which roughly correspond to the historical, traditional regions of the country. The regions are then divided into provinces (province), which are then further divided into town councils (comuni). Five of the regions (Sicily, Sardinia, Trentino-Alto Adige, Friuli-Venezia Giulia and Valle d'Aosta) are semi-autonomous, with special powers granted under the constitution. Their regional assemblies are similar to parliaments and have a wider range of economic and administrative powers than the other 15 regions.

Elections for all three tiers of local government are held simultaneously every five years.

ECONOMY

At the end of WW II, Italy's economy was in ruins, but the country wasted little time in setting about repairing the damage. By the early 1950s much had already been achieved and the country had regained prewar levels of production. The economic boom of the 1950s and early 1960s relied to a great extent on the masses of migrant workers moving from the poorer south of the country to the industrial north, providing a more than ample but low-paid workforce.

Following spectacular economic growth during the 1980s, Italy became the fifth-largest economy in the world, made possible to a large extent by Italy's gift for producing entrepreneurs. There are the 'big ones' such as Agnelli (Fiat), De Benedetti (Olivetti) and Berlusconi (media), and then there are huge numbers of ordinary Italians who run their own small business. Some 90% of Italian firms have fewer than 100 workers and many of these are family businesses.

However, there remains much debate about Italy's ability to perform efficiently in the context of a unified Europe – a debate which has intensified following the country's severe economic crisis in 1992-93. Draconian measures were introduced by the government to control public spending and reduce Italy's massive public debt (106% of GDP in 1992 and rising).

The high public debt was consuming a large proportion of the country's savings, keeping inflation high, stifling the entrepreneurial private sector and forcing the country to borrow even more to service the debt. As part of these measures, the government began the partial privatisation of its huge public sector, including the state railways (Ferrovie dello Stato) and the national electricity commission (ENEL), among many others. One immediate effect was a rise in unemployment, as newly privatised companies, suddenly subject to market forces, began closing down factories considered unprofitable.

The fact that Italy's richer, more industrialised northern regions continue to subsidise the generally poorer regions of the south is becoming an increasingly sore political point. Overall, it is true to say that there remains a significant economic gap between north and south – a gap which, despite years of effort and vast sums of money, continues to grow wider. Although the regions of Apulia, Abruzzo and Molise have experienced significant economic growth and continue to prosper, the fact remains that Italy's richest regions (Piedmont, Emilia-Romagna and Lombardy) are all northern, and its poorest (Calabria, Campania and Sicily) are all southern. Unemployment figures for the south generally run at more than double those of the north, output per head in the south is only about half that of the north, and the southern regions are poorly served by economic infrastructure, compared to the north.

Trillions of lire have been poured into the southern regions in the form of subsidies, grants, loans and tax incentives. The focus initially was on big, state-supported industrial ventures, many of which were abject failures. Private investment is now the target, although investors have been difficult to attract.

It has to be said that the impact of this economic gap is that, generally, things do not work as well in the south as they do in the north – notably in hospitals, banks and public services such as the post office.

POPULATION & PEOPLE

The population of Italy is 57.8 million. The country has the lowest birth rate in Europe (9.6 per thousand in 1987, compared with an EC average of 11.8), a surprising fact, considering the Italians' preoccupation with children and family. Demographers are predicting that the population of Italy will fall by about one million in the next 20 years. More children are born in the south than in the north – for instance, the birth rate in Emilia-Romagna is half that of Campania.

Population density can be high in Italy. The most heavily populated areas are around Rome, Milan and Naples, Liguria, Piedmont and parts of Lombardy, the Veneto and Friuli-Venezia Giulia. The most populous area of Italy – in fact the most populous in the world after Hong Kong – is Portici, a suburb of Naples located directly under Mt Vesuvius.

There is only a small minority of non-Italian-speaking people, which includes German-speakers in Alto Adige (in the province of Bolzano). Slovene is spoken by a small minority near Trieste and, in the south, there are small groups of Greeks and Albanians, descendants of immigrants in the 14th and 15th centuries.

Italy has traditionally been a country of emigrants, as Italians have left their country in search of work, travelling mainly to the USA, Argentina, Brazil, Australia and Canada. Southern Italians have also traditionally moved to the north of the country, to work in the factories of Piedmont and Lombardy.

In recent years, however, it has become a country of immigration. Minimal visa rules and a fairly relaxed attitude to enforcement of immigration laws by Italian authorities has made Italy an easy point of entrance into Europe, particularly for Africans. It is estimated that more than 1.5 million immigrants now live in Italy. Unofficial immigrants are known in Italy as *extracomunitari*. Both African and Asian immigrants have become targets of racist attacks in Italy, although the incidence of such attacks remains limited.

Italians are far more concerned with the traditional hostility of northern Italians towards southerners. Many northerners are resentful that the richer north in effect subsidises the poorer south, and their concerns are finding a strong voice in the success of the Northern League, which has attracted considerable electoral support with its policies opposing the use of tax revenues to pay for public projects in the south. The League's leader, Umberto Bossi, has also called for limitations on immigration of southern Italians to the north, as well as curbs on Third-World immigration to Italy.

EDUCATION

The Italian state-school system is free of charge and consists of several levels. Attendance is compulsory from the ages of six to 14 years, although children can attend an *asilo nido* (nursery school) from the ages of three to five years before starting the *scuola*

elementare (primary school) at six. After five years they move on to the *scuola media* (secondary school) until they reach the age of 14.

The next level, the *scuola secondaria superiore* (higher secondary school), is voluntary and lasts a further five years until the student is 19 years old. It is, however, essential if young people want to continue their studies at university. At this level there are several options: four types of *liceo* (humanities-based school), four types of technical school, and teacher-training school.

The standards of education in the state-run system compare well with those in other countries, although the system does have its problems, compounded by relatively low standards in teacher-training and poor government management.

Private schools in Italy are run mainly by religious institutions, notably the Jesuits.

Italy has a long tradition of university education and can claim to have the oldest university in the world, at Bologna, which was established in the 11th century. Courses are usually from four to six years, although students are under no obligation to complete their courses within that time. Consequently, it is not uncommon for students to take many more years to complete their quota of exams and their final thesis. Actual attendance at lectures is not obligatory, and for scientific courses there are no practical experiments. Students therefore tend to study at home from books.

All state-school and university examinations are oral, rather than written.

ART

Architecture

There is far too much to see in Italy to make a detailed architectural agenda worthwhile. There are 900 churches in Rome alone. Much of the character of Italian architecture, however, can be absorbed by simply wandering through the streets and admiring the richness and wealth on show.

Every Italian town has its square, or *piazza*, a centre for community life and a place where townspeople gather. Rome has some magnificent squares, such as the Piazza Navona, which is one of the city's largest. Originally filled with water for mock battles, it was transformed in the 17th century by the Baroque architect and artist Gian Lorenzo Bernini, who designed and built the Fountain of the Rivers, a masterpiece in which each of the four figures represents one of the four great rivers in the world. The Piazza del Popolo is at the intersection of the three important roads in Rome, and the Piazza di Spagna, with its famous Spanish Steps, is a famous meeting place for lovers and friends.

Roman Roman architecture was a natural successor to the achievements of the Greeks. The Greek temple embodied independent beauty and its legacy can be seen at Paestum, south of Naples, one of the most famous of Italy's Greek archaeological sites.

The Colosseum

The Roman city of Pompeii is frozen in time. South-east of Naples, it is perfectly preserved in the year 79 AD, when Mt Vesuvius erupted violently and buried the entire city in a layer of ash. The Villa of the Mysteries is a must for its excellent examples of Roman frescoes (wall-paintings). It is called the Villa of the Mysteries because archaeologists and historians have been unable to interpret the meaning of the frescoes; the current interpretation is that they represent fertility rituals.

Roman architects tended to construct buildings as part of a group, hence the development of Roman town centres which included temples, a forum or public area, market and other important buildings. The Romans developed the arch, the wall niche and the half-column set into the wall to reduce the isolation of the pure forms of the Greek temple.

Arches are famous in the Roman device for carrying water across the country, the aqueduct, and in Rome's Colosseum, the site of many Christian martyrdoms. Begun by Vespasian in 75 AD, the Colosseum was capable of holding 50,000 people in three tiers of seating and is a monument to Roman architecture.

During the Renaissance and especially during the 18th century, many architects turned to the Roman heritage for inspiration, resulting in Roman-lookalike structures which were referred to as 'classical'.

Byzantine When Constantine recognised Christianity and transferred the seat of the Roman Empire to Constantinople in the 4th century AD, he ushered in the age of Byzantine art. As a result, churches were built everywhere, most in the basilican style. The culmination of this style came during the age of Justinian (527-65) when the grandest of his churches, San Vitale, was built at Ravenna, the Byzantine capital of Italy. San Vitale has outstanding mosaics, predominantly in the Byzantine style, and was constructed in the Eastern manner of a dome over a square plan.

The term 'basilica' derives from the Greek

word meaning royal house. The Romans used the term to denote a rectangular public hall, and later a room for the faithful to gather. A basilican church consists of a nave and aisles separated by a colonnade. At the west end may be an entrance hall (anteroom, vestibule or narthex), or an open courtyard with cloisters, or both. At the east end there is usually an apse (the end of a church behind the choir).

In their mosaics, Byzantine artists created sumptuous works comprising tesserae, or small square tiles of stone. These were irregularly cut to catch the light and covered open vaults, walls and cupolas (domed ceilings). Gold was frequently used to reflect the light in the semidarkness of the churches, adding to the air of mystery.

The Byzantine style is well preserved not only in Ravenna but in St Mark's Basilica in Venice, in Sicily (Cefalù, Palermo) and in Rome. The Church of San Clemente in Rome is a 12th century basilica with fine mosaics, particularly the *Crucifixion* and the *Tree of Life* in the apse.

Romanesque & Gothic The medieval Romanesque and Gothic styles of architecture were at their most prominent from the 11th to the 14th centuries. Influenced by both the Orient and religious art in France, Romanesque architecture flourished, particularly in Lombardy, and spread all over northern and central Italy.

The great vaulted churches had exteriors decorated with elaborately carved façades with bands and arcades, and porches supported by lions, and also had detached bell towers. Romanesque churches are character-

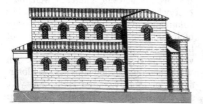

Romanesque basilica

ised by their small, rounded arches resting on massive stone piers. This created a sense of power and weight. Windows were not an option because the weight of the roof would have pushed the walls apart and the church would have collapsed. Not surprisingly, little light penetrates the interiors of such buildings. Romanesque churches also feature typical Romanesque art, which generally took the form of either stylised Byzantine-style images or classical relief sculpture in the stone of the buildings themselves.

Holy Roman Emperor Frederick II's Castel del Monte near Bari in Apulia features an octagonal plan and elements derived from ancient Rome as well as French Gothic. It is regarded as one of the best examples of the Gothic influence on architecture in Europe.

Geometrical decorations based on lozenge configurations and tiers of arcades helped produce a distinctive look for the Pisan style. The Florentine Romanesque style, however, was distinguished by simple lines and the use of white and green marble set alternately on the façades. In southern Italy, influences mingled to produce the Sicilian-Norman style.

Great Italian Romanesque churches include the Cathedral of Pisa, San Miniato in Florence, Sant'Ambrogio in Milan and the cathedral at Massa Marittima in central Tuscany.

The era of the crusades instigated a complete reform in the planning and building of castles. Symmetry as a planning principle was rediscovered and a system of concentric curtain walls with towers at intervals replaced the Norman reliance on architecture for defence of the keep.

Spanning the 12th to 14th centuries, Gothic architecture reached its zenith in the 14th century. The Piedmontese probably invented Gothic vaulting, although its use in Italy was not widespread until the style had been improved and used extensively by the French.

The Gothic style is a combination of pointed arch and flying buttress. Together the buttresses and arches relieved the pressure of the heavy Romanesque wall and allowed the use of the characteristically pointed Gothic window. The cathedrals of Milan and Siena highlight the Gothic style, as does the San Petronio Basilica in Bologna.

Renaissance The Renaissance was a period marked by innovation, a renewed interest in classical works and a rejection of dogmatic religious authority. The Quattrocento or 15th century is the most important in the history of the arts in Italy. During this period many artists of genius emerged, most encouraged by the patronage of the ruling Medici family in Florence.

The two great architects of the early Renaissance are Filippo Brunelleschi (1377-1446) and Leone Battista Alberti (1404-72). Formerly a talented goldsmith and sculptor, Brunelleschi is credited with having designed the first Renaissance building, Florence's Ospedale degli Innocenti. An extraordinary engineer, his place in history was sealed when he designed the first major dome of the Renaissance over the Cathedral of Santa Maria del Fiore in Florence, a beautifully proportioned structure whose design still baffles architects. A traditionalist when it came to building, Brunelleschi derived inspiration from antique sources and exhibited purity and elegance in works such as the Pazzi Chapel, the Church of the Holy Spirit and the San Lorenzo Basilica, all in Florence.

A humanist, poet and theorist, Alberti was the first to place architecture within the context of town planning. He designed the Malatesta Temple in Rimini, and also constructed the churches of San Sebastiano and Sant'Andrea in Mantua and the Rucellai Palace in Florence. The wonderful façade of Florence's Santa Maria Novella church is also his work.

The High Renaissance (about 1490-1520) was dominated by three men known as the triumvirate of the High Renaissance: Leonardo da Vinci (1452-1519), Michelangelo Buonarroti (1475-1564, usually known by his first name), and Raphael (1483-1520).

Da Vinci was a master of many forms – architect, weapons designer, musician, engineer, scientist and artist. He left behind more incomplete projects than finished objects, but still left a legacy of amazing achievements. Michelangelo's designs for St Peter's in Rome elevated Italian architecture to new heights.

Other notable architects working in the 16th century, or Cinquecento, included Bramante (1444-1514) who invented the 'rhythmic bay', a façade composed of alternating windows, pilasters (rectangular columns often attached to a wall) and niches. During this time the style of the Florentine palace emerged with its embossing, ringed columns, curved frontons or pediments and projecting cornices.

A leading figure of this period, Bramante worked in Milan and at the court in Urbino before developing the central plan of St Peter's in Rome. Raphael succeeded as the architect of St Peter's and was followed by Antonio de Sangallo and Michelangelo, who designed the dome while he was completing the city's Farnese Palace.

Andrea Palladio (1508-80) produced his work in the period between the Renaissance and the following Baroque period. He designed many palaces, villas and churches, including the Villa Rotunda at Vicenza and the Church of the Redeemer in Venice. He also composed a series of architectural treatises, Four Books on Architecture, which helped to revive interest in classical Roman architecture. Palladio's work is characterised by the classical, central proportions of his buildings.

Baroque The Baroque style was born as a reaction to the work of the Mannerist period, the art of the Counter-Reformation, which used the principles of the Renaissance but altered them in an extreme or 'mannered' fashion. Governed by irregular contours and generous forms, the Baroque style sought to achieve a combination of the theatrical and picturesque.

Carlo Maderna designed the façade of St Peter's in 1614, while Francesco Borromini (1599-1667) was the most important High-Baroque architect. Borromini revolutionised architectural practice by emphasising the play of space and used light to enhance the effect of illusion.

Rome herself became the Baroque city it predominantly remains today mainly because of the architectural achievements of Gian Lorenzo Bernini (1598-1680), whose work includes the immense colonnade of St Peter's Square. Sculptures such as the central fountain in the Piazza Navona are testament to Bernini's remarkable artistry. Rome's Trevi Fountain (1732) by Nicola Salvi is also one of the great Baroque fountains.

Later Styles The influence of the French led to the decorative Rococo style and the more imposing formalism of neoclassicism which both succeeded Baroque.

Italy's role in the development of architectural styles has continued into the 20th century through the work of the modern and postmodern schools. Architects such as Pier-Luigi Nervi and Gio Ponti were both experts in the use of reinforced concrete and plastics, and Ponti's Pirelli Tower, near Milan's main train station, is regarded as one of Europe's finest skyscrapers. Nervi was responsible for Florence's futurist soccer stadium and the Vatican's Pope Paul VI audience hall.

Mussolini drew on the country's futurist art movement, securing the services of young architects who were happy to oblige the dictator's grandiose plans. His favourite architect, Marcello Piacentini, was responsible for Mussolini's greatest architectural legacy, the huge EUR area in Rome.

Painting & Sculpture

Generally speaking, Italian painting is characterised by soft outlines and light colours which contrast strongly with the formality and spartan qualities of French art and the detailed realism of the Flemish and Germanic nations.

Roman The frescoes taken from the walls of Pompeii are virtually all that remains of Roman painting. As Pompeii was generally regarded as a city of hedonists, the examples tend to reflect the lavish lives of the city's people. The Romans added a vitality and naturalism to the idealised Greek style which preceded them.

The Romans were 'painterly' while the Greeks were 'linear' – they introduced landscape and added depth to the art. Roman sculpture attempted to show the realistic physical appearance of form. Trajan's Column in Rome, dating from the year 106 AD, depicts Trajan's life in a continuous narrative relief. The column is noted for the realism of its elaborate scenes.

Christian, Romanesque & Gothic The adoption of Christianity as the official state religion of the Roman Empire in 323 AD saw the emergence of two styles of art: Early Christian throughout Italy and much of the Western Roman Empire, and Byzantine in the East. The Christians tended to depict the life hereafter and were less concerned with the physical beauty of humans and nature. Byzantine art took the form of mosaics made from small pieces of richly coloured glass and stone. The artists tended not to represent movement or background and depicted a religious awe.

Following the turn of the millennium, Romanesque emerged as the dominant style in Italian art, coming to prominence by the 12th century. Sculpture was essentially religious and decorative, with some French influence. As early as the 12th century, Italian sculptors, unlike the French, were signing their works.

The ability to travel more easily in the late 14th century opened the communication lines between European countries. Italian artists such as Gentile da Fabriano (c 1370-1427) came into close contact with work being carried out in France, the so-called International Gothic, which treated subjects in a more humanistic form even if the style was largely unemotional and decorative.

Andrea Orcagna and Andrea da Firenze were leaders of this period. Da Firenze, also known as Andrea di Bonaiuto, decorated the

Spaniards' Chapel in Santa Maria Novella in Florence and the Camposanto cemetery in Pisa.

While northern Europe was preoccupied with the Gothic movement, artists in central Italy, notably throughout Tuscany, were using a mix of Gothic and Byzantine styles to produce a distinctive, stylised form of painting. Artists such as Duccio di Buoninsegna (c 1255-1318) and Simone Martini (c 1284-1344) were prominent in the Sienese school. Duccio painted profoundly emotional religious subjects in the decorative Byzantine style. Sienese school artists included Taddeo de Bartolo, Sassetta, Giovanni de Paolo and Matteo di Giovanni.

Renaissance By introducing naturalism into his works, Giotto di Bendone (1267-1337), known simply as Giotto, not only revolutionised painting but helped nurture the forces that spawned the Renaissance. Said to have been a shepherd boy, Giotto was discovered by leading Florentine painter Giovanni Cimabue, who worked in St Francis' Basilica in Assisi and later as superintendent of the execution of mosaics at Pisa's cathedral. Guided by Cimabue, Giotto brought passion and poignancy to the heavily formalised themes which had inspired the art of the Gothic world.

Renowned as a humanist, Giotto overturned traditions and challenged the medieval world with his remarkable depictions of human dramas. His most famous frescoes narrating the lives of Mary and Christ are in the Scrovegni Chapel in Padua, a surprisingly modest little building inside what had been a Roman arena. Giotto incorporated movement and light into his work, presenting the viewer with rounded figures who moved in three-dimensional space. His proportions and backgrounds were realistic, and light, atmosphere and emotion were all featured. His *Death of St Francis* in the Bardi Chapel of the Church of Santa Croce, Florence, is another good example of this. Also a sculptor and architect, Giotto was responsible for the exquisitely designed bell tower of the cathedral in Florence.

The 15th and early 16th centuries were a time of unparalleled creativity and visionary accomplishments in all aspects of political, cultural and social life. The Medici family of Florence patronised one of the most remarkable explosions of artistic and literary achievements in recorded history.

It was during the early stages of the Renaissance that artists overcame the problems of perspective, anatomy and movement and began painting their subjects in a realistic, convincing manner. The artist Masaccio (1401-28) was the first to apply to painting the laws of perspective discovered by his contemporary, the architect Brunelleschi. Masaccio used light, shadow and colour with rare skill. Some of his works, including the frescoes in the Brancacci Chapel in Florence's Church of Santa Maria del Carmine, are arguably more dramatic and realistic in their depictions of human drama than Michelangelo was able to accomplish a century later.

Lorenzo Ghiberti (1378-1455), one of the most prominent of the early Renaissance sculptors, drew on Gothic influences to create the magnificent Gates to Paradise, the bronze doors of the Baptistry in Florence. Creating the doors took decades and required the establishment of a workshop for students which eventually produced one of the most influential artists of the 15th century, Donatello (1386-1466).

While revering classical Roman forms, Donatello was an innovator and the first sculptor to give movement to niche statues. His bronze *David* in Florence's Bargello Museum was the first free-standing nude since antiquity. He also cast the first great equestrian statue since Roman times, the *Gattamelata*, which stands in Padua. A close study of anatomy inspired his sculpture and his sculpture in turn inspired realism in subsequent Renaissance painters.

Luca della Robbia, a contemporary of Donatello, specialised in cherubs and developed a new art form in glazed terracotta, which his nephew, Andrea, turned into a commercial industry.

At the end of the Quattrocento (15th century), Florentine school sculptor Andrea del Verrocchio (1435-88) created his famous statue of Bartolomeo Colleoni in Venice.

Preserving the Gothic spirit but adopting the new style, Fra Angelico (1387-1455), a Dominican friar, created altarpieces and frescoes that were fresh, and combined purity of drawing and colour. His *Annunciation* in Cortona's Diocesan Museum and frescoes in Florence's Monastery of St Mark are good examples of his work.

Fra Filippo Lippi (1406-98) displayed a sincere piety combined with pleasing composition and fine quality of drawing. Lippi also taught Sandro Botticelli (1444-1510), who drew on influences of classical art and pagan and Christian subjects and enjoyed the great patronage of the Medicis. His *Birth of Venus* is a seminal work as is his *Spring*, both in Florence's Uffizi Gallery.

Mantegna (1431-1506), the master of the *Dead Christ* now housed in Milan's Brera Gallery, taught his pupils and nurtured his passions for archaeology and anatomy at Mantua.

The Bellini family hailed from Venice, and consisted of Jacopo and his two sons, Gentile and Giovanni. Giovanni Bellini was the brother-in-law of Mantegna and displayed sensitivity and realism in his altarpiece compositions and landscapes.

The Cinquecento (16th century) marked a move away from the religious to the worldly. Da Vinci, Michelangelo and Raphael were the dominant artists of what is known as the High Renaissance.

The patronage of the Medici family helped Michelangelo develop his extraordinary talent. A painter and sculptor of incredible power, the Sistine Chapel is his great achievement in painting. After finishing it, he didn't paint again for 25 years. In sculpture, he bequeathed many great works to the world: his *Pietà* in St Peter's in Rome, the virile *David* in Florence's Accademia Gallery, and *Moses*, a powerful work in Rome's San Pietro in Vincoli. After serving his apprenticeship in Florence, he came to Rome to design the tomb of Pope Julius II.

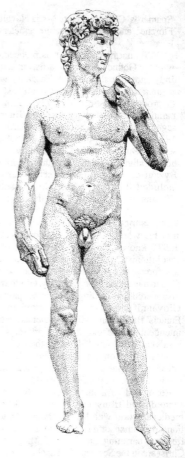

Michelangelo's *David*

He died in Florence after finishing the tombs of the Medicis, in which his genius was allowed free rein.

Da Vinci was nothing if not diverse. His fresco the *Last Supper* in the Vinciano Refectory next to Milan's Church of Santa Maria delle Grazie, is a monumental work. In it, he captures the scene where Christ announces that one of his apostles has betrayed him. The fresco shows the range of emotions – rage, hatred, curiosity, pain – expressed by each.

Da Vinci also set new standards for human proportional definition (helped by his anatomical studies), perfected aerial perspective, and was a virtuoso of *sfumato*, literally 'mist', a technique used to glide from colour to colour. This revolutionised painting in Europe.

Known as the grand master of classicism, Raphael was prolific while striving for technical perfection. His accuracy, attention to detail and brilliant composition laid the foundations of modern painting. He invented the seated three-quarter-length portrait and the group portrait. His frescoes in the Vatican Museum are a must, as is his *Madonna* in Florence's Uffizi Gallery.

Titian (1490-1576), a disciple of Bellini, was equally proficient with mythological or religious compositions and portraiture. His works are dotted around the country, with Venice's Accademia Gallery housing his *Presentation of the Virgin at the Temple.*

Angst-ridden and profound, Tintoretto (1518-94) used light to dramatic effect when working with religious subjects and his more unsettling secular works. *Paradise* in Venice's Doges' Palace is one of his masterpieces and is one of the world's largest paintings.

Baroque Rome was pillaged in 1527 by German and Spanish mercenaries, and the Renaissance ended as a result of political turbulence and instability. The resulting disillusionment contributed to Mannerism, an art movement more concerned with idealised beauty and style rather than the naturalism of the Renaissance. The work of Mannerists – Michelangelo, Tintoretto and others – reflected feelings of tension, discord and violent emotion. Michelangelo's *Last Judgment*, on the altar wall of Rome's Sistine Chapel, is crowded with writhing, agonised figures and is regarded as a reflection of the artist's tortured mind.

Michelangelo da Caravaggio (1573-1610) emerged as Baroque Rome's pre-eminent painter later in the 16th century, a leader of the period which derived from the Counter-Reformation. Defining naturalism as the depiction of nature whether ugly or beautiful, Caravaggio led an outspoken, stormy existence scornful of those who feared ugliness. He invited controversy by framing his subjects with harsh lighting and portraying Christ's Disciples as labouring peasants. His dramatic work is exemplified by *The Descent from the Cross* in the Vatican Museums.

The 18th century was unremarkable except for Tiepolo (1696-1770), who was the last of the great Italian decorative painters. Using a bright palette, he created many vibrant frescoes. His *Virgin In Glory* in the Scuola dei Carmini in Venice displays his talent.

Later Styles Neoclassicism preceded the modern era, marked by the sculptor Canova (1757-1822) and painter Appiani (1754-1817).

Early in the 20th century a group of young, educated Italians formed a movement called futurism. Rebelling against the art of the past and the static nature of cubism, these angry young artists attempted to capture the different phases of movement and discover a new world of art through the mechanical rhythms of machines. Futurism's major artists included Boccioni, Balla, Carra and Severini. Their infatuation with machines led many to join the army during WW I. The movement was brought to an abrupt close in 1920 with the untimely deaths at war of many of the artists.

The two prominent artists of the 20th century are Amedeo Modigliani (1884-1920) and Giorgio de Chirico (1888-1978). Modigliani, a member of a banking family, was fond of women and addicted to drugs and alcohol. These indulgences, combined with tuberculosis and a poverty-stricken life in Paris, killed him at the age of 36. His major works are portraits, featuring characteristically oval faces with elongated necks and sloping shoulders, mostly painted out of Italy.

De Chirico, an Italian artist born in

Greece, was a major influence on the surrealist movement. His eerie streetscapes and unsettling figures – often mysterious, threatening shapes – hovered on the edge of perception or moved in ambiguous space.

Literature

Roman The great Latin poets of antiquity included Virgil, whose *Aeneid* links the founding of Rome with the fall of Troy. Ovid addressed love in his poems, *Amores*, annoyed Emperor Augustus with descriptions of lewd lifestyles in *Ars Amatoria* just after the emperor's daughter had been banished for vice, and wrote about transformation myths in *Metamorphosis*. Horace toed the martial line, Livy chronicled the emergence of the new empire and Julius Caesar recorded his campaigns in Gaul and the disintegration of the Republic.

Cicero took Latin prose to new heights with *Brutus*, and Catullus' love poetry set new standards for passion. Petronius conveyed the decadence of the age of Nero in his *Satyricon*, although only a fragment still exists. The years following the downfall of Nero are detailed in Tacitus' *Histories*, while his *Annales* reveal the astounding court intrigues of the early emperors. Marcus Aurelius' *Meditations* were the musings of the last philosopher-king of the crumbling empire.

Renaissance Literature as an art form disappeared in the Middle Ages, re-emerging during the early Renaissance, in particular with Dante Alighieri (1265-1321), probably the greatest figure in Italian literature. His genius confirmed the Italian vernacular as a serious medium for poetic expression with works such as the *Divina Commedia* (Divine Comedy). His Latin work *De Monarchia* reflects his personal preference for a return of imperial power and his vision for a world where pope and emperor provided complementary reigns.

Another great poet of this time was Petrarch (Francesco Petrarca, 1304-74), the son of a lawyer exiled from Florence at the same time as Dante. Petrarch was crowned poet laureate in Rome in 1341 after earning a reputation throughout Europe as a classical scholar. His epic poem, *Africa*, and the wonderful sonnets of his *Il Canzoniere* exemplify Petrarch as a great lyricist, one who has had a permanent influence on Italian poetry. His talent for self-examination in an individual, personal style was unprecedented in medieval literature.

Dante and Petrarch were two members of a triumvirate completed by Giovanni Boccaccio (1313-75), author of the *Decameron*, 100 short stories ranging from the bawdy to the earnest in chronicling the exodus of 10 young Florentines from their plague-ridden city. Boccaccio is considered the first Italian novelist.

The 15th century produced several treatises on architecture and politics, while serious study of the Greek and more 'modern' Hebrew and Arabic scholars highlighted the literary works of the later 15th century. Marsilio Ficino (1433-99) founded the Platonic Academy in Florence under the patronage of Lorenzo de' Medici. Ficino, although a devout Christian, successfully reconciled the philosophy of Plato with Christianity, and his translation of Plato into Latin gave Western Europe its first full expo-

Pico della Mirandola

sure to the ancient philosopher's great insights into human behaviour and values.

The genius of Ficino's young friend Pico della Mirandola (1463-94) marked one of the great turning points for Renaissance humanism. Pico believed that a grain of truth could be extracted from every system of thought or creed, but the result of the extractions in his case was an immense respect for the place of man in the universe, as evidenced by his famous *Oration on the Dignity of Man*.

The single greatest boost for Renaissance humanism and the widespread debates it inspired was the advent of movable-type printing, which was developed on a commercial scale in Italy, specifically in Venice. Aldo Manuzio (c 1450-1515) flooded the market with Greek classics from his famous Aldine Press in Venice and formed a Greek Academy which published many great scholars. Manuzio introduced italic type in 1501 and also the octavo, which was half the size of a standard quarto page and more suitable for printed books.

In contrast to the mood of the times, Machiavelli's *The Prince* was the first purely secular political work and the most lasting of the Renaissance. Surprisingly for many, Machiavelli (1469-1527) was also the Renaissance's finest playwright.

Michelangelo wrote many sonnets, da Vinci wrote about everything and even Lorenzo de' Medici penned hundreds of poems and songs while ruling Florence.

Giorgio Vasari (1511-74), an architect and painter, was regarded as the first biographer with his *Lives of the Most Excellent Italian Architects, Painters & Sculptors*, a chronicle of the Renaissance's most important figures and one of the most important records of the period.

Later Authors The birth of the modern Italian novel was marked by *I Promessi Sposi* (The Betrothed) by Alessandro Manzoni (1785-1873). Italy was part of the innovative literary explosion of the 20th century in both prose and poetry. The flamboyant escapades of Gabriele d'Annunzio (1863-1938) enhanced his eccentric verse,

while Salvatore Quasimodo, Eugenio Montale and Giuseppe Ungaretti all earned Nobel Prizes for literature after WW II. The novelist Alberto Moravia (1907-90) describes the doings of the bourgeoisie and working people of Rome, while Curzio Malaparte (1898-1957) concentrates on Neapolitans and Tuscans.

One of Italy's most famous modern writers was the Sicilian playwright, Luigi Pirandello (1867-1936). His original style highlighted the crisis in human values and ideals of his time. He was awarded the Nobel Prize for Literature in 1934.

Sicily also produced Giuseppe Tomasi di Lampedusa (1896-1957), who wrote *The Leopard*, based on the struggles of a minor prince trying to retain his holdings in the time of Garibaldi, later filmed by Luchino Visconti.

Recently, Umberto Eco (1932-) wrote the popular *The Name of the Rose*, which was also filmed. He also wrote the obscure *Foucault's Pendulum*.

Music

The Italians have played a pivotal role in the history of music: they invented the system of musical notation in use today; a 16th century Venetian printed the first musical scores with movable type; Cremona produced violins by Stradivari and others; and Italy is the birthplace of the piano.

The 16th century brought a musical revolution with the development of opera, which began as an attempt to recreate the drama of ancient Greece. The first successful opera composer, Claudio Monteverdi (c 1567-1643), drew freely from a variety of sources.

In the 17th and early 18th centuries, instrumental music began to establish itself, helped by the concertos of Arcangelo Corelli (1653-1713) and Antonio Vivaldi (c 1675-1741). Vivaldi, whose best known work is *The Four Seasons*, gave us the concerto in its present form while he was teaching in an orphanage in Venice. Domenico Scarlatti (1685-1757) wrote more than 500 sonatas for harpsichord, and Giovanni Battista

Sammartini (1700-75) experimented with, and developed, the symphony.

Verdi, Puccini, Bellini, Donizetti and Rossini, composers from the 19th and early 20th centuries, are all stars of the modern operatic era. Giuseppe Verdi (1813-1901) was an icon midway through his life and his achievements include *Aida* and one of the most popular operas of all, *La Traviata*. Rossini's *Barber of Seville* is an enduring favourite with a lively score, and *Madame Butterfly*'s angelic music ensures Puccini a firm place in musical history.

The composer Gian Carlo Menotti (1911-) is also famed for creating the Spoleto Festival of Two Worlds at Spoleto in Umbria.

The opera season in Italy runs from December to June. The country's premier opera theatres include La Scala in Milan, San Carlo in Naples, the Teatro dell'Opera in Rome and La Fenice in Venice. Tenor Luciano Pavarotti (1935-) is the current luminary of the Italian operatic world.

Modern Italian music is mostly disappointing, unless you find eurodisco alluring. The country's main pop stars look uncomfortably like parodies of their US and UK counterparts. The 1960s produced the fabulous Mina, an exceptional female vocalist, while the 1970s and 1980s have been largely bereft of international-standard talent.

Film

Italian film stars include the likes of Marcello Mastroianni, who starred in *La Dolce Vita* and countless other films; Anna Magnani, who won an Academy Award for *The Rose Tattoo*; Gina Lollobrigida *(Go Naked in the World* and *Come September)*; and, of course, Sophia Loren, whose films include *It Started In Naples*, *Houseboat* and *Boy On a Dolphin*.

Born in Turin in 1904, the Italian film industry originally made an impression with silent spectaculars. By 1930 it was virtually bankrupt and Mussolini attempted to nationalise the industry. With the fall of Fascism, a new generation of film-makers were free to express themselves. Neorealist cinema

(1943-50) favoured location shoots and authentic emotions verging on the raw, with directors such as Luchino Visconti and Roberto Rossellini having a huge effect on international cinema. Vittorio de Sica's 1949 masterpiece, *Bicycle Thieves*, is a touching yet simple tale which helped usher in the modern age of film-making.

Leaders in the period following neorealism include Federico Fellini, who made *La Dolce Vita*, *Roma* and *Ginger & Fred*; and Michelangelo Antonioni, whose best work includes *Blow-Up*.

Incurring the ire of feminists in 1974 with her best known work, *Swept Away*, was Lina Wertmuller, while Bernardo Bertolucci won Academy Awards for *The Last Emperor* and filmed Marlon Brando's steamiest scenes in *Last Tango in Paris*. The Taviani brothers came to prominence in the 1980s, and a recent hit was Giuseppe Tornatore's *Cinema Paradiso*.

CULTURE

It is difficult to define Italian culture, except by resorting to stereotypes, basically because Italians have lived together as one nation for little over 100 years. Prior to unification, the inhabitants of the Italian peninsula were subject to a variety of masters – kings, popes, colonisers and conquerors – and cultures, who in different periods influenced different areas of the peninsula. Consequently, the people absorbed and adapted a diverse range of cultural influences, while maintaining their own dialects, traditions, customs and practices. Even after unification, it was not until the advent of TV that all Italians began to speak standard Italian. Previously it was not unusual to find farmers and villagers who spoke only their local dialect.

While there exists a national identity and a sense of *patria* (homeland), it is more likely to find its expression in a sense of pride at a World Cup soccer match than in a form of patriotism similar to the American or German style.

Regionalism remains a strong force in Italy and you will find that people identify far more strongly with their region, even their town, than with the concept of nationality. A person is therefore 'Apulian', 'Sicilian' or 'Tuscan' before they are Italian – and certainly their dialect, accent and even their culinary traditions define their own cultures. Others maintain an even further localised identity, being first and foremost Romano, Bolognese, Fiorentino or Napoletano.

But you can be sure that, confronted with a foreigner, Italians will know how to energetically defend their national identity – revealing a national pride that is difficult to detect in the relationship Italians have with each other.

Stereotypes

Foreigners may like to think of Italians as a land of passionate, animated people who gesticulate wildly when speaking, love to eat, drive like maniacs and don't like to work. However, it will take more than a holiday in Italy to understand its vigorous and remarkably diverse inhabitants.

An Italian journalist recently defined his compatriots as a hard-working, resilient and resourceful people, who are optimistic and have a good sense of humour. If there is a national stereotype, this is probably closer to the truth. They are also passionately loyal to their friends and families. The same journalist noted that these were all-important qualities, since 'a happy private life helps people tolerate an appalling public life'.

Italians in general have a strong distrust of authority and, as Italian writer Luigi Barzini observed, when confronted with a silly rule, an unjust law or a stupid order, they don't complain, nor do they try to change it, they simply ignore it and try to find the quickest route around the obstacle.

Complexities

Barzini also wrote that without seeing Sicily one could not get a clear idea of what Italy was. He observed that the Sicilians' best virtues, like those of most Italians, were obviously not those of the anonymous organisation person of today, but those of ancient heroes fighting, with their little

group, against the rest of the world. If most Italians manage at times to weave skilfully in and out of written laws, most Sicilians appear to avoid them completely. They are the supreme masters of this skill, recognised by all Italians as the unbeatable champions.

The most significant lesson for modern political and social history, a lesson epitomised in 'the Italian experience', is that real change can only be wrought if it takes with it the hearts and minds of the people involved. That this has not been the case so far in Italy is obvious in the instability that has marked Italian governance since the Allies restored the democratic republic after WW II: there have been more governments than years passed. Yet Italy was a founding member of the European Economic Community, with the first official documentation that led to its establishment, the Treaty of Rome, being signed in that city in 1957.

One way to understand Italians and the Italy they share is to witness the commonalities of these community-bound people who relish their differences. One clue lies in the nation's reputation for supporting a plethora of administrative rules, regulations and bureaucrats governing every aspect of daily life, producing bylaws which almost strive to anticipate the unexpected. It is not regarded as strange by Italians that many of these laws and regulations are never enforced or, at the very least, are simple to avoid.

Family

In the end, the most important unit for the Italian is not country, state, region, town or even church, but the family. Unlike in the UK, Australia and the USA, most young Italians tend to remain in the family home until they marry. In 1988 only 14% of Italians under the age of 25 lived away from home, although a lack of affordable housing for young singles is a major contributing factor.

Modern attitudes and practices have eroded the traditional institution of family to some extent. Statistics show that one in three married couples have no children and one in nine children is born out of wedlock. In Milan, more than one-third of families are headed by a single parent and two-thirds of these are headed by a woman. Nevertheless, the family remains an important focus for the average Italian.

Avoiding Offence

Italians tend to be very tolerant people, mainly concerned with their private lives, and are generally reluctant to become involved in other people's business (not surprising, since not minding your own business could prove fatal in the Mafia-afflicted south of the country).

Italians do have some tendency towards prudishness. This might seem strange, since every second billboard and TV advertisement uses semi-naked women to promote anything from laxatives to cars, and in public parks and parked cars you will find it difficult not to notice young couples engaged in physical activities that could have them arrested in another country.

On the other hand, if you walk around the streets of the Lido in Venice wearing only a bikini, you will be fined. And don't expect to be allowed into churches if you are wearing a miniskirt or shorts – in some churches you will be kicked out if you have bare arms. Churches which are major tourist attractions, such as St Peter's in Rome and St Francis' in Assisi, are extremely strict in their enforcement of dress rules. Remember that churches are also places of worship, so if you want to visit one during a service, try to be as inconspicuous as possible.

In some parts of Italy, particularly in the south, women will be harassed if they wear skimpy or see-through clothing – in fact, one female traveller reported that she was hissed at, jeered and spat on by locals when she arrived in Assisi wearing a tight miniskirt.

Beach-goers will be likely to cause grave offence if they choose to sunbathe nude or topless (if a woman) at beaches where no Italians are doing so. It is very common for women in Italy to sunbathe topless, but it is always best to check that you will not be alone before removing your own top.

You might find yourself in serious trouble if you offend a member of the police force in Italy. The police and carabinieri (see the Police section under Dangers & Annoyances in the Facts for the Visitor chapter) have the right to arrest you for 'insulting a state official' if they believe you have been rude or offensive to them.

RELIGION

Some 85% of Italians professed to be Catholic in a census taken in the early 1980s. Of the remaining 15%, there were about 500,000 evangelical Protestants, about 140,000 Jehovah's Witnesses, and other, small groups, including a Jewish community in Rome and the Waldenses (Valdesi) – Swiss-Protestant Baptists living in small communities in Piedmont. There are also communities of orange-clad followers of Bhagwan Rajneesh, known in Italy as the *arancioni*.

Strangely enough, while so many Italians are Catholic and the fabric of Italian life is so profoundly affected by Christian values, few Italians practise their religion. Church attendance is low – an average of only 25% attend Mass regularly – and many children are never baptised. But first communion remains a popular event, the majority of Italian couples prefer to be married in a church, and religious festivals never fail to attract a large turnout. Italians are also very well acquainted with the saints and keenly follow the activities of the pope.

Commitment to the church also depends on which part of the country you come from. One could perhaps generalise that southerners are more pious than the people of the more left-wing regions of Umbria and Emilia-Romagna.

THE MAFIA

It is quite an understatement to note that the Mafia knows no limits, but in Italy it is a reality which has led all to question just who runs the country – the government or the Mafia? And that is not an easy question to answer. As a journalist noted recently, 'Everyone knows that the Mafia and the establishment are intertwined, and that this marriage is one of the pillars of political life in Italy. The Mafia is not only omnipotent, it is omnipresent.'

In Italy, the term 'Mafia' can be used to describe five distinct organised crime groups: the original Sicilian Mafia, also known as the Cosa Nostra; the Calabrian 'Ndrangheta; the Camorra of Naples; and two relatively new organisations, the Sacra Corona Unita (United Holy Crown) and La Rosa (the Rose) in Apulia. These groups operate both separately and together.

At a 1989 meeting in Nice, the Sicilian Mafia, the 'Ndrangheta and the Camorra met with representatives of the Colombian and Venezuelan drug cartels and carved up the world's heroin and cocaine markets. The Sicilians retained the heroin trade, with the Calabrians taking on an important role, and the Camorra emerged as the white-powder specialists.

By the early 1990s, the combined estimated worth of the Italian mafia groups was around L100,000 billion, or about 12% of GNP, and the EC shudders at the prospect of Mafia money being laundered legitimately across the community as borders break down.

Cosa Nostra

The Sicilian Mafia has its roots in the oppression of the Sicilian people and can claim a history extending back to the 13th century. Its complex system of justice is based on the code of silence known as *omertà*. Mussolini managed to virtually wipe out the Mafia, but from the devastation of WW II grew the modern version of the organisation, known as Cosa Nostra, which has spread its tentacles worldwide and is far more ruthless and powerful than its predecessor. It is involved in drug-trafficking and arms deals, as well as finance, construction and tourist development, not to forget public-sector projects and Italian politics. Few Italians doubt the claim that the Mafia's tentacles extend into almost every part of the country, and well beyond.

The early 1990s saw a virtual firestorm of Mafia violence in Sicily, seen by many as a push by the Cosa Nostra to once and for all wipe out its opposition. Two anti-Mafia judges were assassinated in Palermo in separate bomb blasts, and the murders were interpreted as messages from the Mafia that it could kill with impunity. The assassinations, however, had a reverse effect, as the Italian government, long lethargic and even reluctant in its efforts to combat the Cosa Nostra, was finally moved to take action.

One early result of this newly found, feverish anti-Mafia activity was the arrest of Salvatore 'Toto' Riina, the Sicilian godfather. Riina, head of the powerful Corleonese clan, had been the world's most wanted man since 1969. When he was arrested, it was discovered that he had never left Sicily and had, in fact, been living in the centre of Palermo with his family.

'Ndrangheta

Until the late 1980s, the 'Ndrangheta was a disorganised group of bandits and kidnappers; today it controls an organised crime network specialising in arms and drug-dealing, as well as construction. In the 1970s, oil heir J Paul Getty III was kidnapped and held by the 'Ndrangheta, having his ear severed before his release. The organisation continues to kidnap for profit. With its base in the villages of Calabria, the 'Ndrangheta is notorious for its savage, raw violence: in the early 1990s there was an average of one execution every day.

Camorra

This secret society grew to power in Naples in the 19th century. It was all but wiped out by severe repressive measures around the turn of the century, but managed to survive and enjoyed a renaissance in the post-WW II period, dealing mainly in contraband cigarettes. It took great advantage of the funds which poured into the region after the devastating 1980 earthquake, diverting hundreds of millions of dollars meant for reconstruction projects to build an organised empire which has diversified into drugs, construction, finance and tourist developments. It has worked closely with the Sicilian Mafia.

Sacra Corona Unita & La Rosa

Apulia had managed to escape the clutches of the organised crime groups which had terrorised the rest of the south, but by the late 1980s the Mafia had arrived in the form of the Sacra Corona Unita in the south of the region and La Rosa in the north. As a natural gateway to Eastern Europe through its main ports of Bari and Brindisi, Apulia was a natural target following the collapse of communism. Apulia has quickly supplanted Naples as a base for the Mafia's smuggling activities, chiefly in contraband cigarettes, and an early consequence of its activities has been a massive upsurge in the number of heroin addicts in the cities of Bari, Brindisi and Taranto.

LANGUAGE

Although many Italians speak some English because they study it in school, English is more widely understood in the north, particularly in major centres such as Milan, Florence and Venice, than in the south. Staff at most hotels, pensioni and restaurants usually speak a little English, but you will be better received if you at least attempt to communicate in Italian.

Italian is a Romance language which is related to French, Spanish, Portuguese and Romanian. The Romance languages belong to the Indo-European group of languages, which include English. Indeed, as English and Italian share common roots in Latin, you will find many Italian words which you will recognise.

Modern literary Italian began to develop in the 13th and 14th centuries, predominantly through the works of Dante, Petrarch and Boccaccio, who wrote chiefly in the Florentine dialect. The language drew on its Latin heritage and the many dialects of Italy to develop into the standard Italian of today. Although many and varied dialects are spoken in everyday conversation, standard Italian is the national language of schools,

media and literature, and is understood throughout the country.

There are 58 million speakers of Italian in Italy; half a million in Switzerland, where Italian is one of the four official languages; and 1.5 million speakers in France, Slovenia and Croatia. As a result of migration, Italian is also ·videly spoken in the USA, Argentina, Brazil and Australia.

Visitors to Italy with more than the most fundamental grasp of the language need to be aware that many older Italians still expect to be addressed by the third person formal, ie *lei* instead of *tu*. Also, it is not considered polite to use the greeting *ciao* when addressing strangers, unless they use it first; it's better to say *buongiorno* (or *buonasera*, as the case may be) and *arrivederci* (or the more polite form, *arrivederla*).

Note that we have included a Food Vocabulary in the Food section of the Facts for the Visitor chapter.

Pronunciation

Italian is not difficult to pronounce once you learn a few easy rules. Although some of the more clipped vowels, and stress on double letters, require careful practice for English speakers, it is easy enough to make yourself understood.

Vowels Vowels are generally more clipped than in English.

a   as the second 'a' in 'camera'
e   as the 'ay' in 'day', but without the 'i' sound
i   as in 'see'
o   as in 'dot'
u   as in 'too'

Consonants The pronunciation of many Italian consonants is similar to that of English. The following sounds depend on certain rules:

c   like 'k' before 'a', 'o' and 'u'. Like the 'ch' in 'choose' before 'e' and 'i'
ch a hard 'k' sound

g a hard 'g' as in 'get' before 'a', 'o' and 'u'. Before 'e' and 'i', like the 'j' in 'job'
gh a hard 'g' as in 'get'
gli as the 'lli' in 'million'
gn as the 'ny' in 'canyon'
h always silent
r a rolled 'rrr' sound
sc before 'e' and 'i', like the 'sh' in 'sheep'. Before 'h', 'a', 'o' and 'u', a hard sound as in 'school'
z as the 'ts' in 'lights' or as the 'ds' in 'beds'

Note that when 'ci', 'gi' and 'sci' are followed by 'a', 'o' or 'u', unless the accent falls on the 'i', the 'i' is not pronounced. Thus the name 'Giovanni' is pronounced *'joh-vahn-nee'*, with no 'i' sound after the 'G'.

Stress Double consonants are pronounced as a longer, often more forceful sound than a single consonant.

Stress often falls on the next-to-last syllable, as in *spa-**ghet**-ti*. When a word has an accent, the stress is on that syllable, as in *cit-**tà**,* 'city'.

Essentials

Please write it down.	*Può scriverlo, per favore?*
Can you show me (on the map)?	*Me lo puo mostrare (sulla carta/pianta)?*
I (don't) understand.	*(Non) Capisco.*
Do you speak English?	*Parla (Parli) inglese?*
Does anyone speak English?	*C'è qualcuno che parla inglese?*
Where are you from?	*Di dove viene? Di dove sei?*
I am from …	*Sono da … Vengo da …*
How old are you?	*Quanti anni ha (hai)?*
I am … years old.	*Ho … anni.*
Just a minute.	*Un momento.*
How much is it?	*Quanto costa?*

name	*nome*
date of birth	*data di nascita*
place of birth	*luogo di nascita*
sex (gender)	*sesso*
nationality	*nazionalità*
passport	*passaporto*
visa	*visto consolare*

Greetings & Civilities

Hello.	*Buon giorno/Ciao.*
Goodbye.	*Arrivederci/Ciao.*
Yes/No.	*Sì/No.*
Please.	*Per favore/Per piacere.*
Thank you.	*Grazie.*
That's fine/You're welcome.	*Prego.*
Excuse me.	*Mi scusi.*
Sorry (excuse me, forgive me).	*Mi scusi. Mi perdoni.*

Small Talk

What is your name?	*Come si chiama?* (formal) *Comé ti chiami?* (informal)
My name is …	*Mi chiamo …*
Are you married?	*È sposata/o lei?*
I am single. I am married.	*(Non) sono sposata/o.*
I (don't) like …	*(Non) Mi piace …*
Just a minute.	*Un minuto.*
How do you say …?	*Come si dice …?*
What does … mean?	*Che vuole dire …?*

Getting Around

What time does … leave/arrive?	*A che ora parte/arriva …?*
the boat	*la barca*
the bus	*l'autobus*
the train	*il treno*
the first	*il primo*
the last	*l'ultimo*
I would like …	*Vorrei …*
a one-way ticket	*(un biglietto di) solo andata/un biglietto semplice*

a return ticket	*(un biglietto di) andata e ritorno*
1st class	*prima classe*
2nd class	*seconda classe*
platform No	*binario no.*
station	*stazione*
ticket office	*biglietteria*
timetable	*orario*
train station	*stazione FS (Ferrovie dello Stato)*
I want to go to ...	*Voglio andare a ...*
I'd like to rent a car.	*Vorrei noleggiare una macchina.*
The train is cancelled/delayed.	*Il treno è cancellato/in ritardo.*

Directions

Where is ...?	*Dov'è ...?*
Go straight ahead.	*Si va/Vai sempre diritto.*
Turn left ...	*Gira a sinistra ...*
Turn right ...	*Gira a destra ...*
at the next corner.	*al prossimo angolo/all'angolo più vicino.*
at the traffic lights.	*al semaforo*
behind/in front of	*dietro/davanti*
far/near	*lontano/vicino*
opposite	*di fronte a*

Useful Signs

Camping Ground	*Campeggio*
Youth Hostel	*Ostello per la Gioventù*
Entrance	*Ingresso/ Entrata*
Exit	*Uscita*
Full/No Vacancies	*Completo*
Guesthouse	*Pensione*
Hotel	*Albergo*
Information	*Informazione*
No Smoking	*Vietato Fumare*
Open/Closed	*Aperto/Chiuso*
Police	*Polizia/Carabinieri*
Police Station	*Questura*
Telephone	*Telefono*

Toilets	*Gabinetti/Bagni*

Around Town

I'm looking for ...	*Sto cercando ...*
a bank	*un banco*
the church	*la chiesa*
the city centre	*il centro (città)*
the ... embassy	*l'ambasciata di...*
my hotel	*il mio albergo*
the market	*il mercato*
the museum	*il museo*
the post office	*la posta*
a public toilet	*un gabinetto/ bagno pubblico*
the telephone centre	*il centro telefonico/SIP*
the tourist information office	*l'ufficio di turismo/ d'informazione*
I want to exchange some money/ travellers' cheques.	*Voglio cambiare del denaro/degli assegni per viaggiatori*
beach	*la spiaggia*
bridge	*il ponte*
castle	*il castello*
cathedral	*il duomo/la cattedrale*
church	*la chiesa*
island	*l'isola*
main square	*la piazza principale*
market	*il mercato*
mosque	*la moschea*
old city	*il centro storico*
palace	*il palazzo*
ruins	*le rovine*
sea	*il mare*
square	*la piazza*
tower	*il torre*

Accommodation

Where is a cheap hotel?	*Dov'è un albergo che costa poco?*
What is the address?	*Cos'è l'indirizzo?*

Could you write the address, please?	*Può scrivere l'indirizzo, per favore?*	It's cheap.	*Non è caro/a.*
		It's too expensive.	*È troppo caro/a.*
Do you have any rooms available?	*Ha camere libere?/ C'è una camera libera?*	small	*piccolo/a*
		big	*grande*
		more	*più*
		less	*meno*
I would like ...	*Vorrei ...*		
a single room	*una camera singola*	**Time & Dates**	
		What time is it?	*Che ora è? Che ore sono?*
a double room	*una camera matrimoniale (double bed)/ doppia (two single beds)*	It is ...	*Sono le ...*
		in the morning	*di mattina*
		in the afternoon	*di pomeriggio*
a room with a bathroom	*una camera con bagno*	in the evening	*di sera*
to share a dorm	*un letto in dormitorio*	today	*oggi*
		tomorrow	*domani*
a bed	*un letto*	yesterday	*ieri*
How much is it per night/per person?	*Quanto costa per la notte/ciascuno?*	Monday	*lunedì*
		Tuesday	*martedì*
Can I see it?	*Posso vederla?*	Wednesday	*mercoledì*
Where is the bathroom?	*Dov'è il bagno?*	Thursday	*giovedì*
		Friday	*venerdì*
		Saturday	*sabato*
		Sunday	*domenica*
Food			
breakfast	*prima colazione*	January	*gennaio*
lunch	*pranzo/colazione*	February	*febbraio*
dinner	*cena*	March	*marzo*
		April	*aprile*
I would like the set lunch.	*Vorrei il menu turistico.*	May	*maggio*
		June	*giugno*
Is service included in the bill?	*È compreso il servizio?*	July	*luglio*
		August	*agosto*
I am a vegetarian.	*Sono vegetariano/a. Non mangio carne.*	September	*settembre*
		October	*ottobre*
		November	*novembre*
Shopping		December	*dicembre*
I would like to buy...	*Vorrei comprare ...*		
I don't like it.	*Non mi piace.*	**Numbers**	
Can I look at it?	*Posso dare un'occhiata?*	0	*zero*
		1	*uno*
I'm just looking.	*(Sto) Solo guardando.*	2	*due*
		3	*tre*
		4	*quattro*
Do you accept credit cards?	*Accetta carte di credito?*	5	*cinque*
		6	*sei*

7	sette
8	otto
9	nove
10	dieci
11	undici
12	dodici
13	tredici
14	quattordici
15	quindici
16	sedici
17	diciassette
18	diciotto
19	diciannove
20	venti
21	ventuno
22	ventidue
30	trenta
40	quaranta
50	cinquanta
60	sessanta
70	settanta
80	ottanta
90	novanta
100	cento
1000	mille
one million	un milione

Health

I'm ...	Sono ...
diabetic	diabetico/a
epileptic	epilettico/a
asthmatic	asmatico/a
I'm allergic ...	Sono allergico/a ...
to antibiotics	agli antibiotici
to penicillin	alla penicillina
antiseptic	antisettico
aspirin	aspirina
condoms	preservativi
contraceptive	anticoncezionale
diarrhoea	diarrea
medicine	medicina
sunblock cream	crema/latte solare
	(per protezione)
tampons	tamponi

Emergencies

Help!	Aiuto!
Call a doctor!	Chiama un dottore/un medico!
Call the police!	Chiama la polizia!
Go away!	Vai via! (informal)
	Mi lasci in pace! (formal)

Facts for the Visitor

VISAS & EMBASSIES

Residents of the USA, Australia, Canada and New Zealand are not required to apply for visas before arriving in Italy, if they are entering the country as tourists only. (Citizens of the UK and other member countries of the European Community are subject to different regulations – see the separate EC Citizens section.) At the point of entry to Italy, residents of the above countries should have their passports stamped with an automatic three-month tourist visa. However, Italian border authorities have adopted the habit of rarely stamping the passports of visitors from Western nations. Even when specifically asked to stamp a passport with the three-month visa they will often remain reluctant to do so. The open-border policy introduced between EC countries in January 1993 may make it almost impossible to procure a stamp if you're coming overland from France or by boat from Greece or Corsica.

But if you are entering Italy for any reason other than tourism (for instance, study), or if you plan to remain in the country for an extended period, you should insist on having the visa stamp. Without it you could encounter problems when trying to obtain a *permesso di soggiorno* (see the separate section on this), which is essential for everything from enrolling at a language school to applying for residency in Italy.

While it is theoretically possible to officially extend a tourist visa in Italy, extensions are rarely granted in practice. In any case it would be extremely unlikely that a tourist would encounter any problems with police or border guards if they happened to remain in Italy for longer than three months. Since the border guard probably didn't stamp your passport when you originally entered Italy, there is, in fact, no way of determining exactly how long you have been in the country anyway.

Tourists wanting to play it safe might find it easier to go to the nearest border post and ask for a new stamp in their passport.

Study Visas

Foreigners who want to study at a university in Italy must have a study visa. Australians and New Zealanders also require a visa to study at a language school (citizens of the USA, Canada and EC countries do not need visas for this). These visas can be obtained from your nearest Italian embassy or consulate. It should be noted that you will normally require confirmation of your enrolment before a visa will be issued and the visa will then cover only the period of the enrolment. This type of visa is renewable within Italy, but again only with confirmation of ongoing enrolment and with proof that you are able to support yourself financially, such as a photocopy of your bank statement.

Work Permits

Non-EC citizens wishing to work in Italy will need to obtain a work permit *(permesso di lavoro)* in their own country. In order to qualify for a work permit they will need to have the promise of work from an employer for a position which could not be filled by an Italian.

A person with a genuine offer of work from an Italian company should ensure that the prospective employer organises the work permit. It is advisable to seek detailed information from an Italian embassy or consulate on the exact requirements before attempting to organise a legitimate job in Italy. Many foreigners, however, don't bother with such formalities, preferring to work 'black' in areas such as English-teaching, bar work and seasonal work. See the section on Work later in this chapter.

Permesso di Soggiorno

Within eight days of arriving in Italy all foreign visitors (including EC citizens) are technically required to report to a *questura* (police headquarters) to obtain a permesso di soggiorno – in effect, permission to remain in the country for a nominated period.

If you are staying in hotels, you need not bother because the hotel proprietor is responsible for registering your details with the police. People planning to stay for more than one week in private accommodation are technically required to report to the police and obtain a permesso di soggiorno. Few tourists bother (generally because they are unaware of the requirement to do so) and, in fact, it is really not necessary if you are a genuine tourist.

Obtaining a permesso di soggiorno only becomes a necessity if you plan to study, work or live in Italy. You can't live without one if you fit into any of these categories. Obtaining one is never a pleasant experience. It involves enduring long queues, rude police officers and the frustration of arriving at the counter (after a two-hour wait) to find that you don't have all the necessary documents.

The exact requirements, such as documents and official stamps (*marche da bollo*), vary from city to city. In general you will need a valid passport, containing a visa stamp indicating your date of entry into Italy (or a visa issued in your own country), four passport-style photographs and proof of your ability to support yourself financially.

It is best to go to the questura to obtain precise information on what is required. Sometimes there is a list posted, otherwise you will need to join a queue at the information counter.

The Rome questura, in Via Genova, is notorious and best avoided if possible. A group of young Australians living in Rome reported that they managed to get their permits only after three mornings of queueing from 4 am.

EC Citizens

Citizens of EC countries require only a passport or national identity card to stay in Italy for as long as they like. Danish, Irish and UK citizens need a valid passport, while for others it may be expired up to a maximum of five years. UK citizens may also use a British Visitor's Passport.

Legally EC nationals are required to obtain a permesso di soggiorno if they want to work. While EC citizens are legally allowed to work in Italy, they still need a letter from an employer promising a job. See the section on Work later in this chapter.

Italian Consulates & Embassies

The following is a selection of Italian diplomatic missions abroad:

Australia
    61-69 Macquarie St, Sydney (☎ 02-247 8442)
    34 Anderson St, South Yarra, Melbourne (☎ 03-867 5744)
Canada
    136 Beverley St, Toronto (☎ 416-977 1566)
    3489 Drummond St, Montreal (☎ 514-849 8351)
Croatia
    Meduliceva ulica 22, 41000 Zagreb (☎ 041-27 7857)
France
    47 Rue de Varennes, 73343 Paris (☎ 1-45.44.38.90)
Germany
    Karl Finkelnburgstrasse 49-51, 5300 Bonn 2 (☎ 0228-82 00 60)
Greece
    Odos Sekeri 2, Athens 106 74 (☎ 01-36 11 722)
New Zealand
    34 Grant Rd, Thorndon, Wellington (☎ 04-729 302)
Slovenia
    Snezniska ulica 8, 61000 Ljubljana (☎ 061-21 4814)
Switzerland
    Elfenstrasse 14, 3006 Bern (☎ 031-44 41 51)
Tunisia
    3 Rue de Russie, 1002 Tunis (☎ 01-34 1811)
UK
    38 Eaton Place, London (☎ 071-235 9371)
USA
    12400 Wilshire Blvd, West Los Angeles (☎ 213-820 0622)
    690 Park Ave, New York (☎ 212-737 9100)
    2590 Webster St, San Francisco (☎ 415-931 4925)

Foreign Diplomatic Missions in Italy

Foreign embassies are all based in Rome, although there are generally British and US consulates in other major cities. The following addresses and phone numbers are for Rome (telephone code 06):

Australia
    Via Alessandria 215 (☎ 85 27 21)
Austria
    Via Pergolesi 3 (☎ 855 82 41)
    Consulate: Viale Liegi 32 (☎ 844 35 29)
Canada
    Via G B de Rossi 27 (☎ 841 53 41)
    Consulate: Via Zara 30 (☎ 440 30 28)
Croatia
    Via SS Cosma e Damiano 26 (☎ 33 25 02 42)
France
    Palazzo Farnese (☎ 68 60 11)
    Visas at Via Giulia 251 (☎ 654 21 52)
Germany
    Via Po 25c (☎ 88 47 41)
    Consulate: Via Francesco Siacci 2 (☎ 88 47 42 86)
Greece
    Via Mercadante 36 (☎ 855 31 00)
    Consulate: Via Tacchini 6 (☎ 808 20 30)
Netherlands
    Via Michele Mercati 8 (☎ 322 11 41)
New Zealand
    Via Zara 28 (☎ 440 29 28)
Slovenia
    Via L Pisano 10 (☎ 808 10 75)
Spain
    Largo Fontanella Borghese 19 (☎ 687 81 72)
Switzerland
    Via Barnarba Oriani 61 (☎ 808 36 41)
Tunisia
    Via Asmara 5-7 (☎ 860 30 60)
UK
    Via XX Settembre 80a (☎ 482 54 41)
USA
    Via Vittorio Veneto 119a-121 (☎ 4 67 41)

For other foreign embassies in Rome and consulates in other major cities throughout Italy, look under *Ambasciate* or *Consolati* in the telephone book, or, in Rome, in the *English Yellow Pages*. Tourist offices will also generally have a list.

DOCUMENTS

A passport is the only important document you will need in Italy as a tourist. It is necessary to produce your passport when you register in a hotel or pensione in Italy. The proprietor, or desk clerk, is likely to want to keep the document long enough to copy out the necessary details. Some proprietors will want to keep your passport for the duration of your stay. This is not a requirement and you are legally entitled to have your passport returned to you if you request it. It is a legal requirement in Italy that everyone carry an identity card (or passport); however, in some parts of Italy, where bag-snatchers prey on tourists, it is probably safer to leave your passport at the hotel.

Vehicle Papers

If you want to rent a car or motorcycle, you will generally need to produce your driving licence. Certainly you will need to produce it if pulled over by the police or *carabinieri*, who, if it's a non-EC licence, may also want to see an Italian translation of the licence (available from the Italian State Tourist Office in your country, or its equivalent, ENIT, in Rome), although this is unlikely. An International Driving Permit, available from automobile clubs throughout the world and usually valid for 12 months, is an acceptable substitute in combination with your proper licence. If you are driving your own car in Italy you will need an International Insurance Certificate, also known as a Green Card *(Carta Verde)*. Your third party insurance company will issue this. For further details, see Car & Motorbike in the Getting There & Away chapter.

Student & Youth Cards

In order to take advantage of the discounts offered to travelling students in Italy, get an International Student Identity Card (ISIC) before leaving home. Recognised in more than 70 countries worldwide, it is probably the safest student ID card to carry, although it might pay in Italy (where the bureaucrats are document-mad) to carry an additional form of student ID.

The cards are available from the following offices:

Australia
    Student Services Australia, 1st Floor, 20 Faraday St, Carlton (☎ 03-348 1777)

Canada
  Travel Cuts, 187 College St, Toronto (☎ 416-977 3703)
  Voyages Campus, Université McGill, 3480 Rue McTavish, Montreal (☎ 514-398 0647)
UK
  CTS, 33 Windmill St, London (☎ 071-580 4554)
USA
  CIEE, 205 East 42nd St, New York (☎ 212-661 1414)
  1093 Broxton Ave, Los Angeles (☎ 213-208 3551)
  312 Sutter St, San Francisco (☎ 415-421 3473)

People who are aged under 26, but not students, can obtain an International Youth Card, issued by the Federation of International Youth Travel Organisations (FIYTO). The card entitles holders to a wide range of discounts on transport, accommodation, entrance fees to museums, car hire and in restaurants.

The head office of FIYTO is in Denmark, at Islands Brygge 81, DK-2300 Copenhagen S, where you can write to request a brochure. Otherwise, the organisations listed above for the USA, UK and Canada will issue the cards. In Italy, any office of the CTS (Centro Turistico Studentesco e Giovanile) will issue them too, as long as you can prove that you are aged under 26 (see the Useful Organisations section).

Photocopies

Make photocopies of all your important documents, especially your passport. This will help speed up replacement if they are lost or stolen. Other important documents to photocopy might include your airline ticket and credit cards. It is also vital to record the serial numbers of your travellers' cheques (cross them off as you cash them in). All of this material should be kept completely separate from your passport, money and other documents, and leave extra copies with someone reliable at home. Keep a small amount of emergency cash with this material. If your passport is stolen or lost, notify the police and obtain a statement, and then contact your embassy or consulate as soon as possible.

CUSTOMS

There is a long list of items which can be imported into Italy by nonresidents without having to pay duty. These include: two still cameras and 10 rolls of film; a movie camera with 10 cartridges of film; a tape recorder or CD player, with a reasonable number of tapes or CDs; sports equipment, including skis; one bicycle or motorbike (not exceeding 50 cc); one portable radio and one portable TV set (both may be subject to the payment of a licence fee on entry to Italy); personal jewellery; up to 400 cigarettes; two bottles of wine and one bottle of liquor. If you are travelling to or from another EC country, however, the open-border policy means that you may carry a generous 800 cigarettes, 90 litres of wine, 110 litres of beer and 10 litres of spirits. There are restrictions on the amount of lire you can import and export without making a declaration. At the time of writing this was 20 million lire.

MONEY
Currency

Italy's currency is the lira (plural: lire). The smallest note is L1000. Other denominations in notes are L2000, L5000, L10,000, L50,000 and L100,000. Coin denominations are L50, L100, L200 and L500. Although smaller coin denominations have been taken out of circulation, you will still often find a worthless L20 or even L10 coin in your change. *Gettoni* (telephone tokens) are legal tender and have the same value as a L200 coin.

Remember that, like other Continental Europeans, Italians indicate decimals with commas and thousands with points.

Exchange rates

A$1	=	L989
US$1	=	L1473
UK£1	=	L2257
NZ$1	=	L809
DM1	=	L907
C$1	=	L1155

Travellers' Cheques

These represent a safe and convenient way to carry money and are easily exchanged at banks and exchange offices throughout Italy. In order to avoid potential problems if your cheques are stolen, always keep the bank receipt listing the cheque numbers separate from the actual cheques and keep a list of the numbers of those you have already cashed.

Before deciding on which travellers' cheques to buy, check the provisions for replacement in the event of loss or theft. Travellers using the better known cheques, such as Visa, American Express and Thomas Cook, will have little trouble in Italy. American Express, in particular, has offices in all the major Italian cities and agents in many other smaller cities.

Deciding which currency to buy will depend on current exchange rates and where you intend to travel. Study currency trends carefully before making your decision, taking into account the value of the lira against your own and other major currencies. In 1992 the lira was devalued and went into free fall against all the major currencies after it was withdrawn from the European Exchange Rate Mechanism. The US dollar and the Deutschmark both appear to be strong against the lira, but it's anybody's guess what the future will hold.

If you plan to spend all of your time in Italy it might be a good idea to investigate buying your travellers' cheques in lire. Generally there should be no commission charge when cashing cheques then.

Credit Cards

Carrying a plastic card or two is an extremely convenient way to organise your holiday funds. By arranging for payments to be made into your card account while you are travelling, enough to cover your expenditure, you can avoid paying interest. Even travellers on a shoestring budget should consider carrying a credit card for use in emergencies.

Major credit cards, such as American Express, Visa and MasterCard , are accepted throughout Italy in shops, restaurants and larger hotels. However, many trattorias, pizzerias and most pensioni and one-star hotels do *not* accept credit cards, particularly in the south of Italy. At large flea markets, such as the leather market around San Lorenzo in Florence, many stallholders accept Visa and MasterCard, but will bargain only if you pay cash.

Apart from the inevitable queueing, it is generally a simple procedure to obtain a cash advance on Visa and MasterCard. Simply go to the exchange *(cambio)* counter at the bank and present your card. Visa is probably the more convenient, since only a limited number of banks will honour MasterCard. The Banca Commerciale Italiana, the Cassa di Risparmio and Credito Italiano will all give cash advances on MasterCard.

If your credit card is lost or stolen, you can telephone toll-free to have an immediate stop put on its use. For MasterCard the number in Italy is ☎ 1678-6 80 86 , or make a reverse-charges call to St Louis in the USA on ☎ 314-275 6690; for Visa, phone ☎ 1678-2 10 01 in Italy.

American Express is also a convenient credit card in Italy. It is widely accepted (though not as widely as Visa or MasterCard) and it is possible to make payments on the card at American Express offices in major Italian cities. The full-service offices (such as in Rome and Milan) will issue new cards if yours has been lost or stolen. The toll-free emergency number to report a lost or stolen American Express card in Italy is ☎1678-7 43 33.

Credit cards can also be used in automatic teller machines (ATMs) to obtain cash 24 hours a day throughout Italy, where ATMs are known as bancomats. You will need to obtain a PIN number from the bank issuing the credit card. Several travellers have reported having difficulties using bancomats, ranging from losing their cards in the machines, to simply having their cards rejected. Ensure that you obtain precise information about using ATMs in Italy, and how to replace your card quickly in the event that it is swallowed by the machine. Generally, if you stick to using bancomats at major banks in city centres, you should have less trouble.

Banking

Anything to do with money and banks is likely to cause significant time-wasting and frustration in Italy. As in post offices and police stations, you will generally need to join long queues to exchange money or draw on your credit card. Banks are the most reliable places to exchange money and generally offer the best rates, but the best advice is to shop around for both good rates and the lowest commission charges. Some places charge a flat fee of up to L8000 to exchange travellers' cheques and it may be best to locate institutions which instead charge a percentage commission.

Because of the high petty crime rate in major Italian cities it is unwise to carry large amounts of cash, so calculate your financial needs carefully before exchanging money. Note that your options for good rates might be limited during the weekend.

It is advisable to obtain a small amount of lire (enough to cover transport, food and accommodation for the first night) before arriving in the country. In this way you can avoid the long queues and poor rates at airports and most train stations.

Sending Money to Italy The fastest and most reliable way to send money to Italy is by 'urgent telex' through the foreign office of a large Italian bank, or through major banks in your own country, to a nominated bank in Italy. It is important to have an exact record of all details associated with the money transfer, particularly the exact address of the Italian bank where the money has been sent. It should be noted that the money will always be held at the head office of the bank in the town to which it has been sent. Urgent-telex transfers should take only a few days, while other means, such as by draft, can take weeks. You will be required to produce identification, usually a passport, in order to collect the money. It is also a good idea to take along the details of the transaction. It is inadvisable to send cheques by mail to Italy, because of the unreliability of the country's postal service.

Costs

Daily expenditure will obviously vary dramatically according to each traveller's personal budget. However, there are some basic guidelines to travelling in Italy which will be useful for everyone from the backpacker to the luxury traveller. Those on a really tight budget will find Italy expensive – accommodation charges and high entrance fees for the major museums and monuments will keep daily expenditure high. A *very* prudent backpacker could get by on less than L40,000 a day, but only by staying in youth hostels, eating one simple meal a day, making your own sandwiches for lunch and minimising the number of museums and galleries visited.

Mid-range travellers will find that they can live reasonably for around L70,000 to L80,000 a day and quite well for under L100,000 (given that they stay in a two-star hotel and still eat only one sit-down meal a day).

A basic breakdown of costs during an average day for the budget to middle-range traveller could be: accommodation L18,000 to L40,000; breakfast L2000 to L3000 (coffee and croissant); lunch (sandwich and mineral water) L3000 to L5000; bottle of mineral water L1000; public transport (bus or underground railway in a major town) L2500; entrance fee for one museum L5000 to L10,000; cost of long-distance train or bus travel (spread over three days) L7000; sit-down dinner L12,000 to L25,000.

Accommodation Budget travellers can save by staying in youth hostels (open to people of all ages) or camping grounds. If travelling with a group of friends and you plan to stay in pensioni or hotels, always ask for triples or quads: the cost per person diminishes dramatically the more people you have in a room. Travellers on a bigger budget should consider sticking to two or three-star pensioni and hotels. Chosen carefully, they provide perfectly adequate accommodation.

Avoid, where possible, pensioni and hotels which charge for a compulsory breakfast. A cappuccino and brioche at a bar could cost considerably less.

Eating Remember that, in Italian bars, prices double (sometimes even triple) if you sit down. Stand at the bar to drink your coffee or eat a sandwich – or buy a sandwich or slice of pizza and head for the nearest piazza. Read the fine print on menus (usually posted outside eating establishments) to check the cover charge (coperto) and service fee (servizio). These can make a big difference to the bill and it is best to avoid restaurants which charge both. Shop in supermarkets and alimentari (grocery shops) for the makings of picnic lunches and for the odd meal in your room.

Travelling Train fares are still relatively cheap in Italy, but intercity buses are generally cheaper. If travelling by train and you have time to spare, take a locale or diretto: they are slower but cheaper than the rapido intercity trains, for which you have to pay a supplement (even if travelling on an Inter-Rail pass, though Eurail pass holders are exempt). See the Getting Around chapter for information about these different types of trains and about various discounts on train travel.

In the cities, buy a daily tourist ticket for urban bus travel: costing around L2500, they are good value. When catching ferries (such as to Sicily, Sardinia or Greece), consider travelling deck class (passaggio ponte). You can only do so in summer and it is not available on all ferries.

Other Cost-Savers Instead of sending postcards or normal letters by air mail, buy aerograms from the post office for L850. At museums, never hesitate to ask if there are discounts for students, young people, children, families or the elderly.

Tipping & Bargaining

You are not expected to tip on top of restaurant service charges, but it is common (although not standard) practice among Italians to leave a small amount. If there is no service charge, the customer might consider leaving a 10% tip, but this is by no means obligatory. In bars, Italians will usually leave any small change as a tip, often only L100 or L200. Tipping taxi drivers is also not common practice, but, if staying in a higher class hotel, you should tip the porter.

Bargaining is common throughout Italy in the various flea markets, but not in shops. At the Porta Portese market in Rome, for instance, don't hesitate to offer half the asking price for any given item. Don't be deterred by stallholders who dismiss you with a wave of the arm: the person at the next stall will be just as likely to accept your offer after a brief (and obligatory) haggle. While bargaining in shops is not acceptable, you might find that the proprietor is disposed to give a discount if you are spending a reasonable amount of money.

It is quite acceptable to bargain for the price of a room in a pension, particularly if you plan to stay for more than a few days, and it is standard practice to bargain with taxi drivers, although you must agree on the price before you get in the cab.

Consumer Taxes

Whenever you buy an item in Italy, you will pay value-added tax, known as IVA in Italy. Tourists who are residents of countries outside the EC are able to claim a refund on this tax if the item was purchased for personal use and cost more than a certain amount (L300,000 at the time of writing). If you want to claim a refund, the relevant goods have to be carried with your luggage and must be unopened and unused when you leave Italy.

The refund offer only applies to items which were purchased at retail outlets affiliated to the system – these shops usually display a 'Tax-free for tourists' sign. Otherwise, ask the shopkeeper. Ensure that the shopkeeper gives you a tax-free shopping form which details the purchase and the amount to be refunded. This form, the fiscal receipt and the actual goods then have to be presented to customs when you leave the country and the form must be stamped. You can then either get your refund at the airport and some border points, or return the form to the vendor within 60 days, who will then make the refund, either by cheque or to your credit card.

Receipts

Laws introduced to tighten controls on the payment of taxes in Italy mean that the onus is on the buyer to ask for and retain receipts for all goods and services. The receipt must be kept until you are a reasonable distance from the establishment where you bought the goods. This applies to everything from a litre of milk to a haircut. Although it rarely happens, you could be asked by an officer of the Fiscal Police (Guardia di Finanza) to produce the receipt immediately after you leave a shop. If you don't have it, you will have to pay a L30,000 fine.

WHEN TO GO

The best time to visit Italy is in the off season, from April to June and in September/ October, when the weather is usually good, prices are lower and there are fewer tourists. The weather is warm enough for beach-goers in most of the country from June to September, but during August (high season) it is very hot, prices are inflated and the entire country swarms with holidaying foreigners and Italians.

Apart from the difficulty of maintaining a rigorous sightseeing schedule in the relentless August heat, tourists will find that a large number of businesses, including shops and restaurants, close down during that month, as most Italians abandon the cities to spend their annual holidays at the beach or in the mountains. Consequently this means that it can be virtually impossible to find accommodation near a beach or mountain in August, unless you have booked months in advance.

July and September are the best months for people interested in hiking in the Alps and Apennines – walking trails and refuges are crowded in August. During these months the weather is generally good, although you should always allow for cold weather. Mountain refuges usually open from late June to the end of September for hikers and at Easter for skiers.

A mild climate makes winter a reasonable time to visit Italy's southern regions and Sardinia. However, the central and northern regions can be very cold and wet – not the best weather for sightseeing.

WHAT TO BRING

Certainly the best advice is to bring as little as possible and the second important consideration is what to carry it in. A backpack is a definite advantage in Italy, for two main reasons: petty thieves prey on tourists who have no hands free because they are carrying too much luggage, and there are endless flights of stairs at most train stations and in many small medieval towns. Travellers with suitcases and portable trolleys will find themselves at a definite disadvantage under these circumstances. However, two people travelling together should be able to overcome most problems if they use only one large suitcase between them.

A small pack (with a lock) for day trips and for sightseeing is preferable to a handbag or shoulder bag, particularly in the southern cities where motorcycle bandits are particularly active. A money belt is an unfortunate necessity in Italy, particularly in major cities and throughout the south of the country, where it is absolutely inadvisable to carry a purse or wallet in your pocket.

When to choosing what to pack, remember that, except in the mountains, Italy is uniformly hot in summer, but the climate varies in winter. For example, in most areas you will need only a light jacket (in case of cool evenings) in July and August. In winter you will need a heavy coat, gloves and scarf for the north of the country, while in Sicily a lined raincoat would be adequate.

Most importantly, bring a pair of hardy, comfortable walking shoes. Apart from the many km you will cover as a sightseer, pavements are uneven in many Italian cities and are often made of cobblestones.

Top Left : Entrance to the Vatican Museums, Rome (GE)
Top Right : Ceiling of the Sistine Chapel, Rome (GE)
Bottom Left : Spanish Steps, Rome (EPT)
Bottom Right : St Peter's Square, Rome (EPT)

Top : Tellaro at dusk, Liguria (JG)
Bottom Left : Fishing nets in Camogli, Liguria (JG)
Bottom Right : Russian Orthodox Church in San Remo, Liguria (JG)

Clothing maintenance is an important consideration when travelling for long periods. Unless you plan to spend large sums of money in dry-cleaners and laundries in Italy, make sure you pack a portable clothesline at the very least. While many pensioni and hotels specifically ask guests not to wash clothes in the room, such rules are rarely enforced. A light travel iron is not a bad idea if you can't bear the thought of crumpled clothes. A more sensible option is to pack crease-proof clothes.

People planning to hike in the Alps should ensure that they bring the necessary clothing and equipment, in particular a pair of hiking boots (lightweight and waterproof). Even in high summer you will need to carry warm clothing on long hikes. Inexperienced hikers should check with a local mountaineering group to get a list of essentials before leaving home.

Essentials

People who need to take regular medication should bring a supply, as well as their prescription. Ask your doctor to write out the prescription using the generic name of the drug, rather than its brand name. Basic drugs, such as headache pills, are easily purchased. Condoms are expensive in Italy, costing up to L30,000 for 12. If they are cheaper in your home country, bring along a supply.

TOURIST OFFICES

The quality of the services offered by tourist information offices throughout Italy varies dramatically. One office might have enthusiastic staff but no useful printed information, while another might have a gold mine of brochures kept hidden under the counter by indifferent and sometimes hostile staff members.

There are three main categories of tourist office: regional, provincial and local. The system has been undergoing a reorganisation, which means that the names of the tourist boards vary throughout the country, but they offer basically the same services. Tourists shouldn't need to have anything

to do with the regional offices, which are concerned with promotion, planning, budget and other projects far removed from the daily concerns of the humble tourist. The provincial and local tourist boards have information offices open to the public, often both in the same town. The provincial offices are known in some parts of Italy as EPT (Ente Provinciale per il Turismo) and in other parts as APT (Azienda di Promozione Turistica, or Tourist Promotion Department). These offices can provide tourist information on both the province and the town.

The local offices are generally known as AAST (Azienda Autonoma di Soggiorno e Turismo), but sometimes as the APT. They specialise in information about the town, but usually also have some provincial information. These offices are the places to go if you want specific information about bus routes, museum opening times etc.

In most of the very small towns and villages the local tourist office is called a Pro Loco. Run by local committees, in some towns these offices are similar to the AASTs, providing a good range of useful information. In others they are little more than a meeting place for the local elderly men, who know nothing about their town's tourist facilities, but might try to sell you a book about the town's cathedral.

Most offices of the EPT, APT and AAST say that they will respond to both written and telephone requests for information about hotels, apartments for rent etc.

Tourist offices are generally open from 8 am to 12.30 or 1 pm, and from 3 to around 7 pm. Hours are usually longer in summer and few offices open on Saturday afternoons or on Sundays.

There are tourist information booths at all major train stations in Italy and at many of the smaller stations. These tend to be open from 8 am to 12.30 pm and from 3 to 7 pm (although opening hours vary from office to office) and can usually provide a map (*pianta della città*), list of hotels (*elenco degli alberghi*) and information on the major sights (*informazioni sulle attrazioni turistiche*). Whether or not they will help you find a hotel will depend on the mood of the staff, but you can generally expect that they will make a few recommendations and mark the locations on a map.

English is usually only spoken at offices in larger towns and in areas which attract large numbers of foreign tourists.

The best advice if you encounter lethargic, unhelpful or hostile staff is to be polite but insistent that they provide you with the information you require.

If you are landing in Rome, you can obtain limited information about the major destinations throughout the country from the EPT office, Via Parigi 11, 00185 Rome, and at the headquarters of Italy's national tourist office, ENIT (Ente Nazionale Italiano per il Turismo), Via Marghera 2, 00185 Rome, both near Rome's central train station, Stazione Termini.

The addresses and telephone numbers of provincial and local tourist offices are listed under towns and cities throughout this book. Addresses are also included for regional offices which might be of assistance.

Italian Tourist Offices Abroad
Information on Italy is available from ENIT offices in the following countries:

Canada
    1 Place Ville Marie, Suite 1914, Montreal, Que H3B 3M9 (☎ 514-866 7667)
UK
    1 Princes St, London W1R 8AY (☎ 071-408 1254)
USA
    630 Fifth Avenue, Suite 1565, New York, NY 10111 (☎ 212-245 4961)
    12400 Wilshire Blvd, Suite 550, Los Angeles, CA 90025 (☎ 310-820 29 77)
    500 North Michigan Ave, Suite 1046, Chicago, IL 60611 (☎ 644 0996)

In Australia, ENIT operates through Alitalia (Italy's national airline) in the Orient Overseas Building, Suite 202, 32 Bridge St, Sydney (☎ 02-247 1308).

CIT (Compagnia Italiana di Turismo), Italy's national travel agency, also has offices throughout the world. They can provide extensive information on travelling in Italy and will organise tours. CIT can also make all rail bookings for Italy, including sector bookings (such as Rome-Naples), and sells Eurail passes and discount passes for rail travel in Italy. CIT offices include:

Australia
    123 Clarence St, Sydney (☎ 02-29 4754)
    Suite 10, 6th Floor, 442 Collins St, Melbourne (☎ 03-670 1322)
Canada
    1450 City Councillors St, Suite 750, Montreal (☎ 514-845 9101)
    111 Avenue Rd, Suite 808, Toronto (☎ 416-927 7206)
UK
    Marco Polo House, 3-5 Lansdowne Rd, Croydon, Surrey (☎ 081-686 0677)
USA
    594 Broadway, Suite 307, New York (☎ 212-274 0596)
    6033 West Century Blvd, Suite 980, Los Angeles (☎ 310-338 8615)

Italian cultural institutes in major cities throughout the world have extensive information on study opportunities in Italy.

USEFUL ORGANISATIONS
The following organisations in Italy might prove useful:

ACI (Automobile Club Italiano)
    If you are driving in Italy, consider joining ACI (around L70,000), which will entitle you to free breakdown assistance. You may already have reciprocal rights through membership of your home-country organisation – enquire about this before you leave, and ask for a letter of introduction. Tourist packages of petrol coupons and discounts for the toll autostradas (freeways) were abolished in 1992, although the system is under review and could be reintroduced. Ask at CIT offices in your country or at ACI border offices on entry to Italy. The club has offices at Corso Venezia 43, Milan (☎ 02-7 74 51); Via Marsala 8, Rome (☎ 06-4 99 81); and throughout Italy.
AIG (Associazione Italiana Alberghi per la Gioventù)
    The Italian youth hostel association, affiliated with the International Youth Hostel Federation, has its head office (☎ 06-487 11 52) at Via Cavour 44, Rome, where you can obtain a list of all hostels in Italy and buy a membership card if necessary.

CAI (Club Alpino Italiano)
This organisation will provide information and maps for hiking and trekking, and phone numbers for refuges in the Alps. It has offices throughout Italy which can provide trekking information, but only for their particular zone. It does not have a central office, although you should be able to get some assistance at the Milan office (☎ 02-86 46 35 16), Via Silvio Pellico 6, and in Rome (☎ 06-656 10 11), Via Ripetta 142.

CIT (Compagnia Italiana di Turismo)
Italy's national tourist agency has offices throughout the country and abroad (see the previous section). You can book train, bus, air and sea travel and obtain information about guided tours of the cities and package tours of Italy.

CTS (Centro Turistico Studentesco e Giovanile)
This agency has offices all over Italy and specialises in discounts for students and young people, but is also useful for travellers of any age looking for cheap flights and sightseeing discounts (you will be required to pay a membership fee of around L30,000). CTS is linked with the International Student Travel Confederation and, with documents proving you are a student, you can get a student card at CTS offices.

TCI (Touring Club Italiano)
The head office (☎ 02-852 62 44) is at Corso Italia 10, Milan. It publishes useful trekking guides and maps, and has offices throughout Italy.

BUSINESS HOURS

Business hours vary between the north and south of Italy and can also vary among cities, but as a rule, the working week runs from Monday to Saturday.

Generally shops and businesses in north and central Italy are open Monday to Saturday from 8 am to 1 pm and 3.30 to 7.30 pm. In the south they usually close for lunch around 12.30 pm and reopen from 4 to 8 pm. In some cities, grocery shops *(alimentari)* might not reopen until 5 pm and, during the warmer months, they could stay open until 9 pm. All alimentari close on Thursday afternoons and often on Saturday afternoons. Shops in smaller towns and on city outskirts often close on Saturday afternoons as well.

Banks tend to be open Monday to Friday from 8.30 am to 1.30 pm and 2.30 to 4.30 pm, although hours can vary. They are closed at weekends, but it is always possible to find an exchange office open in the larger cities and in major tourist areas.

Major post offices open from 8.30 am to 6 or 7 pm Monday to Saturday. Smaller post offices open Monday to Friday from 8.30 am to 2 pm and on Saturdays from 8.30 am to midday.

Pharmacies are usually open from 9 am to 12.30 pm and 3.30 to 7.30 pm. They are always closed on Sunday and alternatively on Saturday or Wednesday. Pharmacies which are open all night and on Sundays and holidays are listed under the individual towns throughout this book.

Bars (in the Italian sense, ie coffee-and-sandwich places) and cafés open from 7.30 am to 8 pm and restaurants open from midday to 3 pm and 7.30 to 11 pm (later in summer and in the south). Restaurants and bars are required to close for one day each week.

Museum and gallery opening hours vary, although many close on Mondays and some close during religious holidays.

HOLIDAYS

Most Italians take their annual holidays in August, deserting the cities for the cooler seaside or mountains. This means that many businesses and shops close for at least a part of the month, particularly during the week around the Feast of the Assumption on 15 August (this holiday is known in Italy as *Ferragosto*). Larger cities, notably Milan and Rome, are left to the tourists, who may be frustrated that many restaurants, clothing and grocery shops are closed until early September.

National public holidays include: Epiphany (6 January); Easter Monday; Liberation Day (25 April); Labour Day (1 May); Feast of the Assumption (15 August); All Saints' Day (1 November); Feast of the Immaculate Conception (8 December); Christmas Day (25 December); and the Feast of Santo Stefano (26 December).

Individual towns also have public holidays to celebrate the feasts of their patron saints. Some of these are: the feast of St Mark on 25 April in Venice; the feast of St John the

Baptist on 24 June in Florence, Genoa and Turin; the feast of Sts Peter & Paul in Rome on 29 June; the feast of San Gennaro (Janarius) in Naples on 19 September; and the feast of St Ambrose in Milan on 7 December.

CULTURAL EVENTS

Italy has a full calendar of religious and cultural events, including colourful traditional festivals, either religious or historical, and festivals of the performing arts, including opera, music and theatre. Events range from the famous Venice Carnevale and Siena's Palio to festivals honouring patron saints, such as the Feast of San Gennaro in Naples and of San Nicola in Bari, and usually involve local people in full traditional costume. Festivals are particularly numerous in Sicily and Sardinia, notably *le feste di Pasqua* (Easter Week celebrations) in Sicily.

There are several important opera seasons, including those held at the Arena in Verona, the Baths of Caracalla in Rome and La Scala in Milan. Major music festivals include Umbria Jazz in Perugia and Maggio Musicale Fiorentino in Florence, while the Festival of Two Worlds in Spoleto is certainly worth including in your itinerary. As well as Carnevale, Venice also offers an international film festival and the Biennale visual arts festival, the latter held every odd year (previously every even year).

If you are interested in timing your visit to coincide with a particular festival, contact the ENIT office in your country or write to ENIT in Rome (see under Tourist Offices in this chapter) for specific dates. ENIT publishes an annual booklet entitled *An Italian Year*, which lists most festivals, music, opera and ballet seasons, as well as art and film festivals.

The following are some of the more interesting and important festivals and events, although they represent only a small proportion of those held in a normal year. Since dates often change from year to year, the events are listed under the relevant month, and dates have been included only when they are fixed, such as for festivals of patron saints.

February/March/April

Carnevale During the period before Ash Wednesday many towns stage carnivals for which locals don masks and costumes and take advantage of their last opportunity to indulge before the 40 days of Lent begin. Traditionally the period started at Epiphany on 6 January and ended on the first day of Lent. The carnival held in Venice during the 10 days before Ash Wednesday is the most famous, but the more traditional and popular carnival celebrations are held at Viareggio on the north coast of Tuscany.

Sartiglia This event is the highlight of carnival celebrations at Oristano in Sardinia on the Sunday and Tuesday before the start of Lent. It involves a medieval tournament of horsemen in masquerade.

Festival of the Almond Blossoms A traditional festival featuring a historical pageant and fireworks held at Agrigento, Sicily, in early March.

Le Feste di Pasqua Holy Week in Italy is marked by solemn processions and passion plays. At Taranto in Apulia on Holy Thursday there is the Procession of the Addolorata and on Good Friday the Procession of the Mysteries, when statues representing the Passion of Christ are carried around the town. One of Italy's oldest and most evocative Good Friday processions is held at Chieti in Abruzzo. The week is marked in Sicily by numerous events, including a Procession of the Mysteries at Trapani and the celebration of Easter according to Byzantine rites at Piana degli Albanesi, near Palermo. Women in colourful 15th century costume give out Easter eggs to the public.

Scoppio del Carro (Explosion of the Cart) Held in Florence in the Piazza del Duomo at noon on Easter Sunday, this event features the explosion of a cart full of fireworks – a tradition dating back to the Crusades. If this works well, it is seen as a good omen for the city.

May

Feast of San Nicola On 2 and 3 May, the people of Bari, in Apulia, participate in a procession in traditional costume to re-enact the delivery of the bones of their patron saint to Dominican friars. The following day a statue of the saint is taken to sea.

Festival of Snakes Held at Cocullo in Abruzzo, this famous festival honours the town's patron, St Dominic. His statue is draped with live snakes and carried in procession.

Feast of San Gennaro Three times a year (on the first Sunday in May, 19 September and 16 December) the faithful gather in Naples' Duomo to wait for the blood of the saint to liquefy – if the miracle occurs it is a good omen for the city.

Corsa dei Ceri (Race of the Candles) This exciting and intensely traditional event is held at Gubbio in Umbria on 15 May. Groups of men carrying huge wooden shrines race uphill to the town's basilica, dedicated to the patron saint, Ubaldo.

Cavalcata Sarda (Sardinian Cavalcade) Hundreds of Sardi wearing colourful traditional costume gather at Sassari on the second-last Sunday in May to mark a victory over the Saracens in the year 1000.

Palio della Balestra (Palio of the Crossbow) Held in Gubbio on the last Sunday in May this is a crossbow contest between men of Gubbio and Sansepolcro, who dress in medieval costume and use antique weapons. There is a rematch at Sansepolcro on the first Sunday in September.

Maggio Musicale Fiorentino An important music festival held in Florence in May and June.

June

Historical Regatta of the Four Ancient Maritime Republics A procession of boats and a race between the four historical maritime rivals – Pisa, Venice, Amalfi and Genoa. The event rotates between the four towns.

Feast of Sant'Antonio Fans of St Anthony, patron saint of Padua and of lost things, might want to attend the procession of the saint's relics held annually on 13 June.

Infiorata To celebrate Corpus Domini on 21 June, some towns decorate a selected street with colourful designs made with flower petals. Towns include Genzano, near Rome, and Spello in Umbria.

Gioco del Ponte (Game of the Bridge) Two groups in medieval costume contend for the Ponte di Mezzo, a bridge over the Arno.

Festival of Two Worlds This major festival of the arts is held in June and July at Spoleto, a beautiful hill town in Umbria. Created by Gian Carlo Menotti, the festival features music, theatre, dance and art exhibitions.

July

Il Palio The pride and joy of Siena, this famous traditional event is held twice a year – on 2 July and 16 August – in the town's beautiful Piazza del Campo. It involves a dangerous bareback horse race around the piazza, preceded by a parade of supporters in traditional costume.

Ardia More dangerous than the Palio, this impressive and chaotic horse race at Sedilo in Sardinia on 6 June (repeated the following day) celebrates the victory of the Roman Emperor Constantine over Maxentius in 312 AD (the battle was actually at the Ponte Milvio in Rome). A large number of horsemen race around the town while onlookers shoot guns into the ground or air.

Festa del Redentore (Feast of the Redeemer) Fireworks and a procession over the bridge to the Church of the Redeemer on Giudecca Island in Venice on the third weekend in July.

Umbria Jazz Festival Held at Perugia in Umbria in July, this week-long jazz festival features performers from around the world.

Opera Seasons start at the Arena (Roman amphitheatre) in Verona and at the Baths of Caracalla in Rome, continuing throughout August.

International Ballet Festival Held at Nervi, near Genoa, this festival features international performers.

August

Quintana This historical pageant features a parade of hundreds of people in 15th century costume, followed by a spectacular jousting tournament. It is held at Ascoli Piceno in the Marches on the first Sunday in August.

I Candelieri (Festival of the Candelabra) Held on 14 August at Sassari in Sardinia, this festival features town representatives in medieval costume carrying huge wooden columns through the town. It celebrates the Feast of the Assumption to honour a vow made in 1652 to end a plague.

Il Palio This is a repeat of Siena's famous horse race on 16 August.

Festa del Redentore Held at Nuoro in Sardinia, this folk festival and parade is attended by thousands of people from all over the island, who dress in traditional regional costume. The actual dates of the festival change each year.

International Film Festival Held at the Lido, Venice, the festival attracts those involved in the international film scene.

September

Living Chess Game The townspeople of Marostica in the Veneto dress as chess figures and participate in a match on a chessboard marked out in the town square. Games are held only in even years on the first weekend in September.

Palio della Balestra A rematch of the crossbow competition between Gubbio and Sansepolcro is held at Sansepolcro.

Regata Storica (Historical Regatta) This race of gondolas along Venice's Grand Canal is preceded by a parade of boats decorated in 15th century style. It is held on the first Sunday in September.

Giostra della Quintana A medieval pageant involving a parade and jousting event with horsemen in traditional costume. Held on the second Sunday in September.

Feast of San Gennaro On 19 September the faithful of Naples gather for the second time to await the miraculous liquefaction of the saint's blood.

POST & TELECOMMUNICATIONS

Italy's postal service is notoriously slow, unreliable and expensive. Don't expect to receive every letter sent to you, or that every letter you send will reach its destination. An air-mail letter will take up to two weeks to reach the UK or the USA, while a letter to Australia will take between two and three weeks. Postcards will take even longer because they are low-priority mail. The service within Italy is no better: local letters take at least three days and up to a week to arrive in another city, although instances of letters taking weeks to arrive are common. A 1988 survey on postal efficiency in Europe found that next-day delivery did not exist in Italy.

Sending letters *espresso* (express) doesn't help much. Though you pay an extra L3000, they generally take the same amount of time.

One way to avoid all of this frustration, but only if you are in Rome, is to use the Vatican post office in St Peter's Square, which has an excellent record for prompt and reliable delivery but doesn't accept poste restante mail.

The cost of sending a letter *via aerea* (air mail) depends on its weight and where it is being sent. An average-size letter on air-mail paper will cost L1350 to send to Australia, L1000 to the USA and L750 to the UK. A postcard will cost around the same, unless you write only five words, in which case it costs significantly less (L850 to Australia). Aerograms are a cheap alternative, costing only L850 to send anywhere. They can be purchased only at post offices.

Stamps *(francobolli)* are available at post offices and at authorised tobacconists *(tabacchi)*, but since letters must be weighed it is best to go to the post office.

If you want to post more important items by registered mail *(raccomandato)* or by insured mail *(assicurato)*, remember that they will take as long as normal mail. Raccomandato costs L3200 on top of the normal cost of the letter and assicurato is an extra L6000. Urgent mail can be sent by EMS (Express Mail Service), also known as CAI Post, a cheaper version of private courier services such as DHL. A letter or parcel weighing up to one kg will cost approximately L30,000 within Europe, L50,000 to the USA and Canada, and L70,000 to Australia and New Zealand. EMS guarantees to deliver mail within a certain period, but even this is not what would qualify as 'urgent' delivery – the period for delivery to Australia is, for instance, within 10 days. Ask at post offices for addresses of EMS outlets.

Poste restante is known as *fermo posta* in Italy. Letters marked 'fermo posta' will be held at the counter of the same name in the main post office in the relevant town. Ask your friends to write your surname in block letters, and to address mail as follows: John SMITH, Fermo Posta, postal code plus name of town or city (postal codes of central-city areas are given throughout this book). You will need to pick up your letters in person and present your passport as identification.

Telephones

It is relatively simple to make a phone call in Italy. However, you will inevitably encounter some minor problems, including the cost – Italy's rates for long-distance calls are the highest in Europe. A local call will cost L200 for around four minutes.

There are four types of public telephones: old-style phones which accept only *gettoni* (telephone tokens which have the same value as a L200 coin – try to avoid these phones since it can sometimes be difficult to get hold of gettoni); normal pay phones, which accept gettoni as well as L100, L200 and L500 coins; card phones, which accept phonecards *(carte telefoniche)* with a value of L5000, L10,000 or L50,000 (if one card starts to run out, you can insert another, as with coin phones); and metred phones, either at offices of ASST (see below) or in a bar or shop in smaller towns – the cost of your call is recorded on a meter and you pay afterwards.

Public telephones are ubiquitous in Italy, both on the street and in bars. Otherwise you can go to the SIP office (SIP is the name of Italy's telephone company) in larger towns, where there are public phones and telephone

Italian telephone card, with illustration of phone rates

books for all of Italy. In many larger towns there are also ASST offices, where you can make long-distance calls and pay afterwards.

Telephone cards can be purchased at tobacconists and newspaper stands, or from vending machines at SIP offices.

Direct international calls can easily be made from public phones using phonecards. You need to dial 00 to get out of Italy, then the relevant country and city codes, followed by the phone number. Useful country codes are: Australia 61, Canada and USA 1, New Zealand 64, and the UK 44. Codes for other countries in Europe include: France 33, Germany 49, Greece 30, Ireland 353, and Spain 34. Other codes are listed in Italian phone books.

Note that it is always cheaper to telephone after 10 pm for long-distance calls within Italy, and after 11 pm for international calls. A toll-free number *(numero verde)* in Italy starts with the code 1678.

If you want to make a reverse-charges or operator-connected call, dial 170 (you may need to insert L200 or a gettone to get through); the operators always speak English. Say clearly that you want to make a collect call. Otherwise you can direct-dial an English-speaking operator in your own country and ask to make your collect call. Numbers for this service are as follows: Australia ☎ 172 10 61, Canada ☎ 172 10 01, New Zealand ☎ 172 10 64, UK ☎ 172 10 44, and USA (through AT&T) ☎ 172 10 11. With any of these reverse-charges or direct-dial services you may have a long wait before getting through.

To call Italy from abroad, dial the international access code (different from each country), followed by Italy's country code (39), the area code for the relevant city (dropping the leading zero), followed by the subscriber number.

Area codes are listed under cities and towns in this book. Important codes include: Rome 06, Milan 02, Florence 055, Naples 081, Cagliari 070, and Palermo 091.

Warning The telephone system in Italy seems to be in a constant state of overhaul, which means that telephone numbers change with alarming regularity. Often there will be a message giving you the new number, but only in Italian. Otherwise dial 12 and hope you find an operator who speaks English. If a phone number is going to change, the new number will often be listed in brackets after the existing number in the telephone book. It will be preceded by the word *prenderà*. At peak periods (such as after 10 pm) you could have difficulty getting a free line and it is simply a matter of being patient.

Fax & Telegraph

Faxes have become an extremely important mode of communication for Italian businesses, as an alternative to the country's unreliable and slow postal system. However, Italy's high telephone charges make faxes an expensive mode of communication for the average tourist. Charges to send a fax are generally around L2000 per page, plus the cost of the telephone call. If the fax is a slow machine the cost can be very high (at least L60,000 to send two or three pages to Australia). You will also pay between L1000 and L2000 per page to receive a fax. Public fax facilities are numerous throughout the country.

Telegrams are sent from post offices and are an expensive, but sure, way of having important messages delivered by the same or next day.

TIME

Italy operates on a 24-hour clock. Daylight-saving time starts on the last Sunday in March, when clocks are put forward one hour. Clocks are put back an hour on the last Sunday in September. Ensure that when telephoning home you also make allowances for daylight-saving in your own country.

European cities such as Paris, Munich, Berlin, Vienna and Madrid have the same time as Italy. Athens, Cairo and Tel Aviv are one hour ahead. When it's noon in Rome, it's 11 pm in Auckland, 11 am in London, 6 am in New York, 7 pm in Perth, 3 am in San Francisco, 9 pm in Sydney, and 6 am in Toronto.

ELECTRICITY

The electric current in Italy is 220 V, 50 Hz, but make a point of checking with your hotel management because in some areas, for instance in parts of Rome, they still use 125 V.

Power points have two or three holes, and plugs have two or three round pins. The middle one is for earth, and many Italians either pull it out or chop it off since often there is no earth in Italian electrical systems, but you'd be wise to seek information before following their example. Some power points have larger holes than others. Italian homes are usually full of plug adapters to cope with this anomaly. Power points do not have their own switches.

If you are bringing any electrical appliances from your own country, you should always check on any extras you might need. People travelling from the USA will need a voltage converter (although many of the more expensive hotels have provision for 110 V appliances such as shavers). The difference in the shape of plug prongs means that many travellers from outside Continental Europe will need an adapter. It is a good idea to buy these *before* leaving home as they are virtually impossible to get in Italy. If you do forget, there is always the option of taking your appliance to an electrical store and having them replace the foreign plug with an Italian one.

LAUNDRY

Laundries in Italy are expensive, and self-service laundrettes are few and far between. Most places charge by the kg and do the laundry themselves, which can make it an expensive proposition. In larger towns, particularly where there are universities, there are more likely to be coin-operated laundries, but a load will still cost around L8000. The best option is to wash your clothes in the basin of your hotel room.

Dry-cleaning is also expensive and the standard of service can be unreliable. Average charges are around L6000 for a shirt and L12,000 for a jacket.

WEIGHTS & MEASURES

Italy uses the metric system. Basic terms for weight include *un etto* (100 grams) and *un chilo* (one kg). Travellers from the USA will have to cope with the change from pounds to kg, miles to km and gallons to litres. A standard conversion table is at the back of this book.

Note that Italians indicate decimals with commas and thousands with points.

BOOKS
History & People

For in-depth research there is Edward Gibbon's masterpiece, *History of the Decline and Fall of the Roman Empire* (available in six hardback volumes, or an abridged, single-volume paperback version). Other, simpler history books include: *The Oxford History of the Roman World* edited by John Boardman, Jasper Griffin & Oswyn Murray (Oxford, paperback); *Daily Life in Ancient Rome* by Jerome Carcopino (paperback); *Italy: A Short History* by Harry Hearder (paperback); *Concise History of Italy* by Vincent Cronin (paperback); *History of the Italian People* by Giuliano Procacci (paperback); *The Oxford Dictionary of Popes* compiled by J N D Kelly (Oxford University Press, paperback); *Rome: Biography of a City* by Christopher Hibbert (paperback), and by the same author, *Venice: The Biography of a City* (paperback) and *The Rise and Fall of the House of the Medici* (paperback).

For background on the Italian people and their culture, there is the classic by Luigi Barzini, *The Italians* (paperback). *Italian Labyrinth* by John Haycraft (paperback) looks at Italy in the 1980s. *Getting it Right in Italy: A Manual for the 1990s* by William Ward (paperback) aims with considerable success to provide easily accessible, useful information about Italy, while also providing a reasonable social profile of the people.

Art

The Penguin Book of the Renaissance by J H Plumb (Penguin, paperback), *Painters of the Renaissance* by Bernard Berenson (paperback), and Giorgio Vasari's *Lives of the Artists* (paperback) should be more than enough on the Renaissance. Other worthwhile books include *A Handbook of Roman Art*, edited by Martin Henig (paperback); *Roman Architecture* by Frank Sear (paperback); and *Art and Architecture in Italy 1600-1750* by Rudolf Wittkower (hardback).

Travellers' Tales

There are endless books written by travellers to Italy. For a potted idea of how the great writers saw the country, it's worth reading *Venice: the Most Triumphant City* compiled by George Bull (hardback) and *When in Rome: the Humorists' Guide to Italy* (paperback).

Three Grand Tour classics are Johann Wolfgang von Goethe's *Italian Journey* (paperback), Charles Dickens' *Pictures from Italy* (paperback), and Henry James' *Italian Hours* (paperback). D H Lawrence wrote three short travel books while living in Italy, now combined in one volume entitled *D H Lawrence and Italy* (paperback).

Others include: *Venice* by James Morris (paperback); *The Stones of Florence* and *Venice Observed* by Mary McCarthy (paperback); *On Persephone's Island* by Mary Taylor Simeti (paperback); *Siren Land* by Norman Douglas (paperback); and *A Traveller in Southern Italy* by H V Morton (paperback). Although written in the 1960s the latter remains a valuable guide to the south and its people. Morton also wrote *A Traveller in Italy* and *A Traveller in Rome*.

Travel Guides

Companion Guides (paperback) are excellent and include *Rome* by Georgina Masson, *Venice* by Hugh Honour, *Umbria* by Maurice Rowdon, *Tuscany* by Archibald Lyall and *Southern Italy* by Peter Gunn.

Lonely Planet publishes *Mediterranean Europe on a shoestring* and *Western Europe on a shoestring* (paperbacks); both books include chapters on Italy and are recommended for those planning further travel in Europe. Also by Lonely Planet, the *Mediterranean Europe phrasebook* lists all the words and phrases you're likely to need when travelling in Italy and other countries in the area.

For information on hiking, try Stefano Ardito's *Backpacking and Walking in Italy* (paperback), published in English. Several walking guides by the same author are published only in Italian, and include *Grandi Sentieri d'Italia* (Istituto Geografico de Agostini).

Self-Catering Italy by Helena Ramsay (paperback) might be useful if you want to rent an apartment, villa etc.

Literature

If you're serious, you might like to start with works of ancient literature, such as *Selected Works* of Cicero (paperback volumes), Livy's *Early History of Rome* (paperback), Ovid's *Metamorphoses* and *Erotic Poems* (both available in paperback) and Virgil's *The Aeneid* (paperback).

You could then progress to Dante's *The Divine Comedy* (paperback), Giovanni Boccaccio's *The Decameron* (paperback) and Niccolò Machiavelli's *The Prince* (paperback).

As far as modern literature is concerned, there are several books which you might like to put in your suitcase. They include: *The Leopard* by Giuseppe di Lampedusa (paperback); *Christ Stopped at Eboli* by Carlo Levi (paperback); and *The Name of the Rose* by Umberto Eco (paperback). Works by Italo Calvino, Alberto Moravia and Elsa Morante are also among the best Italy has produced.

The Mafia

The Honoured Society by Norman Lewis (paperback) is an excellent introduction to the subject.

Food

The Food of Italy by Waverley Root (paperback) is an acknowledged classic.

Bookshops

English-language books are expensive in Italy – expect to pay between L16,000 and L35,000 for novels, history books and trans-

lations of Italian writers. Unless you regard your books as precious items, consider swapping them with fellow travellers. There are several excellent bookshops in Italy which specialise in English-language books, including:

Rome
    The Corner Bookshop, Via del Moro 48, Trastevere
    The Anglo-American Bookshop, Via della Vite 27 & 57
    The Lion Bookshop, Via del Babuino 181
Florence
    The Paperback Exchange, Via Fiesolana 3r
Milan
    The American Bookstore, Via Camperio 16, at Largo Cairoli

Apart from these shops, Feltrinelli bookshops usually have a reasonable selection of English-language books. Other bookshops are listed under the individual towns.

MAPS

For maps of cities, you will generally find those published in this book, combined with those provided by the tourist offices, adequate. However, if you want more detailed maps (such as for the larger cities), you can buy them at Feltrinelli bookshops or at newspaper stands. Excellent road and city maps are published by the Istituto Geografico de Agostini, the Touring Club Italiano and Michelin, and are available in all major bookshops. If you are driving around Italy, invest in de Agostini's *Atlante Stradale Italiano* (L32,000), a complete book of road maps for the country, including city maps for many places.

Maps of walking trails in the Alps and Apennines are available in major bookshops, although you will find it easier to locate maps of specific zones once you are in the area. Recommended maps are published by Tabacco and Kompass. Both series of maps also feature the location of mountain refuges.

MEDIA
Newspapers & Magazines

Each major city has its own daily newspaper,

which tends to have separate sections devoted to larger towns in the surrounding province. There is no 'national' newspaper as such, although Rome's *La Repubblica* and Milan's *Corriere della Sera* give extensive coverage of national and international events and have been 'adopted' as the two national newspapers; they're available throughout the country. Newspapers all have their own political slant, but as far as these two major papers are concerned probably no more so than in the USA or the UK.

The major English-language newspapers available in Italy are the *Herald Tribune* (L2400, US-based and available Tuesday to Sunday) and the *European* (L3000, available Fridays). The *Guardian* (L2200 on airmail paper) and *The Times* (L3000), as well as the various tabloids, are sent from London, so, outside major cities such as Rome and Milan, they are generally a few days old. *Time*, *Newsweek* (both L3700) and the *Economist* (L6200) are available weekly.

TV & RADIO

There are more than 600 TV channels in Italy, although some are obviously very local. There are three national public stations: RAI 1, 2 and 3. Control of these three is handed out to the three main political parties – the Christian Democrats control RAI 1, the Socialists control RAI 2, and the Communists control RAI 3. The differences become really obvious in their news services, which can be quite blatant in their coverage of political news, each station favouring its respective controller.

There are five national private TV stations: ReteA, Telemontecarlo (TMC), Canale 5, Italia 1 and a video music channel. All the other stations are local and private – about 600 licences were issued in early 1993 to 'solve' the world-record proliferation of pirate stations.

The CBS evening news is broadcast every morning from Tuesday to Saturday on Telemontecarlo at 7.30 am and again at 8 am. The station also broadcasts CNN from about 2 am until 7.30 am. On Channel 41 (known as Eurovox) in Rome you can pick up the American PBS News McNair Lehir News Hour between 7.30 and 8.30 pm.

Radio

There are three public radio stations, again run by RAI. All of the rest are private and there are no pirates, since all may transmit until 1995 when about 1000 licences will be issued.

Vatican Radio (526 on the AM dial or 93.3 and 105 on FM) broadcasts the news in English at 7 am, 8.30 am, 6.15 pm and 9.50 pm. On the RAI radio station at 846 on the AM dial, news in English is broadcast hourly throughout the night, from 1 to 5 am at three minutes past the hour.

FILM & PHOTOGRAPHY

A roll of normal Kodak film (36 exposures, 100 ASA) costs L8000. It costs up to L23,000 to have 36 exposures developed and L16,000 for 24 exposures. A roll of 36 slides costs L10,000 and L6000 for development.

Outlets where you can buy films and have your photos processed are numerous. A roll of film is called a *pellicola* but you will be understood if you ask for 'film'. Many places claim to process films in one hour but you will rarely get your photos back that quickly – count on late the next day if the outlet has its own processing equipment, or three to four days if it doesn't.

Enthusiasts should note that the light changes quite markedly throughout Italy. In the south it is stronger and brighter, whereas the regions of Tuscany and Umbria in central Italy are noted for their soft light. As you go farther north the atmosphere is generally misty, a combination of natural effect and air pollution.

HEALTH

It is important to be aware that the quality of medical treatment in Italian public hospitals varies throughout Italy. Basically, the farther north you travel the better the standard of care. You will generally stand a better chance of good, prompt treatment, for instance, in Trentino-Alto Adige than you would in Rome at a public hospital, although standards can vary between institutions. Private hospitals and clinics throughout the country generally provide excellent and reliable services. They are, however, very expensive if you have no medical insurance, although if it is necessary to pay for treatment at a public hospital, costs can also be very high. Your embassy or consulate in Italy will be able to provide a list of recommended doctors in major cities; however, if you have a specific health complaint, it would be wise to obtain the necessary information and referrals for treatment before leaving home.

The public health system is administered by local centres known as Unità Sanitaria Locale (USL), listed under 'U' in the phone book. Each USL centre is responsible for about 15,000 people and therefore they can be very numerous in large cities. Opening hours are limited, from 8 am to 12.30 pm. For emergency treatment, it's better to go straight to the first-aid *(pronto soccorso)* section of a public hospital, where you'll also receive emergency dental treatment. Often, first aid is also available at train stations, airports and ports.

Medical Cover

Citizens of EC countries are covered for emergency medical treatment in Italy on presentation of an E111 form. It is necessary to obtain information about this from your national health service before leaving home. Note that treatment in private hospitals is not covered. Australia also has a reciprocal arrangement with Italy so that emergency treatment is covered; Medicare in Australia publishes a brochure with the details. The USA, Canada and New Zealand do not have reciprocal arrangements, and citizens of these countries will be required to pay for any treatment in Italy themselves. Advise medical staff of any reciprocal arrangements *before* they begin treating you.

Health Insurance

Travellers should seriously consider taking out a travel insurance policy which also covers health care, whether or not a reciprocal arrangement exists, in order to have

greater flexibility in deciding where and how you are treated. Such insurance will usually also cover ambulance expenses as well as the cost of repatriation to your own country.

There is a wide variety of policies and your travel agent will have recommendations. The international student travel policies handled by STA or other student travel organisations are usually good value.

Some policies specifically exclude 'dangerous activities' which can mean scuba diving, motorcycling, and even trekking. If such activities are on your agenda, you don't want that sort of policy.

You may prefer a policy which pays doctors or hospitals direct rather than you having to pay on the spot and claim later. If you have to claim later, make sure you keep all documentation. Some policies ask you to call back (reverse charges) to a centre in your home country where an immediate assessment of your problem is made.

Travel Health Guides

Most books on travel health are geared towards the tropics, where health is a major issue. This is not the case in Italy, although you might consider the following books:

Travellers' Health, Dr Richard Dawood, Oxford University Press. Comprehensive, easy to read and authoritative, this book is highly recommended, though rather large to lug around.
Travel with Children, Maureen Wheeler, Lonely Planet Publications. This includes basic advice on travel health for younger children.

Medical Kit

A small, straightforward medical kit might prove useful, if only to avoid the problem of buying basic items when you are uncertain how to ask for them in Italian. In any case, all necessary medications are available in pharmacies throughout the country.

The kit could include:

- Aspirin or Panadol for pain or fever
- an antihistamine (such as Benadryl), useful as a decongestant for colds, allergies, to ease the itch from insect bites or stings or to help prevent motion sickness

- antiseptic, Mercurochrome and antibiotic powder or a similar 'dry' spray for cuts and grazes
- calamine lotion to ease irritation from bites or stings
- bandages and Band-aids for minor injuries
- scissors, tweezers and a thermometer (note that mercury thermometers are prohibited by airlines)
- insect repellent, sunscreen, suntan lotion and chapstick

Other useful medications might include laxatives and antifungal skin ointments, and Lomotil (or Imodium) for diarrhoea, particularly if you are travelling with children.

General Preparations

Given the potential problems with language, make sure you are healthy before you leave home. If you are embarking on a long trip, make sure your teeth are OK: dentists are particularly expensive in Italy.

If you wear glasses, take a spare pair and your prescription. If you lose your glasses, you will be able to have them replaced within a few days by an optician (ottico).

If you require a particular medication, take an adequate supply as well as the prescription, with the generic rather than the brand name, as it will make getting replacements easier.

No vaccinations are required for entry into Italy, unless you have been travelling through a part of the world where yellow fever or cholera may be prevalent.

Basic Rules

Care in what you eat and drink is the most important health rule; stomach upsets are the most likely travel health problem, but in Italy the majority of these upsets will be relatively minor and probably due to overindulgence in the local food.

Water Tap water should be drinkable throughout Italy, although it is a good idea to check with the locals first as in some areas it can be unreliable. A sign that says *acqua non potabile*, sometimes seen on camping grounds for instance, and in every train toilet, means that the water is not drinkable.

Italians have developed the habit of drinking bottled mineral water, but if you are on a tight budget this can be an expensive proposition. As a rule, if you do drink tap water, you should have no problems apart from a possible reaction to the change of water.

In the hotter climate of southern Italy, make sure you drink enough – don't rely on feeling thirsty to indicate when you should drink. Not needing to urinate or very dark-yellow urine is a danger sign.

Nutrition Make sure your diet is well balanced. You will have little trouble finding good-quality fruit and vegetables in Italy.

Everyday Health A normal body temperature is 98.6°F or 37°C; more than 2°C higher is a 'high' fever. A normal adult pulse rate is 60 to 80 beats per minute (children 80 to 100, babies 100 to 140). You should know how to take a temperature and a pulse rate. As a general rule the pulse increases about 20 beats per minute for each °C rise in fever.

Respiration (breathing) rate is also an indicator of illness. Count the number of breaths per minute: between 12 and 20 is normal for adults and older children (up to 30 for younger children, 40 for babies). People with a high fever or serious respiratory illness (such as pneumonia) breathe more quickly than normal. More than 40 shallow breaths a minute usually means pneumonia.

Many health problems can be avoided by taking care of yourself. Avoid climatic extremes: keep out of the sun when it's hot, dress warmly when it's cold. You can avoid insect bites by covering bare skin when insects are around, by screening windows or beds or by using insect repellents.

Climatic & Geographical Considerations

Sunburn In the south of Italy during summer or at high altitude in the Alps you can get sunburnt surprisingly quickly, even through cloud. Use a sunscreen and take extra care to cover areas which don't normally see sun – eg your feet. A hat provides added protection, and you could also use zinc cream or some other barrier cream for your nose and lips. Calamine lotion is good for mild sunburn.

Prickly Heat Prickly heat is an itchy rash caused by excessive perspiration trapped under the skin. It usually strikes people who have just arrived in a hot climate and whose pores have not yet opened sufficiently to cope with greater sweating. Keeping cool but bathing often, using a mild talcum powder or even resorting to air-conditioning may help until you acclimatise.

Heat Exhaustion Dehydration or salt deficiency can cause heat exhaustion. Take time to acclimatise to high temperatures and make sure you get sufficient liquids. Salt deficiency is characterised by fatigue, lethargy, headaches, giddiness and muscle cramps and in this case salt tablets may help. Vomiting or diarrhoea can deplete your liquid and salt levels.

Anhydrotic heat exhaustion, caused by an inability to sweat, is quite rare. Unlike the other forms of heat exhaustion, it is likely to strike people who have been in a hot climate for some time, rather than newcomers.

Heatstroke This serious and sometimes fatal condition can occur if the body's heat-regulating mechanism breaks down and the body temperature rises to dangerous levels. Long, continuous periods of exposure to high temperatures can leave you vulnerable to heatstroke. You should avoid excessive alcohol or strenuous activity when you first arrive in a hot climate.

The symptoms are feeling unwell, not sweating very much or at all and a high body temperature (39°C to 41°C). Where sweating has ceased, the skin becomes flushed and red. Severe, throbbing headaches and lack of coordination will also occur, and the sufferer may become confused or aggressive. Eventually the victim will become delirious or convulse. Hospitalisation is essential, but meanwhile get patients out of the sun, remove their clothing, cover them with a wet sheet or towel and then fan them continually.

Fungal Infections Hot-weather fungal infections are most likely to occur on the scalp, between the toes or fingers (athlete's foot), in the groin (jock itch or crotch rot) and on the body (ringworm). You get ringworm (which is a fungal infection, not a worm) from infected animals or by walking on damp areas, like shower floors.

To prevent fungal infections, wear loose, comfortable clothes, avoid artificial fibres, wash frequently and dry carefully. If you do get an infection, wash the infected area daily with a disinfectant or medicated soap and water, and rinse and dry well. Apply an antifungal powder, like the widely available Tinaderm. Try to expose the infected area to air or sunlight as much as possible and wash all towels and underwear in hot water as well as changing them often.

Cold Too much cold is just as dangerous as too much heat, particularly if it leads to hypothermia. Cold combined with wind and moisture is particularly risky. If you are trekking at high altitudes or in a cold, wet environment, be prepared.

Hypothermia occurs when the body loses heat faster than it can produce it and the core temperature of the body falls. It is surprisingly easy to progress from very cold to dangerously cold through a combination of wind, wet clothing, fatigue and hunger, even if the air temperature is above freezing. Symptoms of hypothermia are exhaustion, numb skin (particularly toes and fingers), shivering, slurred speech, irrational or violent behaviour, lethargy, stumbling, dizzy spells, muscle cramps and violent bursts of energy. Irrationality may take the form of sufferers claiming they are warm and trying to take off their clothes.

To treat hypothermia, first get the patient out of the wind and/or rain, remove their clothing if it's wet and replace it with dry, warm clothing. Give them hot liquids – not alcohol – and some high-kilojoule, easily digestible food. This should be enough for the early stages of hypothermia, but if it has gone further it may be necessary to place victims in warm sleeping bags and get in with them. Do not rub patients, place them near a fire or remove their wet clothes in the wind. If possible, place a sufferer in a warm (not hot) bath.

Altitude Sickness Acute Mountain Sickness or AMS occurs at high altitudes, where the lack of oxygen affects most people to some extent. There is no hard and fast rule as to how high is too high: AMS can strike at altitudes of 3000 metres, although 3500 to 4500 metres is the usual range. Very few treks or ski runs in the Alps reach heights of 3000 metres or more, so it's unlikely to be a major concern.

Headaches, nausea, dizziness, a dry cough, insomnia, breathlessness and loss of appetite are all signs to heed. Mild altitude problems will generally abate after a day or so, but if the symptoms persist or become worse the only treatment is to descend – even 500 metres can help.

Motion Sickness

Eating lightly before and during a trip will reduce the chances of motion sickness. If you are prone to motion sickness, try to find a place that minimises disturbance – near the wing on aircraft, close to midships on boats, near the centre on buses. Fresh air and a steady reference point like the horizon usually help, whereas reading or cigarette smoke don't. Commercial preparations against motion sickness, which can cause drowsiness, have to be taken before the trip commences; when you're feeling sick it's too late. Ginger is a natural preventative and is available in capsule form.

Diseases of Insanitation

Diarrhoea Despite all your precautions, you may still have a bout of mild travellers' diarrhoea, but a few rushed toilet trips with no other symptoms is not indicative of a serious problem. Moderate diarrhoea, involving half-a-dozen loose movements in a day, is more of a nuisance. Dehydration is the main danger with any diarrhoea, particularly for children, so fluid replenishment is the number one treatment. Weak black tea with

a little sugar, soda water, or soft drinks allowed to go flat and diluted 50% with water are all good. With severe diarrhoea a rehydrating solution is necessary to replace minerals and salts, and you should see a doctor. Stick to a bland diet as you recover.

Diseases Spread by People & Animals

Rabies Rabies is still found in Italy, but only in isolated areas of the Alps. It is caused by a bite or scratch by an infected animal. Dogs are a noted carrier. Any bite, scratch or even lick from a mammal in an area where rabies does exist should be cleaned immediately and thoroughly. Scrub with soap and running water, and then clean with an alcohol solution. If there is any possibility that the animal is infected, medical help should be sought immediately. Even if the animal is not rabid, all bites should be treated seriously as they can become infected or can result in tetanus.

Sexually Transmitted Diseases (STDs)

Sexual contact with an infected partner spreads these diseases. While abstinence is the only 100% preventative, using condoms is also effective. Gonorrhoea and syphilis are the most common of these diseases: sores, blisters or rashes around the genitals, discharges, or pain when urinating are common symptoms. Symptoms may be less marked or not observed at all in women. Syphilis symptoms eventually disappear completely but the disease continues and can cause severe problems in later years. The treatment of gonorrhoea and syphilis is by antibiotics.

There are numerous other STDs, for most of which effective treatment is available, though as yet there is no cure for herpes or HIV/AIDS. The latter has become a considerable problem in Europe, and also in Italy. HIV, the human immunodeficiency virus, may develop into AIDS, acquired immune deficiency syndrome. Apart from abstinence, the most effective preventative is always to practise safe sex using condoms. It is impossible to detect the HIV-positive status of an otherwise healthy-looking person without a blood test.

HIV/AIDS can also be spread through

infected blood transfusions and by dirty needles – acupuncture, tattooing and ear or nose piercing can potentially be as dangerous as intravenous drug use if the equipment is not clean. Needles used in Italian hospitals are reliable.

If you require treatment or tests for a suspected STD, head for the nearest USL or public hospital. Each USL area has its own Family Planning Centre (Consultorio Familiare) where you can go for contraceptives, pregnancy tests and information about abortion; these are listed under each USL office in the phone book, otherwise ask at the USL office.

Cuts, Bites & Stings
Cuts & Scratches Skin punctures can easily become infected in hot climates and may be difficult to heal. Treat any cut with an antiseptic solution and Mercurochrome. Where possible avoid bandages and Band-aids, which can keep wounds wet.

Bites & Stings Bee and wasp stings are usually painful rather than dangerous. Calamine lotion will give relief, or use ice packs to reduce the pain and swelling.

Snakes There is only one dangerous snake in Italy – the viper, which is found throughout Italy (except in Sardinia). To minimise your chances of being bitten, always wear boots, socks and long trousers when walking through undergrowth where snakes may be present. Don't put your hands into holes and crevices, and be careful when collecting firewood.

Viper bites do not cause instantaneous death, and an antivenin is widely available in pharmacies. Keep the victim calm and still, wrap the bitten limb tightly, as you would for a sprained ankle, and attach a splint to immobilise it. Then seek medical help, if possible with the dead snake for identification. Don't attempt to catch the snake if there is even a remote possibility of being bitten again. Tourniquets and sucking out the poison are now comprehensively discredited.

Lice All lice cause itching and discomfort. They make themselves at home in your hair (head lice), clothing (body lice) or in pubic hair (crabs). You catch lice through direct contact with infected people or by sharing combs, clothing and the like. Powder or shampoo treatment will kill the lice, and infected clothing should then be washed in very hot water.

Leeches & Ticks Leeches may be present in damp forest conditions; they attach themselves to your skin to suck your blood. Trekkers often get them on their legs or in their boots. Salt or a lighted cigarette end will make them fall off. Do not pull them off, as the bite is then more likely to become infected. An insect repellent may keep them away. Vaseline, alcohol or oil will persuade a tick to let go.

Always check your body if you have been walking through a tick-infested area.

Women's Health
Some women experience irregular periods when travelling, due to the upset in routine. If you use contraceptive pills, don't forget to take time zones into account, and beware that the pills may not be absorbed if you suffer intestinal problems. Ask your physician about these matters. If you think you've run into problems in Italy, contact the nearest Consultorio Familiare (see the earlier section on Sexually Transmitted Diseases).

Gynaecological Problems Poor diet, lowered resistance through the use of antibiotics for stomach upsets, and even contraceptive pills, can lead to vaginal infections when travelling in hot climates. Maintaining good personal hygiene, and wearing skirts or loose-fitting trousers and cotton underwear will help to prevent infections.

Yeast infections (thrush), characterised by a rash, itch and discharge, can be treated with a vinegar or even lemon-juice douche or with yoghurt. Nystatin suppositories are the usual medical prescription. Trichomonas is a more serious infection; symptoms are a discharge and a burning sensation when urinating, and if a vinegar-water douche is not effective, medical attention should be sought. Flagyl is the prescribed drug. In both cases, sexual partners must also be treated.

WOMEN TRAVELLERS

Italy is not a dangerous country for women, but women travelling alone will often find themselves plagued by unwanted attention from men. This attention usually involves catcalls, hisses and whistles and, as such, is more annoying than anything else. Lone women will also find it difficult to remain alone – you will have Italian men falling at your feet as you walk along the street, drink a coffee in a bar or try to read a book in a park. Usually the best response is to ignore them, but if that doesn't work, politely tell them that you are waiting for your husband (*marito*) or boyfriend (*fidanzato*) and, if necessary, walk away.

Some women wear fake wedding rings, but it is really a bit ridiculous to follow suggestions that you wear thick glasses, have your hair cut short and dress unfashionably.

If you really can't shake off an ardent admirer and he starts to become a serious nuisance or aggressive, it is best to avoid becoming aggressive in return as this almost always results in an unpleasant confrontation. The flirtatious Italian man in full flight can take serious offence at a rude rejection of his advances. If all else fails, approach the nearest member of the police or carabinieri.

Basically most of the attention falls into the nuisance/harassment category. However, women on their own should use their common sense. Avoid walking alone in deserted and dark streets, and look for hotels which are centrally located and within easy walking distance of places where you can eat at night (unsafe areas for women are noted throughout this book). Women should also avoid hitchhiking alone.

Women will find that, the farther south they travel, the more likely they are to be harassed. It is advisable to dress more conservatively in the south, particularly if you are travelling to small towns and villages. In cities where there is a high petty crime rate, such as Rome, Naples, Palermo, Syracuse and Bari, women on their own are regarded as prime targets for bag-snatchers and should be very careful about walking around in deserted streets.

Rome is one of the worst cities when it comes to overattentive males. Watch out for men with wandering hands on crowded buses. Either keep your back to the wall or make a loud fuss if someone starts fondling your backside.

Recommended reading is the *Handbook for Women Travellers* by M & G Moss (Judy Piatkus Publishers, London).

SPECIAL NEEDS

Travellers with special needs should try to seek information in advance about how to make their holiday in Italy as trouble-free as possible. Families, disabled and elderly travellers should book accommodation in advance in order to avoid inconvenience. Local tourist offices might be of some assistance in providing information.

Travel with Children

Successful travel with children can require a special effort. Don't try to overdo things by packing too much into the time available, and make sure activities include the kids as well. Remember that visits to museums and galleries can be tiring even for adults. Children might also be more interested in some of the major archaeological sites, such as Pompeii, the Colosseum and the Forum in Rome, and Greek temples in the south and Sicily. Include children in the planning of the trip – if they have helped to work out where they will be going, they will be much more interested when they get there. Discounts are available for children (usually under 12 years of age) on public transport and admission to museums, galleries etc.

For more information, see Lonely Planet's *Travel with Children* by Maureen Wheeler.

Older Travellers

Senior citizens are entitled to discounts on public transport and on admission fees at some museums in Italy. It is always important to ask. The minimum qualifying age is generally 60 years. You should also seek information in your own country on travel packages and discounts for senior travellers, through senior citizens' organisations and travel agents.

Disabled Travellers

Italy has only recently started to make proper provisions for disabled people, but little can be done about the uneven pavements in most cities, or about the endless flights of stairs at train stations and in many medieval hill towns. If you have a physical disability, get in touch with your national support organisation to see if it has specific information on facilities in Italy. If not, it should at least be able to provide general travel advice. The ENIT in your country will provide advice on facilities for the disabled in Italy, as well as on Italian associations for the disabled.

The UK-based Royal Association for Disability & Rehabilitation (RADAR) publishes a useful guide called *Holidays & Travel Abroad: A Guide for Disabled people*, which gives a good overview of facilities available to disabled travellers throughout Europe. Contact RADAR on ☎ 071-637 5400, or at 25 Mortimer St, London W1N 8AB.

The Italian travel agency, CIT, can advise on hotels which have special facilities, such as ramps etc. By booking rail travel in advance through CIT, you can also request that wheelchair ramps be provided on arrival of your train.

Gay & Lesbian Travellers

Homosexuality is legal in Italy and is well tolerated in major cities and particularly in the north of the country. However, overt displays of affection by homosexual couples could attract a negative response in smaller towns and villages. Generally speaking, friendships between Italian men are very physical anyway, involving physical contact that most Anglo-Saxons would find excessive. As such, the sight of two men (or two women) walking down a street arm in arm is hardly unusual.

Cities such as Rome, Florence and Milan offer several gay discos, which are generally listed in the Leisure sections of the local newspapers. The national organisation for gay men is ARCI-gay (☎ 051-43 67 00), which is affiliated with the Communist Party's youth section, at Piazza di Porta Saragozza 2, P O Box 691, 40100 Bologna. The corresponding organisation for lesbians is based in Rome: ARCI-Co-ordinamento Donne (☎ 06-325 09 21), Via F Carrara 24. The bimonthly newsletter for lesbians, *Bolletino delle Connessioni Lesbiche Italiane*, is available here.

Babilonia is the national gay magazine, published monthly, and *Guida Gay Italia* is published annually. Both provide extensive information and are available at newsstands. General publications include: the *Spartacus Guide for Gay Men*, published by Bruno Gmünder (Berlin), a directory of gay entertainment venues in Europe; and, for lesbians, the international *Gaia's Guide*.

Further information about gay discos can be found throughout this book under the various city sections.

DANGERS & ANNOYANCES

Theft is the main problem for travellers in Italy. Thieves in the form of pickpockets and bag-snatchers operate in most major cities and are particularly active in Naples and Rome. The best way to avoid being robbed is to wear a money belt under your clothing. You should keep all important items, such as money, passport, other papers and tickets in the money belt at all times. If you are carrying a bag or camera, ensure that you wear the strap across your body and have the bag on the side away from the road. This will help deter snatch thieves, who often operate from motorcycles and scooters, although if they use a knife to slash the strap you might not stand much of a chance. Since the aim of young motorcycle bandits is often fun rather than gain, you are just as likely to find yourself relieved of your sunglasses – or worse, of an earring. Motorcycle bandits are very active in Naples, Rome, Syracuse and Palermo.

You should also watch out for groups of dishevelled-looking women and children. They generally work in groups of four of five and carry paper or cardboard which they use to distract your attention while they swarm around and riffle through your pockets and bag. Never underestimate their skill – they are lightning fast and very adept. Their favourite haunts are in and near major train stations, at tourist sights (such as the Colosseum) and in shopping areas. If you notice that you have been targeted by a group, either take evasive action, such as crossing the street, or shout *va via!* (go away!) in a loud, angry voice.

Pickpockets often hang out on crowded buses (the No 64 in Rome, which runs from Stazione Termini to the Vatican, is notorious) and in crowded areas such as markets. There is only one way to deter pickpockets: simply *do not* carry any money or valuables in your pockets, and be very careful about your bags.

Be careful even in hotels and don't leave valuables lying around your room. You should also be cautious of sudden friendships, particularly if it turns out that your new-found *amico* or *amica* wants to sell you something. Parked cars are also prime targets for thieves, particularly those with foreign number plates or rental company stickers. Try removing the stickers, or cover them and leave a local newspaper on the seat to make it look like a local car.

Never leave valuables in your car – in fact, try not to leave anything in the car if you can help it and certainly not overnight. It is a good idea to pay extra to leave your car in supervised car parks, although there is no guarantee that they are completely safe. Throughout Italy, particularly in the south, service stations along the autostradas are favourite haunts of thieves, who can clean out your car in the time it takes to have a cup of coffee. If possible, park the car where you can keep an eye on it. When driving in cities, you also need to be aware of snatch thieves when you pull up at traffic lights. Keep the doors locked, and if you have the windows open, ensure that there is nothing valuable on the dashboard. Car theft is a major problem in the regions of Campania and Apulia, particularly the cities of Naples, Bari, Foggia and Brindisi.

Horror tales abound about women being dragged to the ground by thieves trying to snatch their bags, about people losing wallets, watches and cameras on crowded buses or in a flurry of newspaper-waving children. The problem is that these things really do happen! Certainly even the most cautious travellers are still prey to expert thieves, but there is no need to be paranoid. By taking a few basic precautions, you can greatly lessen the risk of being robbed.

In case of theft or loss, always report the incident to the police within 24 hours and ask for a statement, otherwise your travel insurance company won't pay out.

In case of emergency, you can contact the police throughout Italy on ☎ 113, or the carabinieri on ☎ 112.

Traffic & Pedestrians

Italian traffic can at best be described as chaotic, at worst downright dangerous for the unprepared tourist. Drivers are not keen to stop for pedestrians, even at pedestrian crossings, and are more likely to swerve. Italian pedestrians deal with this problem by simply stepping off the sidewalk and walking through the (swerving) traffic with determination – it is a practice which seems to work, so if you feel uncertain about crossing a busy road, wait for the next Italian. In many cities, roads which appear to be for one-way traffic have special lanes for buses travelling in the opposite direction – always look both ways before stepping onto the road.

Pollution

Italy has a poor record when it comes to environmental concerns. Few Italians would think twice about dropping litter in the streets, illegally dumping household refuse in the country or driving a car or motorbike with a faulty or nonexistent muffler.

Tourists will be affected in a variety of ways by the surprising disregard Italians have for their country, which is of considerable natural and artistic beauty. Noise and air pollution are problems in the major cities, both caused mainly by heavy traffic. A headache after a day of sightseeing in Rome is likely to be caused by breathing carbon monoxide and lead, rather than simple tiredness. While cities such as Rome, Florence and Milan have banned normal traffic from their historic centres, there are still more than enough cars, buses and motorbikes in and around the inner city areas to pollute the air. When booking a hotel room it is a good idea to ask if it is quiet – although this might mean that you will have to decide between a view and sleep.

Italy's beaches are generally heavily polluted by industrial waste, sewage and oil spills from the Mediterranean's considerable sea traffic. The only reliably clean beaches are found in Sardinia, although the beaches of Sicily and the less populated areas of the south are also generally clean.

Italian-Style Service

It requires a lot of patience to deal with the Italian concept of service. What for Italians is simply a way of life, can be horrifying for the foreigner – like the bank clerk who wanders off to have a cigarette just as it is your turn (after a one-hour wait) to be served, or the postal worker who has far more important work to do at a desk than to sell stamps to customers. Anyone in a uniform or behind a counter (including police officers, waiters and shop assistants) is likely to regard you with imperious contempt. Long queues are the norm in banks, post offices and any government offices. But while the Italian queue, as an Australian journalist once observed, is usually 40 people wide and two people deep, Italians usually know their place.

It pays to remain calm and patient. Aggressive, demanding and angry customers stand virtually no chance of getting what they want.

Drugs

Drug laws in Italy are harsh, and anyone (including foreigners) found with even the smallest amount of drugs could find themselves hauled off to prison. The possession of any amount of drugs, including marijuana or hash, is illegal and penalties are harsh. Following a referendum in 1993, the Italian government is changing its 'zero tolerance' drug laws to make penalties less harsh for drug users, but the sensible option will still be to avoid drugs altogether.

Police

If you run into trouble in Italy, you're likely to end up dealing with either the police or the carabinieri. The police *(la polizia)* are a civil force and take their orders from the Ministry of the Interior, while the carabinieri fall under the Ministry of Defence. There is a considerable duplication of their roles, despite a 1981 reform of the police forces which intended to merge the two. Both forces are responsible for public order and security, which means that you can call either in the event of a robbery, attack etc.

The carabinieri wear a dark-blue uniform with a red stripe and drive dark-blue cars with a white stripe. Most of them come from the south and they are the butt of 'dumb-jokes' (much like the Polish and Irish), although they are well trained and tend to be helpful. You are most likely to be pulled over by the carabinieri rather than the police when you are speeding etc.

The police wear powder-blue pants with a fuchsia stripe and a navy-blue jacket and drive the same cars as the carabinieri, but with 'polizia' written on the side. They are generally held to be arrogant and not very helpful. However, tourists who want to report thefts, and people wanting to get a residence permit, will have to deal with them. Their headquarters are called the questura, and addresses and phone numbers are given in the Emergency sections throughout this book.

WORK

It is illegal for non-EC citizens to work in

Italy without a work permit, but trying to obtain one is extremely difficult. You will need to have a firm promise of a job which cannot be filled by an Italian and then you must apply to the Italian embassy in your own country for a work permit.

EC citizens are allowed to work in Italy, but they still need to obtain a permesso di soggiorno from the main police station in the town where they have found work. See the earlier Visas & Embassies section for information about these permits. A letter from the prospective employer promising work is necessary.

The easiest source of work for foreigners is teaching English, but even with full qualifications an American, Australian, Canadian or New Zealander will find it difficult to secure a permanent position. Most of the larger, more reputable schools will hire only people with work permits, but their attitude can become more flexible if demand for teachers is high and they come across someone with good qualifications. The more professional schools will require a TEFL (Teaching English as a Foreign Language) certificate. It is advisable to apply for work early in the year, in order to be considered for positions available in October (language school years correspond roughly to the Italian school year: late September to the end of June).

'Black economy' work (for those without permits) is generally untaxed, but in Italy even illegal workers can pay their taxes. Some employers will be prepared to hire people without permits, but will require them to have a *codice fiscale*, basically a tax number, which means that you are registered as a taxpayer, even though you are working illegally.

Again, teaching English is the first choice for most travellers who want to supplement their funds. There are numerous schools throughout the country which hire people without work permits or qualifications, but the pay is usually low (around L15,000 an hour). It is more lucrative to advertise your services and pick up private students (although rates vary wildly, ranging from as low as L10,000 to up to L50,000 an hour). In a large city like Rome the average rate is around L30,000, while in smaller provincial towns, where the market is more limited, even qualified private teachers will have to charge as low as L15,000 to L20,000 in order to attract students. Although you can get away with absolutely no qualifications or experience, it might be a good idea to bring along a few English grammar books (including exercises) to help you at least appear professional.

Most people get started by placing advertisements in shop windows and on university notice boards, or in a local publication, such as *Wanted in Rome* or *Porta Portese* in Rome or *Secondomano* in Milan. All are available at newsstands.

Many foreigners also find illegal, untaxed work in bars, restaurants, or as baby-sitters. To find this type of work, ask around, or keep an eye on the employment columns in the publications just mentioned. Another option is au pair work. A useful guide is *The Au Pair and Nanny's Guide to Working Abroad* by S Griffith & S Legg (Vacation Work, paperback). By the same publisher is *Work Your Way Around the World* by Susan Griffith (paperback).

Busking is common in Italy, although theoretically buskers require a municipal permit. Although Italians tend not to stop and gather around street performers, they are usually generous. Selling goods on the street is also illegal unless you have a municipal permit, and you are likely to run into trouble unless you manage to find a spot at a flea market.

ACTIVITIES

If the museums, galleries and sights are not enough to occupy your time in Italy, there are numerous options for getting off the beaten tourist track. From mountaineering to courses in the history of art, Italy offers a wide range of outdoor and cerebral pursuits.

Hiking & Mountaineering

The Alps, in particular the spectacular Dolomites, offer well-marked trails and strategically placed mountain refuges for the long-distance hiker. With careful planning it is possible to walk for as many days as you want, without the need to carry large quantities of supplies, as it is possible to obtain both food and accommodation at the refuges. However, hikers still need to be well prepared in the Alps – even at the height of summer the weather can change suddenly. Hikers planning to tackle longer and more difficult trails, particularly at high altitudes, should ensure that they leave basic details of their route with someone. They should also be well informed on weather predictions and prepared for cold weather, rain and snow (the first snow can fall in September). It is also a good idea to carry a lightweight thermal blanket in the event that it is necessary to leave behind an injured person while you seek help, as help might not arrive until the next day. While there are many refuges along the way, hikers should still carry lightweight, high-energy food, such as chocolate or muesli bars, and ensure that they have plenty of water.

Guided treks are a good idea for inexperienced people, although there are also guided treks along more difficult trails, usually involving the use of ropes and which generally require that you have mountaineering skills and the correct equipment (see the Alpine sections of the northern regions for further information).

The Apennines also have good walking trails, and interesting areas include the Abruzzo National Park and the Sila Massif in Calabria. The Alpi Apuane in Tuscany also have well-marked and challenging trails. In Sardinia the rugged landscape offers some spectacular hikes in the eastern ranges, such as Gennargentu, and the gorges near Dorgali. See the relevant sections for further information.

Skiing

There are numerous excellent ski resorts in the Italian Alps and, again, the Dolomites provide the most dramatic scenery. Options include downhill and cross-country *(sci di fondo)* skiing, as well as alpine skiing (only for the adventurous and advanced), where skiers head well away from the organised runs and combine their mountaineering and skiing skills.

Skiing is quite expensive because of the costs of ski lifts and accommodation, but special packages known as *Settimana Bianca* (white week) can reduce the expense. It is not expensive, on the other hand, to hire ski equipment – and this factor should be weighed up against the inconvenience of bringing your own gear. Cross-country skiing obviously costs less because it is not necessary to pay for the lifts.

The season in Italy generally extends from December to late March, although at higher altitudes and in particularly good years it can be longer. On the Marmolada glacier in Trentino-Alto Adige there is year-round skiing.

The five major (read: most fashionable and expensive) ski resorts in Italy are Cortina d'Ampezzo in the Veneto, Madonna di Campiglio, San Martino di Castrozza and Canazei in Trentino, and Courmayeur in the Valle d'Aosta. There are many other, less expensive resorts which also offer excellent facilities (see the Alpine sections of the northern regions for more information).

Water Sports

Windsurfing and sailing are extremely popular in Italy, and at most beach resorts it is possible to rent boats and equipment – generally for a hefty fee. There are also various diving schools, but the scenery above water is much more interesting. See the Things to See & Do and Activities sections throughout this book for boat and windsurfing equipment hire at water resorts.

Cycling

This is a good option for people who can't afford a car but want to see some of the more out-of-the-way places. The only problem is that more than 75% of Italy is mountainous or hilly, so you will need some stamina and a good bike. A mountain bike would be a good idea, enabling you to tackle some of the Alpine trails as well. Cycling is not a particularly popular sport in Italy and consequently it can be difficult to hire bikes for long periods, although mountain biking is growing in popularity and bikes are easy to hire in the mountain regions. People planning to cycle around Italy are advised to bring their own bikes, or might consider buying one once they arrive in Italy (see the Getting Around chapter for details). Bikes can be transported on aeroplanes for a surprisingly low fee and, within Italy, they can be transported free on ferries to Sicily and Sardinia and relatively cheaply on trains.

Good areas to explore by bike include the coastal areas of Sardinia and Apulia and the hills of Tuscany and Umbria.

Courses

Travelling to Italy to study the language is becoming increasingly popular. Courses are offered by private schools and universities throughout Italy and are a great way to learn Italian, while enjoying the opportunity to live in an Italian city or town.

The cheapest option is the Università per Stranieri in Perugia, where the cost per month is L240,000 (compared to an average of L600,000 at a private school in Florence). Individual schools and universities are listed under the relevant towns throughout this book. Accommodation can usually be arranged through the school.

Many schools also offer courses in painting, art history, sculpture, architecture and cooking; however, all of these courses can be expensive at an average of L600,000 a month.

It is also possible to undertake serious academic study at an Italian university, although obviously only if you have a very good command of the language.

Italian cultural institutes will provide information about study in Italy, as well as enrolment forms.

HIGHLIGHTS

Being a serious tourist in Italy can be a mind-numbing experience. There are so many important churches, museums, galleries, and archaeological sights – far too many to take in during the average holiday. Overzealous sightseers will find that after the first two or three major museums they might start to resent the sight of another sculpture or painting. Constant visits to archaeological sites and churches will start to seem like marathon runs and you will find yourself yearning for an armchair and TV.

The secret is not to overdo it. Try to do some research beforehand to determine which museums, galleries, churches etc you particularly want to see – while allowing enough time in your schedule for detours and surprises. Also make time for some long lunches and allow a few hours here and there to enjoy a coffee or wine in one of the country's beautiful piazzas. Instead of making a whirlwind tour of every archaeological site, choose some of the better ones and take along a picnic.

Following are a few of the highlights and 'musts' of a trip to Italy, including some lesser known, out-of-the-way places to visit. Don't take it as a definitive list of things to see, but rather as a start for your own further research.

Museums & Galleries

The Vatican Museums in Rome and the magnificent Uffizi Gallery in Florence are absolutely not to be missed, but try to take your time. The Bargello Museum in Florence, with its excellent sculpture collection, is another must, as is the Accademia Gallery,

Museum entry ticket (note price rise)

which houses Michelangelo's *David*. In Venice the Peggy Guggenheim Gallery of Modern Art is well worth a visit. The Museo Archeologico Nazionale in Naples houses one of the most important archaeological collections in the world (although large sections of the museum are usually closed). A visit to the Museo Nazionale di Villa Giulia in Rome to see its important collection of Etruscan treasures will make a tour of the Etruscan sites in Lazio (see the following section) more enjoyable.

Archaeological Sites

The Colosseum, the Roman Forum and the Palatine Hill are obvious musts in Rome, but also take a look at the Baths of Caracalla and at least one of the catacombs. Near Rome, at Tivoli, is the Villa Adriana, the massive villa of the Roman emperor Hadrian.

The best Etruscan sites are also near Rome and include the painted tombs of Tarquinia and the *tumuli*, tombs under huge mounds of earth, at Cerveteri. Both towns also have small Etruscan museums worth a look.

The excavations at Pompeii should not be missed. Travelling farther south, at Paestum, are the first important relics of Magna Graecia, a group of well-preserved temples. Other temples well worth a visit are at Agrigento, Selinunte and Segesta in Sicily. The backdrop to the Greek theatres at Segesta and at Taormina make them particularly evocative. The archaeological park in Syracuse is also recommended.

Still in Sicily, visit the imperial Roman villa at Casale, just out of Piazza Armerina, to see the fabulous mosaics.

Churches

The phenomenal number of churches in Italy should satisfy even the most obsessive lover of religious architecture. A few highlights include the cathedrals in Florence, Milan, Siena and Orvieto, and that at Monreale, near Palermo, for its beautiful mosaics. The Basilica of San Vitale in Ravenna is notable both for its mosaics and for the design of the church. Apulia has several Romanesque churches worth a visit, the most beautiful being undoubtedly the cathedral at Trani. The Romanesque cathedral in Otranto is worth a visit to see the extraordinary 12th century mosaic of *The Tree of Life* which covers its floor. Most tourists will eventually make their way to St Peter's Basilica in Rome, and you can make the trip even more interesting (depending on your point of view) by attending a mass said by the pope.

Historic Towns

There are so many fascinating and beautiful medieval towns in Italy that it seems a shame to confine your travels to the major cities. In Tuscany visit San Gimignano and Volterra, and in Umbria make a tour of the medieval hill towns, many still surrounded by their walls and crowned with ruined castles. The more interesting towns include Assisi, Spoleto, Gubbio and Orvieto, but also try to visit the villages of Spello and Narni. In the Marches visit the beautiful town of Urbino, birthplace of Raphael. Ravenna, with its extraordinary Byzantine churches and mosaics, is one of the great highlights of a visit to Italy.

In Liguria walk along the coast of the Riviera di Levante to visit the Cinque Terre, five tiny villages linked by a walking track. One of the most fascinating towns in Italy is Matera in Basilicata. Wandering around its famous *sassi* (stone houses) is an experience not easily forgotten. Positano is the most beautiful town on the Amalfi Coast, but it's also worth visiting Ravello.

Natural Parks

If you want to take a break from your grand tour of the tourist sights, head for the Dolomites, in particular the stunning park, Fanes-Sennes-Braies. Near Madonna di Campiglio is one of the more beautiful valleys in the Alps, the Val di Genova in the Parco Nazionale Adamello-Brenta. The Parco Nazionale di Gran Paradiso, straddling the Valle d'Aosta and Piedmont, and the Abruzzo National Park are also worth putting on the itinerary. There are some spectacular locations in Sardinia, including Capo Testa near Santa Teresa di Gallura; the long sandy beaches of the Costa Verde, notably the isolated Piscinas; and the Codula di Luna and the Gola di Gorroppu near Dorgali.

For an unforgettable experience, go on a tour of Sicily's volcanoes. Climb Vulcano and Stromboli in the Lipari Islands, and Mt Etna, one of the world's largest active volcanoes.

General Sights

Italy itself is a virtual museum and in every part of the country you will come across monuments, works of art, views and special places which have the capacity to surprise even the most world-weary traveller. Here are a few of the better ones: Michelangelo's *Pietà* in St Peter's Basilica, Rome; the Grand Canal in Venice; the *Pala d'Oro* (gold altarpiece) in St Mark's Basilica, Venice; the view of Tuscany from the top of the town hall tower in San Gimignano; Giotto's frescoes in the Scrovegni Chapel, Padua; Siena's Piazza del Campo and Pisa's Campo dei Miracoli; the strange meadow named Piano Grande at Monte Vettore, near Castelluccio at the border of Umbria and the Marches; and the Porta Portese market in Rome.

ACCOMMODATION
Camping

Facilities range from major complexes with swimming pools, tennis courts, restaurants and supermarkets, to simple camping grounds. Prices at even the most basic camping grounds can be surprisingly expensive once you add up the various charges for each person, a site for your tent or caravan and a car, but they generally still work out cheaper than a double room in a one-star hotel. Average prices are L6000 to L8000 per adult, L4000 to L6000 for children aged under 12 years, L6000 to L8000 for a site, and the same for a car. There is sometimes a charge for use of the showers, usually around L1000, and for electricity, usually between L2000 and L3000.

Locations are usually good, ranging from beach or lakeside, to valleys in the Alps. In major cities, camping grounds are often far from the historic centres, and the incon- venience, plus the additional cost of needing to use public transport, should be weighed up against the price of a hotel room.

Free camping is generally not permitted in Italy and you might find yourself disturbed during the night by the carabinieri. But out of the main summer tourist season, free campers who choose spots not visible from the road, don't light fires, and who try to be inconspicuous in other ways, shouldn't have too much trouble. Camper vans are very popular in Italy, particularly in Sardinia (see the Getting Around chapter for details on renting them) where they are a useful mode of transport and accommodation for travellers to the island's more isolated and beautiful spots.

Camping grounds are listed throughout this book, and full lists in and near cities and towns are usually available from local tourist offices. In Sicily and Sardinia the regional tourist boards publish annual booklets listing all facilities throughout the islands. The Touring Club Italiano (TCI) publishes an annual book listing all camping grounds in Italy, *Campeggi e Villagi Turistici in Italia* (L20,000), and the Istituto Geografico de Agostini publishes the annual *Guida di Campeggi in Europa* (L20,000), both available in major bookshops in Italy.

Hostels

Hostels in Italy are called *ostelli per la gioventù* and are run by the Associazione Italiana Alberghi per la Gioventù (AIG), which is affiliated with the International Youth Hostel Federation (IYHF). An IYHF card is not always required, but it is recommended that you have one. Membership cards can be purchased at major hostels, from CTS (student and youth travel centre) offices, from AIG offices throughout Italy, and of course from an IYHF-affiliated office in your home country. Pick up a booklet on Italian hostels, with details of prices, locations etc, from the AIG national head office (☎ 06-487 11 52), Via Cavour 44, Rome.

Many Italian hostels are beautifully located, some in castles and villas. Many have bars and with few exceptions they have restaurants, or kitchens (to cook your own meals), or both. Nightly rates vary from L12,000 to L18,000 and the cost per night often includes breakfast. If not, breakfast will cost L2000. In some hostels there is an extra charge for use of heating and hot water, usually around L1000. A meal will cost L12,000.

Accommodation is in segregated dormitories, although some hostels offer family rooms (at a higher price per person).

Hostels are generally closed from 9 am to 6 pm, although there are many exceptions. Check-in is from 6 to 10.30 pm, although some hostels will allow you to check-in in the morning, before they close for the day (it is best to check beforehand). Curfew is 10.30 or 11 pm in winter and 11.30 pm or midnight in summer. It is usually necessary to pay before 9 am on the day of your departure, otherwise you could be charged for another night.

Pensioni & Hotels

Prices charged by hotels and pensioni in Italy were deregulated by the government in 1992. Previously all prices had been controlled by provincial boards, which awarded each establishment a classification based on the service and amenities provided. The system was based on stars, a one-star hotel being the most basic and a five-star the most luxurious.

While the star classification system has been retained, establishments can now set their own prices. This meant that prices skyrocketed by up to 40% in some cities, particularly Rome, Milan and Florence. Travellers reported that lists of prices set by provincial boards remained posted in some hotels, even though they were no longer adhered to. Tourist offices will continue to publish booklets listing pensioni, hotels and prices, but only those establishments which set their room charges in advance and notify the tourist offices will be included. Once the hotels and pensioni have notified the tourist board of charges for the coming year, they will be required by law to adhere to these prices and tourists can report any overcharg-

ing to the tourist office. The catch is that proprietors have two legal opportunities annually to increase prices.

The government expects that market forces and common sense will see prices stabilise by the end of 1993. Meanwhile, the best advice would be to confirm hotel charges before you put your bags down, as well as shopping around to take advantage of the competition that has resulted from the new deregulated system.

Proprietors still employ various methods of bill-padding. These include charges for showers (usually around L2000), a compulsory breakfast (up to L14,000 in the high season) and compulsory half or full board (although this can often be a good deal in some towns).

There is no difference between an establishment that calls itself a *pensione* and one that calls itself an *albergo* (hotel) – in fact, some use both titles. However, a pensione will generally be of one to three-star quality, while a hotel can be awarded up to five stars. *Locande* (similar to pensioni) and *alloggi*, also known as *affittacamere*, are generally cheaper, but not always. Locande and affittacamere are not included in the star classification system, although in some areas (such as the Lipari Islands and in the Alps) the standard of affittacamere is very high.

While the quality of accommodation can vary a great deal, one-star hotels/pensioni tend to be very basic and usually do not have private bathrooms attached to rooms. Standards at two-star establishments are often only slightly better, but rooms will generally have private bathrooms. Once you arrive at three stars you can assume that standards will be high, although quality still varies dramatically. Four and five-star hotels are usually part of a group of hotels and offer facilities such as room service, laundry and dry-cleaning. These types of hotels are generally used by businesspeople and by tour companies which book-in large groups of tourists (thus taking advantage of special low rates). For the average traveller it is really an unnecessary expense in Italy to go above three-star hotels.

Overall, prices are higher in Rome, Florence, Milan and Venice, and at other major tourist destinations. They also tend to be higher in northern Italy than in the south (the deregulation of hotel prices had only minimal impact in most of the south), and prices can skyrocket in the high season at beach resorts and during the ski season in the Alps.

A single room *(camera singola)* is uniformly expensive in Italy, costing from L25,000 to well over L100,000, and many of the cheaper establishments do not even bother to cater for the single traveller. A double room *(camera doppia* for a room with twin beds, and *camera matrimoniale* for a double bed) ranges from around L40,000 to upwards of L250,000. It is much cheaper to share with two or more people. In most parts of Italy, proprietors will charge no more than 15% of the cost of a double room for each additional person.

Tourist offices have booklets listing all pensioni and hotels, including prices (although they might not always be up to date). Ask for lists of locande and affittacamere. It is also possible to telephone many tourist offices to obtain information in advance.

Rental Accommodation

Finding rental accommodation in the major cities can be difficult and time-consuming, but not impossible. There are rental agencies which will assist for a fee (agencies are listed under the individual cities in this book). Prices are higher for short-term rental. A small apartment anywhere near the centre of Rome will cost around L1,800,000 a month and it is usually necessary to pay a bond (generally at least one month in advance). Apartments and houses (villas) for rent are listed in local publications such as the weekly *Porta Portese* in Rome. You will find that many owners want to rent to foreigners only. This is usually because they want to rent their property for the short term, or because they intend to charge a high rent. Another option is to answer an advertise-

ment in any of the local publications to share an apartment.

In major resort areas, such as the Lipari Islands and other parts of Sicily, the coastal areas of Sardinia and in the Alps, the tourist offices have lists of local apartments and villas for rent. Most offices will be more than cooperative if you telephone beforehand for information on how to book an apartment.

People wanting to rent a villa in the countryside can seek information from specialist travel agencies in their own country, or contact an organisation in Italy directly. One of the major companies in Italy, which has villas in Tuscany, Umbria, the Veneto, Sicily and near Rome, is Cuendet. This reliable company publishes a booklet listing all of the villas in its files, many with photos. Prices for a villa for two or three people range from around L350,000 a week in winter to more than L1,000,000 a week in August. For details, write to Signora N Cuendet, Località Il Cereto/Strove, 53035 Monteriggioni, Siena (☎ 0577-30 11 30, fax 0577-30 11 49), and ask for a catalogue (US$15). In London, Cuendet operates through International Chapter (☎ 071-722 9560), 102 St John's Wood Terrace, London NW8 6PL. In the USA it operates in partnership with Destination Italia (☎ 0201-327 2333), 165 Chestnut St, Allendale, NJ 07401.

CIT offices throughout the world also have lists of villas and apartments available for rent in Italy. In Australia, try an organisation called Cottages & Castles (☎ 03-862 1142), 11 Laver St, Kew 3101.

Don't expect to land in Italy and find an apartment or villa immediately – unless you are staying for an indefinite period, you might find that your holiday is taken up with flat-hunting.

Other Accommodation

Agriturismo This is a holiday on a working farm and is becoming increasingly popular in Italy. Traditionally the idea was that families rented out rooms in their farmhouses, and it is still possible to find this type of accommodation. However, the more common type of establishment is a restaurant in a restored medieval farm complex, with rooms available for rent. All establishments are actual farms and you will usually be able to sample the local produce. Agriturismo is well organised in Trentino-Alto Adige, Tuscany, Umbria and parts of Sardinia, and local tourist offices will usually have information.

Two national bodies which publish books listing all facilities in Italy are: Agriturist (☎ 06-6 85 21), Corso Vittorio Emanuele 101, 00186 Rome (the book costs L33,000 and is available in selected bookshops); and Turismo Verde (☎ 06-361 10 51), Via Mariano Fortuny 20, 00196 Rome (the book costs L14,000 and is available at Feltrinelli bookshops in Italy).

Refuges If you are planning to hike in the Alps, Apennines or other mountains in Italy, obtain information on the network of mountain refuges *(rifugi)*. Many are run by the CAI (see the Useful Organisations section) and the average price per person for an overnight stay plus breakfast is around L18,000 (less if you are a member of the CAI). Accommodation is generally in dormitories and meals are available. There are also numerous private refuges, which are more expensive, usually charging prices similar to one-star hotels. The locations of refuges are marked on good hiking maps and it should be noted that most are open only from July to September. It is a good idea, particularly during August, to book a bed in advance. Additional information, including telephone numbers, can be obtained from local tourist offices or from the CAI.

Religious Institutions These institutions offer accommodation in major cities and often in monasteries in the country, although many will accept Catholics only. The standard is usually good, but prices are no longer low. You can expect to pay about the same as for a one-star hotel, if not more. Information can be obtained through local tourist offices, or through the archdiocese in your city. Some religious institutions offering accommodation are listed throughout this

book. Women can seek information from the Associazione Cattolica al Servizio della Giovane (or Protezione della Giovane), which can organise accommodation for women (not men) in hostels. The organisation has offices in most major towns, often at major train stations, although these can be open at irregular hours.

Student Accommodation As already mentioned in the Activities section, people planning to study in Italy can usually organise accommodation through the school or university they will be attending. Options include a room with an Italian family, or a share arrangement with other students in an independent apartment. Some Italian universities operate a *casa dello studente*, which houses Italian students throughout the school year and lets out rooms to others during the summer break (July to the end of September). It can be very difficult to organise a room in one of these institutions. The best idea is to attempt to book a room through your own university, or to contact the relevant Italian university directly.

Warning
Prices for accommodation listed throughout this book are intended as a guide only. In light of the volatile state of affairs following deregulation, prices for hotels and pensioni (particularly in the budget category) will continue to fluctuate and are as likely to fall as to go through the roof. It is recommended that travellers always check room charges before putting their bags down.

FOOD
Eating is one of life's great pleasures for Italians. Be adventurous and never be intimidated by eccentric waiters or indecipherable menus and you will find yourself agreeing with the locals, who believe that nowhere in the world is the food as good as in Italy and, more specifically, in their own town.

What the world regards as Italian cooking is really a collection of regional cuisines *(cucine)*. While the eating habits of Italians are now fairly homogeneous, cooking styles continue to vary notably from region to region and significantly between the north and south. In the north the food is rich and often creamy, while in Sicily, for example, it is spicier.

The regional specialities of Emilia Romagna, including *tagliatelle al ragù* (and its adaptation, *spaghetti bolognese*), *lasagne* and *tortellini*, are among the best known Italian dishes, and the best *prosciutto* (cured ham) comes from Parma, which is also the home of *parmigiano reggiano*.

Liguria is the home of *pesto*, a delicious uncooked pasta sauce of fresh basil, garlic, oil, pine nuts and cheese, ground together with a mortar and pestle. Also try the *farinata*, a tart made with chick-pea flour, and the *focaccia*, a flat bread.

In Piedmont the cuisine is influenced to some extent by nearby France. It is often delicate and always flavoursome. *Tartufo bianco* (white truffle) is used in a wide variety of dishes. Traditional dishes make good use of game birds and animals, including chamois, pheasant and quail, as well as more unusual meats, such as horse, donkey and frog (there is even such a dish as frog risotto).

In Trentino-Alto Adige the cuisine has a heavy Austrian influence, and alongside minestrone and spaghetti, you will find *canerdeli* (a soup with noodles in it), goulash soup and Wiener schnitzel. Local specialities include smoked meats, eaten with heavy, black rye bread.

In the Veneto, try the boiled meats and the bitter red lettuce *(radicchio trevisano)*, eaten baked, or in risotto or with pasta. Risotto comes in many varieties in the Veneto: with mushrooms, zucchini, sausage, quail, trout and various other seafoods, chicken, spring vegetables and, not to be missed, *risotto nero*, coloured and flavoured with the ink of squid.

In Tuscany and Umbria the locals use a lot of olive oil and herbs, and regional specialities are noted for their simplicity, fine flavour and the use of fresh produce.

In Tuscany, try *bistecca fiorentina*, a huge T-bone steak usually three to four centimetres thick. It is quite acceptable, and in fact advisable, to order one steak for two people. Among the staples of Tuscan cuisine are small white beans known as *cannellini*, although all types of beans are widely used. There is also a wide range of Tuscan soups, from the simple *acquacotta*, which translates as 'cooked water', to the rich *minestrone alla fiorentina*, flavoured with pork and chicken giblets. Don't miss the incredibly rich *panforte*, Siena's famous traditional Christmas fruitcake.

In Umbria both the *tartufo* (truffle) and the *porcini* mushrooms (like the French *cèpes*) are abundant and both turn up in pasta, rice and a large number of other dishes. While many Umbrian dishes are based upon vegetables, the locals eat more meat than any other Italians, and a local speciality is *porchetta*, a whole roast piglet stuffed with rosemary. Umbrian cakes and pastries are worth a try, as are the chocolates produced by the Perugina factory at Perugia, notably the famous *baci* (chocolate-coated hazelnuts).

In and around Rome, traditional pasta dishes include spaghetti *carbonara* (with egg yolk) and *alla matriciana* (with a sauce of tomato, onion and bacon). Offal is also popular in Rome – if you can stomach it, try the pasta *pajata*, made with the entrails of very young veal, considered a delicacy since they still contain the congealed mother's milk.

As you go farther south, the food becomes hotter and spicier and the *dolci* (cakes and pastries) sweeter and richer. Don't miss the experience of eating a pizza in Naples (where it was created), or the *melanzane parmigiana* (eggplant layered with a tomato sauce and mozzarella and baked), another classic Neapolitan dish. A favourite *dolce* in Naples is *sfogliatelle*, layers of fine pastry with a ricotta filling.

The food of Apulia is simple and hearty, featuring a lot of vegetables. Try the *orrechiette* (pasta in the shape of 'little ears' with a sauce of sautéed green vegetables). Another popular local dish is made from puréed broad beans topped with chicory. The Pugliesi also eat a lot of seafood.

In Sicily, try the *pesce spada* (swordfish, usually sliced into thick steaks and cooked on an open grill). *Pasta con le sarde* (pasta with sardines) is popular in Palermo. Eggplant is popular in Sicily, turning up in pasta dishes or as *melange alla siciliana*, filled with olives, anchovies, capers and tomato.

The Sicilians are masters when it comes to their dolci. Don't leave the island without trying *cassata*, a rich sponge cake filled with a cream of ricotta cheese, liqueur and candied fruits. Another speciality is *cannoli*, tubes of sweet pastry filled with a rich cream, often made from a mixture of cream cheese, honey and almond paste with bits of candied fruit. Also try the assortment of *paste di mandorle* (almond pastries) and the *zabaione*, native to Marsala. The *granita* is a drink made of crushed ice with fresh lemon or other fruit juices, or with coffee topped with fresh whipped cream. Another speciality is *marzapane* (marzipan), which Sicilian pastry chefs whip into every imaginable shape.

Sardinia's best known dish is *porcheddu*, baby pig roasted on a spit. Try also the *carte musica*, a thin, crisp bread eaten warm and sprinkled with salt and oil.

Vegetarians will have no problems eating in Italy. While there are very few restaurants devoted to them, vegetables are a staple of the Italian diet. Most eating establishments serve a good selection of *contorni* (vegetables prepared in a variety of ways), and the farther south you go, the more excellent vegetable dishes you will find. Vegetarian restaurants and grocery shops are listed throughout this book.

Where to Eat

Eating establishments are divided into several categories. A *tavola calda* (literally 'hot table') usually offers cheap, pre-prepared meat, pasta and vegetable dishes in a self-service style. A *rosticceria* usually offers cooked meats, but often has a larger selection of takeaway food. A *pizzeria* will of course serve pizza, but usually also a full menu. An *osteria* is likely to be either a wine bar offering a small selection of dishes, or a small *trattoria*. A trattoria is basically a cheaper version of a *ristorante* (restaurant), which in turn generally has a wider selection of dishes and a higher standard of service. The problem is that many of the establishments that are in fact ristorantes call themselves trattorias and vice versa for reasons best known to themselves. It is best to check the menu, which is usually posted by the door, for prices.

Don't judge the quality of a restaurant or trattoria by its appearance. You are likely to eat your most memorable meal at a place with plastic tablecloths in a tiny backstreet, a dingy piazza or on a back road in the country.

And don't panic if you find yourself in a trattoria which has no printed menu: they are often the ones which offer the best and most authentic food and have menus which change daily to accommodate the availability of fresh produce. Just hope that the waiter will patiently explain the dishes and how much they cost.

Most eating establishments have a cover charge, usually around L2000 to L3000, and a service charge of 10% to 15%. Restaurants are usually open for lunch from 12.30 to 3 pm, but will rarely take orders after 2 pm. In the evening, opening hours vary from north to south. They eat dinner earlier in the north, usually from 7.30 pm, but in Sicily you will be hard-pressed to find a restaurant open before 8.30 pm. Note that very few restaurants stay open past 11.30 pm.

Numerous restaurants offer tourist menus, with an average price of L18,000. Generally the food is of a reasonable standard, but choices will be limited and you can usually get away with paying less if you want only pasta, salad and wine.

After lunch and dinner, head for the nearest *gelateria* (ice-cream parlour) to round off the meal with some excellent Italian *gelati*, followed by a *digestivo* (digestive liqueur) at a bar.

For a light lunch, or a snack, most bars serve *panini* (sandwiches), and there are numerous outlets where you can buy pizza by the slice. Another option is to go to one of the many alimentari and ask them to make a panino with the filling of your choice. At a *pasticceria* you can buy pastries, cakes and biscuits.

Fast food is becoming increasingly popular in Italy. There are McDonald's outlets throughout the country as well as numerous other chain restaurants and US-style hamburger joints.

Eating Customs

Italians rarely eat a sit-down breakfast *(colazione)*. Their custom is to drink a cappuccino, usually *tiepido* (cool), and eat a brioche, *cornetto* or other type of pastry while standing at a bar. Lunch *(pranzo)* is traditionally the main meal of the day and shops and businesses close for three to four hours each afternoon to accommodate the meal and siesta which generally follows.

A full meal will consist of *antipasto*, which can vary from *bruschetta*, a type of garlic bread with various toppings, to fried vegetables, or *prosciutto e melone* (cured ham wrapped around melon). Next comes the *primo piatto*, a pasta dish or risotto, followed by the *secondo piatto* of meat or fish. Italians often then eat an *insalata* (salad) or contorni, and round off the meal with fruit (occasionally with a sweet) and *caffè*, often at a bar on the way back to work.

The evening meal *(cena)* for many Italians is a simpler affair, but habits are changing because of the inconvenience of travelling home for lunch every day.

If you have access to cooking facilities, it is best to buy fruit and vegetables at open markets (see under individual towns for information), and salami, cheese and wine at alimentari or *salumerie*, which are a cross between grocery stores and delicatessens. Fresh bread is available at a *forno* or *panetteria* and usually at alimentari. There are also supermarkets in most towns and they are listed throughout this book.

Stand or Sit?

Remember that as soon as you sit down in Italy, prices go up considerably, since you have to pay for the service. A cappuccino at the bar will cost around L1200 to L1500, but if you sit down you will pay anything from L2500 to L5000 and more than L10,000 in the Piazza San Marco in Venice. Italians rarely sit down in bars and, consequently, many do not even have seating. In some bars, where it is obvious that no-one is serving the tables, you can sometimes sit down without paying extra.

Food Vocabulary

This is intended as a brief guide to some of the basics and by no means covers all of the dishes you are likely to encounter in Italy. Names and ingredients of dishes often vary from region to region, and even pizza toppings can change. Most travellers to Italy will already be well acquainted with the various Italian pastas, which include spaghetti, fettucine, penne, rigatoni, gnocchi, lasagne, tortellini and ravioli. The names are the same in Italy and no further definitions are given here.

Useful Words

bill/cheque	*il conto*
boiled	*bollito*
cooked	*cotto*
cooked over hot coals	*alla bracia*
firm (as all good pasta should be)	*al dente*
fried	*fritto*
grilled	*alla griglia*
knife/fork/ spoon/teaspoon	*coltello/forchetta/ cucchiaio/ cucchiaino*
menu	*menù*
plate	*piatto*
raw	*crudo*
restaurant	*ristorante*
roasted	*arrosto*
smoked	*affumicato*
waiter/waitress	*cameriere/a*
well done (cooked)	*ben cotto*

Staples

bread	*pane*
butter	*burro*
cheese	*formaggio*
chilli	*peperoncino*
cooked cornmeal	*polenta*
cream	*panna*
eggs	*uova*
honey	*miele*
jam	*marmellata*
lemon	*limone*
oil	*olio*
olives	*olive, ulive*
pepper	*pepe*
rice	*riso*
rice cooked with wine and broth	*risotto*
salt	*sale*
sugar	*zucchero*
vinegar	*aceto*
wholemeal bread	*pane integrale*

Meat & Fish

anchovies	*acciughe*
beef	*manzo*
chicken	*pollo*
clams	*vongole*
cod	*merluzzo*
crab	*granchio*
cutlet or thin cut of meat, usually crumbed and fried	*cotoletta*
dentex (a type of fish)	*dentice*
lamb	*agnello*
liver	*fegato*
lobster	*aragosta*
mackerel	*sgombro*
mussels	*cozze*
octopus	*polpo*
oysters	*ostriche*
prawns	*gamberi*
rabbit	*coniglio*
sardines	*sarde*
sausage	*salsiccia*
sole	*sogliola*
squid	*calamari*
steak	*bistecca*
swordfish	*pesce spada*
tripe	*trippa*
tuna	*tonno*

turkey	*tacchino*
veal	*vitello*

Vegetables

artichokes	*carciofi*
asparagus	*asparagi*
cabbage	*cavolo*
carrots	*carote*
chicory	*cicoria*
eggplant	*melanzane*
onion	*cipolla*
peas	*piselli*
peppers	*peperoni*
potatoes	*patate*
spinach	*spinaci*
string beans	*fagiolini*

Fruit

apples	*mele*
bananas	*banane*
cherries	*ciliegie*
grapes	*uva*
oranges	*arance*
peaches	*pesche*
pears	*pere*
strawberries	*fragole*

Soup *(Zuppa)* & Starters *(Antipasti)*

brodo	*broth*
carpaccio	*very fine slices of raw meat*
insalata caprese	*sliced tomatoes with mozzarella and basil*
insalata di mare	*seafood, generally crustaceans*
minestrina in brodo	*pasta in broth*
minestrone	*vegetable soup*
olive ascolane	*stuffed, deep-fried olives*
prosciutto e melone	*cured ham with melon*
ripieni	*stuffed, oven-baked vegetables*
stracciatella	*egg in broth*

Pasta Sauces

al ragù	*meat sauce (bolognese)*
arrabbiata	*tomato and chilli*

People

Top : Ruins of Taormina's Greek/Roman theatre, Sicily (SC)
Bottom Left : Paestum, Temple of Neptune, Campania (JG)
Bottom Right : Temple of Castor & Pollux, Agrigento, Sicily (HG)

carbonara	egg, bacon and black pepper
matriciana	tomato and bacon
napoletana	tomato and basil
panna	cream, prosciutto and, sometimes, peas
pesto	basil, garlic and oil, often with pine nuts
vongole	clams, garlic and oil, sometimes with tomato

Pizzas

capricciosa	tomato, mozzarella, olives, prosciutto, mushrooms, artichokes
frutti di mare	seafood
funghi	tomato, mozzarella, mushrooms
margherita	tomato, mozzarella and oregano
napoletana	tomato and anchovies
pugliese	tomato, mozzarella and onions
quattro formaggi	with four types of cheese
quattro stagioni	the same as capricciosa, but sometimes with egg
verdura	tomato, mozzarella and mixed vegetables (usually zucchini, eggplant and sometimes carrot and spinach)

DRINKS
Coffee
The first-time visitor to Italy is likely to be confused by the many ways in which the locals consume their caffeine. The following is a basic guide, although there can be variations from north to south.

An *espresso* is a small amount of very strong black coffee. You can ask for a *doppio espresso*, which means double the amount, or a *caffè lungo* (although this can sometimes mean a slightly diluted espresso). If you want a long black coffee (as in a weaker, watered-down version), ask for a *caffè Americano*. If you are in an isolated village in Sardinia where they have no name for diluted coffee, try asking for an *espresso con molta acqua calda* (coffee with a lot of hot water). A *corretto* is an espresso with a dash of grappa or some other spirit, and a *macchiato* is espresso with a small amount of milk – on the other hand, *latte macchiato* is milk with a spot of coffee. *Caffè freddo* is a long glass of cold coffee.

Then, of course, there is the *cappuccino*, coffee with hot, frothy milk – if you want it without the froth, ask for a *caffè latte* or a cappuccino *senza schiuma*. Italians tend to drink cappuccino only with breakfast and during the morning. They never drink it after meals or in the evening and, if you order one after dinner, don't be surprised if the waiter asks you two or three times, just to make sure that he or she heard correctly. You will also find it difficult to convince bartenders to make your cappuccino hot, rather than lukewarm. Ask for it *molto caldo* and wait for the same 'tut-tut' response that you attracted when you ordered a cappuccino after dinner.

Tea
Italians don't drink a lot of tea *(tè)* and generally only in the late afternoon, when they might take a cup with a few *pasticcini* (small cakes). You can order tea in bars, although it will usually arrive in the form of a cup of warm water with an accompanying tea bag. If this doesn't suit your taste, ask for the water *molto caldo* or *bollente* (boiling). Good-quality packaged teas, such as Twinings tea bags and leaves, as well as packaged herbal teas, such as cammomile, are often sold in alimentari and some bars. You can find a wide range of herbal teas in a herbalist's shop *(erboristeria)*, which sometimes also stocks health foods.

Wine & Spirits

While wine *(vino)* is an essential accompaniment to any meal, and digestive liqueurs *(digestivi)* are a popular way to end one, few Italians abuse alcohol. It is usually consumed only with meals, and the foreign custom of going out for a drink is considered quite unusual. It is not considered acceptable to get drunk *(ubriaco/a)*, and at parties many Italians will drink more mineral water than wine or beer.

There are exceptions, however. In some parts of Italy, generally in the country and in Sardinia, it is common to see men starting their day with a grappa for breakfast, and to continue consuming strong drinks throughout the day.

Wine is reasonably priced and you will rarely pay more than L10,000 for a good bottle of wine, although prices range up to more than L20,000 for really good quality. There are two main classifications of wine, DOC *(denominazione di origine controllata)* and *vino da tavola* (table wine) – either classification will be marked on the label. A DOC wine is produced subject to certain specifications, although the label does not certify quality. DOCG *(denominazione d'origine controllata e garantita)* is subject to the same requirements as normal DOC but it is also tested by government inspectors. While there are table wines better left alone, there are also many which are of excellent quality, notably the Sicilian Corvo red and white.

Although some excellent wines are produced in Italy, most trattorias stock only a limited selection of bottled wines and generally only cheaper varieties. Most people tend to order the house wine *(vino della casa)* or the local wine *(vino locale)* when they go out to dinner.

The styles of wine vary throughout the country, so make a point of sampling the local produce in your travels. Try the famous Chianti in Tuscany, but also the Vernaccia of San Gimignano and the reds of Montalcino; the Soave in Verona and Valpolicella around Venice. Piedmont and Trentino-Alto Adige both produce excellent wines, notably the Barolo in Piedmont. The wines of Orvieto in Umbria are good, and in Rome try the local Frascati and Est! Est! Est! In Sicily and Sardinia the wines are sweeter and heavier. Sicily is known as the home of Marsala.

Before dinner, Italians might drink a Campari and soda, or a fruit cocktail, usually pre-prepared and often without alcohol *(analcolico)*. After dinner try a shot of grappa, a very strong, clear brew made from grapes, or an *amaro*, a dark liqueur prepared from herbs. If you prefer a sweeter liqueur, try an almond-flavoured *amaretto* or the sweet aniseed brew, *sambuca*.

Beer

Italy produces its own beer *(birra)* and imports beers from throughout Europe and the world. All of the main German beers are, for instance, available in bottles or cans; English beers are often found on tap *(alla spina)* in *birrerie* (bars specialising in beer), and Australians might be pleased to know that you can even find a Foster's. The main local labels are Peroni, Dreher and Moretti, all very drinkable and cheaper than the imported varieties. If you want a local beer, ask for a *birra nazionale*, which will be either in a bottle or on tap.

Water

While tap water is generally reliable throughout the country, most Italians prefer to drink bottled mineral water *(acqua minerale)*. It will be either sparkling *(frizzante)* or still *(naturale)* and you will be asked in restaurants and bars which you would prefer. If you want a glass of tap water, ask for *acqua dal rubinetto*, although simply asking for *acqua naturale* will also suffice.

ENTERTAINMENT

Whatever your tastes, there should be some form of entertainment in Italy to keep you amused, from the national obsession, soccer *(il calcio)*, to the opera, theatre, classical music concerts, rock concerts, traditional festivals and major entertainment festivals, such as the Festival of Two Worlds in June/July at Spoleto, Umbria Jazz in Perugia in July, and the Venice Biennale in every odd-numbered year (see the Cultural Events section in this chapter). Operas are performed in Verona and Rome throughout summer (for information, see the Entertainment sections for both cities) and at various times of the year throughout the country, notably at the opera houses in Milan and Palermo.

The main theatre season is during winter, and classical music concerts are generally performed throughout the year. Nightclubs, indoor bars and discotheques are more popular during winter and, in fact, some close down for the summer months. Entrance charges to discos are high, usually starting at around L20,000. This usually covers the cost of the first drink, although after that one you will pay up to L6000 just for a glass of wine. There are gay discos and nightclubs in most cities. Information on entertainment is listed under each city and town throughout this book. More detailed listings can be found in the entertainment sections of local newspapers. Tourist offices will also provide information on important events, festivals, performances and concerts.

THINGS TO BUY

Shopping in Italy is probably not what you are used to back home. The vast proportion of shops are small businesses, and large department stores and supermarkets tend to be very thin on the ground. If you need necessities such as underwear, pantyhose, pyjamas, T-shirts, toiletries, condoms etc, head for one of the large retail stores, such as Standa, Upim or Rinascente. Otherwise, pick up underwear, pantyhose and pyjamas in a *merceria* (haberdashery), toiletries and condoms in a *farmacia* (pharmacy) or sometimes in an alimentari, and items such as T-shirts in a normal clothing store. All of these items can also be found in street markets. Hardware items can be purchased at a *ferramenta*, and air-mail paper, note pads, pens, greeting cards etc at a *cartoleria* (paper-goods shop).

Clothing

Italy is synonymous with elegant, fashionable and high-quality clothing. The problem is that most of the better quality clothes are very expensive. However, if you can manage to be in the country during the summer sales in July and August and the winter sales in December and January, you can pick up incredible bargains. By mid-sale, prices are often slashed by up to 60% and 70%. Generally speaking, Rome, Florence and Milan have the greatest variety of clothing, shoes and accessories (main shopping areas are detailed under the relevant cities throughout this book). Fashions tend to be conservative and middle-of-the-range, and cheaper clothing can be downright boring for English, US and Australian travellers accustomed to a wide variety of styles and tastes.

The same applies to shoes. Expect to pay dearly (although still considerably less than at home) for the best quality at shops such as Beltrami and Pollini. Again, prices drop dramatically during the sales, but expect to have some difficulty finding shoes to fit if you take a larger size.

Italy is particularly noted for the quality of its leather goods, so plan to stock up on bags, wallets, purses, belts and gloves. At markets such as Porta Portese in Rome you can find some incredible second-hand bargains. The San Lorenzo leather market in Florence has a vast array of leather goods, including jackets, bags, wallets and belts, although the variety can be limited, and you should check carefully for quality before buying. At San Lorenzo, prices are usually half what you would pay in a shop. A few price examples are: L70,000 for a bag, L15,000 for a belt, L15,000 for suede gloves, and L250,000 to L400,000 for a leather jacket.

Glassware & Ceramics

Some might call the famous and expensive Venetian glass grotesque – and it is certainly an acquired taste. Shops all over Venice are full of it and if you listen to the claims of the shop assistants, most of it (except for the glass in *their* shop) is not the real thing.

Hordes of tourists are taken on guided tours of the larger manufacturers, both in the city of Venice and on the island of Murano (the home of Venetian glass), and encouraged to spend hundreds of thousands of lire on decanter sets, ornaments and lamps which are then specially packaged and sent home at additional expense. If you want to buy Venetian glass, shop around and compare prices and quality. The merchandise at the larger factories is generally not cheaper, but you can be sure that it is authentic. And remember that you will probably have to pay customs duty on your purchase when you arrive home.

Ceramics and pottery are less costly and more rustic. There is a great diversity of traditional styles throughout Italy, associated with villages or areas, where designs have been handed down over the centuries. Major centres include: Deruta, near Perugia in Umbria; Faenza, in Emilia-Romagna; Vietri sul Mare, near Salerno at the start of the Amalfi Coast; and Grottaglie, near Taranto in Apulia. Sicilian pottery is particularly interesting, notably the products of Desimone (see the Palermo section).

Other Items

The beautiful Florentine paper goods, with their delicate flower design, and Venetian paper goods, with a marbled design, are reasonably priced and make wonderful gifts. Specialist shops are dotted around both cities, although it is possible to buy these paper goods in cartolerie throughout the country.

Popular jewellery tends to be chunky and cheap-looking, but if they can afford it, Italians love to wear gold. The best known haunt for tourists wanting to buy gold in Italy is the Ponte Vecchio in Florence, lined with tiny shops full of both modern and antique jewellery. Jewellery and ornaments carved from coral can be found at Torre del Greco just out of Naples, and on the west coast of Sardinia, although overharvesting and pollution threaten this once thriving industry.

Local handicrafts include lace and embroidery, notably on the Isola Maggiore in Lake Trasimene, Umbria, and the woodcarvings of the Val Gardena in Trentino-Alto Adige.

Getting There & Away

If you live outside Europe, flying is the easiest way to get from your country to Italy. Competition between the airlines means that you should be able to pick up a reasonabnly priced fare, even if you are coming from as far away as Australia. The following Air section has more details. If you live in Europe, chances are you'll be going to Italy overland – by train, bus, car or hitchhiking. See the Land section for more information.

Whichever way you are travelling, make sure that you take out travel insurance. This will cover you for medical expenses, luggage theft or loss, and for cancellation of and delays in your travel arrangements. Cover depends on your insurance and type of ticket, so ask both your insurer and ticket-issuing agency to explain where you stand. Ticket loss is also covered by travel insurance, but make sure you have a separate record of your ticket details (see Photocopies under Documents in the Facts for the Visitor chapter). Buy travel insurance as early as possible. If you buy it the week before you fly or hop on the bus, you may find, for example, that you are not covered for delays to your trip caused by strikes or other industrial action.

Paying for your ticket with a credit card often provides limited travel accident insurance, and you may be able to reclaim the payment if the operator doesn't deliver. Ask your credit card company what it will cover.

AIR
Buying a Plane Ticket
The plane ticket will probably be the single most expensive item in your budget, and buying it can be an intimidating business. Start early: some of the cheapest tickets have to be bought months in advance, and some popular flights sell out early. Talk to other recent travellers and look at the ads in newspapers and magazines (not forgetting the Italian press in your home country), consult reference books and watch for special offers. Then phone round travel agents for bargains.

Find out the fare, the route, the duration of the journey and any restrictions on the ticket.

Official cheap tickets include advance-purchase tickets, budget fares, Apex and super-Apex and various other names thought up by the airlines. Unofficial discount tickets are released by the airlines through selected travel agents and it is worth shopping around to find them. Sometimes the discount 'special deals' have bonuses attached, such as a free flight within Europe, free accommodation for the first few nights, or a free stopover. Discounted tickets are available only from travel agents, although airlines can provide information on routes and time-tables, and their low-season, student and senior citizens' fares can be very competitive.

Return tickets usually work out much cheaper than buying two one-way tickets (Italy is not the place to buy your ticket home, because cheap tickets, particularly one-way, can be difficult to find). If Italy is only one stop on your grand world tour, consider buying a Round-the-World (RTW) ticket, which is often an excellent deal. Official RTW tickets usually involve a combination of two airlines and permit you to fly anywhere you want on their route systems, as long as you don't backtrack. You are usually required to book the first sector in advance, and cancellation penalties then apply. There may be restrictions on how many stops you can make, and the tickets are usually valid for 90 days to one year.

Since RTWs can sometimes get a bit complicated, depending on how many stops you want to make and where, it pays to ensure that your travel agent has made your bookings correctly and has filled you in on all of the ticket's restrictions and conditions. Two Australian travellers were recently forced to pay a hefty penalty fee in Italy when they rebooked the third leg of their ticket, after their travel agent had assured them the dates could be changed without any problems.

If you are travelling to Italy from the USA or South-East Asia, or you have decided to fly home from London in the hope of finding a cheaper fare there than would be available in Italy, you will probably find that the cheapest flights are being advertised by obscure agencies whose names haven't yet reached the telephone directory. Many such firms are honest and solvent, but there are a few rogues who will take your money and disappear, to reopen elsewhere a month or two later under a new name. If you feel suspicious about a firm, don't give them all the money at once – leave a deposit of 20% or so and pay the balance when you get the ticket. If they insist on cash in advance, go somewhere else. And once you have the ticket, ring the airline to confirm that you are actually booked on the flight.

Many travellers will prefer to pay more than the rock-bottom fare in order to fly with a major airline, or to avoid 'milk-run' flights which have several stopovers before finally landing in Rome. However, few travellers want to pay full airline fares, and there are numerous better known travel agents which offer bargain fares. Firms such as STA, which has offices worldwide, Council Travel in the USA, Travel CUTS in Canada, and Flight Centres International in Australia, are not going to disappear overnight, leaving you clutching a receipt for a nonexistent ticket.

Use the fares quoted in this book as a guide only. They are approximate and based on the rates advertised by travel agents at the time of writing, and are likely to have changed by the time you read this.

Travellers with Special Needs

If you have broken a leg, you're a vegetarian or require a special diet, are travelling in a wheelchair, taking a baby or your dog, or you are terrified of flying, whatever, let the airline know as soon as possible so that they can make arrangements accordingly. You should remind them when you reconfirm your booking (at least 72 hours before departure) and again when you check in at the airport. It may also be worth ringing round the airlines before you make your booking to find out how they can handle your particular needs. Some airlines publish brochures on the subject. Ask your travel agent for details.

Children aged under two travel for 10% of the standard fare (or free on some airlines), as long as they don't occupy a seat. They don't get a baggage allowance either. 'Sky-cots', baby food and nappies (diapers) should be provided by the airline if requested in advance. Children aged between two and 12 can usually occupy a seat for half to two-thirds of the full fare, and do get a baggage allowance. Pushchairs (strollers) can often be taken as hand luggage.

To/From the USA

The North Atlantic is the world's busiest long-haul air corridor and the flight options are bewildering. Several airlines fly direct to Italy, landing at either Rome or Milan. These include Alitalia, TWA and Delta. However, if your European trip will not be confined to Italy, consult your travel agent on whether cheaper flights are available to other European cities. The *New York Times*, *LA Times*, *Chicago Tribune* and *San Francisco Chronicle Examiner* all have weekly travel sections with plenty of travel agents' ads.

Standard fares on commercial airlines are expensive and probably best avoided. However, travelling on a normal scheduled flight can be more secure and reliable, particularly for older travellers and families, who might prefer to avoid the potential inconveniences of the budget alternatives.

Discount and rock-bottom options from the USA include charter flights, stand-by and courier flights. Stand-by fares are often sold at 60% of the normal price for one-way tickets. Airhitch (☎ 212-864 2000), Suite 100, 2790 Broadway, New York, NY 10025, specialises in this sort of thing. You will need to give a general idea of where and when you want to go, and a few days before your departure you will be presented with a choice of two or three flights.

Courier flights are where you accompany freight or a parcel to its destination. A New York-Rome return on a courier flight can cost under US$300 in the low season (more expensive from the west coast). Generally courier flights require that you return within a specified period (sometimes within one or two weeks, but often up to one month). You will need to travel light, as luggage is usually restricted to what you can carry on to the plane (the parcel or freight you carry comes out of your luggage allowance), and you may have to be a US resident and apply for an interview before they will take you on. Most flights depart from New York.

A good source of information on courier flights is Now Voyager (☎ 212-431 1616), Suite 307, 74 Varrick St, New York, NY 10013. This company specialises in courier flights, although it is necessary to pay an annual membership fee (around US$50) which then entitles you to take as many courier flights as you like. Phone after 6 pm to listen to a recorded message detailing all available flights and prices.

Prices drop as the departure date approaches. It is also possible to organise flights directly through the courier companies. Look in your local Yellow Pages under Courier Services.

Charter flights tend to be significantly cheaper than scheduled flights. Reliable travel agents specialising in charter flights, as well as budget travel for students, include STA and Council Travel, both of which have offices in major cities. Agencies specialising in cheap fares include:

STA
    48 East 11th St, New York, NY 10003 (☎ 212-477 7166)
    914 Westwood Blvd, Los Angeles, CA 90024 (☎ 213-824 1574)
    166 Geary St, Suite 702, San Francisco, CA 94108 (☎ 415-391 8407)
Council Travel
    148 West 4th St, New York, NY 10011 (☎ 212-254 2525)
    205 East 42nd St, New York, NY 10017 (☎ 212-661 1450)
    1093 Broxton Ave, Los Angeles, CA 90024 (☎ 213-208 3551)
    Suite 407, 312 Sutter St, San Francisco, CA 94108 (☎ 415-42 3473)

Other travel agents specialising in budget airfares include Discount Travel International in New York (☎ 212-362 3636), and Way to Go Travel in New York (☎ 212-947 1242), Los Angeles (☎ 213-466 1126) and San Francisco (☎ 415-292 7801).

To/From Canada

Both Alitalia and Air Canada have direct flights to Rome and Milan from Toronto and Montreal. Travel CUTS, which specialises in discount fares for students, has offices in all major cities. Otherwise scan the budget travel agents' ads in the *Toronto Globe & Mail*, the *Toronto Star* and the *Vancouver Province*. See the previous section for information on courier flights. For courier flights originating in Canada, contact FB on Board Courier Services (☎ 514-633 0740 in Toronto or Montreal, or ☎ 604-338 1366 in Vancouver).

To/From Australia

STA and Flight Centres International are major dealers in cheap airfares, although heavily discounted fares can often be found at the travel agent in your local shopping centre. The Saturday travel sections of the Melbourne *Age* and the *Sydney Morning Herald* have many advertisements offering cheap fares to Europe, but don't be surprised if they happen to be 'sold out' when you contact the agents – they are usually low-season fares on obscure airlines with conditions attached.

Discounted return airfares on mainstream airlines through reputable agents can be surprisingly cheap, with low-season fares around A$1600 to A$1800 return and high-season fares up to A$2500.

Qantas flies from Melbourne and Sydney to Rome twice a week and Alitalia has flights three times a week. Asian airlines such as Cathay Pacific, Singapore Airlines and Thai Airways all fly from Melbourne and Sydney to Rome. Flights from Perth are generally a few hundred dollars cheaper.

The following are some addresses for agencies offering good-value fares:

STA
    224 Faraday Street, Carlton, Vic 3053 (☎ 03-347 6911)

    1st Floor, 732 Harris Street, Ultimo, NSW 2007 (☎ 02-281 9866)

    Hackett Hall, University of Western Australia, Crawley, WA 6009 (☎ 09-380 2302)

Flight Centres International
    Bourke Street Flight Centre, 19 Bourke Street, Melbourne, Vic 3000 (☎ 03-650 2899)

    Martin Place Flight Centre, Shop 5, State Bank Centre, 52 Martin Place, Sydney, NSW 2000 (☎ 02-235 0166)

    City Flight Centre, 25 Cinema City Arcade, Perth, WA 6000 (☎ 09-325 9222)

CIT
    123 Clarence St, Sydney, NSW 2000 (☎ 02-29 4754)

    Suite 10, 6th Floor, 442 Collins St, Melbourne, Vic 3000 (☎ 03-670 1322)

    2nd Floor, 43 Ventnor Ave, Perth, WA 6000 (☎ 09-322 1096)

To/From New Zealand

As with Australia, STA and Flight Centres International are popular travel agents in New Zealand. The cheapest fares to Europe are routed through the USA, and an RTW ticket may be cheaper than a return. Otherwise, you can fly from Auckland to pick up a connecting flight in Melbourne or Sydney. Air New Zealand can fly you to Bangkok to connect with a Thai Airways flight to Rome, to Singapore to connect with a Singapore Airlines flight, or to Hong Kong to connect with a Cathay Pacific flight. Garuda flies from Auckland to Rome via Jakarta.

Useful addresses include:

Flight Centres International
    Auckland Flight Centre, Shop 3A, National Bank Towers, 205-225 Queen St, Auckland (☎ 09-309 6171)

STA Travel & International Travellers Centre
    10 High St, Auckland (☎ 09-309 0458)

Campus Travel
    Gate 1, Knighton Rd, Waikato University, Hamilton (☎ 07-856 9139)

To/From the UK

London is the discount flight capital of Europe, and finding a cheap fare to Italy should be no problem. The main airlines flying this route are British Airways (☎ 081-897 4000) and Alitalia (☎ 071-602 7111), which operate regular flights (usually several a day) to Rome, Milan, Venice, Turin, Naples and Pisa, as well other cities, including Palermo, during the summer. Normal fares on a scheduled flight are around £260 one way and £524 return on Alitalia, and £260 and £409 respectively on British Airways. However, Apex and other special fares are a better option and can cost as little as £180 return.

Bucket shops abound in London. They generally offer the cheapest tickets, usually with restricted validity. The listings magazines *Time Out* and *City Limits*, the Sunday newspapers, and the *Evening Standard* and *Exchange & Mart* carry ads for cheap fares. Also look out for the free magazines and newspapers widely available in London, especially *TNT*, *Southern Cross* and *Trailfinder* – you can usually pick them up outside the main railway and tube stations.

The Trailfinders head office in west London is a good place to go for budget airfares and also has a travel library, bookshop, visa service and immunisation centre. STA also has branches in the UK. Both agencies can organise open-jaw return fares, whereby you can fly to one city in Italy and out of another. It isn't even necessary for both of your chosen cities to be in Italy. STA has good-value fares as low as £173 return, or £100 one-way. Campus Travel is helpful and offers many interesting deals for students. These agencies will also be able to provide information on courier flights (see the earlier To/From the USA section), organised by Polo Express, Courier Travel Service and Shades International Travel.

Another option is to take a direct charter flight from London to Rome or Milan. Pilgrim Air in London, part of the Air Travel Group, specialises in charter flights to all major Italian cities. It runs a service called Italy Sky Shuttle, offering unsold tickets on Britannia Airways at heavily discounted rates. A return fare through Pilgrim Air costs around £136. Cheaper tickets are available which combine a one-way charter flight to Italy with a return by bus to London. Pilgrim also has offices in Italy, from where you can buy tickets for charter flights to Britain. There are two other organisations in the Air Travel Group: Magic of Italy, which organises resort holidays, and Italian Escapades, which puts together package deals.

Addresses of these and other agencies include:

Campus Travel
174 Kensington High St, London W8 (☎ 071-730 3402) – tube: High St Kensington
Council Travel
28A Poland St, London W1 (☎ 071-437 7767) – tube: Oxford Circus
Italia Tours Ltd
241 Euston Rd, London NW1 2BU (☎ 071-383 3886)
Pilgrim Air
227 Shepherd's Bush Rd, London W6 7AS (☎ 071-748 1333)
STA
74 Old Brompton Rd, London SW7 (☎ 071-937 9921) – tube: South Kensington
Trailfinders
194 Kensington High St, London W8 (☎ 071-937 5400) – tube: High St Kensington

Most UK travel agents are registered with the ABTA (Association of British Travel Agents). If you have paid for your flight to an ABTA-registered agent who then goes out of business, ABTA will guarantee a refund or an alternative. Unregistered bucket shops are obviously more risky.

The Globetrotters Club (BCM Roving, London WC1N 3XX) publishes a newsletter called *Globe* which contains useful information for travellers and can help you find a travelling companion.

To/From Continental Europe

Air travel between Italy and other places in Continental Europe is worth considering if you are pushed for time. Although relatively short hops can become extremely expensive, for longer journeys you can sometimes find airfares that beat on-the-ground alternatives in terms of cost.

If you want to fly from Greece to Italy, shop around the travel agents in the backstreets between Syntagma Square and Omonia Square. Cheap flights can also be found easily in Amsterdam – another major bucket shop centre.

Across Europe many travel agents have ties with STA. Outlets include: Voyages et Découvertes (☎ 1-42 61 00 01), 21 Rue Cambon, 75001 Paris; SRID Reisen (☎ 069-43 01 91), Berger Strasse 118, Frankfurt; and ISYTS (☎ 01-32 21 267), 2nd Floor, 11 Nikis St, Syntagma Square, Athens.

Several airlines, including Alitalia, Qantas, Air France and Philippine Airlines, offer cut-rate fares on legs of international flights between European cities. These can be remarkably cheap, but the catch is they are often during the night or very early in the morning, and days on which you can fly are severely restricted. Most travel agents will have details of these special fares. For example, at the time of writing, a Rome-Paris fare on Saudi Air was L305,000 return. Alitalia discount fares for the same route were around L470,000. Alitalia was also offering discount fares to major cities in Europe – for example, Rome-Amsterdam L490,000, Milan-Moscow L650,000, and Rome-Vienna L440,000.

Departure Tax

There is no departure tax payable when you leave Italy.

LAND

If you are travelling by bus, train or car to Italy it will be necessary to check whether you require visas to the countries you intend to pass through.

Bus

International bus travel in Europe tends to take second place to going by train. While buses can sometimes be cheaper, they are generally slower, less comfortable and more cramped. Eurolines (☎ 071-730 0202), 52 Grosvenor Gardens, Victoria, London SW1, is the main international carrier, with representatives in Italy and across Europe.

The bus companies operating the service in Italy are: Lazzi in Florence (☎ 055-36 30 41), Via Mercadente 2, and Rome (☎ 06-841

74 58) Via Tagliamento 27r; and Sadem in Turin (☎ 011-561 30 19), Corso Siccadi, 6, and Milan (☎ 02-80 11 61), Piazza Castello 1. Buses leave from Rome, Milan, Turin, Venice and Naples, as well as numerous other towns, for major cities throughout Europe, including Paris, London, Vienna, Prague, Barcelona, Athens, Amsterdam and Istanbul.

Eurolines representatives elsewhere in Europe include: Eurolines/Budgetbus (☎ 020-627 51 51), Rokin 10, Amsterdam; Eurolines (☎ 1-43 54 11 99), 55 Rue Saint Jacques, 75005 Paris; and Deutsche Touring (☎ 089-59 18 24), Arnulfstrasse 3, Munich.

Examples of one-way ticket prices are Rome-Paris L126,000, and Rome-London L205,000. From London to Rome you will pay £85 one way and £136 return. For London to Milan, one-way tickets cost £76 and a return is £117. Considering the small difference in price and the big difference in comfort, it really is preferable to take a train. Most fares carry a L10,000 to L15,000 supplement in July and August.

Information and tickets can be obtained from the above companies, or from any CIT office within Italy.

Train

Train travel is a convenient and simple means of travelling from most parts of Europe to Italy. It is certainly a popular way of getting around for backpackers and other young travellers, and even the more well-heeled travellers will find European trains a comfortable and reliable way to reach their destination.

EuroCity (EC) trains run from major destinations throughout Europe, including Paris, Geneva, Zürich, Frankfurt, Vienna and Barcelona, direct to major Italian cities. On overnight hauls you can book a *cuccetta* (sleeping berth) for L18,500. If travelling from France to Italy, or out of Italy, by train, there is the option of a 1st-class cuccetta, in compartments of four beds or less, or 2nd class, where you will be crammed into a compartment of six beds.

It is always advisable to book a seat on EuroCity trains, or for any long-distance train travel to/from Italy. Trains are often extremely overcrowded, particularly during the summer months, and you could find yourself standing in the passageway for a six-hour trip or longer.

When crossing international borders on overnight trips, train conductors will usually collect your passport and hand it back the following morning.

Examples of prices for normal one-way, 2nd-class fares are: Rome-London L190,000, Rome-Paris L136,800, and Rome-Amsterdam L295,600.

Eurail Passes These passes can be bought by residents of non-European countries and are supposed to be purchased before arriving in Europe. If you have been resident in Europe for more than six months, you are entitled to buy an Inter-Rail pass, which is a better buy if you are aged under 26 (see the following section).

If you are planning to travel only within Italy, forget about buying a Eurail pass, since the relatively modest cost of train travel in Italy would make it difficult to justify the cost of the pass. The pass starts to become good value if you plan to do a reasonable amount of travelling within a short space of time – Eurail itself reckons that its passes only start saving money after 2400 km of travel within a two-week period – a long distance in Europe.

A Eurail Youthpass, for people aged under 26, is valid for 2nd-class travel for one month (US$470) or two months (US$640). The Youth Flexipass, also for 2nd class, is valid for 15 days in a two-month period (US$420). Corresponding passes for people aged over 26 are available in 1st class only. The Flexipass, which is available in five versions, costs from US$280 for five days' travel in a 15-day period, and up to US$610 for 14 days' travel in a one-month period. The standard Eurail pass (also five versions) costs from US$430 for 15 days of unlimited travel up to US$1150 for three months. (See the Getting Around chapter for an idea of train fares within Italy.)

A Eurail pass is also valid for ferries between Italy and Greece.

Inter-Rail Passes These passes are available to residents of European countries and are valid for 2nd-class travel for one month in all of the countries covered by Eurail, as well as several Eastern European countries, Morocco and Turkey. It also gives free travel on shipping routes from Brindisi to Patras in Greece. While these passes are better value than Eurail, it would still pay to weigh up the cost against the cost of individual fares if you plan to do most of your travelling within Italy. A second important consideration is that Inter-Rail passes entitle you to only a 50% discount on train fares in the country where you buy the pass.

The normal pass is limited to people aged under 26 and costs £240 for one month. A pass for people aged over 26, called Inter-Rail 26+, costs £240 for 15 days. It is not as good value and carries various restrictions.

The national rail organisations of Italy and a few other EC countries have been threatening for some time to pull out of the Inter-Rail accord, and in the case of Italy its participation will be reviewed in early 1994. Check what the situation is when buying your pass. Any office of the Italian youth travel agency, CIT, should be able to tell you.

Other Cheap Tickets Travellers aged under 26 can buy BIJ tickets (Billet International de Jeunesse, also known in Italy as BIGE), which cut fares by up to 40% throughout Europe. Examples of one-way fares are Rome-Paris L110,000, Florence-Amsterdam L140,000, and Milan-Munich L51,500. These tickets are valid for two months and, although you must specify your destination, you can make as many stopovers as you like within the period of validity. BIJ tickets can be purchased at Transalpino offices at most major train stations, at other agencies, including Eurotrain (in London at 52 Grosvenor Gardens, SW1), or from any CIT office.

For people aged over 26 there are RIT (Rail Inclusive Tour) tickets. These are for either 1st or 2nd class and carry a discount of 20%. They must be purchased in conjunction with other tourist services, such as a reservation for a minimum of three nights' accommodation at the city of arrival. CIT can also provide information about these tickets.

For information about train discounts within Italy, see the Getting Around chapter.

Security Travellers often tell horror stories about being robbed during train journeys, ranging from whole carriages being gassed through the ventilation system by bandits and the occupants being divested of their belongings, to individual travellers being drugged and robbed. This sort of thing can happen, but it is not nearly as widespread as some people make out. Nevertheless it pays to take basic precautions. Don't leave your belongings unattended, and make sure you lock your compartment doors overnight. If it is necessary to leave your belongings, at least ensure that suitcases or packs are locked and, if possible, secured to the luggage rack.

Car & Motorbike

Travelling with your own vehicle is the best way to get to those more remote places and gives you the most flexibility. In Italy, the drawbacks are that cars can be inconvenient in larger cities, where you will have to deal with heavy traffic and parking problems. In southern Italy car theft is a major problem in some cities, so make sure you are well insured. Also bear in mind that petrol *(benzina)* is expensive in Italy (around L1500 per litre) and that you must pay tolls on the autostradas (see the Getting Around chapter for further details).

Remember that, while Europe might be compact, it can still take a long time to drive to Italy. The distance from Paris to Rome is 1449 km (about 20 hours' drive if you stick to the toll motorways), from Frankfurt 1312 km and from Moscow 3299 km.

The main points of entry to Italy are the Mont Blanc tunnel from France at Chamonix, which connects with the A5 for Turin and Milan; the Grand St Bernard tunnel from

Switzerland, which also connects with the A5; and the Brenner Pass from Austria, which connects with the A22 to Bologna. Mountain passes in the Alps are often closed in winter and sometimes in autumn and spring, making the tunnels a less scenic, but more reliable way to arrive in Italy.

Paperwork & Preparations Proof of ownership of a private vehicle should always be carried (Vehicle Registration Document for UK-registered cars) when driving through Europe. A UK or other European driving licence is acceptable for driving throughout Europe, although in Italy the carabinieri may require an Italian translation or International Driving Permit for non-EC licences (see Documents in the Facts for the Visitor chapter). Although it is unlikely you will have any problems without a translation, in a tight spot it might prove useful.

Third party motor insurance is a minimum requirement in Italy and throughout Europe, and it is compulsory to have a Green Card, an internationally recognised proof of insurance, which can be obtained from your insurer. Also ask your insurer for a European Accident Statement form, which can simplify matters in the event of an accident. Never sign statements you can't read or understand – insist on a translation and sign that only if it's acceptable.

A European breakdown assistance policy is a good investment, such as the AA Five Star Service or the RAC Eurocover Motoring Assistance. In Italy, assistance can be obtained through the Automobile Club Italiano (ACI). See the Getting Around chapter for details.

Every vehicle travelling across an international border should display a nationality plate of its country of registration. A warning triangle (to be used in the event of a breakdown) is compulsory in Italy and throughout Europe. Recommended accessories are a first-aid kit, a spare bulb kit and a fire extinguisher.

In the UK, further information can be obtained from the RAC (☎ 081-686 0088) or the AA (☎ 0256-20123).

Rental There is a mind-boggling variety of special deals and terms and conditions attached to car rental. However, there are a few pointers to help you through. Multinational agencies – Hertz, Avis, Budget Car, and Europe's largest rental agency, Europcar – will provide a reliable service and good standard of vehicle.

However, if you walk into an office and ask for a car on the spot, you will always pay high rates, even allowing for special weekend deals. National and local firms can sometimes undercut the multinationals, but be sure to examine the rental agreement carefully (although this might be difficult if it is in another language).

Planning ahead and prebooking a rental car through a multinational agency before leaving home will enable you to find the best deals. Prebooked and prepaid rates are always cheaper, and there are fly/drive combinations and other programmes that are worth looking into. You will simply pick up the vehicle on your arrival in Italy (or other European city) and then return it to a nominated point at the end of the rental period. Ask your travel agent for information, or contact one of the major rental agencies.

No matter where you rent, make sure you understand what is included in the price (unlimited km, tax, insurance, collision damage waiver etc) and what your liabilities are. The minimum rental age in Italy is 21 years, while in other European countries it can be as high as 23 years. A credit card is usually required.

Motorbike and moped rental is common in Italy and there are specialist rental agencies in most cities (see the Getting Around chapter).

Purchase It is illegal for nonresidents to purchase vehicles in Italy and some other European countries. The UK is probably the best place to buy, as second-hand prices are good and, whether buying privately or from a dealer, the absence of language difficulties will help you to establish exactly what you are getting for your money. Bear in mind that you will be getting a left-hand drive car (ie steering wheel on the right) if you buy in the UK. If you want a right-hand drive car and can afford to buy new, prices are relatively low in Belgium, the Netherlands and Luxembourg. Paperwork can be tricky wherever you buy, and many countries, including Italy, have compulsory roadworthiness checks on older vehicles which can add considerably to initial purchase costs.

SEA

Ferries connect Italy to Greece, Turkey, Tunisia and Malta. There are also services to Albania (Durazzo), Egypt (Alexandria) and Spain (Barcelona). Ticket prices vary according to the time of year and are at their most expensive during summer. Prices for cars, camper vans and motorbikes vary according to the size of the vehicle, and bicycles can sometimes be taken free of charge. Italian rail-pass holders are sometimes entitled to discounts (for example,

Hellenic Lines offers a 30% discount to holders of Italian Flexi Railcards and Italian Tourist Tickets). Eurail pass and Inter-Rail pass holders pay only a supplement on the Italy-Greece route, but must travel with approved companies. Ticket prices are very competitive on the heavily serviced Brindisi-Greece route, and travellers wanting to pick up the best deals can shop around in Brindisi.

For detailed information, see the Getting There & Away sections for Brindisi and Bari (ferries to/from Greece), Ancona (to/from Greece and Turkey), Naples and Trapani (to/from Tunisia), Naples and Syracuse (to/from Malta), Venice (to/from Greece and Egypt), Trieste (to/from Albania), Livorno and the Lipari Islands (to/from Barcelona).

TOURS

See the Getting Around chapter for information about tours to/from Italy.

Getting Around

AIR

Travelling by plane is expensive within Italy and it makes much better sense to use the efficient and considerably cheaper rail and bus services. The main domestic airline, ATI, is the domestic arm of Alitalia. The main airports are in Rome, Pisa, Milan, Naples, Catania and Cagliari, but there are other, smaller airports throughout Italy. Domestic flights can be booked either directly through the airlines or through agencies such as CIT, CTS and normal travel agencies.

Alitalia offers a range of discounts, including for students, young people, families, the elderly and weekend travel. It also offers Apex fares discounted by up to 40%. It should be noted that airline fares fluctuate, and that special deals sometimes only apply when tickets are bought in Italy. The airfares chart on this page will give you an idea of return fares at the time of writing. Barring special deals, a one-way fare is generally half the return fare.

BUS

Bus travel within Italy is provided by numerous companies, and services vary from local routes linking small villages, to those making major intercity connections, which are fast and reliable. It is generally slightly cheaper to travel by bus than by train and, by utilising the local services, it is possible to arrive in just about any location throughout the country. However, services connecting small villages to each other or to larger provincial towns are provided for the local people and are usually not geared to tourist needs. Therefore, while it might be possible to arrive in a tiny village, it might not be possible to leave again until the next day.

It is usually not necessary to make reservations on buses – just arrive early enough to claim a seat (on some major routes the companies will often provide an additional bus if needed). But, for longer trips (such as Rome-Palermo), and certainly during peak season, it is a good idea to buy your ticket in advance to ensure a seat.

Buses can be a cheaper and faster way to get around if your destination is not on major rail lines, for instance from Umbria to Rome and Florence, and in the interior areas of Sicily and Sardinia.

It is usually possible to get bus timetables for the provinces and for intercity services from local tourist offices. If not, staff will be

Italy Airfares

Prices quoted by Alitalia in thousands of lire, for full economy-class return fares in May 1993. One-way fares are generally half the return fare, and special deals may be available within Italy.

able to point you in the direction of the main bus companies. In larger cities most of the main intercity bus companies have ticket offices or operate through agencies, and buses leave from either a bus station (*autostazione*) or from a particular piazza or street. Details are provided throughout this book under the individual towns and cities. In some smaller towns and villages tickets are sold in bars – just ask for *biglietti per l'autobus* – but often tickets are sold on the bus. Note that, unlike trains in Italy, buses almost always leave on time.

Some price examples for intercity bus travel are: Palermo-Rome L68,000, Perugia-Rome L15,000, and Agrigento-Palermo L6000.

TRAIN

Travelling by train in Italy is simple, cheap and generally efficient. The Ferrovie dello Stato (FS) is the state railway and there are several private railway services throughout the country.

The FS runs five types of trains: *locale*, which usually stops at all stations and can be very slow; *diretto*, which stops less frequently and indicates that you do not need to change trains to reach the final destination; *espresso*, which stops only at major stations; *rapido*, which services only the major cities and is also known as an *intercity*; and the ETR450, a new express service between major cities which has 1st class only.

To travel on the rapido and ETR450 trains, you are required to pay a *supplemento*, an additional charge determined by the distance you are travelling. For instance, on the intercity train between Florence and Bologna (about 100 km) you will pay L2700. Between Rome and Perugia (about 250 km) you will pay L6400. Always check whether the train you are about to catch is an intercity, and pay the supplement before you get on the train, otherwise you will pay extra. Note that Eurail pass holders are not required to pay the supplement and that some intercities do not have 2nd-class compartments.

You can catch a EuroCity train (see the Getting There & Away chapter) to travel between major Italian cities, but you must pay a rapido supplement if you do so.

On overnight trips within Italy it can be worth paying extra for a cuccetta (L18,500).

It is not worth buying a Eurail pass or Inter-Rail pass if you are going to travel only in Italy, since train fares are reasonably cheap. The FS offers its own discount passes for travel within the country. These include the Cartaverde for young people aged 26 years and under. It costs L40,000, is valid for one year and entitles you to a 20% discount on all train travel. Children aged between four and 12 years are automatically entitled to a 50% discount, and under four years they can travel for free. BTLC tickets, designed specifically for tourists, are valid for a period of eight, 15, 21 or 30 days and entitle you to unlimited travel and exemption from payment of rapido supplements. A ticket for 21 days costs L260,000, or for 15 days L224,000. Unless you are on a whirlwind tour of the country, you will probably find it difficult to make a saving.

The FS has recently introduced an Italy Flexi Railcard, which offers basically the same advantages as BTLC, but with more flexibility. This pass is for 1st-class travel only and is consequently more expensive than the BTLC.

Some price examples for one-way train fares are: Rome-Milan L43,500, Rome-Palermo L46,800, Rome-Perugia L16,300, Florence-Bologna L10,000, and Naples-Rome L17,400.

Train timetables are posted at all train stations. There often are information booths (generally with long queues), or computerised information facilities. Tourist offices can also usually provide some information about trains. If you are doing a reasonable amount of travelling, it is worthwhile investing in a train timetable. There are several available, including the two volumes, *Sud e Centro Italia* (South & Central Italy) and *Nord e Centro Italia* (North & Central Italy), each costing L4500 and available at newsstands in or near train stations.

There are also several private train lines in Italy, which are noted throughout this book.

TAXI

Try to avoid using taxis in Italy; they are very expensive (even the shortest taxi ride in Rome will cost around L10,000) and it is generally possible to catch a bus instead. If you do need a taxi, you can usually find them on taxi ranks at train and bus stations or you can telephone (radio-taxi phone numbers are listed throughout this book in the Getting Around sections of the major cities). Taxis will rarely stop when hailed on the street.

Rates vary from city to city. A good indication of the average is Rome, where taxis charge L6400 flagfall (plus L3000 night rate from 10 pm to 7 am) plus L500 for each piece of luggage. After three km, the rate is L300 for every 250 metres. If you are stationary for more than nine minutes, the meter will start to tick over L300 every 50 seconds. The limit on the number of people is four or five depending on the size of the taxi.

On long trips, you could try bargaining with the driver before setting off. On other occasions, such as from Rome airport to the city, it is a good idea to agree on the price before getting in – it is not uncommon that trips take a lot longer than necessary and therefore cost a lot more.

CAR & MOTORBIKE

Trains and buses are fine for travelling through most of Italy, but if you want to get off the beaten track, renting a car or motorbike is a good idea, particularly in Sicily and Sardinia, where some of the most interesting and beautiful places are difficult to reach by public transport.

Roads are generally good throughout the country and there is an excellent network of autostradas (freeways). The main north-south link is the Autostrada del Sole, which extends from Milan to Reggio di Calabria (called the A1 from Milan to Naples and the A3 from Naples to Reggio di Calabria). The only problem with the autostradas is that they are toll roads. The toll for the trip from Rome to Bologna is, for example, L28,000.

Travellers with time to spare should consider using the system of state roads (*strade statali*, ss), which are often multi-lane dual carriageways and toll-free. Provincial roads (*strade provinciali*, sp) are sometimes little more than country lanes, but provide access to some of the more beautiful scenery and myriad towns and villages.

Driving in Italian towns and cities is quite a different experience and may well present the unprepared driver with unwelcome headaches. A stopover in a medieval hill town will generally mean that you will have to leave the car in a car park some distance from the town centre. It is always unwise to leave your belongings in an unattended car. Parking, as well as heavy traffic, can pose problems in larger cities. The Italian attitude to driving bears little comparison to the English concept of traffic in ordered lanes (a normal two-lane road is likely to carry three or four lanes of traffic), and the farther south you travel, the less drivers seem to pay attention to road rules. Instead, the main factor in determining right of way is whichever driver is more forceful, or *prepotente*.

If you must drive in an Italian city, particularly in Rome or Naples, remain calm, keep your eyes on the car in front of you and you should be OK. Most roads are well signed, and once you arrive in a city or village, follow the *centro* signs to arrive in the centre of town. Be extremely careful where you park your car. In the major cities it will almost certainly be towed away and you will pay a heavy fine if you leave it in an area marked with a sign reading *Zona Rimozione* (Removal Zone) and featuring a tow truck.

Although the Italian government liberalised petrol prices in 1992, the cost remains relatively high at around L1500 per litre (slightly less for unleaded petrol). Petrol is called *benzina*, unleaded petrol is *benzina senza piombo* and diesel is *gasolio*. If you are driving a car which uses LPG (liquid petroleum gas), you will need to buy a special guide to service stations which have *gasauto*. By law these must be located in nonresidential areas and are usually in the country or on city outskirts.

Rental

It is cheaper to rent a car or camper van before leaving your own country, for instance through some sort of fly/drive deal. Most major firms, including Hertz, Avis and Budget, will arrange this, and you simply pick up the vehicle at a nominated point when you arrive in Italy. Foreign offices of the Italian national travel agency, CIT, can also help to organise car or camper van rental before you leave home.

You will need to be aged 21 years or over (23 years or over for some companies) to rent a car in Italy, and you will find the deal far easier to organise if you have a credit card. Most firms will accept your standard licence, sometimes with an Italian translation (which can usually be provided by the agencies themselves) or International Driving Permit.

At the time of writing, Hertz offered a special weekend rate which compared well with rates offered by other firms: L191,000 for a Fiat Uno or Renault Clio, from Friday 9 am to Monday 9 am. The cost for a week was L643,000. Avis offered a deal on camper van rental, to be organised before you left home, from around US$106 a day for a four-berth van. Details are available through CIT offices abroad. Local operators aren't necessarily cheaper, and none can compete against fly/drive deals organised beforehand.

Rental motorbikes come in two versions: mopeds *(motorini)* under 50 cc, and scooters, such as a Vespa. The average cost for a Vespa is around L60,000 per day and L380,000 per week. For a motorino you will pay L50,000 per day and L300,000 per week. See the following Road Rules section for age, licence and helmet requirements.

Rental agencies are listed under the major cities in this book. Most tourist offices can provide information about where to rent a car or motorbike, otherwise look in the local Yellow Pages (Pagine Gialle).

Purchase

Car It is not possible for foreigners to buy a car in Italy, as the law requires that you must be a resident to own and register one. The only way to get around this is to have a friend who is a resident of Italy buy one for you.

It is possible to buy a cheap small car, around 10 years old, for as little as L1,000,000 to L1,500,000, ranging up to around L6,000,000 for a decent second-hand, five-year-old Fiat Uno, and up to L9,000,000 for a two-year-old Uno. The best way to find a car is to look in the classified section of local newspapers. If you buy a car in another country and need any assistance or advice in Italy, contact the ACI (see the Useful Organisations section in the Facts for the Visitor chapter).

Motorbike The same laws apply to owning and registering a motorbike. The cost of a second-hand Vespa ranges from L500,000 to L1,000,000, and a motorino will cost from L300,000 to L1,000,000. Prices for more powerful bikes start at L1,500,000.

Road Rules

As throughout Europe, driving is on the right side of the road and passing is on the left. Unless otherwise indicated, you must give way to cars coming from the right. It is compulsory to wear seat belts if fitted to the car (front seat belts on all cars, rear seat belts on cars produced after 26 April 1990), and carabinieri spend a lot of time looking for those who break the law. If caught, you will be required to pay a L50,000 fine on the spot.

There are no random breath tests in Italy, but if you're involved in an accident while under the influence of alcohol, the penalties can be severe even if the accident wasn't your fault. The limit on blood-alcohol content is 0.08%.

Speed limits, unless otherwise indicated by local signs, are: on autostradas 130 km/h for cars of 1100 cc or more, 110 km/h for smaller cars and for motorcycles under 350 cc; on all main, non- urban highways 110 km/h; on secondary, non-urban highways 90 km/h; in built-up areas 50 km/h. Speeding fines follow EC standards and are L50,000 for up to 10 km/h over the limit, L200,000 for up to 40 km/h, and L500,000 for more than 40 km/h. Driving through a red light will cost L100,000.

To ride a motorino (moped under 50 cc), you don't need a licence but you should be aged 14 years or over, and a helmet is compulsory up to age 18; passengers are not allowed and you can't ride on autostradas. A new law may be introduced to make a helmet and licence compulsory for anyone riding a motorino – check this when you arrive. The speed limit for a motorino is 40 km/h. To ride a motorcycle or scooter up to 125 cc, you must be at least 16 years old and have a licence (a car licence will do). Helmets are compulsory. Over 125 cc you need a motorcycle licence and, of course, a helmet. There is no lights-on requirement for motorcycles during the day – in fact, this practice is officially illegal in Italy!

BICYCLE
Bikes are available for rent in most Italian towns (see the Getting Around section in each city), but if you are planning to do a lot of cycling, consider buying a bike in Italy. If you shop around, bargain prices range from L190,000 (woman's bike without gears) to L300,000 (mountain bike with 16 gears). Rental costs for a bicycle range from L10,000 to L18,000 a day and up to L90,000 per week. If you plan to bring your own, check with your airline for any additional costs. The bike will need to be disassembled and packed for the journey.

A primary consideration on a cycling tour is to travel light, but you should take a few tools and spares, including a puncture repair kit and a spare inner tube. Panniers are essential to balance your possessions on either side of the bike frame. A bike helmet is a very good idea, as are a very solid bike lock and chain, which you can use to attach your machine to poles, railings etc whenever you leave it unattended.

One organisation that can help you plan your bike tour is the Cyclists' Touring Club (☎ 0483-417 217), Cotterell House, 69 Meadrow, Godalming, Surrey GU7 3HS, Britain. It can supply information to members on cycling conditions, itineraries

and cheap insurance. Membership costs £24 per annum or £12 for people aged under 18.

If you get tired of pedalling and want to put your feet up on a train, you can also organise for your bike to be transported by train. It is quite cheap, although bikes will usually only be accepted as luggage on the slower local trains. Fast trains (IC, EC etc) will generally not accommodate bikes and they will need to be sent as registered luggage. This can take a few days and it might be an idea to send your bike in advance, if possible. See the Activities section in the Facts for the Visitor chapter for some suggestions on places to cycle.

HITCHING
It is illegal to hitchhike on Italy's autostradas, but quite acceptable to stand near the entrance to the toll booths. It is not a major pastime in Italy, but Italians are friendly people and you will generally find a lift. A man and a woman travelling together is probably the best combination. Two or more men must expect some delays, while two women together will make good time. Women travelling alone should be extremely cautious about hitchhiking, particularly in the south, Sicily and Sardinia. It is preferable to find a companion.

Hitching on smaller roads where there is less traffic can be very time-consuming, and don't try to hitch from city centres: take public transport to suburban exit routes or to the nearest point to autostrada entrances. Never hitch where drivers can't stop in good time or without causing an obstruction. You could also approach drivers at petrol stations and truck stops. Look presentable, carry as little luggage as possible and hold a sign in Italian, indicating your destination. It is sometimes possible to arrange lifts in advance – scan student notice boards in colleges and universities, or ask around at youth hostels. Dedicated hitchers might like to invest in Simon Calder's *Europe – a Manual for Hitch-hikers* (paperback).

Although many travellers hitchhike, it is not a totally safe way of getting around. Just because we explain how hitching works doesn't mean we recommend it.

BOAT

Large ferries (*navi*, 'ships') service the islands of Sicily and Sardinia, and smaller ferries (*traghetti*) and hydrofoils (*aliscafi*) service areas such as the Lipari Islands, Capri and Ischia. The main embarkation points for Sardinia are Genoa, Livorno, Civitavecchia and Naples; for Sicily, Naples and Villa San Giovanni in Calabria. The main points of arrival in Sicily are Palermo and Messina; in Sardinia, Cagliari, Arbatax, Olbia and Porto Torres.

Tirrenia Navigazione is the major company servicing the Mediterranean and it has offices throughout Italy. The FS (state railway) also operates ferries to Sicily and Sardinia. Travellers can choose between cabin accommodation (men and women are usually segregated in 2nd class, although families will be kept together) or a *poltrona*, an airline-type armchair. Deck class is available only in summer and only on some ferries, so ask when making your booking.

Detailed information is provided in the Getting There & Away sections for both Sicily and Sardinia. Many services are overnight and all ferries carry vehicles (generally it is possible to take a bicycle free of charge). Restaurant, bar and recreation facilities, including cinemas, are available on the larger, long-haul ferries.

LOCAL TRANSPORT

All of the major cities have good transport systems, including bus and underground railway, although in Venice your only options are by boat or on foot. Efficient bus services also operate between neighbouring towns and villages. Tourist offices will provide information on urban public transport systems, including bus routes and maps of the subway systems.

In the cities, bus services are usually frequent and reliable. You must always buy bus tickets before you board the bus, and validate them once aboard. It is common practice among Italians and many tourists to ride

buses for free by not validating their tickets – just watch how many people rush to punch their tickets when an inspector boards the bus. However, if you get caught with an un-validated ticket, you will be fined up to L50,000 on the spot. While in the past many foreigners pleaded ignorance and got away with it, today inspectors are less likely to accept your story, particularly since, in many cities, the signs telling people to punch their tickets are in English as well as Italian.

Tickets are sold at most tobacconists, at many newsstands and at ticket booths at bus terminals (for instance, outside Stazione Termini in Rome where many of the urban buses stop). Tickets are different from city to city and generally cost from L800 to L1200, although most cities offer 24-hour tourist tickets for around L2500.

On the subways in Milan (MM), Rome and Naples (Metropolitana) you must buy tickets and validate them before getting on the train. They are different from bus tickets, and you can usually get them at tobacconists and newspaper stands.

TOURS

People wanting to travel to Italy on a fully organised tour have a wide range of options, and it is best to discuss these with your travel agent. Foreign offices of CIT (see the Tourist Offices section in the Facts for the Visitor chapter) can provide information and organise package tours. Student or youth travel agencies will be able to recommend companies which specialise in tours for young people. In London these include: Contiki (☎ 081-290 6422), Tracks (☎ 071-937 3028) and Top Deck (☎ 071-370 6487).

For people aged over 60, Saga Holidays offers holidays ranging from cheap coach tours to luxury cruises. You will find offices in Britain (☎ 0800-300 500), Saga Building, Middelburg Square, Folkstone, Kent CT20 1AZ; the USA (☎ 0617-451 6808), 120 Boyleston St, Boston, MA 02116; and Australia (☎ 02-957 4222), Level 4, 20 Alfred St, Milsons Point, Sydney 2061.

Being in a tour group removes most of the

hassles associated with travelling – such as
where to sleep and eat and how to get around.
However, it also takes away your independence and any opportunities to make
interesting detours or to take your time
savouring the sights, so make sure you weigh
up the pros and cons carefully before deciding on a guided tour.

Once in Italy, it is often less expensive and

usually more enjoyable to see the sights
independently, but if you are in a hurry or
prefer guided tours, go to the CIT office (in
all major cities). Apart from package tours of
Italy, they also organise city tours for an
average price of L35,000. Local tourist
offices sometimes offer cheap guided tours
and can generally assist with information on
other local agencies which offer tours.

Rome

Rome

'I now realise all the dreams of my youth,' wrote Goethe on his arrival in Rome in the winter of 1786. Perhaps Rome (Roma) today is more chaotic, but certainly no less romantic or fascinating. In this city a phenomenal concentration of history, legend and monuments coexists with an equally phenomenal concentration of people busily going about everyday life. It is easy to pick the tourists, because they are only the only ones to turn their heads as the bus passes the Colosseum.

In Rome there is visible evidence of the two great empires of the Western world: the Roman Empire and the Christian Church. From the Roman Forum and the Colosseum to St Peter's and the Vatican and in between, in almost every piazza, lies history on so many levels, that the saying 'Rome, a lifetime is not enough' must certainly be true.

It is generally agreed that Rome had its origins in a group of Etruscan, Latin and Sabine settlements on the Palatine, Esquiline, Quirinal and surrounding hills – later the famous seven hills of Rome. Ancient Romans put the date of their city's foundation as 21 April 753 BC and, indeed, archaeological discoveries in our century have confirmed the existence of a settlement on the Palatine in that period. It is, however, the legend of Romulus & Remus which prevails. The twin sons of Rhea Silvia and the war god Mars, they were raised by a she-wolf after being abandoned on the banks of the Tiber (Tevere). The myth says that Romulus killed his brother during a battle over who should govern, and then established the city on the Palatine. Romulus, who had established himself as the first king of Rome, disappeared one day, enveloped in a cloud which carried him back to the domain of the gods.

From the legend grew an empire which eventually controlled almost the entire world known to Europeans at the time, an achievement described by a historian of the day as 'without parallel in human history'. The celebrated historian, Edward Gibbon, wrote that Rome comprised the most beautiful part of the earth and its most civilised people. He further wrote that the most prosperous and happy period of human existence took place between the death of Emperor Domitian in 96 AD and the ascent of Emperor Commodus in 180 AD. Perhaps Gibbon neglected to consider the lives of the thousands of slaves who served the Romans.

But Rome has always inspired wonder and awe in its visitors. The ruined, but still imposing monuments of Rome represent a point of reference for a world which, through the imperial, medieval, Renaissance and Baroque periods, has always regenerated itself without interruption. As such, the cultured and well-to-do Europeans who, from the mid-17th century onwards, rediscovered Rome, found in the 'Eternal City' an example of continuity from the pagan to the Christian worlds. In fact, from the time of the Roman Empire, through the development of Christianity to the present day, a period of more than 2500 years, daily life in Rome has produced an archaeological archive of Western culture.

The historical sites of Rome are only the tip of the iceberg. Tourists wandering around the city with their eyes raised to admire its monuments, should know that everywhere they go, about four metres under their feet

Romulus & Remus with the she-wolf

exists another city, and traces of other settlements even deeper. St Peter's Basilica stands on the site of an earlier basilica built by Emperor Constantine in the 4th century over the necropolis where St Peter was buried. Castel Sant'Angelo was the tomb of Emperor Hadrian before it was converted into a fortress. The form of the Piazza Navona suggests a hippodrome and, in fact, it was built on the ruins of Emperor Domitian's stadium. To know all of this can help you to interpret and understand this chaotic and often frustrating city that, for so many centuries, has resisted with sublime indifference those who would consume it.

To see Rome, it is best to assume the attitude of an explorer and look for traces of Rome's many levels – sometimes as simple as a broken piece of ancient Roman sculpture set into the wall of a medieval church or palace.

Modern-day Rome is a busy city of about four million residents and, as capital of Italy, it is the centre of national government. Tourists will spend their time in the historical centre, thereby avoiding the sprawling and architecturally anonymous suburbs. While the look of central Rome is most obviously defined by the Baroque style of many of its fountains, churches and palaces, there are also the ancient monuments, the beautiful Romanesque churches and buildings of the medieval, Gothic and Renaissance periods, not to forget the architectural embellishments of the post-Risorgimento and Fascist eras.

Realistically a week is probably a reasonable amount of time to explore the city, but whatever time you devote to Rome, put on your walking shoes, buy a good map and plan your time carefully, and the city will seem less overwhelming than it first appears. Remember that it is best to avoid Rome during August, when the weather is suffocatingly hot and humid, making sightseeing a very unpleasant pastime. Most Romans head for the beaches or mountains to take their summer holidays, leaving half the city closed down.

ORIENTATION

Rome is a vast city, but the historical centre is quite small. Most of the major sights are within a reasonable distance of the central railway station, Stazione Termini. It is, for instance, possible to walk from the Colosseum, through the Roman Forum and the Palatine, up to the Spanish Steps and across to the Vatican in one day, although this is hardly recommended even for the most dedicated tourist. One of the great pleasures of Rome is to allow time for wandering through the many beautiful piazzas (squares), stopping now and again for a caffè and *pasta* (cake). All of the major monuments are to the west of the station area, but make sure you use a map. While it can be enjoyable to get lost in Rome, it can also be very frustrating and time-consuming.

It can be difficult to plan an itinerary if your time is limited, but generally it is best to head for museums in the morning, as most close by 2 pm. Sights such as the Colosseum, the Roman Forum and St Peter's Basilica are open in the afternoon, although the Roman Forum closes by 2 pm in winter and 5 pm in summer.

Most new arrivals in Rome will end up at Stazione Termini, the terminus for all international and national trains. The main city bus terminus is in the Piazza dei Cinquecento, directly in front of the station, and many intercity buses arrive and depart from the area between Piazza dei Cinquecento and Piazza della Repubblica.

The main airport is Leonardo da Vinci, also known as Fiumicino Airport, at Fiumicino (about an hour by train or car from the city centre). The new airport train will take you to or from the airport in a fast 20 minutes – the only problem being that the terminal is at the Ostiense train station, which is not in the city centre. From there you need to catch a bus or the subway (see the Getting Around section towards the end of this chapter).

A word of warning: the area around Stazione Termini teems with pickpockets and snatch thieves who prey on confused and lost-looking tourists. On arrival, try to look as though you know where you're going and avoid, at all costs, carrying too much luggage. If attacked by a group of thieves you will need a hand free! (See the Dangers & Annoyances section in the Facts for the Visitor chapter.)

If you're going to arrive in Rome by car, invest in a good road map of the city beforehand so as to have an idea of the various routes into the city centre. Normal traffic is not permitted into the centre of Rome, but tourists are allowed to drive to their hotels. Otherwise, there are numerous small, supervised car parks around the periphery of the historical centre, including between Piazza della Repubblica and Via Parigi (for the tourist office). The main car park is at the Villa Borghese (see the Getting Around section later in this chapter).

The majority of cheap hotels and pensioni are concentrated around Stazione Termini, but if you are prepared to go the extra distance, it is only slightly more expensive and definitely more enjoyable to stay closer to the city centre. The area around the station, particularly to the west, is unpleasant, seedy and can be dangerous at night, but the sheer number of hotels makes it the most popular area for budget travellers and tour groups.

While Rome is nowhere near as chaotic as Naples, many drivers, particularly motorcyclists, do not stop at red lights. Don't expect them to stop at pedestrian crossings either. The accepted mode of crossing a road is to step into the traffic and walk at a steady pace. If in doubt, follow a Roman.

INFORMATION
Tourist Offices

There is a branch office of the EPT (Ente Provinciale per il Turismo) opposite platform No 2 at Termini, open from 9 am to 7 pm, where you can get a map, a full list of all hotels in Rome and other information. The staff will book accommodation or provide a list of hotels and a map. The hotel list gives addresses and phone numbers, but only a vague idea of the location of hotels and pensioni in relation to the station, so ask the staff to point you in the right direction. The office also has an indecipherable brochure on city bus routes, issued by the bus company ATAC – forget it and invest L4000

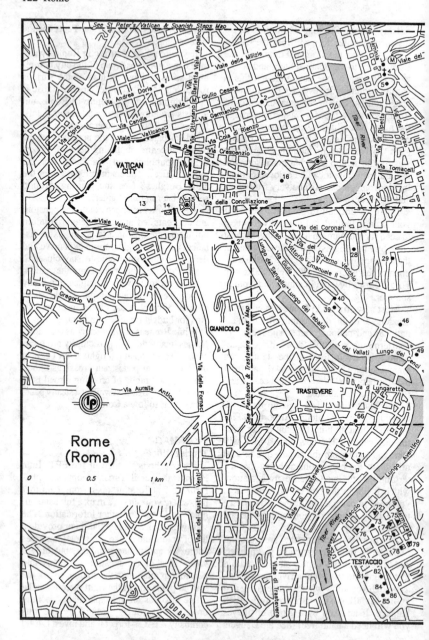

Rome
(Roma)

0   0.5   1 km

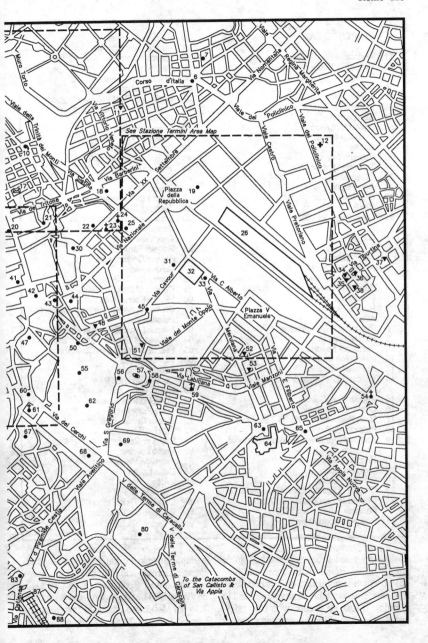

▼ PLACES TO EAT

11	Andrea
34	Pizzeria L'Economica
35	Formula 1
36	Le Maschere
37	Pommidoro
38	Il Dito e La Luna
48	Alle Carrette
51	Hostaria di Nerone
52	Tana del Grillo
53	Galilei
72	Pizzeria Remo
74	Trattoria Da Bucatino
75	Il Canestro
76	Agustarello
78	Da Felice
79	Perilli
81	Checchino dal 1887

OTHER

1	Largo Trionfale
2	Piazza dei Quiriti
3	Piazzale Flaminio
4	Church of Santa Maria del Popolo
5	Piazza del Popolo
6	Piazza Fiume
7	Alien
8	Piazza del Risorgimento
9	Piazza Cavour
10	Piazza di Spagna
12	Policlinico Umberto I
13	St Peter's Basilica
14	Vatican Post Office & Information Office
15	Piazza San Pietro
16	Castel Sant'Angelo
17	Main Post Office & ASST Telephones
18	Palazzo Barberini
19	Baths of Diocletian & Roman National Museum
20	Piazza Colonna
21	Trevi Fountain
22	Quirinal Palace
23	Church of Sant'Andrea al Quirinale
24	Church of San Carlo alle Quattro Fontane
25	Police Headquarters

26	Stazione Termini
27	Piazza delle Rovere
28	Piazza Navona
29	Pantheon
30	Piazza del Quirinale
31	IYHF head office
32	Basilica of Santa Maria Maggiore
33	Piazza Santa Maria Maggiore
39	Farnese Palace
40	Campo de'Fiori
41	Palazzo Doria Pamphili
42	Piazza Venezia
43	Trajan's Forum & Column
44	Trajan's Markets
45	Largo V Venosta
46	Piazza Mattei
47	Piazza del Campidoglio
49	Teatro di Marcello
50	Entrance to Roman Forum
54	Church of Santa Croce in Gerusalemme
55	Roman Forum
56	Arch of Constantine
57	Colosseum
58	Piazza del Colosseo
59	Church of San Clemente
60	Piazza Bocca della Verità
61	Church of Santa Maria in Cosmedin
62	Palatine Hill
63	Piazza San Giovanni in Laterano
64	Basilica of San Giovanni in Laterano
65	Piazza di Porta San Giovanni
66	Piazza Mastai
67	Aventine Hill
68	Circus Maximus
69	Celian Hill
70	Porta Portese Market
71	Porta Portese
73	Piazza Santa Maria Liberatrice
77	Piazza Testaccio
80	Baths of Caracalla
82	Radio Londra
83	Piramide Mausoleum
84	Caffè Latino
85	L'Alibi
86	Caruso Caffè
87	Ostiense Train Station
88	Piazzale dei Partigiani

in the very good street map and bus guide simply titled *Roma*, with a red-and-blue cover, which is published by Editrice Lozzi in Rome; it is available at any newsstand in Termini. It lists all streets, with map references, as well as all bus routes, and provides a simple guide to the major sights, in English, French, German and Italian.

The main EPT office (☎ 06-488 18 51) is at Via Parigi 11 and is open from 8.15 am to 7.15 pm Monday to Friday, to 2 pm Saturday (closed Sunday). Walk directly ahead from

Termini, through Piazza dei Cinquecento and Piazza della Repubblica; Via Parigi runs to the right from the top of the piazza, about five minutes' walk from the station. The office has a good range of brochures, including: *Here's Rome*, an excellent introduction to the city, listing important and useful addresses and phone numbers; *Tutta Roma*, a monthly listing of all current events; the *English Yellow Pages* and the *Italian Yellow Pages for Tourists*, basically English-language phone books for Rome; *Carnet di Roma*, a monthly guide to events in Rome, including summer festivals and concert seasons, published in English; and individual brochures on most of the major sights. The office also has up-to-date information on the opening hours and entrance fees of museums and monuments and is probably the only place in Rome where you can find comprehensive information about provincial and intercity buses (ask to look through the folder containing timetables, prices and addresses of bus companies). Brochures and, sometimes, maps and hotel lists for other Italian cities are available at this office.

Italy's national tourism body, ENIT (☎ 06-4 97 11), is at Via Marghera 2, where you can pick up information on most towns in Italy. Take the north-eastern exit from the central hall of Termini into Via Marsala. The street directly in front is Via Marghera.

Money
Banks are open Monday to Friday from 8.30 am to 1.30 pm and 2.45 to 3.45 pm. You will find a bank and several exchange offices at Termini – one in the main arrival area and one near the exit to Piazza dei Cinquecento – and both are open until the evening. There is an exchange office (Banco di Santo Spirito) at Fiumicino Airport. There are numerous other exchange offices scattered throughout the city, including: Credito Italiano, Piazza di Spagna 20, and Piazza Navona 48; Società Rosati, Via Nazionale 186; and American Express in Piazza di Spagna (see the following Travel Agencies section). Otherwise, go to any bank in the city centre.

If you are using a MasterCard to obtain cash advances, go directly to a branch of the Banca Commerciale Italiana to avoid wasting time (most other banks do not accept MasterCard). The bank's head office is at Via del Corso 226, at Piazza Venezia, which is also a good place to receive money transfers; the closest branch to Stazione Termini is at Largo Santa Susanna 124, through Piazza della Repubblica, just before Via Barberini. Visa card holders should have no problems at most banks.

Post & Telecommunications
See the Facts for the Visitor chapter for detailed information about making calls and posting mail in Italy.

Post The main post office is at Piazza San Silvestro 28, just off Via del Tritone, and is open from 8.30 am to 8 pm Monday to Friday, to noon on Saturdays. Fermo posta (the Italian version of poste restante) is available here. Telegrams can be sent from the office next door (open 24 hours a day). There is also a post office at the station. The Vatican post office in Piazza San Pietro is open Monday to Friday from 8.30 am to 7 pm, Saturdays to 6 pm. The service from here is faster and more reliable, but there's no poste restante.

The postal code for central Rome is 00100.

Telephones The ASST telephone office is next door to the post office in Piazza San Silvestro, and is open Monday to Saturday from 8 am to 11.30 pm, Sundays from 9 am to 8.30 pm. There is also a branch of the ASST downstairs at Termini, open 24 hours a day, seven days a week. The main SIP office is in Corso Vittorio Emanuele 201, near Piazza Navona, open from 8 am to 9 pm daily. Remember that international calls can also be made easily (with a phonecard) from public phones. Phonecards can be purchased at most tobacconists and newsstands.

Rome's telephone code is 06.

Foreign Embassies

For addresses and telephone numbers, see Foreign Embassies in the Facts for the Visitor chapter. All embassies and consulates are listed in the Rome telephone book under *Ambasciate*. The Australian, New Zealand and Canadian embassies can be reached from Stazione Termini on bus No 36, which travels along Via Nomentana. This bus also passes the British Embassy. Both the US and British embassies are easily accessible on foot from the station.

Travel Agencies

There is a CIT office (☎ 488 16 78) in Stazione Termini, where you can make bookings for trains, buses, ferries and planes. The staff speak English and can provide information on fares and discounts for students and young people. The office also handles tours of Rome and surrounding areas.

CTS (Centro Turistico Studentesco, ☎ 4 67 91), Via Genova 16, off Via Nazionale, offers much the same services and will also make hotel reservations, but focuses on discount and student travel. Good deals on airfares are available, but you will need to pay a L30,000 membership fee to take advantage of them and it is a good idea to check first that other agencies are not also offering similar discounts. The staff speak English.

American Express (☎ 6 76 41), Piazza di Spagna 38, has a travel service similar to those just mentioned and can arrange tours of the city and surrounding areas. A full list of all travel agencies in Rome is available at the EPT office.

Bookshops

The best English-language bookshop in Rome is the Anglo-American Bookshop, with two branches in Via della Vite, at No 27 and 57, off Piazza di Spagna. It has an excellent range of literature, travel guides and reference books. The Lion Bookshop, Via del Babuino 181, also has a good selection. Feltrinelli, Via V E Orlando 83, just off Piazza della Repubblica, has mainly classics and an excellent choice of guidebooks and maps for Rome and Italy. The Economy Book & Video Center, Via Torino 136, also has a good selection of books, as well as second-hand paperbacks. The Corner Bookshop, Via del Moro 48, Trastevere, has an excellent range of English-language books and is run by an Australian.

There are also English-language libraries in Rome: the British Council Library (☎ 482 66 41), Via delle Quattro Fontane 20, and the United States Information Service (USIS) (☎ 4 67 41), Via Veneto 119a.

Emergency

Emergency medical treatment is available in the casualty sections of public hospitals, including: Policlinico Umberto I (☎ 4 99 71), Viale del Policlinico 255, near Stazione Termini; Policlinico A Gemelli (☎ 33 01 51), Largo A Gemelli 8 (some distance from the centre); and Santo Spirito (☎ 65 09 01), Lungotevere in Sassia. The Salvator Mundi clinic (☎ 58 89 61), Via della Mura Gianicolense 67, and the Rome American Hospital (☎ 2 25 51), Via E Longoni 69, are both private and you should use their services only if you have health insurance and have consulted your insurance company.

Your embassy will also be able to make recommendations on where to go for medical treatment. Unless you are a citizen of an EC country, or of a country which has a reciprocal health-care arrangement with Italy, you will be required to pay for medical assistance in a public hospital. For an ambulance, call ☎ 51 00, and for first aid, call ☎ 115.

There is a pharmacy in Stazione Termini, open from 7 am to 11 pm daily (closed in August). For recorded information (only in Italian) on all-night pharmacies in Rome, call ☎ 19 21.

The police headquarters (☎ 46 86) are at Via San Vitale 15. The Ufficio Stranieri (Foreigners' Bureau, ☎ 46 86 29 87) is around the corner at Via Genova 2. It is open 24 hours a day and thefts should be reported here. For immediate police attendance, call ☎ 112 or 113.

Other Information

If you need a wash when you arrive in Rome, there are public baths downstairs at the station (follow the *diurno* signs), open from 6.40 am to 8 pm. Showers cost L10,000. To wash your clothes, there is a coin laundry *(lavasecco a gettoni)* at Campo de' Fiori 38 and Via Castelfidardo 29, near the station. Remember that it is expensive to use a laundry: you will pay around L8000 to L10,000 for a medium load and up to L30,000 for a heavy load (around five kg).

The Italian Youth Hostels Association (☎ 487 11 52), Via Cavour 44, will provide information about all the youth hostels in Italy. You can also join the IYHF here.

Dangers & Annoyances

Thieves are very active in the area around Stazione Termini, at major sights such as the Colosseum and Roman Forum, and in the city's more expensive shopping streets, such as Via Condotti. Pickpockets like to work on crowded buses (the No 64 from Stazione Termini to St Peter's is notorious). If approached by a group of scruffy-looking women and children, who are usually carrying pieces of newspaper or cardboard, don't be fooled by their 'up-front' approach: they are highly skilled and very fast. The best way to avoid being robbed is to remain extremely alert and shout *va via!* (go away!) when approached. Never carry a purse, wallet or documents in your pockets and keep a good grip on your bag. Purse and bag-snatchers also use motorcycles in Rome and it is best to wear your shoulder bag on the side of your body away from the road, with the strap across your chest.

THINGS TO SEE & DO

It would take years to explore every corner of Rome, months to even begin to appreciate the incredible number of monuments, and weeks for a thorough tour of the city. The average traveller usually has only a matter of days, but it is possible to cover most of the important monuments in five days, three at a minimum. If you have even less time, try

visiting St Peter's and the Vatican in the morning, then head for the Roman Forum, Palatine and Colosseum in the afternoon (keep in mind that the Roman Forum closes at 2 pm in winter and 5 pm in summer). Try not to overdo it if you have only a short time in Rome, and make the time to have at least one long lunch in one of its many piazzas.

Walking Tour

Try to get hold of the book *Strolling Around Rome*, published by the Lazio Region's Assessorato del Turismo, and occasionally available at the EPT office. Another guide is *Romewalks* by Anya M Shetterly (paperback), which details four walks in the city.

A good, but rather long walk to help orient yourself in Rome is to start from the **Church of Santa Maria degli Angeli** in Piazza della Repubblica and head north-west along Via V E Orlando, turning left into Via XX Settembre, passing the intersection of Via delle Quattro Fontane, named for the fountains on each corner, to reach the **Piazza del Quirinale**, from where you have a lovely view of the city. From the piazza, walk back down Via del Quirinale and turn left into Via delle Quattro Fontane to get to **Piazza Barberini** and Bernini's **Fontana del Tritone**. From here you can wander up **Via Veneto**, or take Via Sistina to the top of the **Spanish Steps**.

Take the high-class shopping street, Via Condotti, down to Via del Corso, turn left and continue until you cross Via del Tritone, then take the second left (Via delle Muratte) to see the **Trevi Fountain**. Return to Via del Corso and cross into the **Piazza Colonna**. Things get a bit complicated here, but use a good map and follow the tourist signs and you won't get lost. Walk through the piazza into the **Piazza di Montecitorio**, continue walking straight ahead along Via del Vicario and buy a gelati at **Giolitti** before turning left at Via della Maddalena to get to the **Pantheon**.

Take Via Giustiniani from the north-western corner of the piazza and follow the signs to the **Piazza Navona**. Leave the piazza at Via Cuccagna, cross Corso V Emanuele and take Via Cancelleria to reach the **Campo de' Fiori**. From here take Via Gallo into the **Piazza Farnese** and then walk directly ahead out of the piazza on Via dei Farnesi into **Via Giulia**.

If you still have the energy, you have two choices. Either continue along Via Giulia and cross the Ponte V Emanuele II to get to **St Peter's Basilica** and the **Vatican**, or cross the **Ponte Sisto** at the southern end of Via Giulia and wander through **Trastevere**.

Another walk to take in the ancient area of Rome starts from Piazza Venezia. To the left off the piazza as you face the Vittorio Emanuele monument is **Trajan's Forum**. Wander around there before returning to Piazza Venezia to climb the steps to the Piazza del Campidoglio. Walk through the piazza and exit to the right for a great view of the Forum, then walk downhill along Via Monte Tarpeo into Piazza Consolazione. Take Via San Giovanni Decollato to Via del Velabro and the Piazza Bocca della Verità, where you can see the **Arco di Giano** (Arch of Janus) and the Romanesque **Church of San Giorgio in Velabro** and the adjacent **Arco degli Argentari** (Arch of the Money-changers), erected in honour of Emperor Septimus Severus. Then walk through the piazza, past the two Roman temples, to place your hand in the famous Mouth of Truth at the beautiful **Church of Santa Maria in Cosmedin**. From there, take either Via dei Cerchi or Via Circo Massimo past the **Circus Maximus** and the **Palatine Hill**, then turn left into Via di San Gregorio and head towards the **Arch of Constantine** and the **Colosseum**. You can choose to enter the Palatine from here, or continue around into Via dei Fori Imperiali to enter the **Roman Forum**.

An interesting deviation from the corner of Via dei Cerchi and Via di San Gregorio is to continue straight ahead along the Viale delle Terme di Caracalla to the **Baths of Caracalla**. Before reaching the baths, on your left is the **Celio**, one of the seven hills of Rome. There is a park at the top of the hill where the Ninfeo (Area of Pleasure) of Nero's Golden House once stood.

Trajan's Forum

Designed by Apollodorus of Damascus for Emperor Trajan and constructed at the beginning of the 2nd century AD, Trajan's Forum was the last of the forums. It was a vast complex extending from what is now the Piazza Venezia and comprising a basilica for the judiciary, two libraries, a temple, a triumphal arch in honour of the emperor, and the **Colonna di Traiano** (Trajan's Column). Restored in the late 1980s, the column was

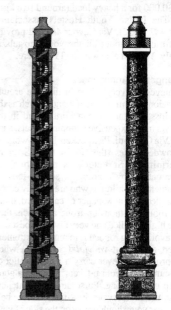

Trajan's Column

erected to mark the victories of Trajan over the Dacians (who lived in what is now Romania). It is decorated with a spiral series of reliefs depicting the battles between the Roman and Dacian armies, which are regarded as among the finest examples of ancient Roman sculpture. A golden statue of Trajan once topped the column, but it was lost during the Middle Ages and replaced with a statue of St Peter. Apart from the column, all that remains of the grand imperial forum are some of the pillars which once enclosed the complex.

By comparison, **Trajan's Markets** (Mercati di Traiano) are relatively well preserved. Also designed by Apollodorus, the markets were constructed on three levels, comprising six floors of shops and offices in a semicircular shape. You can get an idea of their grandeur from the high vaulted roofs. The markets and forum are open from 9 am to 1.30 pm Monday to Saturday, to 1 pm Sundays, and also on summer afternoons on Tuesdays and Thursdays from 4 to 7 pm. Entrance is L4000. The entrance to the markets is at Via IV Novembre 94.

Next to Trajan's forum and markets are the forums of Nerva and Augustus, although very little remains of either complex. Across the Via dei Fori Imperiali is Caesar's Forum, built by Julius Caesar at the foot of the Capitoline Hill. Again, very little remains to give an idea of the original structure.

Colosseum

Originally known as the Flavian Amphitheatre, construction was started by Emperor Vespasian in 72 AD in the grounds of Nero's Golden House and completed by his son Titus. The massive structure could seat 50,000, and the bloody gladiator combat and wild beast shows, when thousands of wild animals were slashed to death, give some insight into Roman people of the day. Historians disagree on whether many early Christian martyrs were fed to lions in the stadium.

In the Middle Ages the Colosseum became a fortress and was later used as a quarry for travertine and marble for the Palazzo Venezia and other buildings.

Opening hours are from 9 am to 3 pm in winter, to 7 pm in summer, and to 1 pm on Sunday, Wednesday and holidays. Entrance costs L6000.

Arch of Constantine

Next to the Colosseum is the triumphal arch built to honour Constantine following his victory over Maxentius at the battle of the Milvian Bridge (near the present-day Zona Olimpica, north-west of the Villa Borghese) in 312 AD. Its decorative reliefs were taken from earlier structures. The arch was recently unveiled after restoration.

Roman Forum & Palatine Hill

The commercial, political and religious centre of ancient Rome, the Forum stands in a valley between the Capitoline and Palatine hills. Originally marshland, the area was drained during the early Republican era and became a centre for political rallies, public ceremonies and senate meetings. The Forum was constructed over a period of about 900 years, with later emperors erecting buildings next to buildings from the Republican era. Its importance declined along with the empire after the 4th century AD, and the temples, monuments and buildings constructed by successive emperors, consuls and senators fell into ruin, eventually leading to the site being used as pasture land.

The area was excavated in the 18th and 19th centuries, and excavations are still continuing. You can watch archaeological teams at work in several locations.

Colosseum cross-section

The Roman Forum in ancient times

You can enter the Forum from Via dei Fori Imperiali, which leads from Piazza Venezia to the Colosseum. It is open in summer from 9 am to 6 pm, to 3 pm in winter, and to 1 pm on Sundays and Tuesdays. Entrance costs L10,000 and covers both the Forum and the Palatine.

To the right as you enter the Forum is the **Basilica Aemilia** built as a two-storey portico lined with shops. Nearby is the **Curia**, once the meeting place of the Roman Senate. It was converted into a Christian church in the Middle Ages, which explains its well-preserved state today. Opposite is the famous **Lapis Niger**, a large piece of black marble, which legend says covered the grave of Romulus. The tomb also contains the oldest known Latin inscription.

The **Arch of Septimus Severus** was erected in 203 AD in honour of this emperor and his sons and is considered one of Italy's major triumphal arches. A recent project to renovate the arch left it exactly half cleaned when the money ran out. To the left is the Rostrum, used by public speakers, which was decorated in ancient times by the rams of captured ships. A circular base stone

marks the symbolic centre of ancient Rome, the *umbilicus urbis*. The nearby **Column of Phocus** was erected in 608 AD in the main square of the Forum in honour of a Byzantine emperor.

Along the Via Sacra lies the **Temple of Saturn**, one of the most important temples in ancient Rome. Eight granite columns remain. The Basilica Julia, opposite, was the seat of justice, and nearby is the Temple of Julius Caesar, which was erected by Octavian in 29 BC on the site where Caesar's body was burned and Mark Antony read his famous speech. The **Temple of Castor & Pollux** was built in 489 BC to mark the defeat of the Etruscan Tarquins and in honour of the Heavenly Twins, or Dioscuri.

The **Church of Santa Maria Antiqua**, near the Palatine, is the oldest Christian church in the Forum, and, although badly damaged, contains frescoes of interest. After walking back to the remains of the Arch of Augustus you find the **House of the Vestals**, home of the virgins who tended the sacred flame in the adjoining **Temple of Vesta**. If the flame went out it was seen as a bad omen. The other major sights are the

Temple of Antoninus & Faustina, of which six columns remain, and the **Arch of Titus**, at the end of the Forum, built in 81 AD in honour of the emperor who conquered Jerusalem.

From here climb the **Palatine**, where wealthy Romans built their homes and where legend says that Romulus founded the city. Cicero lived here and Emperor Augustus built his palace on the hill. His successors followed suit with a series of palaces and temples. Like the Forum, the buildings of the Palatine fell into ruin and in the Middle Ages the hill became the site of convents and churches. During the Renaissance wealthy families established their gardens here. The Farnese villa and gardens were built over the ruins of the Palace of Tiberius.

Worth a look are the **House of Livia**, decorated with frescoes; the **Domus Augustana** (Imperial Residence); the **Palace of the Flavians**, built by Domitian; the **Temple of Magna Mater**, which was built in 204 BC to house the black stone Cybele; and the impressive ruins of the **Baths of Septimus Severus**. Bring a picnic lunch. Opening hours are the same as for the Forum.

Past the Palatine is the **Circus Maximus**. There is not much to see here: only a few ruins remain of what was once a chariot racetrack big enough to hold more than 200,000 people.

From the Arch of Constantine, bus No 118, or a 15-minute walk, will take you to the **Baths of Caracalla** (Terme di Caracalla). A huge complex covering 10 hectares, the baths could hold 1600 people and had shops, gardens, libraries and entertainment. Begun by Septimus Severus in 206 AD and completed by his son Antonius Caracalla, the baths were used until the 6th century AD. For some years they have been an atmospheric venue for opera performances in summer. The baths are open from 9 am to 6 pm in summer, to 3 pm in winter, but to 1 pm on Sundays and Mondays. Entrance is L6000.

Celian Hill

One of the seven hills of Rome, the Celio is accessible either from Via di San Gregorio or, from the other side, the Piazza di Navicella. The **Villa Celimontana** is a large public park, perfect for a quiet picnic. The 4th century **Church of SS Giovanni e Paolo**, in the piazza of the same name along Via di San Paolo della Croce, is dedicated to two Romans, Sts John & Paul, who had served in the court of Emperor Constantine and were beheaded by his anti-Christian successor for refusing to serve as officers in his court. The church was built over their houses. Downhill, along a pretty road under a series of brick arches, is the 8th century **Church of San Gregorio Magno**, built in honour of Pope Gregory the Great on the site where he dispatched St Augustine to convert Britain to Christianity. The church was remodelled in the Baroque style in the 17th century.

Aventine Hill

Cross Viale Aventino to the far side of the Circus Maximus and head up another of Rome's seven hills, the Aventino, by way of Via di Valle Murcia and Clivo dei Publici to Via di Santa Sabina. Along the way, you will pass the **Valle Margia**, a beautiful rose garden, best seen obviously when the roses are in bloom, and the **Parco Savello**, before reaching the **Church of Santa Sabina**, built in the 5th century and now restored to its original state. Note particularly the carved wooden doors, which date from the same period as the church, with panels that depict biblical scenes. Farther along Via Santa Sabina is the Piazza Cavalieri di Malta and the **Priorato di Malta**. Look through the keyhole in the central door of the entrance to the property's private garden for a surprising view.

Piazza del Campidoglio

Designed by Michelangelo in 1538, the piazza is on the Capitoline Hill and is bounded by three palaces: the Palazzo dei Conservatori on the right, the Palazzo dei Senatori at the rear, and the Palazzo Nuovo. The streets on either side of the Palazzo dei Senatori lead down to the Forum. It was on this hill, which has always been the seat of the Roman government, that Brutus spoke of the death of Julius Caesar and that Nelson hoisted the British flag in 1799 to keep Napoleon out of the city.

In the centre of the square stood a bronze equestrian statue of Emperor Marcus Aurelius. The statue, which was originally gilded, was removed for restoration after being badly damaged by pollution. It will eventually be placed in the Roman National Museum and a replica will be erected in the piazza.

The **Museo Capitolino** (Capitoline Museum) is in the Palazzo Nuovo and the Piazza dei Conservatori opposite. The most famous piece in the museum is the *Capitoline Wolf*, an Etruscan bronze statue from the 6th century BC. A statue of Romulus & Remus was added in the early 16th century and is in the Palazzo dei Conservatori. Other interesting works in this wing of the museum include the *Boy with Thorn*, a statue of a boy taking a thorn from his foot, and a bronze bust of Brutus, the man who assassinated Julius Caesar. Works in the Palazzo Nuovo include the impressive *Dying Gaul* and the *Capitoline Venus*, a Roman copy of a 2nd century BC Greek original. Well worth a look is the gallery of busts of Roman emperors and other famous people of the day. The museum is open from 9 am to 1.30 pm Tuesday to Saturday (also 5 to 8 pm Tuesday and Saturday) and 9 am to 1 pm Sunday (closed Monday). Entrance is L10,000.

The Forum is below the piazza, and on the way, along Via di San Pietro in Carcere, is the ancient Roman **Mamertine Prison**, where prisoners were put through a hole in the floor to starve to death. St Peter was believed to have been imprisoned there and to have created a miraculous stream of water to baptise his jailers. It is now the site of the Church of San Pietro in Carcere.

The **Church of Santa Maria d'Aracoeli** is between the Campidoglio and the Victor Emmanuel monument, at the top of a long flight of steps. Built on the site where legend says the Sybil told Augustus of the coming birth of Christ, it features frescoes by Pinturicchio and a statue of the baby Jesus said to have been carved from the wood of an olive tree from the garden of Gethsemane. The statue, in a chapel to the right of the altar, is an object of pilgrimage and is placed in a Nativity scene at the church each Christmas.

Piazza Mattei & the Jewish Quarter

From the bottom of the steps leading up to the Campidoglio, walk to the right along Via del Teatro di Marcello to reach the **Teatro di Marcello**, built around 13 BC to plans by Emperor Augustus. It was converted into a fortress and residence during the Middle Ages, and a palace was built on the site in the 16th century which preserved the original form of the theatre.

Walk back along Via del Teatro di Marcello and turn left into Via Montanara to Piazza Campitelli and then Via dei Funari to Piazza Mattei. In the piazza is the **Fontana delle Tartarughe**, a fountain designed by Giacomo della Porta and sculpted by Taddeo Landini in the 16th century. The tortoises were added in the 17th century.

Take Via della Reginella to Via del Portico d'Ottavia and wander through the area known as the Jewish Ghetto. In the 16th century Pope Paul IV ordered the confinement of Jewish people in this area, marking the beginning of a period of intolerance which continued well into the 19th century.

From the ghetto area, you can reach the **Isola Tiberina** (Tiber Island) across the **Ponte Fabricio**, which was built in 62 BC and is Rome's oldest standing bridge. The island has been associated with healing since the 3rd century BC when the Romans adopted the Greek god of healing as their own and erected a temple to him on the island. Today it is the site of the Fatebenefratelli Hospital. The church of San Bartolomeo was built in the 10th century on the ruins of the Roman temple. It has a Romanesque bell tower and a marble wellhead, believed to have been built over the same spring which provided healing waters for the temple. The **Ponte Cestio**, built in 46 BC, connects the island to Trastevere. The remains of a bridge to the south of the island are part of the **Ponte Rotto** (Broken Bridge), which was ancient Rome's first stone bridge.

Trastevere

The settlement at Trastevere was, in early times, separate from Rome. Although it was soon swallowed up by the growing city, this sense of separation continued during medieval times, when the area, because it was on the other side of the river, developed its own identity. It is said that even today many of the old people of Trastevere will rarely cross the river to go into the city. It's worth wandering through the narrow streets of this busy and bohemian area. It is particularly beautiful at night and is one of the more interesting areas for bar-hopping or a meal.

Of particular note here is **Santa Maria in Trastevere**, in the lovely piazza of the same name, believed to be the oldest place of worship dedicated to the Virgin in Rome. Although the first basilica was built on this site in the 3rd century AD, the present structure was built in the 12th century and features a Romanesque bell tower and façade, with a mosaic of the Virgin. Its interior was redecorated during the Baroque period.

Campo de' Fiori

This is a lively piazza where a flower and vegetable market is held every morning except Sunday. Now lined with bars and trattorie, the piazza was in fact a place of execution during the Inquisition. The famous heretic Giordano Bruno was burned at the stake in the piazza in 1600 and his statue now stands at its centre.

The **Farnese Palace** (Palazzo Farnese), in the piazza of the same name, is just off Campo de' Fiori. A magnificent Renaissance building, it was started in 1514 by Antonio da Sangallo, work was carried on by Michelangelo and completed by Giacomo della Porta. Built for Cardinal Alessandro Farnese (later Pope Paul III), the palace is now the French Embassy. The piazza has two fountains, which were enormous granite baths taken from the Baths of Caracalla.

Via Giulia

This street was designed by Bramante, who was commissioned by Pope Julius II to create a new approach to St Peter's. It is lined with Renaissance palaces, antique shops and art galleries.

Piazza Navona

This is a vast and beautiful square, lined with Baroque palaces. It was laid out on the ruins of Domitian's stadium and holds three fountains, including Bernini's masterpiece, the **Fontana dei Fiumi** (Fountain of the Rivers), in the centre, depicting the Nile, Ganges, Danube and Rio de la Plata. The piazza is a popular gathering place for Romans and tourists alike. Take time to relax on one of the stone benches and watch the artists who gather in the piazza to work, have your tarot cards *(tarocchi)* read, or pay top prices to enjoy a drink at one of the outdoor cafés, such as Tre Scalini. Facing the piazza is the Church of Sant'Agnese, designed by Bernini's bitter rival, Borromini.

The Pantheon

The only building of ancient Rome which remains perfectly preserved, it was built by Marcus Agrippa, son-in-law of Augustus, in 27 BC and dedicated to the most important planetary gods. Although the temple was rebuilt by Emperor Hadrian around 120 AD, Agrippa's name remains inscribed over the entrance.

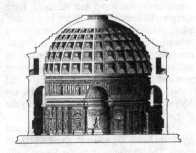

Cross-section of the Pantheon

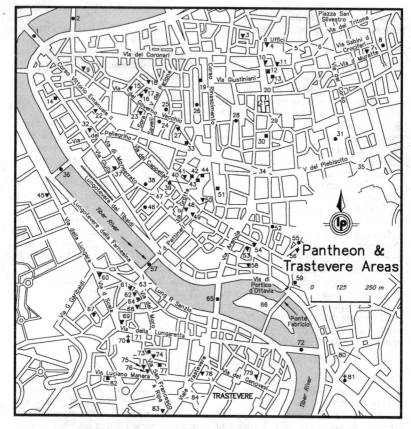

Pantheon & Trastevere Areas

Over the centuries the temple has been consistently plundered and damaged. Pope Gregory III removed the gilded bronze roof tiles, although the original bronze doors remain. The extraordinary dome is considered the most important achievement of ancient Roman architecture. Pagan worship was forbidden by the Christian emperors and in 609 AD the temple was consecrated to the Virgin and Christian martyrs, supposedly the origin of All Saints' Day.

The Italian kings Victor Emmanuel II and Umberto I and the painter Raphael are buried there. The Pantheon is in the Piazza della Rotonda and is open from 9 am to 2 pm Monday to Saturday, to 1 pm Sunday and holidays. Entrance is free.

Trevi Fountain

This high-Baroque fountain was designed by Nicola Salvi in 1732. Its water was supplied by one of Rome's earliest aqueducts. Work to clean the fountain and its water supply was completed in 1991. The famous custom is to throw a coin into the fountain (over your shoulder while facing away) to ensure your return to Rome. If you throw a second coin you can make a wish.

■ PLACES TO STAY

12	Albergo Abruzzi
13	Hotel Senato
14	Cardinal Hotel
30	Pensione Mimosa
33	Pensione Primavera
42	Hotel Campo de'Fiori
43	Albergo del Sole
44	Albergo della Lunetta
51	Albergo Pomezia
77	Hotel Cisterna
82	Albergo Manara

▼ PLACES TO EAT

3	Il Bacaro
4	Giolitti
7	Pizza a Taglio
9	Da Alfredo e Ada
10	Fortunato al Pantheon
11	Tazza d'Oro
15	Nameless Osteria
16	Paladini
17	Pizzeria Corallo
18	Trattoria Pizzeria Da Francesco
22	Trattoria Polese
23	Pizzeria Da Baffetto
27	Cul de Sac
32	Il Cardinale
37	Hostaria Giulio
41	Hosteria Romanesca
45	Da Giovanni
48	Il Grottino
49	Patrizia e Roberto del Pianeta Terra
50	Filetti di Baccala
53	Al Pompiere
54	Sora Margherita
56	Vecchia Roma
58	Piperno
60	Da Gildo
61	Suria Mahal
62	Checco er Carrettiere
64	Mario's
67	Da Lucia
68	D'Augusto
69	Tana de Noiantri
74	Paris
75	Pizzeria Da Vittorio
76	Pizzeria Ivo
78	Panattoni
79	Cul de Sac 2
83	Frontoni

OTHER

1	Ponte Vittorio Emanuele
2	Ponte Sant'Angelo
5	Piazza di Monte Citorio
6	Piazza Colonna
8	Piazza di Trevi & Trevi Fountain
19	Bevitoria Navona
20	Piazza della Rotonda
21	Pantheon
24	Caffè Gardenia
25	Enoteca Piccolo
26	Piazza Navona
28	Bar Sant'Eustachio
29	Piazza della Minerva
31	Palazzo Doria Pamphili
34	Largo di Torre Argentina
35	Piazza Venezia
36	Ponte G Mazzini
38	Caffè Peru
39	Vineria
40	Campo de' Fiori
46	Farnese Palace
47	Piazza Farnese
52	Piazza Mattei
55	Piazza Campitelli
57	Ponte Sisto
59	Teatro di Marcello
63	Piazza Trilussa
65	Ponte Garibaldi
66	Isola Tiberina
70	Basilica of Santa Maria in Trastevere
71	Piazza Santa Maria in Trastevere
72	Ponte Palatino
73	Bar San Calisto
80	Piazza Bocca della Verità
81	Church of Santa Maria in Cosmedin
84	Piazza Mastai

Piazza di Spagna & Spanish Steps

The piazza, church and the famous staircase (the Scalinata della Trinità dei Monti) have long provided a major gathering place for foreigners. Built with a legacy from the French in 1725, but named after the Spanish Embassy to the Holy See, the steps lead to the French church of Trinità dei Monti.

In the 18th century the most beautiful women and men of Italy gathered there, waiting to be chosen as an artist's model. To the right as you face the steps is the house where Keats died in 1921, now the Keats-Shelley Memorial House. It is open from 9 am to 1 pm and 2.30 to 5.30 pm Monday to Friday. Admission is L4000. In the piazza is

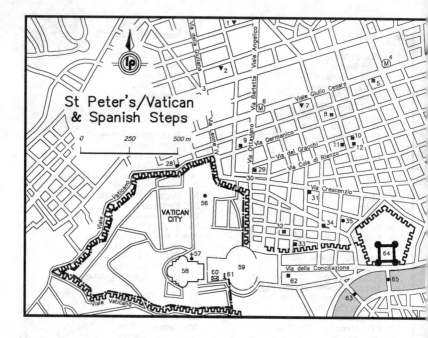

St Peter's/Vatican
& Spanish Steps

■ PLACES TO STAY	76 Hotel Julia

■	PLACES TO STAY
5	Pensione Schiavo & Pensione Valparaiso
8	Giuggioli Hotel, Pensione Lady, Pensione Zurigo & Pensione Nautilus
9	Hotel Amalia
10	Hotel Ticino
11	Pensione San Michele
12	Hotels Joli & Florida
19	Albergo Fiorella
25	Hotel Pensione Merano
27	Hotel Forte
29	Pensione Ottaviano
31	Hotel Prati
32	Hotel Sant'Anna
33	Hotel Bramante
34	Hotel Adriatic
44	Hassler Villa Medici
45	Hotel Gregoriana
47	Hotel Scalinata di Spagna
48	Hotel Pensione Suisse
53	Hotel Sistina
62	Hotel Columbus

76	Hotel Julia

▼	PLACES TO EAT
1	Pizzeria Giacomelli
2	Osteria dell'Angelo
7	Il Tempio della Pizza
18	Dal Bolognese
20	Paneformaggio & Bibo
21	Caffè Sogo
22	Margutta Vegetariano
23	Osteria Margutta
39	Otello alla Concordia
40	Fior Fiore
41	Al 34
50	Pizzeria Il Leoncino
51	Mario
52	Sogo Asahi
55	Tullio
67	El Toulà
68	Il Convivio
69	La Campana
70	Ristorante La Pentola
71	M&M Volpetti

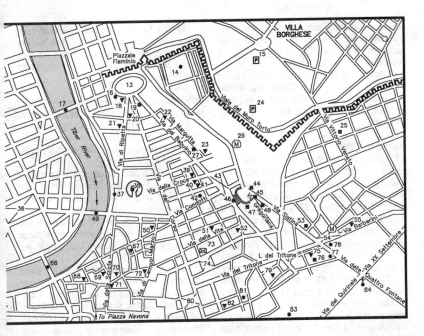

72	Gino in Vicolo Rossini	
75	Colline Emiliane	
79	Golden Crown	
82	Al Moro	

OTHER

3	Largo Trionfale
4	Lepanto Metro Stop
6	Ottaviano Metro Stop
13	Piazza del Popolo
14	Pincio Hill
15	Villa Borghese Car Park
16	Caffè Rosati
17	Ponte Regina Margherita
24	Villa Borghese Car Park
26	Spagna Metro Stop
28	Entrance to Vatican Museums
30	Piazza del Risorgimento
35	Il Castello
36	Piazza Cavour
37	Ara Pacis
38	Mausoleum of Augustus
42	Caffè Greco

43	Piazza di Spagna
46	American Express Office
49	Ponte Cavour
54	Piazza Barberini & Barberini Metro Stop
56	Vatican Museums
57	Sistine Chapel
58	St Peter's Basilica
59	St Peter's Square
60	Vatican Post Office
61	Tourist Office
63	Ponte Vittorio Emanuele II
64	Castel Sant'Angelo
65	Ponte Sant'Angelo
66	Ponte Umberto I
73	Main Post Office & ASST Telephones
74	Piazza San Silvestro
77	Esperimento
78	Palazzo Barberini
80	Piazza Colonna
81	Trevi Fountain
83	Quirinal Palace
84	Church of San Carlo alle Quattro Fontane

the boat-shaped fountain called the **Barcaccia**, believed to be by Pietro Bernini, father of the famous Gian Lorenzo. One of Rome's most elegant shopping streets, **Via Condotti**, runs off the piazza towards Via del Corso. The famous **Caffè Greco** is at No 86, where artists, musicians and the literati used to meet, including Goethe, Keats, Byron and Wagner.

Villa Borghese

This huge and beautiful park was once the estate of Cardinal Scipione Borghese. Take a picnic to the park if the tourist trip starts to wear you down. His 17th century villa houses the **Borghese Museum**, which has been under restoration for almost a decade (work will continue into the 21st century). Only the sculpture section is open, from 9 am to 7 pm Monday to Saturday, to 1 pm Sunday, and entry is free. In the park, near the villa, the **National Gallery of Modern Art**, Viale delle Belle Arti 131, houses a large collection of Italian art from the 19th century to the present day. It is open Tuesday to Saturday from 9 am to 2 pm, Sunday to 1 pm (closed Monday). Entrance is L8000.

Museo Nazionale Etrusco di Villa Giulia

Situated in the 16th century villa of Pope Julius III at the top end of the Villa Borghese in the Piazzale di Villa Giulia, this museum houses the national collection of Etruscan treasures, many found in tombs at sites throughout Lazio. Of particular note are the statue of Apollo found at Veio, and the famous *Sarcofago degli Sposi* discovered in a tomb at Cerveteri. The museum is open from 9 am to 2 pm Monday to Saturday, to 1 pm Sunday, and to 7.30 pm Wednesday. Admission is L8000.

The Vatican

After the unification of Italy, the Papal States of central Italy became part of the new Kingdom of Italy, which caused a considerable rift between the church and the state. In 1929, Mussolini, under the Lateran Treaty, gave the pope full sovereignty over what is now the Vatican City.

The city has its own postal service, currency, newspaper, radio station, train station and army of Swiss Guards – and of course St Peter's Basilica, the most famous church in the Christian world.

Information & Services The tourist office, in Piazza San Pietro to the left of the basilica, is open from 8.30 am to 7 pm and can provide general information about the church and the Vatican. Guided tours of the Vatican can be organised at the office.

The Vatican post office, said to provide a much faster and more reliable service than the normal Italian postal system, is a few doors up from the tourist office (there is another outlet on the other side of the piazza). Letters can be posted in Vatican postboxes only if they carry Vatican stamps.

St Peter's Basilica & Square In the same area where the church now stands, there was once the Circo Vaticano, built by Nero. It was in this stadium that St Peter and other Christians were martyred between 64 and 67 AD. The body of the saint was buried in an anonymous grave next to the wall of the circus, and his fellow Christians built a humble 'red wall' to mark the site. In 160 the stadium was abandoned and a small monument erected on the grave. In 315 the first Christian emperor, Constantine, ordered construction of a basilica on the site of the apostle's tomb. This first St Peter's was consecrated in 326 and completed in 349.

After more than 1000 years, the church was in a poor state of repair and, at the instigation of Pope Julius II, in the first years of the 16th century, it was demolished and plans for a new basilica were prepared. Many great works of art – Byzantine mosaics and frescoes by artists including Giotto – were lost as a result of the demolition. In 1506 work started on a new basilica, designed by Bramante.

It took more than 150 years to realise the completion of the basilica, involving the contributions of Bramante, Raphael, Antonio da Sangallo, Michelangelo, Della Porta and Maderno. It is generally held that

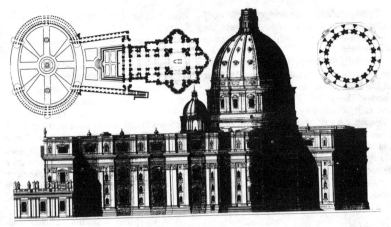

St Peter's Basilica

St Peter's owes most to Michelangelo, who took over the project in 1547 at the age of 72 and was particularly responsible for the design of the dome. He died before the church was completed. The cavernous interior, which can hold up to 60,000 people, contains treasures including Michelangelo's superb *Pietà*, sculpted when he was only 25 years old and the only work to carry his signature (on the sash across the breast of the Madonna). It is now protected by bulletproof glass after having been attacked in 1972 by a hammer-wielding Hungarian.

Bernini's huge Baroque *Baldacchino* – a heavily sculpted bronze canopy over the papal altar – stands 29 metres high in the centre of the church and, although an extraordinary work of art, might not suit all tastes. Another point of note is the red porphyry disk near the central door, which marks the spot where Charlemagne and later emperors were crowned by the pope.

The entrance to the Vatican Grottoes, the resting place of numerous popes, is in the transept of the basilica, to the right as you approach the papal altar. The tombs of many early popes were moved there from the old St Peter's, and later popes, including John XXIII, Paul VI and John Paul I, are buried there. The grottoes are open daily from 7 am to 6 pm (April to September) and 7 am to 5 pm (September to March).

The excavations *(scavi)* beneath St Peter's are of considerable interest. Archaeologists believe they have found the grave of St Peter in these excavations, which have uncovered parts of the original church, an early Christian cemetery and pagan tombs. The excavations can be visited only by appointment, which can be made at the Ufficio Scavi (☎ 698 53 18), to the left of the church in Piazza Braschi, open Monday to Saturday from 9 am to 5 pm. It costs L10,000 to visit the excavations with a guide, which is recommended over the use of a tape and headset for L6000.

Michelangelo's dome soars 119 metres above the papal altar and the site of St Peter's tomb. The entrance to the dome *(cupola)* is to the right as you climb the stairs to the atrium of the basilica. Access to the roof of the church is by elevator (L5000) or stairs (L4000). From there, ascend the stairs to the base of the dome for a view down into the basilica. From here, a narrow staircase leads eventually to the top of the dome and St Peter's lantern, from where you have an unequalled view of Rome. It is well worth the effort, but bear in mind that it is a long and tiring climb.

Dress regulations are stringently enforced at St Peter's. It is forbidden to enter the church in shorts (men included), or wearing a short skirt.

Bernini's **St Peter's Square** (Piazza San Pietro) is considered a masterpiece. Laid out in the 17th century as a place for the Christians of the world to gather, the immense piazza is bounded by two semicircular colonnades, each of which is made up of four rows of Doric columns. In the centre of the piazza is an obelisk brought to Rome by Caligula from Heliopolis in ancient Egypt. When you stand on the dark paving stones between the obelisk and either of the fountains, the colonnades appear to have only one row of columns.

Papal Audiences The pope normally gives a public audience at 11 am every Wednesday in the Papal Audience Hall. For permission to attend, go to the Prefettura della Casa Pontificia, through the bronze doors under the colonnade to the right of St Peter's as you face the church. The office is usually open from 9 am to 1 pm. You can also apply in writing to the Prefettura della Casa Pontificia, 00120 Città del Vaticano. Individuals shouldn't have too much trouble obtaining a ticket to an audience at short notice. The pope also occasionally says mass at the basilica, and information can be obtained at the same office.

People wanting to attend a normal mass at St Peter's can ask for the times of daily masses at the tourist information office in the piazza. The most atmospheric service is conducted on Sundays at 10.30 am during winter and 9.45 am in summer.

The Vatican Museums From St Peter's, follow the wall of the city to the museums, which are open Monday to Saturday from 9 am to 2 pm; in summer, and at Easter, they stay open to 5 pm. Admission is L10,000. They are closed on Sundays and holidays, but open on the last Sunday of every month from 9 am to 2 pm (free entry). A regular bus service runs from outside the tourist office to the Vatican Museums about every half hour

from 8.45 am to 12.45 pm. A ticket costs L2000.

The Vatican Museums contain an incredible collection of art and treasures accumulated by the popes, and you will need several hours to see the most important areas and museums. One visit is probably not enough to appreciate the full value of the collections. Another point to note is that the **Sistine Chapel** comes towards the end of a full visit. If you want to spend most of your time in the chapel, it is possible to walk straight there and then work your way back through the museums. Of great assistance and well worth the L10,000 investment, is the *Guide to the Vatican Museums and City*, on sale at the Vatican Museums.

The **Egyptian Museum** (Museo Gregoriano Egizio) contains many pieces taken from Egypt in Roman times. The collection is small, but there are many important and interesting pieces. Don't miss the mummies in room No 2.

The **Pio-Clementine Museum**, containing Greek and Roman antiquities, is on the ground floor near the entrance. In the Octagonal Courtyard (Cortile Ottagono), which forms part of the gallery, are some of the most important pieces of sculpture in the Vatican collection: the *Apollo Belvedere*, a Roman copy in marble of a 4th century BC Greek bronze; and notably the *Laocoon*, a celebrated sculpture depicting Laocoon, a Trojan priest of Apollo, and his two sons in mortal struggle with two sea serpents. When discovered in 1506 (Michelangelo was said to be present), the sculpture was recognised from descriptions by the Roman writer, Pliny the Elder, and was purchased by Pope Julius II. In the Room of the Muses (Sala delle Muse) is the *Belvedere Torso*, a Greek sculpture of the 1st century BC, much admired by Michelangelo and other Renaissance artists. In the Greek Cross Room (Sala a Croce Greca) are the porphyry sarcophagi of Constantine's daughter, Constantia, and his mother, St Helen.

Up the next flight of the Simonetti staircase is the Etruscan Museum (Museo Gregoriano Etrusco), which contains a collection of artefacts from Etruscan tombs throughout Lazio. There is also a collection of Greek vases and Roman antiquities in the museum.

Through the **Tapestry Gallery** and the **Map Gallery** are the **Stanze di Rafaello** (Raphael's Rooms), the private apartment of Pope Julius II, which was painted by Raphael. Of particular note is the magnificent **Stanza della Segnatura**, which features Raphael's masterpieces, *The School of Athens* and *Dispute over the Sacrament.*

From Raphael's Rooms, go down the stairs to the sumptuous **Borgia Apartments**, painted by Pinturicchio, then go down another flight of stairs to the Sistine Chapel, the private papal chapel, completed in 1484 for Pope Sixtus IV. The chapel is used for some papal functions and for the conclave which elects a successor after the death of a pope. Restoration work on the ceiling has been completed and it is now possible to see Michelangelo's wonderful frescoes, with the *Creation* in the centre, in full, vibrant colour. It took him four years, at the height of the Renaissance, to paint the ceiling. Twenty-two years later he painted the *Last Judgment* on the end wall, now hidden behind covered scaffolding while restoration work is completed (with luck, before the end of 1993). The walls of the chapel were painted by artists including Botticelli, Ghirlandaio, Pinturicchio and Signorelli.

Castel Sant'Angelo

Originally the mausoleum of Emperor Hadrian, the building was converted into a fortress for the popes in the 6th century AD. It was named Castel Sant'Angelo by Pope Gregory the Great in 590 AD, after a vision he saw of an angel above the structure heralded the end of a plague in Rome. It was linked to the Vatican palaces in 1277 by a wall and passageway, used often by the popes to escape to the fortress in times of threat. During the 16th century sack of Rome by Emperor Charles V, hundreds of people lived in the fortress for months. It is open from 9 am to 1 pm Monday to Saturday (also

2 to 6 pm Mondays), to noon on Sunday. Admission is L8000.

Hadrian built the **Ponte Sant'Angelo** across the Tiber in 136 AD to provide an approach to his mausoleum. It collapsed in the Holy Year of 1450 and was rebuilt, incorporating parts of the ancient bridge. In the 17th century, Bernini and his pupils sculpted the figures of angels which now line the bridge.

Ara Pacis

Cross the Ponte Sant'Angelo from the castle and turn left along the Lungotevere to reach the Ara Pacis (Altar of Augustan Peace), sculpted and erected during the four years after the victories of Augustus in Spain and Gaul. The marble altar is enclosed by a marble screen decorated with reliefs – historical scenes on the sides and mythological scenes on the ends. The whole structure is enclosed in a protective glass building. Of particular interest are the stories related to the discovery and eventual reconstruction of the Ara Pacis.

Sculpted marble panels were first unearthed in the 16th century and sections were acquired by the Medici family, the Vatican and even the Louvre. More panels were unearthed in the early 19th century during excavations under a palace at the corner of Via del Corso and Via di Lucina. The Italian government began acquiring the various panels from all over the world and continued excavations until the surrounding palaces were in danger of collapse. It was not until Mussolini ordered the excavation to be resumed that the remainder of the monument was unearthed and the Ara Pacis reconstructed at its present site.

The monument is open from 9 am to 1.30 pm Monday to Saturday, to 1 pm Sunday. In summer it is also open from 4 to 7 pm on Tuesday and Thursday. Entrance is L4000.

Beyond the monument is the **Mausoleum of Augustus**, built by the emperor for himself and his family. It was originally faced with marble and was converted into a fortress during the Middle Ages. It then served various purposes until restored to its original state in 1936.

Piazzas

Apart from those already mentioned, there are several more piazzas worth visiting in Rome. On the Quirinal Hill, the **Piazza del Quirinale** affords a stunning view of Rome and St Peter's. Italy's president lives at the Quirinal Palace.

The **Piazza Venezia** is overshadowed by one of the world's more unusual monuments, dedicated to Victor Emmanuel II. Built to commemorate Italian unity, the monument was completed in 1911 and incorporates the **Altare della Patria** (Altar of the Fatherland) and the tomb of the unknown soldier. Considered out of harmony with its surroundings, there have been many calls to demolish the monument. Also in the piazza is the 15th century **Palazzo Venezia**, which was Mussolini's official residence.

The **Piazza del Popolo** is a semicircular piazza designed in the early 19th century by Valadier. It is at the foot of the **Pincio** hill, which affords a stunning view of the city.

In **Piazza Barberini** is the **Fontana del Tritone** (Triton Fountain), created by Bernini in 1637 for Pope Urban VIII, patriarch of the Barberini family. It features a Triton blowing a stream of water from a conch shell. He is seated in a large scallop shell which is supported by four dolphins. Nearby, at the end of Via Veneto, is another fountain created by the same artist for the Barberini, the **Fontana delle Api** (Fountain of the Bees), featuring two worker bees drinking at a large scallop shell while a queen bee takes flight (the three bees of the Barberini family crest).

At the end of Via del Tritone, across Via del Corso, is **Piazza Colonna** featuring the **Column of Marcus Aurelius**, erected around 190 AD and decorated with bas-relief sculptures depicting military victories by the emperor.

Basilicas & Churches

Apart from St Peter's, there are three other basilicas in Rome. **Santa Maria Maggiore**, down Via Cavour from Stazione Termini, was built in the 5th century, but remodelled several times. Its façade is Baroque and its bell tower is Romanesque. The interior features 5th century mosaics.

San Giovanni in Laterano, south of Stazione Termini, is Rome's cathedral and the most important of Rome's seven pilgrimage churches (the four basilicas, as well as San Lorenzo Fuori le Mura, Santa Croce in Gerusalemme and San Sebastiano). The original church was built in the 4th century and was the home of the popes until the 14th century. Largely destroyed over the centuries, it was rebuilt in the 16th and 17th centuries and Borromini redesigned its interior in 1650. There are important relics in the church, notably the heads of Sts Peter & Paul, contained in a tabernacle over the papal altar.

San Paolo Fuori le Mura is in Via Ostiense some distance from the city centre (take Metro Linea B to San Paolo). The original church was built in the 4th century AD by Emperor Constantine over the burial place of St Paul and, until the construction of the present-day St Peter's, was the largest church in the world. The church was destroyed by fire in 1823 and the present structure was erected in its place. The beautiful cloisters of the adjacent Benedictine abbey, decorated with 13th century mosaics, survived the fire.

Santa Croce in Gerusalemme, in the piazza of the same name (take Metro Linea A to San Giovanni), dates from the 4th century but was completely remodelled in Baroque style in the 18th century. A modern chapel inside the church contains what are said to be fragments of the cross on which Christ was crucified. The fragments were found by St Helen, the mother of Emperor Constantine, in the Holy Land.

San Lorenzo Fuori le Mura is dedicated to the martyred St Lawrence. The original structure was built by Constantine, but the church was rebuilt on many occasions. Of note are the 13th century pulpits and bishop's throne. The remains of St Lawrence and St

Stephen are in the church crypt. See the Catacombs section for information on the church of San Sebastiano.

Other churches of interest include **Santa Maria in Cosmedin**, in the Piazza Bocca della Verità, which is regarded as one of the finest medieval churches in Rome. It has a seven-storey bell tower and its interior was heavily decorated with inlaid marble by the Cosmati family, including the beautiful floor. There are 12th century frescoes in the aisles. The main attraction for the tourist hordes is, however, the **Bocca della Verità** (Mouth of Truth), an ancient Triton mask set into the wall just outside the main door. Legend says that if you put your right hand into the mouth, while telling a lie, it will snap shut. **San Pietro in Vincoli**, just off Via Cavour, houses Michelangelo's *Moses* and his unfinished statues of *Leah* and *Rachel*.

San Clemente in Via San Giovanni in Laterano, near the Colosseum, defines how history in Rome exists on many levels. The 12th century church at street level was built over a 4th century church which was, in turn, built over a Roman house containing a temple to the pagan god of light, Mithras. It is believed that foundations from the period of Republican Rome lie beneath the house. It is possible to visit all three levels. In the medieval church, note the marble choir screen, originally in the older church below, the early Renaissance frescoes by Masolino in the Chapel of Santa Caterina, depicting the life of St Catherine of Alexandria, and the rich mosaics decorating the apse. While little remains of the church below, which was destroyed by invaders in the 11th century, some Romanesque frescoes remain. Descend farther and you arrive at the Roman house and Temple of Mithras.

The Gothic **Santa Maria sopra Minerva**, in Piazza della Minerva just behind the Pantheon, was, as its name suggests, built on the site of an ancient temple of Minerva. It contains Michelangelo's statue of the *Risen Christ*, as well as frescoes by Filippo Lippi in the Chapel of the Annunciation of St Thomas. The relics of St Catherine of Siena are contained in the high altar. In front of the church is a statue of an elephant, carved by Bernini, supporting an Egyptian obelisk.

The Renaissance **Santa Maria del Popolo**, in the Piazza del Popolo, contains artwork by Pinturicchio and Caravaggio.

Two important examples of Baroque architecture are the churches of **Sant'Andrea al Quirinale**, designed by Bernini, and **San Carlo alle Quattro Fontane**, designed by his great rival, Borromini. San Carlo was the first church designed by Borromini in Rome and was completed in 1641. It is considered one of the finest examples of the Baroque style. Sant'Andrea is also considered a masterpiece. Bernini designed it with an oval floor plan, with eight chapels opening onto the central area. The interior is heavily decorated.

The opening hours of Rome's churches vary, but they are generally open from 7 or 8 am to midday, and then from around 4 to 7 or 8 pm.

Palaces

There are numerous palaces to visit in Rome apart from those already mentioned. Among the more interesting is the 17th century **Palazzo Barberini** in Via delle Quattro Fontane. Both Bernini and Borromini worked on its construction for the Barberini family, whose symbol, the bee, adorns many other buildings throughout the city. The palace houses the **Galleria Nazionale di Arte Antica**. The collection includes paintings by Raphael, Caravaggio, Filippo Lippi, Holbein and others. It is open from 9 am to 2 pm Tuesday to Saturday, to 1 pm Sunday (closed Monday). Entrance is from Via delle Quattro Fontane 13 and costs L6000. Note the ceiling of the main salon of the palace (part of the gallery), painted by Pietro da Cortona.

The **Palazzo Doria Pamphili** is on the corner of Via del Corso and Via del Plebiscito. Inside is the **Galleria Doria Pamphili**, containing the private collections of the Doria and Pamphili families, including paintings by Titian, Tintoretto and Caravaggio, as well as sculptures. It's open Tuesday, Friday and weekends from 10 am to 1 pm. Entrance is from Piazza del Collegio Romano 1 and costs L5000.

The **Palazzo Spada**, near the Campo de' Fiori in Piazza Capo di Ferro, has an elaborately decorated façade. Originally built in the 16th century, the palace was restored by Borromini a century later. Note the optical illusion created by the trompe l'oeil colonnade, which he built to give an idea of greater space in linking two courtyards within the palace. The **Galleria Spada** contains the private collection of Cardinal Bernardino Spada and features works by Titian, Andrea del Sarto and Caravaggio. It is open Tuesday to Saturday from 9 am to 2 pm, Sunday to 1 pm (closed Monday). Entrance is L4000.

Via Veneto

This was Rome's hot spot in the 1960s, where film stars could be spotted at the expensive sidewalk cafés. Its full name is Via Vittorio Veneto and it's still the city's most fashionable street, although the atmosphere of Fellini's *Roma* is long dead. **Santa Maria della Concezione**, in Via Veneto, is an austere 17th century building, but the Capuchin cemetery beneath the church (access is on the right of the church steps) features a bizarre display of monks' bones which were used to decorate the walls of a series of chapels.

Baths of Diocletian

Known as Terme di Diocleziano in Italian, these baths, built by Emperor Diocletian, were completed in the 4th century. The complex of baths, libraries, concert halls and gardens covered about 13 hectares and could house up to 3000 people. After the aqueduct which fed the baths was destroyed by invaders in about 536 AD, the complex fell into disrepair. Parts of the ruins are now incorporated into the Church of Santa Maria degli Angeli, which faces onto Piazza della Repubblica, and the Roman National Museum, facing the Piazza dei Cinquecento.

Santa Maria degli Angeli was designed by Michelangelo and incorporates what was the tepidarium ('lukewarm room') of the original baths. During the following centu-

ries his work was drastically changed and little evidence of his design, apart from the great vaulted ceiling of the church, remains. An interesting feature of the church is a double meridian in the transept, one tracing the polar star and the other telling the precise time of the sun's zenith. The church is open from 7.30 am to 12.30 pm and 4 to 6.30 pm. Through the sacristy is an entrance to a stairway which leads to the upper terraces of the ruins. A plaque near the stairway records the traditional belief that the baths were built by thousands of Christians who were forced to do so.

The **Roman National Museum** (Museo Nazionale Romano) houses an important collection of ancient art, including Greek and Roman sculpture. It also contains the *Ludovisi Throne*, an important work of 5th century BC Greek sculpture, and frescoes taken from the Villa of Livia at Prima Porta. The museum is open Tuesday to Saturday from 9 am to 2 pm, to 1 pm on Sundays, and is closed Mondays. Admission is L3000.

Panoramic View

Go to the top of the **Gianicolo**, the hill between St Peter's and Trastevere, for a panoramic view of Rome. Catch bus No 41 from Via della Conciliazione in front of St Peter's. The same bus will take you within easy walking distance of the **Villa Doria Pamphili**, the largest park in Rome and a lovely quiet spot for a walk and a picnic. The actual villa was built in the 17th century for the Pamphili family and is now used for official government functions.

Via Appia

Known to ancient Romans as the *regina viarum* (queen of roads), the Via Appia (Appian Way) extends from the Porta San Sebastiano, in the Aurelian Walls near the Baths of Caracalla, to Brindisi on the coast of Apulia. It was started around 312 BC by the censor Appius Claudius Caecus, but did not connect with Brindisi until around 190 BC. The first section of the road (90 km), to Terracina, was considered revolutionary in its day because it was almost perfectly straight – perhaps the world's first autostrada.

Along the road near Rome are many interesting monuments, including the catacombs, Roman tombs and the palace and **Circus of Maxentius** (Circo di Massenzio). The circus, built around 309 AD by Emperor Maxentius, is better preserved than the Circus Maximus. In front of the circus is the **Tomb of Romulus** (Tomba di Romolo), built by the same emperor for his son, and next to both are the ruins of the imperial residence.

Farther along the Via Appia is the famous **Tomb of Cecilia Metella**, a Roman noblewoman. The tomb was incorporated into the castle of the Caetani family in the early 14th century. It is open from 9 am to 6 pm Tuesday to Saturday in summer, to 3 pm during other months, and to 1 pm on Sundays and Mondays. Entrance is free.

Catacombs

There are several catacombs along and near the Via Appia – kilometres of tunnels carved out of volcanic rock, which were the meeting and burial places of early Christians in Rome. The **Catacombs of San Callisto**, Via Appia Antica 110, are the largest and most famous and contain the tomb of the martyred St Cecilia. In the 20 km of tunnels explored to date, archaeologists have found the sepulchres of some 500,000 people. The catacombs are open from 8.30 am to midday and 2.30 to 5 pm (closed Wednesday). Entry is with a guide only and costs L6000. Catch bus No 118 or 218 from Piazza di Porta San Giovanni.

Nearby is the **Church of San Sebastiano**, believed to have been a safe haven for the remains of St Peter and St Paul during periods of Christian persecution by Roman emperors. The church was built over the site of catacombs, as well as Roman tombs, and the early Christian wall paintings and symbolic decorations are of particular interest. The church and catacombs, at Via Appia Antica 136, are open Friday to Wednesday from 9 am to midday and 2.30 to 5 pm. Entrance is L6000.

The **Catacombs of San Domitilla**, Via delle Sette Chiese 283 (take bus No 218), are interesting for their Christian wall paintings and the underground Church of Sts Nereus & Achilleus. They are open Friday to Wednesday from 8.30 am to midday and 2.30 to 5.30 pm. Entrance is L6000.

EUR

This acronym, which stands for Esposizione Universale di Roma, has become the name of a peripheral suburb of Rome, interesting for its many examples of Fascist architecture, including the **Palazzo della Civiltà del Lavoro** (Palace of the Workers), a square building with arched windows known as the Square Colosseum. Mussolini ordered the construction of the satellite city for an international exhibition to have been held in 1942. Work was suspended with the outbreak of war and the exhibition was never held; however, many buildings were completed during the 1950s.

The **Museo della Civiltà Romana**, Piazza G Agnelli, reconstructs the development of Rome with the use of models. It's open from 9 am to 1.30 pm Monday to Saturday, to 1 pm Sunday, and also from 3 to 6 pm Tuesday and Thursday. Admission is L5000. The suburb is accessible on the Metro Linea B.

ORGANISED TOURS

Carrani Tours (☎ 488 05 10), Via V E Orlando 95, operates half-day tours of the city for L36,000 to L46,000 and full-day tours for L93,000 to L109,000. It also offers tours to Tivoli and the Villa Adriana (L58,000), to Sorrento and Capri (L180,000), and a three-day trip to Naples, Sorrento, Pompeii and Capri (L430,000). American Express (☎ 6 76 41), Piazza di Spagna, also operates tours of the city. The city bus company, ATAC, operates a daily three-hour bus tour of Rome. Buses leave from Piazza dei Cinquecento at 3.30 pm and tickets can be purchased at the ATAC information booth. The CIT office at Stazione Termini also offers guided tours.

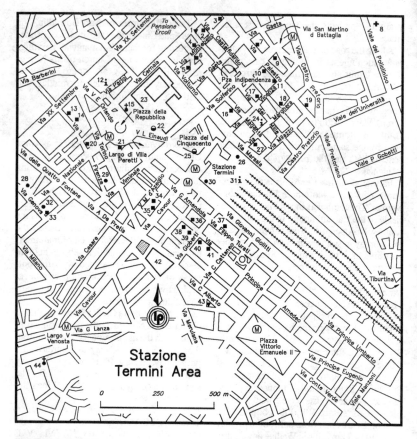

Stazione
Termini Area

0   250   500 m

PLACES TO STAY

There are a vast number of pensioni and
hotels in Rome. Even during summer, rooms
can still be found, although it is advisable to
book ahead in this period. The EPT office at
Stazione Termini will make hotel bookings
or provide a list of hotels. If you want to find
your own room, either ring from the station
to check for vacancies, or check your bags in
and walk the streets either to the left or right
of the station. If the tourist office is closed,
there is a board in the ticket hall which lists
hotels, although the choices given on the
following pages should offer ample choice.
The EPT warns against people at the station

who claim to be tourism officials and offer
to find you a room – ask them for identification.

The Associazione Cattolica Internazionale al Servizio della Giovane, downstairs at
Termini, is open (unreliably) from 9 am to 1
pm and 2 to 8 pm, and will help young
women find accommodation, generally in
religious institutions. If the office is closed,
try contacting the head office (☎ 488 00 56)
at Via Urbana 158, which runs parallel to Via
Cavour.

Most of the budget pensioni and larger
hotels catering for tour groups are located in
the area near Stazione Termini. The area

■ PLACES TO STAY

2   Hotel Castelfidardo
3   Hotel Montecarlo
4   Hotel Floridia
5   Papa Germano
6   Albergo Mary 2
7   Pensione Gexim/Hotel Pensione
    Simonetta
9   Hotel Reatina/Pensione Lachea/
    Hotel Pensione Dolomiti/Tre Stelle
10 Hotel Positano
11 Pensione Restivo/Albergo Mary
13 Hotel Pensione Oceania
14 Hotel Pensione Seiler
16 Pensione Giamaica/
    Pensione Lucy/Hotel New York
17 Hotel Piemonte
18 Hotel Venezia
19 Hotel Pensione Gabriella/
    Hotel Ventura
20 Hotel Elide
21 Pensione Eureka/Pensione Arrivederci
27 Hotel Rimini
33 Hotel Galatea
34 Hotel Giada
35 Argentina/Pensione Everest
36 Hotel Dina

37 Hotel Rizzo
38 Albergo Onella/Hotel Sweet Home
39 Hotel Acropoli
40 Hotel Palladium
41 Hotel Igea

▼ PLACES TO EAT

1   Trimani
43 Agata e Romeo

    OTHER

8   Policlinico Umberto I
12 EPT Tourist Information
15 Church of Santa Maria degli Angeli
22 Intercity Bus Terminal
23 Roman National Museum
24 ENIT Head Office
25 Urban Bus Terminal
26 ASST Telephones
28 Police Headquarters
29 Teatro dell'Opera
30 CIT Office
31 EPT Branch Office
32 CTS
42 Basilica of Santa Maria Maggiore
44 Church of San Pietro in Vincoli

south-west (to the left as you leave the station) can be noisy and unpleasant. It teems with pickpockets and snatch thieves and women may find it an unsafe area at night. To the north-east of the station there is a better standard of accommodation in quieter and somewhat safer streets. However, the historic centre of Rome is far more appealing and the area around the Vatican much less chaotic, and both areas are only a short bus or Metro ride away.

You'll often find three or four budget pensioni in the same building, although most are small establishments of 12 rooms or less which fill quickly in the summer. The sheer number of budget hotels in the area should, however, ensure that you find a room.

Most hotels will accept bookings in advance, although some demand a deposit for the first night. Practices at hotels vary from town to town throughout Italy, and a feature of Roman establishments is the will-ingness of owners to bargain on the price of a room. Generally prices go down if you stay for more than three days.

The liberalisation of hotel prices by the Italian government in 1992 had a dramatic effect in Rome, where prices in many budget establishments jumped by up to 30%. They may come down again once the situation calms down – then again, they may not. The prices listed here were current at the time of going to press.

Places to Stay – bottom end
Unless otherwise stated, the prices quoted for hotels in this section are for rooms without a shower or bath. Many pensioni charge an extra L1000 to L2000 for use of the communal bathroom.

Camping The most convenient camping ground is *Nomentano* (☎ 610 02 96), Via della Cesarina 11, on the corner of Via

Nomentana, a main thoroughfare leading north-east out of the city. Take bus No 36 from Termini, then No 337 from Piazza Sempione. The cost is L8100 per person, per day. It costs L4000 per tent, L16,000 per person for a bungalow and L4000 if you have a car. It is open from 1 March to 31 October. The *Capitol* (☎ 566 27 20), Via di Castel-fusano 195, in Ostia Antica, has a swimming pool. It costs L8500 per person, per day, L7500 per tent and L4500 if you have a car. From the Magliana Metro stop, take the train to Ostia Antica.

Hostels Rome has three youth hostels, all of which are some distance from the historical centre of the city. The main one is *Ostello Foro Italico* (☎ 323 62 67), Viale delle Olimpiadi 61. Take Metro Linea A to Ottaviano, then bus No 32 to Foro Italico. Breakfast and showers are included in the price, which is L18,000 per night. A meal costs L12,000. *Ostello CIVIS* (☎ 324 25 71), nearby at Viale Ministero Affari Esteri 6, is open only from 27 July to 9 September, and bed and breakfast costs L18,000. Follow the same transport directions as for Ostello Foro Italico and get off at Piazzale della Farnesina.

Ostello De Lollis (☎ 324 25 71), Via Cesare de Lollis 20, is also open only from July to September and the cost for bed and breakfast is the same as at CIVIS. From the east exit of Stazione Termini, turn right into Via Marsala and walk to Piazzale Sisto V, then cross into Via dei Ramni which becomes Via de Lollis.

Reservations at the hostels can be made by writing to the Centro Regionale AIG, Via Carlo Poma 2, 00195 Rome. A deposit is required.

Religious Institutions There are a number of religious institutions in Rome, including near the station and the Vatican. However, they have strict curfews. If you want to stay in one, you can apply to the nearest Catholic archdiocese in your town. Otherwise, try the *Domus Aurelia (delle Suore Orosoline)* (☎ 637 64 80), Via Aurelia 218, which has singles/doubles with bath for L45,000/

65,000 but is quite a distance from the city centre. The *Padri Trinitari* (☎ 638 38 88), Piazza Santa Maria alle Fornaci, very close to St Peter's, has singles/doubles/triples without bath for L45,000/80,000/106,000 (breakfast included).

Hotels & Pensioni North-East of Termini
To reach the pensioni in this area, head to the right as you leave the train platforms, onto Via Marsala, which runs alongside the station. At Via Marghera 17 is the *Hotel Rimini* (☎ 446 19 91) with singles/doubles with bathroom for L60,000/80,000. Off Via Vicenza, at Via Magenta 13, there are three pensioni. *Pensione Giamaica* (☎ 49 01 21) has good-quality rooms at L35,000/55,000. *Pensione Lucy* (☎ 445 17 40) has rooms for L35,000/60,000. The two-star *Hotel New York* (☎ 446 04 56) is more expensive, with rooms for L49,000/80,000, or with bathroom for L80,000/125,000. All prices include breakfast.

Farther along Via Vicenza you reach Via Palestro, where there are several reasonably priced pensioni. *Pensione Restivo* (☎ 446 21 72), Via Palestro 55, has singles/doubles for L40,000/60,000. There is a midnight curfew. *Albergo Mary* (☎ 446 21 37), in the same building, has rooms for L40,000/60,000, and with bathroom for L50,000/80,000. *Hotel Positano* (☎ 49 03 60) at No 49 has clean, but more expensive, rooms for L50,000/90,000 and with bathroom for L70,000/120,000. It also offers dormitory accommodation for students at L20,000 a bed. The *Pensione Gexim* (☎ 444 13 11), across Piazza dell'Indipendenza at Via Palestro 34, has singles/doubles for L40,000/55,000, and triples for L25,000 per person. In the same building is the *Hotel Pensione Simonetta* (☎ 444 13 02). Singles are L45,000, doubles L60,000 and triples L90,000 with bathroom. The *Hotel Pensione Gabriella* (☎ 445 02 52), Via Palestro 88, has clean doubles for L60,000. In the same building is the *Hotel Ventura* (☎ 445 19 51) with singles/doubles with bathroom for L60,000/70,000.

Hotel Reatina (☎ 445 42 79), Via San

Martino della Battaglia 11, charges L40,000/80,000 for a single/double. In the same building are several other pensioni. *Pensione Lachea* (☎ 495 72 56) has doubles/triples for L45,000/60,000. *Hotel Pensione Dolomiti* (☎ 49 10 58) has a helpful management and singles/doubles for L40,000/65,000, breakfast included; a triple is L90,000. Downstairs is *Tre Stelle* (☎ 446 30 95) with singles/doubles/triples for L35,000/55,000/75,000. *Albergo Mary 2* (☎ 474 03 71), Via Calatafimi 38, has singles/doubles for L40,000/60,000, or L50,000/80,000 with bathroom. *Papa Germano* (☎ 48 69 19), Via Calatafimi 14a, has rooms for L35,000/50,000, and doubles with bath for L60,000. Nearby, at Via Montebello 45, is *Hotel Floridia* (☎ 474 10 35) with singles/doubles/triples for L40,000/70,000/90,000.

Hotel Castelfidardo (☎ 474 28 94), Via Castelfidardo 31, off Piazza dell'Indipendenza, has singles/doubles for L40,000/55,000, and triples for L25,000 per person (L30,000 with private bath). Across Via XX Settembre, at Via Collina 48 (a 10-minute walk from the station), is *Pensione Ercoli* (☎ 474 54 54) with singles/doubles/triples for L35,000/45,000/65,000. In the same building is *Pensione Tizi* (☎ 474 32 66) with singles/doubles for L30,000/45,000. Triples are L60,000 with private shower.

Hotels & Pensioni South-West of Termini

This area is decidedly seedier, but prices remain the same. As you exit to the left of the station, follow Via Gioberti to Via G Amendola, which becomes Via Filippo Turati. This street and the parallel Via Principe Amedeo harbour a concentration of budget pensioni and you shouldn't have any trouble finding a room.

Hotel Rizzo (☎ 446 73 26), Via F Turati 37, has doubles/triples with bath for L70,000/80,000. The *Hotel Dina* (☎ 481 88 85), which has incorporated the former Pensione Terni, at Via Principe Amedeo 62, is clean with a friendly management. Singles/doubles with bath are L45,000/80,000, and triples L90,000. *Albergo Onella*

(☎ 488 52 57) at No 47 has presentable singles/doubles with bath for L58,000/95,000. The *Hotel Acropoli* (☎ 488 56 85) at No 67 has singles/doubles with bathroom for L50,000/80,000.

At Via Cavour 47, the main street running west from the piazza in front of Termini, there are two budget pensioni. The *Argentina* (☎ 488 32 63) is very clean with big rooms; singles/doubles cost L40,000/70,000, cost of shower included. Downstairs is the *Pensione Everest* (☎ 488 16 29), also clean and simple, with rooms for L35,000/50,000. Directly ahead of the station, at Piazza della Repubblica 47, are the pensioni *Eureka* (☎ 488 03 34) and *Arrivederci* (☎ 482 58 06), run by the same management and with singles/doubles for L37,000/62,000, or L39,000/70,000 with shower. Prices include breakfast.

Hotels & Pensioni – City Centre

Prices go up in the areas around the Spanish Steps, Piazza Navona, the Pantheon and Campo de' Fiori, but for the money you have the convenience and pleasure of staying right in the centre of historical Rome. Budget hotels are few and far between, but there are some pleasant surprises. The easiest way to get to the Spanish Steps is on the Metro Linea A to Spagna. To get to the Piazza Navona and Pantheon area, take bus No 64 from Piazza dei Cinquecento, in front of Termini, to Largo di Torre Argentina.

The cheapest and one of the most centrally located hotels is *Pensione Primavera* (☎ 654 31 09), Piazza San Pantaleo 3, on Via Vittorio Emanuele II, just around the corner from Piazza Navona. A magnificent entrance leads to a pleasant but slightly chaotic establishment where there are no singles and where a double costs L60,000 with an extra L15,000 for a triple. Prices per person go down the more there are in a room, and the owner is more than happy to strike a deal. The *Albergo Abruzzi* (☎ 679 20 21), Piazza della Rotonda 69, overlooks the Pantheon. You couldn't find a better location, but the rooms can be very noisy until late at night when the piazza is finally deserted.

Singles/doubles are L55,000/78,000. The use of the communal shower is free. Bookings are essential at this popular hotel throughout the year.

Pensione Mimosa (☎ 654 17 53), Via Santa Chiara 61 (off Piazza della Minerva), has singles/doubles for L50,000/70,000 and doubles with bathroom for L85,000. The *Albergo della Lunetta* (☎ 686 10 80), Piazza del Paradiso 68, near Campo de' Fiori, has doubles for L70,000, or singles/doubles with shower for L55,000/90,000. Bookings are essential. The *Albergo Pomezia* (☎ 686 13 71), Via dei Chiavari 12 (which runs off Via dei Giubbonari from Campo de' Fiori), is reasonably priced given its location, with doubles/triples for L70,000/90,000. Use of the communal shower is free.

Near the Spanish Steps is *Albergo Fiorella* (☎ 361 05 97), Via del Babuino 196, with very clean singles/doubles for L40,000/70,000, breakfast included.

Hotels & Pensioni – near the Vatican & Trastevere

Bargains do not abound in this area, but it is comparatively quiet and still close to the main sights. Bookings are an absolute necessity because rooms are often filled with people attending conferences etc at the Vatican. The simplest way to reach the area is on the Metro Linea A to Ottaviano. Turn left into Via Ottaviano, and Via Germanico is a short walk. Otherwise, take bus No 64 from Termini to St Peter's and walk away from the basilica along Via di Porta Angelica, which becomes Via Ottaviano after the Piazza del Risorgimento, a five-minute walk.

The best bargain in the area is *Pensione Ottaviano* (☎ 38 39 56), Via Ottaviano 6, near the Piazza del Risorgimento. It has beds in dormitories from L18,000 to L23,000 per person, and the owner speaks good English. *Giuggioli Hotel* (☎ 324 21 13), Via Germanico 198, is a delight, but very small. The woman owner, her dog and cats make it seem like home. There are no singles and a double costs L75,000. Rooms are beautifully furnished. There are three other pensioni in the same building. *Hotel Pensione Lady*

(☎ 324 21 12), on the 4th floor, has large, clean singles/doubles for L55,000/75,000. *Hotel Pensione Zurigo* (☎ 372 01 39), on the 5th floor, has singles/doubles for L45,000/60,000, triples for L75,000 and quads for L100,000. The same management runs the *Pensione Nautilus* on the 2nd floor. Prices are the same as for the Zurigo.

Pensione San Michele (☎ 324 33 33), Via Attilio Regolo 19, off Via Cola di Rienzo, has average singles/doubles for L31,000/49,500. At Via Giulio Cesare 47, near the Lepanto Metro stop, are *Pensione Schiavo* (☎ 321 60 21) and *Pensione Valparaiso* (☎ 321 31 84). Both charge L20,000/30,000.

The *Albergo Manara* (☎ 581 47 13), Via Luciano Manara 25, is right in the heart of Trastevere and has clean, basic singles/doubles for L45,000/68,000; triples are L78,000 and showers cost L3000.

Places to Stay – middle

The establishments in this section are all hotels or pensioni, generally in the two-star category, but including some better quality one-stars. All rooms have private bathrooms unless otherwise stated.

Near Termini To the south of the station, at Via Principe Amedeo 97, is the *Hotel Igea* (☎ 446 69 13). It has clean singles/doubles for L75,000/100,000 and triples for L130,000. At No 47 is the *Hotel Sweet Home* (☎ 488 09 54), with singles/doubles for L75,000/80,000 and triples for L118,000; prices include breakfast. *Hotel Palladium* (☎ 446 69 17), Via Gioberti 36, has large double rooms for L130,000; singles are L80,000 and triples/quads cost L180,000/200,000.

North-west of the station, in Via Firenze, off Via Nazionale, there are three good-value hotels. The *Hotel Elide* (☎ 474 13 67) at No 50 has well-maintained rooms. Singles/doubles are L70,000/90,000 and triples are L121,000; without bathroom, prices are L60,000/75,000 for singles/doubles. Ask for room No 18, which has an elaborate, gilded ceiling. *Hotel Pensione Seiler* (☎ 48 55 50) at No 48 has clean but basic rooms, although all have a TV and the price includes breakfast. Singles/doubles are L75,000/120,000 and triples/quads are L150,000/180,000. *Hotel Pensione Oceania* (☎ 482 46 96) at No 38 is an ideal family hotel. Simply furnished singles/doubles are L80,000/122,000, triples are L168,000, quads L214,000, and a room for five is L260,000. During winter the hotel offers a 20% discount, and a 10% discount can be negotiated at other times.

Hotel Galatea (☎ 474 30 70), Via Genova 24, is through the grand entrance of an old palace. Its well-furnished singles/doubles are good value at L65,000/90,000, or L55,000/70,000 with bathroom. A triple costs around L130,000.

North-east of the station is the *Hotel Piemonte* (☎ 445 22 40), Via Vicenza 34, with reasonable singles/doubles for L60,000/90,000, or L120,000/160,000 with bathroom.

City Centre The *Albergo del Sole* (☎ 654 08 73), Via del Biscione 76, off Campo de' Fiori, used to be one of the best bargains in Rome, but it has been renovated and the prices have gone up accordingly. It has big rooms and a roof terrace. A single costs L70,000 (L60,000 with shower only and L52,500 without bathroom) and a double costs from L75,000 (without bathroom) to L96,000.

Near Piazza di Spagna is *Hotel Pensione Suisse* (☎ 678 36 49), Via Gregoriana 54. It has good-quality singles/doubles without bathroom for L65,000/98,000; doubles with bathroom are L128,000, triples are L165,000 and quads L200,000. Closer to Piazza del Popolo is the *Hotel Margutta* (☎ 322 36 74), Via Laurina 34, off Via del Corso. It has spotless rooms, and prices, which are negotiable, include breakfast. There are no singles and a double costs L113,000, a triple L135,000 and a quad L160,000. The *Hotel Forte* (☎ 320 76 25), Via Margutta 61 (parallel to Via del Babuino), is comfortable and quiet. Singles/doubles/triples are L75,000/ 115,000/150,000.

Hotel Pensione Merano (☎ 482 17 96) is a lovely old place, well located at Via Vittorio Veneto 155. It has singles/doubles for L88,000/126,000 and triples for L165,000. *Hotel Julia* (☎ 488 16 37), Via Rasella 29 (off Via delle Quattro Fontane near Piazza Barberini), is a no-frills establishment but quiet and clean. Singles/ doubles/triples are L94,000/140,000/ 180,000, or L75,000/106,000/135,000 without bathroom; the price includes breakfast and all rooms have TV.

Near the Vatican & in Trastevere Just around the corner from St Peter's is the *Hotel Bramante* (☎ 654 04 26), Vicolo delle Palline 24, virtually next to the Vatican wall off Via de' Corridori. It has rooms of reasonable quality. Singles/doubles without bathroom are L64,000/84,000, doubles with bathroom are L107,000, triples L145,000 and quads L182,000. *Hotel Prati* (☎ 687 53 57), Via Crescenzio 89, has singles/doubles for L79,000/108,000 and triples for L148,000. Singles/doubles without bathroom are L63,000/88,000. *Hotel Adriatic* (☎ 686 96 68), Via Vitelleschi 25 (the continuation of Via Porcari, off Piazza del Risorgimento), has modern rooms and is very good value at L85,000/112,000 for singles/doubles; rooms without bathroom are L64,000/85,000. A triple costs L150,000, or L120,000 without bathroom.

At Via Cola di Rienzo 243 there are two good-quality hotels, both excellent value for their location and prices. *Hotel Joli* (☎ 324 18 54) is on the 6th floor. It has large rooms and is ideal for families. Singles/doubles are L70,000/90,000 and triples L120,000. *Hotel Florida* (☎ 324 18 72) is on the 2nd floor and has singles/doubles for L73,000/94,000 and triples for L150,000; without bathroom, prices are L53,000/74,000/125,000 respectively. Discounts are available out of the high season.

Hotel Ticino (☎ 324 32 51), Via dei Gracchi 161, has comfortable rooms, some big enough for families. There are no toilets in the rooms, but prices include breakfast. Singles/doubles/triples are L62,000/

88,000/122,000; without bathroom, prices are L51,000/73,000/102,000 respectively. A room for four costs L156,000.

Hotel Amalia (☎ 31 45 19), Via Germanico 66 (near the corner of Via Ottaviano), has a beautiful courtyard entrance and clean, sunny rooms. Singles/doubles are L50,000/90,000 with use of the communal shower; triples are L96,000. Singles/doubles are L70,000/110,000, and triples L135,000.

In Trastevere there is the *Hotel Cisterna* (☎ 581 72 12), Via della Cisterna 7-9 (off Via San Francesco a Ripa). It has average, comfortable rooms. Singles/doubles/triples are L75,000/95,000/120,000.

Places to Stay – top end
There is no shortage of expensive hotels in Rome, but many, particularly those near the station, are geared for large tour groups and, while certainly offering all conveniences, tend to be a bit anonymous. The following three and four-star hotels have been selected on the basis of their individual charm, as well as value-for-money and location.

Near Stazione Termini *Hotel Venezia* (☎ 445 71 01), Via Varese 18 (on the corner of Via Marghera), is beautifully furnished in antique style. A single room costs L130,000, a double L180,000 and a triple L250,000. Prices drop in the low season. At *Hotel Montecarlo* (☎ 446 00 00), Via Montebello 109 (on the corner of Via Palestro), singles/doubles cost L120,000/150,000, triples are L200,000 and a quad is L250,000. It also offers generous discounts on rooms in the low season. Across the street, at Via Palestro 19, is the *Artdeco Hotel* (☎ 445 75 88), expensive at L232,000/364,000 for singles/doubles. However, it offers special weekend, summer and other discount tariffs. On the other side of the station is *Hotel Giada* (☎ 488 58 63), Via Principe Amedeo 9. It is a very pleasant establishment with singles/doubles for L118,000/140,000 and triples for L180,000. Discounts are offered in the off season and during August.

The *Grand Hotel* (☎ 47 09), Via Vittorio Emanuele Orlando 3, between the station and Via Veneto, is recognised as one of the best and most elegant hotels in Rome. You can mingle with the jet set for up to L650,000 a double.

City Centre Near the Spanish Steps are several of Rome's better hotels. The *Gregoriana* (☎ 679 42 69), Via Gregoriana 18, has long been an institution for the fashionable set. Its rooms are not numbered, but instead adorned with letters by the 1930s fashion illustrator Erté. Singles/doubles/triples are L156,000/220,000/260,000. Magnificently located at the top of the Spanish Steps, at Piazza Trinità dei Monti 17, is the *Hotel Scalinata di Spagna*, which has a roof terrace overlooking the city. It has rooms for L200,000/260,000/320,000. Opposite is the high-class *Hassler Villa Medici* (☎ 678 26 51), another of Rome's top hotels. Doubles cost up to L650,000 per night. Around the corner at Via Sistina 136 is the small *Hotel Sistina* (☎ 474 41 76) with singles/doubles/triples for L180,000/280,000/340,000.

Hotel Senato (☎ 678 43 43), Piazza della Rotonda 73, overlooks the Pantheon. Its comfortable rooms are L132,000/182,000/240,000. They are also reasonably quiet, considering the hotel's position. *Hotel Campo de' Fiori* (☎ 654 08 65), Via del Biscione 6, is, as its name suggests, just off the Campo de' Fiori. It has nicely furnished rooms on its six floors (but there is no lift), and a roof garden. Doubles are L145,000 (L85,000 without bathroom) and triples are L170,000 (L130,000 without bathroom).

The *Cardinal Hotel* (☎ 654 27 19), Via Giulia 62, is in one of Rome's most beautiful streets. It has singles/doubles for L157,000/263,000, and triples for L345,000.

Near the Vatican *Hotel Columbus* (☎ 686 52 45), Via della Conciliazione 33, is in a restored 15th century palace in front of St Peter's. It has singles/doubles/triples for L175,000/245,000/300,000. The beautiful, elegant *Hotel Sant'Anna* (☎ 654 18 82), Borgo Pio 134, is just near the Vatican and St Peter's. It has double rooms for L140,000 to L230,000 and triples for L160,000 to L240,000.

Rental

Apartments near the centre of Rome are expensive, and you can expect to pay a minimum of L1,500,000 a month. A good way to find a shared apartment is to buy *Wanted in Rome* or *Porta Portese* at newsstands. A room in a shared apartment will cost at least L500,000 a month, plus bills. There are also agencies *(agenzie immobiliari)* specialising in short-term rentals in Rome, which charge a fee for their services. They are listed in *Wanted in Rome*.

PLACES TO EAT

Of all the Italian cities, Rome hosts the most diverse selection of eating places. This does not mean a diversity of international cuisines, as the Italians have regional cooking traditions which are varied enough in themselves. Rather, in Rome, it is possible to sample all of the regional cuisines or, if you prefer, to eat only Roman fare. Meal times are generally from 12.30 to 3 pm and from 8 to 11 pm, although in summer many restaurants stay open later.

Antipasto dishes in Rome are particularly good and many restaurants allow you to make your own mixed selection. Typical pasta dishes include: *fettuccine con panna*, with butter, cream and Parmesan; *penne all'arrabbiata*, which has a hot sauce of tomatoes and chilli; *spaghetti carbonara*, with *pancetta* (cured bacon), eggs and cheese. *Saltimbocca alla Romana* (slices of veal and ham) and *abbachio* (roast lamb seasoned with rosemary) are classic meat dishes, which are followed by a wide variety of vegetables. During winter, try the *carciofi alla Romana* (artichokes stuffed with mint or parsley). Offal is also very popular in Rome, and a local speciality is the *pajata* (pasta with a sauce of chopped veal intestines). Drink a bottle of the local Frascati wine with your meal.

Always remember to check the menu posted outside the establishment for prices, cover and service charges. Expect to pay

under L25,000 per person at a simple trattoria, up to L50,000 at an average restaurant and around L100,000 or more at Rome's top eating places. These prices are for a full meal including entrée, main, dessert and wine. Eating only a pasta and salad and drinking the house wine at a trattoria can keep the bill down to around L15,000, while in restaurants, if you order meat or, particularly, fish, you will push up the bill substantially.

Good options for cheap, quick meals are the hundreds of bars, where panini (sandwiches) cost L2000 to L4000 taken *al banco* (at the bar), or takeaway pizzerias, where a slice of freshly cooked pizza, sold by weight, can cost as little as L2000. Bakeries are particularly numerous in the Piazza Navona/ Campo de' Fiori area and are another good choice for a cheap snack. Try a huge piece of *pizza bianca*, a flat bread resembling focaccia, from around L1000 a slice (see the section on Sandwiches & Snacks later in this chapter).

For groceries and supplies of cheese, prosciutto, salami and wine, shop at alimentari (see the section on Alimentari later in this chapter), and for fresh fruit and vegetables there are numerous outdoor markets, notably the lively daily market in Campo de' Fiori. Other, cheaper food markets are held in Piazza Vittorio Emanuele near the station, in Piazza Testaccio on the other side of the Aventine Hill from the Circus Maximus, and in Via Andrea Doria, near Largo Trionfale, north of the Vatican. The huge wholesale food markets are in Via Ostiense, some distance from the city centre, open to the public from 10 am Monday to Saturday.

Restaurants, Trattorias & Pizzerias

Generally the restaurants near Stazione Termini are to be avoided if you want to pay reasonable prices for good-quality food. The side streets around Piazza Navona and Campo de' Fiori harbour many good-quality, low-priced trattorie and pizzerie, and the areas of San Lorenzo (to the east of Termini, near the university) and Testaccio (across the Tiber near the Piramide mausoleum) are eating districts popular with the locals.

Trastevere might be among the most expensive places to live in Rome, but it still offers an excellent selection of rustic eating places hidden in tiny piazzas, and pizzerias where it doesn't cost the earth to sit at a table on the street.

City Centre – bottom end *Otello alla Concordia* (☎ 679 11 78), Via della Croce 81 (between Via Babuino and Via del Corso), is a popular eating place for tourists and locals alike. You can eat a good Roman meal for around L25,000. Nearby at Via Margutta 82 (which runs parallel to Via Babuino) is *Osteria Margutta* (☎ 320 77 13). It has good-quality food for around the same prices. Across Via del Corso from Via Condotti is *Pizzeria Il Leoncino* (☎ 687 63 06), Via del Leoncino 28, with good pizzas at low prices – eat and drink for under L15,000. Nearby is *Ristorante La Pentola* (☎ 654 26 07), Piazza Firenze 20. Prices are reasonable and it serves pizzas as well as pasta, meat and vegetable dishes. *Gino in Vicolo Rossini* (☎ 687 34 34), Vicolo Rossini 4, off Piazza del Parlamento towards the Pantheon from Piazza Colonna, is popular with politicians and journalists, and a full meal will cost around L25,000.

Cul de Sac 1 (☎ 654 10 94), Piazza Pasquino 73, just off Piazza Navona, is a wine bar (see the Cafés & Bars section later in this chapter) with excellent light meals for around L25,000. The *Pizzeria Da Baffetto* (☎ 686 16 17), Via del Governo Vecchio 11, is a Roman institution. While its pizzas are extra large, they are by no means the best you will eat in Italy. However, expect to join a queue if you arrive after 9 pm and don't be surprised if you end up sharing a table. Pizzas cost around L6000 to L8000, a litre of wine costs L7000, and the cover charge is only L1000. A full meal will cost around L16,000. Farther along the street at No 18 is a tiny, nameless *osteria* (no phone), run by Antonio Bassetti, where you will eat an excellent meal for under L20,000. The consistently good quality of the food and the low prices make it one of the best value eating

places in Rome. There is no written menu, but don't be nervous: even when very busy, the owner/waiter will try to explain (in Italian) the dishes.

At Via Banchi Nuovi 14 (the continuation of Via del Governo Vecchio), there is *Da Alfredo e Ada*, a small trattoria run by an elderly couple. This place might not suit all tastes, as you don't get a choice of what you want to eat – Ada simply puts it in front of you. The food is very basic and the house wine probably best avoided; however, it is worth a visit simply to experience one of Rome's last traditional osterie.

Trattoria Pizzeria Da Francesco, Piazza del Fico 29 (take Via del Corallo from Via del Governo Vecchio), has good pasta dishes for around L9000, and a good range of antipasto and vegetables. Pizzas range in price from around L6000 to L12,000, and a full meal will cost around L20,000. *Pizzeria Corallo* (☎ 68 30 77 03), Via del Corallo 10, off Via del Governo Vecchio, has good pizzas and is open late. A meal will cost around L18,000.

In Piazza della Cancelleria, between Piazza Navona and Campo de' Fiori, is *Grappolo d'Oro* (☎ 686 41 18). It serves excellent quality, traditional Roman food for around L30,000 a full meal.

There are several small restaurants in the Campo de' Fiori. *Hosteria Romanesca* is tiny, so arrive early if you're there in winter, when there are no outdoor tables. A dish of pasta will cost L6000 to L10,000, and a full meal under L25,000. Along Via Giubbonari, off Campo de' Fiori, is *Filletti di Baccalà* (☎ 686 40 18) in Largo dei Librari, which serves only deep-fried cod fillets and wine. You can satisfy moderate hunger and thirst for under L10,000. *Il Grottino*, Via delle Grotte 27 (off Via dei Giubbonari near Campo de' Fiori), serves reasonable pizzas for around L6000 to L9000, a litre of wine costs L5000 and the coperto is L1500. A full meal will cost under L20,000.

On the other side of Via Arenula, in the Jewish quarter, is *Sora Margherita* (☎ 686 40 02), Piazza delle Cinque Scole 30, which serves traditional Roman and Jewish food in very simple surroundings. A meal will cost under L20,000.

Trattoria Polese (☎ 686 17 09), Piazza Sforza Cesarini 39, off Via Vittorio Emanuele towards the Tiber, has good, straightforward and reasonably priced meals. It has outside tables in summer. *Hostaria Giulio* (☎ 654 04 66), Via della Barchetta 19 (off Via Giulia), is another good-value eating place. It has two or three tables outside in summer.

City Centre – middle The very popular *Mario* (☎ 678 38 18), Via della Vite 55, off Piazza di Spagna, offers Tuscan food for around L45,000 a full meal. Another good restaurant in the area is *Al 34* (☎ 679 50 91), Via Mario de' Fiori 34, which has a menu combining Roman cooking with regional dishes from throughout the country. A full meal will cost around L40,000. Near the Trevi Fountain is *Al Moro* (☎ 678 34 95), Vicolo delle Bollette 13, which runs between Via dei Crociferi and Via delle Muratte. A good-quality, traditional Roman meal will come to less than L50,000. *Tullio* (☎ 475 85 64), Via San Nicola da Tolentino 26, which runs off Piazza Barberini, serves Roman and Tuscan dishes. It is of a high standard and a full meal will cost between L50,000 and L60,000. Also near Piazza Barberini is *Colline Emiliane* (☎ 481 75 38), Via degli Avignonesi 22, a spartan-looking trattoria which serves superb Emilia-Romagnan food. A full meal will cost around L50,000.

At Via degli Spagnoli 27, near the Pantheon, is *Il Bacaro* (☎ 686 41 10), a tiny trattoria whose menu reflects what is available fresh on any given day. A meal will cost around L40,000. *Fortunato al Pantheon* (☎ 679 27 88), Via del Pantheon 55, is a popular eating place for politicians. In summer, book a table outside. A good-quality meal will cost more than L50,000.

La Campana (☎ 686 78 20), Vicolo della Campana 18, at the top end of Via della Scrofa, is believed to be Rome's oldest restaurant and is certainly one of its favourites. A full meal will cost around L50,000. *Il Cardinale – GB* (☎ 686 93 36), Via delle Carceri 6, which runs off Via Giulia, is another well-known restaurant with superb and interesting food. A full meal should come to less than L60,000.

In the Jewish quarter is *Al Pompiere* (☎ 686 83 77), at Via Santa Maria de' Calderari 38. Its food is great – try the carciofi alla giudia – and prices are reasonable. A full meal should cost under L40,000.

City Centre – top end The widely known *Dal Bolognese* (☎ 361 14 26), Piazza del Popolo 1, is in a prime position to attract tourists, but maintains high culinary standards and reasonable prices. You must book if you want a table outside in summer. A full meal will cost more than L65,000. *Andrea* (☎ 482 18 91), Via Sardegna 24-28, close to Via Veneto, is one of Rome's best known and most popular top restaurants. A full meal will be in the range of L90,000 to L100,000. *Il Convivio* (☎ 686 94 32), Via dell'Orso 44, near Piazza Navona, is an elegant restaurant with a creative menu. A full meal will cost around L80,000. *El Toulà* (☎ 687 34 98), Via della Lupa 29, is one of Rome's most prestigious restaurants, which is reflected in the prices – around L130,000 for a full meal. Near Campo de' Fiori, at Via dell'Arco del Monte 95, is *Patrizia e Roberto del Pianeta Terra*, considered one of Rome's best restaurants. Again, a full meal will cost around L130,000.

In the Jewish quarter there are two excellent restaurants where prices (depending on what you eat) can move into the higher range. *Vecchia Roma* (☎ 686 46 04), Piazza Campitelli 18, has a well-deserved reputation for good food. Its outside tables are extremely popular in summer. *Piperno* (☎ 654 27 72), Via Monte de' Cenci 9, has a menu combining Roman and Jewish cooking and is considered one of Rome's better mid-range restaurants. At both establishments a full meal will cost as much as L75,000.

West of the Tiber – bottom end The main concentration of good-value restaurants is in Trastevere and the Testaccio district. Most of the establishments around St Peter's and the Vatican are geared for tourists and can be very expensive. *Osteria dell'Angelo* (☎ 38 92 18), Via G Bettolo 24, is in the Trionfale area, along Via Leone IV from the Vatican. A hearty Roman meal can be had for around L30,000. *Pizzeria Giacomelli* (☎ 38 35 11), Via di Bruno Emilia Faà 25, is off Via della Giuliana past Largo Trionfale. The pizzas are good, big and cheap. *Il Tempio della Pizza* (☎ 321 69 63), Viale Giulio Cesare 91, in Prati, is open late and the good-quality food is reasonably priced.

In Trastevere's maze of tiny streets there are any number of pizzerias and cheap trattorias. The area is beautiful at night and most establishments have outside tables. It is also very popular, so arrive before 9.30 pm unless you want to join a queue to wait for a table.

Mario's (☎ 580 38 09), Via del Moro 53, is a local favourite for its cheap pasta dishes (around L6000 to L8000), but you can find better quality. From Viale Trastevere, walk along Via Lungaretta. *D'Augusto* (☎ 580 37 98), Piazza dei Renzi 15, just around the corner from the Basilica of Santa Maria in Trastevere (turn right as you face the church and walk to Via della Pelliccia), is another great spot for a cheap meal. Try the home-made fettucine. If you arrive early there is also a good range of vegetables. A meal with wine will cost around L15,000 to L20,000.

Da Giovanni (☎ 686 15 14), Via della Lungara 41, is a good 10-minute walk from the centre of Trastevere. It is a popular eating place and you will probably have to wait for a table. The food is basic, but the prices are good. *Da Gildo* (☎ 580 07 33), Via della Scala 31, is a pizzeria/trattoria with an interesting range of pizzas and good-quality food. A full meal will cost around L25,000. Nearby, at Vicolo del Mattinato 2, is *Da Lucia* (☎ 580 36 01), which offers an excellent range of antipasto and pasta dishes. A hearty meal will cost around L35,000. *Pizzeria Ivo* (☎ 581 70 82), Via San Francesco a Ripa 158, has outdoor tables and is said to have the best pizza on the west bank; this is an exaggeration and they could be bigger for the price (from L7500 to L10,000). The

bruschetta is an excellent start to the meal. The house wine comes in bottles and is not a bargain at L8000.

From Viale Trastevere, take Via delle Fratte and turn right into Via S Francesco a Ripa. At the other end of the street, across Viale Trastevere on the corner of Piazza San Francesco d'Assisi, is *Hostaria Gran Sasso*, with excellent food, specialising in dishes from Abruzzo. A meal will cost around L25,000. *Pizzeria Da Vittorio*, Via San Cosimato 14a, is tiny and you have to wait if you arrive after 9 pm. A delicious bruschetta and pizza with wine will cost around L13,000. At Viale Trastevere 53 is *Panattoni* (☎ 580 09 19); open late and always crowded, it is one of the more popular pizzerias in Trastevere. You can eat there for around L12,000.

You won't find a noisier, more popular pizzeria in Rome than *Pizzeria Remo* (☎ 574 62 70), Piazza Santa Maria Liberatrice 44, in Testaccio. A meal will cost around L16,000. *Agustarello* (☎ 574 65 85), Via G Branca 98, off the piazza, specialises in the very traditional Roman fare of offal dishes. A full meal should cost around L20,000. *Trattoria Da Bucatino*, Via Luca della Robbia 84, is a popular Testaccio eating place, with pasta dishes from L7000 to L10,000 and pizzas for around the same prices. It also serves traditional Roman fare. A full meal could cost around L30,000. *Da Felice* (☎ 574 68 00), Via Maestro Giorgio 29, has a legendary reputation, both for the standard of its food and the fact that it can be very difficult to get a table. It is essential to book and then to arrive early to claim your table. *Perilli* (☎ 574 21 45), Via Marmorata 39, serves good-quality, traditional fare for around L35,000 a full meal.

West of the Tiber – middle to top end The *Cul de Sac 2* (☎ 581 33 24), Vicolo dell'Atleta 2 (off Via dei Genovesi) in Trastevere, is a relatively new restaurant with creative, high-quality food for around L80,000 for a full meal. *Paris* (☎ 581 53 78), Piazza San Calisto 7, has developed a reputation for excellent cuisine. A meal will cost around L60,000. Just off Piazza Santa Maria in Trastevere, at Via della Paglia 1, is *La Tana de Noiantri* (☎ 580 64 04), which has outside tables in a lovely setting in summer. A full meal will cost L35,000 or more. *Checco er Carrettiere* (☎ 581 70 18), Via Benedetta 10, just off Piazza Trilussa, is very popular with foreigners and Romans alike, but, at around L65,000 for a full meal, prices are a bit high for what you get.

In Testaccio is *Checchino dal 1887* (☎ 574 63 18), Via Monte Testaccio 30, which serves superb, very traditional Roman food, which means lots of offal. A full meal will cost around L75,000.

San Lorenzo & from Stazione Termini to the Forum

San Lorenzo is Rome's university district, and one of the more popular eating places, *Pizzeria L'Economica*, Via Tiburtina 44, serves typical local fare and good pizzas at prices students can afford. *Formula 1* (☎ 445 38 66), Via degli Equi 13, is another good-value pizzeria, as is *Le Maschere* (☎ 445 38 05), Via degli Umbri 8, both popular with students. One of the area's more famous trattorias is *Pommidoro* (☎ 445 26 92), Piazza dei Sanniti 44; an excellent meal will cost around L30,000.

If you have no option but to eat near Stazione Termini, try to avoid the tourist traps offering overpriced full menus. There are many tavole calde in the area, particularly to the west of Termini, which offer panini and pre-prepared dishes for reasonable prices. There are a few good-quality, good-value restaurants in the area. *Da Gemma alla Lupa* (☎ 49 12 30), Via Marghera 39, is a simple trattoria with prices to match: a full meal will cost around L20,000. *Galilei* (☎ 731 56 42), Via Galilei 12, between the station and the church of San Giovanni in Laterano, is a good pizzeria and prices are reasonable. Towards the Colosseum, at Via delle Terme di Tito 96, is *Hostaria di Nerone* (☎ 474 52 07). Popular with tourists, it has good food and a full meal will cost under L25,000. Another decent pizzeria is *Alle Carrette* (☎ 679 27 70), Vicolo delle Carrette 14, off Via Cavour near the Roman Forum; a pizza and wine will come to around L12,000.

Going up the price scale, *Tana del Grillo* (☎ 731 64 41), Via Alfieri 4-8, off Via Merulana near Piazza San Giovanni in Laterano, offers examples of the cuisine of Ferrara, as well as the usual Roman fare. A full meal will cost from L35,000 to L40,000. *Agata e Romeo* (☎ 446 61 15), Via Carlo Alberto 45 (off Piazza Santa Maria Maggiore), is an elegant restaurant with a mix of creative and classic dishes. A full meal will cost around L80,000. *Il Dito e La Luna* (☎ 494 07 26), Via dei Sabelli 47-51, in the San Lorenzo district, serves hearty, quality meals for around L35,000 to L40,000.

Non-Italian Restaurants

These are not exactly abundant, but there are some very good restaurants in Rome which serve the cuisine of other nationalities. Chinese food is very popular, but approach Chinese restaurants with some care because the food is often heavily salted and can leave a lot to be desired.

Golden Crown (☎ 678 98 31), Via in Arcione 85, between Via del Tritone and the Quirinal Palace, is a good choice; a solid meal will cost up to L30,000. For an excellent Japanese meal, head for *Sogo Asahi* (☎ 678 60 93), Via di Propaganda 22, near the Spanish Steps. It is expensive, however, at around L70,000 a head. There's a sushi bar, for which you have to book. *Suria Mahal* (☎ 589 45 54), Piazza Trilussa, in Trastevere, is an Indian restaurant where a delicious meal will cost around L30,000.

If all you really want is a Big Mac, you'll find McDonald's outlets in Piazza della Repubblica (with outside tables), Piazza di Spagna, and Viale Trastevere (between Piazza Sonnino and Piazza Mastai).

Vegetarian Restaurants

All trattorie serve a good selection of vegetable dishes, but there are several other options for vegetarians in Rome. They tend to be expensive, in line with their 'trendy' image – count on paying over L30,000. *Centro Macrobiotico*, Via della Vite 4, is a relatively cheap exception: there's a L5000 membership fee and dishes start at L8000. At *Margutta Vegetariano* (☎ 678 60 33), Via Margutta 19, which runs parallel to Via del Babuino, décor and prices suggest up-market standards and a meal will cost no less than L40,000. *Il Canestro*, Via Luca della Robbia 47, Testaccio, specialises in vegetarian food and is also expensive.

Cafés & Bars

Remember that prices skyrocket in bars as soon as you sit down, particularly near the Spanish Steps, where a cappuccino at a table can cost as much as L5000. The same cappuccino taken at the bar will cost around L1500. The narrow streets and tiny piazzas in the area between Piazza Navona and the Tiber offer a good number of popular small cafés and bars. For those on a tight budget, there is *Caffè Peru*, in Piazza di Santa Caterina della Rota, just down the street to the right as you face the Palazzo Farnese. Here, serious local drinkers mingle with young bohemians and students, and you can buy beer by the bottle at rock-bottom prices and sit at a table for no extra charge. The occasional art show brightens the walls of this otherwise seedy (but interesting) bar. Hold on to your bag at all times.

The *Vineria* in Campo de' Fiori, also known as *Giorgio's*, has a wide selection of wine and beers and was once the gathering place of the Roman literati. Today it is less glamorous, but is still a good place to drink, although cheap only if you stand at the bar. *Goldfinch* is a good, cheap bar which stays open late; it is near the Campo de' Fiori in the Piazza del Teatro di Pompeo. *Caffè Gardenia*, Via del Governo Vecchio 98, has snacks for L3500 to L5000, and live jazz. Nearby is *Enoteca Piccolo* at No 75, a pleasant wine bar with snacks available. Off Via del Governo Vecchio, in Via della Pace, is the *Bar della Pace*, a popular place for the young 'in' crowd, but you pay high prices to drink there. *Cul de Sac 1*, Piazza Pasquino 73, just off Piazza Navona at the start of Via del Governo Vecchio, is a popular wine bar which also serves excellent food.

There are numerous cafés and bars (with outdoor tables in summer) in Piazza Navona, near the Spanish Steps, Piazza della Rotonda and Piazza Santa Maria in Trastevere, which are extremely popular with tourists. Expect to pay a lot of money to sit down and drink your coffee, wine or beer. The *Bevitoria Navona*, Piazza Navona 72, is one which charges reasonable prices (around L2500 for a glass of average wine and up to L10,000 for better quality wine). *Trimani*, Via Cernaia 37, near Stazione Termini, is another good wine bar and serves good-quality food.

Those seeking the best coffee in Rome go to the *Tazza d'Oro*, just off the Piazza della Rotonda in Via degli Orfani, and *Bar Eustachio*, Piazza Sant'Eustachio, near the Pantheon. Fashionable (and expensive) places to drink your coffee or tea are the *Caffè Greco*, Via Condotti 86, near Piazza di Spagna, and *Caffè Rosati* in Piazza del Popolo.

In Trastevere there is the *Bar San Calisto* in the piazza of the same name, with tables outside. Again, this bar is seedy, but cheap and interesting and you can sit down without paying extra. A much more comfortable place to drink is the *San Michele aveva un Gallo* in Via San Francesco a Ripa, across Viale Trastevere near the corner of the Piazza San Francesco d'Assisi.

Sandwiches & Snacks

Paladini, Via del Governo Vecchio 29, might look like a run-down alimentari, but they make mouth-watering pizza bianca on the premises and fill it with whatever you desire for L3000. Try the bresaola and rucola. *Bar La Penna*, Via Giulia 21, is another place whose looks can be deceiving. It has good sandwiches for around L2500 and a cappuccino costs less than L1000. In Via di Ripetta, which runs off Piazza del Popolo, parallel to Via del Corso, there are several bars and takeaways with good fare. *Caffè Sogo*, Via di Ripetta 242, has Japanese snacks, as well as coffee etc. Next door is a tiny Japanese grocery store. *M & M Volpetti*, Via della Scrofa 31, near Piazza Navona, is a well-known rosticceria where you can buy great lunch-time snacks.

Among the more famous sandwich outlets in Rome is *Frontoni* in Viale Trastevere, on the corner of Via Francesco a Ripa, opposite Piazza Mastai. It makes its panini with both pizza bianca and bread and you can choose from an enormous range of fillings. Sandwiches are sold by weight, and a generously filled one will cost around L4000. It also has excellent pizza by the slice (*a taglio*).

Takeaway pizza by the slice is very popular in Rome and there are numerous outlets all over the city. Usually you can judge the quality of the pizza simply by taking a look. Some good places are *Pizza Rustica* in Campo de' Fiori and *Pizza a Taglio* in Via delle Muratte, just off the Piazza di Trevi. Near Piazza di Spagna, at Via della Croce 18, is *Fior Fiore*.

Gelati

Giolitti, Via degli Uffici del Vicario 40, has long been a Roman institution. It was once the meeting place of the local art crowd and writers. Today it remains famous for its fantastic gelati. *Gelateria della Palma*, around the corner at Via della Maddalena 20, has a huge selection of flavours, and some say the gelati is better than at Giolitti; a cone with three flavours costs around L2500. Both establishments also have cakes and pastries. *Pica*, Via della Seggiola 12, near Largo di Torre Argentina, is another of Rome's better ice-cream bars, where you can try some unusual flavours. *La Fontana della Salute*, Via Cardinal Marmaggi 2-6 in Trastevere, is a good place to buy excellent gelati late at night.

Bread & Pastries

Bernasconi, Largo di Torre Argentina 1, is a reasonably good and well-known pasticceria. *Bella Napoli*, a bar/pasticceria that specialises in Neapolitan pastries, is at Via Vittorio Emanuele 246. *Valzani*, Via del Moro 37 in Trastevere, is a good pasticceria, as is *Antonini*, Via Sabotino 21-29, near Piazza Mazzini in Prati. *La Dolceroma*, Via del Portico d'Ottavia 20 (between the Teatro

di Marcello and Via Arenula), specialises in Austrian cakes and pastries. In the same street at No 2 is *Il Forno del Ghetto*, a very popular outlet for cakes and pastries. It is a kosher bakery and you will need to look for the street number, because no sign indicates the place. Near Stazione Termini is *Panella l'Arte del Pane*, Largo Leopardi 2-10 (on Via Merulana), with a big variety of pastries and breads.

Grocery Shops

There are hundreds of small outlets in the centre of Rome where you can buy cheese, salami, bread and grocery supplies. The following are some of the better known gastronomic establishments.

Billo Bottarga, Via di Sant'Ambrogio 20, near Piazza Mattei, specialises in kosher food. It is famous for its bottarga (roe of tuna or mullet). *Castroni*, Via Cola di Rienzo 196, in Prati near the Vatican, has a wide selection of gourmet foods, packaged and fresh, including international foods. *Franchi*, in the same street at No 204, is a salumeria (delicatessen), as well as an excellent takeaway. *Gino Placidi*, Via della Maddalena 48, near the Pantheon, is one of central Rome's best alimentari. *Ruggeri*, Campo de' Fiori 1, has a good range of cheese and meats, and *Strega Cavour*, Via Marianna Dionigi 19, near Piazza Cavour in the Vatican area, combines a bar and well-stocked alimentari. *Volpetti*, Via Marmorata 47, in Testaccio, has high-quality cheese and meats.

Health Foods

Buying muesli, soy milk and the like can be expensive in Italy. The following outlets have a good range of products, including organic fruit and vegetables at relatively reasonable prices.

L'Albero del Pane, Via Santa Maria del Pianto 19, in the Jewish quarter, has a wide range of health foods, both packaged and fresh. It has an outlet for organic fruit and vegetables at Via dei Baullari 112, just off the Campo de' Fiori. *Emporium Naturae*, Viale Angelico 2 (take Metro Linea A to Ottaviano), is a well-stocked health-food supermarket. *Il Canestro*, Via Luca della Robbia 47, in Testaccio near the market, also has a large selection of health food, as well as fresh fruit and vegetables and takeaway food.

ENTERTAINMENT

Rome's primary entertainment guide is *Trovaroma*, a weekly supplement in the Thursday edition of the newspaper *La Repubblica*. Considered the bible for what is happening in the city, it provides a comprehensive listing, but in Italian only. The newspaper also publishes a daily listing of cinema, theatre and concerts. All this information is in Italian, but it is pretty easy to understand. *Carnet di Roma*, published monthly by the EPT in both English and Italian, gives information on the sights, as well as listing exhibitions and musical and theatrical events. *This Week in Rome* is another excellent guide (in English) to what's happening in the city. *Metropolitan* is a free fortnightly magazine which reviews what is happening in Rome's English-speaking community. It also has entertainment listings (for English speakers), as well as bars and pubs etc. The magazine is available at various outlets, including the Lion Bookshop and the Economy Book & Video Center (see the Rome Information section for addresses) as well as various newsstands in the centre of Rome.

Festivals & Music

Although Romans desert their city in summer, particularly in August, when the weather is relentlessly hot and humid, cultural and musical events liven up the place and many performances and festivals are held in the open. In July and August, opera is performed at the Baths of Caracalla. A summer festival, organised by the Commune of Rome and the EPT, features concerts, dance and folklore, including various events held in the city's many piazzas (information available from the EPT). A series of concerts is performed in Piazza del Campidoglio during July.

The Festa de Noantri, in honour of Our Lady of Mt Carmel, is held in Trastevere in the last two weeks of July and is not much more than a line of street stalls. Some street theatre and music is performed and meals are eaten in the street. The Festa di San Giovanni is held on 23 and 24 June in the San Giovanni district of Rome and features much dancing and eating in the streets. Part of the ritual is to eat stewed snails and suckling pig.

During June and July, Tevere Expo takes place on the banks of the Tiber, featuring an exhibition of the crafts and products of Italy's regions. In July at the Castel Sant'Angelo, on the Tiber, two huge screens are erected to show films (in Italian, free entry). Free jazz concerts are also held here – check daily papers for listings.

Out of season the entertainment moves indoors to the nightclubs, bars, theatres and concert halls. There is a season of concerts in October and November at the Accademia di Santa Cecilia, Via della Conciliazione 4, and the Accademia Filarmonica, Via Flaminia 18. The opera season at the Teatro dell'Opera, Piazza Beniamino Gigli, starts in November. Ballet is also performed at the Teatro dell'Opera. Other musical events in this period feature performances by the RAI Symphonic Orchestra.

At Christmas the focus is on the many churches of Rome, each setting up its own Nativity scene, notably the 13th century crib at Santa Maria Maggiore and the crib at Ara Coeli. During Holy Week, at Easter, the focus is again religious and events include the famous procession of the cross between the Colosseum and the Palatine on Good Friday, and the pope's blessing of the city and the world in St Peter's Square on Easter Sunday.

The Spanish Steps become a sea of flowers during the Spring Festival in April.

Rock concerts are held throughout the year and are advertised on posters plastered all over the city. Concerts by major performers are usually held at the Palazzo dello Sport or Stadio Flaminia, both a good distance out of the city centre. For information and bookings, contact the ORBIS agency (☎ 475 14 03) in Piazza d'Esquilino near the station.

Top Left : The Dolomites, Trentino (SC)
Top Right : Val di Genova in Adamello-Brenta National Park, Trentino (SC)
Bottom Left : Mountain hut near Merano, Alto Adige (SC)
Bottom Right : Moonrise over the Sesto Dolomites, Alto Adige (SC)

Top Left : Juliet's Balcony, Verona (JG)
Top Right : Canal scene in Venice (JG)
Bottom Left : Venice Carnival (APT)
Bottom Right : Courtyard of Doges' Palace, Venice (JG)

Nightlife

Nightclubs and discotheques are popular mainly during winter. Among the more interesting and popular Roman live music clubs is Radio Londra, Via di Monte Testaccio, in the Testaccio area. Entrance is free, but you might find it hard to get in here because the bouncers tend to pick and choose. There are several other good nightclubs and bars in the same street, including Caruso Caffè Concerto at No 36 and Caffè Latino at No 96.

The Uonna Club is a long way from the centre at Via Cassia 871. Its crowd tends towards New Wave and there are often live concerts by foreign groups fitting that description. The Druid's Den, Via San Martino ai Monti 28, is an Irish pub serving Guinness where you can meet other English speakers.

Esperimento, Via Rasella 5, near Piazza Barberini, is a rock club which often stages live concerts by young English, and even Australian, bands. Membership is L10,000. One of Rome's newer nightclubs is Alpheus, Via del Commercio 36, near the Piramide mausoleum, where you can listen to a variety of music in different rooms. It costs L10,000 to get in, and up to L25,000 on Saturday nights or when there is a concert. Il Castello is a music club which often has live underground bands at Via Porta Castello 44, just near Castel Sant'Angelo. For jazz, try Alexander Platz, Via Ostia 9 (open nightly), and Music Inn, Largo dei Fiorentini 3.

Roman discos are expensive. Expect to pay up to L30,000 to get in (although women are sometimes allowed in free of charge), which may or may not include one drink. Hot spots include Alien, Via Velletri 13, and Piper, Via Tagliamento 9. Rome's best gay disco is L'Alibi, Via di Monte Testaccio 44. Women are allowed in only if accompanied by a man. Another choice for gays is the bar/disco L'Angelo Azzurro, Via Cardinal Merry del Val 13.

Films

The cinema Pasquino (☎ 580 36 22), Vicolo del Piede 19, in Trastevere, screens films in English. It is just off Piazza Santa Maria. On Monday nights you can see English-language films at Alcazar (☎ 588 00 99), Via Merry del Val, off Viale Trastevere. The Nuova Sacher (☎ 581 81 16) at Largo Ascianghi, between the Porta Portese area and Trastevere, shows films in their original language on Mondays and Wednesdays. A new cinema complex with three screens, the Greenwich (☎ 574 58 25), Via G B Bodoni 59, in Testaccio, also shows films in their original language.

Theatre

The Agora (☎ 686 85 28), Via della Penitenza 33, has seasons of English-language theatre.

THINGS TO BUY

The first things that come to mind when thinking of shopping in Rome are clothing and shoes. But it can be difficult to find bargains here. The city's main shopping areas are not as compact as Florence, or as impressive as Milan, but, if you have the money, the quality is certainly there.

It is probably advisable only to window-shop in the expensive Ludovisi district, the area around Via Veneto. The major fashion shops are in the Via Sistina and Via Gregoriana, heading towards the Spanish Steps, as well as in Via Condotti and the parallel streets heading from the Piazza di Spagna to Via del Corso. However, in these streets you will also find moderately expensive clothing and footwear boutiques, as well as shops selling accessories. Via del Corso is also a major shopping street. It is cheaper, but not as interesting, to shop along Via del Tritone and Via Nazionale. There are some interesting second-hand clothes shops along Via del Governo Vecchio. Across the river, near St Peter's, the best shopping street is Via Cola di Rienzo.

If clothes don't appeal, wander through the streets around Via Margutta, Via Ripetta, Piazza del Popolo and Via Frattina to look at the art galleries, artists' studios and antiquarian shops. There are antique shops in Via Coronari, between Piazza Navona and Tor di

Nona, but the antique shops along Via del Babuino are expensive.

Everyone flocks to the famous Porta Portese market every Sunday morning. Hundreds of stalls line the streets of Porta Portese, near Trastevere, selling anything you can imagine. Here you can pick up a genuine 1960s evening dress for L1000, an antique mirror for L10,000, or a second-hand leather jacket for L40,000. Take time to rummage through the piles of clothing and bric-a-brac and you will find some incredible bargains. The market extends for a few km along the side streets parallel to Viale Trastevere from the Trastevere station. The market becomes very crowded by around 11 am.

The market in Via Sannio, near Porta San Giovanni, sells new and second-hand clothes. For prints, antiques and books, head for the market at Piazza Fontanella Borghese, held every morning except Sunday.

GETTING THERE & AWAY
Air
The main airport is Leonardo da Vinci (☎ 6 01 21), also known as Fiumicino (the name of the town near which it is located). The other airport is Ciampino, where many national and some international, including charter, flights arrive. See the following Getting Around section for details on how to get to/from the airports, and see the Getting There & Away chapter earlier in this book for information on flights to/from Rome.

All of the airlines have offices in the departure hall at Fiumicino, but their main offices are located in the area around Via Veneto and Via Barberini, north of Stazione Termini. They include:

Alitalia
Via Bissolati 13 (☎ 4 68 81, or ☎ 6 56 43 for general information)
Air New Zealand
Via Bissolati 54 (☎ 488 07 62, or ☎ 1678-7 61 26 for general information)
British Airways
Via Bissolati 54 (☎ 47 99 91)
Cathay Pacific
Via Barberini 3 (☎ 487 01 50)
Delta Airlines
Via Bissolati 46 (☎ 47 73)
Qantas
Via Bissolati 35 (☎ 48 65 58)
Singapore Airlines
Via Bissolati 24-26 (☎ 481 89 43)
TWA
Via Barberini 67 (☎ 4 72 11)

Bus
The main terminal for intercity buses is in Viale Einaudi, between Piazza della Repubblica and Piazza dei Cinquecento, north of the train station. Buses connect with major cities including Florence, Milan, Naples, Palermo and many smaller towns and cities throughout the country. Numerous buses also connect Rome with towns and villages throughout the province of Rome, as well as provincial cities throughout Italy. These depart from various points throughout the city and it is necessary to obtain information directly from the bus companies or from the EPT office at Via Parigi 11, where they have a full list of all bus services to and from Rome. Information about the intercity buses can also be obtained from the CIT office at the train station.

The following is a brief list of agencies for some of the bus companies operating services to/from Rome:

ACOTRAL
Via Ostiense 131 (☎ 722 24 70 or ☎ 591 55 51)
Services to towns and villages throughout Lazio
ARPA
Information at Eurojet, Piazza della Repubblica 54 (☎ 474 45 21)
Services to Abruzzo, including L'Aquila and Pescara
Bonelli
Bar Piccarozzi, Piazza della Republicca 62 (☎ 488 59 24)
Services to Emilia-Romagna, including Ravenna and Rimini
CIAT
Information at Eurojet (see ARPA)
Services to Naples, the Amalfi Coast and Salerno
Lazzi
Via Tagliamento 27r (☎ 841 74 58)
Services to other European capitals, via various places in the Alps

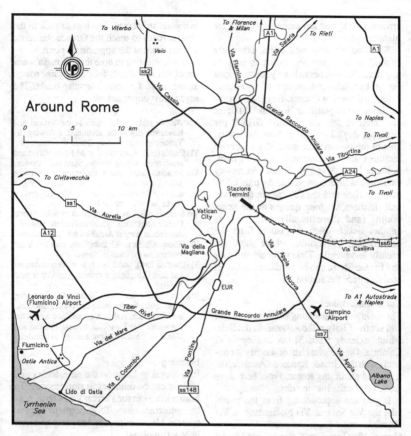

Around Rome

0   5   10 km

To Viterbo

To Florence & Milan

To Rieti

To Naples

To Tivoli

To Tivoli

To Civitavecchia

To A1 Autostrada & Naples

Veio

ss2

Via Cassia

Via Flaminia

Via Salaria

Grande Raccordo Annulare

Via Tiburtina

Via Aurelia

ss1

A12

Vatican City

Stazione Termini

Via della Magliana

Via Casilina

ss6

Leonardo da Vinci (Flumicino) Airport

Flumicino

Ostia Antica

Lido di Ostia

Tyrrhenian Sea

Tiber River

EUR

Via del Mare

Via C. Colombo

Via Pontina

Via Appia Nuova

Grande Raccordo Annulare

Via Appia

Ciampino Airport

ss7

Albano Lake

ss148

Lirosi
Information at Eurojet (see ARPA)
Services to Calabria

Marozzi
Information at Eurojet (see ARPA)
Services to Bari and Brindisi, via towns including Alberobello and Matera

SAIS
Information at Bar Piccarozzi (see Bonelli)
Services to Sicily

Segesta
Information at Bar Piccarozzi (see Bonelli)
Services to Sicily

SULGA
Information at Eurojet (see ARPA)
Services to Perugia, Assisi and other places in Umbria

Train

Almost all trains arrive at and depart from Stazione Termini. There are regular connections to all major cities in Italy and Europe, including Florence (takes two to four hours), Venice (six to eight hours), Milan (four to seven hours), and Naples (three to four hours). For train timetable information, phone ☎ 47 75 (from 7 am to 10.40 pm), or go to the information office at the station, where English is spoken. Official timetables are available free of charge, but are generally difficult to come by. Privately produced timetables can be bought at newsstands for around L4000 and are extremely useful for planning your travel.

Stazione Termini will seem extremely chaotic to new arrivals, but it is easy to negotiate. Remember to keep your eyes open for pickpockets and groups of pint-sized, cardboard-waving thieves. Baggage storage facilities are at platform No 1 and at the far end, next to the last platform (L1500 per item, per day). Downstairs from the central area of the station there are ASST telephone facilities and the entrances to the Metropolitana lines A and B. Postal and money exchange facilities, as well as the train information office and the CIT, are in the ticket hall. If there are long queues at the ticket booths (and there usually are), there is another ticket office downstairs from the central part of Termini where there are usually less people. Tickets for urban buses and for the Metro can be purchased at tobacconists inside the station.

Car & Motorbike

The main road connecting Rome to the north and south of Italy is the Autostrada del Sole, which extends from Milan to Reggio di Calabria. On the outskirts of the city it connects with the Grande Raccordo Anulare, the ring road encircling Rome. From here there are several exits into the city.

If you are approaching from the north, take the Via Salaria, Via Nomentana or Via Flaminia exits. From the south, Via Appia Nuova, Via Cristoforo Colombo and Via del Mare (which connects Rome to the Lido di Ostia) all provide reasonably direct routes into the city. The Grande Raccordo and all of the arterial roads in Rome are clogged with traffic on weekday evenings from about 5 to 7.30 pm, and on Sunday evenings, particularly in summer, all approaches to Rome are subject to traffic jams as Romans return home after weekends in the country or by the sea.

The A12 connects the city to Civitavecchia and then along the coast to Genoa (it also connects the city to Fiumicino Airport). Signs from the centre of Rome to the autostradas can be vague and confusing, so invest in a good street map. It is best to stick to the arterial roads to reach the Grande Raccordo and then exit at the appropriate point.

It is interesting to note that the main roads out of Rome basically follow the same routes as the ancient Roman consular roads. The seven most important are:

Via Aurelia (ss1), which starts at the Vatican and leaves the city to the north-east, following the Tyrrhenian coast to Pisa, Genoa and France;

Via Cassia (ss2), which starts at the Ponte Milvio and heads north-west to Viterbo, Siena and Florence;

Via Flaminia (ss3), which also starts at the Ponte Milvio, and goes north-west to Terni, Foligno and over the Apennines into the Marches, ending on the Adriatic coast at Fano;

Via Salaria (ss4), which heads north from near Porta Pia in central Rome to Rieti and into the Marches, and ends at Porto d'Ascoli on the Adriatic coast;

Via Tiburtina (ss5), which links Rome with Tivoli and Pescara, on the coast of Abruzzo;

Via Casilina (ss6), which heads south-east to Anagni and into Campania, terminating at Capua near Naples;

Via Appia (ss7), the most famous of the consular roads, which heads south along the coast of Lazio into Campania, and then goes inland across the Apennines into Basilicata, through Potenza and Matera to Taranto in Apulia and on to Brindisi.

Hitching

It is illegal to hitch on the autostradas and Italians can be reluctant to stop anyway. To head north, wait for a lift on Via Salaria, near the autostrada entry. To go south to Naples, take the Metropolitana to Anagnina and wait in Via Tuscolana.

GETTING AROUND
To/From the Airports

Fiumicino Access to the city is via the airport-Ostiense train, which costs L6500. The train station is opposite the airport arrivals hall and signs direct the way. Trains depart approximately every 20 minutes and arrive at the Ostiense station. Underground tunnels connect the station to the Piramide Metropolitana stop (Linea B), from where you can catch the metro to Stazione Termini. The process is simple, but there is a fair amount of walking involved, which can be difficult if you have a lot of luggage. During the night, from around 2 to 6 am, the route is serviced by ACOTRAL buses approximately every hour and a quarter, from the airport to Piazzale dei Partigiani, in front of the Ostiense station.

Taxis from the airport are quite expensive: expect to pay upwards of L60,000, and agree on the price *before* you get in the taxi. Note that there is a special surcharge on taxi rides between the city centre and the airport.

The airport is connected to the city centre by an autostrada. Follow the signs for Rome out of the airport complex, and exit from the autostrada at EUR. From there, follow the signs marked 'centro' to reach Via Cristoforo Colombo, which will take you directly into the centre.

The EPT branch at the airport, open from 8.15 am to 5 pm Monday to Saturday, will provide maps and information about accommodation.

Ciampino If you arrive at Ciampino Airport, ACOTRAL buses (from 5.45 am to 10.30 pm) will take you to the Anagnina Metropolitana stop, from where you can catch the subway to Stazione Termini. If you arrive late or very early, you have little option other than to catch a taxi.

The airport is connected to Rome by the Via Appia Nuova.

Bus

The city bus company is ATAC and most of the main buses terminate in Piazza dei Cinquecento at Stazione Termini. At the information booth in the centre of the piazza you can obtain a map detailing bus routes, otherwise the EPT has a free (but largely indecipherable) map. The previously mentioned Lozzi map of Rome (see the Rome Information section) provides a good enough guide to bus routes. Generally, ATAC staff at the information booth are more than happy to provide information and advice on which buses to catch.

Another central point for the main bus routes in the city centre is Largo di Torre Argentina, near Piazza Navona. Buses run from about 6 am to midnight, with limited services continuing throughout the night on some routes.

Tickets cost L800 and are valid for 90 minutes. They must be purchased *before* you get on the bus and then validated in the machine as you enter. The fine for travelling without a validated ticket is L50,000, and inspectors are tiring of the same old explanations from tourists that they 'didn't know'. Tickets are available in Piazza dei Cinquecento, at any tobacconist and at newsstands. Daily tourist tickets cost L2800 and weekly tickets cost L10,000.

Useful buses include:

No 64, from Stazione Termini to St Peter's
No 27, from Termini to the Colosseum
No 44, from Piazza Venezia to Trastevere
No 118, from the Colosseum to the Baths of Caracalla, the Catacombs and Via Appia Antica
No 3 or 910, from Termini to the Villa Borghese
No 36, from Termini along Via Nomentana (for foreign embassies)

Pickpockets are active on crowded buses, particularly those popular with tourists. The No 64, for example, is notorious, but the No 27 is also a popular route for thieves.

Metropolitana

The Metropolitana (Metro) has two lines, Linea A and Linea B. Both pass through Termini. Take Linea A for Piazza di Spagna and Flaminio (the Villa Borghese), and for Ottaviano (the area near the Vatican). Linea B will take you to the Colosseum, Circus Maximus and Piramide (for Stazione Ostiense and trains to the airport and the Lido di Ostia), as well as to EUR. Metro tickets are different from bus tickets and cost L800, or L7000 for a block of 10, and can be purchased at ticket offices downstairs at Termini, from tobacconists, or from vending machines at Metro stations. Trains run approximately every five minutes.

Taxi

Taxis are on radio call 24 hours a day in Rome. Phone numbers include ☎ 35 70 for Cooperativa Radio Taxi Romana, and ☎ 49 94 for La Capitale. Major taxi ranks are at the airports and Termini. Taxis are not as abundant in Rome as they are in New York or London, so it is a good idea to order one by phone, or go to the nearest rank, rather than attempt to hail one in the street. There are surcharges for luggage, night service, public holidays and travel to and from Fiumicino Airport. The taxi flagfall is L6400.

Car & Motorbike

Negotiating Roman traffic by car is difficult enough, but you may be taking your life in your hands if you ride a motorbike in the city. The rule in Rome is to look straight ahead to watch the vehicles in front, and hope that the vehicles behind are watching you.

Most of the historic centre of Rome is closed to normal traffic, although tourists are permitted to drive to their hotels. Traffic police *(vigili)* control the entrances to the centre, and should let you through if you have a car full of luggage and mention the name of the hotel you're going to. Once there, inform the hotel management that you have a car and they will provide a pass which allows you to drive and park in the centre. If you manage to enter without a pass, you are likely to return to find a brace on a wheel of your car or, at worst, that the car has been towed away. In the event that your car goes missing after it was parked illegally, always check first with the traffic police (☎ 6 76 91 or ☎ 676 98 38). You will have to pay about L180,000 to get it back.

Rather than having the hassle of driving around Rome, it is a much better idea to leave your vehicle in a car park (unless you are lucky enough to find a legal parking spot in the centre) and use public transport. There are numerous small car parks scattered around the centre on vacant blocks of land that are attended during the day, but for longer periods it's safer to use one of the larger, covered car parks. The major parking area closest to the centre is at the Villa Borghese; entry is from Piazzale Brasile at the top of Via Veneto. There is also a supervised car park at Stazione Termini. Other car parks are at Piazzale dei Partigiani, just outside the Ostiense station and connected to the centre

on the Metropolitana nearby at Piramide, and at Stazione Tiburtina, from where you can also catch the Metro into the centre.

The EPT at Via Parigi 11 has a list of car parks in the suburbs of Rome, run by the ACI. All are accessible to the city centre by Metro or bus and they are generally cheap (around L1000 an hour for those closer to the centre and as cheap as L2000 a day for those on the periphery of the city).

Car Rental To rent a car, you will need to be at least 21 years old and have a valid driving licence. It is cheaper to organise a car in advance if you want one for a long period. For a guide to rental costs, see the Getting Around chapter earlier in this book. The multinational operators in Rome (Avis, Europcar and Hertz) are slightly cheaper than the locals. The major companies are:

Avis – Fiumicino Airport (☎ 65 01 15 79), Stazione Termini (☎ 470 12 19), Piazza Esquilino 1 (☎ 470 12 16), or toll-free ☎ 1678-6 30 63
Dollaroexpres – Viale delle Milizie 9D (☎ 37 51 59 44, or toll-free ☎ 1678-6 51 10)
Euronolo – Via Valle Vermiglio 21 (☎ 88 64 01 85)
Europcar – Fiumicino Airport (☎ 65 01 08 79), Stazione Termini (☎ 488 28 54), or central phone ☎ 52 08 12 00
Hertz – Fiumicino Airport (☎ 65 01 14 48), Stazione Termini (☎ 474 03 89), or toll-free ☎ 1678-2 20 99
Maggiore – Fiumicino Airport (☎ 65 01 06 78), Stazione Termini (☎ 488 00 49), or toll-free ☎ 1678-6 70 67

Scooter & Bicycle Rental For scooters and bicycles, contact Scooters for Rent (☎ 488 54 85), Via della Purificazione 66. For a guide to rental costs, see the Getting Around chapter earlier in this book.

Lazio

Rome demands so much of your time and concentration that most tourists forget that the city is part of the Region of Lazio. Declared a region in 1934, the geographical area of Lazio (also known as Latium in English) has, since ancient Roman times, been an extension of Rome. Through the ages, the rich built their villas in the Lazio countryside, and many of its towns developed as the fiefs of noble Roman families, such as the Orsini, Barberini and Farnese. Even today, Romans build their weekend and holiday homes in the picturesque areas of the region (the pope, for instance, has his summer residence at Castelgandolfo, south of Rome) and Romans continue to migrate from their chaotic and polluted city to live in the Lazio countryside. This means that the region is relatively well served by public transport, and tourists can take advantage of this to visit places of interest.

While the region does not abound in major tourist destinations, it does offer some interesting places within easy day-trip distance of the city. A tour of Etruria, the ancient land of the Etruscans, which extended into northern Lazio, is highly recommended. Visits to the tombs and museums at Cerveteri and Tarquinia provide a fascinating insight into Etruscan civilisation. The ruins of Hadrian's villa, near Tivoli, and of the ancient Roman port at Ostia Antica, are both easily accessible from Rome, as is the interesting medieval town of Viterbo, north of the capital. In summer, tired and overheated tourists can head for the lakes north of Rome, including Bracciano and Vico, which are somewhat preferable to the polluted beaches near the city.

OSTIA ANTICA

The Romans founded this port city at the mouth of the Tiber River in the 4th century BC and it became a strategically important centre of defence and trade. It was populated by merchants, sailors and slaves, and the ruins of the city provide a fascinating contrast to the ruins at Pompeii, which was populated by wealthy Romans. After barbarian invasions and the appearance of malaria it was abandoned, but Pope Gregory IV re-established the city in the 9th century AD.

Information about the town and Roman ruins is available at the EPT office in Rome.

Things to See & Do

The ruins are quite spread out and you will need a good few hours to wander through them. Entrance to the city is through the **Porta Romana**, which leads you onto Ostia Antica's main thoroughfare, the **Decumanus Maximus**. The Porta Marina, at the other end of the road, once opened onto the seafront. Of particular note in the excavated city are the **Terme di Nettuno** (Neptune's Baths), to your right just after entering the city. Take a look at the black-and-white mosaic depicting Neptune and Amphitrite. Next is a **Roman theatre** built by Augustus. It was restored in 1927 and is now used for staging classical performances and concerts. Behind the theatre is the **Piazzale delle Corporazioni**, where Ostia's merchant guilds had their offices, distinguished by mosaics depicting their wares.

Returning to the Decumanus Maximus, you reach the **forum**, the **Tempio di Roma e Augusto**, dedicated to the goddess Rome, and the **Tempio Rotondo**. Follow the Vico del Pino and Via del Tempio Rotondo to the Cardo Maximus to reach the **Domus Fortuna Annonaria**, the heavily decorated home of one of Ostia's wealthier citizens. Opposite, in the area next to the **Grandi Horrea** (warehouses), are private houses, including the well-preserved **Casa di Diana**. Continue along the Via dei Dipinti to reach Ostia Antica's **museum**, which houses statues, mosaics and wall paintings found at the site.

The ruins are open daily from 9 am to 6 pm in summer, and to 3 pm in winter. Entrance is L10,000.

Getting There & Away

To get to Ostia Antica, take the Metro Linea B to Magliana and then the Ostia Lido train. Trains leave every half hour and the trip takes about 20 minutes. Buy a L1000 ticket which covers both the Metro and Ostia train. The ruins are also easy to reach by car from

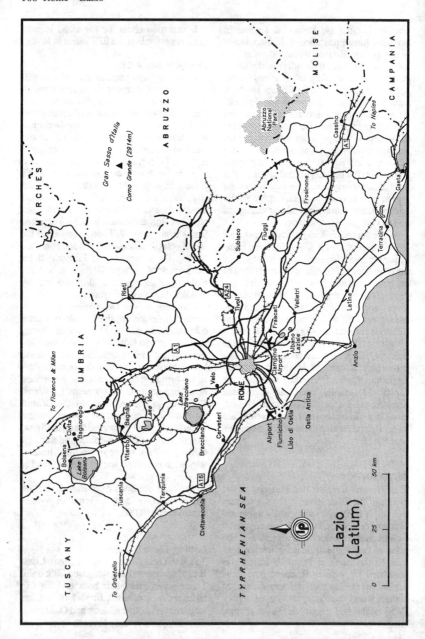

Rome. Take the Via del Mare, which is the continuation of Via Ostiense.

TIVOLI

Set on a hill by the Anio River, Tivoli was a resort town of the ancient Romans and again became popular as a summer playground for the rich during the Renaissance. While the majority of tourists are attracted by the terraced gardens and fountains of the Villa d'Este, the ruins of the spectacular Villa Adriana, built by the Roman emperor Hadrian, are far more interesting.

The local AAST tourist office (☎ 0774-2 12 49) is in Largo Garibaldi, near the ACOTRAL bus stop. It is open from 8 am to 6 pm in summer, and to 2 pm in winter.

Things to See & Do

Hadrian built his summer villa in the 2nd century AD, influenced by the architecture of the famous classical buildings of the day. It was successively plundered by barbarians and Romans for building materials, and many of its original decorations were used to embellish the Villa d'Este. However, enough remains to give an idea of the incredible size and magnificence of the villa. You will need about four hours to wander through the vast ruins, and you will find that you are tired before you have seen even half of the villa. Take a break for a picnic, or lunch at the bar in the visitors' centre before resuming your tour.

Highlights include **La Villa dell'Isola** (The Villa of the Island), where Hadrian spent his pensive moments, the **Imperial Palace** and its **Golden Square** (Piazza d'Oro), and the floor mosaics of the **Hospitalia**. Although very little remains of Hadrian's **Piccole e Grandi Terme** (Small & Large Baths), it is easy to work out their layout and imagine their former grandeur. Take a look at the model of the villa in the small visitors' centre to get an idea of the extent of the complex. The villa is open from 9 am to 7 pm (last entry 6 pm) in the warmer months, and to 4 pm in winter. Entrance is L8000.

The Renaissance **Villa d'Este** was built in the 16th century for Cardinal Ippolito d'Este, grandson of the Borgia Pope Alexander VI, on the site of a Franciscan monastery. The villa's beautiful gardens are decorated with numerous fountains, which are its main attraction. You will wander through the cardinal's villa on the way to the gardens. Rather than paying too much attention to the fairly drab rooms, take a look out of the windows to get a bird's-eye view of the gardens and fountains. Opening hours vary for each season – in summer from 9 am to 6.30 pm and in winter to 4.30 pm. Entrance is L5000.

Getting There & Away

Tivoli is about 40 km east of Rome and accessible by ACOTRAL bus which leaves from Via Tiburtina. Take Metro Linea B from Stazione Termini to Rebibbia; the bus leaves from outside the station every 15 minutes (L4600 return). The bus also stops at the Villa Adriana, about one km from Tivoli. You can catch the same bus from the Villa Adriana to the Villa d'Este. The fastest route by car is on the Rome-L'Aquila autostrada.

ETRUSCAN SITES

There are several important Etruscan archaeological sites in Lazio, most within easy reach of Rome by car or public transport. These include Tarquinia (one of the most important cities of the federation of city-states known as the Etruscan League), Cerveteri, Veio and Tuscania. The tombs and religious monuments discovered throughout the area have yielded the treasures which can now be seen in museums including the Villa Giulia and the Vatican, although the smaller museums at Tarquinia and Cerveteri are well worth a visit.

The sheer number of tombs in the area has long supported the illegitimate industry of the *tombaroli* (tomb robbers), who have been plundering the Etruscan sites for centuries and selling their 'discoveries' on the black market. It is said that, since many tombs are still to be excavated, a good number of tombaroli are still active. Prospective buyers

Etruscan roof ornament, 5th century BC

of illicit Etruscan artefacts should, however, beware: another notorious activity of the tombaroli has been the manufacture of fake treasures.

If you have the time, a few days spent touring at least Tarquinia and Cerveteri, combined with visits to their museums and the Villa Giulia, should constitute one of your more fascinating experiences in Italy. A useful guide to the area, called *The Etruscans*, is published by the Istituto Geografico de Agostini and comes with a map. Free copies are sometimes available at the EPT office in Rome. If you really want to lose yourself in a poetic journey, take along a copy of D H Lawrence's *Etruscan Places* (published by Penguin in the compilation *D H Lawrence and Italy*).

Tarquinia

Believed to have been founded in the 12th century BC, and home of the Tarquin kings who ruled Rome before the creation of the republic, Tarquinia was an important economic and political centre of the Etruscan League. The major attractions here are the painted tombs of its necropoli (burial grounds).

Orientation & Information By car or bus (see the Getting There & Away section that follows) you will arrive at the Barriera San Giusto, just outside the main entrance to the town. The tourist information office (AAST, ☎ 0766-85 63 84) is on your left as you walk through the medieval ramparts, at Piazza Cavour 1. It's open Monday to Saturday from 8.30 am to 12.30 pm and 4 to 6 pm. It is possible to see Tarquinia on a day trip from Rome, but if you want to stay overnight in the medieval town, it is advisable to make a booking.

Tarquinia's telephone code is 0766.

Things to See The 15th century Palazzo Vitelleschi, in Piazza Cavour, houses the **National Museum** and a large collection of Etruscan treasures, including frescoes removed from the tombs. There is a beautiful terracotta frieze of winged horses, taken from the Altar of the Queen (see later in this section). Numerous sarcophagi found in the tombs are also on display. At any one time, sections of the museum are likely to be closed to the public. The museum is open Tuesday to Sunday from 9 am to 2 pm (closed Mondays). Admission costs L8000.

The same ticket admits you to the **necropolis**, also open from 9 am to 2 pm (ask for directions from the museum, a 15 to 20-minute walk). Only a small number of the thousands of tombs have been excavated and only a handful of these are open on any given day. You must wait until a guide is available to open the tombs and it could be a long wait in summer, when thousands of tourists visit the necropolis daily. The tombs are richly decorated with frescoes, although many are seriously deteriorated, and they are now maintained at constant temperatures to preserve the remaining decorations. This means that it is possible to see them only through glass partitions.

D H Lawrence, who studied the tombs before measures were taken to protect them, wrote extensive descriptions of the frescoes he saw, and it is well worth reading his *Etruscan Places* before seeing the tombs of Tarquinia. Entering the famous Tomb of the Leopards, Lawrence noted how, despite the extensive destruction of the tombs through vandalism and neglect, the colours of the wall paintings were still so fresh and alive:

The walls of this little tomb are a dance of real delight. The room seems inhabited still by Etruscans of the sixth century before Christ, a vivid life-accepting

people, who must have lived with real fullness. On come the dancers and the music-players, moving in a broad frieze towards the front wall of the tomb, the wall facing us as we enter from the dark stairs, and where the banquet is going on in all its glory. Above the banquet, in the gable angle, are the two spotted leopards, heraldically facing each other across a little tree. And the ceiling of rock has chequered slopes of red and black and yellow squares, with a roof-beam painted with coloured circles, dark red and blue and yellow. So that all is colour, and we do not seem to be underground at all, but in some gay chamber of the past.

If you have a car, ask for directions to the remains of Etruscan Tarquinia, on the crest of the Civita hill nearby. There is little evidence of the ancient city, apart from a few limestone blocks which once formed part of the city walls. However, a large temple, the **Altar of the Queen**, was discovered on the hill and has been excavated this century. It is enclosed by a wire fence because archaeological work is still underway, but it can be seen through the fence.

If you have time, wander through the pleasant medieval town of Tarquinia. There are several churches worth a look, including the late 13th century San Francesco, in Via Porta Tarquinia, and the beautiful Romanesque Santa Maria di Castello, in the citadel at the north-west edge of the town.

Places to Stay & Eat There is a camping ground by the sea at Tarquinia Lido, *Tusca Tirrenia* (☎ 8 82 94), Viale Neriedi.

There is only one budget option in the town if you want to stay overnight, and it can be difficult to find a room if you don't book well in advance. *Affittacamere di Benedetti Alessandra* (☎ 85 52 67) has rooms for L20,000 per person. Go to the tobacconist's at Piazza Cavour 12. The only moderately priced hotel in the medieval town, the *Hotel San Marco*, was closed for restoration at the time of writing. Check with the tourist office for details. Otherwise try the *Hotel all'Olivo* (☎ 85 73 18), Via Togliatti 15, in the newer part of town about 10 minutes' walk downhill from the medieval centre. Singles/doubles are L55,000/80,000. Closer to the centre, but more expensive, is *Hotel Tar-*

conte (☎ 85 65 85), Via Tuscia 23, with rooms for L75,000/110,000, including breakfast.

There are few places to eat in Tarquinia, but for a good, cheap meal, go to *Cucina Casareccia* at Via G Mazzini 5, off Piazza Cavour, where a full meal with wine will cost around L17,000.

Getting There & Away Buses leave approximately every hour for Tarquinia from Via Lepanto in Rome, near the Metro Linea A Lepanto stop, arriving at Tarquinia a few steps away from the tourist office. You can also catch a train from Rome, but Tarquinia's station is at Tarquinia Lido (beach), approximately three km from the centre. You will then need to catch one of the regular local buses to the Barriera San Giusto. Buses leave from the Barriera for Tuscania every few hours. If you are travelling by car, take the autostrada for Civitavecchia and then the Via Aurelia. Tarquinia is about 90 km from Rome.

Cerveteri

Ancient Caere was founded by the Etruscans in the 8th century BC and enjoyed a period of great prosperity as a commercial centre from the 7th to 5th centuries BC. The main attractions here are the tombs known as *tumoli*, great mounds of earth with carved stone bases. Treasures taken from the tombs can be seen in the Vatican Museums, the Villa Giulia Museum and the Louvre. The Pro Loco tourist office is at Piazza Risorgimento 19.

The main necropolis area, **Banditaccia**, is open daily from 9 am to 4 pm in winter and 9 am to 7 pm in summer, and entrance is L8000. It's accessible by local bus in summer only from the main piazza in Cerveteri, otherwise it is a pleasant three-km walk west from the town. You can wander freely once inside the area, although it is best to follow the recommended routes in order to see the best preserved tombs. One of the more interesting is the Tomba dei Rilievi, which is decorated with painted reliefs of household items. The tomb has been closed in order to avoid further damage to its paintings, but it can be viewed through a glass window. Follow the signs also to the Tomba dei Capitali and the Tomba dei Vasi Greci. Signs detailing the history of the main tombs are in Italian only.

There is also a small **museum** in Cerveteri which contains an interesting display of pottery and sarcophagi. It is in the Palazzo Ruspoli and is open from 9 am to 2 pm (closed Monday). Entrance is free.

Cerveteri is only about 40 minutes from Rome and accessible by ACOTRAL bus from Via Lepanto, outside the Lepanto stop on Metro Linea A. By car take either Via Aurelia or the Civitavecchia autostrada.

Veio

Another stopover on your visit to Etruria could include Veio (Veii as it was known to the Etruscans), which is very close to Rome. This proximity meant that there was a traditional rivalry between the two cities, and, after a long siege, it finally fell under Rome's dominion in 396 BC. It became a municipium under Augustus, but eventually declined in importance and was abandoned.

Very little evidence remains of what was once the largest city in southern Etruria. The only things to see are the remains of a swimming pool and the lower section of a temple. However, important finds were made during excavations of the site, including the famous

Etruscan tomb in Cerveteri

statue of Apollo, now in the Villa Giulia museum.

By car, leave Rome on the Via Cassia and exit at Isola Farnese. Signs will point you towards Veio. Otherwise, take bus No 201 (for Olgiata) from Piazza Mancini, near the Ponte Milvio, to Isola Farnese and ask the bus driver to let you off at the road to Veio (although it should be noted that, for the trouble of catching public transport, there is little to see at Veio).

CIVITAVECCHIA

There is little to recommend this busy port and industrial centre to tourists, other than the ferries which leave daily for Sardinia. Established by Emperor Trajan in 106 AD as the port town of Centumcellae, it was later conquered by the Saracens, but regained importance as a papal stronghold in the 16th century. The medieval town was almost completely destroyed by bombing during WW II.

Orientation & Information

The port, and therefore the departure point for ferries, is a quick walk from the train station. As you leave the station, turn right into Viale Garibaldi and follow it along the seafront. The EPT tourist information office (☎ 0766-2 53 48) is at Viale Garibaldi 42 and is open Monday to Saturday from 8.30 am to 12.30 pm and 3.30 to 7 pm.

Places to Stay & Eat

There should be no need to spend the night in Civitavecchia. It is easily accessible from Rome and, to save time and money, it is better to catch a night ferry to Sardinia. If stuck, try the *Albergo Miramare* (☎ 0766-2 61 67), on the waterfront at Viale della Repubblica 6. Singles/doubles cost L35,000/50,000.

For a meal, head for one of the pizzerias along the waterfront, or try the *Trattoria da Vitale* at Viale Garibaldi 26. It is not overly expensive to eat on the ferry (full restaurant meals, as well as snacks, are available), but it is a good idea to bring supplies on board if you want to save money. There is a grocery shop near the station at Civitavecchia and a market every morning from Monday to Saturday in Via Doria.

Getting There & Away

Civitavecchia is on the main train line between Rome (1½ hours) and Genoa (2½ hours). By car it is easily reached from Rome on the A12 autostrada. If arriving from Sardinia with your car, simply follow the A12 signs from the Civitavecchia port to reach the autostrada for Rome.

Ferries to/from Sardinia Tirrenia operates ferries to Olbia (seven hours), Arbatax (nine hours) and Cagliari (12 hours). From late September to early June there is one ferry a day to each destination (in the evening), and during the summer months services are increased to two ferries a day to Arbatax and Cagliari, and three to Olbia (including a morning ferry). Departure times and prices change annually and it is best to check with a travel agent, or with Tirrenia directly, for up-to-date information. At the time of writing, a one-way fare to Olbia was L27,000 for an airline-type chair, L40,000 for a 2nd-class cabin and L110,000 for a small car. Tickets can be purchased at travel agents, including CIT, or at the Tirrenia offices in Rome (☎ 06-474 20 41), Via Bissolati 41, and at the Stazione Marittima in Civitavecchia.

The Ferrovie dello Stato also runs several ferries a day to Sardinia, docking at Golfo Aranci (about 20 km north of Olbia and accessible by bus or train). Tickets can be purchased at travel agents, including CIT, at Stazione Termini in Rome, or the Stazione Marittima in Civitavecchia.

VITERBO

Founded by the Etruscans and eventually taken over by Rome, Viterbo developed into an important medieval centre and in the 13th century became the residence of the popes. Papal elections were held in the town's Gothic Papal Palace and stories abound about the antics of impatient townspeople, anxious for a decision. In 1271, when the college of cardinals had failed to elect a new pope after three years of deliberation, the Viterbesi first locked them in a turreted hall of the Papal Palace and then removed its roof and put the cardinals on a starvation diet. Only then did the cardinals manage to elect Gregory X.

Although badly damaged by bombing during WW II, Viterbo remains Lazio's best preserved medieval town and it is a pleasant base for exploring northern Lazio. For travellers with less time, Viterbo is an easy day trip from Rome.

Apart from its historical appeal, Viterbo is famous for its therapeutic hot springs. The best known is the sulphurous Bulicame pool, mentioned by Dante in his *Divine Comedy*.

Orientation & Information

As with most historic centres in Italy, the town of Viterbo is neatly divided between newer and older sections. The bus and train stations, as well as hotels, are in the newer part of town, and you will cross the Piazza del Plebiscito and its 15th and 16th century palaces before reaching medieval Viterbo and the real reason for your visit.

Viterbo's EPT tourist office (☎ 0761-34 63 63) is in the newer part of town at Piazza dei Caduti 16, and is open Monday to Saturday from 8 am to 2 pm. From the train and bus stations, turn right into Viale Trieste and follow the city walls to the Porta Fiorentina and then walk along Via Giacomo Matteotti to Piazza Verdi. Turn right again into Via G Marconi to reach the EPT. There is another branch in Via San Lorenzo, just off Piazza della Morte, which is open the same hours.

The main post office is in Via F Ascenzi, just off Piazza del Plebiscito. The SIP telephone office can be found at Via Cavour 28, off the other side of the piazza.

Viterbo's postal code is 01100 and its telephone code is 0761.

Things to See & Do

Start your tour in the **Piazza del Plebiscito**, enclosed by 15th and 16th century palaces. The most imposing is the **Palazzo dei Priori**, with an elegant 17th century fountain in its courtyard. Many rooms are decorated with frescoes, notably the Sala Reggia, which is decorated with a late-Renaissance fresco depicting the myths and history of Viterbo. There is also the lovely *Pietà* by Sebastiano del Piombo. Note the Roman sarcophagus outside the Church of Sant'Angelo, said to have been the tomb of Galiana, a beautiful and virtuous woman murdered by a Roman baron after she refused his advances.

From the piazza, walk along Via San Lorenzo to reach medieval Viterbo. In Piazza San Lorenzo is the 12th century **San Lorenzo Cathedral**, rebuilt in the 14th century to a Gothic design, although the interior has just been restored to its original

---

■ PLACES TO STAY	
6	Hotel Milano
7	Hotel Roma
9	Hotel Tuscia

▼ PLACES TO EAT	
14	Il Richiastro
17	All'Archetto
28	Il Ciuffo

OTHER	
1	Intercity Bus Station
2	Train Station
3	Porta Fiorentina
4	Piazza San Francesco
5	Church of San Francesco
8	Piazza Verdi
10	EPT Tourist Office
11	Urban Bus Station
12	Main Post Office
13	Palazzo dei Priori
15	Piazza del Plebiscito
16	SIP Telephones
18	Papal Palace
19	San Lorenzo Cathedral
20	Piazza San Lorenzo
21	Palazzo Farnese
22	Church of Santa Maria Nuova
23	EPT Tourist Office
24	Piazza della Morte
25	Fontana Grande
26	Porta Romana
27	Piazza San Pelligrino

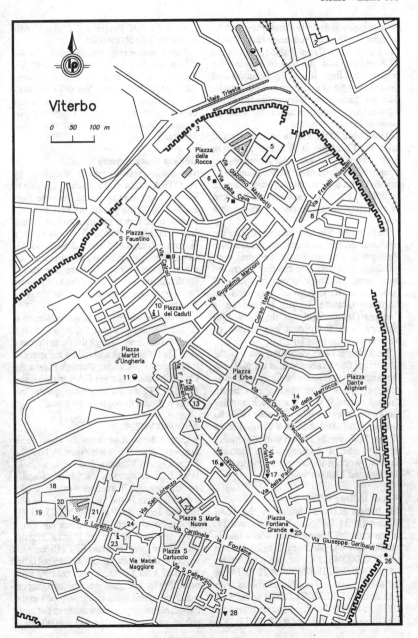

Viterbo

0   50   100 m

Via Trieste

Piazza della Rocca

Piazza S Faustino

Piazza dei Caduti

Piazza Martiri d'Ungheria

Piazza d'Erbe

Piazza Dante Alighieri

Piazza S Maria Nuova

Piazza Fontana Grande

Piazza S Carluccio

Via Giacomo Matteotti

Via della Cava

Via Caroli

Via Guglielmo Marconi

Corso Italia

Via F. Ascenzi

Via dell'Orologio Vecchio

Via della Marrocca

Via S Cristoforo

Via della Pace

Via Fratelli Rosselli

Via Cavour

Via San Lorenzo

Via S Lorenzo

Via Cardinale la Fontaine

Via Macel Maggiore

Via S Pellegrino

Via Giuseppe Garibaldi

Romanesque simplicity (they may still be working on it when you read this). Also in the piazza is the **Papal Palace**, built in the 13th century with the aim of enticing the popes away from Rome. Its beautiful and graceful loggia is in the early Gothic style. The part facing the valley collapsed in the 14th century and you can see the bases of some of the columns.

Head back to the Piazza della Morte and take Via Cardinale la Fontaine to Piazza Santa Maria Nuova. The Romanesque church of the same name was restored to its original form after sustaining bomb damage in WW II. The cloisters, which are believed to date from an earlier period, are worth a visit.

Head down Via San Pellegrino into the medieval quarter to reach the **Piazza San Pellegrino**. The extremely well-preserved buildings which enclose this tiny piazza are considered the finest group of medieval buildings in Italy. Also of interest is the **Fontana Grande**, in the Piazza della Fontana Grande. Built in the early 13th century, it is the oldest and largest of Viterbo's Gothic fountains.

Back at the entrance to the town is the **Church of San Francesco**, in the piazza of the same name, a Gothic building which was restored after suffering serious bomb damage during WW II. The church contains the tombs of two popes: Clement IV (who died in 1268) and Adrian V (who died in 1276). Both tombs are lavishly decorated, notably that of Adrian, which features Cosmati work, a mosaic technique used in the 12th and 13th centuries.

Places to Stay & Eat

For budget accommodation try the *Hotel Milano* (☎ 34 07 05), Via della Cava 54, which runs off Piazza della Rocca and is parallel to Via G Matteotti. Singles/doubles are L30,000/45,000, or with bathroom L45,000/65,000. The *Roma* (☎ 22 72 74), in the same street at No 26, has rooms with bathroom for L50,000/71,000, or without for L33,000/49,000. For three-star accommodation there is the *Tuscia* (☎ 22 33 77), Via

Cairoli 41 (off Piazza dei Caduti), with rooms for L60,000/90,000.

For a reasonably priced meal, try *All'Archetto*, Via San Cristoforo, off Via Cavour. A full meal will cost around L20,000. *Il Richiastro*, Via della Marocca 18, is slightly more expensive and has outside tables in summer. *Il Ciuffo* is a pizzeria in Piazza Capella, just off Piazza San Pellegrino.

Getting There & Away

The easiest way to get to Viterbo is by ACOTRAL bus from Rome. There are several a day, leaving Rome from the Saxa Rubra stop on the private rail line, Ferrovia Roma-Nord. Catch the train to Saxa Ruba from Piazzale Flaminio. You can catch a Ferrovia Roma-Nord train directly to Viterbo, although it is slower than the bus. See the earlier Orientation & Information section for details on how to get to the town centre from both the train and bus stations in Viterbo.

By car, the easiest way to get to Viterbo is on the Cassia-bis (about 1½ hours' drive). Enter the old town through the Porta Romana onto Via G Garibaldi and follow the street as it becomes Via Cavour, through Piazza del Plebiscito, and on to Via F Ascenzi to reach the EPT. There are numerous public car parks scattered throughout the town.

AROUND VITERBO

Viterbo's **thermal springs** are about three km out of town. They were used by both the Etruscans and Romans, and the latter built large bath complexes, of which virtually nothing remains. Travellers wanting to take a cure or relax in the hot sulphur baths will find the Terme dei Papi (☎ 0761-25 00 93) the easiest to reach. Take urban bus No 2 from the bus station in Piazza Martiri d'Ungheria, near the main EPT office.

At Bagnaia, a few km out of Viterbo, is the beautiful **Villa Lante**, a 16th century villa noted for its fine gardens. The two, superficially identical, palaces are not open to the public, although you can wander in the large public park for free, or pay L4000 for a guided tour of the gardens. They are open from 9 am to 7.30 pm in summer, and to 4 pm in winter. Guided tours leave every half hour. Unfortunately, picnics are not permitted in the park. From Viterbo, take urban bus No 6 from Piazza Martiri d'Ungheria.

The **Parco dei Mostri** at Bomarzo will be particularly interesting for people with young children. The 16th century palace (Palazzo Orsini) and park, created for the Orsini family, is scattered with gigantic and grotesque sculptures including an ogre, a giant and a dragon. Also of interest are the octagonal *tempietto* (little temple) and the crooked house, built without use of right angles. The park is open from 8.30 am to 7 pm in summer, and until 4 pm in winter. Entrance is L8000. To get there from Viterbo, catch the ACOTRAL bus (from the stop near Viale Trento) to Bomarzo, then follow the signs to Palazzo Orsini.

Another interesting detour from Viterbo is the tiny, hill-top medieval town of **Civita di Bagnoregio**, near its newer, basically Renaissance counterpart, Bagnoregio. In a picturesque area of tufa ravines, Civita is known as the 'dying town' because continuous erosion of its hill has caused the collapse of many of its buildings. Eventually abandoned by its residents, who moved to Bagnoregio, most of the town's buildings were purchased by foreigners and artisans, and, in recent years, Civita has been restored and has developed into a minor tourist attraction. Regular ACOTRAL buses connect Bagnoregio with Viterbo. From the bus stop, ask for directions to Civita, which has been recently connected to Bagnoregio's outskirts by a pedestrian bridge.

THE LAKES

There are three large lakes north of Rome – extremely popular recreational spots in summer for hot Romans. The shores of the lakes never seem to get as crowded as Lazio's beaches, and their hilly, leafy environment makes them more attractive swimming destinations. **Lake Bracciano** is the closest to Rome and easily accessible by ACOTRAL buses, which depart roughly every half hour from outside the Lepanto Metro stop, arriving in Piazza Roma in the centre of the town of Bracciano. Walk to nearby Piazza Dante to catch one of the regular buses to the lake. For picnic supplies there is an alimentari in Piazza Roma, or you can dine by the lake at *Da Alfredo*.

Closer to Viterbo is **Lake Vico**, a nature reserve with various recreational facilities, including canoeing. There is a camping ground, *Natura* (☎ 0761-64 70 27), at the lakeside about four km from the town of Caprarola. It is open from June to December and bookings are essential in summer. The town is accessible by train from Rome's Trastevere station. Catch the Viterbo train and change at Capranica-Sutri. Otherwise catch an ACOTRAL bus from Viterbo to Caprarola.

Lake Bolsena is too far from Rome to warrant a day trip for swimming; however, it is close to Viterbo, from where you can catch one of the regular ACOTRAL buses to the town of Bolsena. There are several camping grounds around the lake, including *La Pineta* (☎ 0761-79 90 81), Via A Diaz 48, open April to October, and *Il Lago* (☎ 0761-79 91 91), Viale Cadorna 6 and open March to September.

Northern Italy

Italy's northern regions are its wealthiest and offer many and varied attractions to travellers. A tour of the north could take you from the beaches of the Italian Riviera in Liguria, to Milan for a shopping spree, through countless medieval and Renaissance towns and villages, and into the Alps to ski or trek in the Dolomites, before taking a boat trip down the Grand Canal of timeless Venice.

Liguria

The coastline of Liguria was inhabited by Neanderthals about a million years ago, and many of their remains have been unearthed in the area. The locals claim that the prehistoric humans were attracted to the beautiful beaches. And indeed, stretching from La Spezia in the east to the French border in the west, this narrow coastal region, encompassing the once great maritime power of Genoa, offers a feast for the traveller – from magnificent beaches to skiing, mountain climbing and skin diving.

The overdeveloped Riviera di Ponente, west of Genoa towards the French border, has some of the most expensive holiday resorts in Europe. East of Genoa, the Riviera di Levante offers beautiful untouched villages set in mountain terrain.

Liguria has been ruled by the Greeks, Saracens, Romans, Venetians, Lombards and the French, and strong influences from Sicily, Northern Africa and Spain, through early trade, are evident.

The regional cuisine features the products of the warm Mediterranean climate – fresh herbs, the sweet, extra virgin olive oil and plenty of seafood. Among its more famous creations are pesto, focaccia and farinata. The Cinque Terre is a famous wine-producing area and a visit there is not complete without trying the delicious but rare dessert wine, Sciacchetrà. The Riviera di Ponente is also well known as a wine-producing area.

GENOA (GENOVA)

Travellers who think of Genoa as simply a dirty port town and bypass it for the coastal resorts don't know what they're missing. This once powerful maritime republic, birthplace of Christopher Columbus (1451-1506) and now the capital of Liguria, can still carry the title *La Superba*, The Proud. It is a fascinating city, full of contrasts. Here you can meet crusty old seafarers in the markets and trattorie of the port area, where some of the tiny streets are so narrow it is difficult for two people to stand together. But, go round a corner and you will find young Genoese in the latest Benetton gear strolling through streets lined with grand, black-and-white marble palaces.

History

Genoa was founded in the 4th century BC, but the origins of its name are in dispute – one theory is that it derives from the Latin *janua*, meaning door. An important Roman port town, it later became a maritime power in its own right, although it was often subject to the domination of other powers. It was occupied by the French in 774, the Saracens in the 10th century and even by the Milanese in 1353. Genoa's greatest victory, against Venice in 1298, led to a period of rapid political and economic growth, but quarrels between the city's noble families – the Grimaldis, the Dorias and the Spinolas – caused much internal disruption.

Genoa reached its peak in the 16th century under the leadership of Andrea Doria and, in this period, helped to finance Spanish exploration of the New World. This golden period, which extended into the 17th century, produced innumerable magnificent palaces and great works of art. The artistic activity attracted many well-known artists to the city, among them Rubens, Caravaggio and Van

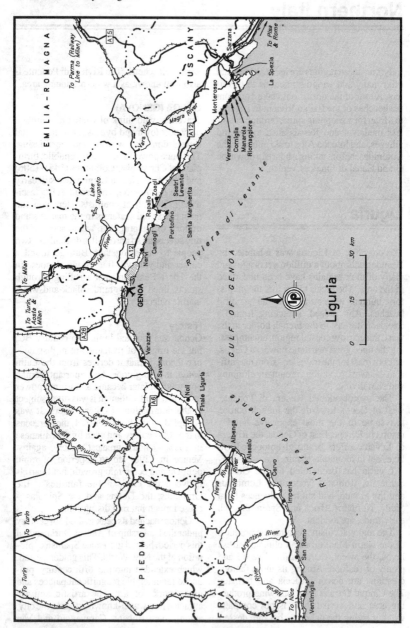

Dyck. Galeazzo Alessi (1512-72), who designed many of the city's splendid palaces, is now considered an equal of Palladio. The city was an active revolutionary centre for propaganda during the Renaissance, a tradition that carried through to WW II when, as a well-organised partisan centre, it was the first north Italian town to rise against the combined might of Nazis and Fascists, obtaining liberation before the arrival of the Allied troops.

Genoa's historical centre is regarded as one of the best preserved in Europe. The city expanded as the pressures of industry grew, and the villages of Voltri and Nervi have been drawn into its environs. In 1992 the city celebrated the 500th anniversary of the voyage of discovery of its most famous citizen, Christopher Columbus. Vast sums of money were spent restoring much of the decaying waterfront area and the city, a project which came under intense criticism after the usual budget blow-out. A huge flood in the autumn of 1992 left two people dead and destroyed sections of the town.

Orientation

Genoa stretches along the Ligurian coast for more than 27 km and is served by 15 train stations. Trains from La Spezia and Rome generally stop at Stazione Brignole, and from Savona and France at Stazione Principe, the two main train stations. Trains from Bologna and Milan usually stop at both. The city centre lies between the two stations and extends to the waterfront. The area around Brignole offers more pleasant accommodation and is considered safer than Principe, which is close to the port.

Directly in front of Brignole station is Piazza Verdi, a square and garden leading to one of the city's grandest monuments, the Piazza della Vittoria. As you exit Brignole, Via Brigate Bisogno is to the left, marked by three modern glass towers. This major business thoroughfare leads to the waterfront and away from the city centre. From Brignole, walk directly ahead along Via Fiume to Via XX Settembre (Genoa's main thoroughfare for the evening stroll, or *passeggiata*), and

follow the road to Via Roma, the tourist office and the historical centre.

From Principe, head for Via Balbi, directly in front of the station, which leads into Piazza della Nunziata and then Via Garibaldi. Most banks are based around here and farther along towards Via Roma and the Piazza de Ferrari, which is at the head of Via XX Settembre. Just south of the station are Via Prè (notorious home to Genoa's low life) and the ports.

Information

Tourist Offices Genoa's main APT office (☎ 010-54 15 41) is on the 2nd floor at Via Roma 11 and is open Monday to Friday from 8 am to 1.30 pm and 2 to 5 pm, Saturday to 1.30 pm. There are branch offices at the train stations and the airport, which are open Monday to Saturday from 8 am to 8 pm, and smaller offices in Nervi and Arenzano, which have irregular opening hours.

The APT produces a booklet of walking tours through the centre, taking in significant churches and palaces, entitled *Genoa, The Old City*.

Money Most banks will give cash advances and change travellers' cheques. Opposite Stazione Brignole, the Cassa di Risparmio Genova e Imperia is open Monday to Friday from 8.20 am to 1.20 pm and 2.30 to 4 pm. Near the Piazza de Ferrari, the Credito Italiano has similar opening hours and is open until 6 pm Wednesdays. American Express operates through an agent, Viatur (☎ 010-56 12 41), Piazza Fontane Marose 3, and offers limited services.

Post & Telecommunications The main post office is in Via Dante, just off the Piazza de Ferrari. It opens from 8.15 am to 7.40 pm Monday to Saturday. Genoa's postal code is 16100.

The most convenient public telephone office is the ASST at the main post office. Other offices are at Stazione Brignole and at Via XX Settembre 139. All are open from 8 am to midnight daily (the Brignole office is

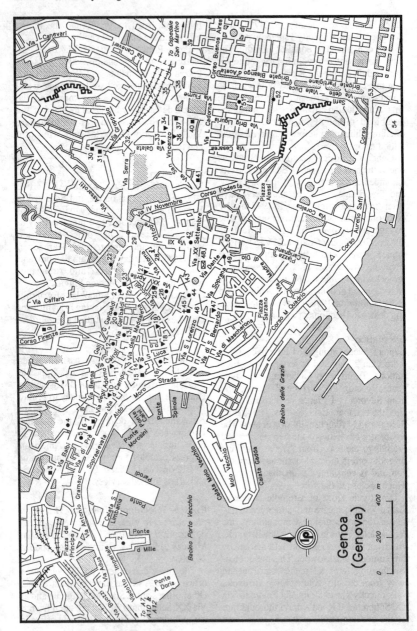

Genoa (Genova)

■ PLACES TO STAY

3	Pensione Balbi
6	Albergo Parigi
7	Albergo Armonia
9	Hostel Genova
15	Albergo Riviera Ligure
23	Hotel Metropoli
25	Minerva Italia
30	Albergo Rita
31	Pensione Valle, Pensione Mirella & Pensione Carola
37	Pensione Nido
39	Albergo Vittoria
40	Albergo Fiume
41	Hotel Bel Soggiorno

▼ PLACES TO EAT

10	Trattoria Rita
11	Ristorante San Siro
14	Trattoria Walter
18	Osteria d'Agostino Vincenzo
19	Imperial
27	Trattoria da Maria
33	Raggio Alfredo
34	Al Rustichello
36	Trattoria da Guglie
47	Trattoria Casalinga

OTHER

1	Stazione Principe
2	Stazione Marittima
4	University
5	Palazzo Reale
8	Piazza della Nunziata
12	Palazzo Bianco
13	Palazzo Rosso
16	Piazza Caricamento
17	Palazzo Spinola
20	Palazzo Doria Tursi
21	Viatur (American Express)
22	Oriental Art Museum
24	Piazza Fontane Marose
26	Opera House
28	APT Tourist Information Office
29	Piazza Corvetto
32	Piazza Brignole
35	Stazione Brignole
38	Piazza G Verdi
42	ASST Telephones
43	Piazza de Ferrari
44	Palazzo Ducale
45	Cathedral of San Lorenzo
46	Piazza Matteotti
48	Main Post Office
49	House of Columbus
50	Piazza Dante
51	Piazza della Vittoria
52	Police Headquarters
53	Piazzale Kennedy
54	Palazzo della Sport

closed Sunday). Genoa's telephone code is 010.

Foreign Consulates The British Consulate (☎ 56 48 33) is at Via XII Ottobre 2. The US Consulate (☎ 28 27 41) is at Piazza Portello 6.

Travel Agencies CTS (☎ 56 43 66) is at Via San Vincenzo 117. CIT (☎ 29 19 51) has an office at Via XXV Aprile 16.

Bookshops Bozzi, Via Cairoli 2, has a good selection of English-language books.

Gay & Lesbian Information Arci Gay (☎ 28 14 30), Via San Luca, is the city's hotline and provides a variety of information.

Emergency The police headquarters are at Via Diaz (☎ 5 36 61), or for immediate attendance, call ☎ 113. For an ambulance, call ☎ 5 70 59 51. The hospital, the Ospedale San Martino (☎ 51 67 48), is at Via Benedetto XV. The Guardia Medica Regione Liguria (☎ 35 40 22) operates an after-hours, home-visit medical service from 8 pm to 8 am. For information about all-night pharmacies, call ☎ 192.

Dangers & Annoyances The area around the port and Stazione Principe is considered very dangerous, particularly at night. Although the ugly reputation of the area around the waterfront and Via Prè tends to be exaggerated, it is seedy and single women are advised to avoid the area at night. It's quite interesting, though, and a daytime visit is a must.

Things to See & Do

Museums & Galleries Start with Genoa's two most important and well-known galleries, housed in the historic palaces, the Palazzo Rosso and Palazzo Bianco, opposite each other on Via Garibaldi. The **Galleria di Palazzo Rosso** is open Tuesday to Saturday from 9 am to 7 pm (although it's likely to close around the middle of the day for a short period), and Sunday morning, and entrance costs L4000. It features works from the Venetian and Genoese schools and several canvasses by Van Dyck. The **Galleria di Palazzo Bianco** has the same hours and entry fee, and features works by Flemish, Spanish and Dutch masters, displaying Genoa's international cultural links.

Close by is the **Galleria Nazionale di Palazzo Spinola**, Piazza Superiore di Pellicceria 1, in a 16th century mansion housing Italian and Flemish Renaissance works. It is open Tuesday to Saturday from 9 am to 5 pm, Sunday and Monday to 1 pm. Entrance is L4000. The **Galleria di Palazzo Reale**, Via Balbi 10, also features Renaissance works. It is open daily from 9 am to 1.30 pm and entrance is L4000.

The **Oriental Art Museum**, Villetta Dinegro, is set in gardens with city views and has one of the largest collections of Oriental art in Europe. It is open Tuesday to Saturday from 9 am to 5 pm, Sunday to 12.30 pm. Entrance is L4000. The city also boasts a **Modern Art Museum** at Nervi, and a museum of pre-Columbian art, the **Museo Americanistico F Lunardi**, in the Villa Gruber on Corso Solferino.

Churches The **Cathedral of San Lorenzo**, Piazza San Lorenzo, was built between the 12th and 16th centuries and features a magnificent black-and-white marble Gothic façade in the typical Genoese style. Inside is the **Cappella della Battista**, which once housed the bones of St John the Baptist in the sarcophagus. There is also a museum housing the famous *Sacro Catino*, a cup

given to Solomon by the Queen of Sheba, said to have been used by Jesus at the Last Supper. Other relics include the polished quartz platter upon which Salome is said to have received John the Baptist's head. It's open Tuesday to Saturday from 9.30 to 11.45 am and 3 to 5.45 pm.

The **Santissima Annunziata del Vestato**, Piazza della Nunziata, is a rich example of 17th century Genoese architecture and is still being restored after the church was virtually destroyed in WW II bombing raids. The trompe l'oeil in the dome features remarkable use of perspective. The **Church of San Siro**, Via San Siro, which was also badly damaged in WW II, dates back to the 4th century, but was rebuilt in the 16th century.

The **Church of San Donato**, Via San Bernardo, was built in the 11th century in pure Romanesque style, but was enlarged in the 12th and 13th centuries. The church of the Doria family, **San Matteo**, in Piazza Matteotti, was founded in 1125. Andrea Doria's sword is preserved under the altar and his tomb is in the crypt.

Monuments & Villas Alessi's famous **Via Garibaldi** is lined with splendid palaces now mainly used by banks and other financial institutions. Wander in if the gates are open. At No 9, the **Palazzo Doria Tursi**, Genoa's town hall since 1848, was built in 1564. Apart from the city council, it houses the relics of two famous Genoese – fragments of the skeleton of Christopher Columbus, and one of the violins of another favourite son, Niccolò Paganini, which is used occasionally at concerts. The **Palazzo Podestà**, Via Garibaldi 7, has magnificent frescoes in the courtyard.

On the west side of Piazza Dante is the **House of Columbus**, in which the explorer was born. The original house was destroyed in a French naval bombardment in 1684 and was partly rebuilt in the 18th century. Close to the house, at Via Porta Soprana, are two towers and a gateway known as the **Porta Soprana**. One tower originally housed a guillotine.

Christopher Columbus

Just beyond the gate and along Via di Porta Soprana is Piazza Matteotti and the **Palazzo Ducale**. Once the residence of the city's rulers, it is now occupied by the law courts.

Places to Stay – bottom end

Camping There are camping grounds on the outskirts of the city, all easily accessible by bus from Stazione Brignole. *Villa Doria* (☎ 68 06 13), Via Vespucci 25, on the way to Pegli, is open all year and can be reached on bus No 1, 2 or 3. Farther on is the *Caravan Park La Vesima* (☎ 63 57 72), Via Aurelia. Catch bus No 95 from Pegli.

Hostels & Hotels The new IYHF *Hostel Genova* (☎ 58 64 07), Via Costanzi, at Righi, is just north of Genoa's old centre. Bed and breakfast is L18,000 and a meal L12,000. Catch bus No 40 from Stazione Brignole, which stops almost outside the hostel's door. It is closed from 16 December to 14 January. The *Casa della Giovane* (☎ 20 66 32), Piazza Santa Sabina 4, off Piazza Nunziata, a short walk east of Stazione Principe, has beds for women at only L10,000 a night.

Hotels and pensioni near Stazione Brignole include a group in a lovely old building at Via Groppallo 4. Turn right as you leave Stazione Brignole and walk up to Piazza Brignole. To your right is Via Groppallo. The *Pensione Valle* (☎ 88 22 57) with singles/doubles for L30,000/35,000, while at the *Pensione Mirella* (☎ 89 37 22) you will pay L30,000/ 45,000, plus an extra L2000 for a shower. The *Pensione Carola* (☎ 89 13 40) has rooms for L30,000/46,000. Next door at No 8 is the *Albergo Rita* (☎ 87 02 07) with rooms from L22,000/35,000.

Turn left from the station and you come across *Albergo Vittoria* (☎ 58 15 17), Largo Archimede 1. Situated on the top floor, the rooms are large, have character and a view. They cost L20,000 per person and most rooms sleep three people. There are several pensioni across from the station, along Via Fiume. *Pensione Nido* (☎ 54 21 16) at No 4-6 has singles/doubles for L37,000/47,000. A few doors up, *Albergo Fiume* (☎ 59 16 91) has rooms for L35,000/65,000; single rooms with a shower are L55,000, breakfast costs L3000 and it's one of the few budget hotels to accept credit cards.

Near Stazione Principe is *Pensione Balbi* (☎ 28 09 12), Via Balbi 21, with singles/doubles for L24,000/38,000, or L43,000 for a double with a bathroom. Near the port is the *Albergo Riviera Ligure* (☎ 20 19 96), Via Colalanza 2, off Via Santa Luca near Piazza Caricamento. Singles/doubles are L15,000/30,000.

If you want to mix it with prostitutes, sailors and so forth, head for Via Prè. *Albergo Parigi* (☎ 25 21 72), Via Prè 72, has doubles for L40,000 and is very secure. *Albergo Armonia* (☎ 20 76 60), at No 46, has singles/doubles for L40,000/60,000 and all rooms have a bathroom.

Places to Stay – middle

If you want to spend a little more, you cannot go past *Hotel Bel Soggiorno* (☎ 58 14 18) on Genoa's gracious main street, Via XX Settembre 19. Singles/doubles are L48,000/ 65,000 with bathroom. The *Minerva Italia* (☎ 20 09 41), Via XXV Aprile 14, has rooms from L50,000/70,000. *Albergo Rio* (☎ 29 05 51), Via Ponte Calvi 5, charges L74,000/108,000. The *Firenze e Zurigo* (☎ 25 69 87), Via Gramsci 199r, near Via Prè has rooms for L86,000/110,000.

Places to Stay – top end

The *Hotel Metropoli* (☎ 28 41 41) in Piazza delle Fontane Marose has rooms from L125,000/150,000, including breakfast. The hotel offers generous weekend packages.

Places to Eat

Don't leave town without trying pesto genovese (pasta with a sauce of basil, garlic, parmesan cheese and pine nuts), *torta pasqualina* (made with artichokes and eggs), *pansoti* (spinach ravioli with a thick, creamy hazelnut sauce) and, of course, focaccia.

Two of the best deals in town are at *Trattoria Da Maria*, Vico Testa d'Oro 14, where a meal costs L11,000, including wine, and *Trattoria Casalinga*, Vico San Pollaiuoli 7, which has two set-price menus for vegetarians for L10000 and L15000. *Ristorante San Siro*, Via Cairoli 22, specialises in seafood and offers a set-price lunch for L15,000. If you want really cheap food, head for *Osteria d'Agostino Vincenzo*, Vico dietro il Coro delle Vigne 15r, where lunch could cost L5000. At *Trattoria Rita*, Via del Campo 33, just near Via Prè, the farinata is good and cheap.

Carlo Brusaca, the owner of *Trattoria Walter*, at Vico Colalanza 2r, concentrates on Genoese specialities. Pasta starts at L5000. For a cheap pizza, *Trattoria Da Guglie*, at Via San Vincenzo 64r near Stazione Brignole, is a pleasant, family-run restaurant with pizzas from L6000. *Al Rustichello*, opposite Da Guglie at Via San Vincenzo 59r, is one of the few restaurants open on Sunday. Pizzas start at L5000.

An excellent restaurant is *Raggio Alfredo*, Via Galata 35, which specialises in local fare and has a takeaway service. A meal will cost around L20,000 to L25,000. The *Imperial*, Piazza Campetto, in the former Palazzo di Gio Vincenzo Imperiale, features magnificent frescoes and stucco. Prices start at L7000 for pasta and L15,000 for main courses.

One of Genoa's more famous restaurants is *Zeffirino*, Via XX Settembre 20. A meal here will cost more than L50,000 a head.

Mangini & C, on Via Roma at Piazza Corvetto, is renowned as Genoa's finest bar and pasticceria. *A Ved Romanengo Fabbrica*, Via Orefici 31, has been serving scrumptious pastries since 1805.

Entertainment

Theatre is performed by the acclaimed Genoa Theatre Company throughout the year at the Teatro Genovese (☎ 89 35 89), Via Piaggio, and at the Teatro della Corte (☎ 570 24 72), Corte Lambruschini. The main season is from January to May.

Posters around the city advertise concerts at the Teatro Margherita (☎ 58 93 29), Via XX Settembre. The city's opera house, Teatro Carlo Felice (☎ 5 38 11), Piazza de Ferrari, opened in 1991 on the site of the original opera house, which was heavily bombed in WW II, and has year-round programmes.

The city has three cinema clubs which show films in their original language (usually in English) on selected nights. They are: Cineclub Chaplin (☎ 88 00 69), Piazza Cappuccini 1; Fritz Lang (☎ 21 97 68), Via Acquarone 64; and Cineclub Lumière (☎ 50 59 36), Via Vitale 1. They cost L4000 to join and then about L4000 to see a film.

A nightclub that's popular with heterosexuals as well as gays is Company, Via Smirne 2r.

Getting There & Away

Air Cristoforo Colombo International Airport at Sestri Ponente, six km west of the city, serves regular domestic and international flights to Rome, Venice, southern Italy, Paris, Amsterdam, London and other major European centres as well as New York. For flight information, ring ☎ 5 49 38.

Train Genoa is directly connected by train to Turin, Milan, Pisa and Rome, making it reasonably accessible to all other major Italian cities. Phone ☎ 28 40 81 for train information.

Car & Motorbike The A12 autostrada connects Genoa with Livorno in Tuscany and with the A11 for Florence. The A7 goes to Milan, the A26 to Turin and the A10 to Savona and the French border. From the A7, take the exit marked 'Genova', which will take you into the centre. Hitchers should ask at Brignole for bus routes to desired autostrada on/off ramps, or at the APT for main road maps.

Boat The city's busy port is a major embarkation point for ferries to Sicily, Sardinia, Corsica and Tunisia. Major companies are:

Corsica Ferries, Piazza Dante 5 (☎ 59 33 01)
    for Corsica and Sardinia
Tirrenia, Ponte Colombo (☎ 25 80 41)
    for Sicily and Sardinia
Grandi Traghetti, Via Fieschi 17 (☎ 58 93 31)
    for Sardinia

See also the Getting There & Away sections for Sicily and Sardinia.

It is possible to catch a ferry to towns along the Riviera di Levante, including Camogli, Portofino, the Cinque Terre, Santa Margherita and San Fruttuoso. Cooperativa Battellieri del Porto di Genoa (☎ 26 57 12) ferries leave from Ponte dei Mille, near the Stazione Marittima, several times a day and cost up to L15,000 return. The company also operates trips around the port.

Getting Around
To/From the Airport An airport bus service, the Volabus (☎ 24 11), leaves from Piazza della Vittoria, outside Stazione Brignole, and stops at Principe usually an hour before flight departures.

Bus AMT buses (☎ 5 99 71), Via d'Annuncio 8, operate services throughout the city. Most pass through Piazza Acquaverde, outside Stazione Principe. Several buses link the stations, including Nos 33 and 37.

Car & Taxi It is easier to walk around the old city as most traffic is banned from the centre. Car parks are well signed, but it is probably a good idea to park at your hotel and forget the car for the duration of your stay. For a taxi, call ☎ 26 96.

AROUND GENOA
On Genoa's eastern edge, **Nervi** was absorbed into the city as the metropolis grew. Renowned for its outdoor International Ballet Festival at the Teatro ai Parchi in July, and an outdoor cinema in the rose garden (Cinema nel Roseto) at the same venue in August, Nervi is by no means overshadowed and retains much of its own identity. Also there is the Galleria d'Arte Moderna, Via Capolungo, in the Villa Serra. The place is worth a visit. Contact the APTs in Genoa or Nervi for information.

Hidden behind the industrial wasteland of Genoa's west is **Pegli**, another victim to the city's growth. Popular with the British, Pegli is in a sheltered harbour and offers magnificent views of the city and coastline. The Museo Navale is in the Villa Doria at Piazza Bonavino. The Museo Archeologico, Via Pallavicini, in the Villa Pallavicini, has a comprehensive collection of Ligurian archaeology. The Villa itself is set in a magnificent park modelled on the Genoese gardens of the Renaissance.

RIVIERA DI LEVANTE
This area, stretching from Genoa to La Spezia on the border with Tuscany, has a spectacular coastline to rival that of Amalfi. It has several resorts, such as Santa Margherita, Camogli and the enchanting Cinque Terre, which, despite attracting thousands of summer tourists, manage to remain unspoiled.

La Spezia
La Spezia sits at the head of the gulf that bears its name, a body of water more commonly known as the Gulf of Poets – a celebration of Byron, Dante, D H Lawrence, Shelley, George Sand and others who were drawn by its beauty. Today it is home to the

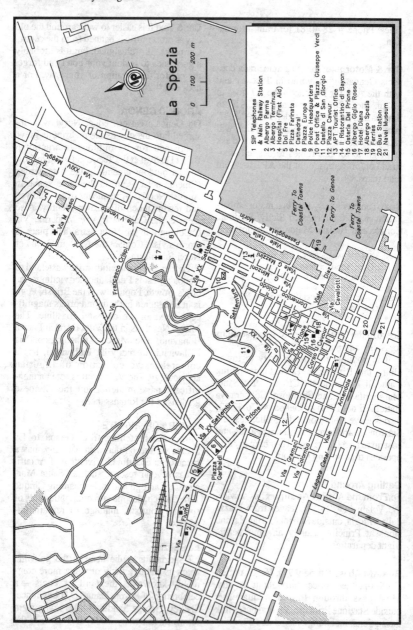

La Spezia

0   100   200 m

1   SIP Telephones
    & Main Railway Station
2   Albergo Parma
3   Albergo Terminus
4   Hospital (First Aid)
5   Poi Fre
6   Pizza Farinata
7   Cathedral
8   Piazza Europa
9   Police Headquarters
10 Post Office & Piazza Giuseppe Verdi
11 Castello di San Giorgio
12 Piazza Cavour
13 APT Tourist Office
14 Ristorantino di Bayon
15 Osteria Del Prione
16 Albergo Giglio Rosso
17 Hotel Diana
18 Albergo Spezia
19 Ferries
20 Bus Station
21 Naval Museum

Ferry To Coastal Towns

Ferry To Genoa

Ferry To Coastal Towns

country's largest naval base, and sits on the Riviera di Levante, regarded as one of Italy's most beautiful stretches of coastline. It also makes a good base for further travel.

Orientation & Information The city is sandwiched between the naval base to the west and the commercial port to the east. The main street, along which locals parade in the evenings, is Via Prione, running through the centre of town from the main train station to palm-lined Viale Italia along the waterfront.

The APT (☎ 0187-3 60 00), on the 1st floor at Viale G Mazzini 47, near the waterfront, is open Monday to Saturday from 7.30 am to 1 pm and 3.30 to 6.30 pm (closed afternoons on Wednesday and Saturday).

The post office is in Piazza G Verdi and is open Monday to Friday from 8.15 am to 7.40 pm. La Spezia's postal code is 19100. An SIP public telephone office is at the train station and is open 24 hours a day. The telephone code for La Spezia is 0187.

For emergency police attendance, call ☎ 113. The police headquarters (☎ 3 61 30) are at Via XX Settembre 4. For medical attention, call ☎ 53 32 27 or, at night, ☎ 51 15 11.

Things to See The city's **Naval Museum**, Piazza Domenica Chiodo, is open Monday to Saturday from 9 am to midday and 2 to 6 pm. It was founded in 1870, following the transfer of the Genoese maritime museum to La Spezia. The adjoining naval base is open to the public on one day a year, 19 March, the festival of the town's patron saint, San Giuseppe.

La Spezia is home to the **National Transport Museum**, north-east of the city centre at Via del Canaletto 100, housing an anthology of the country's transport history.

Activities La Spezia is a centre for several walking clubs which offer information on medium to long walks around the coast and into the mountains. Natura Trekking and Università Verde, both sharing the same phone number (☎ 3 83 11) and office at Via

Paleocapa 19, provide maps and information, as does the APT.

The province, which takes in Calice, Luni and Varese Liguria, has more than a dozen horse-riding clubs and many tracks. For information contact the APT or the Associazione Nazionale Turismo Equestre in Provincia della Spezia (☎ 93 55 87).

Scuba diving is also popular in the area. The Federazione Italiana Pesca Sportiva (☎ 51 10 26), Via V Veneto 173, can advise you on locations and direct you to hire places. La Spezia SUB Centro Immersioni Dyria Sub (☎ 2 74 41), Piazza San Bon 15, is one of several clubs in town. The APT produces a rough map showing diving locations.

Places to Stay La Spezia is an oasis of reasonably priced accommodation in a sea of expensive tourist resort towns. Its proximity to the Cinque Terre, Portovenere, Lerici and beyond makes it a perfect base for travel. There is no camping ground in La Spezia, but plenty in the surrounding towns.

Albergo Giglio Rosso (☎ 3 13 74), Via Carpenino 31, has singles/doubles for L18,000/23,000. The *Albergo Spezia* (☎ 3 51 64), Via Felice Cavallotti 31, is one street from the waterfront and has only large doubles from L34,000. Opposite the train station, *Albergo Terminus* (☎ 3 72 04), Via Paleocapa 21, has singles/doubles from L25,000/38,000. *Albergo Parma* (☎ 743 01 00), Via Fiume 143, has rooms from L35,000/54,000. *Hotel Diana* (☎ 2 51 20), Via Colombo 30, is near the naval base and has only doubles from L50,000.

Places to Eat Most restaurants and cafés are along Via Prione, with a few decent bars and gelaterie dotted along the waterfront. *Pizza Farinata*, Piazza Garibaldi 27, is a good place for lunch, selling pizza by the slice for about L1500. It is open until 9.30 pm. *Osteria Con Cucina 'Del Prione'*, Via Prione 270, has good pizzas from L5000. *Doi Fre*, Via Fiume 6, has pasta from L7000. The *Il Ristorantino di Bayon*, Via Felice Cavallotti

23, has a set menu including wine for L20,000.

Getting There & Away La Spezia is on the Rome-Genoa rail line, which follows the coast, and is also connected to Milan, Turin and other northern cities. The Cinque Terre and other coastal towns are easily reached by train, but other towns, such as Portovenere, Sarzana and Lerici, are best reached by ATC buses (☎ 52 25 22) which leave from outside the train station or the post office at 10-minute intervals.

La Spezia is on the A12 autostrada, and the A15 connects the city with the main north-south route, the A1. Hitchhikers can catch the Lerici bus along Viale San Bartolomeo and get off at Via Valdilocchi in the ports area, a main access to the A12 and A15.

Ferries leave La Spezia for coastal towns and Genoa during the summer months. Navigazione Golfo dei Poeti (☎ 96 76 76) at Imbarcadero Lato Sud, Gruppo Battellieri (☎ 28 06 66) at Banchina Revel, and In Tur (☎ 3 03 87) at Viale Mazzini all offer services. Some services between Genoa, Lerici and Portovenere operate all year.

Lerici

At the southern end of the Riviera, 10 km from La Spezia, Lerici is an exclusive summer refuge for wealthy Italians. It is a town of villas with manicured gardens set into the surrounding hills, with equally well-kept bathing boxes built into the cliffs along the beach. Make your way up to the 12th century **Lerici Castle** overlooking the town and take in the superb view from its roof.

If you plan to stay in the area, jump off the bus at **San Terenzo**, a much more pleasant little village where accommodation and food are both cheaper. Lerici is only a 10-minute walk away. It was from San Terenzo that Shelley set sail on the voyage that cost him his life.

A pleasant walk or bus ride from Lerici along the Fiascherino road takes you past some magnificent little bays. When you reach a huge illuminated sign reading 'Ecco del Mare', head down to one of the glorious

and secluded inlets along the route. Many beaches are private, so beware.

Tellaro, four km from Lerici, is a quiet fishing village with houses painted in hues of pink and orange, where cars are banned from the tiny centre. Walk the cobbled paths that weave through the village to the Church of San Giorgio, sit on the rocks and watch the world go by.

Places to Stay & Eat Three camping grounds dot the hills around Lerici. The *Gianna* (☎ 0187-96 61 11), Via Fiasherino-Tellaro, opens from Easter to the end of September. *Maralunga* (☎ 0187-96 83 96) at Via Carpanini 61, and *Senato Park* (☎ 0187-98 83 96), Via Senato 1, both open in May and close at the end of September. The camping grounds can be reached by bus from Piazza P G Garibaldi in Lerici.

Hotels include the *Albergo Emiliano* (☎ 0187-97 05 92), Via Garibaldi 40, with singles/doubles for L40,000/50,000. Outside Tellaro at Via Fiasherino 57 is the affittacamere *Armando Sarbia* (☎ 0187-96 50 49), with doubles for L50,000.

Trattoria Da Sandro, Via Roma 62, at San Terenzo, faces the water and has pasta from L4000. *Bar Shelley*, Via Matteotti 12, an inexpensive café on the waterfront, is perfect for breakfast or lunch.

Sarzana

Situated in the Magra Valley, a short bus ride from La Spezia, Sarzana lies at the southernmost tip of Liguria and was once an important outpost of the Genoese republic. The **cathedral** features the oldest existing crucifix painted on wood in the world. On display in the chapel is a phial which is said to have contained the blood of Christ.

The **Castruccio Castracani**, the fortress of Sarzanello, offers magnificent views. Catch a bus from Sarzana to **Luni**, an ancient Etruscan city which became a Roman colony in 177 BC and prospered because of its now long extinct port. The town features a well-preserved 1st century Roman amphitheatre, temple and forum.

Top Left : A street in Assisi, Umbria (JG)
Top Right : View from San Gimignano, Tuscany (JG)
Bottom Left : The Duomo, Bergamo (JG)
Bottom Right : Alleyway in Siena, Tuscany (JG)

Top Left : Late-Gothic cathedral in Ostuni, Apulia (SC)
Top Right : Duomo doorway in Assisi, Umbria (JG)
Bottom Left : Church of Madonna della Grazie, Gravina, Apulia (SC)
Bottom Right : Duomo in Trani, Apulia (JG)

Portovenere

It is worth catching the bus from La Spezia for razor-clam soup, Portovenere's contribution to Ligurian fare. The village is on the western shore of the Gulf of La Spezia and was founded as a Roman base, Portus Veneris, on the route from Gaul to Spain. Wander past the brightly coloured houses along the waterfront and up any of the steep and narrow staircases into the village, with its maze of cobbled paths following the contours of the hillside.

Head to the top to the **Church of San Lorenzo**, in the shadow of the **Castello Doria** with its magnificent terraced gardens and superb view along the coast. At the end of the waterfront quay is the **Church of San Pietro**, built in the Genoese Gothic style with black and white bands of marble, and the **Grotta Arpaia**, once a haunt of Byron, with views towards the Cinque Terre.

Fishing is the mainstay of this village (or at least the locals will have you believe it isn't tourism) and it is possible to hire gear and head out with one of the locals. Expect to pay handsomely. To hire a kayak or motor boat, go to Lucky Nautica Sport (☎ 0187-90 21 98), Calata Doria 38. Kayaks cost L7000 an hour and boats up to L80,000 a day.

Places to Stay & Eat Only 12 km from La Spezia, Portovenere is a cheap day trip. If you want to stay there, *Albergo Il Genio* (☎ 0187-90 06 11), in a former castle at the start of the waterfront quay, has singles/ doubles from L52,000/72,000.

Ristorante Miramare and *Taverna del Corsaro*, beside each other on the waterfront quay, Calata Doria, are both good, although expensive. If you are day-tripping, try *Bar al Naviglio*, Via Olive 73, away from the quay and a cheap place for lunch.

Cinque Terre

Miss the five magnificent villages of the Cinque Terre (Five Lands) – Monterosso, Riomaggiore, Vernazza, Manarola and Corniglia – and you will be missing some of Italy's most beautiful countryside. But blink as the train zips between tunnels and miss

them you will. Wedged into the impossibly mountainous countryside, the five tiny fishing villages appear to remain untouched by the tourist invasion which has blighted much of the Ligurian Coast. But their economies are as dependent on tourist dollars as the rest of the region. The towns are connected by a scenic pathway which winds along the terraced hillside, through olive groves and the vineyards which produce the area's nationally renowned white and dessert wines, Morasca, Chiaretto del Faro and the heavenly sweet wine, Sciacchetrà.

It is easy to find reasonably priced accommodation, particularly if you ask locals on the street or bar owners for a room in a private home. Eating is a different story, with most restaurants and trattorias charging high prices for average food.

It is possible to drive to all the five villages of the Cinque Terre, but cars are not permitted beyond the entrance to each town. There are no buses, but the local La Spezia-Genoa train stops at each town and this is the most convenient way to get to the Cinque Terre.

The telephone code for the area is 0187.

Riomaggiore Overlooking a tiny cove, Riomaggiore is a mess of houses wedged into the steep hillside, with tiny fishing boats lining the shore and stacked in the town's small square. The train stops in a newer part of the small village. The older part is a few minutes' walk south, through a long tunnel which starts just outside the station. The old centre can also be reached by walking through the newer part next to the station, and over the small hill, although most of this trip is an uphill climb. Riomaggiore is probably the cheapest and best of the villages for food and accommodation.

Set into the hillside high above the village is *Soggiorno Alle Cinque Terre* (☎ 92 05 87), Via De Gasperi 1. The owners have other rooms in the town. Signora Anna Michielini (☎ 92 04 11) rents rooms at Via Colombo 63, and has apartments, each with kitchen and bathroom, all for L25,000 per person. Most restaurants are along Via Colombo, which runs from the waterfront through the centre of the village. Try *Veciu Muin*, Via Colombo 31, for a good pizza.

Manarola Connected to Riomaggiore by the Via dell'Amore, or Lovers' Lane, Manarola is the most picturesque of the five villages. Head up into the village from the station, and if you're game, take the path off Via Rollandi, near Piazza Castello, through vines to the top of the mountain. On a clear day you can see all the villages. The affittacamere run by Gianni Capellini (☎ 2 23 68), Via Discovolo 6, has big, modern rooms with views for L50,000 a double. He also has an apartment with a kitchen and terrace overlooking the town for L60,000 a day.

Corniglia Not for the faint-hearted, this town is high above the water and quite a hike up stairs from the station. It gives the impression of being more untouched than the other villages. On the path to Manarola, behind the train station, is the *Villaggio Marino Europa* (☎ 81 22 79), a row of self-contained bungalows sleeping up to six people. Open from June to the end of September, they can be rented for three/seven days (L250,000/ 350,000) or 15/30 days (L950,000/ 1,500,000) and are cheaper in the shoulder months of June and September. Local wine maker Domenico Spora (☎ 81 22 93) offers rooms and apartments, some sleeping up to six, with views for L30,000 per person.

Vernazza Of the five villages, Vernazza makes the most of the ocean, with a promenade and a piazza on the water. *Da Sandro* (☎ 81 22 23), Via Roma 62, has doubles for L45,000, as does *Del Capitano* (☎ 81 22 01), Piazza G Marconi 21 (ask at the bar of the same name). *Sorriso* (☎ 81 22 24), Via Gavino 4, offers full board only for L55,000 a person. All have restaurants, but *Da Sandro* is the best value and has a marvellous pasta al gambero with whole prawns for L9000.

Monterosso Huge statues carved into the rocks overlook the only real beach on the Cinque Terre. One of the largest of the villages and also the least attractive with its modern section, Monterosso gets its name from the unusual red colouring of the cliff faces near the village. *Hotel La Spiaggia* (☎ 81 75 67), Monterosso Al Mare, right on the beach and near the station, has rooms for L25,000/50,000, or slightly more with bathrooms.

Rapallo
Rapallo is a major resort town, just minutes by train and road from Santa Margherita and Portofino. As such, it is often bypassed for its more famous neighbours. But the historic centre, right on the waterfront, with its cobbled paths and beautifully decorated food shops, give Rapallo the feel of a much less commercialised town. The Thursday food market at Piazza Cile adds a real provincial flavour to the town.

Rapallo has Roman origins and boasts attractions such as the **castle** on the Lungomare Vittorio Veneto, and **Hannibal's Bridge**, supposedly used by the Carthaginians during their invasion of Italy in 218 BC. But Rapallo's prominence is more recent, being the location for the signing of the Italo-Yugoslav Treaty in 1920 which defined the two countries' borders, and the Russo-German Treaty of 1922, which marked peace between the two nations.

The APT office (☎ 0185-5 12 82) is through the town centre at Via Diaz 9 and is open every day. The telephone code for the area is 0185.

Off Corso Assereto is a *funivia* (cable car) to **Montallegro** (every half hour, L4500 one way, L7000 return), the sanctuary built on the spot where the Virgin Mary reportedly appeared on 2 July 1557. It can also be reached by road from Rapallo and by foot (enquire at the APT).

Places to Stay & Eat Camping grounds in the hills near Rapallo are easily reached by taking the bus for Savagna from the train station. *Miraflores* (☎ 5 07 39), Via Savagna 10, is open all year, while *Rapallo* (☎ 6 02 60), Via San Lazzaro 4, opens only in summer. The pick of the hotels at Rapallo is *Bandoni* (☎ 5 04 23), Via Marsala 24, right on the waterfront with singles/doubles for L23,000/46,000. The *Duomo* (☎ 5 16 27), Via San Filippo Neri 12, has rooms from L25,000/50,000.

Vesuvio, Lungomare Vittorio Veneto 29, is a cheap trattoria, and the *Sailor's Club*, Via Montebello 11, serves food until late.

Getting There & Away Regular buses connect Rapallo with Santa Margherita (every 20 minutes) and Camogli. The trip in both directions is more pleasant than by train.

Santa Margherita

In a sheltered bay on the east side of the Portofino Promontory in the Gulf of Tigullio, Santa Margherita is a pleasant and attractive resort town. The old fishers' houses facing onto the port make for a lovely promenade and you can admire the million-dollar yachts at their moorings.

Santa Margherita was once a base for a considerable coral-fishing fleet which used to sail to the coast of Africa, but is now more famous for its orange blossoms and its lace. It can be used as base for excursions to Portofino, San Fruttuoso and Camogli. The tourist office boasts that surfers try their hardest off Santa Margherita, but here as elsewhere along the Ligurian Coast the conditions aren't good at all.

Orientation & Information From the train station, head downhill into the town and then north along the waterfront on Via Gramsci and into Piazza Martiri della Libertà, the main square, from where most buses depart.

The APT (☎ 0185-28 74 85), Via XXV Aprile, is between the train station and the sea. It is open Monday to Saturday from 8.45 am to midday and 3 to 6 pm, with extended hours in summer.

The post office is at Via Roma 36 and is open Monday to Friday from 8.45 am to 6.45 pm, and Saturday mornings. The postal code is 16038. There are public telephones at the train station and around the city. The telephone code is 0185.

For the police, call ☎ 113, otherwise go to the police headquarters (☎ 28 71 21) in Via

Vignolo. For medical assistance, the Ospedale Civile di Rapallo (☎ 6 03 33) is at Rapallo in Piazza Molfino.

Activities Santa Margherita is a sporting playground, with the list headed by sailing, water-skiing and diving. Ask at the tourist office, at the concierge desks at the Grand Hotel Miramare (see the following section), or at the Hotel Helios, Via Gramsci 6.

Places to Stay & Eat The *Pensione Corallo* (☎ 28 67 74), Via XXV Aprile 20, has singles/doubles for L20,000/40,000. *Albergo Nuovo Riviera* (☎ 28 74 03), Via Belvedere 10, has rooms from L30,000/45,000; full board (L75,000 per person) is compulsory in the high season. The friendly owners impose a strict no smoking rule. *Albergo Fasce* (☎ 28 64 35), Via L Bozzo 3, has only doubles from L50,000. The *Europa* (☎ 28 71 87), Via Trento 5, has singles/doubles for L50,000/60,000. One of the town's best hotels is the *Grand Hotel Miramare* (☎ 28 07 13), Lungomare Milito Ignoto 30, but you will pay more than L150,000 a double.

At *Trattoria San Siso*, Corso Matteotti 137 (about 10 minutes from the seafront), a full meal will cost around L20,000. Try the panzotti (small ravioli in a walnut sauce). *Trattoria da Pino*, Via Jacopo Ruffini, is quite cheap, while at *Ristorante da Alfredo*, Piazza Martiri della Libertà 38, overlooking the water, pizzas start at L6000. *Simonetti*, Via Bottaro 51, has great gelati.

Getting There & Away Santa Margherita is on the Genoa-La Spezia train line. By car, the A12 autostrada passes Rapallo before cutting inland towards Santa Margherita. Viale E Rainusso, which runs off Piazza Vittorio Veneto, joins the Via Aurelia, the secondary road to Genoa, which is the best bet for hitchhikers. Buses leave Piazza Martiri della Libertà for Portofino, and Servizio Marittimo del Tigullio (☎ 28 46 70) operates ferries from near the bus stop to Portofino (L9000 return). Other ferries service Camogli (L16,000 return) and the Cinque Terre (L25,000 return).

Portofino

Almost certainly the most picturesque of the small fishing villages along the coast, Portofino is a charming and beautiful spot and should be visited. In summer, the famous portside piazza is awash with glitterati as film stars flock to the most 'happening' spot in all of Liguria. Near the **Church of San Giorgio** a flight of stairs leads up to the **Castello San Giorgio**, which was used during the French, Spanish and Napoleonic wars and has a great view. Continue on to the **lighthouse**, an hour's walk there and back, for an even better view.

The APT tourist office (☎ 0185-26 90 24), Via Roma 35, just back from the port, is open from 9 am to midday and 3 to 6 pm daily. It has maps of walks, including the 2½-hour trek to **San Fruttuoso**, a magnificent walk along the cliff face overlooking the ocean. It can also advise on water sports and accommodation, which is scarce and expensive. Boats can be hired from Mussini Giorgio & C (☎ 0185-26 93 27), Portofino Mare 39.

Places to Stay & Eat The cheapest lodgings are at *Eden* (☎ 0185-26 90 91), Vico Dritto 18, set appropriately in a garden, for L100,000 a double. The cover charge alone at most restaurants would equal the daily meal allowance of some travellers. But don't despair. If your trip is quick, try the cheese focaccia, a local speciality, at *Panificio Canale*, Via Roma 30 – not bad at L3000 per 100 grams. *The American Bar*, on the waterfront promenade is both cute and expensive.

Getting There & Away Portofino can be reached by bus from Santa Margherita, and ferries crisscross the gulf from most towns along the coast. Servizio Marittimo del Tigullio runs ferries to San Fruttuoso (L10,000 return), Rapallo (L9000 return) and Santa Margherita (L7000 return). Drivers must park at the entrance to town (L3000 first hour, L25,000 a day) as cars are banned from the tiny village.

San Fruttuoso

Accessible only on foot from Camogli or Portofino (about 2½ hours from each), or by ferry, San Fruttuoso is a fascinating village dominated by the **Abbey of San Fruttuoso di Capodimonte**, a Benedictine abbey and monastery with medieval origins. Built as a resting place for the martyred bishop, St Fructuosus, the abbey was rebuilt in the mid-1200s with the assistance of the Doria family, who used it as a family crypt. It fell into decay with the decline of the abbey, and in the 1800s was divided into small living quarters by the local fishers. The Dorias donated the abbey and hamlet to the Italian Environmental Protection Foundation in 1983, and it was renovated three years later at a cost of L3.5 billion.

Perhaps more fascinating is the bronze statue of Christ *(Il Cristo degli Abissi)*, lowered 50 feet to the sea bed off the headland by locals in 1954 to bless the waters and as a tribute to divers who had lost their lives at sea. You must dive to see it, but locals claim if the waters are calm it can be viewed from a boat. A replica in a fish tank is on show in the church adjoining the abbey.

Camogli

Wander through the narrow alleyways and the long, cobbled streets of Camogli and you will see some of the finest trompe-l'oeil works in Liguria, with house after house featuring meticulously painted columns, balustrades and even windows. The town is famous for its annual Sagra del Pesce in May, when local fishers fry hundreds of fish in pans measuring three metres across, for the townsfolk (and the tourists), as a celebration of the year's bounty.

Camogli retains an air of simplicity despite its reliance on tourism. The name Camogli means House of Wives *(casa delle mogli)* and comes from the days when the women would run the town while their husbands were at sea for lengthy periods. The town was also a naval power and at one stage boasted a fleet of ships larger than Genoa's.

Orientation & Information To the right of

the train station is the APT tourist office (☎ 0185-77 10 66) at Via XX Settembre 29. It's open Monday to Saturday from 9 am to 12.30 pm and 3.30 to 6.30 pm (except Friday afternoon), and has extended hours in summer. From there, a labyrinth of dark and narrow stairs weaves down to the waterfront promenade, Via Garibaldi. Camogli's telephone code is 0185.

Activities Luigi Simonetti Barche da Diporto, Via Garibaldi 59, hires canoes, pedal boats, rowing and motor boats by the hour, half day or full day. Canoes are L7000 an hour or L35,000 a day, and boats are more expensive. Bob Mare Sport (☎ 77 02 54), Via Garibaldi 197A, operates a diving centre.

Places to Stay & Eat The *Albergo La Camogliese* (☎ 77 14 02), Via Garibaldi 55, has singles/doubles from L35,000/55,000. The *Augusta* (☎ 77 05 92), Via P Schiaffino 100, has rooms from L40,000/55,000, and closer to the train station is *Selene* (☎ 77 01 49), Via Cuneo 15, with rooms from L42,000/69,000.

Eating out is expensive, with most of the waterfront restaurants charging high prices for ordinary food. Try *Il Faulo*, which specialises in traditional Genoese fare and has a vegetarian menu. Pasta starts at L12,000. Smaller, less expensive trattorias are tucked into the laneways away from the water, so you'll need to explore.

RIVIERA DI PONENTE

This section of the Ligurian Coast, stretching west to the French border, is more heavily developed and is a favourite destination for large package tour groups from Germany and other parts of Europe.

Savona

Savona is not the greatest introduction to the Riviera di Ponente. Its centre is well preserved and quite beautiful, and its attractions and history are as alluring as other cities in Liguria, but it is totally dominated by the industrial sprawl which surrounds it. A regional capital and the see of a bishop,

Savona has a busy port and was bombed heavily in WW II.

Orientation & Information The train station is in a newer part of town, east of the waterfront and over the river. Via Collodi, to the right of the station, and Via Don Minzoni, to the left, both cross the river and meet the massive Piazza del Popolo and Via Paleocapa, Savona's main and grandest street, which runs to the water. Buses for towns inland and along the coast leave from outside the station and Piazza Popolo.

The APT tourist office (☎ 019-82 05 22), Via Paleocopa 23, is open from 8 am to 1 pm and 3 to 6 pm, Monday to Saturday. The telephone code for Savona is 019.

Places to Stay & Eat Savona has two youth hostels. The *Fortezza Priamar* (☎ 81 26 53), Corso Mazzini, is on the waterfront and charges L16,000 for bed and breakfast. *Villa de' Franceschini* (☎ 26 32 33), Via alla Strà 29, Conca Verde, charges L14,000 for bed and breakfast; telephone on arrival in Savona for its private bus. Both hostels are open all year.

The *Albergo Cacciatori* (☎ 3 76 23), Via XX Settembre 7, has singles/doubles from L22,000/40,000. The *Nazionale* (☎ 85 16 36), Via Astengo 55R, has rooms for L35,000/52,000.

Most restaurants are along Via Paleocapa, where you can expect to pay reasonably high prices. The bars and cafés, however, are quite cheap. *Ristorante Da Nicola*, Via XX Settembre 43, offers local specialities, with pasta from L8000.

Around Savona

Noli The small, well-preserved medieval village of Noli, with modern additions, can only be reached by bus from Savona or Finale Ligure (L1600) and is definitely worth the diversion. With one of the better beaches along the Ponente, Noli is dominated by **Genoese ruins**, particularly the fort and wall which runs from the hill top to the outskirts of the village. The view from the top of the hill is almost as good as the *troffie*, a local pasta made from potato flour. Fishers set up stalls along the beach and in summer the waterside promenade transforms into a food market.

The APT tourist office (☎ 019-74 89 31) is at Corso Italia 8, on the waterfront. Take the Finale Ligure bus from the Savona train station. For even better beaches, make a stop-off in **Varigotti**, past Noli on the way to Finale Ligure.

Other Destinations Situated in the Savonese Apennines, about a 40-minute bus ride or 20-km drive from Savona, **Sassello** is a mountain resort close to the Ligurian-Piedmontese border and is one of the more interesting inland towns. It has skiing, both on water and snow, at Alberola, and its monuments include the Bastia Soprano, a Doria family castle.

Acqui Terme, in neighbouring Piedmont, is an ancient spa built around the ruins of a Roman water system and is 32 km farther north-east. Enjoy a 75°C bath in the natural hot-water spring.

Finale Ligure
With a pleasant, village-like atmosphere, a good beach and affordable accommodation, Finale Ligure is worth considering as a base for the Riviera di Ponente. If climbing rocks is your idea of fun, pack your ropes and head for the hinterland, where several areas offer good free-climbing, and where well-organised clubs produce maps of the best climbs.

Orientation & Information Finale Ligure is divided into three areas. Finalborgo, away from the coast on the Pora River, is the old town and original centre of the region. Also quite historic is the Finalmarina area, which is on the waterfront and where most accommodation and restaurants can be found, while Finalpia, towards Genoa, runs along the Sciusa River and is rather suburban. The train station is at Piazza Vittorio Veneto, at the western edge of Finalmarina. Walk straight ahead along Via Saccone and you

will hit the ocean. All buses stop outside the station.

The APT tourist office (☎ 019-69 25 81), opposite the beach at Via San Pietro 14, is open every day and can recommend accommodation and provide details on rock climbing and other sporting activities. The telephone code for Finale Ligure is 019.

Activities Climbers meet at weekends in the bars of Finalborgo and Calice. To reach these towns, take the Rialto bus. Rockstore in Via Nicotera, Finalborgo, hires climbing gear and gives free advice. If cycling along the beach is more your speed, Oddone, Via C Colombo 20, hires bicycles for L3500 an hour or L10,000 a day.

Places to Stay & Eat There are two camping grounds open all year: *Del Mulino* (☎ 60 16 69), Via Castelli; and *Tahiti* (☎ 60 06 00), Via Varese, although neither is close to train or bus routes. The APT can advise on private rooms, or mini-apartments with kitchens in private houses close to the beach, for over L15,000 per person. *Adele Tiranti* (☎ 60 07 73), Via Veneto 39, has reasonably priced rooms, which are booked out in summer.

The town boasts 130 hotels. *Marita* (☎ 69 29 04), Via Saccone 17, is close to the train station with singles/doubles for L25,000/40,000, although prices go up in the high season.

Eating is surprisingly cheap and rather good. *Pizzeria Forno a Legna*, Via San Pietro 4, has specials galore, pizzas starting at L6000 and an ocean view. *Trattoria La Tavernetta*, Via C Colombo 42, does a great troffie with pesto.

Albenga
From an archeological point of view, this town is considered the most important in Liguria. It flourished under the Romans but was destroyed by the barbarians, again achieving significance during the early medieval period when it became the see of a bishop. Its magnificent **Diocesan Museum**, featuring a painting by Caravaggio, is near the 5th century **baptistry** and Romanesque

cathedral. The nearby **Roman Naval Museum**, Via Cavour, has a collection of 1st century amphoras, or wine urns, recovered in 1950 from the wreck of a Roman cargo vessel four km offshore. It is one of the oldest discovered shipwrecks.

The APT tourist office is at Viale Martiri della Libertà 1, and is open Monday to Saturday from 9 am to midday and 3 to 7 pm, closing at 6 pm on Saturday.

Places to Stay & Eat The camping grounds, *Florida* (☎ 0182-5 06 37) and *Delfino* (☎ 0182-5 19 98), both on Via Aurelia, are reasonably close to the train station. For a decent hotel try *Il Gabbiano* (☎ 0182-5 03 77), Via Genova 71. It has only doubles for L30,000 and is closed during winter. *Da Romano* (☎ 0182-5 04 08), Piazza Corridoni 1, has singles/doubles for L38,000/55,000.

Trattoria Bar La Bifora, Via delle Medaglie d'Oro 20, is in the historic heart and has pizzas starting at L3500. *Bar La Bocca*, Via Roma 74, does great things with swordfish and other fruits of the sea and has a set menu for L18,000.

Alassio

Apart from its beaches, this town also boasts the famous Baci, a delicious chocolate concoction that falls somewhere between a truffle and a biscuit. Each town in the region has a local version but none as good as Alassio's. Indulge at *Caffè Talmone*, Via Mazzini 107, or nibble one while reclining on some of the coast's best beaches – three km of white sand.

The APT tourist office (☎ 0182-64 03 46) is at Via Gibb 3, and a prominently placed billboard outside the station lists accommodation and other information. The SAR Autolinee bus information office (☎ 0182-64 04 52) at Piazza della Libertà has tourist information and can organise trips to Gallinara Island, as well as day trips inland and to Monte Carlo.

Imperia

Dominated by the massive olive-oil vats dotting the coastline and the hothouses which scar its hillside, Imperia is the main city of the province of the Riviera dei Fiori. It has the busiest olive-oil factories in Italy and claims to be Europe's largest flower-growing area. Imperia was founded in 1923 by Mussolini when he bridged the Imperio River and unified the towns of Porto Maurizio (to the west) and Oneglia. However, Imperia remains pretty much divided into two towns.

Porto Maurizio contains an appealing historical section, dominated by the **Church of San Maurizio**, a large neoclassical cathedral in Piazza Duomo at the highest point on the hill. One of the city's main cultural attractions is the **Museo Navale Internazionale del Ponente Liguria**, Piazza Duomo 11, open Monday and Tuesday mornings and Wednesday and Saturday evenings.

Orientation & Information Trains stop at both the Oneglia and Porto Maurizio stations, and it is most convenient to get off at the latter. Most food outlets and accommodation are located around the old town. From the station, head up the hill to Viale G Matteotti, the main street, or through an underpass to the waterfront area, which eventually leads to Corso Garibaldi. Buses connect both train stations, and the No 3 runs through Porto Maurizio.

The APT tourist office (☎ 0183-6 07 30) is at Viale G Matteotti 22. Imperia's telephone code is 0183.

Places to Stay & Eat The camping grounds, *Eucalyptus* (☎ 6 15 34) and *La Pineta* (☎ 6 14 98), both on Via Littardi, are close to the A10 autostrada and can be reached by bus No 2 or 3 from both train stations. The *Pensione Paola* (☎ 6 29 96), Via Rambaldo 30, has singles/doubles from L25,000/38,000, while *Pensione Amo* (☎ 6 38 78), Via Aurelio Saffi 32, is close to Stazione Porto Maurizio and has doubles only for L40,000.

The *Ristorante Il Gabbiano*, near the waterfront at Via Scarincio 46, has cheap, traditional food. *Chez Marcello*, Via Scarincio 96, charges L15,000 for a meal.

Pizzamania, Via XX Settembre 39, has pizza by the slice and is good for lunch.

Around Imperia

North of Imperia at Pontedassio, a six-km bus ride from Porto Maurizio station, is one of the more quirky attractions on the coast: a private **Spaghetti Museum**, which belongs to the Agnesi family whose name appears on packet pasta in every Italian kitchen. It opens according to the family's whim, so check with the Imperia APT before setting out.

Past Capo Cervo, heading east from Imperia, is the small fishing village of **Cervo**, with its well-preserved ring of medieval walls and towers.

San Remo

San Remo gained prominence as a resort for the continent's social elite, particularly from Britian and Russia, in the mid-1800s when the likes of Empress Maria Alexandrovna of Russia (mother of Nicholas II, the last tsar) sunned themselves on the sandy shore. Today, while a few hotels continue to thrive as luxury five-star resorts for the mega-rich, many built in that period are long past their prime and are now cut off from the beach by the railway line.

Orientation The old centre, La Pigna, is just north of Corso Matteotti, San Remo's main strip, where the wealthy take their evening stroll. Just past Piazza Colombo and Corso Garibaldi to the east, is the city's seedier area. Corso Matteotti meets San Remo's other famous strip, Corso Imperatrice, at Piazzale Battisti and the train station. Corso Trento e Trieste, which runs along the waterfront east of the train station, features the Villa Nobel, in which the Swedish inventor of dynamite and originator of the Nobel prizes, Alfred Nobel, lived and died.

Information The APT tourist office (☎ 0184-57 15 71) is at Largo Nuvoloni 1. It's open Monday to Saturday from 8 am to 7 pm, Sunday to 2 pm.

The main post office is at Via Roma 156 and opens from 8 am to 7.40 pm Monday to Saturday, to 1 pm Sunday. The postal code for central San Remo is 18038.

Public telephones are located at the train station and on Via Roma near Corso Mombello, open from 8 am to 10 pm. San Remo's telephone code is 0184.

In case of an emergency, you can ring the police on ☎ 113. The police headquarters (☎ 50 77 77) are at Via del Castillo 5. For medical assistance, head for the Pronto Soccorso (☎ 53 61), Via Giovanni Borea 56.

Things to See & Do The **Russian Orthodox Church** in Piazza Nuvolino was built as a place of worship for the Russian community who followed Tsarina Alexandrovna to San Remo. The church, with its onion domes, was designed in 1906 by artist Josef Choussef, who 20 years later went on to plan Lenin's mausoleum in Moscow's Red Square. It is open daily from 7 am to 12.45 pm and 3 to 7 pm. Italy's principal **flower market** is held in Corso Garibaldi from June to October, daily from 6 am to 8 am. Go along and watch the frenetic bidding.

In February, hundreds of people come to compete in the San Remo Festival della Canzone Italiana, Italy's famous song contest, watched by 30 million TV viewers annually.

Monte Bignone is a short drive from the centre, or a cable-car ride from Corso Inglesi, and offers views over San Remo and as far as Cannes.

Activities For the water-sport enthusiast, San Remo has two windsurfing schools which hire gear: Morgana (☎ 50 36 47), Corso Salvo d'Acquisto, and Paradiso (☎ 66 78 75), Lungomare Vittorio Emanuele.

Bianchi Emilio (☎ 54 13 17), Corso Cavalotti 39, hires scooters and motorbikes, and Oasi Hire (☎ 50 22 42), Giardino Vittorio Veneto, has pedalos (four-seated pedal cars), and bicycles.

Places to Stay & Eat Accommodation is surprisingly cheap in parts of San Remo, although you can forget it during the summer unless you've booked ahead. There are three

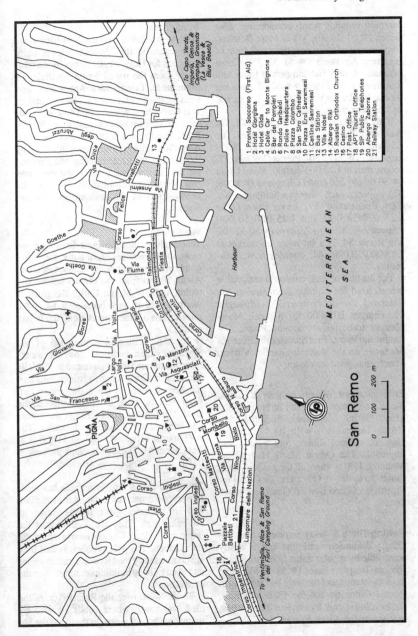

San Remo

1 Pronto Soccorso (First Aid)
2 Hotel Sanremo
3 Hotel Giorgiana
4 Hotel Gilda
5 Cable Car to Monte Bignone
6 Bar del Pompieri
7 Rondo Garibaldi
8 Police Headquarters
9 Piazza Colombo
10 San Siro Cathedral
11 Piazza Eroi Sanremesi
12 Cantina Sanremesi
13 Bus Station
14 Villa Nobel
15 Albergo Riki
16 Russian Orthodox Church
17 Casino
18 Post Office
19 APT Tourist Office
20 SIP Public Telephones
21 Albergo Zaborra
22 Railway Station

MEDITERRANEAN SEA

0   100   200 m

camping grounds worth considering: *Blue Beach* (☎ 51 32 00), Via al Mare Bussana, five km east of town near the small town of Bussana; *La Vesca* (☎ 51 37 75), Corso Mazzini 74, only two km east of town; and *San Remo e dei Fiori* (☎ 6 06 35), two km west at Via Tiro al Volo 3. All can be reached by bus from the train station.

The *Albergo Riki* (☎ 50 69 24), Via Astraldi 3, has singles/doubles for L20,000/35,000. At the *Albergo Internazionale* (☎ 50 45 50), Piazza Colombo 17, rooms start at L20,000/40,000. *Hotel Gilda* (☎ 50 66 89) and *Hotel Giorgiana* (☎ 50 69 30), opposite each other in a building at Via San Francesco 37, have rooms for L23,000/34,000 and L25,000/50,000 respectively. *Albergo Zaborra* (☎ 50 31 70), Via Roma 54, is a bit more up-market at L35,000/70,000. All doubles have bathrooms.

For the best of local cuisine at reasonable prices, head for *Cantina Sanremesi* at Via Palazzo 7. *Bar dei Pompieri*, Via Marsaglia 55, charges L15,000 for a meal. Many cheaper trattorias are around Piazza Colombo and Piazza Eroi Sanremesi. *Gelateria Manuela*, on the water at Giardini Vittorio Veneto, has good ice cream.

Entertainment With more than 20 clubs, San Remo jumps. First and foremost is the grand Casino Municipale di San Remo, Corso Inglesi 18, with its 'American Games', cabaret shows, roof garden and nightclub. The Odeon Music Hall, Corso Matteotti 178, is where all the groovy young things go to dance. Otherwise they head for Pipistrello, Piazza Borea d'Olmo 8, to watch bands.

Getting There & Away San Remo is on the Genoa-Ventimiglia rail line and is easily accessible by regular trains from either city. Riviera Trasporti buses (☎ 53 40 81) leave from the station and the main bus terminal at Piazza Colombo for the French border, Imperia and inland. By car, San Remo is best reached on the A10 autostrada.

Bordighera

Following a tradition which dates back to the 16th century, the Vatican selects palm branches for Holy Week celebrations exclusively from the palms lining Bordighera's promenade, **Lungomare Argentina**, and from the town's plantations. The train station is at Piazza Eroi della Libertà and the medieval part of town is to the east. From Viale F Rossi you can reach the **Church of Sant' Ampelio**, built over a cave once inhabited by the saint. In the gardens along Via Romana are the International Library and the **Bicknell Museum**, founded in 1888 as the headquarters of the Institute of Ligurian Studies.

Ventimiglia

Ventimiglia is not the most inviting town along the Riviera dei Fiori, but it does offer good, reasonably priced accommodation. About 10 km from the French border and within sight of Monte Carlo, the town is worth a visit if only because it lacks the tourist gloss of other towns along the Italian coast.

The train station is at the head of Via Stazione, which continues along the waterfront and through the main centre as Via della Repubblica. Corso Genova, which runs past the Roman ruins, is the main eastern exit from the city, while its continuation to the west, Via Cavour, runs through the centre and heads towards the French border. The APT tourist office (☎ 0184-35 11 83) is at Via Cavour 61. The town's telephone code is 0184.

Things to See & Do Ventimiglia has well-preserved **Roman ruins** dating from the 2nd and 3rd centuries, when it was known as Albintimulium. They are north-east of the urban area along Corso Genova from the train station. The only problem is that they are dominated by road flyovers, railway lines and even railway buildings perched over the excavations.

To the west, over the Roia River, is the medieval town, where roads flanked by unrestored houses weave to the top of the hill and meet Via Garibaldi, the old centre's main street. The 12th century **cathedral** and **Church of San Michele** stand side by side, and there are magnificent views of the coast from farther along the road.

Eurocicli (☎ 35 18 79), Via Cavour 86A, hires bicycles and tandems, starting at L2000 an hour.

Places to Stay & Eat Ventimiglia makes a good base, as accommodation is quite cheap. The camping ground, *Roma* (☎ 3 35 80), Via Peglia 1, is near the centre. The *Albergo Via XX Settembre* (☎ 35 12 22), Via Roma 16, has singles/doubles for L16,000/28,000. Its restaurant also offers a good meal for L16,000 and is popular among stallholders from the fruit and vegetable market opposite. *Cavour* (☎ 35 13 66), Via Cavour 3, has doubles only from L31,000. *Abbo* (☎ 35 11 04), Via Cavour 33, has singles starting at L10,000 and doubles from L25,000.

Cheaper restaurants can be found around Via Roma and Piazza della Libertà or along Via Cavour. Try *Pizza al Giro* at Via Cavour 62, which has pizza by the slice (L1500 to L2000) or limited sit-down service. *Pizzeria 4 Assi*, Passeggio Oberdan 19, on the beach, has cheap pizzas, while *Il Vesuvio*, Via Trossarelli 14, on the river, has a L16,000 menu.

Getting There & Away By bus, Riviera Trasporti (☎ 35 12 51), Via Cavour 61, operating from next to the tourist office, connects the city with towns along the coast and into France. Trains connect the city with towns along the coast, including Genoa, Nice, Cannes and Marseilles. The A10 autostrada connects the city with Genoa and Nice, the ss20 leaves the city to the north for France, and the ss1 (Via Aurelia) hugs the coast between the French border and Genoa.

Around Ventimiglia

About eight km from Ventimiglia towards France by bus from the train station is **Balzi Rossi**, considered one of the most significant palaeontological sites in Liguria, where you can view the remains of Cro-Magnon man. The **Museo di Balzi Rossi**, Ponte San Ludovic, near the seaside, features the Triple Burial (a grave of three Cro-Magnon men), pots of weapons, and remains of fauna from the period. It is open from 9 am to midday and 2.30 to 6 pm.

A few stops before, on the same bus, is **Villa Hanbury** and its important botanical gardens, featuring one of Italy's largest collections of exotic plants. It is open from 10 am to 6 pm, except Wednesday (L10,000 admission).

Piedmont

Nestling beneath the French and Swiss Alps in the north-west corner of Italy, Piedmont (Piemonte) offers a feast of activities for both the budget traveller and the more well heeled. From the sophisticated and exclusive cafés lining the grand squares in Turin, to the hiking tracks and skiing runs through the mountains, Piedmont's diversity and relatively low ranking as a tourist destination make the region well worth a visit.

The House of Savoy, which ruled Piedmont from early in the 11th century and made Turin their capital in 1574, built for themselves one of the grandest cities in Europe. The Savoys, under King Victor Emmanuel II and Piedmontese statesman Camillo Cavour, were instrumental in achieving Italian unification, and succeeded in making Turin the capital of Italy, albeit briefly, from 1861.

Much of Italy's industrial boom this century has its roots in the region, particularly in Turin, where the industrial giant Fiat started making cars. Today, the region is second only to Lombardy in industrial production and remains one of the country's wealthiest regions.

Piedmont's cuisine is heavily influenced by French styles of cooking, and uses marinated meats and vegetables. *Bagna caoda* (meats dipped in a bath of oil, anchovies and garlic) is popular during winter, and the white truffles of Piedmont are considered the best in Italy. The region produces two-thirds

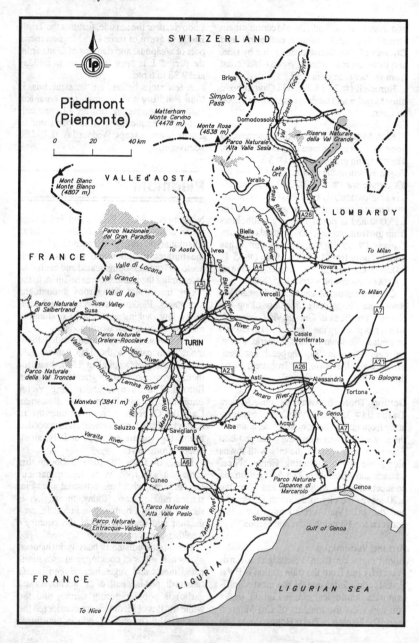

of Italy's rice, and risotto is very popular. Piedmont produces some of Italy's best red wines, notably those from the vineyards of Barolo and Barbera, and, of course, the sparkling wines from Asti.

As a transportation hub, Turin makes a good base for day trips to most cities in the region, in particular the beautiful town of Saluzzo to the south, and Asti, the home of Italy's sparkling wine industry, to the east. For walkers, the area's main attraction is the Grande Traversata delle Alpi, a walk of more than 200 km through the Alps from the Ligurian border to Lake Maggiore in the north.

TURIN (TORINO)

One of the most beautiful cities in Italy, Turin's grandeur is often compared to that of Paris. The House of Savoy which ruled the region for hundreds of years, and Italy until 1945, built for themselves a gracious Baroque city and filled it with treasures from across Europe and North Africa. Italy's industrial expansion began here, with companies like Fiat (Fabbrica Italiana di Automobili Torino) and Olivetti luring hundreds of thousands of impoverished southern Italians, who were housed in vast company-owned and built suburbs, such as Mirafiori to the south. Fiat is Italy's largest company, and its owner, Gianni Agnelli, is one of the country's most powerful men (he publicly admitted that Fiat, too, had been involved in the corruption scandals that rocked the country in 1992-93). Industrial unrest on the company's factory floors spawned the Italian Communist Party and, in the 1970s, the left-wing terrorist group, the Red Brigades.

Turin is generally overlooked by tourists because of the misconception that it is a dirty industrial city, but it is definitely worth visiting. It is bitterly cold in winter and can be very hot in summer.

History

The city's history is in dispute, with some believing it to be of Ligurian origin and others claiming it was Celtic. Known as Taurisia in ancient times, the region was a fierce enemy of Rome but eventually became an ally. Like most of northern Italy, it was controlled by the Romans, followed by the Goths, the Lombards and the Franks.

Marriages in the 11th century planted the seeds for the House of Savoy, which endured a turbulent existence, culminating in its reign over Italy from 1861 to 1945. Turin was annexed to France in 1536, but the House of Savoy was restored in 1562 and the city became home to its court thereafter. The Savoys won control of Sardinia in 1720 but their empire faltered when the city was again occupied by the French in 1798 and later by Austrians and Russians. The House was restored when Victor Emmanuel I entered Turin in 1814.

The movement for Italian unification was born in the north, particularly in Turin, where the final stages were played out under King Victor Emmanuel II and the driving force behind the Risorgimento, the Piedmontese prime minister, Camillo Cavour. In 1859 the Austrians were driven out and, in 1860, Garibaldi handed over Sicily and Southern Italy. Turin was proclaimed capital of Italy in 1861, a glory that lasted until 1864 when the capital moved to Florence and eventually Rome.

Turin adapted quickly to its loss of political significance, becoming a centre for industrial production during WW I and later a centre for trade-union activity. Antonio Gramsci, one of the founders of the Italian Communist Party, led actions at the Fiat factories. Today, it is Italy's second-largest industrial city after Milan.

Orientation

The north-facing Porta Nuova train station is the point of arrival for most travellers. Trams and buses out the front connect with most parts of the historic centre, which is quite spread out. From the station, walk straight ahead over the main east-west route, Corso Vittorio Emanuele II, through the grand Piazza Carlo Felice and along Via Roma until you come to the massive, café-lined Piazza San Carlo. Piazza Castello and the Duomo with the famous Shroud of Turin are

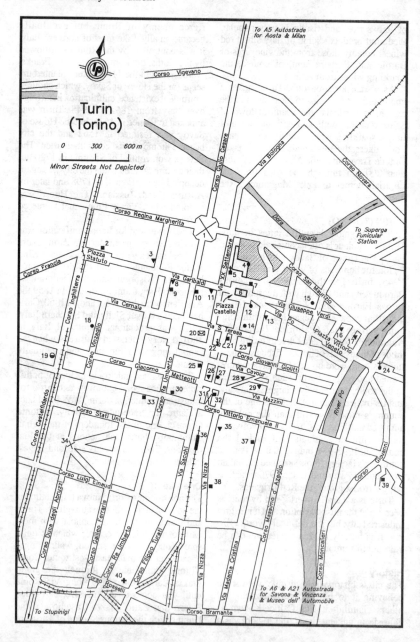

■ PLACES TO STAY		26	Lullaby
		28	Pizzeria alla Baita
2	Albergo Florida	29	Pizzeria Italo
7	Albergo Europa	35	Ristorante del Chianti
9	Albergo Canelli		
10	Albergo Kariba		OTHER
21	Albergo San Carlo		
23	Albergo Alfieri	1	Piazza della Repubblica
25	Albergo Campo di Marte	4	Palazzo Reale & Royal Gardens
30	Albergo Bologna	5	Duomo
32	Albergo Roma & Rocca Cavour	6	Palazzo Madama
33	Albergo Magenta	12	Palazzo Carignan
37	Albergo Edelweis	14	Palazzo dell'Accademia delle Scienze
38	Albergo la Consolata	15	Mole Antonelliana
39	Ostello Torino	18	Police Headquarters
		19	Bus Station
▼ PLACES TO EAT		20	Main post office
		22	APT tourist information office
3	Ristorante Lanternin	24	Gran Madre di Dio
8	Pizzeria da Luigi	27	SIP telephones
11	La Grangia	31	Piazza Carlo Felice
13	Monterosso	34	Piazza Duca d'Aosta
16	Ristorante Otto Colonne	36	Porta Nuova railway station
17	Trattoria Alba	40	Ospedale Mauriziano Umberto I

farther north along Via Roma. The Mole Antonelliana dominates the horizon to the east, leading to Via Po (the student area), Piazza Vittorio Veneto and the mighty River Po.

Information

Tourist Office The APT (☎ 011-53 51 81) is at Via Roma 226, under the colonnade at the south-west corner of the Piazza San Carlo. There is a smaller office at the main train station, and both are open Monday to Saturday from 9 am to 7.30 pm. Informa Giovani (☎ 011-57 65 35 76), Via Assarotti 2, publishes a magazine for young people, *Città di Torino Informa Giovani*, and has a range of information from travel to services for the handicapped.

Money There is an exchange booth at the main train station, open until 9.30 pm seven days a week. Banks are located along Via Roma or in Piazza San Carlo. The Banca d'America e d'Italia at Corso Vittorio Emanuele II 197, has a bancomat that accepts Visa cards. The agent for American Express is Viaggi Quick (☎ 011-51 71), Via Arsenale 25.

Post & Telecommunications The main post office is at Via Alfieri 10 and opens from 8.15 am to 2 pm Monday to Saturday. A post office at the main station has longer opening hours. The postal code for central Turin is 10100.

SIP public telephones are at Via Roma 18 and are open from 8 am to 10 pm seven days a week. Others are at Via XX Settembre 65 and at the station. The telephone code for Turin is 011.

Emergency The main police headquarters (☎ 5 58 81) are at Corso Vinzaglio 10, or ring ☎ 113 in case of emergency. Contact SSUT (☎ 57 47) for an ambulance or night and holiday medical attention; otherwise go to the Ospedale Mauriziano Umberto I (☎ 5 08 01), Largo Turati 62. The Boniscontro pharmacy, Corso Vittorio Emanuele 66, is open 24 hours a day.

Foreign Consulates The UK has a representative in Turin (☎ 68 39 21) at Corso d'Azeglio 60.

Bookshops Libreria Luxembourg, Via C Battisti 7, has a good range of British and American books and newspapers.

Other Information For gay and lesbian information, contact Arci Gay Maurice (☎ 650 98 60), Via O Moragari 17, or Informagay (☎ 436 50 00). The Club Alpino Italiano (☎ 53 92 60) is at Via Barbaroux 1. CTS (☎ 53 43 88), for student travel, is at Via Camerana 3. There's an Alba laundrette at Via S Secondo 1, or you can also go to Bruno Maria, Via Dandolo 33.

Dangers & Annoyances The APT advises all tourists, most importantly single women, against visiting the area around Via Nizza, particularly at night.

Things to See & Do

The massive **Porta Nuova** railway station built by Mazzucchetti in 1865 is one of Italy's grandest. It opens out on to **Piazza Carlo Felice**, an elegant garden surrounded by porticoes (there are about 18 km of porticoes in Turin's centre). North of the station is Via Nizza, once elegant but now home to the city's seedier side. Visit during the day but certainly not at night, unless you're in a group. Via Roma, Turin's main shopping and most gracious boulevard, heads north from the piazza. It was laid out in 1615, but was completely rebuilt between 1931 and 1936.

About halfway along Via Roma is Piazza San Carlo, which is known as Turin's drawing room and features many of the city's better cafés. At the southern end are the Baroque churches of **San Carlo** and **Santa Cristina**, the latter designed by Filippo Juvarra. Continuing north, Via Roma ends at **Piazza Castello**, the centre of historic Turin. In the middle of the piazza is the **Palazzo Madama**, named because it was the residence of Vittorio Amedeo I's widow, Maria Cristina. The palace is a sumptuous reminder of the Savoys' wealth. It was built in the 13th

century on the site of the old Roman gate and has been altered many times. It houses the **Museo Civico d'Arte Antica**, which opens from 9 am to 5 pm Tuesday to Saturday, and Sunday mornings. Entrance is L5000.

At the north-west corner of the square is the **Church of San Lorenzo**, designed by Guarini, and farther along, through the massive gates with their statues of the ancient Roman deities, Castor & Pollux, is the **Palazzo Reale**, an austere, apricot-coloured building constructed for Carlo Emanuele II around 1646. Its interior is in stark contrast to its exterior, with gilded walls and eccentric collections ranging from Chinese vases to tasteless pieces that belonged to the royal family. The Royal Gardens, east of the palace, were designed by Louis le Nôtre in 1697, whose other work includes the gardens at Versailles. The **Armeria Reale**, the Savoys' royal armoury, houses what is believed to be the best collection of arms in Europe. The palace and the armoury cost L10,000 each and are open most days, as are the gardens, which are free.

The **Cathedral of San Giovanni**, west of the Palazzo Reale off Via XX Settembre, houses the famous, but disputed, **Shroud of Turin**, the linen cloth that the faithful believe was used to wrap the crucified Christ. Carbon dating carried out during the 1980s dates the shroud somewhere in the 13th or 14th century, but the thousands who flock to see it don't seem to mind. The shroud is in the **Capella della Santa Sindone** (Chapel of the Holy Shroud), topped by Guarini's honeycomb-like black marble dome, while a copy adorns the walls of a nearby chapel. Despite the carbon dating, no-one has been able to explain the shroud's markings. Luigi Gagna's copy of Leonardo da Vinci's *Last Supper*, above the doors, is considered the best copy of the painting ever produced. The chapel is open from 9 am to midday and from 3 to 6 pm daily except Mondays.

The **Palazzo Carignano**, Via Accademia delle Scienze 5, is in pure Baroque style and has great historical significance as the birthplace of Carlo Alberto and Victor Emmanuel II and as the seat of the Italian parliament from 1861 to 1864. The palace houses the **Museo Nazionale del Risorgimento Italiano**, which is open from 9.30 am to 6.30 pm Tuesday to Saturday and from 9 am to 12.30 pm on Sunday. Entrance is L10,000, free on Sunday.

The **Palazzo dell'Accademia delle Scienze** on the street of the same name houses the city's impressive **Egyptian Museum**, established in the late 18th century and now considered one of the world's best after those of London and Cairo. It is open Tuesday to Saturday from 9 am to 2 pm, and 3 to 7 pm and entrance is L10,000. In the same building is the **Galleria Sabauda**, housing the Savoy collection, which features works by many Italian, French and Flemish artists. It's open Tuesday to Saturday from 9 am to 2 pm and 3 to 7.30 pm, and entrance is L10,000.

The **Galleria d'Arte Moderna**, Via Magenta 31, boasts an impressive collection of 19th and 20th century works, including pieces by Renoir, Courbet, Klee and Chagall.

Along Via Giuseppe Verdi from Piazza Castello is the impressive **Mole Antonelliana**, originally intended as a synagogue when it was started in 1863. Its chequered history (mostly as a white elephant) can be studied at the small museum, but a trip to the highest platform, at about 110 metres, is well worth it for the view of the city and Alps. It's open Tuesday to Sunday from 9 am to 7 pm, and entrance is L4000. Walking south along the River Po, you will come to **Valentino Castle**, a Disneyland-like medieval castle built in the 19th century for an exposition.

East from Piazza Vittorio Veneto, across the Po, is the **Gran Madre di Dio** church, built between 1818 and 1831 to commemorate King Victor Emmanuel's return from exile. Set into the hills, its dome dominates the area and acts as a landmark. The church is generally closed to the public.

The **Museo dell'Automobile**, south along Via Nizza, has an impressive collection of cars, including one of the first Fiats and the Isotta Franchini driven by Gloria Swanson in the film *Sunset Boulevard*. The museum can be reached by bus No 34 from

beside the station. It's open Tuesday to Sunday from 9.30 am to 12.30 pm and 3 to 7 pm, and entrance is L10,000.

Overlooking Turin, set into the hills across the river where most wealthy Turinese reside, is the **Basilica di Superga**. In 1706, King Vittorio Amedeo promised to build a basilica to honour the Virgin Mary if Turin was saved from the besieging French and Spanish armies. The city was saved and the church was built by Filippo Juvarra as the resting place of the Savoys, whose lavish tombs make for interesting viewing. The spot is probably more popular, however, as a football shrine. The tomb of the Torino football team, all killed when their plane crashed into the basilica in 1949, is at the rear. The basilica is reached by No 15 tram (to the end of the line) and connecting funicular.

A visit to the city is not complete without viewing **La Palazzina di Caccia di Stupenigi**, the Savoys' luxurious hunting lodge, which is now nestled in the outer edge of the Fiat plants and Mirafiori suburb. It is slowly being restored with Fiat money and many parts of the building are in original condition. Check with the APT because opening times vary. Take bus No 41 from Corso Vittorio Emanuele II, left of Porta Nuova.

Places to Stay – bottom end

Finding a room can be difficult in Turin, and finding a cheap one even harder. Call the APT in advance for a suggestion, although the staff won't make a reservation. The APT at the station will give you a map and directions to your hotel.

Camping & Hostel The *Campeggio Villa Rey* (☎ 819 01 17), Strada Superiore Val San Martino 27, is away from the centre. Check with the APT for directions and opening times.

The *Ostello Torino* (☎ 660 29 39), Via Alby 1, is in the hills east of the River Po and can be reached by bus No 52 from Porta Nuova. Ask the driver for the right stop. Bed and breakfast is L16,000, and a meal

L12,000, but things are more expensive without an IYHF card.

Hotels Hotels include *Albergo Alfieri* (☎ 839 59 11), Via Pomba 7, which has singles/doubles from L40,000/50,000. The *Canelli* (☎ 54 60 78), Via San Dalmazzo, 7, off Via Garibaldi, has rooms for about the same price. In the same pleasant area, *Albergo Kariba* (☎ 54 22 81), Via San Francesco d'Assisi 4, charges L35,000/50,000. *Albergo La Consolata* (☎ 669 89 79), Via Nizza 21, is clean and safe despite the location. Rooms start at L34,000/45,000. *Albergo Florida* (☎ 562 89 16), Piazza Statuto 9, at the western end of Via Garibaldi, has rooms from L40,000/50,000. *Albergo Edelweis* (☎ 650 72 08), Via Madama Cristina 34, has rooms from L45,000/55,000. *Albergo San Carlo* (☎ 55 35 22), overlooking the piazza of the same name, has rooms from L50,000/60,000. *Albergo Magenta* (☎ 54 26 49) is close to Porta Nuova at Corso Vittorio Emanuele II 67, with rooms, including breakfast, from L50,000/68,000.

Places to Stay – middle to top end
The *Albergo Campo di Marte* (☎ 54 53 61), Via XX Settembre 7, has singles/doubles from L75,000/95,000. *Albergo Europa* (☎ 54 42 38), Piazza Castello 99, has rooms for about the same price, as does *Albergo Bologna* (☎ 562 01 91), Corso Vittorio Emanuele II 60, near the main station. The three-star *Albergo Roma & Rocca Cavour* (☎ 561 27 72), Piazza Carlo Felice, 60, charges about L110,000 for a single and L140,000 for a double – all in sumptuous style. The *Stazione e Genova* (☎ 562 94 00), Via Sacchi 14, is of the same standard and charges about the same price. The *Venezia* (☎ 562 33 84), Via XX Settembre 70, has rooms from L110,000/140,000, although it halves its prices in winter months.

The city's most luxurious hotel is the *Turin Palace* (☎ 562 55 11), Via Sacchi 8, with singles/doubles starting at L280,000/330,000.

Places to Eat
Turin's cuisine is heavily influenced by the French style of cooking, and the massive migration to the city of southern Italians brought traditions of cooking unmatched anywhere else in the north. The city's cafés are traditional and many could claim to be among Europe's most elegant. As with their politics, the Turinese are progressive with their dining habits, and many of the city's finer restaurants have banned smoking. Try a *risotto alla piemontese* (with butter and cheese) or *zuppa canavesana* (turnip soup) and finish with a Savoy favourite, *panna cotta* (baked cream). The area around Via Po is great for cheaper restaurants full of students. The wines come largely from the Asti region, or the well-known Barolo vineyards.

One of the better self-service restaurants is *La Grangia*, Via Garibaldi 21, where you can eat a full meal for L10,000. Another is *Monterosso*, Via Bogono 2, off Via Po, open for lunch only with pasta from L2500. Close to the station, *Ristorante del Chianti*, Via Saluzzo 13 (parallel to Via Nizza), has a set menu for L18,000, including wine.

A typical and cheap place to eat is *Ristorante Otto Colonne*, Via G Barolo 5, near Via Po, with pasta from L5000 and meat dishes from L12,000. *Pizzeria alla Baita dei Sette Nani*, Via A Doria 5, is said to be the best in Turin, with cheap wine and pizzas from L3500. Crowds queue for hours to get in. *Pizzeria da Luigi*, Via S Dalmazzo 1, near Via Garibaldi, has main courses from L5000, good steaks and great calzone.

Trattoria Alba, Via Bava 2, off Piazza Vittorio Veneto, is dirt cheap, with good serves of pasta from L2500. *Lullaby*, Via XX Settembre 6, has a range of local specialities, with main courses from L6000. *Pizzeria Italo*, Via Botero 7, has very good pizzas, done in the Turinese style, and is good for vegetarians as it has great salads.

Ristorante Lanternin, Via Consolata 1, is more expensive, with pasta from L7000, but has an adventurous menu.

Cafés The *Leri*, Corso Vittorio Emanuele II 64, is near Porta Nuova, and has jazz performances. *Caffè Fiorio*, Via Po 8, in the student area, is a bit more accessible for ordinary folk, although still sophisticated. *Baratti and Milano*, Piazza Castello, is very highbrow but worth a look if you can handle coffee for L5000. *Caffè San Carlo*, Piazza San Carlo, is popular with the city's powerful.

Gelati The *Gelateria delle Alpi*, Via Po 18, and *Gelateria Fiorio*, Via Po 8, are among the best, while *Gelateria Copa Rica*, near Porta Nuova, has great semifreddo gelati.

Entertainment
On Fridays, the newspaper *La Stampa* has an entertainment insert, *Torino Sette*, which lists everything. The city organises Punta Verdi – a series of summer concerts and films in various parks and theatres from June until August. There are usually free midday concerts from February to April, and locally produced video-opera is shown, also for free, from November to June at 1 pm most days at the Teatro Piccolo Regio in Piazza San Carlo.

The cheapest tickets for the opera season at Teatro Regio Torino sell for L25,000, but there is generally a queue.

Cinema Massimo, near the Mole Antonelliana, offers an eclectic mix of films, mainly in English, or with subtitles.

The city's nightclubs are among the country's best, but most require membership (although they usually let you join temporarily). Charming Club, Via P Clotilde, 82, is very popular, although it is exclusively gay on Saturdays. Epic Club, Via Martiri della Libertà, and La Cage aux Follies, Via Garibaldi 11, are also popular. Doctor Sax, Lungo Po Cadorna 4, near the river, is a nightclub and jazz venue.

Getting There & Away
Air Turin is serviced by Caselle International Airport (☎ 577 83 61), with flights to European and national destinations.

Bus Buses terminate at the Autostazione (☎ 44 25 25), Corso Inghilterra 3. Buses

serve the Valle d'Aosta, most towns and ski resorts in Piedmont, and major Italian cities.

Train The main train station (☎ 561 33 33) is at Porta Nuova, Piazza Carlo Felice. Regular trains connect Turin with Milan, Aosta, Venice, Genoa and Rome.

Car & Motorbike Turin is a major autostrada junction. The A4 connects with Milan, the A5 with Aosta, the A6 with Savona and the Ligurian Coast, and the A21 with Piacenza. For hitchhikers, the ss29 heads for Asti, the ss24 for Susa and the ss11 east for Milan.

Getting Around
To/From the Airport The SADEM bus company (☎ 30 16 16) runs a service to the airport every half hour from the bus station in Corso Inghilterra.

Bus & Tram The city is large and is well served by a network of buses and trams run by Trasporti Torinesi (TT, ☎ 53 83 76), which has an information booth at Porta Nuova. A map of public transport routes is available from the APT. Single-trip tickets are available, but day tickets (L3500) are the best bet. The company also runs Navigazione sul Po (☎ 83 02 44), which operates boat rides on the river.

Car Rental Major rental agencies include Avis (☎ 50 11 07), Corso Turati 15, and Europcar (☎ 650 36 03), Via M Buonarroti 17. Most other agencies are represented in the city.

AROUND TURIN
Allow yourself a couple of weeks to complete the Grande Traversata delle Alpi (GTA), or a couple of days to complete smaller sections of this walk that starts in the area of Viozene, in the south of Piedmont, and follows a network of Alpine refuges north through the province of Cuneo, the Susa Valley, the Gran Paradiso National Park, through the north of the region before ending on the banks of Lake Maggiore at Cannobio. A fold-out map entitled *Percorsi*

e Posti Tappa GTA (literally, 'Routes & and Places to Stop'), which lists the names and locations of refuges and emergency information, is available from the APT or the CAI in Turin. If the APT does not have a copy of the map, ask for a contact at the Regione Piemonte tourism section, which produced it. Unfortunately, the information is in Italian only, but addresses and details are easily deciphered.

The Alpitrek map, *A Cavallo Tra Valsusa & Valsangone*, provides similar information for horse-riding tracks through the Piedmontese Alps. It is available from the Valle di Susa APT in Oulx. A second map, *In Piemonte a Cavallo*, with routes starting at Albissola on the Ligurian coast, is available from the APT in Turin or the Associazione Nazionale Turismo Equestre Piemonte (☎ 011-54 74 55) in Turin, Via Bertola 39.

THE SUSA VALLEY (VALLE DI SUSA)

West of Turin and easily accessible by car, bus and train, the Susa Valley takes in the Susa ski resort and the more glamorous but overdeveloped resort of Sestriere. Parts of this area are very beautiful, although it is very busy and populated, especially on weekends and during the skiing season. Walking possibilities are good, but better in the north and the Gran Paradiso.

The main APT for the Susa Valley is in Oulx (☎ 0122-83 15 96), Piazza Garambois 5, and can help with lodgings, White Week packages and walking details.

The **Sacra di San Michele**, one of the region's best attractions, is perched atop Monte Pirchiriano at the mouth of the Susa Valley. Dating back to the 11th century, the Gothic-Romanesque abbey is a creepy reminder of medieval Piedmont. The closest town is Avigliana, a short train ride from Turin, which is connected to the abbey by bus (about three a day). A better route is to continue by train to Sant'Ambrogio, at the foot of the hill, and tackle the 90-minute walk up to the abbey. Check the opening times with the APT in Turin before setting out.

Susa

On the busiest route between Turin and France, Susa is a busy regional centre of Celtic origin which eventually became Roman, and still bears a well-preserved collection of Roman ruins. It is worth a visit and makes a good stopover for the resorts farther along the valley.

The **Cathedral of San Giusto**, built in the early 11th century, is one of the finest churches in Piedmont. Other features in the city are primarily Roman: **Augustus's Arch** and the **Castle of Marian Adelaide**, a short walk uphill from the cathedral, provide magnificent views. In the city, the ampitheatre and baths are worth finding.

The *Albergo Sole* (☎ 0122-62 21 92) in Piazza IV Novembre has doubles for under L30,000. *Giardini* (☎ 62 20 79) is nearby and has singles/doubles for L23,000/32,000.

Sestriere

Conceived by Mussolini and built by the Agnelli clan (of Fiat fame), Sestriere is a cultural desert that has grown to become one of Europe's most fashionable ski resorts. It is as important for the wealthy Turinese to be seen swooshing past here as it is for them to be seen sipping tea in the capital's Piazza San Carlo.

The APT (☎ 0122-7 68 65) is in Piazza G Agnelli, and has good information about skiing and accommodation, as does the Ski Club Sestriere (☎ 0122-7 63 06), Piazza Agnelli 4. The resort is reached by bus from Turin or Susa or by lift from Sauze d'Oulx. The Borgata Sestriere Ski School is at Via al Colle, and the Sestriere school is at Piazzale Kandahar. Both are expensive.

In summer, the resort is still popular and offers a range of activities, including free climbing, mountain-bike riding, horse riding and walking, details of which are available from the APT.

The *Albergo La Torre* (☎ 0122-7 71 23) has singles/doubles from L30,000/40,000.

Getting There & Away

There are frequent local train services between Porta Nuova in Turin and Modane in France, passing through Susa, Oulx and Bardonecchia. The rail line is also the main Turin-Lyons route and it is possible to catch express trains between some of the towns. See Getting There & Away under Turin for buses. The A4 autostrada, also known as the T4 after Turin, weaves its way through the valley and most of the towns to Bardonecchia, the French border and Lyons. Hitchers should take the ss24 road from Turin, but be well prepared for freezing conditions during winter.

SOUTHERN PIEDMONT
Cuneo

The main regional centre in the south of Piedmont, Cuneo is a modern city with a few interesting buildings. However, the city's main attraction is that it is a major transport hub for the many valleys and smaller cities in the area. This part of Piedmont is one of the least popular with tourists, despite the beauty of the many valleys that radiate away from the city. These include the Valle Stura, noted for its rare species of flowers, and the Valle Nermenagna, which leads to three national parks – the Parco Naturale Argentera, the Riserva Naturale Bosco e Laghi di Palanfre and, farther east, the Parco Naturale Alta Valle Pesio. The valleys also offer about 20 smaller skiing areas. Although the mountains might not be as high as those farther north, the area is begging to be explored.

Orientation & Information The main train station is at the western edge of town on Corso IV Novembre. Cross Piazzale Libertà in front of the station and walk east along Corso Giolitti until it intersects Corso Nizza, the city's main thoroughfare. To the north is Piazza di Duccio Galimberti and the city's older area, with the Duomo and most buildings of historical significance.

The APT (☎ 6 66 15) is at Corso Nizza 17, and has extensive information about the province. The town's telephone code is 0171.

Places to Stay & Eat The *Albergo Ciriegia* (☎ 69 27 03), Corso Nizza 11, has singles/

doubles from L30,000/40,000; the *Cavallo Nero* (☎ 6 20 17), Piazza Seminario 8, charges slightly more. This hotel also has a restaurant, which is quite cheap, with pasta from L5000. *Ristorante Tre Citroni*, Via Bonelli 2, is more expensive and serves local dishes and wines.

Getting There & Away ATI buses (☎ 0175-4 37 44) connect Cuneo with towns to the north. The Provincia di Cuneo – Settore Trasporti (☎ 44 51), Via Nizza 21, or the APT can provide a complete bus timetable. The city is on the train line between Ventimiglia and Turin and also connects with Asti. There is a second station for the Cuneo-Gesso line, serving small towns in the valley. By car, take the A6 autostrada from Turin towards Savona and exit at Fossano. Follow the signs for Cuneo.

Saluzzo

Between Cuneo and Turin, Saluzzo is a pleasant village set in the lush Po Valley. On the valley's western edge, with Mt Monviso (3841 metres) rising behind, the town is one of the most picturesque villages in Piedmont. The APT (☎ 0175-4 67 10), Via Griselda 6, has a range of information about the surrounding valleys. The Comunità Montana Valle Varaita (☎ 0175-9 61 52), Piazza della Vittoria 52, in Sampeyre, has information about the valley.

Albergo Luna (☎ 4 37 07), Via Martiri della Liberazione 10, has singles/doubles from L28,000/36,000.

EASTERN PIEDMONT
Asti

The region gives its name to Italy's best known sparkling wine, the Asti Spumante. Significant palaeontological discoveries have been made around the town of Asti and the area is considered one of the world's most important sites. Asti is a pleasant and attractive town set in the rolling Monferrato hills, but only really comes to life during its Palio in mid-September, when the Campo del Palio in the city's centre is transformed from car park to race track, and during wine festi-

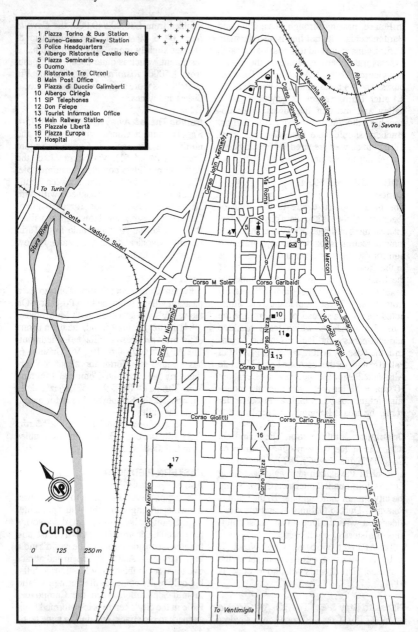

1 Piazza Torino & Bus Station
2 Cuneo–Gesso Railway Station
3 Police Headquarters
4 Albergo Ristorante Cavallo Nero
5 Piazza Seminario
6 Duomo
7 Ristorante Tre Citroni
8 Main Post Office
9 Piazza di Duccio Galimberti
10 Albergo Cirlegia
11 SIP Telephones
12 Don Felepe
13 Tourist Information Office
14 Main Railway Station
15 Piazzale Libertà
16 Piazza Europa
17 Hospital

Cuneo

0   125   250 m

vals held later in the year. The city is worth visiting, particularly as a base for a tour of the many family-owned vineyards within easy driving distance.

The APT (☎ 0141-5 03 57), Piazza Alfieri, in the centre of town, has information about the town and can also assist with itineraries for the wine areas. The town's telephone code is 0141.

The **cathedral**, Piazza Cattedrale, is a large 14th century Gothic construction and one of the most important churches in Piedmont. The city's other noteworthy church is the **Church of San Secondo**, Asti's patron saint. During the late 13th century, the region became one of Italy's wealthiest, and some 100 towers of the period stand as reminders of its glorious past.

Places to Stay & Eat Accommodation is loaded in the multistar category, catering to the wine business rather than the tourist. *Campeggio Umberto Cagni* (☎ 27 12 38), Via Valmanera 78, off Corso Volta, has sites from L6000. Hotels include the *Albergo Antico Paradiso* (☎ 21 43 85), Corso Torino 329, which has singles/doubles from L25,000/46,000; and the *Genova* (☎ 5 31 97), Corso Alessandria 26, which is slightly more expensive.

Restaurants in Asti are not cheap, but there are plenty of shops selling picnic essentials around Piazza Alfieri. At *La Grotta*, Corso Torino 336, typical dishes are served, with main courses from L10,000.

Getting There & Away The city is reached by train from Turin and can be reached from Genoa. Autolinee Giachino (☎ 0141-93 71 55), in Villanova d'Asti, runs bus services to towns throughout the region. By car, take the A21 autostrada which runs between Turin and Piacenza and exit at either Asti Ovest or Asti Est, and then follow signs to the centre.

Around Asti
Costigliole d'Asti, in the centre of the wine-growing area and a short bus ride from Asti, is a cheaper accommodation alternative, although eating can still be expensive.

Albergo Penna Nera (☎ 0141-96 61 02), Regione Sabbionassi, has singles/doubles from L25,000/33,000.

NORTHERN PIEDMONT

The obvious reason to head north is for the mountains. There is also Lake Maggiore, which straddles the region's boundary with Lombardy, and there are several natural reserves, the most popular and beautiful being around Monte Rosa. This area provides a feast of year-round activities, with excellent skiing in the winter and exceptional walking and horse riding in summer.

Varallo
This town, at the start of the Valsesia, makes a good base or starting point for adventures in the mountains. The APT della Valsesia (☎ 0163-5 12 80), Corso Roma 41, has detailed information about the area, including skiing, although Monterosa Ski in Alagna is the best place for information about Alpine activities. *Albergo Monte Rosa* (☎ 0163-5 11 00) has singles/doubles from L30,000/50,000.

Domodossola
Farther north, along the Val d'Ossola, is this regional centre for the north of Piedmont. The APT delle Ossola information office (☎ 0324-48 13 08), Corso P Ferraris 49, has detailed information about walking and skiing. Most of the resorts in the area are well organised and offer White Week accommodation packages, details of which are available at the APT. The Comunità Montane Valle Ossola (☎ 0324-4 63 91) is also a useful place to get information.

Albergo Domus (☎ 0324-24 23 23), Via Cuccioni 12, is about the town's cheapest hotel, with singles/doubles from L25,000/40,000. *Albergo La Pendola* (☎ 0324-24 37 04) has rooms for slightly more. *Trattoria Romana*, Via Binda 16, is cheap, with main courses from L8000, and specialises in French/Roman cuisine. *Pizzeria Rugantino*, Via Giovanni XXIII, is cheaper, with pizzas from L5000.

Getting There & Away Trains from Milan or Turin connect with local trains at Novara. Domodossola is closer to Milan than Turin, and can be reached by taking the A4 autostrada which connects the two cities. Exit the autostrada just north of Novara.

Valle d'Aosta

Covering a mere 3262 sq km and with a population of 117,000, Valle d'Aosta (literally, Valley of Aosta) is the smallest of the Italian regions, but one of the wealthiest. Its origins are Roman, although the Italian language arrived only in 1861 with unification. The Valdestans, as they are called, still speak the Franco-Provençal patois, and French is afforded equal rights with Italian. To the east, small villages cling to a German dialect called Tich. The region remained isolated until the opening of the Mont Blanc tunnel in 1965, connecting Courmayeur to the French city of Chamonix. As a result, the quiet valley became a major road-freight thoroughfare and one of Europe's premier skiing areas. Unfortunately, the problems of overdevelopment and pollution soon followed.

Valle d'Aosta enjoys self-governing status, stemming from its binational origins, which means 90% of local taxes are spent in the province. It has the nation's most efficient public services and is less antagonised by the traditional northern bias against the south. In practice, autonomy means Valdestans receive substantial tax advantages not shared by other Italians.

Valle d'Aosta shares Europe's highest mountain, Mont Blanc (4807 metres, known as Monte Bianco in Italy), with France, and the Matterhorn (4478 metres, known as Monte Cervino in Italy) with Switzerland. The small province also takes in Monte Rosa (4638 metres) and parts of Gran Paradiso (4061 metres), which adjoins Piedmont. Its resort towns – Courmayeur, Breuil-Cervinia, La Thuile, Gressoney and Cogne – and the valleys running off the central Aosta Valley offer a feast of year-round activities. The area provides some of Europe's best skiing, and the Gran Paradiso National Park reputedly offers the country's best hiking.

The region's origins date back to 3000 BC, and several human settlements of the Neolithic period and early Bronze Age have been discovered. Early Roman sites dot the valley, and Aosta is known as the Rome of the Alps. Alpine castles dating from the 11th to 15th centuries, the forts and residences of the Challant family, which ruled the region for seven centuries, line the valley floor.

AOSTA

Aosta is the capital and only major city of the province, with a population of about 37,000. It lies at the centre of the valley on the Dora Baltea River and is the main transport hub. It has limited attractions, but is a jumping-off point to the 11 valleys and their resorts.

Orientation

From Piazza Manzetti, outside the train station, Via G Carducci to the left and Via Giorgio Carrel to the right follow the Roman wall around the city. Via Ribetel and Viale della Stazione lead from the station into the centre, the former into Piazza Narbonne, which houses the main post office and bus station, and the latter to Piazza Chanoux, the main square.

The city is laid out on a grid following the Roman pattern, and most of the historic centre is closed to traffic. Via De Tillier, west of Piazza Chanoux, is Aosta's main boulevard and has a good selection of restaurants, bars, cafés and fashion shops. Via Porte Pretoriane to the east is the main Roman thoroughfare heading to the Roman gate, Porta Pretoria, and is now the main tourist strip.

Information

Tourist Office The APT (☎ 0165-3 56 55) is at Piazza Chanoux 8 and is open from 9 am to midday and 3 to 8 pm every day except Sunday. It has information on the entire province and can assist with accommodation and information on skiing conditions and

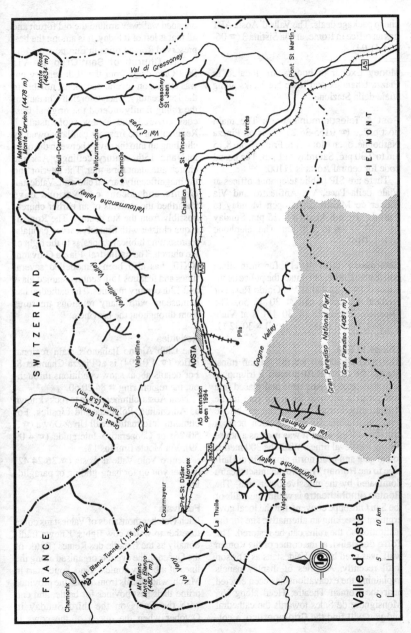

Valle d'Aosta

cheap package deals. The Valle d'Aosta APT has an office in Rome, at Via Sistina 3 (☎ 06-474 41 04).

Money Exchange booths are located in Piazza Chanoux and there are banks along Viale della Stazione.

Post & Telecommunications The main post office (☎ 0165-36 22 87) is on Piazza Narbonne, open Monday to Friday from 8.15 am to 7.30 pm, Saturday to 1 pm. The postal code for central Aosta is 11100.

There are SIP public telephone offices at Viale della Pace, Via Anfiteatro and Via Xavier de Maistre 28A, open Monday to Saturday from 8.45 am to 7.15 pm, Sunday from 10.30 am to 5.30 pm. The telephone code is 0165.

Emergency Dial ☎ 113 for immediate police attendance, or contact the police headquarters (☎ 3 21 41) at Via Guido Rey. For medical attention, call ☎ 30 42 56. The Ospedale Regionale (☎ 30 41) is at Viale Ginevra. For an ambulance, call ☎ 30 42 11.

Things to See
The main attractions are the Roman ruins. Start at the **Arch of Augustus**, a triumphal arch dedicated to Augustus and placed in a straight axis between the main gate to the Roman city, Porta Pretoria, and the bridge over the Buthier River. The arch bears a crucifix, added when it was used as a house during medieval times. Walk the 300 metres to the gate and head north along Via di Baillage to the **Roman Theatre**, an intact theatre dominated by the massive outer wall. The **Roman Amphitheatre** is within the walls of the San Giuseppe convent, but the local government is seeking an alternative site for the institution so the ruins can be restored. The **Torre dei Balivi**, at the corner of the Roman wall, was used by the Valdestans as a prison until recently. A series of display panels explaining the excavations has been erected near the Roman Theatre. Head along Via Monsignore de Sales towards the cathedral and you will find the **Criptoportico**, a col-

onnaded walkway around the old forum and all that is left of it today. It is among the best preserved Roman ruins in Europe.

The **Church of Sant'Orso** in Via Sant'Orso dates from the 10th century but was altered on several occasions, notably in the 15th century, when Giorgi di Challant of the ruling family ordered the original frescoes covered and a new roof installed. Remnants of the frescoes can be viewed by climbing up into the cavity between the original and 15th century ceilings. Ask the church attendant for a tour. The interior and the magnificently carved choir are Valdestan Gothic and recent excavations have unearthed the remains of an earlier church, possibly from the 8th century. The Romanesque cloister with ornately carved capitals, representing biblical scenes, is to the right of the church. The **cathedral**, Piazza Giovanni XXIII, has also been remodelled several times and features 15th century stained glass and 12th century mosaics. The cathedral has a museum with many religious treasures from throughout the province.

Activities
The Club Alpino Italiano's main regional office (☎ 4 01 94) is at Piazza Chanoux 8. For details about snow conditions throughout the region, ring ☎ 84 20 60.

Near Aosta, climbers cling to rocks known as Adrénaline, Polyester and Lipstick. For climbing information, call Up & Down (☎ 3 50 26) or Cooperativa Interguide (☎ 4 09 39), Via Monte Emilius 13.

Centro Volo Valle d'Aosta (☎ 36 24 42) can set you up for hang-gliding or paragliding.

Festivals
Each October thousands of Valdestans come together to watch cow fights. Known traditionally as the Bataille des Reines (Battle of the Queens), the event is organised along the lines of a beauty contest. Knockouts start in March, when locals from across the province prime their best bovines for battle, and end with the finals on the third Sunday in October when the queen of the cows is

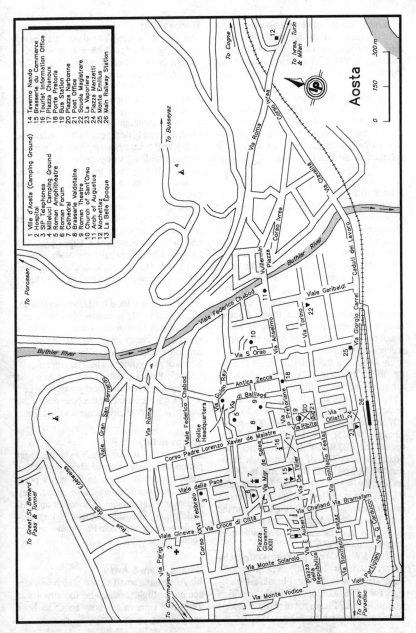

1   Ville d'Aosta (Camping Ground)
2   Hospital
3   SIP Telephones
4   Milleluci Camping Ground
5   Roman Amphitheatre
6   Roman Forum
7   Cathedral
8   Brasserie Valdôtaine
9   Roman Theatre
10 Church of Sant'Orso
11 Arch of Augustus
12 Mochettaz
13 La Belle Époque
14 Taverno Nando
15 Brasserie du Commerce
16 Tourist Information Office
17 Piazza Chanoux
18 Porte Pretoria
19 Bus Station
20 Piazza Narbonne
21 Post Office
22 Scuola Magistrale
23 La Vaperiera
24 Piazza Manzetti
25 Monte Emilius
26 Main Railway Station

Aosta

0   150   300 m

crowned. This might seem a bit strange, but it is a tradition from the days when cows returning from mountain fields would tussle with each other. The losing cow is not injured, the match ends when one pulls away. The queen sells for millions of lire.

The Foire de Sant' Orso, the annual wood fair held on 30-31 January, brings together craftspeople from all over the valley who display their carvings and then present an item to the saint at the church of his name. It is held near the Porta Pretoria.

Places to Stay

Accommodation in Aosta is generally expensive and difficult to find, particularly during the high season around Christmas and Easter. Cheaper and more pleasant lodgings can be found in the hinterland, usually accessible by bus. Check with the APT. There are no hostels in the province.

There are camping facilities at *Ville d'Aosta* (☎ 3 28 78), Viale Gran San Bernardo 76, just out of the town. Another camping ground, *Milleluci* (☎ 4 42 74), is about one km north-east of Aosta and can be reached by bus No 11.

In Aosta, try the hotel *La Belle Époque* (☎ 36 22 76), Via d'Avise 18, which has singles/doubles without bathrooms for L26,000/46,000, slightly cheaper in the low season. *Mochettaz* (☎ 4 37 06), Corso Ivrea 107, has rooms for L27,000/45,000. *Monte Emilius* (☎ 3 56 92), Via G Carrel 9, has rooms for L22,000/40,000 and offers full board for L50,000 per person. *Gran Paradiso* (☎ 4 06 54), Via Binel 12, at the better end of the scale, has rooms for L60,000/93,000, less in the low season. If you have a car, *Hirondelle* (☎ 5 11 10), eight km into the hills from Aosta at Arpuilles, has great views of the city and mountains. Singles/doubles start at L26,000/42,000.

A good White Week package is offered by *Albergo Joli* (☎ 3 57 47), Via delle Valli Valdostane, with bed-and-breakfast packages for L196,000/266,000 in the low/high season. The APT has a list of about 30 hotels offering weekly packages.

Places to Eat

The cuisine of the Valle d'Aosta is based largely on the local cheese, Fontina, a curious cross between Gouda and brie. Traditional local dishes include *valpelinentse*, a thick soup of cabbage, bread, brodo and Fontina, and *carbonada con polenta*, a dish traditionally made with the meat of the chamoix, although beef is now generally used. *Mocetta* (dried meats) are popular. The valley also boasts numerous small, government-subsidised cooperative vineyards, most producing fewer than 200,000 bottles of white, red and *rosato* (rosé). The wines produced in these vineyards, Europe's highest, are dry and fruity.

At the cheaper end of the scale, Aosta has several self-service restaurants that are good and well patronised. *La Vaporiera*, Via Giorgio Carrel, opposite the train station, and *Scuola Magistrare*, Viale Garibaldi, near the Arch of Augustus, are both open for lunch only.

For traditional local food, *Taverno Nando*, Via de Tillier 41, is reasonably priced, and *Brasserie du Commerce*, Via de Tillier 10, is good for a cheap meal. At the top end is *Brasserie Valdotaine*, Via Xavier de Maistre 8, one of the province's best restaurants.

Boch, Piazza Chanoux, has Aosta's best gelati and is where the local youth hang out, while *Café Nazionale*, at the other end of the piazza, is where their parents drink coffee.

Things to Buy

Tradition has it that Sant'Orso, the local patron saint, gave carved shoes known as *sabo*, not unlike clogs, to the city's poor. Valdestans continue to carve shoes, tiny houses and ceremonial pots which are still widely used. Shops throughout the city, particularly along Via Porte Pretoriane, sell the goods.

Getting There & Away

Air Aosta has a small airport which services commuter flights, otherwise the airports at Turin and Geneva are both about an hour away by car.

Bus Buses to several major European cities leave from the bus station (☎ 36 20 27) in Piazza Narbonne. The extensive regional bus service, connecting Aosta with most resorts in the region, also operates from the piazza.

Train The town is serviced by trains from most parts of Italy, via Turin and Milan. Most travellers to and from Milan must change trains at Chivass. There is a limited train service from Aosta to Pré-St Didier, about five km from Courmayeur.

Car & Motorbike The A5 from Turin and Milan terminates east of the city and continues along its northern edge as Via Roma and then Via Parigi, which connects with the Mont Blanc tunnel. Viale Gran San Bernardo, also to the north, connects Aosta with the Great St Bernard Tunnel and Switzerland. A continuation of the A5, bypassing Aosta to the south, is expected to open in late 1993, but only as far as Morgex, two towns before Courmayeur. Aosta has several large car parks, including one opposite the train station.

Hitchers should have no trouble on Viale Gran San Bernardo, Via Roma or Via Parigi.

Getting Around

The town is quite small and all sites are easily reached on foot. The SVAP (☎ 4 11 25) bus No 1 connects the train station with Piazza Arco d'Augusto and Piazza Chanoux in the town centre. Coop Taxis can be reached on ☎ 4 43 55.

AROUND AOSTA

Apart from the slopes, the Aosta region is worth visiting for its impressive Romanesque and Gothic castles. The valley is virtually a living museum tracing the development of the Alpine castle, but seeing them really requires a car. At the few castles which are open to the public, you must visit in groups of about 25, which can mean waiting until more people turn up. At some, tickets (mostly L4000) are usually only sold for a short period in the morning. Enquire at the APT.

Each castle is within eyesight of the next, and messages used to be flagged along the valley. Heading east from Aosta is the magnificently restored **Fénis Castle**, formerly of the Challant family and featuring rich frescoes, as well as period graffiti. The ruined **Castle of Ussel** is close to the town of St Vincent, and past the town is the **Castle of Verrès**. About one km south of the Dora River is the **Castle of Issogne**, built in the 15th century and recently restored. Towards the Mont Blanc tunnel from Aosta, near the village of Introd, is the **Castle of St Pierre**, which also houses a museum of natural history.

Probably the only reason to visit **St Vincent**, Valle d'Aosta's second-biggest city, is for its casino and as a stopping-off point for the Val d'Ayas and Valtournenche, which leads to the Matterhorn. (The town is also a magnet for prostitutes and drug addicts, a feature the locals try hard to ignore.) With one of the few casinos in Italy, it features the valley's best hotel, the *Billia* (☎ 0166-34 36), with singles from L250,000 and doubles from L350,000. The *Albergo Panoramique* (☎ 0166-51 28 25) has singles/doubles from L24,500/40,000, and the *Riviera* (☎ 0166-51 25 57) has rooms starting at L26,000/45,000.

PILA

This is the closest resort to Aosta (about 18 km south) and prices are quite good. There is a reasonably sized village at Pila, but most services, such as the tourist office, police and medical services, are handled from Aosta. The telephone code is 0165.

Activities

Skiing Pila is among the largest ski areas in the valley, with more than 80 km of runs, including about 10 km for cross-country skiers. It is serviced by 15 lifts, including four cable ways, one of which connects the village with Aosta. It offers challenging and difficult black runs and has a competition slalom course, but also caters for beginners with many easy runs. The highest slope reaches 2700 metres, in the shadow of Gran Paradiso.

Hiking This is not one of the best areas for walking if you like high Alpine country, but the lower slopes leading down into the Dora River valley provide picturesque and easy walks. There are only two refuges in the Charvensod area, with one open all year. Some of the lifts operate in summer for walkers or day trippers.

Horse Riding Contact Maison de Jean (☎ 52 10 93) for horse riding in July and August.

Places to Stay

It is cheaper to stay in Aosta than it is in Pila. There are camping facilities at *Soleil et Neige* (☎ 5 99 48), which is open all year, about seven km from the resort. *Hotel La Nuova* (☎ 52 10 05) has singles/doubles for L40,000/55,000 in the low season or L45,000/60,000 in peak. *Chacaril*, (☎ 52 12 15) has rooms for L35,000/64,500. The best White Week deals are in Aosta (see the Aosta Places to Stay section).

Getting There & Away

Two roads, one from Aosta and the other from Gressan, about six km west of Aosta, lead to Pila. A cable car (☎ 0165-52 10 45 in Aosta) connects Aosta with the village. SVAP bus Nos 8 and 9 go from Aosta to Charvensod and Gressan respectively, but there is no bus service to Pila.

COURMAYEUR

With much of the original village intact and restrictions governing further building, this is the most picturesque of the skiing resorts in the Aosta Valley. It is also the most expensive. Out of season, wealthy Milanese and Turinese women leave their fur coats in a local furrier's vault – minks and ermines too valuable to be worn in the streets of their home cities. In the shadow of Mont Blanc, Courmayeur has more than 140 km of downhill and cross-country skiing runs and a feast of summer activities, including skiing, horse riding, hang-gliding, canoeing and 280 km

of mountain paths. Courmayeur's phone code is 0165.

Information

Tourist Office The APT (☎ 84 20 60) is at Piazzale Monte Bianco and is open from 9 am to 12.30 pm and 3 to 6.30 pm Monday to Saturday and 9.30 am to 12.30 pm Sunday. The Associazione Operatori Turistici del Monte Bianco (☎ 84 23 70), Piazzale Monte Bianco 3, can assist with accommodation.

Emergency For the police, phone ☎ 113, or go to the headquarters (☎ 84 42 35) at Strada della Margherita. For medical attention and ambulance, phone ☎ 84 25 60 or go to the Pronto Soccorso at the Ospedale Regionale d'Aosta (☎ 4 14 00).

Activities

Skiing The Ski Club Courmayeur Monte Bianco (☎ 84 24 41) is at Piazzale Monte Bianco, and there is a skiing school (☎ 84 24 77) at Strada Regionale 51. Lessons start at L40,000 an hour for one or two people.

Four cable cars leave the Courmayeur area for the slopes from La Palud, Courmayeur, Dolonne and Val Veny. Cars from La Palud stop at Pavillion, where another cable car connects with the *Rifugio Torino* and **Punta Helbronner** (the Italian-French border). From there it is possible to catch a cable car to Chamonix. La Palud to Helbronner costs L23,000/33,000 one way/return. Expect to pay up to L60,000 for the Courmayeur-Chamonix trip.

Most ski runs, chair lifts and ski lifts can be reached via the Courmayeur, Dolonne and Val Veny cable cars. For details, check with the APT or the cable-way station in Val Veny (☎ 84 35 66), or Cableways Mont Blanc in La Palud (☎ 8 99 25). Ski passes for six days cost L160,000 in the low season or L190,000 in the high season, or up to L40,000 a day.

Summer Skiing Summer runs can be reached via the La Palud cable car and are serviced by three ski lifts. Contact Cableways Mont Blanc or the skiing school (☎ 84 24 77) at Strada Regionale 51.

Walking, Hiking & Climbing The Mountain & Alpine Guide Association can be contacted on ☎ 84 20 64. The APT publishes a map of walks in the Mont Blanc area, and the cable cars from the valley operate during summer, taking hordes of walkers, family groups and climbers into the Alpine ranges. Val Veny is the starting point for many climbs and hiking trails, while Val Ferret, north-east of Courmayeur, is also a popular starting point for walks. Even in summer, when the valley experiences sweltering heat, temperatures can plunge below zero in the mountains, so make sure you are dressed properly and are well prepared for all weather conditions. Popular climbing spots are La Saxe, Entrelevie and Bec de l'Aigle.

There are almost 30 Alpine refuges in the mountains around Courmayeur, located along walking trails. They are marked on all walking maps and most open all year. You should book in advance. The APT can advise on walking trails and provide a list of refuge locations and phone numbers.

Mountain Bikes To rent a bike, go to Noleggio Ulisse (☎ 84 22 55), in front of the Courmayeur chair lift, or Club des Sports (☎ 8 95 70), Planpincieux.

Other Activities The Scuola di Canoa e Rafting Courmayeur (☎ 80 00 88) can advise

Alpine ibex (stambecca)

on canoeing possibilities. If you want to go ballooning, contact the Club Aérostatique Mont Blanc (☎ 76 55 25).

Places to Stay
During peak seasons, accommodation in Courmayeur is extremely expensive, but the surrounding towns of La Palud, Dolonne, Entrèves, La Saxe, Plan Ponquet, Val Ferret, Pré-St Didier and Morgex, along the valley, offer reasonably priced rooms. Alpine refuges, camping and White Week packages make the area accessible. You will need to book accommodation months ahead. Contact the APT for assistance, or the hotel association (☎ 84 23 70) at Piazzale Monte Bianco 3, and call the hotel for directions.

Campers can head for *Cai-uget Monte Bianco* (☎ 8 92 15) in Val Veny, and *Val Veny-Cuignon* (☎ 84 28 61), both within easy reach of Courmayeur. In Courmayeur, try the *Motel AGIP* (☎ 84 24 27), Strada Regionale 76, which has singles/doubles from L20,000/35,000, or L35,000/50,000 in the peak season. *Ferrato* (☎ 84 22 49) has doubles for L43,000, and *La Pigna* (☎ 84 23 17) has singles/doubles starting at L25,000/39,000. The *Serena* has rooms from L22,000/40,000.

In La Palud there is *La Quercia* (☎ 8 99 31), which has rooms from L28,000/45,000, and *Albergo Funivia* (☎ 8 99 24) which charges L25,000/44,000.

In Pré-St Didier, the *Albergo Alpechiara* (☎ 8 78 22) has singles/doubles from L40,000/55,000.

Many hotels offer seven-day White Week packages. Check with the APT, or try the Albergo Alpechiara just mentioned, which offers the best deal, with prices from L280,000. Contact Mont Blanc Tour Operators (☎ 84 23 70), Piazzale Monte Bianco 3, for more details or bookings.

Places to Eat
Eating in Courmayeur is expensive. There are good food shops along Via Roma, through the old part of town, if picnicking or eating in your room are the only options. Most restaurants are also along Via Roma,

but you'll find cheaper ones in the surrounding towns. *Café des Guides*, Viale Monte Bianco 2, is the most popular spot in town, and the *American Bar*, Via Roma 43, is also worth visiting.

Getting There & Away

Three trains a day from Aosta terminate at Pré-St Didier, with bus connections to the main bus terminus at Piazzale Monte Bianco, outside the tourist office. Courmayeur is serviced by buses from Milan, Turin and Geneva, and buses operate into the valleys. Phone the bus terminus (☎ 84 29 60) for information. By car, Courmayeur is reached from Aosta on the ss26. The trip from Chamonix through the Mont Blanc tunnel costs L30,000.

VALTOURNENCHE

Stretching from the Aosta Valley to Monte Cervino, as the Italian side of the Matterhorn is known, the Valtournenche Valley takes in several smaller and reasonably priced skiing areas – Antey-St André, Chamois, La Magdeleine and Torgnon – and culminates in the resorts of Valtournenche and Breuil-Cervinia. The latter is the second-largest resort area in Valle d'Aosta and is modern, purpose-built, expensive and somewhat unattractive although it offers some of the best skiing in Europe.

Information

Tourist Office The Matterhorn Central Valley APT office (☎ 0166-4 82 66) is in Antey-Saint-André; the Breuil-Cervinia office (☎ 0166-94 91 36) is at Via Carrel 29. In the town of Valtournenche, the APT office (☎ 0166-9 20 29) is at Via Roma. The telephone code for the valley is 0166.

Mountain & Alpine Guides For guides, contact the Society of Cervino Guides (☎ 94 87 44).

Emergency For the police, phone ☎ 113 in an emergency, or otherwise ☎ 94 90 73.

Activities

Skiing Chamois can be reached only by cable car from the Valtournenche road. It has six lifts and is the second-highest resort in the valley, featuring extensive downhill and cross-country runs. Contact the Matterhorn Central Valley APT office or the cable-way station (☎ 4 84 46) for details.

Torgnon is reached by bus No 30 from Châtillon (five a day), which is accessible by bus from Aosta. It is marginally cheaper than the main resorts towards Cervino. For information about the resort, contact the Central Valley APT office or the ski-lift office (☎ 4 85 20). There is a skiing school (☎ 4 03 22) in Torgnon.

Valtournenche is a slightly cheaper option than Breuil-Cervinia. It has nine lifts and dozens of long runs of all standards. It is possible to ski from this area to Cervinia. Contact the tourist office or the lift operator, Cime Bianche (☎ 9 22 21), for details.

From Breuil-Cervinia, eight cable ways and 18 lifts take skiers into some of Europe's most breathtaking terrain. Summer skiing is also possible as several cable ways and lifts continue to operate, taking skiers on to the Plateau Rosa. This resort introduced Valle d'Aosta to night skiing, on the Campetto area. For details, contact the tourist office or Ski-lift Crétaz (☎ 94 86 76). Breuil-Cervinia has two skiing schools, the Matterhorn Ski-School (☎ 94 84 51) and Ski-School Cielo Alto (☎ 94 84 51). For night-skiing information, call Crétaz Val Furggen (☎ 94 86 76).

Hiking Make your way to the APT in Breuil-Cervinia or Aosta for a complete walking map of the area. About 30 refuges are dotted along the Valtournenche, making long walks possible. Many open all year but are in constant demand.

One of the better, and more demanding, walks takes you north of Breuil-Cervinia and around the slopes of the Matterhorn. A popular three-hour walk takes in the Colle Superiore delle Cime Bianche at almost 3000 metres, with great views to the east.

Places to Stay

There is a camp site in Valtournenche, called the *Glair-Lago Di Maen* (☎ 9 20 77). In Breuil-Cervinia, try *Hotel Du Soleil* (☎ 94 95 20), which has singles/doubles from L18,000/28,000, with prices doubling in the high season. It also offers good deals on White Week packages. Also in Breuil-Cervinia, *Leonardo Carrell* (☎ 94 90 77) has rooms for L29,000/50,000 year round. In Valtournenche, try *Albergo Meynet* (☎ 9 20 75), where rooms are L26,500/45,500 year round.

Getting There & Away

Buses operate from Aosta to the resorts and most ski areas in the valley. SAVDA (☎ 0165-36 12 44) operates services from Courmayeur, Aosta and Cervinia, and from Châtillon to Cervinia. Dinotours (☎ 015-222 15) also operates several bus services in the valley.

GRAN PARADISO

Situated in one of Italy's most important national parks, and offering excellent hiking possibilities, the Gran Paradiso is also a superb skiing area. In its shadows, the lesser known valleys of Cogne (with the best cross-country skiing in Valle d'Aosta), Valsavarenche, Rhêmes, Soana and Orco on the Piedmontese side of the mountain offer unspoiled countryside dotted with villages not yet gentrified. The area has always been popular with the highest and mightiest – in the 1870s, Italy's King Victor Emmanuel II hunted on the Gran Paradiso massif, and, more recently, Pope John Paul II has occasionally taken a smallish house in Le Combe, near Introd in the Valsavarenche Valley, and, according to reports, has often enjoyed a lengthy hike.

Information

Tourist Offices The Gran Paradiso Mountain Community Tourist Office (☎ 0165-9 50 55) is at Loc Champagne 18, Villeneuve. There is an APT office in Cogne (☎ 0165-7 40 40). Both have excellent information about summer and winter activities. The Mountain Guide Society has offices in Cogne (☎ 0165-740 40), Rhêmes-Notre-Dame (☎ 0165-9 61 04), Valgrisenche (☎ 0165-9 71 68) and Valsavarenche (☎ 0165-9 59 20). Les Amis du Paradis (the Friends of Paradise Association, ☎ 0165-7 48 35) offers reams of information about the area. The telephone code for the area is 0165.

Emergency For police attendance, call ☎ 113, or ☎ 7 40 26 in Cogne, and ☎ 9 50 25 in Villeneuve. First aid is available in Saint-Pierre (☎ 90 38 11) and Cogne (☎ 74 91 07).

Activities

Skiing Cogne has more than 90 km of cross-country tracks and about 10 km of downhill runs. The Cogne-Montzeuc cable car takes skiers to 1219 metres and the bulk of the downhill runs. The Ski School (☎ 7 43 00) gives lessons in Cogne. A ski pass (requiring a photo) can cost as little as L25,000 a day or L112,000 a week.

Valgrisenche is a small resort and very cheap. It has only 18 km of runs and a six-day ski pass costs L60,000. For all skiing information in Valgrisenche, contact the town hall (☎ 9 71 05). Rhêmes-Notre-Dame is a slightly bigger resort and slightly more expensive – contact the town hall (☎ 9 61 14) for skiing information.

Hiking Offering the best hiking in Aosta, the Gran Paradiso is a mecca for walkers, hikers and climbers. There are 15 popular refuges in the park. The tourist offices have the useful *Guide to Walks & Excursions* which provides detailed information about walking in the park.

Horse Riding Cooperativa Pegaso (☎ 74 92 08), c/o Bar du Village, Cogne, operates year round.

Places to Stay

Camping facilities are available at *Al Sole* (☎ 7 42 37) in Cogne (open all year). In Valsavarenche there is *Camping Pont Breuil* (☎ 9 54 58), open only during summer.

Hotels in Cogne include the *Albergo Stambecco* (☎ 7 40 68), which has singles/

doubles from L15,000/24,000 in the low season and L29,000/49,000 in the high season. Good White Week packages are available at *Du Soleil* (☎ 7 40 33) for upwards of L225,000. In Valsavarenche, try the *Edelweiss* (☎ 90 59 70), which is conveniently close to transport and has rooms for L31,000/50,000.

Getting There & Away

All of the valleys are reached from Aosta or through the Mont Blanc tunnel by car or a good network of buses. SAVDA (☎ 36 12 44) operates bus No 36 to Rhêmes-Notre-Dame, and Autoservizi Benvenuto (☎ 5 76 68) runs the No 46 to Valgrisenche. SVAP (☎ 4 11 25) operates bus No 18 to Cogne and No 20 to Valsavarenche. Cogne can also be reached by cable car from Pila (☎ 7 40 08 in Pila).

MONTE ROSA

The massive Monte Rosa dominates this area, which takes in the Val d'Ayas and Val di Gressoney, with the smaller, cheaper resorts of Antagnod and Champoluc in the former and La Trinité and St Jean in the latter.

Information

Tourist Offices APT offices are in Champoluc (☎ 30 71 13), Brusson (☎ 30 02 40), La Trinité (☎ 36 61 43) and St Jean (☎ 35 51 85). The Club Alpino Italiano has an office in La Trinité (☎ 36 62 59) at the Hotel Castore. For information about mountain guides, contact the tourist offices. The telephone code in the lower valley is 0166, but higher up (including Champoluc, Brusson, La Trinité, St Jean and Verrès) it becomes 0125.

Emergency Call ☎ 113 for police attendance, or ☎ 30 01 23 in Brusson, ☎ 35 53 04 in St Jean, and ☎ 92 90 10 in Verrès.

Activities

Skiing In the Val d'Ayas, the main skiing areas are Challand, Col de Joux and Emarèse in the lower valley, Brusson at mid-valley and Champoluc, Frachey and Antagnod higher up. Prices increase as you go up the mountain, although this whole area is con-

siderably cheaper than the more glamorous resorts of Courmayeur and Breuil-Cervinia.

The lower valley runs offer decent, unadventurous skiing. For skiing information, contact the St Vincent APT (☎ 0166-22 39), or the Emarèse town hall (☎ 0166-7 51 03). Col de Joux has a cross-country skiing school (☎ 0166-3 70 33).

Brusson is probably the cheapest place to stay and ski in the valley. For skiing information, contact the APT. In the upper valley, contact the Champoluc APT. Skiing schools are located in Champoluc (☎ 0125-307 11 30) and Antagnod (☎ 0125-30 66 41).

One skiing area in the Val di Gressoney is Gressoney-La-Trinité, with runs at almost the same height as neighbouring Breuil-Cervinia, to which it is a good, cheap alternative. Farther down the valley is the smaller skiing area of St Jean. Together they have 18 lifts and some good, challenging downhill and cross-country runs. Contact the respective APTs for ski information. Both have branches of the Monte Rosa Ski School (☎ 0125-36 62 65 in La Trinité, ☎ 0125-35 52 91 in St Jean).

Hiking The two valleys have many smaller walking tracks and about 20 refuges. Gressoney-La Trinité is the starting point for a walk that crosses Valle d'Aosta's northern limits and finishes at Courmayeur. Designed to take eight days, the walk is featured in a small booklet, *Valle d'Aosta Alte Vie 1 & 2*. Some ski lifts operate during the summer months.

Places to Stay

Accommodation is reasonable in some mountain areas but good options are St Vincent, Verrès or Brusson, all close to the base of the Val d'Ayas. There is cheap accommodation along the Val di Gressoney. Camping is available in the Val d'Ayas at *Sole e Neve* (☎ 0125-30 66 10) in Morenex, open all year. In the Val di Gressoney, in Gressoney-La-Trinité, try *Staffal* (☎ 0125-36 62 01), also open all year.

Hotels in the Val d'Ayas include *Albergo Cre-Forne* (☎ 0125-30 71 97) in Crest, with singles/doubles from L19,000/25,000 and slightly more during peak season.

In Gressoney-La-Trinité try the *Monte Rosa* (☎ 0125-36 61 20), which has singles/doubles from L25,000/37,500, or *Albergo Castore* (☎ 0125-36 61 31), where rooms start at L21,000/42,000. In Verrès there is the *Bon Accueil* (☎ 0125-92 90 15) which has rooms from L25,000/34,000.

Good White Week packages are available at *Refuge Vieux Crest* (☎ 0125-30 79 83) in the Val d'Ayas, which offers packages from L250,000 all year. In Gressoney-La-Trinité the *Casa dei Larici* (☎ 0125-36 62 84) has packages from L175,000.

Getting There & Away
The train to Aosta stops in St Vincent and Verrès, from where you can catch a bus to either of the valleys. SAVDA (☎ 0165-361244) operates bus No 33 along the Val di Gressoney and bus No 35 from Verrès to Champoluc. Bus No 40 connects Aosta with Champoluc, via Col de Joux. Leave the A5, ss26 or Aosta-Turin/Milan train at Pont-St-Martin for the Val di Gressoney, which is also accessible by SAVDA buses.

Lombardy

Extending from the Alps to the lush plains of the River Po, Lombardy's natural attributes are as diverse as its political history. Italy's richest and most developed region, Lombardy (Lombardia) offers much for the traveller. With the magnificent lakes of Orta, Maggiore, Como, Iseo and Garda nestling below the mountains along the region's northern reaches, landlocked Lombardy is both a summer and a winter playground.

Lombardy formed part of the Roman province of Gallia Cisalpina before it fell to barbarian tribes and later to the Germanic Langobards (Lombards). It was ruled by the Franks, united under the Lombard League, and eventually divided among some of Europe's most powerful families – the Viscontis, Sforzas, Gonzagas and Scaligers.

It was later invaded by the Venetians, then the Austrian Hapsburgs and the French under Napoleon.

Milan is more than just the Lombard capital, it is the country's economic and fashion centre, and in many ways is closer to the rest of Europe than it is to the south it despises. The main cities of Mantua, Cremona, Bergamo, Brescia and Pavia exude wealth and style, and while they are worth visiting, may seem a little staid, particularly if you are coming from the south.

The cuisine of Lombardy draws heavily on rice and polenta and features butter, cream and cheese from the Alpine pastures. Gorgonzola cheese originated just outside Milan. The pasta of the region is fresh and is usually stuffed with winter squash, meat, cheese and spinach, or, as a dessert, can contain raisins or candied fruit. The meats are predominantly pork and veal – *cotoletta alla milanese*, fillet of veal fried in breadcrumbs, is famous around the country.

Whether for snob value or not, the locals, and in particular the Milanese, tend to drink wines from other regions. Lombardy's sparkling wines, however, are among Italy's best – the Franciacorta red is mellow and the white is fruity and dry. The region around Lake Garda also produces good wines.

Public transport is excellent and almost every town can be reached easily.

MILAN (MILANO)
Obsessed with work and money, the Milanese have created for themselves a well-

organised metropolis run in a businesslike manner – a feat which is quite un-Italian. The city is home to a magnificent cathedral, or duomo (the world's fourth-largest church), and to Leonardo da Vinci's *Last Supper*, and holds the enviable position of being the world's leading centre for design and an international fashion capital.

It was not long ago that Milan was Italy's largest city, a position since taken over by Rome which, as the national capital, expanded in the boom years after WW II. The Romans outnumber the Milanese almost two to one, but Milan remains the financial hub, home to Italy's stock market and most of the country's major corporations as well as the nation's largest concentration of industry. The city and surrounds generate almost a quarter of Italy's tax revenue.

Milan's business and political leaders have long criticised what they regard as a corrupt and inefficient Roman government, particularly the disproportionate level of subsidy it channels to the country's south. In the late 1980s, Milan spawned a right-wing party, the Lega Lombarda (Lombard League), which quickly captured 3% of the national vote and pushed that to an astonishing 7% in the 1992 election (it captured 20% of the local vote), campaigning mainly on the promise of breaking the cycle of corruption that characterises Italian politics.

However, Milan itself is not exempt from corruption. In 1992 and 1993, leaders of its government were sacked and some jailed in a scandal over illegal payments, known as *tangenti*. Ongoing investigations showed that the bribes and kickbacks extended to the highest levels of national government, leading to the downfall of many senior politicians. See the History and Government sections in the Facts about the Country chapter for details about this affair.

Milan is one of Italy's most sophisticated cities. Its shopping is the country's best, its nightclubs, bolstered by the country's largest gay community, are the most diverse, and its restaurants offer cuisine from around the country and Europe. The city has a strong provincial cuisine. Polenta (a cornmeal porridge similar to American grits) is served with almost everything, and risotto dominates the first course of the city's menus. Try a *bistecca milanese*, a veal fillet fried in breadcrumbs, or *ossobuco*, veal shank. Polenta also figures on the sweets menu, but *torta di tagliatelle*, a cake made with egg pasta and almonds, might be more inviting.

The Milanese pride themselves on their city, although outsiders can easily be fooled into thinking it is dull and uninviting. Spend a few days and wander around the shopping arcades and backstreets, the grimy student areas near the central train station, the exclusive boutique area of Monte Napoleone or the groovier Navigli to the south. But avoid the city in August – it virtually closes down as the locals take holidays, and very few shops or restaurants are open. Summers are very hot and winters can be bitterly cold.

History

Milan is believed to have been founded by Celtic tribes who settled around the 7th century BC along the banks of the River Po. Romans invaded the territory in 222 BC, defeating the Gallic Insubres, and named the town Mediolanum, meaning in the middle of the plain. The town prospered because of its position between Rome and the rest of

Europe, and in 313 AD, Constantine I chose it as the location to make his famous edict granting Christians freedom of worship.

A period of decline due to barbarian invasions ended early in the 11th century when the city formed a *comune*, a government involving all classes, which led to a period of rapid growth. Forming an alliance with other Lombard towns envious of Milan's wealth and importance, the Holy Roman emperor Frederick Barbarossa besieged and devastated Milan in 1162. The city and its allies formed the Lombard League and exacted revenge in 1176.

From the mid-13th century, the city was ruled by a succession of important families – the Torrianis, the Viscontis and finally the Sforzas. Under the latter two it enjoyed considerable wealth and power. It came under Spanish rule in 1535, but was passed to Austria in accordance with the terms of the Treaty of Utrecht of 1713, signed at the end of the War of the Spanish Succession. Legacies of the reign of Maria Theresa of Austria are still evident, particularly the dull-yellow (her favourite colour) façades of the Scala opera house and the royal palacd.

Napoleon made Milan the capital of his Cisalpine Republic in 1797, and five years later of his Italian Republic, crowning himself King of Italy and Milan there in 1805. Austrians again occupied the town in 1814, but were defeated during the Battle of Magenta in 1859 when troops of Victor Emmanuel II and Napoleon III brought its liberation and incorporation into the Kingdom of Italy. The city was heavily bombed during WW II, but was rebuilt and quickly grew to industrial prominence.

Orientation

Milan is a sprawling metropolis, but most attractions are concentrated in a small area in the centre, between the Duomo and the Castello Sforza. Apart from the centre, the main areas of interest for tourists are the Brera, immediately north of the Duomo, which takes in many galleries and fashionable shopping streets, and Navigli to the south. The city is serviced by an efficient

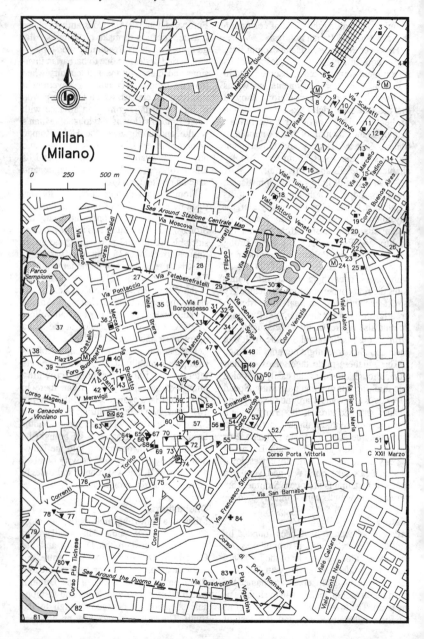

■ PLACES TO STAY

3	Hotel Valley
10	Hotel Italia
11	Albergo Salerno
12	Hotel Paradiso
13	Hotel Due Giardini
15	Hotel Nettuno
16	Hotel Verona
18	Hotel Casa Mia
19	Hotels Kennedy, Canna & San Tomaso
22	Hotel Fenice
25	Albergo Tris
34	Albergo Manzoni
36	Albergo Commercio
40	Hotel London
54	Hotel Ambasciatori
56	Hotel Nuovo
58	Hotel Duomo
63	Albergo Vecchia Milano
68	Hotel Speronari
69	Albergo Rio
79	Albergo Cantore

▼ PLACES TO EAT

4	Ristorante Primavera d'Oriente
9	Brek
20	Ciao
21	Trattoria di Polpetta
33	Alemagna
41	Vecchia Napoli
42	Ciao
43	San Tomaso
46	Don Lisander
47	Casa Fondata
51	La Baia
53	Trattoria da Bruno
55	Popeye
65	Peck Delicatessen
66	Dai Dan II
67	Amico Motta
70	Pizzeria Dogana
77	Berlin Café
78	Café Guarany
80	Trattoria Artisti
81	El Brellin
83	Quadronno

OTHER

1	Porta Garibaldi Railway Station
2	Stazione Centrale
5	Piazza Caiazzo & Caiazzo Metro Station
6	APT Tourist Information Office
7	Stazione Centrale Metro Station
8	Piazza Duca d'Aosta
14	Piazza Lima
17	Piazza della Repubblica
23	Piazzale Oberdan
24	Porta Venezia Metro Station
26	Piazza VIII Novembre
27	Piazza San Marco
28	Police Headquarters
29	Piazza Cavour
30	Galleria d'Arte Moderna
31	Centrodomus
32	Design Gallery of Milano
35	Brera Palace
37	Castello Sforza
38	Piazzale Cadorna
39	Cairoli Metro Station & Largo Cairoli
44	La Scala Opera House
45	Piazza della Scala
48	Museum of Milan
49	Autosila Parking
50	Piazza San Babila & San Babila Metro Station
52	Largo Augusto
57	Duomo
59	Galleria V Emanuele II
60	Piazza del Duomo & Duomo Metro Station
61	Piazza Cordusio
62	Main Post Office & ASST Telephones
64	Ambrosiana Art Gallery
71	APT Tourist Information Head Office
72	Palazzo Reale
73	Piazza Diaz
74	Underground Car Park
75	Piazza Missori
76	Largo Carrobbio
82	Piazza XXIV Maggio
84	Ospedale Maggiore Policlinico

underground railway, the Metropolitana Milanese (MM), with three lines (the red MM1, green MM2 and yellow MM3), which is the most convenient way to get around. It is easy to get lost in the city, so a map is essential.

The Piazza Duca d'Aosta is immediately outside Stazione Centrale, the central train station, as is the closest MM station. To your right as you leave the train station is the Pirelli Building, a slender skyscraper which serves as a good reference point. The area behind it is predominantly occupied by offices, and most of the city's better hotels are clustered there as well. To the south-east of Stazione Centrale, Via Vitruvio leads to the main area for budget hotels. It meets Piazza Lima at the intersection of Corso Buenos Aires and becomes Via Plinio.

From Piazza Duca d'Aosta, walk straight ahead along Via Pisani, through the enormous park-lined Piazza della Repubblica, and continue along Via F Turati, which winds to the left and becomes Via Manzoni. This takes you through the exclusive Monte Napoleone shopping and residential area and into Piazza della Scala, home to the Scala opera house. From there the glass-domed Galleria Vittorio Emanuele II leads to Piazza del Duomo, and the tourist office is at the south-east corner. Corso Vittorio Emanuele, at the north-east end of the piazza, leads to Corso Venezia, which eventually becomes Corso Buenos Aires. Via Torino and Via Orefici are at the south-west corner of the piazza, the latter leading to the Castello Sforza.

Information

Tourist Office The main branch of the APT (☎ 02-80 96 62) is at Via Marconi 1, in Piazza del Duomo, where you can pick up the very useful *Milan is Milano*, *What's On In Milan* and *Milano Mese*. It's open from 8 am to 8 pm Monday to Saturday, and on Sundays and holidays from 9 am to 12.30 pm and 1.30 to 5 pm. There is a branch office (☎ 02-669 05 32) at Stazione Centrale, open daily from 8 am to 8 pm.

The Milan City Council operates an information office in Galleria V Emanuele II, just off Piazza del Duomo.

Money Banks in Milan are open Monday to Friday from 8.30 am to 1 pm and for one hour in the afternoon, usually from 2.45 to 3.45 pm. Exchange offices at weekends include: Banca Ponti, Piazza del Duomo 19, open from 9 am to 1 pm Saturdays; Banca delle Comunicazioni, Stazione Centrale, open from 8 am to 7 pm weekdays, to 6.30 pm Saturdays and 9 am to 1.30 pm Sundays.

There are also weekend exchange offices at both airports. There is an American Express office (☎ 02-8 55 71) at Via Brera 3.

Post & Telecommunications The main post office is at Via Cordusio 4, off Via Dante near Piazza del Duomo. Poste restante is here. The office is open from 8 am to 8 pm Monday to Friday, to 2 pm Saturdays. There are also post offices at Stazione Centrale and both airports. The postal code for central Milan is 20100.

ASST telephone offices are at the main post office and at Stazione Centrale, open from 7 am to 7.45 pm daily. The main SIP telephone office is in Galleria V Emanuele II (where you will also find a Reuters news service in English).

SIP is currently changing telephone numbers in Milan, a process which is taking several years to complete. Some numbers have been changed twice recently. If a number has changed, call directory enquiries on ☎ 12. The telephone code for Milan is 02.

Foreign Consulates Quite a number of countries have consulates in Milan, including the following:

Australia
    Via Turati 40 (☎ 659 87 27)
Canada
    Via Vittorio Pisani 19 (☎ 669 74 51)
UK
    Via San Paolo 7 (☎ 896 34 42)
USA
    Via P Amadeo 2-10 (☎ 65 28 41)

Travel Agencies Il Pavone Viaggi (☎ 698 79 33), Via Gustavo Fara 33, can book hotels and travel. For student and budget travel, CTS has offices at Via S Antonio 2 (☎ 58 30 41 21) and Corso di Porta Ticinese 83 (☎ 837 26 74). CIT (☎ 58 30 41 21) is in the Galleria V Emanuele II.

Bookshops The American Bookstore, Largo Cairoli, has a good selection, as does the English Bookshop, Via Mascheroni 12.

Other Information For information on gay

activities, call Arci Gay/Centro d'Iniziativa Gay (☎ 839 46 04), Via Toricella 19, between 3 and 8 pm. The staff can advise on other associations in Milan. Babilonia (☎ 569 64 68) publishes several magazines for gays, including the monthly *Babilonia*, which is available at most newsstands.

The Lavanderia Automatica, Corso Porta Vittoria 51, behind the Duomo, is one of the few coin-operated laundrettes in the city centre.

Emergency For police emergency, call ☎ 113. The police headquarters (☎ 6 22 61) are at Via Fatebenefratelli 11. The staff speak English. For an ambulance, call ☎ 77 33, and for emergency first aid, call the Italian Red Cross on ☎ 38 83. The Ospedale Maggiore Policlinico (☎ 551 35 18) is at Via Francesco Sforza 35, close to the city centre. There are all-night pharmacies in Stazione Centrale (☎ 669 07 35) and in Piazza del Duomo (☎ 87 22 66). To find out which other pharmacies are open all night, call ☎ 192. For lost property, contact the Milan City Council (☎ 87 08 21).

Dangers & Annoyances Milan's main shopping areas are popular haunts of pickpockets and thieves, including the ubiquitous groups of dishevelled-looking women and children. They are as numerous here as in Rome and also lightning fast. They use the same technique of waving cardboard or newspaper in your face to distract your attention while they head for your pockets. The same streets are also patrolled by plainclothes police, so don't hesitate to make a racket if you are swamped.

Things to See
Around the Duomo Start with the extraordinary **Duomo** (MM1: Duomo), which was commissioned by Gian Galeazzo Visconti in 1386, now the world's fourth-largest church. The first glimpse of this spiky, tumultuous structure is certainly memorable, with its marble façade shaped into pinnacles, statues and pillars. All Milanese pay a special tax to fund the ongoing construction of the unfinished church. There are some 135 spires and 3200 statues built on the roof and into the façade, but masons add a new piece every few years. The huge brass doors at the front bear the marks of bombs which fell near the church in WW II. Inside are 15th century stained-glass windows on the right and newer, painted copies on the left. You will notice a definite contrast between the colours of the two sets. A nail stored high above the altar is said to have come from Christ's Cross and is displayed once a year, in September. Originally lowered using a device made by Leonardo da Vinci called the *nigola*, it is now retrieved with more modern means. The Nigola is stored near the roof on the right-hand side as you enter the church. Note the ceiling which appears carved – it is actually trompe l'oeil.

The **Museo della Fabbrico del Duomo**, Piazza del Duomo 14, is worth a visit to view the church's six centuries of history. It is open from 9.30 am to 12.30 pm and 3 to 6 pm, except Mondays, and entrance is L5000.

The **Museo Civico d'Arte Contemporanea**, in the recently restored Palazzo Reale, south of the Duomo, contains works by Italian futurists and by lesser known Italian artists.

The graceful **Galleria Vittorio Emanuele II** at the northern edge of Piazza del Duomo was virtually rebuilt after it was destroyed by heavy bombing in WW II. One of the first buildings in Europe to use iron and glass as structural elements, the galleria was designed by Giuseppe Mengoni following the plan of a Latin cross. The four mosaics around the central octagon represent four continents – Europe, Asia, Africa and North America. The galleria gained the title of 'il salotto di Milano' (Milan's living room) thanks to its famous cafés such as Savini (now opposite a hamburger outlet).

Walk through the galleria to Piazza della Scala and **La Scala**, Milan's renowned opera house. In the centre of the piazza stands a statue of Leonardo da Vinci by Pietro Magni and four of his pupils. La Scala, considered one of the world's best opera houses, opened on 3 August 1778. Toscanini travelled to

Around the Duomo

0   200   400 m

Milan to reopen the theatre in 1946 after bombing destroyed much of it during the war. Visit the **Museo Teatrale alla Scala** on the site, which boasts such curiosities as Verdi's death mask (complete with the maestro's facial hairs). Visitors can wander into the opera house from the museum. The museum is open Monday to Saturday from 9 am to midday and 2 to 6 pm, Sundays from 9.30 am to midday and 2.30 to 6 pm. Admission is L5000.

The **Palazzo Marino**, between Piazza della Scala and Piazza San Fedele, is considered one of the city's most beautiful private palaces. Started in 1558 by Galeazzo Alessi,

it is one of the best examples of 16th century residential architecture. The **Church of San Fedele**, in the piazza of the same name, was started in the 16th century and only completed last century.

The **Museo Poldi Pezzoli** collection was bequeathed to the city in 1871 by nobleman Giacomo Poldi Pezzoli and features works by Raphael and Bellini.

The **Pinacoteca Ambrosiana**, Piazza Pio XI 2 (MM1: Cordusio), is one of the city's finest galleries and contains Caravaggio's famous *Fruit Basket*, Italy's first real example of a still life, as well as works by Tiepolo, Titian and Raphael.

■ PLACES TO STAY

9	Albergo Manzoni
10	Albergo Commercio
16	Hotel London
27	Hotel Duomo
31	Hotel Rosa
32	Hotel Ambasciatori
33	Hotel Nuovo
36	Albergo Vecchia Milano
41	Hotel Speronari
42	Albergo Rio

▼ PLACES TO EAT

8	Alemagna
12	Casa Fondata
17	Vecchia Napoli
19	Don Lisander
20	San Tomaso
24	Ciao
34	Trattoria da Bruno
38	Peck Delicatessen
39	Amico Motta
40	Dai Dan II
43	Pizzeria Dogana
46	Popeye
51	Café Guarany
52	Berlin Café

OTHER

1	Police Headquarters
2	Piazza San Marco
3	Piazza Cavour
4	Galleria d'Arte Moderna
5	Brera Palace
6	Centrodomus
7	Design Gallery of Milano
11	Castello Sforza
13	Museum of Milan
14	Piazzale Cadorna
15	Cairoli Metro Station & Largo Cairoli
18	La Scala Opera House
21	Piazza della Scala
22	Autosila Parking
23	San Babila Metro Station & Piazza San Babila
25	Piazza Cordusio
26	Galleria V Emanuele II
28	Main Post Office & ASST Telephones
29	Piazza del Duomo
30	Duomo
35	Largo Augusto
37	Ambrosiana Art Gallery
44	APT Tourist Information Head Office
45	Palazzo Reale
47	Piazza Diaz
48	Underground Car Park
49	Largo Carrobbio
50	Piazza Missori
53	Ospedale Maggiore Policlinico

Nearby is the **Church of San Sepolcro**, established in 1030 and featuring a Romanesque crypt. It was dedicated to the Holy Sepulchre during the second crusade and features some important local artworks.

South of the Duomo is one of Milan's more memorable skyscrapers, the **Torre Velasca**, a 20-storey building topped by a six-storey protruding block. A classic late-1950s design by Studio BBPR, this building should be seen. Apparently the Duomo offered some inspiration.

Around the Castello Sforza At the end of Via Dante is the huge **Castello Sforza**, also known as the Castello Sforzesco (MM1: Cadorna or Cairoli, or MM2: Cadorna). It was originally a Visconti fortress, but was entirely rebuilt by Francesco Sforza in the 15th century. Its museums hold excellent sculpture collections, including Michelangelo's *Pietà Rondanini*. It is open Tuesday to Sunday, from 9.30 am to 12.15 pm and 2.30 to 5.15 pm, and admission is free. Behind the castle is the **Parco Sempione**, a 47-hectare park featuring an arena which was inaugurated by Napoleon.

Nearby, in Via Brera, is the 17th century Brera Palace, which houses the **Brera Gallery** (MM2: Lanza). Its large collection of paintings includes Andrea Mantegna's masterpiece, the *Dead Christ*. It is open Tuesday to Saturday from 9 am to 2 pm and Sunday to 1 pm, and admission is L8000. The **Museum of Milan**, Via Sant'Andrea 6 (MM1: San Babila), is open from 9.30 am to 5.30 pm and details the city's history.

An absolute must is Leonardo da Vinci's *Last Supper*, in the Vinciano Refectory (Cenacolo Vinciano) next to the **Church of Santa**

Maria delle Grazie, noted for Bramante's tribune (MM1: Conciliazione, or MM2: Cadorna). Painted between 1495 and 1498 in the refectory of the Santa Maria delle Grazie convent, da Vinci's famous work is believed to capture the moment when Jesus uttered, 'One of you will betray me'. Recently, it has become evident that da Vinci subscribed to a theory that Jesus had a twin. The basis for this contention can be seen in the painting, which depicts two virtually identical Christs.

Restoration began in 1977 and is proceeding slowly, but centuries of damage from floods, bombing and decay have left their mark. Ironically, it was the method employed by restorers last century that has caused most damage. Their alcohol and cotton wool removed a layer from the painting. A photo display shows the incredible post-WW II scene of the building virtually destroyed. All that was left standing was the wall bearing da Vinci's work. It is open Tuesday to Saturday from 9 am to 1.15 pm and 2 to 6.15 pm, Sundays and Mondays from 9 am to 1.15 pm. Admission is L6000.

The Science & Technology Museum (Museo della Scienza e della Tecnica), Via San Vittore 21, open from 9.30 am to 4.50 pm (closed Mondays), is one of the world's largest technology museums and features a room dedicated to da Vinci's scientific work.

The city's Civico Museo Archeologico, Corso Magenta 15 (MM2: Cadorna), features substantial Roman, Greek, Etruscan, Gandhara (ancient north-west Indian) and medieval sections. It is open from 9.30 am to 5.30 pm, and entrance is free. It is housed in the Monastero Maggiore, which is attached to the Church of San Maurizio and features frescoes by B Luini.

Left along Via Sant'Agnese is the Lombard Romanesque-style Basilica of Sant'Ambrogio, dedicated to Milan's patron saint, St Ambrose. Founded in the 4th century by Ambrose, Bishop of Milan, the church has been rebuilt several times since.

Around Piazza Cavour The Galleria d'Arte Moderna, Via Palestro 16 (MM1: Palestro), in the former Royal Villa which once housed Napoleon, has a wide range of 19th century works including works from the Milanese neoclassical period. The nearby Church of San Babila is said to have been built on the site of an earlier church, dating back to 46 AD.

The Design Gallery of Milano, at Via Manzoni 46, features exhibitions of local design works. The gallery is closed Tuesdays and admission is free.

Around Navigli The San Lorenzo Maggiore, Piazza Vetra, is an early Christian church which was built between 355 and 372 AD on the site of a Roman building, and features several 3rd century columns in front of the church. The Church of Sant'Eustorgio, Piazza Sant'Eustorgio, was built in the 9th century and altered in the 11th century, and features a 15th century Portinari Chapel, or Chapel of St Peter Martyr. Bramante designed the baptistry.

Courses
The Linguadue School of Italian (☎ 29 51 99 72), Corso Buenos Aires 43, offers individual or group courses in the Italian language. The Milan-based Noi Blu sailing school (☎ 282 67 66), Via Cavalcanti 1, runs weekend courses on Lake Como for L290,000 and L390,000.

Organised Tours
The VAMI (Voluntary Associates for Italian Museums, ☎ 76 02 21 52) charges a small fee for guided visits to the Duomo Museum, Castello Sforza and other sites. Call from 9 am to 1 pm. CIT organises day trips to lakes Maggiore and Como by bus and ferry. Buses leave at 8.10 am (☎ 80 11 61) and 8.45 am (☎ 669 69 23).

Festivals
One of the major festivals is on 7 December, St Ambrose's Day, and features a traditional street fair near the Basilica of Sant'Ambrogio.

Places to Stay
Milan has the most expensive and heavily

booked hotels in Italy. The area around Stazione Centrale abounds with cheapish one and two-star hotels and pensioni, but quality can vary dramatically. The popularity of the city as a trade-fair and exhibition venue means hotel owners charge what they like – and get away with it.

The tourist offices will make recommendations, but will not make bookings. The Associazione Lombardia Albergatori (hotel association, ☎ 76 00 60 95), Via Palestro 24, will book you a room in any category hotel, while Hotel Reservation Milano (☎ 76 00 79 78) will reserve rooms only at four and five-star hotels.

The APT has an extensive list of private rooms, student accommodation, religious institutions and boarding houses. Most are generally rented by the month. The APT offers a deal called Weekend Milano, which operates for most of the year and provides substantially discounted weekend accommodation packages in some of the city's better hotels.

Places to Stay – bottom end
Camping The *Campeggio Città di Milano* (☎ 48 20 01 34) is a fair distance out of the centre at Via G Airaghi 61. It is near the MM1 De Angeli station. By car, exit the Tangenziale Ovest at San Siro-Via Novara.

Hostels & Religious Institutions The IYHF youth hostel, *Ostello Piero Rotta* (☎ 36 70 95), is at Viale Salmoiraghi 2. Bed and breakfast is L20,000, or L22,000 per bed for family accommodation. Take the MM1 in the direction of Molino Dorino and get off at QT8 (the name of the station and surrounding area). An IYHF card is compulsory, but you can buy it there (L20,000). The *Casa Famiglia* (☎ 29 00 01 64), Corso Garibaldi 123, is run by nuns and is only for women aged 29 years and under. Bed and shower is L18,000 a night.

The *Pensione Benefica Giovani* (☎ 87 36 48), Via Formentini 8, is a small hostel for women only. It is classified as student accommodation but travellers can stay during the summer holidays for about

L15,000 a night. The *Protezione della Giovane* (☎ 29 60 01 64), Corso Garibaldi 123, near Stazione Centrale, is for women aged between 16 and 24. Beds cost from L15,000.

The *Fondazione Sacro Cuore* (☎ 214 00 51), Via Rombone 78, near Stazione Centrale, is a religious hostel for men only. Full board for one month is L675,000, but rooms are sometimes available for one night.

Around Stazione Centrale & Corso Buenos Aires
Most of the cheaper hotels near the station will not take bookings. The *Nettuno* (☎ 29 40 44 81), Via Tadino 27, is a 10-minute walk along Via D Scarlatti (to the left as you leave the station) and has singles/doubles for L38,500/53,500. Nearby, *Hotel Paradiso* (☎ 204 94 48), Via Benedetto Marcello 85, has rooms for L40,000/60,000.

In Via Vitruvio, to the left of Piazza Duca d'Aosta as you leave the station, there are two good budget options. The *Salerno* (☎ 204 68 70) at No 18 has doubles with bathroom for L50,000. The *Italia* (☎ 669 38 26) at No 44 has singles/doubles for L27,000/40,000. The *Due Giardini* (☎ 29 52 10 93), Via Lodovico Settala 46 (which intersects Via Vitruvio), has singles/doubles for L40,000/60,000 and triples for L80,000. Across Corso Buenos Aires at Via Gaspare Spontini 6 is *Del Sole* (☎ 29 51 29 71), with singles/doubles/triples for L38,000/ 53,000/70,000. The *Verona* (☎ 66 98 30 91), at Via Carlo Tenca 12 (just off Piazza della Repubblica), has singles/doubles for L40,000/50,000.

About halfway between the station and the centre is a concentration of hotels around Corso Buenos Aires and Viale Tunisia. Take the MM1 and get off at Porta Venezia. *Hotel Casa Mia* (☎ 657 52 49), Viale Vittorio Veneto 30, is a short walk from the MM1 stop. It has singles/doubles for L45,000/ 60,000; a triple is L80,000.

At Viale Tunisia 6, just off Corso Buenos Aires, there are several hotels. The *Hotel Canna* (☎ 29 52 40 55) is the cheapest, with singles/doubles for L38,000/56,000, and triples with private shower for L28,000 per

Around Stazione Centrale

1	Hotel Valley	11	Hotel Paradiso
2	Stazione Centrale	12	Del Sole
3	Ristorante Primavera d'Oriente	13	Hotel Due Giardini
4	APT Tourist Information Office	14	Piazza Lima
5	Piazza Caiazzo & Caiazzo Metro Station	15	Hotel Verona
6	Stazione Centrale Metro Station	16	Hotel Nettuno
7	Porta Garibaldi Railway Station	17	Hotel Casa Mia
8	Brek	18	Hotels Kennedy, Canna & San Tomaso
9	Hotel Italia	19	Ciao
10	Albergo Salerno		

person; a double with private bath is L70,000. *Hotel Kennedy* (☎ 29 40 09 34) has singles/doubles for L45,000/60,000; a double with private bathroom is L75,000, and triples are L30,000 per person. This hotel accepts bookings. *Hotel San Tomaso* (☎ 29 51 47 47) has singles/doubles for L35,000/53,000, and triples for L25,000 per person. Closer to the city centre, off Piazza G Oberdan, is *Hotel Tris* (☎ 29 40 06 74), Via Sirtori 26, with singles/doubles from L40,000/55,000.

City Centre The *Albergo Commercio* (☎ 86 46 38 80), Via Mercato 1, has singles/doubles for L40,000/50,000 with shower. From Piazza Cordusio, walk down Via Broletto, which becomes Via Mercato. The entrance to the hotel is around the corner in Via delle Erbe. Very close to Piazza del Duomo is *Hotel Speronari* (☎ 86 46 11 25), Via Speronari 4, eccentrically decorated, but comfortable. Singles/doubles are L38,000/53,000, and triples L72,000. *Hotel Nuovo* (☎ 86 46 05 42), Piazza Beccaria 6, is in a great location just off Via Vittorio Emanuele. Singles/doubles are L40,000/60,000, but the management can be abrasive.

Around Navigli The *Albergo Cantore* (☎ 835 75 65), Corso Genova 25, is close to one of Milan's trendy areas. It has no single rooms but doubles/triples are L55,000/80,000.

Places to Stay – middle to top end

Around Stazione Centrale & Corso Buenos Aires The *Hotel Fenice* (☎ 292 55 41), Corso Buenos Aires 2, in the three-star category, has singles/doubles from L60,000/85,000.

City Centre The *Albergo Vecchia Milano* (☎ 87 50 42), Via Borromei 4, between the Duomo and Castello Sforza, has singles/doubles/triples for L75,000/110,000/160,000 and all rooms have bath. *Hotel London* (☎ 72 02 01 66), Via Rovello 3, looks swanky but charges reasonable rates. Singles/doubles are L50,000/80,000,

and L75,000/110,000 with a shower. *Albergo Manzoni* (☎ 76 00 57 00), Via Santo Spirito 20, is close to Piazza Cavour. Rooms are L100,000/140,000. *Albergo Rio* (☎ 87 41 14), Via Mazzini 8, in a great location just off Piazza del Duomo, has singles/doubles/triples for L80,000/145,000/200,000.

The *Hotel Duomo* (☎ 88 33) is right behind the Duomo and is one of the city's better hotels. Singles start at about L170,000 and doubles from L230,000. The *Hotel Ambasciatori* (☎ 76 02 02 41), Galleria del Corso 3, off Corso Vittorio Emanuele II, is pure luxury with rooms starting at L230,000. *Hotel Rosa* (☎ 88 31), Via Pattari 5, is in the same league and price bracket.

Places to Eat

Italians say that the cuisine of Lombardy is designed for people who don't have time to waste because they are always in a hurry to work. Fast-food outlets and sandwich bars are very popular in the city and are cluttered around Stazione Centrale and the Duomo. However, the city is Italy's window for foreign cuisine as well as that of various regions, in particular Tuscany and Calabria.

Via Speronari is one of the better areas to shop for bread, salami, cheese and wine. Bar snacks are an institution in Milan and most lay out their fare from 5 pm daily.

Around Stazione Centrale The *Ciao*, Corso Buenos Aires 7, is part of a chain (there are others in Corso Europa and at Via Dante 5), but the food is good quality and relatively cheap, with pasta dishes around L5000 and salads for around L3000. *Brek*, Via Roberto Lepetit 20 (turn right off Via Vitruvio from the station), has pasta from L4000. *L'Osteria del Treno*, Via San Gregorio 46-48, serves good, reasonably priced food. *Trattoria di Polpetta*, on the corner of Via Tadino and Via Panfilo Castaldi, is a small local eating place with pasta from L6000.

Pizza '90, Via Paganini 2, is a great pizzeria, with pizzas from L5000. For an alternative, *Ristorante Primavera d'Oriente*,

Via Palestrina 13, offers Chinese meals from L13,500.

Around the City Centre The *Alemagna*, Via Manzoni, on the corner of Via Croce Rossa, is an elegant, buffet-style restaurant, with main courses from L5000.

The first time the Milanese tasted pizza it was cooked at *Di Gennaro*, Via S Radegonda 3, although today you can eat a better pizza at *La Baia*, Via Cellini 3. *Pizza del Circo*, Via Circo 10, makes a great vegetarian pizza. *Dai Dan II*, Via Torino 34, is close to the Duomo and serves pizzas from L6000.

The *Trattoria da Bruno*, Via Cavallotti 15, off Corso Europa, is popular and has a set-price lunch for L13,000. *Pizzeria Dogana*, on the corner of Via Capellari and Via Dogana, near the Duomo, has pasta and pizza for around L7000.

Popeye, Via S Tecla 8, is reputed to have the best pizza in Milan. Pizzas cost around L7000 to L10,000. *San Tomaso*, Via San Tomaso 5 (near Via Rovello), features live jazz and specialises in salads, which range in price from L5000 to L12,000. Close by is *Vecchia Napoli*, Via San Tomaso on the corner of Via Rovello, with pizzas from L5000.

One of the city's better restaurants is *Don Lisander*, Via Manzoni 12A, which serves Milanese risotto and a host of Tuscan dishes. It is relatively expensive, with dishes starting at L18,000. But perhaps the city's most traditional restaurant is *Savini* in the Galleria V Emanuele II, with its plush red velvet, chandeliers and matching prices. Its risotto giallo is famous in the city.

Around Navigli The *Berlin Café*, Via G Mora 5 (off Corso Porta Ticinese), has a set-price brunch for L10,000 and a small menu at night (L10,000 for one dish). Nearby is *Café Guarany*, Via G Mora 9, open from 7 am to 7 pm except Sunday, which serves pasta from L3000. *El Brellin*, Via Casale 5, serves traditional Milanese food, and many dishes are vegetarian. A meal could cost L20,000. *Trattoria Artisti*, Corso Porta Ticinese 16, is a popular hang-out for Milanese bohemians. It serves a set-menu lunch for L15,000.

Cafés & Sandwich Bars One of Milan's oldest fast-food outlets is *Luini*, Via S Radegonda 16, just off Piazza del Duomo, which sells panzerotti (pizza dough stuffed with tomatoes, garlic and mozzarella) for L2000. *Le Tre Marie*, on the corner of Via Cesare Cantù and Via Armorai, has great bar snacks.

One of the best sandwich bars is *Quadronno*, on the corner of Via Quadronno and Porta Vigentina, which specialises in unusual concoctions. Another is *Bar Assodi Cuori*, Piazza Cavour, which is crowded at lunch time, but the sandwiches, starting at L2000, are great.

For gourmet takeaway, head for *Peck*. Its rosticceria is at Via C Cantù 11, where you can buy cooked meats and vegetables; another outlet is at Via Spadari 9. Several other outlets are dotted around the area, including a snack bar and restaurant at Via Victor Hugo 4.

The *Casa Fondata*, Via Monte Napoleone 8, in the city's fashionable and expensive Monte Napoleone shopping district, is an elegant but expensive tearoom where you can mix it with wealthy Milanese. Close by is the slightly less expensive *Sunflower Bar*, Via Pietro Verri, another haunt of the fashion-conscious.

In the Stazione Centrale area is *Pattini & Marinoni*, Corso Buenos Aires 53, which sells bread, and pizza by the slice for about L1500. *Gran Caffè Doria*, Viale Andrea Doria, is a creperie and makes a great breakfast place.

South of the Duomo area, in Navigli, *Le Scimmie*, Via A Sforza 49, is a music bar which is very popular with younger people.

Gelati East of the Duomo, near Piazza Wagner, is *Gelateria Marghera*, Via Marghera 33, with a permanent queue. For the ultimate in healthy ice cream, how about soya gelati from *Gelateria Odeon*, Via Marghera 51 (MMI: Marghera)?

Near Stazione Centrale, at Viale Andrea

Doria, on the corner of Via Palestrino, is *Gelateria Grasso*, a fine tribute to 1970s architecture and an even better one to good gelati. *Milanodoc*, Piazzale Antonio Cantore 4 in Navigli, has tables and chairs set up in the piazza.

Entertainment
The city has Italy's best clubs (although still poor by international standards), a host of cinemas screening English-language films, and a fabulous year-round cultural calendar, topped, of course, by the famous La Scala opera season which opens each year on 7 December. If you happen to be in the city then, watching the line-up of furred, bejewelled society matrons can be more exciting than the opera itself.

The tourist office in Piazza del Duomo has complete listings for the city's entertainment, as do most of the daily newspapers. Pick up *What's On In Milan* or *Milano Mese*, both monthly entertainment guides from the tourist office.

Music & Theatre La Scala's season runs until early June and the theatre is closed from mid-July to the end of August. During June and September, it is host to musical performances and ballet. The box office (☎ 72 00 37 44) is in the portico in Via Filodrammatici, on the left-hand side of the building, and is open from midday to 7 pm daily and until 15 minutes after curtains on performance nights. Book well in advance, even from another city if you are travelling to Milan, as most performances sell out months before. Your only hope may be the 200 standing-room tickets that go on sale 45 minutes before scheduled starting time at the entrance to the opera house museum. CIT offices abroad will book tickets.

In March/April and October/November there are organ concerts performed at the Church of San Maurizio in the Monastero Maggiore. In April/May there is a jazz festival, Città di Milano (☎ 76 11 00 93), and in summer the city stages the Milano d'Estate, a series of concerts, theatre and dance performances. This is followed in August by the Vacanze a Milano, another special programme of theatre and music.

The main season for theatre and concerts opens in October. The Conservatorio Giuseppe Verdi (☎ 76 00 17 55), Via Conservatorio 12, is the venue for many classical music concerts.

Cinema English-language films are shown at the following cinemas: Anteo (☎ 659 77 32), Via Milazzo 9 (MM2: Moscova); Arcobaleno (☎ 29 40 60 54), Viale Tunisia 11, (MM1: Lima); Mexico (☎ 48 95 18 02), Via Savona 57 (MM2: Porta Genova); and Angelicum (☎ 655 17 12), Piazza Sant'Angelo 2 (MM3: Turati). The Marconi (☎ 36 27 31), Viale Dante 32, screens gay films.

Nightclubs After Dark, Viale Certosa 134, is young and about as hip as Milan gets. You must become a member to get in. HD, Via Tajani 11, is a small disco playing mainly American music. Killer Plastic O, Viale Umbria 120, is gay on Thursday and straight other nights. Contatto, Corso Sempione 76, is gay, but women are allowed in. Membership is required and it is free on Wednesday. Falk, Via Santa Maria Segreta 7, is gay only on Wednesday and straight other nights.

Soccer Milan's two teams, Inter and AC Milan, play on alternative Sundays during the football season, at San Siro Stadium, also known as Meazza because it is in Piazza Meazza. Tram No 24 and bus Nos 95, 49 and 72 go direct. Tickets are available at the stadium, or for AC Milan matches, from Milan Point (☎ 78 27 68), Largo Corsia dei Servi 11. For Inter matches, get tickets at Banca Popolare di Milano branches.

Car Racing The Italian Grand Prix is held at the Monza Autodrome each September. The track is several km out of town and can be reached along Viale Monza from Piazzale Loreto.

Things to Buy
Every item of clothing you ever wanted to

buy, but could never afford, is in Milan. The main streets for clothing, footwear and accessories are behind the Duomo around Corso Vittorio Emanuele II, and between Piazza della Scala and Piazza San Babila.

For up-market and exclusive fashions, head for Via Borgospesso and Via della Spiga or the understated boutique mecca of Via Monte Napoleone. Versace is at Via della Spiga 4; Gianfranco Ferré is along the road at No 11; Krizia at No 23, while around the corner in Via Sant'Andrea you will find Armani, Fendi, Trussardi, Kenzo and Comme des Garçons. Valentino, Ungaro, Ferretti and Daniel Hechter are cluttered along Via Monte Napoleone.

The areas around Via Torino, Corso XXII Marzo and Corso Buenos Aires are less expensive.

Markets are held in the areas around the canals, notably on Viale Papiniano on Tuesday and Saturday mornings. A flea market is held in Via Calatafimi on Saturdays, and decent antique markets are held in Brera at Via Fiori Chiari on every third Saturday of the month, and on the Navigli Canal, Ripa di Porta Ticina (tram No 19) on the third Sunday of the month.

Design Milan is the world's design capital, although you have to search it out as shops and galleries are spread throughout the city, and most products are made for export. The magazine *Interni* publishes a fold-out guide called *Interni Annual* which lists the names and addresses of most design shops and galleries, as well as a list of upcoming design fairs and exhibitions (of which there are many). It is available with the magazine, on sale at most newsstands, or for free from various furniture and other design-oriented shops and galleries. The *Milano Design Guide*, published by Abitare, sells at most bookshops and contains 'design itineraries'. Centrodomus, Via Manzoni 37, operated by the architectural and design magazine *Domus*, is a bookshop and gallery space, and is a good place to start a design tour of the city.

Getting There & Away

Air International flights use Malpensa Airport, about 50 km north-west of the city. Domestic and European flights use Linate Airport, about seven km east. The city is served by an increasing number of flights from the USA and from many cities in Europe.

Some of the major airlines in Milan include: Alitalia (☎ 6 28 11), Corso Como 15; British Airways (☎ 80 98 92), Piazza Diaz 7; and TWA (☎ 7 79 61), Corso Europa 9-11. Call ☎ 28 36 for domestic flight bookings and ☎ 28 37 for international bookings.

Bus Buses are not as convenient as trains and are more expensive. SAL, Autostradale and several other companies operate from Piazza Castello (MM2: Cairoli) for national and international destinations.

Train You can catch a train from Stazione Centrale to all of the major cities in Italy, Western Europe and, increasingly, to Eastern Europe. Most of the trains from Rome are intercities, for which you pay the rapido supplement. There are regular trains for Venice, Florence (and Bologna), Genoa, Turin and Rome. The city has several train stations, although most trains use Stazione Centrale. For train information, phone ☎ 6 75 00.

The Stazione Nord (☎ 851 16 08) in Piazzale Cadorna (MM1 and MM2) connects Milan with Como, Erba and Varese. The Porta Genova station (☎ 58 10 01 43) (MM2) connects the city to the west of Lombardy and parts of Piedmont. Porta Garibaldi (☎ 655 20 78) connects Milan with Lecco, Valtellina and the north-west.

Car & Motorbike Milan is the major junction of Italy's motorways, including the Autostrada del Sole (A1) to Reggio di Calabria; the A4, also known as the Milano-Torino (to Turin) and the Serenissima (to Verona and Venice); the A7 to Genoa; and the A8 and A9 north to the lakes and Swiss border. The city is also a hub for smaller national roads,

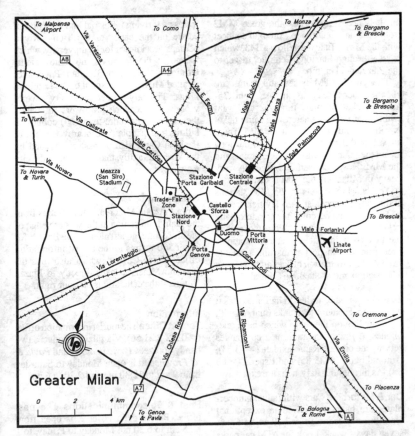

Greater Milan

0   2   4 km

including the ss7 (Via Emilia), which runs through Emilia-Romagna, and the ss11, which runs east-west from Turin to Brescia.

All these roads converge onto the Milan ring road, the Tangenziale Est and Tangenziale Ovest. From here, follow the signs into the city centre. It should be noted that the A4 in particular is an extremely busy road, where numerous accidents can hold up traffic for hours. In winter all roads in the area become extremely hazardous because of rain, snow and fog.

Getting Around
To/From the Airports An airbus service leaves from Stazione Centrale (outside the Doria Agency) for Malpensa daily every half hour, stopping also at the Porta Garibaldi train station. Tickets cost L8000 from the agency. Extra services are run to coincide with flights. Buses for Linate leave from outside the Doria Agency every 20 minutes and cost L2500, otherwise take bus No 73 from Piazza San Babila (Corso Europa) for L800.

Public Transport Milan's public transport system is extremely efficient. The underground MM has three lines. The red MM1 provides the easiest access to the city centre, but it is necessary to take the green MM2 from Stazione Centrale to Loreto to connect with the MM1. Take the yellow MM3, which passes through Stazione Centrale, to get to the Piazza del Duomo.

The city's ATM buses and trams are cheaper, because you can use your 75-minute ticket as many times as you want within that period, whereas the same ticket is valid for only one ride on the MM. There are a few different-looking tickets but they are all the same and valid on buses, trams and the MM. However, traffic is generally very heavy in Milan and the MM is faster.

You can buy tickets in the MM stations and at any tobacconist. All-day tickets cost L3500. Take some coins for the automatic ticket machines – they are much quicker than the ticket-window queues at MM stations. Free public transport maps are available from ATM information offices at the Duomo MM station and at Stazione Centrale.

Taxi Don't bother trying to hail a taxi, as it won't stop. Head for taxi ranks (marked with a yellow line on the road) which have telephones. A few of the radio-taxi companies serving the city are Radiotaxidata (☎ 53 53), Autoradiotaxi (☎ 85 85) and Esperia (☎ 83 88). As throughout Italy, taxis are expensive.

Car & Motorbike Cars with Italian number-plates are banned (with some exceptions) from the city centre from 7.30 am to 6 pm, seven days a week. Look for ATM car parks on the outskirts of the city centre (represented by a white P on a blue background). They are numerous and supervised, but they are expensive. There is also an underground car park in Piazza Diaz, near the Duomo. A cheaper alternative is to use one of the supervised car parks at the last stop on each MM line.

Hertz, Avis, Maggiore and Europcar all have offices at Stazione Centrale. To rent a bicycle, try Cooperativa Il Picchio (☎ 837 79 26), Corso San Gottardo 42.

PAVIA

Virtually a satellite of Milan, Pavia is none-theless a thriving industrial and agricultural centre on the banks of the Ticino River, perhaps best known for its university, which is one of the country's most prestigious. Originally the Roman Ticinum, Pavia later rivalled Milan as the capital of the Lombard kings. The city gained notoriety several years ago when one its towers (of which there used to be more than 100) collapsed, killing four people. The nearby Certosa di Pavia, a Carthusian monastery founded by the Visconti family, makes a visit to the city a must.

Orientation

From Piazzale Minerva, a few metres from the main train station at the western edge of the city centre, go left along Viale Battisti for about 500 metres to the tourist information office. Corso Cavour, which also runs off Piazzale Minerva, leads directly to Piazza Vittoria – the cathedral is on your right.

Information

Tourist Office The tourist information office (☎ 0382-2 21 56), Via Filzi 2, produces two handy booklets, *Pavia in a Day* and *Pavia & its Province*. It is open Monday to Saturday from 9 am to 12.30 pm and 2.30 to 6 pm.

Post & Telecommunications The post office, Piazza della Posta 2, is open from 8.15 am to 6.30 pm Monday to Friday, to 1 pm Saturday. The postal code for central Pavia is 27100.

There is an SIP public telephone office at Via Galliano, near the post office, which is open from 9 am to 12.30 pm and 2.30 to 7.30 pm Monday to Saturday, 9 am to 2 pm Sunday. The telephone code for Pavia is 0382.

Emergency For police emergency, call ☎ 113. The police headquarters (☎ 30 12 04) are at Piazza Italia 5. For medical assistance, go to the Ospedale San Matteo (☎ 38 81), Piazza Golgi; for emergencies, ring ☎ 38 84 21, and at night, ☎ 2 96 00.

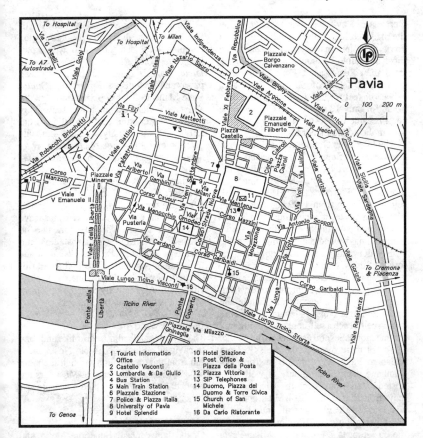

Map Legend

1 Tourist Information Office
2 Castello Visconti
3 Lombardia & Da Giulio
4 Bus Station
5 Main Train Station
6 Piazzale Stazione
7 Police & Piazza Italia
8 University of Pavia
9 Hotel Splendid
10 Hotel Stazione
11 Post Office & Piazza della Posta
12 Piazza Vittoria
13 SIP Telephones
14 Duomo, Piazza del Duomo & Torre Civica
15 Church of San Michele
16 Da Carlo Ristorante

Things to See

Start at the northern end of Corso Strada Nuova at the **Castello Visconti**, a harsh-looking complex with four corner towers built in 1360 for Galeazzo II Visconti. Inside are the Museo Civico, Museo del Risorgimento and a small modern-art gallery. The castle is open Tuesday to Saturday from 9.30 am to 1.30 pm and from 10 am to 5 pm on Sunday, with shorter hours during winter. Entrance is L6000.

Along Corso Strada Nuova is the **University of Pavia**, dating from the early 1400s and built by the Visconti family. Among its notable graduates are Christopher Columbus (whose ashes are purportedly kept in a safe in the director's office), Petrarch and the physicist Alessandro Volta, after whom the volt is named. Examples of his work are on show.

The **Duomo**, started in 1488, features the third-largest dome in Italy. Both da Vinci and Bramante contributed to the church's design. The **Church of San Michele**, the city's oldest Romanesque church, dates from the 7th century and was the preferred spot for coronations among northern Italian kings for many centuries. Charlemagne was crowned here in 774.

Certosa di Pavia Nine km from Pavia, on the road to Milan, is the splendid Certosa di Pavia, a Carthusian monastery and one of the most incredible buildings produced during the Italian Renaissance. Founded by Gian Galeazzo Visconti of Milan in 1396 as a private chapel for the Visconti family and a home for only 12 monks, the Charterhouse soon became one of the most lavish buildings in the country's north.

The interior is Gothic, although traces of Renaissance influence can be detected. Note the trompe l'oeil high on the nave giving the impression that people were watching the monks. In the former sacristy is a mammoth sculpture dating from 1409 and made from hippopotamus teeth, including 66 small bas-reliefs and 94 statuettes. Other features include inlaid-wood stalls dating from the 15th century, early plumbing devices and the tombs of the Viscontis.

The small cloisters to the right offer good photo angles of the church, particularly from behind the Baroque fountain, while the immense larger cloisters feature 122 arches and 24 cells, each a self-contained living area for one monk. Several are open to the public.

To get there by car, take the ss35 from Milan to Pavia and turn off at Torre del Mangano. The Charterhouse is well sign-posted. SGEA buses for the Charterhouse leave from Piazza Castello in Milan and from Via Trieste in Pavia, near the train station. The Charterhouse is a 10-minute walk from the bus stop. It is also on the Milan-Pavia train line.

Places to Stay & Eat

It is better to stay in Milan and make the short trip to Pavia, as accommodation is expensive and in short supply.

The *Camping Ticino* (☎ 52 53 62), Via Mascherpa 10, opens from April to September and charges L5000 per person and L4000 per tent. The *Hotel Stazione* (☎ 3 54 77), Via B de Rossi 8, is the cheapest hotel, with singles/doubles from L35,000/52,000. The *Hotel Splendid* (☎ 2 47 03), Via XX Settembre 11, is about the same price and offers board from L66,000 a person.

The local area provides about one third of Italy's rice, so risotto is very popular. Try the favoured local dish of risotto with small frogs. *Da Carlo Ristorante Pizzeria Santa Lucia*, Piazzale Ponte Ticino 3, has cheap pizzas and local dishes. *Pizzeria Da Giulio*, Viale Matteotti 39, has pizzas from L5000, and *Lombardia* next door is a reasonably priced trattoria with local specialities from L7000. The university's 22,000 students give the city a few good bars and a lively atmosphere, particularly around the campus.

Getting There & Away

The city's bus station is on Via Trieste, to the left of the train station. SGEA buses run to Milan and the Certosa di Pavia. Trains leave hourly for Milan. The city can also be reached direct from Genoa, Mantua and Cremona. By car, take the A7 autostrada from Milan and exit at the Bereguardo or Gropello C turn-off. Follow the signs to the city centre. Alternatively, take the ss35 from Milan, a better bet for hitchhikers.

Getting Around

The town is small, almost grid-like and easy to navigate on foot. SGEA bus Nos 3 and 6 run from the train station through the main square, Piazza della Vittoria. Most cars are banned from the centre and there are car parks near the station.

MANTUA (MANTOVA)

On the shores of lakes Superiore, Mezzo and Inferiore in the lush Po Valley, Mantua is a serenely beautiful and well-preserved city. However, the surrounding industrial sprawl of Mantua's booming petrochemical industry is encroaching on the old town centre and has left the lakes heavily polluted. The city can be easily visited as a day trip from Milan, but to do it justice, spend the night.

Mantua was settled by the Etruscans in the 10th century BC and later prospered under Roman rule. It passed to the House of Gonzaga in 1328, flourishing under one of the foremost Renaissance dynasties and attracting the likes of Petrarch, Pisanello, Mantegna, Giulio Romano and Rubens.

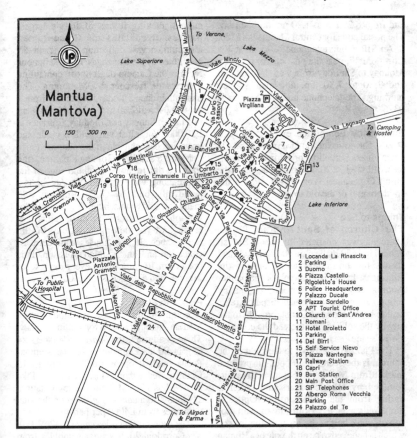

Mantua (Mantova)

0   150   300 m

1 Locanda La Rinascita
2 Parking
3 Duomo
4 Piazza Castello
5 Rigoletto's House
6 Police Headquarters
7 Palazzo Ducale
8 Piazza Sordello
9 APT Tourist Office
10 Church of Sant'Andrea
11 Romani
12 Hotel Broletto
13 Parking
14 Del Birri
15 Self Service Nievo
16 Piazza Mantegna
17 Railway Station
18 Capri
19 Bus Station
20 Main Post Office
21 SIP Telephones
22 Albergo Roma Vecchia
23 Parking
24 Palazzo del Te

Orientation

The old part of the city is on a small peninsula at the southern edge of the three lakes, with the newer parts spread around their shores. From the train station in Piazzale Don Leoni, head a short distance to the right for Piazza Belfiore. From there, take a sharp left and walk along Corso Vittorio Emanuele II for the city centre. The walk takes 10 minutes.

Information

Tourist Office The APT (☎ 0376-35 06 81), Piazza Mantegna 6, produces a range of information about trips throughout the province. It opens from 9 am to midday and 3 to 6 pm, every day except Sunday.

Money Banks are located right throughout the city centre, and open from 8.20 am to 1.20 pm and 3.20 to 4.20 pm. Some banks have extended hours on Thursdays.

Post & Telecommunications The main post office is in Piazza Martiri Belfiore, along Via Roma from Piazza Marconi. It is open Monday to Friday from 8 am to 7 pm, and from 8.20 am to 1.20 pm on Saturday. The postal code for central Mantua is 46100.

An SIP public telephone office is at Via Corridoni 17, near the post office. It's open Monday to Saturday from 9 am to 12.30 pm and 2.30 to 7.30 pm, and also Sunday morning. The telephone code for Mantua is 0376.

Emergency For police emergency, call ☎ 113. The police headquarters (☎ 32 63 41) are in Piazza Sordello. For medical emergencies, call ☎ 33 72 20. The public hospital, the Istituti Ospedalieri, is on Via Albertoni, at the southern end of the old town.

Things to See

The **Church of Sant'Andrea**, Piazza Marconi, was designed by Leon Battisti Alberti in 1472 in the pure classical style and shows the boundless ambitions of the Gonzagas. Inside is the tomb of the painter Andrea Mantegna, a Baroque cupola by Filippo Juvara, and a much disputed relic, said to be the blood of Christ, brought to the city by the soldier who pierced the crucified Christ's side.

The Piazza delle Erbe, to the right of the church, is the scene of an open-air produce market from Monday to Saturday. It is surrounded by marble pillars and columns dating from the 15th century. Opposite Sant'Andrea is the **Rotunda of San Lorenzo**, sunk below the level of the piazza, which is believed to be on the site of a Roman temple dedicated to Venus.

Past the 13th century Palazzo della Ragione is the **Palazzo Broletto**, which dominates the Piazza del Broletto. In a niche on the façade is a figure, said to represent Mantua's favourite son, Virgil.

Continuing on is the Piazza Sordello and the 10th century **Duomo**, containing paintings by the Mantegna school. **Rigoletto's House**, Piazza Sordello 23, was used by Verdi as a set model for most of his operas.

The **Castello dei Gonzaga** is a massive complex of buildings and gardens, including the **Palazzo Ducale**, with 450 rooms, 12 courtyards and gardens, three piazzas and a

church, making it one of Italy's largest palaces. It contains the **Greco-Roman Museum**, a vast collection of ancient art assembled by the Gonzagas. Its most famous room is the Camera degli Sposi, containing a series of frescoes by Mantegna. The museum is open Tuesday to Saturday from 9 am to 1 pm and 2.30 to 5 pm, and from 9 am to 1 pm on Sunday and Monday. Entrance is L10,000. You must visit with a guide and leave any bags outside in the piazza.

Mantua's other Gonzaga palace, the **Palazzo del Te**, at the southern edge of the centre along Via Roma and Via Acerbi, is a grand villa built by Giulio Romano with many splendid rooms, including the **Sala dei Giganti**, described as one of the most fantastic and frightening creations of the Renaissance. It also houses a modern art collection and an Egyptian Museum. It is open from 10 am to 6 pm every day except Monday and entrance is L10,000.

Places to Stay

Accommodation prices are moderate in Mantua – another reason for visiting the city. There is a hostel, the *Sparafucile* (☎ 37 24 65), in Strada Legnaghese on the Mantua-Padua road. It opens from 1 April to 15 October. Bed and breakfast is L15,000. Take APAM bus No 2M from the train station. There is also a *camping ground* on the site, with rates from L4000 per person.

The *Albergo Roma Vecchia* (☎ 32 21 00), Via Corridoni 20, has singles/doubles from L30,000/L42,000. It is closed in August and during the second half of December. The *Locanda La Rinascita* (☎ 32 06 07), Via Concezione 4, charges about the same as the Roma Vecchia and opens all year. Do it in style at *Hotel Broletto* (☎ 32 67 84), Via Accademia 1, off Piazza Sordello, with rooms for L75,000/110,000.

Places to Eat

Over a million pigs are reared in the province of Mantua each year, and many local dishes incorporate them. Try the *salumi* (salt pork), *pancetta*, *prosciutto crudo* or *salamella* (small sausages), or perhaps risotto with the locally grown *vialone nano* rice. Local wines from the hills around Lake Garda are becoming more appreciated. Try the red Rubino dei Morenici Mantovani.

The *Self Service Nievo*, Via Nievo 8 (closed weekends), has good, cheap dishes, with pasta from L4000. *Capri*, Via Bettinelli 8, opposite the train station, has good pizzas and other local dishes, with pasta from L6000. *Dei Birri*, Piazza Broletto 8, is another good, cheap restaurant. *Romani*, Piazza Erbe 13, is one of the city's better restaurants and is still quite cheap; a full meal could cost L30,000.

Getting There & Away

APAM (☎ 23 01) operates bus services to many cities in Lombardy from the bus station in Piazzale Mondadori. Trains link Mantua with Milan, Verona, Modena, Pavia, Cremona, Padua and Ferrara. By road, Mantua is close to the A22 autostrada – take either Mantova Nord or Sud exits and follow the 'centro storico' signs.

Getting Around

The easiest way is to walk around the city – the centre is only 10 minutes from the train station. However, APAM bus Nos 2M and 4 will also get you from the station to the centre.

CREMONA

Home of the violin and the dynasties of violin-makers – Amati, Guarneri and Stradivari – Cremona is a world centre for violin-making with over 100 craftspeople still working in the city. It attracts violin-lovers and musicians from all over the world, but if that is not for you, Cremona can be a little dull.

Orientation

The town is small and easy to navigate. From the train station in Piazza Stazione (near the bus station), walk straight ahead along Via Palestro to the central area around Piazza Cavour, Piazza della Pace and Piazza del Comune. Bus No 1 goes to the centre from the station.

Information

Tourist Office The APT office (☎ 0372-2 32 33) is at Piazza del Comune 5, opposite the cathedral, and is open from 9.30 am to 12.30 pm and 3 to 6 pm.

Post & Telecommunications The main post office is at Via Verdi 1, open from 8 am to 7 pm Monday to Friday, to 1 pm on Saturday. The postal code for central Cremona is is 26100.

The SIP public phone office is at Piazza Cavour 1, open daily from 9 am to 6 pm. The telephone code for Cremona is 0372.

Emergency For police emergency, call ☎ 113. The police headquarters (☎ 25 274) are at Via Tribunali 6. For an ambulance, call ☎ 43 44 45. The public hospital (☎ 40 51) is east of the town centre along Via XX Settembre.

Things to See

If you are here for the violins, pick up a copy of the APT's *Cremona in Violin Terms*, an itinerary of the city's violin sites. The **Piazza del Comune** is the hub of Cremona's life, and was named in memory of the city's period as a commune, from the 11th to the 14th centuries, after which it fell to the Viscontis.

The **Duomo**, or cathedral, was started in the early 12th century and features a richly decorated Gothic façade. The interior features frescoes by Boccaccio, Bembo and others. The church is connected to the adjoining **Torrazzo** (Bell Tower) by a Renaissance loggia, the **Bertazzola**. At 111 metres, the Torrazzo is claimed to be Italy's tallest tower. It is open from 10 am to midday and 3 to 6.30 pm, and entrance is L5000. To the south is the **baptistry**, begun in 1167 by architect Teodosio Orlandino.

Past the **Loggia dei Militi**, the medieval base for the town's militia, is the **Palazzo Comunale** (Town Hall), which features an arched portico. Visit the town-hall violin collection, featuring two Amatis, two Guarneris and a Stradivarius which dates from 1689. A local maestro plays the instruments at 11 am on some days, but you must book ahead. Phone ☎ 40 71 to make an appointment.

As the name suggests, the **Museo Stradivariano**, Via Palestro 17, features items from the Stradivari workshop. It is open Tuesday to Saturday from 9.30 am to 12.30 pm and 3 to 6 pm, and entrance is L6000. It is also open from 9.30 am to 12.30 pm on Sundays, for free. Next door is the **Museo Civico**, which has more violins and an unusual array of other exhibits. If you want to see violins being made, visit **Riccardo Bergonzi** at Corso Garibaldi 45.

Places to Stay & Eat

Cremona is only a short distance from Milan by train or road and can be visited as a day trip, or on the way to Mantua.

The *Camping Parking al Po* (☎ 2 71 37), Via Lungo Po Europa, has sites from L5000. Head south-west from Piazza Cavour.

The *Albergo Touring* (☎ 2 13 90), Via Palestro 3, is near the train station and has singles/doubles for L30,000/42,000. The *Brescia* (☎ 43 46 15), Via Brescia 7, has rooms from L34,000/L45,000, and the *Albergo Bologna* (☎ 2 42 58), Piazza Risorgimento 7, has rooms for about the same

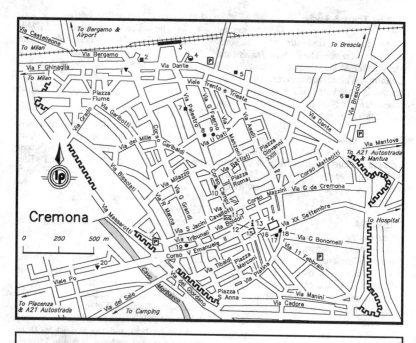

1	La Bersagliera	8	Museo Stradivariano	14	Duomo & Torrazzo
2	Albergo Bologna	9	Museo Civico	15	Palazzo Comunale
3	Train Station	10	Marechiaro	16	Piazza del Comune
4	Bus Station	11	Main Post Office	17	Loggia dei Militi
5	San Giorgio	12	Piazza Cavour	18	Baptistry
6	Brescia	13	APT Tourist	19	Police Headquarters
7	Albergo Touring		Information Office	20	Bella Napoli

price. The *San Giorgio* (☎ 2 04 62), Via Dante 20, is more up-market with rooms from L50,000/70,000.

The *Marechiaro*, Corso Campi 49, has traditional local dishes, and a full meal could cost L20,000. Try its occasional local speciality, marubini in broth, also known as boiled meats. *La Bersagliera*, Piazza Risorgimento 12, is slightly more expensive and has good local dishes from L6000. *Bella Napoli*, Viale Po 121, has pizzas from L6000. *Mocchino*, Via Mocchino 11, is a self-service restaurant with pasta from L3500.

Getting There & Away

The bus station (☎ 2 92 12) is in Via Dante, east of the train station, and serves Milan and other cities around Cremona. By rail (☎ 2 22 37), the city can be reached from Milan via Treviglio, from Mantua, Pavia and Brescia, or from the south, by changing at Piacenza.

By car, take the Cremona exit from the A21 autostrada, which connects Milan with Brescia. The city can also be reached by the A1, which connects with the A21 at Piacenza.

BRESCIA

Situated at the foot of the Lombard Pre-Alps and on the western plain of Lake Garda, Brescia is a mosaic of Italian development – Roman ruins, medieval, Renaissance and Fascist architecture, a historically important arms manufacturing centre, rich museums and a thriving economic centre.

The site of modern-day Brescia had been settled for several centuries before it was captured in 200 BC by the Romans, who called it Brixia. From 1426 to 1797 it was controlled by Venice and then the Austrians. In 1849, it won the nickname 'Lioness of Italy' after holding out against the Austrian army for 10 days during an uprising.

Orientation

The easiest way to reach the city centre from the train or bus station, both near each other at the old city centre's south-western edge, is to take Via Stazione to the huge Piazza della Repubblica and then follow Corso dei Martiri della Libertà to Piazza della Vittoria. The centre is a 10-minute walk from the stations, but buses operate as well.

Information

Tourist Office Known as IAT in Brescia, the tourist information office (☎ 030-4 34 18) is at Corso Zanardelli 34. It opens from 9 am to midday and 3 to 6.30 pm Monday to Friday, and from 9 am to midday on Saturday. There is a second office on the A4 autostrada near the city, which opens from 8 am to 8 pm April to September.

Post & Telecommunications The main post office is in Piazza della Vittoria and opens from 8 am to 6.30 pm Monday to Friday, and from 8.30 am to 12.30 pm Saturday. The postal code for central Brescia is 25100.

The SIP public telephone office is at Via Moretti 46. The telephone code for Brescia is 030.

Emergency The police headquarters (☎ 4 25 61) are at Via dei Musei. The Ospedale Civile (☎ 3 99 51) is in Piazzale Ospedale at the northern edge of the city.

Things to See

From the Fascist-inspired **Piazza della Vittoria**, laid out in 1932 by Piacentini, walk to the **Piazza della Loggia**, the heart of Renaissance Brescia. On the west side is the **loggia**, said to have been partly built in 1489 by Bramante, with the upper floor by Palladio. A Venetian-style loggia forms part of the **Monte di Pietà** to the south side of the square, complete with the **Torre dell'Orologio**, the clock tower reminiscent of the one in St Mark's Square in Venice. Passing under the clock tower, you will enter **Piazza del Duomo**, with two fountains, two cathedrals and loads of atmosphere.

The **Rotunda** or Duomo Vecchio (Old Cathedral), an 11th to 12th century Romanesque structure on the site of an earlier building dating from the 6th century, is, as the name suggests, built on a circular base.

Brescia

	PLACES TO STAY
15	Servizio della Giovane
16	Albergo
18	Regina e Due Leoni
19	Albergo Mansione & Rigamonti
23	Albergo Solferino

▼	PLACES TO EAT
1	Nuovo Livio
3	La Trattoria
4	Wimpy
5	Biondi
13	Ciao
20	Don Rodriguez

OTHER

2	Castle
6	Piazza della Loggia
7	Broletto
8	Museo Romano
9	Police Headquarters
10	Main Post Office
11	Piazza del Duomo
12	Duomo
14	Piazza della Vittoria
17	Tourist Information Office
21	SIP Telephones
22	Pinacoteca Tosio Martinengo
24	Main Bus Station
25	Main Railway Station

The **Duomo Nuovo** (New Cathedral), dating from 1604, is richly classical and has an ornate white marble façade. Both churches have strict dress requirements. The **Broletto**, a communal palace from the 13th century, is dominated by the massive Torre del Popolo.

To the north, through Piazza Tito Speri, named after the hero of the 1849 revolt against the Austrians, is Via dei Musei and the archaeological zone. The remains of the Capitolium (literally, 'capital hill') house the **Museo Romano**, with a small collection of antiquities. It is open Tuesday to Sunday from 10 am to 12.30 pm and 2 to 6 pm, and entrance is L6000. Farther along is the Church of Santa Giulia and the **Museo dell'Età Cristiana** (Museum of Christian Art), containing specimens of pre-Romanesque and Renaissance art, including *intagli* (engraved designs) adorning the spectacular 8th century Cross of Desiderio. It is open daily from 10 am to 6 pm; entrance is L6000.

The **Pinacoteca Tosio-Martinengo**, off Via F Crispi, near Corso Magenta, features works by artists of the Brescian school as well as Raphael. It is open Tuesday to Sunday from 9 am to 12.30 pm and 2 to 5.30 pm, and entrance is L6000. The **castle**, at the old town's northern edge, is worth a visit if you like armaments as its museum has the country's most extensive collection.

Festivals
The Stagione di Prosa runs from December to April and features many theatrical performances. The International Piano Festival, held from early April until June, is staged with nearby Bergamo, while during summer there is the Estate Aperta festival of music and other activities.

Places to Stay
There should be no problems finding accommodation here, particularly in summer. A hostel, the *Servizio della Giovane* (☎ 5 53 87), Via F Bronzetti, not far from the train station, is for women only and charges L12,000 a night.

Most one-star hotels charge L30,000 for a single and L50,000 for a double. The *Albergo Solferino* (☎ 4 63 00), Via Solferino 1, is near the station and has singles/doubles from L30,000/44,000. The *Albergo Rigamonti* (☎ 4 03 32), Contrada Mansione 6, is between the station and the centre and has rooms for the same price. The two-star *Albergo Mansione* at the same address is more expensive at L44,000/60,000, with services. The *Regina e Due Leoni* (☎ 59 276), near the IAT tourist office, has rooms from L30,000/L44,000.

Places to Eat
The locals head for Piazza del Mercato for fresh produce on most days. Risotto and beef dishes are common in Brescia, as in most of Lombardy. The region offers many good wines, including those from the Botticino, Lugana and Riviera del Garda vineyards.

Head for *Bar Duomo* in Piazza del Duomo for a cheap drink. *Ciao*, Via Porcellaga above Corso Palestra, is cheap, with pasta from L4000. *Don Rodriguez*, Via Cavallotti 6, has pizzas from L6000. *Biondi*, Contrada Santa Chiara, north of Piazza Rovetta, is a good, cheap trattoria. At *Nuovo Livio*, Via S Rocchino 90, a meal of local dishes could cost L30,000. *La Trattoria*, Via Milano 55, has main courses from L10,000.

Getting There & Away
If you're coming by train from Rome, change at Verona. From Milan, frequent trains take 50 minutes. The bus station (☎ 5 82 37) is near the train station, and SIA buses connect Brescia with Milan, the lakes and other cities in Lombardy. By car, take the A1 autostrada to Modena Nord, the A22 to Verona and the A4 from Milan.

BERGAMO
Virtually two cities, Bergamo's magnificent ancient *città alta* (upper town), the walled, hill-top city, is surrounded by the *città bassa* (lower town), the sprawling modern additions to this attractive former outpost of the Venetian empire. Although Milan's skyscrapers are visible on a clear day, the city's dialect and traditions echo those of Venice, which controlled Bergamo for 350 years

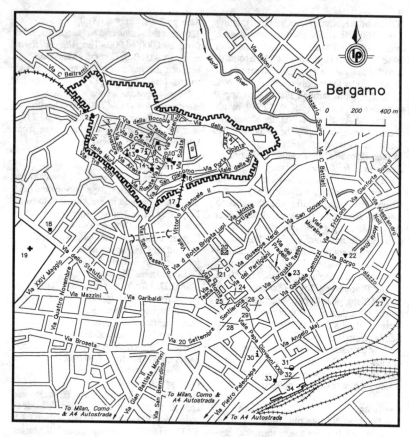

until the Napoleonic period. Despite its wealth of medieval, Baroque and Renaissance architecture, the city is not a big tourist destination. This factor makes it well worth visiting.

Orientation

The main train station in Piazzale Marconi, and the nearby bus station, are at the southern end of Viale Papa Giovanni XXIII. The tourist office is on the left as you approach Piazza Matteotti and the adjoining Piazza Vittorio Veneto, the centre of the lower town. Viale Papa Giovanni XXIII then becomes Viale Roma and soon Viale Vittorio

Emanuele II, which leads to the funicular for the upper town. The road continues up the hill to Piazzale Sant'Agostino at the eastern edge of the old city. Piazza Vecchia, about 500 metres west, past the Rocca (fortress), is the centre of the upper town.

Information

Tourist Office In the lower town, the APT is at Viale Papa Giovanni XXIII 106 (☎ 035-24 22 26), and in the upper town at Vicolo Aquila Nera 2 (☎ 035-23 27 30). Both open from 9 am to 12.30 pm and 2.50 to 6.30 pm Monday to Friday. The upper town office also opens at weekends.

■ PLACES TO STAY		8	Piazza Vecchia
		9	Rocca (Fortress)
6	Albergo Sole	12	Baptistry
10	Agnello d'Oro	13	Church of Santa Maria Maggiore
18	Novacento	14	Piazza Duomo
33	Albergo Stazione	15	Duomo
		16	Funicular Station
▼ PLACES TO EAT		17	Funicular Station
		19	Hospital
5	Franco	20	Main Post Office
11	Da Ornella	21	Piazza della Libertà
22	Öl Giopì e la Margì	23	Police Headquarters
27	Gennaro e Pia	24	Piazza Dante
		25	Piazza Vittorio Veneto
OTHER		26	Piazza Cavour
		28	Piazza Matteotti
1	Funicular to Mt San Vigilio	29	Largo Porta Nuova
2	Porta S Alessandro	30	Tourist Information Office
3	Piazza Citadella	31	Bus Station
4	Piazzale Sant'Agostino	32	Piazzale Marconi
7	Tourist Information Office	34	Main Train Station

The Club Alpino Italiano (☎ 035-24 42 73) is at Via Ghisilanzoni 15.

Post & Telecommunications The main post office is at Via Masone 2A, beyond Piazza della Libertà. It opens from 8.15 am to 8 pm Monday to Friday, and from 8.30 am to 12.30 pm Saturday. The postal code is 24100.

SIP public telephones are in Largo Porta Nuova, near Piazza Vittorio Veneto, open from 9 am to 12.30 pm and 2.30 to 7 pm. There is a 24-hour office at Via Pignolo 58. In the upper town, the office is in Piazzetta San Pancrazio. The telephone code for Bergamo is 035.

Emergency For police emergency, call ☎ 113. The police headquarters are on Via Torquato Tasso, north-east of Piazza Cavour. The Ospedale Maggiore (☎ 26 91 11) is at the western edge of town, along Via Garibaldi and its continuation, Via Mazzini. For an ambulance, call ☎ 25 02 46. There is a pharmacy at Via XXIV Maggio 67 in the upper town, open 24 hours a day, or ring ☎ 34 44 34 for urgent night service.

Things to See
The tourist office produces a series of brochures simply entitled *Bergamo – The Monuments, Museums* and *Donizetti Places*, a tour of sites related to the operatic composer Gaetano Donizetti who was born here.

Most attractions are located in the upper town, but start in Piazza Matteotti, completely redesigned in 1924 by the Fascist-era favourite, Marcello Piacentini. Over Viale Papa Giovanni XXIII, whose namesake was born near Bergamo, is the **Sentierone**, a promenade lined with cafés and fashionable expensive shops. The **Teatro Donizetti**, near Piazza Cavour, was built in the shape of a horseshoe in the 18th century and dedicated to the artist on the centenary of his birth in 1898. The **Church of Santo Spirito**, Via T Tasso, was built in 1309 and has a significant Renaissance interior.

Continue along Viale Vittorio Emanuele II, past the funicular railway for the upper town, and turn right into Via D Noca for the **Accademia Carrara**, one of Italy's most important galleries. Founded in 1807 by a local nobleman in a fine neoclassical building, the gallery boasts an early *St Sebastian* by Raphael and works by Botticelli, Lorenzo

Lotto, Mantegna, Tiepolo, Titian, Canaletto and other Venetian masters. It opens from 9.30 am to 12.30 pm Tuesday to Sunday and 2.30 to 5.30 pm Tuesday to Saturday, and entrance is L5000.

Return to the funicular station to reach the upper town, or walk through the **Porta Sant'Agostino**, with its relief of the winged lion of St Mark. The funicular deposits you at Piazza del Mercato delle Scarpe (the shoe market square), at the southern end of the upper town. From there, head up the small laneway to the right for the Parco delle Rimembranze and the **Rocca**, the 14th century fortress which houses two war-related museums. From the parklands, you can look across the Lombard plains and over the city.

Return to Via Gombito and you will pass the **Torre di Gombito**, dating from 1100, before entering **Piazza Vecchia**, surrounded by the city's finest buildings. Straight ahead is the **Palazzo della Ragione** (1198), bearing the lion of St Mark, a testament to the Venetian presence. To the right is the **Torre del Comune**, with its 15th century clock that still strikes a 10 pm curfew.

On Sunday afternoons in summer, the arcades under the Palazzo della Ragione become the stage for traditional puppeteers. Their art dates back to the 16th century and contributed much to the Venetian commedia dell'arte. Through the arches is the Piazzetta del Duomo, with the Duomo, the Colleoni Chapel, the Baptistry and the Church of Santa Maria Maggiore. The sumptuous **Colleoni Chapel** was built for Bartolomeo Colleoni, the Venetian condottiere (commander), as a burial chapel, although he was not interred here. It features the fresco *Life of John the Baptist* by Tiepolo, and is open from 9 am to midday and 2 to 6.30 pm (to 4.30 pm in winter). Entry is free.

The **Baptistry**, by Giovanni da Campione, is a well-proportioned octagon built in 1340 inside the **Church of Santa Maria Maggiore** but transferred to its present site in 1898. The Romanesque church dates from the 12th century and is a magnificent structure heavily embellished with stucco in the late 16th century. It houses Donizetti's tomb and features Tuscan and Flemish tapestries depicting scenes from the Bible.

The **Duomo**, to the right as you exit Santa Maria Maggiore, was begun in the 15th century and rebuilt several times, and was dedicated to St Alexander, whose remains are here. The cathedral features works by Tiepolo.

Take Via Bartolomeo Colleoni from Piazza Vecchia, through the Porta Sant'Alessandro, for the funicular to Mt San Vigilio for the best view of the city.

Activities

The Club Alpino Italiano (see the earlier Information section) has details about winter sports, hiking and more gentle walks in the Bergamo Alps, which rise to 1000 metres close to the town.

The tourist office produces a series of bicycle itineraries called *Passeggiate Fuori Porta*, with maps, but they're only in Italian. Bikes can be rented from near the train station.

Places to Stay

Cheaper hotels are clustered around the train station, although it is more pleasant, and more expensive, to stay in the upper town. However, the city is easily reached as a day trip from Milan. The APT has an extensive list of camping grounds, refuges in the nearby Bergamo Alps, and agriturismo farms and houses throughout the province.

The *Ostello Bergamo* (☎ 34 23 49), Via Galileo Ferraris 1, is several km from the lower town. Take bus No 14 from the train station. Bed and breakfast is L16,000.

Lower Town One of the budget hotels is *Novecento* (☎ 25 52 10), Via dello Statuto 23, near the corner of Via Damiano Chiesa, with singles/doubles from L30,000/40,000. *Albergo Stazione* (☎ 21 83 21), Piazzale G Marconi 1, opposite the station, has rooms from L35,000/60,000.

Upper Town The *Agnello d'Oro* (☎ 24 98 83), Via Gombito 23, is a short walk from the funicular station and has rooms from L40,000/65,000. The *Albergo Sole* (☎ 21 82 38), Via Rivola 2, near Piazza Vecchia, has rooms from L50,000/70,000.

Places to Eat

Like the Venetians, the people of Bergamo are fond of polenta (cornmeal porridge) and eat it as a side dish or dessert. They contributed *casonsei*, a ravioli stuffed with meat, to the Italian table, and the area is noted for its fine red wines, including Valcalepio.

Lower Town For a good, cheap meal, head for *Ciao*, Piazza Vittorio Veneto, with main courses from L6000. *Gennaro e Pia*, Via Borgo Palazzo 41, has pizzas from L5000. *Öl Giopì e la Margì*, Via Borgo Palazzo 25G, is a bit expensive (L50,000 for a meal) but the waiters wear traditional costume.

Upper Town For a selection of local cakes, including polenta e ösei, head for *Messi*, Via Gombito 32. It also sells pizza by the slice. *Gelateria Balzerino*, Piazza Vecchia, has a huge selection of granita (ice drinks).

Franco, Via B Colleoni 8, has pizzas from L5000. *Da Ornella*, Via Gombito 15, offers traditional foods, and a full meal will cost around L35,000.

Getting There & Away

Frequent trains leave from Milan, and from most other areas you will need to connect at Brescia. The bus station (☎ 24 81 50) in Piazzale G Marconi is serviced by SAB, which operates to the lakes and mountains, and by Autostradale, which operates to Milan, Trieste and other cities. By car, take the A4 autostrada from Milan or Venice. Hitchhikers should take the ss11 from Milan, or the ss42 from the south.

Getting Around

From the station, city bus No 1 passes through the lower town and connects with the funicular railway. Bus No 3 travels from the station to the upper town. Tickets for both are L1000 and can be purchased from machines at the train station. Bikes can be rented from near the train station.

AROUND BERGAMO

There are several small ski resorts in the Bergamo Alps, notably around the **Val Brembana**, reached from Bergamo along Via Nazario Sauro, and **Val Seriana**, reached by way of Via Santa Caterina from the lower town. Each resort has about seven Alpine refuges for summer and winter activities (details are available from the Bergamo APT or Club Alpino Italiano), many walking tracks and good, reasonably priced accommodation. Pick up the *Orobie Estate* and *Orobie Inverno* brochures, which list details of activities and accommodation for summer and winter, although they are both written in Italian only.

VALTELLINA

Covering the band of Alps across Lombardy's north, this area is one of Italy's least attractive Alpine regions. Despite this, the region has some good skiing areas and is very well set up for walking.

The APT Valtellina has offices in Bormio (☎ 0342-90 33 00), Via Stelvio 10; in Sondrio (☎ 0342-51 25 00), Via C Battisti 12; in Aprica (☎ 0342-74 61 13), Corso Roma 161; in Madesimo (☎ 0343-530 15); and in Livigno (☎ 0342-99 63 79). Pick up a copy of *Trekking in Valtellina*, which details walks and provides refuge information for the whole area.

Trains leave Milan for Sondrio, a regional transport hub, and buses connect with the resorts and towns.

The Lakes District

Dotted across Northern Italy, where the Lombard plains rise up into the Alps, are dozens of lakes, including Garda, Como and Maggiore. This area is regarded as one of the country's most beautiful regions. The only problem is that millions of tourists think so too – and prices reflect this. Notably, the lakes are the playground of the Milanese rich.

Most of the lakes are easily reached from Milan or nearby provincial centres such as Bergamo and Brescia. There are plenty of camping grounds, some hostels and hotels in all categories, and in the more Alpine areas, many refuges.

LAKE COMO (LAGO DI COMO)
Marie Henri Beyle first set foot on the shores of Lake Como as a 17-year-old soldier serving under Napoleon. Years later, when he had taken on the pseudonym Stendhal, the celebrated French author, he wrote in *La Chartreuse de Parme* that the blue-green waters of the lake and the grandeur of the Alps made it the most beautiful site in the world. Roman authors Pliny the Elder and Pliny the Younger were born here.

Known also as Lake Lario, this immense body of water is enchantingly beautiful, as are its tiny waterside villages, some accessible only by boat. Today, the waters are murky and swimming is permitted only in parts, but it is not advisable.

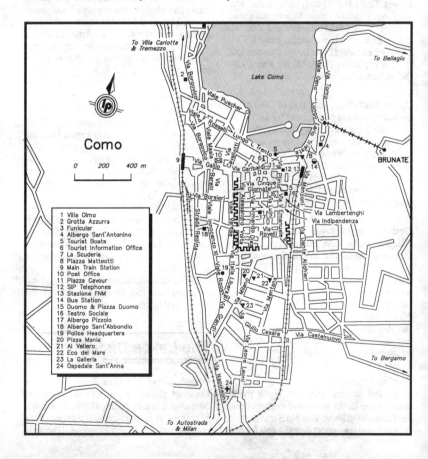

Como

0   200   400 m

1 Villa Olmo
2 Grotta Azzurra
3 Funicular
4 Albergo Sant'Antonino
5 Tourist Boats
6 Tourist Information Office
7 La Scuderia
8 Piazza Matteotti
9 Main Train Station
10 Post Office
11 Piazza Cavour
12 SIP Telephones
13 Stazione FNM
14 Bus Station
15 Duomo & Piazza Duomo
16 Teatro Sociale
17 Albergo Pizzolo
18 Albergo Sant'Abbondio
19 Police Headquarters
20 Pizza Mania
21 Al Veliero
22 Eco del Mare
23 La Galleria
24 Ospedale Sant'Anna

Como

Despite its impressive historic walled centre, the town of Como is becoming increasingly developed and unpleasant. However, it makes a good base from which to explore the lake.

Orientation From the main train station at Piazzale San Gottardo, walk straight ahead to Piazza Cacciatori delle Alpi, and continue along Via Garibaldi to Piazza Volta. The main square, Piazza Cavour, which overlooks the lake, is about 50 metres farther along Via Fontana. Tourist boats depart from near the piazza. From Piazza Cavour, walk east along the waterfront boulevard, Lungo Lario Trieste, to Stazione Ferrovia Nord Milano (FNM), a smaller train station, and the bus station. The funicular for the mountain settlement of Brunate is farther along.

Information The APT tourist office (☎ 031-26 20 91) is at Piazza Cavour 17, open from 9 am to 12.30 pm and 2.30 to 6 pm every day except Sunday. It operates a foreign exchange booth. There is a smaller information office in the central train station.

The main post office is at Via Gallio 6, and opens Monday to Friday from 8 am to 7.30 pm, and from 8.30 am to 2 pm on Saturday. The postal code for central Como is 22100.

The SIP public telephone office is at Via Bianchi Giovini 4, and opens from 9 am to 12.30 pm and 2.30 to 5.30 pm daily. The telephone code for Como is 031.

For police emergency, call ☎ 113. The police headquarters (☎ 27 23 66) are at Viale Roosevelt 7. The Ospedale Sant'Anna (☎ 58 52 49) is at Via Napoleona 60.

Things to See & Do From Piazza Cavour, walk along the arcaded Via Plinio to Piazza del Duomo and the exuberant marble **Duomo**, built and rebuilt between the 12th and 18th centuries. The cathedral combines elements of Romanesque, Gothic, Renaissance and Baroque design and is crowned with a high octagonal dome. To the left of the Duomo is the polychromatic **Broletto** (town

hall), altered in 1435 to make way for the cathedral.

The 12th century Romanesque **Church of San Fedele**, with its medieval sculpture, is along Via Vittorio Emanuele, as are the Palazzo Giovio and Palazzo Olginati – the former housing the **Municipal Museum**, with important prehistoric and Roman remains, and the latter housing the **Museum of the Risorgimento**, with relics of Garibaldi's period. Both open from 9 am to midday and 2 to 5 pm daily, except Monday and Sunday afternoons. The **Pinacoteca Civica** is at Via Diaz 84.

Return to Piazza Cavour and walk east along the waterfront to the funicular railway station for Brunate. Tickets are L3300 one way or L5800 return. Check the timetable for the last car before you leave. Brunate overlooks Como and the lake and offers a pleasant walk and excellent views from the small town of San Maurizio.

The tourist office has produced a hiking map of the area with a 50-km walk from Cernobbio, near Como, to Sorico, near the lake's northern edge. It can be broken into four stages. The map shows the locations of refuges and some camping grounds. Maps for other walks are available, but mostly in Italian. Try also the Club Alpino Italiano (☎ 26 41 77), Via Volta 56.

Places to Stay Accommodation in the town is reasonably expensive, but the hostel in Como, and two along the lake, make a visit inexpensive for the budget conscious.

The *International* camping ground (☎ 52 14 36), Via Cecilio, is away from the centre and the lake, and should probably be overlooked for better grounds along the lake. The *Villa Olmo* hostel (☎ 57 38 00), Via Bellinzona 2, fronting the lake, is one km from the central train station and 20 metres from the closest bus stop. Take bus No 1, 6, 11 or 14. Bed and breakfast is L13,000 and a meal is L12,000.

The *Albergo Sant'Abbondio* (☎ 26 40 09), Via S Abbondio 7, has singles/doubles starting at L20,000/30,000. *Teatro Sociale* (☎ 26 40 42), Via Maestro Comacini 8, near the

Duomo, has rooms from L30,000/50,000. *Albergo Pizzolo* (☎ 27 21 86), Via Indipendenza 65, is right in the centre, with rooms from L50,000/70,000. *Albergo Sant'Antonino* (☎ 30 42 77), Via Coloniola 10, is close to the funicular railway station and has rooms from L45,000/60,000. *Grotta Azzurra* (☎ 57 26 31), Via Borgovico 161, is at the other end of town, near the youth hostel. It has a good pizzeria downstairs, with pizzas from L5000.

Places to Eat Como's fare is dominated by nearby Milan, and caters primarily to the tastes of the Milanese who flock to the city for weekends and holidays. Hence, food is generally good, offers the same specialities as Milan, and can be quite expensive. There are, however, many sandwich bars and self-service restaurants. There is a large food market at Via Mentana 15, open mornings from Monday to Saturday.

Pizza Mania, outside the city wall at Via Milano 20, sells pizza by the slice and is quite cheap. *La Galleria*, Via G Cesare 2, near the corner of Via Milano, is a self-service restaurant with dishes from L5000. *Al Veliero*, at Via Milano 204, has pizzas from L5000. *Eco del Mare*, Via Mentana near Via G Giulini, specialises in typical Lombard dishes, with main courses starting at L10,000. *La Scuderia*, Piazza Matteotti 4, is a popular trattoria and reasonably cheap.

Getting There & Away SPT buses (☎ 30 47 44) leave from Piazza Matteotti for destinations along the lake and cities throughout the region. Trains from Milan's Stazione Centrale arrive at Como's main train station, and go to many cities throughout Western Europe. Trains from Milan's Stazione Nord are more frequent and arrive at Como's Stazione FNM. By car, Como is on the A9 autostrada which connects with the Milan ring road, as does the ss35, the best bet for hitchhikers.

The lake is crisscrossed by *battelli* (boats) and *aliscafi* (hydrofoils). Navigazione Lago di Como (☎ 30 40 60), Piazza Cavour, operates boats all year. Check with the APT because services are reduced on holidays and during winter. A day ticket allowing unlimited trips is L25,000, a day ticket with lunch on the boat is L39,000, and a three-day ticket is L46,500.

Other Destinations

Looking like an inverted 'Y', Lake Como is 51 km long and lies at the foot of the Rhetian Alps. Its myriad towns can easily be explored by boat, or bus from Como, and are worth at least a two-day visit. Highlights include the **Villa d'Este** at Cernobbio, a monumental 16th century villa that is now a hotel; the **Comacina Island**, the lake's sole island, where Lombard kings took refuge from invaders; and the **Villa Carlotta** near Tremezzo, with its magnificent gardens. The towns farther north are lesser tourist attractions.

There are two youth hostels along Lake Como, numerous camping grounds and many reasonably priced hotels. The *Ostello La Primula* (☎ 0344-3 23 56), Via IV Novembre 38, at Menaggio, about halfway up the lake on the western side, is close to the bus stop on the route from Como. It charges L12,000 a night. Farther north is the *Ostello Domaso* (☎ 0344-960 94), Via Case Sparse 4, at Domaso, which is the same price and on the same bus route. Both open from March to October/November. Check with the APT in Como for lists of the 50 or so camping grounds, hotels and agriturismo facilities along the lake.

LAKE MAGGIORE (LAGO MAGGIORE)

The largest and generally regarded as the most beautiful of all the Northern Italian lakes, Maggiore, or Lake Verbano as it is also known, could be a bit of a disappointment. Although stunning in parts, notably the Borromean Islands, Maggiore's shores are flatter and less spectacular than other pre-Alpine lakes, and the area becomes overcrowded in the high season with British and German tourists. Fed by a number of rivers and streams, principally the Ticino and Tresa rivers, Lake Maggiore is about 65 km long.

Information

The APT del Lago Maggiore (☎ 0323-3 01 50) is at Via Principe Tomaso 70, Stresa, one of the main tourist spots, on the lake's western edge. Other tourist offices are at Arona, Baveno and Verbania. The lake's northern reaches are Swiss, as are some of the better walking areas, so consult the Swiss Government Tourist Office (☎ Switzerland 093-31 03 33) for details, or write to the Ente Turistico di Locarno e Valli, Largo Zorzi, 6601 Locarno, Switzerland.

Getting There & Away

Navigazione Lago Maggiore (☎ 0323-3 03 93) in Stresa operates boats and hydrofoils to most towns on the lake and to the Borromean Islands. Single-trip tickets and day tickets are available. For about L10,000, you can buy a day pass allowing unlimited trips between the islands and the shore.

The main rail line between Milan and Switzerland passes through Arona, Stresa and Baveno on the lake's west coast. By car, the A8 autostrada connects Milan with Varese, south-east of the lake. Exit at Legnano for the ss33 road which passes the lake's west and continues to the Simplon Pass. The A26 from Milan has an exit for Lago Maggiore, via Arona.

Stresa

This resort town is one of the best places to start exploring Lake Maggiore. The Borromean Islands are nearby and other features include the **Villa Pallavicino**, a huge garden with a zoo where the animals roam relatively freely (a rarity in this country). The grounds of the villa offer superb views of the lake and the surrounding mountains. The **Villa Ducale** was the summer home of the Turinese Savoys until 1912. From Stresa, you can get to **Mt Mottarone** by cable car or bus from the city centre, or by the road to Armeno. It is a small skiing resort, and a good place to begin walks in the area. It has fabulous views across the lake and over the Monte Rosa Massif.

Camping is available at *Sette Camini Residence* (☎ 0323-201 83), a few km from Stresa at Gignese. Check with the Stresa APT for other grounds in the area. Hotels are plentiful in the area, but must be booked well in advance for summer or long weekends. *Orsola Meublé* (☎ 0323-3 10 87), Via Duchessa di Genova 45, has singles/doubles from L30,000/40,000. *Albergo Flora* (☎ 0323-305 24), Strada Statale del Sempione 26, has rooms from L35,000/ L50,000. The three-star *Speranza au Lac* (☎ 3 11 78), Piazza Imbarcadero, has rooms from L85,000/120,000.

The Borromean Islands (Isole Borromeo)

The islands can be reached from various points around the lake, but Stresa and Baveno are the best step-off points. The four islands, Bella, Pescatori (or Superiore), Madre and San Giovanni, form the lake's most beautiful region.

Isola Bella is the most popular and also the most famous, and has played host to many famous holiday-makers – Wagner, Stendhal, Byron and Goethe among them. The **Palazzo Borromeo** is Isola Bella's major attraction. The sumptuous palace, built in the 17th century for the Borromeo family, contains artworks by Tiepolo and van Dyck, Flemish tapestries and sculptures by Canova. The gardens are magnificent and contain plants from around the world – although you must pay L10,000 to see it all.

Isola Pescatori, also known as Isola Superiore, retains some of its original fishing-village atmosphere. Isola Madre contains Italy's tallest palm trees, an 18th century palace and even more lavish gardens than Isola Bella.

The *Albergo Elvezia* (☎ 0323-3 00 43) on Isola Bella has singles/doubles from L40,000/60,000. Most hotels on the islands are expensive.

LAKE GARDA (LAGO DI GARDA)

The largest and most popular of the Italian lakes, Garda is situated between the Alps and the Po Valley plain. As a result its climate is one of the country's most temperate, with pleasant summers and mild winters. At its northern reaches, Garda is hemmed in by craggy mountains and resembles a fjord. As it broadens towards the south, the lake takes on the appearance of an inland sea.

There are many large villages around the lake, but most are heavily developed and unpleasant. The picturesque but Disneyland-like resort of Sirmione is worth visiting, as is Gardone Riviera on the lake's western edge. At the northern end, Riva del Garda is a good base for walking in the nearby Alps.

Getting There & Away

Buses leave Verona, Brescia, Mantua and Milan for the main towns on the lake. Desenzano del Garda is on the main Milan-Venice train line. By car, the A4 autostrada which connects Milan with Venice passes the southern edge of the lake, and the A22 runs parallel with the lake's eastern shore, connecting Verona with Trento. Riva can be reached by exiting the A22 at Rovereto Sud.

Getting Around

Navigazione sul Lago di Garda (☎ 030-914 13 21), Piazza Matteotti, in Desenzano, operates ferries between most towns on the lake. It has offices or booths in all towns it serves, and operates all year. Ask at tourist offices for timetables. A day ticket is L15,000 and a single journey L2000.

Sirmione

Catullus, the Roman poet, already celebrated Sirmione in his writings, and the village became a favourite bathing spot through the centuries. The remains of a Roman villa and baths (the Grotte di Catullo) and the Rocca Scaligera (a castle built in 1250 for the Scaliger family) make up the historical aspect of this mega-tourist destination. Entering the city's gates is rather like entering Disneyland – the town is picture-book pristine, and well worth visiting.

The tourist information office (☎ 030-91 62 45) is at Viale Marconi 2, and has information on hotels as well as activities such as walking, skiing and horse riding. Pick up a copy of *Garda Pocket*, which features a seven-day tour of the area. The telephone code for Sirmione is 030.

It is possible to swim at the small beaches on the town's eastern side and there is an array of water activities that can be arranged in the town. Windsurfers can try Grumelli (☎ 919 61 30), while the Yachting Club Sirmione (☎ 919 60 72) can assist with boating.

Places to Stay & Eat Looking at this small-ish village, it is hard to believe there are close to 100 hotels. Book ahead or stay away in summer and at long weekends. There are four camping grounds near the town and the APT can advise on others around the lake. *Campeggio Sirmione* (☎ 91 90 45), Via Sirmioncino 9, is the largest and is lakeside. Hotels include the *Albergo Regina* (☎ 91 60 92), Via Antiche Mura 11, east of the centre. It is cute and one of the cheapest, with singles/doubles from L25,000/36,000. The *Albergo Progresso* (☎ 91 61 08), Via Vittorio Emanuele 16, has rooms from L30,000/ 45,000. *Albergo Sirmione* (☎ 91 63 31), Piazza Castello, has rooms from L90,000/ 150,000.

The *Osteria al Pescatore*, Via Piana 20, is one of the better, reasonably priced restaurants and there is loads of takeaway food to be found.

Around Sirmione

Sirmione is about five km east of Desenzano del Garda, the lake's largest town and a main transport hub (but not really worth a visit). Farther north from Desenzano del Garda is Salò, which became the seat of Mussolini's Fascist republic in 1943, after the dictator was rescued from the south by the Nazis. The Club Alpino Italiano has an office in Salò, at Via San Carlo 17, with good information on walks and Alpine refuges in the surrounding mountains.

Gardone Riviera

On the western edge of the lake at the head of a small inlet, Gardone Riviera is an extremely popular resort that retains a hint of its gloriously sophisticated past. Once the lake's most elegant holiday spot, Gardone Riviera has succumbed to development and the problems of being a group tourist destination, particularly for Germans and British.

The APT tourist office (☎ 0365-203 47) is at Corso Repubblica 35. The town's telephone code is 0365.

Things to See A visit to the town is a must to see **Il Vittoriale**, the exotic villa of Italy's controversial 20th century writer, Gabriele d'Annunzio. The villa was a gift from Mussolini, whom d'Annunzio supported fervently, but it was located away from Il Duce's base at Salò because the writer's extreme antics became somewhat of an embarrassment. D'Annunzio was more than a writer: he led an outrageous lifestyle as a socialite and soldier. He died in 1938 and is buried near the villa among his WW I companions.

One of his most triumphant and more bizarre feats was to capture, with a band of his soldiers, a battleship from the fledgling Yugoslavia. Its bow protrudes from the villa's gardens and adds to the kitsch flavour of the Hollywood-style residence. The villa is at the north-eastern edge of town and is open from Tuesday to Sunday, and costs L16,000 for entrance to both the grounds and the house. The town also features **botanical gardens**, on the road to d'Annunzio's villa.

Places to Stay & Eat The *Albergo Nord* (☎ 2 07 07), Via Zanardelli 18, has singles/doubles from L30,000/42,000 and is in a good location. *Villa Fiordaliso* (☎ 2 01 58), Via Zanardelli 132, has rooms from L50,000/90,000 and was a favourite of Mussolini's mistress, Clara Petacci. It is also one of the lake's most beautiful hotels and best restaurants (although it is very expensive). *Pizzeria San Souci*, near the tourist office and Corso Repubblica, has pizzas from L5000.

Riva del Garda

By far the most popular of the resort towns around Lake Garda, Riva, at its northern edge, has a pleasant old centre of cobbled laneways and squares, although it focuses almost entirely on tourism. Situated in Trentino-Alto Adige, Riva has a strong Austrian heritage and was under the control of the Hapsburgs until it was incorporated into Italy after WW I.

The town's APT tourist office (☎ 0464-55 44 44) is in the Giardino di Porta Orientale, opposite the castle. It has extensive information on sporting activities and can advise on accommodation, including apartments for rent. The town's telephone code is 0464.

Activities Riva is one of Italy's most popular spots for windsurfing and has four schools that hire equipment. Try Bouwmeester Windsurfing Centre (☎ 55 42 30), c/o the Hotel Pier, or Nautic Club Riva (☎ 55 44 40), Viale Rovereto 132. Fraglia della Vela (☎ 55 24 60) can point you in the right direction for sailing information. The tourist office can also provide information about mountain cycling, horse riding and walking.

The town is a great starting point for walks around Mt Rocchetta, which dominates the northern end of Lake Garda.

Places to Stay & Eat Several camping grounds dot the waterfront, including *Campeggio Bavaria* (☎ 55 25 24), Viale Rovereto 100. There is an IYHF youth hostel, the *Benacus* (☎ 55 49 11), at Piazza Cavour 10, in the centre of town. It charges L14,000 for bed and breakfast, and opens from early March to mid-October.

Hotels are plentiful, but during summer it is advisable to book. *La Montanara* (☎ 55 48 57), Via Montanara 18, is one of the cheapest places in town, with singles/doubles for L22,000/42,000 and doubles with bathroom for L44,000. It also offers half and full board and has a pleasant trattoria. *Albergo Alpino* (☎ 55 22 45), Via Cerere 10, has rooms for L28,000/48,000 and also offers half and full board. *Hotel Portici* (☎ 55 54 00) Piazza III Novembre 19, offers half board for up to L75,000 and full board for up to L83,000.

The town has many takeaway food places and good delicatessens where you can pick up picnic supplies. *Vaticano*, Via Santa Maria 8, has pasta and some local dishes and a meal could cost L20,000. Try the small trattoria at the hotel *La Montanara*, or the pizzeria *Alla Torre*, Via Maffei 10.

Getting There & Away The town's bus station is in Viale Trento, in the newer part of town, a 10-minute walk from the lake. Regular APT buses connect Riva with Verona, leaving Verona from the Porta Nuova bus station. Atesina buses connect Riva with Trento.

OTHER LAKES
Lake Orta (Lago d'Orta)
Only 15 km long and about 2.5 km wide, Lake Orta is one of the smallest of the Italian lakes. It is dominated from the north-east by Mt Mottarone and, set in lush woodlands, is probably the most unspoilt lake. Tourist numbers are much lower here than at other lakes, even in the high season.

The lake's main town, **Orta San Giulio**, rises from a lakefront piazza and is a beautiful, traffic-free village extending up the slopes of the Sacro Monte. On the mountain itself are many chapels, dating from 1591, which contain frescoes depicting the life of St Francis.

The APT del Lago d'Orta (☎ 0322-9 03 54), Via Olina 9-11, has information about the lake and ferry services, as well as walking and hiking.

There are only a couple of budget hotels, and finding a room can be difficult, particularly in the high season. *Camping Cusio* (☎ 0322-9 02 90), Via G Bosco, is near the shore of the lake. *Taverna Antica Agnello* (☎ 0322-902 59) is about the cheapest hotel, with singles/doubles from L30,000/40,000. *Pizzeria Elesir Amaro*, Via Giacomo Giovanetti, has about the cheapest food in town.

The small village of **Armeno**, at the foot of Mt Mottarone, is worth visiting, not least for its umbrella museum, but also for accommodation. The *Madonna di Luciago* (☎ 0322-90 01 92) has singles/doubles from L40,000/L60,000, although cheaper rooms can be found by asking the locals.

The **Isola San Giulio**, the lake's main attraction, owes its name to a Greek who arrived to evangelise the island in 390 AD only to find it inhabited by snakes and monsters. He earned his sainthood by driving them away and creating a sanctuary. A 12th century basilica dominates the island.

Getting There & Away Orta San Giulio is on the Novara-Domodossola rail line, and can also be reached by bus from Stresa. The town is about 10 km from Stresa via Gignese or Mt Mottarone. From the south, take the ss32 from Novara, or the road to Borgomanero, also from Novara, which is not as good but much quicker.

Lake Iseo (Lago d'Iseo) & Valle Camonica
Probably the least known of the large Italian lakes, Iseo is almost entirely surrounded by mountains, and looks like a typical Alpine lake. It is at the southern end of the Valle Camonica and is fed by the Oglio River. South of the lake is the area known as Franciacorte, rolling countryside producing good wines. The lake is less popular with tourists than the other lakes, although mountains surrounding it have many excellent walking tracks. Check with the APT in the lake towns, or at Bergamo or Brescia, for more detailed information.

The town of **Iseo**, at the lake's southern edge, is a small, pleasant spot fronting the lake, and features the first monument erected to Garibaldi. The APT del Lago d'Iseo (☎ 030-98 02 09) is at Lungolago Marconi 2.

Sarnico, at the south-western edge of the lake, is worth a visit if just to catch a ferry to Monte Isola, the largest lake island in Europe. The APT (☎ 035-91 09 00) is at Via Buelii 18.

The area is well supplied with accommodation, particularly camping grounds. Iseo has about 10 camping grounds, including the *Belvedere* (☎ 030-98 90 48), Via Risorgimento. *Campeggio Monte Isola* (☎ 030-98 81 26), Via Croce, is on the island. *Albergo Il Cenacolo* (☎ 030-98 01 30), Via Mirolte 13, at Iseo, has singles/doubles from L20,000/30,000.

Navigazione sul Lago d'Iseo operates ferries between Iseo, Monte Isola, Lovere and Sarnico.

The **Valle Camonica** weaves its way from the north of Lake Iseo to the vast Adamello-Brenta Natural Park and farther north, to the Stelvio National Park. The area borders on Trentino-Alto Adige and takes in the better parts of the Lombard Alps. The two national parks offer many walks of varying difficulty and are dotted with Alpine refuges (see the Trentino- Alto Adige section).

The area is part of the province of Brescia, and Brescia's APT is a good place to obtain walking, camping and refuge information. In the valley there are tourist information offices at Darfo Boario Terme (☎ 0364-53 16 09), Edolo (☎ 0364-7 10 65) and Ponte di Legno (☎ 0364-9 11 22).

Trentino-Alto Adige

This semiautonomous Alpine region, incorporating the spectacular limestone mountain range known as the Dolomites, is best thought of as two regions. Its two provinces, Trentino and Alto Adige, are culturally, linguistically and historically separate. The northern part, Alto Adige, or Südtirol (South Tyrol), was part of the Tyrol area of Austria until 1918, when it was ceded to Italy. Its population is predominantly of Germanic descent and their first language is German. Trentino was a reluctant part of the Austrian and Austro-Hungarian empires for about a century, until it was returned to Italy after WW I. The population in this part of the region is strongly Italian and, while German is widely spoken, Italian is the preferred language.

The less than comfortable relationship of the two cultural groups has at times been characterised by extreme politics. The right-wing (neofascist) Italian party, the MSI (Movimento Sociale Italiano), has strong support in the region. Its opposition is the SVP (Südtiroler Volkspartei), which encompasses those who want to secede from Italy. Terrorist bombings associated with the more radical secessionists shook the region in the 1960s and again during the 1980s.

On the more positive side, tourism in the region is highly organised and travellers will have little difficulty finding good-value accommodation, as well as extensive information and advice on their choice of activity, including walking, trekking and skiing. You will find that the types of accommodation are slightly different here. While there are still hotels and pensioni (which tend to insist on half or full board), there are also *garnis*, which are basically B&Bs, and *rifugi*, mountain refuges which range from expensive and touristy hotel/restaurants at the top of cable-car and chair-lift routes, to simple Alpine refuges as you go higher into the mountains. Prices charged at all establishments can vary greatly according to the season, and it should be noted that Alpine refuges are generally open only from late June to late September. If you plan to go walking in the mountains during August, it is best to book a bed at the refuges before you set out, since they are often full.

The two provincial tourist offices are the APT del Trentino at Trento and the APT for South Tyrol at Bolzano (see under those towns for details), both of which are extremely helpful and have loads of information in English about the region. There are also APT Trentino offices in Rome (☎ 06-679 42 16), Via Poli 47, and in Milan (☎ 02-87 43 87), Piazza Diaz 5.

Trentino-Alto Adige has an excellent public transport network. The two main bus companies for the region are SAD in Alto Adige and Atesina in Trentino. The main towns and many of the ski resorts are also accessible from major cities throughout Italy, including Rome, Florence, Bologna, Milan and Genoa, by a network of long-haul buses operated by three companies, Lazzi, SITA and STAT. Information about the services is available from tourist offices and *autostazioni* (bus stations) throughout Trentino-Alto Adige, or from the following offices: Lazzi Express (☎ 06-884 08 40), Via Tagliamento 27B, Rome; SITA (☎ 055-21 47 21), Autostazione, Via Santa Caterina di Siena 17, Florence; and STAT (☎ 0142-78

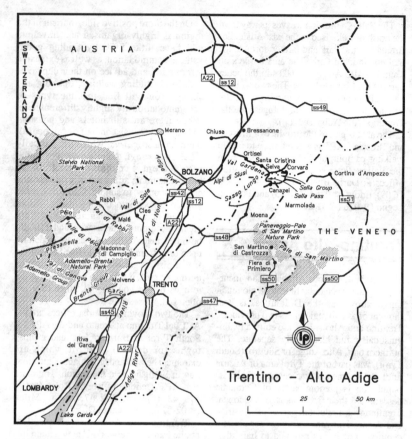

Trentino – Alto Adige

16 60, or 010-58 71 81), Piazza della Vittoria 30, Genoa.

TREKKING IN THE DOLOMITES

Without doubt, the Dolomites, stretching across Trentino-Alto Adige into the Veneto, provide the most spectacular opportunities for walkers in the Italian Alps – from a half-day stroll with the kids to walks/treks which you can plan for as many days as you like, and demanding treks which combine walking with mountaineering skills. There is a vast network of trails, which are generally well marked with numbers on red-and-white painted bands (which you will find on trees

and rocks along the trails), or by numbers inside different coloured triangles for the Alte Vie (High Routes, see the following Where to Go section). There are numerous refuges where you can buy refreshments or spend the night. Tourist offices usually have maps which roughly mark out trails and are generally sufficient as a guide for short walks (less than a day). Staff will also be happy to give advice on the grade of difficulty of the various trails.

Preparations

If you plan to embark on a serious trek, it is recommended that you invest in a good map, such as Kompass or Tobacco 1:50,000 maps, which give extensive detail on trails, altitudes and gradients. These maps are widely available throughout the Dolomites.

The season for walking is from the end of June to the end of September and, depending on weather conditions, sometimes into October – although it should be noted that refuges will close by around 20 September. Trekkers should check weather predictions before setting out and ensure that they are prepared for high-altitude weather conditions. Remember that, in the Alps, the weather can suddenly change from hot and sunny to cold and wet even in mid-August. Weather changes usually occur in the afternoon, so it is always best to set out early in the day. Even if you plan to walk for only a short distance, it is advisable to be prepared.

The following is a list of recommended items to carry on high-altitude treks of more than one day (although items such as good walking shoes, a warm jacket and water are essential even for short walks):

- Comfortable, waterproof walking/trekking boots (already worn-in)
- Light, comfortable backpack
- Anorak (or pile/wind jacket)
- Change of T-shirt, underwear and socks (wool and cotton)
- Short and long pants
- Gloves, wool or pile hat
- Water bottle with at least one litre per person
- Hooded raincoat, or poncho
- Torch (flashlight) and batteries, a lightweight thermal blanket (for emergencies), tissues, sunglasses and (if necessary) a sheet or sleeping bag. You could also bring along a pair of slippers or thongs to wear at the refuge.

Where to Go

The best areas to walk in the Dolomites include the following:

The Brenta Group (Dolomiti di Brenta), accessible from either Molveno to the east or Madonna di Campiglio to the west

The Val di Genova and the Adamello Group, accessible also from Madonna di Campiglio (the Brenta and Adamello groups form the Adamello-Brenta Natural Park)

The Sella Group, accessible from either the Val Gardena to the west or the Val Badia to the east

The Pale di San Martino, accessible from San Martino di Castrozza

The area around Cortina, which straddles Trentino and the Veneto and features the magnificent Parco Naturale di Fanes-Sennes-Braies, and, to the south, Mt Pelmo and Mt Civetta

The Sesto Dolomites north of Cortina towards Austria

The vast Stelvio National Park, accessible from either the Val di Rabbi or the Valle di Péio

There are four Alte Vie in the Dolomites – treks which can take from 10 days to two weeks to complete. The routes link up pre-existing trails and, in some places, have created new trails to make difficult sections easier to traverse. Each route links a chain of refuges and can be traversed either completely or in sections:

Alta Via No 1 crosses the Dolomites from north to south, from the Lago di Braies to Belluno.

Alta Via No 2 extends from Bressanone to Feltre and is known as the High Route of Legends, because it passes through Odle, the mythical kingdom of ancient Ladino fairy tales.

Alta Via No 3 links Villabassa and Longarone.

Alta Via No 4 goes from San Candido to Pieve di Cadore.

The Alte Vie are marked by numbers inside triangles – blue for No 1, red for No 2 and orange/brown for No 3 (No 4 is marked by the normal numbers on red and white bands). Booklets which map out the routes in detail are available at the APT of Belluno, in the Veneto, or ask for information at the APT in Trento.

People wanting to undertake guided treks, or who want to tackle the more difficult trails which combine mountaineering skills with walking (with or without a guide), can seek information at Alpine guide offices in most towns in the region (see under the various towns for further details).

A Basic Trek

The following is a basic guide for a three-day trek, accessible from Cortina d'Ampezzo or Corvara, which incorporates a section of Alta Via No 1, starting from the Passo Falzarego and ending at the Passo Cimabanche. It should be used as an outline only and detailed maps should also be used. Times mentioned are intended as a guide for walkers who maintain a steady pace. Those who tend to meander could double the time taken to complete each stage and this should be taken into account when aiming for specific refuges. The trek is suitable for people with little trekking experience.

Day One This first stage will take you from the Passo Falzarego to the Rifugio Fanes (four to five hours). The Passo Falzarego (2105 metres) is easily accessible by public transport or car from Cortina. Bus services are run by Dolomiti Bus and three a day leave from the Cortina bus station; the trip takes 40 minutes. Buses also leave for the Passo Falzarego from Corvara. A cable car will then take you up to the Rifugio Lagazuoi (2752 metres). Enjoy the spectacular view across to the Marmolada glacier, because this is the highest altitude you will reach during the trek.

From the refuge, head downhill into the wide valley, always following the trail marked with a No 1 inside a blue triangle. On reaching the small lake, you will find, to the right, the beautiful but tiring ascent to the Forcella del Lago (2486 metres), from where you start the long descent into the Piano Grande, with a magnificent view of the Conturines mountains to your left. Once in the Piano Grande, a pretty valley of Alpine pastures, take the trail to the right. At the end of the Piano Grande, past Passo Tadega, follow the triangle signs along the dirt road to eventually reach the Lago di Limo (2159 metres) at the foot of the Col Bechei. Follow the trail to the left and you will descend to the picturesque *Rifugio Fanes* (2060 metres), or slightly farther along the trail, the less expensive *Rifugio La Varella* (2042 metres). You can eat a meal and spend the night at either one. If you still have the energy, explore the beautiful Fanes high plain, taking trail No 12 to Lago Paron through enchanting scenery of limestone white and a thousand shades of green, dotted with the colours of Alpine flowers.

Day Two This stage will take you from Rifugio Fanes to Rifugio Biella (five to six hours). Again following the blue triangular Alta Via signs, head down into the small valley of the Rio San Vigilio until you reach Lago Picodel on your right. Shortly after the lake, again on your right, is a trail that can be taken in preference to the Alta Via route, which, at this point, becomes a long descent to the Rifugio Pederù (1548 metres), from where you would have to ascend to 2000 metres following a road heavily used by 4WD vehicles ferrying tourist groups to the refuge. (For those who want to finish their trek at this point, there is a road from the refuge that descends into the Val Badia.) The detour, on the other hand, is an atmospheric route which, although tiring at times, is not difficult. The trail, which is not numbered, heads off to the right just after a river of gravel, and follows the lake before ascending into the heart of the semi-wilderness, Banc Dal Se. You will arrive at the *Rifugio Fodara Vedla* (1966 metres), where you can relax on the terrace with a drink while enjoying the magnificent scenery. From here you rejoin the Alta Via route, heading in the direction of Rifugio Sennes (2116 metres). After a few hundred metres there is another recommended detour to your right, which crosses a high plain where it is not uncommon to encounter the wild animals of the area.

Once you rejoin the Alta Via route, follow it to the left until you reach Rifugio Sennes, situated by a lake of the same name, and surrounded by a small village of *malghe*, Alpine huts where graziers make butter and cheese in summer. From here, follow the Alta Via in the direction of Rifugio Biella, or take trail No 6, which crosses a beautiful high plain where it is not impossible to find pieces of twisted metal remaining from WW I. These mountains were the scene of some of the more ferocious battles along the Alpine front line. From trail No 6 you will descend to rejoin the Alta Via, within view of the old wooden *Rifugio Biella* (2327 metres), set in a fascinating and unforgettable lunar landscape. Here you can eat a meal and spend the night. If you have the energy, make the easy climb up the Croda del Becco (two to three hours total).

Day Three This stage goes from Rifugio Biella to the Passo Cimabanche (five to six hours). Ascend trail No 28, which follows the crest above the refuge. At this point the trek no longer follows the Alta Via route, which descends to the Lago di Braies, a short distance north. Our trek instead heads southeast towards the majestic Croda Rossa, a beautiful mountain inhabited by golden eagles. Trail No 28 continues to follow the crest until it reaches the forcella Cocodain, a mountain pass at 2332 metres. From here you descend to the left, in a northerly direction on the slope of the Prato Piazza. After a short distance you will pick up trail No 3 and continue the descent until an intersection with trail No 4. Continuing to follow No 3 to the right, you will reach the Casera Cavallo di sopra, a malgha at 2164 metres. From here the trail starts an ascent, always towards the right. It follows the face of the Croda Rossa where there's a narrow point with a sheer drop to one side. Here you will find a fixed iron cord to hold onto for security. This section might be a bit frightening for those who are afraid of heights, but presents no technical difficulty. Continuing to follow trail No 3, you will descend towards the valley to meet trail No 18 (at this point ensure that you do not take No 3A, which descends to the Prato Piazza). Follow the No 18 south, towards the Valle dei Canopi, where there is a slippery descent to the ss51 road and the Passo Cimabanche. Here there is a bar and bus stops for Cortina (to the right), which is only 15 km away, and Dobbiaco (to the left). It is also possible to hitchhike.

SKIING IN THE DOLOMITES

There are innumerable excellent ski resorts in the Dolomites, including the expensive and fashionable Cortina d'Ampezzo, Madonna di Campiglio, San Martino di Castrozza and Canazei, as well as the extremely popular resorts of the Val Gardena. Accommodation and ski facilities are abundant throughout the region and there

are numerous opportunities to choose between downhill and cross-country skiing, as well as *sci alpinismo*, which combines skiing and mountaineering skills on longer ski excursions through some of the region's most spectacular territory.

Tourist offices throughout the region have extensive information on facilities. Probably the best offices to visit for brochures and general information are the APT del Trentino in Trento and the APT for Alto Adige/ Südtirol Dolomiti in Bolzano (see the Trento and Bolzano sections). Staff speak English at both offices and it is possible to write or phone requesting brochures which detail prices for accommodation, ski passes etc.

The high season is generally from Christmas to early January and then from early February to April, when prices go up considerably. A good way to save money is to buy a Settimana Bianca (White Week) package through the CIT or CTS, and travel agencies throughout the country. This will cover accommodation, food and ski passes for seven days.

If you want to go it alone, but plan to do a lot of skiing, invest in a ski pass. Most resort areas offer their own passes for unlimited use of lifts at several resorts for a nominated period (average price in the 1992/93 high season for a seven-day pass was L214,000). However, the best value is the Superski Dolomiti pass which allows access to 450 lifts and more than 1100 km of ski runs. In the 1992/93 high season a Superski pass for seven days cost L234,000. Ring Superski Dolomiti (☎ 0471-79 53 98) for information, or pick up brochures at tourist offices throughout the region.

The average cost of ski hire is L9000 to L15,000 a day for downhill skis and L7000 to L11,000 for cross-country. In an expensive resort like Cortina, however, prices jump to L18,000 to L22,000 a day for downhill skis.

There are ski schools at all of the resorts.

TRENTO

This calm, well-organised provincial town is a good place to start any exploration of the region. Its tourist offices can provide extensive information, both about the town itself and about Trentino in general, and it is a convenient central point for public transport throughout the province.

Known as Tridentum under the Romans, it later passed from the Goths to the Lombards and was eventually annexed to the Holy Roman Empire, when it was known as Trent or Trient. For eight centuries from 1027 it was an episcopal principality, a period marked by constant political and territorial conflict with the rulers of Tyrol. The famous Council of Trent (1545-63) considered the restructure of the Catholic Church and launched the Counter-Reformation.

Orientation

The train station and the adjacent bus terminal are close to Trento's compact historical centre, as well as to most accommodation. To get to the centre, turn right as you leave the station (or bus terminal) and follow Via Andrea Pozzo, which becomes Via Cavour, to Piazza del Duomo.

Information

Tourist Offices Cross the small park directly in front of the train station and turn right to reach the APT tourist information office (☎ 0461-98 38 80) at Via Alfieri 4. It's open from 9 am to midday and 3 to 6 pm Monday to Friday, to midday on Saturdays. The office has loads of information about the town, including maps and glossy brochures in English.

The provincial tourist office, the APT del Trentino (☎ 0461-90 00 00), Corso III Novembre 134, has extensive information on Trentino and can advise on skiing facilities, walking, trekking and climbing, as well as other activities. It can also provide good road maps of the province, with suggested itineraries.

Post & Telecommunications Trento's main post office is in Via Calepina, at Piazza Vittoria, east of Piazza del Duomo. The postal code for central Trento is 38100.

There are SIP public telephones in Piazza della Portella, on Via Torre Vanga, to the right off Via A Pozzo near the train station. Trento's telephone code is 0461.

Emergency For police attention, call ☎ 113, or go to the police station (☎ 98 61 13), Piazza della Mostra, near the Castello Buonconsiglio. The public hospital is Ospedale Santa Chiara (☎ 90 31 11), Largo Medaglie d'Oro, south-east of the centre, off Corso III Novembre.

Things to See & Do

The Piazza del Duomo is the natural place to start a tour of Trento. The piazza is flanked by a Romanesque **cathedral** and the 13th century **Palazzo Pretorio** and tower. The Council of Trent was held in the cathedral (as well as in the Church of Santa Maria Maggiore). Inside the cathedral are fragments of medieval frescoes in the transept, and two colonnaded staircases flank the nave. Underneath the cathedral are the foundations of an early Christian church, discovered in the late 1970s. The area is open Monday to Saturday from 10 am to midday and 2.30 to 6 pm, and entrance is L2000.

The ticket also used to be valid for entrance to the **Diocesan Museum** in the Palazzo Pretorio, which houses paintings depicting the Council of Trent, as well as a collection of Flemish tapestries, but it's closed for restoration and is expected to reopen by 1994.

On the other side of the piazza are two Renaissance houses, known as the **Case Rella**, their façades decorated with frescoes. In the centre of the piazza is the 18th century **Fountain of Neptune**.

From the piazza, head north along Via Belenzani or Via Oss Mazzurana and turn right into Via Manci to reach the **Castello di Buonconsiglio**. Along these streets are several palaces of interest. The castle was the home of the bishop-princes who ruled Trento and incorporates the 13th century Castello Vecchio and the Renaissance Magno Palazzo. Inside the castle is the **Museo Provinciale d'Arte**. The castle and museum are

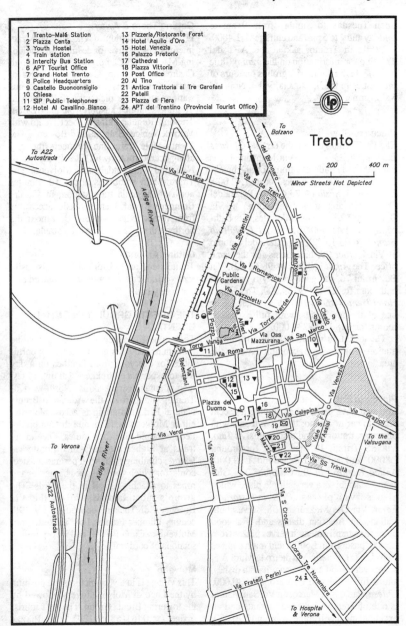

1 Trento-Malé Station
2 Piazza Centa
3 Youth Hostel
4 Train station
5 Intercity Bus Station
6 APT Tourist Office
7 Grand Hotel Trento
8 Police Headquarters
9 Castello Buonconsiglio
10 Chiesa
11 SIP Public Telephones
12 Hotel Al Cavallino Bianco
13 Pizzeria/Ristorante Forst
14 Hotel Aquilo d'Oro
15 Hotel Venezia
16 Palazzo Pretorio
17 Cathedral
18 Piazza Vittoria
19 Post Office
20 Al Tino
21 Antica Trattoria ai Tre Garofani
22 Patelli
23 Piazza di Fiera
24 APT del Trentino (Provincial Tourist Office)

Trento

0   200   400 m

Minor Streets Not Depicted

To Bolzano
To A22 Autostrada
To Verona
To Hospital & Verona
To the Valsugana

Adige River

Via del Brennero
Via S da Trento
Via Fontana
Via Segantini
Via Romagnosi
Via Manzoni
Public Gardens
Via Gazzoletti
Via Torre Verde
Via Oleslo
Via Alfieri
Via Pozzo
Via Oss Mazzurana
Via San Marco
Via Torre Vanga
Via Roma
Via Belenzani
Via Verdi
Piazza del Duomo
Via Rosmini
Via Calepina
Via Mazzini
Via Venezia
Via Grazioli
Via S F d'Assisi
Via SS Trinità
Via S Croce
Corso Tre Novembre
Via Fratelli Perini

open Tuesday to Sunday from 9 am to midday and 2 to 5 pm, and entrance is L4000.

While in Trento, ask at the APT del Trentino for information on the *trenini* (little trains) which take tourist groups on tours of the castles in the Valsugana, Val di Non and Vallagarina.

Places to Stay
The IYHF youth hostel, the *Ostello Giovane Europa* (☎ 23 45 67), Via Manzoni 17, is really the only budget option. Bed and breakfast is L15,000 and a meal costs L12,000. The *Hotel Venezia* (☎ 23 41 14), Piazza del Duomo 45 and around the corner at Via Belenzani 70, has singles/doubles with bathroom for L45,000/70,000. *Al Cavallino Bianco* (☎ 23 15 42), off Piazza del Duomo at Via Cavour 29, has rooms for the same price. The *Aquilo d'Oro* (☎ 98 62 82), Via Belenzani 76, has good-quality rooms with bathroom for L88,000/139,000. The *Grand Hotel Trento* (☎ 98 10 10), Via Alfieri 1-3, is one of the top hotels, with fully serviced rooms for L180,000/230,000.

The local tourist office can provide information on agriturismo accommodation in the area.

Places to Eat
You will have no problem finding a decent place to eat in Trento: the town teems with pizzerias, trattorias and restaurants. *Al Tino*, Via SS Trinità 10, has pasta for around L8000 and salads for around L10,000. *Antica Trattoria ai Tre Garofani*, Via Giuseppe Mazzini, is a very simple place which also serves pizzas. *Pizzeria/Ristorante Forst*, Via Oss Mazzurana 38, serves both Italian and Austrian dishes and is a good place for a family meal. It serves pizzas from L5000, pasta from L6000, and main courses from L9000. *Patelli*, Via dietro le Mura A 5, serves very good and unusual Italian dishes, and a full meal will cost around L30,000. *Chiesa*, Parco San Marco, on Via San Marco, is one of Trento's better restaurants and an excellent meal will come to around L70,000.

Getting There & Away
From the bus station in Via Andrea Pozzo, intercity buses leave for destinations including Madonna di Campiglio, San Martino di Castrozza, Molveno, Canazei and Riva di Garda. Timetables are posted at the bus station, otherwise pick up a full guide to Trentino's public transport from the APT del Trentino. Regular trains connect Trento with Verona, Venice, Bologna and Bolzano. The Trento-Malé train line connects the city along scenic routes with Cles in the Val di Non, and with Andalo and Molveno. The Trento-Malé station is about 10 minutes north of the main train station, in Via del Brennero. By car, Trento is easily accessible from Verona in the south and Bolzano in the north on the A22 Brennero autostrada.

Getting Around
Trento's compact historical centre is easily seen on foot and you will have no need of a car or city buses.

THE BRENTA GROUP (DOLOMITI DI BRENTA)
This majestic group of spiky limestone mountains provides good walking opportunities for everyone from families on a day trip to experienced trekkers wanting to test their mountaineering skills. North-west of Trento, and part of the Adamello-Brenta Natural Park, the group is accessible from either Molveno or Madonna di Campiglio. People should plan their routes, since many trails at higher altitudes incorporate *vie ferrate*, climbing trails with permanent steel cords, for which you will need harnesses and ropes to attach yourself to the cords. The group's most famous trail is the Via Bocchetta di Tuckett, opened up by 19th century climber Francis Fox Tuckett, from Molveno to Cima Brenta, and incorporating sections of cord trail.

Molveno
This village is in a very picturesque position by the Lago di Molveno, overshadowed by the towering Brenta Group. The APT tourist office (☎ 0461-58 69 24) is at Piazza

Marconi 7 and is open Monday to Saturday from 9 am to 12.30 pm and 3 to 6.30 pm, Sunday from 10 am to midday. The staff will help you find accommodation (although in August you should book in advance) and will advise on walking trails. Also in the piazza is the office of the Alpine Guides Group (Gruppo Guide Alpine, ☎ 0461-58 60 86), which organises guided treks for groups of four to five people for L240,000 a day (for the group).

The telephone code for the village is 0461.

Activities From the top of the village, a *cabinovia* (two-seater cable car) will take you up to the Rifugio Pradel (1400 metres), from where you can catch the chair lift to the Rifugio Montanara (1525 metres). From here, take trail No 340bis, which connects with trail No 340 (which starts at the Rifugio Pradel) and will take you to the Rifugio Croz dell'Altissimo (1430 metres), a pleasant and easy one-hour walk. Take trail No 340 to the Rifugio Selvata (1630 metres), then trail No 319 to the refuges Tosa and Tommaso Pedrotti (2491 metres and about four hours' walk).

From here, follow trail No 318 to the Via delle Bocchette (trail No 305), which incorporates sections of cable trail for which you will need to be equipped with harnesses and ropes. Otherwise, you can continue along No 318, passing the Rifugio dei Brentei (2182 metres), until you reach trail No 328, heading to the right to the Rifugio del Tuckett (2272 metres). Trail No 316 then heads for the Passo Grosté, from where a cable car will take you down to Madonna di Campiglio. From the Rifugio Pedrotti to the Passo Grosté the walk will take at least six hours.

For a less demanding walk, there is a path around the lake which starts at the camping ground. Making the entire circle of the lake will take from four to six hours.

Places to Stay & Eat The tourist office will provide a list of the mountain refuges and their phone numbers to help you plan your trek. If you want to stay in Molveno, there is

Camping Spiaggia Lago di Molveno (☎ 58 69 78), which charges up to L7000 per person and L12,000 for a space.

Prices do not vary greatly among the various hotels in town, and at most you will be required to take full board. Average prices are from L50,000 per person in May and June, and from L80,000 per person in the high season (August). Try the *Zurigo* (☎ 58 69 47, Via Rio Massò 2, or *Europa* (☎ 50 60 62), Via Nazionale 11. The *Grand Hotel Molveno* (☎ 58 69 34) is in a lovely position out of town by the lake. Full board is from L90,000 to L130,000.

Getting There & Away Molveno is accessible by bus from Trento. Atesina buses also connect Molveno with Milan, leaving from Piazza Castello in Milan (ring ☎ 02-80 11 61 in Milan for details).

Madonna di Campiglio

One of the top ski resorts in the Alps, Madonna di Campiglio (often simply called Madonna) is in the Valle Rendena, on the other side of the Brenta Group. It is extremely well equipped with ski lifts and runs, and there are excellent opportunities for cross-country and alpine skiing.

The APT tourist office (☎ 0465-4 20 00) is in the centre of the village, off Piazza Brenta Alta. It has loads of information about skiing and walking in the area, and will advise on accommodation. The office of the Alpine Guides Group (☎ 0465-4 12 62) is across the street (open only after 4 pm), and brochures on its summer excursions are available at the tourist office.

The telephone code for the village is 0465.

Activities A network of chair lifts and cable cars will take you from the village to the numerous ski runs. A few km out of the village at Campo Carlo Magno is a cable car (in two stages) up to the Passo Grosté, from where trekkers can set off into the Brenta Group. The Via delle Bocchette (trail No 305) leaves from the Rifugio Grosté at the cable-car station. The return trip on the cable car will cost L22,000.

Near Madonna is the Val di Genova, often described as one of the most beautiful valleys in the Alps. The valley extends up into the striking Adamello mountain range, where there are some challenging walking trails. There are four refuges in the valley, each costing around L35,000 a person per night. During August the valley is closed to normal traffic, and half-hourly buses ferry walkers and tourists to the Rifugio Adamello at the end of the road, from where you can take trail No 241 to the end of the valley (2000 metres) beneath a huge, receding glacier. The trail then makes the steep ascent to the Rifugio Caduti dell'Adamello (3020 metres) at the edge of the glacier.

Places to Stay & Eat There are numerous hotels and garnis in Madonna, none of which will suit the pockets of budget travellers. Most require that you pay for half or full board, and in the high season may be reluctant to accept bookings for less than seven days. *Garni La Montanara* (☎ 4 11 05), on the main road, at Via Cima Tosa, opposite Piazza Brenta Alta, is one where you can pay only for the room. Singles/doubles are L30,000/50,000. The *Bellavista* (☎ 4 10 34), a very pleasant establishment, uphill from the tourist office, near the Funivia Pradalago, charges from L70,000 to around L115,000 per person per day for full board, depending on the season. *La Fontanella* (☎ 4 13 98) is a few km out of town towards the Val di Genova and has a magnificent view of the Brenta Group. Its prices are much lower, from around L58,000 per person per day to L75,000 for full board.

Try *Ristorante/Pizzeria Le Roi*, Via Cima Tosa, near Piazza Brenta Alta, where a full meal will cost around L20,000 to L25,000. Around the corner is *Bar Dolomiti*, where hot sandwiches for L4500 should be sufficient for lunch.

Getting There & Away Madonna di Campiglio is accessible from Trento by Atesina bus. It is also accessible from cities including Rome, Florence and Bologna by Lazzi (in Rome and Florence) and SITA buses.

VAL DI NON

The Val di Non is a picturesque valley of apple orchards and castles, accessible from Trento by Trento-Malé train or bus. The main town is Cles, dominated by the Castel Cles. The Pro Loco tourist office is in Corso Dante, just off the main road through town. If you want to stay here on your way north, try the *Antica Trattoria* (☎ 0463-2 16 31), Via Roma, which has singles/doubles for L38,000/52,000 with bath. The *Cristallo* (☎ 0463-2 13 53), Corso Dante, has rooms for L48,000/72,000 with bathroom.

STELVIO NATIONAL PARK

Heading east along the Val di Sole, you will reach two valleys, the Val di Rabbi and the Valle di Péio, which head up into the Stelvio National Park (Parco Nazionale dello Stelvio). This is one of Italy's major national parks, encompassing the Ortles mountain range and extending into Lombardy.

From Péio (also spelt Péjo) Terme (1393 metres) there are chair lifts to the Rifugio Doss dei Cembri (2400 metres), from where you can pick up trail No 105 to the Rifugio Mantova al Vioz (3535 metres) at the edge of the Forni glacier. If you want to climb Mt Vioz (3645 metres) or continue onto the glacier, you will need the appropriate equipment.

The tourist office at Malé (☎ 0463-90 12 80), Piazza Regina Elena, has extensive information on all three valleys, including accommodation, transport and sporting activities, and will advise on walking trails and ski facilities.

Ferrovia Trento-Malé buses connect Péio Terme with Madonna di Campiglio and with Malé in the Val di Sole. Malé is accessible on the Trento-Malé train line from Trento and from Cles.

SAN MARTINO DI CASTROZZA

East of Trento, this important ski resort is at the foot of the Pale di San Martino, an imposing group of Dolomite mountains, so stark in their pale grey-white colour that they virtually glow in the dark. The mountains are part of the Paneveggio-Pale di San Martino nature park, noted for its Alpine vegetation and wildlife, including the roe deer, chamois, marmot, wildfowl and birds of prey such as the golden eagle. It is a magnificent area in which to ski or walk, and both San Martino di Castrozza and nearby Fiera di Primiero are well equipped for tourists.

Information

San Martino's APT tourist office (☎ 0439-76 88 67) is at Via Passo Rollo 167. It has extensive information on accommodation, transport and skiing facilities, and can advise on walking trails. You can telephone or write to request information about hotels or apartments. The office is open Monday to Saturday from 9 am to midday and 3 to 7 pm, Sunday from 9.30 am to 12.30 pm. Information about Alpine guides is also available at the office from 5 to 7 pm daily. A two-day trek with a guide costs L100,000 per person. Rock-climbing and cord-trail courses are also offered.

The nearest hospital is at Feltre, although a tourist medical service is available during the summer and winter months. Full details are available at the tourist office.

San Martino's telephone code is 0439.

Activities

The area has excellent ski runs and is part of the extensive Superski Dolomiti system, and during winter a special ski bus connects the valley with the various runs. For walkers, the Pale di San Martino has well-marked trails, and a reasonable map is available at the tourist office. A chair lift followed by cable car will take you to the Rifugio Rosetta (2600 metres), from where you can choose between several walks, or more difficult treks requiring mountaineering skills.

For an enjoyable three-hour walk, take trail No 707 from the nearby Rifugio Pedrotti and, after a short distance, veer to the right on trail No 708, which eventually becomes trail No 718 and descends to the Rifugio Canali. From here, take the path to the right, which heads down into the pretty Canali Valley and will eventually bring you to Fiera

di Primiero, from where you can catch a bus back to San Martino.

Places to Stay & Eat

Prices vary according to the season, and many places will require that you pay for half or full board. They may also be reluctant to accept bookings for less than seven days. The tourist office will advise on apartments to rent and has a full list of refuges in the area.

The *Suisse* (☎ 6 80 87), Via Dolomiti 1, has singles/doubles for L38,000/48,000 (room only). *Biancaneve* (☎ 6 81 35) is nearby at No 14 and charges L35,000 per person for bed and breakfast. The newly renovated *Hotel Plank* (☎ 76 89 76), Via Laghetto, charges from around L55,000 to L90,000 per person for full board.

For meals in San Martino, try *Lo Sfizio*, a creperie just off Via Passo Rollo, near the tourist office. Slightly out of town, along Via Fontanelle, are *Ristorante Le Fontanelle* and *Caffè Col*. Typical food of the area is served at the various malghe around San Martino, which have developed into proper restaurants. Try the *Malga Venegiota* (☎ 6 46 57), accessible by a short trail from the Malga Juribello near Passo Rolle, or *Malga Ces*, about two km east of town. A meal at either will cost less than L30,000.

Getting There & Away

San Martino is accessible directly from Florence and Rome (change at Florence) by Lazzi and SITA buses. From Bologna you can catch a Dolomiti Express bus from the bus station in Via XX Settembre. San Martino is also accessible from Trento by Atesina bus (leaving from the bus station in Via Pozzo, Trento), and from Canazei by SITA bus.

THE SELLA GROUP

The Sella Group (Gruppo di Sella), in the western Dolomites, straddles the border between the provinces of Trentino and Alto Adige, and is close to Cortina d'Ampezzo and the Parco Naturale di Fanes-Sennes-Braies in the Veneto. To the west of the group is the spiky Sasso Lungo, which extends to the Alpi di Siusi, overshadowing the Val Gardena in Alto Adige. To the east is the Val Badia and Corvara, its main town, while to the south are the Val di Fassa, its popular ski resort, Canazei, and the Marmolada, where there is glacier skiing in summer.

The entire zone is extremely well equipped for skiers, and, by following a network of runs known as the Sella Ronda, you can make a day-long skiing tour of the valleys surrounding the Sella Group. Full details on the tour are available at all tourist offices in the area.

The walking trails of the Sella and Sasso Lungo are most easily accessible from Canazei, or from the resorts of the Val Gardena by SAD (Servizi Autobus Dolomiti) bus to Passo Sella or Passo Pordoi. At Passo Sella (2240 metres), where there is a magnificent view across the Alps, there is a cable car to the Rifugio T Demetz (2996 metres) on the Sasso Lungo. From here you can pick up trail No 525, which traverses the mountain's jagged peaks. From Passo Pordoi (2242 metres), take the cable car up to Sasso Pordoi (2952 metres). Here you can take the Alta Via No 2, which crosses the group, or detour on No 638, which will take you up to the Rifugio Piz Fass on Piz Boé (3152 metres). Continuing along No 638 you will reach a cable-car service down to Corvara in the Val Badia.

Canazei

This popular ski resort is fairly modern, and very well equipped for tourists. Skiing possibilities include a range of downhill and cross-country runs, as well as some very challenging alpine tours and the Sella Ronda network of runs. The AAST tourist office (☎ 0462-6 11 13) has loads of information on ski runs, lifts and schools, and will advise on accommodation as well as walking trails.

The telephone code for Canazei is 0462.

Places to Stay & Eat Hotels are numerous, but it is advisable to book in August and during the peak ski season. There are also rooms and apartments for rent, and the tourist office can provide details on request.

The *Camping Marmolada* (☎ 6 16 60) is in the town centre and is open in both summer and winter. Prices are L7000 per person and L10,000 for a site. *Pensione Genzianella* (☎ 6 11 43), Via Roma 15, charges L25,000 per person for bed and breakfast and L45,000 for half board. It closes in October and November. The *Stella Alpina* (☎ 6 11 27), Via Antermont 4, charges L33,000 per person for bed and breakfast and L47,000 for half board. *Pensione Rita* (☎ 6 12 19), Via Pareda, charges up to L78,000 per day and up to L530,000 per week half board in the high season.

There is a supermarket at Via Dolomiti 120, and numerous bars and panini shops can be found in the town. The *Osteria La Montanara*, Via Dolomiti 147, serves good meals for around L25,000. Opposite is the *Pizzeria/Ristorante Italia*, where pizzas cost from L6000 to L10,000 and a full meal will come to under L25,000.

Getting There & Away Canazei can be reached by Atesina bus from Trento and by SAD bus from Bolzano and the Val Gardena. It should be noted that services do not cross the high mountain passes (such as Sella) in winter.

The Val Gardena

This picturesque valley in Alto Adige is enclosed by the Sella Group – Sasso Lungo and the Alpi di Siusi to the south, and the mountains of the Parco Naturale Puez-Odle to the north. It is one of the more popular skiing areas in the Alps, because of its relatively reasonable prices and excellent facilities. However, during the ski season its runs are packed with skiers and you may prefer to avoid the valley for this reason. Its main towns are Ortisei, Santa Cristina and Selva, all offering lots of accommodation and easy access to ski facilities.

The Val Gardena has two great traditions: the Ladin language and woodcarving. Ladin is derived from a Latin dialect traceable to the Roman legions, and is still spoken by many people in the valleys surrounding the Sella Group. The traditional woodcarvers of the Val Gardena are famous for their statues, figurines, altars and toys. If you plan to buy a woodcarving, choose carefully to ensure that your purchase is handcrafted rather than mass-produced.

Information There are tourist offices in each of the towns, and those at both Santa Cristina (☎ 0471-79 30 46) and Selva (☎ 0471-79 51 22) have extensive information on the valley, its accommodation and ski facilities, as well as information on walking trails in the area. Pick up a guide to each town (available in English), which details all useful tourist information. Information on guided treks and rock-climbing schools can also be obtained at the tourist offices.

The telephone code for the valley is 0471.

Activities Apart from the extensive downhill runs, there is also excellent cross-country skiing in the Alpi di Siusi and in the Vallunga (near Selva). Alpine skiers should consult the tourist office for detailed information. There are some stunning trails in the zone, in the areas of Forcella Pordoi and Val Lasties in the Sella Group, and on the Sasso Lungo.

Walkers are in a virtual paradise in this area, literally surrounded by endless possibilities, from the challenging High Routes of the Sella Group to picturesque walks in the Alpi di Siusi. The Vallunga is a perfect place for a family walk. Just behind Selva, the valley is home to some overfriendly horses who like to harass picnicking tourists. The walk to the end of the valley and back will take three to four hours. It is possible to continue from the end of the valley, up along trail No 14, to pick up the Alta Via No 2, on which you can continue up into the Odle Group, or double back into the Puez Group and on to the Sella.

Places to Stay & Eat The valley has hundreds of hotels and pensioni, but it is still advisable to book during August and at Christmas. Many places will require that you pay half or full board, but there are also plenty of B&Bs and affittacamere. The tourist offices have full lists, including photos and prices, so write or phone to request a booklet in advance.

In Santa Cristina, try *Affittacamere Desirée* (☎ 79 65 18), Via Chemun 60, which charges up to L26,000 for bed and breakfast. *Garni Cir* (☎ 79 33 58), Via Paul 22, charges around L30,000 per person for bed and breakfast. *Haus Walter* (☎ 79 33 37), Via Val 6, is very simple and charges up to L33,000 for bed and breakfast. *Pensione Bellavista* (☎ 79 20 39) is set back from the town at Via Plesdinaz 65 and offers half board for up to L62,000 per person. In the centre of town is *Hotel della Posta* (☎ 79 20 79), which offers half board for up to L105,000 per person and full board for up to L120,000.

In Selva, try *Villa Thëres* (☎ 79 54 65), back from the town at Via Rainel 47, which charges around L27,000 per person, with breakfast and private bathroom. *Garni Katiuscia* (☎ 7 55 08) is near the Vallunga, a fair walk from the town, but in a lovely position, at Via Larciunëi 38. Bed and breakfast is L30,000 a person. *Garni Zirmei* (☎ 79 52 12), Via Col da Lech 60, charges up to L40,000 for bed and breakfast.

There are not many restaurants in the valley, since most hotels require that their guests pay for half or full board. In Santa Cristina, try *Pizzeria da Peppi*, Via Chemun 52, and in Selva, try *Caffè Sal Fëur*, a pizzeria at Streda Pueze 6.

Getting There & Away The Val Gardena is accessible from Bolzano by SAD bus, as well as from Canazei (only in summer). Regular buses also connect the towns along the valley, and you can reach the Alpi di Siusi either by bus or cable car. Full timetables are available at the tourist offices. Information about long-distance bus services (Lazzi, SITA and STAT) to major cities throughout Italy can be obtained at Tourdolomiti Viaggi (☎ 79 53 24) in Selva.

Corvara

This ski resort is in the Alta Badia, in Alto Adige, in a beautiful position surrounded by the mountains of the Parco Naturale Puez-Odle to the west and the magnificent Parco

Naturale Fanes-Sennes-Braies to the east. Corvara was the central town of the Ladin tribes and the area has a rich tradition of legends about giants, kings, witches, fairies and dragons, many centred on the majestic Fanes Group. Today it is a pleasant little town, with a well-organised tourist office and plenty of accommodation.

Corvara is on the Sella Ronda ski trail. From the town, you can reach the Passo Falzarego by SAD bus and then take the cable car up into the Fanes-Sennes-Braies park (see the earlier section on Trekking in the Dolomites).

The AAST tourist office (☎ 0471-83 61 76) is in the town's main street and open Monday to Saturday from 8 am to midday and 3 to 7 pm, Sunday from 10 am to midday. It has extensive information on ski facilities, walking trails, accommodation and transport.

Corvara's telephone code is 0471.

Places to Stay & Eat The tourist office will assist if necessary, but otherwise try the *Garni Laura* (☎ 83 63 40), back from the main road near the tourist office, which has bed and breakfast for L22,000 per person. *Garni Granval* (☎ 83 60 64) offers bed and breakfast for L30,000 per person. Full meals at *Ristorante/Pizzeria La Tambra* cost under L25,000.

Getting There & Away SAD buses connect Corvara with Bolzano, the Val Gardena, the Passo Sella and Passo Pordoi, Canazei, the Alpi di Siusi and the Passo Falzarego (note that buses do not cross the high passes in winter). Full timetable details are available at the tourist office.

CORTINA D'AMPEZZO

Across the Fanes-Conturines mountains from the Val Badia is the jewel of the Dolomites, Cortina d'Ampezzo. Italy's most famous, fashionable and expensive ski resort, Cortina is also one of its best equipped and certainly the most picturesque. If you are on a tight budget, the prices for accommodation and food will be prohibitive, even in the

low season. However, camping grounds and Alpine refuges (open only during summer) provide more reasonably priced alternatives.

Situated in the Ampezzo bowl, Cortina is surrounded by some of the most stunning mountains in the Dolomites, including Mt Cristallo, the Marmarole Group, Mt Sorapiss and the Tofanes. To the south are Mt Pelmo and Mt Civetta. Facilities for both downhill and cross-country skiing are first class and the small town's population swells dramatically during the ski season, as the rich and famous pour in. The town is also busy during the summer months, since the area offers great possibilities for trekking and climbing, with well-marked trails and numerous refuges.

Information
The main APT tourist information office (☎ 0436-32 31) is at Piazzetta San Francesco 8, in the town centre. It has information on accommodation, ski facilities and hiking trails. It can also provide, on request, a full listing of apartments and rooms for rent. There is a small information office at Piazza Roma 1.

Cortina's Alpine Guides Group (☎ 0436-47 40) is based at Piazzetta San Francesco 5, open from 8 am to midday and 4 to 8 pm.

Cortina's telephone code is 0436.

Trekking
Apart from the three-day trek through Fanes-Sennes-Braies detailed in the Trekking in the Dolomites section, the Dolomites around Cortina offer a network of spectacular trails. A series of three cable cars (L33,000 return) will take you from Cortina up to the Tofana di Mezzo (3243 metres), from where all of the trails are difficult and incorporate cord trails, for which you will need to be properly equipped. You can link up with the Alta Via No 1 either at the Passo Falzarego, or at the evocative Passo Giau, with the spiky Croda da Lago to the east and the Cinque Torri to the north-west. To get to the Passo Giau, you will need to catch a bus from Cortina to Pocol and then hitch a ride.

Another interesting possibility is to take

the local bus from Cortina east to Passo Tre Croci (1805 metres) and take trail No 215 (which is a section of Alta Via No 3) up to the Rifugio A Vandelli (1928 metres) in the heart of the Sorapiss Group. From here the Alta Via No 3 continues up to 2316 metres and then to the left, as trail No 242. This section incorporates a section of cord trail, as does trail No 215, which heads off to the right.

Places to Stay

The *International Camping Olympia* (☎ 50 57) is a few km north of Cortina at Fiames. Open all year, it charges L6000 per person and from L9000 to L20,000 for a site, depending on the season. The camping ground has an excellent restaurant/pizzeria, which is worth eating at even if you are not camping there.

There are no budget hotels in Cortina, and the lowest you can expect to pay is around L80,000 a double in the low season and L100,000 in the high season. *La Ginestrina* (☎ 86 02 55), Via Roma 55, has doubles from L90,000 to L116,000. *Albergo Cavallino* (☎ 26 14), Corso Italia 142, is in the heart of the town and charges from L43,000 up to L82,000 per person, with breakfast. *Albergo Villa Alpina Dolomiti* (☎ 21 18) is in Via Roma near La Ginestrina. Charges for full board range from L50,000 to L120,000 per day. *Fanes* (☎ 34 27), Via Roma 136, charges from L60,000 to L200,000 for full board.

Places to Eat

There are numerous good eating places in and around Cortina, though many are very expensive. The Standa supermarket in Via Franchetti is a good place to shop if you have access to a kitchen. For a good pizza, head for *Il Ponte*, Via Franchetti 8, or *Pizzeria Olympia* at the International Camping Olympia at Fiames, as previously mentioned. The *Ristorante Croda Caffè*, Corso Italia 186, has reasonably priced meals. *Il Meloncino* overlooks Cortina on the road to Passo Falzarego and is one of the town's best known eating places. A full meal will cost L40,000 to L50,000.

Getting There & Away

Cortina's bus station is in Via Marconi. Pick up a timetable at either the bus station or the tourist office. SAD buses connect Cortina with Bolzano, Brunico and Dobbiaco. Dolomiti Bus travels to Belluno. There are also bus services to Venice and Padua (ATVO), Bologna and Milan (Zani), and Florence and Rome (a combination of Lazzi and SITA). Local services connect the town with Passo Falzarego, the camping ground at Fiames, and Pocol (from where you can hitch to Passo Giau).

BOLZANO

The capital of the province of Alto Adige (South Tyrol), Bolzano – known as Bozen in German – is unmistakably Austrian. Even though its inhabitants speak both German and Italian (both languages are compulsory subjects in school), and its street names, hotels and restaurants are identified in both languages, you will find little evidence of an Italian influence here. The town's historic centre, with its typical Tyrolean architecture and arcaded streets, harbours numerous outdoor cafés and good restaurants, making it a very pleasant place to spend a few days.

Orientation

The old-town centre is Piazza Walther, a few minutes' walk along Via Stazione from the train station on Via Garibaldi. The intercity bus station is between the station and the square.

Information

Tourist Offices The town's APT tourist office (☎ 0471-97 56 56) is at Piazza Walther 8 and is open Monday to Friday from 8.30 am to 12.30 pm and 2 to 6 pm, Saturday from 9 am to 12.30 pm. The staff have extensive information on the town and will advise on accommodation. The provincial tourist office for Alto Adige (☎ 0471-99 38 08) is at Piazza Parrocchia 11 and is open Monday to Friday from 9 am to midday and 3 to 5.30 pm. Here you can pick up information about accommodation, as well as walking and trekking possibilities throughout Alto Adige.

Money It is possible to change money at all the banks in Bolzano. On weekends, from 7 am to 8 pm, there is an exchange office open at the train station.

Post & Telecommunications The main post office is in Via della Posta, just off Piazza Walther. There is an SIP public telephone office in Piazza Parrocchia, open Monday to Saturday from 8.30 am to 12.15 pm and 3.30 to 7.45 pm, Sunday from 8 am to 1 pm. The postal code for central Bolzano is 39100 and the telephone code is 0471.

Emergency For immediate police attendance, call ☎ 113. The main police station (☎ 94 76 11) is in Via Marconi. The public hospital, the Ospedale Regionale San Maurizio (☎ 90 81 11), is in Via Lorenze Böhler, some distance from the town centre off the road to Merano, and accessible on city bus No 8 from the train station.

Things to See & Do

While away a few hours at one of the outdoor cafés in Piazza Walther, or along the side streets leading to Piazza delle Erbe. The city offers a free bike 'rental' service in Viale Stazione (between the train station and Piazza Walther), where you can use a bike for half a day free of charge (although you must leave a L10,000 deposit). The service operates from Easter to November. The APT tourist office offers a free Visitor's Pass (Carta di Ospite), which entitles you to free entrance to some of the sights as well as a guided walking tour of the town, among other things.

Start with the Gothic **Duomo** in Piazza Walther and the nearby **Dominican Church**, with its cloisters and chapel featuring frescoes of the Giotto school. The 13th to 14th century **Franciscan Church** in Via dei Francescani features beautiful cloisters and a magnificent Gothic altarpiece, carved by Hans Klocker in 1500. There are two castles in the town: the 13th century **Castel Mareccio**, along Via della Roggia from Piazza delle Erbe, and the **Castel Roncolo**, along Via Weggenstein and Via Beato Arrigo

from the old centre. The free bikes will come in handy for visiting both (the APT Visitor's Pass entitles you to free entrance to the Castel Roncolo).

While wandering around the old town, take a look at **Via Portici**, a street lined with arcades, extending from the open-air market in Piazza delle Erbe to the town hall.

Places to Stay

There is a wide choice of accommodation in Bolzano, including hotels and pensioni, as well as rooms for rent and agriturismo – the tourist office has full listings. There is a camping ground, *Moosbauer* (☎ 91 84 92), at Via San Maurizio 83, out of town towards Merano.

The *Croce Bianca* (☎ 97 75 52), Piazza del Grano 3, off Via Portici, has singles/doubles for around L29,000/45,000, or doubles with bathroom for L60,000. The *Hotel Bahnhof Stazione* (☎ 97 32 91) is in a less pleasant position to the right of the train station, at Via Renon 23; it has rooms with bath for L27,500/54,000. The *Capello di Ferro* (☎ 97 83 97), in the picturesque Via Bottai in the centre, has rooms for L30,000/55,000 with bathroom. You will need to book in advance. The *Figl* (☎ 97 84 12), also in Piazza del Grano, has good-quality rooms for L80,000 a double, or L90,000 with bathroom. Triples are L115,000 with bathroom. *Hotel Feichter* (☎ 97 87 68), Via Grappoli 15, has doubles with bathroom and breakfast for L90,000. More up-market is the *Hotel Luna Mondschein* (☎ 97 56 42), Via Piave 15, which charges L97,000/146,000 for singles/doubles with bathroom.

Places to Eat

You can pick up supplies of fruit and vegetables, bread and cheese etc from the open-air market, held every morning from Monday to Saturday in and around Piazza delle Erbe. In the same area are numerous bakeries, pastry shops and cafés. While you can eat pizza and pasta if you wish, Bolzano's best restaurants specialise in Tyrolean food. The *Cavallino Bianco*, Via dei Bottai, is extremely popular and the food is great, as well as reasonably priced at around L20,000 to L25,000 for a full meal. *Zum Bogen*, Via Dr Streter 31, off Via Bottai, also serves Tyrolean food and a full meal should cost about the same. One of Bolzano's best restaurants is *Grifone*, in the hotel of the same name on Piazza Walther. The food is very good, although you will pay around L50,000 or more for a full meal.

Getting There & Away
Bolzano is a major transport hub for Alto Adige. SAD buses leave from the bus terminal in Via Perathoner near Piazza Walther, for destinations throughout the province, including the Val Gardena, the Alpi di Siusi, Merano, Brunico and the Val Pusteria, and to the valleys leading up into the Stelvio National Park. SAD buses also head for resorts outside the province, such as Cortina d'Ampezzo and Canazei (though it is necessary to make several changes). Full timetable details are available from the bus terminal or at the tourist office.

Regular trains connect the town with Trento, Verona and Merano and, less regularly, with Milan.

The town is easily accessible from the north and south on the A22 Brennero autostrada.

MERANO
Two key words can be used to describe Merano (Meran in German): sedate and relaxing. The town's centre is clean, well tended and features characteristic Tyrolean architecture. Its main attraction is the Terme di Merano, a large complex of therapeutic baths and treatments, and a majority of the town's many tourists tend to be of older age groups. Merano is close to the Parco Naturale Gruppo di Tessa (the Tessa Group, or Texalgruppe in German) and to the Stelvio National Park with the spectacular Ortles mountain range.

The train and intercity bus stations are in Piazza Stazione, a 10-minute walk to the right along Via Europa to Piazza Mazzini and then along Corso della Libertà to the town centre.

Information
The tourist office, the AAST (☎ 0473-3 52 23), is at Corso della Libertà 45, where you can pick up a map of the town, a brochure of useful information and advice on accommodation and restaurants.

The main post office and SIP telephones are at Via Roma 2, on the other side of the river from the historic centre. The town's telephone code is 0473.

For police emergency, call ☎ 113. The public hospital, the Ospedale Provinciale (☎ 4 61 11), is at Via Goethe 50, along Via O Huber from Corso della Libertà.

Things to See & Do
The historic centre of the town is around the arcaded Via Portici and the Piazza del Duomo – take any of the streets off Corso della Libertà near the tourist office (leading away from the river). However, as mentioned, the town's main attraction is the complex of therapeutic baths, which offers the full range of treatments, including thermal (L8500) and radioactive baths (L25,000), mud baths (L28,000), massages (L30,000) and physiotherapy. The complex is open all year from Monday to Saturday.

There is an office of the Club Alpino Italiano (☎ 4 89 44) at Corso della Libertà 188 for people seeking information about walking trails. A free bike service is also offered here and is based at the Alpina car park in Via delle Terme, across the river from the town centre.

Places to Stay
Accommodation is abundant in Merano, including rooms and apartments for rent, as well as hotels and guesthouses. Ask at the tourist office for assistance in finding a room. Almost without exception, the establishments in and around the centre are expensive, although the *Albergo Dolomiten* (☎ 3 63 77), off Piazza del Duomo at Vicolo Haller 4, has reasonably priced rooms at L30,000 per person, including breakfast.

Other, cheaper places are outside the centre, and include *Villa Pax* (☎ 3 62 90), Via Leichter 3, which charges up to L23,000 per person. From Corso della Libertà, cross the river at Piazza D Rena and follow Via Cavour to Via Dante, turn right and then left into Via Leichter. *Pensione Tyrol* (☎ 4 97 19), Via XXX Aprile 8, has rooms for L37,000 per person. *Villa Fanny* (☎ 3 35 20), Winterpromenade 30, charges up to L50,000 per person for bed and breakfast.

Places to Eat
The *Ristorante Forsterbräu*, Corso della Libertà 90, has an internal garden/courtyard and serves typical Tyrolean food at reasonable prices. A full meal could cost well under L20,000. *Picnic Grill*, Via delle Corse 26, is even more economical, with pizzas and pre-prepared food. Two restaurants in Via Portici serve excellent Tyrolean fare at higher prices: *Algunder Weinstube* at No 232 and *Terlnaer Weinstube* at No 231. A full meal at either will cost around L30,000.

Getting There & Away
Merano is easily accessible by bus or train from Bolzano (about 40 minutes). SAD buses also connect the town with Katharinaberg and other villages which give access to the Tessa Group, and to Silandro and the valleys leading up into the Ortles range and the Stelvio National Park.

The Veneto

A trip through the Veneto can be a trip through Italian history. Travellers swarm to this north-eastern region for the majesty of Venice, the incredible Giotto frescoes at Padua, or to take in an opera at Verona's magnificent Roman Arena. Then there are the beaches of the Adriatic and some of the best walking in the country in the Dolomites.

Certainly Venice is the main drawing card, but visitors to the Veneto should plan to spend a couple of weeks exploring the far reaches, from the Po delta in the south, to

Coat of arms of Venice

Lake Garda in the west (see the Lakes section), the Palladian villas around Vicenza and the splendid medieval towns around Belluno, and up into the mountains to the north (see the Trentino-Alto Adige section).

The Romans colonised the various Venete tribes; later, the onslaught of barbarian invasions forced thousands of people into the lagoons to form Venice. The city looked eastward to the Byzantine Empire and the Orient, and as its maritime power grew, expeditions returned to the city with booty and influences that are clearly evident today.

The region's cuisine is founded on rice and corn. Polenta is served with hearty game stews, is fried or turns up with almost every main-course dish across the region. Risotto is cooked with almost everything the countryside and lagoon have to offer, from baby peas to shellfish and game. But the Veneto's greatest contribution to the Italian table is *tiramisù*, a rich dessert of mascarpone cheese, Marsala wine, sponge and chocolate. The wine list provides some of Italy's most popular brands, including the Soave, a fine white that is well known in the USA, the UK and Australia. The light, sparkling *prosecco* and the *bardolino* wines are also known widely. Of course, the Bellini, a cocktail of prosecco and fresh peach juice, has come a long way since Giuseppe Cipriani first mixed one at Harry's Bar in Venice in the 1950s.

Getting around is easy. The A4 autostrada,

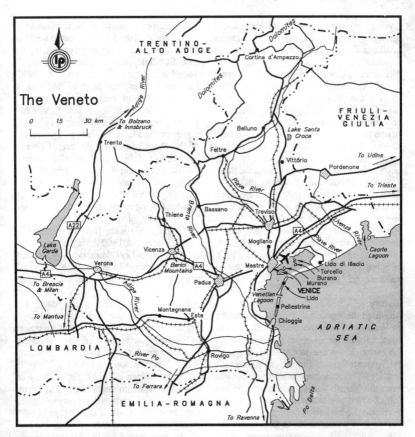

which runs from Turin to Venice, bisects the region, and an efficient bus and train network mean that few parts of the region are out of reach. Unfortunately, accommodation and food prices are highly inflated in Venice, but generally, staying in the Veneto is no more expensive than other parts of the north.

VENICE (VENEZIA)

Perhaps no other city in the world has inspired the superlatives heaped upon Venice by great writers and travellers through the centuries. It was, and remains, a phenomenon, La Serenissima, the Most Serene Republic.

Forget that Venice is no longer a great maritime republic, that its buildings are in serious decay and constantly threatened by rising tides. Today Byron would be reluctant to take his daily swim along the Grand Canal: it is too dirty. But the thoughts of Henry James are as true today as they were a century ago: 'Dear old Venice has lost her complexion, her figure, her reputation, her self-respect; and yet, with it all, has so puzzlingly not lost a shred of her distinction.'

It is said that the history of Venice has been one of continuous, remorseless decline, but who cares? In this uniquely splendid city you will have no need of a lover to feel romantic.

Byron observed that 'everything about Venice is, or was, extraordinary – her aspect is like a dream, and her history is like a romance'.

The secret to really seeing and discovering the romance and beauty of Venice is to *walk*. Parts of Dorsoduro and Castello are empty of tourists even in the high season. You could become lost for hours in the narrow, winding streets between the Accademia and the train station, where the signs pointing to San Marco and the Rialto never seem to make any sense – but what a way to pass the time!

Venice floods during winter, making a holiday unpleasant, but the crowds are much smaller than during the hotter months. In midsummer the high temperature can be oppressive and, on occasions, the canals smell disgusting. The busiest months are June to September and during the Carnevale in February, but it is always a good idea to make a hotel booking.

History

Although the lagoons and islands that make up Venice had been inhabited by fishers and hunters for hundreds of years, it wasn't until the barbarian invasions and the collapse of the Western Roman Empire during the 5th century AD that the population grew. Settlers from the Veneto and Roman towns on the Adriatic fled to the marshy islands in terror to escape the barbarian hordes from central Europe who were pouring in from across the Alps. With each successive wave, more people fled to the lagoons in the hope the invaders would be deterred by the expansive stretch of water between the islands and the mainland.

In the 6th century, the islands began to form a type of federation, with each community electing representatives to a central authority, though its leaders were subject to the Byzantine rulers in Ravenna. Byzantium's hold over Italy grew weaker early in the 8th century and in 726 the people of Venice elected their first doge, a type of magistrate whose successors would lead the city for more than 1000 years. As a symbolic measure of the city's growing strength,

Venetian merchants stole the remains of St Mark, the apostle, from Alexandria in 828 and brought them triumphantly to the lagoon city. St Mark displaced the Byzantine St Theodore as patron saint, and St Mark's Basilica was erected next to the Doges' Palace to house his remains.

By late in the 10th century, Venice had become an important trading city and a power on the Mediterranean, prospering out of the chaos caused by the First Crusade, launched in 1095. During the 12th century, the city took part in the Fourth Crusade under Doge Enrico Dandolo, consolidating a maritime might that made it the envy of other powers. During much of the 13th century, the Venetians struggled with Genoa for maritime supremacy, a tussle that culminated in Genoa's defeat in 1380 during an epic siege at Chioggia. In 1271, Venetian merchant and explorer Marco Polo set out for his overland trip to China, returning by sea over 20 years later.

Their maritime power consolidated, the Venetians turned their attentions to dominating the mainland, but the increasing power of the Turks forced the Venetians to deploy forces to protect their interests elsewhere. When Constantinople fell to the Turks in 1453 and Morea in 1499, the Turks won control of access to the Adriatic. The Portuguese Vasco da Gama's discovery of the sea route around the Cape of Good Hope in 1498 meant that traders no longer needed to cart goods across land to the Venetian ports, thereby diminishing their importance.

Further successes by the Turks in the 16th century and a dispute with Rome in 1606 over papal jurisdiction damaged the republic's standing. In 1669, after a 25-year battle, Venice lost Crete to the Turks, its last stronghold in the Mediterranean. The republic declined during the 18th century, and in 1797 its Great Council abolished the constitution and acceded to Napoleon, who in turn handed Venice to the Austrians during the signing of the Campo Formio Treaty that year. Napoleon returned in 1805, incorporating the city into his Kingdom of Italy, but it reverted to Austria after his fall.

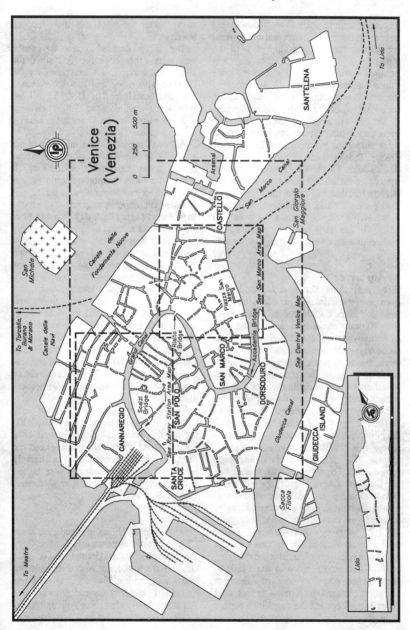

Venice
(Venezia)

0   250   500 m

To Lido

San Michele

To Torcello,
Burano
& Murano

Canale delle Navi

To Mestre

Canale delle Fondamenta Nuove

SANT'ELENA

Arsenal

San Marco Canal

San Giorgio Maggiore

CASTELLO

San Marco Canal

See San Marco Area Map

San Marco
Piazza San Marco

SAN MARCO

Accademia Bridge

Rialto Bridge

DORSODURO

See Central Venice Map

Grand Canal

SAN POLO

See Railway Station Area Map

Scalzi Bridge

CANNAREGIO

SANTA CROCE

Giudecca Canal

GIUDECCA ISLAND

Sacca Fisola

Lido

The movement for Italian unification spread quickly through the Veneto, and after several rebellions, the city was united with the Kingdom of Italy in 1866. The city was bombed during WW I but received only minor damage during WW II, when most of the attack was aimed at the neighbouring industrial regions of Mestre and Marghera.

The city's prestige as a tourist destination grew during the 19th century, while its ports were surpassed in importance by those of Trieste. Today it is one of Italy's main tourist destinations. There is a permanent population of about 80,000 people living on the islands, less than half that of the 1950s' level, but Venice's total population, including those living on the mainland, is around 350,000. The city attracts more than 23 million tourists a year, most on day trips.

Saving Venice

Fifty years ago, Venice was flooded an average of three times a year. Now, the city's famous Piazza San Marco is awash more than 70 times annually, a result of the push by industry in the 1960s to develop the mainland and regain some maritime power for the city's mainland ports. When the local government ordered the industrial town of Marghera to stop draining the area's underground water supplies in the mid-1960s, Venice was sinking at a rate of 13 cm a year.

The average yearly decline is around two cm now, but the problem has become so severe that the Italian government, under intense international pressure, has been forced to act. To protect the city, three massive floodgates have been proposed at the lagoon's main entrances. However, environmentalists believe they will create as many problems as they are intended to rectify. Until 20 years ago, the Adriatic's natural tidal currents flushed the lagoons and kept the canals relatively clean. But the dredging of a 14-metre-deep canal in the 1960s to allow tankers access to the giant refinery at Marghera changed the currents. In fact, tidal flows have deepened the canal by a further eight metres, confounding scientists who

worry about the effects of the proposed floodgates.

The city has decided to clean the canals, which have not been dredged since the 1960s, but Rome is stalling funds for the US$112-million job and has not allocated the first instalment of US$75 million, approved by parliament in 1990. Then there is the problem of where to dump the heavily polluted waste.

Although tourists are the mainstay of the economy, Venetians are becoming more concerned about their effect on the city. St Mark's Basilica resembles a train station more than an important religious shrine, and thousands of tourists stomp across its mostly unprotected paving each day. Plans to limit the number of tourists have been vetoed by locals who fear the city could become a museum, and a grand scheme to host Expo 2000 was dumped after a huge public outcry. Plans for a subway beneath the lagoons are on hold pending further investigation.

The city has benefited through international exposure generated by preservation groups including the New York-based Save Venice. Similar organisations have sprung up around the globe, including in Australia and the UK, which raise money for restoration projects. Most of these groups believe that tourists take too much and give nothing to the city.

But the city is fighting back. In the early 1990s it imposed fines of up to L2,000,000 for littering and vandalism, as well as a L30,000 fine for wearing a bathing costume on the street. In a more peculiar but heavily publicised scheme, residents were issued with cameras to photograph misbehaving tourists. So watch out.

Orientation

Venice is built on 117 small islands, has some 150 canals and more than 400 bridges. Only three bridges cross the Grand Canal (Canale Grande): the Rialto, the Accademia and the Scalzi at the station. The city is divided into six *sestieri* (sections): Cannaregio, Castello, San Marco, Dorsoduro, San Polo and Santa Croce. A street is called a *calle* (sometimes shortened to *ca')* or *salizzada*, a canal is a *rio*, and a quay is a *riva* or *fondamento*. The only square in Venice called a piazza is San Marco – all the others are called a *campo*. On maps you will find the following abbreviations: Cpo for Campo, Sal for Salizzada, cl for Calle and Fond for Fondamenta.

If all that isn't confusing enough, Venice also has its own style of street numbering. Instead of a system based on individual streets, there is instead a long series of numbers for each sestiere.

There are no cars on the islands, although ferries transport cars to the Lido, and all public transport is via the canals, on a *vaporetto*. To cross the Grand Canal between the bridges, use a *traghetto*, a cheap way to get a short gondola ride, although there are only five operating. Signs will direct you to the traghetto points. The other mode of transportation is *a piedi* (on foot). To walk from the train station to San Marco along the main thoroughfare, the Lista di Spagna (whose name changes several times), will take a good half hour – follow the signs to San Marco.

From San Marco, the routes to other main areas, such as the Rialto, Accademia and the train station, are well signposted but can be confusing, particularly in the Dorsoduro and San Polo areas. The free map provided by the tourist office provides only a vague guide to the complicated network of streets. Pick up a cheap de Agostini map, simply entitled *Venezia*, which lists all street names with map references.

Information

Tourist Offices Venice's main APT office (☎ 041-522 63 56) is at the western end of Piazza San Marco under the porticoes, and opens from 8.30 am to 8.30 pm. There are smaller offices at the train station (☎ 041-71 90 78), which opens Monday to Friday from 9 am to midday and 3 to 6 pm, Saturday to 12.30 pm, and on the Lido (☎ 041-526 57 21) at Viale Santa Maria Elisabetta. The staff are generally unhelpful unless you insist, but there is a range of information, including the useful booklet *Un Ospite di Venezia* (A Guest

in Venice). See the following Places to Stay section for details about the Venetian Hoteliers' Association office next to the APT at the station, which will book you a room.

Take your passport and a colour mug shot to the tourist office and join up for the Carta Giovani (Youth Pass) if you are aged under 26, or the Rolling Venice card for others. Both offer significant discounts on food, accommodation, entertainment, museums and galleries for a small charge.

Youth Information There is an Informa Giovani (Youth Information) office (☎ 041-534 62 68) at Mestre, Viale Garibaldi 155, which can provide information on a range of topics from assistance for the disabled to courses offered in the city.

Money Banks are always the most reliable place to change money and they offer the best rates. Most of the main banks have branches in the area around the Rialto Bridge and San Marco. There is an exchange office on Salizzada San Moisé, near San Marco, open Monday to Saturday from 9 am to 7 pm, Sunday to 1 pm. Thomas Cook, in Piazza San Marco and close to the Rialto, opens Monday to Saturday from 9 am to 7 pm, Sunday to 5 pm. There is a bank with endless queues at the train station, and an Exact Change booth in the platform area offering good rates, which opens from 8 am to 10 pm daily. Avoid changing money at the train ticket office, which offers bad rates.

The American Express office (☎ 041-520 08 44) is at Salizzada San Moisé (exit from the western end of Piazza San Marco on to Calle Seconda dell'Ascensione). For American Express card holders there's also an express cash machine. The office is open Monday to Friday from 9 am to 5.30 pm, Saturday to 12.30 pm.

Post & Telecommunications The main post office is at Salizzada del Fontego dei Tedeschi, just near the Rialto Bridge on the main thoroughfare between San Marco and the station. It opens Monday to Saturday from 8.15 am to 7 pm. Stamps are available

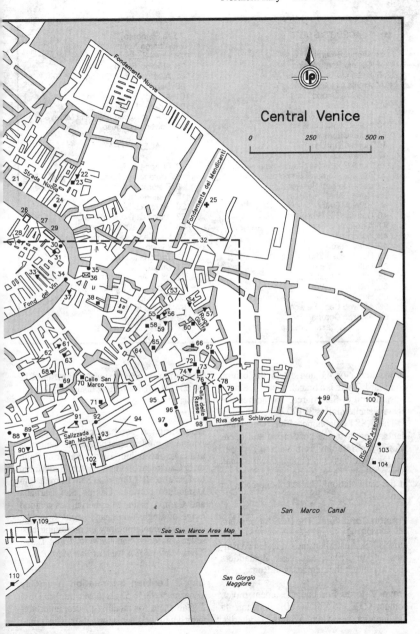

Central Venice

Fondamenta Nuove

Strada Nuova

Fondamenta dei Mendicanti

Fond. del Vin

Fond. del Vin

Calle San Marco

Riva degli Schiavoni

Salizzada San Moisè

Rio dell'Arsenale

San Marco Canal

See San Marco Area Map

San Giorgio Maggiore

0   250   500 m

■ PLACES TO STAY

3 Alloggi Smeraldo
4 Ostello Santa Fosca
5 Hotel Marte
7 Archie's House
9 Hotel Al Gobbo
10 Hotel Rossi
11 Hotel Minerva & Nettuno
13 Hotel Santa Lucia
14 Hotel Caprera
16 Hotel Atlantide
17 Locanda Antica Casa Carettoni
18 Hotel Edelweiss Stella Alpina
23 Albergo Bernardi Semenzato
38 Locanda San Salvador
39 Hotel Canal
43 Hotel Al Gallo
46 Domus G B Giustinian
47 Albergo Da Bepi
48 Hotel Falier
49 Casa Peron
50 Hotel della Mora
55 Hotel Da Bruno
58 Istituto San Giuseppe
60 Locanda Piave
65 Hotel Riva
66 Albergo Casa Verado
67 Albergo Corona
69 Locanda Casa Petrarca

70 Al Gambero
71 Albergo Noemi
72 Hotel Bridge
73 Albergo Tiepolo
81 Albergo Antico Capon
98 Danieli
101 Albergo San Maurizio
104 Albergo Paganelli
105 Albergo Accademia Villa Maravege
110 Pensione Seguso

▼ PLACES TO EAT

2 Pizzeria Al Faro
6 Trattoria alla Palazzina
8 Ristorante al Ponte
15 Trattoria Nuova
20 Pizzeria all'Anfora
22 Antica Carbonera
33 Trattoria alla Madonna
37 Self Service al Ponte di Rialto
45 Il Volto
47 Trattoria Da Bepi
51 Crepizza
52 Da Silvio
54 Pizzeria da Egidio
56 Cip Ciap
57 Osteria al Mascaron
59 Alle Testiere
61 Colusse il Fornaio

at window Nos 11 and 12 in the central courtyard. There is a branch post office at the western end of San Marco. The address for poste restante mail is 30100 Venezia.

The ASST telephone office, with attendants, is next to the post office and opens Monday to Saturday from 8 am to 7.45 pm, but there are banks of phones down a small lane opposite. There is another ASST office at the train station. The telephone code for Venice is 041.

Foreign Consulates The British Consulate (☎ 522 23 92) is at Dorsoduro 1051. The closest US, Australian and Canadian consulates are in Milan, and New Zealanders should contact their embassy in Rome.

Travel Agents For budget student travel, contact CTS (☎ 520 56 60), Fondamenta Tagliapietra, near Campo Santa Margherita.

Transalpino is near the train station, and CIT (☎ 504 00 33), for budget deals, is in Mestre at Via Mestrina 67.

Bookshops A good selection of English-language guides and books on Venice is available at Studium, on the corner of Calle de la Canonica, on the way from San Marco to Castello. Il Libraio a San Barnaba, in Dorsoduro between Campo San Barnaba and Campo Santa Margherita has a good range of English-language books from the classics to contemporary literature and best sellers, as does San Giorgio, Calle Larga XXII Marzo 2087, west of San Marco.

Gay & Lesbian Information Arci Gay Venezia (☎ 98 36 53) is in Mestre, Via Olivi 2. Call them for meeting-places, entertainment details or other information. The Italian

63 Italy & Italy, Black Jack Bar
68 Zorzi
74 Pizzeria Conca d'Oro
76 Trattoria Rivietta
82 Bar La Sosta
83 L'Incontro
86 Trattoria da Memi
89 Vino Vino
90 La Caravella
91 Cantina do Mori
109 Linea d'Ombra

OTHER

1 Ghetto
12 Campo San Geremia
19 APT Tourist Office
21 Ca d'Oro
24 Palazzo Michiel dalle Colonne
25 Hospital
26 Pescheria
27 Campo della Pescaria
28 Campo Beccarie
29 Fabbriche Nuove
30 Produce Market & Public Toilet
31 Fabbriche Vecchie
32 Campo SS Giovanni e Paolo
34 Rialto Bridge
35 ASST Telephones
36 Main Post Office

40 Parking
41 Parking
42 Bus Station
44 Campo San Polo
53 Campo Santa Maria Formosa
62 Campo San Luca
64 Campo San Zulian
75 Campo SS Filippo e Giacomo
77 Campo San Provolo
78 Police Headquarters
79 Campo di San Zaccaria
80 Campo Santa Margherita
84 Campo San Barnaba
85 Palazzo Grassi
87 Campo F Morosini
88 Teatro la Fenice
92 English Language Bookshop
93 APT Tourist Information Office
94 Piazza San Marco
95 St Mark's Basilica
96 Bridge of Sighs
97 Doges' Palace
99 Church of San Giovanni in Bragora
100 Arsenal Gateway
102 Harry's Bar
103 Naval Museum
106 Accademia Bridge
107 Galleria dell'Accademia
108 Peggy Guggenheim Collection

gay magazine *Babilonia* can be picked up from the newsstand at the train station.

Lost Property Call ☎ 71 61 22 for the main lost-property office at the station, or ☎ 78 03 10 for goods left on ACTV vaporetti.

Medical Services The Ospedale Civili Riuniti di Venezia (☎ 520 56 22) is at Campo SS Giovanni e Paolo. For an ambulance, call ☎ 523 00 00. Current information on all-night pharmacies is listed in *Un Ospite di Venezia*.

Emergency For police emergencies, call ☎ 113. The police headquarters (☎ 520 32 22), where you can report thefts etc, are at Parrocchia di San Zaccaria, Castello. If you are in trouble, police patrol the area around San Marco day and night.

Things to See & Do

Before organising yourself to visit the main monuments, churches and museums, catch the No 1 vaporetto along the Grand Canal. When the boat deposits you at San Marco, take a long walk around the piazza and then head for the Accademia Bridge to reach the narrow, tranquil streets and squares of Dorsoduro and San Polo. It is in these sestieri that you will be able to appreciate just how beautiful and seductive Venice can be. Arm yourself with a guidebook and a good map. *A Day in Venice*, published by Bonechi, is available for L5000 at all the souvenir stands. Virtually all galleries and museums mentioned here are closed on Mondays. Check with the APT for exceptions.

The Comune di Venezia has arranged a special ticket costing L16,000 that covers entry to the Doge's Palace, Museo Correr

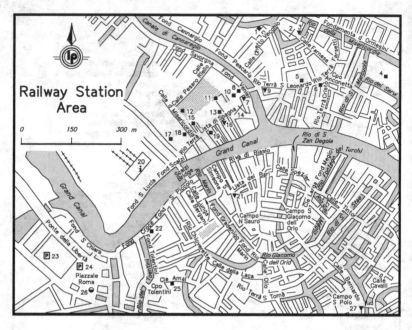

Railway Station Area

0   150   300 m

and seven other main sites. It can be purchased from any of the city's museums.

The Grand Canal Described by French writer Philippe de Commines in the 15th century as 'the finest street in the world, with the finest houses', the Grand Canal is a little dilapidated these days but still rivals the great boulevards of the world. It weaves for 3.5 km through the city like a huge, upside-down S, is about six metres deep and ranges from 40 metres to 100 metres across. Taking a vaporetto is the only way to see the incredible parade of buildings, from brightly coloured houses to stone palaces, dating from every period in the city's history and representing various architectural styles. Board the vaporetto No 1 in Piazzale Roma and try to grab a seat on the deck at the back.

Santa Lucia train station stands on the site of a former Palladian church dedicated to St Lucy, demolished in the mid-19th century to make way for the railway line. The present white building beside the older

station, opened in 1954, was conceived during the Fascist era.

A short distance after the **Church of San Simeone Piccolo**, with its huge copper dome, on the left after the train station, is the opening for the **Canale di Cannaregio**, the second-largest in the city after the Grand Canal. Farther on, to the right, is one of the most celebrated Venetian-Byzantine-style buildings, the **Fondaco dei Turchi**, recognisable by the three-storey towers on either side of its colonnade. Originally built in the 12th century as headquarters for Oriental merchants stationed in Venice, this building was remodelled in the 19th century and now houses the **Museum of Natural History**.

Past the Rio della Maddalena to the left is the **Palazzo Vendramin Calergi**, one of the finest examples of Renaissance architecture in the city and the place where Wagner died on 13 February 1883. Farther on and to the right is the **Ca' Pesaro**, the Baroque masterpiece of Baldassarre Longhena, which was built between 1679 and 1710. It is said the

■ PLACES TO STAY

4	Ostello Santa Fosca
5	Alloggi Smeraldo
6	Archie's House
8	Hotel Marte
10	Hotel Al Gobbo
11	Hotel Rossi
12	Hotel Santa Lucia
13	Hotel Minerva & Nettuno
15	Hotel Caprera
17	Hotel Edelweiss Stella Alpina
18	Hotel Atlantide
19	Locanda Antica Casa Carettoni
22	Hotel Canal
25	Hotel Al Gallo

▼ PLACES TO EAT

3	Pizzeria Al Faro
7	Ristorante al Ponte
9	Trattoria alla Palazzina
16	Trattoria Nuova
21	Pizzeria all'Anfora
27	Il Volto

OTHER

1	Ghetto
2	Campo Ghetto Nuovo
14	Campo San Geremia
20	APT Tourist Office
23	Parking
24	Parking
26	Bus Station

builder died worrying about the cost of the building, recognisable by its rusticated stone base which is surmounted by a double tier of windows set off by clusters of columns. It houses the city's **Gallery of Modern Art** and **Oriental Art Museum**

To the left, a short distance farther on, is the **Ca' d'Oro** (Golden House), acclaimed as the most elegant palace in Venice. Built in 1440 in the late-Gothic style, the building was originally gilded all over. The building and its art collection were donated to the state in 1916 by Baron Giorgio Franchetti after whom the collection is named. To the right as the boat turns to approach the **Rialto Bridge** is the **Pescheria** (Fish Market) on the Campo della Pescaria, built in 1907. Opposite the fish market is the **Palazzo Michiel dalle Colonne**, with its distinctive ground-floor colonnade; 'dalle Colonne' (of the Columns) was added, say some, because a family member brought the columns standing in Piazza San Marco to the city from the East.

On the right bank, just after the fish market, are the **Fabbriche Nuove di Rialto**, built in 1552 by Jacopo Sansovino as public offices for trade and commerce. Next door is the city's produce market and then the **Fabbriche Vecchie di Rialto**, built in 1522 as a courthouse. Facing the two buildings is the 13th century **Ca' da Mosto**, one of the most serene palaces in Venice. The **Fondaco dei Tedeschi** was built in 1515 by Scarpagnino and served as a German storehouse and is now the main post office. The Rialto Bridge spans the canal ahead.

Past the bridge on the left is the 12th century **Palazzo Farsetti**, a fairly typical building for its time, now housing the Venice town hall. Farther on as the canal swings to the left is the **Ca' Foscari** (on the right and beside the Rio Ca' Foscari), a 15th century Gothic palace commissioned by Doge Francesco Foscari and acclaimed as being one of the finest in the city. Farther on, to the left, is the **Palazzo Grassi**, built in 1718 for the Grassi family of Bologna. Opposite is the **Palazzo Rezzonico**, a splendid three-storey building set on a rusticated façade. The last of the canal's three bridges, the **Accademia Bridge** (Ponte dell'Accademia), approaches. The bridge dates from 1930 and is on the site of a 19th century, all-metal bridge, pulled down because it clashed with the canal's harmonious style. Past the bridge on the right is the **Palazzo Venier dei Leoni**, once home to American heiress Peggy Guggenheim and which now houses her collection of modern art.

Facing the gallery is the **Casina delle Rose**, where sculptor Canova lived in the 18th century and writer D'Annunzio earlier this century. The **Ca' Grande**, to the left, with its ivy-covered wall, was built in 1535 by Sansovino and was later occupied by the Austrian governor. On the right, before the canal broadens out into the expanse facing San Marco, is the magnificent **Church of Santa Maria della Salute** by Baldassarre Longhena.

Piazza & Basilica di San Marco One of the most famous squares in the world, San Marco was described by Napoleon as the finest drawing room in Europe. Enclosed by the basilica, the old Law Courts and the Libreria Vecchia (Old Library), the piazza hosts flocks of pigeons and tourists, both competing for space in the high season. Stand and wait for the famous bronze *mori* (Moors) to strike the bell of the Law Courts' 15th century clock tower, or sit and enjoy a coffee at the two remaining 18th century cafés, Florian and Quadri, opposite each other – expect to pay up to L10,000 (an extra L3000 if there is music).

The **basilica** stands on the site of an earlier 10th century church, built to house the body of St Mark which had been stolen from its burial place in Egypt by two Venetian merchants. Doge Giustiniano Partecipazio had bequeathed a huge sum of money to build a basilica fitting such a considerable relic, and his brother, Giovanni, was given the task of building it alongside the Doges' Palace. The church took 60 years to complete, but was badly damaged during a fire in 976. Despite rebuilding, Doge Domenico Contarini decided in 1000 that the building was poor in comparison to the splendid Romanesque churches being built in mainland cities, and had it demolished.

The new basilica was started in 1063 on the plan of a Greek cross, and took 10 years to complete. Topped by five bulbous domes, the church is modelled on Constantinople's Church of the Twelve Apostles and was intended to compete with St Peter's in Rome. Over the next 500 years, the church was enlarged and embellished and the resulting building is a blending of influences from

Marble relief, St Mark's Basilica

Byzantine, European and Islamic cultures. It is important to note that the basilica was not intended as the cathedral of Venice but rather as a private chapel of the doges, who made their public appearances here.

The four bronze horses over the central door are copies of those stolen from Constantinople by Doge Dandolo during the famous sack of that city in 1204 during the Fourth Crusade. Napoleon removed them to Paris in 1797, but they were returned after the fall of the French Empire. The originals are in the museum inside the basilica. The interior of the church is a sea of mosaic colour. Some of the best works are above the **chancel**, over the tomb of St Mark. Scenes depict the life of St Mark and the Venetian theft of his body from Alexandria. The **Pala d'Oro** behind the chancel is a magnificent gold-and-jewel-encrusted altarpiece, made in Constantinople in 976.

Buy a L2000 ticket at the right of the chancel to visit the basilica and the **Treasury**, which contains most of the booty from the raid on Constantinople, including a supposed thorn from the crown of thorns worn by Christ. Go up through the narthex to reach the **Basilica Museum**, which costs L2000 and where you can get a better view of the mosaics and see the original four horses.

Pick up one of the invaluable brochures describing the mosaics as you enter the church, and remember that all Venetian churches have strict dress guidelines. Although the church opens longer hours, tourists are restricted to 9.30 am to 5.30 pm Monday to Saturday and 2 to 5.30 pm Sunday and holidays. The best (but most crowded) times to go are from 11.30 am to 12.30 pm Monday to Saturday, and Sunday afternoons, when the mosaics are illuminated.

Venice's trademark **Campanile** (bell tower) in the piazza stands 99 metres tall. It was built in the 10th century but suddenly collapsed on 14 July 1902 and was later rebuilt. You can pay L2000 to climb it.

The Law Courts' **Clock Tower** (Torre dell'Orologio), facing the church to the left,

was built between 1496 and 1499 and comprises two bronze figures (dubbed the 'Moors' because of their dark colouring) which strike the hour. To the left is the **Procuratie Vecchie**, once the residence of the Procurators of St Mark, the magistrates who were responsible for the upkeep of the church. The Procuratie Nuove on the south side of the square was begun by Scamozzi and completed by Longhena in 1640. Napoleon converted this building into his Royal Palace (Palazzo Reale), demolishing the church of San Geminiano at the western end of the piazza to build the wing commonly known as the **Ala Napoleonica**, which housed his ballroom. This wing now houses the **Museo Correr**, an immense museum outlining Venice's history, but it can be a little dull compared to the city's other offerings. The building also houses the **Quadreria**, a picture gallery with several notable works by artists including Carpaccio. The **Risorgimento Museum**, also in the Ala Napoleonica, has a good array of artefacts relating to the fall of the Venetian empire and Italian unification.

The area between San Marco and the Molo (waterfront), known as the **Piazzetta di San Marco**, features two of the city's most famous landmarks: the two columns bearing the statue of the Lion of St Mark and the statue of St Theodore, the two emblems of the city. Originally a marketplace, the area was later used by politicians to gather before meetings. The area between the two columns was also used for public executions.

The 16th century **Marciana Library**, taking up the entire west side of the Piazzetta, was described by Palladio as the most sumptuous palace ever built. If you want to visit the main reading room, which has an impressive collection of illustrated manuscripts, call ☎ 520 87 88. The **Archaeological Museum**, housed in part of the building, has an impressive collection of Greek and Roman sculpture. It opens Monday to Saturday from 9 am to 2 pm, Sunday to 1 pm, and costs L4000. Around the corner, facing the lagoon, is the **Zecca** (Mint), built in 1537.

■ PLACES TO STAY

10	Hotel Da Bruno
15	Locanda Piave
19	Albergo Casa Verado
21	Locanda Casa Petrarca
23	Albergo Noemi
24	Albergo Corona
26	Albergo Tiepolo
36	Albergo San Maurizio
46	Danieli

▼ PLACES TO EAT

4	Trattoria alla Madonna
8	Self Service al Ponte di Rialto
9	Cip Ciap
11	Alle Testiere
13	Pizzeria da Egidio
14	Osteria al Mascaron
17	Colusse il Fornaio
18	Italy & Italy, Black Jack Bar
20	Zorzi
22	Ristorante da Ivo
25	Pizzeria Conca d'Oro
27	Trattoria Rivietta
33	Cantina do Mori
37	La Caravella
51	Linea d'Ombra

OTHER

1	Campo della Pescaria
2	Fabbriche Nuove
3	Fabbriche Vecchie
5	Rialto Bridge
6	ASST Telephones
7	Main Post Office
12	Church of Santa Maria Formosa
16	Church of San Salvatore
28	Police Headquarters
29	Church of San Zaccaria
30	Clock Tower
31	St Mark's Basilica
32	Teatro La Fenice
34	English Language Bookshop
35	Procuratie Vecchie
38	Ala Napoleonica
39	Tourist Information Office
40	Campanile
41	Procuratie Nuove
42	Marciana Library
43	Doges' Palace
44	Bridge of Sighs
45	Old Prisons
47	Zecca (Mint)
48	Piazzetta Columns
49	Harry's Bar
50	Peggy Guggenheim Collection

Doges' Palace The Doges' Palace (Palazzo Ducale), next to the basilica, was the residence of the doges, the republic's rulers, who were elected for life. It also housed most of the government, many of the republic's government workers and even the prisons. The building assumed its present form in 1340, after having been built and rebuilt several times, originally over a Byzantine palace on the site. After much of the building was destroyed by a fire in 1577, a competition to rebuild the palace was held, which attracted many of the day's celebrated architects. The winner was Antonio Da Ponte, architect of the Rialto Bridge, who restored the building to its 14th century appearance.

Despite its imposing bulk, the palace's pink and white marble and the rows of Gothic arches give it an impression of lightness. The main entrance, the 15th century **Porta della Carta** (literally, the Door of Paper), to which government decrees were fixed, is attributed to Giovanni and Bartolomeo Bon. From the courtyard, the **Scala dei Giganti** (Giants' Staircase) takes its name from the huge statues of Mars and Neptune by Sansovino, which flank the landing.

Up Sansovino's **Scala d'Oro** (Golden Staircase) are rooms dedicated to the various doges, including the **Sala delle Quattro Porte**, its ceiling designed by Palladio. The room features a painting by Tiepolo and frescoes by Tintoretto. The splendid **Sala del Senato** has better lighting to view the superb artworks by Tintoretto and Sansovino. The immense **Sala del Maggiore Consiglio** (Grand Council Chamber) features Tintoretto's *Paradise*, one of the world's largest oil paintings, measuring 22 by seven metres.

The route through the palace takes you across the famous **Bridge of Sighs** (Ponte dei Sospiri) and into the prisons. The name of the bridge derives from the sighs released by prisoners crossing into the dungeons,

San Marco Area

0   50   100 m

including, no doubt, Casanova, who was condemned by the magistrates responsible for security, the Council of Ten.

The palace opens daily from 9 am to 4 pm and entry is L8000. Hire an infrared radio receiver which looks like a mobile phone and picks up an audio-loop commentary in each room; it costs L5000 and can be found in the first room after the Golden Staircase.

San Marco to Cannaregio Leading away from San Marco, starting at the Clock Tower is a string of streets known as the **Mercerie**.

They form the quickest route between the piazza and the Rialto and have traditionally been merchants' streets, although these days most of them concentrate on fast food and tourist souvenirs. The **Church of San Salvatore**, built on the plan of three Greek crosses end to end, features Titian's *Annunciation* and Bellini's *Supper in Emmaus*. North of the church is the **Campo San Bartolomeo**, featuring a statue of Carlo Goldoni, Italy's most celebrated comic playwright. Farther north, the **Church of San Giovanni Grisostomo**, built in 1504 on a Greek plan, features works by Bellini.

Cross the Bridge of San Giovanni Grisostomo for the **Chiesa di SS Apostoli** (Church of the Holy Apostles), at the southern edge of the Strada Nuova. The church has a reasonably dull exterior, but is worth visiting for the Cappella Corner, which features a painting by Tiepolo. North of here, along the Rio Terrà SS Apostoli, is the **Chiesa dei Gesuiti**, a high-Baroque building with a sculpture by Titian and an *Assumption* by Tintoretto.

Return to the Strada Nuova and turn left into the Calle della Ca' d'Oro for the **Galleria Franchetti**, housed in the Ca' d'Oro. The gallery has an impressive collection of bronzes, tapestries and paintings, with works by Van Dyck, Filippino Lippi and Mantegna, and opens from 9 am to 2 pm. Entry costs L4000.

Continuing along the Strada Nuova and then west along the path beside the Rio di San Felice is the **Church of Santa Marziale**, worth a look-in for its works by Titian and Tintoretto. Farther west across the Ponte della Sacca is the Gothic **Church of Madonna dell'Orto**, dating from the 14th century. Its most notable work is *John the Baptist with Four Saints* by Cima da Conegliano. There are also works by Bellini and Tintoretto, whose tomb is to the right of the altar.

Venice has the distinction of having the world's first **ghetto**, reached from the north along the Fondamenta degli Ormesini. Originally a foundry (the word 'ghetto' comes from the Venetian dialect *geto*, meaning foundry), this small island became an enclave after Jews were ordered to move here in 1516 and were locked in at night by Christian soldiers. However, Venice was more lenient towards Jews than were other European states, allowing them to practise their religion. The **Jewish Museum** in Campo Ghetto Nuovo opens from 10 am to 4 pm daily, and entry costs L4000.

After crossing the **Canale di Cannaregio**, the city's widest after the Grand Canal, head to the right for the **Church of San Giobbe**, an elegant church in the Gothic-Renaissance style, containing the family tombs of Doge Cristoforo Moro. Walk along the Lista di Spagna, named after the former Spanish embassy which stood at No 168, but now the domain of the city's souvenir and tourist-menu pedlars, for the **Chiesa degli Scalzi** (Church of the Barefooted), built from 1670 for the barefoot order of Carmelite nuns of the same name. The train station is now straight ahead.

Rialto Bridge to San Polo Some of the first settlers in Venice established themselves around the high bank *(riva alta)* near where the bridge stands today. The area later became the centre of Venice's commercial activities. The Rialto Bridge was completed in 1592.

To the right of the bridge as you step into San Polo is the **Church of San Giacomo di Rialto**. According to local legend it was founded on the same day as the city (25 March 421 AD). Straight ahead and over the Rio delle Beccarie, follow the signs for the Palazzo Pesaro, which houses the **Museum of Modern Art** (Galleria d'Arte Moderna). Started in 1897, the collection comprises works mainly from the Venice Biennale art festival held every even-numbered year, and is one of the largest collections of modern art in Italy. The gallery is open from 9 am to 2 pm and entry is L8000. The **Oriental Museum** (Museo Orientale), in the same building, features a collection of Asian and Eastern oddments put together in the 19th century. It opens the same hours, but entry is only L4000.

Continuing north-west, past the **Church of San Stae**, and along Calle del Megio, is the Fondaco dei Turchi, originally a warehouse used by Turkish merchants and now the **Museum of Natural History**, which opens from 9.30 am to 1.30 pm. Entrance is L3000. Heading south, the **Church of San Giacomo dall'Orio**, near the piazza of the same name, features a ceiling painting by Veronese and a fine bell tower in the Romanesque Byzantine style. The **School of San Giovanni Evangelista**, near Calle dell'Olio, has a number of notable features, including a grand double staircase by Mauro Codussi.

The **Church of Santa Maria dei Frari**, south along Calle della Chiesa, is one of the city's finest churches. Nicola Pisano started the church for the Franciscans in 1251. It contains the tombs of Titian and Canova and features works by an illustrious line-up, including a statue of John the Baptist by Donatello and an *Assumption* by Titian. Behind the Frari is the **Church of San Rocco**, featuring works by Tintoretto, depicting the life of the saint. The **Scuola Grande di San Rocco** beside the church is one of the many schools in the city and is worth a visit for the 56 Old Testament scenes painted by a young Tintoretto.

Calle dei Saoneri leads to the **Church of San Polo**, dating from the 9th century and featuring works by Tintoretto, Tiepolo and Veronese.

San Marco to Dorsoduro Start at the southwest corner of San Marco and take the Calle Larga XXII Marzo, one of the city's more well-heeled strips. Take the Calle del Sartor, cross a canal and walk into the Campo San Fantin to see the Renaissance **Church of San Fantin**, topped with a dome by Sansovino. Over the campo is the **Teatro La Fenice**, the city's oldest and largest theatre, which opened in 1792. Pop in if there is a performance that day and the staff might let you see the plush interior.

Return to Larga XXII Marzo for the **Church of Santa Maria del Giglio**, also known as Santa Maria Zobenigo. Its façade features maps of European cities as they were in 1678. Continue on to reach Campo Francesco Morosini and the **Church of Santo Stefano**, featuring the bronze tomb of the doge after whom the piazza is named. It also features a brilliant series by Tintoretto in the sacristy. The church's Renaissance bell tower has the most pronounced lean of the towers in Venice. South-west from the piazza, past the 18th century **Church of San Vitale** and across the Accademia Bridge, is the **Galleria dell'Accademia**, housing the city's finest art collection.

In the former church and convent of Santa Maria della Carità, which has additions by Palladio, the collection follows the progression of Venetian art from the 14th to the 18th centuries and is displayed in chronological order. Room 1 contains a work by Paolo Veneziano, the *Coronation of the Virgin*. The highlight of Room 2, containing works of the late 15th and early 16th centuries, is Carpaccio's gruesome *Crucifixion & Glorification of the 10,000 Martyrs of Mt Ararat* and works by Giovanni Bellini. Rooms 4 and 5 feature some of the collection's best work – Mantegna's *St George* and a series of Madonnas by Giovanni Bellini. Rooms 6 to 10 contain works of the high Renaissance and feature Tintoretto and Titian. One of the highlights of the collection is Paolo Veronese's *Christ in the House of Levi* in Room 10. Originally called *The Last Supper*, the painting's name was changed after leaders of the Inquisition demanded to know why it featured such irreverence as drunkards, Germans and dwarfs. The room also contains Titian's last work, a *Pietà*. The 18th century begins in Room 11, and Tiepolo, the city's most prominent painter of the time, is featured. The collection is rounded off with works by Canaletto, Gentile Bellini, Carpaccio, Vivarini and Titian. The gallery opens from 9 am to 2 pm Monday to Saturday, to 1 pm Sunday, and entry is L8000.

From the Accademia, take Calle Gambara to the **Church of San Barnaba**, featuring Veronese's *Holy Family*, to reach the **Ca' Rezzonico** (1660), one of the city's most magnificent palaces. It now houses the **Museo del Settecento Veneziano** (Museum of the 18th Century) and is worth visiting for the palace and the curiosities. It's open daily from 9 am to 4 pm, and entry is L5000. South-west along Callelunga San Barnaba is the **Church of San Sebastiano**, where Veronese sought refuge in 1555 after he fled Verona. He painted many works for the church, and is buried here.

Walk along the Fondamenta di San Biagio to the Fondamenta delle Zattere, which runs along the Giudecca Canal (Canale della Giudecca). Its name changes to Zattere ai Gesuati near the **Chiesa dei Gesuati**, which contains ceiling frescoes by Tiepolo. Continuing along to the point of Dorsoduro and returning along the Grand Canal, you come across the **Church of Santa Maria della Salute**. Built by Longhena and dedicated to the Virgin Mary, who is believed to have saved the city from plague, it is the scene of a procession from San Marco to the church every 21 November to give thanks for the city's good health. Inside the sacristy are works by Titian.

The **Peggy Guggenheim Collection** is to the west of here. It is housed in the unfinished Palazzo Venier dei Leoni, where Peggy Guggenheim lived for 30 years until her death in 1979. It is her personal collection and features pieces from her favourite modern artists, including Pollock, Dali, Chagall, Brancusi, Malevich and Kandinsky. It is open from 11 am to 6 pm daily but is closed on Mondays, and entry is L7000. Admission is free during special Saturday openings, usually held from 6 to 9 pm during winter. Take a wander around the sculpture

Façade of Santa Maria del Giglio

garden, where Miss Guggenheim and many of her pet dogs are buried.

San Marco to Castello Weave a path northeast for the Campo **Santa Maria Formosa** and the church of the same name. On the site of a 7th century church, the present building dates from 1492. The painting *St Barbara & the Four Other Saints* by Palma Vecchio is supposed to depict the ideal image of female beauty. To the right of the church and over the small canal is the **Palazzo Querini-Stampalia**, housing a picture gallery that contains 14th to 18th century Venetian works donated to the city in 1868 by Count Gerolamo Querini. It has been closed for restoration but should reopen by late 1993.

North of the Campo Santa Maria Formosa is the **Church of SS Giovanni e Paolo**, in the piazza of the same name. The Venetian Gothic building was started in 1246 for the Dominicans and took 200 years to complete. It contains the tombs of many doges and features splendid paintings by Veronese. On the north side of the piazza is the **Scuola Grande di San Marco**, built in the Lombard style and now a hospital.

Returning south is the **Church of San Zaccaria**, which dates from 1444, although it was built on the site of an earlier church. Most of the Gothic façade is by Antonio Gambello, and the upper part, in Renaissance style, is by Codussi. The second altar inside features Giovanni Bellini's masterpiece, *Madonna with Saints & Angel Musician*.

Continue south to reach the the Riva degli Schiavoni and then head east along the waterfront for the **Church of Santa Maria della Pietà**, with a ceiling fresco by Tiepolo. Take a left along Calle del Dose into Campo Bandiera e Moro for the **Church of San Giovanni in Bragora**, rebuilt in 1475 on the site of a much earlier church, where you can buy a copy of Antonio Vivaldi's birth certificate.

Farther along the waterfront, across the Rio dell'Arsenale, is the **Arsenal**, the city's huge naval dockyard, which is said to have been founded in 1104. Covering 32 hectares, the Arsenal employed up to 16,000 people during the republic's peak. Its entrance, through the imposing Renaissance gateway by Gambello, is surmounted by the Lion of St Mark, with larger lions either side brought to the city as spoils of war. The **Naval Museum**, back towards the San Marco Canal on the far side of the Rio dell'Arsenale, covers the republic's maritime history with a huge exhibition of paraphernalia, model boats, costumes and weapons, and is well worth visiting. Among the exhibits are Peggy Guggenheim's gondola, one of the oldest remaining in the city. It is open from 9 am to 1 pm and entry is L2000. Most of the Arsenal is closed to the public, and some sections are derelict. But wander around the Castello district for glimpses into the site. Farther east are the **Biennale Gardens** where the city's famous biennial art exhibition has been held since 1895.

At the eastern edge of Venice, the small islands of **San Pietro** and **Sant'Elena** are worth walking through to see how average Venetians live. Both islands are quite gloomy, although the **Church of San Pietro** on the island of the same name deserves a visit.

Islands of the Lagoon From Fondamenta Nuove, take boat No 12 for the islands, or vaporetto No 5 for San Michele and Murano.

San Michele, the city's island cemetery, was established under Napoleon and is maintained by the Franciscans. The island's **Church of San Michele in Isola**, started by Coducci in 1469, was among the city's first Renaissance buildings.

The people of **Murano** have been working glass since 1292 but now they work the tourists as well. The island is worth visiting, but the produce is not any cheaper here than in Venice. Signs direct you to glass-blowing exhibitions. Visit the **Museo Vetrario** (Glass Museum), which contains some exquisite pieces and opens from 9 am to 4 pm; entry costs L4000. The **Church of SS Maria e Donato** dates from the 7th century although it was mostly rebuilt in the 12th century, and features a work by Tiepolo.

The island of **Burano** is famous for its lace, which locals are more than keen to sell you. But its brightly painted houses facing the small canals give the impression that the island has remained unaffected by the tourist hordes. The **Consorzia Merletti di Burano** is a museum of the craft of lace-making and opens from 9 am to 6 pm Tuesday to Saturday and from 10 am to 4 pm on Sunday. Entry is L5000. The bell tower beside the island's **Church of San Martino** has a pronounced lean.

Torcello, farther on from Burano, reached its zenith in the mid-7th century when it was the seat of the Bishop of Altinum and home to 20,000 people. Today, fewer than 80 people call the island home. Its **cathedral** was founded in the 7th century, rebuilt early in the 11th century and contains magnificent Byzantine mosaics, including a depiction of the Last Judgment. The adjacent **Museo dell'Estuario** in the Palazzo del Consiglio outlines the history of the island and features paintings by Veronese. It opens mornings and afternoons, except Monday, and entry is L3000.

Giudecca Island Reached by vaporetto No 5 from San Marco or near Zattere ai Gesuati,

the island features the **Chiesa del Redentore** (Church of the Redeemer) by Palladio. It was built in 1577 after the city was saved from the plague, and, on the third Saturday in July, there is a procession from the Zattere across a pontoon bridge to the church. The church, which features a painting by Tintoretto, is the island's main attraction, although the old stores at its western end make for good exploring. They are soon to be turned into expensive residential complexes.

Island of San Giorgio Maggiore The island can be reached from San Marco by vaporetto No 5 and should not be missed for the view from the top of the **Church of San Giorgio Maggiore**. The church was built by Palladio between 1565 and 1580 and is considered one of his most famous works. The austere interior is a little dull after gazing at the bold exterior, but it contains impressive works by Tintoretto and Carpaccio. Head for the elevator to take in the 60-metre-high view. It is open from 9 am to 7.30 pm daily and costs L2000.

The Lido The main draw here is the beaches, although why anybody would want to swim in the disgustingly polluted waters is beyond comprehension. The expanse of beach along Venice's outermost islands – the land barriers between the lagoon and the Adriatic – was once Italy's most fashionable. For centuries, the doges trekked out here to fulfil Venice's Marriage to the Sea ceremony by dropping a ring into the shallows, and its more glorious days are depicted in Thomas Mann's novel, *Death in Venice*.

A visit to the beach these days means paying a fortune (between L20,000 and L80,000) to rent a space (with chair and umbrella) on the so-called public beaches. You can also hike to the Lido's extremities where you can bask for free. The rows of modern apartments and hotels ensure the beaches are crowded, particularly with holidaying Italians and Germans.

The Lido's snappy **Palazzo del Cinema** hosts the city's international film festival each September and the **casino** packs them in during the summer months. Apart from that, there is little to draw you here, unless you are passing through on your way to Chioggia. The Lido can be reached by vaporetto Nos 1, 2 and 6, and ferry No 17 from San Marco.

Chioggia Chioggia reached its peak in the 13th century when the Genoese seized this small town on the southern tip of the Venetian lagoon. The town was virtually destroyed in the ensuing battle with the Venetians, which resulted in Genoa's retreat. The small medieval section is worth visiting, although the two-hour trip by ferry/bus from San Marco could bite heavily into your schedule. Chioggia remains one of Italy's main fishing ports, but its beach, the Sottomarina, is grubby and uninspiring. City bus No 1, 2, 6 or 7 connects Chioggia with the Sottomarina, saving you the 15-minute walk.

One highlight of the trip is the bus ride from Lido, which takes you along the giant sea wall. Take bus No 11 from Gran Viale Santa Maria Elisabetta, outside the tourist office on the Lido, which connects with a ferry for Chioggia at Caroman, south of Pellestrina. The APT (☎ 40 10 68) is on the waterfront at the Sottomarina and can assist with accommodation.

Courses
The Società Dante Alighieri (☎ 528 91 27), Ponte del Purgatorio, Arsenale, offers intensive and longer Italian-language courses from September to June. Monthly courses start at L330,000.

The Cini Foundation (☎ 528 99 00) runs short seminars on a host of subjects relating to the city, in particular Venetian music and art. From April to November, a local cultural association, Artfluence (☎ 524 17 68), arranges an evening slide show and talk called the 'Art & History of Venice', in the 18th century Ca' Favretto palace.

Organised Tours
A local group organises guided visits to St Mark's Basilica daily from Monday to Saturday at 11 am. Call ☎ 520 48 88 for information. Consult *Un Ospite di Venezia* for details of visits to other churches and sites in the city. The APT has an updated list of authorised guides, who will take you on a walking tour of the city. The going rate is L105,000 for a three-hour tour for 20 people.

Ital-Travel (☎ 522 91 11), San Marco 72B, under the colonnade at Piazza San Marco's western end, organises a variety of sightseeing trips, including Venice on Foot for L28,000, and a tour of the city by motorboat for L22,000. It also offers a half-day bus trip to the Venetian villas along the Brenta Riviera at a cost of L65,000.

Festivals
The major event of the year is the famous Carnevale, held during the 10 days before Ash Wednesday, when Venetians don spectacular masks and costumes for what is literally a 10-day street party.

The APT publishes a list of annual events which includes the plethora of religious festivals staged by almost every church in the city. One of the main religious festivals is held in early July at the Church of the Redeemer (see the previous Giudecca Island section), and another is celebrated at the Church of Santa Maria della Salute each November (see the San Marco to Dorsoduro section).

The city next hosts the Historical Regatta of the Four Ancient Maritime Republics in 1996. The former maritime republics of Genoa, Pisa, Venice and Amalfi take turns to host this colourful event. The annual Redentore Regatta on the Grand Canal is another regatta celebrating the city's former maritime supremacy and is held each July.

Places to Stay
Simply put, Venice is expensive. The average cost of a single room without bath is L35,000, or L50,000 for a double. There are cheaper places but, apart from the hostel, they are generally of a low standard.

Hotel proprietors here are inclined to pad the bill by demanding extra for a compulsory breakfast and, almost without exception, they increase prices in the high season. It is advisable in Venice, probably more than for any other Italian city, to make a booking before you arrive. In the high season, if you arrive without a booking, you could find yourself backtracking to Padua or Verona.

As previously mentioned, Venice does not have a traditional street-numbering system. The best idea is to ring your hotel when you arrive and ask for specific directions.

The Venetian Hoteliers' Association at the train station will book you a room, but you must leave a small deposit. It opens from 8 am and does not accept phone reservations. Also, the station can be like a cattle yard during the peak seasons when agents for many of the city's hotels descend on newly arrived tourists. Many are legitimate, but check the hotel's reputation with the APT or Hoteliers' Association before booking.

Places to Stay – bottom end

Camping There are numerous camping grounds at the Litorale del Cavallino, the coast along the Adriatic north-east of the city. Many have bungalows. The tourist office in San Marco has a full list, but you could try the *Marina di Venezia* (☎ 96 61 46), Via Montello 6, at Punta Sabbioni. On the Lido is *San Niccolò* (☎ 526 74 15); take bus A as you get off at the Lido vaporetto stop.

Hostels The IYHF *Ostello Venezia* (☎ 523 82 11) is on the island of Giudecca, at Fondamenta delle Zitelle 86. It's open to members only, although you can buy a card there for L30,000. Bed and breakfast is L18,000 and full meals are available for under L12,000. Take vaporetto No 5 sinistra (the left circle line) from the station (L1800 one way) and get off at Zitelle. The *Istituto Canossiano* (☎ 522 21 57), nearby at Ponte Piccolo 428, has beds for women only from L15,000 a night. Take vaporetto No 5 to Sant'Eufemia on Giudecca. The *Istituto San Giuseppe* (☎ 522 53 52), Castello 5402, has dormitory beds for L25,000 per person, but it's not the simplest place to find. From Campo San Zulian, near Piazza San Marco,

walk through Campo della Guerra, go across the bridge and take the first left, where you will see the sign.

The *Suore Mantellate* (☎ 522 08 29), Calle Buccari, Castello 10, offers relatively expensive accommodation at L32,000 for B&B. It's at the far end of Castello, away from San Marco. Take vaporetto No 1 or 2 from the station to Sant'Elena, east of the centre. *Domus G B Giustinian* (☎ 522 50 67), Santa Croce 326A is near the Rio Terrà dei Pensieri and has beds for L16,000 a night.

The *Ostello Santa Fosca* (☎ 71 57 75), Cannaregio 2372, is about halfway between the station and San Marco. Follow the signs for San Marco and you will see signs directing you to the hostel, which charges L16,000 a night and less for subsequent nights. Check in between 6 and 11.30 am.

Around Cannaregio This is the easiest area to find a bed because of the sheer number of pensioni, locande and alloggi. One of the cheapest is *Archie's House* (☎ 72 08 84), Cannaregio 1814B. Follow the Lista di Spagna from the station, through Campo San Geremia, go across the bridge and along Rio Terrà San Leonardo to the Campiello Anconetta (about 10 minutes' walk). Beds in somewhat dingy dormitories are L18,000 a night, or L20,000 per person for a double.

Closer to the station is *Locanda Antica Casa Carettoni* (☎ 71 62 31), Lista di Spagna 130. Singles/doubles are L26,000/46,000 and there's no extra charge for use of the communal shower. The place is full of cats cared for by the pleasant and rather eccentric owner.

Just off the Lista di Spagna, at Calle Misericordia 358, is *Hotel Santa Lucia* (☎ 71 51 80), in a newish building which has rooms for L45,000/65,000. Nearby is the *Hotel Atlantide* (☎ 71 69 01), Calle Misericordia 375, which has singles/doubles from L68,000/84,000 and triples from L116,000. All prices include breakfast.

At *Al Gobbo* (☎ 71 50 01), in Campo San Geremia, the compulsory breakfast bumps up the prices. Singles/doubles are L42,000/

L58,000. The *Hotel Marte* (☎ 71 63 51), in the same campo, has rooms from L45,000/70,000.

Along the Rio Terrà San Leonardo, at No 1333, is the *Alloggi Smeraldo* (☎ 71 78 38), located in an old palace which retains some signs of its former splendour. Singles/doubles are L35,000/50,000 and triples are L79,000.

The *Hotel Minerva & Nettuno* (☎ 71 59 68), Lista di Spagna 230, has rooms for L47,000/68,000.

The *Albergo Bernardi Semenzato* (☎ 522 72 57), just off the Strada Nuova at Campo SS Apostoli, has cheap rooms for L28,000/43,000, but many of them are dark and uninviting. If you don't want to undertake the 20-minute walk from the station, catch the No 1 vaporetto to Ca' d'Oro.

Around San Marco One of the nicest places to stay in this area is *Locanda Casa Petrarca* (☎ 520 04 30), San Marco 4386, with singles/doubles for L40,000/70,000 and triples for L95,000; doubles/triples with bathroom are L100,000/120,000; use of the communal shower is L2000. The friendly owner speaks English. If you can find Campo San Luca, follow Calle dei Fuseri, take the second left and then turn right into Calle Schiavine. The *Locanda San Salvador* (☎ 528 91 47), San Marco 5264, is run by the same family and charges about the same. It is just off Campo San Bartolomeo, near the Rialto Bridge.

Around Castello This area is to the east of San Marco, and though close to the piazza, is less heavily touristed. The easiest way to get there from the station is to catch the No 1 vaporetto.

A stone's throw east of San Marco, *Hotel Bridge* (☎ 520 52 87), just off Campo SS Filippo e Giacomo, has doubles/triples for L67,000/93,000, breakfast included. The *Albergo Corona* (☎ 522 91 74), north-east of Campo SS Filippo e Giacomo at Calle Corona 4464, has singles/doubles from L34,000/48,000 and triples from L65,000;

showers are L3000, and an electric baggage carrier whisks cases up the four flights.

Albergo Tiepolo (☎ 523 13 15), just off the Campo SS Filippo e Giacomo, looks a bit shabby but the rooms are good. Singles/doubles L40,000/52,000.

Around San Polo & Santa Croce The *Hotel Al Gallo* (☎ 523 67 61) on Calle Amai, just off Campo Tolentini and a couple of minutes' walk from Piazzale Roma, has singles/doubles from L45,000/80,000, all with showers. *Albergo Da Bepi* (☎ 522 67 35), Fondamenta Minotto, just south of the Al Gallo, has singles/doubles from L45,000/70,000 and triples from L100,000, all including breakfast.

The *Locanda Sturion* (☎ 523 62 43), Calle Sturion 679, is two minutes from the Rialto Bridge. It has been a hotel on and off since the 13th century. Prices include breakfast. The one, tiny single is no bargain at L45,000. Doubles/triples are L63,000/83,500, and for four or five people, L104,000/124,000.

Albergo Casa Peron (☎ 528 60 38), Salizzada San Pantalon 84, has singles/doubles for L43,000/70,000, with breakfast and private bathroom. From the station, cross the Scalzi Bridge and follow the signs to San Marco/Rialto until you reach the Rio delle Muneghette, then cross the wooden bridge.

Chioggia The fishing-village atmosphere makes an alternative to the hustle and bustle of Venice. *Albergo Clodia* (☎ 40 08 13), Via Forno Filippini 876, has singles/doubles from L33,000/50,000. The *Val d'Ostriche* (☎ 40 05 27), Calle Sant'Andrea 763, is slightly more expensive.

Staying at Sottomarina, Chioggia's answer to the Lido, can be less expensive than its northern counterpart. The *Adige* (☎ 40 16 69), Via Adige 4, one block inland from the tourist office, has singles/doubles from L25,000/33,000.

Mestre You should consider staying here, particularly if you have a car, as parking on the islands can be prohibitively expensive.

Adria (☎ 98 97 55), Via Cappuccina 34, near the centre, has singles/doubles from L40,000/66,000 and offers parking. *Da Tito* (☎ 531 45 81), Via Cappuccina 67, has rooms for about the same price and also offers parking.

Places to Stay – middle
Around Cannaregio The *Hotel Caprera* (☎ 71 52 71), Cannaregio 219, in a small street to the left after Calle Misericordia, has singles/doubles from L45,000/65,000 and triples for L80,000, all including breakfast. Prices are higher during summer months.

The *Hotel Rossi* (☎ 71 51 64) is also near the station in the tiny Calle delle Procuratie, off the Lista di Spagna. It is good value with singles/doubles in the high season for L43,000/61,000 and triples/quads for L90,000/120,000. In the low season, singles/doubles are L35,000/55,000.

Close to the station, on Calle Priuli ai Cavalletti 99, is the *Hotel Edelweiss Stella Alpina* (☎ 71 51 79), with singles/doubles from L67,500/90,000, including breakfast. Prices drop in the low season.

Around San Marco The *Albergo Noemi* (☎ 523 81 44) on Calle dei Fabbri 909, from San Marco towards the Rialto, has singles/doubles from L38,000/55,000 and triples for L78,000 all year. Farther along towards the Rialto is the *Albergo Al Gambero* (☎ 522 43 84), with singles/doubles from L35,000/52,000; triples are L101,200.

The *Albergo San Maurizio* (☎ 528 97 12) in the piazza of the same name has singles/doubles for L45,000/55,000, slightly higher during the peak season. *Albergo Casa Verado* (☎ 528 61 27), at Ponte Storto 4765, just north of Campo SS Filippo e Giacomo, has rooms from L35,000/65,000, more for a room with conveniences.

Around Castello The *Locanda Piave* (☎ 528 51 74), Ruga Giuffa 4838/40, is tucked away in a maze of tiny streets. Singles/doubles are L50,000/71,000, and triples are L100,000, all including breakfast. From the Campo San Provolo (near the Albergo Tiepolo), go through the passageway, cross the bridge and follow Calle Rota to the end.

Hotel Riva (☎ 5227034), Ponte del-l'Angelo 5310, is on a lovely side canal. Doubles/triples with breakfast and private bathroom are L70,000/130,000. From San Marco, walk along the Calle San Marco and turn left into Calle Angelo.

Hotel Da Bruno (☎ 523 04 52), Salizzada San Leo 5726, just west of Campo Santa Maria Formosa, has singles/doubles from L88,500/123,000 and triples from L161,000, all including breakfast and showers in the rooms.

One of the best deals in Venice is at the *Albergo Paganelli* (☎ 522 43 24), Riva degli Schiavoni 4182, on the waterfront near the Arsenal. Singles/doubles are L75,000/95,000 and most rooms overlook the water.

Around San Polo & Santa Croce The *Hotel Canal* (☎ 523 84 80), Fondamenta dei Tolentini, is a few minutes' walk from Piazzale Roma and overlooks the Grand Canal. Singles/doubles are L90,000/150,000 and triples/quads are L187,500/225,000.

Just south on Salizzada San Pantalon is the *Hotel della Mora* (☎ 523 57 03), with singles/doubles from L55,000/72,000 and triples/quads from L93,000/98,000, all including breakfast. A few doors down is the *Hotel Falier* (☎ 522 88 82), with singles/doubles from L60,000/80,000, all with showers and breakfast. Prices go up by 30% in summer.

Around Dorsoduro The *Albergo Antico Capon* (☎ 528 52 92) on Campo Santa Margherita has singles/doubles from L60,000/80,000 and is only a few minutes' walk from Piazzale Roma. The *Albergo Accademia Villa Maravege* (☎ 521 01 88) on Fondamenta Bollani has rooms from L70,000/90,000.

Lido In summer this area is expensive, but good bargains can be found in the low season, when the weather is still warm. The *Pensione La Pergola* (☎ 526 07 84), Via

Cipro 15, has doubles/triples for L64,000/85,000, including breakfast. It is open all year and has a shady terrace. Turn left off the Gran Viale Santa Maria Elisabetta into Via Zara, then right into Via Cipro. *Villa Edera* (☎ 526 07 91), Via Negroponte 13, left of the main street near the sea, has singles/doubles in the high season for L45,000/65,000, including breakfast; in the low season, rooms are L35,000/50,000 and the owner is happy to strike a deal.

Mestre The three-star *Tritone* (☎ 93 09 55), Viale Stazione 16, is close to the centre and the station but does not have free parking. Singles/doubles are L65,000/85,000.

Places to Stay – top end
Around San Marco Just along the waterfront Riva degli Schiavoni from San Marco towards Castello are some of the city's finest hotels. The four-star *Londra Palace* (☎ 520 05 33) has singles/doubles from L150,000/220,000, and most rooms have views over the water. The five-star *Danieli* (☎ 522 64 80) next door has rooms from L350,000/450,000 and most of them look out over the canal.

Around Dorsoduro The *Pensione Seguso* (☎ 522 23 40) on Fondamenta delle Zattere, facing the Giudecca Canal, usually offers room and half-board for two people from L175,000.

Giudecca The *Cipriani* (☎ 520 77 44) is more like a resort set in lavish grounds on the island of Giudecca, with unbeatable views across to San Marco. Singles/doubles start at L400,000/500,000 a night, but it is recognised as one of Italy's finest hotels. Take the hotel's private boat from San Marco.

Torcello The *Locanda Cipriani* (☎ 73 07 57), Piazza Santa Fosca, is run by the owners of Harry's Bar and provides luxury accommodation in splendid isolation. Singles/doubles start at L160,000/280,000, but the

hotel generally offers packages that include meals.

Lido The grand *Excelsior* (☎ 526 02 01), Lungomare Marconi 41, is one of the city's finest hotels, with singles/doubles from L400,000/600,000 a day; apartments cost L1,400,000 a week.

Mestre The *Plaza* (☎ 92 93 88) nearby at Viale Stazione 36 has rooms from L110,000/140,000 and also provides parking.

Places to Eat
Eating in Venice can be an expensive pastime unless you choose very carefully. Many restaurants, particularly around the station and San Marco, are tourist traps, where prices are high and the quality is low. Be careful to read the fine print if you want to eat seafood as most fish is sold by weight.

The best areas to look for places to eat are in the side streets of Castello, and around Campo San Barnaba and Campo Santa Margherita in Dorsoduro. Many bars serve filling snacks with lunch-time and pre-dinner drinks. Most also have a wide range of Venetian panini, with every imaginable filling. *Tramezzi* (sandwich triangles) and huge bread rolls cost from L3000 to L5000 if you eat them standing up. A cheaper alternative can be the many *baccari* (small bars serving local wines and snacks) that are usually crammed with locals.

The staples of the Veneto region's cuisine are rice and beans. Try the *risotto con piselli* (risotto with peas), the *minestra di pasta e fagioli* (pasta-and-bean soup), and don't miss a risotto or pasta dish with *radicchio trevisano* (chicory). The rich dessert, tiramisù, is a favourite here.

There are fruit and vegetable stalls lining the main thoroughfare from the station to San Marco, but the prices are inflated for the tourists. The main markets are in the streets around the Rialto Bridge (on the San Polo side). Grocery shops, for salami, cheese and bread, are concentrated around Campo Beccarie. There is a Standa supermarket on

Strada Nuova and a Mega 1 supermarket in Campo Santa Margherita.

Cannaregio & around the Station There are few decent options in this area. *Trattoria alla Palazzina*, Cannaregio 1509, is just over the first bridge after Campo San Geremia. It has a garden at the rear and serves good pizzas for L6000 to L7000. A full meal will cost around L25,000. Otherwise there are numerous bars which serve panini and takeaway pizza by the slice.

Locals say that the best pizza and pasta in Venice is served at *All'Anfora*, across the bridge from the station at Lista dei Bari 1223. It has a garden at the rear. Try the pizza ottombrina, with brie and spek. Pizzas cost from L6000 to L10,000, pasta is L6000 to L9000 and a main course from L9000 to L15,000. The wine, however, is expensive. To get there, walk straight ahead from the bridge, turn left at the second street and follow the signs to the Rialto.

Trattoria Nuova, Lista di Spagna 189, just before the Canale di Cannaregio, is pleasant and small with an excellent, L15,000 tourist menu. *Antica Carbonera*, Calle Bembo off Strada Nuova, is a small trattoria catering more to locals than tourists. Main dishes start at L8000.

Pizzeria al Faro is at the eastern edge of the Ghetto and has pizzas from L4500 and pasta from L5000, with a L1500 cover charge. On the Canale Cannaregio near Ponte Guglie is *Ristorante al Ponte*, with a set-meal price of L12,500.

Around San Marco The self-service *Italy & Italy*, in Campo San Luca, off Calle dei Fabbri, has pasta from L6000 and great hamburgers, with no cover charge. The *Colusse il Fornaio* in the campo has pizza by the slice from L1500 as well as breads, and is good for lunch or a snack.

Vino Vino, San Marco 2007, is a popular bar/osteria at Ponte Veste near Teatro La Fenice. The menu changes daily and the pre-prepared food is good quality. A pasta or risotto costs L6000, a main dish L12,000, and there is a good selection of vegetables.

Wine is sold by the glass for L1200. Just off the Riva del Carbon at Calle Cavalli, near the Rialto, is *Il Volto*, one of the city's most popular wine bars, where you can grab a panino from L2500. Nearby, on Calle dei Fuseri, near Campo San Luca, is *Zorzi*, a vegetarian restaurant with main courses from L8000.

Ristorante Da Ivo, Calle dei Fuseri, near the canal, is an excellent restaurant specialising in local cuisine, and a meal will cost upwards of L30,000.

A popular place for cakes and pastries is *Pasticceria Marchini* on the other side of Piazza San Marco, just off Campo Santo Stefano, at Calle del Spezier 2769. *Trattoria da Memi*, Campiello Santo Stefano, just off Campo Santo Stefano, has a good-value tourist menu for L20,000 and serves pizzas for L5000 to L7000.

If you get really desperate for a change, *Wendy's*, of the hamburger chain, is at Calle Larga, north of San Marco.

Noemi, beneath the hotel of the same name on Calle dei Fabbri, offers excellent food at reasonable prices. Pasta starts at L10,000 and main courses from L15,000. West of San Marco, on Calle Larga XXII Marzo, is one of the city's best restaurants, *La Caravella*; a meal could cost up to L80,000.

Castello The *Trattoria Rivetto*, Salizzada San Provolo, just before Campo San Provolo, serves typical Venetian food. A pasta dish costs around L9000, a main dish around L15,000; wine is expensive at L11,000 a litre.

In this area there are several bars which serve excellent and cheap panini. One is on the corner of Calle delle Rasse, just off Campo SS Filippo e Giacomo, another is *Al Vecchio Penasa*, just around the corner at Calle delle Rasse 4586. *Trattoria Rivietta*, in Campo SS Filippo e Giacomo, near the canal bridge, serves local dishes, with main courses from L8000. *Trattoria Pizzeria Conca d'Oro* in the campo is one of the city's best pizzerias, with pizzas from L5000.

Pizzeria Da Egidio in Campo Santa Maria Formosa has pizzas from L5000 and you can sit in the piazza. Just off the campo is *Cip Ciap*, at the Ponte del Mondo Nuovo. It serves fantastic and filling pizza by the slice. *Osteria al Mascaron*, on Calle Lunga, east of the campo, is a traditional bar where you can eat a meal for L14,000 or have a snack while drinking. *Alle Testiere*, nearby on Calle del Mondo Nuovo, has a great antipasto and daily pasta specials which start at L4000.

Il Golosone, nearby on Salizzada San Lio 5689, is one of the best cake shops in Venice.

San Polo & Santa Croce This is the best area for small, cheap trattorias and pizzerias. *Self Service al Ponte di Rialto*, Riva del Ferro, on the San Marco side of the Rialto Bridge, looks very tacky but the food is good and reasonably cheap. Pasta dishes start at L5000.

Cantina do Mori, on Sotoportego dei do Mori, off Ruga Rialto, is a small wine bar where you can grab a good panino for lunch, or a meal at night for about L15,000. The *Trattoria alla Madonna*, Calle della Madonna, two streets west of the Rialto, is hard to find and there is not a tourist in sight. Main dishes start at L8000.

Trattoria Da Bepi, Fondamenta Minotto 159, is small and family run and offers a good, L16,000 set-price menu.

Dorsoduro Typical regional fare is served in *L'Incontro* along Rio Terrà Canal, between Campo San Barnaba and Campo Santa Margherita, which is one of the better deals in the city. The menu alters daily and a full meal will cost L25,000 to L30,000. *Antica Locanda Montin*, off Fondamenta di Borgo near Campo San Barnaba, has good, simple food and a shady garden. A full meal will cost around L30,000.

Linea d'Ombra, near Fondamenta della Salute and the Guggenheim Collection, offers excellent food and a view out to San Marco. Expect to pay L8000 for a first course and from L16,000 for a main dish.

In Campo Santa Margherita is *Bar La Sosta*, a student favourite. Panini cost from L1500 to L4000 and you can sit outside for

no extra charge. *Crepizza*, Calle San Pantalon 3757, past Campo Santa Margherita, serves pasta for L8000, pizza for L8000 to L10,000, and fantastic crêpes for L8000 to L10,000. Around the corner at Crosera San Pantalon 3817 is *Da Silvio*, which serves pizzas for around L7000 in a garden setting. A full meal here will cost under L25,000.

Giudecca *Harry's Dolce*, Fondamenta San Biagio, is run by the owners of the infamous Harry's Bar but is considerably cheaper and has wild desserts. A meal could still cost over L50,000 but the restaurant is considered one of Venice's best. *All'al Tanella*, Calle delle Erbe 269, is a cheaper alternative, where a meal will cost about L25,000.

Lido The *Self Service Pilla*, Gran Viale Santa Maria Elisabetta, near the APT, is cheap, with pasta dishes from L4000. *Trattoria da Scarso*, Piazzale Malamocca 4, is one of the better restaurants near the beach, and offers a L15,000 set menu.

Murano The *Osteria dalla Mora*, Fondamenta Manin 75, looks out over the island's canal and is worth considering for lunch or dinner. A meal will cost L16,000.

Burano *Da Romano*, Piazza Galuppi 221, is a small, family-run trattoria, where main courses cost about L8000.

Torcello The *Osteria del Diavolo*, between the ferry stop and the cathedral, makes staying on the island for an early dinner worth the effort. First courses start at L8000 and main courses from L15,000.

Chioggia *La Plaza Pizza*, Piazza XX Settembre, has good pizzas from L4500, and *Trattoria al Bersagliere*, Via Cesare Battisti, off Corso del Popolo, is recognised by the APT as serving typical Chioggia cuisine. Pasta dishes start at L5000 and main courses at L10,000.

Mestre There is a *Brek* self-service restaurant at Via Carducci 54, where pasta starts at

L4000 and main courses are priced from L6000. *Da Bepi*, Via Sernaglia 27, serves some traditional dishes and a meal could cost L25,000.

Bars & Cafés If you can cope with the idea of paying L10,000 for a cappuccino, spend an hour or so sitting at an outdoor table in Piazza San Marco, listening to the orchestra. *Caffè Florian* is the most famous of San Marco's cafés. Although a bit faded these days, it is still an atmospheric place. Lord Byron, Henry James and friends took breakfast here before crossing the piazza to *Caffè Quadri* for lunch. Both cafés have bars, where you will pay normal prices for a coffee or drink and still enjoy the elegant surroundings. *Al Todaro*, facing the canal from Piazzetta San Marco and opposite the Doges' Palace, is a cheaper alternative with a fabulous view.

The famous *Harry's Bar*, Calle Vallaresso 1323, off Salizzada San Moisé at the western edge of San Marco, is the most likely place to find British travel writer Jan Morris. The Cipriani family which started the bar claims to have invented many Venetian specialities, including the Bellini cocktail, which sells for L10,000. A meal at the restaurant upstairs will cost you at least L80,000, but it is one of the few restaurants in the city to have been awarded a Michelin star.

The *Black Jack Bar*, Campo San Luca, serves a decent Bellini for L3500 and is a great place for a cheap drink. *Nave de Oro*, Calle del Mondo Nuovo, off Salizzada San Lio, is open from 8 am to 1 pm and 5 to 8 pm and specialises in wines from the Veneto that are sold by the glass. In the market area at Campo Beccarie is *Vini da Pinto*, a small bar frequented by stall holders.

Bar Paradiso in the Giardini della Biennale, Castello 1260, faces the water and offers great views back towards San Marco.

Gelati The best ice cream in Venice is at *Gelati Nico*, Fondamenta delle Zattere 922. The locals take their evening stroll along the fondamenta, while eating their gelati. *Il Doge*, Campo Santa Margherita, also has excellent gelati. The *Boutique del Gelato*, Salizzada San Lio, is one of the best.

Entertainment

The famous Venice Carnevale (see the earlier Festivals section) provides one of the best forms of entertainment in Italy, but exhibitions, theatre and musical events continue throughout the year in Venice. Information is available in the weekly *Un Ospite di Venezia*, and the tourist office also has brochures listing events and performances for the entire year.

The Venice Biennale, a major exhibition of international visual arts, started in 1895 and has been held every even-numbered year since early this century. However, the 1992 festival was postponed until 1993 so there would be a festival on the Biennale's 100th anniversary in 1995. At this stage, the organisers are unsure if the event will revert to even years. The Venice International Film Festival is held every year in September at the Palazzo del Cinema on the Lido.

Concerts and opera are performed throughout the year at Teatro La Fenice (☎ 521 01 61), and concerts of symphony and chamber music are staged in the Church of Santa Maria della Pietà. Tickets can be purchased from Agenzia Kele & Teo (☎ 520 87 22), Ponte dei Baratteri, San Marco, or from the church two days before the event. Major art exhibitions are held at the Palazzo Grassi and you will find smaller exhibitions in various venues throughout the city throughout the year. A Contemporary Music Festival is held annually in October at the Goldoni Theatre.

The Casino Municipale di Venezia has two locations. In winter it is at the Palazzo Vendramin Calergi, on the Grand Canal, and in summer it moves to the Palazzo del Casino at the Lido. Vaporetto No 2, the so-called Casino Express, takes you to both locations.

The city is without an English-language cinema, but Summer Arena, a cinema-under-the-stars in Campo San Polo during July and August, features British and American films, but they are generally dubbed.

As far as nightclubs go, the city's spread

is pretty dismal. El Souk, Calle Corfu near the Accademia, is a bar by day and a club by night – but don't expect too much. A drive to Mestre is the best bet, or a boat to the Lido, but clubs tend to close there during winter.

Things to Buy

Who can think of Venice without a picture of its elaborately grotesque Venetian glass coming to mind? There are several workshops and showrooms, particularly in the area between San Marco and Castello, and on the island of Murano, designed mainly for large tourist groups. If you want to buy Venetian glass, shop around carefully, because quality and prices vary dramatically. The high number of shops around Piazza San Marco means that competition for tourist dollars is fierce. Remember to haggle, as the marked price is usually much higher than what the seller expects to get.

The famous Carnevale masks are beautiful though expensive souvenirs. A small workshop and showroom in a small street off Campo SS Filippo e Giacomo, towards San Marco, is worth a look, as is Mondo Nuovo, Campo Santa Margherita, which will design and make you a mask. Venice is also noted for its *carta marmorizzata* (marbled paper), sold at many outlets throughout the city. Veneziartigiana, Calle Larga San Marco 412, is a collective selling works by 45 Venetian artists.

The main shopping area for clothing, shoes, accessories and jewellery is in the narrow streets between San Marco and the Rialto. Shop hours are roughly the same as throughout Italy, although many outlets open on Sundays during the tourist season.

Getting There & Away

Air Marco Polo Airport (☎ 66 11 11) is just east of Mestre and is served by flights from most major Italian cities, most major European cities and New York.

Alitalia (☎ 521 63 33) is at San Marco, Fondamenta Orseolo 1166; the Padua office of British Airways (☎ 049-66 04 44) is the closest to Venice; Qantas, Canadian Airways

and TWA are handled by Gastaldi Tours (☎ 98 97 55), Via Verdi 34 in Mestre.

Bus ACTV buses (☎ 528 78 86) leave from Piazzale Roma for surrounding areas including Mestre and Chioggia. There are also bus connections to Padua and Treviso. Tickets and information are available at the office in the piazza.

Train The Stazione Santa Lucia (☎ 71 55 55), known in Venice as the *ferrovia*, is directly linked to Padua, Verona, Trieste, Milan and Bologna and thus is easily accessible from Florence and Rome. You can also leave from Venice for major points in Germany, Austria and the former Yugoslavia.

Orient Express The Venice Simplon Orient Express runs between Venice and London via Verona, Zürich and Paris twice weekly, although in winter there is only one service each week. Any travel agent in Venice can assist, or call the headquarters in London on ☎ 071-928 5100.

Car & Motorbike The A4 autostrada passes through Mestre and is the quickest way to reach Venice. Take the Venezia exit and follow the signs for the city. The A4 connects Trieste with Turin, passing through Milan. From the south, take the A13 from Bologna, which connects with the A4 at Padua. A more interesting route is to take the ss11 road from Padua to Venice. This is also the best road for hitchhikers.

Once you cross the bridge from Mestre, the Ponte della Libertà, cars must be left at one of the huge car parks in Piazzale Roma, or on the island of Tronchetto. Parking is not cheap and you will pay over L25,000 for every 24 hours. A cheaper alternative is to leave the car at Fusina near Mestre and catch the No 16 vaporetto to Zattere and then the No 5 either to San Marco or the station. Ask for information at the tourist information office just before the bridge to Venice.

Avis (☎ 522 58 25) is in Piazzale Roma,

Europcar is at Marco Polo airport (☎ 541 50 92) and in Piazzale Roma (☎ 523 86 16).

Boat Kompas Italia (☎ 528 65 45), San Marco 1497, operates some ferry and hydrofoil services to Croatia. Most services were suspended because of the unrest there, so call first to see what is available. Kompas also operates day trips to the towns of Porec, Rovinj and Pula on the Istrian Peninsula, all L40,000 one way.

Ferries run from Venice to Alexandria in Egypt via Bari and stop at Piraeus in Greece. The company operating the ferries is Adriatica (☎ 78 18 61). It has an office at Porto di Venezia, Stazione Marittima Molo 103. The ferries do not have deck class or airline-type armchairs. At the time of writing, cabins (with four beds) in the high season were L415,000 per person to Piraeus and L830,000 to Alexandria.

Getting Around

To/From the Airport The airport is accessible by regular *motoscafo* (motorboat) from San Marco and the Lido (L15,000), operated by the Cooperativa San Marco (☎ 522 23 03). There are also buses operated by the Società ATVO (☎ 520 55 30) from Piazzale Roma, which cost L5000, or you can take the regular ACTV city bus No 5, also from Piazzale Roma. A water taxi from San Marco will cost more than L83,000.

Local Transport As already mentioned, there are no cars in Venice proper. Vaporetti are the city's mode of public transport. However, car ferry No 17 departs from Tronchetto, near Piazzale Roma, for the Lido, which enables you to take your car to the islands along the Adriatic.

From Piazzale Roma or Tronchetto, vaporetto No 1 zigzags up the Grand Canal to San Marco and then the Lido. There are faster and more expensive alternatives if you are in a hurry. Vaporetti also head from the station to Murano, Burano and Torcello. A full timetable is available at the tourist office. Tickets cost L2200 for most routes or L2500 for

faster vaporetti. A 24-hour ticket costs L10,000 and a three-day ticket is L17,000.

Traghetti The cheap way to ride a gondola, traghetti are used by locals to cross the Grand Canal away from the bridges. As they are unprofitable, they are slowly being phased out and only five remain. Signs direct you to the locations. They operate between Calle Traghetto, near San Marco, and Fondamenta della Salute; between Campo San Samuele, north of the Accademia Bridge, and Calle Traghetto; between Calle Mocenigo, farther north, and Calle Traghetto; between Fondamenta del Vin and Riva del Carbon, near the Rialto Bridge; and between Campo Santa Sofia and Campo Pescaria, near the produce market. The ride costs L500.

Water Taxis Water taxis are prohibitively expensive, with a set L27,000 charge for a maximum of seven minutes, an extra L8000 if you order one by phone, and various surcharges which make a gondola ride seem cheap.

Gondolas These might represent the quintessential romantic Venice, but at L70,000 for 50 minutes they aren't cheap, and the price goes up to L90,000 after 8 pm. It is possible to squeeze up to five people into one gondola and still pay the same price, which is less romantic but more affordable.

Gondolas are available near main canals all over the city, or can be booked in the following areas: San Marco (☎ 520 06 85), Rialto (☎ 522 49 04), Piazzale Roma (☎ 522 05 81) and the train station (☎ 71 85 43).

Porters Getting from the vaporetto stop to your hotel can be quite difficult if you are heavily laden with luggage. There are several porter stands around the city, with baggage carriers who will escort you to your hotel. They charge L8350 for one or two items and L2350 for each subsequent item. They can be found at the Accademia Bridge (☎ 522 48 91), the train station (☎ 71 52 72), Piazzale Roma (☎ 520 30 70), the Rialto

Bridge (☎ 520 53 08), and San Marco (☎ 523 23 85).

THE BRENTA RIVIERA
Dotted along the Brenta River, which passes through Padua and spills into the Venetian lagoon, are more than 100 villas, built by wealthy Venetian families as summer homes, although most are closed to the public. The most outstanding are the **Villa Foscari** (1571), built by Palladio at Malcontenta, and the **Villa Pisani**, also known as the Villa Nazionale, at Strà. Buses running between Padua and Venice stop at or near the villas. The one at Strà was built for Doge Alvise Pisani, was used by Napoleon and was the site of the first meeting between Hitler and Mussolini. See the Around Vicenza section later in this chapter for more Venetian villas.

The luxurious *Burchiello* barge plied the Brenta River between Venice and Padua in the 17th and 18th centuries. Today an imitation ferries tourists for about L100,000, including lunch and short tours. Call ☎ 049-66 09 44 for information. The bus, or road ss11 for drivers, are cheaper alternatives.

PADUA (PADOVA)
Although famous as the city of St Anthony and for its university, one of the oldest in Europe, Padua is often seen as merely a convenient and cheap place to stay while visiting Venice. The city, however, offers a rich collection of art treasures, including Giotto's incredible frescoed chapel, and its many piazzas and arcaded streets are a pleasure to explore.

The city's wealth grew during the 13th century when it was controlled by the counts of Carrara, who encouraged cultural and artistic prosperity and established the Stadium, the forerunner of the city's university, which is regarded as one of the country's most prestigious.

Orientation
The main train station is at the northern edge of the centre in Piazzale della Stazione. Walk south along Corso del Popolo, through the city wall and continue along Corso Gari-

baldi, through piazzas Eremitani and Garibaldi and into Corso Cavour. It continues into Piazza della Frutta and Piazza delle Erbe, separated by the Palazzo della Ragione.

Information
Tourist Offices There is an APT at the train station (☎ 049-875 20 77) and one closer to the city centre at Riviera Mugnai 8 (☎ 049-875 06 55). There is a small office in Piazza Eremitani (☎ 049-875 11 53). The main offices open Monday to Saturday from 8 am to 6 pm, Sunday from 8.30 am to 12.30 pm, and produce the useful *Padova Today* brochure, which is free, or *Padova Benvenuti* which costs L1000. The APTs will also change money at good rates.

Post & Telecommunications The post office is at Corso Garibaldi 33, and the ASST telephone office is a few doors away at No 7. Other phones are at Riviera dei Ponti Romani 40. Address poste restante mail to 35100 Padua. The city's telephone code is 049.

Emergency For a police emergency, call ☎ 113. The police headquarters (☎ 83 31 11) are at Via Santa Chiara, on the corner of Riviera Ruzante. Medical assistance is provided by the Ospedale Civile (☎ 821 11 11), Via Giustiniani 1.

Things to See
The city offers a special ticket that allows you entry to the main monuments and sells for L10,000. It can be purchased at the main sites.

Start at the **Scrovegni Chapel** with its magnificent series of frescoes by Giotto – for many, the main reason for going to Padua. Inside the Arena Gardens, named after the ruins of a Roman amphitheatre, the Scrovegni Chapel was commissioned by Enrico Scrovegni in 1303 as a burial place for his father, who had been denied a Christian burial because of his usury. Giotto created the 38 frescoes between 1304 and 1306 to

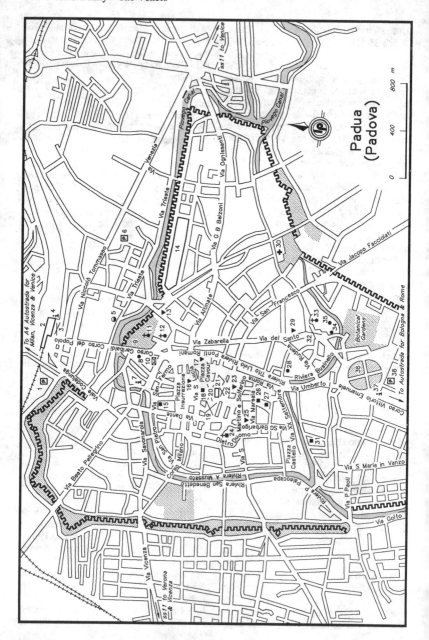

Padua (Padova)

■ PLACES TO STAY		5	Bus Station
		6	Parking
15	Albergo Sant'Antonio	7	Riviera Mugnai Tourist Office
18	Leon Bianco	8	SIP Telephones
26	Albergo Pace	9	Arena Gardens
27	Albergo Pavia	10	Main Post Office
31	Ostello Città di Padova	11	Scrovegni Chapel
		12	Church of the Hermits & Tourist Office
▼ PLACES TO EAT		14	University
		19	Piazza dei Signori
13	Pizzeria Eremitani	20	Piazza della Frutta
16	Trattoria al Pero	21	Palazzo della Ragione
17	Brek	22	Piazza delle Erbe
23	Osteria dei Fabbri	24	Duomo & Baptistry
25	Antica Desiderio	28	Police Headquarters
29	Pizzeria Al Santo	30	Ospedale Civile
		32	Piazza del Santo
OTHER		33	Basilica of St Anthony
		34	Municipal Museum
		35	Oratorio di San Giorgio
1	Parking	36	Prato della Valle
2	Main Train Station	37	Tourist Information Office
3	Piazzale della Stazione	38	Parking
4	APT Tourist Office		

illustrate the lives of Mary and Christ. Take a confusing but adequate plan of the frescoes from the entrance. The most famous scenes are the *Kiss of Judas* and the *Entombment*. The series ends with the *Last Judgment* on the entrance wall, and the Vices and Virtues are depicted around the lower parts of the walls. The chapel is invariably full, and in busier times attendants enforce strict time limits, usually of 30 minutes. It is open from 9 am to 7 pm daily except Monday, until 6 pm in winter, and entry is L8000. The ticket is also valid for the adjacent Museo Civico, a largely forgettable collection of archaeological artefacts and 19th century art.

Just outside the gardens is the 14th century **Church of the Hermits** (Chiesa degli Eremitani), which was destroyed during WW II and subsequently rebuilt. It contains a series of frescoes, which had been removed before the war, depicting the lives of St James and St Christopher by Mantegna when he was in his early 20s. The church is open from 8.15 am to midday, and in the afternoon on religious holidays.

Take Corso Garibaldi into the centre of the city, and continue along Via VIII Febbraio

for the city's **university,** the main part of which is housed in the Palazzo Bò ('Ox' in Venetian dialect, named after an inn which previously occupied the site). Established in 1221, the university is Italy's oldest after Bologna's institution. Europe's first anatomy theatre was opened here in 1594. The building may still be closed for restoration when you read this.

Continue along for Piazza delle Erbe and Piazza della Frutta, separated by the majestic **Palazzo della Ragione,** also known as the Salone for the grand hall on the upper floor. Built in the 13th and 14th centuries, the building features frescoes by Giusto de' Menabuoi and Niccolò Mireto demonstrating the astrological theories of Pietro d'Abano. The palace is open from 10 am to 6 pm except Monday, and closes earlier in winter. Entry is L4000.

West from here is the Piazza dei Signori, dominated by the 14th century **Palazzo del Capitanio,** the former residence of the Venetian ruler of the city. Heading south is the city's **Duomo,** built from plans drawn by Michelangelo. The building was altered during construction and rebuilt in 1552, so there is little left of Michelangelo's design. The 13th century **Baptistry** features a series of frescoes of the Old and New Testaments by Giusto de' Menabuoi, which were influenced by Giotto. The baptistry and cathedral are open from 9.30 am to 12.30 pm and 2.30 to 5.30 pm, but are closed on Mondays. Entry to the baptistry is L2000.

Walk along Via del Santo for Piazza del Santo, in the centre of which is Donatello's equestrian statue of *Gattamelata*, or the Honeyed Cat, as the Venetian condottiere Erasmos da Narni was known. Created by Donatello in 1453, it is believed to have been the first statue cast in bronze in Italy since antiquity.

The city's most celebrated monument, the **Basilica of St Anthony**, is at the far side of the square. Known simply to the people of Padua as **Il Santo**, the church was started in 1231 and is in the Romanesque and Gothic styles, crowned by eight domes in the Byzantine style. St Anthony, the city's patron saint and also patron saint of lost things, is buried in the sumptuous Cappella del Santo, left of the basilica's high altar. The Cappella del Beato Luca Belludi has frescoes by de'Menabuoi and the high altar has bronze bas-reliefs by Donatello. The adjoining cloisters are worth visiting for fragments of frescoes by Giotto.

On the south side of the piazza is the **Oratorio di San Giorgio**, the burial chapel of the Lupi di Soranga family of Parma, with 14th century frescoes. Next door is the **Scuola di Sant'Antonio** (St Anthony's School), containing works believed to be by Titian. The two open from 9 am to 12.30 pm and 2.30 to 4.30 pm, and entry is L1000. The **Municipal Museum**, next to the school, houses a collection of 14th to 18th century art from throughout the Veneto. The collection includes works by Giotto, Mantegna and Tintoretto. It is open from 9 am to 1.30 pm except Monday and entry is L2000.

The street next to the gallery leads to the **Botanical Gardens**, the oldest in Europe. They open from 9 am to 1 pm and 3 to 6 pm, with shorter hours in winter, and entry costs L3000.

Activities

For information about walking in the areas around the city, particularly the Euganean Hills to the south-west (see the following Around Padua section), the Club Alpino Italiano (☎ 875 08 42) has an office in Padua at Galleria San Bernardino 5.

For kayaking and canoeing, the Kayak Polo Padova (☎ 69 32 23), Via Ognissanti 69, and the Canoa Club (☎ 63 32 15), Via SS Fabiano e Sebastiano, can offer information and will advise on hiring equipment. For information about the many horse-riding tracks south of the city, contact the Scuola Padovana Equitazione (☎ 871 72 44), Via Libia 20.

Places to Stay

Padua has no shortage of budget hotels, but they fill up quickly in summer with the overflow from Venice. University holidays can mean some cheaper accommodation in student quarters, but usually for a minimum of one week. Contact the Centro Universitario (☎ 65 42 99), Via Zabarella 82, or the Cattolici Popolari (☎ 828 31 11, ext 399).

The closest camping ground, *Montegrotto Terme* (☎ 79 34 00), Strada Romana Aponense 104, is 15 km from the city at Montegrotto Terme and can be reached by city bus M. Sites are L5000 a person and there is a small charge for a tent and car. The *Ostello Città di Padova* (☎ 875 22 19), Via A Aleardi 30, is non-IYHF. Bed and breakfast is L15,000. Take bus No 3, 8, 12 or 18 from the station to Prato della Valle and then ask directions.

The *Verdi* (☎ 66 34 50), Via Dondi dell'Orologio 7, has basic, clean singles/doubles for L30,000/38,000. *Albergo Pavia* (☎ 66 15 58), Via dei Papafava 11, has rooms from L32,000/40,000. The *Albergo Pace* (☎ 875 15 66), a few doors down at No 3, has rooms for the same price. To reach the hotels, follow Corso del Popolo until it becomes Via Roma, then turn right into Via Marsala.

The *Albergo Sant'Antonio* (☎ 875 13 93), Via San Fermo 118, at the northern end of Via Dante, has rooms from L38,000/50,000, and the three-star *Leon Bianco* (☎ 875 08 14), Piazzetta Pedrocchi 12, near Piazza della Frutta, has rooms from L94,000/118,000.

Places to Eat

The city's cuisine mimics that of other cities in the Veneto. Some of the local specialities include *risi e bisi* (risotto with peas) and thick pasta known as *bigoli*. The area is a large chicken producer and many dishes are based on poultry. The nearby Euganean Hills produce excellent wines, in particular the Colli Euganei whites.

Daily markets are held in the piazzas around the Palazzo della Ragione, with fresh produce sold in the Piazza delle Erbe and Piazza della Frutta, and bread, cheese and salami sold in the shops under the porticoes.

The cheapest place to eat a meal is *Brek* in Piazza Cavour, a self-service restaurant with pasta dishes from L4000 and main courses from L5000. *Pizzeria al Santo*, Via del Santo 63, has good pizzas from L5000. *Pizzeria Eremitani*, at the end of Via Porciglia near the bus station, has excellent pizzas from L5000. *Antica Desiderio*, Via S G Barbarigo 3, is a small trattoria/pizzeria serving some traditional meals. Main courses start at L6000 and the cover charge is L1500. *Trattoria Al Pero*, Via Santa Lucia 38, is great for a cheap meal, and features several typical dishes from L7000. *Osteria dei Fabbri*, Via dei Fabbri 13, has a good atmosphere and pasta from L7000.

The city's famous *Caffè Pedrocchi*, just off Via Cavour, was the meeting place for 19th century liberals and one of Stendhal's favourite haunts. It warrants a visit, although it has lost most of its grandeur. A cheaper and equally atmospheric alternative is *Vescovi*, in the market building in Piazza delle Erbe.

Entertainment

The city hosts the Notturni d'Arte festival from July to September each year, featuring concerts and outdoor events, many for free. The APT has details. Each summer, Italian and some foreign films are shown from 8 pm at an outdoor cinema in the Arena Gardens.

Some opera and theatrical performances are held at the Teatro Comunale Verdi (☎ 3 94 79), Via Livello 32. One of the better nightclubs is New Lola-Lola, Riviera Ponti Romani.

Getting There & Away

Autotrasporti Padova (ATP) buses (☎ 820 68 11) depart from Piazzale Boschetti, 200 metres south of the train station, for Montegrotto, the Euganean Hills, Trieste, Venice, Este, Mantua, Piacenza and Genoa. By train (☎ 875 18 00), the city is connected to Milan, Venice and Bologna, and is easily accessible from most other major cities.

By car and motorcycle, the A4 Turin-Venice autostrada passes to the north, while the A13, which connects the city with Bologna, starts at the southern edge of town. The two autostradas are connected by a ring road. The Padova Ovest exit will take you to a major car park near the train station and the Padova Sud exit connects with a car park near Prato della Valle. Hitchhikers can take the ss11, which connects Vicenza with Venice and passes through the city. The ss16 connects the city with southern towns, including Rovigo.

Getting Around

To reach the centre of town from the station, take ATP bus No 10 along Corso del Popolo, which becomes Corso Garibaldi, to the historic centre, otherwise it is a 10-minute walk. A 24-hour tourist bus ticket, allowing unlimited travel, is available for L2500.

AROUND PADUA

Just south-west of Padua, along the A13 autostrada or the ss16, are the **Euganean Hills** (Colli Euganei), dotted with vineyards and good walking trails. The Club Alpino Italiano in Padua can provide information about trails and accommodation. The Consorzio Vini DOC dei Colli Euganei (☎ 049-521 18 96), Via Vescovi 35 in Luvigliano, can provide details of the vineyards.

If you are driving, follow the Euganean Hills Wine Road (Strada dei Vini dei Colli

Euganei), identified by special signposts throughout the hills, which will take you on a tour of many vineyards. Pick up a map and itinerary book from the APT in Padua. Most of the vineyards are open to the public and some offer accommodation.

The medieval town of **Montagnana** has a tourist information office (☎ 0429-8 13 20), Piazza Trieste, which can assist with information about the region. The city also has a youth hostel, the *Rocca degli Alberi* (☎ 0429-81 07 62), Castello degli Alberi, housed in a former castle and open from April to October. Bed and breakfast is L12,000 and it is close to the town's train station.

TREVISO

A small, pleasant city with historical importance as a Roman centre, Treviso is worth a stopover when heading north for the Dolomites. However, the complete absence of one-star accommodation means there are no cheap rooms in the city. If you are prepared to pay higher rates, it can make a good base from which to see Venice and the smaller towns leading up into the Alps. It is an extremely prosperous town, and claims Luciano Benetton as its favourite son. The

company's factories can be found around the city.

The APT tourist office (☎ 0422-54 76 32) is in the Palazzo Scotti, Via Toniolo 41, south of Piazza dei Signori along Via Santa Margherita. It opens Monday to Friday from 8.30 am to 12.30 pm and 3 to 6 pm, Saturday to midday. The city's telephone code is 0422.

Things to See & Do

The APT promotes Treviso as the *città d'acqua* (city of water) and compares it with Venice. While the Sile River, which weaves through the centre, is quite beautiful in parts, the city is not a patch on La Serenissima. Boat cruises on the *Silis* (☎ 78 86 63) and *Altino* (☎ 78 86 71) operate on the Sile between Treviso and the Venetian lagoon, but only in summer.

The city's other claim to fame as the *città dipinta* (frescoed city) is a little more worthy. Pick up a copy of *Treviso Città Dipinta* from the APT and follow the fresco itinerary, which takes in the **Cathedral of San Pietro**, with frescoes by Pordenone, and the **Church of San Pietro**, with frescoes by Tomaso.

Places to Stay & Eat

The best accommodation options are at *Al*

■ PLACES TO STAY

9 Albergo Due Mori
12 Albergo Vicenza
24 Albergo Italia
25 Casa San Raffaele

▼ PLACES TO EAT

8 Osteria Torre Vecchia
16 Pizzeria Bella Vicenza
20 Polenta e Baccala
27 Pizzeria al Pellegrino

OTHER

1 Olympic Theatre
2 Olympic Theatre & Tourist Office
3 Church of the Holy Crown

4 Police Headquarters
5 Palazzo Thiene
6 Palazzo Valmarana
7 Municipal Museum
10 Piazza dei Signori
11 Main Post Office
13 SIP Telephones
14 Piazza del Duomo & Duomo
15 Basilica Palladiana
17 Tourist Office
18 Palazzo Porto Breganze
19 Car Park
21 Bus Station
22 Piazzale Stazione
23 Railway Station
26 Piazzale della Vittoria
28 Mt Berico Basilica
29 Villa Valmarana
30 La Rotonda

Cuore (☎ 41 09 29), Piazzale Duca d'Aosta, which has singles/doubles from L35,000/45,000 and also has a good, cheap restaurant, or the *Beccherie* (☎ 54 08 71), Piazza Ancillotto 10, with rooms for about the same price. Its restaurant is one of the city's best and a meal could cost L40,000 per person. *Ristorante Al Dante*, Piazza Garibaldi 6, is one of the better budget options, with pasta dishes from L6000.

Getting There & Away

The bus station (☎ 54 58 47), Lungosile Mattei, near the train station, serves Lamarca Trevigiani coaches which run between Venice and Treviso, and Ferrari coaches which operate to Turin, Padua, Belluno, Venice, Udine and smaller towns in the area. Trains (☎ 54 13 52) arrive at Piazzale Duca d'Aosta and connect the city with Venice, Belluno, Padua and major cities to the south and west. By car, the ss53 connects the city with Venice, Padua and the A27 autostrada.

VICENZA

This city is the centre for Italian textile manufacture and a leader in the development and production of computer components,

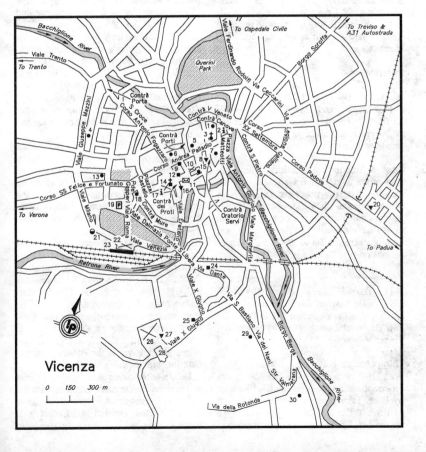

Vicenza

0   150   300 m

making it one of the country's wealthiest cities. However, most people come to Vicenza to see the work of Andrea di Pietro della Gondola, better known as Palladio, whose designs have influenced architects worldwide. Vicenza flourished as the Roman Vicentia and in 1404 became part of the Venetian Republic, sharing the city's fortunes, as the many Venetian Gothic palaces demonstrate.

Orientation

From the train station, in the gardens of the Campo Marzo, walk straight ahead along Via Roma into Piazzale De Gasperi. From here, the main street, Corso Andrea Palladio, leads into the centre. Piazza Duomo and the main tourist office are to the right, about 200 metres along.

Information

Tourist Office The Piazza Duomo office of the APT (☎ 0444-54 41 22) is not as useful as the office at Piazza Matteotti 12 (☎ 0444-32 08 54). The latter opens from 9 am to 12.30 pm and 2.30 to 6 pm daily, except Sunday afternoons.

Post & Telecommunications The main post office is at Contrà Garibaldi near the Duomo. Address poste restante mail to 36100 Vicenza. The SIP telephone office is just around the corner in Contrà Vescovado, or at Piazzale Giusti (the main office), and both open from 8 am to 9.30 pm. The telephone code for Vicenza is 0444.

Emergency For a police emergency, call ☎ 113. The police headquarters (☎ 54 33 33) are at Viale Mazzini 24. For medical assistance, go to the Ospedale Civile (☎ 99 37 23), Via Rodolfi, north of the city centre from Piazza Matteotti.

Things to See & Do

From 16 March to 15 October, the tourist office sponsors a programme called Vicenza by Bike. Take your passport to the Piazza Matteotti office and they'll give you a bike for the day, for free, and a map and guide to the city's Palladian buildings. It is the best way to see the city. De Val Viaggi (☎ 32 24 14), Via Giuriolo 26, organises city tours on Saturday and Sunday from L15,000.

Start in Piazza Castello, which features several grand palaces, including the **Palazzo Porto-Breganze**, on the western side, designed by Palladio and built by Scamozzi, one of the city's leading 16th century architects. The city's main street, Corso Andrea Palladio, runs north-east from the square and is lined with palaces. Several hundred metres along is Piazza dei Signori, reached by Corso Cavour, and dominated by the immense **Basilica Palladiana**, built by Palladio from 1549 over an earlier Gothic building and recognised as one of his finest works. The adjoining 12th century bell tower gives an idea of the basilica's original appearance. The basilica is open Tuesday to Saturday from 9.30 am to midday and 2.30 to 5 pm, Sunday from 10 am to midday. Palladio's **Loggia del Capitanio**, on the north-western side of the piazza on the corner of Via del Monte, was left unfinished at his death and shows his flair for colour.

South-west from the basilica is the **Duomo**, a dull church destroyed during WW II and later rebuilt, although some of its artworks were saved. North-west along Corso Fogazzaro from the cathedral is the Palladian Palazzo Valmarana, built in 1566. Contrà Porti, reached by way of Contrà Riale, is one of the city's most majestic streets. The **Palazzo Thiene** at No 12, by Lorenzo da Bologna, was originally intended to occupy the entire block. Palladio's **Palazzo Porto-Barbaran** at No 11 features a double row of columns. His **Palazzo Valmarana** at No 16 is considered one of his more eccentric creations, and he also built the **Palazzo Isoppo da Porto** at No 21, which remains unfinished. Across the Bacchiglione River is the **Palazzo Capra-Querini**, with the city's largest park.

Return to the centre along Contrà Zanella and into the Piazza Santo Stefano, with the church of the same name. North along Corso Andrea Palladio and left into Contrada di Santa Corona is the **Church of the Holy**

Top Left : Entrance to the Galleria from the Piazza del Duomo, Milan (JG)
Top Right : Colle di Val d'Elsa, Tuscany (JG)
Bottom Left : Roman aqueduct, Spoleto, Umbria (JG)
Bottom Right : The Rialto Bridge in Venice (APT)

Landscapes

Crown (Chiesa della Santa Corona), built from 1261 by the Dominicans to house a relic from Christ's crown of thorns. Inside are the *Baptism of Christ* by Giovanni Bellini and *Adoration of the Magi* by Veronese.

Corso Andrea Palladio ends at the **Olympic Theatre**, started by Palladio in 1580 and completed by Scamozzi after Palladio's death. Considered one of the purest creations of Renaissance architecture, the theatre design was based on Palladio's studies of Roman structures. Scamozzi's street scene is modelled on the ancient Greek city of Thebes. He created an impressive illusion of depth and perspective by slanting the streets upward towards the rear of the set. It was inaugurated in 1580 with a performance of *Oedipus Rex* and operas are still performed here. It should not be missed. It is open from 9.30 am to 12.30 pm and 3 to 5.30 pm daily, except Sunday when it opens from 9.30 am to midday. Entry is L5000. The ticket is also valid for the nearby **Municipal Museum** in the Palazzo Chiericati, open the same hours, which contains works by local artists as well as Tiepolo and Veronese.

South of the city, along Via Dante or Viale X Giugno, is the **Mt Berico Basilica** and the Piazzale della Vittoria, set on top of the hill, with a magnificent view over the city. The basilica was the site of two alleged appearances by the Virgin Mary in 1426. The current 18th century building incorporates a 15th century Gothic church. An impressive 18th century colonnade runs most of the way along Viale X Giugno to the church at the top of the hill. Catch city bus No 8.

A 10-minute walk back along Viale X Giugno is the **Villa Valmarana 'ai Nani'**, featuring brilliant frescoes by Giambattista and Giandomenico Tiepolo. The 'ai nani' ('dwarves' in Italian) refers to the statues perched on top of the gates surrounding the property. The villa opens from 10 am to midday on Wednesday, Friday, Saturday and Sunday and all afternoons except Monday. Hours vary, so call ☎ 22 18 03 to check. Entry is L5000.

Signs mark the path to Palladio's Villa Capra, better known as **La Rotonda**. Considered one of the finest buildings ever constructed, the Rotonda is also one of the most copied, with architects using it as a base for Palladian buildings in Europe and the USA. The gardens open Tuesday, Wednesday and Thursday from 10 am to midday and 3 to 6 pm, and the villa opens the same hours but only on Wednesdays. Entry to the gardens is L3000, and L5000 to the villa. Bus No 8 stops nearby.

Palladio's Rotonda

Places to Stay

Many hotels close during the summer, particularly in August, so never arrive without a booking. At other times you should have no problems getting a room.

The closest camping, the *Campeggio Vicenza* (☎ 58 23 11), Strada Pelosa, is near the Vicenza Est exit from the A4 autostrada. Sites, with car, are L17,500 plus L6,800 per person. The city has a hostel, the *Madonna di Monte Berico* (☎ 54 38 30), Contrà San Marco 3, with bed and breakfast for L30,000. It is not an IYHF hostel. Bus Nos 4 and 9 will drop you off close by.

The *Albergo Italia* (☎ 32 10 43), Viale Risorgimento, near the train station, has singles/doubles from L30,000/35,000. *Vicenza* (☎ 32 15 12), Stradella dei Nodari 5-7, near Piazza dei Signori, has rooms from L30,000/40,000. The *Due Mori* (☎ 32 18 86), nearby at Contrà Do Rode 26, has rooms from L39,000/51,000. One of the best choices is the *Casa San Raffaele* (☎ 32 36 63), Viale X Giugno 10, in a former convent behind the colonnade leading to Mt Berico, with rooms from L45,000/60,000.

Places to Eat

A large produce market is held each Tuesday

and Thursday in Piazza delle Erbe. *Vini al Chiampo*, Contrà Pescherie Vecchie near Piazza delle Erbe, is an old wine bar with cheap local wines. *Pizzeria Bella Vicenza*, Contrà dei Proti, has excellent pizzas from L6000, as does *Pizzeria al Pellegrino* at Piazzale della Vittoria. *Polenta e Baccalà*, Viale della Pace 7, is a typical trattoria and a meal could cost L15,000. *Osteria Torre Vecchia*, Contrà Oratorio dei Servi 23, serves good local dishes and a meal will cost over L30,000.

Entertainment
Vivi Vicenza is the city's summer concert festival and features international jazz artists and classical performances for free in the city's churches and piazzas. For information, call ☎ 32 71 41. For details about performances in the Olympic Theatre, contact the APT or call ☎ 32 37 81.

Getting There & Away
FTV buses (☎ 54 43 33) operate from Viale Milano near the train station for Padua, Thiene, Asiago, Bassano, Verona and into towns throughout the nearby Berici Mountains. Trains (☎ 32 50 46) connect the city with Venice, Milan, Padua, Verona, Treviso and with smaller towns in the north. By car, the city is on the A4 autostrada connecting Milan with Venice. The ss11 connects the city with Verona and Padua, the best route for hitchhikers. There is a large car park near Piazza Castello and the station.

Getting Around
The city is best seen on foot, but bus Nos 1, 2, 3 and 7 connect the train station with the city centre.

AROUND VICENZA
As Venice's maritime power waned in the 15th century, the city's wealthy inhabitants turned their attentions inland, acquiring land to build sumptuous villas (see also the Brenta Riviera section earlier in this chapter). Forbidden from building castles by the Venetian senate which feared a landscape dotted with well-defended forts, the city's patricians set about building thousands of villas, of which about 3000 remain. Most are inaccessible to the public and many are run down.

The APT in Vicenza can provide reams of information about the villas, including a booklet entitled *Vicenza – the Villas*. The de Agostini map, *Ville Venete*, sells for about L7000 from newsstands and is one of the few complete maps. Drivers should have little trouble planning an itinerary. Otherwise, a good route is to take the FTV bus north from Vicenza to Thiene, passing through Caldogno and Villaverla, and then to continue on to Lugo.

The Villa Godi-Valmarana, now known as the **Malinverni**, at Lonedo di Lugo, was Palladio's first villa. A good driving itinerary is to take the ss11 through Montecchio Maggiore and continue south for Lonigo, Pojana Maggiore and then head north for Longare and back to Vicenza. A round trip of 100 km, the route takes in about a dozen villas.

There is an IYHF hostel a few km south of Pojana Maggiore at Montagnana, reached by bus from Vicenza, which enables you to plan a trip through the region. It's called the *Rocca degli Alberi* (☎ 0429-81 07 62) and is in the Castello degli Alberi, a 500-metre walk from the train station, or west of Piazza Vittorio Emanuele along Via Matteotti. A bed is L12,000 a night.

Check with the APT in Vicenza for details of the Concerti in Villa Estate, a series of classical concerts held in villas around Vicenza each summer. Also ask about accommodation, which is available in some villas.

BELLUNO
Belluno is a beautiful little town at the foot of the Dolomites and makes a good base for exploration into the mountains. It is worth a day trip from Venice either by train or bus and is also easily accessible from Treviso.

The tourist office, the Azienda di Promozione Turistica delle Prealpi e Dolomiti Bellunesi (☎ 0437-94 00 83), Via Rodolfo Psaro 21, produces a feast of information on walking, trekking, skiing and other sporting endeavours, and should be visited if you are planning to head into the Dolomites. The Comunità Montana Bellunese (☎ 0437-94 02 83), Via San Lucano 7, can assist with details on Alpine refuges and mountain guides. The town's telephone code is 0437.

The *Camping Park Nevegal* (☎ 90 81 43), Via Nevegal 347, is about 10 km from the town at Nevegal and is reached by Autolinee Dolomiti bus from Belluno. The *Casa per Ferie Giovanni XXIII* (☎ 94 44 60), Piazza Piloni 11, near the centre of Belluno, has beds from L14,000 a night. The *Albergo Taverna* (☎ 2 51 92), Via Cipro 7, has singles/doubles from L15,000/25,000, while the three-star *Mirella* (☎ 94 18 60), Via Don Minzoni 6, has rooms from L50,000/65,000. Most of the town's restaurants are around the central Piazza dei Martiri.

Autolinee Dolomiti bus services (☎ 94 12 37), Piazzale della Stazione, depart from the station at the western edge of town for Agordo, Cortina d'Ampezzo, Feltre and smaller towns in the mountains and south of town. Trains (☎ 94 44 38) are less regular to northern towns but there are services to Cortina as well as Treviso and Venice.

VERONA

Forever associated with Romeo and Juliet, Verona has much more to offer than the relics of a tragic love story. Known as *piccola Roma* (little Rome) for its importance as a Roman city, its golden era was during the 13th and 14th centuries under the rule of the Scaliger family, a period noted for the savage family feuding on which Shakespeare based his play. It is one of Italy's most beautiful cities, and is definitely worth visiting.

Orientation

Old Verona is small, but there is much to see and it is a popular base for exploring surrounding towns. The train station and bus depot are both in Piazza XXV Aprile. Turn right as you leave the station, and walk along Corso Porta Nuova to Piazza Brà, 15 minutes away. From the piazza, walk along Via Mazzini and turn left at Via Cappello to reach Piazza delle Erbe.

Information

Tourist Office The APT has two branches, at Via Dietro Anfiteatro 6B (☎ 045-59 28 28), just off Piazza Brà and facing the Roman Arena, and at Piazza delle Erbe 42 (☎ 045-803 00 86). Both open from 8 am to 8 pm, except Sunday, when they open from 8.30 am to 12.30 pm. They offer concise and useful information on the city and its frequent cultural events.

Money The Banca d'America e d'Italia at Porta Nuova 135 has an exchange facility and will also advance cash on Visa and MasterCard. On weekends and holidays, currency exchange booths are at the APT near the Arena and at the station.

Post & Telecommunications The main post office is at Piazza Viviani 7. It opens from 8 am to 6.30 pm Monday to Friday, to 12.30 pm Saturday. Address poste restante mail to 37100 Verona. SIP telephones are at Via Leoncino 45, near the Arena, and they are open until midnight. Verona's telephone code is 045.

Emergency For a police emergency, call ☎ 113. The police headquarters (☎ 59 67 77) are at Lungadige Porta Vittoria, near Via San Francesco. The city's Guardia Medica (☎ 91 32 22) provides medical services from 8 pm to 8 am and usually comes to you. Otherwise, the Ospedale Civile Maggiore (☎ 93 11 11) is at Piazza A Stefani, north-west from Ponte Vittoria.

Things to See & Do

The pink marble Roman amphitheatre, known as the **Arena**, in Piazza Brà, was built in the 1st century AD and is now Verona's opera house. It was one of the largest Roman amphitheatres and survived a 12th century earthquake which destroyed most of its outside wall. The interior, which can seat 22,000, survived intact. The arena is open from 8 am to 6.30 pm and entry is L6000.

Walk along Via Mazzini to Via Cappello and **Juliet's House** (Casa di Giulietta), and rub the left breast of the bronze statue of

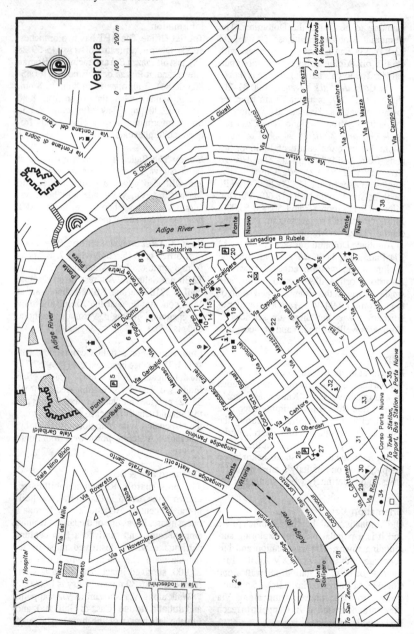

■	**PLACES TO STAY**	14	Piazza dei Signori
		15	Palazzo degli Scaligeri
3	Villa Francescatti	16	Tombs of the Scaligers
6	Casa della Giovane	17	Tourist Information Office &
10	Albergo Mazzanti		Piazza delle Erbe
18	Albergo Aurora	19	Lamberti Tower
29	Albergo Ciopeta	20	Parking
		21	Main Post Office
▼	**PLACES TO EAT**	22	Bottega del Vino
		23	Juliet's House
9	Ristorante Maffei	24	Former Arsenal
12	Osteria al Duca	25	Porta Borsari
13	Osteria Sottoriva	26	Parking
30	Pizzeria Liston	27	SS Apostoli
		28	Castelvecchio
	OTHER	31	Piazza Brà
		32	Tourist Information Office
1	Castel San Pietro	33	Arena
2	Roman Theatre	34	Teatro Filarmonico
4	Cathedral	35	SIP Telephones
5	Parking	36	Porta Leoni
7	Palazzo Forti & Gallery of Modern Art	37	Church of San Fermo
8	Church of Sant'Anastasia	38	Police Headquarters
11	Loggia del Consiglio		

Juliet by the entrance if you require a new lover (or so the locals say). Shakespeare created the characters of Romeo and Juliet, but the Capulets and Montagues did exist in the city. The Capulets' name is derived from Cappello, as they were a family of hatters, hence the street name. The house and famous balcony are open from 8 am to 6.30 pm and entry is L5000.

Farther along the street is the **Porta Leoni**, one of the gates to the old Roman Verona. The other is the **Porta Borsari** at the bottom end of Corso Porta Borsari. At the end of Via Leoni is the **Church of San Fermo**, which is actually two churches: the upper building was added in the 13th century by the Benedictines over the original 8th century Romanesque structure.

North of the Arena is **Piazza delle Erbe**, the former site of the Roman forum. Lined with the characteristic pink marble palaces of Verona, the piazza today remains the lively centre of the city, but the permanent market stalls in its centre detract from its beauty. In the piazza is the **Fountain of Madonna Verona**. The square is lined with some of Verona's most sumptuous palaces,

including the **Palazzo Maffei**, at the northwestern end, with the adjoining 14th century **Torre del Gardello** and the **Casa Mazzanti**, with impressive 16th century murals.

Separating the Piazza delle Erbe from the Piazza dei Signori is the **Arco della Costa**. Suspended in this archway is a tusk which locals believe will fall on the first 'just' person to walk beneath it. In several centuries, it has never fallen, not even on the various popes who have paraded beneath it.

In the Piazza dei Signori, the 15th century **Loggia del Consiglio**, the former city council building, is regarded as Verona's finest Renaissance building. Opposite is the **Palazzo degli Scaligeri**, the Scaligers' residence now used by the local government, which was partly decorated by Giotto. Ascend the **Lamberti Tower** by elevator or on foot for a great view of the city. It is open from 8 am to 6.30 pm daily and costs L3000.

Pass under the arch at the far end of the piazza for the **Tombs of the Scaligers** (Arche Scaligere), superb Gothic mausoleums. The tombs feature portrayals of ladders, the Scaliger family emblem. In the doorway of the adjacent **Church of Santa**

Maria Antica is the tomb and an equestrian statue of Cangrande I ('Big Dog', as the popular Scaliger leader was known). The statue is a copy, the real one is in the Castelvecchio.

Nearby at Via Arche Scaligere 2 is the former home of Romeo and the Montecchi family, upon whom Shakespeare based the Montague characters of his play. It is now a restaurant, the Osteria al Duca (see the following Places to Eat section).

North from here in Piazza Sant'Anastasia is the church of the same name. The city's largest church, the Sant'Anastasia was started in 1290 and is mainly in the Gothic style. Inside are numerous art works, including Pisanello's St George Setting out to Free the Princess. Walk along Via Ponte di Pietra for the city's cathedral, with its Romanesque main doors and Titian's Assumption.

Across Ponte di Pietra is the Roman Theatre, one of Italy's best preserved, now used for performances of Shakespeare plays. It sits beneath the Castel San Pietro, built by the Austrians on the site of a Roman castle. The summit view is worth the 10-minute walk. The San Girolamo Convent on the hill houses the city's Archaeological Museum. Both the museum and theatre open from 8 am to 6.30 pm in summer, to 1.30 pm in winter, except Monday, and entry to both is L5000.

The city's Gallery of Modern Art, housed in the Palazzo Forti, Via Forti 1, features a collection of 20th century Italian and other European art. It opens from 8 am to 6.30 pm except Monday and entry is L4000.

South-west from Piazza delle Erbe, along Corso Cavour, is the Castelvecchio, the Scaligers' residence and fortress. The building was used by Napoleon as a barracks, but now houses a museum and gallery. Among the paintings are works by Bellini, Tiepolo, Carpaccio and Veronese's Descent from the Cross. The museum opens from 8 am to 6.30 pm, except Mondays, and entry is L5000. The Ponte Scaligero spanning the Adige River was rebuilt after being destroyed by the Germans during WW II.

North-west along Rigaste San Zeno, about one km from the Castelvecchio, is the Church of San Zeno Maggiore, a masterpiece of Romanesque architecture. This church in honour of the city's patron saint was founded in the 5th century, although the current church dates from the 12th century. One of the highlights is Mantegna's Madonna & Saints, near the high altar.

Places to Stay

The beautifully restored IYHF youth hostel, the Villa Francescati (☎ 59 03 60), Salita Fontana del Ferro 15, should be your first choice. Bed and breakfast is L14,000 a night and an IYHF card is not necessary. Next door is a camping ground run by the hostel management. Catch bus No 2 from the station to Piazza Isolo, then follow the signs. The Casa della Giovane (☎ 59 68 80), Via Pigna 7, is for women only and costs L11,000 a night. It's just off Via Garibaldi – catch bus No 2 and ask the driver where to get off.

One of the best located hotels in the city, overlooking Piazza delle Erbe, is the Albergo Aurora (☎ 59 47 17), Via Pelliciai 2, with singles/doubles from L40,000/50,000. The Albergo Mazzanti (☎ 800 68 13), Via Mazzanti 6, just off Piazza dei Signori has rooms for about the same price. Otherwise, try Albergo Ciopeta (☎ 800 68 43), Vicolo Teatro Filarmonico 2, near Piazza Brà, with singles/doubles from L45,000/60,000.

Places to Eat

Known for its fresh produce, its crisp Soave (a dry white wine) and its boiled meat, Verona offers good-quality eating at reasonable prices. The best bet for cheap meals is Brek, facing the Arena in Piazza Brà. Pasta dishes start at L4000 and the view across the piazza to the Arena is unbeatable. The city also has one of Italy's few McDonald's, just south of Piazza Brà, outside the wall. Pizzeria Liston, Via dietro Listone 19, near the Castelvecchio, has pizza with mascarpone cheese and rucola (a type of lettuce) for L8500, but the cover charge is L2000.

The Osteria al Duca, Via Arche Scaligere 2, in Romeo's family home, has a good set menu for L14,000. Osteria Sottoriva, on the

Adige River between Ponte Navi and Ponte Nuovo, is a small traditional restaurant, popular with locals. A meal could cost L15,000. The *Bottega del Vino*, Vicolo Scudo di Francia 37, has pasta dishes from L10,000 and the frescoes are worth seeing. The excellent *Ristorante Maffei* in the Palazzo Maffei, Piazza delle Erbe 38, has pasta dishes from L10,000 and main dishes from L20,000.

Try the small bar, *Birreria Mazzini*, Via Mazzini, near the Arena, which serves local wines for L1500 a glass and panini from L3000. Giovanni Zampieri's *wine bar* at Via Alberto Mario 23, near the Arena, has local wines from L600 a glass.

Entertainment
Throughout the year the city hosts musical and cultural events, culminating in the season of opera and ballet from July to September at the Arena. The cheapest tickets are L17,000. There is a lyric-symphonic season in winter at the 18th century Teatro Filarmonico (☎ 800 28 80), Via Mutilati 4, just south of Piazza Brà, and Shakespeare is performed at the Roman Theatre in summer. Information and tickets for these events are available at the Ente Lirico Arena di Verona (☎ 59 01 09), Piazza Brà 28.

Getting There & Away
Verona-Villafranca Airport (☎ 51 30 39) is 10 km south-west of the city and serves flights from major Italian cities and Paris. City buses depart for the airport from the bus station near Porta Nuova.

The main Azienda Provinciale Trasporti bus terminal (☎ 800 41 29) is in the piazza in front of the station. Buses leave for surrounding areas, Mantua, Ferrara and Brescia. By train, Verona is directly linked to Milan, Venice, Padua, Mantua, Modena, Florence, Rome, Austria and Germany. By car, the city is at the intersection of the Serenissima A4 (Milan-Venice) and Brennero A22 autostradas.

Getting Around
AMT bus (☎ 52 12 00) Nos 1, 2 and 8

connect the station with Piazza Brà, and No 32 with Piazza delle Erbe. Cars are banned from the city centre in the mornings and early afternoon, but are permitted if you are staying at a hotel. There are free car parks at Via Città di Nimes near the train station, and Piazza Cittadella just south of Piazza Brà. For a taxi, call ☎ 803 05 65.

Friuli-Venezia Giulia

This region's complex ethnic make-up matches its geographic diversity. Although strongly Italian, pockets of Friuli-Venezia Giulia bear influences of other cultures which have dominated life since Roman times.

It is a region of mountains, hills, plains and lagoons, and is wedged between the Adriatic Sea, Slovenia, Austria and the Veneto. After the Romans came the Visigoths, Attila's Huns, the Lombards and Charlemagne's Franks, each leaving their mark on the countryside. The Patriarchate of Aquileia, formed in the second half of the 10th century, unified the local church and remained autonomous from the church in Rome and from other states for several centuries. Friuli lost its independence to Venice in 1420, and in 1797 it fell to the Austrians. Western Friuli joined Italy in 1866, but it was not until after WW I that Eastern Friuli, comprising Gorizia, Trieste, Istria and Dalmatia, joined the unified country and the name Friuli-Venezia Giulia was coined.

A long-running border dispute with Tito's Yugoslavia was settled in 1947, following a long period of Allied occupation, when the Istrian peninsula was ceded to Yugoslavia. The Italians kept Trieste but the town of Gorizia was divided between the two countries.

Today, the old Friulian dialect is spoken is small areas south of the Alps. Udine's appearance is vaguely Venetian; Trieste, which was rebuilt by the Hapsburgs, looks Austrian; Aquileia preserves Roman ruins; and Gorizia is strongly Slavonic.

AUSTRIA

CARNIC ALPS

Mt Zoncolan
(1740 m)

Tarvisio

CARNIA

Forni di
Sopra

Tolmezzo

Sella
Nevea

Lago di
Cavazzo

JULIAN ALPS

SLOVENIA

Lago di
Cà Zul

Lago di
Tramonti

Lago di
Cà Selva

THE
VENETO

A23

Cividale
del Friuli

Udine

Pordenone

Meduna River

Tagliamento River

A23

Gorizia

A4

A28

Stella River

Como River

Monfalcone

Duino

Aquileia

Isonzo River

Gulf
of
Panzano

Friuli-Venezia
Giulia

Marano
Lagoon

Grado
Lagoon

Miramare

Villa Opicina

Lignano
Sabbiadoro

Grado

Muggia
Bay

TRIESTE

0   15   30 km

ADRIATIC SEA

The region is small and most parts are easily accessible, although the northern reaches can be difficult to get to by public transport. Nevertheless, it offers good beaches along the Adriatic and good to excellent walking and climbing in the Alps. Dozens of Alpine refuges and myriad WW I mule trails will ensure enjoyment for hardened walkers. It is one of the few Italian regions where tourism has yet to take a strong hold on both the countryside and the economy.

TRIESTE

Sitting on Italy's border with Slovenia,

Trieste is where Latin and Slavonic cultures meet. Its streets are lined with opulent neo-classical palaces, a reminder of its maritime importance to the Austrian Hapsburgs during the 18th century. Trieste is worth visiting briefly as it falls a little short on attractions. However, as a transport hub it makes a logical point to start a trip into Eastern Europe. The city closes down almost completely in August, including many restaurants and hotels.

History

Known in antiquity as Tergeste, Trieste was originally a fortified settlement occupied by people of various origins, including tribes from across the Veneto, Gauls and Celts. It grew to prominence under the Romans in the 2nd century BC as an important port and trading centre. However, when the Romans founded Aquileia to the west, Trieste fell into an obscurity that was to last until the 18th century, when Austrian empress Maria Theresa saw the potential of the Adriatic city as a port. Much of the city's medieval heart was levelled to make way for fine neoclassical buildings. When Trieste became Italian in 1918, the government discovered that the city was no match for the major Adriatic ports to the south, and again it fell into decline.

Its position between the Slavonic and Latin lands has meant that the city has also been a political hotbed. The Allies occupied the city from 1945, with a watchful eye over the dispute for its possession between Italy and Yugoslavia, which was resolved in 1954 with the Italians winning the city and the Yugoslavs gaining disputed parts of the region's hinterland. Today, traffic through the city's port is growing, although its main purpose is for the massive oil tankers supplying a pipeline to Austria.

Orientation

The main train station is at the northern edge of Trieste's historic centre, in Piazza della Libertà. A 10-minute walk along Viale Miramare, which runs past the station, will take you to Via Roma, which runs through the centre to Corso Italia. Viale Miramare first leads into Piazza Dalmazia and Piazza Oberdan, from where you can catch the tram for Villa Opicina (see the Around Trieste section). An alternative route is to walk south from the station through the disused port area to Corso Cavour which leads into the main waterfront boulevard, the Riva III Novembre and Riva del Mandracchio.

Information

Tourist Office The main APT (☎ 040-42 01 82) is at the train station, and opens daily from 9 am to 1 pm and 4 to 7 pm, although it is closed on both Saturday afternoon and Sunday from October to the start of June. There is another, less useful office at Via San Niccolò 20.

Money The Banca d'America e d'Italia, Via Roma 7, is best for cash advances on credit cards and offers good exchange rates. Cambiavalute Ghega, Via Ghega 8, near the station, is open longer hours. Paterniti Viaggi SNC (☎ 040-36 61 61), Corso Cavour 7, is an American Express agent.

Post & Telecommunications The main post office is at Piazza Vittorio Veneto 1 and opens Monday to Friday from 8.30 am to 6 pm, Saturday to 12.30 pm. Poste restante mail can be addressed to 34100 Trieste.

The ASST telephone office is at Via Pascoli 9, near Piazza Garibaldi, and is open 24 hours a day. There is an SIP telephone office in Piazza Oberdan. The telephone code for Trieste is 040.

Foreign Consulates The British Consulate (☎ 30 28 84) is at Vicolo delle Ville 16; the USA has a consular agency (☎ 91 17 80) at Via Pellegrini 42. Trieste has a Consulate of the Federal Republic of Yugoslavia (☎ 41 01 25) at Strada Friuli 54 and a Consulate of Slovenia (☎ 63 61 61) at Via Carducci 29. Australian, Canadian and New Zealand residents should contact offices in Rome or Milan.

Travel Agencies The Student Travel Centre (☎ 36 18 79), Piazza Dalmazia 3, can advise on travel to the former Yugoslavia.

Medical Services The Ospedale Maggiore (☎ 77 61) is in Piazza dell'Ospedale, southeast of Via Carducci. There is a centrally located pharmacy at Via dell'Orologio 6, near Piazza dell'Unità d'Italia, or else call ☎ 192 for a 24-hour pharmacy.

Emergency For a police emergency, call ☎ 113. The police headquarters (☎ 3 79 01) are at Via del Teatro Romano.

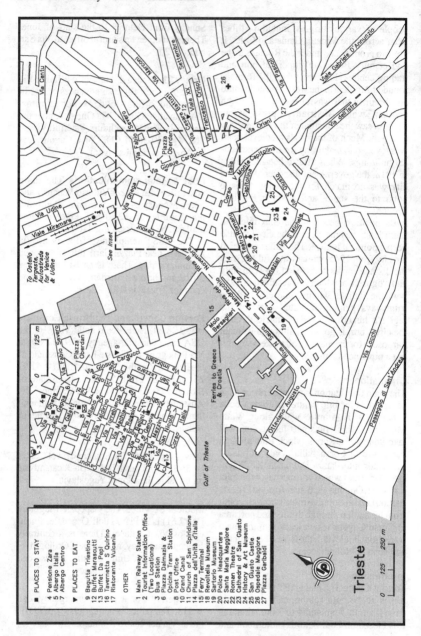

PLACES TO STAY
4 Pensione Zara
5 Albergo Italia
7 Albergo Centro

▼ PLACES TO EAT
9 Bagutta Triestino
12 Buffet Marascutti
13 Buffet Da Pepi
16 Tavernetta S Quirino
17 Ristorante Vulcania

OTHER
1 Main Railway Station
2 Tourist Information Office
   (Two Locations)
3 Bus Station
6 Piazza Dalmazia &
   Opicina Tram Station
8 Post Office
10 Grand Canal
11 Church of San Spiridione
14 Piazza dell'Unità d'Italia
15 Ferry Terminal
18 Revoltella Museum
19 Sartorio Museum
20 Police Headquarters
21 Santa Maria Maggiore
22 Roman Theatre
23 Cathedral of San Giusto
24 History & Art Museum
25 San Giusto Castle
26 Ospedale Maggiore
27 Piazza Garibaldi

Trieste

Things to See

Start in the city's grand **Piazza dell'Unità d'Italia** which features some of the city's finest buildings, and walk away from the waterfront to Via del Teatro Romano, the main cluster of Roman ruins. The theatre, built during Trajan's reign, was discovered in 1938 and is in quite bad condition. The nearby Baroque **Church of Santa Maria Maggiore** is one of Trieste's finest. From here, Via F Venezian, Via San Michele and Via San Giusto lead up to the city's only major tourist attraction, the **Hill of San Giusto**.

The **castle**, which opens from 8 am to sunset, was started in 1470 on old fortifications and expanded during Venetian rule during the next century. Inside is a museum with a small collection of armaments and antiques. It opens Tuesday to Sunday from 9.30 am to 12.30 pm. The **Cathedral of San Giusto**, completed in 1400, is the synthesis of two earlier Christian basilicas and blends northern Adriatic and Byzantine styles. The interior contains 14th century frescoes depicting St Justus, the town's patron saint. The **History & Art Museum** has religious artefacts and Egyptian oddments and opens from 9 am to 1 pm daily. Entrance is L4000. The Garden of Inscribed Stones, behind the museum, has a collection of bits of classical statues and pottery.

Going back down Via Capitolina you come to Corso Italia, the main business thoroughfare. The area of straight boulevards to the north, known as the Borgo Teresiano, was designed by Austrian urban planners in the 18th century for Empress Maria Teresa and features the pathetic-looking Grand Canal. The Serbian Orthodox **Church of San Spiridione**, on the street of the same name, was completed in 1868 and features interesting mosaics.

The city's chief museum, the **Revoltella Museum**, is at Via Diaz 27. The museum section is closed for restoration, but the art gallery opens from May to September and has a reasonable collection of modern art. It opens from 10 am to 1 pm and 3 to 7 pm except Mondays, and entry is L5000. The

other museum worth a look-in is the **Sartorio Museum** at Via Papa Giovanni XXIII 1, with a collection of Byzantine and early Greek art. It opens from 9 am to 1 pm daily, except Monday, and entry is L4000.

The **Risiera di San Sabba**, at the southern end of Trieste on Via Valmaura, was a rice-husking plant until 1943, when the occupying Germans turned it into Italy's only concentration camp and installed a crematorium, in which up to 20,000 people are believed to have been killed. The Yugoslavs closed it when they liberated the city in 1945, and in 1965 it became a national monument and a museum was established on the site. It is open Tuesday to Sunday from 9 am to 1 pm and can be reached by bus No 10.

Activities

The APT runs a walking tour each Sunday starting at 8.45 am which costs L10,000. Meet at the Stazione Marittima, Molo Bersaglieri 3. Also on Sundays, local boat operators run harbour tours from just opposite the Piazza dell'Unità d'Italia from L5000 a person.

The Club Alpino Italiano (☎ 6 03 17), Via Macchiavelli 17, can advise on walking and skiing, particularly in the region's north.

Places to Stay

Finding a room is generally easy, although in August many hotels close, so you should call ahead for a booking. The closest camping ground to the city centre is *Obelisco* (☎ 21 16 55) on the ss58 road in Villa Opicina, with sites for L4000 a person and L4000 per vehicle. Take bus No 2 or 4 from Piazza Oberdan. The *San Bartolomeo* (☎ 27 41 82), Lazzaretto di Punta Sottile, at Muggia, can be reached by bus No 7. The IYHF *Ostello Tergeste* (☎ 22 41 02), Viale Miramare 331, is five km from the station towards Venice and can be reached by bus No 36. Bed and breakfast is L17,000 and it opens all year.

The *Pensione Zara* (☎ 366 89 11), Via Rittmeyer 2, is a short walk from the station and has singles/doubles from L25,000/40,000. Closer to the city centre, *Albergo*

Centro (☎ 63 44 08), Via Roma 13, has rooms from L28,000/48,000. The two-star *Albergo Italia* (☎ 36 99 00), Via della Geppa 15, has rooms from L60,000/93,000. The *Albergo Riviera* (☎ 22 41 36), Strada Costiera 22, which is on the waterfront at the nearby town of Grignano, has rooms from L80,000/140,000. Ask at the APT about 'T For You', an innovative weekend discount deal involving some of the city's better hotels.

Places to Eat

The Friulian cuisine has been influenced by many cultures but poverty has contributed most to the region's table. Cooking over an open fire is the most traditional way of cooking, and a typical dish of *brovada* could see you eating turnips fermented with the dregs of pressed grapes. Otherwise gnocchi (potato, squash or bread dumplings) are popular, as are polenta and boiled meats, eaten in restaurants called buffets. Wines from the Eastern Hills of Friuli, stretching from near the city on the border up into the Alps, are considered the region's best. Finish dinner with a *resentin*, coffee in a cup rinsed with grappa.

Buffet Marascutti, Via Cesare Battisti 2B, is a typical restaurant specialising in boiled meats and is quite cheap. *Buffet Da Pepi*, Via Cassa di Risparmio 3, has a more varied menu, but is still cheap.

Ristorante Vulcania, Riva Nazario Sauro, on the waterfront opposite the ferry terminal, has pasta and pizzas from L6000. *Tavernetta S Quirino*, nearby at Via A Diaz 3B, is a small trattoria where a meal could cost about L15,000. *Bagutta Triestino*, Via Carducci 33, is a better restaurant and a meal will cost L30,000.

The elegant *Caffè San Marco*, Via Cesare Battisti 18, and *Caffè Tommaseo*, Piazza Tommaseo, preserve some of the city's grandeur, while Viale XX Settembre should not be missed for its gelati shops. *Zampolli*, at No 25, turns out ice-cream creations shaped like pasta and meat dishes. They look bad, but taste great.

Entertainment

The Teatro Verdi (☎ 36 66 36), Piazza Verdi, is the venue for the city's November-to-May opera season, but the International Operetta Festival, a six-week series, is held at the Teatro Politeama Rossetti (☎ 56 72 01), Viale XX Settembre 45, from June. Most of the nightclubs are pretty tacky but the Mexico Club, Via XXX Ottobre 4, is one of the better night spots. Il Mandracchio, Passo di Piazza 1, is very popular.

Getting There & Away

Air Some international flights and domestic flights to Rome, Genoa and southern Italy land at Ronchi dei Legionari International Airport (☎ 42 27 11) on Via Aquileia.

Bus All national and international buses operate from the bus terminal (☎ 37 01 60) in Piazza della Libertà. Autolinee Triestine (☎ 42 50 20) and Saita (☎ 42 50 01) operate services to Udine, Gorizia, Duino, Cividale del Friuli, Venice, Genoa and places in Slovenia and Croatia.

Train The station (☎ 41 82 07) in Piazza della Libertà handles trains to Gorizia, Udine, Pordenone, Mestre and main cities to the east and in the south. Most trains to Slovenia and Croatia depart from here while some also depart from the Villa Opicina train station (☎ 21 16 82).

Car & Motorbike Trieste is at the end of the A4 autostrada and near the A23, which connects the A4 with Austria. The ss14 road follows the coast and connects the city with Venice. It continues into Slovenia, as does the ss15.

Avis (☎ 42 15 21) and Hertz (☎ 77 70 25) rent cars from Piazza della Libertà.

Boat Agemar (☎ 36 37 37), Via Rossini 2, is a good place to enquire about ferries to Croatia, Albania and Greece. Jadrolinija ferries depart from Trieste at 4 pm on Saturday to Igoumenitsa, Wednesday to Dubrovnik and Sunday to Mali Losinj, but only from June until September. Anek Lines runs a summer service to Igoumenitsa and Corfu, leaving every Saturday at 1.30 pm.

Getting Around

An airport bus runs from the bus terminal in Piazza della Libertà at regular intervals.

ACT buses (☎ 7 79 51) operate extensive routes throughout the city. Bus No 30 connects the train station with Via Roma and the waterfront. Services operate to Miramare and Villa Opicina.

Taxi Radio Trieste (☎ 30 77 30) or Autotassametri Cooperativa Alabarda (☎ 5 45 33) are the main taxi companies.

AROUND TRIESTE

About seven km north-west of Trieste is **Miramare Castle**, a grand white castle that dominates the coastline and is touted as the area's main tourist attraction. It was ordered by Archduke Maximilian of Austria in the mid-19th century, but he never occupied it. After a brief stint as emperor of Mexico for Napoleon III, he was executed by the Mexicans in 1867. His widow, Carlotta, who remained at the castle, went mad. It was subsequently rumoured that anyone spending a night at Miramare would come to a bad end. A son et lumière (sound and light show) recreates the lives of Maximilian, Carlotta and the emperor's Mexican tragedy each July and August. The APT in Trieste sells the tickets at L7000. Take bus No 36 from Trieste, or the train.

Villa Opicina, five km from Trieste, boasts the **Grotta Gigante**, the world's largest accessible cave. The interior is spotlit with coloured globes, and the 90-metre-high cavern is worth visiting. Take the Villa Opicina tram from Piazza Oberdan and then the No 45 bus for L9500, which includes the entrance fee. The cave is open from 9 am to midday and 2 to 7 pm during the summer, but opening hours are shorter in winter.

GORIZIA

A short distance from Trieste by bus or train, Gorizia's **castle**, perched atop the hill dominating the town, is a testament to its historic strategic importance as a transport junction between Friuli-Venezia Giulia and the Danube basin. Signs of Austrian patronage are obvious, as are Venetian influences. The town was literally torn apart in the 1947 border settlement with Yugoslavia. The town remained Italian, but its eastern regions, the Nova Gorica, became Yugoslav, and Gorizia has declined. The town has a few sights worth visiting and is a good side trip if you are driving between Trieste and Udine.

The tourist office (☎ 0481-53 38 70) at Corso Verdi 100 provides good information about the town. If you are planning to stay, the *Albergo Driussi* (☎ 0481-53 16 93), Via Duca d'Aosta 27, has singles/doubles from L28,000/45,000.

AQUILEIA

Founded in 181 BC by the Romans, Aquileia's strategic importance as a trading centre was soon obvious. Within 100 years, it had earned the name 'Second Rome' and figured prominently in the empire's dealings with lands over the Alps and to the east. By 10 BC, it was the richest market town in Italy and surpassed in importance only by Rome, Milan and Capua. Early in the 4th century AD, the important Patriarchate of Aquileia was founded, adding to the town's glory. Successive raids by Attila and the Lombards, and a period of Venetian control, caused decline.

The town is small, but worth visiting on the way to Trieste. It features impressive Roman ruins, and the 11th century **basilica**, on the site of a 4th century church, is a conglomeration of architectural and artistic influences. The 4th century mosaic floor offers a feast of religious and maritime symbols not seen in any other early Christian church. Visit the Distilleria Aquileia, Via Julia Augusta 87A, where you can sample local products (for free), and view the grappa-making process.

The APT tourist office (☎ 0431-91 94 91), Piazza Capitolo, opens daily from April to October. There is a main office in Grado (☎ 0431-8 00 35), on the Adriatic, at Viale Dante Alighieri 68, which opens all year and has information about Aquileia.

The *Camping Aquileia* (☎ 0431-9 10 42 in summer and ☎ 0431-9 10 37 in winter), at Via Gemina 10, charges L5500 a person and L8500 a site. The town is only a short distance from Trieste by bus or train and slightly farther from Udine.

LIGNANO SABBIADORO

If you want beaches, this area at the western edge of the Marano Lagoon is for you. Lignano Sabbiadoro, at the tip of a peninsula facing the lagoon to the north and the Adriatic to the south, is the main town of the area, a purpose-built resort popular with German tourists. Other towns include Lignano Pineta and Lignano Riviera, both south along the peninsula. None is very attractive, but the waters are generally clean and spared the pollution pumped into the Adriatic by the River Po, farther south. The APT tourist office (☎ 0431-7 18 21), Via Latisana 42, at Lignano Sabbiadoro, can assist with hotels and camping grounds, most of which fill during summer months.

UDINE

The region's second-largest city, Udine has an impressive medieval centre which makes it a worthy destination. The city is a mix of Italian, German and Croatian cultures, and some inhabitants still speak the local Friulian dialect.

Udine's history dates back to imperial Roman times, when it was founded as a military post. In the early 15th century it came under Venetian control. After a brief period under Napoleon, the city was passed to Austria in 1788 and joined Italy in 1866. The city survived WW II intact, but a catastrophic earthquake in 1976 caused heavy damage and cost hundreds of lives, although subsequent rebuilding has left little evidence of the disaster. The great Renaissance painter Giambattista Tiepolo lived in the city for many years.

Orientation

The main train station is on Viale Europa Unità at the southern edge of the old city centre. Walk straight ahead along Via Roma, through Piazza Repubblica and along Via Carducci for the Duomo. An alternative route from Piazza Repubblica is to veer to the left along Via Dante and continue along for Piazza della Libertà. The massive Piazza I Maggio is to the north-east.

Information

Tourist Office The APT (☎ 0432-29 59 72) is at Piazza I Maggio 7. It opens Monday to Friday from 9 am to 12.30 pm and 2.30 to 6 pm, Saturday to 12.30 pm. It produces a good city map, and a booklet, *Udine Il Giracittà*, featuring walking itineraries.

Money The Banca Commerciale Italiana is centrally located in Piazza del Duomo.

Post & Telecommunications The main post office is at Via Vittorio Veneto 42 and opens Monday to Saturday from 8.15 am to 7.30 pm. Poste restante mail can be addressed to 33100 Udine.

SIP telephones are at Via Savorgnana 15 and at Via Piave 17. Both open from 9 am to 12.30 pm and 3.30 to 8 pm daily. The telephone code for Udine is 0432.

Emergency For a police emergency, call ☎ 113. The police headquarters (☎ 50 28 41) are at Via Prefettura 16. For medical attention, go to the Ospedale Civile (☎ 55 21), north of the city centre in Piazza Santa Maria della Misericordia.

Gay & Lesbian Information Arci Gay (☎ 2 68 59), Via Manzini 42, can be contacted between 6 and 8 pm daily.

Things to See & Do

Most sights are clustered around the central Piazza della Libertà, one of the most beautiful Renaissance squares in Italy. The 15th century town hall, also known as the **Loggia del Lionello** after its architect, is a clear reminder of Venetian influence, as is the **Loggia di San Giovanni** opposite, featuring

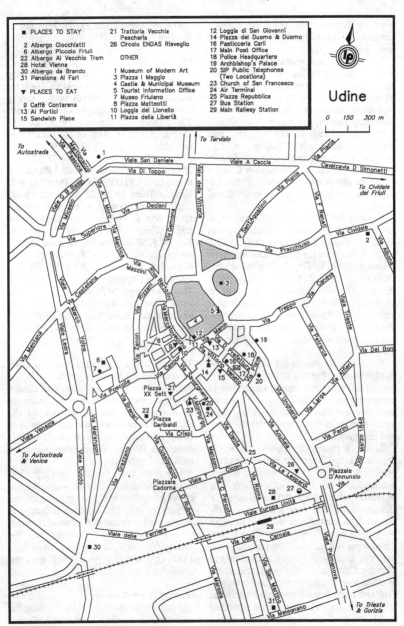

■ PLACES TO STAY

2 Albergo Ciocchiatti
6 Albergo Piccolo Friuli
22 Albergo Al Vecchio Tram
28 Hotel Vienna
30 Albergo da Brando
31 Pensione Al Fari

▼ PLACES TO EAT

9 Caffè Contarena
13 Ai Portici
15 Sandwich Place

21 Trattoria Vecchia
Pescheria
26 Circolo ENDAS Risveglio

OTHER

1 Museum of Modern Art
3 Piazza I Maggio
4 Castle & Municipal Museum
5 Tourist Information Office
7 Museo Friulano
8 Piazza Matteotti
10 Loggia del Lionello
11 Piazza della Libertà

12 Loggia di San Giovanni
14 Piazza del Duomo & Duomo
16 Pasticceria Carli
17 Main Post Office
18 Police Headquarters
19 Archbishop's Palace
20 SIP Public Telephones
(Two Locations)
23 Church of San Francesco
24 Air Terminal
27 Bus Station
29 Main Railway Station

Udine

0   150   300 m

Moorish figures that strike the hours – similar to the Mori of Venice's Torre dell'Orologio.

The Bollani Arch next to the clock tower was designed by Palladio in 1556 and leads up to the **castle**, which was used by the Venetian governors. It now houses the **Municipal Museum** with an extensive art collection including works by Caravaggio, Carpaccio and Tiepolo. The museum opens Tuesday to Sunday from 9.30 am to 12.30 pm and 3 to 6 pm, and entrance is L3200. Also on the hill is the 12th century **Church of Santa Maria del Castello**, which originally stood within the walls of the medieval castle.

Returning to Piazza della Libertà and continuing along Via Vittorio Veneto you will reach the Piazza del Duomo and the 13th century Romanesque-Gothic **Duomo**, with several frescoes by Tiepolo. The **Museo del Duomo**, in the bell tower, contains some frescoes by Viale da Bologna and opens on Wednesday, Thursday and Saturday from 9 am to midday. To the right of the cathedral is the **Oratorio della Purità**, with a beautiful ceiling painting of the Assumption by Tiepolo.

North-east of Piazza del Duomo is the **Archbishop's Palace** (Palazzo Arcivescovile) on Piazza Patriarcato, where Tiepolo completed an incredible series of frescoes depicting the Old Testament. The palace opens from 9 am to midday except weekends and entry is free.

South of Piazza del Duomo on Via B Odorico is the **Church of San Francesco**, considered the city's most beautiful church, although it is used only as a gallery. The **Museum of Modern Art** in Piazzale P Diacono features a wide selection of well-known 20th century art and also displays works by modern Friulian artists. The gallery opens from 9.30 am to 12.30 pm and 3 to 6 pm, but is closed Sunday afternoon and Monday. Entry is L3200. One other museum worth a visit if time permits is the **Museo Friulano delle Arti e Tradizioni Popolari** at Via Viola 3, which boasts various aspects of traditional local life, including costumes. It opens the same hours as the Museum of Modern Art.

Places to Stay

The city is without a hostel or camping ground, and many cheap hotels exist only for workers, so call ahead to book. A map outside the train station pinpoints all hotels. The *Albergo da Brando* (☎ 50 28 37), Piazzale Cella 16, west of the station, has singles/doubles from L22,000/38,000. The *Albergo Piccolo Friuli* (☎ 50 78 17), Via Magrini 9, west of Piazza della Libertà, has rooms from L30,000/48,000. The *Albergo Al Vecchio Tram* (☎ 50 25 16), near Piazza Garibaldi, north-west of the train station along Via C Percoto, has rooms from L35,000/50,000, as does the *Pensione Ai Fari* (☎ 52 07 32), south of the station at Via Melegnano 41. *Albergo Clocchiatti* (☎ 50 50 47) is east of the city centre at Via Cividale 29, and has rooms from L36,000/52,000. The *Hotel Vienna* (☎ 29 44 46), Viale Europa Unità 47, is almost opposite the station and has singles/doubles from L50,000/80,000 and triples/quads for L100,000/110,000.

Places to Eat

The city has a vegetarian restaurant, the *Circolo ENDAS Risveglio* (☎ 29 72 43), Via Aquileia 103, open for lunch and dinner, although a reservation is required for dinner. *Ai Portici*, Via Veneto 10, behind the Duomo, is a snack bar/restaurant where pasta dishes start at L5000. The *Trattoria Vecchia Pescheria*, Piazza XX Settembre, is a cheap, traditional restaurant.

One of the city's best cafés is *Caffè Contarena*, Piazza della Libertà, where the 'in' crowd hangs out. It is also very elegant and very expensive. The Austrian influence is clearly visible in the city's cakes; for great cakes and a coffee, try *Pasticceria Carli*, Via Vittorio Veneto 36, in a building dating from 1392. Opposite is a good lunch spot, the *Sandwich Place* at No 27.

Getting There & Away

The bus station (☎ 50 69 41) is opposite the train station, slightly to the east. Ferrari

(☎ 50 40 12) operates services to smaller towns in the north of the region, and to Trieste and Lignano. Saita (☎ 50 24 63) also serves Trieste and Grado.

The train station (☎ 50 36 56) is on the main Trieste-Venice line and services are regular. Connections can be made to Milan and beyond as well as Vienna.

By car, the A23 autostrada passes the city to the west. It connects the A4 with Austria. For hitchhikers, the ss56 connects the city with Trieste and the ss13 heads north to Austria. There is a major car park in Piazza I Maggio. Hertz (☎ 50 34 03) is near the train station at Viale Europa Unità 127.

Getting Around

The station is only a few minutes from the city centre, but all ATM buses (☎ 50 30 45) pass outside. Take No 1 or 3 for Piazza del Duomo. Radiotaxi (☎ 50 34 00) serves the city all hours.

CIVIDALE DEL FRIULI

A trip to Cividale del Friuli is a must if you make it to Udine. One of the most picturesque towns in the region, Cividale has a well-preserved medieval centre, despite several devastating earthquakes. Julius Caesar founded it in 50 BC and in the 6th century it became the seat of the first Lombard duchy. About 200 years later, its growing reputation drew the patriarch of Aquileia to the town.

The APT tourist office (☎ 0432-73 13 98) at Largo Boiani 4 has information about the town and also about the Natisone Valley, as well as the mountains to the north and east which contain many good walking tracks.

Although few tourists venture to Cividale, the town boasts a fine array of sights, including the **Tempietto Longobardo**, on Borgo Brossano. This 'little temple', or the Oratorio di Santa Maria in Valle as it is also known, was largely destroyed in a 13th century earthquake, but was later rebuilt. It is a fine example of Lombard architecture, although Romanesque and Byzantine influences are clearly evident. The **Duomo**, to the west, once again is a mix of architectural styles,

but inside is the Altar of Ratchis, a magnificent example of 8th century Lombard sculpture.

The town has no camping, and only three hotels, so a short trip from Udine is the best alternative option. The *Albergo Pomo d'Oro* (☎ 0432-73 14 89), Piazza San Giovanni 20, has singles/doubles from L30,000/44,000.

Trains and infrequent buses connect the town with Udine and Trieste, or you can drive the 17 km from Udine on the ss54.

CARNIA

The area stretching from Udine north to Tarvisio on the Austrian border is known as Carnia, after the Celtic tribes who settled in the region around the 4th century BC. It is of little interest unless you are driving to or from Villach in Austria, or unless you are a walker. The area is crisscrossed with good paths, and many old WW I mule tracks weave their way through crumbling fortifications, which should appeal to both day-tripping walkers or seasoned trekkers.

The Carnic Alps and the eastern Dolomites cover the top of Friuli-Venezia Giulia and have played host to a number of national and international skiing events, an indication that the area has some good runs, particularly around Forni Savorgnani, a small skiing area around Forni di Sopra; the resort at Mt Zoncolan, farther north-east; and Sella Nevea, north-east of Udine, which has good cross-country runs. Compared to other resort areas, skiing can be quite cheap.

For walkers, the Traversata Carnica crosses the Alps from Tarvisio to the western edge of the region near Forni di Sopra. Enquire at any of the tourist offices, including at Udine, about the Carta Neve, an annual ski pass valid for all ski lifts in Friuli which sells for L400,000.

The AAST tourist office has branches in the towns of Tarvisio (☎ 0428-21 35), Via Roma 10; at Forni di Sopra (☎ 0433-8 80 24); Sella Nevea (☎ 0433-5 40 60); and at Mt Zoncolan (☎ 0433-6 60 33). The Azienda Regionale delle Foreste (☎ 0432-29 47 11) at Via Manzini 41 in Udine can assist with maps and other information.

Central Italy

Central Italy

The landscape in central Italy is a patchwork of textures bathed in a beautiful soft light – golden pink in Tuscany, and a greenish gold in Umbria and the Marches. The people remain close to the land, but in each of the regions there is also a strong artistic and cultural tradition which means that even the smallest medieval hill town can harbour extraordinary works of art; and then there is the remarkable cuisine of Emilia-Romagna.

For geographical convenience, Emilia-Romagna has been included in central Italy in this book even though culturally and economically it belongs very much to the north.

Emilia-Romagna

Despite its convenient location between the big tourist drawing cards of Tuscany in the south and Lombardy and the Veneto in the north, Emilia-Romagna is largely overlooked by the visiting masses. The capital of the region, Bologna, became one of the most important Renaissance cities; its university is Europe's oldest and graduated the likes of Dante and Petrarch. It has long been regarded as the country's culinary capital, drawing on produce from the fertile plains along the Po Valley that have added Parmesan, prosciutto and Lambrusco wines to the Italian table. In short, it is a sophisticated city well worth several days, and makes a good base for short trips to Ferrara, Modena and Parma, each important Renaissance towns.

The Adriatic towns of Ravenna, which boasts one of the world's best collection of Byzantine mosaics, and Rimini, with its beaches and tacky nightlife, add to the region's diversity, as does the marshland of the Po delta, which Emilia-Romagna shares with the Veneto.

A highlight for walkers is the Grand'Escursione Appenninica, a 25-day hike that cuts a path through the Apennines, taking in refuges and many of the dozens of medieval castles dotting the range.

Emilia, west of Bologna, and Romagna to the east were only joined at Italian unification. Former papal states, the regions retain their own identity: the Emilians are an industrious people while the Romagnoli are still known for their blood feuds – maybe more in memory than practice, even though Mussolini was a native of the area.

The region was settled by the Etruscans, but it was not until 187 AD when the Romans built the Via Emilia that Emilia-Romagna prospered. With the exception of a period of Byzantine rule along the Adriatic coast, most of Emilia-Romagna's wealth and prosperity dates from the Renaissance, when some of the country's most notable families ruled the various towns – the Farnese in Parma and Piacenza, the Este in Ferrara and Modena – and built opulent palaces and courts.

Transport along the Via Emilia is excellent and bus connections allow exploration into the mountains and north along the River Po. However, hotel bookings are advisable throughout the year as rooms can be difficult to find. The region's prosperity means that prices are relatively high, but thanks to several youth hostels dotted throughout Emilia-Romagna even a budget traveller can see the entire region without too much trouble.

BOLOGNA

Elegant, intellectual and wealthy, Bologna also has an arrogance which makes it stand out among the many beautiful cities of Italy. The capital of Emilia-Romagna, Bologna is famous for its porticoes, its harmonious architecture, its university (one of the oldest in Europe) and, above all, its gastronomic tradition. The Bolognese have given the world tortellini, lasagne, mortadella and the ubiquitous spaghetti bolognese, hence one of the city's nicknames, La Grassa, The Fat.

Bologna is the bastion of what used to be

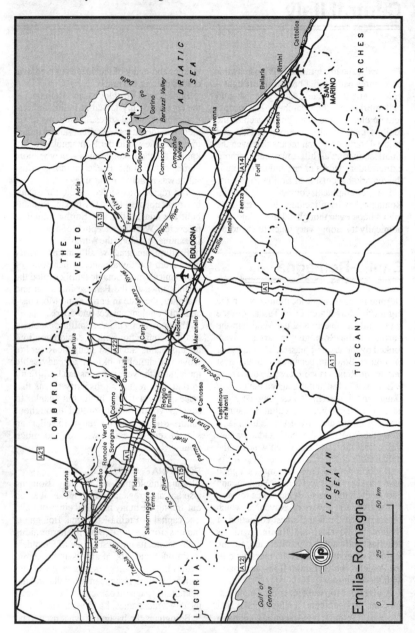

Emilia–Romagna

the Italian Communist Party, earning it the name Red Bologna (also for the red colour of its buildings), and the city was a major centre of anti-government student protests in the late 1970s. The left-wing terrorist organisation, the Red Brigades, had a strong base of support here. In 1980, right-wing terrorists planted a bomb at the city's train station which killed 85 people and wounded 200. But left-wing politics have given Bologna an enlightened city government with a social conscience (uncommon in Italy) which constantly organises a variety of events, particularly in summer.

History

Bologna was settled by the Etruscans in the 6th century BC as Felsina and was the capital of the Etruscan territories in the Po plain. About 200 years later, Gauls known as Boii occupied the city and renamed it Bononia, but were evicted as the Romans expanded northward. In later years, Bologna was sacked and occupied by a succession of Visigoths, Huns, Goths and Lombards.

A commune was established around the start of the 13th century, and Bologna flourished as the most important university town in Europe. To mark the city's wealth during this period, its most important families built more than 180 towers, of which only 15 remain. Bologna was caught up in the conflict between Guelphs, who supported papal rule, and the Ghibellines, who favoured rule by the Germanic emperors. The city was under papal rule from early in 16th century until the French Revolution. It was incorporated into Piedmont and the emerging Kingdom of Italy in 1859. During WW II, about 40% of its buildings were destroyed. Today, it is a centre for Italy's high-tech industries.

Orientation

Bologna is an easy city to find your way around, as most attractions are clustered in a small area around the central Via Ugo Bassi, Piazza Nettuno and Piazza Maggiore, and they are best seen on foot. From the train station in Piazza delle Medaglie d'Oro, walk left through Piazza XX Settembre, where the bus station is located, and then south along Via dell'Indipendenza, one of the city's main boulevards, for Piazza Nettuno and Piazza Maggiore. An alternative is to exit the train station and turn right, heading south along Via Giovanni Amendola, which becomes Via Guglielmo Marconi and eventually intersects Via Ugo Bassi. If you are driving, all main roads meet the city's ring road, and routes to the centre are clearly marked with the familiar 'centro' target symbol.

Information

Tourist Office The most useful APT office is on the western side of Piazza Maggiore (☎ 051-23 96 60) and also goes by the name of Centro di Informazione Comunale. It opens from 9 am to 7 pm Monday to Saturday, to 1 pm Sunday. The main APT office is at Via G Marconi 45 (☎ 051-23 74 13), and other offices are at the train station and airport. Staff will assist with finding rooms, but will not make bookings.

Bologna's APT is the among country's most organised and produces a range of publications, including *A Guest in Bologna* in English. If the Piazza Maggiore office is closed, there is computerised information in the foyer.

Post & Telecommunications The main post office is in Piazza Minghetti, south-east of Piazza Maggiore. It opens from 8.15 am to about 7 pm Monday to Friday, to 12.30 pm Saturday. Poste restante mail can be addressed to 40100 Bologna.

ASST telephone offices, with attendants, are at Piazza VIII Agosto 24 and the station. Bologna's telephone code is 051.

Emergency For police emergency, call ☎ 113. The police headquarters (☎ 33 71 11) are in Palazzo Caprara, on Piazza F D Roosevelt, and there's an office for foreigners (☎ 33 74 75). For medical attention, the Ospedale Sant'Orsola (☎ 636 31 11) is on Via Massarenti, at the eastern edge of Via San Vitale. Zarri Pharmacy, Via Ugo Bassi 1, is open 24 hours a day.

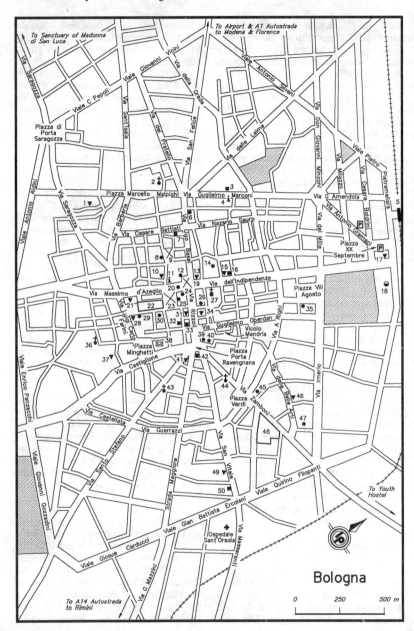

Bologna

0   250   500 m

■ PLACES TO STAY

3	Albergo Marconi
7	Albergo Panorama
16	Albergo Donatello
32	Albergo Apollo
33	Albergo Garisenda
50	Albergo Perla

▼ PLACES TO EAT

1	Osteria Senzanome
10	La Mela
13	Self Service Al Centro
15	Diana
17	Terminal
21	Ristorante Torre
28	Zanarini
31	Osteria del Sole
34	Analcolico
37	Osteria dei Poeti
41	Vanes
46	Pizzeria Bell'Arti
49	Osteria du Madon

OTHER

| 2 | Church of San Francesco |
| 4 | Main APT Tourist Information Office |

5	Railway Station & Tourist Office
6	Zarri Pharmacy
8	Palazzo Caprara & Police
9	Piazza F D Roosevelt
11	Tourist Information Office
12	Communal Palace
14	Medieval & Renaissance Museum
18	Main Bus Station
19	Piazza Nettuno
20	Fountain of Neptune
22	San Petronio Basilica
23	Piazza Maggiore
24	King Enzo's Palace
25	Podestà Palace
26	SIP telephones
27	Cathedral of San Pietro
29	Archiginnasio
30	Municipal Archaeological Museum
35	ASST Telephones
36	San Domenico Basilica
38	Post Office
39	Linen Drapers' Palace
40	Feltrinelli Bookshop
42	Leaning Towers
43	Santo Stefano Basilica
44	Church of San Giacomo Maggiore
45	Municipal Theatre
47	National Picture Gallery
48	University & Poggi Palace

Money A booth at the train station gives reasonable rates and is open from 8 am to 7.45 pm daily. Otherwise, branches of the major banks are on Via Rizzoli, the continuation of Via Ugo Bassi.

Other Information The CIT travel agency (☎ 26 89 81) is in Piazza Nettuno, and CTS (☎ 26 48 62), for student travel, at Via delle Belle Arti 20.

Feltrinelli bookshops (one Italian, one foreign) are a few doors apart on Via dei Giudei, near the two leaning towers.

Arci Gay Cassero (☎ 43 33 95), Piazza di Porta Saragozza 2, arranges events and provides information for gay people.

There is a coin laundry at Via Schiavonia 2, near Via N Sauro, two blocks east of Via G Marconi.

Dangers & Annoyances

The city is only just starting to have problems with street crime such as bag theft and pickpocketing. However, the area around the university, particularly Piazza Verdi, is a haunt for drug addicts and their suppliers and can be unsafe at night.

Things to See

Piazza Maggiore is the centre of Bologna's old city and a logical place to start. Visit the tourist office and pick up a city map which indicates piazzas and many of the 200 churches, 300 palaces and other features of the city. In the area between the piazza and Piazza Nettuno is the **Fountain of Neptune**, sculpted in 1566 in bronze by a French artist who became known as Giambologna. The four angels represent the winds and the four sirens the then known continents. It is considered a little risqué, particularly if you stand on the ATC grate about 20 metres behind Neptune and observe the placement of his thumb. Locals say Giambologna was poking fun at the church which restrained his design, and created a phallic illusion with the giant's first digit.

On the western side of the piazza is the **Communal Palace** with its immense staircase, attributed to Bramante, which leads to the 1st-floor apartments. It was wide enough for horse-drawn carriages so the occupants could be chauffeured from ground level. The building houses parts of the local government and features a bronze statue of Pope Gregory XIII, a native of Bologna who created the Gregorian calendar.

Inside, a wooden building erected and used for the restoration of the Fountain of Neptune has a gangway that enabled the public to watch the process. It is used for other restorations and is worth seeing. The palace also contains the city's art collections and is open from 9 am to 2 pm (closed Tuesdays).

Across the piazza and bordering Piazza Nettuno is **King Enzo's Palace**, named after Enzo, King of Sicily, who was confined here for 20 years from 1249. The **Podestà Palace** next door is a fine example of Renaissance architecture. Beneath the palace and behind the cafés facing Piazza Maggiore are so-called whisper chambers. Stand diagonally opposite another person and whisper – the acoustics are amazing.

The **San Petronio Basilica**, named after the city's patron saint, was started in 1392 to plans by Antonio di Vicenzo but was never finished. It is Bologna's largest church. Originally intended to be larger than the first St Peter's in Rome (the structure which was destroyed to make way for the present St Peter's Basilica), the building suffered at the hands of the papacy, which decreed that it could not be larger than St Peter's and decided that much of the land should be used for the city's original university. Walk along Via dell'Archiginnasio along the eastern side of the basilica and you will see the beginnings of apses poking out oddly from the basilica and the incomplete façade. Even so, the basilica is one of the largest in the world, and is a fine example of Gothic architecture. The central doorway, by Jacopo della Quercia, dates from 1425 and features carvings from the Old and New Testaments and a beautiful *Madonna & Child*. The chapels inside contain frescoes by Giovanni da Modena and Jacopo di Paolo. A giant sundial, designed by Cassini in 1656, lines the floor of the north aisle. Sun beams through an aperture in the roof and marks out hours, days and months on the brass device.

The **Municipal Archaeological Museum** is south along Via dell'Archiginnasio (entrance on Via de' Musei), and has impressive collections of Egyptian and Roman remains and one of Italy's best Etruscan displays, featuring two burial chambers unearthed near the city. It is open from 9 am to 2 pm Tuesday to Sunday, and entry is L10,000.

The **Archiginnasio**, first site of the city's university and now its library, contains an anatomy theatre carved entirely from wood in 1647. It was destroyed during WW II but was completely rebuilt. Both the theatre and the Stabat Mater room, named after Rossini's hymn which had its first playing here in 1842, can be visited for free. Just find the attendant.

On Via dell'Indipendenza, north from Piazza Nettuno, is the **Cathedral of San Pietro**, dating from the 10th century but rebuilt many times since. On Via Manzoni is the **Medieval & Renaissance Museum**, housed in the Palazzo Ghislardi-Fava, which contains some armour and a few frescoes by della Quercia. It is open Monday and Wednesday to Saturday from 9 am to 2 pm, Sunday to 12.30 pm, and entry is L4000.

Returning to Via Rizzoli, walk east to the two leaning towers. The area just north of Piazza Porta Ravegnana, particularly around Vicolo Mandria and Via Tubertina, is the city's former ghetto and was long derelict, but is now having a resurgence as a trendy housing area.

Piazza di Porta Ravegnana features Bologna's main landmarks, the Torre degli Asinelli and the Torre Garisenda, the two **leaning towers**. The former reaches 97.6 metres, leaning about 1.3 metres off centre, and was built by the family of the same name in 1109. Climb its 498 steps for a great view of the city. Entry is L4000. The Garisenda family were less cautious with foundations when building their tower, designed to compete with its neighbour, and stopped at 48 metres because of its 3.2-metre lean. The Linen Drapers' (or Strazzaroli) Palace, built in the 15th century, and the Loggia della Mercanzia, built in 1384, face the piazza.

North-east along Via Zamboni is the **Church of San Giacomo Maggiore**, in Piazza Rossini. Built in the 13th century and remodelled in 1722, the church contains the Bentivoglio Chapel with frescoes by Lorenzo Costa. Next is the **Municipal Theatre**, where Wagner's works were performed for the first time in Italy.

Farther along is the university area, worth visiting just for the cafés and bars. The university has many specific museums that are open to the public, mostly in the **Poggi Palace**, on the corner of Via Zamboni and Via San Giacomo, details of which can be obtained from the APT. North of the university, at Via delle Belle Arti 56, is the **National Picture Gallery**, which concentrates on works by Bolognese artists. The gallery opens Monday and Wednesday to Saturday from 9 am to 2 pm, Sunday to 12.30 pm, and entry is L5000.

Back to the two towers, head south-east along Via Santo Stefano to the **Santo Stefano Basilica**, a complex originally consisting of seven churches, now reduced to four. On the right is the 11th century Romanesque Church of the Crucifix and the octagonal Church of the Holy Sepulchre, which contains the bones of St Petronius, Bologna's patron saint. The basin in the small courtyard is supposed to be the one in which Pilate washed his hands after he condemned Christ to death. The city's oldest church, the San Vitale e Agricola, features many recycled Roman ruins, and the Church of the Trinity features a museum. The complex is open from 9 am to midday and 3.30 to 6 pm.

South-west in Piazza San Domenico is the **San Domenico Basilica**, built in the early 16th century to house the remains of St Dominic, the founder of the Dominican order. Head straight for the San Domenico Chapel, containing his sarcophagus by Nicola Pisano. The angel on the right of the altar was carved by Michelangelo when he was 19 and bears a resemblance to *David*, which he carved years later. Mozart spent one month in the city's musical academy and played on the church's organ. Ask an attendant for permission to see the inlaid wood of the choir stalls behind the altar, or to visit the small museum.

At the western end of Via Ugo Bassi, at Piazza Marcello Malphigi, is the **Church of San Francesco**, which features the tombs of the glossators (law teachers), elaborate edifices standing in the church grounds. Inside the church, one of the first in Italy to be built in the French Gothic style, is the tomb of Pope Alexander V.

In the hills overlooking the city is the **Sanctuary of the Madonna of San Luca**, about four km south-west of the city centre but connected by a long portico with 666 arches. Each April a statue of the Virgin Mary is carried from the church along the portico in an effort to stop the rains and bring on summer. Take bus No 21 from the station to the start of the portico at Via Sturzo, or bus No 20 from the city centre to Via Porrettana.

Festivals

Each summer, the city sponsors Bologna Sogna ('Bologna Dreams'), a three-month festival of events involving museums and galleries, the university and local and national performers. Torri da Estate is another summer programme and includes discos. Most events are free and a schedule is available at the APT.

Places to Stay

Budget hotels in Bologna are virtually non-existent and it is almost impossible to find a room for one person only. Call before you arrive in the city, as Bologna's booming trade-fair calendar usually fills most hotels for at least one week a month.

There are several *camping* grounds within driving distance of the city. Check with the

APT. Also ask at the tourist office for student accommodation, but only during university holidays.

Hostel The best option is the IYHF youth hostel, the *Ostello San Sisto* (☎ 51 92 02), Via Viadagola 14, with bed and breakfast for L16,000 and a meal for L12,000. Take bus No 93 from the train station, No 301 from the bus station or No 19 from Via dell'Indipendenza, and ask the driver where to get off, then follow the signs. The hostel produces a series of walking-tour maps.

Hotels – bottom end The pick of the city's cheaper hotels is the *Albergo Garisenda* (☎ 22 43 69), Via Rizzoli 9, off the Galleria del Leone, with rooms looking out over the leaning towers. Prices for singles/doubles range from L40,000/60,000. *Albergo Perla* (☎ 22 45 79), Via San Vitale 77, at the eastern edge of the city centre, has rooms from L40,000/60,000. The *Albergo Apollo* (☎ 22 39 55), Via Drapperie 5, off Via Rizzoli (extension of Via Ugo Bassi), has rooms from L36,000/60,000.

Several cheaper hotels can be found on Via G Marconi. The *Albergo Marconi* (☎ 26 28 32), at No 22 has rooms for about the same price. A small pensione run by *Angela Cancellaro* (☎ 26 22 30) at No 24 has doubles/triples from L70,000/90,000. The *Albergo Panorama* (☎ 22 18 02), Via Livraghi 1, off Via Ugo Bassi, has singles/doubles for L40,000/65,500 and triples for L80,000.

Hotels – middle to top end The city is jammed with expensive hotels catering to businesspeople, but standards are sometimes poor. The *Albergo Donatello* (☎ 24 81 74), Via dell'Indipendenza 65, has singles/doubles from L90,000/130,000.

Places to Eat
As the epithet La Grassa suggests, the Bolognese are very serious about food and are particularly fussy about their pasta. The best pasta is *tirata a mano*, hand-stretched and rolled with a wooden pin, not a machine.

It is cooked in many ways and eaten with a multitude of sauces. Everyone knows spaghetti bolognese, but the Bolognese in fact call the meat sauce *ragù* and tend to eat it with fresh fettuccine, made with eggs. *Mortadella*, known around the globe (sometimes as Bologna sausage or baloney), hails from the area. The hills near Bologna produce the Riesling Italico and the full, dry Sauvignon.

Fortunately it is cheap to eat in Bologna, particularly in the university district north of Via Rizzoli. The city has many good bars and osterias, where you can get cheap drinks and snacks. Some serve full meals and rarely levy a cover charge. A cheaper way to eat is to buy panini and eat them standing at the bar, or to take advantage of the generous bar snacks provided for pre-dinner drinkers in most bars.

Shop at the Mercato Ugo Bassi, Via Ugo Bassi 27, a vast covered market offering all the local fare, or the immense daily produce market west and east of the Piazza Maggiore, centred around speciality food shops on Via de' Fusari, Via Drapperie, Via Marchesana and Via Clavature.

Self Service Al Centro, Via dell'Indipendenza, near Piazza Nettuno, is very cheap, with pasta from L3000. *Terminal*, also on Via dell'Indipendenza, near the train station, is similarly cheap.

Osteria del Sole, Via Ranocchi 1D, is 500 years old and the oldest restaurant in the city. Drinks start at L2000 and cheap meals are served at the whim of the owner. *Osteria du Madon*, Via San Vitale 75, at the road's eastern edge, serves mainly pasta dishes and is quite cheap, with courses starting at L6000. *Osteria Senzanome*, Via Senzanome 42, is one of the best osterie and a full meal could cost L20,000. *Osteria dei Poeti*, Via dei Poeti, near the San Domenico Basilica, is slightly more expensive but the food is excellent.

The Ristorante Self-Service Naturista Vegetariano, Via degli Albari 6, off Via Rizzoli, goes by the name *Analcolico* and specialises in cheap vegetarian fare.

Locals say the city's best pizza comes from *La Mela*, Via de' Fusari 5, and they start at L5000. *Vanes*, Strada Maggiore 5C, near the two towers, specialises in pasta, which is made at the restaurant. Pasta dishes cost from L7000, pizzas from L5000 and the cover charge is L2500.

Ristorante Torre de' Galluzzi, Piazza Galluzzi behind the San Petronio Basilica, has a L50,000 set menu featuring local specialities. But if you're aiming for the top, hit *Diana*, Via dell'Indipendenza, near Piazza Nettuno, considered the city's best restaurant, where a full meal will cost at least L60,000.

Cafés & Bars The *Zanarini*, Via Luigi Carlo Farini 2, behind the San Petronio Basilica, is one of the city's finest tearooms, specialising in unusual cakes. Some of its past glory is lost, but the grand décor makes a visit worthwhile, if a little expensive. *Bar Vittorio*, opposite the San Petronio Basilica in Piazza Maggiore, is the city's most famous bar, but a beer will cost L10,000. *Gelateria Montegrappa*, Via Montegrappa, north of Via Ugo Bassi, is one of the city's best ice-cream places.

Entertainment

The tourist office has several what's-on brochures. The *Young People's Handbook* and *Notte in Bologna* list bars, clubs, restaurants and concerts, and other useful details such as the local political parties. *Bologna Spettacolo News* is also available at the tourist office or at any newsstand (L1000) and is a more comprehensive guide. The Municipal Theatre (☎ 22 29 99), Piazza Verdi, is the main venue for opera, theatre and concerts.

English-language films are screened at Tiffany (☎ 33 07 57), Porta Saragozza 5, and Lumiere (☎ 52 35 39), Via Pietralata 55A.

The best nightclubs are Kinki, Via Zamboni 1, which goes lesbian and gay on Saturday nights, and Cassero, Porta Saragozza, which is run by the gay community. Sporting, Galleria del Toro, varies the entertainment from disco to ballroom dancing.

Getting There & Away

Bologna's Guglielmo Marconi Airport (☎ 31 15 78), north-west of the city on Borgo Panigale, is serviced by mainly European airlines and there are flights to Rome, Venice, southern Italy, Pisa and London, Paris and Frankfurt.

Buses to major cities depart from the depot in Piazza XX Settembre, around the corner from the train station.

Bologna is a major transport junction for northern Italy, and trains from virtually all major cities stop here. The only hitch is that many are intercity trains, which means you have to pay a supplement. Call ☎ 24 64 90 for information.

The city is linked to Milan, Florence and Rome by the A1 Autostrada del Sole. The A13 heads directly for Venice and Padua, and the A14 for Rimini and Ravenna. The city is also on the original Roman Via Emilia, also known as the ss9, which connects Milan with the Adriatic coast.

Getting Around

ATC bus no 91 connects the city centre with the airport, and bus No 25 will take you from the train station to the historical centre. Traffic is limited in the city centre, and major car parks are at Piazza XX Settembre and Via Antonio Gramsci.

The city centre is best seen on foot. However, Bologna has an efficient bus system, run by ATC (☎ 24 70 05), which has an information booth at the bus depot on Piazza XX Settembre and another on Via Marconi, near Via Ugo Bassi. Bus Nos 11, 25 and 27 are a few of the many connecting the train station with the city centre.

For a taxi, call ☎ 37 27 27. For car hire, all major companies are represented in the city and most have offices at the airport. Avis (☎ 55 15 28) is at Via Pietramellara, and Europcar (☎ 24 71 01) is at Via Boldrini 3B.

MODENA

This city, some 40 km north-west of Bologna, was one of the many established along the Via Emilia, but it was not until the House of Este, banished from Ferrara in 1597, resettled its court in Modena that the city began to prosper. Home to Italy's

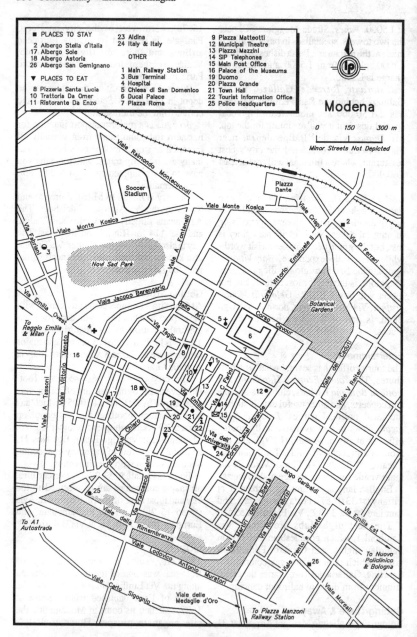

PLACES TO STAY
- 2 Albergo Stella d'Italia
- 17 Albergo Sole
- 18 Albergo Astoria
- 26 Albergo San Gemignano

PLACES TO EAT
- 8 Pizzeria Santa Lucia
- 10 Trattoria Da Omer
- 11 Ristorante Da Enzo

- 23 Aldina
- 24 Italy & Italy

OTHER
- 1 Main Railway Station
- 3 Bus Terminal
- 4 Hospital
- 5 Chiesa di San Domenico
- 6 Ducal Palace
- 7 Piazza Roma

- 9 Piazza Matteotti
- 12 Municipal Theatre
- 13 Piazza Mazzini
- 14 SIP Telephones
- 15 Main Post Office
- 16 Palace of the Museums
- 19 Duomo
- 20 Piazza Grande
- 21 Town Hall
- 22 Tourist Information Office
- 25 Police Headquarters

Modena

0   150   300 m

Minor Streets Not Depicted

favourite tenor, Luciano Pavarotti, and famous car makers like Ferrari, Maserati, Bugatti and De Tomaso, the city has ridden the wave of Italy's boom and its people enjoy one of Italy's highest standards of living.

Orientation

From the main train station in Piazza Dante, head down Viale Crispi, to the left, for Corso Vittorio Emanuele II, which leads to the Ducal Palace. Walk around the palace to Piazza Roma, and then straight ahead along Via L C Farini for Via Emilia, the main street. Piazza Grande and Piazza Mazzini are to the right, and Piazza Matteotti is farther along to the right.

Information

Tourist Office The IAT tourist office (☎ 059-22 24 82), Via Scudari 30, is one block east of Piazza Grande. Informa Giovani (☎ 059-20 65 83), Via Scudari 8, provides a range of information for young people.

Post & Telecommunications The main post office is at Via Emilia 86 and opens from 8.30 am to 7.30 pm. Poste restante mail can be addressed to 41100 Modena. SIP telephones are at Via Farini 26. The telephone code for Modena is 059.

Emergency For a police emergency, call ☎ 113. The police headquarters (☎ 22 51 72) are at Viale delle Rimembranze 14. For medical attention, the Nuovo Policlinico (☎ 36 10 24) is at Via del Pozzo 17, east of the city centre along Via Emilia. The main city hospital (☎ 23 62 39) is at Piazzale Sant'Agostino, opposite the Palace of the Museums.

Things to See

Start in Piazza Grande at the **Duomo**, dedicated to San Geminiano, which was started in 1099 and is recognised as one of the finest Romanesque cathedrals in Italy, even if it and its bell tower, the Torre Ghirlandina, are both sinking. Barricades erected around

Piazza Grande fence off the church, but it is possible to enter the building. The façade features bas-relief sculpture depicting scenes from Genesis by the 12th century sculptor Wiligelmo. Much of his work has been removed to the Duomo Museum, adjoining the cathedral at Via Lanfranco 6 (open Monday to Saturday from 9 am to 7 pm, Sunday to 1 pm, entry by donation). The bas-reliefs adorning the façade are excellent copies. The cathedral's interior is solemn and simple in its Romanesque style. The rood screen (balustrade) over the nave was carved in the 12th century and shows scenes from Christ's Passion.

The **Torre Ghirlandina** was started in 1269 and rises to 87 metres, although it now has quite a lean. It is topped with a Gothic spire, while at the base a memorial has been erected to commemorate Modenese killed by the Nazis and Fascists.

West along Via Emilia is the **Palace of the Museums**, Piazzale Sant'Agostino, which makes visiting the city easy. It houses several galleries, including the city's art collection and the Este Library. The Lapidary Museum contains Roman stoneworks including sarcophagi. The Este Gallery, featuring most of the Este family collection, comprises works by Cosimo Tura, Veronese, Correggio and Tintoretto. The Este Library has one of Italy's most valuable collections of books, letters and manuscripts, and includes the *Bible of Borso d'Este*, 1200 pages illustrated by Ferrarese artists and considered the most decorated Bible in existence. It can be seen, but you must leave your passport at the desk. The Risorgimento Museum is worth visiting for its documents such as letters, newspapers and photographs chronicling the lead-up to Italian unification, but may be closed for restoration. The Civic Museum contains an impressive collection of Italian and Oriental fabrics. Opening times vary for each museum, so check first at the APT.

The **Ducal Palace** on Piazza Roma was started in 1634 for the Este family and now houses Modena's military academy, whose cadets wear fuchsia-coloured uniforms (and look like they've stepped off a Quality Street chocolate tin) but are considered Italy's crack soldiers.

South of the city, in the town of Maranello, is the **Ferrari Automobile Factory** (☎ 0536-94 32 04), difficult but not impossible to visit. Call well in advance, beg a little and you might be lucky. The company has opened a museum nearby, the Ferrari Gallery, Via Dino Ferrari 43, also in Maranello. It features one of the largest collections of Ferraris on show in the world. Take bus No 2 or the bus bound for Sassulo from the bus station and ask the driver for the right stop. It is open from 9.30 am to 12.30 pm and 3 to 6 pm daily except Monday, and entry is L6000.

Activities

The Apennines south of Modena offer a host of activities, including walking, horse riding, canoeing and skiing. The Club Alpino Italiano (☎ 24 31 30) in Modena and the town's tourist information office have many brochures, such as *Modena Altro Turismo*, *Modena Trekking*, *Modena's Apennine* and *Skiing on Modena's Mountains*, which list activities and give details of clubs. About 12 mountain refuges are located in the mountains and there are many walking tracks.

Places to Stay

Modena is close enough to Bologna to make it a short day trip, although the city does have reasonably cheap accommodation. To be safe, you should book before you arrive. If you're driving, signposts on the main roads into the city direct you to hotels. *International Camping Modena* (☎ 33 22 52), Via Cave di Ramo 111, is a couple of km west of the city in Bruciata. Take bus No 19.

The *Albergo Sole* (☎ 21 42 45), Via Malatesta 45, west of Piazza Grande, has singles/doubles from L27,000/45,000. The *Albergo Astoria* (☎ 22 55 87), Via Sant'Eufemia 43, one block back from Via Emilia near the Duomo, has rooms from the same price. *Albergo Stella d'Italia* (☎ 22 25 84), Via Paolo Ferrari 3, has rooms from L36,000/55,000, and the *Albergo San Geminiano* (☎ 21 03 03), Viale Moreali 41, a

10-minute walk east of the city centre, has rooms from L38,000/50,000. It also has free parking.

Places to Eat

Like Bologna and Parma, Modena produces excellent *prosciutto crudo* (cured ham). The city's main gastronomic delight is *zampone* (stuffed pig's trotter). It also produces the bulk of Italy's balsamic vinegar, a rich aromatic vinegar using grapes grown locally which is sprinkled liberally over salads and meat dishes. Tortellini are a speciality and served only in broth, and the area produces Lambrusco, one of the more famous Italian sparkling reds, which should be drunk chilled and with everything. The city's Consorzio Tutela del Lambrusco (☎ 23 50 05), Viale Martiri della Libertà, can help with information about vineyards and advise on tastings and opening times.

Italy & Italy, Via dell'Università, off Corso Canal Grande, is one of the country's better fast-food chains, with the country's best hamburgers. Pasta dishes start at L4000. *Aldina*, Via Albinelli 40, is a typical trattoria where a meal could cost L15,000. *Pizzeria Santa Lucia*, Via Taglio, north of Piazza Matteotti, has pizzas from L6000. *Trattoria Da Omer*, Via Torre 33, also serves typical dishes, but a meal will cost over L35,000. *Ristorante Da Enzo*, Via Coltellini 17, is one of the better restaurants, with main courses from L10,000. The pizzeria at Albergo San Geminiano is also good, with pizzas from L5000.

Entertainment

The city's better bars are along Via Emilia, near the Duomo, but check prices, as a beer could cost L10,000. The city's Sipario in Piazza, held during July and August, features outdoor concerts and ballet centred around Piazza Grande, with tickets starting at L10,000. Posters advertise events. The opera season each winter sometimes attracts Pavarotti to the Municipal Theatre (☎ 22 51 83), Corso Canal Grande 85. Cinema Embassey, Vicolo dell'Albergo 8, screens

Top : The Trevi Fountain, Rome (EPT)
Bottom Left : Fountain of the Rivers, Piazza Navona, Rome (GE)
Bottom Right : One of the many fountains in Rome (GE)

Top Left   : Domes of St Mark's Basilica, Venice (APT)
Top Right   : Rooftops, Urbino, Marches (JG)
Bottom Left : Garden in the Certosa di Pavia, Lombardy (JG)
Bottom Right : View from the Torre degli Asinelli, Bologna (JG)

English-language films from September to May. Check with the tourist office for discos.

Getting There & Away

Buses arrive at the bus terminal (☎ 30 88 00) along Via Fabriani. ATCM (☎ 30 80 11) connects Modena with most towns in the region and other cities including Cremona and Milan.

The main train station is in Piazza Dante (☎ 21 82 26) and serves trains from Bologna, Rome, Parma and Milan. A second train station in Piazza Manzoni (☎ 30 80 11) serves smaller towns in the region.

By car, the city is at the junction of the A1 Autostrada del Sole, which connects Rome with Milan, and the A22, which heads north for the Brenner Pass. There is a car park at Viale Trento e Trieste 39 (L1500 an hour), a few minutes' walk from the centre.

Getting Around

ATCM buses provide services through the city. Bus No 6 connects the train station with the city centre. For a taxi, call ☎ 37 42 42. Bicycles can be rented from next to the station for L1000 an hour.

REGGIO EMILIA

Although it may have less to offer than other towns in Emilia-Romagna, Reggio Emilia's pleasant centre, built mostly by the Este family which controlled the city for more than 400 years, is worth stopping for. The city attracts few tourists, but its youth hostel makes it a good base for exploring, particularly into the Apennines to the south.

Information

The IAT tourist information office (☎ 0522-45 11 52) in Piazza Camillo Prampolini is about one km west of the train station in Piazza Marconi, along Via Emilia San Pietro. The main post office is at Via Sessi 3, and poste restante mail can be addressed to 42100 Reggio Emilia. The city's telephone code is 0522.

The police headquarters (☎ 113 or 43 58 41) are at Via Dante Alighieri 6, and for medical emergencies, the Ospedale Santa Maria Nuova (☎ 29 64 38) is at Viale Risorgimento 80.

Things to See

The city's sites are concentrated around Piazza Cesare Battisti, on Via Emilia, Piazza Prampolini to the south and Piazza San Prospero to the east, which are separated by the **Duomo**. Built in the 13th century and in the Romanesque style, the cathedral was completely remodelled in the 16th century.

On the south side of Piazza Prampolini, in the town hall's Sala del Tricolore, the Italian flag was devised during a conference which established Napoleon's Cispadane Republic in 1797.

North from Piazza Battisti, facing the Piazza Martiri del VII Luglio, are the **Civic Museums**, four in all, with a collection of 18th century artworks and archaeological discoveries. The **Parmeggiani Gallery** at Corso Cairoli 2 should be open after extensive renovations by the time you read this, and contains some important Italian and Flemish works.

Places to Stay & Eat

The *Reggio Emilia* youth hostel (☎ 45 47 95), Via dell'Abbadessa 8, about 500 metres from the train station in the city centre, has bed and breakfast for L14,000. For a hotel, try the *Albergo Stella* (☎ 43 22 80), Via Blasmatorti 5, near Piazza Roversi, which has singles/doubles from L30,000/40,000. The *Albergo Morandi* (☎ 45 43 97), Via Emilia San Pietro 64, near the station, has rooms from L35,000/55,000, as does the *Cairoli*, Piazza XXV Aprile, near the bus station. *Albergo Reggio* (☎ 4 00 56), Via San giuseppe 7, has singles/doubles from L70,000/95,000 and is in the centre.

There is a produce market each Tuesday and Friday in Piazza San Prospero. The hostel restaurant, the *Casa dello Studente*, is the best bet for budget meals, with main courses from L4000. *Trattoria La Favella*, Via Monzermone 2, is traditional and reasonably cheap, while *Boiardo*, Galleria San Rocco, and *L'Altro Condor*, Via Secchi 17, are good pizzerias, with pizzas from L5000.

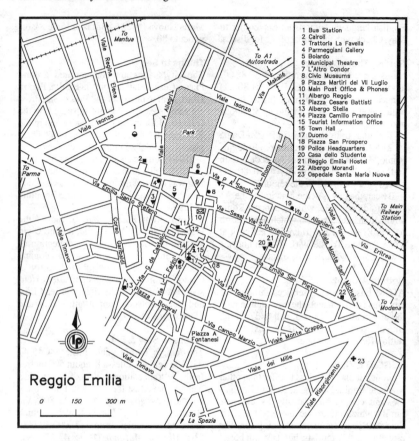

Reggio Emilia

1 Bus Station
2 Cairoli
3 Trattoria La Favella
4 Parmeggiani Gallery
5 Boiardo
6 Municipal Theatre
7 L'Altro Condor
8 Civic Museums
9 Piazza Martiri del VII Luglio
10 Main Post Office & Phones
11 Albergo Reggio
12 Piazza Cesare Battisti
13 Albergo Stella
14 Piazza Camillo Prampolini
15 Tourist Information Office
16 Town Hall
17 Duomo
18 Piazza San Prospero
19 Police Headquarters
20 Casa dello Studente
21 Reggio Emilia Hostel
22 Albergo Morandi
23 Ospedale Santa Maria Nuova

0   150   300 m

Getting There & Away

The city is on the Via Emilia (the ss9), and the A1 autostrada passes to the north. Most trains from Milan to Bologna stop here (☎ 43 96 50 for information), and ACT buses (☎ 51 44 22) serve the city and region from the bus station in Viale Allegri. There is a huge car park at Viale Monte Grappa, charging L4000 a day.

AROUND REGGIO EMILIA

South of the city along the ss63 road is a national park spread along the region's share of the Apennines. The tourist information office at **Castelnovo ne' Monti** (☎ 0522-81

04 30), Piazza Martiri della Libertà, can provide details of activities. For walkers, there are several refuges dotted along the trails. Contact the Club Alpino Italiano in Reggio Emilia (☎ 3 66 85), Corso Garibaldi 14, for information.

Exploring the area north of the city, along the banks of the River Po, has been made easier by the establishment of a youth hostel at Guastalla (☎ 0522-82 49 15), Via Lido Po 11, reached by the ss63 road from Reggio Emilia.

PARMA

Straddling the banks of a Po tributary, the

Parma River, this city is one of the most serene in the north of Italy. Its people are among the country's wealthiest, ensuring a high standard of living and, unfortunately, expensive restaurants and hotels. However, the city has a hostel and should not be missed.

Stendhal lived here, Verdi lived nearby and composed many of his greatest works in the city, and the 20th century composer Toscanini also lived here. The city gives its name to Parmesan cheese, sprinkled liberally over pasta and other local dishes, and what is generally considered Italy's best prosciutto, also known as Parma ham.

Originally Etruscan, Parma achieved importance as a Roman colony following the construction of the Via Emilia. With the fall of Rome, Parma lapsed into obscurity, later prospering under the Gothic king Theodoric. The city was headed by various important families through the early period of the Renaissance, including the Viscontis, Estes and Sforzas, before it was presented to the Farnese family by Pope Paul III. The Bourbons took control in 1731 as did Napoleon later that century. Correggio and Parmigianino, two great Renaissance painters, worked extensively in the city.

Orientation

From the train station in Piazzale dalla Chiesa, head south along Via Verdi for the huge Palazzo della Pillotta. Cross Via Garibaldi for the Duomo area, or walk south for Piazza Garibaldi, the main square.

Information

Tourist office The APT tourist office (☎ 0521-23 47 35) is in Piazza del Duomo and opens from 9 am to 12.30 pm and 3 to 5 pm Monday to Friday, to 12.30 pm Saturday. Informa Giovani (☎ 0521-21 87 48), Viale Toscanini 2, can help on a range of topics, including information for gay, lesbian and disabled travellers.

Post & Telecommunications The main post office is at Via Melloni, off Via Garibaldi, and opens from 8.15 am to 7 pm

Monday to Friday, to 12.30 pm Saturday. Poste restante mail can be addressed to 43100 Parma. SIP telephones are in Piazza Garibaldi and open from 7 am to 11.30 pm daily. The telephone code for Parma is 0521.

Emergency For a police emergency, call ☎ 113. The police headquarters (☎ 23 88 88) are at Borgo della Posta. For medical attention, the Ospedale Maggiore (☎ 9 67 20) is at Via Gramsci 14, west of the centre.

Things to See

Piazza Garibaldi, with its expensive cafés, is the centre of Parma. The Governor's Palace at the northern end, dating from the 17th century, hides the **Madonna della Steccata** church, containing frescoes completed by Parmigianino before he died, and tombs of the Farnese and Bourbons.

A few minutes' walk along Strada Cavour, lined with cafés, banks and expensive shops, is the Piazza del Duomo. One of the most beautiful churches in Italy, the 11th century Lombard-Romanesque **Duomo** houses brilliant frescoes, including the *Assumption of the Virgin* by Correggio in the cupola. The sculpture *Descent from the Cross*, completed in 1178 by Benedetto Antelami, is in the south transept. The cathedral is undergoing restoration, but remains open. It is closed from midday to 3.30 pm daily.

The pink marble **Baptistry** was completed in 1260 by Antelami, who was also responsible for the reliefs inside. It is considered his best work. It opens daily from 9 am to 12.30 pm and 3 to 6 pm, and entry is L3000.

The **Church of San Giovanni Evangelista**, behind the cathedral, contains more works by Correggio and Parmigianino. Other Correggio works can be seen in the refectory of the **Convent of San Paolo** to the west, off Via Melloni.

West from the Duomo across Strada Cavour is the **Glauco-Lombardi Museum**, housing a collection of pieces belonging to Marie-Louise of Austria, wife of Napoleon,

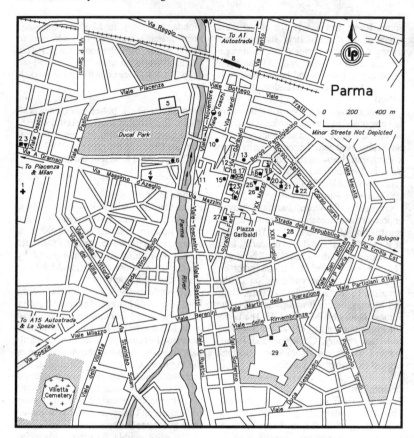

who ruled the city after her husband's defeat at Waterloo. It is open daily from 9.30 am to 12.30 pm and 3 to 7 pm, and entry is free.

Across Via Garibaldi is the immense **Pillotta Palace**, several walls of which still stand alone after WW II bombing caused heavy damage. Built for the Farnese family between 1583 and 1622, and named after the Spanish ball game of pelota played within its walls, the palace now houses several museums and picture galleries. The National Gallery includes works by Correggio and Parmigianino, as well as Fra Angelico, van Dyck and a figure of Marie-Louise by Canova. The gallery opens from 9 am to 2

pm except Monday, and entry is L10,000, which includes entry to the Farnese Theatre. The theatre, a copy of Palladio's Olympic Theatre in Vicenza, is housed in the palace's fencing school. It was completely rebuilt after being destroyed during WW II. Upstairs in the National Archaeological Museum is an impressive collection of Etruscan artefacts excavated from the Po plain. It is open daily from 9 am to 2 pm, except Monday, and entry is L4000. The Palatine Library has an important collection of volumes, while the Bodoni Museum is devoted to the life of Giambattista Bodoni, who designed the typeface that bears his

■ PLACES TO STAY

2 Albergo Sole
7 Albergo Moderno
26 Albergo Lazzaro
27 Croce di Malta
29 Citadel Youth Hostel &
   Camping Ground

▼ PLACES TO EAT

3 Blu Moon
4 Pizzeria Il Gattopardo
25 Le Premier & San Biagio

OTHER

1 Ospedale Maggiore
5 Ducal Palace

6 Toscanini House
8 Main Railway Station
9 Main Bus Station
10 Pilotta Palace
11 Piazza Ghiaia
12 Piazza della Pace
13 Convent of San Paolo
14 Main Tourist Information Office
15 Teatro Regio
16 Glauco-Lombardi Museum
17 Main Post Office
18 Episcopal Palace
19 Piazza del Duomo
20 Baptistry
21 Duomo
22 Church of San Giovanni Evangelista
23 Church of Madonna della Steccata
24 SIP Telephones
28 Police Headquarters

name. The museum is closed until early 1994.

Opposite the palace across the river is the Ducal Palace and **Ducal Park**, an immense garden dating from the 18th century, built around a Farnese palace. The palace opens daily except Sunday from 8 am to midday, while the gardens open from 7 am to 5.30 pm; both have free admission.

Just south of the palace at Via R Tanzi is **Toscanini House**, the birthplace of one of Italy's greatest 20th century composers. Farther south, along Strada Nino Bixio, is the **Villetta Cemetery**, with a tomb of composer Niccolò Paganini.

Places to Stay

Cheap accommodation can be difficult to find most of the year, so bookings are advisable. Located within the walls of the giant former fortress, the city's youth hostel, the *Ostello Cittadella* (☎ 58 15 46), Parco Cittadella 5, charges L13,000 a night. Take bus No 6 or 9 from the train station or city centre and ask the driver for directions. There is a *camping ground* inside the fortress, run by the same management.

The *Albergo Sole* (☎ 99 51 07), Via Gramsci 15, has singles/doubles from L33,000/45,000. Take bus No 10 from the station. *Albergo Lazzaro* (☎ 20 89 44), Via XX Marzo, the street leading away from the Baptistry, has rooms from L33,000/50,000. The *Croce di Malta* (☎ 23 56 43), Borgo Palmia 8, south of Piazza Garibaldi, has rooms from L38,000/58,000. The two-star *Albergo Moderno* (☎ 77 26 47), near the station at Via A Cecchi 4, has rooms from L38,000/60,000.

Places to Eat

There is a produce market in Piazza Ghiaia, near the river south of the Pillotta Palace, open daily in the morning and afternoon. For eats at the cheaper end, the self-service restaurant *Le Premier*, Borgo San Biagio 6, is worth finding. A meal could cost less than L10,000. *San Biagio*, a couple of doors down, is an excellent place to sample local fare at reasonable prices.

Pizzeria Il Gattopardo, Via M d'Azeglio 63, is considered one of the city's best, with pizzas from L5000. If you are staying at Albergo Sole, *Blu Moon*, a couple of doors towards the city centre on Via Gramsci, has everything from seafood to pizzas. Main courses start at L8000 and the cover charge is L2000.

Entertainment

The city's opera calendar features top Italian performers and is staged at the Teatro Regio (☎ 79 56 78), Via Garibaldi 16. Parma's theatre companies are highly regarded and perform at Teatro Due (☎ 23 02 42), Viale Basetti 12. The city sponsors the *Musica e Stelle* festival during summer, featuring classical music and opera in Piazza del Duomo.

Getting There & Away

TEP (☎ 21 41) operates bus services throughout the city and region, including into the Apennines and to Soragna and Busseto (see the following section) from Viale P Toschi, three blocks south of the train station. By train (☎ 77 11 18), the city is connected by frequent services to Milan, Bologna and Rome.

By car, the city is just south of the A1 autostrada and east of the A15, which connects the A1 to Genoa. It is on the Via Emilia (ss9), while the ss62 provides an alternative route parallel to the A15. The ss63 heads south-west to the Riviera di Levante. There is a major car park surrounding the Pillotta Palace and plenty of metered parking near the station.

AROUND PARMA

The area north of Parma makes for an interesting drive. Take Via Emilia west from Parma and head north on the road for Soragna at Fidenza. The **Rocca di Soragna**, a sumptuous castle dating from the 15th century, was built for the Sanvitale family, whose descendants still occupy it. There are frescoes by Parmigianino and original furniture. It opens from 9 am to midday and 3 to 7 pm from Thursday to Sunday.

Continuing north-west is Roncole Verdi, the birthplace of the great composer, and then **Busseto**, Verdi's home. Busseto boasts the splendid Verdi Theatre, where the master performed regularly (unfortunately closed for restoration until 1994), and his apartment. A small Verdi museum inside the run-down Villa Pallavicino is worth a visit, as is his villa just north-west of Busseto at

Sant'Agata. The L5000 ticket gains entry to all the Verdi sites.

There are 25 castles in the province of Parma, most below the city. The **Bardi Castle**, south-west of the city, dates back to 898, although most of the structure was built in the 15th century. Contact the APT in Parma for a road map with locations of the castles.

The **Parma Apennines** south of the city offer walking tracks of varying difficulties, and the many mountain refuges allow longer treks. Contact the tourist office in Parma for details, or the Gestione Servizi Turistico Sportivi (STS, ☎ 9 12 60) in Parma, Via Rapallo 2, which arranges sporting trips and can advise on hiring sporting equipment. The Centro Turismo Equestre at Tarsogno (☎ 0525-892 66), south of Salsomaggiore Terme (ask the Parma APT for directions), hires horses and arranges horse treks.

PIACENZA

At the north-western corner of Emilia, Piacenza is another prosperous Italian town generally overlooked by tourists. It features several significant Renaissance monuments and is worth a stopover. The city is on the Via Emilia and is close to the A1 autostrada.

Orientation & Information

The train station is at the eastern edge of town. The IAT tourist information office (☎ 0523-293 24) in Piazza dei Mercanti opens in the mornings and afternoons but is closed on Thursdays and Sundays. It provides information on the city's main attractions and the medieval castles dotting the Emilian countryside. Poste restante mail can be addressed to 29100 Piacenza, and the telephone code for Piacenza is 0523.

Things to See

The central Piazza dei Cavalli is dominated by the town hall, also known as **Il Gotico**. The 13th century building is one of the country's finest Gothic palaces. In front of the palace, the two equestrian statues of Farnese dukes Ranuccio and Alessandro, by Francesco Mochi, date from 1625 and are

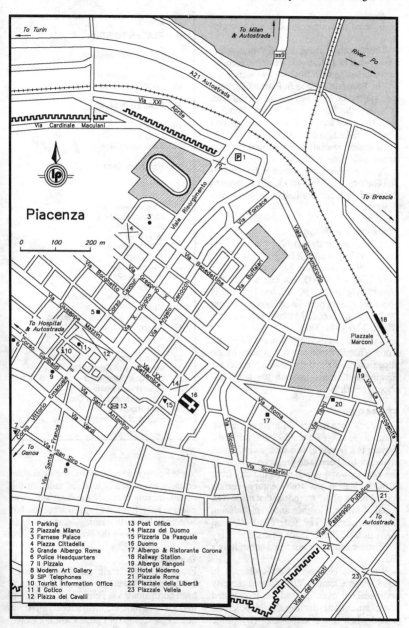

Piacenza

0   100   200 m

To Turin

To Milan
& Autostrada

River Po

To Brescia

To Hospital
& Autostrada

To Genoa

Piazzale
Marconi

To
Autostrada

1 Parking
2 Piazzale Milano
3 Farnese Palace
4 Piazza Cittadella
5 Grande Albergo Roma
6 Police Headquarters
7 Il Pizzaio
8 Modern Art Gallery
9 SIP Telephones
10 Tourist Information Office
11 Il Gotico
12 Piazza dei Cavalli
13 Post Office
14 Piazza del Duomo
15 Pizzeria Da Pasquale
16 Duomo
17 Albergo & Ristorante Corona
18 Railway Station
19 Albergo Rangoni
20 Hotel Moderno
21 Piazzale Roma
22 Piazzale della Libertà
23 Piazzale Vellela

considered masterpieces of Baroque sculpture.

The **Duomo**, along Via XX Settembre, was started in 1122 and is a sombre Romanesque building with frescoes by Guercino.

The **Farnese Palace** in Piazza Cittadella was started in 1558 but was never finished. It houses the Municipal Museum, home to the Etruscan *Piacenza Liver*, a bronze liver used for divining the future. The museum has been under restoration but should be open again some time in 1993.

At the southern end of town is the **Modern Art Gallery**, Via San Siro 13, which contains 18th and 19th century Italian art and sculpture.

Places to Stay & Eat

Budget accommodation is not one of Piacenza's strong points. *Albergo Corona* (☎ 2 09 48), Via Roma 141, has singles/doubles from L30,000/40,000, but call ahead. The *Hotel Moderno* (☎ 2 92 96), Via Tibini 31 is about the same price. The *Albergo Rangoni* (☎ 2 17 78), Piazzale Marconi 1, has rooms from L32,000/44,000.

If you are just passing through, *Il Pizzaio*, Corso Vittorio Emanuele II, has pizza by the slice from L1500, or else grab a pizza at the *Ristorante Corona*, beneath the hotel, for about L6000.

FERRARA

On the northern fringes of Emilia-Romagna, close to the River Po and its delta wetlands, Ferrara is a beautiful and serene city whose character has been well preserved. Home to the Este dynasty, which ruled the city from 1260 to late in the 16th century, Ferrara retains much of the splendour that made it an equal of Milan, Florence and Venice during the Renaissance. The Este court attracted many notable Renaissance artists, and today the historic centre is considered one of Italy's finest.

When the House of Este collapsed in 1598, Pope Clement VIII claimed the city and presided over its decline. It regained some splendour during the Napoleonic period when it was made chief city of the

■	PLACES TO STAY
2	Albergo Bergamasco
3	Youth Hostel
18	Albergo Nazionale
20	Casa degli Artisti

▼	PLACES TO EAT
13	Al Brindisi
19	Le Grazie
21	Fantastico Giovedi
22	Il Cucco
30	Ristorante Orazio

	OTHER
1	Main Railway Station
4	National Picture Gallery
5	Police Headquarters
6	Main Post Office
7	SIP Telephones
8	Este Castle
9	Piazza Castello
10	Main Bus Station
11	Piazza Municipio & Tourist Information Office
12	Municipal Palace
14	Cathedral & Piazza Cattedrale
15	Piazza Trento Trieste
16	Ghetto
17	Parking
23	Casa Romei
24	Monastery of Corpus Domini
25	Ospedale Sant'Anna
26	Palazzina di Marfisa
27	Piazzale Medaglie d'Oro
28	Schifanoia Palace
29	Palace of Ludovico the Moor

lower Po, and in recent years, the local government has carefully restored much of the centre, making it one of the most attractive cities in Italy. It is not a big tourist centre but is definitely worth visiting, particularly if you want to explore the Po delta.

Orientation

From the main train station in Piazza Stazione at the western edge of the centre, head north along Via Felisatti and turn right into Viale Cavour, the main street. Turn right at the Este Castle for Piazza Castello. Corso

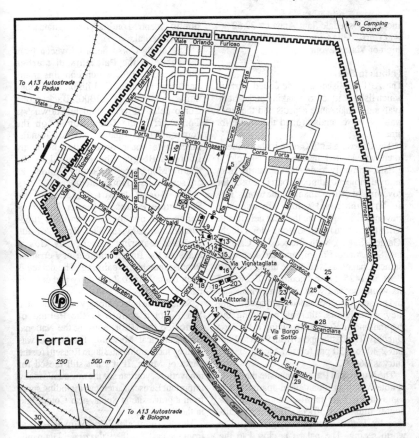

Ferrara

0   250   500 m

Martiri della Libertà, at the far end of the castle, runs into Piazza Cattedrale and Piazza Trento Trieste, the centre of town. Piazza Municipio and the tourist office are reached through a gateway opposite the front entrance of the cathedral. The piazza can also be reached along Via Cassoli and Via Garibaldi, a more direct route from the station.

Information

Tourist Office The APT tourist office (☎ 0532-20 93 70) is in Piazza Municipio, and has good information about the region, including the Po delta.

Post & Telecommunications The post office is at Viale Cavour 27, near the castle. It's open Monday to Friday from 8.15 am to 7 pm, Saturday from 8.30 am to 1 pm. Poste restante mail can be addressed to 44100 Ferrara.

SIP telephones are in Largo Castello 30, and open until 7.30 pm. Next door are ASST phones with attendants, open until midnight. The telephone code for Ferrara is 0532.

Emergency The police headquarters (☎ 2 69 44) are at Corso Ercole I d'Este 26, and the staff speak English. For medical assistance, the Ospedale Sant'Anna (☎ 39 52 36) is at Corso della Giovecca 203, the continuation of Viale Cavour.

Things to See

The APT publishes a guide called *Ferrara* which lists six itineraries, taking in the medieval and Renaissance aspects and the city's wall, which extends around the centre for nine km.

The imposing **Este Castle** in the centre of town was started in 1385 for Niccolo II d'Este, primarily to defend the family from unloyal subjects. Although parts are used for government offices, many of the rooms, particularly the royal suites, are open for viewing. Highlights are the Sala dei Giganti (Giants' Room) and Salone dei Giochi (Games' Salon), with frescoes by Camillo and Sebastiano Filippi, and the Renée de France Chapel, as well as the dungeon cells. Here, in 1425, Duke Nicolò III d'Este had his young second wife, Parisina Malatesta, and his son, Ugo, beheaded after discovering they were lovers, thereby providing the inspiration for Robert Browning's *My Last Duchess*. The castle opens from 9 am to 1 pm and 2.30 to 6.30 pm (closed Monday), and entry is L6000.

The **Municipal Palace** opposite the castle is noteworthy as it contained apartments of some of the Este family, although it now houses municipal offices. The grand staircase by Pietro Benvenuti degli Ordani is worth seeing. The palace is closed to the public, but you can see some of the rooms if you ask the attendant.

South-east is the **cathedral**, consecrated early in the 12th century, featuring a mixture of Renaissance and Gothic styles. Note also the array of columns along its south façade. Inside is the Cathedral Museum, containing a superb collection of Renaissance pieces such as 15th century illustrated missals, and works by Jacopo della Quercia and other Renaissance masters. It opens daily from 10 am to 2 pm and 3.30 to 5 pm, and admission is by donation. The bell tower was started in 1412 by the important Florentine architect, Leon Battista Alberti. The city's former

ghetto is centred on Via Vignatagliata south of the cathedral.

East along Corso della Giovecca from the castle is the **Palazzina di Marfisa d'Este** at No 170, which contains many important frescoes by Filippi. It is open daily and entry is L2000. Back along Corso della Giovecca and left down Via Corramari is the **Casa Romei**, on the corner of Via Savonarola, a typical Renaissance-style house once called home by Lucrezia Borgia. She is buried in the nearby Monastery of Corpus Domini, as are several Este family members.

Via Borgo di Sotto leads to the **Schifanoia Palace**, a former Este residence and one of the family's most sumptuous palaces. The Room of the Months, featuring frescoes by Cossa, ranks as the finest example of Ferrarese Renaissance mural painting. The palace is open from 9 am to 7 pm daily and entry is L2,500.

South of the palace along Via Mellone and Via Porta d'Amore is the **Palace of Ludovico the Moor**, housing the National Archaeological Museum. The palace was built by local architect Biagio Rossetti for the Duke of Milan. If it's not still closed for renovations, you can see the museum's many important Etruscan artefacts, including some from a grave site at Spina, near Comacchio in the Po delta.

Heading north along Corso Ercole I d'Este from the castle is the Palazzo dei Diamanti, the Palace of the Diamonds, named after the shape of its rusticated façade and built for Sigismondo d'Este late in the 15th century by Biagio Rossetti. Regarded as the family's finest palace, the building now houses the **National Picture Gallery**, featuring works by artists of the Ferrarese and Bolognese schools, and a series of prints by Mantegna. The gallery is open from 9 am to 2 pm Tuesday to Saturday, to 1 pm Sunday, and entry is L6000. The **Modern Art Gallery**, also in the building, features works by prominent Italian contemporary artists. Next door at No 19 is the **Risorgimento & Resistance Museum**.

Festivals

The Ferrara Buskers' Festival, held late each August, attracts buskers from around the globe, primarily because the city pays travel and accommodation expenses for 20 lucky aspirants. Entry forms are available from the festival (☎ 4 93 37, fax 75 41 91), or write to the festival, c/o the Istituto di Cultura, Casa G Cini, Via Santo Stefano 24.

Places to Stay

Accommodation is easy to find most of the year, although many hotels close during August. The city's only camping ground is *Estense* (☎ 75 23 96), Via Gramicia, north of the centre outside the wall. Take bus No 3 from the station. The IYHF youth hostel, the *Ostello Estense* (☎ 2 10 98), Via Benvenuto Tisi 5, is about 10 minutes from the station towards the castle. Take bus No 1, 2 or 9. Bed and breakfast is L12,000 and it closes from October to April.

The best hotel deal is at *Casa degli Artisti* (☎ 76 10 38), Via Vittoria 66, a few minutes from the cathedral, with singles/doubles for L25,000/38,000. Book ahead. The *Albergo Bergamasco* (☎ 20 49 56), Corso Porta Po 170, has rooms from L26,000/40,000. The *Albergo Nazionale* (☎ 20 96 04), Corso Porta Reno 32, is near the station and has rooms from L33,000/43,000.

Places to Eat

The cuisine is similar to that of most of the region, incorporating meats and cheeses. One of the local specialities is *cappellacci*, a pasta pouch filled with pumpkin, available at *Il Cucco*, Via Voltacasotto, where a meal could cost up to L25,000. Another traditional dish is *tigella*, a mixture of cheeses and meats served with bread, available at *Ristorante Orazio*, Via Passega, south-west of the city centre; the dish costs L15,000 and is a full meal. *Le Grazie*, Via Vignatagliata 61, in the ghetto, specialises in Jewish dishes. Main courses start at L8000. *Al Brindisi*, Via Adelardi 11, next to the cathedral, dates from 1435 and serves a salami-and-red-wine dish. This restaurant is more expensive.

Getting There & Away

The bus station is at Via Rampari di San Paolo. ACFT buses (☎ 20 52 35) operate services within the city and to surrounding towns such as Comacchio as well as the Adriatic beaches. By train (☎ 3 76 49 for information) there are frequent services to Bologna, Venice, Ravenna and other towns in the region. By car, the city is close to the A13 autostrada which connects Bologna with Padua.

Getting Around

Normal traffic is banned from the city centre, and there are parking stations at the southern end of the centre on Via Bologna, and the eastern edge near Piazzale Medaglie d'Oro. ACFT runs bus Nos 1, 2 and 9 from the station to the centre.

THE PO DELTA

Considering the incredibly polluted state of the River Po, the Po delta, which straddles Emilia-Romagna and the Veneto, should be an unpleasant and uninviting place. However, the stretch of coast where the mighty Po meets the Adriatic Sea is strangely alluring, particularly because the wetlands surrounding the two large lagoons – the Comacchio Valleys in the south and the Bertuzzi Valley in the north – have been designated as nature reserves. The area provides some of Europe's best bird-watching, and after many years of neglect by tourist authorities is now drawing quite a crowd. Despite this, swimming is banned in the river, and many beaches on the coast have perennial problems with sludge-like algae plagues caused by the high phosphate levels from the polluters upstream.

If you want to stay in the area, try *Albergo Luciana* (☎ 0533-71 21 40), Via Roma 66, in Codigoro, which charges L25,000/40,000 for a single/double.

Information

Most towns in the area have IAT or APT tourist offices, including at Adria (☎ 0426-4 25 54), Piazza Bocchi; Comacchio (☎ 0533-31 28 44), Palazzo Patrignani; and at the splendid Pomposa Abbey (☎ 0533-71 01 00) near Codigoro. They produce a wealth of information, including cycling itineraries, walking and horse-riding details, and boat excursions, the best way to see the area.

Things to See & Do

The **Pomposa Abbey**, 50 km east of Ferrara, near Codigoro, is one of the oldest Benedictine abbeys in Italy, with a church dating from the 7th century. It is believed the monk Guido d'Arezzo invented the musical scale here. Inside, the church is adorned with frescoes from the 14th century Rimini school and works by Vitale di Bologna, and it contains a small (free) museum. Musica Pomposa (☎ 0533-72 95 85 for information) is a music festival staged at the abbey each July. Buses connect the abbey with Ferrara and Comacchio.

Comacchio is a small fishing village which has but one attraction – the Trepponti (Triple Bridge) built in 1635, which crosses three canals. Don't stop unless you must, as the city's claim to be a mini Venice is not worthy.

The tourist office at Ca' Vecchia (☎ 0544-44 68 66), Via Fossatone, produces a map detailing the types of birds likely to be found in the Po Delta Regional Park near San Vitale, and the sanctuaries at Punte Alberete and Valle Mandriole. The World Wide Fund for Nature in Ferrara (☎ 0532-6 00 09), Viale Alfonso I d'Este 7, can provide information about the wildlife.

For boat trips, try the boat *Delfinus* (☎ 0533-38 12 65), which leaves from Lido degli Scacchi east of Comacchio, or the *Principessa* (☎ 0533-99 98 15), which leaves from Gorino.

RAVENNA

This city is famous for the early Christian and Byzantine mosaics which adorn its churches and monuments, many of them dating from the mid-6th century when Ravenna was the capital of the Byzantine Empire's western regions during the reign of Emperor Justinian and Empress Theodora. The city had been the capital of the Western

■	PLACES TO STAY
3	Al Giaciglio
25	Albergo Italia
33	Albergo Perla Nera

▼	PLACES TO EAT
5	Scai'
10	La Gardella
11	Free Flow Bizantino
22	Guidarello
23	Enoteca dei Vini di Romagna

	OTHER
1	Theodoric's Mausoleum
2	Tourist Information Office
4	Piazza Baracca
6	National Museum
7	Basilica of San Vitale
8	Mausoleum of Galla Placidia
9	Tourist Information Office
12	Piazza Andrea Costa
13	Baptistry of the Arians & Church of the Holy Spirit
14	Piazza Farini
15	Railway Station
16	Piazza del Popolo
17	Police Headquarters
18	Post Office
19	Piazza Garibaldi
20	SIP Telephones
21	Piazza Kennedy
24	Basilica of Sant'Apollinare Nuovo
26	Piazza del Duomo
27	Neoni Baptistry
28	Cathedral
29	Episcopal Museum
30	Piazza Caduti
31	Church of San Francesco
32	Ospedale Santa Maria delle Croci

Roman Empire from 402 AD when Emperor Honorius moved his court from Rome because Ravenna's surrounding marshes made it easier to defend from northern invaders. Rome fell to the Goths soon after, and Ravenna succumbed in 473. Byzantine rule came in 540 and lasted until 752, when the city was conquered by the Lombards. Venetians controlled the city from 1441 to 1509, when it was incorporated into the Papal States.

Under the Romans, Goths and Byzan-

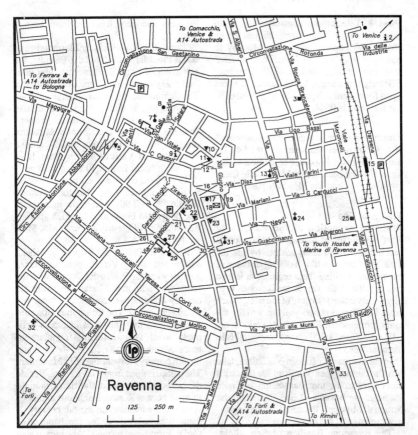

Ravenna

0   125   250 m

tines, Ravenna grew to become one of the most splendid cities on the Mediterranean, and its mosaics are considered the best outside Istanbul; in his *Divine Comedy*, Dante described them as a symphony of colour. The city is close to Adriatic beaches, but prospective swimmers should first check pollution levels, as the Po spews out industrial effluent to the north.

Orientation

From the train station, on the eastern edge of town in Piazza Farini, it's a short walk along Viale Farini and its continuation, Via Diaz, into the central Piazza del Popolo. Via di Roma, which crosses Viale Farini, heads north to Venice and the A14 autostrada, and south to Rimini.

Information

Tourist Offices The APT (☎ 0544-3 54 04) is at Via Salara 8. Walk north along Via Matteotti from Piazza XX Settembre, adjoining Piazza del Popolo, turn left into Via C Cavour and right into Via Salara. It opens daily from 8.15 am to 1.45 pm and 3.30 to 6.30 pm. A second office (☎ 0544-45 15 39) is at Theodoric's Mausoleum, Via delle Industrie 14, and opens from March to September.

Post & Telecommunications The main post office is in Piazza Garibaldi, just before Piazza del Popolo, and opens Monday to Saturday from 8 am to 7 pm. Poste restante mail can be addressed to 48100 Ravenna. SIP telephones are in Via G Rasponi 22, and open from 8 am to 8 pm. The telephone code for Ravenna is 0544.

Emergency For a police emergency, call ☎ 113. The police headquarters (☎ 54 41 11) are in Piazza del Popolo. For medical assistance, the Ospedale Santa Maria delle Croci (☎ 40 91 11) is at Via Missiroli 10.

Things to See

With the exception of the Basilica of Sant'Apollinare in Classe, five km southeast of the city and easily reached by bus, the main sites are all within walking distance of each other. Visiting them requires at least a full day. The best way to see Ravenna is to buy a daily ticket from any of the sites, which costs L9000 and allows you entry to the six main monuments. Remember to take some L100, L200 and L500 coins for spotlights in the churches.

From the tourist office in Via Salara, take Via Cavour and then Via Fanti for the city's main attractions, the Mausoleum of Galla Placidia, the Basilica of San Vitale and the National Museum, clustered on the northwestern edge of the city centre.

The Byzantine **Basilica of San Vitale**, consecrated in 547 by Archbishop Maximian, is built on an octagonal plan. Its exterior belies the dazzling interior, regarded as one of Italy's marvels. The marble decoration and Byzantine columns lead the eye to the mosaics around the chancel, constructed between 521 and 548. The mosaics on the side and end walls represent scenes from the Old Testament; to the left, Abraham and the three angels and the sacrifice of Isaac are depicted; and on the right are the death of Abel and the offering of Melchizedek. Inside the chancel are the finest mosaics of the series, depicting the Byzantine emperor Justinian with Maximian, and to the right,

Empress Theodora. It is open from 9 am to 7 pm.

Through the basilica is the **Mausoleum of Galla Placidia**, built by Galla Placidia, the half-sister of Emperor Honorius, who initiated many of Ravenna's grandest buildings. The light inside, filtered through the alabaster windows, is dim but good enough to illuminate the city's oldest mosaics. It opens from 9 am to 7 pm. The **National Museum** contains Roman, Christian and Byzantine artefacts and various items from later periods; it opens from 8.30 am to 1.30 pm.

To see local artisans constructing mosaics in the traditional way, visit the **Mosaics Studio** (☎ 3 60 90), next to the museum at Via Benedetto Fiandrini 14, which specialises in copies of the city's finer works. Most are for sale.

Return to Piazza del Popolo and head south-west along Via Rasponi to Piazza Kennedy and the Piazza del Duomo with the **cathedral**, built in 1733 after the earlier 5th century building was completely destroyed by an earthquake. The **Episcopal Museum** next door in the Episcopal Palace is definitely worth visiting for the fragments of mosaics gathered from around the city, and the 6th century ivory throne of St Maximian. The palace is open from 9 am to 7 pm. Beside the cathedral is the **Neoni Baptistry**, thought to have been a Roman bathhouse and converted into a baptistry in the 5th century. It features mosaics depicting the baptism of Christ, surrounded by the 12 Apostles. It also opens from 9 am to 7 pm.

Through Piazza Caduti is the **Church of San Francesco**, built in the 5th century, and the **Tomb of Dante**, who fled to Ravenna in 1317 after being driven out of Florence. He wrote much of the *Divine Comedy* in Ravenna. The tomb opens from 8 am to 7 pm, and a small museum next door, dedicated to his life, opens from 7 am to 12.30 pm and 3 to 6 pm. Entry is L3000, but free on Sundays.

Heading north through Piazza Garibaldi with the Teatro Alighieri and right into Via Diaz, you will come to the **Baptistry of the Arians** and Church of the Holy Spirit. The baptistry was built by the Goths and features fine mosaics. South along Via di Roma is the **Basilica of Sant'Apollinare Nuovo**, originally built by the Goths in the 6th century. The high walls on the nave are completely covered with mosaics – on the right depicting a procession of 26 martyrs, and on the left a procession of virgins. It opens from 9 am to 7 pm.

Five km south-east of the city centre along Via Romea Sud, the continuation of Via di Roma and Via Cesarea, is the **Basilica of Sant'Apollinare in Classe**. Built in the 6th century on the burial site of Ravenna's patron saint, St Apollinaris, who converted the city to Christianity in the 2nd century, the basilica is regarded as one of the city's finest and features a brilliant mosaic over the altar. By train, the basilica is one stop out of town, or take bus No 4 from the city centre.

Mosaic Courses

The Centro Internazionale di Studi per l'Insegnamento del Mosaico runs a series of two-week mosaic courses during June, July and August each year starting at L400,000, where you can learn to make your own Byzantine wonder. Contact CISIM (☎ 48 23 78), Via Corrado Ricci 29, for information.

Places to Stay

The city is a day trip from Bologna, but its hostel and cheap hotels make staying no problem, except in summer. The APT can provide a list of the hundreds of hotels lining the beaches near Ravenna, and Terranostra (☎ 3 32 15), Via Massimo d'Azeglio 38, can arrange accommodation on farms in the province.

The closest camping is at Marina di Revenna on the beach (take the ATM bus or follow the ss67). *Camping Piombino* (☎ 53 02 30), Viale Lungomare, and *Campeggio Riva Verde* (☎ 53 04 91), Viale della Nazione 301, have reasonably priced sites.

The IYHF youth hostel, the *Ostello Dante* (☎ 42 04 05), Via Aurelio Nicolodi 12, is one km from the train station towards the beach, and is served by bus No 1. Bed and breakfast is L16,000 and a meal L12,000.

The *Albergo La Perla Nera* (☎ 6 20 55),

Via Cesarea 191, is one of the cheapest hotels, with singles/doubles from L22,000/35,000. *Al Giaciglio* (☎ 3 94 03), Via Rocca Brancaleone 42, is slightly more expensive. *Albergo Italia* (☎ 21 70 04) near the station at Viale G Pallavicini 4, has singles/doubles from L35,000/55,000.

Places to Eat

The city's fresh-produce market in Piazza Andrea Costa, north of Piazza del Popolo, is the best bet for budget food, while the self-service *Free Flow Bizantino*, in the same piazza, is very cheap. *Pizzeria Altero*, Via Cavour 31, has pizza by the slice from L1000, and the hamburger fast-food restaurant *Burghy* in Piazza del Popolo has a great view and cheap beers.

To try local wines, the *Enoteca dei Vini di Romagna*, Via Corrado Ricci 24, has a good selection and serves traditional food at reasonable prices. At *La Gardella*, Via Ponte Marino 1, and *Scai'*, Via Maggiore 2, you can eat a meal for about L23,000, while *Guidarello*, Via Gessi 9, specialises in local dishes and charges from L6000 for main courses.

Entertainment

The city hosts a blues festival each July which attracts big US names. There is also a busy summer concert calendar using many of the churches as venues. Enquire at the APT.

Getting There & Away

ATM buses (☎ 3 52 88) depart from the train station for towns along the coast and north, in the Po delta area. Frequent trains (☎ 3 64 50 for information) connect the city with Bologna, Ferrara (where you can change for Venice), Rimini and the south coast. By car, Ravenna is reached by a branch of the A14 Bologna-Rimini autostrada. Major car parks are behind the train station and near the Basilica of San Vitale, and charge L1500 an hour.

Getting Around

Ravenna is fairly compact and easy to cover

on foot. To see the city by bicycle, hire one at Coop San Vitale in Piazza Farini to the left of the station for L1000 an hour or L7000 a day.

RIMINI

Originally Umbrian, then Etruscan and Roman, Rimini sits at the centre of the Riviera del Sole and is now inhabited by beach-goers. Little is left of the old city centre, and what remained was badly damaged or destroyed during 400 bombing raids in WW II. There is little to draw you to the town, unless you are interested in some of Italy's best beaches and having a bit of fun after dark – the city's massive holiday crowds throng to the 120 mostly tacky night-clubs or gawk at the booming transsexual prostitution trade.

Orientation

The main train station is in Piazzale Cesare Battisti, at the northern edge of the old city centre. Via Dante leads to Via IV Novembre and Piazza Tre Martiri. Corso d'Augusto connects that piazza with the city's other main square, Piazza Cavour. To get to the beach, walk to the north-western edge of Piazzale Battisti and turn right into Viale Principe Amedeo di Savoia, which broadens out into the Parco dell'Indipendenza (and the piazzale of the same name) at the waterfront.

Information

Tourist Offices The main APT office (☎ 0541-5 11 01) is at Piazzale dell'Indipendenza 3 and opens daily from 8 am to 8 pm. There is a second office at the station. The Comune di Rimini (☎ 0541-70 41 10) also operates an information office in the city centre at Corso d'Augusto 156, which opens Monday to Friday from 8 am to 1 pm and 2 to 7 pm, and Saturday morning. Both provide an array of informative brochures, including the *Book Istantaneo*, a very useful annual guide to the city.

Post & Telecommunications The main post office is at Largo Giulio Cesare, with a branch at Via Gambalunga, leading into Piazza Cavour. Both open from 8.30 am to 1.30 pm and 3 to 4 pm Monday to Friday, from 8 am to midday Saturday. Poste restante mail can be addressed to 47037 Rimini.

SIP telephones are at post offices and at Piazza Ferrari 22, and open from 8 am to 10 pm daily. The telephone code for Rimini is 0541.

Emergency For police emergency, call ☎ 113. The police headquarters (☎ 5 10 00) are at Corso d'Augusto 152. For medical assistance, the Ospedale Civile (☎ 70 51 11), Viale Luigi Settembrini 2, is south-east of the city centre along Viale di Roma and Viale Ugo Bassi. The city offers free medical attention for tourists (☎ 2 21 03) during summer months at Viale Mantegazza 13, near Parco dell'Indipendenza.

Things to See

The central Piazza Cavour is lined with the city's finest palaces, including the Communal Palace, built in 1562 and subsequently rebuilt after being almost completely destroyed during WW II. The Gothic

1	Main APT Tourist Office
2	Piazzale Kennedy
3	Fiore Garni
4	Filadelfia Garni
5	Main Railway Station
6	Cardellini Meublé
7	Main Bus Station
8	Roman Amphitheatre
9	Branch Post Office & Telephones
10	Piazza Ferrari
11	Malatesta Temple
12	Bridge of Tiberius
13	Picnic
14	Caffè Imperiale
15	Police Headquarters
16	Comune Tourist Information Office
17	Piazza Cavour
18	Piazza Tre Martiri
19	Main Post Office
20	Arch of Augustus & Largo Giulio Cesare
21	Osteria di Santacolomba
22	Piazza Malatesta
23	Sigismondo Castle

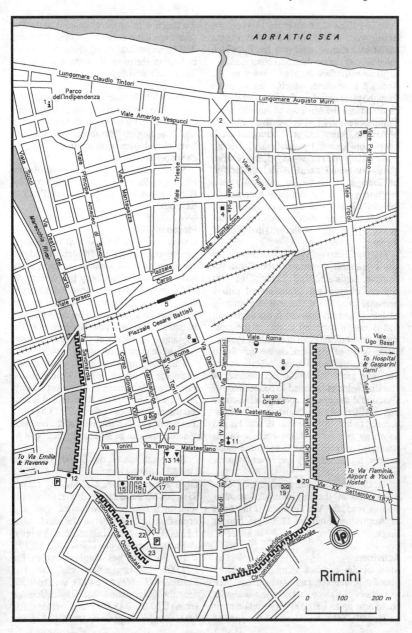

ADRIATIC SEA

Lungomare Claudio Tintori

Parco dell'Indipendenza

Lungomare Augusto Murri

Viale Amerigo Vespucci

Viale Principe Amedeo di Savoia

Viale Mantegazza

Viale Trieste

Viale Pola

Viale Flume

Viale Montalcone

Viale Parisano

Viale Tripoli

Marecchia River

Via Destra del Porto

Viale Succi

Viale Perseo

Piazzale Carso

Piazzale Cesare Battisti

Viale Roma

Viale Ugo Bassi

To Hospital & Gasparini Garni

Via Savonarola

Corso Giovanni

Via Gambalunga

Viale Roma

Via Tonini

Via Dante

Via Clementini

Largo Gramsci

Via Castelfidardo

Via Bastioni Orientali

Via IV Novembre

Via Tonini

Via Templo Malatestiano

To Via Emilia & Ravenna

Corso d'Augusto

To Via Flaminia, Airport & Youth Hostel

Via XX Settembre 1870

Via Garibaldi

Circonvallazione Occidentale

Circonvallazione Meridionale

Via Bastioni Meridionale

Rimini

0   100   200 m

Podestà Palace was built in the 14th century. South-west of Piazza Cavour is Piazza Malatesta, named after the family which ruled the city during the 15th century, and the **Sigismondo Castle**, also known as the Rocca Malatestiana, which takes its name from the most notorious family member. The castle houses the Museum of non-European Cultures, featuring an impressive collection of African, Asian and pre-Columbian art. It opens from 9 am to 1 pm and entry is L6000.

Heading north-west along Corso d'Augusto from Piazza Cavour is the **Bridge of Tiberius**, built in the 1st century AD at the beginning of the Via Emilia as testament to the city's importance to the empire. Piazza Tre Martiri, south-east along Corso d'Augusto, is the site of the original Roman forum.

Just north-east on Via IV Novembre is the city's grandest monument, the **Malatesta Temple**. Dedicated to St Francis, the 13th century church was transformed into a personal chapel for the evil Sigismondo Malatesta and his beloved Isotta degli Atti, and is now recognised as one of the most significant buildings of the Italian Renaissance. Most of the work on the unfinished façade was by Leon Battista Alberti, one of the great architects of the Renaissance. A crucifix inside is believed to be the work of Giotto and the church contains a fresco by Piero della Francesca. Sigismondo was condemned to hell by Pope Pius II, who burned an effigy of him in Rome because of his shameful crimes, which included rape, murder, incest, adultery and severe oppression of his people.

At the south-eastern edge of Corso d'Augusto at the beginning of another Roman road, the Via Flaminia, is the **Arch of Augustus**, built in 27 BC to honour Emperor Augustus.

Activities

Most of the beaches along the coast are rented to private companies which rent space to bathers. At some, a chair and umbrella could cost up to L80,000 a day, while most go for L20,000 a day. Head for the parts of the beach without the ubiquitous umbrellas (there are three small areas near the Parco dell'Indipendenza) or sit close to the shore in front of the rows of paying beach-goers. They can't stop you unless you try to erect your own umbrella.

The River Po pumps its heavily polluted waters into the Adriatic north of Rimini and this occasionally results in sludge-like green algae washing onto the shores. Beaches have been closed over summer in the past, so check before you swim.

Sailboards can be hired from Bagno Nettuno on the beach near Piazzale Kennedy. Bicycles can also be hired from Piazzale Kennedy.

Places to Stay

Unless you have booked well in advance, accommodation can be difficult to find and very expensive in summer, as proprietors make full board compulsory. In winter, many of the area's 1500 hotels close and the city is dead. Your only hope in summer are the room-hawkers, sanctioned by the APT, who frequent intersections on the outskirts of the city and offer rooms at so-called 'bargain' rates, which can be excessive.

The camping ground *Maximum Internazionale* (✆ 37 26 02) on Viale Principe Piemonte at Miramare, south-east of the city, is accessible by bus No 10 or 11 and is near the water. *Camping Italia* (✆ 73 28 82), Via Toscanelli 112, is north-west of the centre at Viserba, and can be reached by bus No 4 or 8.

The youth hostel, the *Ostello Girometti* (✆ 37 32 16), Via Flaminia 300, is beside the city's airport south-east of the city centre. Take bus No 9 and ask the driver, or take the train to Stazione FS Miramare. Bed and breakfast is L16,000 and a meal costs L12,000. The hostel is closed during winter.

The hotel *Filadelfia Garni* (✆ 2 36 79), Viale Pola 25, has singles/doubles for L22,000/44,000 and triples for L66,000. The *Cardellini Meublé* (✆ 2 64 12), Via Dante 50, near the train station, has singles/doubles from L30,000/45,000 and triples for L60,000. *Gasparini Garni* (✆ 38 12 77), Via

Boiardo 3, has rooms from L25,000/40,000 and triples for L60,000 all year. The *Fiore Garni* (☎ 39 06 32), Via Parisano 22, has singles/doubles from L30,000/50,000 and triples for L66,000.

Places to Eat
The city is not noted for its culinary contributions to the Italian table and many restaurants offer cheap tourist menus. The city's produce market is at Via Castelfidardo, near the Malatesta Temple. The self-service restaurant *Picnic*, Via Tempio Malatestiano is one of the better budget deals. The nearby *Caffè Imperiale*, on the corner of Via Tempio Malatestiano and Via Sella Mentana, is a bar serving some takeaway food. *Osteria di Santacolomba*, Via di Duccio 2, off Piazza Malatesta, serves traditional cuisine, with dishes starting at about L7000.

Entertainment
The city's clubs and bars are mainly located along the waterfront. Ask at the tourist office for your type of club – they range from strip and sleazy cabaret to vaguely groovy.

Getting There & Away
By air, the city's Aeroporto Civile (☎ 37 31 32), Via Flaminia, is served by flights from Rome and Milan. ATR buses (☎ 2 44 79) depart from Viale di Roma near the Roman amphitheatre for most towns in the region, including San Marino. The main train station (☎ 5 35 12) has frequent services to Bologna, Milan, Ravenna and south along the coast. By car, the city is close to the A14 autostrada. Parking is available in Piazza Malatesta for L1000 an hour, near the train station and near Piazzale Kennedy.

Getting Around
ATAM buses (☎ 39 04 44) operate services throughout the city and to the airport. Bus Nos 10 and 11 pass the station and go through Piazza Tre Martiri, before heading for Parco dell'Indipendenza. Taxis (☎ 5 00 20) charge a minimum of L6000, then L1650 a km. You can hire bicycles at Piazzale Kennedy, on the waterfront.

San Marino

Supposedly the world's oldest republic, San Marino is more like Disneyland than a typical medieval town. It was formed in 300 AD when a stone-cutter was given the land on top of Monte Titano by a rich Roman woman whose son he had cured.

From the moment you step into this medieval tinseltown you are swept up in the frenzy of its highly organised tourism industry, on which the town depends entirely for its income. It has a small population, mints its own coins and stamps, and even boasts an army of soldiers who do little more than pose for photos. The republic is not worth visiting, except for the splendid views it offers of the coastline. Note that on weekends San Marino becomes extremely crowded, making a visit even more unpleasant.

The Ufficio di Stato per il Turismo (☎ 0549-88 29 98), Palazzo del Turismo, Contrada Omagnano 20, will stamp your passport for a fee. There is a misconception that the republic is a duty-free zone, but prices for alcohol are normal and in some cases higher than in nearby Italy.

The republic has some accommodation, but if the traffic wardens make you park at the base of the mountain (highly likely), you must lug your belongings up in the cable car (L3500 return) from Borgo Maggiore, the main access to the town.

From Rimini, you can catch an ATR bus or drive along Via Nazionale, which becomes the ss72. There is no train to San Marino.

Tuscany

The people of Tuscany (Toscana) can rightly claim to have just about the best of everything – art, architecture, archaeological wonders, countryside bathed in soft pink hues, and some of Italy's best and most well-known wines. It was in Tuscany about 600

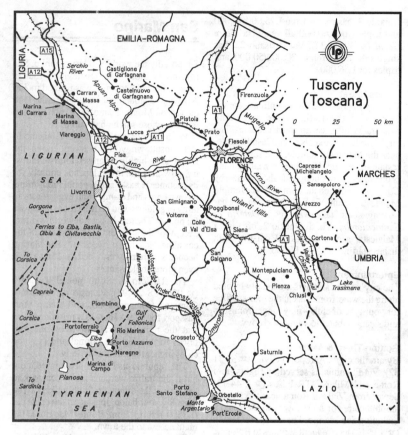

Tuscany (Toscana)

years ago that the Renaissance began, and its effects have been felt throughout the world. The works of Michelangelo, Donatello, Leonardo da Vinci and other 15th and 16th century Tuscan masters still influence artists across the globe. Tuscan architects – notably Brunelleschi, responsible for the magnificent dome of Florence's cathedral, and Alberti, who designed the façade of the city's Santa Maria Novella church – have influenced architects through the centuries. Dante Alighieri, Petrarch and Boccaccio planted the seeds for the Italian national language in the region, and today there is somewhat of a sense of rivalry between the Sienese and the

Florentines as to who speaks the purest Italian.

The Etruscans, who had been in Tuscany since the 8th century BC, were usurped by the Romans and eventually the Lombards. During the 10th century, many towns in Tuscany became free communes – a period that led to intense suspicion between many of these city-states and the subsequent fortification designed to protect them from invaders, and each other. The Medicis in Florence presided over the flowering of the Renaissance, supporting and indulging artists, but the ongoing dispute between the Vatican-backed Guelphs and the Ghibellines, supported by the Holy Roman emperor, maintained this suspicion and eventually led to a period of decline among the major cities.

Most people are drawn to Tuscany by the Renaissance splendour of the art cities of Florence and Siena, or perhaps Pisa's leaning tower. Obviously these cities are the drawing cards, but Tuscany features some of Italy's most impressive hill towns, including Montepulciano in the south-east, and Massa and Carrara near the coast in the north-west, with their marble quarries where Michelangelo selected blocks of the famous white marble for his works. The Etruscan cities of the south – Saturnia, Sovana and others – will take you away from the mainstream tourist itinerary. There is also excellent walking in the area known as the Mugello, north-east of Florence, and on the island of Elba, Napoleon's place of exile.

The Tuscan cuisine is dominated by bread and the extra virgin olive oil produced in the region's hills, which is perhaps Italy's finest. Bread features in every course, including dessert, where it can be topped with egg yolk and orange rind and sprinkled with a heavy layer of powdered sugar. *Crostini*, minced chicken liver canapés, and *bruschetta*, a slab of toasted bread rubbed with garlic and dipped in oil, are popular antipasti, and hearty soups, such as *ribollita*, thickened with bread, are common starters. Meat and poultry are grilled, roasted or fried, and may come simply with a slice of lemon which the Tuscans refer to as sauce. Traditional desserts are simple, such as biscuits flavoured with nuts or spices and served with a glass of the dessert wine *vin santo*.

The region's wines are perhaps the country's best known: Chianti, *vino nobile* and Vernaccia. Traditionally, most Tuscan wines were red, and for some reason whites have never been given much prominence, but in recent years the vineyards around San Gimignano have produced Vernaccia, a crisp white that is becoming more popular.

Travelling in Tuscany is easy. The A1 autostrada and the main north-south train line ensure good north-south connections,

and there are excellent train and bus services within the region. Most areas are easily accessible by public transport, but the flexibility of a car can mean you will get to parts of Tuscany few tourists see. Many of the cities have hotel associations which will book a room for you, although at certain times of the year – Palio time in Siena, for example – finding a room is almost impossible unless you have booked months in advance.

FLORENCE (FIRENZE)

Cradle of the Renaissance, home of Dante, Machiavelli, Michelangelo and the Medicis, Florence is at once overwhelming in its wealth of art, culture and history, and yet one of the most atmospheric and pleasant cities to visit in Italy. The central area of Florence still bears strong resemblance to the small city that contributed so much to the cultural and political development of Europe.

Situated on the banks of the Arno River and set among low hills clad in olive groves and vineyards, Florence is immediately captivating. And despite the traffic, some of the more modern alterations to buildings in the city centre, the intense and unrelenting summer heat, the pollution and the industrial sprawl on the city's outskirts, Florence still attracts millions of tourists each year who come to gaze at Michelangelo's *David*, or stand in awe of Brunelleschi's immense and magnificent Duomo, and Giotto's accompanying bell tower. The French writer Stendhal expressed a feeling of culture shock, of giddy faintness that left him unable to walk after being dazzled by the magnificence of the Church of Santa Croce. This condition is now known as Stendhalismo, or Stendhal's Disease, described by Florentine doctors who treat up to 12 cases each year.

Don't plan to do Florence in a couple of days. You will need at least four or five to get more than just a tourist's impression, which can leave you both overwhelmed and a little disappointed. Many people leave the city unsatisfied, perhaps expecting a pristine Renaissance museum. What you get is a functioning city – even if most businesses are directed towards the tourist dollar – complete with run-down palaces, chaotic traffic, pollution and street litter.

If possible, avoid visiting Florence during August when the weather is extremely hot, still and unrelenting, and when most Florentines depart for the coast. The best times to visit are May, June, September and October.

History

Although Florence's origins are hazy, it is believed that the city was founded as a colony of the Etruscan city of Fiesole in about 200 BC. Development of Florence started after it was settled as Florentia by the Romans in the 1st century BC, probably in the year 59 BC when Julius Caesar chose the banks of the Arno as a settlement for a garrison of the Roman army, whose purpose was to control the Via Flaminia which linked Rome to northern Italy and Gaul. The city grew rapidly under the Romans, largely to serve the trading vessels which used the river.

Around 550 AD the city succumbed during the barbarian invasions, and 20 years later it was occupied by the Lombards, who ruled the city from Lucca. Late in the 8th century the city became part of the Frankish Carolingian empire, which also had its Italian base in Lucca, and later it came under the control of the Germanic Holy Roman emperors. The city prospered during the next three centuries, and in 1115, when Countess Matilda (from the German house of the Marquises of Tuscany) died, control of the city

passed to a body of officials known as the Good Men, and Florence became a free commune. By 1138 the city was ruled by 12 consuls who were assisted by a Council of Hundred, drawn mainly from the prosperous merchant class. Agitation among differing factions in the city led to the appointment of a foreign head of state in 1207, known as the *podestà*, who replaced the council.

The first dissension among the pro-papal Guelphs and the pro-imperial Ghibellines started towards the middle of the 13th century. The Guelphs formed their own constitution and instituted a body of nobles, the Capitano del Popolo, to oversee it. This in effect meant that the city was divided into two republics: the commune under the podestà and the *popolo*, as the new constitution was known, under the capitano. In 1260, the Guelphs were defeated by the Ghibellines at the battle of Montaperti, but the Guelphs returned and took control of the city in 1266.

By 1292, the increasingly turbulent nobility had been excluded from government and by the turn of the century, factions among upper-class Guelphs grouped themselves into two parties, the Neri (Blacks) and the antipapal Bianchi (Whites). When the latter were defeated, one of the many members driven into exile in 1302 was Dante Alighieri. During his time in Florence, and later in exile, Dante established the use of the Italian vernacular in a number of his works and helped to supplant Latin as the language of writers. It was he who formed the basis of the Italian national language that came about almost 600 years later.

In the period leading up to the mid-14th century, the system of government was further democratised until the city became a commercial republic, controlled by the merchant class, which was strongly Guelph.

The plague cut the city's population by one-third in 1347. Subsequent financial problems caused great discontent among workers, who were eventually granted representation on the city's government. However, their representation was short-lived, as from 1382 an alliance between the

Guelphs and the city's wealthiest merchants seized control of the city for over 40 years.

During the latter part of the 14th century, the city was ruled by a caucus of Guelphs under the leadership of the Albizzi family. Opposed to them were the Ricci, Alberti and Medici families, who had the support of the lower classes. During this period, Florence acquired Arezzo, Pisa, Cortona, Livorno and Montepulciano, and it was during this time that the Medicis consolidated their influence, eventually becoming the papal bankers, with branches in 16 cities. After making claims to the leadership of the party in opposition to the Albizzi, Cosimo de' Medici was banished.

His political fortunes grew in his absence, mostly because of the Medici family's sympathies with the lower classes. He returned a year later and became the city's ruler. He was described as serious but unassuming, had a deep understanding of the arts and letters, and was a magnificent patron. His eye for talent and his tact in dealing with artists drew the likes of Alberti, Brunelleschi, Ghilberti, Donatello, Fra Angelico and Filippo Lippi to the city, and many of the city's finest buildings are testimony to his tastes.

Upon Cosimo's death in 1464, rule was assumed by his son, Peter the Gouty, and then his grandson, Lorenzo the Magnificent. Lorenzo's rule (1469-92) ushered in the most glorious period of Florentine civilisation and of the whole Italian Renaissance. His court saw a great flowering of art, music and poetry, achieving a splendour unrivalled in history. Lorenzo favoured Botticelli, Ghirlandaio and Benozzo Gozzoli, and encouraged Leonardo da Vinci, although in 1483, the young Leonardo sought the patronage of the Sforzas in Milan. Lorenzo also encouraged the young Michelangelo, who worked under Bertoldo, Donatello's pupil.

Just before Lorenzo's death in 1492, the Medici bank failed. In 1494, his son Piero fled Florence after surrendering to the French invaders under Charles VIII. The city fell under the control of Girolamo Savonarola, a Dominican monk who instituted a puritanical republic until he fell from public favour and was burned as a heretic in 1498. At about this time, Lorenzo the Magnificent's efforts to gain closer relations with the papacy were coming to fruition. Pope Innocent VIII married his son to Lorenzo's daughter and gave the cardinal's hat to Lorenzo's second son, Giovanni, at the age of 14. Giovanni went on to become Pope Leo X. After Florence's defeat by the Spanish in 1512, the Medicis returned to the city, were expelled in 1527, and returned again two years later. They then ruled the city until 1737, gaining control of all of Tuscany in that period.

After the Medicis, the Grand Duchy of Tuscany passed to the House of Lorraine, and from 1799 to the French under Napoleon. In 1814 it returned to the Lorraines, who remained in control until the Italian drive for unification. Florence was incorporated into the Kingdom of Italy in 1860 and became capital a year later until Rome assumed the mantle in 1875.

The city was badly damaged during WW II by the retreating Germans, who bombed all bridges except the Ponte Vecchio. The floods of 1966 left the city under several metres of water and caused inestimable damage to its buildings and artworks, some of which are still being restored. However, it was the cleanup programme after the floods that led to the widespread use of present-day restoration techniques which have saved artworks across the country.

In 1993, the world-famous Uffizi Gallery was damaged by a car-bomb explosion. See Around Piazza della Signoria in the following Things to See section for details about the gallery and the explosion.

Orientation

Whether you arrive by train, bus or car, the central train station, Santa Maria Novella, is a good reference point. The main thoroughfare to the city centre is Via de' Panzani and then Via de' Cerretani, about a 10-minute walk. You will know you've arrived when you first glimpse the Duomo.

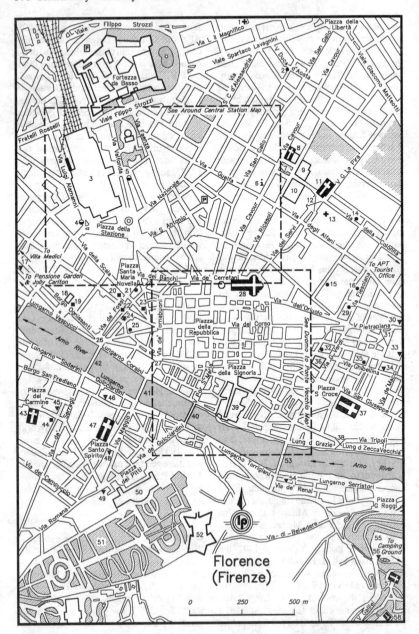

Florence
(Firenze)

0   250   500 m

■ PLACES TO STAY

19 Excelsior
20 Pensione Ottaviani & Albergo Visconti
22 Albergo Palmer
23 Pensione Toscana & Pensione Sole
44 Ostello Santa Monaca

▼ PLACES TO EAT

17 Ristorante Da Mario &
   Pizzeria Carolina
24 Da Il Latini
30 Sant'Ambrogio Caffè
33 Trattoria la Maremmana
34 Enoteca Pinchiorri
45 Trattoria I Raddi
46 Il Cantinone di Gatto Nero
48 Trattoria Casalinga
49 La Mangiatora
54 I Tarocchi
56 La Loggia

   OTHER

1 Tourist Medical Service
2 Police Headquarters
3 Central Railway Station
4 SITA Bus Terminal
5 CLAP, Lazzi & COPIT Bus Terminal
6 Comune di Firenze Tourist Office
7 Piazza San Marco
8 Church of San Marco & Museum
9 University

10 Accademia Gallery
11 Church of the Santissma Annunziata
12 Piazza della Santissima Annunziata
13 Ospedale degli Innocenti
14 Archaeological Museum
15 Pergola Theatre
16 Rex Café
18 All Saints' (Ognissanti) Church
21 Fiddler's Elbow
25 Rucellai Palace
26 Piazza Goldini
27 Piazza Santa Trinità
28 Duomo
29 Paperback Exchange Bookshop
31 Piazza dei Ciompi
32 Antica Enoteca
35 Casa Buonarroti
36 Verdi Theatre
37 Santa Croce
38 Piazza dei Cavalleggeri
39 Uffizi Gallery
40 Ponte Vecchio
41 Ponte Santa Trinità
42 Ponte alla Carraia
43 Church of Santa Maria del Carmine
47 Church of the Holy Spirit
50 Pitti Palace
51 Boboli Gardens
52 Belvedere Fort
53 Ponte alle Grazie
55 Piazzale Michelangelo
57 Church of San Salvatore al Monte
58 Church of San Miniato al Monte

Once at the Piazza del Duomo you will find Florence easy to negotiate. Most of the major sights are within easy walking distance, and you can walk from one end of the city centre to the other in about 30 minutes. From Piazza San Giovanni around the Baptistry, Via Roma leads to Piazza della Repubblica and continues as Via Calimala to the Ponte Vecchio. Take Via de' Calzaiuoli from Piazza del Duomo for Piazza della Signoria, the historic seat of government – don't be fooled by Michelangelo's *David* outside the Palazzo Vecchio, the real one is housed in the Accademia Gallery, elsewhere in the city. The Uffizi Gallery is at the piazza's southern edge, near the Arno River bank. Cross the Ponte Vecchio, or the Ponte alle Grazie farther east, to reach Piazzale Michelangelo in the south-east for a view over the city, one of the best views in Italy.

The imposing Fortezza da Basso is just north of the train station, and the IYHF youth hostel is on the city's north-eastern fringe, accessible by bus from the station.

Like many Italian cities, Florence has two street-numbering systems: red or brown numbers indicate a commercial premises and black or blue numbers denote a private residence. When they are written, black or blue addresses are denoted by the number only, while red or brown addresses usually carry an 'r' after the number. Of course, there are exceptions, but check the colouring if you are trying to find an address.

Information

Tourist Offices To complicate things, there are several autonomous tourist offices in the city. The APT office (☎ 055-234 62 86) is in a former convent at Via Manzoni 16, just off Piazza Beccaria, which is a 15-minute walk east of the Duomo. The office opens Monday to Friday from 8 am to 1.30 pm and 4 to 6.30 pm, Saturday from 8.30 am to 1.30 pm. The APT also opens a small booth in Piazza della Repubblica over the summer months.

The city council, known as the Comune di Firenze, also operates a service. The main office (☎ 055-276 03 82), Via Cavour 1r, is just north of the Duomo. It opens Monday to Saturday from 8 am to 2 pm. For people arriving at the train station, there is a small branch tourist office (☎ 055-21 22 45) just outside near where buses stop. There is a small office (☎ 055-230 21 24) at Chiasso Baroncelli 17, just south of Piazza della Signoria. Both offices open Monday to Saturday from 8 am to 7.30 pm.

All tourist offices offer similar information, but the APT map is a more convenient pocket size. You can also stop in at any of the city's better hotels or bars for one of the invaluable booklets available at the counter, in particular the quarterly *Florence Concierge Information* or *Firenze Oggi*, which should also be available from tourist offices. None of the tourist offices will book you a room, but see the Places to Stay section for details about the Consorzio ITA office at the station, which will do so.

There is an Informa Giovani office (☎ 21 83 10) at Vicolo Santa Maria Maggiore 1, which provides information for young, disabled and other travellers.

Money To change money it is always best to use a bank. Most of the main ones are concentrated around Piazza della Repubblica. Avoid using the service at the station because it offers bad rates and generally charges a fee. Thomas Cook has an exchange office (☎ 055-28 97 81) at Lungarno Acciaioli 6r, near the Ponte Vecchio. There's a full American Express office and travel service (☎ 055-28 87 51) at Via de' Guicciardini 49r.

Post & Telecommunications The main post office is in Via Pellicceria, off Piazza della Repubblica, open Monday to Friday from 8.15 am to 7 pm, Saturday to midday. Poste restante mail can be addressed to 50100 Firenze.

The ASST telephone office is in the post office building and is open 24 hours a day. Another ASST office is at the train station, open Monday to Saturday from 8 am to 9.45 pm. There is an SIP office at Via Cavour 21, near the Duomo, where the public phone booths are open 24 hours a day, seven days a week. The city's telephone code is 055.

Consulates The US Consulate (☎ 239 82 76) is at Lungarno Vespucci 38 and operates the US Information Service (USIS, ☎ 29 49 21) Monday to Friday from 8.30 am to 1.30 pm and 2 to 5.30 pm. Call ahead, because you can only visit the USIS office by appointment. The British Consulate (☎ 28 41 33) is at Lungarno Corsini 2. Other English-speaking nationalities can choose between embassies in Rome or consulates in Milan.

Travel Agencies The CIT office (☎ 29 43 06), Via Cavour 56r, is central Italy's main office. A smaller branch (☎ 239 69 63) is at the train station. For budget student travel, the Student Travel Service (☎ 29 20 88) is at Via Zanetti 18r.

Bookshops The Paperback Exchange, Via Fiesolana 31r, has a vast selection of new and second-hand books, including classics, contemporary literature, reference books and best sellers, as well as travel guides (closed Sunday). Internazionale Seeber, Via de' Tornabuoni 70r, also has a good selection of English and American classics and contemporary literature, as well as a reasonable range of books by Australian authors.

Medical Services The huge Santa Maria Nuova hospital on Via Bufalini is just behind the Duomo, but the APT advises tourists to contact the Tourist Medical Service (☎ 47 54 11), Via Lorenzo il Magnifico 59. This is open 24 hours a day and doctors speak English. The city has a volunteer organisation called the Associazione Volontari Ospedalieri (☎ 40 31 26 or 234 45 67), which, once you've found a doctor, provides a free translation service. There is an ambulance station (☎ 21 22 22) in Piazza del Duomo. All-night pharmacies include the Farmacia Comunale (☎ 21 67 61) inside the train station, and Molteni (☎ 21 54 72) in the city centre at Via Calzaiuoli 7r.

Emergency For police emergency, call ☎ 113. The police headquarters (☎ 4 97 71) are at Via Zara 2. There is an office for foreigners, where you can report thefts etc.

Other Services Lost property (☎ 36 79 43) can be collected (if you're lucky) from Via Circondaria 19. Towed-away cars can also be collected here (note that if you park illegally in Florence your car will be towed away and you risk getting a large fine, if not getting arrested).

One of the cheapest laundries is at Via Pietrapiana 34, east of the Duomo, which costs L3000 a kg. Lavamatic, Via degli Alfani 44r, has coin-operated machines.

Arci Gay (☎ 28 81 26), Via Montebello 6, operates a phone information service from 5 to 7 pm. The Edicola Balsanelli newsstand in Piazza Santa Maria Novella opens late and has all Babilonia gay publications.

Dangers & Annoyances

The most annoying aspect of Florence is the crowds, closely followed by the summer heat. Beware in the crowds and particularly on buses because the city is notorious for pickpockets whose deft skills could leave you without your wallet in a flash. Carry a money pouch or wear a money belt and never carry money in your pockets. The city has a small problem with motorino bandits who will try and grab handbags.

Things to See

The APT produces *One, three, five... days in Florence*, a map and itinerary which can assist you in prioritising your time. Do not miss the Uffizi Gallery or the Duomo and Baptistry. Also, the churches of Santa Maria Novella, Santa Croce and SS Annunziata should not be missed. Make sure you carry plenty of L100, L200 and L500 coins to illuminate the usually dimly lit frescoes in the churches.

Around Piazza del Duomo The remarkable **Duomo**, with its dome and pink, white and green marble façade, dominates the skyline of Florence. At first sight, no matter how many times you have visited the city, the Duomo will take your breath away. Called the Cathedral of Santa Maria del Fiore, it was started in 1296 by the Sienese architect Arnolfo di Cambio but took almost two centuries to complete. It is the fourth-largest cathedral in the world.

The Renaissance architect Brunelleschi won a public competition to design the enormous dome, the first since antiquity. Although now severely cracked and under restoration, it remains a remarkable achievement of design. When Michelangelo left Florence for Rome to build the Vatican, he said, 'I go to build a greater dome, but not a fa.rer one.' The dome was decorated with frescoes by Vasari and Zuccari, and stained-glass windows by Donatello, Andrea del Castagno, Paolo Uccello and Ghiberti. However, the scaffolding erected for the dome's restoration more than 20 years ago now obscures the works, and you must climb into the dome to see them. Enter to the left as you face the altar. The view from the summit over Florence is unparalleled. The dome is open from 10 am to 5.40 pm Monday to Saturday and the climb costs L5000.

The sacristies on each side of the altar feature enamelled terracotta lunettes over their doorways by Luca della Robbia. A stairway near the main entrance of the cathedral leads to the crypt, where excavations have unearthed parts of the 5th century Basilica of Santa Reparata, which originally stood on the site, and Brunelleschi's tomb. The Duomo's marble façade was built in the 19th century to replace the original, uncompleted façade, which was destroyed in the 16th

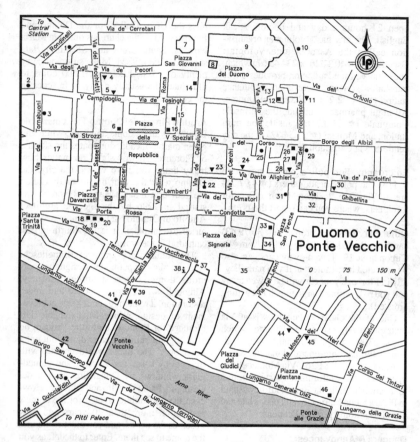

century. The cathedral opens daily from 10 am to 5 pm, and strict dress standards are enforced.

Giotto designed and began building the **bell tower** (campanile) next to the cathedral, but died before it was completed. The first tier of bas-reliefs around the base of the tower depict human arts and activities, and are by Andrea Pisano and Luca della Robbia. Those on the second tier depict the planets, cardinal virtues, the arts and the seven sacraments. All are copies – the originals are in the cathedral's museum. The Campanile is 82 metres high and you can climb its stairs for L5000 between 9 am and 7.30 pm daily.

The Romanesque-style **Baptistry**, believed to have been built in the 8th century, was originally a pagan temple converted to Christian use. It is one of the oldest buildings in Florence and is famous for its gilded bronze doors, particularly the east doors facing the cathedral, the *Gates of Paradise* by Lorenzo Ghiberti. The south door, by Andrea Pisano, is the oldest. The north door is also by Ghiberti, who won a public competition in 1401 to design it, but the *Gates of Paradise* remain his consummate masterpiece. Dante was baptised in the Baptistry. Most of the doors are copies – the originals are being removed to the Cathedral Museum

■ **PLACES TO STAY**

6   Albergo Pendini
12 Albergo Firenze
14 Locanda Colore
15 Maxim
16 Savoy
18 Pensione TeTi & Prestige
19 Soggiorno Davanzati
26 Pensione Maria Luisa de' Medici
27 Brunori
33 Bernini Palace
40 Aily Home
46 Albergo Rigati

▼ **PLACES TO EAT**

4   Self Service Leonardo
5   Al Campidoglio
11 Trattoria Le Mossacce
13 Osteria Il Caminetto
23 Ristorante Paoli
24 Chiodo Fisso
28 Trattoria del Pennello
30 Osteria del Gallo e Volpe
39 L'Orafo
42 Osteria del Cinghiale Bianco
44 Angie's Pub
45 Trattoria da Benvenuto

OTHER

1   Student Travel Service
2   Informa Giovani
3   Internazionale Seeber
7   Baptistry
8   Campanile
9   Duomo
10 Cathedral Musuem
17 Strozzi Palace
20 Florentine House Musuem
21 Post Office & ASST Telephones
22 Orsanmichele
25 Dante's House
29 Pazzi Palace
31 Badia
32 Bargello Palace & National Museum
34 Gondi Palace
35 Palazzo Vecchio
36 Uffizi Gallery
37 Loggia della Signoria
38 Comune di Firenze Tourist Office
41 Thomas Cook Exchange Office
43 American Express

as copies are completed. The Baptistry is open from 1 to 6 pm Monday to Saturday and 9.30 am to 12.30 pm Sunday, and entrance is free.

The **Duomo Museum**, behind the cathedral at Piazza del Duomo 9, features most of the art treasures from the Duomo, Baptistry and Campanile, and shows equipment used by Brunelleschi to build the dome, as well as his death mask. Perhaps its best piece is Michelangelo's *Pietà*, which he left unfinished. It has been removed from the Duomo during restoration of the dome. The collection of sculpture is considered the city's second-best after that in the Bargello Museum. Donatello's carving of the prophet Habakkuk and his wooden impression of Mary Magdalene are considered among the museum's best works. It opens from 9 am to 7.30 pm daily except Sunday, and entry is L5000.

Take Via Calzaiuoli from Piazza del Duomo to the Church of St Michael in the Garden, more commonly known as the **Orsanmichele**. Originally a 9th century church, the building was rebuilt in the 14th century as a grain store. The church is noteworthy because many of its statues were removed to the Bargello Museum. However, many splendid pieces remain in the façade, including *John the Baptist* by Ghiberti and a copy of Donatello's *St George*. The main feature of the interior is the immense Gothic tabernacle by Andrea Orcagna.

Just west along Via degli Speziali is the Piazza della Repubblica. Originally the site of a Roman forum, it is now home to Florence's most fashionable and expensive cafés. Return to Via Calzaiuoli and continue towards the river for Piazza della Signoria.

Around Piazza della Signoria The hub of the city's political life through the centuries and surrounded by some of the city's most celebrated buildings, the piazza takes on the appearance of an outdoor sculpture gallery. Ammannati's huge Fountain of Neptune sits beside the Palazzo Vecchio, as copies of Michelangelo's *David* and Donatello's *Marzocco* (the Florentine lion) watch over tourists queueing to enter the palace. An equestrian statue of Cosimo I by Giam-

Giambologna's *Rape of a Sabine*

bologna stands towards the centre of the piazza, and a bronze plaque marks the spot where Savonarola was burned at the stake in 1498.

Obscured by scaffolding, the **Loggia della Signoria** was originally built in the late 14th century as a platform for speakers. It eventually filled with sculpture, and features Benvenuto Cellini's magnificent statue of Perseus holding the head of Medusa. Also on show through the steel poles is Giambologna's *Rape of a Sabine*, his last work.

The **Palazzo Vecchio**, built by Arnolfo di Cambio between 1299 and 1314, was, and remains, the seat of the Florentine government. Its **Arnolfo Tower** reaches 94 metres and is as much a symbol of the city as Brunelleschi's dome. In the 16th century it became the ducal palace of the Medicis, before they moved to the Pitti Palace. Giorgio Vasari was commissioned by the

Medicis to reorganise the interior and created a series of sumptuous rooms. Visit the beautiful courtyard by Michelozzo just inside the entrance, and the lavishly decorated apartments upstairs. The Salone dei Cinquecento housed the Great Council and features frescoes by Vasari and Michelangelo's *Genius of Victory*, originally destined for Rome and Pope Julius II's tomb. The Studiolo, or Francis I's study, was designed by Vasari and decorated by several of the city's Mannerist artists. Farther on, the Signoria Chapel decorated by Ghirlandaio in 1514. The palace opens Monday to Friday from 9 am to 7 pm and Sunday from 8 am to 1 pm, and entry is L10,000.

Designed by Vasari at the request of Cosimo I, the **Uffizi Gallery** originally housed the city's administrators, judiciary and guilds which had been scattered over the city. Cosimo wanted to bring them all closer to his residence in the Palazzo Vecchio. Upon Vasari's death, Buontalenti continued the buildings but altered the upper floor at the request of Francesco I to house the Medicis' growing art collection. The Medicis were great art patrons and the gallery grew out of their private collection, and in 1737 it was bequeathed to the city by the last Medici ruler, Anna Maria Ludovica.

Over the years, sections of the collection have been moved to the Bargello Museum and the city's Archaeological Museum, leaving the world's best collection of Italian Renaissance paintings in the gallery.

Sadly, several of its artworks were destroyed and others badly damaged when a car bomb exploded outside the gallery's western wing in May 1993. A family of four – including two girls aged nine months and eight years – were among the six killed when the bomb exploded. The Mafia was blamed for the attack (although it did not claim responsibility) which was widely seen as payback for the Italian government's ongoing purge of the criminal organisation.

The Torre delle Pulci outside the gallery's western wing took the full brunt of the explosion and was destroyed. The exit staircase by Buontalenti sustained structural damage, and the Vasari corridor over the Arno was also damaged. Several paintings were destroyed, including Gerrit van Honthorst's *Birth of Christ* and *Good Fortune*, and *Scenes of Life* by Bartolomeo Manfredi. Documents which made up the 10-year effort by gallery staff to catalogue the Uffizi's collection were destroyed. Paintings by Rubens, Giotto and Van Dyck were damaged but could be repaired. Bullet-proof glass installed to protect important works from vandal attacks saved dozens of paintings. The Uffizi was closed for about a month, and parts of the gallery are expected to remain closed until well into 1994.

The gallery is arranged to illustrate the evolving story of Italian, and in particular Florentine, art. However, the gallery has its problems: poor funding (despite the incredible box-office takings) means that rooms have to be closed every day, and many paintings are hung in unsuitable locations or are lit by inadequate lighting. To avoid the crowds, be there when the gallery opens, go during the lunch-time hours, or later in the afternoon. One visit is not enough – you will come away remembering the highlights but little else. Several guidebooks to the gallery are on sale at vendors all over the city, and outside the entrance.

The first rooms feature works by early Tuscan masters, in particular Cimabue's *Virgin in Majesty*, Giotto's *Virgin & Child with Angels & Saints* and Simone Martini's *Annunciation*, which show the beginning of the Renaissance. Room 7 features 15th century Florentine works, including one panel from Paolo Uccello's *Battle of San Romano* (the other two are in the Louvre and London's National Gallery) and Piero della Francesca's *Portrait of the Duke of Urbino*. The next room contains one of Filippo Lippi's most famous works, his *Virgin & Child*.

The Botticelli rooms, Nos 10 to 14, are considered the gallery's most spectacular. Highlights are the well-known *Birth of Venus* and *Primavera*. Room 15 features Leonardo da Vinci's *Annunciation*. Room 18 contains paintings by Raphael and portraits of the Medicis, but you will have to queue to get in, primarily for the *Medici Venus*, carved by a Greek sculptor in the 3rd century BC. Continuing on, Room 20 features works from the

Botticelli's *Birth of Venus*

German Renaissance, including Dürer's *Adoration of the Magi*. Room 21 is devoted to Giovanni Bellini and Giorgione. Peek through the railings to see the 15th to 19th century works in the Miniatures Room and then cross into the western wing, which features works of Italian masters dating from the 16th century.

Room 25 features Michelangelo's *Holy Family* and in the next room is Raphael's *Leo X*. Room 28 features Titian's *Urbino Venus*, and in rooms 31 to 35 are works by Venetian artists, including Veronese, whose *Holy Family with St Barbara* is hung in Room 34. Canaletto features in Room 42 and Caravaggio's *Bacchus as a Youth* is in Room 43. Room 44 is dedicated to Dutch painters and features two Rembrandts. The gallery is open Tuesday to Saturday from 9 am to 7 pm, Sunday to 1 pm, and admission is L10,000.

Ponte Vecchio From the Uffizi Gallery, wander along the bank of the Arno for the Ponte Vecchio. This famous 14th century bridge, lined with the shops of gold- and silversmiths, was the only one to survive Nazi bombing in WW II. The shops originally housed butchers until Cosimo I ordered them removed in favour of jewellers whose trade was considered more appropriate. A corridor along the 1st floor was built by the Medicis to link the Pitti Palace and the Uffizi Gallery.

Around Santa Trinità Continuing along the Arno bank, the next bridge, the **Ponte Santa Trinità**, was completely destroyed by the Nazis and subsequently rebuilt. The original plan was believed to have been drawn by Michelangelo, and the bridge was built by Ammannati. Head back towards the Duomo, along Via de' Tornabuoni, one of the city's main streets and home to most of the city's banks during the 15th century. It features the **Mercato Nuovo**, a series of arcades built in the mid-16th century to house the city's gold and silver trade and which today host the ubiquitous leather vendors.

The 13th century **Santa Trinità** church, in the piazza of the same name, features several

significant works, including frescoes by Ghirlandaio. Opposite the church, along Via Porta Rossa, is the Palazzo Davanzati, a well-preserved 14th century mansion that now houses the **Florentine House Museum** (Museo dell'Antica Casa Fiorentina), featuring many of the original fittings, linen and domestic items of the time. It is open Tuesday to Sunday from 9 am to 1 pm, and entry is L5000.

Return to Via de' Tornabuoni and head north for the **Strozzi Palace**, one of the most impressive Renaissance palaces in the city. The palace is used for art exhibitions. Via della Vigna Nuova branches off to the southwest for the 15th century **Rucellai Palace**, built to a design by Leon Battista Alberti and featuring a beautiful courtyard. The palace houses a photographic museum dedicated to the vast collection compiled by the Alinari brothers. It is open Tuesday to Sunday from 10 am to 7.30 pm and entry is L5000.

The **All Saints' Church** (Chiesa Ognissanti) was founded in the 13th century by a Benedictine order but was completely remodelled, with the exception of the bell tower, when the church went to the Franciscans. The church contains frescoes by Ghirlandaio and Sandro Botticelli, and a highlight is Ghirlandaio's *Last Supper*, which covers most of a wall in the former monastery's refectory. The church opens daily from 8 am to midday and 4 to 7 pm.

Around Santa Maria Novella Walk northeast from Piazza Goldini, along Via de' Fossi towards the train station, for the **Church of Santa Maria Novella** facing the piazza of the same name (originally used by the Romans for chariot races). The Santa Maria Novella was started in 1246 by the Dominicans and was the Florentine base for their order. The green and white marble façade, partly designed by Alberti, was erected in the 15th century. Along the north is one of the church's highlights, Masaccio's fresco of the *Trinity*, one of the first artworks to use the newly discovered techniques of perspective and proportion.

The first chapel to the right of the choir,

the Filippo Strozzi Chapel, features beautiful frescoes by Filippino Lippi. One of the highlights is Ghirlandaio's series of frescoes behind the altar, painted with the help of a young student, Michelangelo. The cloisters feature some of the city's best frescoes, including those in the Green Cloister, so named because of the predominant colour in Uccello's series. The impressive Spaniards' Chapel has frescoes by Andrea di Bonaiuto which depict the triumph of the Catholic church. The church is open daily from 7 to 11.30 am and 3.30 to 6 pm, except Sunday morning. The cloister is open from 9 am to 2 pm daily except Friday and entry is L5000.

Around the Bargello Museum Return to Piazza del Duomo and take Via del Proconsolo in the direction of the Arno River. Near the intersection of Borgo degli Albizi is the **Pazzi Palace**, an important building attributed to Brunelleschi which now houses offices. You can wander into the courtyard. Head west along Via del Corso for Via Santa Margherita and **Dante's House** at No 1, with a small museum that examines his life. It is open Monday to Friday except Wednesday from 9.30 am to 12.30 pm and 3.30 to 6.30 pm, weekends to 12.30 pm. Entry is free.

Return to Via del Proconsolo and continue towards the river for the Bargello Palace. Started in 1254, the palace was originally the residence of the governing podestà and then the city's police headquarters. During its days as a police complex, many people were tortured near the well in the centre of the medieval courtyard. It now houses the **Bargello Museum**, and its collection contains the most comprehensive range of medieval and Renaissance sculpture in Italy. Notable works include Michelangelo's drunken *Bacchus*, painted when he was 22, many works by Benvenuto Cellini, and Donatello's stunning bronze *David*, the first sculpture since antiquity to depict a fully nude man. The museum should not be missed, and part of the attraction is its relative unpopularity compared to the Uffizi and Accademia galleries, as it attracts smaller crowds. It is open Tuesday to Friday from 9

am to 2 pm, weekends to 1 pm, and entry is L6000.

The 10th century **Badia**, facing the Bargello across Via del Proconsolo, was the church of a monastery and features Filippino Lippi's *Appearance of the Virgin to St Bernard*. Wander into the Renaissance cloister. Piazza San Firenze to the south features several significant buildings, including the **Gondi Palace** built late in the 15th century.

Around Santa Croce Take any of the streets heading east for Piazza Santa Croce, once a popular residential area but now the domain of leather shops and tacky souvenir stalls. In Savonarola's day, the piazza was used for the execution of heretics.

Attributed to the architect of the Duomo, Arnolfo di Cambio, the Franciscan **Santa Croce** (Church of the Holy Cross) was started in 1294, although the façade and bell tower were added in the 19th century. The floor is paved with 276 tombstones and more line the walls. The interior is renowned for its simplicity and the church is considered one of Italy's most beautiful.

Along the south wall is Michelangelo's tomb, designed by Vasari, and a cenotaph dedicated to Dante, who is buried in Ravenna. Farther along is a monument to Alfieri by Canova, a monument to Machiavelli and a bas-relief *Annunciation* by Donatello. The Castellani Chapel features frescoes by Gaddi and other works by 14th century artists. Adjoining the sacristy is a corridor by Michelozzo which leads to the Medici Chapel, featuring a large altarpiece by Andrea della Robbia. The Bardi and Peruzzi chapels, to the right of the chancel, are completely covered in works by Giotto.

The cloisters were designed by Brunelleschi just before his death in 1446 and are noted for their serenity. Brunelleschi's Pazzi Chapel, at the end of the first cloister, is a masterpiece of Renaissance architecture. The Santa Croce Museum, off the first cloister, features a crucifix by Cimabue, badly damaged during the 1966 floods.

The church is open from 7.30 am to 12.30 pm and 3 to 6.30 pm daily. The museum opens from 10 am to 12.30 pm and 2.30 to 6.30 pm, except Wednesdays, and entry is L4000.

North from Piazza Santa Croce along Via de' Pepi is the **Casa Buonarroti**, Via Ghibellina 70, which Michelangelo owned but never lived in. Upon his death, the house went to his nephew and eventually became a museum in the mid-1850s. The collection of memorabilia is mostly copies of Michelangelo's works and portraits of the master. On the 2nd floor is Michelangelo's earliest known work, *The Madonna of the Steps*. The museum opens daily, except Tuesday, from 9.30 am to 1.30 pm and entry is L5000.

Around SS Annunziata Return to the Duomo and head north-east along Via dei Servi for the Piazza della Santissima (SS) Annunziata, considered the city's most beautifully proportioned square. In the centre is Giambologna's equestrian statue of Ferdinand I.

Up until the 17th century, the city's year started on Annunciation Day (25 March), and so the **Church of the SS Annunziata** is one of the city's most popular. It dates from the 13th century and was rebuilt by Michelozzo in the 15th century. The main doorway features a mosaic by Ghirlandaio and the interior is decorated with beautiful frescoes by Bartolomeo and several Florentine artists.

The **Ospedale degli Innocenti** on the south-east side of the square was designed by Brunelleschi and opened in 1445 as Europe's first orphanage; it is now a children's hospital. A small gallery inside features works by Florentine artists, including Luca della Robbia. It opens daily from 9 am to 1 pm, except Wednesday, and entry is L5000.

About 100 metres south-east of the church along Via della Colonna is the entrance to the **Archaeological Museum**, considered to be one of Italy's best. Most of the Medici collection of antiquities is on show, including well-preserved Etruscan artefacts. The museum also features an impressive collection of Egyptian, Greek and Roman items.

Many exhibits were badly damaged in the 1966 floods, and the museum is still undergoing renovation. It opens daily from 9 am to 2 pm, except Monday, and entry is L6000.

Take Via Cesare Battisti from Piazza della SS Annunziata to Piazza San Marco. The **Accademia Gallery** is to the left along Via Ricasoli. Europe's first drawing academy, the gallery features works by some of the greatest masters of the Renaissance. Michelangelo's *David* is here, as are many of his sketches and models. The gallery also features a good collection of paintings, including works by Botticelli. It is open Tuesday to Saturday from 9 am to 2 pm, Sunday to 1 pm. Entry is L10,000.

Around San Marco Piazza San Marco is the centre of the city's university area and is also one of the most pleasant squares in the city. The **Church of San Marco** was founded in 1299, rebuilt by Michelozzo in 1437, and again remodelled by Giambologna some years later.

It features several significant paintings, but pales in comparison to the treasures contained in the adjoining **San Marco Museum**, housed in the former Dominican convent whose occupants included Fra Angelico, Antonino, Savonarola and Fra Bartolomeo. The first rooms feature many of Fra Angelico's paintings on wood, including the outstanding *Last Judgment*. The chapterhouse features more works by Fra Angelico, including his *Crucifixion*. Upstairs are the monks' dormitory cells, all covered in frescoes by Fra Angelico and his assistants. The 'extras' in many of the biblical scenes are St Peter Martyr, represented with an axe embedded in his skull, and St Dominic, with a star over his head. The museum is open Tuesday to Saturday from 9 am to 2 pm, Sunday to 1 pm, and entry is L6000.

If you have the time and inclination, the city's university across the road houses three museums – the Botanical, Mineralogy and Geology & Palaeontology museums – which are considered among the country's best in their fields. The entrance is at Via La Pira 4, just north of Piazza San Marco.

North-west along Via Arazzieri and then Via XXVII Aprile is the **Fortezza da Basso**, built in 1534 by Antonio da Sangallo, who also built the Farnese Palace in Rome and collaborated on Rome's St Peter's Basilica. It's not open to the public. Return to the Duomo along Via Faenza and you will come to the Piazza Madonna degli Aldobrandini.

Around Piazza San Lorenzo The **San Lorenzo Basilica** in the adjoining piazza of the same name was started by Brunelleschi in 1425 on the site of a 4th century church and is regarded as one of the city's purest Renaissance churches. It was the Medici family's parish church and many of the family members are buried here. The two bronze pulpits are by Donatello, who is buried in the chapel featuring Filippo Lippi's *Annunciation*. The church is open daily from 7 am to 12.30 pm and 3.30 to 5.30 pm.

Visit the **Laurenziana Library**, reached through the cloister. It was commissioned by Cosimo I to house the family's library and contains 10,000 volumes. The magnificent staircase was designed by Michelangelo. It opens from 9 am to 1 pm daily except Sundays and entrance is free.

The **Medici Chapels** are entered via Piazza Madonna degli Aldobrandini. The Princes' Chapel, sumptuously decorated with precious marble and semiprecious stones, was the principal burial place of the Medici rulers. The graceful and simple New Sacristy was designed by Michelangelo and was his first architectural work, although he left Florence for Rome before its completion. It contains his beautiful sculptures *Night & Day*, *Dawn & Dusk* and the *Madonna with Child*, which adorn the Medici tombs. It is open Tuesday to Friday from 9 am to 2 pm, weekends to 1 pm, and admission is L8500.

The **Medici-Riccardi Palace** to the east is typical of the Florentine Renaissance style and was started by Michelozzo for Cosimo I in 1444. The Medici residence from 1459 to 1540, it was the prototype for other buildings in the city, such as the Pitti Palace. However, it was remodelled in the 17th century by the Riccardi family. The chapel upstairs has beautiful frescoes by Benozzo Gozzoli, with regal scenes featuring members of the Medici clan. The Luca Giordano Room was built by the Riccardis and is sumptuously decorated. The palace opens Monday to Friday, except Wednesday, from 9 am to 1 pm and 3 to 5 pm, to midday on weekends, and entry is free.

South of the Arno In medieval times, the inhabitants on the more fashionable northern side of the Arno River referred to the southern side as the Oltre Arno, or the other side of the Arno. The Oltrarno is very pleasant and worth wandering through, particularly for the incredible view from Piazzale Michelangelo.

Cross the Ponte Vecchio and head west along the river for the Piazza del Carmine and the **Church of Santa Maria del Carmine**. The church was severely damaged in a late 18th century fire, although the magnificent frescoes in the Brancacci Chapel by Masaccio were not damaged. Completed in 1427 when the artist was in his late 20s, the frescoes are important because Masaccio was one of the first artists to employ techniques such as perspective in painting. The church and chapel are open from 10 am to 5 pm daily except Tuesday, and entry is L6000.

Wander east along Via Sant'Agostino for the **Church of the Holy Spirit** (Chiesa del Santo Spirito), one of Brunelleschi's last commissions and one of the most evenly proportioned churches in Italy. It features several significant artworks including a *Madonna & Saints* by Filippino Lippi. The piazza outside has developed somewhat of a bohemian feel to it, even if it is still a little seedy.

The immense and imposing **Pitti Palace** was designed by Brunelleschi for the Pitti family, who were rivals of the Medicis. When the Medicis eventually removed the Pittis, Eleanora di Toledo, wife of Cosimo I, expanded the palaces by adding two wings. It houses several museums. The Palatine Gallery has 16th and 17th century works by Raphael, Filippo Lippi, Tintoretto, Veronese

■ PLACES TO STAY

3	La Romagnola & La Gigliola
7	Pensione Montreal
13	Pensione Margareth
14	La Scala
15	Croce di Malta
17	Albergo Palmer
18	La Mia Casa
19	Polo Nord
20	Giotto
21	Albergo Majestic
22	Pensione Accademia
23	Grand Hotel Baglioni
27	Pensione Bellavista, Albergo Ester & Pensione Le Cascine
29	Tony's Inn & Hotel Apollo
30	Ostello Spirito Santo
32	Atlantic Palace
33	Pensione Kursaal & Pensione Ausonia & Rimini
34	Daniel & Soggiorno Nazionale
37	Albergo Roxy & Albergo Mary
39	Albergo Tina
45	House for Tourists Aglietti
46	Giada

▼ PLACES TO EAT

2	Trattoria il Giardino
5	Il Biribisso
6	La Grotta di Leo
8	Super Tripperia
9	Vini Buffet Freddo
10	Trattoria Da Giorgio
11	Ristorante Dino
12	Trattoria il Contadino
25	Caffè Cristallo
26	Italy & Italy
31	Bondi
35	Trattoria da Giovanni
36	Caffè degli Innocenti
38	Le Fonticine
43	Mario's
44	Café Za Za

OTHER

1	ASST Telephones
4	SITA Bus Terminal
16	Church of Santa Maria Novella
24	Comune di Firenze Branch Office
28	CLAP, Lazzi & COPIT Bus Terminal
40	Comune di Firenze Tourist Office
41	SIP Telephones
42	Mercato Centrale
47	Medici-Riccardi Palace
48	Medici Chapels
49	San Lorenzo Basilica
50	Baptistry
51	Duomo

and Rubens, hung in lavishly decorated rooms. The Apartments of the Medicis, and later of the Savoys, show the splendour in which the rulers lived. The Modern Art Gallery covers Tuscan works from the 18th century until the mid-20th century, and the Silver Museum, entered from the garden courtyard, has a collection of glassware, silver and semiprecious stones from the Medici collections. All of the galleries have the same opening hours: Tuesday to Friday from 9 am to 2 pm, Saturday and Sunday to 1 pm. Admission to the Palatine Gallery and the Apartments is L8000, a ticket for admission to the other museums is L6000.

The **Palazzo dei Vini** (Wine Palace) opposite the Pitti Palace entrance displays Tuscan wines, particularly those grown around Florence and Siena, and, of course, the famous Chianti wines. It is worth visiting for its interesting displays, and also for the oc-

casional free tastings. The palace is open Wednesday to Saturday from 10 am to midday and 4 to 7 pm.

After the Pitti and Wine palaces, visit the Renaissance **Boboli Gardens**, designed in 1549 by Tribolo, and enjoy the view of Florence. As they are the only gardens near the city centre, they can become very crowded. The star-shaped **Belvedere Fort**, built in 1590 at the southern end of the gardens, is worth wandering past on your way to Piazzale Michelangelo.

Via di Belvedere eventually leads to the **Piazzale Michelangelo** from the Pitti Palace; from the Ponte Vecchio, walk along the river and head south at Piazza Giuseppe Roggi. The Piazzale Michelangelo offers one of the most beautiful views in the world, and should not be missed at any cost. Behind the piazza is the austere Church of San Salvatore al Monte. Farther along, the **Church**

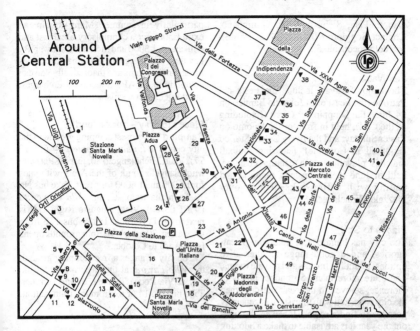

Around Central Station

0   100   200 m

of **San Miniato al Monte**, with its green and white marble façade, is one of the best examples of the Florentine-Romanesque style. The church was started in the early 11th century, and the façade features a mosaic depicting Christ between the Virgin and St Minius, which was added 200 years later. The interior has a crucifix, above the altar, by della Robbia, and the Portogallo Chapel has a tomb by Rossellino and terracottas by della Robbia. It is possible to wander through the cemetery outside.

Cycling
The Globetrotter's Club in Florence (☎ 24 59 22) arranges cycling holidays around the city each spring, with most tours taking in Siena and stopping for accommodation at various agriturismo farms. If you are interested in cycling, pick up a copy of *Viaggio in Toscana – Discovering Tuscany by Bike* from the APT. It is produced by the Tuscan government, and details this growing industry, including where to hire bikes. For other

rental possibilities, see Car & Motorbike in the following Getting Around section.

Language Courses
The city is jammed with language schools, some less reputable than others, so contact your embassy in Rome or the Italian Cultural Institute in your own country to help you find a suitable school. The British Institute of Florence (☎ 28 40 31), Lungarno Guicciardini 9, or Eurocentro (☎ 21 30 30), Piazza Santo Spirito 9, both have short or longer courses, starting at about L1,000,000 for a month. Eurocentro also offers tuition/accommodation packages.

Organised Tours
The best advice is to check for the range of tours at the desks of any major hotels, particularly those around Piazza della Repubblica. Several companies offer walking and bus tours of the city, and also operate day tours to cities throughout Tuscany. United Sightseeing Service operates tours of the city and

also to Pisa, Siena and San Gimignano. Contact Soggiorno Brunori (☎ 28 96 48), Via del Proconsolo 5.

Festivals

The major festivals include the Festa del Patrono (the Feast of St John the Baptist) on 24 June; the Scoppio del Carro (Exploding of the Cart), held in front of the Duomo on Easter Sunday; and the lively Calcio Storico (Football in Costume), featuring football matches played in 16th century costume, held in June in Piazza della Signoria and ending with a fireworks display over Piazzale Michelangelo.

Places to Stay

The city has hundreds of hotels in all categories, and a good range of alternative options, including hostels and private rooms. There are more than 150 budget hotels in Florence, so even in the peak season, when the city is packed with tourists, it is generally possible to find a room. However, throughout the year it is advisable to make a booking and arrive by late morning to claim your room. Hotels and pensioni are concentrated in three main areas: near the train station, near Piazza Santa Maria Novella and in the old city from the Duomo to the river.

If you arrive at the train station without a booking, the Consorzio Informazioni Turistiche e Alberghiere (☎ 28 28 93), inside the station on the main concourse, can probably find you a room. Using a computer network, the accommodation office will check the availability of rooms and book you a night for a small fee. This will require a deposit that will be credited against your bill. Contact the APT for a list of private rooms, which generally charge L19,000 per person in a shared room and L25,000 per person in a single room. Most fill with students during the year, but are a good option if you are staying for a week or longer.

When you arrive at the hotel, always ask for the full price of a room before putting your bags down. Florentine hotels and pensioni are notorious for their bill-padding,

particularly in summer. Many require an extra L5000 for a compulsory breakfast and will charge L3000 and more for a shower. By law they can charge no more than the prices posted in the rooms and theoretically you can complain to the APT if a hotel overcharges, but don't expect a satisfactory outcome.

Places to Stay – bottom end

Camping The closest camping ground to the city centre is *Italiani e Stranieri* (☎ 681 19 77), Viale Michelangelo 80, just off Piazzale Michelangelo south of the Arno, with sites for L6000 and L6000 for a tent. Take bus No 13 from the train station. *Villa Camerata* (☎ 61 03 00), Viale Augusto Righi 2-4, is next to the IYHF hostel (take bus 17B from the station, 30 minutes). Both grounds opens from April to October.

The city arranges a free camping ground, the *Villa Favard*, at the eastern edge of the city at Via Rocca Tedalda, during summer. Take bus No 14 or 62 from the train station.

Hostels The IYHF *Ostello Villa Camerata* (☎ 60 14 51), Viale Augusto Righi 2-4, is considered one of the most beautiful in Europe. Bed and breakfast is L18,000, dinner L12,000 and there is a bar. Members only are accepted and reservations can be made by mail. Take bus 17B, which leaves from the left of the station (track No 5). The trip takes 30 minutes.

The private *Ostello Santa Monaca* (☎ 26 83 38), Via Santa Monaca 6, is a 15 to 20-minute walk from the train station, through Piazza Santa Maria Novella, along Via de' Fossi, across the Ponte alla Carraia and directly ahead along Via de' Serragli. Via Santa Monaca is on the right. A bed costs L15,000, and sheets cost an extra L2000.

The *Ostello Spirito Santo* (☎ 239 82 02), Via Nazionale 8, is a religious institution near the train station. The nuns accept only women and families, and charge L40,000 per person or L60,000 for a double. Call ahead to book. The hostel opens from July to October.

Around the Station This area is noted for its seedy one-star hotels, although many of the hotels are very well run, clean and safe. The area includes the streets around Piazza della Stazione and those east of the station, across to Via Cavour.

Some of the cheapest rooms in Florence are at the *Daniel* (☎ 21 12 93), Via Nazionale 22. Doubles cost L30,000, triples/quads are L45,000/60,000, and showers cost L1500 extra. The hotel is pleasant but dark, and the owner will not take bookings, so arrive very early. In the same building is *Soggiorno Nazionale* (☎ 26 22 03), which has singles/doubles from L33,000/50,000 or, with private shower, L43,000/60,000. The *Pensione Kursaal* (☎ 49 63 24), next door at Via Nazionale 24, has singles/doubles from L28,000/35,000, although sometimes it makes breakfast compulsory and charges an extra L8000 per person.

The *Pensione Bellavista* (☎ 28 45 28), Largo Alinari 15, at the start of Via Nazionale, is small, but a knockout bargain if you can manage to book one of the two double rooms with balconies and a view of the Duomo and Palazzo Vecchio. Singles/doubles cost L38,500/53,500, although you will be hit for L3500 to use the bath. *Albergo Ester* (☎ 21 27 41) is accessible by the same entrance and offers singles/doubles for L33,000/49,000. A shower costs L2000.

Albergo Roxy (☎ 47 29 28), Piazza della Indipendenza 5, has views over the gardens in the piazza and large, modern rooms from L37,000/60,000, slightly cheaper in winter. Compulsory breakfast is included in the price. The *Albergo Mary* (☎ 49 63 10) in the same building has rooms for slightly more, and triples/quads for L92,000/118,000. All prices include compulsory breakfast.

The *House for Tourists Aglietti* (☎ 28 78 24), Via Cavour 29, is on the 4th floor and there is no elevator. Singles/doubles are L36,000/49,000.

Around Piazza Santa Maria Novella This area is just south of the train station and includes Piazza Santa Maria Novella, the

streets running south to the Arno and east to Via de' Tornabuoni. It is a very pleasant area, and is close to all the sites.

La Mia Casa (☎ 21 30 61) at Piazza Santa Maria Novella 25 is a rambling place, filled with antiques and backpackers. The owner is friendly, helpful and speaks English, and singles/doubles are L29,000/43,000 and triples/quads L58,000/73,000.

Via della Scala, which runs off the piazza, is lined with pensioni. *La Romagnola* (☎ 21 15 97) at No 40 has large, clean rooms and a helpful management. Singles/doubles are L30,000/45,000, or L42,000/57,500 with bathroom. A triple room is a good deal at L58,500. The same family runs *La Gigliola* (☎ 21 15 97) upstairs, with rooms for about the same price. *La Scala* (☎ 21 26 29) at No 21 is small and has singles/doubles from L37,000/50,000, slightly more with a bathroom. Rooms for three and four people cost L25,000 per person. There is a midnight curfew.

The *Pensione Margareth* (☎ 21 01 38) at No 25 is pleasantly furnished with singles/doubles from L35,000/45,000, or L38,000/49,000 with bathroom. It charges only L10,000 for a third person and L2500 for use of the communal shower. *Pensione Montreal* (☎ 238 23 31) at No 43 has singles/doubles from L33,000/47,000.

The *Polo Nord* (☎ 28 79 52), Via de' Panzani 7, pads prices in the high season by charging L9500 for a basic continental breakfast, but from November to April it is not compulsory. Rooms are L35,000/53,000, and use of the communal bathroom is free; rooms with bathroom are L39,000/58,000.

The *Pensione Sole* (☎ 239 60 94), Via del Sole 8, is on the 3rd floor and there is no lift. Some rooms are very noisy. Singles/doubles start at L33,000/48,000 and extra beds are L21,000. *Pensione Ottaviani* (☎ 239 62 23), Piazza degli Ottaviani 1, just off Piazza Santa Maria Novella, has rooms from L30,000/42,000 including breakfast. *Albergo Palmer* (☎ 238 23 91), Via degli Avelli 2, close to Santa Maria Novella, has only doubles from L48,000, or L60,000 with bathroom.

Between the Duomo & the Arno This area is a 15-minute walk from the train station and covers the heart of old Florence. One of the best deals is at the small *Aily Home* (☎ 239 65 05), Piazza Santo Stefano 81, just near the Ponte Vecchio. The owners charge L20,000 per person throughout the year, but their five rooms generally fill fast. The centrally located *Locanda Colore* (☎ 21 03 01), Via de' Calzaiuoli 13, is right next to the Duomo. One of its double rooms has an evocative view of the cathedral. Clean and simple, it has singles/doubles for L36,000/49,000. Keep a L100 coin handy for the elevator. The *Soggiorno Davanzati* (☎ 28 34 14) at Via Porta Rossa 15 is run down, but the rooms are clean. Rooms are L29,000/42,000, and a double with bathroom is L53,000. The hotel might close in late 1993 or early 1994 for restoration.

The *Albergo Firenze* (☎ 21 42 03), Piazza dei Donati 4, just south of the Duomo, has rooms from L41,000/64,000, all including breakfast. The helpful owners of *Brunori* (☎ 28 96 48), Via del Proconsolo 5, charge L32,000/53,000 for rooms and an extra L5000 for showers, but only in summer.

Places to Stay – middle
Around the Station The *Pensione Le Cascine* (☎ 21 10 66), Largo Alinari 15 near the station, is a two-star hotel with beautifully furnished rooms, some with balconies. Singles/doubles are L45,000/60,000. A triple with bathroom is L95,000.

The *Pensione Ausonia & Rimini* (☎ 49 65 47), Via Nazionale 24, is run by a young couple who go out of their way to help travellers. Singles/doubles are L41,000/60,000 and a triple is L80,000. The price includes breakfast, and use of the communal bathroom is free. They offer a 5% discount from May to October.

Pensione Accademia (☎ 29 34 51), Via Faenza 7, is pricey, but the rooms are beautiful and the hotel is in an 18th century palace replete with magnificent stained-glass doors and carved-wooden ceilings. Singles/doubles are L46,000/74,000 in the high season and include breakfast; rooms are

about one-third cheaper in winter. *Tony's Inn* (☎ 21 79 75) at Via Faenza 77 has rooms from L66,000/90,000. Upstairs and owned by the same people is the *Hotel Apollo* (☎ 28 41 19), with rooms from L80,000/120,000.

The *Albergo Tina* (☎ 48 35 19), Via San Gallo 31, has rooms from L50,000/65,000, although you should add L14,000 per person for breakfast during summer months. The *Pensione Garden* (☎ 21 26 69) at Piazza Vittorio Veneto 8 is near the river, west of the station. Rooms start at L35,000/52,000 and are very good value.

Around Piazza Santa Maria Novella The *Pensione Toscana* (☎ 21 31 56), Via del Sole 8, is an eccentrically decorated place and all rooms have a bathroom. Prices for singles/doubles are L48,000/62,000, triples are L90,000 and quads are L120,000. The *Albergo Visconti* (☎ 21 38 77), Piazza degli Ottaviani 1, is very elegant and has a beautiful roof garden. Singles/doubles are L36,000/52,000, although the owners generally add L12,000 per person for breakfast. The *Giotto* (☎ 28 98 64), Via del Giglio 13, has rooms from L45,000/75,000, and the *Giada* (☎ 21 53 17), nearby at Via Canto de' Nelli 2, has rooms from L55,000/83,000.

Between the Duomo & the Arno The *Pensione TeTi & Prestige* (☎ 239 84 35), Via Porta Rossa 5, has singles/doubles for L40,000/L74,000 and charges an extra L12,000 per person for breakfast. The *Maxim* (☎ 21 74 74), Via dei Medici 4, has rooms from L48,000/68,000 and offers substantial discounts in the low season. The *Albergo Rigati* (☎ 21 30 22), Lungarno Generale Diaz 2, is in a superb location overlooking the Arno and has rooms from L48,000/68,000. Call ahead because the owners are planning to close the hotel for restoration.

The *Maria Luisa de' Medici* (☎ 28 00 48), Via del Corso 1, is in a 17th century palace and its historically important entrance staircase features a fresco believed to have been painted by Alessandro Gherardini. It has no singles – with large rooms for up to five people, the management caters for families. A double is L67,500, or L78,000 with bathroom, a triple is L95,000, or L110,000 with bathroom. Family rooms for four can cost as little as L22,000 per person, and a room for five, with bathroom, is L172,000 (prices include breakfast). Prices drop in the low season. The accommodating management speaks English.

South of the Arno The *Albergo Goffredo* (☎ 68 79 24), Via di Ripoli 169, is south-east of the city centre and has singles/doubles from L40,000/68,000.

Places to Stay – top end
Around the Station The *Villa Medici* (☎ 238 13 31), Via il Prato 42, just west of the station, has singles/doubles from L210,000/320,000. The *Atlantic Palace* (☎ 29 42 34), Via Nazionale 12, has rooms from L120,000/180,000. The *Jolly Carlton* (☎ 27 70), Piazza Vittorio Veneto 4A, has rooms from L160,000/250,000.

Around Piazza Santa Maria Novella The *Albergo Majestic* (☎ 26 40 21), Via del Melarancio 1, has singles/doubles from L140,000/180,000. *Grand Hotel Baglioni* (☎ 21 84 41), Piazza dell'Unità Italiana 6, has rooms from L120,000/170,000. The *Croce di Malta* (☎ 21 83 51), Via della Scala 7, has rooms from L150,000/240,000.

Between the Duomo & the Arno The *Albergo Pendini* (☎ 21 11 70), Via Strozzi 2, overlooks Piazza della Repubblica and has singles/doubles from L96,000/147,000, cheaper in the low season. One of the city's best hotels is the five-star *Excelsior* (☎ 26 42 01), Piazza Ognissanti 3, which has rooms from L220,000/350,000. The *Savoy* (☎ 28 33 13), Piazza della Repubblica 7, charges from L210,000/300,000, and the *Bernini Palace* (☎ 28 86 21), Piazza San Firenze 29, from 150,000/200,000.

Places to Stay – apartments
If you want an apartment in Florence, save your pennies and start looking well before

you arrive. Apartments are difficult to come by and can be very expensive. A one-room apartment with kitchenette in the city centre will cost from L600,000 to L1,000,000 a month. Florence & Abroad (☎ 48 70 04), Via Zanobi 58, handles rental accommodation. Florence House-finding (☎ 247 66 20) also arranges apartments. Another option is to watch the notice board at the university for people looking for someone to share a flat.

Places to Eat
Simplicity and quality appropriately describe the cuisine of Tuscany. In a country where the various regional styles and traditions have provided a richly diverse cuisine, Tuscany is known for its fine cooking. The rich green olive oil of Tuscany, fresh fruit and vegetables, tender meat and, of course, the classic wine, Chianti, are the basics of a good meal in Florence.

No meal should begin without *bruschetta*, a thick slice of toasted bread, rubbed with garlic and soaked with olive oil. Try the *acquacotta* (literally, cooked water), a vegetable soup served with a slice of bread and an egg, topped off with Parmesan, or the deliciously simple *fagiolini alla Fiorentina*, green beans and olive oil. Florence is noted for its excellent *bistecca* (beefsteak) – thick, juicy and big enough for two people.

Eating at a good trattoria can be surprisingly economical, but many tourists fall into the trap of eating at the self-service restaurants which line the streets of the main shopping district between the Duomo and the river. Be adventurous and seek out the little eating places south of the Arno and near the Mercato Centrale in San Lorenzo. The market, open from 7 am to 2 pm Monday to Saturday (also from 4 to 8 pm Saturday), offers fresh produce, cheeses and meat at reasonable prices.

Between the Duomo & the Arno The streets between the Duomo and the Arno harbour many pizzerias where you can buy pizza by the slice to take away for around L2000 to L3000, depending on the weight. The *Self Service Leonardo*, on the corner of

Via de' Pecori and Via dei Vecchietti, is one of the better self-service restaurants and has pasta from L2500 and main courses from L5500. The snack bar *L'Orafo*, Via Por Santa Maria 8, on the way to the Ponte Vecchio, is another good choice for a quick, light and cheap lunch.

Trattoria da Benvenuto, Via Mosca 16r, on the corner of Via dei Neri, is considered one of the best trattorie in Florence. Its menu changes regularly and the excellent food is typical of the region. A full meal will cost under L17,000. A quick meal of pasta, bread and wine will cost around L8000. It is wise to reserve a table. *Osteria Il Caminetto*, Via dello Studio 34, south of the Duomo, has a small, vine-covered terrace. A pasta dish costs around L7000, and a main from L9000 to L10,000. The L2000 cover charge plus a 10% service charge bumps up the price of a meal.

Trattoria Le Mossacce, Via del Proconsolo 55r, just off Piazza del Duomo, serves pasta for around L6000, and a full meal with wine will cost up to L18,000.

Trattoria del Pennello, Via Dante Alighieri 4, is popular and quite cheap. Pasta dishes start at L5000 and a set meal costs L20,000. Just down the road at No 16 is *Chiodo Fisso*, a Mexican wine bar with Gypsy Kings-type entertainment. A meal could cost L25,000.

Ristorante Paoli, Via dei Tavolini 12, has magnificent vaulted ceilings and frescoed walls, and food to match. It offers a L28,000 set menu, pasta from L8000 and the cover charge is L2500. *Al Campidoglio*, Via del Campidoglio 8r, is an excellent restaurant specialising in Tuscan fare, where a meal could cost L40,000.

South of the Arno Just past the Pitti Palace is *La Mangiatora*, Piazza San Felice 8-10r. The upstairs section is called a tavola calda and downstairs a ristorante, but the prices are the same and downstairs is more pleasant. A pasta will cost L5000 to L6000, a main dish up to L8000 and a pizza from L5000 to L7000. A half-litre of Chianti is L3000 and

the cover charge is L1500. *Osteria del Cinghiale Bianco*, Borgo San Jacopo 43, to the right as you exit the Ponte Vecchio, specialises in Florentine foods and offers a delicious onion soup and wild boar with polenta. Pasta dishes start at L5000 and main courses from L9000, and the cover charge is L1500.

Trattoria Casalinga, Via dei Michelozzi 9r, is a bustling, popular local eating place. The food is great and a filling meal of pasta, meat or vegetables plus wine will cost you around L17,000. Don't expect to linger over a meal, as there is usually a queue of people waiting for your table.

I Tarocchi, Via de' Renai 12-14r, serves an excellent pizza from L6000, dishes typical of the region, including a good range of pasta, from L6000 to L9000, and plenty of salads and vegetable dishes from L4000 to L7000. The cover charge is only L1500. Expect to wait for a table at this popular restaurant.

Trattoria I Raddi, Via Ardiglione 47, just near Via de' Serragli, serves traditional Florentine meals and has pasta from L6000 and main courses from L12,000. *Il Cantinone di Gatto Nero*, Via di Santo Spirito 6r, specialises in crostini, thick Italian bread topped with a variety of ingredients. They start at L3500, pasta from L4500 and the cover charge is 1500.

La Loggia, Piazzale Michelangelo, is a very good restaurant, where a meal could cost L40,000.

Around Santa Maria Novella The *Caffè Cristallo*, Piazza della Stazione 44, opposite the train station, offers American and English breakfasts from L13,000. *Italy & Italy*, Piazza della Stazione, near Largo Alinari, makes a good alternative if you want a hamburger or other takeaway. *Caffè degli Innocenti*, Via Nazionale 57, near the famous leather market in the streets around the Mercato Centrale, has a great selection of prepared panini and cakes for around L3000 to L4000.

La Grotta di Leo, Via della Scala 41, is a pleasant trattoria with a L15,000 set menu, or pizzas and pasta from L7000. *Trattoria il Giardino* at No 67 has an L18,000 set menu, and serves typical dishes and cheap wine. The food is hearty and good. *Trattoria da Giovanni*, Via Guelfa 94r, offers a L15,000 set menu, or entrées from L2000 and pasta from L4000. *Il Biribisso*, Via dell'Albero 16, has a L13,000 set menu. *Super Tripperia*, Via dell'Albero 3A, specialises in tripe dishes and also does takeaway; a tripe panino will cost you L2500.

Bondi, Via dell'Ariento 85, specialises in focaccia and offers a variety of toppings. They start at L2500, and pizza by the slice is also L2500.

Le Fonticine, Via Nazionale 79r, is one of the city's better restaurants and a meal could cost L40,000.

Around Santa Croce Among the great undiscovered treasures of Florence is *Angie's Pub*, Via dei Neri 35r, east of the Palazzo Vecchio, which offers a vast array of panini and focaccia, as well as hamburgers, Italian-style with mozzarella and spinach, and hot dogs with cheese and mushrooms. A menu lists the panini, but you can design your own from the extensive selection of fillings; try one with artichoke, mozzarella and mushroom cream. Prices range from L4000 to L5500. There is a good range of beers and no extra charge to sit down.

Osteria del Gallo e Volpe, on the corner of Via Ghibellina and Via de' Giraldi, has pizzas from L5000 and pasta from L6000, and the cover charge is L2500. The *Sant'Ambrogio Caffè* at Piazza Sant'Ambrogio 7 is a groovy bar and restaurant, where you can get a panino from L3000 or pasta from L7000.

Trattoria la Maremmana at Via de' Macci 77r, behind Santa Croce, is a bit out of the way but worth seeking out for its good, hearty food and variously priced menus, starting at L18,000.

One of the city's finest restaurants, *Enoteca Pinchiorri*, Via Ghibellina 87, is both excellent and expensive. The mixed-seafood tortellini is very good and a meal could cost L100,000 a head.

Around Piazza Ognissanti The *Vini Buffet Freddo*, on the corner of Via Palazzuolo and Via dell'Albero, is a small restaurant that offers pasta from L3500, but it only opens during lunch time and into the early afternoon. Nearby is the *Trattoria il Contadino* at Via Palazzuolo 55, with a L13,000 set menu, including wine. *Trattoria Da Giorgio*, at No 54, also has a L13,000 set menu and the food is very good.

Ristorante Dino, Via Maso Finiguerra 6-8, is a good little trattoria, with pasta dishes from L6000 and main courses from L10,000. The L2500 cover charge bumps up the price. *Ristorante Da Mario*, Via Montebello 59, is cheap, with pasta from L5000, main courses at about L10,000, and a cover charge of L1400. *Pizzeria Carolina* is almost opposite at No 69 and has pizzas and pasta from L5000.

Da Il Latini, Via dei Palchetti 4, just off Via del Moro, is an attractive trattoria serving pasta from L6000 and main courses from L12,000.

Around San Lorenzo *Mario's*, a small bar and trattoria at Via Rosina 2r, near the Mercato Centrale, is open only at lunch time and serves pasta dishes for around L6000 to L8000, mains for L7000 to L9000. It is very popular. A few doors down, at Piazza del Mercato Centrale 20, is *Caffè Za Za*, another popular local eating place. Prices are around the same as at Mario's.

Bars & Cafés The *Antica Enoteca*, Via Ghibellina 142, is one of the city's oldest bars and features hundreds of wines. The owners will gladly open any bottle, and engage in a chat if you have the time. Wines start at L1500 a glass. The *Fiddler's Elbow*, Piazza Santa Maria Novella, opens from 4 pm to 1 am and is a popular spot for UK and US expats. *Rex Café*, Via Fiesolana 25r, in the Sant'Antonio area, is popular with the city's arts community.

Gilli, Piazza della Repubblica, is one of the city's finest cafés, and is reasonably cheap if you stand at the bar: a coffee at the bar is L1200, but at a table outside it is

L5000. *Giacosa*, at the intersection of Via de' Tornabuoni and Via della Vigna Nuova, is also very elegant, and a coffee at the bar is L1800. *Caffè Rivoire*, Piazza della Signoria 5r, is very expensive but in a lovely location.

Gelati People queue outside *Bar Vivoli*, Via dell'Isola delle Stinche, near Via Torta, to delight in the gelati that is widely considered the city's best. *Il Triangolo di Bermude*, Via Nazionale 61, near the leather market, and *Perché No?*, Via dei Tavolini 19r, off Via de' Calzaiuoli, are both excellent. *Festival del Gelato*, Via del Corso 75, just off Via de' Calzaiuoli, offers an incredible 90 flavours, including a good selection of semifrozen ice creams. *Gelateria dei Neri*, Via dei Neri 22r, has excellent flavours and is cheaper than most gelaterias. Try its Ferrero Rocher flavour.

Entertainment
There are several publications which list the theatrical and musical events and festivals held in the city and surrounding areas, including *Florence Today*, distributed bimonthly; a monthly news sheet, *Firenze Information*; and *Firenze Spettacolo*, all available from the tourist information office. Posters at the university and in Piazza della Repubblica advertise current concerts and other events.

A more sedate pastime is the evening stroll in Piazzale Michelangelo, overlooking the city (take bus No 13 from the station or the Duomo). In May, visit the city's iris garden nearby, when the irises are in full bloom. The city has many small art galleries, and hosts important travelling art shows. Check with the APT. The area around Piazza Sant'Ambrogio has many small galleries.

The city hosts the Internazionale Antiquariato, a biennial antique fair attracting 100 exhibitors from across Europe, at the Strozzi Palace, Via de' Tornabuoni. Call ☎ 28 26 35 for information.

Concerts, opera and dance are performed year-round at the Municipal Theatre, Corso Italia 16, with the main seasons running from September to December and January to April. Contact the theatre's box office (☎ 277 92 36). The Centro Culturale Dantesco (☎ 21 50 44) stages organ concerts each April, May and June at the Chiesa di Dante, Via Santa Margherita 2, and the Church of Santa Maria de' Ricci, Via del Corso.

Ballet is generally performed at the Verdi Theatre (☎ 21 23 20), Via Ghibellina 101. In summer there is the Florentine May Music Festival, a series of classical music concerts at the Municipal Theatre and Pergola Theatre, featuring important musicians from around the world. Book at the festival box office (☎ 24 23 61), Via della Pergola 10Ar.

The Astro Cinema in Piazza San Simone, near Santa Croce, runs films in English every night except Monday. There is no telephone, so check with the APT, or watch for street posters advertising upcoming movies.

As for nightclubs, La Dolce Vita, Piazza del Carmine, south of the Arno, is frequented by foreigners and Italians alike. Circus, Via delle Oche 17, is one of the better nightclubs. The Café Be Bop, Via dei Servi 76r, is a bit tacky; your feet will stick to the carpet but it really jumps from 11 pm. Both charge L10,000 entry, but the price includes one drink. Dr No, Via dei Benci 19r, is a popular club and features rock bands, flamenco and other types of live music.

Things to Buy
It is said that Milan has the best clothes and Rome the best shoes, but Florence without doubt has the greatest variety. The main shopping area is between the Duomo and the river, with boutiques concentrated along Via Roma, Via de' Calzaiuoli and Via Por Santa Maria, leading to the goldsmiths lining the Ponte Vecchio. Window-shop along Via de' Tornabuoni, where the top designers, including, Gucci, Saint-Laurent and Pucci, sell their wares.

The open-air market (Monday to Saturday) in the streets off San Lorenzo near the Mercato Centrale offers leather goods, clothing and jewellery at low prices, but quality can vary greatly. You could pick up the bargain of a lifetime here, but check the item carefully before paying. It is possible to bargain, but not if you want to use a credit card. The flea market (Monday to Saturday) at Piazza dei Ciompi, off Borgo Allegri near Santa Croce, is not as extensive, but there are great bargains.

Florence is famous for its beautifully patterned paper, which is stocked in the many stationery shops throughout the city and at the markets. One of the better shops is opposite the Pitti Palace in the Piazza dei Pitti.

Getting There & Away

Air The city is served by two airports, Amerigo Vespucci (☎ 37 34 98), a few km north-west of the city centre at Via del Termine 11, and Aeroporto Galileo Galilei (☎ 21 60 73), about an hour train or car from the city in Pisa. Vespucci serves domestic flights only, and there are services to Bari, Milan, Naples, Palermo, Rome and Turin. Galileo Galilei is one of northern Italy's main international and domestic airports, with regular flights to London, Paris, Zürich, Frankfurt and major Italian cities.

Most major European and some US airlines are represented in the city. Alitalia (☎ 2 78 88) is at Lungarno Acciaiuoli 10-12r; British Airways (☎ 21 86 55) is at Via Vigna Nuova 36r; and TWA (☎ 239 68 56) is at Via dei Vecchietti 4.

Bus The SITA bus terminal (☎ 21 47 21), Via Santa Caterina da Siena, is just to the west of the train station. Buses leave for Colle di Val d'Elsa, Poggibonsi (where there is a connecting bus to San Gimignano), Siena, Arezzo, Castellina in Chianti, Faenza, Marina di Grosseto, Volterra and other smaller cities throughout Tuscany. Several bus companies, including CLAP (☎ 28 37 34), Lazzi (☎ 239 88 40) and COPIT (☎ 21 54 51), operate from a terminal on Piazza Adua, east of the station. CLAP serves Lucca and other smaller cities; Lazzi operates to Empoli, La Spezia, Massa, Pistoia and Prato, and COPIT serves Pistoia and some smaller villages.

Train Florence is on the main Rome-Milan line, which means that most of the trains for Rome, Bologna and Milan are the fast intercities, for which you have to pay a supplement. There are also regular trains to and from Venice (three hours) and Trieste. For Verona you will generally need to change at Bologna. To get to Genoa and Turin, a change at Pisa is necessary. For train information, ring ☎ 27 87 85, or pick up the handy train timetable booklet available at the station.

There is a porter service operating from the train station. Porters will escort you to your hotel and charge L2500 per article.

Car & Motorbike Florence is connected by the Autostrada del Sole (A1) to Bologna and Milan in the north, and Rome and Naples in the south. The motorway to the sea, the Autostrada del Mare (A11), joins it to Prato, Lucca, Pisa and the Mediterranean coast, and a superstrada (dual carriageway) joins the city to Siena. Exits from the autostradas into Florence are well signed and there are tourist information offices on the A1 to both the north and south of the city.

The more picturesque ss67 connects the city with Pisa to the west and Forlì and Ravenna to the east. Hitchhikers from the south can follow the ss71, which runs parallel to the A1.

For car-rental details, see the following section.

Getting Around

To/From the Airports SITA operates direct buses between Vespucci Airport and the company's terminal west of the train station, from 6.55 am to 9.05 pm. The trip takes 15 minutes.

The best way to get to Galilei Airport is to check in at the air terminal (☎ 21 60 73) inside the train station near platform No 5. Check-in your luggage 15 minutes before the train departs. Hourly services begin at 5.55 am, with the last train leaving at 8 pm.

Alitalia and the state railways operate an airport train which connects Florence with Rome's Fiumicino Airport. Enquire at the Alitalia office.

Bus ATAF buses service the city centre and Fiesole, and the terminal for the most useful buses is in a small piazza to the left as you exit from the train station onto Via Valfonda. Bus No 7 leaves from here for Fiesole, also stopping at the Duomo. Bus No 91 Notturno connects the station, Duomo and Via Ghibellina from midnight to 6 am at half-hourly intervals. ATAF tickets must be bought at tobacconists or automatic vending machines at major bus stops before you get on the bus (L1000 for 70 minutes, L1300 for 120 minutes).

There are good-value tourist tickets which cost L5000 and are valid for 24 hours. The Carta Arancio is a seven-day tourist ticket allowing unlimited travel throughout the province of Florence on trains and buses (not sightseeing buses). Tickets are available at any of the bus-ticket offices around the station.

Car & Motorbike Traffic is restricted in the city centre, and the main car parks are in the Piazza del Mercato Centrale (expensive and only for daytime parking) and at the Fortezza da Basso, Viale Fillipo Strozzi, just behind the train station (L1000 an hour for all-night parking). There is a major underground car park near the train station but it is expensive.

The city and local car-park operators sponsor an innovative scheme whereby you will be given two free bicycles for two hours if you park in car parks at the Porta Romana, Piazza Vittorio Veneto, Piazza della Libertà, Piazza Cavalleggeri, Viale Mazzini (on the corner of Viale Gramsci) and Piazza Stazione. For more information, or to confirm the deal, contact Ciao & Basta (☎ 234 27 26), Costa dei Magnoli.

Rental Avis (☎ 234 66 68) is at Lungarno Torrigiani 33, Europcar (☎ 29 41 30) at Borgo Ognissanti 10r, and Eurodollar (☎ 29 31 86) at Via della Scala 48Ar. Alinari (☎ 28 05 00) rents scooters and larger motorini as well as bicycles from three locations: Via Guelfa 85r, Via de' Bardi 35 (south of the Arno River, near the Ponte Vecchio), and

from Piazza dei Cavalleggeri (south of Santa Croce).

Taxi You can find taxis outside the train station, or call ☎ 47 98 or 43 90. As always in Italy, taxis are very expensive.

AROUND FLORENCE
Fiesole
Perched in hills about eight km north-east of Florence, between the valleys of the Arno and Mugnone rivers, Fiesole has attracted the likes of Boccaccio, Carducci, Giovanni Dupré, Marcel Proust, Gertrude Stein and Frank Lloyd Wright, all drawn by the lush olive groves and valleys – not to mention the spectacular view over Florence. Fiesole was founded in the 7th century BC by the Etruscans and remained the most important city in northern Etruria. It is well worth visiting for the views and is a fabulous spot for a picnic and short walk.

Fiesole is easily reached from Florence. ATAF bus No 7 from the Florence train station passes through the centre of Florence and connects with Piazza Mino da Fiesole, the centre of this small town. If you are driving, find your way to Piazza della Libertà north of the Duomo and then follow the signs to Fiesole. The APT in Florence, or in Fiesole (☎ 055-59 87 20), Piazza Mino da Fiesole 37, can assist with general information about the town and can advise on accommodation, walks and other activities. Most other services are located around the tourist office.

Things to See & Do Opposite the tourist office in Piazza Mino da Fiesole is the **Duomo**, started in the 11th century and altered in the 13th century, although a 19th century renovation has eradicated many earlier features. Behind the Duomo is the **Bandini Museum**, featuring an impressive collection of early Tuscan Renaissance works, including Gaddi's *Annunciation* and Petrarch's beautifully illustrated *Triumphs*.

Opposite the entrance to the museum on Via Portigiana, the **Archaeological Zone** features a 1st century BC Roman theatre which is used during July and August for the

Estate Fiesolana, a series of concerts and performances. Also in the complex is a small Etruscan temple and Roman baths, which date from the same period as the theatre. The small archaeological museum is worth a look-in if you have the time, as it includes finds ranging from the Bronze Age to the Roman period. A cumulative ticket costing L6000 allows you entry to the archaeological zone and museum and the Bandini Museum. Check with the APT, as opening times for all sites vary considerably during the year.

If you are planning a picnic, or just want a refreshing walk, head uphill along the main street from Piazza Mino da Fiesole to Via Corsica. Take Via Pelagaccio, which eventually becomes a dirt track as it weaves a small trail around the mountain overlooking Florence and winds back into Fiesole. You'll probably get lost but there is no shortage of locals to redirect you. Beware of *il Mostro* (the Monster), a real-life villain who police believe stalks the hills over Florence and has murdered several couples. He hasn't been heard of since the mid-1980s but the tourist office warns that he has not been caught. The APT advises that you camp in provided areas.

Places to Stay & Eat There is a camping ground at Fiesole, the *Campeggio Panoramico* (☎ 055-59 90 69), Via Peramonda 1, which also has bungalows. Take bus No 70 from Piazza Mino da Fiesole to reach the ground.

The city has several hotels but most are quite expensive. The *Bencistà* (☎ 055-5 91 63), Via Benedetto da Maiano 4, about one km from Fiesole on the road to Florence, is an old villa and from its terrace there is a magnificent view of Florence. Half-pension is compulsory at L74,000 per person, or L90,000 with private bathroom. It might bust the budget, but for one or two days it is well worth it.

The *Casa del Popolo di Fiesole*, Via Antonio Gramsci 25, up the hill from Piazza Mino da Fiesole, is a cheap pizzeria with great views over the mountains to the north and east from the terrace. Piazza Mino da

Fiesole is full of expensive bars, but the *Blu Bar* is one of the more popular.

The Medici Villas
The Medicis built several opulent villas throughout the countryside around Florence as their wealth and prosperity grew during the 15th and 16th centuries. Most are now enclosed by the city's suburbs and its industrial sprawl, and many are easily reached by taking various ATAF buses from the train station. Ask for details at the APT in Florence about bus numbers and opening times.

The **Villa della Petraia**, about 3.5 km north of the city, is one of the finest. Commissioned by Cardinal Ferdinand de' Medici in 1576, this former castle was converted by Buontalenti and features a magnificent garden. The **Villa di Castello**, farther north of the city, was the summer home of Lorenzo the Magnificent, while the **Villa di Poggio a Caiano**, about 15 km from Florence on the road to Pistoia, was built for Lorenzo – and it shows.

The Mugello
The area north-east of Florence leading up to Firenzuola, near the border with Emilia-Romagna, is known as the Mugello and features some of the most original villages in Tuscany. The Sieve River winds through the area and its valley is one of Tuscany's premier wine areas after the Chianti region.

Start with the APT in Florence, or contact the Comunità Montana del Mugello by telephone (☎ 055-845 65 51) for information. The APT should have several brochures on the area including *Sorgenti di Firenze Trekking*, which details 22 walks in the area. Apart from trekking, the area is popular with free-climbers and offers plenty of trails for horse riders. The Sieve's rapids are also popular with canoeists.

PRATO
Virtually enclosed in the urban and industrial sprawl of Florence, Prato is 17 km north-west of the city and is one of the country's main centres for textile production. Founded by the Ligurians, the city fell to the Etruscans

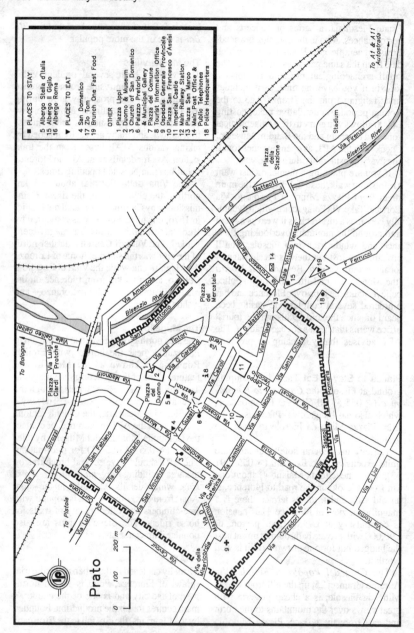

Prato

0   100   200 m

PLACES TO STAY
5 Albergo Stella d'Italia
15 Albergo Il Giglio
16 Albergo Roma

PLACES TO EAT
4 San Domenico
17 Zio Tom
19 Brunch One Fast Food

OTHER
1 Piazza Lippi
2 Duomo & Museum
3 Church of San Domenico
6 Palazzo Pretorio
7 Municipal Gallery
8 Piazza del Comune
9 Tourist Information Office
10 Ospedale Generale Provinciale
11 Piazza San Francesco d'Assisi
12 Main Railway Station
13 Imperial Castle
14 Piazza San Marco
16 Main Post Office &
     Public Telephones
18 Police Headquarters

To A1 & A11
Autostrada

To Bologna

To Pistoia

Stadium

Bisenzio River

Piazza
della
Stazione

Piazza del
Mercatale

Piazza del
Duomo

Piazza
Ciardi

and later the Romans, and by the 11th century was an important centre for wool production. It is worth visiting on your way to the more picturesque cities of Pistoia, Lucca and Pisa to the west.

Orientation

The old city centre is small and surrounded by the city wall. The main train station, in Piazza della Stazione, is to the east. From the station, cross the Bisenzio River and walk west along Viale Vittorio Veneto, through Piazza San Marco, and continue along Via Mazzini, which becomes Via Cairoli. The central Piazza del Comune is ahead and Piazza del Duomo is just to the north along Via G Mazzoni. Another cluster of piazzas, including Piazza San Francesco d'Assisi, is to the south of Via Cairoli.

Information

The APT tourist office (☎ 0574-2 41 12) is at Via Cairoli 48-52 and opens Monday to Saturday from 8.30 am to 1.30 pm. The office also opens afternoons during summer months.

The city's main post office and telephones are at Via Arcivesco Martini 8. The postal code for Prato is 51100, and the telephone code 0574.

The police headquarters (☎ 113 or 2 77 77) are at Via Baldinucci. For medical emergencies, the Ospedale Generale Provinciale (☎ 49 42 54) is in Piazza dell'Ospedale, south-west of Piazza del Comune.

Things to See

Start in Piazza del Comune, which has several of the city's finest palaces. On the north side is the town hall, and on the south side is the Palazzo Pretorio, which now houses the city's **Municipal Gallery**, featuring a small but impressive collection of paintings. Among those represented are Filippo and Filippino Lippi and Vasari. The gallery is closed Sunday and Tuesday but opens other days from 9 am to 12.30 pm and 3.30 to 6.30 pm, and entry is L5000.

Take Via Mazzoni to Piazza del Duomo for the city's 12th century **Santo Stefano**

Cathedral. The façade features a lunette by Andrea della Robbia, and the Pergamo del Sacro Cingolo (Pulpit of the Holy Girdle) on the right-hand side of the façade as you face the main entrance. The pulpit is a copy, the original is in the **Cathedral Museum** next door, and is used five times a year (Easter, 1 May, 15 August, 8 September and 25 December) to display the Virgin's girdle, apparently dropped by the Virgin and given to St Thomas and bought to the city from Jerusalem after the Second Crusade. The interior of the church features magnificent frescoes by Filippo Lippi, Paolo Uccello and Gaddi. The museum opens the same hours as the Municipal Gallery and entry is L6000.

From Piazza del Comune, Via C Guasti leads to the Gothic **Church of San Domenico**, with frescoes by Uccello. South of Via Cairoli is the **Imperial Castle**, built during the 13th century and incorporating parts of an earlier fortification. The castle opens Tuesday to Saturday from 9.30 am to midday and 3 to 5 pm, and Sunday mornings.

Places to Stay & Eat

The *Albergo Stella d'Italia* (☎ 2 79 10), overlooking the cathedral at Piazza del Duomo 8, has singles/doubles from L35,000/50,000, while the *Albergo Roma* (☎ 3 17 77), Via Carradori 1, has rooms from L50,000/70,000. *Albergo Il Giglio* (☎ 3 70 49), Piazza San Marco 14, has rooms from L45,000/68,000.

There is a produce market in Piazza Lippi next to the Cathedral Museum, open daily (except Sunday) from 8 am to 1 pm. If you want good, cheap food, head for *Brunch One Fast Food*, Via F Ferrucci 43A, with pasta from L4000. *Zio Tom*, Via Roma 75, has pizzas from L5000, and *San Domenico*, Via Guasti 62, is a good trattoria where a meal could cost L30,000.

Getting There & Away

CAP buses (☎ 60 82 24), Piazza del Duomo 23, operate regular services to Florence and Pistoia. The train station (☎ 2 66 17) is in Piazza della Stazione, and Prato is on the Florence-Bologna and Florence-Lucca lines.

By car, take the A1 and exit at Calenzano, or the A11 from Florence to the sea and exit at Prato Est or Ovest. The ss325 connects the city with Bologna. Several CAP buses, including No 5, connect the train station with the cathedral.

PISTOIA

One of the most pleasant cities in Tuscany, Pistoia is generally overshadowed as a tourist destination by Florence, about 30 minutes away by train. At the foot of the Apennines, the city has grown beyond its well-preserved medieval ramparts and is today one of the world's main centres for the manufacture of trains. In the 16th century the city's metalworkers created the pistol, named after the city.

Orientation & Information

The old city centre is quite large, but easy to negotiate. From the train station in Piazza Dante Alighieri, head north along Via XX Settembre through Piazza Treviso and turn right into Via Cavour. Via Roma, to the left, takes you to Piazza del Duomo and the APT tourist information office (0573-2 16 22), which opens daily from 9 am to 12.30 pm and 3.30 to 6 pm.

The main post office is at Via Roma 5, near Via Cavour, and SIP telephone offices are in Via del Molinuzzo, near Piazza San Francesco d'Assisi, and on Corso Gramsci, just north of Via della Madonna. The telephone code for Pistoia is 0573.

For police emergencies, call ☎ 113, or contact the police headquarters (☎ 2 13 44) at the western edge of the city centre along Via Sacconi. For medical emergencies, call ☎ 2 03 21.

Things to See

The most 'happening' part of Pistoia is around Piazza del Duomo. The **San Zeno Cathedral** dates from the 5th century but was rebuilt in the 12th and 13th centuries, and is a blending of Pisan Romanesque and Florentine Renaissance styles. The green and white marble façade features terracotta reliefs by della Robbia, and the bell tower

has three tiers of loggias by Giovanni Pisano. Inside the San Jacopo Chapel is the altar of St James, one of the finest works of silver in Italy. The **Baptistry**, elegantly banded in green and white marble, was started in 1337 to a design by Andrea Pisano.

Opposite is the austere 15th century **Podestà Palace**, and next to the cathedral is the late 14th century town hall, which houses the city's **Municipal Museum** featuring artworks from the 13th to the 19th centuries. On the ground floor is a permanent collection dedicated to life of Pistoia-born artist Marino Marini. Both the museum and Marini collection are open Tuesday to Saturday from 9 am to 1 pm and 3 to 7 pm as well as Sunday morning, and entry is L6000. Entry is free on Saturday afternoon.

Wander north to Piazza dell'Ospedale for one of Giovanni della Robbia's most serene works. Adorning the façade of the hospital, the **Ospedale del Ceppo**, is a glazed terracotta frieze depicting the *Seven Works of Mercy*. Some churches worth visiting are the **Church of San Giovanni Fuorcivitas** on Via Cavour, notable for terracotta reliefs by della Robbia and a font by Giovanni Pisano. The **Church of the Madonna dell'Umiltà**, south-west of Piazza del Duomo on Via della Madonna, was designed by Vasari and pays homage to Brunelleschi's dome on the Duomo in Florence.

Places to Stay & Eat

Accommodation is reasonably cheap and generally easy to find in peak months. The *Albergo Autisti* (☎ 2 17 71), Viale Pancinotti 93, has singles/doubles from L30,000/40,000, and the *Albergo Appennino* (☎ 3 22 43), Via XX Settembre 21, has rooms from L44,000/60,000.

There is a produce market most days in Piazza della Sala, south-west of the cathedral. For a cheap pizza or a snack, try *Pizzeria del Duca*, Via del Duca 7. *Tonino*, Corso Gramsci 159, is a pleasant trattoria where a meal could cost L25,000. *Leon Rosso*, Via Panciatichi 4, is very good and slightly more expensive, with pasta from

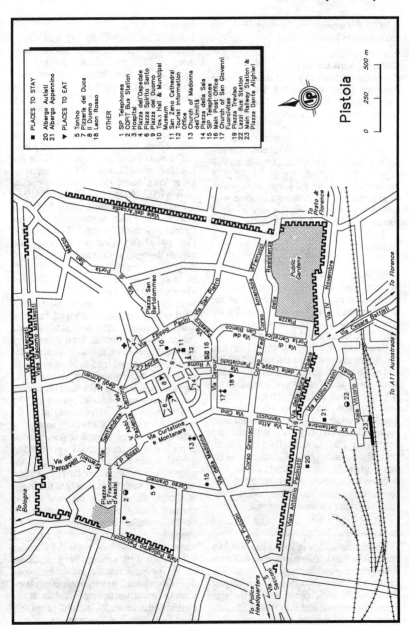

Pistoia

0   250   500 m

PLACES TO STAY
20 Albergo Autlati
21 Albergo Appennino

▼ PLACES TO EAT
5 Tonino
7 Pizzeria del Duca
8 Il Duomo
18 Leon Rosso

OTHER
1 SIP Telephones
2 COPIT Bus Station
3 Hospital
4 Piazza dell'Ospedale
6 Piazza Spirito Santo
9 Piazza del Duomo
10 Town Hall & Municipal Museum
11 San Zeno Cathedral
12 Tourist Information Office
13 Church of Madonna dell'Umiltà
14 Piazza della Sala
15 SIP Telephones
16 Main Post Office
17 Church of San Giovanni Fuorcivitas
19 Piazza Treviso
22 Lazzi Bus Station
23 Main Railway Station & Piazza Dante Alighieri

L7000. *Il Duomo*, Via Braccioloni 5, has main courses from L8000.

Getting There & Away

Buses connect the city with most towns in Tuscany. Lazzi buses (☎ 2 51 32) serve Prato, Florence and Pisa from Viale Vittorio Veneto, east of the train station. COPIT (☎ 2 11 70) also serves Florence, from Via del Molinuzzo, off Piazza San Francesco d'Assisi. Trains (☎ 2 07 89) connect the city with Florence, Bologna, Lucca and Viareggio. By car, the city is on the A11 autostrada, and the ss64 and ss66, which head north-east for Bologna and north-west for Parma respectively. The city is easily explored on foot, although COPIT bus No 10 or 12 connects the train station with the cathedral.

LUCCA

With its imposing Renaissance walls and medieval street plan, Lucca is one of the most serene cities in Tuscany. Situated at the base of the Apuan Alps and only a short trip from Pisa, Lucca should not be missed.

Originally founded by the Ligurians, Lucca became a Roman colony in 180 BC and a free commune during the 12th century, setting off a period of prosperity based on the silk trade. Many of the city's finest buildings date from the 14th century when the town developed under Castruccio Castracani degli Anterminelli. The city later fell under the control of Pisa, and in 1805, Napoleon created the principality of Lucca, placing his sister Elisa in control. In 1817 the city became a Bourbon duchy before it was incorporated into the Kingdom of Italy. Lucca remains a strong agricultural centre.

Orientation

From the train station in Piazza Ricasoli, just outside the walls to the south, walk to Piazza Risorgimento and through the Porta San Pietro. Via Vittorio Veneto will take you past the main APT tourist office, through the huge Piazza Napoleone and into Piazza San Michele – the centre of the city.

Information

The APT (☎ 0583-49 36 39), Via Vittoria Veneto 40, is open Monday to Saturday from 9 am to 12.30 pm. There's another APT office on Via Sant'Andrea, near the Torre delle Ore. A third tourist office, the Centro Accoglienza Turistica (☎ 0583-5 35 92), is at the western edge of the walled city in an old city gate, the Vecchia Porta San Donato, Piazzale Verdi, and is more useful. This office opens daily from 9 am to 7.30 pm.

The main post office is in Via Vallisneri, just north of the Duomo, and SIP telephones are at Via Cenami 15. The city's telephone code is 0583 and the postal code is 55100.

For police emergencies, call ☎ 113, or head for the police headquarters on Viale Cavour, near the train station. The main hospital (☎ 97 01) is on Via dell'Ospedale, outside the walls to the east.

Things to See & Do

Start in Piazza Napoleone, a grand square lined with expensive hotels and bars that doubles as a car park. To the west is the Ducal Palace, which houses the local government and is not open to the public. Walk along Via Duomo to get to Piazza San Martino and the cathedral dedicated to St Martin, the **Duomo**, which dates from the 11th century but was completely rebuilt between the 13th and 15th centuries. The façade is in the Lucca-Pisan style and was built around the existing bell tower. Note the columns in the upper part of the façade: each was carved by a local artisan and all are different. In the north aisle is the Temple of the Holy Visage, containing a crucifix said to bear the image of Christ. Nicodemus is believed to have carved the image at Calvary, and each year on 13 September it is carried through the streets in a procession at dusk. In the north transept is the tomb of Ilaria del Carretto, wife of the 15th century Lord of Lucca, Paolo Guinigi, which was carved by Jacopo della Quercia and is recognised as a masterpiece of funerary sculpture. The church also contains other artworks, including a magnificent *Last Supper* by Tintoretto.

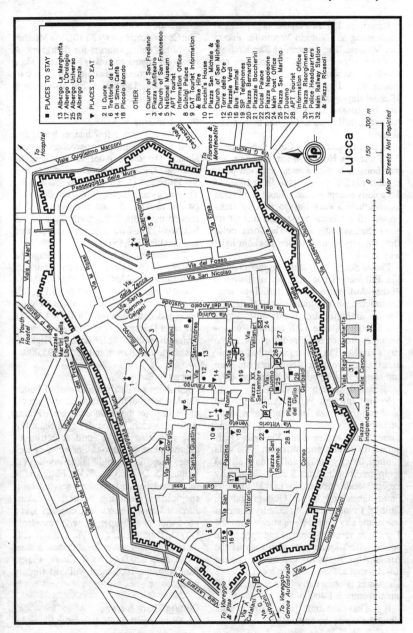

PLACES TO STAY
- 13 Albergo La Margherita
- 17 Albergo L'Orologio
- 25 Albergo Universo
- 29 Albergo Cinzia

PLACES TO EAT
- 2 Il Cuore
- 6 Trattoria da Leo
- 14 Di Simo Caffè
- 18 Piccolo Mondo

OTHER
- 1 Church of San Frediano
- 3 Piazza Anfiteatro
- 4 Church of San Francesco
- 5 National Museum
- 7 APT Tourist
     Information Office
- 8 Guinigi Palace
- 9 Centro Tourist Information
     & Bike Hire
- 10 Puccini's House
- 11 Piazza San Michele &
      Church of San Michele
- 12 Torre delle Ore
- 15 Piazzale Verdi
- 16 Bus Terminal
- 19 SIP Telephones
- 20 Piazza Bernardini
- 21 Piazza Boccherini
- 22 Ducal Palace
- 23 Piazza Napoleone
- 24 Main Post Office
- 26 Piazza San Martino
- 27 Duomo
- 28 APT Tourist
      Information Office
- 30 Piazza Risorgimento
- 31 Police Headquarters
- 32 Main Railway Station
      & Piazza Ricasoli

Lucca

0   150   300 m

Minor Streets Not Depicted

Return to Piazza Napoleone and head north along Via Vittorio Veneto for Piazza San Michele. The **Church of San Michele in Foro** dates from the 12th century and stands on the site of the Roman forum. The façade, topped by a figure of the Archangel Michael slaying a dragon, contrasts with the simple Romanesque interior. Look for Andrea della Robbia's *Madonna* in the south aisle.

Opposite the church at Corte San Lorenzo 9 is **Puccini's House**, where the composer was born. It houses a small museum dedicated to his life, which opens from 10 am to 4 pm daily except Monday. East from Piazza San Michele is **Via Fillungo**, the city's best preserved medieval street and one of its most characteristic areas. The **Torre delle Ore**, the city's clock tower, is about halfway along.

Piazza Scarpellini, at the northern end of Via Fillungo, leads into the oval-shaped **Piazza Anfiteatro**, whose buildings were constructed on the foundations of the old Roman amphitheatre. North-west, across Via Fillungo, is the 12th century Romanesque **Church of San Frediano**, one of the city's largest. The white façade has marble cannibalised from the Roman amphitheatre and features a 13th century, Byzantine-style mosaic depicting the Ascension.

Return through Piazza Anfiteatro and head east for Piazza San Francesco with the attractive 13th century church of the same name, then continue along Via della Quarquonia for the **National Museum** in the Villa Guinigi, the city's major collection of art and sculpture. It opens from 9 am to 2 pm daily except Monday, and entry is L6000. Via della Fratta takes you to Via Guinigi and the **Guinigi Palace**, the 15th century home of one of the city's main Renaissance families. The tower, recently restored and open to the public, offers spectacular views across the Apuan Alps. Roots from an oak tree on the tower's roof are visible in the room beneath. The tower is open daily from 9 am to 7.30 pm and entry is L4000.

If you have the time, do the four-km walk along the top of the city wall.

Language Courses
The Centro Koinè (☎ 49 30 40), Via Mordini 60, offers Italian courses for foreigners. A two-week summer course is L460,000, while month-long courses, available all year, start at L590,000. The school can also arrange accommodation.

Places to Stay
The city has only a few budget hotels and most fill with students or workers, so call ahead. The city's hotel association, the Sindicato Lucchese Albergatori (☎ 4 41 81), Via Fillungo 121, will help you find a room. The city's youth hostel, the *Ostello Il Serchio* (☎ 34 18 11), Via del Brennero 673, is outside the walls to the north. Take CLAP bus Nos 1, 2 or 7 from the train station. Bed and breakfast is L15,000.

The best budget option is the *Albergo La Margherita* (☎ 4 41 46), Via Sant'Andrea 8, with singles/doubles from L22,000/40,000. The *Albergo L'Orologio* (☎ 5 34 19), Via San Pierino 7, has rooms for about the same price, as does the *Albergo Cinzia* (☎ 4 13 23), Via della Dogana 9. The three-star *Albergo Universo* (☎ 49 36 78), Piazza del Giglio 1, has singles/doubles from L60,000/95,000.

Places to Eat
Food shops are easily found around Piazza San Michele, but for an abundance of atmosphere, head for the produce market in Piazza Anfiteatro each Wednesday and Saturday. The city also has a good selection of relatively cheap trattorias. For pizza-by-the-slice, there is a small takeaway at Via Fillungo 5. *Di Simo Caffè*, Via Fillungo 58, is a grand bar and gelateria serving local specialities including buccellato cakes. *Piccolo Mondo*, Piazza dei Cocomeri 5, is a good spot for a cheap meal, with pasta from L4000. *Trattoria da Leo*, Via Tegrimi 1, is quite cheap and serves local dishes; a meal could cost L20,000. At *Il Cuore*, Piazza Sant'Agostino 10, a meal will cost slightly more.

Getting There & Away
CLAP buses (☎ 58 78 97) serve Florence,

Massa, Viareggio and several towns in the Garfagnana, the mountains north of the city. Lazzi (☎ 58 48 76) operates buses to Florence, La Spezia, Carrara, Pisa, Prato, Pistoia, Turin and Rome. Both companies operate from Piazzale Verdi.

The city is on the Florence-Viareggio-Pisa train line, and there are also services into the Garfagnana. By car, the A11 autostrada passes to the south of the city, connecting it with Pisa and Viareggio. The ss445 connects the city with the Garfagnana. Most cars are banned from the city centre, although tourists are allowed to drive into the walled city. There are parking areas in piazzas Bernardini, San Martino and Napoleone. For a taxi, call ☎ 4 49 89.

Getting Around

The city is best seen on foot or by bicycle, which can be rented from the tourist office in Piazzale Verdi from L1500 an hour, or L10,000 a day. Several CLAP buses connect the train station, Piazza del Giglio and Piazzale Verdi.

THE GARFAGNANA

Much of the Apennines above Lucca form an area known as the Garfagnana, which is one of the best areas in Tuscany for trekking, horse riding and a host of other sporting pursuits. The area is also stunningly beautiful and parts of it look like the Dolomites of Trentino Alto-Adige.

The Garfagnana is based around the valley formed by the Serchio River and its affluents, and its tourist infrastructure is highly organised. The tourist offices in Lucca or Pisa can provide a range of information, as can the Club Alpino Italiano in Lucca (☎ 0583-58 26 69), which is housed in the Ducal Palace. In the Garfagnana, the most useful organisation is the Comunità Montane at Castelnuovo di Garfagnana (☎ 0583-65 89 90), Via Vittorio Emanuele 9. Many small towns have Pro Loco tourist offices which can give details about accommodation and the mountain refuges dotted throughout the mountains.

If you are interested in walking, pick up a copy of *Garfagnana Trekking*, which details a 10-day walk. Another booklet, *Garfagnana a Cavallo*, lists details of guided horse-riding treks which can cost L18,000 an hour or L90,000 a day. Details of these and other aspects of the mountains, including farm holidays, are available from the Azienda Agrituristica La Garfagnana (☎ 0583-6 87 05), Le Prade 25, in Castiglione di Garfagnana.

MASSA & CARRARA

These two towns in the northern reaches of Tuscany don't really warrant a visit unless you are interested in seeing Italy's most famous marble quarries. Massa is the administrative centre of the province and is rather unattractive, although the beachfront extension, Marina di Massa, is very popular with holidaying Italians. You might wonder why, if you happen to stumble on to the overpopulated shores.

Carrara, however, is quite picturesque. At the foothills of the Apuan Alps, the town appears to be dominated by snowcapped mountains – an illusion created by limestone formations and the vast quarries which virtually cover the hills. The texture and purity of Carrara's white marble is unrivalled and was chosen by Michelangelo for many of his masterpieces. He travelled to the quarries on many occasions to personally select blocks for his works.

The APT has offices at Marina di Massa (☎ 0585-24 00 46), Viale Vespucci 24, at Carrara (☎ 0585-84 33 70), Viale XX Settembre, and at Marina di Carrara (☎ 0585-63 22 18), Piazza Menconi 5B. The hotel association in Massa, the Associazione Commerciati (☎ 0585-4 17 96), Viale Chiesa, will help you find a room. There is a youth hostel on the coast at Marina di Massa, the *Ostello della Gioventù* (☎ 0585-78 00 34), Via delle Pinete, which charges L10,000 for a bed.

Both towns are accessible from the A12 autostrada and the ss1 Via Aurelia, and signs direct you to quarries you can visit and other attractions, such as museums.

PISA

Once a maritime power to rival Genoa and Venice, Pisa now seems content to have one remaining claim to fame: its leaning tower. Situated on the banks of the Arno River, near the Ligurian Sea, it was a busy port, the site of an important university and the home of Galileo Galilei (1564-1642). Devastated by Genoa in the 13th century, its history eventually merged with that of Florence. Today Pisa is a pleasant town, but there is not a lot to see after you have explored the main square, the Campo dei Miracoli, also known as the Piazza del Duomo, and taken a walk around the old city centre.

Duomo & Leaning Tower

History

Possibly a settlement of Greek origin, Pisa became an important naval base during Roman times and remained a significant port for many centuries. The city's greatest period, its so-called Golden Days, began late in the 9th century when the city became an independent maritime republic and a rival of Genoa and Venice, and peaked during the 12th and 13th centuries when Pisa controlled Corsica, Sardinia and most of the Italian coast as far south as Civitavecchia. Most of the city's finest buildings date from this period.

Pisa supported the Ghibellines during the tussles between the Holy Roman emperor and the pope when much of Tuscany supported the Guelphs. As such, the city came into conflict with Siena, Lucca, Florence and Genoa, whose fleet inflicted a devastating defeat on Pisa during the naval battle of Meloria in 1284. The city eventually fell to Florence, and the Medicis encouraged great artistic, literary and scientific endeavour. The city was badly damaged during WW II but almost no evidence remains.

Orientation

From Stazione Pisa Centrale, the city's main train station, at the southern edge of the old city centre, walk north along Viale Gramsci and through Piazza Vittorio Emanuele II, and continue along Corso Italia, one of the city's main shopping boulevards. Cross the river

over the Ponte di Mezzo and continue walking north along Borgo Stretto, Via Oberdan and Via Carducci, and then left into Via Cardinale Maffi, which will take you to the Campo dei Miracoli (Field of Miracles) with the Duomo, Baptistry and famous tower. Most sights, hotels and restaurants are clustered around this route.

Information

Tourist Office The main APT (☎ 050-54 18 00) is on the river at Lungarno Mediceo 42 and is open Monday to Friday from 9 am to 12.30 pm. More useful offices are located at Piazza del Duomo (☎ 050-56 04 64) and outside the train station (☎ 050-4 22 91). Both these offices open Monday to Saturday from 8 am to 8 pm in summer, and from 9.30 am to midday and 3 to 5.30 pm Monday to Saturday in the off season. The Duomo office generally only opens in the summer months.

Money Avoid the exchange booths near the Duomo. Change money at banks along Corso Italia, or at the train station.

Post & Telecommunications The main post office is in Piazza Vittorio Emanuele II. Poste restante mail can be addressed to 56100 Pisa.

There are telephones at the train station, and there's an SIP telephone office at Via Carducci 15 which stays open late. The city's telephone code is 050.

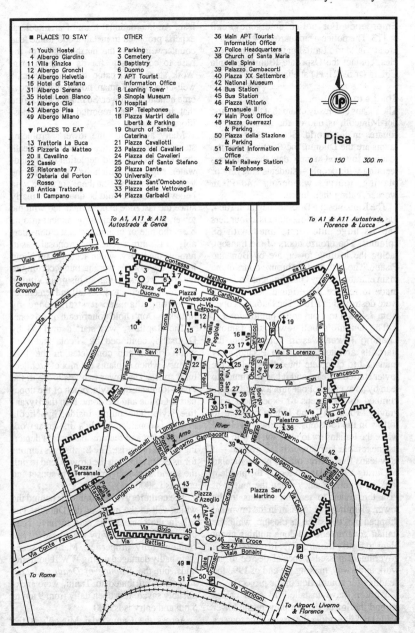

PLACES TO STAY

1 Youth Hostel
4 Albergo Giardino
11 Villa Kinzica
12 Albergo Gronchi
14 Albergo Helvetia
16 Hotel di Stefano
31 Albergo Serena
35 Hotel Leon Bianco
41 Albergo Clio
43 Albergo Pisa
49 Albergo Milano

PLACES TO EAT

13 Trattoria La Buca
15 Pizzeria da Matteo
20 Il Cavallino
22 Cassio
26 Ristorante 77
27 Osteria del Porton Rosso
28 Antica Trattoria Il Campano

OTHER

2 Parking
3 Cemetery
5 Baptistry
6 Duomo
7 APT Tourist Information Office
8 Leaning Tower
9 Sinopia Museum
10 Hospital
17 SIP Telephones
18 Piazza Martiri della Libertà & Parking
19 Church of Santa Caterina
21 Piazza Cavallotti
23 Palazzo dei Cavalieri
24 Piazza dei Cavalieri
25 Church of Santo Stefano
29 Piazza Dante
30 University
32 Piazza Sant'Omobono
33 Piazza delle Vettovaglie
34 Piazza Garibaldi

36 Main APT Tourist Information Office
37 Police Headquarters
38 Church of Santa Maria della Spina
39 Palazzo Gambacorti
40 Piazza XX Settembre
42 National Museum
44 Bus Station
45 Bus Station
46 Piazza Vittorio Emanuele II
47 Main Post Office
48 Piazza Guerrazzi & Parking
50 Piazza della Stazione & Parking
51 Tourist Information Office
52 Main Railway Station & Telephones

Pisa

0   150   300 m

Emergency For police emergency, call ☎ 113. The police headquarters (☎ 58 35 11) are at Via Mario Lalli. For medical emergencies, contact the Ospedale Riuniti di Santa Chiara (☎ 59 21 11) at Via Roma 67.

Things to See

The Pisans can justly claim that their Campo dei Miracoli, is one of the most beautiful squares in the world. Set in its sprawling lawns are the Duomo, the Baptistry and the leaning tower. On any day the piazza is teeming with people – students studying or playing, tourists wandering and Pisan workers eating their lunch.

The Romanesque **Duomo**, begun in 1064, has a beautiful façade of columns in four tiers and its huge interior is lined with 68 columns. The bronze doors of the transept, facing the leaning tower, are by Bonanno Pisano. The 16th century bronze doors of the main entrance are by Giambologna and were made to replace the original doors, which were destroyed in a fire. The Duomo is open from 7.45 am to 1 pm and 3 pm to sunset.

The Duomo's bell tower, the famous **Leaning Tower**, was in trouble from the start. Its architect, Bonanno Pisano, only managed to complete three tiers before the tower started to lean, and it has continued to lean by an average of one mm a year. Galileo climbed its 294 steps to experiment with gravity. Today it is no longer possible to follow in his footsteps. The tower is closed while the Italians try to work out how to stop its inexorable lean towards the ground – it now leans five metres off the perpendicular.

During 1992, plans to rectify the problem took on a new urgency when the mayor of Pisa threatened to readmit tourists to the tower, claiming that tourism in the town had dropped by 20% since its closure, while the Italian government had done nothing about plans to fortify the structure. In response, the government passed a special decree to get work underway, making the end of 1993 the deadline for completion of the project.

Workers have installed 18 steel cables around the lower tiers to prevent the lower walls buckling under the strain of the tower's lean. An international team of architectural experts proposed to install a 600-tonne lead counterweight on the northern side of the base to compensate for its southern lean. Work started but came to a halt when a well-preserved Roman house was discovered beneath the tower. So intact was the find that archaeologists reported cups still positioned on tables.

Many agree that the tower's problems stem from the geological formation beneath the city and the rapid depletion of groundwater supplies, which has added to the tower's instability. But there are some who believe nothing should be done, particularly since the last time experts meddled with the tower, in 1934, by injecting cement into its base, the rate of incline increased considerably to 1.2 mm a year. One proposal was to remove the belfry, which accounts for about half of the tower's weight, but according to the controversial Italian art historian Vittorio Sgarbi, it is 'better to see it fall and remember it leaning than see it straightened by mistake'. Don't hold your breath on this one.

The **Baptistry** was started in 1153 by Diotisalvi, continued by Nicola and Giovanni Pisano and completed in the 14th century, which explains the mix of architectural styles. The lower two levels are in the Pisan-Romanesque style, much of the upper part is Gothic and the dome is in the Byzantine style. The pulpit inside, by Nicola Pisano, is considered Italy's first great work of Gothic art and features bas-reliefs depicting the life of Christ. The Baptistry is famous for its echo, although the crowds tend to dull the sound. It is open from 9 am to sunset and entry is L5000.

The **cemetery** (camposanto) is behind the white wall to the north of the Duomo. The soil in the cemetery is said to have been brought from Calvary by the crusaders and contains holy properties. Many frescoes were badly damaged during WW II bombing raids, but the *Triumph of Death* and *Last Judgment*, attributed to Traini, were inexplicably saved. It is open daily from 9 am to 5 pm and entry is L5000.

Across the Campo dei Miracoli is the

Sinopia Museum, a museum housing sinopias, reddish-brown sketches drawn onto walls as the base for frescoes, which were discovered in the cemetery after the WW II bombing raids. They have been restored and provide a fascinating insight into the process of creating a fresco. The museum opens daily from 9 am to 1 pm and 3 pm to sunset, and entry is L5000.

The **Duomo Museum** in Piazza Arcivescovado, near the Leaning Tower, features many artworks from the tower, Duomo and Baptistry, including a magnificent ivory carving, the *Madonna & Crucifix* by Giovanni Pisano. It opens daily from 9 am to 1 pm and 3 pm to sunset, and entry is L5000.

Head south along Via Santa Maria from the Campo dei Miracoli and turn left at Piazza Cavallotti for the splendid **Piazza dei Cavalieri**, which was remodelled by Vasari in the 16th century and is now the seat of the city's premier university, which spreads through surrounding streets. The **Palazzo dell'Orologio** by Vasari is decorated with frescoes. The **Palazzo dei Cavalieri** on the north-east side of the piazza, also by Vasari, features busts of grand masters of the Knights of St Stephen, a religious and military order founded by Cosimo de' Medici. The **Church of Santo Stefano** by Vasari is brilliant with its green, white and pink marble façade. The **Church of Santa Caterina**, to the east along Via San Lorenzo on Piazza Martiri della Libertà, is a fine example of Pisan Gothic architecture and contains works by Nino Pisano.

Wander south for the area around Borgo Stretto, the city's most authentic medieval section. East along the waterfront boulevard, the Lungarno Mediceo, is the **National Museum**, one of Tuscany's finest galleries, featuring the work of Giovanni and Nicola Pisano, Donatello and Simone Martini. The gallery opens Tuesday to Saturday from 9 am to 7 pm, Sunday to 1 pm, and entry is L6000.

Cross the **Ponte di Mezzo** for Piazza XX Settembre, dominated by the **Gambacorti Palace**, now the local-government building, and head west for the

Church of Santa Maria della Spina, built in the early 14th century to house a thorn from Christ's crown.

Places to Stay

Pisa has a reasonable number of budget hotels for a small town, but many double as residences for students during the school year, so it can be difficult to find a cheap room. A camping ground, the *Camping Torre Pendente* (☎ 56 06 65), Via delle Cascine 86, is west of the Duomo. There is a youth hostel, the *Ostello per la Gioventù* (☎ 89 06 22), north-west of the Duomo on Via Pietrasantina 15. A bed costs L12,000. Take bus No 3 from the train station.

The *Albergo Serena* (☎ 2 44 91), Via D Cavalca 45, just off Piazza Dante, has singles/doubles from L20,000/28,000. The *Helvetia* (☎ 55 30 84), Via Don Gaetano Boschi 31, near the Duomo, has rooms from L26,000/38,000. *Hotel di Stefano* (☎ 55 35 59), Via Sant'Apollonia 35, near Via Oberdan, has rooms from L30,000/44,000. The *Albergo Gronchi* (☎ 56 18 23), Piazza Arcivescovado 1, just near the Campo dei Miracoli, is a great bargain offering rooms for L28,000/44,000, and triples/quads for L60,000/74,000. The *Albergo Giardino* (☎ 56 21 01), Via Carlo Cammeo, just west of the Piazza del Duomo, has rooms for the same price.

South of the river is the *Albergo Clio* (☎ 2 84 46), Via San Lorenzino 3, which has singles/doubles from L26,000/44,000. Near the train station is the *Albergo Milano* (☎ 2 31 62), Via Mascagni 14, with comfortable rooms and a friendly owner. Singles/doubles cost L32,000/46,000, and triples cost L66,000.

The two-star *Albergo Pisa* (☎ 4 45 51), Via Manzoni 22, has rooms from L35,000/50,000. The *Hotel Leon Bianco* (☎ 54 36 73), Piazza del Pozzetto 6, off Piazza Garibaldi, has rooms from L40,000/68,000. More up-market is the *Villa Kinzica* (☎ 56 04 19), Piazza Arcivescovado 2, with views of the Leaning Tower and rooms from L70,000/110,000.

Places to Eat

Being a university town, Pisa hosts a good range of cheap eating places. Head for the area around Borgo Stretto and the university. There is an open-air food market in Piazza delle Vettovaglie, off Borgo Stretto.

For a lunch-time snack, *Specchio*, Via Domenica Cavalca 11, has pizza by the slice from L1000 a piece. The *Osteria del Porton Rosso* next door has pasta from L6000 and main courses from L10,000, and offers some local Pisan dishes. The *Trattoria la Mescita* in Piazza delle Vettovaglie is appealing, cheap and features a menu loaded with Pisan dishes. The *Antica Trattoria Il Campano*, in an old tower at Vicolo Santa Margherita, is slightly more expensive and a meal could cost about L20,000. The *Trattoria Sant'Omobono* in Piazza Sant'Omobono does wonders with tripe, a local speciality. Otherwise, pasta dishes start at L6000.

Heading north, the *Ristorante 77*, Via Santa Cecilia 34, is reasonably expensive but the food is considered excellent. *Il Cavallino*, facing Piazza Martiri della Libertà, has pasta from L6000 and main courses from L9000.

Trattoria La Buca in Piazza del Duomo has pizzas from L4000 and the cover charge is only L1000. *Cassio*, Piazza Cavallotti, is a pizzeria/bar with pizzas from L3000 and pasta from L4000. *Pizzeria da Matteo*, Via Santa Maria 20, has a good deal of a beer and pizza for L6000.

One of the city's finest bars is the *Caffè Federico Salza*, Borgo Stretto 46, with fabulous cakes, gelati and chocolates. Prices inside are one-third of those charged if you eat at the tables outside. Another is *Bar Duomo*, facing the Leaning Tower and very expensive. For a great gelati, head for *La Bottega del Gelato* in Piazza Garibaldi, near the river.

Entertainment

The tourist office has a list of nightclubs and events in the city. Opera and ballet are staged at the Teatro Verdi (☎ 94 11 11), Via Palestro 40, from September to November. Cultural and historic events include the Gioco del Ponte on the last Sunday in June, a festival of traditional costume. On 17 June, the Arno River comes to life with the Regata Storica di San Ranieri, a rowing competition commemorating the city's patron saint.

Getting There & Away

Air The city's Galileo Galilei Airport (☎ 50 07 07), about two km south of the city centre, is Tuscany's main international airport and handles flights to major cities in Europe as well as New York.

Alitalia (☎ 4 80 27) has an office at Via Corridoni, while British Airways (☎ 50 18 38) and other major airlines are all based at the airport.

Bus Lazzi (☎ 4 62 88), Piazza Vittorio Emanuele II, operates services to Lucca, Florence, Prato, Pistoia, Massa and Carrara. APT (☎ 2 33 84), Piazza Sant'Antonio, near the train station, serves Volterra, Livorno and Lucca.

Train The station is in Piazza della Stazione (☎ 4 13 85) at the southern edge of town. The city is connected to Florence and is also on the main Rome-La Spezia line, with frequent services running in all directions.

Car & Motorbike The city is close to the A12 autostrada, which connects Livorno in the south to Parma. It is currently being extended to Rome, but that will take several years to complete. The city is also close to the A11, connecting it with Florence. The north-south ss1, the Via Aurelia, connects the city with La Spezia and Rome, while the ss67 connects it with Florence.

Large car parks are all around Pisa and are denoted by a white 'P' on a blue background. A large car park is just north of the Duomo and perfect for day-trippers.

Getting Around

To get to the airport, take a train from the main station in Pisa for the four-minute journey to the Stazione FS Pisa Aeroporto, or take city bus No 7, which passes through the city centre on its way to the airport. For a taxi to the airport, call ☎ 2 85 42.

To get from the train station to the Duomo, take city bus No 1 or walk the 1.5 km.

LIVORNO

Tuscany's second-largest city, Livorno (also known as Leghorn in English) is not worth a visit unless you are catching a ferry to Sardinia, Corsica, Sicily or Spain. The city is a modern industrial centre and was heavily bombed during WW II.

Orientation & Information

From the train station in Piazza Dante at the eastern edge of the city centre, walk west along Viale Carducci and then Via Grande into the central Piazza Grande. The main APT tourist office (☎ 0586-89 81 11) is at Piazza Cavour 6 to the south. From Piazza Grande, continue west towards the waterfront, through Piazza Micheli for Piazza Arsenale and a smaller APT (☎ 0586-89 53 20). A third office is at the main ferry terminal, known as Calata Carrara, near the Stazione Marittima train station. The main office opens Monday to Friday from 9 am to 2 pm, Saturday to 1 pm, and the smaller offices open mornings and afternoons during the summer months only.

The main post office is at Via Cairoli 46, and SIP telephones are at Largo Duomo and Scali A Saffi 21. The city's postal code is 57100 and the telephone code is 0586.

For police emergency, call ☎ 113, or go to the police headquarters (☎ 89 86 11) in the Palazzo del Governo, Piazza Unità d'Italia. The Ospedale Civile (☎ 40 33 51) is on Viale Alfieri near the train station.

Things to See

If you have some time, the city does have a few worthy sights. The **New Fortress** (Fortezza Nuova), in the area known as Piccola Venezia because of its small canals, was built for the Medici family in the late 16th century. Close to the waterfront is the city's other fort, the **Old Fortress** (Fortezza Vecchia), built 60 years earlier on the site of an 11th century building.

The city has two galleries of note: the **Museo Civico Giovanni Fattori**, Viale della Libertà 30, which features works by a 19th century Livorno-based movement led by the artist Giovanni Fattori; and the **Museo Progressivo d'Arte Contemporanea**, also known as the Centro di Documentazione Visiva, Via Redi 22, which has a smattering of well-known 20th century works. Both galleries open Tuesday to Sunday from 9 am to 1 pm and entry is L6000 each. The city's unspectacular cathedral is just off Piazza Grande.

Places to Stay & Eat

Finding accommodation shouldn't be a problem. The *Albergo Stazione* (☎ 40 23 07), Viale Carducci 301, is near the train station and has singles/doubles from L32,000/43,000. *Albergo L'Amico Fritz* (☎ 40 11 49) is nearby at Viale Carducci 180 and has rooms for the same price, as does the *Pensione Dante* (☎ 89 34 61), near the waterfront at Scali d'Azeglio 28.

For produce, the market is on Via Buontalenti, and the area around Piazza XX Settembre is great for bars and cafés. *Pizzeria Tavola Calda*, Via dell'Angiolo 12, has pizzas from L4000 and is a good place for a cheap lunch. *L'Angiolo d'Oro*, Piazza Mazzini 15, is an inexpensive trattoria with pasta from L6000. The *Cantina Senese*, Borgo dei Cappuccini, is also cheap and serves some local dishes.

Getting There & Away

ATL buses (☎ 89 61 11) depart from Piazza Grande for Cecina, Piombino and Pisa, and Lazzi (☎ 89 95 62) departs from Piazza Manin for Florence, Pisa, Lucca and Viareggio.

The main train station in Piazza Dante is on the Rome-La Spezia line and the city is also connected to Florence and Pisa. There is a second station, called Stazione Marittima, near the main port area, but trains are less frequent. It is usually easier to catch a train to the main train station and then a bus to the ports.

By car, the A12 autostrada passes through

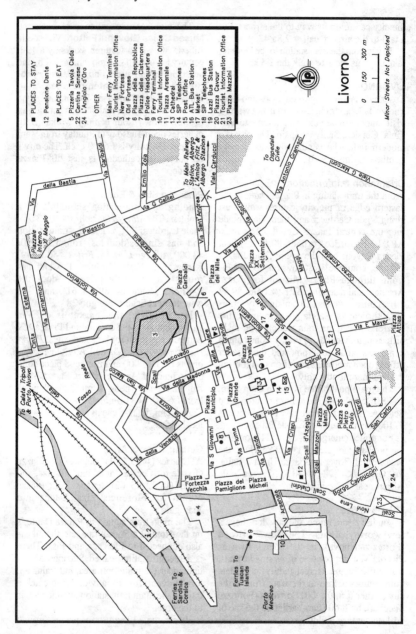

Livorno

0   150   300 m

Minor Streets Not Depicted

■ PLACES TO STAY
12 Pensione Dante

▼ PLACES TO EAT
5 Pizzeria Tavola Calda
22 Cantina Senese
24 L'Angiolo d'Oro

OTHER
1 Main Ferry Terminal
2 Tourist Information Office
3 New Fortress
4 Old Fortress
6 Piazza della Repubblica
7 Piazza delle Cisternone
8 Police Headquarters
9 Ferry Terminal
10 Tourist Information Office
11 Piazza Arsenale
13 Cathedral
14 SIP Telephones
15 Post Office
16 ATL Bus Station
17 Market & Fritz
18 SIP Telephones
19 Lazzi Bus Station
20 Piazza Cavour
21 Tourist Information Office
23 Piazza Mazzini

the city and the ss1 connects Livorno with Rome. There are several car parks near the waterfront.

Boat Livorno is one of the main ferry ports on the west coast. The city has two main ferry terminals: the major terminal, the Stazione Marittima, is in an area called Calata Carrara and is just north of the Old Fortress; the smaller ferry terminal is near Piazza Arsenale and is called the Molo Mediceo. Both can be reached by bus from the main train station. There is a third ferry terminal, known as the Porto Nuovo, at Calata Tripoli, several km north of the city along Via Sant'Orlando. It is not easily reached by public transport (ask at the tourist office for directions).

Ferry companies operating from Livorno are as follows:

Alimar (☎ 88 07 33) serves Barcelona and Sicily from the Stazione Marittima.
Compagnia Sarda Navigazione Marittima (☎ 40 99 25) at Varco Galvani, Calata Tripoli, operates ferries to Olbia.
Corsica Ferries (☎ 88 13 80), at the Stazione Marittima on Calata Carrara, operates regular services to Bastia.
Navarma (☎ 89 33 27), Via Veneto 24, serves Bastia, Bonifacio and Santa Teresa di Gallura from the Stazione Marittima.
Sardinia Ferries (☎ 88 13 80) in the Stazione Marittima building operates services to Olbia.
Sicil Ferry (☎ 40 98 04) at the Porto Nuovo, Calata Tripoli, serves Palermo.

Getting Around

To get from the train station to Piazza Arsenale and the Porto Mediceo, take ATL bus No 1. To reach the Stazione Marittima, take bus No 18. To reach the city centre, take bus No 1, 2 or 8.

SIENA

Beautiful, gentle Siena is built on three hills and is still surrounded by its historic ramparts. Its medieval centre has streets lined with majestic Gothic buildings in various shades of the reddish-brown colour known as burnt sienna. The city became one of

Europe's major centres during the 13th and 14th centuries and flourished as a result of its extensive trade links and pre-eminent banking houses – the country's richest at the time.

Today, Siena thrives as much on tourism as any other industry, and is host to the famous Palio, a medieval festival culminating in a bareback horse race around the magnificent Piazza del Campo. Siena is also home to the Monte dei Paschi di Siena bank, the world's oldest bank and the city's largest employer.

History

According to legend, Siena was founded by the sons of Remus (one of the founders of Rome). Probably of Etruscan origin, Siena came under the rule of the Gauls around the 5th century. The city reached it peak in the early 13th century, bolstered by a victory against the more superior Florence at the Battle of Montaperti in 1260. The Ghibelline Sienese had long been the rivals of the Florentine Guelphs who exacted their revenge in 1269 and occupied the city. Under Florence, the city's merchants ruled the city and brought about rapid urban growth. The city reached its architectural peak during the years between 1320 and 1340 when the governing Council of Nine ordered the building of the city's cathedral and the Piazza del Campo – Italy's finest medieval square – with its incredible town hall.

The outbreak of the plague in 1348 left the cathedral unfinished, killed 65,000 of the city's 100,000 people and led to a period of decline. At the end of the 14th century, the city came under the control of Milan's Visconti family and then in the 15th century was ruled by the autocratic leader Pandolfo Petrucci. Holy Roman Emperor Charles V conquered the city in 1555 after a two-year siege that left thousands dead. Cosimo de' Medici absorbed the city into his Grand Duchy of Tuscany, barring the inhabitants from operating banks and thus curtailing Siena's power for good.

The city produced important works of art

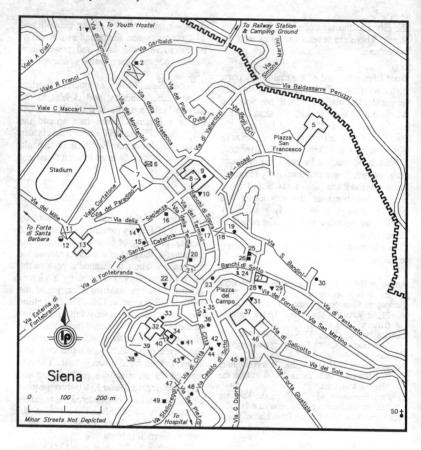

Siena

0   100   200 m

Minor Streets Not Depicted

by painters of the Sienese school and was home to St Catherine and St Benedict.

Orientation

Siena is well geared for tourism. Signs direct you through the modern town to the medieval city, and within the walls there are easy-to-follow signs to all the major sights. The main train station is in Piazza F Roselli, north of the city centre. Walk along Viale Giuseppe Mazzini, through the city wall at the Barriera San Lorenzo, and continue along Via Garibaldi, which eventually runs into Via dei Montanini. Piazza Salimbeni is

to the left and Piazza del Campo is about 250 metres farther south.

Information

Tourist Office The APT office (☎ 0577-28 05 51) is at Piazza del Campo 56 and is open Monday to Saturday from 8.30 am to 7.30 pm in summer and from 9 am to 12.30 pm and 3.30 to 7 pm for the rest of the year. There is another office at Via di Città 43 (☎ 0577-4 22 09).

Money The main branch of the Monte dei Paschi di Siena is in Piazza Salimbeni. The

■ PLACES TO STAY

2	Piccolo Hotel Il Palio
16	Albergo Bernini
20	Albergo La Perla
25	Piccolo Hotel Etruria
26	Tre Donzelle
45	Locanda Garibaldi
49	Albergo Duomo

▼ PLACES TO EAT

1	Da Titti
10	Nannini
14	La Chiacchiera
22	Osteria La Grotta del Fantino
28	Osteria Le Logge
29	Pizzeria del Gallo Nero
31	Il Barbero
42	Hostaria Il Carroccio
43	Ai Marsili

OTHER

3	Piazza del Sale
4	Piazza Gramsci
5	Church of San Francesco
6	Main Post Office
7	Piazza Matteotti
8	Piazza Salimbeni
9	Monte dei Paschi di Siena Bank
11	Piazza San Domenico
12	Tra-in & Sita Bus Terminal
13	Church of San Domenico
15	St Catherine's House
17	SIP Telephones
18	Piazza Tolomei
19	CTS Travel office
21	Piazza Indipendenza
23	Loggia dei Mercanti
24	APT Tourist Information Office
27	Piccolomini Palace
30	Language School
32	Duomo
33	Baptistry of San Giovanni
34	Duomo Museum
35	APT Branch office
36	Ricama
37	Town Hall
38	Ospedale Santa Maria della Scale
39	Piazza del Duomo
40	Piazza Jacopo della Quercia
41	Police Headquarters
44	Palazzo Chigi-Saracini
46	Piazza del Mercato
47	Piazza di Postierla
48	National Picture Gallery
50	Church of Santa Maria dei Servi

bank has an automatic exchange service nearby on Via Montanini near the piazza.

Post & Telecommunications The main post office is at Piazza Matteotti 1. Poste restante mail can be addressed to 53100 Siena. The SIP telephone office is at Via dei Termini 40. Siena's telephone code is 0577.

Travel Agency For budget travel, CTS (☎ 28 50 08) has an office at Via Cecco Angiolieri.

Emergency For police emergency, call ☎ 113. The police headquarters are at Via del Castoro, near the Duomo. The Foreigners' Office is in Piazza Jacopo della Quercia and opens from 10 am to midday Monday to Saturday. In a medical emergency, call ☎ 2 99 11, or for an ambulance, ☎ 28 01 10. There is a hospital south of the city centre at Via dei Tufi, near the Porta Tufi.

Things to See & Do

The **Piazza del Campo**, known simply as the Campo, is a magnificent, shell-shaped, slanting piazza, its paving divided into nine sectors representing the nine-member council which ruled Siena during the 13th and 14th centuries. At the upper part of the piazza is the **Fountain of Joy** (Fonte Gaia), a copy of the original by Jacopo della Quercia.

At the lowest point of the piazza is the imposing **town hall** (the Palazzo Pubblico, also known as the Palazzo Comunale), which dates from 1297 and is considered one of the most graceful Gothic buildings in Italy. The adjacent **Mangia Tower** stands 102 metres and with the town hall forms the city's emblem. Inside the town hall are numerous important Sienese works of art, including Simone Martini's *Maestà* and Ambrogio Lorenzetti's frescoes, the *Effects of Good & Bad Government*, and Jacopo della Quercia's original Fonte Gaia. There is also a chapel with frescoes by Taddeo di Bartolo. The town hall opens daily from 9.30 am to 7.45 pm in summer, to 1.45 pm in winter, and entry is L6000, or L3000 for students. Climb to the top of the tower for a spectacular view. It opens roughly the same hours as the town hall and entry is L4000.

Leave the Campo through the Loggia dei Mercanti and follow Via di Città past the 14th century Gothic **Palazzo Chigi-Saracini**. Continue along to the Piazza di Postierla and wander up the hill along Via del Capitano to Piazza del Duomo and the city's stunning **Duomo**. Next to the cathedral in Orvieto, Siena's cathedral is one of the most beautiful in Italy. Its black-and-white striped marble façade has a Romanesque lower section, with carvings by Giovanni Pisano. The cathedral reached its present stage of completion in 1215, although its upper section is 14th century Gothic and there are 19th century mosaics at the top. There were plans to create one of Italy's largest churches, evident by the incomplete exposed curtain walls in Piazza del Duomo, but structural problems and the plague put paid to much further work. The cathedral's interior features an inlaid-marble floor, with various works depicting biblical stories. The beautiful pulpit was carved in marble and porphyry by Nicola Pisano, the father of Giovanni Pisano. Other important artworks include a bronze statue of St John the Baptist by Donatello and statues of St Jerome and Mary Magdalene by Bernini.

Through a door from the north aisle is the **Piccolomini Library**, which Pope Pius III (pope during 1503) had built to house the books of his uncle, the former pope Pius II. It features frescoes by Pinturicchio and a Roman statue of the three Graces. Entry is L2000.

The **Duomo Museum** is just off Piazza del Duomo. It houses many important works of art that formerly adorned the cathedral. These include 12 statues of prophets, philosophers and the *Sybil* by Giovanni Pisano; the famous *Maestà* by Duccio di Buoninsegna, formerly used as a screen for the cathedral's

high altar; and works by artists such as Ambrogio, Lorenzetti, Simone Martini and Taddeo di Bartolo. The collection also inlcudes tapestries and manuscripts. The museum is open daily from 9 am to 7.30 pm and admission is L6000.

The **San Giovanni Baptistry**, which is behind the cathedral, has a Gothic façade and is decorated with 15th century frescoes, a font by Jacopo della Quercia, and sculptures by artists such as Donatello and Ghiberti. On the south-west side of Piazza del Duomo is the **Ospedale Santa Maria della Scala**, a former hospital with frescoes by Domenico di Bartolo in the main ward. An appointment for a visit must be made on ☎ 29 94 10. The building is soon to house the **Etruscan Archaeological Museum**, with an impressive collection of Roman and Etruscan remains.

In the 15th century Palazzo Buonsignori, a short walk south of the Duomo at Via San Pietro 29, is the **National Picture Gallery** with innumerable masterpieces by Sienese artists, including the *Madonna of the Franciscans* by Duccio di Buoninsegna, *Virgin & Child* by Simone Martini and a series of Madonnas by Ambrogio Lorenzetti. The gallery is open from 8.30 am to 2 pm Monday, to 7 pm Tuesday to Saturday, and to 1 pm Sunday in summer, with shorter hours in winter. Admission is L8000.

From the Loggia dei Mercanti north of the Campo, take Banchi di Sotto to the east for the **Piccolomini Palace**, regarded as the city's finest Renaissance palace. The building houses the city's archives and a small museum which opens Monday to Saturday from 9 am to 1 pm. Entry is free. Farther east are the 13th century **Church of Santa Maria dei Servi** with a fresco by Lorenzetti, and the 14th century **Porta Romana**.

Return to the Loggia dei Mercanti and head north along Banchi di Sopra and past Piazza Tolomei, dominated by the 13th century **Palazzo Tolomei**. Farther along Banchi di Sopra is the Piazza Salimbeni featuring the **Palazzo Tantucci** to the north, the Gothic **Palazzo Salimbeni** to the east and the Renaissance **Palazzo Spannocchi**, all housing the head office of the Monte dei Paschi di Siena bank. North-east of here, along Via Rossi, is the Gothic **Church of San Francesco**.

West along Via del Paradiso is Piazza San Domenico from where you can see the massive **Forte di Santa Barbara** built for Cosimo de' Medici. The **Church of San Domenico** was started in the 13th century and features the Cappella delle Volte where St Catherine had visions and took her vows. One of the church's most prized possessions is St Catherine's head.

A little way from here along Via della Sapienza is **St Catherine's House** on Costa di Sant'Antonio, with paintings by several prominent Sienese artists. The house where the saint was born is open daily from 9.30 am to 12.30 pm and 3.30 to 6 pm, and entrance is free.

Study Courses

Language It is generally held that the Sienese speak the purest form of Italian, and it is a popular place to study the language. The School of Italian Language & Culture for Foreigners (☎ 4 92 60) is in Piazzetta Grassi 2, Siena 53100. The school is open all year and the only requirement for enrolment is a high-school graduation/pass certificate. There are three areas of study: Italian language and literature; archaeology and the history of art; and Italian history and institutions. Courses cost L500,000 for 10 weeks and brochures can be obtained by making a request by letter or telephone to the secretary, or from the Italian Cultural Institute in your country.

Music The Accademia Musicale Chigiana (☎ 4 61 52), Via di Città 89, offers classical-music classes every summer, as well as seminars and concerts performed by visiting musicians, teachers and students as part of the Settimana Musicale Senese. Classes are offered for most classical instruments and start at L100,000. Enrolments must be completed by 4 April.

The Associazione Siena Jazz (☎ 27 14 01), Strada di Santa Regina 6, offers courses

in jazz which start at L380,000; it's one of Europe's foremost institutions of its type.

Festivals

Siena is famous for the Palio, which is held twice yearly, on 2 July and 16 August, and is generally considered Italy's most spectacular festival. It is a bareback horse race around the Campo that lasts barely a minute but is preceded by pomp and medieval pageantry. The race dates back to the 11th century, is dedicated to the Virgin Mary and was originally run through the city's streets. The current format, three laps of the Campo, was introduced late in the 16th century, and only mattresses and other barriers have been added since as protection for horses and riders alike.

The city was originally divided into about 60 *contrade* ('districts'), but now there are only 17 of these wards covering the old city centre. Each year 10 are chosen by lot (as are the jockeys) to compete in the Palio. There is one official rule, that riders are not to interfere with the reins of other horses, but cheating has always been prevalent. The actual Palio is the richly ornamented banner presented to the winner.

The race is basically run by the Sienese for the Sienese (even if jockeys are rarely local) and the city eschews outsiders. Efforts by the Benetton to sponsor the race have been unsuccessful, and the Sienese place incredible demands on the national TV network, RAI, for rights to televise the event. Book well in advance for a room, and join the crowds at least four hours before the event for a spot on the fence, although you can generally see some of the race from anywhere in the Campo if there's any room left. The event is free.

Places to Stay

Although there is a good range of budget accommodation in Siena, you should book well in advance for August, particularly during the Palio, when accommodation is impossible to find for miles around the city. For assistance in finding a room, contact Siena Hotels Promotion (☎ 28 80 84), Piazza

San Domenico, which is open daily from 9 am to 8 pm in summer and shorter hours during winter. Agriturismo is well organised around Siena. The tourist office has a list of more than 60 establishments which rent rooms by the week or month.

The *Colleverde* camping ground (☎ 28 00 44) is north of the historical centre at Strada di Scacciapensieri 47 (take bus No 8 from Piazza Gramsci near the city centre). The cost for one night is L10,000 for adults and L5000 for children. The IYHF youth hostel *Guido Riccio* (☎ 5 22 12), Via Fiorentina, Stellino, is about two km north-west of the city centre (leave the city along Via Vittorio Emanuele, which starts at the end of Via di Camollia). Bed and breakfast is L18,000. Take bus No 15 from Piazza Gramsci.

In town, try the *Tre Donzelle* (☎ 28 03 58), Via delle Donzelle 5, which has singles/doubles for L30,000/50,000. The *Piccolo Hotel Etruria* (☎ 28 80 88), close by at Via delle Donzelle 1, has rooms from L37,000/48,000. The *Locanda Garibaldi* (☎ 28 42 04), Via Giovanni Dupré 18, has doubles for L48,000 (no singles). It also has a small trattoria with a L15,000 tourist menu.

The *Albergo Bernini* (☎ 28 90 47), Via della Sapienza 15, has clean, simple singles/doubles with shower for L40,000/53,000. The *Albergo La Perla* (☎ 4 71 44) is on the 2nd floor at Via delle Terme 25, a short walk from the Campo. Small but clean rooms with shower are L40,000/55,000.

The *Piccolo Hotel Etruria* mentioned earlier also has a two-star hotel on its premises, with rooms from L45,000/55,000. The *Piccolo Hotel Il Palio* (☎ 28 11 31), Piazza del Sale 19, has rooms from L60,000/85,000, while the three-star *Albergo Duomo* (☎ 28 90 88), Via Stalloreggi 34, has rooms from L60,000/105,000.

Places to Eat

The Sienese claim that most Tuscan cuisine has its origins in Siena, and that the locals are still using methods introduced to the area by the Etruscans, namely simple cooking methods and the use of herbs. Beans are very popular and are included in many dishes, and

bread is made without salt. *Panforte*, a rich cake of almonds, honey and candied melon or citrus fruit, has its origins in the city. Loosely translated, panforte is heavy bread, and it was created as sustenance for the crusaders.

Il Barbero in Piazza del Campo is a cheap self-service restaurant, where a pasta will cost L4000. *Hostaria Il Carroccio*, Via Casato di Sotto 32, off the Campo, has excellent pasta for around L7000; a bottle of house wine is only L4500, but a full meal will come to around L28,000. *Osteria La Grotta del Fantino*, Via di Fontebranda 5 (off Via di Città), has meals for around the same price. *Pizzeria del Gallo Nero*, Via del Porrione 67, has good pizzas from L5000, and the *Osteria Le Logge*, Via del Porrione 33, is an inexpensive, typical restaurant.

La Chiacchiera, Costa di Sant'Antonio 4, off Via Santa Caterina, is very small, but it has a good menu with local specialities. Pasta dishes cost from L5000 and a litre of house wine is L4500. A full meal will cost about L17,000. *Al Marsili*, Via del Castoro 3, is one of the city's best restaurants and has typical dishes from L7000.

About 10 minutes' walk from the Campo, in a less frenetic neighbourhood, are several trattorias and alimentari. *Da Titti*, Via di Camollia 193, is a no-frills establishment with big wooden bench-tables where full meals with wine cost around L20,000. *Pizzeria Il Riccio*, nearby at Via Malta 44, has pasta for around L7000 and big pizzas from L6000.

At the local grocery shops near Piazza Matteotti you can buy panini, as well as pre-prepared food, such as marinated vegetables, salads etc. In the city centre near the Campo, head for the *Bar Pomo d'Oro* in Piazza Indipendenza and then go next door to the bakery for a piece of panforte. *Nannini*, Banchi di Sopra 22, is one of the city's finest cafés.

Entertainment

The Accademia Musicale Chigiana holds the annual Settimana Musicale Senese each July and concerts are frequently held at the San

Galgano Abbey, a former abbey about 20 km south-west of the city and regarded as one of Italy's finest Gothic buildings. For information, call ☎ 4 61 52. See also the separate San Galgano Abbey section.

The city hosts Siena Jazz, an international festival each July and August. For information, call ☎ 27 14 01.

Things to Buy

The shop Ricama, Via di Città 61, promotes the typical crafts of Siena, in particular embroidery, and is worth a visit.

Getting There & Away

Tra-in and Sita buses (☎ 22 12 21) leave from Piazza San Domenico for Florence, San Gimignano and other main cities in Tuscany, and Rome. Siena is not on a major train line, so from Rome it is necessary to change at Chiusi, and from Florence at Empoli, making buses a better alternative. Trains arrive at Piazza F Rosselli, north of the city centre. By car, there is a branch of the A1 autostrada connecting Florence with Siena, or, alternatively, take the ss2 which runs between Florence and Rome.

Getting Around

Tra-in (☎ 22 12 21) operates city bus services from a base in Piazza Gramsci. From the train station, catch bus No 2, 4 or 15 to Piazza Matteotti, from where it takes about five minutes to walk to the Campo. From the bus terminal in Piazza San Domenico it's also a five-minute walk. No cars, apart from those of residents, are allowed in the medieval centre. For a taxi, call ☎ 4 92 22, or after 9 pm, ☎ 28 93 50.

CHIANTI

Much of central Tuscany, from just south of Florence to the Umbrian border near Lake Trasimene, forms the area known as Chianti. The Chianti Hills, which rise up into the Apennines, form Chianti's eastern boundary and comprise some of Tuscany's most beautiful countryside. Most famous for its internationally known wines, Chianti features some of Tuscany's most beautiful

towns, including Siena, Arezzo and Montepulciano.

Getting information about the area is easy. Virtually every tourist office in Tuscany has good information, but the best bets are the APTs in Florence, Siena, San Gimignano and other main centres. Also check with these tourist offices for accommodation and restaurants. Available at most tourist offices and other locations throughout the area is the newspaper *Chianti News*, which lists itineraries, transport information, accommodation and tourist highlights by district. It is also a valuable source of information if you are planning to visit vineyards and gives details of visiting times.

One of the better known Chianti wines is the Chianti Classico, a crisp white. Other popular drops include the Chianti Rufino and the Chianti Colli Senesi, which comes from around Montepulciano. Pick up a copy of the *Map of Tuscan Wines*, which identifies the main growing areas and details 10 itineraries.

SAN GIMIGNANO

From a distance, the towers of San Gimignano dominate the Elsa Valley, a lush landscape of wheat and vines. Only 14 of the original 72 towers remain, but the city still carries the name San Gimignano of the Fine Towers.

Little is known about its origins, but it is believed to date back to the 3rd or 2nd century BC as an Etruscan site. The name comes from the bishop of Modena, St Gimignano, who is said to have saved the city from the barbarians. It became a free commune in 1199, but internal fights between the Ardinghelli family (Guelph) and the Salvucci family (Ghibelline) over the next two centuries caused deep divisions and rivalry. Most towers were built during this period as status symbols, the height depending on the family's wealth.

A serious plague in the 14th century caused the city to fall under the control of Florence in 1353, but its importance as a stop on the road to France ensured continued prosperity. Today, San Gimignano is one of

Europe's best preserved medieval cities and has the feel of a museum.

Orientation

The manicured gardens of Piazzale dei Martiri di Montemaggio, at the southern end of San Gimignano, are outside the medieval wall and next to the main gate, the Porta San Giovanni. From the gate, Via San Giovanni heads north until it meets Piazza Cisterna and to the left, Piazza del Duomo, in the city centre. The other major thoroughfare, Via San Matteo, leaves Piazza del Duomo for the main northern gate, Porta San Matteo. The walled city is small and dominated by the cathedral, also known as the Collegiata, in Piazza del Duomo. One of the city's tallest towers, the Rognosa Tower (51 metres), stands opposite.

Information

Tourist Office The Associazione Pro Loco (☎ 94 00 08) is at Piazza del Duomo 1, on the left as you approach the cathedral. It opens daily from 9.30 am to 12.30 pm and 2.30 to 6 pm, 30 minutes later in summer.

Post & Telecommunications The post office is in Piazza delle Erbe 8, on the north side of the cathedral. Poste restante mail can be addressed to 53037 San Gimignano.

An SIP telephone office is at Via San Matteo 15 and is open 24 hours a day. The telephone code for San Gimignano is 0577.

Emergency For police emergency, call ☎ 113. The carabinieri office (☎ 94 03 13) is behind the bus stop in Piazzale dei Martiri di Montemaggio. For medical assistance, call the Confraternita della Misericordia (☎ 94 03 67), Via San Matteo. The Farmacia Comunale is in Piazza della Cisterna, or call ☎ 95 50 80 for the night chemist.

Things to See & Do

Before you set out, buy the L10,000 ticket from any of the city's sights which allows you entry into most of San Gimignano's museums. All museums open daily from 9.30 am to 12.30 pm and 3 to 6 pm, except

Mondays. During winter months, the closing time is 5.30 pm.

Start in the triangular Piazza Cisterna, named after the 13th century cistern in its centre. The piazza is lined with houses and towers dating from the 13th and 14th centuries. Adjoining it to the north is Piazza del Duomo, dominated by the **Mayor's Palace** (Palazzo del Podestà), which dates from early in the 13th century, and its tower, known as **La Rognosa**. The crenellated **Palazzo del Popolo** is still the city's town hall, and its tower, the **Torre Grossa**, is the tallest in town (54 metres). Climb it for a fabulous view. To the left stand the twin Salvucci towers. Inside the palace, on the ground floor, is the Dante Room, where Dante addressed the locals in 1299, urging them to join the Guelphs. The **Municipal Museum** upstairs features paintings from the 12th to 15th century Sienese and Florentine schools.

The city's cathedral, known as the **Collegiata**, dates from the 13th century and is in the Romanesque style. The interior is almost completely covered in frescoes, and highlights include Taddeo di Bartolo's *Last Judgment* on the wall with the main doors. The Santa Fina Chapel was magnificently decorated with frescoes by Ghirlandaio.

The Sacred Art Museum and the Etruscan Museum, just south of the cathedral, house good collections and are popular with busking musicians in summer. The ruins of the **fortress** are a short walk to the west of Piazza del Duomo and offer great views.

North from the cathedral is Via San Matteo, one of the best preserved streets in the city, which ends at the Porta San Matteo. Nearby is the **Church of Sant'Agostino**, whose main attraction is the fresco cycle depicting the life of St Augustine by Benozzo Gozzoli.

The A Uncinetto e Ricami, Via degli Innocenti 1, produces and sells traditional local embroidery.

Places to Stay

San Gimignano has only a handful of hotels with eye-popping prices. However, the hostel, a camping ground and the Sant'Agostino Convent, with cheap rooms in the city centre, come to the rescue. The well-organised Cooperativa Hotels Promotion (☎ 94 08 09), Via San Giovanni, just inside the gate of the same name, can place you in one of the dozens of private rooms, flats or villas in and around the city. It will make arrangements months in advance and charges no fee.

The camping ground, *Borchetto di Piemma* (☎ 94 03 52), is at Santa Lucia, a couple of km south of the Porta San Giovanni, and is open only in summer. Buses leave from Piazzale dei Martiri di Montemaggio. The *Ostello della Gioventù* (☎ 94 19 91), Via delle Fonti 1, is at the northern edge inside the wall. Bed and breakfast is L15,000.

The best room deal is at the *Foresteria Convento di Sant'Agostino* (☎ 94 03 83), Piazza Sant'Agostino 4, with singles/doubles for L25,000/35,000. The hotel *Locanda Il Pino* (☎ 94 04 15), Via San Matteo 102, has doubles for L60,000, or L70,000 with a bath. *Hotel La Cisterna* (☎ 94 03 28) in the magnificent Piazza Cisterna has singles/doubles from L60,000/90,000. Ask for a room in the medieval section, with a view across the valley.

Places to Eat

The city's cuisine is traditional Tuscan, as the stuffed wild boars adorning the walls of many restaurants indicate. The local cakes and sweets, including the famous panforte, beckon from bars and cake shops along Via San Giovanni. The produce market is held on Thursday mornings in Piazza Cisterna. Try the Vernaccia white wine, or the red Brunello from the hills of Montalcino. Try wines at *Il Castello*, Via del Castello 20, a wine bar and restaurant which stays open until midnight. Pasta dishes start at L5000.

The cheapest option is *Fast Food*, Viale Roma, just outside Porta San Giovanni, with a good selection of local dishes from L5000. Inside the gate and to the left, *Rosticceria Chiribiri*, Piazzetta della Madonna 1, has pizza by the slice from L2000. *Gelati Giulebbe*, Via San Giovanni 113, and *Gelateria di Piazza*, Piazza della Cisterna 4, are great; the latter turns the local wine, Vernaccia, into a delicious ice cream.

Pizzeria Pizzoteca, Via dei Fossi, is one of the best in town, with pizzas from L5000. *La Stella*, Via San Matteo 77, offers traditional dishes from L4500. A meal could cost L25,000. *Trattoria La Mangiatoia*, Via Mainardi 5, is one of the city's better restaurants, with pasta from about L7000.

Getting There & Away

Regular SITA and Tra-in buses run from Florence to Poggibonsi, where you need to change for San Gimignano (only 20 minutes away). A direct bus runs from Piazza San Domenico in Siena. Buses arrive in Piazzale dei Martiri di Montemaggio at the Porta San Giovanni. The closest train station is in Poggibonsi to the east, 20 minutes by Tra-in bus.

To reach San Gimignano by car, take the ss68 from Colle di Val d'Elsa (which is on the ss2 between Florence and Siena) and follow the signs. The city is small and easily seen on foot. Signs direct you to large car parks outside the Porta San Giovanni.

COLLE DI VAL D'ELSA

About 20 km north of Siena, Colle di Val d'Elsa is worth visiting for its impressive medieval section, set atop a hill overlooking the more modern parts of the town. The town is surrounded by some of Tuscany's most beautiful countryside and is dotted with restored farms that offer reasonably priced lodging. Contact the APT in Siena, or the tourist office representative in the town, Agenzia Arnolfo Tour (☎ 0577-92 39 25), Piazza Arnolfo, for information.

For a hotel in the town, try *Olimpia* (☎ 0577-92 16 62), Via A Diaz, which has singles/doubles from L25,000/40,000. In the old section, the *Sapia Bar*, Bastione di Sappia, has a terrace overlooking the countryside and serves light, inexpensive meals.

Buses from all directions stop in the central Piazza Arnolfo, in the new town.

SAN GALGANO ABBEY

About 20 km south-west of Siena on the ss73 is the ruined 13th century San Galgano Abbey, one of the country's finest Gothic buildings in its day. A former Cistercian abbey, its monks were among Tuscany's most powerful, forming the judiciary and acting as accountants for the communes of Volterra and Siena. They ruled over disputes between the cities, played a significant role in the construction of the Duomo in Siena, and built for themselves an opulent church. By the 16th century the monks' wealth and importance had declined, and the church deteriorated to the point of ruin. The walls remain standing but the roof collapsed long ago. The abbey is definitely worth a diversion if you are driving, but visiting by public transport is quite difficult. The Accademia Musicale Chigiana in Siena sponsors concerts at the abbey during summer (see the Siena Entertainment section).

VOLTERRA

The Etruscan settlement of Velathri was an important trading centre, a status that continued under the Romans, who renamed the city Volaterrae. A long period of conflict with Florence starting in the 12th century ended when the Medicis took possession of the city in the 15th century.

Perched on top of a huge rocky plateau, the city looks impressive from a distance, and its well-preserved medieval ramparts are equally impressive. The city has long had a strong alabaster industry which sadly has degenerated into a tourist sideshow.

Orientation & Information

If you arrive by car, head for the main car park in Piazza Martiri della Libertà, on the south side of the city, where all buses arrive. From here it is only a short walk to the central Piazza dei Priori.

There is a small tourist office (☎ 0588-8 61 50) at Via Turazza 2, which offers only an incomplete hotel list and little information about the town. The main post office and SIP telephones are on the northern side of Piazza dei Priori. The city's postal code is 56048, and the telephone code is 0588. For emergencies, call ☎ 113 or visit the police station in the Palazzo Pretorio in Piazza dei Priori.

Things to See

The Piazza dei Priori is recognised as one of Italy's finest medieval squares and is surrounded by austere palaces. The 13th century **Palazzo dei Priori** is the oldest communal palace in Tuscany and is believed to have been a model for Florence's Palazzo Vecchio. The **Palazzo Pretorio**, also dating from the 13th century, is dominated by the Piglet's Tower, so named because of the wild boar sculpted on its upper section.

Behind the Palazzo dei Priori, along Via Turazza, is the **Duomo**, originally built in the Pisan-Romanesque style, although it has been rebuilt several times. Highlights include a fresco by Benozzo Gozzoli, the *Adoration of the Magi*, and the tabernacle by Mino da Fiesole. The 13th century **Baptistry** features a font by Sansovino. Items from the Duomo, Baptistry and other churches in Tuscany are in the **Duomo Museum** at Via Roma 13, and in the **Picture Gallery** in the Palazzo Minucci Solaini, Via dei Sarti 1, which contains works by Andrea della Robbia. Both museums open from 9.30 am to 6.30 pm Tuesday to Sunday, with slightly shorter hours during the winter months. Admission is L6000 for the Duomo Museum and L8000 for the Picture Gallery.

From Piazza XX Settembre, head southeast for the **Etruscan Museum** at Via Don Minzoni 11, the city's premier museum and one of the country's best in its field. It houses 600 Etruscan funerary urns, carved in alabaster and other materials, which date mostly from the 3rd century BC. The museum opens Tuesday to Sunday from 9.30 am to 1 pm and 3 to 6.30 pm in summer, from 10 am to 4 pm in winter, and entry is L6000.

Farther along Via Minzoni is the **Fortezza Medicea**, built in the 14th century and altered by Lorenzo the Magnificent, which is now a prison. Near the fort is the pleasant **Archaeological Park**, whose archaeological remains have suffered with the passage

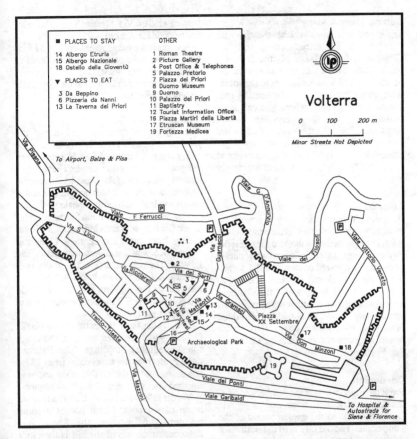

PLACES TO STAY
14 Albergo Etruria
15 Albergo Nazionale
18 Ostello della Gioventù

PLACES TO EAT
3 Da Beppino
6 Pizzeria da Nanni
13 La Taverna dei Priori

OTHER
1 Roman Theatre
2 Picture Gallery
4 Post Office & Telephones
5 Palazzo Pretorio
7 Piazza dei Priori
8 Duomo Museum
9 Duomo
10 Palazzo dei Priori
11 Baptistry
12 Tourist Information Office
16 Piazza Martiri della Libertà
17 Etruscan Museum
19 Fortezza Medicea

Volterra

0   100   200 m

Minor Streets Not Depicted

of time. Little remains, but it's a good place for a picnic. At the city's northern edge is the **Roman Theatre**, a well-preserved complex which includes a Roman bath.

The **Balze**, a deep ravine created by erosion, about a 20-minute walk north-west of the city centre, has claimed several churches since the Middle Ages which have fallen into the deep gullies. A 14th century monastery is perched close to the precipice and is in danger of collapsing into the ravine.

Places to Stay & Eat

The best deal is at the *Ostello della Gioventù* (☎ 8 55 77), Via Don Minzoni, near the Etruscan Museum, which has beds for L14,000. The *Albergo Etruria* (☎ 8 73 77), Via Matteotti 32, has singles/doubles from L45,000/65,000, and the *Albergo Nazionale* (☎ 8 62 84), Via dei Marchesi 7, has rooms from L50,000/80,000 and a restaurant, considered one of the city's best, with pasta dishes from L7000.

The restaurant *Da Beppino*, Via delle Prigioni 13, has good pasta from L6000 but hits you with a L2500 cover charge. *Pizzeria da Nanni*, opposite at No 40, has pizzas from L5000. *La Taverna dei Priori*, Via Giacomo Matteotti 19, is a self-service restaurant with pasta from L4000.

Getting There & Away

Tra-in and Sita buses connect the city with Pisa, Siena, Florence, Cecina and San Gimignano from Piazza Martiri della Libertà. There is a small train station in the nearby town of Saline, nine km to the southwest, which is connected to Volterra by bus. Trains run to Cecina, where you can catch trains on the main Rome-Pisa line. By car, take the ss68 which runs between Cecina and Colle di Val d'Elsa. The easiest way to get around Volterra is to walk. Cars are banned from the city centre, and car parks are clearly marked.

AREZZO

In eastern Tuscany, Arezzo was one of the most important Etruscan settlements before it fell to the Romans. In the Middle Ages, the city prospered as an independent republic until Florence seized control in 1384. Luminaries such as Vasari, Petrarch and Guido d'Arezzo lived here, and Michelangelo nearby at Caprese, near Sansepolcro, yet all left the city. It was an outsider, Piero della Francesca, who painted one of Italy's most beautiful cycles of frescoes in the Church of San Francesco.

Orientation

From the train station at the southern edge of the walled city, walk north-east along Via Guido Monaco to the garden piazza of the same name. The old city is to the north-east and the modern parts are to the south-east along Via Roma.

Information

There is an APT tourist office (0575-37 76 78) at the train station in Piazza della Repubblica, which opens Monday to Saturday from 9 am to 1 pm and 4 to 7 pm. The main office (☎ 0575-2 39 52) is at Piazza Risorgimento 116 and opens about the same hours but is closed Saturday afternoon.

The main post office is at Via Guido Monaco 34, and the city's postal code is 52100. SIP telephones are in Piazza Guido Monaco and are open late. Others are at the bottom end of Via Margaritone. The telephone code for Arezzo is 0575.

For police emergencies, call ☎ 113 or head for the police headquarters on Via Fra Guittone near the bus station. The Ospedale Civile (☎ 35 67 57) is outside the city walls on Via F Veneziana.

Things to See & Do

The city's main attraction, and one of the great contributions to the Renaissance, is the 14th century **Church of San Francesco** in the piazza of the same name. The famous fresco cycle *Story of the Cross* by Piero della Francesca is, sadly, under continuous restoration and large sections are sealed off.

Wander along Corso Italia for the Romanesque **Church of Santa Maria della Pieve**, dating from the 12th century. Over the central doorway are representations of the months. The bell tower, erected in the 14th century, has 40 windows and has become something of an emblem for the city. Inside is a polyptych by Pietro Lorenzetti, which is worth seeking out.

The church faces the harmonious Piazza Grande, which features some of the city's finest medieval buildings. The **Palazzo della Fraternità dei Laici** dates from 1375. It was started in the Gothic style and was finished after the onset of the Renaissance.

Via dei Pileati leads to **Petrarch's House**, home of the poet, which houses a small museum and institute, the Accademia Petrarca. At the top of the hill is the city's 13th century **cathedral**, a dull brown building housing Piero della Francesca's fresco of Mary Magdalene and terracotta reliefs by Andrea della Robbia.

Take Via Ricasoli and Via Sassoverde for the 13th century **Church of San Domenico**, which features a magnificent painted crucifix by Cimabue. South on Via XX Settembre is **Vasari's House**, built and sumptuously decorated by Vasari. The house is open Monday to Saturday from 9 am to 7 pm, Sunday to 1 pm, and entry is free. Down the hill on Via San Lorentino is the **Museum of Medieval & Modern Art** with a collection of works by local artists spanning the 13th to

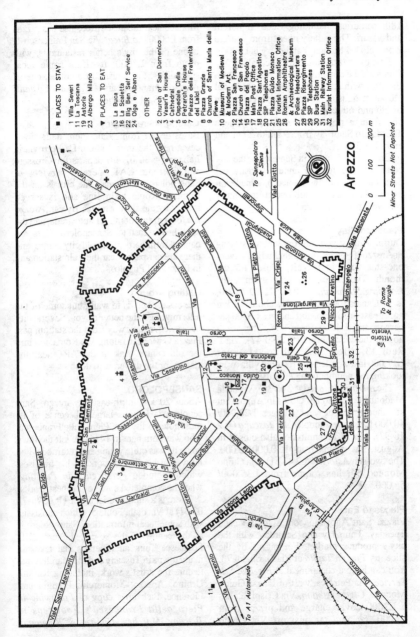

Arezzo

0   100   200 m

Minor Streets Not Depicted

To Sansepolcro
& Siena

To Rome
& Perugia

To A1 Autostrada

PLACES TO STAY
1   Villa Severi
11 La Toscana
19 Astoria
23 Albergo Milano

PLACES TO EAT
13 La Buca
16 La Scaletta
22 Big Ben Self Service
24 Olga e Albano

OTHER
2   Church of San Domenico
3   Vasari's House
4   Cathedral
5   Ospedale Civile
6   Petrarch's House
7   Palazzo della Fraternità
    dei Laici
8   Piazza Grande
9   Church of Santa Maria della
    Pieve
10 Museum of Medieval
    & Modern Art
12 Piazza San Francesco
14 Church of San Francesco
15 Piazza del Popolo
17 Main Post Office
18 Piazza Sant'Agostino
20 SIP Telephones
21 Piazza Guido Monaco
25 Tourist Information Office
26 Roman Amphitheatre
    & Archaeological Museum
27 Police Headquarters
28 Piazza Risorgimento
29 SIP Telephones
30 Bus Station
31 Main Railway Station
32 Tourist Information Office

18th centuries, including Luca Signorelli and Vasari. The gallery opens from 9 am to 2 pm (closed Monday) and entry is L5000.

East of Piazza Guido Monaco along Via Roma are the remains of the **Roman Amphitheatre**, with an adjoining **Archaeological Museum** housing an impressive collection of 5th and 6th century BC Etruscan statues and Roman pottery. The museum opens Tuesday to Saturday from 9 am to 2 pm and entry is L5000.

On the first Sunday in September, the city comes to life for the annual Giostra del Saracino (Joust of the Saracen), a medieval event performed in traditional 14th century costume in Piazza Grande.

Places to Stay

During August you can forget about staying in Arezzo if you are on a tight budget – every one-star hotel in the city closes for the month. The closest camping ground, the *Camping Michelangelo* (☎ 0575-79 38 86), is in Caprese Michelangelo, about 20 km north-east of Arezzo, and charges L3300 per person and L4600 for a site. The youth hostel, the *Villa Severi* (☎ 2 90 47), Via F Redi 13, offers bed and breakfast for L17,000 in a wonderfully restored villa overlooking the neighbouring countryside.

The *Albergo Milano* (☎ 2 68 36), Via della Madonna del Prato 83, closes in August but at other times of year charges L28,000/40,000 for singles/doubles. *La Toscana* (☎ 2 16 92), Via M Perennio 56, also closed in August, has rooms from L30,000/46,000. The two-star *Astoria* (☎ 2 43 61), Via Guido Monaco 54, has rooms from L35,000/56,000.

Places to Eat

Piazza Sant'Agostino comes to life each Tuesday, Thursday and Saturday with the city's produce market. For pizzas by the slice, try *Pizza a Taglio* at Via Garibaldi 73. You can have a cheap meal at *Big Ben Self Service*, Via Petrarca, west of Piazza Guido Monaco. *Olga e Albano*, Via Crispi 32, has a L2000 cover charge and pizzas from L6000. *La Scaletta*, just off Via Guido

Monaco near the post office, also has pizzas from L6000. *La Buca*, Via San Francesco 1, is one of the city's better restaurants, with pasta from L8000; it offers some local specialities. For a drink or a coffee, one of Arezzo's grandest bars is *Caffè dei Costanti* in Piazza Sant'Agostino.

Getting There & Away

Buses depart from Viale Piero della Francesca near the train station. La Ferroviaria Italiana (☎ 30 07 48) departs for Grosseto and Cortona. CAT operates services to Sansepolcro and Siena. The city is on the Florence-Rome train line and is served mostly by the slower trains. By car, Arezzo is a few km east of the A1 autostrada, and the ss71 heads east to Sansepolcro. Cars are banned from parts of the old city centre, and there are car parks near the train station and in Piazza del Popolo.

Getting Around

The easiest way is to walk, but some of the hills might get the better of you. Several city buses weave their way from the station, past Piazza G Monaco, along Via Roma and into the old centre. Ask at the APT near the station, or the driver, if in doubt.

SANSEPOLCRO

About 20 km north-east of Arezzo, Sansepolcro is famous largely because of its most noteworthy son, Piero della Francesca, who was born here in 1416. He left the town when he was quite young and returned when he was in his 70s to work on his treatises, which included *Perspective in Painting*, when he completed some of his best works.

There is a small tourist office (☎ 0575-73 02 31) at Via della Fonte 5, which can assist with some local information. Sansepolcro is at the centre of the so-called Piero della Francesca Tour, an itinerary that takes in many towns in Tuscany and the Marches that feature the artist's work, including Rimini, Urbino, Arezzo, Monterchi, Perugia and Florence. Pick up a copy of *Following in Piero della Francesca's Footsteps in Tuscany, Marches, Umbria & Romagna*, unfortunately only available in Arezzo and Sansepolcro.

The **Municipal Museum**, Via Aggiunti 65, is the pride of the town. Occupying rooms in the former town hall, it features one of the masterpieces of the Renaissance, Piero della Francesca's *Resurrection*.

If you need to stay in the town, there are several reasonably priced hotels, including the *Orfeo* (☎ 0575-74 22 87), Viale A Diaz 12, with singles/doubles from L25,000/ 35,000. The three-star *Fiorentino* (☎ 0575-74 03 50), Via L Pacioli 60, has rooms from L35,000/60,000.

CAT buses connect Arezzo with Sansepolcro hourly, and the town is on the Terni-Perugia train line. By car, take the ss71 or ss73 from Arezzo, or the ss3b from Perugia.

The small town of **Monterchi**, about halfway between Sansepolcro and Arezzo on the ss73, is worth visiting for Piero della Francesca's *Madonna with Child*, one of the few examples of the pregnant Virgin. The painting is the main exhibit in the cemetery chapel, which is easily found. The CAT bus between Sansepolcro and Arezzo stops a couple of km from Monterchi.

CORTONA

Set into the side of a hill clad with olive groves, Cortona has changed little since the Middle Ages. From the city, there are stunning views across the Tuscan countryside and as far south as Lake Trasimene. Cortona was a small settlement when the Etruscans moved in during the 8th century BC and later became a Roman town until it was razed by the Goths in about 450 AD. Little is known of the city's history until it was taken by Florence in the 15th century. In the late 14th century, it attracted the likes of Fra Angelico, and Luca Signorelli was born here. The city is small, easily seen in a couple of hours and well worth visiting for the sensational view.

Orientation

Piazzale Garibaldi, at the southern edge of the walled city, is where buses arrive, and it has a large car park. It also offers some of the best views in the city. From the piazza, walk straight up Via Nazionale for Piazza della Repubblica, the centre of town.

Information

The APT (☎ 0575-63 03 52), Via Nazionale 72, can assist with a hotel list and the useful *Cortona*, a complete guide to tourist essentials. It opens Monday to Saturday from 8 am to 1 pm and 3 to 6 pm. For police emergencies, call ☎ 113.

Things to See

Start in Piazza della Repubblica with the crenellated **town hall**, which was renovated in the 16th century. To the north is Piazza Signorelli, named after the artist and dominated by the 13th century **Praetorian Palace**, also known as the Casanova Palace, whose façade was added in the 17th century. Inside is the **Museum of the Etruscan Academy**, which displays substantial local Etruscan finds, including a curious 5th century BC oil lamp. The museum opens from 10 am to 1 pm and 4 to 7 pm (closed Mondays), and entry is L5000.

Little is left of the Romanesque character of the **cathedral** north-west of Piazza Signorelli, which was completely rebuilt late in the Renaissance and again in the 18th century. Opposite is the Chiesa del Gesù, which houses the city's other museum, the **Diocesan Museum**. Among its collection is Fra Angelico's *Annunciation* and several works by Signorelli.

At the eastern edge of the city centre is the **Church of Santa Margherita**, which features the magnificent Gothic tomb of St Margaret. Farther up the hill is the 16th century **fortress**, built by the Medicis and offering the best views in town, over the ruins of the Etruscan and Roman walls.

Places to Stay & Eat

The city has several cheap hotels and a hostel, and finding a room shouldn't be a problem at any time of the year. The *Ostello San Marco* (☎ 0575-60 13 92), Via Maffei 57, just a short walk east of Piazzale Garibaldi, has bed and breakfast for L12,000. The

Betania (☎ 0575-6 28 29), Via Severini 50, is a monastery which offers rooms from L24,000 a person. The *Albergo Italia* (☎ 0575-60 32 54), Via Ghibellina 5, has singles/doubles from L30,000/44,000.

There is a produce market in Piazza della Repubblica each Saturday and there are several grocery shops around the area. *Trattoria Dardano*, Via Dardano 24, is a good trattoria where you can eat a meal for L16,000. *Il Cacciatore*, Via Roma 11, is one of the city's better restaurants and offers local specialities. A meal could cost over L30,000.

Getting There & Away

LFI buses connect the city with Arezzo from Piazzale Garibaldi at regular intervals. The city is served by two train stations. Trains from Arezzo stop at the Camucia-Cortona station, in the valley below Cortona, and trains for Rome stop at Terontola, about five km to the south. Shuttle buses connect both stations with Piazzale Garibaldi, and a board opposite the APT entrance details schedules. By car, the city is on the north-south ss71 which runs to Arezzo, and it is close to the superstrada that connects Perugia to the A1 autostrada.

MONTEPULCIANO

Set atop a narrow ridge of volcanic rock, Montepulciano combines the best of Tuscany's superb countryside with some of the region's finest wines. This medieval town is extremely beautiful and is the perfect place to spend a few days admiring the view across Lake Trasimene. A highlight is the number of *fattorie*, shops or restaurants in Montepulciano serving wines and other products from the farms around the town. Most offer free wine tastings.

Orientation & Information

However you arrive at Montepulciano, you will probably end up at the Porta al Prato at the town's northern edge. From here, buses take you through the town to Piazza Grande. The 15-minute walk is mostly uphill but well worth the exercise. The tourist office

(☎ 0578-75 74 42) is at Via Ricci 9, just off Piazza Grande, where you can pick up *Montepulciano Perla del Cinquecento*, a useful guide to the town.

Things to See

Most of the main sights are clustered around Piazza Grande, although the town's streets provide a wealth of medieval palaces and other fine buildings. It is virtually impossible to get lost, so go for a wander. To the left as you enter the Porta al Prato is the 18th century **Church of San Bernardo**. Nearby on your right is the **Palazzo Avignonesi** by Vignola. Several other palaces line the street, including the **Palazzo Bucelli** at No 73 whose façade features Etruscan and Latin inscriptions.

You then come to Piazza Michelozzo, which has the **Church of Sant'Agostino** by Michelozzo, and the 16th century **Pulcinella Tower**, a clock tower surmounted by a bizarre figure of a clown, the Pulcinella (the Italian name for Punch, of Punch and Judy fame), which strikes the hours.

Continue up the hill and take the first left past the **Loggia** for Via del Poggiolo, which eventually becomes Via Ricci. The tourist office is on one side, in the Renaissance Palazzo Ricci, and the town's **Civic Museum** is opposite in the Palazzo Neri-Orselli. The small collection features terracotta reliefs by della Robbia and some Gothic and Renaissance paintings. It opens from 9.30 am to 1 pm and 3.30 to 5 pm from Wednesday to Sunday, and entry is L5000.

Piazza Grande marks the highest point of the town and features the austere **town hall**, a 13th century Gothic building remodelled in the 15th century by Michelozzo. From the top of the 14th century tower, you can see the Monti Sibillini to the east and the Gran Sasso to the south, and the towers of Siena to the north-west, but only on a clear day. The tower opens from 8 am to 1.30 pm Monday to Saturday and the climb is free.

The other palaces in the square are the **Palazzo Contucci**, used as a *cantina*, a wine shop, and the **Palazzo Tarugi** attributed to Vignola, near the fountain. The unfinished

cathedral, dating from the 16th century, is attributed to Sangallo and features several interesting Renaissance works, including Taddeo di Bartolo's altarpiece.

Outside the town wall, about one km from the Porta al Prato, is the **Church of San Biagio**, a fine Renaissance church built by Sangallo and consecrated in 1529 by the Medici pope Clement VII.

Places to Stay & Eat

You might consider visiting Montepulciano on a day trip when you discover the hotel prices. The *Albergo Il Marzocco* (☎ 0578-75 72 62), Piazza Savonarola 18, has singles/doubles from L45,000/75,000. The *Albergo Il Borghetto* (☎ 0578-75 75 35), Via Borgo Buio 5, is very appealing and has rooms for about the same price.

Lo Spuntino, Via Roma 25, sells pizza by the slice, and the *Caffè Poliziano* is a great place for breakfast, lunch or dinner and offers superb views to the north of the town. *Ristorante Dal Cittino* (☎ 0578-75 73 35), Vicolo della Via Nuova, off the Corso, has pasta from L5000 and main dishes from L8000. The owners also have rooms at L20,000 per person.

Of the many wine cellars, the *Cantine di Fognano*, Via del Sasso 3, is worth a look because it bottles on site. You can also try the local wines at *Le Cantine Contucci*, in the Palazzo Contucci on Piazza Grande. The *Fattoria Azienda Agricola Pulcino*, Via di Gracciano nel Corso 96, offers free samplings of wines, sheep's-milk cheese and salamis. There is a restaurant next door specialising in local dishes. The local wines include the excellent Nobile di Montepulciano and the Chianti Colli Senesi.

Getting There & Away

By bus, Tra-in operates eight services daily between the town and Siena, via Pienza. Other services operate to Florence and Chiusi.

The most convenient train station is at Chiusi-Chianciano Terme, 10 km south-east, which is on the main Rome-Florence line. Only the slow local and some direct trains

stop here, and buses for Montepulciano meet each train. Another station, at Stazione di Montepulciano about five km to the north-east, has less frequent services, and there are less frequent bus services from here to Montepulciano.

By car, exit the A1 autostrada at Chianciano Terme and follow the ss166 for the 18-km trip to Montepulciano. Most cars are banned from the town centre and there are car parks near the Porta al Prato. Small town buses weave their way from here to Piazza Grande, or take a taxi (☎ 0578-75 78 05).

ETRUSCAN SITES

Many towns in southern Tuscany, in the area bordering with Lazio, have significant Etruscan remains that are well worth visiting. Getting around can be difficult as bus connections are infrequent, especially to the smaller towns.

Information

Grosseto is the main town in the Maremma area, which includes many of the Etruscan sites, so the APT there (☎ 0564-45 45 10), Via Monterosa 206, is the best place to start. Other useful organisations are the Associazione Albergatori (☎ 0564-2 63 15), Via Matteotti 55, the local hotel association which can assist you in finding a bed in the province; and the main bus company, Autoservizi RAMA (☎ 0564-45 41 69), which operates services from the town's train station to Terme di Saturnia, Pitigliano and Sovana.

Pick up a copy of *Gli Etruschi in Maremma* from the APT in Grosseto, a series of brochures enclosed in a folder, which provides comprehensive information and itineraries and also describes the history of the Etruscans in the Maremma area.

Things to See

Take the ss1 south from Grosseto and head inland on the ss74 for the town of **Marsiliana**, where archaeologists have unearthed several significant Etruscan burial sites. Sadly, many of the best pieces have been shipped off to museums in Florence.

Follow the road east and then head north on the ss322 for **Terme di Saturnia**. The town is more famous for its sulphur spring and baths, but its Etruscan remains, including part of the town wall, are worth a diversion. A tomb at Sede di Carlo, just north-east of the town, is one of the area's best preserved.

Follow the signs east for **Sovana**. Situated on the banks of the Fiora River, Sovana was an important centre during Etruscan times and features some of the province's most impressive tombs. The medieval centre was built over much of the Roman and Etruscan remains, although several Etruscan features remain. The Church of San Mamiliano in Piazza del Pretorio was built over a Roman temple, which itself was built over an Etruscan temple. Parts of the Etruscan wall are visible in the medieval structure.

About one km to the south of the town are a set of Etruscan tombs, the best preserved being the **Ildebranda Tomb**. Take a flashlight (torch) if you are serious about visiting the tomb, as the lighting is virtually non-existent. Sovana is also famous as the birthplace of Pope Gregory VII, whose family built the Aldobrandesca Castle, which sits outside the town wall.

About nine km to the south is the small town of **Pitigliano**, built on a tufa outcrop and featuring an incredible aqueduct. As so few tourists trek to the town, the locals are likely to stare at you as though you've just arrived from outer space. An important Etruscan burial site was discovered just outside the town walls, which features several types of tombs. Parts of the old Etruscan wall are visible near the Porta Capisotto.

ELBA

Made famous by Napoleon, who spent a year in exile on the island from May 1814, Elba now attracts more than one million tourists a year who come to swim in its glorious blue waters or lie on the white sandy beaches. Elba is also growing in popularity among walkers, and the mountainous terrain can provide some tough treks.

Just 28 km long and 19 km wide, Elba is easily seen on a day trip, although there are hundreds of hotels and plenty of camping grounds if you plan to stay longer. The tourist hordes have only arrived in recent years, so the island retains an air of authenticity – peasant farmers still walk the hills, their donkeys laden with wine. However, the main beachfront towns of Portoferraio and Marina di Campo, while they have some character, could be anywhere on the Italian coast.

Orientation & Information

Most ferries arrive at Portoferraio, Elba's main town and its main transport hub. Ferries from Piombino arrive less frequently at Rio Marina, Marina di Campo and Porto Azzurro. The main APT for the island (☎ 0565-91 46 71) is at Portoferraio, at Calata Italia 26, and can assist with general tourist and accommodation information. If you plan to stay and want to visit during the summer months, book well in advance. The local hotel association, the Associazione Albergatori Isola d'Elba (☎ 0565-91 47 54), Calata Italia 20, will find you a room.

If you are planning to walk, pick up a copy of *Trekking all'Elba*, a publication that lists walking trails and details each itinerary. For more information about walking, contact Il Genio del Bosco – Centro Trekking Isola d'Elba (☎ 0565-93 03 35) at Portoferraio. Also, the Comunità Montana at Viale Manzoni 4 in the town has contour maps of the island, with paths clearly marked.

The postal code for the island is 57037, and the telephone code is 0565.

Portoferraio

The island's capital, Portoferraio, is divided in two. The new part includes the port, but the old part, enclosed by a medieval wall, is much more interesting. The **Napoleonic Museum** was one of the residences where Napoleon lived in exile. It features a splendid terraced garden and his library. The museum is open from 9 am to 5 pm Tuesday to Saturday and entry is L5000.

The ticket also allows you entry to the **Villa Napoleonica di San Martino**, his summer residence, set in hills about five km south-west of the town. Take bus No 1 to reach the villa, which houses a modest collection of Napoleonic paraphernalia and also hosts an annual exhibition based on a Napoleonic theme. The villa opens the same hours as the museum.

If you plan on staying, the closest camping grounds are about four km west of Portoferraio in Acquaviva. *Campeggio La Sorgente* (☎ 91 71 39) and *Acquaviva* (☎ 91 55 92) are easily found and have sites from L7000 plus L5000 per person. The *Albergo Le Ghiaie* (☎ 91 51 78), Viale de' Gasperi, has singles/doubles from L35,000/52,000. The *Ape Elbana* (☎ 91 42 45), Salita de' Medici, has rooms from L40,000/75,000.

Restaurants are expensive, but bars selling panini and other snacks are popular. The *Ristorante Villa Ombrosa* on Viale de' Gasperi serves typical Tuscan dishes, and a full meal could cost L30,000.

Marciana Marina

About 15 km west of Portoferraio, Marciana Marina is slightly less popular with the hordes of tourists and is fronted by some fabulous pebble beaches. This town is also a perfect base for walking in the island's western region, where many of the best walking tracks are to be found. The inland villages of Marciana and Poggio are far more interesting, and are easily visited (jump on the only bus). From Marciana you can take the cable car to the summit of Mt Capanne, from where you can see all over Elba and as far as Corsica to the west.

In Marciana Marina, the *Albergo Villa Maria* (☎ 9 90 20), Piazza Sanzio, has rooms from L50,000/73,000. Farther west along the coast is the small town of Sant'Andrea, a pleasant spot with several good hotels.

Marina di Campo

Elba's second-largest town, Marina di Campo, is on Campo Bay on the island's southern side. The beaches are among Elba's best and most crowded. Many camping grounds are located around the town and along the coastline, which means you

shouldn't have too much trouble finding a site, except in the middle of summer. The *Albergo Thomas* (☎ 97 77 32), Viale degli Etruschi, is one of the cheapest hotels here and has singles/doubles from L55,000/80,000. The *Elba* (☎ 97 62 24), Via Mascagni, has rooms for about the same price. There are many cheap eateries near the beach, including a couple of decent self-service restaurants.

Porto Azzurro

Dominated by its fort, built in 1603 by Philip III of Spain, and now a prison, Porto Azzurro remains a pleasant fishing village, despite the number of tourists who visit the town. *Albergo Villa Italia* (☎ 9 51 19), Viale Italia, has singles/doubles from L45,000/73,000. From Porto Azzurro, take a short trip south to Capoliveri, one of the island's most picturesque villages.

Getting There & Away

Unless you have your own boat, the only way to get to Elba is by ferry from Piombino. Toremar (☎ 91 80 80), Calata Italia 22, operates regular ferry and hydrofoil services, as does Navarma (☎ 91 81 01), Viale Elba 4, both in Piombino. Ferries depart from Piazzale Premuda, about two km east of the centre of Piombino (buses connect the two).

Getting Around

The best way to get around Elba is to rent a mountain bike, scooter or motorcycle from Rent Ghiaie, which has offices in all main towns. The Portoferraio office (☎ 91 46 66), Via Cairoli 26, will provide addresses for the other offices. Mountain bikes start at L15,000 a day, scooters from L25,000 a day and motorcycles from L55,000 a day.

The island's bus comany, ATL (☎ 91 43 92), Viale Elba 20, runs services between the main towns.

ARGENTARIO PENINSULA
Orbetello

Situated on an isthmus some 120 km north-west of Rome, the central one of three narrow bands of sand connecting the

Argentario Peninsula to the mainland, Orbetello is a pleasant place popular with Romans who desert the metropolis on weekends.

Ortbetello's main attraction is its **cathedral**, which retained its Gothic façade despite being remodelled in the Spanish style in the 16th century. Other reminders of the Spanish garrison stationed in the city during the 16th century include the fort and city wall, parts of which are the original Etruscan wall. But the main attraction is the increasingly popular Argentario Peninsula and its two harbour towns, Port'Ercole and Porto Santo Stefano, both crammed with incredibly expensive boats and yachts.

Around the Peninsula

The Argentario Peninsula is popular with Romans, but not many tourists make the trek out. Porto Santo Stefano and Port'Ercole are reminiscent of some of the wealthy playgrounds along the Ligurian coast, but still remain largely unspoilt. The main tourist office (☎ 0564-81 42 08) is in Porto Santo Stefano, in the Monte dei Paschi di Siena building, Corso Umberto 55.

For a pleasant drive, follow the signs to Il Telegrafo, one of the highest mountains, and turn off at the **Frati Passionati Convent**, a church and convent with sensational views across to the mainland.

Places to Stay & Eat

Accommodation on the peninsula is generally expensive, although there is a *camping ground* (☎ 0564-83 10 90) near Port'Ercole, on the northern fringe at the Feniglia beach.

In Porto Santo Stefano, *Pensione Weekend* (☎ 0564-81 25 80), Via Martiri d'Ungheria 3, is a cosy place with singles/doubles from L40,000/65,000. *Hotel La Caletta* (☎ 0564-81 29 39), Via G Civinini 10, is a luxurious complex overlooking the water, with rooms from L80,000/110,000 in the high season and L40,000/55,000 during the low season.

Trattoria Da Zirio, Via del Molo 5, on the waterfront in Porto Santo Stefano, has pizzas and pasta from L7000, and *Pizzeria Rossi* at Via del Molo 9 has pizza by the slice from L1500 apiece.

Getting There & Away

Rama buses (☎ 0564-86 70 57) connect most towns on the Argentario Peninsula with Orbetello and Grosseto. Follow the signs to Monte Argentario from the ss1, which connects Grosseto with Rome.

Umbria

One of the few landlocked Italian regions, Umbria has earned and deserves its reputation as Italy's green heart. From the rolling mountains of the Apennines in the north and east, the countryside flattens out into lush valleys along the Tiber River. Umbria is one of Italy's most beautiful regions, and with the exception of the industrial blight around Terni in the south, most towns are unspoilt and have conserved their medieval centres.

The Romans named Umbria after the Umbrii, the Italic tribe who occupied the region. Little is known about them, except that the Roman naturalist Pliny described the Umbrii as the oldest tribe in Italy. The Etruscans later settled the west bank of the Tiber, founding the towns of Perugia and Orvieto, and they eventually created their 12 powerful city-states. Roman rule ended with the barbarian invasions of the 5th and 6th centuries AD, when the Umbrians retreated to the hill towns that gave rise to fortified medieval cities such as Gubbio and Todi. The central piazza in Todi is regarded as Italy's most perfect medieval square. Domination by the Goths, the Lombards and various ruling families, as well as centuries of Guelph-Ghibelline rivalry, led to a long period of decline that left Umbria ripe for papal domination from the early 16th century.

St Francis, one of the country's most famous saints, was born in Assisi, and after his death, the town was transformed with the construction of St Francis' Basilica and its stupendous frescoes by Renaissance painters such as Giotto, Cimabue and Simone Martini. Perugia, a short distance away and the region's capital, is a stunningly beautiful

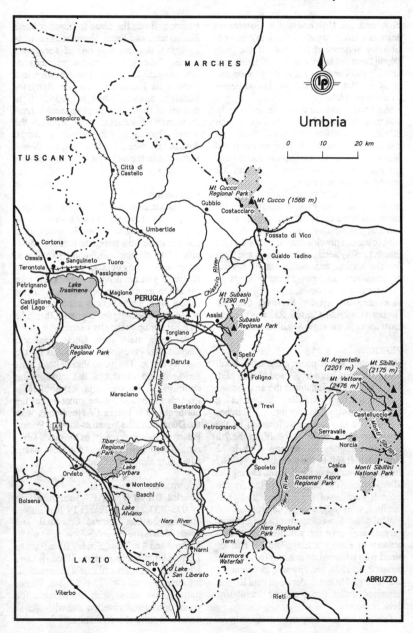

Umbria

0   10   20 km

MARCHES

TUSCANY

Sansepolcro

Città di
Castello

Mt Cucco
Regional Park

Gubbio

Mt Cucco (1566 m)

Costacciaro

Umbertide

Fossato di Vico

Cortona

Gualdo Tadino

Ossaia

Sanguineto

Tuoro

Terontola

Passignano

Petrignano

Lake
Trasimene

Magione

PERUGIA

Chiascio River

Mt Subasio
(1290 m)

Castiglione
del Lago

Assisi

Subasio
Regional Park

Torgiano

Pausillo
Regional Park

Deruta

Spello

Foligno

Mt Argentella
(2201 m)

Mt Sibilla
(2175 m)

Marsciano

Barstardo

Trevi

Mt Vettore
(2476 m)

Tiber River

Petrognano

Castelluccio

A1

Tiber
Regional Park

Todi

Serravalle

Norcia

Monti Sibillini

Orvieto

Lake
Corbara

Spoleto

Casica

Coscerno Aspra
Regional Park

Monti Sibillini
National Park

Montecchio

Baschi

Bolsena

Lake
Alviano

Nera River

Nera River

Terni

Nera Regional
Park

LAZIO

Narni

Orte

Lake
San Liberato

Marmore
Waterfall

ABRUZZO

Viterbo

Rieti

city, and its University for Foreigners ensures a lively nightlife. Spoleto's internationally renowned Festival of the Two Worlds and the beauty of the Valnerina area provide more reasons for visiting the region, as does Lake Trasimene, the Italian peninsula's largest lake.

As a rule, Umbrian cuisine is very simple, and most dishes only contain three or four ingredients. Truffles are popular in many of the southern towns, and *porchetta* (roast piglet) and salami are typical foods. The golden wines from around Orvieto are served around the country.

Umbria is also noted for its extensive range of farm-holiday destinations, also known as agriturismo. Several organisations can suggest destinations, and the APT in each town can provide lists of farms. See the Places to Stay sections in Perugia and Todi for the names and addresses of several organisations that arrange farm holidays.

Extensive bus routes, state railway services and the private Ferrovia Centrale Umbra (Umbrian Central Railway) makes most areas of the region easily accessible.

PERUGIA

One of Italy's best preserved medieval hill towns, Perugia has a lively and bloody past. The Umbrii tribe inhabited the area around Perugia and they controlled land stretching from present-day Tuscany into the Marches region. The city itself was founded by the Etruscans and reached its zenith in the 7th and 6th centuries BC as one of their 12 city-states. It fell to the Romans in 310 BC and was given the name Perusia. During the Middle Ages the city was racked by the internal feuding of the Baglioni and Oddi families, who fought for its control, and the violent external wars against its neighbours. Perugia also gave rise around the mid-13th century to Europe's Flagellants, a curious breed who whipped themselves for religious penance. In 1538, the city was incorporated into the Papal States under Pope Paul III, and remained under papal control for almost three centuries.

Perugia has a strong artistic and cultural tradition. It was the home to fresco painters Pinturicchio and Pietro Vannucci, known as Perugino. Raphael was one of Perugino's pupils. The city also attracted great Florentine painters, including Fra Angelico and Piero della Francesca. The University for Foreigners, established in 1925, offers courses in the Italian language and attracts thousands of students from all over the world. The city is at its most lively for 10 days in July during Umbria Jazz, an international music festival which usually features top jazz performers.

Orientation
The main train station, Stazione Fontivegge, is a few km downhill and south-west of the city centre in Piazza Vittorio Veneto. Unless you are extremely energetic it is not advisable to tackle the steep uphill walk and, fortunately, plenty of buses connect with the centre. If you are driving, either park your car at the train station and catch a bus, or follow the signs to the city centre and park in one of the well-signed car parks, then take an escalator up to the city centre.

Perugia's main strip, Corso Vannucci (named after Perugino), is the focus for the old city centre. The grand Piazza Italia at its southern end overlooks the surrounding countryside, Piazza della Repubblica is towards the middle of the street and at the northern end is Piazza IV Novembre, with the Duomo and the Venetian-looking Priors' Palace. A map is essential as the city's labyrinth of medieval alleyways and lanes makes navigating almost impossible.

Information
Tourist Office The APT tourist office (☎ 075-2 33 27) is in Piazza IV Novembre, opposite the San Lorenzo Cathedral, and opens Monday to Saturday from 8.30 am to 1.30 pm and 4 to 7 pm, Sunday from 9 am to 1 pm. The monthly *Perugia What, Where, When* lists all events and useful information. Informa Giovani (☎ 075-6 17 24), Piazza Italia 1, can assist with information for young or disabled travellers and with educational and cultural information.

Money The exchange booth at the main train station opens from 6.30 am to 8.30 pm daily, otherwise Corso Vannucci is lined with banks. The Cassa di Risparmio di Perugia at No 39 has an automatic exchange machine.

Post & Telecommunications The main post office is in Piazza Matteotti and opens from 8.30 am to 7.30 pm Monday to Saturday. Poste restante mail can be addressed to 06100 Perugia.

There is an ASST telephone office in the post office open from 8 am to 8 pm daily, while SIP telephones are at Corso Vannucci 76, open from 8 am to 10 pm daily. The telephone code for Perugia is 075.

Other Information The CIT travel agency (☎ 2 60 61) is at Corso Vannucci 2, while CTS (☎ 6 16 95), for budget and student travel, is at Via del Roscetto 21.

La Libreria bookshop, Via Oberdan 52, has a selection of English-language books.

Emergency For police emergency, call ☎ 113. The police headquarters (☎ 2 80 00) are in Piazza dei Partigiani, down the escalators in the fortress at Piazza Italia.

The Ospedale Riuniti-Policlinico (☎ 57 81) is at Viale Bonacci Brunamonti, northeast of the city centre. For night and holiday doctor service, call ☎ 3 40 24. The Farmacia San Marino at Piazza Matteotti 26 opens 24 hours a day.

For lost property, call ☎ 577 35 73. If you park illegally and return to find your car gone, chances are it has been towed away. Call the Auto Impound Lot (☎ 577 53 75) to check.

Things to See

At the top of Corso Vannucci is the grand Piazza IV Novembre, surrounded by some of the city's finest buildings. The austere **San Lorenzo Cathedral** was started in 1345 and completed in 1430, although its red and white marble façade was never finished. The Gothic cathedral's impressive size is about its main attribute – there is little inside to cause excitement, apart from the 16th century doorway by Alessi, which faces the fountain out in the square. If you are in the city on 30 July, grab a pew for the annual unveiling of the city's prized relic: the Virgin Mary's wedding ring, which is normally locked away in 15 boxes, fitted inside each other for added security.

Outside is the **Great Fountain** (Fontana Maggiore), which was designed by Fra Bevignate in 1278 and carved by Nicola and Giovanni Pisano. The bas-relief statues represent scenes from the Old Testament and of the 12 months of the year. A female figure on the upper basin and facing Corso Vannucci is called Perugia, because the fruit she bears represents fertility, one of the symbols of the city.

The **Priors' Palace** houses the **National Gallery of Umbria**, with works by Pinturicchio, Perugino and Fra Angelico. In typical Italian tradition, 31 of the gallery's 33 rooms are closed for renovation and no opening date has been set. However, the two rooms that are open contain the gallery's best works. Opening times are from 8.45 am to 1.45 pm and 3 to 7 pm Monday to Saturday, from 9 am to 1 pm Sunday. Entry is L8000. Also in the building is a recently opened science museum. The **Notaries' Hall** (Sala dei Notai) on the 1st floor was built in 1296 for the city council and contains unimportant frescoes that are, however, still worth a look. Entry is free and the building opens from 9 am to 1 pm and 3 to 7 pm daily except Monday.

Still in the palace, but on the Corso Vannucci side, is the **Chamber of Commerce** (Collegio della Mercanzia), the seat of the city's merchants who were powerful during the Renaissance. Inside is impressive early 15th century carved-wood panelling. Also in the building is the **Exchange Building** (Collegio del Cambio), constructed in 1450 for the city's moneychangers. Various rooms inside feature magnificent frescoes by Perugino, considered among his best. Both parts of the building open Tuesday to Saturday from 9 am to 12.30 pm and 2.30 to 5.30 pm, Sunday to 12.30 pm, and entry to both is L2000.

■ PLACES TO STAY

19 Youth Hostel
25 Hotel Morlacchi
28 Pensione Anna
29 Pensione Paola
38 Pensione Lory
47 Piccolo Hotel
49 Hotel Brufani
52 Albergo Aurora

▼ PLACES TO EAT

4 Ristorante dal mi'cocco
10 Ubu Re
11 Tavola Calda
24 Tit-Bit
27 L'Oca Nera
31 Pizza Takeaway
37 Ricciotto
39 Sandri
44 Medio Evo
55 Iris

OTHER

1 Church of Sant'Angelo
2 Porta Sant'Angelo
3 Church of Sant'Agostino
5 University for Foreigners
6 Piazza Fortebraccio
7 Etruscan Arch
8 View Point
9 Church of Santa Maria Nuova
12 Piazza Danti

13 Church of San Severo
14 Augustus Library
15 Church of San Severo
16 Piazza Piccinino
17 San Lorenzo Cathedral
18 Etruscan Well
20 Church of San Francesco al Prato
21 Oratory of San Bernardino
22 Piazza San Francesco
23 Church of Madonna della Luce
26 Via dei Priori Escalator
30 Perugino's House
32 Church of Sant'Agata
33 Great Fountain
34 Priors' Palace & National Gallery
    of Umbria
35 APT Tourist Information Office
36 Piazza IV Novembre
40 Piazza Matteotti
41 Main Post Office
42 Covered Market
43 Piazza della Repubblica
45 SIP Telephones
46 La Libreria Bookshop
48 Piazza Italia
50 Paolina Fortress & Carducci Gardens
51 Paolina Fortress Escalator
53 Archaeological Museum
54 Church of San Domenico
56 Sant'Anna Railway Station
    (Local Trains)
57 Police Headquarters
58 Piazza dei Partigiani
59 ASP Buses
60 Porta San Pietro

Wander from the cathedral to Via del Sole, where you can visit the **Augustus Library**, the city's main library. Farther on is a small piazza with a superb view over the city's north. Walk down Via del Prome for Piazza Fortebraccio to get to the **University for Foreigners** (Università Italiana per Stranieri), housed in the Baroque Gallenga Palace, and the immense **Etruscan Arch**. Only the lower part is Etruscan and dates from the 3rd century BC, one of the few Etruscan remnants in the city; the upper part was added by the Romans in the 1st century BC. An **Etruscan Well** is between Piazza Danti and Piazza Piccinino.

North along Corso G Garibaldi is the **Church of Sant'Agostino**, with a beautiful 16th century choir by Baccio d'Agnolo. Small signs denote the many artworks which were carried off to France by Napoleon. At the end of Via del Tempio, off Corso G Garibaldi to the north, is the **Church of Sant'Angelo**, a 5th century round church with 24 columns from an earlier building that once stood on the site. Corso G Garibaldi continues through the 14th century wall by way of the **Porta Sant'Angelo**. A 10-minute walk takes you to the **Villa Monteripido**, home of the Giuditta Brozzetti fabric company where you can see and buy hand-woven linens, produced using techniques that are centuries old.

East from Piazza Fortebraccio is Via Pinturicchio, named after the painter, who

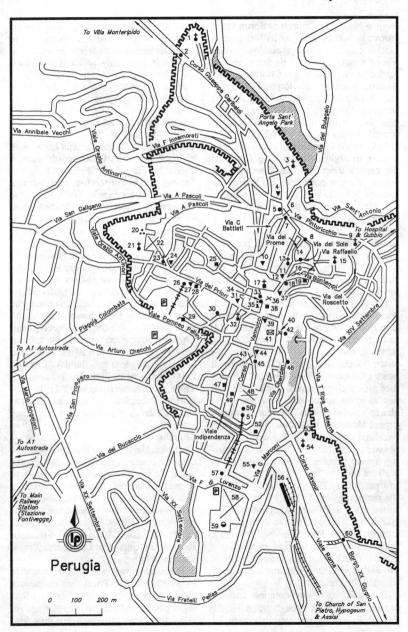

Perugia

0   100   200 m

lived at No 7. The **Church of Santa Maria Nuova** is worth visiting for its 15th century Gothic carved-wooden choir. Walk along Via del Roscetto, then Via Bontempi and Via Raffaello to arrive at the **Church of San Severo**, which features Raphael's magnificent *Trinity with Saints*, probably his first fresco, and other frescoes by Perugino. The chapel opens from 10.30 am to 5.50 pm daily except Monday and entry is L3000.

Head to the opposite end of the city for a cluster of sights. Start in the **Carducci Gardens**, at the end of Corso Vannucci, from where you can see across Umbria to the mountains of Tuscany. Below the gardens is the **Paolina Fortress**, a massive 16th century fortress built by Pope Paul III, who used materials from the palaces and homes of the powerful families of the day. Destroyed by the Perugians after the declaration of the Kingdom of Italy in 1861, the ruins remain a symbol of their defiance against oppression.

Go along Viale Indipendenza which becomes Corso Cavour to see the **Church of San Domenico**, the city's largest church. It dates from the early 14th century, but its Romanesque interior was replaced by austere Gothic fittings in the 16th century. It houses the tomb of Pope Benedict XI, who died after eating poisoned figs in 1325, and has immense stained-glass windows. In the church's cloisters is the **National Archaeological Museum of Umbria**, which has an excellent collection of Etruscan art and remains from various Etruscan tombs throughout Umbria. It opens from 9 am to 1.30 pm and 3 to 7 pm Monday to Saturday, to 1 pm Sunday. Entry is L4000.

Continuing along Corso Cavour you come to the Porta San Pietro. Keep going along Borgo XX Giugno for the 10th century **Church of San Pietro**, reached through a frescoed doorway in the first courtyard you come to. The interior is an incredible mix of gilt and marble, and contains a *Pietà* and paintings by Perugino.

Returning to Corso Vannucci and the centre of town, walk through the arch in the Priors' Palace as you get to Piazza IV Novembre, and wander along Via dei Priori and other medieval streets in this area. Some of the features include spikes protruding at low levels from many buildings, once used for displaying the decapitated heads of thieves and other criminals. The Gothic **Church of Sant'Agata** has traces of 14th century frescoes, while farther on, at Via Deliziosa 5, is **Perugino's House**.

Near the end of Via dei Priori is the **Church of the Madonna della Luce**, with its impressive Renaissance façade. Farther down, on Piazza San Francesco, is the **Oratory of San Bernardino**, with Duccio's rich 15th century façade. The ruins of the 13th century **Church of San Francesco al Prato** next door are all that remains of the immense church. A restoration attempt in 1927 partially rebuilt the façade.

About five km south-east of the city is the Etruscan **Hypogeum**, a burial site discovered in 1840 and traced back to the 2nd century BC. It features an underground chamber with a series of recesses holding the funerary urns of the Volumnio family, and retains most of the original objects found when first discovered. It opens from 9.30 am to 12.30 pm and 4.30 to 6.30 pm Monday to Saturday, to 12.30 pm Sunday. Entry is L4000 and visits are limited to five people at a time, so there can be delays. Take the ASP bus from Piazza Italia to Ponte San Giovanni and walk the short distance from there.

Courses

The Italian University for Foreigners (☎ 5 74 61) is the country's foremost academic institution for foreigners and offers courses in language, literature, history, art and other fields. It runs a series of degree courses as well as one, two and three-month courses and intensive courses. For information, write to the Università Italiana per Stranieri, Palazzo Gallenga, Piazza Fortebraccio 4, Perugia 06100.

The Istituto Europea di Arti Operative (☎ 6 50 22), Via dei Priori, runs courses for foreigners in graphic design, drawing, painting, fashion, industrial and interior design. To study at either institution, you may need to apply for a student visa in your country before arriving in Italy.

Activities

The Club Ippica Santa Sabina (☎ 528 01 98), Via Sodi di Sabina, or the Associazione Ippica San Martino (☎ 69 48 97), Strada Montebello 2, can assist with information on horse riding around Perugia. The Associazione Guide dell'Umbria (☎ 6 51 24) offers guides anywhere in Umbria from L90,000 for three hours.

Festivals

The Umbria Jazz Festival attracts international performers for 10 days each July, usually around the middle of the month. Check with the APT for details. Some events are free, but most cost L10,000.

Places to Stay

Perugia has a good selection of reasonably priced hotels, but if you arrive unannounced during Umbria Jazz in July, or during August, expect problems. For farm accommodation (agriturismo) throughout Umbria, try Agriturist Umbria (☎ 3 20 28), Via Savonarola 38; Terranostra Umbria (☎ 7 45 59), Via Campo di Marte 10; and Turismo Verde Umbria (☎ 500 29 53), Via Campo di Marte.

The city has two camping grounds, both in Colle della Trinità, five km north-west of the city and reached by bus No 36, but the grounds near Lake Trasimene are a better alternative. The *Paradise d'Etè* (☎ 79 51 17) and *Il Rocolo* (☎ 79 85 50) both have sites for L6000 a person and L5000 a tent.

The non-IYHF youth hostel, the *Centro Internazionale per la Gioventù* (☎ 2 28 80), Via Bontempi 13, charges L10,000 a night. Sheets (for the entire stay) are an extra L1000. Its TV room has a frescoed ceiling and its terrace has one of the best views in Perugia.

Pensione Lory (☎ 2 42 66), fabulously located at Corso Vannucci 10, has singles/doubles from L30,000/40,000, as does the *Pensione Anna* (☎ 6 63 04), Via dei Priori 48, off Corso Vannucci. The *Pensione*

Paola (☎ 2 38 16), Via della Canapina 5, is five minutes from the centre, down the escalator from Via dei Priori; it has rooms for L30,000/45,000. Just off Corso Vannucci, at Via Bonazzi 25, is the *Piccolo Hotel* (☎ 2 29 87), with only doubles for L40,000; showers cost an extra L3000.

The two-star *Albergo Aurora* (☎ 2 48 19), Viale Indipendenza 21, has singles/doubles from L38,000/48,000. The *Hotel Morlacchi* (☎ 2 03 19), Via Tiberi 2, has rooms for L35,000/50,000, or L90,000 for a triple with bathroom. When Britain's royalty visits Perugia, they stay at the sumptuous *Hotel Brufani* (☎ 6 25 41), Piazza Italia 12, where a room could set you back L200,000/300,000.

Rental Accommodation If you are planning to study in Perugia, the University for Foreigners will organise accommodation for over L300,000 a month. The weekly *Cerco e Trovo*, L3000 at newsstands, lists all available rental accommodation, and the APT publishes a list of *Casa per Ferie* and *affittacamere*, rooms rented on a weekly or monthly basis.

Places to Eat

Being a student city, Perugia offers many budget eating options. For great pizza-by-the-slice, there is a small *pizza outlet* with no name on Via dei Priori, just below Corso Vannucci. The best places for pizza are *Medio Evo*, Via Baldo 6, just behind the bar on Corso Vannucci, and *Tit-Bit*, Via dei Priori 105. A pizza will cost from L5000 to L6000 at either restaurant. For a cheap meal, try the *tavola calda* in Piazza Danti. *L'Oca Nera*, Via dei Priori 80, has a huge vegetarian range and also offers good hamburgers. Salads start at L4000 and burgers at L5000.

For a traditional Umbrian meal and lots of vegetables, try *Ubu Re*, Via Baldeschi 17, where a full meal will cost around L35,000. *Ristorante dal mi'cocco*, Corso G Garibaldi 12, has an L18,000 set menu featuring local specialities and is a popular student restaurant. *Iris*, Viale Marconi 37, is an excellent restaurant with a balcony looking south. A meal will cost over L25,000. *Ricciotto*, Piazza Danti 20, is also very good, although slightly expensive.

There is a covered market open daily (except Sunday) from 7 am to 1.30 pm, downstairs from Piazza Matteotti, for fresh produce, bread, cheese and meat.

Cafés The *Sandri*, Corso Vannucci 32, retains a medieval air and is the city's finest café. Don't be put off by the ambience – prices are very reasonable. *Café del Cambio* at No 29 is one of the city's trendiest bars. For great ice cream, try *La Fonte Maggiore*, Piazza IV Novembre, beside the APT tourist office.

Entertainment
The city's summer Estate Perugina programme features concerts during August. The box office is in Piazza della Repubblica and opens from 5 pm to 8 pm daily, and venues are close by. The Contrappunto Jazz Club, in Via Scortici 4, is one of the best clubs. Ask the APT for directions.

Getting There & Away
Bus Buses leave from Piazza dei Partigiani, at the end of the Paolina Fortress escalators, for Rome (and Fiumicino Airport), Florence, Siena and cities throughout Umbria, including Assisi, Gubbio and nearby Lake Trasimene. The bus to Rome is faster and cheaper than the train. ASP (☎ 6 18 07) operates most services, or pick up a timetable from the tourist office.

Train The state railway (☎ 500 12 88) operates through Stazione Fontivegge in Piazza Vittorio Veneto, south-west of the city centre. The city is not on the main Rome-Florence train line, so you need to connect at Foligno for Rome or at Terontola for Florence and the north. A private railway, the Ferrovia Centrale Umbra (☎ 2 91 21), operates from Stazione Sant'Anna in Piazzale G Bellucci and serves Umbertide, Sansepolcro, Terni and Todi.

Car & Motorbike From Rome, leave the A1

autostrada at the Orte exit and follow the signs for Terni. Once there, take the ss3bis for Perugia. From the north, exit the A1 at Valdichiana and take the dual-carriageway ss75b for Perugia. The ss75 to the east connects the city with Assisi. Hertz (☎ 500 24 39) is at Stazione Fontivegge in Piazza Vittorio Veneto.

Getting Around
The main train station, Stazione Fontivegge, is a few km downhill from the historical centre. Catch any bus heading for Piazza Matteotti or Piazza Italia to get to the centre (tickets cost L800 and must be bought before you get on the bus).

Most of the city centre is closed to normal traffic, although tourists are allowed to drive to their hotels. Escalators from the historical centre will take you to large car parks downhill, including the escalator in Via dei Priori and the series of escalators which take you down through the Paolina Fortress to Piazza dei Partigiani. The supervised car park at Piazza dei Partigiani costs L7500 a day.

LAKE TRASIMENE (LAGO TRISIMENO)
The fourth-largest lake in Italy, Lake Trasimene is a good alternative if you can't make it to the country's northern lakes. Like the rest of Umbria the lake is very beautiful, although this can't be said for the autostrada route along its northern shore. Because tourism is the mainstay, the lake and its surrounds are kept clean, and swimming, fishing and other water sports are possible.

The lake's northern fringes were the site of one of the bloodiest battles in Roman history when in 217 BC Carthaginian forces led by Hannibal routed Roman troops under the command of Consul Flaminius, killing 16,000. The battlefield extended from Cortona in Tuscany to the small towns of Sanguineto ('the bloody') and Ossaia ('the place of bones'), just north of the lake.

Passignano (full name: Passignano sul Trasimeno) is the most popular spot by the lake for holidaying Italians, so call ahead for a room in summer months. The nicest and most picturesque town on the lake is

Castiglione del Lago, situated on a chalky promontory jutting into the water, dotted with olive trees and dominated by the 14th century castle.

Information

In Passignano, the tourist office (☎ 075-82 76 35), Via Roma 36, can assist with accommodation, water sports and a multitude of publications on the lake. In Castiglione del Lago, the tourist office (☎ 075-95 21 84), Piazza Mazzini 10, is open from 8.30 am to 1 pm and 3 to 7 pm Monday to Friday, as well as Saturday and Sunday mornings. It can advise on the many farm-holiday options and point out good walking tracks.

The telephone code for the lake region is 075.

Things to See & Do

Water sports, walking and horse riding are the main reasons to visit the lake, and apart from the beautiful scenery, there aren't any particular things you should go out of your way to see. Castiglione del Lago's **cathedral** features several frescoes by Perugino.

The lake's only inhabited island, **Isola Maggiore**, near Passignano, was reputedly a favourite spot of St Francis. It can be reached by boat from the main towns, and although there are no camping grounds, you can pitch a tent. The island is noted for the production of lace and embroidery.

Ask at any of the tourist offices in the area for *Tourist Itineraries in the Trasimeno District*, a booklet of walking and horse-riding tracks. If you want to go horse riding, you could contact the Maneggio Trasimeno (☎ 82 79 50) in San Donato about one km east of Passignano, or Poggio del Belveduto (☎ 84 52 29) at Passignano. Both offer lessons and guided tours.

Places to Stay

Passignano Two camping grounds, the *Europa* (☎ 82 74 03) in San Donato, and the *Kursaal* (☎ 82 71 82), are near Passignano, and both charge L7500 per person for a site. The *Albergo Beaurivage* (☎ 82 73 47), Via A Pompili 3, has doubles only from L35,000.

Del Pescatore (☎ 82 71 65), Via San Bernardino 5, has singles/doubles from L42,000/58,000.

Castiglione del Lago The *Listro* camping ground (☎ 95 11 93), Via Lungolago, opens from April to September and has sites for L5000 per person and L5000 for a tent. Other accommodation is not cheap, but try *Elvira* (☎ 958 91 32), Via Nova 20, which has singles/doubles from L38,000/54,000. The *Vittorio* (☎ 95 10 71), Via della Stazione 5, has rooms from L40,000/60,000.

Getting There & Away

Passignano is close to the autostrada and is served by regular trains from Perugia and Terontola, making it the most accessible part of the lake. The ASP bus from Perugia to Tuoro also stops here.

Castiglione del Lago is on the Florence-Rome train line, but make sure you board a local train. You can also take the ASP bus from Perugia bound for Petrignano.

Getting Around

SPNT (☎ 82 71 57) operates regular ferry services between the main towns. The company has information offices on the waterfront at each town, where you can pick up a timetable.

DERUTA

About 15 km south of Perugia, on the ss3bis connecting the city with Terni, is Deruta. The town is famed for its pottery which is regarded as the country's best, known for the richness of its colours and the intensity of its patterns. The Etruscans and later the Romans worked the clay around Deruta, but it was not until the majolica glazing technique, with its bright blue and yellow metallic oxides, was imported from Majorca in the 15th century that the town's ceramics industry took off.

Commercialism has created a downside: most pieces are mass-produced and can be of poor quality. However, the pottery is still beautiful and Deruta is the place to buy it, as prices are cheaper than in Perugia and other towns.

If you have some time, the **Majolica Museum** in the town hall on Piazza dei Consoli houses Umbrian ceramics and features a good collection of pottery. It is open from 10 am to 12.30 pm and some afternoons but is closed Monday, and entry is L5000. The AAST is in the same piazza, but isn't much help. ASP buses connect the town with Perugia.

TODI

Todi's reputation as one of the best preserved medieval towns in Italy is well deserved. The small city was originally an Etruscan frontier settlement, then Roman, and a free commune in the early Middle Ages. It prospered during this period and now claims what is regarded as one of Italy's most perfect medieval squares, the Piazza del Popolo.

Set atop a craggy hill, Todi seems to have ignored the 20th century, although tourist numbers are growing. The city is worth visiting, although getting there by public transport can be quite a slog.

Information

The APT del Tuderte (☎ 075-894 33 95) in Piazza Umberto I is open mornings and late afternoons, and has information about the city and surrounding area.

Things to See

The 13th century **Palazzo del Capitano** in Piazza del Popolo features an elegant triple window and houses the city's Picture Gallery and Archaeological Museum, although both have been closed for restoration since 1977 and nobody seems to know when they will reopen. The square also features the 13th century **Palazzo del Popolo** and the gloomy-looking **Priors' Palace**.

The **Duomo** at the north-western end of the square has a magnificent rose window and intricately decorated doorway. The 8th century crypt is worth visiting for the inlaid wooden stalls in the chancel. The city has several churches worth visiting, and the best

way to do this is to spend an hour or so wandering through the medieval labyrinth.

Festivals

The Todi Festival, held each August and September, is a mixture of classical and jazz concerts, theatre, ballet and cinema.

Places to Stay & Eat

If you are planning to stay, expect to spend a lot of money on accommodation. For farm accommodation in the area, contact Agritop-Umbria (☎ 075-894 26 27), Via Paolo Rolli 3. The cheapest hotel in Todi is the *Zodiaco* (☎ 075-894 26 25), Via del Crocefisso 23, with singles/doubles from L38,000/48,000. The *Villa Luisa* (☎ 075-894 85 71), Via A Cortesi 147, has rooms from L65,000/90,000.

The *Ristorante Umbra*, Via Santa Bonaventura 13, behind the tourist office, is reasonably expensive but worth it for the view from the terrace over the Umbrian countryside.

Getting There & Away

ASP buses from Perugia terminate in Piazza Iacopone, just south of Piazza del Popolo. The city is on the Ferrovia Centrale Umbra, the region's private railway which operates infrequent services to Terni and Perugia. The station is inconveniently located three km from the centre in the valley, although city bus No B makes connections. By road, the city is easily reached by taking the ss3bis main road that runs between Perugia and Terni.

ASSISI

Despite the millions of tourists and pilgrims it attracts every year, Assisi, home of St Francis, manages to remain a beautiful and tranquil refuge (as long as you keep away from the main tourist drags). From Roman times its inhabitants have been aware of the visual impact of the city, perched halfway up Mt Subasio. From the valley its pink and white marble buildings shimmer in the sunlight.

St Francis was born here in 1182 and his

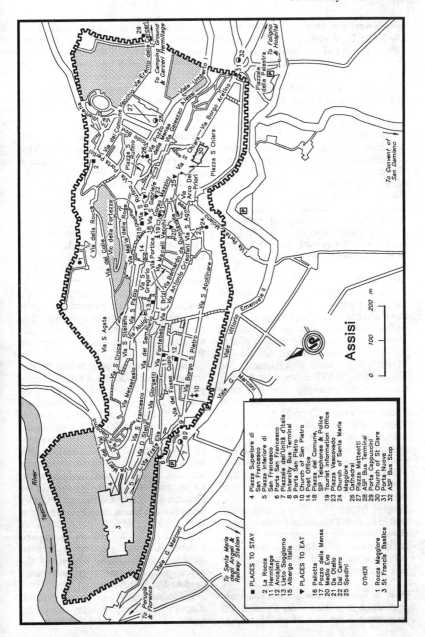

Assisi

0   100   200 m

■ PLACES TO STAY

2   La Rocca
11 Hermitage
12 Ancajani
13 Lieto Soggiorno
15 Albergo Italia

▼ PLACES TO EAT

16 Pallotta
17 Pozzo della Mensa
20 Medio Evo
21 Da Otello
22 Dal Carro
25 Spadini

OTHER

1   Rocca Maggiore
3   St Francis Basilica
4   Piazza Superiore di
    San Francesco
5   Piazza Inferiore di
    San Francesco
6   Porta San Francesco
7   Piazzale dell'Unità d'Italia
8   Intercity Bus Terminal
9   Porta San Pietro
10 Church of San Pietro
14 Post Office
18 Piazza del Comune,
    SIP, Telephones & Police
19 Tourist Information Office
23 Piazza Vescovado
24 Church of Santa Maria
    Maggiore
26 Cathedral
27 Piazza Matteotti
28 ASP Bus Terminal
29 Porta Cappuccini
30 Church of St Clare
31 Porta Nuova
32 ASP Bus Stop

spirit hovers over every aspect of the city's life. He gave up his father's wealth in his late teens to pursue a life of chastity and poverty, founding the order of mendicant friars known as the Order of Minors, or as the Franciscans after his death, which gained a huge following in Europe. One of his disciples, St Clare, born in 1193, was the founder of the Franciscans' female order, the Order of the Poor Clares.

St Francis' Basilica, started two years after his death in 1228, is the city's, and possibly Umbria's, main drawing card. Don't be put off by the prospect of huge crowds: the basilica is one of the country's most impressive churches and is definitely worth a visit. However, check before you visit Assisi that your trip doesn't coincide with a religious celebration of any sort, when hotels are likely to be booked out by pilgrims.

Orientation

Piazza del Comune is the centre of Assisi. At the north-western edge of this square, Via San Paolo and Via Portica eventually lead to St Francis' Basilica, although Via Portica is slightly more direct. Via Portica also leads to the Porta San Pietro and the Piazzale dell'Unità d'Italia, where most intercity buses stop, although ASP buses from smaller towns in the area terminate at Piazza Matteotti. In a southerly direction from Piazza del Comune, Corso Mazzini leads to Piazza Santa Chiara and eventually the Porta Nuova, while Via San Rufino leads to the Duomo. The train station is four km southwest of the city, in Santa Maria degli Angeli; a shuttle-bus service runs every 30 minutes.

Information

Tourist Office The APT tourist office (☎ 075 81 25 34), Piazza del Comune 12, has all the information you need on hotels, sights and events in Assisi. There is a small office in Piazzale dell'Unità d'Italia, where you can pick up a map.

Post & Telecommunications The main post office is in Piazza del Comune and opens from 8 am to 6.30 pm Monday to

Friday, to 1 pm Saturday and Sunday. Poste restante mail can be addressed to 06081 Assisi.

ASST telephones, open from 8 am to 8 pm daily, are in the post office, and SIP telephones, open from 8 am to 10 pm daily, are in Piazza del Comune. The telephone code for Assisi is 075.

Emergency For police emergency, call ☎ 113. The police headquarters (☎ 81 22 15) are in Piazza del Comune. The Ospedale di Assisi (☎ 81 28 24) is about one km southeast of the Porta Nuova, in Fuori Porta.

Things to See

St Francis' Basilica The basilica comprises two churches, one built on top of the other. The lower church was started in 1228 and the upper church two years later, on a patch of land formerly know as the Hill of Hell because death sentences were carried out here. The two churches were erected as a compromise after dissent among the Franciscans, who protested against plans to build an enormous monument. Appropriately, the name of the hill was changed to Paradise Hill.

Entering the **upper church** from the picturesque Piazza Superiore di San Francesco, you are immediately overwhelmed by the colour of frescoes which cover almost every surface. Giotto's sequence of 28 frescoes depicting the life of St Francis is recognised as one of the finest creations of Italian painting. Starting on the right wall near the altar and running around the church, the frescoes start with a young St Francis and finish with his ascension to heaven. The frescoes by Cimabue in the apse and transept are badly deteriorated (a recent clean improved them only slightly), and the poor choice of pigment has left some frescoes looking like photographic negatives. Scenes depicted include the *Crucifixion*, *Visions of the Apocalypse*, *Life of the Virgin* and *Scenes from the Life of St Peter*.

The **lower church** is even more splendid, although quite poorly lit. Bring along quite a few L100, L200 and L500 coins for illumination. Frescoes by Simone Martini showing the Life of St Martin, in the first chapel on the left as you face the altar, are considered the highlight.

Along the left wall of the church are frescoes by Lorenzetti depicting scenes from the Gospel and the life of St Francis. In the transept are frescoes, again showing scenes of St Francis' life, originally thought to have been by Giotto but now attributed to a pupil of his, Maestro delle Vele. In the right transept are more works by Cimabue, and below, more scenes by Simone Martini. A small chapel, reached by stairs on the right side of the church, features various artefacts of St Francis' life, including his shirt and sandals, and fragments of his famous *Canticle of the Creatures*. Descend the stairs in the middle of the church for the crypt with St Francis' tomb and those of four of his companions. The crypt was rediscovered in 1818 after St Francis' coffin was hidden in the 15th century because of fear of desecration.

Dress rules are applied rigidly in the churches – absolutely no shorts, miniskirts or low-cut dresses. The complex opens from 6.30 am to 7 pm daily, although is closed on religious holidays.

The **Basilica Treasury** in the church grounds contains a collection of reliquaries given to the Franciscans over the years. It opens April to October from 9.30 am to midday and 2 to 6 pm, except Sundays, and entry is L3000.

Other Sights From the basilica, take Via San Francesco back to Piazza del Comune, which was the site of the **Roman forum**, parts of which have been excavated. Access is from Via Portica, and entry is L2500. The piazza also contains the **Temple of Minerva**. It is now a church, but retains its impressive pillared façade. Wander into some of the shops, which open their basements to reveal Roman ruins. The city's **Picture Gallery** in the town hall on the western side of the piazza features Umbrian Renaissance art and frescoes from Giotto's school. It opens from 9.30 am to 1 pm and 3 to 7 pm Monday to Saturday, with slightly shorter hours on Sunday, and entry is L2500.

Via Bernardo da Quintavalle leads to Piazza Vescovado and the Romanesque **Church of Santa Maria Maggiore**, formerly the city's cathedral. To the west, near the Porta San Pietro, is the **Church of San Pietro**, worth visiting for its dome. South of Piazza del Comune along Corso Mazzini and Via Santa Chiara is the pink-and-white 13th century **Church of St Clare**, with a deteriorating but nonetheless impressive façade. The gruesome, blackened body of St Clare herself is in the crypt. Also in the church is the Byzantine Crucifix said to have spoken to St Francis in what is now the Convent of San Damiano outside the city, telling him to re-establish the moral foundations of the Church.

North-east of the church, in Piazza San Rufino, is the 13th century Romanesque **cathedral**, remodelled by Galeazzo Alessi in the 16th century and containing the font at which St Francis was baptised.

Dominating the city is the massive 14th century **Rocca Maggiore** (Grand Fortress), a hill fortress offering fabulous views over the valley and back to Perugia. It opens daily from 9 am to 8 pm and entry is L3000, although most of the fortress is closed for a long restoration that will eventually create an immense art gallery.

A good 30-minute walk south from the Porta Nuova, or by car from the Porta San Pietro, is the **Convent of San Damiano**, built on the spot where the Crucifix spoke to St Francis and where he wrote his *Canticle of the Creatures*. The convent on the site was founded by St Clare.

About four km east of the city and reached via the Porta Cappuccini is the **Carceri Hermitage** (literally, Hermitage of the Prisons), where St Francis retreated to after hearing the word of God. The 'prisons' refers to the caves which functioned as hermits' retreats for St Francis and his followers. Apart from a few fences and tourist paths, everything has remained as it was in St Francis' time, and a few Franciscans actually live here.

In the valley south-west of the city, near

the train station, is the **Basilica of Santa Maria degli Angeli**, a huge church built around the first Franciscan monastery. It features the Transito Chapel, where St Francis died in 1226.

Activities

The APT has a map produced by the Club Alpino Italiano of walks on nearby Mt Subasio. None is too demanding, and the smattering of religious shrines and camping grounds could make for an enjoyable couple of days.

Festivals

The Festival of St Francis falls on 4 October and is the main religious event of the city's calendar. Easter week is celebrated with processions and performances. The Ars Nova Musica Festival is held from late August to mid-September and features local musicians and some national performers. The Festa di Calendimaggio celebrates May Day and the coming of spring.

Places to Stay

Assisi is well geared for tourists and there are numerous budget hotels and private rooms. Peak periods, when you will need to book well in advance, are Easter, August/September and the feast of St Francis on 3 and 4 October. The tourist office has a full list of private rooms and religious institutions.

It is possible to stay at the Carceri Hermitage and share the austere conditions with the Franciscan monks who live there. Call the hermitage on ☎ 81 23 01 before you arrive in Italy, and you must have a letter of recommendation from your local parish priest. They usually accept only one or two people at a time.

There is a non-IYHF *hostel* and *camping ground* just east of town at Fontemaggio (☎ 81 36 36 for both), reached by walking about two km uphill along Via Eremo dei Carceri. Beds are L14,000 at the hostel and sites start at L5000 a person. The IYHF youth hostel, the *Ostello della Pace* (☎ 81 67 67), Via Valecchi, is small and opens all year. Bed and breakfast is L16,000. It is on the bus line between Santa Maria degli Angeli and Assisi.

La Rocca (☎ 81 22 84), Via Porta Perlici 27, has singles/doubles for L27,000/38,000, and half-board for L42,000 per person. *Albergo Italia* (☎ 81 26 25), Vicolo della Fortezza, just off Piazza del Comune, has rooms for L30,000/44,000. *Ancajani* (☎ 81 24 72), Via degli Ancajani 16, near the Porta San Pietro, has rooms from L32,000/40,000. The two-star *Lieto Soggiorno* (☎ 81 61 91), Via A Fortini, near Piazza del Comune, has rooms from L38,000/45,000. The three-star *Hermitage* (☎ 81 27 64), Via del Pozzo 1, near the Porta San Francesco, has rooms from L65,000/95,000 and offers car-parking.

Places to Eat

In the same complex as the camping ground at Fontemaggio is *La Stalla*, where you can eat a filling meal under an arbour for about L20,000. The restaurant at *La Rocca* hotel has home-made pasta for L5000 to L6000. *Dal Carro*, Vicolo Nepis 2, has cheap pasta dishes, while *Da Otello*, Piazzetta Chiesa Nuova, has the cheapest pizzas in town. For some traditional local cooking, try *Spadini*, Via Sant'Agnese 6, where a good meal will cost L20,000. Try also *Pallotta*, Via San Rufino 4, where a meal will cost from L25,000 to L30,000. *Pozzo della Mensa*, Via Pozzo della Mensa 11, also specialises in local foods and is about the same price. One of the city's better restaurants is *Medio Evo*, Via Arco dei Priori 4, where an excellent meal will cost about L50,000.

Getting There & Away

ASP buses connect Assisi with Perugia, Foligno and other local towns, leaving from Piazza Matteotti. Piazzale dell'Unità d'Italia is the terminus for buses for Rome, Florence and other major cities. ASP buses terminate in Piazza Matteotti and most of them also stop in Largo Properzio, just outside the Porta Nuova.

Assisi's train station is in the valley at Santa Maria degli Angeli, four km southwest of the city. It is on the Foligno-Terontola

Top : View of Bologna, Emilia Romagna (JG)
Bottom Left : View of St Peter's Square from St Peter's Basilica (GI)
Bottom Right : Amalfi by night, Campania (COASIT)

Top Left : Michelangelo's David, Florence, Tuscany (GE)
Top Right : Statues at the Olympic Village, Rome (JG)
Bottom Left : Angel by Bernini on the Ponte Sant'Angelo, Rome (SC)
Bottom Right : The Triton Fountain in Piazza Barberini, Rome (SC)

line and is about 35 minutes from Perugia. Change at Terontola for Florence and at Foligno for Rome.

By car, take the ss75 from Perugia, exit at Ospedalicchio and follow the signs. The largest and most convenient car park is near the Porta San Pietro.

Getting Around

A shuttle-bus service operates between Assisi and the train station, with departures every 30 minutes. Most cars are banned from the city centre, and buses depart every 20 minutes from all external parking areas to the major monuments.

SPELLO

Spello's proximity to both Perugia and Assisi makes it well worth a quick morning or afternoon trip to see its many Roman remains. Emperor Augustus developed much of the land in the valley, but the Roman ruins are some distance from the present town, which crept farther up Mt Subasio as hostilities grew in the valley during the Middle Ages and Renaissance.

There is a small tourist office at Via Garibaldi 17, although if you are coming from Assisi, you can pick up better information from the APT office there.

The Augustan gate, the **Porta Venere**, leads to the **Church of Sant'Andrea**, with beautiful frescoes by Pinturicchio. Nearby is the 12th century **Church of Santa Maria Maggiore**, with the Baglioni Chapel featuring more frescoes by Pinturicchio, and a pavement (dating from 1566) made of tiles from Deruta.

The people of Spello celebrate the feast of Corpus Domini (21 July) by decorating a long stretch of the town's main street with fresh flowers in colourful designs.

Hotels here are very expensive and there are cheaper options in Assisi and Perugia. The best deal is at *Paolucci* (☎ 0742-65 14 64), Via Brodolini 4, with singles/doubles from L40,000/60,000.

ASP buses running between Perugia and Foligno serve the town, and there are also connections to Assisi. An irregular train service connects the town with Perugia and Terni, and buses operate between the station in the valley and the town. By car, Spello is on the ss75 which runs between Perugia and Foligno.

GUBBIO

Perched on the steep slopes of Mt Ingino, overlooking a picturesque valley, Gubbio looks as if time has passed it by. The ochre colouring of its stone buildings, the tint of the Romanesque tiled roofs and the absence of trees from the paved streets make it possible to imagine you have just stepped into the Italian Middle Ages.

The city is famous for its *Eugubian Tables*, which date from the 4th century BC and feature the best example of ancient Umbrian script in existence. The city was an important ally of imperial Rome and a key stop on the Via Flaminia, but declined during the barbarian invasions. In the 14th century it fell into the hands of the Montefeltro family of Urbino and was later incorporated into the Papal States.

Like many other hill towns in Tuscany and the Marches, Gubbio has taken on the feel of a museum. The city is worth visiting, although there is not a lot to keep you here for more than a day trip.

Orientation

The city is small and easy to explore. The immense traffic circle known as Piazza Quaranta Martiri, at the base of the hill, is where buses to the city terminate, and it also has a large car park. It was named in honour of 40 local people who were killed by the Nazis during the war. From here, it is a short walk along Via della Repubblica for the city's main square, Piazza Grande, also known as the Piazza della Signoria, which is set like a ledge into the hill. Corso Garibaldi and Piazza Oderisi are to your right as you head up the hill.

Information

The APT tourist information office (☎ 075-922 06 93) in Piazza Oderisi produces a good street map and can assist with accommodation. The office opens from 8.30 am to 1.30 pm and 3.30 to 6.30 pm Monday to Saturday, from 9 am to 1 pm Sunday. There is a city-run information office on Via della Repubblica, near Piazza Quaranta Martiri.

The main post office is at Via Cairoli 11 and opens Monday to Saturday from 8.15 am to 7 pm. Telephones are at Easy Gubbio, Via della Repubblica 13, and the telephone code for Gubbio is 075.

For police emergencies, call ☎ 113, or contact the police headquarters (☎ 927 37 31) at Via Perugina. The Ospedale Civile (☎ 9 23 91) is in Piazza Quaranta Martiri.

Things to See

The **Church of San Francesco**, in Piazza Quaranta Martiri is attributed to Perugia's Fra Bevignate and features impressive frescoes by a local artist, Ottaviano Nelli. The **Franciscan Museum** in the adjoining convent features a collection of sacred art, as well as Greek and Apulian ceramics. Ask one of the attendants to let you in (entry is free).

From the piazza, follow Via della Repubblica up the hill to Piazza Grande, also known as Piazza della Signoria, which features the city's grandest collection of buildings. It's dominated by the 14th century **Consuls' Palace**, attributed to Gattapone. The crenellated façade and tower can be seen from most parts of the city.

The building houses the **Municipal Museum & Picture Gallery**. The museum contains the *Eugubian Tables*, which were discovered in 1444 near the Roman Theatre west of Piazza Quaranta Martiri. The seven bronze tablets date from 300 to 100 BC and have provided linguists with the main source for their research into the ancient Umbrian language. Upstairs is the picture gallery, which features works from the Gubbian school. The museum and gallery open from 9 am to 1 pm and 3 to 7 pm daily from October to March, slightly shorter hours for the rest of the year, and entry is L4000. Across the square is the lesser **Pretorian Palace**, built along similar lines to its grander counterpart and now the city's town hall.

Via Ducale leads up to the 13th century pink **Duomo**, featuring a fine 12th century stained-glass window, and a fresco attributed to Pinturicchio. The **Ducal Palace** opposite was built by the Montefeltro family as a scaled-down version of their grand palace in Urbino, and features an impressive Renaissance courtyard. It should reopen in late 1993 after restoration.

From Piazza Grande, Via dei Consoli leads north-west to the 13th century **Bargello Palace**, the city's medieval police station and prison, and in front of it is the **Fountain of the Mad**, so named because of a traditional belief that if you walk around it three times, you will go mad. At Via San Giuliano 3, just south of the Bargello Palace, is the **Antica Fabbrica Artigiana**, a former palace, now a gallery-cum-shop for the city's ceramic artisans – one of Gubbio's main industries during the Middle Ages.

South of Piazza Quaranta Martiri, off Viale del Teatro Romano, are the remains of the 1st century AD **Roman Theatre**. Not much of this reconstructed edifice is original, but it's still an impressive sight.

Back in town, walk south-east along Corso Garibaldi for Via Nelli and the Gothic **Church of Santa Maria Nuova** with the fresco *Madonna del Belvedere* by Ottaviano Nelli. Ask the custodian at Via Dante 66 to let you in the church.

From here, continue along for the funicular station in Via San Gerolamo where you can ride the curious birdcage funicular for the **Basilica of Sant'Ubaldo**, an uninspiring church which houses the city's main religious attraction, the three *ceri*, or massive wooden pillars (literally, candles). These come into play during the annual Corsa dei Ceri on 15 May, which starts at 5.30 am and involves three teams, each carrying a *cero* and racing through the city's streets. It is all very complicated, but there is lots of festivity, all intended to commemorate the city's patron saint, St Ubald. The area around the church offers spectacular views over the city and valley, and you can eat at the bar at the funicular station.

Places to Stay

Many locals rent rooms to tourists, so ask at the APT about private rooms. Otherwise, you might consider making a day trip from Perugia, as accommodation in Gubbio is generally expensive. For camping, try the *Città di Gubbio* (☎ 927 20 37) at Ortoguidone, a southern suburb of Gubbio, about three km south of Piazza Quaranta Martiri along the ss298 (the Via Perugina).

The cheapest hotel option is *Galletti* (☎ 927 42 47), Via Piccardi 3, which has singles/doubles from L32,000/47,000. The *Grotta dell'Angelo* (☎ 927 17 47), Via Gioia 47, has rooms from L47,000/65,000, as does the *Dei Consoli* (☎ 927 33 35), Via dei Consoli 59. The up-market *San Marco* (☎ 927 23 49), Via Perugina 5, has rooms from L70,000/90,000.

Places to Eat

If you want to try some local specialities, *Ristorante San Martino*, Piazza Giordano Bruno, occasionally features traditional dishes at a reasonable price. Pasta dishes start at L6000. *Il Giardino*, Piazza Quaranta Martiri, is also quite cheap and a meal could cost L25,000. *Fabiani*, in the same piazza, is a good, traditional trattoria and a meal will cost L30,000. One of the city's better restaurants, *Alla Fornace di Maestro Giorgio*, in Via Maestro Giorgio, is also one of the more expensive, with main courses starting at L15,000. The *Tipici Prodotti Gastronomici* shop, Via dei Consoli 41, features a wide range of locally produced foods and wines.

Getting There & Away

ASP buses (☎ 927 15 44) connect the city with Perugia (nine a day), Fossato di Vico, Gualdo Tadino and Umbertide, and the company operates daily services to Rome and Florence. Most buses stop in Piazza Quaranta Martiri, but some terminate at the bus station (☎ 927 39 27) in Via San Lazzaro.

Gubbio is not on a train line; the closest station is at Fossato di Vico, about 20 km south-east of the city. Trains connect with Rome and Ancona, Perugia, Terontola, Arezzo and Florence. ASP buses connect Gubbio with the station, usually an hour before each train.

By car and motorcycle, take the ss298 from Perugia, or the ss76 from Ancona, and follow the signs. There is a large car park in Piazza Quaranta Martiri, which costs L1000 an hour.

Getting Around

The easiest way is to walk around this small city, although ASP buses connect Piazza Quaranta Martiri with the funicular station and most main sights. Taxis (☎ 927 38 00) operate from Piazza Quaranta Martiri.

AROUND GUBBIO

The area east of Gubbio, the **Mt Cucco Regional Park** around Mt Cucco, is a veritable haven for various types of outdoor activities and is dotted with caves, many of which can be explored. It is well set up for walkers, rock climbers, horse riders and so on and has many hotels and mountain refuges. **Costacciaro**, reached by bus from Gubbio, is a good place to start exploring the area, and a walk to the summit of Mt Cucco begins there.

Information is available from the APT in Gubbio. The Centro Operativo della Scuola Nazionale di Speleologia del Club Alpino Italiano (☎ 075-917 02 36), Corso Mazzini 9, in Costacciaro, can help with information about exploring local caves. The Club Alpino Italiano also produces a walking map entitled *Carta dei Sentieri Massiccio del Monte Cucco*. It is possible to rent mountain bikes in Costacciaro at the local swimming pool (☎ 075-917 06 18) from L25,000 a day.

There are several horse-riding schools around Gubbio that arrange lessons or treks. Rio Verde (☎ 075-917 01 38) is just north of the city in a small town called Fornace. A farm where you can stay is the *Azienda Agraria Allevamento San Giovanni* (☎ 075-925 66 46), south-east at Torre Calzolari. Ask for directions when you arrive in these towns.

	PLACES TO STAY	11	Roman Amphitheatre
		12	Teatro Nuovo
9	Albergo Fracassa	14	Piazza della Signoria
10	Albergo Anfiteatro	15	Duomo Museum
13	Il Panciolle	16	Piazza del Duomo
27	Hotel Gattapone	17	Duomo
40	Eremo delle Grazie	18	Piazza Mentana
42	Monteluco Camping Ground	19	Church of San Filippo
		20	Piazza Pianciani
▼	PLACES TO EAT	21	Church of Sant'Eufemia
		22	Roman House
3	Da Sportellino	23	Picture Gallery
8	Due Porte	24	Piazza del Municipio
31	Il Pentagramma	25	Piazza Campello
29	Osteria Mon Cherí	26	La Rocca
39	Dei Duchi	28	Bridge of Towers
		30	Porta San Matteo
	OTHER	32	Drusus' Arch
		33	Archaeological Museum
1	Main Railway Station	34	Piazza della Libertà
2	Carabinieri	35	Roman Theatre
4	Basilica of San Salvatore	36	Piazza Fontana
5	SIP Telephones	37	Tourist Information Office
6	Bus Terminal	38	Main Post Office & Telephones
7	Piazza della Vittoria	41	Church of San Pietro

SPOLETO

Each June and July, this normally quiet medieval hill town in the green heart of Umbria takes centre stage for a parade of cultural and often snobbish sophistication, the Festival of the Two Worlds. The Italian-American composer Gian Carlo Menotti selected Spoleto in 1958 after inspecting more than 30 other towns for their suitability, and set up the festival with his American friend, Thomas Schippers. It has given the city a worldwide reputation and has brought great wealth to the small population who bask under the glory of the country's leading international festival of drama, music and dance. Menotti has since expanded the festival to include Charleston in South Carolina and, briefly, Melbourne in Australia.

Interestingly, Menotti has avoided the political *lottizzazione*, whereby the country's political parties divide up senior positions in everything from cultural events to government-owned media. Whereas political meddling has almost grounded Venice's Biennale, Menotti has been lucky. A couple

of years ago he told journalists he hoped this would continue, saying:

In a country in which is it openly and shamelessly admitted that in the state-run theatres, if the artistic director is a Communist, then the superintendent must be a Socialist and so on, it's a miracle that in Spoleto the political parties are all agreed to leave the festival out of their political rivalries and that in these 30 years, no mayor has ever asked me what party I belong to or about my political ideas.

If you are planning to visit Spoleto during the festival, ensure that you book accommodation and tickets months in advance. If you want to make day trips during the festival, the only problem you will have is finding a place to park the car, if you have one. See the following Festivals section for more details.

Apart from the festival, the town is enchantingly beautiful and is well worth a visit for its many art treasures, medieval architecture and well-preserved Roman remains.

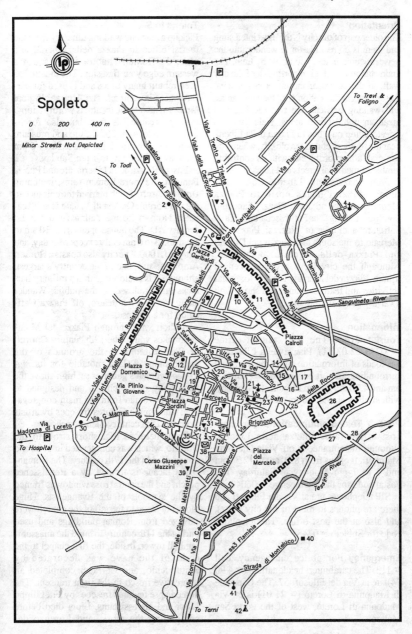

Spoleto

0   200   400 m

Minor Streets Not Depicted

Orientation

The older part of the city is the most interesting and there is no real reason to wander into the newer section, unless you arrive by train. The main station is half a km north-east of the city wall, in the centre of the city's newer area. Buses connect the station with the older areas, and walking between the two sections will mean an uphill climb along Viale Trento e Trieste. Jump on a bus to Piazza della Libertà near the southern end of the old city, where you can grab a map of the city with its confusing jumble of medieval streets and lanes.

From Piazza della Libertà, Corso Giuseppe Mazzini heads north to Piazza Mentana and the adjacent Piazza Pianciani. South-east along Via Fontesecca and Via A Saffi are a cluster of piazzas: Piazza del Mercato to the south and Piazza del Duomo and Piazza della Signoria to the east. Although the city lacks a distinct central square, Piazza del Mercato is a hub for social activities and features many food shops with a variety of local products.

Information

Tourist Office The APT tourist office (☎ 0743-22 03 11), Piazza della Libertà 7, has loads of information about the town and surrounding area. It is open from 9 am to 1 pm and 4.30 to 7.30 pm Monday to Saturday, with slightly shorter hours on Sunday.

Post & Telecommunications The main post office faces Piazza della Libertà, although the entrance is off Viale Giacomo Matteotti. It opens from 8.30 am to 12.30 pm and 3 to 7 pm Monday to Saturday. The postal code for the town centre is 06049.

SIP telephones are at Via dei Filosofi and there are phones in most of the city's bars, and also at the post office. The telephone code for Spoleto is 0743.

Emergency For police emergency, call ☎ 113. The carabinieri headquarters (☎ 4 90 44) are at Via dei Filosofi 57. The Ospedale di Madonna di Loreto (☎ 21 01) is on Via Madonna di Loreto, west of the Porta San Matteo.

Things to See

Pick up a map and walking itinerary from the tourist office in Piazza della Libertà, and make the **Roman Theatre** on the square's western edge your first stop. The theatre has been rebuilt many times and is used for performances in summer. The **Archaeological Museum** next to the theatre is worth visiting, mainly because it's free, but also for its ceramic collection. The theatre and museum open from 9 am to 1 pm and 2.30 to 6 pm Monday to Saturday, to 1 pm Sunday.

East of Piazza della Libertà, around Piazza Fontana, are more Roman ruins, including **Drusus' Arch**, which marked the entrance to the old Forum. On Via di Visiale is an excavated **Roman house** dating from the 1st century AD. The house opens from 10 am to 1 pm and 3 to 6 pm daily except Monday, and entry is L1000. The city also boasts a **Roman Amphitheatre**, one of the country's largest, although it is enclosed within a military barracks and is closed to the public. Wander along Via dell'Anfiteatro, off Piazza Garibaldi, for a glimpse.

A short walk through Piazza del Municipio takes you to the 12th century **Church of Sant'Eufemia** in the grounds of the Archbishop's Palace, notable for its *matronea*, women's galleries set high above the main body of the church and designed to segregate women from the main congregation. The church features frescoes by artists from the 15th century Sienese school.

From here, is it a short stroll to the **Duomo**, which was consecrated in 1198 and remodelled in the 17th century. The Romanesque façade is fronted by a Renaissance porch, and the central rose window is framed by the symbols of the Evangelists. Huge blocks of stone to the left of the church were salvaged from Roman buildings and used during the 11th century to build the unassuming bell tower. Inside, the first chapel to the right of the nave was decorated by Pinturicchio, and Carracci completed an impressive fresco in the right transept. The domed apse features frescoes by Fra Filippo Lippi and his assistants. Lippi died before completing the work, and Lorenzo de'

Medici travelled to Spoleto from Florence and ordered Lippi's son, Filippino, to build a mausoleum for the artist. This now stands in the right transept of the cathedral.

A couple of other features in Piazza del Duomo are the Spoleto Shop, which opens during the festival and sells posters, T-shirts etc, and Gian Carlo Menotti's house at No 8. The **Duomo Museum**, also in the piazza, features a less than impressive collection of religious oddments. It opens from 10 am to midday and 3 to 6 pm (closed Monday), and entry is L3000.

The city's **Picture Gallery** is in the town hall in Piazza del Municipio and was recently renovated. Unfortunately, you must be guided around the gallery, although the sumptuous building and some impressive works by Umbrian artists make a visit worthwhile. The **Modern Art Gallery** in the Rosari-Spada Palace in Corso Mazzini has a permanent collection, but is used mainly for changing exhibitions. Both galleries open from 10 am to 1 pm and 3 to 6 pm (closed Monday), and a L5000 ticket gains entry to both.

Dominating the city is **La Rocca**, a former papal fortress which, until recently, was one of the country's highest security prisons, housing such notables as Pope John Paul II's attempted assassin, Ali Agca. It is currently closed for restorations that started around 1976 and are expected to keep the building off limits for several more years.

Along Via del Ponte is one of the city's most stunning monuments, the **Bridge of Towers** (Ponte delle Torri), which dates from the 14th century although it was built on the foundations of a Roman aqueduct. The bridge is named after the towers on the far side.

If you feel like a walk, cross the bridge and follow the lower path, Strada di Monteluco, for the **Church of San Pietro**. If a long walk doesn't appeal to you, follow Via del Ponte around La Rocca and back into Spoleto. San Pietro's 13th century façade, the church's main attraction, features many sculpted animals.

Festivals

Events at the Festival of the Two Worlds in June and July range from cinema and theatre to ballet and art exhibitions. Tickets range from L10,000 to L200,000 and generally sell out months in advance – tickets for most performances sell out by March. The festival has an office in Rome (☎ 06-321 02 88) at Via Cesare Beccaria 18; in Spoleto, tickets can be purchased at the Teatro Nuovo (☎ 4 02 65) in Largo B Gigli.

Places to Stay

The city is well served with cheap hotels, private rooms, hostels and camping grounds, although if you're going for the festival you will need to book a room months in advance. At other times, you should have no problem.

The closest camping ground is *Monteluco* (☎ 0743-22 03 58), just behind the Church of San Pietro, open from April to September. It charges L6000 for a tent and L4500 per person. *Il Girasole* (☎ 0743-5 13 35) is about 10 km north-west of Spoleto in Petrognano. Buses connect with the town from Spoleto's train station.

The *Istituto Bambino Gesù* (☎ 4 02 32) is a religious hostel, just behind the APT at Via Monterone 4; it has singles/doubles for L25,000/50,000. An IYHF youth hostel, the *Fulginium* (☎ 0742-35 28 82), is 26 km north of Spoleto in Foligno, easily reached by bus; bed and breakfast is L13,000.

The best hotel option is the *Albergo Fracassa* (☎ 22 11 77), Via Focaroli 15, which has singles/doubles for L30,000/37,000. The *Albergo Anfiteatro* (☎ 4 98 53), Via dell'Anfiteatro 14, has rooms from L35,000/45,000. *Il Panciolle* (☎ 4 55 98), Via del Duomo 3, is in a good location and has rooms from L45,000/60,000.

One of the best located hotels is the *Hotel Gattapone* (☎ 22 34 47) at Via del Ponte 6, overlooking the Bridge of Towers, which has rooms from L105,000/120,000. The *Eremo delle Grazie* (☎ 4 96 24) set into the hills at Strada di Monteluco is pure luxury and has rooms from L250,000/350,000; it's the chosen hotel of visiting heads of government.

Places to Eat

Spoleto is one of Umbria's main producers of black truffles, and they are used in a variety of dishes. However, trying them can be a costly exercise. *Due Porte*, Piazza della Vittoria 14, is a good, cheap restaurant with pizzas from L5000. *Osteria Mon Cherí*, Piazza del Mercato 27, is also cheap, with some traditional dishes. *Il Pentagramma*, Via A Martani, is a good trattoria where you can eat a meal for L20,000. *Dei Duchi*, Viale G Matteotti 4, has pizzas from L6500, and *Da Sportellino*, Via della Cerquiglia 4, is a typical Umbrian restaurant, with main courses from L5000.

You can get a great ice cream at *Gelateria Primavera*, Piazza del Mercato 6, and pizza by the slice from *Pizzeria dell'Orologia*, opposite the gelateria. The *American Bar* in Piazza del Duomo is one of the city's best bars.

Getting There & Away

Società Spoletina Trasporti (SSIT) buses (☎ 22 19 91) depart from Piazza della Vittoria for Monteluco, Foligno, Terni, Rome, Bastardo, Assisi, Perugia and dozens of smaller towns. Trains from the train station (☎ 4 85 16) in Piazza Polvani connect with Rome, Ancona and Perugia. By car and motorcycle, the city is on the ss3 which runs from Terni to Foligno, basically the old Roman Via Flaminia. From Terni, it's a short trip to the A1 autostrada. Car parks are at all main approaches to the city.

Getting Around

The city is easily seen on foot, although SSIT buses weave through the streets. Bus Circolare C connects the train station with Piazza della Libertà, and Circolare D runs between the train station and Piazza Garibaldi.

ORVIETO

Orvieto's magnificent cathedral is one of the country's finest Gothic buildings and the city's main tourist attraction. The city's location on the autostrada between Rome and Florence means that tourists flock to see the church. Situated on the top of a volcanic hill overlooking the Paglia Valley, Orvieto is worth visiting for a few hours. If you have a car, the local vineyards producing the internationally renowned Orvieto wines are worth visiting. Orvieto was the site of one of the 12 city-states of Etruria, and a papal stronghold throughout the Renaissance period.

Orientation

The modern section at the base of the hill offers little more than the train station. It is possible to drive up to the old city and park in the large areas outside the city wall – there's plenty of parking in Piazza Cahen. A funicular railway connects the train station with Piazza Cahen, from where you can take Corso Cavour to Piazza della Repubblica. About halfway along on your left, Via del Duomo leads up to Piazza del Duomo and the cathedral.

Information

The APT tourist office (☎ 0763-4 17 72) is at Piazza del Duomo 24 and opens from 10 am to 2 pm and 4 to 7 pm Monday to Saturday, from 10 am to midday and 4 to 6 pm Sunday. The main post office is at Via Cesare Nebbia, just off Corso Cavour, and opens Monday to Saturday from 8.30 am to 6.30 pm. The postal code for the town centre is 05018. SIP telephone card dispensers and phones are west of the entrance to the Cathedral Museum, beside the APT. The telephone code for Orvieto is 0763.

In a police emergency, call ☎ 113, or contact the police headquarters (☎ 4 00 88) in Piazza Cahen. The city's hospital (☎ 4 20 71) is on Piazza del Duomo.

Things to See

The **cathedral** dates back to 1290, and was built to house the blood-stained Corporal, a Eucharist altar cloth which featured in the so-called Miracle of Bolsena. In this episode, a Bohemian priest's doubts about transubstantiation – the process where bread and wine change into the body and blood of Christ when consecrated in the Eucharist –

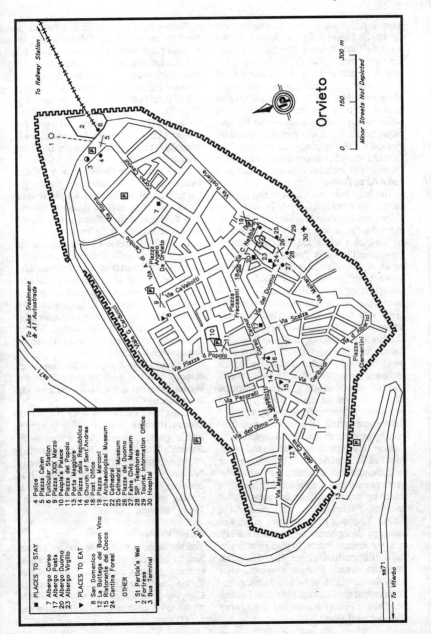

Orvieto

Minor Streets Not Depicted

0   150   300 m

To Railway Station

To Lake Trasimene
& A1 Autostrada

To Viterbo

ss71

ss71

Corso Cavour

Via Postierla

Via Malabranca

Via dell'Olmo

Via Pecorelli

Via Magalotti

Via Garibaldi

Via Scalza

Via del Duomo

Via Maitani

Via d'Alberici

Via delle Cave

Via A. B.

Via Ca Vallotti

Via C. Nebbia

Piazza
Angelo
Da Orvieto

Piazza
Fracassini

Piazza
Clementini

Piazza
del Popolo

Viale G. Carducci

PLACES TO STAY
- 7 Albergo Corso
- 17 Albergo Posta
- 20 Albergo Duomo
- 23 Albergo Virgilio

PLACES TO EAT
- 8 San Domenico
- 12 La Bottega del Buon Vino
- 15 Ristorante del Cocco
- 24 Cantina Foresi

OTHER
- 1 St Patrick's Well
- 2 Fortress
- 3 Bus Terminal
- 4 Police
- 5 Piazza Cahen
- 6 Funicular Station
- 9 Piazza XIX Marzo
- 10 People's Palace
- 11 Piazza del Popolo
- 13 Porta Maggiore
- 14 Piazza della Repubblica
- 16 Church of Sant'Andrea
- 18 Post Office
- 19 Piazza Marconi
- 21 Archaeological Museum
- 22 Cathedral
- 25 Cathedral Museum
- 26 Palace of the Duomo
- 27 Faina Civic Museum
- 28 SIP Telephones
- 29 Tourist Information Office
- 30 Hospital

were dispelled when blood dripped from the Host to the Corporal during a service in 1263 just near Lake Bolsena. The linen was presented to Pope Urban IV, in Orvieto at the time, who declared the event a miracle and set the wheels in motion for the construction of the cathedral. The building took 30 years to plan and three centuries to complete, and while mostly Gothic, bears strong Romanesque influences. It was probably started by Perugia's Fra Bevignate and continued by Lorenzo Maitani, responsible for Florence's Duomo, and includes frescoes by Orcagna and Andrea Pisano.

The **façade** is the highlight and appears completely unrelated to the black-and-white striped marble church behind it. The three huge doorways and gables are decorated with mosaics which are stunning, particularly when the sun is shining on the façade, or at night under spotlights. The areas between the doorways feature 14th century bas-reliefs of scriptural scenes by Maitani and his pupils. The rose window by Orcagna gives way to the finely carved representations of the Evangelists on the pillars.

After the splendour of the exterior, the interior can be something of a disappointment. Banded by black and white marble, the cathedral features impressive 14th century stained-glass windows. The **Corporal Chapel** features the stained linen, preserved in a silver reliquary, decorated by artists of the Sienese school. The walls feature frescoes by Ugolino di Prete Ilario depicting the miracle. The **New Chapel**, at the end of the south aisle, contains the church's greatest treasure: frescoes depicting the *Last Judgment*, painted by Luca Signorelli from 1499, which are believed to have had a great influence on Michelangelo, who painted the Sistine Chapel cycle 40 years later. The cathedral closes during the middle of the day.

In the Soliano Palace, to your right as you face the cathedral, is the **Cathedral Museum**, which features religious relics from the cathedral, as well as Etruscan antiquities and works by artists such as Simone Martini and Pisano. Restoration should keep it closed until 1994.

North-east of the Cathedral Museum, in the 13th century Papal Palace, is the **Archaeological Museum**, which contains a full-size Etruscan tomb and other relics. It is open from 9 am to 1 pm and 3 to 7 pm Tuesday to Sunday, and entry is L4000. The palace itself is of historic and religious significance as it was here in 1527 that Pope Clement VII rejected Henry VIII's plea for divorce from Catherine of Aragon and inadvertently set in motion the foundation of the Church of England.

The **Faina Civic Museum**, in the Faina Palace opposite the cathedral, houses yet more Etruscan goodies and a collection of Greek vases. It opens from 9 am to 1 pm and 3 to 6.30 pm daily, although it is closed Sunday afternoons, and entry is free.

Turn left into Corso Cavour and wander along to Piazza della Repubblica, with the 11th century **Church of Sant'Andrea**, featuring the remains of 14th century frescoes. The crypt reveals remains of an earlier church, and at a lower level are remains of a Roman, and prior to that Etruscan, temple. The square was the site of the ancient Roman forum, and the surrounding area is Orvieto's most authentic medieval quarter.

North of Corso Cavour is the Piazza del Popolo and the 13th century **People's Palace** (Palazzo del Popolo), built in the Romanesque-Gothic style.

At the town's easternmost tip is the 14th century **fortress**, part of which is now a public garden. Below the fortress is **St Patrick's Well**, sunk in 1527 on the orders of Pope Clement VII to ensure that the city had a supply of water in case of siege. It is open daily from 10 am to 7 pm and entry is L5000, which includes admission to the Greek Museum.

Places to Stay

You should have no trouble getting a room here at any time of the year. The closest camping grounds are about 10 km towards Rome, on Lake Corbara, near Baschi. *Camping Scacco Matto* (☎ 0744-95 01 63) on the ss448 charges L5000 per person and L5000 a tent.

In Orvieto, one of the best deals is the *Albergo Duomo* (☎ 4 18 87), Via di Maurizio 7, and some rooms overlook the cathedral; singles/doubles are L35,000/45,000. *Albergo Posta* (☎ 4 19 09), Via L Signorelli 18, has rooms for about the same price. *Albergo Corso* (☎ 4 20 20), Corso Cavour 343, has singles/doubles from L55,000/75,000, and the three-star *Albergo Virgilio* (☎ 4 18 82), Piazza del Duomo 5, overlooks the cathedral and rooms are L70,000/100,000.

Places to Eat

One of the most pleasant places to eat is at *Cantina Foresi*, Piazza del Duomo – a wine cellar with local wines, tables in the piazza and some cheap dishes for lunch or dinner. *San Domenico* is a pizzeria at Piazza XXIX Marzo 18, with pizzas from L5000. *La Bottega del Buon Vino*, Via della Cava 26, has a L16,000 tourist menu. *Ristorante del Cocco*, Via Garibaldi 4, has some local dishes, and a meal will cost L20,000.

Dai Fratelli, Via del Duomo 11, is a small shop selling an incredible range of Orvietan foods, and *L'Archetto*, Piazza del Duomo 14, has great ice creams.

Getting There & Away

All buses depart from Piazza Cahen. ACOTRAL (☎ 0761-22 65 92 in Viterbo) connects the city with Viterbo and Bagnoregio. ATC buses (☎ 4 22 65), Piazza Cahen, connect with Baschi, Montecchio, Bolsena, Perugia and Todi. SIRA (☎ 06-4173 00 83) runs a daily service to Rome.

Trains run to Rome and Florence, and you can change at Terontola for Perugia. By car, the city is on the A1 autostrada, and the ss71 heads north for Lake Trasimene. Make sure you have plenty of coins for the parking metres in Piazza Cahen.

Getting Around

A funicular railway connects Piazza Cahen with the train station, with carriages leaving every 15 minutes from 7.15 am to 8.30 pm daily. Once in the city, the easiest way to see it is on foot, although ATC bus No A connects

Piazza Cahen with Piazza del Duomo, and No B with Piazza della Repubblica.

AROUND ORVIETO

The Etruscans produced wine in the district, the Romans continued the tradition, and today the Orvieto Classico wines are among the country's most popular. You can visit 17 vineyards and sample the produce. Unfortunately, you need a car, as ATC bus services to most small towns near the vineyards are not regular.

Grab a copy of *Andar per Vigne* from the APT tourist office, or pop into the Consorzio Tutela Vino Orvieto Classico e Orvieto (☎ 4 37 90), Corso Cavour 36, for details of its driving tour of the local vineyards.

TERNI

Terni is one of Umbria's most important industrial cities, and as such, it was virtually obliterated in WW II bombing raids. The city has charm, although it falls a long way behind the region's starlets of Perugia, Assisi and Spoleto. It does, however, make a good base for exploration into the Valnerina (the area along the Nera River in Umbria's southeast), and into the beautiful Monti Sibillini range which stretches into the neighbouring Marches.

The city was the birthplace of St Valentine, who was bishop of Terni until his martyrdom in 273 AD. About six km east of Terni is the Marmore Waterfall, created by the Romans in 270 BC when they diverted the Velino River. It is worth catching a bus to see it.

Orientation & Information

The main train station is in Piazza Dante Alighieri at the northern edge of the centre. Walk south along Viale della Stazione to Piazza Cornelio Tacito and continue south along Corso C Tacito for the central Piazza della Repubblica.

The tourist office (☎ 0744-4 30 47) is just west of Piazza C Tacito at Viale Cesare Battisti 7, near Largo Don Minzoni. It closes during the middle of the day and is not open on Sundays.

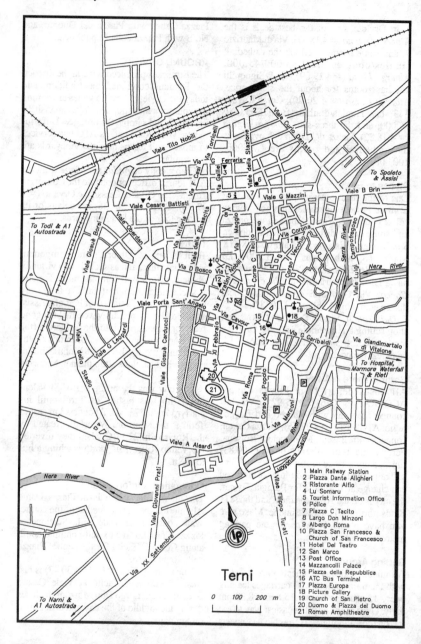

Terni

0   100   200 m

1   Main Railway Station
2   Piazza Dante Alighieri
3   Ristorante Alfio
4   Lu Somaru
5   Tourist Information Office
6   Police
7   Piazza C Tacito
8   Largo Don Minzoni
9   Albergo Roma
10 Piazza San Francesco &
    Church of San Francesco
11 Hotel Del Teatro
12 San Marco
13 Post Office
14 Mazzancolli Palace
15 Piazza della Repubblica
16 ATC Bus Terminal
17 Piazza Europa
18 Picture Gallery
19 Church of San Pietro
20 Duomo & Piazza del Duomo
21 Roman Amphitheatre

The main post office is in Piazza San Giovanni Decollato. Poste restante mail can be addressed to 05100 Terni. SIP telephones are nearby in Piazza della Repubblica. The telephone code for Terni is 0744.

For police emergencies, call ☎ 113, or contact the police headquarters in Piazza C Tacito. The city's hospital (☎ 0744-45 51) is in Via T di Joannuccio, east of the city centre.

Things to See & Do

The city has a few sights worth considering. West from Piazza della Repubblica on Via Cavour is one of Terni's finest buildings, the 14th century **Mazzancolli Palace**, with a magnificent courtyard. South along Via XI Febbraio in the city's **Duomo**, the most interesting component being the remains of its 12th century porch. The interior was renovated in the 17th century. Behind the cathedral are the remains of the **Roman Amphitheatre**, which was in reasonably good condition until the bombing raids of WW II.

Return to Piazza della Repubblica and head north-east along Corso Vecchio for the Romanesque-Gothic **Church of San Pietro**, which features some 14th and 15th century frescoes. The city's **Picture Gallery**, on Via Manassei, has works by Benozzo Gozzoli and lesser known artists such as Spagna, Melanzio and Alunno. The gallery opens from 10 am to 1 pm and 4 to 7 pm, and entry is L3000. The 13th century Gothic **Church of San Francesco**, on Viale A Fratti, features frescoes on Dantesque themes.

At 165 metres, the **Marmore Waterfall** is Italy's highest waterfall and is regarded as one of the most spectacular in Europe, even though it's artificial. The Romans created the falls by diverting the Velino River into the Nera, and it was expanded in the 1930s with the creation of Lake Piediluco to the south-east as part of a hydroelectricity scheme. Curiously, the waterfall can be stopped: a dam at the top diverts the water if the hydro-electric plant is not working. Check with the APT in Terni for operating times. The falls operate most nights between 5 and 6.30 pm,

and the Italians have installed a sound-and-light show which illuminates the water. Whenever the fall is switched on, the ss79 road connecting Terni with Rome resembles a car park as drivers stop to watch the spectacle.

Places to Stay & Eat

The city has many cheap hotels, making it a good base for travel in the surrounding district. The *Albergo Roma* (☎ 40 61 17), Corso Tacito 5, has singles/doubles from L28,000/35,000, as does the *Hotel del Teatro* (☎ 5 60 73), Corso Vecchio 124.

The *Lu Somaru* restaurant, Viale Cesare Battisti 106, features some traditional Umbrian dishes, and a meal will cost between L20,000 and L30,000. *Ristorante Alfio*, Via Galilei, is a pizzeria where a meal will cost L20,000. One of the city's better restaurants is *San Marco*, Via San Marco 4, where a meal costs L40,000.

Getting There & Away

ATC buses (☎ 5 95 41) terminate in Piazza Europa. Bus No 24 goes to the Marmore Waterfall, and timetables at the office list all other destinations.

The city is on the private Umbrian train line connecting the city with Perugia. An FS line runs between Terni and Orte, where you can connect with trains for Rome and Florence. For train information, call ☎ 40 12 83.

The ss3bis superstrada connects the city with Perugia, and the ss204 connects it with the A1 autostrada for Rome and Florence. To the east, the ss209 will get you to Norcia (see the Valnerina section). There is a large car park on Corso del Popolo, south of Piazza della Repubblica.

Getting Around

ATC buses run frequent services from the train station into the city centre. Bus Nos 1 and 2 leave the train station for Piazza della Repubblica and Piazza Europa.

THE VALNERINA

Incorporating most of the lower eastern parts

of Umbria, along the Nera River, the Valnerina is one of the most beautiful areas in the region. Stretching up to the barren summit of Mt Sibilla in the neighbouring Marches, the area is a haven for walkers. It also offers a couple of hang-gliding schools in what is considered to be the best area in Europe to learn this sort of thing.

Travelling into and around the area can be difficult unless you have your own transport. If you are driving, the Field of Flowers on the Castelluccio Plain north-east of Norcia should not be missed; the vast basin under Mt Vettore becomes a sea of purple, yellow, red and blue as flowers bloom from March to May.

The town of Norcia is the region's administrative centre, and a transport hub of sorts. The town preserves some beautiful 13th century architecture and these days is one of the country's major salami-producing areas. There is a small tourist office in the central Piazza San Benedetto.

Activities

Fly Castellucci (☎ 0743-87 02 09), Via del Pian Perduto, in Norcia, can arrange hang-gliding, mountain trekking and winter skiing, and can rent mountain bikes and horses. On offer is a five-day hang-gliding course from L550,000 for beginners or more advanced gliders, and the school can arrange high flights. Pupils can also get accommodation on site for L10,000 a night, with their own sleeping bag.

The area is dotted with mountain refuges, many of which offer guides and sell trekking maps. If you plan to do some walking, pick up a copy of *20 Sentieri Ragionati in Valnerina*, the aptly titled '20 Well-Thought-Out Routes in Valnerina'.

If you are driving, the APT Valnerina-Cascia (☎ 0743-7 14 01), Via Vespasia Polla 1, in Cascia, is a good place to start. Tourist bodies in Umbria and the Marches have erected road signs which identify driving itineraries, and have provided a telephone number (☎ 0736-9 91 22) which gives driving tips on places to visit and the area's highlights.

Places to Stay

There is a free camping ground just outside Castelluccio at Monte Prata (☎ 0737-98 28), which opens from 15 June for the summer months; the best way to find it is to ask a local. There is a small hotel/restaurant in Castelluccio, the *Albergo Sibilla* (☎ 0743-87 01 13), with singles/doubles from L25,000/50,000. In Norcia, the *Da Benito* (☎ 0743-81 66 70) has rooms from L45,000/60,000.

Getting There & Away

Spoleto is the best point from which to head into the area. Spoleto's SSIT bus company (☎ 0743-22 19 91) operates several buses a day to the terminal at Via della Stazione in Norcia, and also operates services to Cascia, Castelluccio, Serravalle and about 10 other small towns in the mountains. Most are served by only one bus per day.

By car, the ss395 from Spoleto or ss209 from Terni connect up with the ss320 and then the ss396, which passes through Norcia. The area can also be reached from Ascoli Piceno in the Marches.

The Marches

A narrow band between the Apennines and the Adriatic, the Marches (Le Marche) is one of Italy's most attractive and least spoilt regions. Most people come for the Renaissance splendour of Urbino, or to catch a ferry from Ancona. But the region deserves a few days' exploration.

The treeless Monti Sibillini range in the south-west corner is considered one of the most impressive stretches of the Apennines, and could keep even the most die-hard walker busy for days. Most of the coastline has been overdeveloped, evident by the ubiquitous rows of beach umbrellas, but some of the beaches north of Ancona around Senigallia and Pesaro are considered among the Adriatic's best. However, it is the small medieval hill towns that are the Marches' most endearing feature. Urbino, Macerata and Ascoli Piceno are the more well known,

The Marches
(Le Marche)

0   10   20 km

but there are hundreds of towns worth exploring. The region is also becoming popular with Romans and foreigners intent on buying old farm houses for renovation, now that Tuscany has outpriced itself.

One of Italy's oldest tribes, the Piceni, were the first inhabitants of the region, and the Marches later fell under Roman control. The region prospered in the Middle Ages and boomed during the 15th and 16th centuries when the powerful Montefeltro family ruled Urbino. The Marches attracted great Renaissance architects and painters, and Urbino itself spawned Raphael and Bramante.

The cuisine draws inspiration and ingre-

dients from two sources. Inland mountain dishes comprise freshwater fish, beef, lamb, mushrooms and truffles, while on the coast, sole and prawns resembling lobsters are popular. *Brodetto* is a tempting fish stew that is common along the coast, while *vincisgrassi*, a rich lasagna with meat sauce, chicken livers and black truffles, is popular inland. The region is a small wine producer, with one of the best drops being the Vernaccia di Serrapetrona, a sparkling red.

The A14 autostrada hugs the coast, and the inland roads are good and provide easy access to all towns. Bus services are excellent and trains connect most towns with the coast.

ANCONA

The main reason to visit Ancona is to catch a ferry to Croatia, Greece or Turkey. Since the Middle Ages, Ancona has been a major port for trade with the East, but these days tourists and not spices have made it the mid-Adriatic's largest port.

The city was founded in 400 BC by settlers from Syracuse, and reached importance during imperial Roman times, particularly under Emperor Trajan, who saw its maritime potential. The city was heavily bombed during WW II, and subsequent redevelopment has created an unattractive industrial town. But its older centre warrants a visit if you have some hours to spare while waiting for a boat.

Orientation

Trains arrive at the main train station in Piazza Nello e Carlo Rosselli, just over one km south-west of the ferry terminal, Stazione Marittima, which is also known as the Molo Santa Maria. Buses connect the two. From Piazza della Repubblica, near the ferry terminal, walk uphill to the central Piazza Roma and then on to the city's grand Piazza Cavour.

Information

The main APT tourist office (☎ 071-3 49 38) is at the eastern edge of the old city centre at Via Thaon de Revel 4, although more convenient offices are at the train station (☎ 071-4 17 03) and at the ferry terminal (☎ 071-20 11 83), all of which open Monday to Friday from 8 am to 1 pm and 3.30 to 7 pm, Saturday to 1 pm. They offer free coupons during summer for guided tours, entry into various museums and discounts at hotels and restaurants.

The main post office is at Piazza XXIV Maggio, and is open Monday to Saturday from 8 am to 7 pm. Poste restante mail can be addressed to 60100 Ancona. ASST telephones are opposite the train station, and the SIP office is in Corso Stamira, near Piazza

1	Duomo
2	Piazza Dante Alighieri
3	National Archaeological Museum
4	Stazione Marrittima (Ferry Terminal) & Tourist Information Office
5	Picture Gallery
6	San Francesco delle Scale
7	Church of Santa Maria della Piazza
8	Osteria del Pozzo
9	La Cantineta
10	Piazza della Repubblica
11	Piazza Kennedy
12	Piazza del Plebiscito
13	Produce Market
14	Albergo Astor
15	SIP Telephones
16	Ospedale Civile
17	Piazza Cavour & Bus Departures
18	Post Office
19	Citadel
20	Osteria No 1
21	Main Railway Station & Tourist Information Office
22	Albergo Dorico
23	Albergo Fiore
24	SIP Telephones

Roma. The telephone code for Ancona is 071.

For police emergency, call ☎ 113, or contact the police headquarters (☎ 5 63 51), Via Gervasoni 19, south of the city centre. The Ospedale Civile (☎ 20 20 95) is in Largo Cappelli.

Things to See

Starting in Piazza del Plebiscito is the **Prefettura**, the former police headquarters, housed in a 15th century palace noted for its Renaissance arcade and beautiful courtyard. Just to the east is the Baroque **Church of San Domenico**, which features several superb artworks, including the *Crucifixion* by Titian and *Annunciation* by Guercino. Near the church is the 13th century city gate, the Arco Ferretti.

Take Via Pizzecolli from the Prefettura through the old city's ramparts to the Bosdari Palace at No 17, which houses the **Picture Gallery**, whose notable works include the *Madonna & Saints* by Titian as well as works

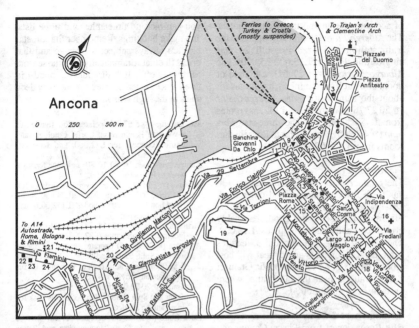

Ancona

0   250   500 m

by Guercino, Crivelli and Lotto. The gallery opens from 9 am to 7 pm Tuesday to Saturday, when entry is L5000, and to 1 pm Sunday, when entry is free.

Continue along Via Pizzecolli for the **Church of San Francesco delle Scale**, noted for its 15th century Venetian-Gothic doorway by Orsini. Beyond San Francesco is Vanvitelli's Chiesa del Gesù, and nearby, the city's 13th century **university** in the Palazzo degli Anziani. On Via Ferretti is the **National Archaeological Museum of the Marches**, housed in the Palazzo Ferretti, which has been restored twice this century, after WW II bombing and a 1972 earthquake. It includes impressive collections of Greek vases and artefacts from the Iron Age as well as Celtic and Roman remnants. It is open Monday to Saturday from 9 am to 1 pm and Sunday from 2.30 to 7.30 pm. Entry is L5000.

Take the Strada Panoramica Giovanni XXIII up Mt Guasco for the city's **Duomo** on the Piazza del Duomo, which is the best place to go for a view of the port and Adriatic. The Romanesque cathedral was built on the site of a Roman temple and has Byzantine and Gothic features. The small museum adjoining the church contains the sarcophagus of Flavius Gorgonius, dating from the 4th century and regarded as a masterpiece of early Christian art.

Leaving the cathedral, walk south along Via Giovanni XXIII to Piazza Dante Alighieri and then head north along Lungomare Luigi Vanvitelli for **Trajan's Arch**, erected in 115 AD. Vanvitelli's **Clementine Arch**, dedicated to Pope Clement XII, is farther on. Return along Lungomare Vanvitelli for Piazza Santa Maria and the **Church of Santa Maria della Piazza**, which has 5th and 6th century mosaic pavements and a *Madonna & Child with Four Saints* by Lorenzo Lotto.

Places to Stay

Many people tend to bunk down in the ferry terminal, although the city has a good range of accommodation and many cheap hotels. The *Albergo Fiore* (☎ 4 33 90), opposite the train station at Piazza Rosselli 24, has singles/doubles for L25,000/35,000. The *Albergo Dorico* (☎ 4 27 61), a couple of doors away at Via Flaminia 8, has rooms for about the same price. The *Albergo Astor* (☎ 20 27 76), Corso Mazzini 142, has rooms from L35,000/50,000. The three-star *Fortuna* (☎ 4 26 65), also in Piazza Rosselli, has rooms from L60,000/90,000.

Places to Eat
The *produce market* at Corso Mazzini 130 has fresh fruit, vegetables and other food. *Osteria del Pozzo*, Via Bonda 2, just of the Piazza del Plebiscito, has good, reasonably priced food and a meal could cost L16,000. The *Osteria No 1*, Via Marconi 3, features some local specialities and a meal will cost around L15,000. *La Cantineta*, Via Gramsci 1, is a trattoria near the old centre, where pasta dishes start at L6000.

Getting There & Away
Bus Buses depart from Piazza Cavour and also from the train station for cities in the Marches. Reni (☎ 20 25 96) operates services to Numana, Senigallia, Fano and Rimini as well as Milan. Marozzi (☎ 0734-859118) runs services between Ancona and Rome.

Train Ancona is on the Bologna-Lecce train line and is thus easily accessible from major places throughout Italy. It is also directly linked to Rome, via Foligno in Umbria. For information, contact the station on ☎ 4 39 33.

Car & Motorbike Ancona is on the A14, which links Bologna and Bari. The ss16 coastal road runs parallel to the autostrada and is a more pleasant alternative. The ss76 connects Ancona with Perugia and Rome. There is some free parking near the ferry terminal, and the Garage Fortuna, in front of the train station, is open 24 hours a day.

Boat All ferry operators have booths at the Stazione Marittima, off Largo Dogana. Here you can pick up timetables and price lists, and make bookings. Remember that timetables are always subject to change and that prices fluctuate dramatically with the season. Most lines offer 10% discount on round-trip fares. Prices listed here are for one-way deck class in the high season:

Minoan Lines (☎ 5 67 89) operates about five ferries a week to Igoumenitsa, Corfu, Cefalonia and Patras (Greece) for L82,000, and Kusadasi (Turkey) for L155,000.

Karageorgis Lines (☎ 20 10 80) has four ferries a week to Patras for L82,000.

Marlines (☎ 5 00 62) operates several services a week to Corfu, Igoumenitsa, Patras (L74,000 each), Heraklion (L111,000), Rhodes (L152,000), and Limassol in Cyprus (L210,000).

Strintzis Lines (☎ 286 44 31) goes to Corfu, Igoumenitsa and Patras (L82,000).

Adriatica (☎ 20 49 15) operates several services a week to Split, Zadar and Dubrovnik in Croatia (L88,000); check at its desk or with the APT for an update on current services.

Jadrolinija (☎ 20 28 05) operates regular services to Zadar and Split (L58,000); check at its desk for an update on services.

Anek Lines (☎ 20 20 33) operates several services each week to Corfu, Igoumenitsa and Patras (L82,000), and charges L172,000 for a small car.

European Seaways (☎ 207 31 92) operates regular services to Igoumenitsa and Corfu (L74,000) where you can make connections for Paxi, Cefalonia, Patras and Athens.

Turisthotel (☎ 20 27 73) operates regular hydrofoil services to Bozava and Zadar in Croatia for L65,000; call ahead or check with the APT for current schedules.

Getting Around
ATMA bus No 1 connects the train station with the ferry terminal and the city centre. For a taxi, call ☎ 4 33 21.

FRASASSI CAVES
About 40 km inland from Ancona, along the ss76, are the incredible Frasassi Caves, the largest discovered cave complex in Europe and the one of the largest in the world. Discovered only in 1971, the caves extend for 18 km of spectacular stalactites and stalagmites. A 1.5-km trail has been carefully carved, and the effect is like walking through an immense opera or theatre set. The first

chamber you enter, the Ancona Abyss, is almost 200 metres high, 180 metres wide and 120 metres long, and could easily accommodate Milan's Duomo.

Take the ss76 from Ancona, or the train from Falconara Marittima, near Ancona, for Genga, where buses connect with the caves. Don't be alarmed at the sideshow array of stalls in the car park, it is just Italians cashing in on one of the country's greatest natural formations. Buy your L15,000 ticket (the price is worth the experience) from the ticket office in the car park and walk one km to the cave's entrance for the 90-minute odyssey. The Consorzio Frasassi (☎ 0732-9 00 80) manages the caves and can assist with tourist information.

URBINO

One of the most beautiful and harmonious towns in all of Italy, Urbino enjoyed a period of great splendour under the Montefeltro family from the 12th century onwards. It reached its zenith under Duke Federico da Montefeltro, who brought some of the greatest Renaissance artists and architects to construct and decorate his palace and other parts of the town. The architects Bramante, who was born in Urbino, and Francesco di Giorgio were among his favourites, as were the painters Piero della Francesca, who developed his theories on mathematical perspective in Urbino, Paolo Uccello, Justus of Ghent and Giovanni Santi, father of Raffaello d'Urbino, the great Raphael, who was born in the city.

Duke Federico lost his right eye and had his nose broken in a tournament and subsequently would only be portrayed in profile. The most famous portrait of him was painted in 1466 by Piero della Francesca and hangs in the Uffizi in Florence.

The city can be difficult to reach by public transport, but it should not be missed. The area north of the city, particularly the road to San Marino and up into Emilia-Romagna, is particularly beautiful, and there are plenty of hotels in small townships along the way. The town of San Leo has been the site of a fortress since Roman times, used most recently by the Fascists as an aircraft-spotting post during WW II.

Orientation

Buses arrive at Borgo Mercatale on the walled city's western edge. From there it is a short walk along Via G Mazzini to Piazza della Repubblica and then along Via Veneto for Piazza Duca Federico and the giant Piazza Rinascimento. If you are driving, you will most likely arrive at Piazzale Roma on the city's northern edge. Via Raffaello connects the piazzale with Piazza della Repubblica.

Information

Tourist Office The APT (☎ 0722-24 41) is at Piazza Duca Federico 35, and opens Monday to Saturday from 9 am to 1 pm and 3.30 to 6.30 pm.

Post & Telecommunications The main post office is at Via Bramante 18 and opens Monday to Saturday from 8.30 am to 5.30 pm. The postal code for the town centre is 61029.

SIP telephones are at Via Puccinotti 4, next to the tourist office and opposite the Metropolitana Basilica, and open from 8 am to 10 pm. The telephone code for Urbino is 0722.

Emergency For police emergency, call ☎ 113. The police headquarters (☎ 26 45) are at Piazza della Repubblica 1, and the Ospedale Civile (☎ 32 93 51) is at Via B da Montefeltro. There is a pharmacy at Piazza della Repubblica 9.

Things to See

Pick up a map from the tourist office and make your way across Piazza Duca Federico for the city's cathedral, also known as the **Metropolitana Basilica**, rebuilt in the early 1800s in the neoclassical style after an earthquake destroyed Francesco di Giorgio Martini's original Renaissance building. The interior is far more enticing than the ordinary exterior, notably for artworks by the likes of

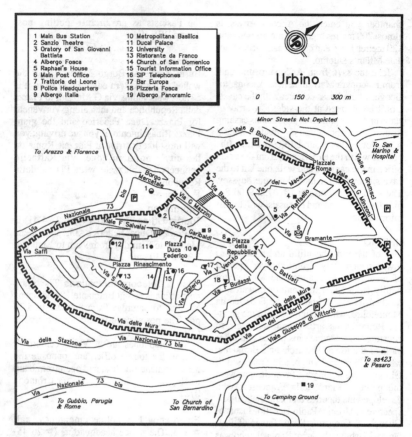

Urbino

1 Main Bus Station
2 Sanzio Theatre
3 Oratory of San Giovanni Battista
4 Albergo Fosca
5 Raphael's House
6 Main Post Office
7 Trattoria del Leone
8 Police Headquarters
9 Albergo Italia
10 Metropolitana Basilica
11 Ducal Palace
12 University
13 Ristorante da Franco
14 Church of San Domenico
15 Tourist Information Office
16 SIP Telephones
17 Bar Europa
18 Pizzeria Fosca
19 Albergo Panoramic

Minor Streets Not Depicted

Andrea da Bologna and Barocci, whose *Last Supper* is outstanding.

Next to the church is the magnificent **Ducal Palace**, designed by Laurana and completed in 1482. The best view is from Corso Garibaldi to the north, from where you can appreciate the size of the building and see its towers and loggias.

Enter the palace from Piazza Duca Federico for the **National Gallery of the Marches**, one of Italy's finest galleries. In Room 9 is a remarkable portrait of Federico da Montefeltro and his son Guidobaldo, possibly by Justus of Ghent or Berruguete. In one of the rooms known as the Ducal

Apartments is Piero della Francesca's *Flagellation*, regarded as one of the greatest paintings of the Renaissance. The collection also features two Titians – the *Last Supper* and *Resurrection* – and farther on is Raphael's *Portrait of a Lady*, which is behind glass and hard to see. Along the way you will pass through Federico's Studiolo, the duke's study, a masterpiece of inlaid wood panelling where cupboard doors seem to be hanging open, books seem real and a letter appears to be lying on a desk.

The palace also houses the **Archaeological Museum**, on the far side of the harmonious Cortile d'Onore, the palace's courtyard. The collection is worth a look-in, although it offers nothing spectacular. The gallery and museum are open from 9 am to 7 pm daily, except Monday when they close at 2 pm, and Sunday when they close at 1 pm. Entry is L8000.

Opposite the palace is the medieval **Church of San Domenico**, notable for its lunette, the panel above the 15th century doorway by Luca della Robbia. North of Piazza della Repubblica is **Raphael's House** at Via Raffaello 57, where the master was born. It is open from 9 am to 1 pm and 3 to 7 pm daily, except Sunday when it closes at 1 pm. Entry is L4000.

The 14th century **Oratory of San Giovanni Battista** on Via Barocci features brightly coloured frescoes by Lorenzo and Giacomo Salimbeni. It's open from 10 am to midday and 3 to 5 pm, except Sunday when it closes at 12.30 pm. Entry is L2000. The **Church of San Bernardino**, outside the city walls to the east along Viale Giuseppe di Vittorio, houses the mausoleum of the Dukes of Urbino which was designed by Bramante and Francesco di Giorgio.

There is a concert season at the Sanzio Theatre from May to September. Pick up a brochure at the tourist office.

Language Courses

The city's university offers an intensive course in language and culture for foreigners during August at a cost of L400,000, and can arrange accommodation at the rate of L220,000 for the month. For information, contact the Segreteria dell'Università, Via Saffi 2, Urbino 61029, or call ☎ 30 52 26.

Places to Stay

Urbino's university means that many cheap beds are taken up by students during the school year. The tourist office has a full list of private rooms. *Campeggio Pineta* (☎ 47 10), the only camping ground, is two km east of the city in San Donato. The *Albergo Fosca* (☎ 32 96 22), Via Raffaello 67, has singles/doubles for L30,000/42,000. *Albergo Italia* (☎ 27 01), Corso Garibaldi 32, is next to the Ducal Palace and has rooms

for L33,000/41,000. *Albergo Panoramic* (☎ 26 00) has rooms from L28,000/45,000.

Places to Eat

There are numerous bars around Piazza della Repubblica in the town centre and near the Ducal Palace which sell good panini. Try *Il Cortigiano* in Piazza Rinascimento, or *Pizzeria Galli*, Via Vittorio Veneto 19, for takeaway pizza by the slice. *Bar Europa*, Via Vittorio Veneto 34, also has pizza by the slice. *Ristorante da Franco*, just off Piazza Rinascimento next to the university, has a self-service section with a set-price lunch for L12,000 in the low season, which jumps to L16,000 in summer. *Trattoria del Leone*, Via Cesare Battisti 5, offers some traditional dishes and a meal will cost L20,000. *Pizzeria Fosca*, Via F Budassi 64, serves pizzas from L6000.

Getting There & Away

The city's bus station (☎ 28 26) is in Borgo Mercatale. SAPUM operates frequent services between Urbino and Pesaro, and to Arezzo and smaller towns in the region. Check with the APT or consult the board under the portico near Café Belpassi for bus schedules. Buses operate to Rome twice a day. There is no train station in Urbino, but the city is connected by bus to the closest train station at Fossato di Vico, on the Rome-Ancona line.

By car, a superstrada and the ss423 connect the city with Pesaro, and the ss73 connects the city with the ss3 for Rome. Car parks are outside all city gates and charge L1000 an hour.

Getting Around

All cars are banned from the walled city, with the exception of residents. Small shuttle buses operate between Piazzale Roma, Borgo Mercatale and Piazza Rinascimento. A taxi service (☎ 25 50) operates from Piazza della Repubblica.

PESARO

Like other resort towns on the Adriatic, Pesaro offers an expanse of beach, the remains of a medieval centre and not much else. However, its position as a regional capital ensures good transportation links, especially to the marvellous city of Urbino, an hour's bus ride inland.

Orientation

The main train station is at the southern edge of the centre, away from the beach. Walk along Viale del Risorgimento, through Piazza Lazzarini and continue for Piazza del Popolo, the town's main square. Via Rossini takes you to Piazza della Libertà and the waterfront.

Information

The town is overloaded with tourist offices, none of them very helpful. The APT (☎ 0721-6 36 90) at Via Rossini 41 near Piazza del Popolo is open Monday to Saturday from 8 am to 1 pm and 3 to 6 pm. Smaller offices are in Piazza della Libertà (☎ 0721-6 93 41) and at the train station (☎ 0721-6 83 78), but both open only in summer.

The main post office is in Piazza del Popolo and opens Monday to Saturday from 8.30 am to 6 pm. The postal code for the town centre is 61100. SIP telephones are in Piazzale Matteotti, south-east of Piazza del Popolo, and open daily from 8 am to 8.30 pm. The telephone code for Pesaro is 0721.

For police emergencies, call ☎ 113, or else contact the police headquarters (☎ 3 39 91) in Piazza Cinelli, near the train station. The main hospital (☎ 3 14 44) is in the same square.

Things to See

The 15th century **Ducal Palace**, dominating Piazza del Popolo, housed the ruling Della Rovere family. Today it houses bureaucracy and is closed to the public. You can enjoy the splendid windows by Domenico Rosselli, which grace its façade.

Head north-west along Corso XI Settembre for Via Toschi Mosca and the town's **Municipal Museum**, which also houses the town's picture gallery. The museum component features a worthy collection of Italian ceramics, while the gallery's prize is

Giovanni Bellini's magnificent altarpiece depicting the *Coronation of the Virgin*. The complex opens Tuesday to Saturday from 9 am to 7.30 pm, Sunday to 1 pm, and entry is L5000. The **Church of Sant'Agostino** on Corso XI Settembre features intricate 15th century inlaid-wood choir stalls.

Via Branca leads from Piazza del Popolo to Piazza Olivieri and the **Rossini Conservatory**, dedicated to one of Italy's greatest composers, who was born in the town. The small museum opens irregular hours, so check with the APT. Behind the museum is the **Oliverano Archaeological Museum**, which contains many finds from the local area, including a child's tomb from the Iron Age, complete with miniature utensils, such as eating implements. Apply for entry at the adjoining library, which has a collection of ancient coins, manuscripts and medals.

In honour of Rossini, the town hosts a series of concerts each August at the theatre bearing his name in Piazza Lazzarini. The APT has programmes.

Activities

The Società Canottieri Pesaro (☎ 40 00 10), Calata Caio Duilio 103, can help with the hire of sailboards and canoes, while the Club Nautico (☎ 2 56 57), Molo Strada Tra i due Porti 20, can arrange sailing lessons. If you want to go horse riding, the Agenzia Ippica (☎ 3 01 58), Via Venturini 4, can set you in the right direction, as can the Club Alpino Italiano (☎ 3 48 05), Via Bramante 21, if you want to go trekking in the Marches.

If you want relatively uncrowded beaches, then the Strada Panoramica Adriatica, the road north from Pesaro to Cattolica in Emilia-Romagna, will take you to them. The town of Gradara can be as crowded as Pesaro, but the smaller fishing towns of Castel di Mezzo and Fiorenzuola are appealing and quiet, even during summer.

Places to Stay

The town's hotel association, the Associazione Pesarese Albergatori (☎ 6 79 59), has an office at Via G Rossini 41 and will help you find a room. The APT has a lengthy list of private rooms, although most are more expensive than hotels.

The closest camping grounds are about five km south of the town centre at Fosso Sejore. The *Marinella* (☎ 5 57 95) on the ss16 has sites for L6000 a person and L6000 a tent, as does the nearby *Norina* (☎ 5 57 92). The IYHF *Ardizio* hostel (☎ 5 57 98), Strada Panoramica dell'Ardizio, is also at Fosso Sejore and has bed and breakfast for L14,000. Take the AMANUP bus to Fano for the camping grounds and the hostel.

The *Albergo Splendour* (☎ 3 10 77), Via Romagnosi 39, has singles/doubles for L20,000/28,000 in the low season and L30,000/45,000 during summer. *Guglielmo Tell* (☎ 3 24 45), near the waterfront at Viale Trento 195, has rooms from 25,000/37,000, and the *Aurora* (☎ 6 18 12), Viale Trieste 147, even closer to the water, has rooms from L35,000/55,000. The *Excelsior* (☎ 3 27 20) on the beach at Lungomare N Sauro, has rooms from L50,000/68,000.

Places to Eat

There is a produce market and several food shops at Via Branca 5, off Piazza del Popolo. *Ristorante C'era una Volta*, Via Cattaneo 26, is a good pizzeria, with pizzas from L6000. *Taverna delle Sfingi*, Viale Trieste 219, is one of the better restaurants near the beach, and a meal could cost L20,000. *La Tartaruga*, Viale Trieste 31, serves some typical dishes and a meal will also cost about L20,000.

Getting There & Away

The main bus station is in Piazza Matteotti. AMANUP buses (☎ 3 47 68) connect the town with Gradara, Cattolica, Carpegna, Fosso Sejore, Fano, Ancona, Senigallia and most small towns in the region. They also operate an hourly service to Urbino from 7.15 am until 7.45 pm.

The town is on the Bologna-Lecce train line and you can connect for Rome by changing trains at Falconara, just before Ancona; for information, call ☎ 3 30 09. If you're coming by car, the town is on the A14 autostrada as well as the ss16.

Getting Around

Most AMANUP buses connect the train station with Piazza Matteotti, including bus Nos 1, 3, 4, 5, CD and CS. For a taxi in the centre, call ☎ 3 14 30, and at the station, ☎ 3 11 11.

FANO

On the ss16 and A14, Fano is one of the most popular resorts on the Adriatic and, while it has several reminders of its origins as a Roman city, it is the beaches that draw the tourists. The APT (☎ 0721-80 35 34) is at Viale Cesare Battisti 10 in Fano, and other offices are at the more pleasant and less touristed towns of Torrette (☎ 0721-88 47 79) and Marotta (☎ 0721-9 65 91).

The only problem with Fano is that accommodation can be pricey, so you are better off staying in Pesaro, or at the camping grounds, details of which are available at the APT. The *Fano* (☎ 0721-80 26 52), is by the sea near the town.

SENIGALLIA

Senigallia's main attraction is the aptly named Spiaggia di Velluto (Velvet Beach), reputedly one of the Adriatic's best beaches. However, the city also boasts the incredible Roveresca Fortress, built by the architect of Urbino's Ducal Palace, Luciano Laurana, for Federico da Montefeltro's son-in-law. The austere exterior belies a plush Renaissance interior, well worth a visit if you have a spare hour or two. Avoid the city in summer, or book a room well in advance.

The city's AAST tourist office (☎ 071 792 27 25) in the Palazzo del Turismo, Piazzale Morandi 2, is quite helpful, while the hotel and camping association (☎ 6 53 43), Via Brofferio 4, will gladly assist you in finding lodging in one of the city's 50,000 beds and camping spots.

The *Helios* camping ground (☎ 69 87 31), Lungomare Italia 3, has sites from L3500 a person and L5000 a tent. The *Liana* (☎ 6 52 06), Lungomare Leonardo da Vinci 54, is about the same price. The *Albergo Simona* (☎ 6 04 28), Via Pisa 4, is one of the cheapest hotels in town, with singles/doubles from

L27,000/45,000. The slightly more up-market *Fano* (☎ 792 35 13), Lungomare Mameli 110, has rooms from L32,000/50,000.

Autolinee Bucci buses (☎ 6 03 32), Via Carducci 24, operate along the ss16 road to Ancona, Fano and Pesaro.

MACERATA

This bustling provincial capital is one of Italy's best kept secrets. Situated atop a hill between the Potenza River valley to the north and the Chienti River in the south, Macerata is every bit as impressive as Umbrian and Tuscan hill towns but lacks the tourists, and makes a good base for exploration into the surrounding countryside – some of the Marches' most picturesque.

The city's Lyric Festival (Stagione Lirica) is one of the country's most prestigious musical events, attracting big names to the superb open-air Arena Sferisterio.

Orientation & Information

ATAC bus Nos 2, 6 and 8 connect the train station, south of the old centre, with the massive Giardini Diaz and the Porta Romana, the main entrance to the city, and also to Piazza della Libertà, the city's main piazza. The city is small and easily navigated on foot. Cars are permitted in the centre and most piazzas double as car parks.

The main APT (☎ 0733-23 48 07) is at Via Garibaldi 87, above the Standa supermarket, and opens Monday to Friday from 9 am to midday and 4 to 6 pm. A second office is in Piazza della Libertà, open about the same hours, although it is closed Monday and Sunday. The city's telephone code is 0733. For all emergencies, call ☎ 113.

Things to See & Do

Piazza della Libertà boasts one of the city's finest buildings, the 16th century Renaissance **Loggia dei Mercanti**, built by the Farnese pope Paul III. In the courtyard of the town hall are archaeological remains from Helvia Ricina, a Roman town five km from Macerata, which was destroyed by the Goths.

Some of the city's finest cafés, bars and shops are along Corso della Repubblica, a grand boulevard where locals take their late-afternoon strolls. At the end of the corso is Piazza Vittorio Veneto and the city's **Municipal Picture Gallery**, with a good collection of early Renaissance works, including a *Madonna* by Carlo Crivelli and a 15th century panel of the *Madonna with Angels & Saints* by Pietro di Montepulciano. The gallery opens Tuesday to Sunday from 9 am to midday and 4.30 to 7.30 pm.

Just off Piazza Mazzini is the neoclassical **Arena Sferisterio**, an impressive venue originally used for sport and now the domain of the city's Lyric Festival held each July and August. The city's rather ordinary Baroque cathedral is unfinished and worth visiting only if you have some spare time.

Places to Stay & Eat

The city's university, one of the country's largest, and a transient worker population mean that most hotels in the city have permanent bookings, and some do not accept tourist bookings. Try the *Arena* (☎ 23 09 31), Vicolo Sferisterio 16, with singles/doubles from L34,000/50,000. The *Arcadia* (☎ 23 59 61), Via Ricci 134, has rooms from L50,000/80,000.

If you are only here for lunch, *Paninoteca Funny Bread*, Via Roma 4, has cheap panini and pizza by the slice. *Pizzeria Da Alberto*, Viale Don Bosco 14, has pizzas from L6000, and *Da Secondo*, Via Pescheria Vecchia 26, is one of the city's best restaurants, where a meal could cost L30,000.

Getting There & Away

The city is served by several bus companies operating services to Rome, Ancona, Ascoli Piceno, Civitanova Marche and Foligno. CONTRAM (☎ 24 02), Piazza Neghelli, is one of the main companies. The main train station (☎ 29 21 12) is in Via Corridoni. The ss77 connects the city with the A14 to the east and with roads for Rome in the west.

ASCOLI PICENO

Many legends surround the founding of this

town in the southern Marches, the most questionable being that a woodpecker led settlers to the site. Most probably settled by the Piceni tribe in the 6th century BC, Ascoli Piceno came under Roman control in 268 BC. The old centre is bounded by the Tronto River to the north and the Castellano River to the south, and is dominated by nearby mountains leading up into the Apennines.

Orientation & Information

The train station is in the newer section of the town, a short walk from the old town centre over the Ponte Maggiore and the Castellano River. After crossing the river, walk along Corso Vittorio Emanuele, past the cathedral, and head north along any of the small streets for the central Piazza del Popolo.

Corso Mazzini leads off from the northwest corner for the main APT tourist office (☎ 0736-25 81 15) at No 229, which opens Monday to Friday from 9 am to 1 pm and 3.30 to 6 pm, and Saturday from 8 am to midday. A small office opens daily in Piazza del Popolo (☎ 0736-25 52 50) but only from April to September.

The main post office is at Via Crispi, east along Corso Mazzini from Piazza del Popolo, open Monday to Saturday from 8.30 am to 7.30 pm. The postal code for the town centre is 63100.

Telephones are at the post office, or else in bars around the main piazzas. The telephone code for Ascoli Piceno is 0736. For all emergencies, call ☎ 113.

Things to See & Do

Piazza del Popolo is the town's central square and features the town's finest architecture. The 13th century **People's Captain's Palace** burned to the ground in 1535 during a bitter family rivalry and was rebuilt about 10 years later. The statue of Pope Paul III was erected as a tribute to the pope who brought peace to the town. At the piazza's eastern end is the **Church of San Francesco**, started in 1262 and featuring a 15th century wooden crucifix and 16th century works by Cola dell'Amatrice. To the

south of the church is the **Loggia dei Mercanti**, built in the 16th century and showing strong Tuscan influence.

The town's **Old Quarter** (Vecchio Quartiere) stretches from Corso Mazzini to the Tronto River, and its main street is the picturesque Via delle Torri, which eventually becomes Via Solestà. The **Church of San Pietro Martire** dates from the 14th century and is dedicated to the saint who founded the Dominican community at Ascoli. The **Ercolani Tower** in Via Soderini, behind San Pietro, is, at 40 metres, the tallest of the town's feudal towers. Abutting the tower is the **Palazzetto Longobardo**, a 12th century Lombard-Romanesque defensive house, which is now the town's youth hostel. Just north is the well-preserved **Ponte di Solestà**, a single-arched Roman bridge.

South of Piazza del Popolo, in Piazza Arringo, is the **cathedral**, a lavish example of Baroque architecture which has been embellished in a less than tasteful manner. It houses Carlo Crivelli's best work, a *Virgin & Saints*, in the Cappella del Sacramento. The baptistry next to the cathedral has remained unchanged since it was constructed in the 12th century.

The **picture gallery** in the Communal Palace is the Marches' largest gallery and one of its most important, featuring works by Van Dyck, Titian and Crivelli, and even a Turner. The gallery opens Tuesday to Saturday from 9 am to 1 pm, Sunday from 10 am to 1 pm, and entrance is L4000. The town's **Archaeological Museum** across the piazza has a collection of implements used by the ancient Ascoli tribe. It is open about the same hours as the gallery and is free.

The town's major festival is the Quintana, a medieval pageant each July that attracts hundreds of locals dressed in traditional costume for jousting, parades and so on.

Places to Stay & Eat

The town's IYHF *Ostello de' Longobardi* (☎ 25 90 07) at Via Soderni 26 charges L10,000 for a bed. Call ahead because the hostel tends to close for lengthy periods. The *Albergo Nuovo Picchio* (☎ 5 10 51), Via

Cesare Battisti 11, has singles/doubles from L20,000/30,000. The *Hotel Pavoni* (☎ 34 25 75), Via Navicella 135, is a short distance from the town centre but can be reached by bus No 3 from Piazza Arringo. Rooms are L26,000/42,000.

Pasticceria Sestili, Corso Mazzini 175, off Piazza del Popolo, has cheap panini and alcohol. *Pizzeria al Teatro*, Via delle Ette Sogli 1, has pasta from L5000 and pizzas from L4000, and is open late. *Ristorante L'Orchidea*, Largo dei Cataldi, serves typical dishes and a meal will cost L20,000.

There is an outdoor market in Piazza San Francesco, near Piazza del Popolo, every morning except Sunday.

Getting There & Away

Buses leave from Viale Alcide de Gasperi, near Via Alighieri. Bucci (☎ 0721-3 20 41) operates services to Rome and Urbino, and ATAM (☎ 32 26 44) runs buses to Arezzo and Ancona. Mazzuca (☎ 40 22 67) serves Montemonaco and Amandola, near the Monti Sibillini range. A spur train line connects Ascoli Piceno with Porto d'Ascoli and San Benedetto del Tronto on the Adriatic, which is on the Bologna-Lecce line. By car, the ss4 connects the town with Rome and the coast.

MONTI SIBILLINI

Located in the lower south-west portion of the region, and stretching into neighbouring Umbria, the Monti Sibillini range is one of this area's greatest assets and one of the most beautiful stretches of the Apennines. Dotted with caves and walking trails, the Monti Sibillini also offer a wide array of sporting activities such as hang-gliding and horse riding. To reach the range, take the ss4 from Ascoli Piceno and follow the signs. Buses connect the range with Ascoli Piceno and various cities throughout the Marches. See also the Valnerina section in Umbria for details about hang-gliding and how to get to the mountains from Umbria.

Information

If you are approaching the area from the south, stop at the AAST tourist office in Acquasanta Terme (☎ 0736-80 12 91), Via Salaria 2, and ask for information prepared by the Consorzio Turistico Monti Sibillini. If you are approaching from the north, along the ss78 from Ancona, stop at the AAST in Sarnano (☎ 0733-65 71 95). Both offices can provide limited walking and climbing information.

Activities

Amandola makes a good base to start exploring the area, but it lacks cheap accommodation. It is one of the prettiest villages in the Marches and is just north of Montefortino, which makes a good base for walking. Montefortino is reasonably close to the Monti Sibillini's serious walking areas, around Montemonaco, which is at the base of Mt Sibilla.

Montemonaco is an out-of-the-way town and not easily reached by public transport, although you'll be surprised at the number of tourists in summer, there for the Gola dell'Infernaccio (Gorge of Hell), one of the easiest and most spectacular walks in the Marches. The range is dotted with mountain refuges and also offers reasonable skiing during winter.

Places to Stay

There is a camping ground just south of Montefortino at Cerrentana. The *Montespino* (☎ 0736-85 92 38) has sites for L5000 a person and L5000 a tent, and opens only in summer. Go straight to Montemonaco for accommodation, as there are quite a few rooms at good rates. The *Rifugio della Montagna* (☎ 0736-96 03 27), in Foce, just near the town, has singles/doubles from L18,000/38,000. The *Albergo Sibilla* (☎ 0736-96 01 44), Via Roma 51, has rooms for slightly more. The *Albergo Simoni* (☎ 0736-9 62 88), Via Campo Sportivo, in the town of Comunanza, near Amandola, has rooms for the bargain rates of L8000/12,000. Call ahead, because it is a small and very popular hotel.

Abruzzo

A region once famous for its witches and snake charmers, Abruzzo still has an air of mystery. Together with the neighbouring region of Molise, it is probably the last area of Italy which has not been inundated by tourists. Certainly neither region is as rich in artistic and cultural heritage as other parts of the country. Instead, the attraction here is the unspoiled countryside and the wild beauty of the region's mountainous terrain – notably the Gran Sasso d'Italia mountain range with the Corno Grande, at 2914 metres the highest mountain in the Apennines, and the Abruzzo National Park, where wolves and bears, among the last in Italy, roam protected. Even if you don't want to explore the region's mountains, visit Abruzzo for the pleasant historic towns of L'Aquila and Sulmona and, if you have the time, some of its isolated hill towns.

Until 1963, Abruzzo and Molise formed one region which was referred to in the plural as *gli Abruzzi*, the Abruzzi, and the term is still sometimes used to describe the geographical area which includes Molise. The region is very earthquake-prone and was devastated by a massive quake in 1915 which left 30,000 people dead.

In ancient times Abruzzo was noted for its witches, wizards and snake charmers – members of a tribe known as the Marsi, who lived in the area around what is now Avezzano. The practice of snake charming persisted into the 20th century and, even today, in the mountain village of Cocullo, near Sulmona, there is a bizarre annual religious festival which features the use of live snakes.

Abruzzo has traditionally been a region of farmers and pastoralists, and sheep farming still plays an important role in the local economy. One of the region's most productive agricultural areas is the Fucino Plain, south of L'Aquila, which was created by draining the vast Fucino Lake in the late 19th century. The project was undertaken by Prince Torlonia, on the condition that he would have title to the land, and was completed during the Fascist period. It was not until the 1950s that the Italian government took over the plain and handed it to local peasants as smallholdings.

The ancient Romans were the first to attempt to drain the lake. In what was both a remarkable and disastrous feat of engineering under the orders of Emperor Claudius, the Romans constructed a tunnel about 10 km long to drain the lake into a neighbouring valley. Unfortunately, when the outlet tunnel was opened it proved too small for the massive volume of water in the lake and thousands of spectators, including the emperor himself, almost drowned.

L'AQUILA

Certainly the most appealing city to visit in Abruzzo, L'Aquila is overshadowed by the Gran Sasso d'Italia mountain range, which has the Corno Grande, the tallest peak in the Apennines. L'Aquila has been hit many times by earthquakes, but enough monuments remain to make it an interesting city to explore. Emperor Frederick II founded the town in 1240, it is said, by drawing together the citizens of 99 villages. Whether historically correct or not, the number 99 became a symbol for the town. Its citizens established 99 churches and 99 piazzas, as well as a fountain with 99 spouts. Earthquakes have destroyed most of the churches and piazzas, but the medieval fountain survives and, every evening, the town-hall bell chimes 99 times.

Orientation

L'Aquila's train station is some distance from the historical centre, but regular urban buses (Nos 1 and 3) will take you uphill to the town centre. Get off in Corso Federico II, the continuation of the old town's main street, Corso Vittorio Emanuele. The intercity bus terminal is in Piazza Battaglione Alpini L'Aquila, and from there it's a short walk down Corso Vittorio Emanuele to the tourist offices and, farther along the Corso, to Piazza del Duomo and the centre of town.

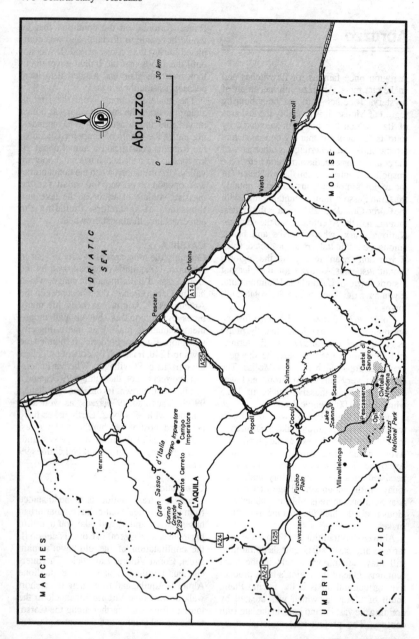

Information

Tourist Offices There is an EPT information office (☎ 0862-41 08 08) at Piazza Santa Maria Paganica, to the right off Corso V Emanuele as you head down from the bus terminal. It is open Monday to Friday from 8 am to 1.50 pm and 4 to 6 pm, Saturday to 1 pm, and can provide information about the town as well as the Gran Sasso range. The AAST tourist office (☎ 0862-41 08 59) at Corso Vittorio Emanuele 49, near Piazza del Duomo, is open Monday to Friday from 9 am to 1 pm and 3 to 6.45 pm, Saturday to 1 pm only. Here you can pick up a map and useful information about the town.

Post & Telecommunications The main post office is in Piazza del Duomo. The postal code for central L'Aquila is 67100.

There is an SIP public telephone office at Via XX Settembre 77, open Monday to Saturday from 8.30 am to 1 pm and 3.30 to 7 pm, Sunday from 9 am to 12.30 pm and 3.30 to 6.30 pm. The town's telephone code is 0862.

Emergency For immediate police attendance, call ☎ 113. The public hospital, the Ospedale San Salvatore (☎ 77 81), is north of the old town centre along Corso Vittorio Emanuele.

Things to See

Start at the 16th century **castle** off Piazza Battaglione Alpini, built by the Spanish after a rebellion by the locals. The square structure, with its massive bastions, houses the **National Museum of Abruzzo**. The museum has a good collection of local religious artworks, but its main attraction is the skeleton of a mammoth, found near the town in the early 1950s.

Off Corso Vittorio Emanuele, in Piazza San Bernardino, is the 15th century **Basilica of San Bernardino**. It has a grand façade and a magnificent Baroque wooden ceiling. The decorations of St Bernardino's mausoleum were the work of local sculptor, Silvestro dell'Aquila. St Bernardino, orig-

inally of Siena, spent his last years in L'Aquila, where he died.

The other church of interest in L'Aquila is the Romanesque **Basilica of Santa Maria di Collemaggio**, south-east of the town centre along Viale di Collemaggio. It has a memorable façade of pink and white marble with rose windows. The basilica was built at the instigation of a hermit, Pietro da Morrone. The 80-year-old recluse was elected pope in 1294, after the College of Cardinals had for two years failed to reach agreement on a successor to Pope Nicholas IV. Pietro da Morrone became Pope Celestine V, but unfortunately this unworldly and trusting man was prey to the manipulations of courtiers and politicians and was eventually forced to abdicate. Regarded as a threat by his successor, Pope Boniface VIII, Celestine was imprisoned and died. As founder of the Celestine Order he was canonised seven years later and his tomb is inside the basilica.

The **Fountain of the 99 Spouts** is near the station, behind the Porta Rivera. Constructed in the late 13th century, the fountain features 99 stone masks, which have spouted water continuously over the centuries. It provided the town's main water source and local women went there to wash their clothes until after WW II.

There is an annual season of concerts from October to May, run by the Società Aquilana dei Concerti. The AAST tourist office can provide information.

Places to Stay

Unfortunately, hotel closures in recent years have left L'Aquila with only one budget establishment. All other hotels in town are in the three-star category and therefore charge at least L100,000 a double. The *Pensione Aurora* (☎ 2 20 53), just off Piazza del Duomo at Via Cimino 21, has singles/doubles for L26,000/36,000. The hotel is reluctant to take bookings, but try anyway. Otherwise, plan to arrive early to claim a room. The *Hotel Duomo* (☎ 41 08 93), Via Dragonetti 6, the next street along from Via Cimino, has rooms with private bathroom, phone and TV for L80,000/120,000. The

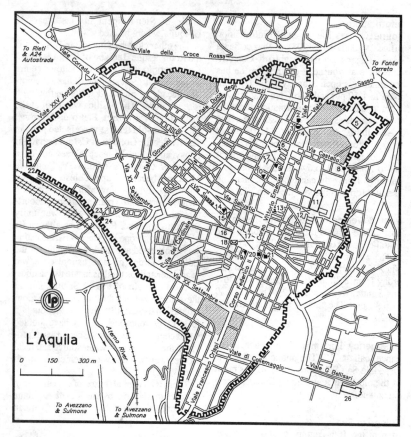

L'Aquila

Hotel Castello (☎ 41 91 47) in Piazza Battaglione Alpini has rooms with the same facilities for around the same price.

Places to Eat

Traditional local dishes include *maccheroni alla chitarra*, thick macaroni cut with a characteristic instrument resembling a guitar, and lamb, either roasted or grilled.

At *Trattoria San Biagio*, Piazza San Biagio, along Via Sassa from Piazza del Duomo, you can eat a good-quality meal for around L20,000. Another good choice for a low-priced meal is *Trattoria del Giaguaro*, Piazza Santa Maria Paganica 4. *Ristorante*

La Mimosa, Via Navelli 22, is more expensive at around L35,000 for a full meal, but offers excellent food. Another, more expensive option is *Ristorante Renato*, Via dell'Indipendenza 9.

Getting There & Away

ARPA buses for Rome and Pescara leave from Piazza Battaglione Alpini – for information about buses from Rome, go to the EPT tourist office in Via Parigi, Rome. ARPA buses also connect L'Aquila with Avezzano and Sulmona. By train, the town is accessible from Rome via Sulmona or Terni, and from Pescara via Sulmona. From

■ PLACES TO STAY

2 Hotel Castello
20 Hotel Duomo
21 Pensione Aurora

▼ PLACES TO EAT

9 Trattoria del Giaguaro
10 Ristorante La Mimosa
14 Trattoria San Biagio
19 Ristorante Renato

OTHER

1 Hospital
3 Intercity Bus Stop
4 Piazza Battaglione Alpini L'Aquila
5 Castle
6 EPT Tourist Office
7 Piazza Santa Maria Paganica
8 Porta Castello
11 Basilica of San Bernardino
12 Piazza San Bernardino
13 AAST Tourist Office
15 Piazza San Biagio
16 Duomo
17 Piazza del Duomo
18 Post Office
22 Train Station
23 Porta Rivera
24 Fountain of the 99 Spouts
25 SIP Telephones
26 Basilica of Santa Maria di Collemaggio

the train station, take urban bus No 1 or 3 to reach the town centre. L'Aquila is easily reached by car from Rome on the A24 autostrada, and from Pescara on the A25.

GRAN SASSO D'ITALIA

The rocky peaks of the Gran Sasso d'Italia range are easily accessible from L'Aquila. Details on walking trails and refuges can be obtained at L'Aquila's EPT (see the L'Aquila Tourist Offices section). There is a cable car at Fonte Cerreto which provides access to some decent walking trails. The Gran Sasso also offers the new and popular, but small and modestly equipped, ski resort of Campo Imperatore in the Campo Imperatore mountain group.

There is a camping ground, the *Funivia del Gran Sasso* (☎ 0862-60 61 63), at Fonte Cerreto, and a network of mountain refuges in the area. Hotel accommodation at Fonte Cerreto and Campo Imperatore is limited to the relatively expensive three-star category, and includes the *Nido dell'Aquila* (☎ 0862-60 66 43) at Fonte Cerreto, which has singles/doubles for L65,000/80,000, and the *Campo Imperatore* (☎ 0862-60 61 32) at Campo Imperatore, which has doubles for L160,000.

From L'Aquila, take urban bus No 6 (six daily) from Via Castello to the cable car at Fonte Cerreto.

SULMONA

Sulmona, the birthplace of the Roman poet Ovid, is a pleasant town with an interesting medieval centre. The town's other claim to fame is its *confetti* industry – the making of elaborate flower-shaped arrangements of sugar-coated almonds, which are a must at every traditional Italian wedding throughout the world.

Orientation & Information

The town's main street, Corso Ovidio, runs from the small public park at Piazzale Tresca, to the vast Piazza Garibaldi, a five-minute walk.

Sulmona's AAST tourist office (☎ 0864-5 32 76) is at Via Roma 21, which runs off Corso Ovidio. Open Monday to Saturday from 9 am to 1.45 pm, the office can provide information on accommodation and transport. The town's telephone code is 0864.

Things to See

Sulmona's main attraction is the **Palazzo dell'Annunziata** on Corso Ovidio, which combines Gothic and Renaissance styles. Note the beautifully carved frieze halfway up the façade. The palace houses a small museum of the work of Sulmona's Renaissance goldsmiths. Next to the palace is the Baroque church of the same name. Also along Corso Ovidio, in Piazza XX Settembre, is a statue of the Roman poet.

Piazza Garibaldi is the scene of a colourful

market every Wednesday and Saturday morning. In the piazza are the austere Renaissance **Fontana del Vecchio** and the medieval **aqueduct**, which borders the piazza on two sides. Note also the Gothic doorway of the **Church of San Martino**. In the adjacent Piazza del Carmine, the Romanesque portal is all that remains of the Church of San Francesco della Scarpa, which was destroyed in an earthquake in 1703.

Places to Stay & Eat

The *Locanda di Giovanni* (☎ 5 13 97) at Via Peligna 8, along Via Mazara from Corso Ovidio, has singles/doubles for L25,000/40,000. The pleasant *Hotel Italia* (☎ 5 23 08) in Piazza San Tommaso, through Piazza XX Settembre from Corso Ovidio, has rooms with private bathroom for L50,000/60,000. *Hotel Artù* (☎ 5 27 58) is at the entrance to the old town, just before the park, in Viale Roosevelt. It has rooms for L40,000/55,000, or L50,000/65,000 with private bathroom.

For a reasonable meal, try the *Ristorante Stella* in Via Mazara, or the *Ristorante Italia* in Piazza XX Settembre.

Getting There & Away

Sulmona is accessible from L'Aquila and Pescara by ARPA bus. From Piazza Tresca, walk along Via di Circonvallazione Orientale to reach the bus station, off Via Japasseri. ARPA buses also head for Castel di Sangro and Pescasseroli in the Abruzzo National Park, and to Scanno and Cocullo. Regular trains connect the town with Rome and Pescara. The station is about two km downhill from the historic centre, and half-hourly urban buses (No A) will take you between the two.

AROUND SULMONA
Cocullo

The tiny mountain village of Cocullo warrants a visit only on one day of the year – the first Thursday in May, when its inhabitants celebrate the feast day of St Dominic in original and weird fashion. A statue of the saint is draped with live snakes and carried in procession through the town, accompanied by townspeople also carrying live snakes. Known as the Processione dei Serpari (Procession of the Snake-Charmers), the festival has pagan origins and is certainly an unforgettable experience if you can manage to be there.

The village has no accommodation, but is close to both Sulmona and Scanno and accessible from both towns by ARPA bus. You should plan to arrive in the village as early as possible on the day of the festival, since it has attracted increasingly large crowds in recent years. Festivities usually start around 10 am, culminating in the procession around midday and then continuing throughout the afternoon.

Ask at the tourist offices in Sulmona and Scanno for details on buses to Cocullo on the day of the festival, since services are augmented for the event.

Scanno

The small mountain resort town of Scanno is worth a stopover for a look at its medieval centre and the nearby lake, Lake Scanno. Italian tourists pack out the village in August, but at other times of the year it provides a quiet refuge. There is an AAST tourist office (☎ 0864-7 43 17) in Piazza Santa Maria della Valle, at the edge of the medieval town centre, which can provide information on accommodation and transport. The telephone code for Scanno is 0864.

If you plan to stay overnight, there is a camping ground by Lake Scanno, the *Camping I Lupi* (☎ 74 01 00), which charges L6500 per person and L12,000 for a site. In Scanno, try the *Pensione Nilde* (☎ 7 43 59), which has singles/doubles for L35,000/55,000, the *Pensione Margherita* (☎ 7 43 53), which has rooms for L45,000/70,000, or the *Hotel Vittoria* (☎ 7 43 98), which has pleasant rooms for L80,000/100,000; all prices quoted here are for rooms with bathroom.

For a meal, try *Ristorante Gli Archetti*, or *Ristorante La Porta*, both in the medieval village.

Top Left : Trompe l'oeil, Camogli, Liguria (JG)
Top Right : Window sill in Gerace, Calabria (JG)
Bottom Left : Cliff-top housing, Calabria (JG)
Bottom Right : Street scene in Camogli, Liguria (JG)

Top & Bottom : The Dolomites, Trentino-Alto Adige (SB)

Scanno is accessible by ARPA bus from Sulmona. An ARPA bus also leaves from Piazza della Repubblica in Rome for Scanno. Contact the EPT tourist office in Via Parigi, Rome, for timetable information.

ABRUZZO NATIONAL PARK

Established in 1923 with a former royal hunting reserve as its nucleus, the Abruzzo National Park now incorporates about 40,000 hectares of the Apennines (plus an external protected area of 60,000 hectares). It is the last refuge in Italy of the Marsican brown bear and the Apennine wolf, although it is very difficult to spot one of these now rare native animals. It is also home to golden eagles, a herd of chamois and the odd wildcat. There are also plans to reintroduce the lynx, another native animal, which became extinct in this area around the turn of the century. The park's forests and meadows are perfect for family excursions and long-distance walks, although it is forbidden to leave the marked trails.

The most convenient base is the town of **Pescasseroli**, in the centre of the park, where there is a visitor's centre and tourist office, as well as accommodation. The visitor's centre, open daily from 10 am to midday and 3 to 6 pm (entrance L5000) features a museum and small zoo, where some of the park's native animals including a wolf, a Marsican brown bear and a lynx are housed in depressingly small enclosures.

The tourist office (☎ 0863-91 04 61) is at Via Piave, open daily from 9 am to 1 pm and 4.30 to 6.30 pm, and can provide information on accommodation and transport. Before setting off into the park, it is recommended that you buy a detailed map of the park, which includes the walking trails and locations of refuges, available at the Ufficio di Zona (☎ 0863-9 19 55), Viale Gabriele d'Annunzio, just off the town's main square, the Piazza Sant'Antonio.

Although it is strictly forbidden to free-camp in the park, there are several camping grounds, including the *Campeggio dell'Orso* (☎ 0863-9 19 55), just south of Pescasseroli on the road to the village of Opi. There are

also refuges in the park, but very few are open and it is necessary to obtain permission to use them, as well as a key, from the Ufficio di Zona at Villavallelonga (☎ 0863-94 92 61). You can obtain information at the visitor's centre in Pescasseroli.

Two km uphill from Pescasseroli is the *Locanda Valle del Lupo* (☎ 0863-91 05 34), which has doubles for L45,000. A short distance away is the lovely *Hotel Pinguino* (☎ 0863-91 25 80), which has doubles with bathroom for L80,000, and the *Hotel Cristiana* (☎ 0863-91 07 95), which has doubles for L70,000 with bathroom and breakfast.

The best place to eat in Pescasseroli is the *Ristorante Pizzeria Picchio*, Via Lungo Sangro, where a full meal will cost up to L35,000. The *fast-food* outlet at Via Vittorio Veneto 11, near Piazza Sant'Antonio, is open for lunch and serves good-quality pasta dishes, as well as sandwiches.

Another possible base is the small mountain village of **Civitella Alfadena**, on the park's eastern edge. It is less touristy than Pescasseroli and a very pleasant place to stay. It also has a visitor's centre and a large enclosure housing six wolves. In a smaller enclosure there is a pair of lynx, which have been under observation since 1991 to determine their suitability for release into the park.

If you want to stay overnight in Civitella Alfadena, the best choice is the *Albergo Ostello La Torre* (☎ 0864-89 01 21), in the centre of the old hill-top town, which has rooms for L22,500 per person. Half-board is available for L45,000 a head.

Pescasseroli, Civitella Alfadena and other villages in the park are accessible by ARPA bus from Avezzano (which is accessible by ARPA bus from L'Aquila), or from Castel di Sangro (which can be reached from Sulmona by train). In summer an ARPA bus leaves from Piazza della Repubblica in Rome for Pescasseroli (go to the EPT tourist office in Via Parigi, Rome, for information).

PESCARA

A heavily developed beach resort and

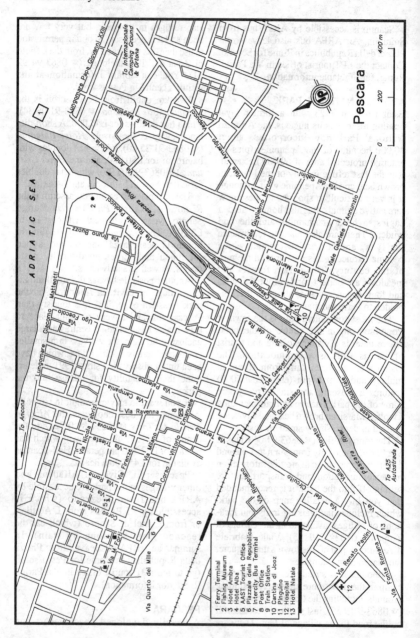

Pescara

ADRIATIC SEA

To Ancona

Pescara River

To Internazionale
Camping Ground
& Ortona

To A25
Autostrada

1   Ferry Terminal
2   Fishing Museum
3   Hotel Ambra
4   Hotel Alba
5   AAST Tourist Office
6   Piazzale della Repubblica
7   Intercity Bus Terminal
8   Post Office
9   Train Station
10   Cantina di Jozz
11   Pinguino
12   Hospital
13   Hotel Natale

commercial centre, and an important transport hub on the Adriatic coast, Pescara's only attraction is the beach and even that is nothing to write home about. However, travellers to Abruzzo are likely to pass through Pescara since it is also the main transport hub of the region, with trains connecting it to Bologna, Ancona, Rome and Bari, and buses connecting it with towns throughout Abruzzo.

There is a jazz festival in the second half of July at the Teatro D'Annunzio, in the public park by the sea east of the city centre. The tourist office can provide information, and tickets cost L25,000 to L30,000. There's a Fishery Museum on the waterfront at Via Raffaele Paolucci, but you'd have to be pretty desperate.

Orientation & Information

From the train station and intercity bus terminal in Piazzale della Repubblica, the beach is a short walk down Corso Umberto I.

There is an AAST tourist information office (☎ 085-37 81 10) at Piazza Salotto 22, just off Corso Umberto I on the way from the station to the beach. During summer, it is open Monday to Saturday from 8.30 am to 12.30 pm and 5 to 7 pm, Sunday from 10 am to midday and 5 to 7 pm. From September to June it opens Monday to Saturday from 8.30 am to 12.30 pm.

The post office is at Corso Vittorio Emanuele II 106, to the right off Piazzale della Repubblica. The postal code for central Pescara is 65100. There are SIP public telephones in the train station and an ASST office at Corso Umberto I 21 (open 24 hours a day). The telephone code for Pescara is 085.

In a police emergency, call ☎ 113. The public hospital, the Ospedale Civile (☎ 37 31 11), is at Via Renato Paolini, south-west of the train station, off Via del Circuito.

Places to Stay & Eat

There is a camping ground, the *Internazionale* (☎ 6 56 53), by the sea on Lungomare Cristoforo Colombo (take bus No 10 from the station). Near the station, at

Via Michelangelo Forti 14, is *Hotel Alba* (☎ 2 82 58), which has singles/doubles with bathroom for L45,000/70,000. The *Hotel Natale* (☎ 421 21 80), Via del Circuito 175, has pleasant singles/doubles for L35,000/55,000 and triples for L75,000. The *Hotel Ambra* (☎ 37 82 47), Via Quarto dei Mille 28, off Via M Forti, has singles/doubles for L40,000/75,000.

For a reasonably priced meal, try the *Pinguino*, Corso Manthonè, across the Pescara River. A meal at *Cantina di Jooz*, in the parallel Via delle Caserme, will cost around L40,000.

Getting There & Away

Buses leave from Piazzale della Repubblica for L'Aquila, Sulmona, Termoli and Rome. Timetables are posted at the bus stop and there is a ticket office in the piazza.

Pescara is on the main train line along the Adriatic coast and is easily accessible to and from towns such as Bologna, Ancona, Foggia and points farther south, as well as L'Aquila, Sulmona and Rome.

A ferry service operates to Split in Croatia from Pescara's port, although services were suspended in 1993. For the latest information, go to Agenzia Sanmar (☎ 6 52 47) at the ferry terminal, next to the Pescara River that divides the city.

Molise

This small, mountainous region is well off the beaten tourist track and with fairly good reason. Its meagre offerings for the tourist pale in comparison with the neighbouring regions, and its towns are generally anonymous concrete jumbles. However, it does offer the interesting ruins of a Roman provincial town, Saepinum, not far from Campobasso, and there are good walking opportunities in the Matese Mountains. Excavations in the town of Isernia have unearthed what is believed to be the oldest village in Europe. Termoli, a small beach resort, is a jumping-off point for the Tremiti

Islands, a small group of islands off the coast of northern Apulia (see Tremiti Islands in the Apulia section).

CAMPOBASSO

The capital of the region, Campobasso is predominantly modern and basically unappealing. The national training school for the carabinieri is here, as is a high-security prison, but Campobasso is a good base for exploring nearby Saepinum.

The town's EPT tourist office (0874-41 56 62) is at Piazza della Vittoria 14, open Monday to Saturday from 8.30 am to 2 pm. From the train station, turn left into Via Cavour, right into Via Gazzani and then left again into Corso Vittorio Emanuele to reach the office.

While in Campobasso, wander up into the older part of town to take a look at the Romanesque churches of **San Bartolomeo** (13th century) and **San Giorgio** (12th century).

If you need a bed for the night, try the *Hotel Belvedere* (☎ 0874-6 27 24), Via Colle delle Api 32, which has singles/doubles for L23,000/35,500, or L29,000/41,000 with bathroom. From the train station, take bus No 1N and ask the driver to let you off at the hotel.

Campobasso is accessible by bus from Termoli, Isernia and Pescara. By train it can be reached from Rome via Sulmona, or from Naples via Benevento.

AROUND CAMPOBASSO

One of the least visited Roman ruins in Italy, **Saepinum** is well worth a visit. A relatively unimportant provincial town, it survived into the 9th century before being sacked by Arab invaders. Surrounded by small farms, the ruins are quite well preserved and include the town walls, a temple, a triumphal arch and the foundations of numerous houses.

To reach Saepinum by public transport, you will need to take one of the infrequent provincial buses to either Altilia, next to the archaeological zone, or Sepino, although from there the zone is a three-km walk.

The **Matese Mountains** south-west of

Campobasso offer good hiking in summer and skiing in winter. Take a bus from Campobasso to Campitello Matese, or a train from Campobasso or Isernia to Boiano. From either point there are trails into the mountains.

Campitello Matese is the centre for winter sports and has several hotels. The cheapest is *La Pinetina* (☎ 0874-78 42 07), with doubles for L36,000, or L40,000 with bathroom. Otherwise try *Lo Sciatore* (☎ 0874-78 41 37), which has singles/doubles for L60,000/80,000.

ISERNIA

About an hour by train from Campobasso, Isernia is a reasonable base for exploring the small hill towns of the area. It has been devastated on several occasions by earthquakes and is therefore a modern town. However, in 1979 evidence of a village thought to be up to 700,000 years old, and believed to be the oldest settlement in Europe, was discovered here. Excavations continue, and stone tools discovered at the site are on display at the town's small **archaeological museum** on Via Marcelli (head to the left along Corso Garibaldi from the train station).

Isernia's EPT tourist office (☎ 0865-39 92) is at Via M Farinacci 11, a short walk from the station (turn left into Corso Garibaldi and right into Via Farinacci). It is open from 9 am to 1 pm Monday to Friday.

For a place to stay, try the *Hotel Sayonara* (☎ 0865-5 09 92), Via G Berta 131, which has singles/doubles with bathroom for L45,000/60,000.

Isernia is easily reached by bus from Campobasso and Termoli and by train from Sulmona, Pescara and Campobasso.

AROUND ISERNIA

Provincial buses will take you to local hilltop villages. Of interest are the remains of a pre-Roman village just outside the town of **Pietrabbondante**, about 30 km north-east of Isernia. It was settled by the Samnites, the people who inhabited the area of Molise

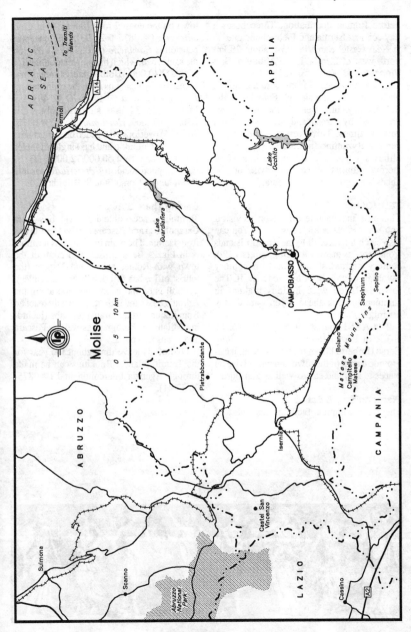

before Roman domination. Three buses a day connect Isernia and Pietrabbondante.

Near Castel San Vincenzo, about 20 km north-west of Isernia, is the **Abbey of San Vincenzo al Volturno** (take the bus for Castel San Vincenzo from Isernia and then walk one km to the abbey). Founded in the 8th century, this Benedictine abbey was destroyed by Arabs and has been rebuilt several times. However, a cycle of 9th century Byzantine frescoes survived in the abbey's crypt and these merit a visit. Isernia's tourist office can advise on the abbey's irregular opening hours.

TERMOLI

This pleasant beach resort is worth a visit if you want to relax for a few days. You can also catch a hydrofoil to the Tremiti Islands from here. Its medieval section offers a 12th century **cathedral** and the 13th century **Swabian castle**, built by Frederick II. The town is filled with holiday-makers in summer, so book ahead if you want to stay overnight.

The AAST tourist office (☎ 0875-70 67 54) is in Piazza Bega, a short walk along Corso Umberto I from the train station. It can provide a map of the town and will advise on places to stay and eat, as well as transport.

Places to Stay & Eat

There are camping facilities just west of town on the coastal road (the ss16) at *Cala Saracena* (☎ 0875-5 21 93). The cheapest pension is *Caminetto* (☎ 0875-5 21 39), on the same road, which has singles/doubles for L20,000/40,000. Both establishments are accessible by local bus from the train station. *Pensione Porreca* (☎ 0875-70 42 48), Via Mascilongo 34, has singles/doubles for L30,000/50,000. *Hotel Meridiano* (☎ 0875-70 59 46) overlooks the beach on Lungomare Cristoforo Colombo and has singles/doubles with bathroom for L50,000/72,000.

For a good meal, try *Pizzeria/Ristorante Il Galeone* at Corso Fratelli Brigida 124.

Getting There & Away

Termoli is accessible by SATI bus from Campobasso and Pescara and by Cerella bus from Isernia. The main intercity bus terminal is in Piazza Bega. Buses also connect the town with Rome, Milan and Naples (the tourist office has full details on timetables). Termoli is on the main train line along the Adriatic coast and is therefore easily reached from major northern transport hubs (including Milan and Bologna), as well as Pescara and towns in Apulia.

Hydrofoils leave throughout the year for the Tremiti Islands. Bookings can be made through Agenzia Intercontinental (☎ 0875-70 53 41).

Southern Italy

Southern Italy

The land of the mezzogiorno (midday sun) will surprise even the most world-weary traveller. Rich in history and cultural traditions, the southern regions are poorer than those of the north, and certainly the wheels of bureaucracy grind increasingly slower as you travel closer to the tip of the boot. The attractions here are simpler and more stark, the people more vibrant and excitable, and myths and legends are inseparable from official history. Campania and Basilicata cry out to be explored, and absolutely nothing can prepare you for Naples. Less well known by foreigners, Calabria has beautiful beaches and the striking scenery of the Sila Massif to offer visitors.

Campania

Campania has everything a traveller could want, from the peak of Mt Vesuvius to the splendour of the Royal Palace at Caserta, modelled on the grand Versailles and built for the Bourbons. The largely unspoiled beauty of the south, the hectic, colourful chaos of Naples, and the sheer wonder of the islands in the Bay of Naples – Capri, Ischia, Procida – make Campania one of Italy's most attractive and interesting regions.

Campania is the beginning of the Italian south, and Naples is the best place from which to explore the area. The city has a vibrancy to match the notoriety of its Mafia, the Camorra, and is worth a visit of at least three days. The region itself could draw you for weeks.

From Naples it is only a short distance to Pompeii and Herculaneum, or to the Phlegraean Fields of volcanic lakes and mud baths, which inspired both Homer and Virgil in their writings. The Greek colony of Cumae, and Sophia Loren's hometown, Pozzuoli, are in this area. The magnificent Amalfi Coast separates the Bay of Naples and the Gulf of Salerno. Farther south is Paestum with its important Greek temples; but less known, and perhaps more enjoyable to visit because it is not overrun by tourists, is the ancient town of Velia. The coast of Cilento is not as beautiful as the coast of Amalfi, but it offers some lovely scenery and secluded beaches.

Campania is alive with myth and legend. Sirens lured sailors to their deaths off Sorrento, the islands in the Bay of Naples were the domain of mermaids, and Lake Avernus, in the Phlegrean Fields, was believed in ancient times to be the entrance to the underworld.

The history of the region centres around Naples, which was founded as Neapolis (New Town) by the Greeks around 600 BC, although legend says it was originally called Parthenope after the siren. It was conquered by the Romans, but retained its Greek traditions, and the area became a favourite holiday destination of Roman emperors, including Augustus and Nero. In later years it was ruled by a succession of foreign invaders, including the Arabs, Normans, French, Austrians and Spanish. After a particularly brutal 200-year period under Spanish rule, the region alternated several times between Spanish, French and Austrian rule before becoming part of the Kingdom of Italy in 1860.

Naples is on the main train line from Rome and is a major regional transportation hub, making travel both easy and cheap. However, like much of the south, even catching a bus can sometimes be a trauma. For the more adventurous, the Club Alpino Italiano in Salerno has details of many walks on the islands, the Sorrento Peninsula and in the Picentini Mountains, and farther south in the mountains along the Cilento coast. Salerno, in particular, has a multitude of sporting clubs offering everything from horse riding to windsurfing, even though there is little else to draw you to the town.

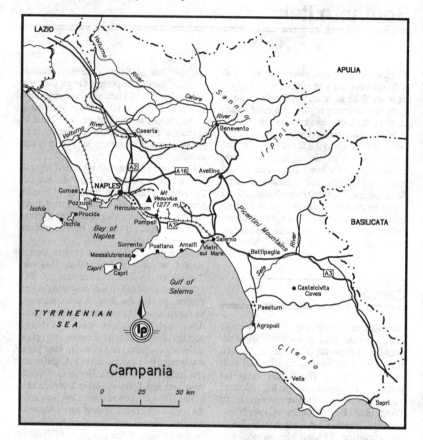

NAPLES

It was Goethe who said that a man who has seen Naples can never be sad. The third-largest city in Italy, Naples almost defies description. Its disastrous, run-down state presents it as a city in decay. Indeed, the city has held the dubious title as Europe's dirtiest city. But the life and vitality of its people, coupled with its own particular identity, give Naples the feel of a real metropolis – Italy's version of New York. It is exciting but scary, and should be approached with care.

Nothing is orderly and regulation is observed with absolute discretion. Red lights are routinely ignored (the government assists in this by leaving lights at even the busiest intersections flashing amber), as are one-way signs and just about every other road rule. It is not unusual to see a whole family aboard a single Vespa, or a child buzzing around dangerously fast on a motorino.

Naples is the centre of a booming clothing counterfeiting racket and is the base for most of Italy's contraband cigarette smuggling operations. This industry involves the Camorra, Naples' brand of the Mafia, whose specialities are bank hold-ups, controlling the local fruit and vegetable markets, and the massive *toto nero* (illegal football pools). Ironically, most of its actions are unofficially

Coat of arms of Naples

sanctioned because of the employment they bring to the city.

The benevolence of Naples' monarchs, notably 'Good King' Robert of Anjou of the early 14th century, attracted many poets and artists from all over Italy including Boccaccio, Petrarch and Giotto. After his arrival in 1607, Caravaggio inspired the founding of the Neapolitan School of Painting, and regarded the city as his new Rome. Naples' Baroque architecture is regarded as some of the country's grandest.

Street food is among Italy's best. *Misto di frittura* – deep-fried potato, eggplant and zucchini flowers – tempt from tiny stalls in tiny streets, as does *mozzarella in carozza* – mozzarella deep-fried in bread. Naturally, seafood is a speciality (although it is best to avoid uncooked shellfish as the bay is extremely polluted), and, of course, Naples is home to pizza. The city's sweets, in particular the *sfogliatelle* (light, flaky pastry filled with ricotta), are delectable.

History

Soon after founding Cumae in 1000 BC, colonists from Rhodes established a settlement on the west side of Mt Vesuvius and, according to legend, named it after the siren Parthenope. Several centuries later, Phoenician traders and Greeks from Athens, attracted by the splendour of the coastal area, gave it the name Neapolis. The city prospered as a centre of Greek culture and later, under Roman rule, became a favourite for such notables as Pompey, Caesar and Tiberius.

After successive waves of invasion by the Huns, the Lombards and others, the city came under Norman rule in 1139. The Normans, under Roger I, were overthrown by the German Hohenstaufens, whose Swabian dynasty lasted until 1269 and gave the city many new institutions, including the university. After an initial period of lawlessness and disorder under the Spanish Aragons, the city later prospered, particularly under Alfonso I of Aragon, who introduced laws and modern styles of justice, and promoted the arts and sciences.

It was during the period of Spanish rule in the 16th century and later under the Bourbons that the city gained much of its high splendour and magnificence, evidence of which can still be seen today. After a brief reign by Joachim Murat from 1806 to 1815, during the Napoleonic Wars, the Bourbons returned and remained until 1860, when Garibaldi ended Naples' reign as seat of the Kingdom of the Two Sicilies. In that year, he conquered Sicily and Calabria, and incorporated Naples and much of southern Italy into the Kingdom of Italy. During the period of Bourbon rule Naples had become one of Europe's grandest cities, and it was a candidate (albeit unsuccessful) to become the capital of united Italy.

The city sustained incredible damage during WW II in more than 100 bombing raids, and marks can still be seen in many monuments. A severe earthquake in 1980 and a dormant, but not extinct, Mt Vesuvius looming to the east, remind the Neapolitans of the city's vulnerability.

Orientation

Naples stretches out along the waterfront and is divided into *quartieri* (quarters). Although the city seems to lack any discernible organisation, most street signs bear the name of the quarter as well. The main train station and bus terminal are off Piazza Garibaldi, just east of the historic Spaccanapoli, the old city. For the recently arrived, the piazza outside the central train station, or Stazione

Centrale, is an enormous and somewhat unwelcoming transport conglomeration, as well as a street market and centre for Naples' more seedy side.

West of the train station, the city's recently added financial and business district is recognisable by the forest of new skyscrapers, and is located near the main industrial and commercial port areas. On the bay to the south-west are the more fashionable areas of Santa Lucia and Mergellina, with its semi-grand waterfront boulevard, Via Caracciolo. Rising up from Mergellina is the up-market Vomero district, dominated by the Castel Sant'Elmo and the Certosa (Carthusian monastery) of San Martino, which can be seen from all over the city.

From Piazza Garibaldi, Corso Umberto I to the south-west leads to Piazza Bovio and eventually to the huge Piazza Municipio, which contains the Castel Nuovo. The Palazzo Reale, the former royal palace, is next to the castle. From the palace, head north for Naples' main street, Via Toledo, which becomes Via Roma for a short stretch after it crosses Piazza Carità, and you will reach Piazza Dante, in the centre of Spaccanapoli. The road continues as Via Santa Teresa degli Scalzi and then Corso Amedeo di Savoia before reaching the Parco di Capodimonte north of the centre.

The extensions of two of Naples' more original and interesting streets, Via B Croce and Via dei Tribunali, eventually meet Via Roma. Most street life, many of the city's artisans and a host of good, cheap restaurants can be found in this area. Via B Croce is useful because it's part of a straight run from near the central train station (starting as Via San Biagio dei Librai) to the foot of the hilltop Castel Sant'Elmo and Certosa of San Martino, where it becomes Via Pasquale Scura.

Information

Tourist Offices Naples has several tourist offices, all providing the extremely useful monthly publication, *Qui Napoli*, which contains generally up-to-date information about happenings in the city, as well as trans-

---

■ **PLACES TO STAY**

2   Pensione Oasi
8   Pensione Margherita
14 Linda
15 Pensione Ruggiero
19 Pensione Ausonia
23 Pensione Astoria & Albergo Teresita
24 Hotel Rex
25 Santa Lucia

▼ **PLACES TO EAT**

4   Mario Daniele
5   Acunzo
6   Frasco
7   Renzo e Lucia
16 Più Focacle
26 Trattoria da Patrizia &
    Antica Trattoria da Pietro

OTHER

1   Botanic Gardens
3   Piazza delle Medaglie d'Oro
9   Castel Sant'Elmo
10 Certosa of San Martino
11 Villa Floridiana
12 Funicolare di Chiaia
13 Piazza Amedeo
17 Pignatelli Museum
18 Piazza dei Martiri &
    EPT Tourist Information
20 Piazza della Repubblica
21 Aquarium
22 Piazza Vittoria
27 Castel dell'Ovo

---

port information. Another publication, the weekly *Postounico*, details entertainment. You can also pick up a good map and free guides to the city's churches and monuments.

The most central office, the AAST (☎ 081-552 33 28), is in Piazza del Gesù Nuovo and opens from 9 am to 7 pm (although it usually closes in the afternoon), and Sundays to 3 pm. Other offices are at the Mergellina hydrofoil terminal and at the entrance to the Borgo Marinari, the little island off Santa Lucia.

There is an office of the EPT at Stazione Centrale and also at Piazza dei Martiri 58

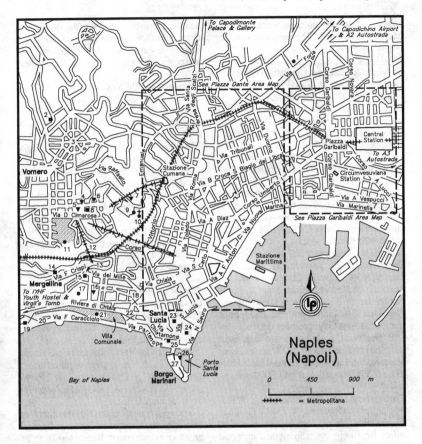

Naples
(Napoli)

Bay of Naples

0   450   900   m

+++++ = Metropolitana

(☎ 081-40 53 11), the Mergellina terminal and the airport. Opening times vary, but are generally from 8 am to 7 pm, with the station and airport offices remaining open during the siesta.

Money The city is dotted with change offices, although the rates are consistently lower than at banks. Some banks charge L3000 to change travellers' cheques, so ask first. The Banca d'America e d'Italia at Via Santa Brigida 10, off Via Toledo, has a bancomat which accepts Visa cards. All banks open from about 8.20 am to 1.30 pm and then 3.10 to 4.20 pm. American Express operates an agency at Ashiba Professional Travel, Via Vittorio Emanuele III 55, near the Castel Nuovo.

Post & Telecommunications The main post office is at Piazza G Matteotti, off Via A Diaz, in a grand, Fascist-era palace. It is open Monday to Friday from 8.30 am to 7.30 pm, and to midday Saturday. The postal code for central Naples is 80100.

There is an ASST telephone office at Stazione Centrale, which is open 24 hours a day. The main SIP office is in Galleria

Umberto I and opens from 9 am to 5 pm, Monday to Saturday. The telephone code for Naples is 081.

Foreign Consulates The British Consulate (☎ 66 35 11) is at Via Crispi 122 – ring ☎ 0337-86 02 70 for after-hours emergencies. The US Consulate (☎ 761 43 03) is on Piazza della Repubblica. There are no diplomatic representations of Australia, Canada or New Zealand in Naples.

Other Information The Associazione Italiana Alberghi per la Gioventù (☎ 552 00 84), Piazza Carità 40, provides information on IYHF hostels and offers travel discounts to IYHF members and young people. The student travel centre, CTS (☎ 552 79 60), is at Via Mezzocannone 25.

Arci Gay Antinoo (☎ 552 88 15), Vico San Geronimo 17-20, provides information of interest to gay travellers, but the phones are generally staffed only from 6 pm to 9 pm. Naples has a big lesbian community, and Orchidea Blu (same address and phone number as Arci Gay) provides details.

If you want to do some washing, most laundries charge L4000-L5000 per kg. Near Vomero, the Lavasecco at Via Mario Fiore 2D, off Via Bernini, charges L3000 per kg.

Emergency For police emergency, ☎ 113. The police headquarters (☎ 794 11 11) are at Via Medina 75, off Via A Diaz. It has an office for foreigners where you can report thefts etc. For stolen cars, ring ☎ 794 14 35.

For an ambulance, call ☎ 752 06 96. The city offers a Guardia Medica Permanente (☎ 751 31 77) – a night and holiday emergency medical service. The Ospedale Monaldi (☎ 545 14 17), Vico L Bianchi, is centrally located, a short walk from the city's grand cathedral, the Duomo. The pharmacy at Stazione Centrale is open from 8 am to 8 pm, or call ☎ 192 for addresses of all-night pharmacies.

Dangers & Annoyances The key word in this city is precaution, as the petty crime rate is extremely high. Beware the motorino bandits who will rip even the sunglasses from your face (as happened to us). Carry your money and documents in a money belt and never carry a bag or purse if you can help it.

Women should be careful about walking alone in the streets at night, particularly near Stazione Centrale and Piazza Dante. Never venture into the dark side streets at night unless you are in a group. The area west of Via Toledo and as far north as Piazza Carità can be particularly threatening.

Take great care when crossing roads. There are few functioning traffic lights and pedestrian crossings, and the Neapolitans never stop at them anyway. When facing a green light they drive with caution, believing that those facing the red light will not stop.

Car and motorbike theft are also major problems in Naples, so think twice before bringing a vehicle to the city.

Things to See

Spaccanapoli The best place to start investigating Naples is right in the historic centre, which spreads from Via Duomo in the east to Piazza Dante in the west. At Piazza Dante you will find the **Port'Alba**, a city gate dating back to 1625. Start your exploration of Spaccanapoli at Piazza del Gesù Nuovo, where you can collect a swag of information from the tourist office.

The 16th century **Gesù Nuovo** church on the north side of the piazza is one of the city's greatest examples of Renaissance architecture, particularly the lozenge-shaped rustication of its imposing façade. The interior was fully redecorated in the Neapolitan-Baroque style by Cosimo Fanzango after a fire in 1639 destroyed its Renaissance interior.

The **Church of Santa Chiara**, a church and convent across the piazza, partly incorporates a Roman wall which was later extended to surround the convent completely in order to protect the nuns. The church was built between 1310 and 1328 and suffered considerable damage during earthquakes over the centuries. Heavy bombing in 1943 destroyed much of the building, which was then restored in its original Gothic style. The **nuns' cloisters** behind the church consist of four paths that form a cross shape, bordered by a long parapet entirely covered in decorative ceramic tiles, depicting 64 different scenes of the nuns.

Via B Croce, its continuation Via San Biagio dei Librai and the parallel Via dei Tribunali are home to many of the city's artisans and craftspeople. It is in these streets and the labyrinth of side alleyways that you will find the many goldsmiths and makers of the famous Neapolitan *presepi* (cribs). The **Ospedale delle Bambole**, Via San Biagio dei Librai 81, is a doll hospital, and from the outside takes on a macabre appearance with dolls' heads piled in the windows. Leaving Piazza del Gesù Nuovo, on the left just after Via San Sebastiano, is the former **Filomarino Palace** with its grand Renaissance entrance hall and courtyard.

The **Church of Sant'Angelo a Nilo**, with its entrance on Vico Donnaromita 15, off Via San Biagio dei Librai, was built in 1385 and remodelled in the 18th century. It contains the monument of Cardinal Brancaccio by Donatello. Farther along you will find the **Palazzo di Carafa di Maddaloni** and the nearby **Church of SS Filippo e Giacomo** with their contrasting Renaissance and Rococo styles. The grand Cappella di Monte di Pietà is worth visiting for its frescoed vault and façade. The **Palazzo Marigliano**, over Via San Gregorio Armeno, features a magnificent Renaissance entrance hall and façade.

The **Church of San Giorgio Maggiore**, where Via San Biagio dei Librai meets Via Duomo, is worth visiting for its austere interior. Opposite is the 15th century **Cuomo Palace**, built by Tuscan artists. The whole building was moved several metres in 1881 when the street was being widened. The palace now contains the Gaetano Filangieri Museum, with an extensive collection of arms, furniture and china. It opens Tuesday to Saturday from 9 am to 2 pm and until 1 pm on Sunday, and entrance is L4000.

The **Church of San Domenico Maggiore**, along Via B Croce in the piazza bearing its name, was built in the 14th century by the Dominican order and was favoured by the city's nobility. It contains 45 coffins of the princes of Aragon and is a mixture of Baroque and 19th century neo-Gothic.

The **San Severo Chapel**, to the east of the church, contains some of the city's most superb sculpture, including the *Veiled Christ* by Giuseppe Sanmartino, a stunning work that still confounds experts, who cannot agree on how the apparently translucent veil was created. It's open from 10 am to 1 pm and then 5 to 7 pm, and to 1 pm on Sundays. Entrance is L4000.

The **Church of San Lorenzo Maggiore**, off Via dei Tribunali in Piazza San Gaetano, bears the influences of many periods, including a Roman road and shops. It contains the mosaic-covered tomb of Catherine of Austria, and a museum housing relics discovered during excavations. Entrance is free. Opposite is the **Church of San Paolo Maggiore**, built in the late 16th century on the site of a temple of the Dioscuri. It contains the tomb of San Gaetano (St Cajetan).

Farther along Via Tribunali and left into Via Duomo stands the city's grand cathedral, the **Duomo**. Started by Charles I, the Angevin king, in 1294, the building was destroyed in 1456 by an earthquake. The façade was altered to the neo-Gothic style in the late 19th century. The famous San Gennaro Chapel (also known as the Chapel of the Treasury), dedicated to St Januarius, the city's patron saint, contains two phials of Bishop Januarius' congealed blood which are kept behind the high altar. St Januarius was martyred at Pozzuoli, near Naples, in 305 AD, and tradition holds that two phials of his congealed blood liquefied in his hands when his body was transferred back to Naples. He is said to have saved the city from disaster, and on the first Sunday in May, on 19 September and on 16 December each year, thousands gather to pray for a miracle, namely that the blood will liquefy and save the city from disaster again. The blood regularly turns to liquid (or so they say); in 1941 the miracle failed to occur and was followed

■ PLACES TO STAY

6   Albergo Tortora
7   Alloggio Fiamma
10 Bellini
16 Soggiorno Imperia
19 Duomo
45 Candy
47 Oriente Grand Hotel

▼ PLACES TO EAT

9   Ristorante Bellini
11 Trattoria da Carmine
12 Pizzeria di Matteo
22 Frittura Fiorenzano
24 Cinese Hong Kong
31 La Campagnola
36 Pizza Fritte
37 Da Luigi
39 Trattoria Franco
40 Pizzeria al 22
43 Giuliano
50 Trianon

    OTHER

1   National Archaeological Museum
2   Piazza Cavour
3   Ospedale Monaldi
4   Church of San Gerolamini
5   Duomo
8   Piazza Bellini
13 Piazza San Gaetano
14 Church of San Lorenzo Maggiore
15 Piazza Dante
17 Church of San Domenico Maggiore

18 San Severo Chapel
20 Church of San Giorgio Maggiore
21 Cuomo Palace
23 Piazza Montesanto &
    Stazione Cumana
25 Il Gesù Nuovo
26 Piazza del Gesù Nuovo
27 AAST Tourist Office
28 Church of Santa Chiara
29 Filomarino Palace
30 Piazza San Domenico Maggiore
32 Church of Sant'Angelo a Nilo
33 Ospedale delle Bambole
34 Church of SS Filippo e Giacomo
35 Mineralogical & Zoological Museums
38 University
41 Church of Sant'Anna dei Lombardi
42 Piazza Carità
44 Associazione Italiana Alberghi per la
    Gioventù
46 Main Post Office
48 Police Headquarters
49 Piazza Bovio
51 Parking
52 Otto Jazz Club
53 Piazza Municipio
54 Funicular for Vomero
55 SIP Telephones
56 Galleria Umberto I
57 Castel Nuovo
58 Stazione Marittima
59 Piazza Trento e Trieste
60 San Carlo Theatre
61 Palazzo Reale
62 Piazza del Plebiscito
63 Church of San Francesco di Paola

by Mt Vesuvius' most recent eruption. The Duomo is open from 8 am to 1 pm and 4.30 to 7.30 pm.

The **Church of San Gerolamini**, or San Filippo Neri, opposite the Duomo, is a rich Baroque church with a beautiful façade. It features the Gerolamini Picture Gallery with works from the 16th and 18th centuries. It is open from 9.30 am to 12.30 pm and 2 to 5.30 pm and entrance is free.

Head north along Via Duomo to Via Foria and turn right to reach the **Botanic Gardens** (☎ 44 97 59) at No 223, near Piazza Carlo III. The gardens were founded in 1807 by Joseph Bonaparte and are now part of the University of Naples. Visits are by appointment only.

The **Church of Sant'Anna dei Lombardi**, south-west of Piazza del Gesù Nuovo, was founded in 1414 by Origlia and features fine Renaissance sculpture, including a superb terracotta *Pietà* (1492) by Guido Mazzoni.

Near the train station, the **Church of Santa Maria del Carmine**, on the waterfront in Piazza del Carmine, was the scene of the 1647 Neapolitan Revolution led by Masaniello. It contains the much-worshipped *Madonna Bruna* (Brown Madonna), and each year on 15 July a fireworks display

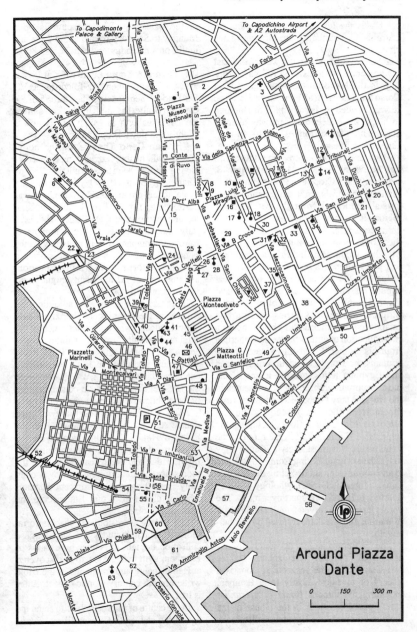

Around Piazza
Dante

0   150   300 m

celebrates the festival of the Madonna del Carmine by simulating the burning of the church.

About one km along the waterfront east of the centre, in a restored railway building, is the **National Railway Museum** at Corso San Giovanni a Teduccio, in Pietrarsa. It was founded by Ferdinand II of Bourbon to house his collection of railway memorabilia and opens from 9 am to midday. Entrance is free.

Back in the town centre, the **Mineralogical Museum** on Via Mezzocannone 8, between Via B Croce and Corso Umberto I, features minerals, meteorites and quartz crystals collected from the Mt Vesuvius region. It is open from 9 am to 2 pm and entrance is free. The building also contains the **Zoological Museum**, which is open Monday, Wednesday and Friday from 9 am to 1 pm. Entrance is free.

Just on the northern fringe of Spaccanapoli, on Piazza Museo Nazionale, near Capodimonte, is the **National Archaeological Museum**. Charles of Bourbon established this museum in 1837 to house a rich collection of antiquities he had inherited from his mother, Elizabeth Farnese. It also contains the Borgia Collection of Etruscan and Egyptian relics, making it one of the most important archaeological museums in the world. Many Graeco-Roman items from the Farnese collection of sculpture are featured on the ground floor, including the impressive *Farnese Bull* in the room of the same name. It is most likely a Roman copy of a Greek original dating from 150 BC, and is an enormous group depicting the death of Dirce, a figure in Greek mythology who was tied to a bull and torn apart over rocks. The whole group was carved from a single block of marble and was later restored by Michelangelo.

The 1st floor is largely devoted to discoveries from Pompeii, Herculaneum, Stabiae and Cumae. On the mezzanine floor is a gallery of mosaics, mostly from Pompeii, including the famous *Battle of Alexander* which paved the floor in the House of the Faun at Pompeii. The Egyptian collection is in the basement. The museum is open Monday to Saturday from 9 am to 2 pm and until 1 pm on Sunday, and entrance is L8000.

City Centre & Santa Lucia Start at Piazza Trieste e Trento, where Via Toledo meets Via San Carlo. The imposing glass atrium of the **Galleria Umberto I**, built in 1890, resembles the larger galleria in Milan and is now a slightly run-down shopping arcade.

The **San Carlo Theatre**, on the northeastern side of the piazza, is recognised as having perfect acoustics. Built in 1737 by Charles of Bourbon (40 years before La Scala, locals proudly boast), San Carlo was destroyed by fire in 1816. Restored since, it features one of the oldest ballet schools in Italy. Stendhal wrote, 'There is nothing in Europe to compare with it, or even give the faintest idea of what it is like.' It is open in the early morning and mid-afternoon, although one of the attendants might escort you in at other times.

In Piazza Plebiscito, and adjoining the theatre, is the magnificent **Palazzo Reale** (Royal Palace), which contains much of the original Bourbon furniture, paintings, porcelain and statues. Built around 1600, it was completely renovated in 1841, but suffered extensive damage during WW II. Niches in the late-Renaissance façade contain statues of the eight most important kings of Naples.

After entering the courtyard, a huge double staircase under a dome leads to the **Palazzo Reale Museum**, housed in the former royal apartments. Works by Filippino Lippi, Titian and Vasari can be seen in the rooms next to the museum, which is open daily from 9 am to 2 pm except Sundays when it closes at 1 pm. Entrance to the museum is L6000.

The palace also contains the **National Library**, which includes the vast Farnese collection brought to Naples by Charles of Bourbon, with over 2000 papyri discovered at Herculaneum and fragments of the Bible written in 5th century Coptic dialect. Entry is free.

In the centre of Piazza Plebiscito stand the equestrian statues of Charles III and Ferdinand I of Bourbon. Opposite the palace is the **Church of San Francesco di Paola**, founded by Ferdinand I in 1817 to celebrate the restoration of his kingdom from the Bonapartes. Flanked by semicircular colonnades, the church is based on Rome's Pantheon and is a popular wedding spot.

The **Castel Nuovo**, known also as Maschio Angioino, in Piazza Municipio, was begun by Charles I of Anjou in 1279 and was given the name 'nuovo' (new) to distinguish it from other castles in the city. It was completely restored prior to WW II. The two-storey triumphal arch at the entrance, the Torre della Guardia, built in 1467, depicts Alfonso I of Aragon's triumphal entry into Naples. The castle contains the **Museo Civico**, which features 14th and 15th century sculptures and frescoes, and paintings, silver and bronze works dating from the 15th century. It is open from 9 am to 1 pm weekdays and entrance is free.

North-east of the Castel Nuovo by Via Agostino Depretis, a business thoroughfare, is Piazza Bovio and the **Fountain of Neptune**. Dating from 1601, its sea creatures were sculpted by Bernini, and the figure of Neptune by Naccherini.

The **Castel dell'Ovo** (Castle of the Egg) is on the small rocky island off Santa Lucia known as Borgo Marinari and connected by bridge from Via Partenope. Folklore has it that the name came about after part of the island collapsed, likened by locals to Virgil's story of the breaking of an egg. The castle occupies the site of a Roman villa. Built in the 12th century by the Norman king, William I, the castle became a fortress defending the whole of Campania. You can wander through the small lanes on the island (mostly occupied by restaurants), but the castle, restored in the 1970s, is opened only for special exhibitions.

The **Fontana dell'Immacolatella**, where Via Partenope meets Via N Sauro, dates from the 17th century and features statues by Bernini and Naccherini.

Mergellina & Vomero Continuing along the waterfront from Borgo Marinari are the various streets making up the Riviera di Chiaia. The **Villa Comunale**, a large park, and the **Aquarium** are along the water. Founded in the late 19th century by German naturalist Anton Dohrn, the aquarium is one of the largest in Europe, with 30 tanks. It is open Monday to Saturday from 9 am to 5 pm, to 6 pm on Sundays in summer and until 2 pm in winter, and entrance is L2000.

Just north of Via F Caracciolo, a short walk from Piazza Sannazzaro, are the **Tombs of Virgil & Leopardi** at Salita della Grotta. Virgil is buried in a Roman vault dating back to the Augustan age. Both can be visited daily from 9 am to 1 pm and entrance is free.

Close by on Riviera di Chiaia is the **Pignatelli Museum**, an old patrician residence containing mostly 19th century furnishings and china. A pavilion set in gardens houses the Coach Museum and contains English and French carriages. Both museums are open from 9 am to 2 pm and until 1 pm on Sundays, and entrance is L4000.

The **Villa Floridiana**, Via Domenico Cimarosa 77, was built in 1817 by Ferdinand I for his lower ranked wife, the Duchess of Floridia. It is set in some of Naples' most beautiful parkland (free entrance daily, except Monday, from 9 am to one hour before sunset) and houses the Duca di Martina Museum, which contains European, Chinese and Japanese china, ivory, enamels and majolica (Renaissance Italian earthenware). This is open from 9 am to 2 pm and until 1 pm on Sundays, and entrance is L4000.

Rising above Spaccanapoli, the Vomero hill can be seen from all over the city. It is capped with the **Certosa of San Martino** and the **Castel Sant'Elmo**, the former a 14th century Carthusian monastery and the latter a star-shaped castle built also in the 14th century, originally as a palace for Robert of Anjou. The monastery was rebuilt in the 17th century by Fanzango in Neapolitan Baroque style, and now contains the San Martino Museum, featuring a section on naval history, an area dedicated to the history of the

Kingdom of Naples, and other interesting collections. There is a magnificent view from the terraced gardens, or if you don't go in, from Largo San Martino (the car park) outside. It is open Monday to Saturday from 9 am to 2 pm and until 1 pm Sunday, and entrance is L6000. The castle is closed to the public, but can be visited. Enquire at the AAST tourist office in the Piazza del Gesù Nuovo.

Capodimonte At the northern end of the city, the **Capodimonte Palace**, a former royal estate built by Charles of Bourbon, is set in extensive parklands which formed the nobles' hunting grounds. It now houses the **Capodimonte National Gallery**, which consists mostly of the lavish Farnese collection. Featured are several Titians and works by Goya, Botticelli and Caravaggio, as well as an impressive range from the 18th century Neapolitan school. The museum, housed in the royal apartments, has an extensive collection of arms, ivories, bronzes, porcelain (including more than 3000 pieces from the palace's original porcelain factory) and other works of art. It's open Monday to Saturday from 9 am to 2 pm and until 1 pm on Sunday, and entrance is L8000. Entrance to the gardens is free and they are open from 9 am to one hour before sunset.

Just below the palace are the **Catacombs of San Gennaro** – enter from Via di Capodimonte and down an alley running beside the Chiesa di Madre del Buon Consiglio, a recently built Vatican lookalike. The catacombs date from the 2nd century and contain the body of the martyred St Januarius. Guided tours are available only on Friday, Saturday and Sunday at 9.30, 10.15, 11 and 11.45 am, costing L3000.

The **Catacombs of San Severo** (☎ 45 46 84), Piazzetta San Severo e Capodimonte, are near those of San Gennaro but can only be visited by appointment.

Activities

The Centro di Lingua e Cultura Italiana (☎ 552 43 31), Vico Santa Maria dell'Aiuto

1	Prati
2	Casanova Hotel
3	Albergo Ginevra
4	Piazza Principe Umberto
5	Hotel Zara
6	Castel Capuano
7	EPT Tourist Information
8	Intercity & Urban Bus Terminal
9	Central Railway Station
10	Trattoria Avellinese
11	Piazza V Calenda
12	Trianon
13	Piazza Nolana
14	Parking
15	Circumvesuviana Station
16	Piazza Mercato
17	Piazza del Carmine
18	Church of Santa Maria del Carmine

17, is one of several language schools in the city.

If you want to go diving, contact the Subacquei Napoletani (☎ 764 49 21), Piazza Santa Maria degli Angeli 11, for details.

For sailing, the Club Nautico (☎ 764 58 29), Borgo Marinari, is a private club but the staff should be able to suggest where you can hire equipment.

Organised Tours

Excursions to the islands and inland to Pompeii and Mt Vesuvius are organised by the CIT (☎ 552 54 26), Piazza Municipio 70; Cima Tours (☎ 554 06 46), Piazza Garibaldi 114; and Tourcar (☎ 552 33 10), Piazza Matteotti 1. A half-day tour to Pompeii is about L50,000. The AAST organises tours of city sights every Sunday at 10.30 am. Details are inside the back cover of *Qui Napoli*, or you can enquire at the AAST branch on Piazza Gesù.

Festivals

The big festival surrounds San Gennaro, when throngs gather in the chapel bearing his name to see his blood liquefy (as explained in the previous Things to See section). Get there early, as police turn back the crowds when the Duomo is full. Other important festivals are the Madonna del Carmine on 15 July, held in Piazza del Carmine, which cul-

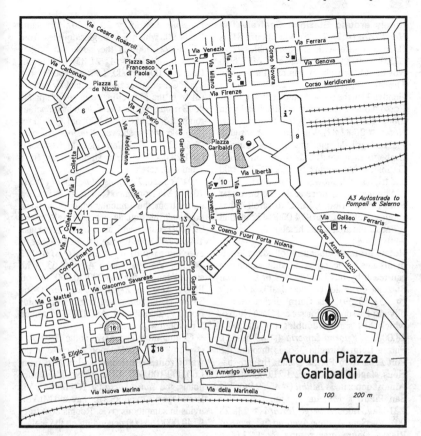

Around Piazza Garibaldi

minates in a fireworks display, and the Madonna di Piedigrotta in early September. Around Christmas, thousands of cribs are erected around the city.

Places to Stay

Naples is surprisingly cheap compared with the north of the country, although most of the budget hotels are clustered around Stazione Centrale in a rather unsafe area. Singles should head for the Spaccanapoli/city centre area. The EPT tourist office at Stazione Centrale will recommend hotels, and you should avoid the hawkers who will harass you around the station – they are on commission and are generally pushing less reputable establishments. The closest *camping ground* is in Pozzuoli – see the Pozzuoli section for details.

Hostel The IYHF *Ostello Mergellina Napoli* (☎ 761 23 46), Salita della Grotta 23, in Mergellina, is modern and safe. Bed and breakfast is L16,000, and L21,000 without an IYHF card. Dinner is L12,000. It is open all year and imposes a minimum three-night stay in summer. Take bus No 152 from Stazione Centrale or the Metropolitana to Mergellina and follow the signs.

Hotels around Stazione Centrale The *Hotel Zara* (☎ 28 71 25), Via Firenze 81, is clean and safe with singles/doubles from L25,000/50,000. Via Firenze is off Corso Novara, to the right as you exit the station. The *Albergo Ginevra* (☎ 28 32 10), Via Genova 116, the second street to the right off Corso Novara, is another reliable hotel with rooms for L30,000/50,000. The *Casanova Hotel* (☎ 26 82 87), Via Venezia 2, through Piazza Garibaldi and past Piazza Principe Umberto in a small side street off Corso Garibaldi, has rooms for L28,000/52,000 and triples with shower for L75,000.

Moving up the price scale, the three-star *Prati* (☎ 554 18 02), Via C Rosaroll 4, has singles/doubles from L74,000/142,500 and is one of the area's best hotels.

Hotels around Spaccanapoli Many hotels in this area are near Piazza Dante, which you can reach by bus No 185, CS or CD from Stazione Centrale. The best deal is at *Candy* (☎ 552 13 59), Via Carrozzieri a Monteolivieto 13, south of Piazza del Gesù Nuovo, which has singles/doubles for L11,000/18,000. *Soggiorno Imperia* (☎ 45 53 82), Piazza Luigi Miraglia 386, is through the Port'Alba from Piazza Dante. Bright, spacious singles/doubles are L21,000/34,000. Almost opposite is *Bellini* (☎ 46 59 96), Via San Pietro a Maiella 6, with rooms for L21,000/37,000. *Albergo Tortora* (☎ 738 28 00), Via Sant'Andrea Avellino 2C, west of Piazza Dante, has rooms for L23,000/33,000. *Alloggio Fiamma* (☎ 45 91 87), Via Francesco del Giudice 13, is nearby. It has very basic rooms at L20,000/38,000, or L40,000 for a double with shower. Just down from the Duomo is the *Duomo* (☎ 26 59 88), Via Duomo 228, with rooms for L32,000/56,000. Don't be put off by the entrance.

Higher in price and quality, the *Oriente Grand Hotel* (☎ 552 11 33), Via A Diaz 44, is one of the city's finest hotels, with rooms starting at about L150,000 for a single and L170,000 for a double.

Hotels in Mergellina, Vomero & Santa Lucia Near the bridge to Borgo Marinari is *Pensione Astoria* (☎ 20 19 20), Via Santa Lucia 90, which has singles/doubles from L12,500/21,000. In the same building is *Albergo Teresita* (☎ 41 21 05) with rooms from L33,000/48,000. *Linda* (☎ 66 80 48), Via F Crispi 104, can be reached by bus No C4 from the Mergellina train station or No 404S from Stazione Centrale. It has spacious rooms from L35,000/55,000, or L65,000 for a double with a shower. *Pensione Ausonia* (☎ 68 22 78), Via F Caracciolo 11, has rooms for L28,000/41,500, or slightly more for a room with services.

At Vomero, *Pensione Margherita* (☎ 556 70 44), Via Domenico Cimarosa 29, is a few doors from the funicular station. Singles/doubles/triples/quads are L40,000/72,000/99,000/126,000 and all include breakfast. Take a L50 coin for the lift. Farther out (if everything is full), try *Pensione Oasi* (☎ 578 74 56), Via Mariano d'Amelio 63, with singles/doubles for L45,000/60,000. Just off Piazza Amedeo, *Pensione Ruggiero* (☎ 66 35 36) is very clean and bright with rooms from L29,000/49,000. Add L4000 a person for a room with a shower.

Getting more expensive is the *Hotel Rex* (☎ 41 63 88), Via Palepoli 12, close to the waterfront, with singles/doubles from L60,000/100,000. One of Naples' better hotels, the *Santa Lucia* (☎ 764 06 66), Via Partenope 46, overlooks the bay and Mt Vesuvius in sumptuous style. Rooms cost from L140,000/166,000 depending on the view.

Places to Eat
Food Stalls If you want to grab a snack in the morning, head for *Giuliano*, Calata Trinità Maggiore 33, just off Piazza Carità, where they make what could well be the world's biggest doughnut. *Pizza Fritte*, Via Candelora 4, near the university, is recognisable only by the small cardboard sign at its brown door, but sells deep-fried pizzas filled with ricotta and tomato for L2000. It's open from 8.30 am to 2 pm.

Near the Riviera di Chiaia, *Più Focacle*, Vico del Vasto a Chiaia, has pizza by the slice for L1500. *Frittura Fiorenzano* in Piazza

Montesanto has deep-fried vegetables for L200 apiece.

For Naples' best gelati, head for *Gelateria Scimma*, Piazza Carità 4, or *Gelati Otranto*, in Vomero at Via M Kerbaker 43.

Around Spaccanapoli & City Centre The *Trattoria da Carmine*, Via dei Tribunali 92, is one of the dozens of small family trattorias in this area. It has pasta from L3000, main dishes from L4000, and cheap alcohol. It is open for lunch but, unfortunately, closes around 8 pm. *Pizzeria di Matteo*, Via dei Tribunali 94, is one of the city's best with pizzas from L3000 – try the pizza lasagna with ricotta, and the misto di frittura (deep-fried vegetables). It also does takeaway. *Da Luigi*, near the university entrance on the corner of Largo Girolamo Giusso and Largo San Giovanni Maggiore, serves pasta and risotto, with all dishes under L4000, but is open for lunch only. Close by is *Trattoria La Campagnola*, Piazzetta del Nilo, a studenty-looking place with pasta from L5000 and main dishes from L8000. It's closed Sunday.

The *Trianon*, Via Pietro Colletta 46, has a wide selection of pizzas from L5000 and is close to Stazione Centrale. There is another *Trianon* to the south-west, near the port area, at Via della Principessa Margherita. *Trattoria Avellinese*, Via Silvio Spaventa 31-35, is just off Piazza Garibaldi and specialises in cheap seafood.

Ristorante Bellini, Via Santa Maria di Costantinapoli 79-80, is one of Naples' better restaurants and a full meal will cost upwards of L25,000.

Across Via Toledo, *Trattoria Franco*, Vico Basilico Puoti 8, specialises in seafood and is cheap, with fish from L8000 and spaghetti vongole at L4500. It's closed Sunday. *Pizzeria al 22*, off Piazza Carità at Via Pignasecca 22, has takeaway pizzas from L4000.

If you want something other than Italian, *Cinese Hong Kong*, Vico Quercia 5A, off Via Roma near Piazza Dante, does good Chinese for about L15,000 a head.

Santa Lucia Don't be put off if you see locals fishing for *cozze* (mussels) from the bay: they're destined for their own tables, not yours; the restaurateurs frequent the city's markets instead. The restaurants on Borgo Marinari are generally overpriced, but try *Trattoria da Patrizia*, Via Luculliana, with the red Coke chairs, which offers pasta from L6000. *Antica Trattoria da Pietro* is a couple of doors down and offers much the same.

Mergellina & Vomero In front of the Certosa of San Martino, *Renzo e Lucia*, Via Tito Angelini 33A, offers spectacular views over the city and lofty prices to match. Pasta costs from L10,000 and pizza from L5000, with a L3000 cover charge. To reach the restaurant, you could take a 30-minute uphill walk (not recommended at night) from Via Roma or take bus No VS, VD or V3 from Piazza Vanvitelli.

The *Acunzo*, Via Domenico Cimarosa 60, has pizzas and pasta, and a full meal can cost L12,000. It's closed Sunday. *Frasco*, nearby at Via Morghen 12, is one of Vomero's more popular spots, with pizzas from L4000 and pasta from L6000. *Mario Daniele*, Via A Scarlatti 104, is a bar with a restaurant upstairs. *Gran Bar Riviera*, Riviera di Chiaia 183, is supposedly one of the city's grandest. Multiply prices by three if you want to sit outside.

Entertainment

The monthly *Qui Napoli* and the weekly *Postounico*, both from tourist offices, are the best guides to what's on. *Naples by Night* sells at newsstands for L10,000 and reviews the latest clubs etc. The main box office for sporting or cultural events (☎ 551 91 88) is at Galleria Umberto I 15-16.

Young, hip Italians stand around their cars and motorini eating gelati at Piazza Amedeo, which can be fun to watch, and the city jumps with jazz joints and trendy (some might say tacky) clubs. Some clubs charge hefty entrance or membership fees, which usually include a drink.

The San Carlo Theatre has year-round performances of opera, ballet and concerts. Tickets start at L15,000 and spiral upwards, and always sell quickly. The booking office is at the theatre (☎ 797 23 31). Adjacent to the theatre in the Palazzo Reale (to the left of the main entrance and up the grand staircase) is the Teatro di Corte, which is slightly avant-garde but still expensive. Watch out for posters and book at the theatre.

In July, there is a series of free concerts called Luglio Musicale a Capodimonte outside the Capodimonte Palace. If sitting around in a bar is your idea of fun, one of the more interesting is *Intra Moenia*, Piazza Bellini 69-70, an arty/gay/leftist café/book-shop in one of the city's more beautiful piazzas.

Check the listings for what's hot in clubs, and try Exclusive, otherwise known as Kiss Kiss, Via Sgambati 47, a long way from the city centre in Vomero. The Otto Jazz Club, Piazzetta Cariati 23, features Neapolitan jazz, while La Belle Epoque, Via Andrea d'Isernia 33, near the Riviera di Chiaia, has rock, blues, jazz and soul on different nights.

Soccer matches are played at the Stadio San Paolo in the western suburb of Mostra d'Oltremare. Call ☎ 61 56 23 for details.

Things to Buy

Naples is renowned for its gold, *presepi* (cribs), *bambole* (dolls) and religious arte-facts. Most artisans are in Spaccanapoli, in particular along Via dei Tribunali, Via B Croce and the side streets and lanes. Many goldsmiths and *gioiellerie* (jewellery shops) are clustered in an area around Via San Biagio dei Librai, and their wares are well advertised. Be warned, some inflate prices for tourists.

The city's better shops are in Santa Lucia, behind Piazza del Plebiscito, along Via Chiaia to Piazza dei Martiri and down to the waterfront. Young people shop along Via Roma and Via Toledo, and the grand Galleria Umberto I is but a shadow of its former self. Street markets selling just about everything are in Piazza Garibaldi and off Piazza Carità.

Getting There & Away

Air Capodichino Airport (☎ 780 57 63), Viale Umberto Maddalena, about five km north-east of the city centre, is southern Italy's main airport and links Naples with most Italian and several major European cities.

The airlines represented in Naples include:

Alitalia (☎ 542 53 33), Via Medina 41-42
British Airways (☎ 780 30 87), at the airport
TWA (☎ 764 58 28), Via Partenope 23
Qantas, handled by Gastaldi Travel (☎ 552 12 63), Via Depretis 108

Bus Buses leave for Italian and some European cities from Piazza Garibaldi in front of the train station. Look carefully or ask, because there are no signs. The Naples Public Transport Board (☎ 700 50 91, with several information offices in Piazza Garibaldi), SITA (☎ 552 21 76, Via Pisanelli 3-7), and Curreri (☎ 879 85 24) operate most routes throughout the region. There are regular services to Sorrento and Salerno (SITA); Benvenuto, Caserta and Avellino (Naples Public Transport Board); and other small towns around Naples, as well as a Capodichino Airport-Sorrento service (Curreri).

Train Naples is the major hub for the south, and many trains originating in the major northern cities pass through Rome and ter-minate here. The city is served by regionale, diretto, espresso, intercity, EuroCity and the superfast ETR 450 trains. They arrive and depart from Stazione Centrale (☎ 553 41 88) at Piazza Garibaldi.

Car & Motorbike Naples is on the major north-south Autostrada del Sole, known as the A1 to Rome and Milan and the A3 to Salerno and Reggio di Calabria. The A30 acts as a ring road through Campania, while the A16 heads east from the city to Bari.

When approaching the city, the autostra-das meet the Tangenziale di Napoli, a major ring road around the city. The multi-laned Tangenziale Ovest di Napoli hugs the city's northern fringe, meeting the A1 and A17 autostradas for Rome and Capodichino Airport in the east, and continues for Pozzuoli and the Phlegrean Fields to the west. The A3 autostrada for Salerno and Calabria can be reached from Corso Arnaldo Lucci, southeast of Piazza Garibaldi.

For rental information, see the following Getting Around section.

Boat Ferries and hydrofoils leave for Capri, Sorrento, Ischia, Procida, Forio and Casamicciola from the Molo Beverello in front of the Castel Nuovo. Ferries to Palermo, Cagliari, Reggio di Calabria, Catania, Syracuse, Milazza and the Aeolian Islands leave from the Stazione Marittima, next to the Molo Beverello. Some hydrofoils leave for the bay islands from Mergellina, and Alilauro and SNAV also operate to most destinations from Mergellina.

Ferry companies and the routes they service are as follows:

Alilauro (☎ 761 10 04) operates boats to Sorrento (L12,000 return).

Caremar (☎ 551 38 82) serves Capri (L13,000 return), Ischia (L9800 return) and Procida (L6400 return).

Linea Lauro operates boats to Ischia (L7800 return).

Navigazione Libera del Golfo (☎ 552 72 09) services Capri (L6800 return).

Siremar (☎ 551 21 13) operates a service to the Aeolian Islands and Milazzo on Tuesday and Thursday.

SNAV (☎ 761 23 48) services Capri.

Tirrenia (☎ 551 21 81) has a daily service to Palermo (L60,000 one way), to Cagliari (L45,000 one way) on Thursday, and to Reggio di Calabria, Sicily and Malta (L58,900) on Wednesday.

Getting Around

To/From the Airport Take bus No 14 from Stazione Centrale, or CLP's airport bus (☎ 531 17 06) every 30 minutes from Via Marina, Piazza Municipio, Via Depretis, Piazza Borsa or Piazza Garibaldi.

Bus & Tram Most city ATAN buses operating in the central area depart from and terminate in front of Stazione Centrale, although the bus stops there are not well signposted. The city does not prepare a bus map, and it is impossible to find decent infor-

mation. There is an ATAN bus information office at Stazione Centrale and another at Piazza Dante. For the only list of routes, pick up a copy of *TuttoCittà* at an SIP telephone office.

A useful bus is the No CA, which starts and terminates at Stazione Centrale and passes Via Diaz, Via Toledo and Corso Umberto I in the city centre. Other buses and their routes include:

CD & CS – round trips in opposite directions from Stazione Centrale through the city centre to Piazza Dante

C1 – from Piazza Gesù to Corso Umberto and back

C4 – around Mergellina, along the waterfront to the city centre, Piazza Diaz, Piazza Amedeo and back to Mergellina

FT – from Stazione Centrale through the city centre and Chiaia to Piazzale Tecchio near Stadio San Paolo

14 & 14R – from Piazza Garibaldi to the airport and the city's north

24 – from the Parco Castello and Piazza Trieste e Trento along Via Toledo, Via Roma to Capodimonte

102, 112 & 112RB – from Parco Castello, along the Riviera di Chiaia and westwards, past Mergellina

109 – from Parco Castello through Piazza Dante past the museum, Capodimonte and farther north

110 – from Stazione Centrale to the museum, Capodimonte and the Castel Caracciolo

127R – from Stazione Centrale to Piazza Cavour, the museum, Capodimonte and Marianella

137R – from Piazza Dante north to Capodimonte, farther north and then back to Piazza Dante

Night buses include:

401 – connects Stazione Centrale with the Riviera di Chiaia, through the city centre, and returns to the station

403S – operates from Stazione Centrale to Mergellina through the city centre, and returns along the same route

404S, 406D & 406S – operate round trips from Stazione Centrale through the city centre

Tram Nos 1 and 1B operate from east of Stazione Centrale, through Piazza Garibaldi, the city centre and along the waterfront to Riviera di Chiaia. Tram No 2B travels from Stazione Centrale to the city centre along Corso Garibaldi.

Train The city has four other railway systems. The Metropolitana (underground railway) operates one line from Gianturco, east of Stazione Centrale, with stops at Stazione Centrale, Piazza Cavour, Piazza Amedeo, Mergellina, Fuorigrotta, Campi Flegrei (the Phlegrean Fields), Pozzuoli and Solfatara.

The Circumvesuviana (☎ 779 24 44), about 400 metres south-west of Stazione Centrale in Corso Garibaldi (take the underpass from Stazione Centrale), operates trains to Sorrento via Pompeii, Herculaneum and other towns along the coast. There are about 40 a day between 5 am and 11 pm.

The Ferrovia Cumana and the Circumflegrea (☎ 551 33 28), based at Stazione Cumana in Piazza Montesanto, 300 metres south-west of Piazza Dante, operate services to Pozzuoli and Cumae every 20 minutes.

Funicular Railways The Funicolare Centrale from Via Toledo connects the city centre with Vomero (Piazza Fuga). The Funicolare di Chiaia travels from Via del Parco Margherita to Via Domenico Cimarosa, also in Vomero. The Funicolare di Montesanto travels from Piazza Montesanto to Via Morghen. All three can be used to reach the Certosa of San Martino and the Vomero area. The Funicolare di Mergellina connects the waterfront at Via Mergellina with Via Manzoni.

Car & Motorbike Forget it unless you have a death wish. Park your car at one of the garages, most of which are staffed, and walk around the city centre. Try Supergarage, Via Shelley 11, in the city centre; Grilli, Via Galileo Ferraris 40, near Stazione Centrale; and Mergellina, Via Mergellina 112 at the hydrofoil terminal there.

Apart from the headaches you will suffer trying to negotiate the city's chaotic traffic, you will also need to remember that car theft is a major problem in Naples. Although it is said that Neapolitans observe some caution when driving behind or near cars with foreign numberplates, the risk of being in an accident is quite high if you fail to understand immediately the local system of not stopping at traffic lights.

Rental Avis has offices at Via Partenope 32 (☎ 764 56 00) and Stazione Centrale (☎ 28 40 41); Europcar (☎ 40 14 54) is at Via Partenope 38. Both also have offices at the airport.

Most companies charge an average L15,000 a day extra because of the city's theft problem, and many will not allow you to drive a car hired in Rome or the north into the city for this reason.

It is impossible to rent a motorino in Naples for reasons of theft. You can hire them at Sorrento.

Taxi Taxis generally ignore kerb-side arm wavers. You can arrange one through Radiotaxi (☎ 556 44 44) or else at taxi stands on most piazzas in the city. The minimum fare is L5000, and a short trip can cost up to L20,000 because of traffic delays.

AROUND NAPLES
The Phlegrean Fields (Campi Flegrei)
The area west of Naples is known as the Phlegrean ('Fiery') Fields, a classical term for the volcanic activity which has made it one of the globe's most geologically unstable areas. It includes the towns of Pozzuoli, Baia and Cumae, and it was through this region that Greek civilisation arrived in Italy. The area was much celebrated in the writings of Virgil and Homer who believed it to be the entrance to Hades. Now part of suburban Naples, it is dirty and overdeveloped, but it bears some well-preserved reminders of the Greeks and Romans, is easily accessible and is worth a half-day trip.

Getting There & Away Take the ATAN bus from Piazza Garibaldi in Naples for Pozzuoli. CTP and SEPSA also run buses to Pozzuoli from near Stazione Centrale.

See the Naples Getting Around section for details of the Metropolitana, Ferrovia Cumana and Circumflegrea rail services to the area.

The Tangenziale di Napoli, the city's ring

road, runs through the area. Exit at Pozzuoli. Alternatively, take Via Caracciolo along the Naples waterfront for Posillipo.

Caremar (☎ 081-526 14 81) runs services from Pozzuoli to Ischia (L10,800).

Pozzuoli Grubby-looking and now just a suburb of Naples, Pozzuoli has lost much of its beauty. However, this major town in the the Phlegrean Fields contains an impressive collection of Roman ruins. The tourist office (☎ 081-526 24 19), Via Campi Flegrei 3, is about one km uphill from the train station and has a reasonable map of the area.

Close to the remains of the Roman port of Puteoli is the **Temple of Serapis** (Tempio di Serapide), which was simply a market of shops and, according to some sources, skilfully designed toilets. It has been badly damaged over the centuries by the seismic activity known as bradyseism (literally 'slow earthquake') which slowly raises and lowers the ground level over long periods. The nearby church of Santa Maria delle Grazie, along Via Roma, is sinking at a rate of about two cm a year because of this.

The **cathedral**, also known as the Temple of Augustus, contains six columns from a temple dedicated to Augustus that once stood in the area. North-east along Via Rosini is the **Flavian Amphitheatre**, which had seating for 40,000 people and could be flooded for mock naval battles. It's open from 9 am to one hour before sunset, and entrance is L6000.

Farther along, Via Rosini becomes Via Solfatara and continues to the **Solfatara Crater**, about a two-km walk (or jump on any city bus heading uphill). Known to the Romans as the Forum Vulcani and bearing some remnants of ancient spa buildings, the Solfatara Crater occasionally ejects steam jets and bubbling mud. The entire crater is a layer of rock supported by the steam pressure beneath. Pick up a boulder, cast it into the air and listen to the rumblings as it hits the ground. Entrance to the site is L4000. The crater area includes a crowded *camping ground* (☎ 081-526 74 13) at Via Solfatana

161. Sites cost L7300 per person and L6600 per tent, plus car fees.

To the south of the crater is the **Church of St Januarius**, where Naples' patron saint was beheaded in 305 AD.

Baia & Cumae Twenty minutes north-west of Pozzuoli, on the Ferrovia Cumana or by SEPSA bus, is Baia, once a fashionable Roman bathing resort, the remains of which are now submerged about 100 metres from the shore. On a clear day, ask one of the local fishers to take you out. They might charge up to L10,000, but the remains are quite large and worth a look.

Beyond Baia is Bacoli with more Roman remains, and Cumae, the site, according to Virgil's account in the *Aeneid*, where Aeneas, the legendary Trojan prince who is said to have laid the foundations from which Rome grew, landed in Italy. A visit to **Sibyl's Cave** is a must. Inland is **Lake Avernus**, the mythical entrance to the underworld where Aeneas is said to have eventually descended to meet his father.

Caserta

Reached by SITA bus from Piazza Garibaldi in Naples (L4200), by train from Stazione Centrale, or via the A1 autostrada or ss87, Caserta has one attraction: the **Royal Palace** (Palazzo Reale) built by the Bourbons of Naples and modelled on the French Versailles. There is a tourist information office (☎ 0823-32 11 37) in the palace, which produces a guide to the site.

The building and its gardens are definitely worth a visit and are only a short trip from Naples. Work started in 1752 after Charles III of Bourbon decided he would build himself a palace similar to Versailles. Neapolitan Luigi Vanvitelli, commissioned for the job, established his reputation as one of the leading architects of the time after working on the palace.

Covering a massive 51,000 sq metres, with a façade stretching 250 metres, the building is of massive proportions, with 1200 rooms, 1790 windows and 34 staircases. After entering by Vanvitelli's immense staircase, you follow a path through the royal apartments, most of them richly decorated with tapestries, furniture, mirrors and crystal. After the library rooms is a room containing a vast collection of Nativity scenes played out in several huge cabinets, featuring hundreds of hand-carved characters.

A walk in the **gardens** is a must. Take a picnic lunch and stroll through the series of fountains – the Daisy Fountain, the Dolphin Fountain and the Fountain of Ceres. At the end of the gardens are the Fountains of Venus and Diana which rise up into the hills. There is a magnificent view of the parkland and palace from high on the hill, which can be reached by a staircase. A bus runs through the grounds (L1000).

Also visit the **Santa Leucio silk factory**, two km north-west of the palace and reached by bus from the train station, which was built by Ferdinand IV and still operates today.

Benevento

A provincial capital about 60 km from Naples, Benevento is on the Via Appia, the old Roman road. After a period as a Lombard duchy, when it controlled much of southern Italy, the town was transferred to the control of the papacy in the 11th century and remained mostly under papal rule until 1860.

The tourist information office (☎ 0824-31 06 61), Via Sala 31, has information about the town and the region.

The town was heavily bombed in WW II and the **cathedral** had to be largely rebuilt. Its 13th century Pisan façade has been preserved and there are a number of Roman stones used in its construction. South of the cathedral is a well-preserved Roman theatre, dating from Hadrian's time. The **Arch of Trajan** built in 114 AD commemorated the opening of the Via Traiana. The **obelisk** in Piazza Matteotti is a reminder of the Napoleonic period. The **Church of Santa Sofia**, near the piazza, adjoins what was once a Benedictine abbey. It contains the **Samnite Museum**, which houses remnants of a temple dedicated to Isis, dating from 88 AD.

The town can be reached by SITA buses or by rail from Naples, and is close to the A16 autostrada. It is also on the ss7 (the Via Appia).

THE BAY OF NAPLES
Capri

Despite the boatloads of British and German tourists who pour onto the Marina Grande each day and restaurants that boast *Würstl*, real English butter and Maxwell House coffee, Capri is a beautiful and relatively unspoilt dot in the Bay of Naples. Its breath-taking caves, luxuriant vegetation and charming narrow laneways of its small towns have attracted visitors for centuries. The best times to visit the island are during April, May, June and October, when the weather and prices are better than in the high season from July to September.

History Capri was occupied by the Greeks and then the Romans, when it became the playground of Emperor Augustus and his successor, Tiberius. Augustus freed Capri from its dependence on Naples and turned it into his private estate. He is believed to have founded the world's first palaeontological museum, in the Villa Augustus, to house fossils and Stone-Age artefacts unearthed by his workers. Tiberius spent his last years on the island, and his debauched lifestyle is said to still haunt the ruins of the Roman palaces and villas on the island.

Orientation About five km from the main-land, Capri is a mere six km long and 2.7 km wide. As you approach the island, there is a lovely view of the town of Capri, with the dramatic slopes of Mt Solaro (589 metres) to the west hiding the other village, Anacapri.

All hydrofoils and ferries arrive at Marina Grande, a small settlement that is virtually part of Capri. Buses connect the port with Capri and Anacapri, departing from Via Marina Grande (L1500), just to the right as you leave the pier. A funicular (L1500) connects the marina with Capri. Otherwise, follow Via Marina Grande for a three-km uphill hike into Capri.

Via Marina Grande reaches a junction at

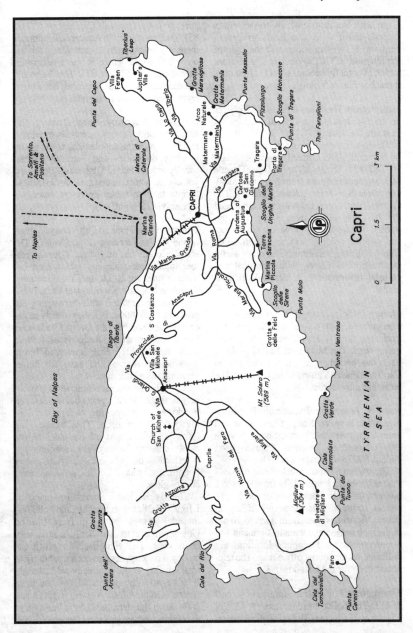

Capri

Capri with Via Roma, which, to the left, is Capri's main strip and leads to Piazza Umberto I, its main square. To the right of the junction is Via Provinciale di Anacapri, which eventually becomes Via G Orlandi as it reaches Piazza Vittoria.

Information There are three AAST offices on the island: at Marina Grande, Bachina del Porto on the dock (☎ 081-837 06 34); Piazza Umberto I, in the centre of Capri (☎ 081-837 06 86); and Via G Orlandi 19A in Anacapri (☎ 081-837 15 24). The Marina Grande office generally opens from 8 am to midday and about 3 to 8 pm (closed Sunday). The Capri office is open from 8 am to 8 pm, and the Anacapri office from 9 am to 3 pm (closed Sunday). They provide a vague map and walking guide as well as a publication, *Capri È*, listing restaurants and other useful information. *A Capri*, with historical and cultural information, is available periodically.

Money Official exchange operations are everywhere, but watch the charges and exchange rates, which are usually below the going rates. The Monte dei Paschi di Siena bank has branches at Via V Emanuele in Capri and Piazza Vittoria 12 in Anacapri. The latter has a bancomat.

Post & Telecommunications The main post office is on Via Roma, to the left as you enter Capri. Another post office is at Viale De Tommaso in Anacapri. Capri's postal code is 80073, Anacapri's 80071.

There is an SIP public telephone office at Piazza Umberto I, open daily from 9 am to 1 pm, and then 3 to 8 pm in winter and 3 to 11 pm in summer. The Anacapri office, in Piazza Vittoria, is open from 8 am to 10 pm in the high season and 9 am to 1 pm and 3 to 8 pm otherwise. Telephone locations are indicated on the tourist office map. The telephone code for the island is 081.

Emergency For police emergency, call ☎ 113. The police headquarters (☎ 837 72 45) are at Via Roma 70. For medical assist-ance, go to the Ospedale Capilupi (☎ 837 05 85), Via Provinciale, in Anacapri. In summer there is a tourist medical emergency service on ☎ 837 20 91. There is also a helicopter ambulance (☎ 584 14 81). The Farmacia Barile, Piazza Vittoria, Anacapri, has a night service but only for prescriptions.

Dangers & Annoyances During the summer months, and occasionally in winter, hundreds of young people flock to the island to party on Friday and Saturday nights, usually around Piazza Umberto I. Beware if you choose a hotel in that area, because these people tend to make noisy nuisances of themselves all night.

Things to See Think of Capri and you think of the **Grotta Azzurra** (Blue Grotto). The island actually has more than a dozen grottoes, most accessible and spectacular, but none as stunning as this one. Two Germans, Augustus Kopisch, a writer, and Ernst Fries, a painter, are credited with discovering the grotto in 1826, but in fact they merely rediscovered and renamed the Grotta Gradola, as locals had known it. Remains of Roman work inside, including a carved ledge towards the rear of the cave for better viewing, were later discovered.

It is believed the cave sank to its present height, about 15 to 20 meters below sea level, blocking every opening except the 1.3-metre-high entrance. This causes the refraction of sunlight off the sides of the cavity, creating the magical blue colour and a reflection of light off the white sandy bottom, giving anything below the surface a silvery glow.

The overinflated admission price of L16,900 (L18,050 on Sundays and holidays) includes a motorboat trip from Marina Grande, transfer to a smaller boat and a very short visit. The visit itself is worth the money. The 'captains' expect a tip, but try to avoid paying – you've already paid enough. It is slightly cheaper to take a bus from Anacapri to the Grotta Azzurra (L1500) and walk down the steps behind the bus stop to the entrance where you meet the small boats, but you are still up for L10,000 admission (plus L500 on Sundays and holidays). Tours start at 9 am.

Although it is not illegal to swim into the grotto, the tourist office says it is a monument and should be respected. It can be done, but only after the last tourist boat at about 5 pm, and only when the water is extremely calm. Because of tidal flows through the small entrance, it is quite dangerous, but locals, despite their fear of the dragons and witches that are believed to inhabit the cave, have swum in it for centuries.

From Piazza Umberto I, in the centre of Capri, an afternoon can be whiled away wandering through the narrow laneways with their tiny houses and villas. In the square itself, the 17th century **Church of Santo Stefano** contains remnants from the Roman villas. Head down Via D Birago, or Via V Emanuele, for the **Certosa di San Giacomo**, a Carthusian monastery with sections, including cloisters, dating from the 14th century. It is open Tuesday to Sunday from 9 am to 2 pm. Nearby are the **Gardens of Augustus** (Giardini di Augusto), offering one of the better views of the **Faraglioni**, the rock formations along the south coast. A path below the gardens leading to Marina Piccola is closed for reconstruction and has been so for a long time.

Head east from the town centre to Via Tiberio and **Jupiter's Villa** (Villa Jovis), the residence of Emperor Tiberius. It is open from 9 am to one hour before sunset and entry is L4000. The walk takes about one hour. The stairway behind the villa leads to **Tiberius' Leap** (Salto di Tiberio), a cliff from where he is believed to have had out-of-favour subjects thrown. A pleasant walk down Via Matermania passes the **Arco Naturale**, a rock arch formed by the pounding sea.

The **Museo del Centro Caprese I Cerio** at Piazzetta Cerio 8A houses a collection of Neolithic and Palaeolithic fossils discovered on the island. It is open Tuesday to Sunday from 9 am to 2 pm and costs L4000.

From Piazza Vittoria in Anacapri, take the chair lift to the top of Mt Solaro (L4500 one way, L5500 return, from 9 am to two hours

before sunset) where on a (rare) clear day you can see for miles.

North from Piazza Vittoria is the **Villa San Michele di Axel Munthe**, built by the Swedish writer and doctor on a former Roman villa. It is open from 9 am to 6 pm in summer, 10.30 am to 3.30 pm in winter, and entrance is L4000. It houses Roman sculptures from Tiberius' rule. The pathway behind the villa offers superb views, and the (usually closed) stairway of 800 steps was the only link between Anacapri and the rest of the island until the mountain road was built in the 1950s. From Anacapri, take a bus to Faro (L1500), a less crowded spot with one of Italy's tallest lighthouses.

Activities For scuba diving, canoeing or boat hire, try the Sea Service Centre (☎ 837 02 21), Marina Piccola, Via Mulo 63, which represents a host of companies, including the Capri Diving Club. Canoes can be rented from L9000 an hour or L32,000 a day; motorised dinghies can be rented from L45,000 to L250,000 an hour and L120,000 to L620,000 a day. The centre offers water skiing from L44,000 for 15 minutes. Alberino Gennaro (☎ 837 71 18) also rents scuba equipment. For sailboards and Hobie Cats, contact Banana Sport (☎ 837 51 88) at Marina Grande. For a real treat, call Gorgonia (☎ 837 75 77) and ask about its submarine voyages around the island.

The main places to swim are at a small inlet west of Marina Grande; Bagno di Tiberio, where the emperor dipped; a rocky area at Marina Piccola; off concrete ledges at the Blue Grotto (only after 5 pm); and, farther west of the grotto, below the restaurants. There are no private beaches on the island, and the best areas can only be reached by hired boat or by traversing rough tracks, particularly around Pizzolungo.

Places to Stay Hotel rooms are at a premium in the summer months, and many close during winter. Beware of the compulsory breakfast in summer and during the off season, haggle for a better price. Camping is strictly forbidden and offenders are either prosecuted or 'asked' to relocate to a hotel. There is no hostel on the island.

Marina Grande The *Villa Marina* (☎ 837 91 76), Via Marina Grande, has singles/doubles from L40,000/56,000. The *Italia* (☎ 837 06 02), Via Marina Grande, has rooms from L45,000/67,500, or more with a shower. Nearby, the *Belvedere e Tre Re* (☎ 837 03 45), Via Marina Grande, has good views, with rooms from L40,000/65,000.

Capri All rooms have views over the bay at *ABC* (☎ 837 06 83), Via M Serafina, at L40,000/70,000, breakfast included. *Stella Maris* (☎ 837 04 52), Via Roma, also has views from every room, with prices starting at L40,000/65,000 for singles/doubles, and L90,000/120,000 for triples/quads. Facing the south side, the Liberty-style *Esperia* (☎ 837 02 62), Via Sopramonte, is a crumbling villa with spectacular views. Rooms start at L55,000/100,000, including breakfast.

Anacapri The *Loreley* (☎ 837 14 40), Via G Orlandi, is one of the better deals at L30,000/60,000, with views over Naples from some rooms. *Caesar Augustus* (☎ 837 14 21), Via G Orlandi, has the best view in town and a terrace overlooking the bay. The hotel has three stars, but discounts empty rooms to L30,000/60,000. *Biancamaria* (☎ 837 10 00), Via G Orlandi, has rooms from L51,000/54,000. Anacapri virtually closes during winter.

Places to Eat Food is good and reasonably priced on the island, and even the expensive-looking bread and cheese dishes aren't exorbitant. *Insalata caprese*, a delicious salad of fresh tomato and mozzarella, has its origins here. Some of the local wines are a bit rough but are generally good. The *Sfizi di Pane*, Via Le Botteghe 4, has local breads and cakes, and the cheese shop opposite sells caprese cheese, a cross between mozzarella and ricotta.

Capri The *Longano*, Via Longano 11, just off

Piazza Umberto I, has a bay view, and pizzas and pasta from L7000. *La Cisterna*, Via M Serafina 5, has only two types of pizza, napoletana and margherita, for L5000, and pasta from L7000. *Il Tinello*, nearby at Via l'Abate 1-3, has pizzas from L5000. *Da Giorgio* and *Moscardino*, beside each other at Via Roma 34 and 28, have the best views in town and a cover charge to match (L3000). Their pizzas start at L6000. One of the island's best traditional restaurants is *La Capannina*, where a meal could cost up to L70,000 a person.

On the way to Arco Naturale, *Ristorante Le Grottelle*, Via Arco Naturale, has pasta from L6500 and meat dishes from L9000. Locals do their fruit and vegetable shopping at the small market, the *mercatino*, below the Capri bus stop (take the stairs).

Anacapri *Il Solitario*, Via G Orlandi 54, set in a garden, has pasta from L7000. *Trattoria Il Saraceno*, Via Trieste e Trento 18, serves ravioli caprese at L7000, and the owners serve their own wine. *Materita Pizzeria*, Via G Orlandi 140, has pizzas from L7000 and faces onto Piazza Diaz, as does *Mamma Giovanna*, Via Boffe 3-5, with pasta from L6000.

Entertainment For a drink with a lot of English people, head for Maxim's Pub, Via Oratorio 9, in Capri, or else hang out with locals at Guarracino, Via Castello 7. In Anacapri, sit on Piazza Diaz or shoot pool at Bar Materita, Via G Orlandi 140, at very reasonable prices. Nightlife is a bit thin on the ground, but try Atmosphere or Number Two, both in Via Camerelle, and the slightly more modern (if that is possible) New Pentothal, Via Vittorio Emanuele 45, all in Capri.

The main non-religious festival is from 1 to 6 January when local folk groups perform in Piazza Diaz and Piazza Umberto I.

Things to Buy The island is covered with ceramic tiles displaying street names and numbers and romantic scenes. Massimo Goderecci, Via P Serafino Cimino 8, just off Piazza Umberto I, takes credit for most of these and will bake you a tile for about L100,000.

The island is famous for its perfume and lemon liqueur. The former smells like lemons and the latter tastes like vodka. Visit Limoncello Capri, Via Capodimonte 27, in Anacapri, and taste the liqueur. The perfumeries are ubiquitous.

Getting There & Away See the Naples Getting There & Away section for details of ferries and hydrofoils. Call EliAmbassador (☎ 789 62 73) for helicopter flights between the island and Naples, which can cost several hundred thousand lira.

Getting Around You can take your car or motorino to Capri, but there is no hire service on the island. The best way to get around is by bus, with most tickets costing L1500 on the main runs between the Marina Grande, Capri, Anacapri, Grotta Azzurra and Faro. Buses run between Capri and Anacapri until past midnight. Tickets are no cheaper if bought in bulk (call SIPPAC on ☎ 837 04 20). A funicular links Marina Grande with Capri (L1500).

A taxi ride between any of the villages can cost up to L20,000, and from the Marina to Capri about L12,000, and the open-topped 1950s Fiats are very inviting. For a taxi in Capri, call ☎ 837 05 43; in Anacapri, call ☎ 837 11 75.

Ischia

The largest and most developed of the islands in the Bay of Naples, Ischia manages to retain a sense of its past, despite its 300 or so hotels. Away from the uglier towns on the island, people still work the land as if they'd never seen a tourist. The island is noted for its thermal springs and 'curative' muds.

The main centres are the touristy town of Ischia and Ischia Porto, Casamicciola Terme, Forio and Lacco Ameno, which are all fairly unattractive and overcrowded compared to the pleasant, picturesque towns of Ischia Ponte, Serrara Fontana, Barano d'Ischia and Sant'Angelo. Hotel prices and camping make the island affordable, and its size

means you can get away from the August crowds.

The ruins of the **Castello d'Ischia**, an Aragonese castle on a small islet, make for an interesting visit (L5000 plus L1000 for the lift). Mt Epomeo (788 metres) is the island's highest mountain and can be reached on foot from Panza and Serrara Fontana (about 1½ hours). It offers superb views of the Bay of Naples.

Orientation & Information Ferries dock at Ischia Porto, the main tourist centre of the island. It is possible to walk from the pier area to Ischia Ponte, the less commercialised area adjoining the port, and on to the Castello Aragonese.

The tourist office (☎ 081-99 11 46), Banchina Porto Salvo at the main port, is open from 9 am to 8 pm Monday to Saturday and until 1 pm on Sunday. Get a hotel list, which features the only decent map that the tourist office has.

The telephone code for the island is 081.

Places to Stay & Eat Call the tourist office well in advance for room availability during the summer months. From October to May, prices drop considerably, although many hotels close. During the peak period, watch out for the compulsory breakfast and extra charge for showers.

Camping The island has several camping grounds. *Camping Internazionale* (☎ 99 14 49) and *Camping del Sole* (☎ 90 11 53) are both in Via M Mazzella, near the castle. On the other side of the island, try *Camping Mirage* (☎ 99 05 51), Piazza Maronti, which offers good views and is close to the better beaches.

Ischia The *Locanda Sul Mare* (☎ 99 15 08), Via Jasolino 68, has singles/doubles from L25,000/L35,000. *Villa Antonio* (☎ 98 26 60), Via San Giuseppe della Croce, has rooms for L50,000/80,000, or L70,000/L120,000 in August.

The *Cicco e Domingo*, Via Luigi Mazzella 80, is a pleasant trattoria with pasta from

L7000. *Pirozzi*, Via Seminario 53, Ischia Ponte, has pizzas from L7500.

Barano & Sant'Angelo On the more attractive side of the island, in Barano, the *Casa Gennaro* (☎ 90 71 18), Via Pezzapiano 50, has doubles for L40,000 and offers triples/quads. *Conchiglia* (☎ 99 92 70), Via Chiaia delle Rose, has rooms for L35,000/50,000, most with ocean views.

On the promontory of Sant'Angelo, the *Pensione Francesco* (☎ 99 93 76), Via Nazario Sauro 42, has doubles only for L65,000, including breakfast. *Da Franceschina*, Via Corrado Buono 51, has rooms for L30,000/56,000, and obligatory half-pension for L38,000 per person in August.

Getting There & Away See the Naples Getting There & Away section for details.

Getting Around Bus services depart from Ischia Porto, and the most useful buses are the CS (Circo Sinistra, Left Circle) and CD (Circo Destra, Right Circle), which circle the island in opposite directions, passing through each town, and leaving every 30 minutes. All hotels and camping grounds can be reached by these buses, but ask the driver for the closest stop.

The best way to see the island is by car or motorino. You can bring either on to the island, but there are two places that rent them. Autonoleggia Ischia (☎ 99 24 44), Via A De Luca 59, has Fiats from L40,000 and scooters from L35,000 a day, with free helmets. Fratelli del Franco (☎ 99 13 34), Via A De Luca 121, has motorini from L15,000 and cars for L50,000. Both hirers also have mountain bikes for L20,000 a day and offer weekly deals. Unfortunately, the vehicles cannot be taken off the island.

Procida

The pinks, whites and yellows of Procida's tiny Mediterranean-style houses cluttered along the waterfront make the island worth a visit. The beauty of the Bay of Naples' smallest island is immediately apparent. There are only three hotels and six camping grounds, making it attractive for backpackers, particularly during the peak tourist season in July/August when the other islands are very crowded.

The 16th century Palazzo Reale d'Avalos, more recently a prison, dominates the island and is worth exploring. Vivara, a smaller island reached by bridge, is now a nature reserve and is a good location for viewing birds and other remaining wildlife and simply walking.

Orientation & Information Marina Grande is the hop-off point for ferries, and forms most of the tourist showcase. Follow signs from the port to the ENTE tourist office (☎ 081-896 99 62), which is at Via Principe Umberto I, uphill behind the port area, and opens mornings and afternoons. There is also an APT tourist office at Via Roma 92 on Ischia.

The telephone code for the island is 081.

Places to Stay & Eat Camping sites are dotted around the island. The *Vivara* (☎ 896 92 42), Via IV Novembre, and *La Caravella* (☎ 896 92 30) are on the eastern side of the island, while *Privato Lubrano* (☎ 896 71 88) and *Graziella* (☎ 896 77 47), both in Via Salette, are near the better beaches of Ciraccio on the western side.

For a hotel, try the *Savoia* (☎ 896 71 97) near Centane, one of the cheapest with singles/doubles for L25,000/45,000, and the *Riviera* (☎ 896 71 97) at Chiaiolella, which is owned by the same people. Ask at the port, or the bus driver, for directions.

Cheap restaurants can be found along the waterfront near the port, and grocery shops are in the area around Via Vittorio Emanuele.

Getting There & Away See the Naples Getting There & Away section for details.

Getting Around The island has a limited bus service, with the L2 and C1 buses making round trips to most parts of the island from the port, where the ferries and hydrofoils arrive. The small APE open-top taxis can be hired for two to three hours for about

L20,000 or L30,000, depending on how hard you bargain. You can hire boats from Barcheggiando (☎ 810 19 34), although the local fishers will take you out for L10,000 to L20,000 per person, depending on the size of your group.

SOUTH OF NAPLES
Herculaneum (Ercolano)
Herculaneum is a suburb of Naples, about 12 km from the centre of the city, and has much the same history as nearby Pompeii. Oscan in origin, later Samnite and eventually Roman, it too was destroyed by an earthquake in 63 AD and completely submerged in the 79 AD eruption of Mt Vesuvius. First discoveries were made in 1719, and excavations began in 1738 and continued until 1874, when most of the booty was carted to Naples to decorate houses and palaces. Work recommenced in 1927 under the government's archaeological authorities. Though smaller and less impressive than Pompeii, Herculaneum is better preserved because it was covered in a torrent of volcanic mud, not the tufa stone that rained on Pompeii. Most inhabitants died in the disaster.

Orientation Herculaneum's main street, Via Panoramica, leads from the Circumvesuviana station at the modern town's eastern edge to Piazza Scavi and the main ticket office for the excavations. The site is easily reached on foot from the station. There is little else in the largely industrial Herculaneum that warrants a visit.

Information Although not strictly a tourist office, the Collegio Regionale Guide Alpine Campania (☎ 081-777 57 20) at Via Panoramica 302 has some information about the site and about Mt Vesuvius. It can also assist with walking and climbing expeditions. The *Amedeo Maiuri* guide to Herculaneum sells at most tourist stands for L10,000, and is considered to be one of the best guides to the site.

Things to See & Do The site is divided into 11 *insulae*, or islands. It sounds confusing, but it is possible to weave a less disorienting path through more than a dozen houses and other ruins. Many sites are closed, but wandering attendants will open doors upon request.

To your right as you enter the site is the **Casa dell'Albergo**, featuring a terrace that once overlooked the sea. Opposite is the **House of Argus** where you can see the remains of a garden. The **House of the Mosaic Atrium** is a magnificent mansion with impressive wall paintings and a mosaic floor that have been well preserved. The **House of the Wooden Partition**, as the name suggests, features a large atrium separated from the main living area by a wooden partition with three doors.

Farther along the main street, Cardo IV, is the **House of the Deer**, another sumptuous, two-storey villa built around a central courtyard. Wander through the corridors – many feature brilliant still-life paintings. In one of the rooms stands a statue of a drunken Hercules.

Continuing along, you will find the **Terme del Foro**, baths with most sections easily identifiable. The **House of the Carbonised Furniture** contains an intact bed and pictures of a variety of domestic items, while the **House of Neptune**, once belonging to a wine merchant, has an extremely well preserved mosaic floor.

Head right onto Decumanus Maximus from Cardo IV. On the south side is the **House of the Bicentenary**, so named because it was excavated 200 years after the ruins were discovered. A room upstairs contains a crucifix, indicating that there might have been Christians in the town before 79 AD. As you exit the ruins, to the left along Corso Ercolano, are the remains of the **Theatre**, dating from the Augustan period.

The archaeological area is open daily from 9 am to one hour before sunset, and entrance is L10,000.

Places to Stay & Eat Like Pompeii, Herculaneum is a convenient day trip from Naples. Otherwise, the *Albergo Belvedere* (☎ 081-739 07 44) is close to the station and has singles/doubles for L40,000/60,000. There are many bars around the entrance where you can buy panini and other snacks. *La Piadina*, Via Cozzolino 10, is one of the better restaurants in town and you can eat a full meal for about L25,000.

Getting There & Away SITA buses stop at Herculaneum on the Naples-Pompeii route. However, the easiest way to get from central Naples or Sorrento to Herculaneum is by train on the Circumvesuviana (see the Naples Getting Around section). By car, take the A3 autostrada from Naples, exit at Ercolano Portici, and follow the signs to car parks near the main entrance to the site.

Mt Vesuvius

If a picture is worth a thousand words, the image of Mt Vesuvius warrants volumes. The still active volcano dominates the landscape, looming ominously over Naples. Soon after its last eruption in 1944, the plume of smoke which had always hung over the cone disappeared, easing the minds of the millions who live in its shadow. This is false relief however, as scientists still expect the volcano to erupt every 30 to 40 years.

Its name is probably derived from the Greek *besubios* or *besbios*, which means fire. The volcano erupted with such ferocity on 24 August 79 AD that it all but destroyed the surrounding towns of Pompeii and Herculaneum, and pushed the coastline out several km. Since then, a massive eruption shook the region in 1631; the town of Torre del Greco was destroyed in 1794; a violent eruption in 1906 caused little damage; and there was a smaller outburst in 1944.

To reach Mt Vesuvius by car, take the A3 autostrada and exit at Ercolano Portici. Follow the signs through the town, but a road map is a must. By train, get off the Circumvesuviana line from Naples at Herculaneum and await the SITA bus (L3000), which runs services from the train station to the volcano. The first bus leaves the station at 8.15 am and the last leaves the mountain at 5.45 pm. They run about every two hours. A taxi ride up and back could cost L150,000.

The bus takes you to the summit car park, from where you walk a distance of about 1.5 km (30 minutes if you're quick). A new chair lift from the car park is due to open by 1994. You must pay L3000 to enter the summit area and visit with a guide, though it is possible to sneak through unaccompanied. Once there, you can walk around the top of the crater. There are several bars at the summit car park.

The **Vesuvius Observatory**, on the road to the summit, was commissioned by Ferdinand II of Bourbon in 1841 and is open to the public. Seismologists monitor the volcano around the clock.

Pompeii

A required stop on any tourist itinerary south of Naples, or even as a long day trip from the city, Pompeii offers one of the few insights into the life, passions, customs and vices of the ancient Romans, even if it is not well maintained. Much of the site is open to the public and requires at least three or four hours to visit. There is only one snack bar, charging excessive prices. The modern town of Pompeii, south-east of the excavations, is not really worth a visit.

History Founded in the 7th century BC by the Campanian Oscans on a prehistoric lava flow of Mt Vesuvius, Pompeii eventually fell under Greek control, and later, in the 5th century BC, under the influence of the Samnites, a southern Italian people related to the

Plaster cast of a Pompeii victim

Oscans. It became a Roman colony in 80 BC and prospered with the construction of many grand temples, villas and palaces until 63 AD when it was devastated by an earthquake. Pompeii had been largely rebuilt when Mt Vesuvius, overshadowing the town to the north, erupted in 79 AD and buried it under a layer of lapilli (burning fragments of pumice stone). Although the town was completely covered by the shower, most of its 20,000 inhabitants are believed to have escaped and only about 2000 died.

Pompeii was abandoned during the period of Saracen raids and its remains were further ruined by subsequent earthquakes. They were accidentally rediscovered in 1594 by architect Domenico Fontana, during the construction of a canal. The discovery was recorded but substantial excavation was not conducted until 1748, in the time of Charles of Bourbon, who was only interested in retrieving items of value. Credit for most of the major discoveries belongs to Giuseppe Fiorelli, who worked under the auspices of the Italian government from 1860. It is said that while Rome gives an insight into the monumental architecture of the Romans and a sense of their civilisation, Pompeii gives an insight into their everyday life.

Work still goes on at the site but most of the ancient city has been uncovered. In the interests of preservation, most of the mosaics and murals have been removed to the National Archaeological Museum in Naples and other museums around the world. The exception is the Villa of Mysteries (Villa dei Misteri), which has its frescoes intact *in situ*. They are the single most important series on the whole site.

Orientation & Information Arriving by train, you are deposited at either of the main entrances to the site; by car, signs direct you to the excavations and car parks.

There are two AASTs, one in modern Pompeii at Via Sacra 1 (☎ 081-850 72 55), and the other just outside the excavations at Piazza Porta Marina Inferiore 12 (☎ 081-861 09 13), near the Porta Marina entrance. Pick up a map and a copy of the handy *NTR (Notiziario Turistico Regionale)*.

A good guidebook is essential as it is very easy to miss important sites. *How to Visit Pompeii* (L7000) is small but comprehensive. The *Guide d'Agostini – Pompeii* is probably the best (L12,000).

The tourist office warns against the dozens of unauthorised guides who swoop at tourists. They charge exorbitant prices for brief and generally inaccurate tours. Authorised guides wear official identification tags and charge L86,000 for three hours, for groups of up to 15 people. Also be warned that some of the official attendants on the site, who should open many of the closed sites upon request, are more than keen to escort women on their own to out-of-the-way ruins, a situation that could turn nasty.

The post office is near Piazza Esedra, near the Porta Marina entrance. The telephone code for the area is 081.

For police emergency, call ☎ 113; for the Polizia Urbana tourist section, call ☎ 861 40 98. Medical first aid (☎ 850 61 93) is available at Via Ravellese, near the Piazza Anfiteatro entrance.

Things to See The town was surrounded by a wall with towers and eight gates. Enter the excavations from the west by the gate to the sea, the **Porta Marina**, which was considerably closer to the water before the eruption. Immediately as you enter you will see the remains of an imperial villa, with its long porticoes. Above is an **Antiquarium**, a museum featuring some remnants from the site. One of the rooms features body casts formed by hollows left in the hardened tufa by decayed corpses, depicting their final moments of horror.

Continuing along Via Marina, you will pass the **Temple of Apollo**, one of Pompeii's most striking monuments, and enter the **forum**, the centre of the city's life. To the right as you enter the forum is the **basilica**, architecturally one of the most important buildings of the site, which was both a law court and an exchange. To the left as you enter are fenced areas containing many

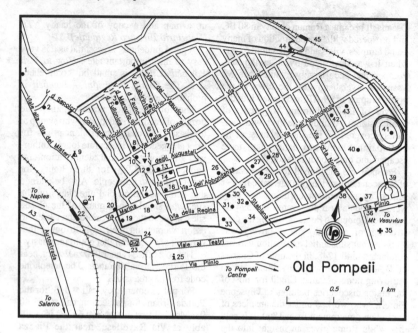

Old Pompeii

1	Villa of the Mysteries	24	Piazza Esedra & Main Entrance
2	Villa of Diomedes	25	Tourist Office
3	House of Apollo	26	Stabian Baths
4	Porta di Vesuvio	27	House of the Cryptoportico
5	House of the Vettii	28	House of the Priest Amandus
6	House of the Faun	29	House of Menander
7	Lupanaro	30	Temple of Isis
8	House of the Tragic Poet	31	Great Theatre
9	Camping Zeus	32	Small Theatre
10	Forum Baths	33	Triangular Forum
11	Snack Bar	34	Gladiators' Barracks
12	Temple of Jupiter	35	First Aid Post
13	Macellum	36	Vesuvio
14	Temple of Vespasian	37	Necropolis
15	Forum	38	Porta Nocera
16	Building of Eumachia	39	Piazza Anfiteatro & Entrance
17	Temple of Apollo	40	Great Palaestra
18	Basilica	41	Amphitheatre
19	Antiquarium	42	House of Venus
20	Porta Marina Entrance	43	House of Julia Felix
21	Main Bus Station	44	Porta Nola Entrance
22	Villa dei Misteri Circumvesuviana Railway Station	45	Pompei Scavi Circumvesuviana Railway Station
23	Post Office & Telephones		

remnants, including more of the gruesome body casts. The various buildings around the forum include the **Temple of Jupiter**, flanked by two triumphal arches, the **Macellum** (market), where you can see the remains of a series of shops, and the **Building of Eumachia**, which features an imposing marble doorway.

Taking the street to the right of the Building of Eumachia, Via dell'Abbondanza, wander along and turn right into Via dei Teatri and enter the **Triangular Forum**, which is surrounded by the remains of a Doric colonnade. To your left is the entrance to the **Great Theatre**. Adjoining it is the **Small Theatre**, also known as the Odeon. Behind the theatres are the **Gladiators' Barracks**, surrounded by a portico of about 70 columns. Wander through the theatres, but note that the attendants become a bit testy if they see you climbing on the ruins.

From the **Temple of Isis**, built as a place of worship for the Egyptian goddess, return to Via dell'Abbondanza, which intersects with Via Stabiana. The **Stabian Baths** are a large complex with many rooms, some featuring original tiling and murals. Several body casts are located here. Farther along Via dell'Abbondanza are the newer excavations. As you wander, you will see that several buildings have murals, protected behind glass, and other artefacts, which have

been saved from removal to museums. Look for the **House of the Cryptoportico**, the **House of the Priest Amandus** and the **House of Menander**, all of which are well preserved.

Continuing along is the **House of Venus**, with a fresco of the goddess standing in her conch shell, and the **Villa of Julia Felix**. Behind is the **Amphitheatre**, where the gladiators fought wild beasts, and close by, the **Great Palaestra**, an athletic field with an impressive portico and the remains of a swimming pool.

Return along Via dell'Abbondanza and turn right into Via Stabiana (which becomes Via Vesuvio) to see some of Pompeii's grandest houses. The **House of the Faun**, one of the best, featured a magnificent mosaic which is now in the Naples Archaeological Museum. Opposite, along Vicolo Storto, is the **Lupanaro**, a brothel with eye-opening murals. Nearby is the **House of the Vettii**, with well-preserved paintings and statues.

To the south in Via Terme are the **Forum Baths** and the **House of the Tragic Poet**, which contains many fine mosaics.

Walking along Via Consolare, at the north-western edge, you leave the town wall through the Porta Ercolano, pass the Villa of Diomedes and come to the **Villa of the Mysteries** (Villa dei Misteri), a remarkable

Pompeii's walls in ancient times

building with many rooms intact. The Dionysiac Frieze around the walls of the large dining room depicts the preparations for the great revelation, or the initiation into the cult of Dionysus (the Greek god of wine), including the moments before and the rites after.

The **Museo Vesuviano**, Via San Bartolomeo, south-east of the excavations, contains an interesting array of artefacts.

Opening times of the archaeological zone change monthly, but are roughly from 9 am to 3 pm in winter, to 7 pm in summer. Entrance is L10,000.

Places to Stay & Eat Pompeii is best visited on a day trip from Naples, Sorrento or Salerno as, apart from the excavations, there is little else to do.

The *Camping Zeus* (☎ 861 53 20) is near the Villa dei Misteri Circumvesuviana stop and has sites from L2000. *Camping Pompei* (☎ 862 28 82), Via Plinio, towards the eastern edge of the excavations, has bungalows from L50,000 a double. *Motel Villa dei Misteri* (861 35 93), near the villa itself, has singles/doubles from L40,000/55,000.

Much to the horror of just about everybody, *McDonald's* has opened a restaurant in the shadow of the city wall. *Ristorante Tiberius*, Villa dei Misteri 1B, near the villa, has pasta from L6000, while *Vesuvio*, Via Plinio 83, near the eastern edge of the excavations, has pasta from L5000.

Getting There & Away Pompeii is easily accessible by most means of transport.

Bus SITA (see the Naples Getting There & Away section) operates regular services between Naples and Pompeii. ATACS (see the Salerno Getting There & Away section) runs regular services from Salerno. CIAT (see also under Salerno) runs services between Pompeii and Rome. Buses arrive at the Villa dei Misteri Circumvesuviana station.

Train The quickest route from Naples is via the Circumvesuviana (see the Naples Get-

■	PLACES TO STAY
2	Loreley et Londres
15	Albergo City
16	Albergo Nice
22	Ostello Surriento
24	Albergo Linda

▼	PLACES TO EAT
3	Foreigners' Club
7	Giardinello
10	La Stalla
12	Gatto Nero
18	Self Service Angelina Lauro
26	Caruso

	OTHER
1	Hydrofoil Terminal
4	Church of San Francesco
5	Tourist Information Office
6	Piazza Sant'Antonino
8	Ospedale Civile
9	Cathedral
11	Palazzo Correale
13	Piazza Tasso
14	SIP Telephones
17	Piazza Angelina Lauro
19	Main Post Office
20	Main Railway Station
21	Bus Station
23	Police Headquarters
25	Car Park

ting Around section) to Sorrento. Get off at the Pompeii-Villa dei Misteri stop, which is near the Porta Marina entrance. Tickets cost L2400. Alternatively, take the Circumvesuviana for Poggiomarino, exiting at Pompeii Santuario. A less frequent service, operated by the state railways from the main station in Naples, goes to the new town.

Car & Motorbike The quickest way is via the A3 autostrada from Naples, a trip of about 23 km. Use the Pompeii exit, and follow the signs to Pompei Scavi. Car parks are clearly marked. Hitchhikers should leave Naples from around the Piazza Duca dell'Abruzzi and follow signs for the ss268 main road, which goes inland and reaches Pompeii.

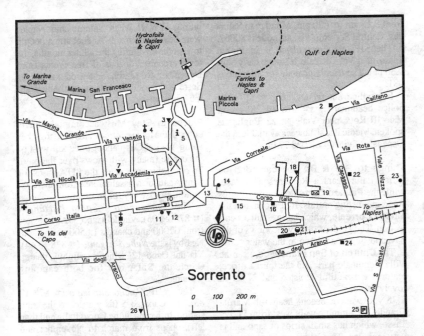

Sorrento

Alternatively, follow the ss145, which hugs the coast.

Sorrento

One of the most famous of all Italian beach resorts, Sorrento is a mecca for German and British tourists, but bears few reminders of its heyday earlier this century. Despite this, Sorrento is a good spot from which to visit Capri and even the Amalfi Coast. Parts of the coast between Pompeii and Sorrento are beautiful, although generally it is heavily residential and industrial.

Sorrento sits at the site of what is known in Greek mythology as the Temple of the Sirens, from where these sirens, or sea monsters with the head and bust of a woman and body of a bird, were supposed to roam the coastline bringing death and destruction. Legend has it that Odysseus (Ulysses) strapped himself to the mast of his ship to resist the fatal draw of their melodious chants.

Orientation Piazza Tasso, in the centre of town, is bisected by Corso Italia, Sorrento's main street, which becomes the ss145. It continues east to Naples, and becomes the Via del Capo to the west. The train station is about 250 metres east of the piazza, along Corso Italia, while the Marina Piccola, where ferries and hydrofoils arrive, is a similar distance northwards along Via Luigi de Maio. A walk from the port involves climbing about 200 stairs to reach the piazza.

Information The APT (☎ 081-878 22 29), Via Luigi de Maio 35, is inside the Circolo dei Forestieri office/restaurant complex. Pick up the what's-on publication, *Surrentum*. The office is open Monday to Saturday from 8.30 am to 12.30 pm and 4.30 to 8 pm.

The Banca d'America e d'Italia, Piazza Angelina Lauro, has a bancomat which accepts credit cards.

The post office at Corso Italia 210 is open

from 8.15 am to 7.20 pm, Monday to Saturday. Central Sorrento's postal code is 80067.

The SIP telephone office is in Piazza Tasso, near Via Correale. It's open daily until 9.30 pm. The telephone code for Sorrento is 081.

For police emergency, ring ☎ 113. The police headquarters (☎ 878 14 38) are at Vico III Rota, near Viale Nizza. English is spoken. Medical assistance is available at the Ospedale Civile (☎ 807 28 77 or 533 11 11).

Things to See & Do The **cathedral** on Corso Italia bears a Romanesque façade, while the **Palazzo Correale** nearby features some interesting murals. It also contains the **Museo Correale**, which has a small art collection. The gardens offer wide views of the bay, and steps lead down to the water.

The **Church of San Francesco**, near the Villa Comunale park and the tourist office, features a beautiful cloister and is set in lovely gardens.

If you want a beach, head for Marina Grande, a 15-minute walk west from Piazza Tasso, which has small strips of sand and is very popular. The jetties nearby with the ubiquitous umbrellas and deck chairs will cost you up to L15,000 a day. Bagni Regina Giovanna, a 20-minute walk west along Via del Capo (or catch the bus for Massalubrense), is more picturesque, set among the ruins of the Roman Villa Pollio Felix. To the east is a small beach at Marinella. It is possible to hire pedal cars at Marina Grande.

Forza 7 (☎ 878 90 08) at Marina Piccola hires a variety of boats from L40,000 a day and organises boat cruises. Goldentours International (☎ 878 10 42), Corso Italia 38E, offers package tours to the Amalfi Coast (L24,000), Pompeii (L34,000), Capri (L40,000) and other destinations.

Festivals The Sorrento Film Festival, regarded as the most important in the country for Italian-produced cinema, is usually held each September/October. The city's patron, Sant'Antonio, is remembered each 15 February with processions and huge markets. The saint is credited with saving Sorrento

during WW II when Salerno and Naples were heavily bombed. To encourage people to visit the city during the winter months, the town organises dozens of free events from December to March, a period known as Sorrento Inverno. Details are available from the tourist office.

Places to Stay Most accommodation is either in the town centre or clustered together along Via del Capo about three km west of the centre (many with views over the bay). To reach this area, catch the SITA buses for Sant'Agata or Massalubrense from the train station. Book early for summer.

The *Campogaio – Santa Fortunata* (☎ 878 24 05), Via del Capo 39A, has sites from L7000 and charges L6500 per person. Nearby is the *Nube d'Argento* (☎ 878 13 44), Via del Capo 12, which is slightly dearer. Catch the SITA bus for both camping grounds.

The IYHF *Ostello Surriento* (☎ 878 17 83), Via Capasso 5 (as you leave the train station, turn right along Corso Italia and then left), opens from march to November and bed and breakfast is L15,000.

Natural arch at Viro Eguen, near Sorrento

The *Albergo City* (☎ 877 22 10), Corso Italia 221, has singles/doubles from L35,000/50,000 and triples/quads for L70,000/100,000. *Albergo Nice* (☎ 878 16 50), Corso Italia 249, has rooms for L40,000/66,000, and charges L5000 per person for a compulsory breakfast during summer. *Albergo Linda* (☎ 878 29 16), Via degli Aranci 125, has rooms for L40,000/55,000. *Loreley et Londres* (☎ 807 31 87), Via Califano 12, overlooks the water and has rooms from L35,000/60,000.

Near Marina Grande is *Elios* (☎ 878 18 12), Via del Capo 33, which has rooms with views from L35,000/55,000. *Desirée*, next door at Via del Capo 31, has singles/doubles from L52,000/94,000 and triples/quads from L119,000/144,000, all including breakfast and private bathrooms. The hotel has an elevator which services its private beach. *La Tonnarella* (☎ 878 11 53), at the same address, charges L45,000 a person a night, or L70,000 for half-board.

Places to Eat One of the cheapest options is *Self Service Angelina Lauro*, Piazza Angelina Lauro, offering pasta from L5000. *Giardinello*, Via dell'Accademia 7, has pizzas from L4000. *Osteria La Stalla*, Via Pietà, has main courses from L9000. *Gatto Nero* in the same street could cost L10,000 for a full meal. *Caruso*, Via Sant'Antonio 12, one of the best restaurants, could cost L40,000 per person.

The *Foreigners' Club* is at Via Luigi de Maio 35, in the same building as the APT. It offers bay views and cheap food.

Entertainment Outdoor concerts are held during the summer months in the cloisters of San Francesco. Nightclubs include the Kan Kan, Piazza Sant'Antonino 1, which is about the best of a bad bunch and is not overrun by the tourist hordes.

Getting There & Away For bus and train, see the Naples Getting There & Away and Getting Around sections. By car, the city can be reached by the ss145, which meets a spur from the A3 at Castellammare. See the following section for information on rental cars in Sorrento.

Caremar (☎ 878 12 82), near the Marina Piccola, operates ferries and hydrofoils to Capri (L5000 and L9000) and hydrofoils to Naples (L10,000).

Getting Around SITA buses leave from outside the train station, and their office is located near the bar in the station. They service the Amalfi Coast (L3300 to Positano), Naples and Sant'Agata. It is possible to catch the buses throughout the town, although you must buy tickets from shops bearing the blue SITA sign.

Sorrento Rent a Car (☎ 878 13 86), Corso Italia 210, rents cars from L56,000 and scooters from L22,000. Thomas (☎ 878 58 61), Piazza Sant'Antonino, rents cars from L55,000 and scooters from L31,000. Both provide free helmets. For a taxi, call ☎ 878 22 04.

THE AMALFI COAST (COSTIERA AMALFITANA)

The 50-km stretch of coastline from Sorrento to Salerno is probably the most beautiful in Europe. The coast road bends and winds along the cliffs, overlooking crystal-clear blue waters and connecting the beautiful towns of Positano, Amalfi and the hillside village of Ravello. The coast is jam-packed with wealthy tourists in summer, prices are inflated and finding a vacancy is impossible. During spring and autumn, it is possible to find reasonably priced accommodation and relatively few tourists. The coast all but shuts down over winter. Shoppers and collectors will be interested to note that the coast is also famous for its characteristic ceramics, but shop around.

Getting There & Away

Bus SITA operates a service along the Amalfi Coast from the Sorrento train station to Salerno and vice versa, with buses leaving every 50 minutes. Tickets must be bought in advance from the bar at the Sorrento station or the SITA depot in Salerno, or else in bars near the stops in the towns along the coast

(Piazza Flavio Gioia in Amalfi and Via G Marconi in Positano).

Train Take the Circumvesuviana from Naples to Sorrento or the train to Salerno, and then the SITA bus along the coast.

Car & Motorbike The road is breathtakingly beautiful, if a little hairy at times as buses from each direction crawl past each other on narrow sections. In summer, it becomes a 50-km traffic jam and can take hours to navigate as the hordes flock to the coast. From Naples, take the A3 and exit near Castellammare, or follow the signs to Sorrento. The coast road, the ss145, passes through Sorrento and becomes the ss163 Amalfitana. A short cut over the hills beyond Meta can save about 30 minutes. Follow the signs to Vietri sul Mare or Amalfi if you are going to approach the coast from Salerno. If hitching, it is generally easy to get a lift.

Boat Navigazione Libera Del Golfo (☎ 081-552 72 09), which is based in Naples, operates hydrofoils between Amalfi, Positano and Capri, and Alilauro (☎ 081-761 10 04) serves the coast from both Salerno and Naples. Amalfi Navigazione (☎ 089-87 31 90), Via Nazionale 17, Amalfi, operates services between Amalfi and Positano, Capri and Salerno, as does Avenire (☎ 089-87 76 19), also in Amalfi. Most companies operate these services only during the summer months.

Positano

Bearing a strong Moorish influence, Positano is the most picturesque of the towns along the coast, and the most precious, with its cute houses and expensive shops.

Orientation The town is virtually divided in two by the cliff bearing the Torre Trasita tower. West is the smaller and more pleasant Spiaggia del Fornillo beach area and the less expensive side of town, and east is the Spiaggia Grande beach area, which gives way to the main centre of the village. Navigating the town is easy. Via G Marconi

breaks from the coast road, and weaves a high path before rejoining it at the town's eastern edge. Viale Pasitea runs off Via G Marconi, and passes through the Fornillo side, becoming Via Cristoforo Colombo before meeting Via G Marconi near the Spiaggia Grande.

Information The small APT tourist office (☎ 089-87 50 67) is at Via del Saracino 4, just near the Spiaggia Grande. It caters mainly to Italians and Germans, but the map the staff will give you speaks English too. It is open 8 am to 2 pm daily all year.

For money exchange, the Ufficio Cambio is in Piazza dei Mulini, although the Banca d'America e d'Italia, Via C Colombo 75, will offer better rates.

The main post office is on Via G Marconi where it meets Viale Pasitea. It's open Monday to Saturday from 8.20 am to 2 pm. The postal code for Positano is 84017.

An SIP telephone office is on Via dei Mulini, just near Via Cristoforo Colombo. Positano's telephone code in 089.

For police emergency, call ☎ 113. The carabinieri (☎ 87 50 11) are on Via G Marconi where it intersects with Viale Pasitea. For medical emergencies at night, on Sundays or holidays, ring ☎ 81 14 44. The Guardia Medica is on Via G Marconi, near Via Cristoforo Colombo.

Things to See & Do Positano's main sight is the **Church of Santa Maria Assunta**, on Via G Marconi near Viale Pasitea, which features a 13th century Byzantine *Black Madonna*. The church is closed in the afternoons.

In the hills overlooking Positano are two hamlets, Montepertuso and Nocelle, which can both be reached by established walking paths from the centre of the town. Montepertuso is a hard 45-minute walk and Nocelle is about 30 minutes farther on. From Nocelle, the **Sentiero degli Dei** (Trail of the Gods) heads directly up into the hills and the small town of Agerola, halfway between Positano and Amalfi. From Montepertuso, you can reach Santa Maria al Castello and

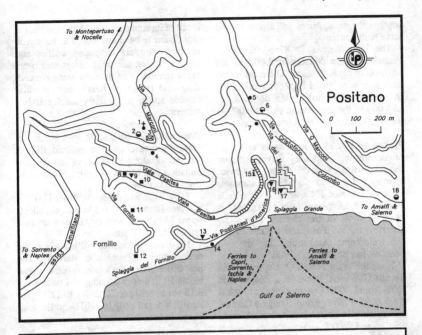

1	Church of Santa Maria Assunta
2	SITA Bus Stop Western Edge of Town
3	Post Office
4	Carabinieri
5	Guardia Medica
6	Bus to Montepertuso
7	SIP Telephones
8	Villa delle Palme
9	Il Saraceno d'Oro
10	Villa Nettuno
11	Villa Maria Luisa
12	Hotel Pupetto
13	Lo Guarracino
14	Torre Trasita
15	Tourist Information Office
16	O' Capurale
17	Chez Black
18	SITA Bus Stop Eastern Edge

Mt Sant'Angelo e Tre Pizzi (1444 metres). The latter is quite a hike.

Boating can be quite expensive. Head for the 'to rent' signs on the Spiaggia Grande, and expect to pay L15,000 an hour for a small rowing boat or L30,000 an hour for a small motor boat, both cheaper by the half or full day.

Hiring a chair and umbrella on the fenced-off beaches can cost L10,000, while the crowded public areas are free.

Places to Stay Positano has several one-star hotels, although in summer they are usually booked well in advance. Out of peak season, haggle with the guest-starved proprietors. Ask at the tourist office about rooms in private houses, which are generally expensive, or apartments for rent.

The pick of hotels is the *Villa Maria Luisa* (☎ 87 50 23), Via Fornillo 40, which has large rooms with terraces and magnificent views for L27,500 per person. Half-board at L55,000 per person is obligatory in late July and August. The *Villa delle Palme* (☎ 87 51 62), around the corner, charges the same prices and is run by the same management.

The *Villa Nettuno* (☎ 87 54 01), Viale Pasitea 208, has doubles for L60,000 and L80,000 in the high season and most rooms have balconies. *Hotel Pupetto*, overlooking the beach at Fornillo, has doubles for L74,000 in the low season and L94,000 in the high season, and all rooms have views.

Places to Eat Most restaurants are over-priced for the food they serve, and you should always check the cover and service charges before you sit. Many restaurants close over winter. *Il Saraceno d'Oro*, Viale Pasitea 254, has pizzas from L5000, and is close to most of the cheaper hotels. *Lo Guarracino*, Via Positanesi d'America, on the waterfront path connecting the two beaches, has pasta from L5000.

Near the main beach, *O' Capurale*, Via Regina Giovanna, serves local dishes, with pasta from L7000. Overlooking the beach is *Chez Black e Da Peppino*, Spiaggia Grande, specialising in seafood. A full meal could cost up to L45,000 although pasta starts at L7000.

Getting Around Dozens of small stairways throughout the town make walking relatively easy, if you don't mind a climb. A small orange bus does a complete circuit of the town, passing along Viale Pasitea, Via C Colombo and Via G Marconi. Stops are clearly marked, and tickets are L1000 and can be bought on board. The bus also stops near the Amalfitana road at the town's western edge, where you can meet the SITA bus.

Amalfi

At its peak in the 11th century, Amalfi was a supreme naval power, a bitter enemy of the northern maritime republics, Pisa and Genoa, and had a population of 70,000. Its *Tavole Amalfitane* navigation tables formed the world's first maritime code and governed all shipping in the Mediterranean for centuries.

Amalfi was founded in the 9th century and soon came under the rule of a doge. As a result of its connections with the Orient, the city claims to have introduced to Italy such modern wonders as paper, coffee and carpets. Today, the small resort still bears many reminders of its early trade connections and is one of Italy's most popular seaside spots, particularly among Italy's glitterati.

Orientation & Information Most hotels and restaurants are located around Piazza Duomo, or along Via Genova and its continuation, Via Capuano, which heads north from the Duomo.

The APT tourist office ☎ 089-87 11 07) is at Corso Roma 19, on the Marina Grande. It opens Monday to Saturday from 8 am to 2 pm and 4.30 to 7 pm.

The Banca d'America e d'Italia is at Via delle Antiche Repubbliche Marinare. The post office is near the tourist office at Corso Roma 29. It's open Monday to Friday from 8.15 am to 6.30 pm, Saturday to 12.15 pm. Amalfi's postal code is 84011 and the telephone code is 089.

Emergency For police emergency, ring ☎ 113, or go to the police headquarters (☎ 87 10 22) at Via Casamare 19. For medical treatment, go to the Municipio Pronto Soccorso (☎ 87 27 85), Piazza Municipio, near the tourist office.

Things to See The **Duomo Sant'Andrea**, an imposing sight at the top of a long flight of stairs, dates from early in the 10th century, although the façade has been rebuilt twice. The interior is mainly Baroque and the altar features statues believed to be by Bernini and Naccherini, and 12th and 13th century mosaics. The **Chiostro del Paradiso** next door was built in the 13th century in Arabic style to house the tombs of noted citizens, and is worth a visit. Entrance is L1000.

The **Municipal Museum**, near Corso Roma, contains the *Tavole Amalfitane* and other historical documents. The restored **Arsenal** of the former republic, the only one of its kind in Italy, is to the left of Porta della Marina.

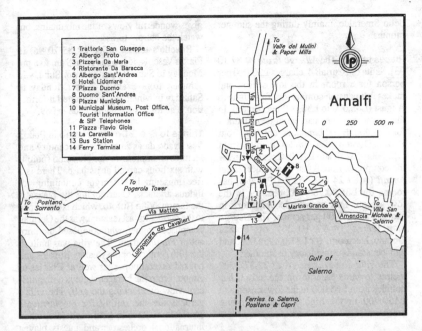

1 Trattoria San Giuseppe
2 Albergo Proto
3 Pizzeria Da Maria
4 Ristorante Da Baracca
5 Albergo Sant'Andrea
6 Hotel Lidomare
7 Piazza Duomo
8 Duomo Sant'Andrea
9 Piazza Municipio
10 Municipal Museum, Post Office,
   Tourist Information Office
   & SIP Telephones
11 Piazza Flavio Gioia
12 La Caravella
13 Bus Station
14 Ferry Terminal

Amalfi

To Valle dei Mulini
& Paper Mills

To Pogerola Tower

To Positano
& Sorrento

Via Matteo

Lungomare dei Cavalieri

Marina Grande

To Villa San
Michele &
Salerno

Amendola

Gulf of
Salerno

Ferries to Salerno,
Positano & Capri

Two paper mills still operate in Amalfi – one at Via Cartoleria 2, and another farther away from Piazza Duomo, also on Via Cartoleria, called the Cartier d'Amatruda, which still makes paper in the traditional way. The latter can be visited. The city's paper museum in Valle dei Mulini is situated in a 13th century paper mill (the oldest in Amalfi), but is usually closed.

The city also has a tradition of ceramic-making, and there are dozens of shops displaying their wares, mainly clustered around Piazza Duomo. Visit the **Studio d'Arte Fusco Giovanna**, at the Bottega d'Arte Fusco Alfonso shop in Piazza Duomo, and see items being made and glazed.

About six km before Amalfi is the **Grotta dello Smeraldo**, the Emerald Grotto for the colour of its sandy bottom; it is but a shadow of the more famous Blue Grotto at Capri. It can be reached by SITA bus from either direction along the Amalfi coast, and entrance is L6000. On 24 December and 6 January, skin divers make their traditional pilgrimage to the ceramic underwater crib in the grotto.

The Regatta of the Four Ancient Maritime Republics, rotating between Amalfi, Venice, Pisa and Genoa, is held on the first Sunday in June and features a host of floating craft. Amalfi hosted it in 1993 and will do so again in 1997.

Activities In the hills above Amalfi, on the way to Ravello, are dozens of small paths and stairways connecting the towns with the small villages that dot the mountainside. Many walks can take several hours. The Club Alpino Italiano in Salerno publishes a map with eight long walks in the area stretching from Salerno to Sorrento. A book titled *Walks from Amalfi – The Guide to a Web of Ancient Italian Pathways* (L10,000) is available from most bookshops in the town.

Boats can be hired at the Marina Grande area, the Spiaggia Santa Croce and the Grotta dello Smeraldo, mainly during the summer months.

Places to Stay The *Albergo Proto* (☎ 87 10 03), Salita dei Curiali 4, charges L20,000 per person for a room in the low season and makes full pension compulsory from June to August (L45,000 to L50,000 per person). In the low season, you can eat in its restaurant for L13,000. *Hotel Lidomare*, entrance from Piazza Duomo, has singles/doubles from L42,000/65,000; add L10,000 per person for the compulsory breakfast in summer. *Hotel Amalfi* (☎ 87 24 40), Via dei Pastai 3, has rooms for L36,000/60,000, cheaper in the low season. Full pension is obligatory in summer at L50,000 per person. The *Albergo Sant'Andrea* (☎ 87 10 23), off Piazza Duomo, has rooms for L31,000/56,000, and half-pension is compulsory in summer.

The *Villa San Michele* (☎ 87 22 37), 500 metres towards Salerno on the ss163, has doubles from L65,000 in the low season and L150,000 in the high season, including breakfast.

Places to Eat Eating is generally an expensive pastime in Amalfi, but there are a number of cheaper establishments at the northern end of Via Capuano.

The *Green Bar*, Via Capuana 46, is very cheap, and a meal could cost L12,000. Nearby is a *tavola calda* with no name, but it serves good pasta from L5000. *Trattoria San Giuseppe*, Salita Fra' Gerardo Sasso, off Via Amalfi, is a typical trattoria with pasta from L5000. *Pizzeria Da Maria*, Via Lorenzo d'Amalfi, has pizzas from L4500. *Ristorante Da Baracca*, overlooking Piazza dei Dogi, has pasta from L5000. *La Caravella*, Via Matteo Camera 12, is one of the city's finest restaurants, where a meal could cost L45,000 per person.

Ravello

Ravello sits like a balcony overlooking the Gulf of Salerno, from where you can peer down on Amalfi and the picturesque towns of Minori and Maiori. The seven-km drive from Amalfi along the Valle del Dragone

gives wonderful views of the mountains, but watch the hairpin turns.

Ravello's tourist office (☎ 85 70 96) in Piazza Vescovado is open from 8 am to 8 pm Monday to Saturday and to 2 pm Sunday in summer, from 8 am to 7 pm Monday to Saturday in winter, and has limited information. The town's telephone code is 089.

Things to See & Do The **Duomo** in Piazza Vescovado dates from the 11th century and features an impressive marble ambo (pulpit) with six lions carved at its base. There is a free museum in the crypt containing religious artefacts. Overlooking the piazza is the famous **Villa Rufolo**, which is now open to the public. Its last resident was the German composer Wagner, who composed the third act of *Parsifal* there. The villa was built in the 13th century for the wealthy Rufolos and housed several popes, as well as Charles of Anjou. From the terraces there is a magnificent view overlooking the gulf. The villa's gardens are the setting for the Festivale Musicale di Ravello held each July, when international orchestras and guests play a selection that always features Wagner. Tickets start at L10,000. The city hosts a smaller Wagner festival in early July, and the patron saint, San Pantaleon, is celebrated with fireworks in late July.

Away from the Piazza Vescovado is the **Villa Cimbrone**, which was built in this century and is set in beautiful gardens.

You can visit the city's vineyards: the Casa Vinicola Caruso, Via della Marra; Vini Episopio, at the Hotel Palumbo, Via Toro; and Vini Sammarco, Via Nazionale.

Places to Stay & Eat Ravello is worth a day trip, but accommodation and food are too expensive to make the town a consideration for most budget travellers. The *Toro* (☎ 85 72 11), Viale Wagner 3, has singles/doubles from L36,000/72,000. *Parsifal* (☎ 85 71 44), Via d'Anna 5, in a former convent, has rooms for L70,000/100,000, with compulsory half-pension at L120,000 in summer.

The *Pizzeria La Colonna*, Via Roma 20, serves typical cuisine, with pasta from

L6000. *Cumpà Cosimo*, Via Roma 42-44, is a little more expensive and a meal will cost L20,000.

Getting There & Away To reach the town by car, take the Amalfitana for Salerno and turn off about two km after Amalfi. SITA operates about 15 buses in each direction daily from Piazza Flavio Gioia in Amalfi, from 6 am to about 9 pm. Cars are not permitted in the town centre, but there is adequate parking in supervised car parks.

SALERNO

Originally Etruscan, Salerno was later an important Roman town. It flourished during the 10th to 13th centuries when its Medica Salernitana, one of Europe's first medical schools, was established. In 1943 the Allies landed at the beaches just south of Salerno and the city sustained extraordinary damage in the battles that followed. It is still a major university town, but there is little reason to visit, unless you plan to use its extensive transportation links to visit the Amalfi Coast and the Greek ruins at Paestum.

Orientation

Salerno is a major stop on the railway line from Naples to Reggio di Calabria and Sicily. The train station is in Piazza Vittorio Veneto, at the eastern end of town. Salerno's main shopping and business strip, the car-free Corso Vittorio Emanuele, leads off to the north-west to the medieval section. Corso Garibaldi, parallel to Corso V Emanuele and nearer the sea, continues as Via Roma to the north-west. Tree-lined Lungomare Trieste runs along the unattractive waterfront from the massive Piazza della Concordia, which doubles as a car park. Lungomare Marconi runs from the other end of the piazza to the south-east.

Information

Tourist Office The EPT (☎ 089-23 14 32), near the train station in Piazza Vittorio Veneto, produces the useful weekly *Memo*, with a host of information. There is another tourist office (☎ 089-25 25 76) at the other

end of town, at Via Roma 258. Both are open from 9 am to 1.30 pm and 2.30 to 8 pm, except Sunday.

Money The Banca d'America e d'Italia is at Corso Garibaldi 152, and the Banca Nazionale del Lavoro is at Corso Garibaldi 208.

Post & Telecommunications The main post office is at Corso Garibaldi 203 and is open Monday to Saturday from 8.15 am to 7.15 pm. The postal code for central Salerno is 84100.

The SIP telephone office is at Corso Garibaldi 31 and is open daily from 8.15 am to 8 pm. The telephone code for Salerno is 089.

Emergency For police emergency, call ☎ 113. The police headquarters (☎ 22 40 00) are on Via Roma, before Via G d'Agostino. The Ospedale Ruggi d'Aragona is at Via San Leonardo. For medical emergencies, ring ☎ 24 12 33 or 22 83 83, or ring ☎ 23 33 30 for an ambulance.

Things to See

The city's **Duomo**, Piazza Alfano 1°, is dedicated to St Matthew the Evangelist, whose remains were brought to the city in 954 and later buried in the crypt. Flanked by a Romanesque bell tower and an atrium featuring 28 Roman columns, the church was built in the Norman style and remodelled in the 18th century. It sustained severe damage in the 1980 earthquake. The Chapel of Gregory VII, or of the Crusaders, was so named because it is where the crusaders' arms were blessed. Pope Gregory VII, who lived in exile in Salerno before he died in 1085, is buried under the altar. The **Museo Diocesano** is at the Duomo and is open from 9 am to 1 pm and 4 to 7 pm.

A walk to the Castello di Arechi along Via Risorgimento is rewarded with good views, if you ignore the industrial sprawl beneath you. The castle is open daily and entrance is free.

The city's **Provincial Museum**, Via San Benedetto 28, contains archaeological finds

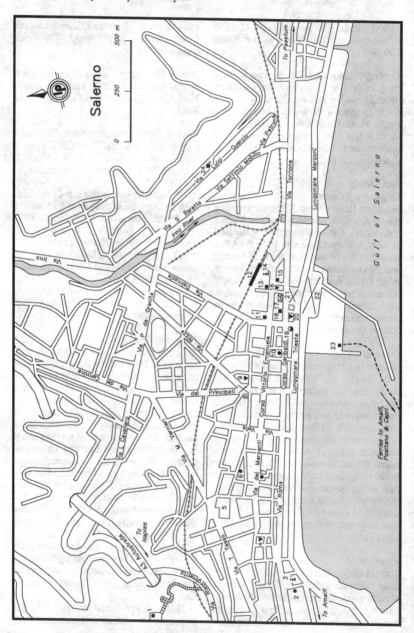

Salerno

■ PLACES TO STAY

11	Albergo Cinzia
13	Albergo Santa Rosa
15	Albergo Salerno
18	Hotel Garibaldi
24	Irno Youth Hostel

▼ PLACES TO EAT

4	Vicolo delle Neve
9	Papio
16	Trattoria da Italia
20	Da Gigino

OTHER

1	Castle
2	Police Headquarters
3	Tourist Information
5	Duomo
6	Provincial Museum
7	Piazza Matteotti
8	Piazza XXIV Maggio
10	SIP Telephones
12	Railway Station
14	Tourist Information
17	Post Office
19	SITA bus terminal
21	Piazza Mazzini
22	Piazza della Concordia
23	Ferry Terminal

from the region and opens from 9 am to 1 pm. The other museum worth a visit is the **Ceramics Museum**, Largo Casavecchia, open Tuesday, Thursday and Saturday from 9 am to 12.30 pm.

Activities

Check with the tourist office about the myriad activities on offer in and around Salerno. The following are just some of them.

Walking In conjunction with the Club Alpino Italiano (☎ 25 27 88), Via Porta di Mare 26, the city's free what's-on magazine, *Memo*, publishes walking excursions around Salerno, along the Amalfi Coast and in the nearby Picentini mountain range. The CAI also arranges mountain-climbing expeditions.

The Centro Documentazione Trekking (☎ 79 09 14), Via G de Caro 47, and Myricae (☎ 79 24 46), Via F Crispi 51, can provide information and assistance with treks.

Free-Climbing Contact Fly Surf (☎ 73 32 97), Via R Cocchia 181-185, or Duegi Sport (☎ 95 14 02), Via Ferreria 213, for details.

Diving Several clubs offer tuition. Try the Centro Attività Subacquee (☎ 22 23 40), Piazza Umberto I, or check *Memo* for others.

Windsurfing Contact Club Gigi Pezzullo (☎ 72 32 97), Porto di Cetara, for details.

Places to Stay

The IYHF *Ostello per la Gioventù Irno* (☎ 79 02 51), Via Luigi Guercio 112, is about 500 metres east of the train station. Bed and breakfast is L15,000 and a meal is L12,000, and it's open all year. The *Albergo Santa Rosa* (☎ 22 53 46), Corso Vittorio Emanuele 14, about 200 metres from the station, has singles/doubles for L30,000/46,000. Opposite is the *Albergo Salerno* (☎ 22 42 11), Via G Vicinanza 42, with rooms from L28,000/50,000. *Cinzia* (☎ 23 27 73), Corso V Emanuele 74, has rooms for L20,000/40,000. The three-star *Garibaldi* (☎ 22 83 00), Via Torrione 54, has rooms from L35,000/60,000.

Places to Eat

The *Trattoria da Italia*, Via Vicinanza, is a takeaway restaurant but serves cheap dishes upstairs. *Da Gigino*, Via Piacenza 117, has good pizzas from L5000. The 500-year-old *Pizzeria del Vicolo delle Neve*, Vicolo delle Neve 24, off Via Mercanti, serves traditional fare, and a meal could cost about L20,000. *Papio*, Via Papio 33, near the train station, is a self-service restaurant charging L3000 for good pasta.

Getting There & Away

Bus The SITA office (☎ 22 66 04) is at Corso Garibaldi 117. Buses for the Amalfi Coast depart from Piazza della Concordia, usually every 30 minutes, while buses for Naples depart from outside the SITA office. SITA is opening a new terminal on Via Martiri, which intersects Corso Garibaldi near Piazza Mazzini. ATAC (☎ 24 10 43), Piazza M Luciani and Piazza Ferrovia, operates bus Nos 4 and 41 to Pompeii from outside the train station, and also services Paestum (catch the bus for Sapri) and other towns along the southern coast from Piazza della Concordia. CIAT (☎ 0774-39 08 15), based in Subiaco east of Rome, operates a bus to Rome (L27,000), leaving Piazza della Concordia at 2.30 pm daily.

Train Salerno is a major stop between Rome/Naples and Calabria and is served by all types of trains. It also has good services to the Adriatic coast and inland.

Car & Motorbike Salerno is on the A3 autostrada between Naples and Calabria, which becomes toll-free after the town as a government concession to the south. Be warned, the government is considering imposing a toll, but wheels turn slowly in this country. From Rome, you can bypass Naples by taking the A30.

Boat Scarano (☎ 22 53 22), Corso Garibaldi 126, runs hydrofoils to Amalfi (L6000), Positano, Sorrento, Ischia, Capri and Naples (L20,000). It also serves Agropoli (L14,000) and other towns on the Cilento Coast.

Helicopter Elicampania (☎ 738 72 57) flies helicopters to the islands in the Bay of Naples, starting at L190,000 a person.

Getting Around
Most hotels are around the train station, and Corso Vittorio Emanuele, the main drag, is a mall, so walking is the most sensible option. ATAC runs bus services though the town. Bus No 11 or 11r runs from the station to the city centre.

PAESTUM
The evocative image of three Greek temples standing in fields of poppies gives an insight into the ancient world of Magna Graecia, when Greeks occupied much of southern Italy. Paestum should not be missed, particularly since its three Doric temples are better preserved than the more famous Parthenon in Athens. The small town is close to some of Italy's better beaches and just south of where the US forces landed in 1943. The new town of Capaccio, about three km from the temples, is to be renamed Paestum some time this decade.

Paestum, or Poseidonia as the city was known, was founded in the 6th century BC by Greek settlers from Sybaris, on the Gulf of Taranto farther south. Conquered by the Lucanians from Basilicata in the 4th century BC, it came under Roman control in 273 BC and became an important trading port. The town was gradually abandoned after the fall of the Roman Empire, periodic outbreaks of malaria and savage raids by the Saracens in 871. The temples were rediscovered in the late 18th century by road builders, who subsequently built right through the ruins.

The site is easily traversed by foot and all public transport is within walking distance. The tourist information office (☎ 0828-81 10 16), Via Aquilia, is opposite the site and provides maps and other details.

Things to See
The first temple you come across when you enter the site from the northern end, near the tourist office, is the **Temple of Ceres**, which dates from the 6th century BC. It is the smallest of the three and was used as a Christian church for a time. The basic outline of the **Forum** is evident as you head south. Among the buildings, parts of which remain, are the Italic Temple, the Greek Theatre, the Bouleuterion, where the senate met, and farther south, the Ampitheatre, which was cut by the road.

The **Temple of Neptune**, dating from about 450 BC, is the most impressive of the remains, the largest and best preserved with only parts of the inside walls and roof missing. From a distance, its structure gives the impression that the columns are leaning outward. The **Basilica** is the oldest surviving monument, dating from the middle of the 6th century BC, and is impressive because of its massive dimensions – nine columns across and 18 along the side.

The city's walls extended 4.7 km and show Lucanian and Roman reconstruction. The most intact section is west of the site, but the area east of the site provides a pleasant walk through typical Italian farmland.

The **Museum of Paestum**, opposite the site, houses a collection of metopes, including 33 of the original 36 from the **Temple of Argive Hera**, nine km north of Paestum, making up one of the best collections of ancient architecture in the world. It also features wall paintings from tombs on the site. Entrance to both the museum (closed Mondays) and the site is L8000.

Places to Stay & Eat

Paestum is a short trip from Salerno, which has more budget accommodation. Camping facilities are at *Intercamping Apollo* (☎ 0828-81 11 78), Via Principe di Piemonte, close to the ruins and near the beach.

Metope relief from the Temple of Argive Hera

Albergo Villa Rita (☎ 0828-81 10 81), Via Principe di Piemonte 39, has singles/doubles from L35,000/50,000. The *Ristorante Il Tempio*, Via Laura, has pizzas from L6000, and a full meal could cost L25,000.

Getting There & Away

Bus ATAC runs buses from Salerno to Paestum (catch the Sapri bus), usually every 35 minutes from 8.15 am to 8.15 pm. There is no marked bus stop near the site – just ask the driver to drop you off. When leaving, just hail the driver and the bus will stop.

Train Paestum is on the train line from Naples through Salerno to Reggio di Calabria. Many trains stop at the Stazione di Capaccio, nearer the new town (about three km from the site), and less frequently at the Stazione di Paestum, a short walk from the temples.

Car & Motorbike Take the A3 autostrada from Salerno and exit for the ss18 at Battipaglia. Paestum is about 35 km from Salerno.

AROUND PAESTUM

The World Wide Fund for Nature has established a wildlife sanctuary about 12 km inland from Paestum on the Sele River, one of the few protected natural environments in the south of Italy. It consists mainly of wetlands and is home to a wide variety of birds. The area is known as the **Woods of Diana**, the Roman goddess of the hunt. Virgil wrote about the area, describing the roses of Paestum and the woodlands. The sanctuary (☎ 0828-97 46 84) is open from September to April, and signs direct you there from the ss18.

Forty km east of Paestum, the **Castelcivita Caves** were discovered late last century, and are heavily promoted as a tourist destination. Recent lighting improvements allow you to wander for about 1700 metres through the labyrinth of chambers, shafts, stalagmites and stalactites. The **Great Waterfall** (Grande Cascata) is magnificent. The caves can be reached via the ss166, which leaves the ss18 north of Paestum. The caves are open all year. For information, call ☎ 0828-97 23 97.

THE CILENTO COAST

Below the Gulf of Salerno, the straight coastline breaks into a craggy, rocky territory which marks the beginning of the Cilento Coast. The beaches are better for skin-divers than swimmers and are not as popular as those farther north and south, into Basilicata and Calabria. ATAC buses leave Salerno for Sapri, the Cilento Coast's southernmost town; trains from Salerno stop at most towns; by car, take the ss18 which connects Agropoli with Velia via the inland route, or the ss267, which hugs the coast.

Agropoli

A pleasant town south of Paestum, Agropoli has a small medieval section nestling at the top of a hill overlooking the more modern section. It could make a good base for travel to the temples at Paestum and also to the clean, sandy beaches to the north.

The *Camping Villaggio Arco delle Rose* (☎ 0974-83 82 27), Via Isca Solofrone, is a tacky tourist resort village but has camping sites. The *Hotel Carola* (☎ 0974-82 30 05), Via Pisacane 1, near the harbour, has singles/doubles for about L35,000/50,000.

The *Ristorante Nuova Gestione*, Piazza Umberto I, in the old section of town, has pizzas from L3000 and pasta from L4500, with a great view of the water.

Velia

The ruins of the Greek settlement of Elea, which was founded in the mid-6th century BC and became a popular spot for wealthy Romans, are well worth a visit if you have the time. Its decline matches that of Paestum (although the ruins are in a far worse state than those of Paestum), but as the town was never an important trading centre, it was considerably smaller than its northern rival.

The nearby town of Ascea has several camping grounds and hotels. *Camping Alba* (0974-97 23 31) is near Marina di Ascea, close to the sea. The *Albergo Sant'Anna*

(☎ 0974-93 11 50) has rooms for about L40,000 and is near the water.

Apulia

Apulia (Puglia) encompasses the 'spur' and 'heel' of Italy's boot, and is bordered by two seas, the Adriatic to the east and the Ionian, known here as the Gulf of Taranto, to the south. Apulia's strategic position as the Italian peninsula's gateway to the east made the region both an important thoroughfare and a target for colonisers and invaders. Greeks founded the Magna Graecia civilisation on the Ionian coast, including Taranto, which was settled by Spartan exiles; Brindisi was, and still is, the point marking the end of the Roman Appian Way; the Norman legacy is seen in the magnificent Romanesque churches which dot the region; Foggia and its province were favoured by the great Swabian king, Frederick II, and several of his castles remain; and Lecce, known as the Florence of the Baroque, displays the architectural mark of the Spanish colonisers.

For the dedicated traveller, Apulia offers many rich experiences. Apart from the contrasts provided by its diverse history, the region holds many other surprises, including the fascinating sanctuary dedicated to St Michael the Archangel at Monte Sant' Angelo; the conical-roofed, stone houses known as *trulli* in the area around Alberobello; the strange tradition of tarantism, a phenomenon from which evolved the tarantella folk dance (see the Galatina section); and the extraordinary floor mosaic in Otranto's cathedral. Then there are the Tremiti Islands, which remain unspoiled by tourism, the ancient Umbra Forest of the Gargano Promontory, and the pleasant beaches of the Salentine Peninsula at the tip of the heel.

Apulia today is the richest of Italy's southern regions, the result of significant industrial development and economic growth in the past 30 years, as well as intensive efforts by the government to develop

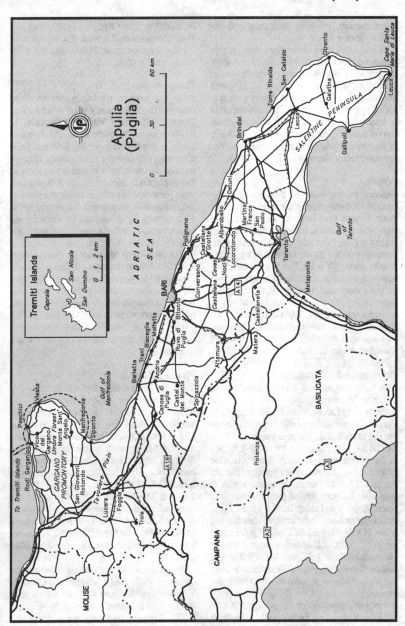

Apulia (Puglia)

0   30   60 km

Tremiti Islands

Caprala

San Nicola

San Domino

0   1 2 km

ADRIATIC SEA

To Tremiti Islands

Peschici

Vieste

Rodi Garganico

Vico del Gargano

Monte Sant'Angelo

Umbra Forest

GARGANO PROMONTORY

San Giovanni Rotondo

Manfredonia

Siponto

Gulf of Manfredonia

Lucera

Foggia

Troia

Tavoliere Plain

MOLISE

CAMPANIA

A16

A2

Barletta

Trani

Bisceglie

Molfetta

Canosa di Puglia

Andria

Castel del Monte

Spinazzola

Ruvo di Puglia

BARI

Bitonto

Altamura

Matera

Castellaneta

BASILICATA

Potenza

A3

Polignano

Conversano

Castellana Grotte

Castellana Caves

Alberobello

Noci

Locorotondo

A14

Ostuni

Martina Franca

San Paolo

Metaponto

Gulf of Taranto

Taranto

Brindisi

Torre Rinalda

San Cataldo

Otranto

Galatina

Lecce

Gallipoli

SALENTINE PENINSULA

Leuca

Cape Santa Maria di Leuca

infrastructure, improve education and increase literacy levels.

If you want to really explore Apulia, you will need either your own mode of transport or lots of time, since many of the more interesting sights are in or near small towns and villages which are not always well serviced by public transport. The best option is to base yourself in the main towns and set out on daily expeditions. For instance, many of the more important Romanesque churches are reasonably close to Bari.

FOGGIA

Situated in the north of the region in the patchwork landscape of the broad Tavoliere Plain, Foggia is an important transport junction. It is a pleasant, basically modern town (most of its historic monuments were destroyed either by earthquake or by Allied bombs during WW II). The town itself is not much of a tourist destination, but it is close to the forest and beaches of the Gargano Promontory. Near Foggia are two towns of considerable interest, Troia and Lucera, the former famous for its beautiful Apulian-Romanesque cathedral, and the latter for its Swabian-Angevin castle.

Orientation & Information

The train station and bus terminal are in Piazzale Vittorio Veneto. From here, walk directly ahead along Viale XXIV Maggio to Piazza Cavour and turn right into Via Lanza for the town's main shopping area.

The EPT tourist office (☎ 0881-2 36 50) is inconveniently located some distance from the town centre, at Via Senatore Emilio Perrone 17, but it might be worth a visit if you want information on the province. It is open Monday to Friday from 8 am to 2 pm. From the station, walk straight ahead along Viale XXIV Maggio to Piazza Cavour and continue straight ahead along Corso P Giannone. Turn left into Via Cirillo and follow it to Piazza Puglia – Via Perrone is on the right. Otherwise, take bus MD from the station.

Foggia's post office is in Viale XXIV Maggio, and there is an SIP public telephone office at Via Conte Appiano 14-18 (take Via Torelli from Piazza Cavour). The postal code for the town centre is 71100, and the telephone code is 0881.

Things to See

Since the town is predominantly modern, there is little to see of any great interest. The **Duomo**, off Corso Vittorio Emanuele, is worth a look. Its lower section is Romanesque, while the Baroque top half was built after an 18th century earthquake. Though most of the cathedral's treasures were lost in the earthquake, there remains a Byzantine icon, preserved in a chapel inside the church. According to legend, it was discovered in the 11th century by shepherds, in a pond over which burned three flames. The flames are now the symbol of the city.

The **Municipal Museum** in Piazza Nigri (take Via Arpi to the right off Corso Vittorio Emanuele) houses archaeological finds from the province, including relics from the Roman and medieval town of Siponto. Three portals incorporated into the side of the building, one featuring two suspended eagles, are all that remains of Frederick II's local palace.

Places to Stay & Eat

There are several decent places to stay very close to the station. *Albergo Venezia* (☎ 7 09 03), Via Piave 40, is very basic, with singles/doubles for L18,000/32,000, or L25,000/45,000 with private shower; triples are L60,000 with bathroom. *Albergo Bologna* (☎ 62 13 41), Via Monfalcone 53, has basic singles/doubles/triples for L25,000/44,000/57,000. *Hotel ASI* (☎ 2 33 27), Via Monfalcone 1, has rooms for the same prices; doubles/triples with bathroom are L65,000/86,000. The *Hotel Europa* (☎ 62 10 57), Via Monfalcone 52, has more up-market singles/doubles for L90,000/130,000.

For a snack, try *Tuttopizzapanini* on the corner of Viale XXIV Maggio and Piazzale Vittorio Veneto. There are lots of little trattorias in the side streets to the right off Viale XXIV Maggio (walking away from the station). *Trattoria Sorrento*, Via Trieste 37, is run by an elderly couple. The food is simple and traditional and for under L20,000 you will eat very well. *Ristorante/Pizzeria Nuova Italia*, on the corner of Via Piave and Via Podgora, has good pizzas for under L10,000, as well as a full menu.

Getting There & Away
Buses leave from Piazzale Vittorio Veneto for towns and locations throughout the province of Foggia. ATAF, the regional bus company, runs buses to Troia every half hour to an hour, and to Manfredonia (about 10 a day) as well as numerous other locations. Timetables are posted on the porticoes on the corner of the piazzale and Via Bainsizza. Tickets can be purchased at the tobacconist at Viale XXIV Maggio 47. SITA buses connect Foggia with Lucera, Vieste, Manfredonia, San Giovanni Rotondo and Monte Sant'Angelo, as well as other towns throughout the province. There is a SITA office (☎ 2 36 18) in Piazzale Vittorio Veneto, where you can pick up a full timetable. Buses depart from outside the office. Ferrovie dello Stato (FS) buses also connect Foggia and Lucera, leaving from outside the station.

Foggia is connected by train to other major towns in Apulia, including Bari, Brindisi and Lecce. The town is easily accessible from points along the Adriatic coast, including Ancona and Pescara.

Arriving in town by car will seem confusing once you reach the system of one-way streets in the main shopping area. If you are staying in one of the hotels listed previously, it is best to follow the 'stazione' signs for the train station.

LUCERA
The town of Lucera stands on a plateau rising above the patchwork landscape of the Tavoliere Plain. In Roman times it was an important town, known as Luceria, but it fell into ruin in later years. Then, in the 13th century, King Frederick II was confronted with the problem of bands of Arabs attacking travellers in Sicily (also part of his domain), so he rounded them up and simply moved

them to Apulia, settling 20,000 of them in Lucera and allowing them to build mosques and live in religious freedom. He recruited his famous Saracen bodyguard from the Arabs of Lucera, who accompanied him on his journeys between castles and to the crusades.

In his book *A Traveller in Southern Italy*, H V Morton wrote of what he described as the 'half oriental life of the most luxurious and civilised court in Europe':

Frederick's passage from castle to castle, from Palermo through the Calabrian mountains into Apulia, must have resembled the progress of Barnum and Bailey. The imperial elephant had been taught to bear the standard of the Hohenstaufen; the imperial treasure was carried upon the backs of camels and dromedaries; the covered litters of the harem were guarded by mounted archers of the Saracen guard; the emperor's hawks and hounds travelled like Princes, and so did the hunting leopards, riding on horseback behind their keepers.

In the late 13th century, Lucera was conquered by Charles II of Anjou. The French replaced many of the town's mosques with Gothic churches, but lived harmoniously with the town's Arab occupants until Charles decided to have them slaughtered.

The town's main attraction is the massive **castle**. Originally built by Frederick II in 1223, its external walls were added by Charles of Anjou, forming a pentagon topped by 24 towers. The remains of Frederick's castle are in the north-east corner of the enclosure. In the central area are excavations which have brought to light the remains of Roman buildings. The castle is open daily until dusk. Entrance is free, but the elderly guard will expect a small tip.

Things to See
The **cathedral**, in the centre of the old town, was started by Charles of Anjou in 1300 and is considered the best example of Angevin architecture in southern Italy. Also of interest is the Gothic **Church of San Francesco**, also built by Charles of Anjou.

On the town's eastern outskirts is a 1st century BC **Roman amphitheatre**, open from 7 am to 1 pm and 2 pm until dusk. The ruins are badly maintained, but interesting enough. Admission is free, but you will need to leave a small tip for the guard.

Places to Stay

Try the *Albergo Gioia* (☎ 0881-94 52 24), Viale Ferrovia 15, just off Piazza del Popolo, outside the walls of the old city. It has singles/doubles for L45,000/70,000.

Getting There & Away

Lucera is easily accessible from Foggia (a 30-minute trip) by SITA and FS buses. Buses stop in Piazza del Popolo.

TROIA

About 18 km south of Lucera is the town of Troia, accessible by bus from either Foggia or Lucera. The attraction here is the beautiful Apulian-Romanesque **cathedral**. Its façade is splendidly decorated with a rose window, and the fantastic Romanesque-style creatures and carvings of the doorway show an Oriental influence. Of particular note are the bronze doors.

If you want to stay here, try the *Albergo Alba d'Oro* (☎ 0881-97 09 40) at Viale Kennedy 30, on the way out of town towards Lucera. It has singles/doubles for L30,000/50,000 with bathroom.

MANFREDONIA

Founded by the Swabian king Manfred, the illegitimate son of Frederick II, this town has little to attract tourists, other than being a useful transport junction on the way to the Gargano Promontory. Intercity buses terminate in Piazza Marconi, and it is then a short walk along Via Manfredi to the AAST tourist office at No 26, open Monday to Saturday from 8.30 am to 1.30 pm, where you can pick up accommodation and transport details, and limited information on the Gargano Promontory.

Of interest is the **castle**, started by Manfred and completed by Charles of Anjou. About two km south of the town is **Siponto**, an important town from Roman to medieval times, which was abandoned in favour of

Manfredonia because of earthquakes and malaria. The only remaining building here is the Church of Santa Maria di Siponto, an 11th century Romanesque church with Byzantine influences.

If you plan to spend a night in Manfredonia, try the *Albergo Santa Maria delle Grazie* (☎ 0884-2 24 65), Piazza d'Acquisto, off Piazza Marconi, which has singles/doubles for L25,000/45,000. *Albergo Svevo* (☎ 0884-2 38 54), Viale di Vittorio 96, has rooms for L32,000/46,000, or with bathroom for L44,000/65,000. For a good meal, try *Al Fuego*, Via dei Celestini, just off Corso Manfredi.

SITA buses connect Manfredonia with Foggia, Vieste and Monte Sant'Angelo, leaving from Piazza Marconi. Bus tickets and timetable information are available at Bar Impero in Piazza Marconi, near the corner of Corso Manfredi.

GARGANO PROMONTORY

This area of limestone mountains, ancient forest and beautiful beaches forms what is often called the 'spur' of the Italian boot. For centuries an important destination for religious pilgrims, the promontory has also become an increasingly popular tourist playground. Its beach resorts, including Vieste and Peschici, are developing rapidly to accommodate the annual influx of beachgoers.

The Umbra Forest in the promontory's mountainous interior is a forest of ancient beech and oak trees, one of the last remaining original forests in Italy. It has a visitor's centre, complete with stuffed examples of the forest's wildlife, and there are numerous well-marked paths for leisurely walks, as well as many picnic areas. Those without their own transport will find that catching public transport to and from the forest can be tricky, but not impossible.

The promontory has two important religious sanctuaries: the Sanctuary of St Michael the Archangel at Monte Sant'Angelo, and the burial place of Padre Pio at San Giovanni Rotondo. Padre Pio was a priest who gained a large following after developing mysterious scars resembling the wounds of Christ. He died in the late 1960s.

Monte Sant'Angelo

Perched on a long, narrow hill close to the promontory's southern coast, this town is famous for the Sanctuary of St Michael the Archangel, built over a grotto where the archangel is said to have appeared to the Bishop of Siponto in 490 AD. The legend goes that a local man who had lost his prize bull eventually found it standing at the entrance to a cave. When he could not make the animal move, he shot an arrow at it. Instead of hitting the bull, the arrow turned and hit the man, who then went to the bishop for advice. St Michael later appeared to the bishop at the grotto, ordering him to consecrate a Christian altar there. Interestingly, the grotto had previously been a pagan shrine with an oracle that performed dream cures.

During the Middle Ages, the sanctuary was the end of one of the most important pilgrim routes, the Route of the Angel, which departed from Normandy, passed through Rome and led to Monte Sant'Angelo. In the year 999 AD, Holy Roman Emperor Otto III made a pilgrimage to the sanctuary to ask that the prophecies about the world ending in the year 1000 would not be fulfilled. The sanctuary's fame grew after the much predicted apocalypse did not eventuate.

Information There is a Pro Loco tourist office in the town's main street, Via Reale Basilica, which can provide limited information about the town. It's open from 9 am to 1 pm and 2.30 to 5 pm Monday to Saturday.

Things to See Today, the **Sanctuary of St Michael** remains an important place of pilgrimage, but it has also become a major tourist attraction. Dress rules are strictly enforced (absolutely no shorts, miniskirts or revealing tops – even bare arms are frowned upon), and you shouldn't be surprised if you are asked to put on a special coat to cover offending exposed skin. You will enter through a double archway, above which is carved a Latin inscription that translates into

'This is an awesome place; it is the House of God and the Gate of Heaven'.

Once inside the sanctuary gates, a flight of stone steps leads down to the grotto. As you descend, note the graffiti which fills the walls, some of it the work of 17th century pilgrims. Since St Michael is said to have left a footprint in stone inside the grotto, it became customary for pilgrims to carve outlines of their feet and hands and leave accompanying messages. The grotto itself is entered through magnificent Byzantine bronze and silver doors.

Inside the grotto, note the famous statue of St Michael, which covers the place where the archangel is said to have left his footprint. The main altar stands at the site of the first altar consecrated by the Bishop of Siponto to St Michael, and behind it is a small fountain of legendary 'healing' waters, which you can no longer drink. Also in the grotto is a beautiful marble bishop's chair, resting on two lions.

Once outside, head down the short flight of steps opposite the sanctuary to visit the **Tomb of Rotari**, thought to be the tomb of a 7th century Lombard king, but more likely a 12th century baptistry. Next door is the **Church of San Pietro**, which was destroyed in a 19th century earthquake. Its façade remains standing and features an interesting rose window. The adjacent 11th century **Church of Santa Maria Maggiore** is closed to the public.

There is also a Norman **castle**, which stands at the town's highest point. It has been closed to the public for some years because of restoration works, but check if it has reopened. Take the time to wander around Monte Sant'Angelo's narrow side streets.

Places to Stay & Eat Try the *Albergo Moderno* (☎ 0884-6 13 31), Via Leone Garganico 34, just off Piazza Duca d'Aosta, where SITA buses terminate. It has singles/doubles for L25,000/50,000. The three-star *Rotary Hotel* (☎ 0884-6 21 46), Via Pulsano, one km downhill from town, has rooms for L50,000/70,000.

Via Reale Basilica is lined with takeaways

and trattorias, including the *Trattoria San Michele* at No 59, and *Ristorante Garden Paradise* at No 51. While in town, try the local sweets, ostie ripiene (literally, 'stuffed Hosts') – two wafers of bread (like Hosts used in the Catholic Communion) with a filling of almonds and honey.

Getting There & Away Monte Sant'Angelo is accessible from Foggia, Manfredonia, Vieste and San Giovanni Rotondo by SITA bus. If you have your own transport, you can take the road to/from Vico del Gargano, which cuts through the Umbra Forest.

Peschici

Set high on rocky cliffs overlooking a pretty bay, Peschici is a fast-developing seaside resort town, but remains relatively unspoiled by tourism. It has a charming medieval section, made up of a maze of narrow streets lined with whitewashed houses. Its sandy beaches become very crowded in summer, as do its hotels, so book well in advance.

Orientation & Information While the medieval part of town clings to the cliff top at the point of the bay, the newer parts of town extend inland and around the bay. Buses arrive at the sporting ground just uphill from the town's main street, Corso Garibaldi. Turn right into the Corso and walk straight ahead to reach the old town.

The Pro Loco tourist office (☎ 0884-96 44

Romanesque Churches

There are 18 important Romanesque churches in Apulia, although only nine are considered to have been preserved in the original style. These include the cathedrals at Bari, Altamura, Barletta, Bitonto, Molfetta, Ruvo di Puglia and Trani. Another church which should be added to this list is the Basilica of San Nicola in Bari, which is considered of exceptional architectural value since it was used as a model for many of the churches built in the Apulian-Romanesque style.

With some careful planning, all of these churches can be visited on day trips from Bari, although the town of Trani is worth a visit in its own right. If you want to make a full tour of the towns and cities in which the churches are located, consider hiring a car for two or three days. This would also enable you to take in a couple of the less important Romanesque churches in the province, as well as including a visit to the Castel del Monte, the stunning octagonal castle of Frederick II of Swabia, about 40 km west of Bari.

The itinerary starts in **Bari** with the Basilica of San Nicola, built in the 11th century on the ruins of a Byzantine palace to house the bones of the miracle-working St Nicholas, which had been stolen by Bari mariners from their resting place in Myra (in what is now Turkey). The basilica has a stark, imposing façade, simply decorated with blind arches and mullioned windows, and flanked by two bell towers. Look for the Lion's Doorway on the basilica's north side, a door decorated with beautiful sculptures and bas-reliefs depicting chivalric scenes. Inside the three-naved interior, there is a splendid 12th century tabernacle, as well as a bishop's throne, known as Elia's Pulpit, sculpted in the second half of the 12th century. The remains of St Nicholas are housed in the crypt, under the transept.

Bari's 12th century cathedral was built on the remains of a Byzantine cathedral. It retains its elegant Romanesque shape and bell tower, but has been much altered and added to over the centuries.

The cathedrals of Bitonto, Ruvo di Puglia and Molfetta are to the west of Bari and are easily accessible by public transport. **Trani** and **Barletta** are farther along the coast, and Trani is a better base for seeing the cathedral there and in Barletta – see the Trani and Around Trani sections for more details. If you have the time, take a look also at the cathedrals in **Conversano** and **Palo del Colle**.

The cathedral of **Bitonto** is a particularly stunning example of Apulian-Romanesque architecture and one of the most beautiful in the region. Built in the late 12th century on the model of Bari's Basilica of San Nicola, it is dedicated to St Valentine. Note the carved animals and plants which decorate the capitals on the side walls. The cathedral has been closed for

25) is just off Corso Garibaldi near the entrance to the old town, on the corner of Via Magenta and Via Mulino a Vento. It can provide information about accommodation, but little else. The town's telephone code is 0884.

Places to Stay Peschici has numerous hotels and pensioni, but prices are usually on the expensive side, particularly in summer. There are numerous camping grounds along the coast on both sides of Peschici. Try the *Baia San Nicola* (☎ 96 42 31), close to town, or *Camping Parco degli Ulivi* (☎ 96 42 42), a few km west of town on the road to Rodi Garganico.

In the medieval section of town is the *Locanda al Castello* (☎ 96 40 38), Via Castello 29, which has singles/doubles for L30,000/60,000. *Albergo La Pineta* (☎ 96 41 26), Via Libetta 77, has rooms for L35,000/55,000, while the *Hotel Timiama* (☎ 96 43 21) next door has rooms for L50,000/70,000.

Places to Eat To stock up on supplies, shop at the Crai supermarket at the far end of Corso Garibaldi from the medieval section. The *Locanda al Castello* is a good, reasonably priced pizzeria and trattoria. Other restaurants in the old part of town include *Ristorante La Taverna*, just off Via Castello, where a full meal will cost up to L30,000, and *Ristorante Vecchia Peschici*, Via Roma

---

some time and is not expected to reopen in the foreseeable future, because of works under its main pavement. Bitonto is accessible from Bari on the private Bari-Nord train line. From the station, walk directly ahead along Via Matteotti (about one km) until you reach the medieval part of town. From here, there are signs directing you to the cathedral, and there are tourist maps posted at various points.

The graceful cathedral in **Ruvo di Puglia** is considered to have one of the most beautiful façades of the region's Romanesque churches. Built at the end of the 12th century, it has a fine rose window and three portals. The finely carved central portal features columns supported by griffins, resting on (now very worn) lions, themselves supported by telamons. Ruvo is on the Bari-Nord train line. It is also accessible from Bari's Piazza Eroi del Mare by Ferrotranviaria bus (approximately every half hour daily, except Sunday), which arrives at Corso Cortugno, just off Ruvo's main piazza. The same bus also goes to Bitonto, Andria and Barletta. From the bus stop, walk to the left through the piazza and turn right into Corso Giovanni Jatta. Once you reach the park, turn right and then right again when you reach the tower, which is at the rear of the cathedral.

Molfetta is worth visiting not only for its impressively simple cathedral, but also for its largely abandoned, tumbledown medieval centre. The cathedral, known as the Duomo Vecchio, was started in 1150 and completed at the end of the 13th century. It has a stark white undecorated façade flanked by two bell towers. Its interior is a mix of Romanesque, Byzantine and Muslim architecture. The medieval quarter, known as the Borgo Vecchio, stretches out behind the cathedral and is in a state of great disrepair, although sections are now being restored. It is interesting to wander through the quarter. Molfetta is on the main Bari-Foggia train line, only about 20 minutes from Bari. From the station, ask for directions to Via Dante and the port. The cathedral is at the port in Largo Chiesa Vecchia.

Altamura is about 45 km south-west of Bari and easily accessible on the Apulo-Lucane train line (see the Bari Getting There & Away section for details). Its 13th century cathedral was built during the reign of Frederick II, but was badly damaged during an earthquake in 1316 and later suffered some Baroque additions. The beautiful medieval main portal and elegant rose window were moved from their original position to what had been the apse. Both survived with little or no ill effect and can be admired today. The cathedral is in the old town's main street, Via Federico II di Svevia. From the train station, walk straight ahead along Viale Regina Margherita to Piazza Unità d'Italia and enter the old town through the Porta Bari. Ferrovie Apulo-Lucane buses also connect Bari and Altamura, arriving in Piazza Santa Teresa. From the piazza, turn right and walk to Piazza Unità d'Italia. ■

31, where an excellent meal on the terrace overlooking the sea will cost around L35,000.

Getting There & Away Peschici is accessible by Ferrovie del Gargano buses from Vieste and Rodi Garganico. From April to September, daily boats leave Peschici's port for the Tremiti Islands at 9.15 am, returning at 6.15 pm. For information and tickets, go to Ondazzurra (☎ 9 42 34) at Corso Umberto I.

Vieste

This is the most popular seaside resort on the promontory and is therefore the most heavily developed and best equipped with tourist facilities. The best beaches are out of town, between Vieste and Peschici, particularly in the area known as La Salata, where there are three camping grounds (see the following Places to Stay section). Vieste has a pleasant historic centre.

Orientation & Information Intercity buses terminate in Piazza Manzoni, a few minutes' walk along Via XXIV Maggio from the entrance to the old town and the tourist office (☎ 0884-70 88 06) in Piazza Kennedy, by the sea. The office is open in summer from 8.30 am to 1.30 pm and 4 to 9.30 pm Monday to Saturday, to 1 pm Sunday. Out of season it opens Monday to Saturday from 8.30 am to 1.30 pm and 3 to 8 pm.

The post office is in Piazza Vittorio Veneto, and there are rows of public telephones both in Piazza Veneto and outside the tourist office. The town's telephone code is 0884.

Things to See & Do The old town, with its whitewashed houses and typical medieval streets, offers a couple of sights of interest, although tourists come here for the beaches rather than the history. The **Duomo** is Apulian-Romanesque, but underwent alteration in the 18th century.

Head down Via Cimaglia to the **Chianca Amara** (Bitter Stone), on which thousands of locals were beheaded when the Turks

sacked Vieste in the 16th century. Nearby, at the town's highest point, is a **castle**, built by Frederick II and now occupied by the military and not open to the public.

If you want to head for the beach and don't have your own transport, the **Spiaggia del Castello** is just south of the town.

Places to Stay Vieste has numerous hotels and pensioni, most of them along the beachfront roads to the north and south of the town. There are also abundant camping grounds in the area, particularly along Lungomare E Mattei to the south of the town. Locals say that the best camping ground in the area is *Campeggio Capo Vieste* (☎ 70 63 26), at La Salata on the road between Vieste and Peschici. It is accessible by Ferrovie del Gargano bus.

The *Pensione al Centro Storico* (☎ 70 70 30) is at Via Mafrolla 32 in the medieval centre (from Via XXIV Maggio, walk through Piazza Vittorio Emanuele and then follow Via Pola). It has singles/doubles for up to L45,000/75,000, and triples for up to L85,000. The *Hotel Vela Velo* (☎ 70 63 03) is at Lungomare Europa 19, north of the old town. It charges by the person, up to L55,000 in the high season, which covers bed and breakfast, use of the private beach and use of a bicycle; out of season you should be able to negotiate to pay for the room only. The *Hotel Seggio* (☎ 70 81 23) is at Via Vieste 7, in the old town. A pleasant hotel, it has a private pool and sunbathing terraces. It charges up to L110,000 a double in the high season, and up to L93,000 per person for full board.

Places to Eat For a snack, try *Il Fornaio*, Piazza della Libertà, at the end of Via Fazzini near the entrance to the old town, which serves pizza by the slice. A panoramic spot for a cool drink is *Le Café*, overlooking the sea in Piazzetta Petrone, downhill along Via Cimaglia. *La Ripa*, Via Cimaglia 16, is a pleasant, rustic little trattoria, where a full meal will cost under L20,000. Otherwise try *Taverna al Cantinone*, Via Vico Caruso (which crosses Via Mafrolla), where a good meal will cost around L30,000. *Vecchia Vieste*, Via Mafrolla 32, is one of the town's better restaurants in the 'reasonable' price range; a full meal, including fish, will cost around L40,000.

Getting There & Away SITA buses connect Vieste with Foggia and Manfredonia, while the Ferrovie del Gargano bus and train network connects the town with Peschici and Rodi Garganico, as well as other towns on the promontory. Buses terminate in Piazza Manzoni and timetables are posted outside the town hall nearby.

Vieste's port is just north of the old town, about five minutes' walk from the tourist office, from where you can catch boats to the Tremiti Islands. They're run by two companies, Adriatica and Motonave, both of which have ticket offices at the port (return tickets cost L33,800). It is also possible to make a boat tour of the coast near Vieste, which includes visits to some of the area's grottoes. Enquire at the port for timetables and tickets (L15,000).

THE TREMITI ISLANDS

This small archipelago about 40 km north of the Gargano Promontory consists of three main islands: San Domino, San Nicola and Capraia. The islands are an increasingly popular summer tourist resort, but remain relatively undeveloped and unspoiled, at least for now. Out of season most of the islands' tourist facilities close down and the 370 or so permanent residents resume their isolated, quiet lives.

The islands have an ancient history. Legend says that Diomedes, a Greek hero of the Trojan War, was buried here and that a rare species of bird which inhabits the island, the Diomedee, continues to mourn his death. At the beginning of the 11th century, the Abbey of Santa Maria was founded on San Nicola by Benedictine monks, who wielded power in the region until the arrival of the Spanish Bourbons in the 18th century. King Ferdinand IV used the abbey as a penal colony, a tradition continued by the Fascists, who sent political exiles to the islands in the 1920s and 1930s.

San Nicola was always the administrative and residential centre of the islands because of the ease with which it could be defended, while the lusher San Domino was used to grow crops. Today, since there is no longer the risk of pirate attacks, you will find most of the islands' accommodation and other tourist facilities on San Domino.

Depending on which ferry or hydrofoil you catch, you will arrive on either San Domino or San Nicola. Don't panic if you think you have been dropped off on the wrong island, since small boats make the brief crossing on a regular basis (L1500 one way – no exact timetable, you just have to wait). Be sure to confirm the departure point of your boat.

Things to See & Do

San Nicola It is interesting to wander around the abbey on San Nicola, noting in particular the **Church of Santa Maria**, which features an 11th century floor mosaic, a painted wooden Byzantine crucifix, brought to the island in 747 AD, and a black Madonna, which was almost certainly transported to the abbey from Constantinople in the Middle Ages.

San Domino San Domino has the only sandy beach on the Tremiti Islands, and it becomes extremely crowded in summer. But there are numerous small coves which dot the San Domino coastline, where you can swim off the rocks. Some are accessible on foot, while others can be reached only by boat.

If you are feeling energetic, there is a walking track around the island which starts at the far end of San Domino village, past Pensione Nassa. Alternatively, you could hire a bicycle from IBIS Cicli (☎ 0882-66 30 58) at Piazzetta San Domino. Motorised rubber dinghies are available for hire at the port for L100,000 a day (go to the Il Piràta bar). Boats leave from San Domino's small port on tours of the island's grottoes; tickets cost L12,000.

Places to Stay & Eat

You will need to book well in advance for summer. If you intend to arrive out of season, you should phone to check that hotels are open. In the high season, most hotels require that you pay for full board – a good idea, since the options for eating out are not extensive.

On San Domino, *Il Faro* (☎ 0882-66 30 72), Via della Cantina Sperimentale, has singles/doubles for around L40,000/70,000, while *Locanda La Nassa* (☎ 0882-66 30 75) has doubles for up to L90,000. *Hotel Gabbiano* (☎ 0882-66 30 44) has a terrace restaurant overlooking San Nicola from San Domino, and very pleasant rooms for around L130,000 a double, or L105,000 per head for full board.

On San Nicola, you could eat at *Diomedea*, where a simple meal will cost around L20,000.

Getting There & Away

Adriatica Navigazione runs small ferries and hydrofoils, as well as a fast boat known as a *monostab*, to the Tremiti Islands from several points along the Adriatic coast, including Vieste, Peschici, Rodi Garganico (the closest point) and Manfredonia, as well as Termoli in Molise.

Services are frequent during the high season, and include the ferry from Vieste (L28,000 return), the monostab from Rodi Garganico (L30,000 return), and the hydrofoil from Termoli (L39,400 return). Tickets can be purchased at ticket offices at the relevant ports, although it should be noted that in summer you will need to buy your ticket 24 hours in advance. In Vieste, you can do this at Gargano Viaggi (☎ 0884-70 85 01), Piazza Roma 7, or at the Adriatica and Motonave offices at the port; in Peschici at Ondazzurra (☎ 0884-9 42 34), Corso Umberto I; in Manfredonia at Ditta Antonio Galli e Figlio (☎ 0884-2 28 88), Corso Manfredi 4; and in Termoli at Intercontinental Viaggi (☎ 0875-70 53 41), Corso Umberto I 93.

TRANI

Along the Adriatic coast towards Bari, this ancient fishing port is a worthwhile stopover on your way south and could even be used in preference to Bari as a base for exploring surrounding towns, such as Barletta and Molfetta, and the Castel del Monte.

Trani was an important medieval town – the modern world's oldest written maritime code, the *Ordinamenta Maris*, was drawn up here – and it flourished during the rule of Frederick II. The town's medieval harbour area was, until recently, semi-abandoned and in a poor state of repair. Fortunately, the past 10 years or so have seen a rejuvenation of this picturesque area and it is now a focus for tourists and the town's nightlife.

Trani's main attraction is certainly its magnificent cathedral, one of the finest examples of Apulian-Romanesque architecture.

Orientation & Information

The train and bus stations are in Piazza XX Settembre. Head down Via Cavour to the large Piazza della Repubblica, where there is a tourist information booth in the far left corner of the park in the piazza's centre. The booth is open Monday to Saturday from 8.30 am to 12.30 pm and 3.30 to 5.30 pm. The helpful staff can provide information about accommodation and places to eat, as well as assistance with bus routes and timetables. Continue along Via Cavour to reach Piazza Plebiscito and the public gardens and, to the left, the port area. Across the small harbour is the cathedral, spectacularly located by the sea on a small promontory.

The town's telephone code is 0883.

Things to See

Started in 1097 on the site of a Byzantine church, the **cathedral** was not completed until the 13th century. Dedicated to St Nicholas the Pilgrim (San Nicola Pellegrino), it is without doubt one of the most beautiful churches in Italy. Its simple but imposing façade is decorated with blind arches. The beautiful bronze doors of the main portal (removed for renovation at the time of writing) were cast in 1180 by Barisano da Trani, an accomplished artisan of whom little is known, other than that he also cast the bronze doors of the cathedral at Ravallo and the side doors of the cathedral at Monreale.

The grand interior of the cathedral was recently restored to its original Norman austerity. Light shines through alabaster windows, giving the interior an eerie glow. Near the main altar, note the remains of a 12th century floor mosaic, similar in style to the mosaic at Otranto. Underneath the main church is the crypt, a forest of ancient columns, where the bones of St Nicholas are kept underneath the altar.

The crypt opens onto the Byzantine **Church of Santa Maria della Scala**. Of note here is the *Madonna Dolorata*, a life-size statue of the Madonna, dressed in black velvet, a dagger protruding from her heart. Down another flight of stairs is the **Tomb of San Leucio**, a chamber believed to date back to the 6th century.

Near the cathedral is the 13th century **castle**, built by Frederick II. It was altered by the Angevins and used as a prison until recently.

There are several palaces and churches of interest around the port area. Note the 15th century Gothic **Caccetta Palace** and the nearby 12th century **All Saints' Church**, both in Via Ognissanti close to the cathedral. The church was built by the Templars as part of a complex used as a hospital for knights injured in the crusades. Also take a look at the **Quercia Palace**, in Piazza Quercia at the other end of the port area.

Places to Stay

The cheapest hotel in town is *Albergo Lucy* (☎ 4 10 22), Piazza Plebiscito 11, which has doubles/triples for L60,000/80,000. About three km out of town (accessible by blue bus for Corato from the station) is *Albergo Capirro* (☎ 58 07 12), a pleasant place with singles/doubles for L25,000/50,000. The *Hotel Duomo* (☎ 58 45 27), Piazza del Duomo 2, is next to the cathedral and has doubles/triples for L70,000/105,000. All

rooms in these establishments have private bathrooms.

Places to Eat

To pick up supplies, shop at the market, held every morning Monday to Saturday in Piazza della Libertà, to the left along Via Pagano from Piazza della Repubblica.

Attached to the Hotel Duomo is a restaurant/pizzeria, the *Antica Cattedrale*, where you can eat a reasonably priced meal. *Pizzeria Al Faro*, Via Statuti Marittimi 50, at the port, is another good choice, while *La Darsena*, in the 18th century Palumbo Palace at the port, is more expensive.

The *Caffè Nautico Club*, Via Statuti Marittimi 18, is actually a private club but also an excellent little restaurant. If you are lucky, you might find that the owner/chef is willing to whip you up a delightful seafood meal for around L35,000.

Getting There & Away

AMET buses connect Trani with points along the coast and inland, including Barletta, Canosa di Puglia, Ruvo di Puglia and Andria. Timetables and tickets are available at Agenzia Sprint, opposite the train station in Piazza XX Settembre.

A special, connecting bus service operates between Trani and the Castel del Monte. It leaves from Piazza XX Settembre at 6.55 am, arriving in Andria at 7.20 am, with a connecting bus to the castle at 8.30 am. The bus then returns to Andria at 3 pm. Check with the tourist office for updated times. Otherwise, catch one of the regular buses to Andria, then hitchhike the 18 km to the castle.

Trani is on the main train line between Bari and Foggia and is therefore easily reached from towns along the coast.

AROUND TRANI
Barletta

About 13 km north-west along the coast from Trani is Barletta, worth a quick visit to see its cathedral and a massive bronze statue known as the *Colossus*.

Orientation & Information From the train

station, turn right into Corso Garibaldi to reach Barletta's centre. From the bus terminal in Via Manfredi, walk to Piazza Plebiscito and turn left into Corso Vittorio Emanuele. The town's tourist office could still be inside the municipal offices in Via Municipio, off Corso Vittorio Emanuele, but at the time of writing new premises were being sought.

Things to See The 12th century Apulian-Romanesque **Duomo**, along Corso Garibaldi from the town centre, is among the region's best preserved examples of this architectural style. It was being restored at the time of writing. Nearby is the imposing **castle**, built by the Normans, rebuilt by Frederick II and fortified by Charles of Anjou. It is closed to the public.

Back in the town centre, just off Corso Garibaldi in Corso Vittorio Emanuele, is the *Colossus*, a 4.5-metre-high Roman statue believed to be of the Emperor Valentinian I. The statue was part of the plunder from the sack of Constantinople in 1203 and was acquired by Barletta after the ship carrying it sank off the Apulian coast. The statue stands next to the 12th century **Basilica of the Holy Sepulchre**. Originally Romanesque, it was altered in the Gothic style in the 13th century and has a Baroque façade.

Festival The main event of the town's annual calendar is the Disfida (Challenge) of Barletta, held annually on the last Sunday in July. One of the country's more famous medieval pageants, it re-enacts a duel between 13 Italian and 13 French knights on 13 February 1503, when the town was besieged by the French. The Italians won the challenge.

Getting There & Away From the bus terminal in Via Manfredi, ATAF buses connect Barletta with Foggia; there are regular AMET buses to Trani and Molfetta; and SITA buses head for Manfredonia and Bari. Barletta is on both the Bari-Foggia coastal train line and the Bari-Nord line and is easily accessible from Trani and other points along the coast, as well as inland towns.

Castel del Monte

The Castel del Monte, standing like a royal crown on a hill top, is one of Apulia's most prominent landmarks. It is situated in the Murge, a long limestone plateau which extends west and south of Bari. You have to be fairly enthusiastic to make the journey to the castle without your own transport, but it is certainly worth the effort.

The octagonal castle was built by Frederick II, probably for his own pleasure and to his own design, in the early 13th century during the last 10 years of his life. It was perhaps used as a hunting lodge, since the surrounding hills and plains were at that time heavily forested and teeming with game.

The castle has eight octagonal towers and no moat or other system of defence, apart from its high walls and slit windows. In recent years it was completely restored and you can wander through the interconnecting rooms admiring the decorative marble columns and fireplaces, and the doorways and window frames decorated with corallite stone. The castle is open in summer from 8.30 am to 7 pm Monday to Saturday, and from 9 am to 1 pm Sunday. From October to March it opens from 8.30 am to 2 pm Monday to Saturday, and from 9 am to 1 pm Sunday, although opening times can vary slightly at the whim of the guards.

Getting There & Away The easiest way to get to the castle is via the nearby town of Andria. A bus leaves from the town's Piazza Municipio at 8.30 am Monday to Saturday for the castle, returning at 3 pm. Andria is easily accessible by bus from Trani, or on the Bari-Nord train line from Bari. The Andria-Spinazzola bus (several a day) passes close to the castle – ask the driver to let you off at the right spot. See also the Trani Getting There & Away section.

BARI

Unless you are planning to catch a ferry to Greece or Croatia, Bari is probably not going to be high on your list of places to go in Apulia. However, it does have some interesting sights to offer, and, particularly if you are aged under 30 and take advantage of the Stop Over in Bari programme (see under Tourist Office in the following Information section), it provides an excellent base for exploring neighbouring towns such as Ruvo di Puglia, Molfetta, Bitonto, Altamura and even Alberobello and the trulli area.

Bari is the capital of Apulia and the second-most important city in the south, after Naples. It was an important Byzantine city and flourished under the Normans and later under Frederick II. Its greatest claim to fame is the remains of St Nicholas of Myra, otherwise known as Father Christmas. The remains, which are contained in a liquid known as the Manna, said to have miraculous powers, were stolen from Myra (in what is now Turkey) by a group of Bari seamen in 1087. The Basilica of San Nicola, built to house his remains, is still an important place of pilgrimage.

The city was occupied by the Allies during WW II and was heavily bombed by the Germans.

Orientation

Bari is a fairly easy town to negotiate. The FS and Bari-Nord train stations are at the vast Piazza Aldo Moro, in the newer (19th century) section of the city, about 10 minutes' walk south of the old town, known to locals as Bari Vecchia. Intercity buses also terminate in and near the piazza.

This newer part of Bari is on a grid plan and any of the streets heading north from Piazza Aldo Moro, including Via Sparano, will take you to Corso Vittorio Emanuele II, which separates the old and new cities. Corso Cavour, which runs parallel to Via Sparano, three streets to the east, is the main shopping strip.

Information

Tourist Offices The EPT information office (☎ 080-524 22 44) is to the right as you leave the train station, just off Piazza Aldo Moro, and opens from 9 am to 1 pm and 4 to 8 pm

Monday to Saturday. It has a reasonable amount of information about the town and province of Bari and can advise on accommodation.

If you are under 30 years old, you can take advantage of Stop Over in Bari, the remarkably generous initiative of Bari's local government and other organisations, which aims to attract youth tourism to the city. The programme operates annually from June to September, offering a stopover package which includes low-priced accommodation in small hotels or private homes, or free accommodation in the Pineta San Francesco camping ground; free use of the city's buses; free admission to the town's museums; cut-rate meals; a free bike service; and three information centres for young travellers. In the 1992 season, the package cost L30,000 for two nights' accommodation.

Stop Over's main office, OTE (☎ 080-521 45 38), is at Via Dante Alighieri 111, and there are information booths at the main train station and at the Stazione Marittima. At all outlets you will find the staff extremely helpful and friendly (they speak English), and they have loads of information about the town. While only under-30s can take advantage of the packages, anyone is welcome to seek information. Ring the above number to make a booking, or go to one of Stop Over's outlets when you arrive in town.

Money You will find the main banks in the central shopping district around Corso Cavour. Alternatively, there are exchange booths at the main train station and the Stazione Marittima.

Post & Telecommunications The main post office is in Piazza Cesare Battisti, on Via Cairoli. From Piazza Aldo Moro, turn left at Via Crisanzio and right at Via Cairoli. The postal code for central Bari is 70100.

There is an SIP public telephone office at Via Oriani, a bit out of the way near the castle, and an ASST office at the train station. Otherwise, there are abundant public telephones throughout the city. Bari's telephone code is 080.

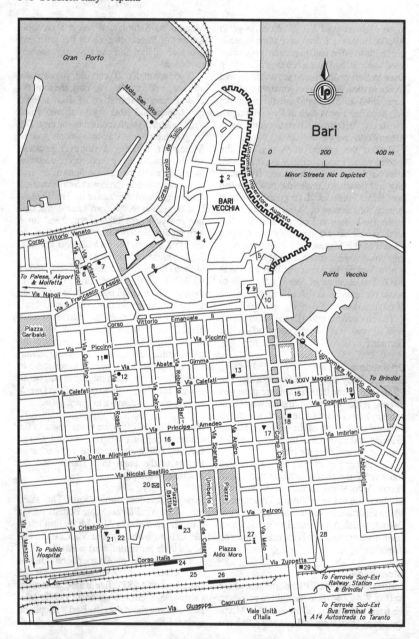

Gran Porto

Molo San Vito

Corso Antonio de Tullio

Lungomare Imperatore Augusto

† 2

BARI VECCHIA

LP

Bari

0   200   400 m

Minor Streets Not Depicted

Corso Vittorio Veneto

Via Carducci

To Palese, Airport
& Molfetta

Via Napoli

Via Orlani

Via S Francesco d'Assisi

3

† 4

5

7

8

9

10

Porto Vecchio

14

Corso   Vittorio   Emanuele   II

Piazza
Garibaldi

Via Piccinni

Via Quintino

11

Via Piccinni

Abate   Gimma

Via Calefati

13

Via XXIV Maggio

Via Roberto da Bari

Via

12

Via Calefati

De Rossi

15

19

Via Cognetti

18

Via Imbriani

17

Corso Cavour

Lungomare Nazario Sauro

To Brindisi

Via Calefati

Via Cairoli

Principe   Amedeo

Via Spirito

Via Argiro

16

Via Dante Alighieri

Via Nicolai Beatillo

20

Piazza
C. Battisti

Umberto I

Piazza
Umberto I

Via Abbrescia

Via Crisanzio

21 22

23

Via de Cesare

Via Petroni

27

Via Melo

28

To Public
Hospital

Via A Manzoni

Corso Italia

24

Piazza
Aldo Moro

Via Zuppetta

29

25   26

To Ferrovie Sud-Est
Railway Station
& Brindisi

Via   Giuseppe   Capruzzi

Viale Unità
d'Italia

To Ferrovie Sud-Est
Bus Terminal &
A14 Autostrada to Taranto

■ PLACES TO STAY

11	Residenza Universitaria
18	Grand Hotel d'Oriente
22	Grand Hotel Moderno
23	Albergo Romeo & Pensione Giulia
29	Hotel Adria

▼ PLACES TO EAT

8	Al Pescatore
9	Vini e Cucina
17	Ristorante Porta d'Oro da Enzo
19	Trattoria Verde
21	Bar Mokambo

OTHER

1	Stazione Marittima
2	Basilica of San Nicola
3	Swabian Castle
4	Cathedral
5	Piazza Mercantile, Sedile & Column of Justice
6	SIP Public Telephones
7	Police Headquarters
10	Piazza del Ferrarese
12	CIT Office
13	Air Terminal
14	Piazza Eroi del Mare & Bus Stops for AMET & Ferrotranviaria
15	Teatro Petruzzelli
16	OTE Office (Stop Over in Bari)
20	Post Office
24	Apulo Lucane Railway Station
25	Bari Nord Railway Station
26	Main Railway Station
27	EPT Tourist Office
28	Piazza Luigi di Savoia

Travel Agency There is a CIT office at Via Abate Gimma 150-152, on the corner of Via De Rossi. OTE (see under Tourist Office) can also assist with budget travel arrangements.

Emergency For immediate police attendance, call ☎ 113. The police headquarters (☎ 29 11 11) are at Via G Murat, near the castle. For medical assistance, go to the Ospedale Consorziale Policlinico (☎ 22 15 14), Piazza Giulio Cesare, south of the town centre, on the other side of the train lines.

Dangers & Annoyances Bari is fast developing a reputation as a major drug and crime centre in the south, and tourists need to be on the alert since there is also a very high petty crime rate. Be extremely careful when visiting the town's historic centre – even during the day, women are best advised not to enter this area alone, and at night most local people avoid it altogether. The town's spiralling drug problem means that, in the old town, you are likely to encounter open drug use. There is a strong police presence around the area's main sights and, if you exercise normal precautions, such as keeping valuables in a money belt and avoiding deserted side streets, you should be able to minimise any potential problems.

Things to See & Do
Bari's main churches, **San Nicola** and the **cathedral**, are discussed in the separate section on Romanesque Churches elsewhere on these pages. Both are in the old town – San Nicola in the piazza of the same name, and the cathedral nearby, off Piazza Odegitria.

Start your exploration of Bari Vecchia at Piazza Mercantile, at the top of Corso Cavour. In the piazza is the **Sedile**, the medieval headquarters of Bari's Council of Nobles, and to one corner of the piazza is the **Column of Justice** to which it is thought debtors were tied. A fresh-produce market is held in the piazza every morning from Monday to Saturday. Head along Via della Vecchia Dogana and the Lungomare Imperatore Augusto to reach the **Basilica of San Nicola**.

You should exercise care while wandering around the narrow streets of Bari Vecchia, but don't let paranoia stop you from really exploring the area. It is interesting to note, for instance, that there are around 40 churches in the old town and more than 120 little shrines dedicated to the Madonna and various saints.

Close to the cathedral is the **Swabian Castle** (Castello Svevo), which represents four levels of history. The original Norman structure was built over the ruins of a Roman fort (now being excavated). Frederick II incorporated parts of the Norman castle into his own design, including two towers which are still standing. The bastions with corner towers overhanging the moat were added in the 16th century during Spanish rule. The castle is open Tuesday to Sunday from 9 am to 1 pm and 4 to 7 pm, and entrance is L5000. Most of the castle is, however, closed to the public.

Festival

The main event on Bari's annual calendar is the Festival of St Nicholas during the first weekend in May. If you can manage to be in town at the time, it is quite a spectacle. On the Saturday evening a procession of people in Norman costume leave the Swabian Castle for the Basilica of San Nicola, where they re-enact the delivery of the saint's bones to the Dominican friars. The next day, a statue of the saint is taken to sea, having pride of place in a procession of boats which make their way along the coast.

Places to Stay

If you are aged under 30, you should certainly take advantage of the Stop Over programme. If not, there are several reasonably priced options. There is an IYHF youth hostel, the *Ostello del Levante* (☎ 32 02 82), just west of Bari by the sea at Palese. Bed and breakfast is L12,000 a night and a meal costs L12,000. The hostel is closed from 20 December to 15 January. It is accessible by the No 1 bus from outside Teatro Petruzzelli on Corso Cavour.

If you choose to stay in a hotel, it is best to pay a bit more for security. The following are all reliable establishments. The *Residenza Universitaria* (☎ 23 52 26) is run by nuns and is for women only. A good, safe option, it is at Via De Rossi 23, not far from the station, and rooms cost L35,000 per person per night.

Albergo Romeo (☎ 523 72 53), Via Crisanzio 12, has singles/doubles for L35,000/60,000 and triples for L75,000, all with bathroom. In the same building is Pen-

sione Giulia (☎ 521 66 30), with singles/doubles with bathroom for L55,000/73,000. *Hotel Adria* (☎ 54 06 99), Via L Zuppetta 10, to the right of the station, has rooms for L65,000/100,000, while *Grand Hotel Moderno* (☎ 521 33 13), Via Crisanzio 60, has rooms for up to L70,000/120,000. The *Grand Hotel d'Oriente* (☎ 54 44 22), Corso Cavour 32, is a lovely old-style hotel, with grand prices: L120,000/190,000 for singles/doubles with full services.

Places to Eat

You will find it difficult to eat a meal more cheaply in Bari than at *Vini e Cucina*, Strada Vallisa, just off Piazza del Ferrarese in the old city. You can't get much more basic than its cave-like atmosphere and paper tablecloths. Head here for lunch (set price L12,000 with wine). *Trattoria Verde*, Largo Adua 18, has excellent pizzas and very reasonably priced pasta and main dishes. A full meal will come to under L25,000.

Ristorante Porta d'Oro da Enzo, Via Principe Amedeo 12, off Corso Cavour, has excellent food for less than L25,000 a full meal. *Al Pescatore*, Piazza Federico II di Svevia 8, is next to the castle and specialises in seafood and Apulian dishes. A full meal here will cost around L40,000.

For excellent ice cream, head for *Bar Mokambo*, Via Crisanzio 72.

Getting There & Away

Air Bari's airport is several km west of the city centre and services domestic flights. You can get there on the Bari-Nord train line. There is also an Alitalia airport bus, which leaves from the air terminal at Via Calefati 87.

Bus Intercity buses leave from several different locations around the town, depending on where you are going and with which company. SITA buses depart from Piazza Aldo Moro for towns including Andria, Bitonto, Castellana and Ruvo di Puglia. Ferrovie Apulo-Lucane buses leave from Corso Italia 6 (to the left out of the main train station) for Altamura, while Ferrovie del Sud-Est (FSE) buses leave from Largo Ciaia, south of Piazza Aldo Moro, for places including Polignano, Ostuni and Taranto. AMET buses leave Piazza Eroi del Mare for Andria, Barletta, Molfetta and Trani, and Ferrotranviaria buses leave from the same piazza for Barletta, Ruvo di Puglia, Trani and Bitonto.

Marozzi buses for Rome leave from Piazza Aldo Moro. The company's office is at Corso Italia 3.

Train As with intercity buses, there is an array of different train lines connecting Bari with the outside world.

Bari is easily accessible by national FS trains from Milan, Bologna, Pescara, Rome and cities throughout Apulia, including Foggia, Brindisi, Lecce and Taranto.

There are also private train lines. The Bari-Nord line connects the city with the airport, Bitonto, Andria and Barletta, and the station is next to the main train station in Piazza Aldo Moro. The Apulo-Lucane connects Bari with Altamura and with Matera and Potenza in Basilicata. The station is in Corso Italia, just off Piazza Aldo Moro. FSE trains head for Alberobello, Castellana, Locorotondo, Martina Franca and Taranto, leaving from the station in Via Oberdan – cross under the train tracks south of Piazza Luigi di Savoia and head east along Via Giuseppe Capruzzi for about half a km.

Boat Ferries leave from Bari's port for Croatia, but services and timetables should be checked since they were cancelled because of the unrest there. They also sail to Greece, Egypt and Albania. All ferry companies have offices at the Stazione Marittima at the port (accessible from the train station on bus No 20). Although prices for passage to Greece are cheaper than what is available at Brindisi, the trip is two hours longer. Note that there is a L11,000 embarkation tax per person.

Once you have bought your ticket and paid the embarkation tax, you will be given a boarding card, which must be stamped by the police at the Stazione Marittima. There is an office of Stop Over in Bari at the Adriatica counter in the Stazione Marittima, and the staff will be happy to assist you with information.

The main companies and the routes they service are as follows:

Adriatica Navigazione (☎ 33 15 55), c/o Agestea at the Stazione Marittima and at Via Liside 4. Adriatica has services roughly every 10 days to Piraeus in Greece and Alexandria in Egypt. It also has a service every 10 days to Dürres in Albania (L85,000 for an airline-type chair; L120,000 shared cabin). Adriatica had suspended its services to Croatia at the time of writing.

Ventouris Ferries (☎ 524 43 88), c/o Pan Travel at the Stazione Marittima, or at Via San Francesco d'Assisi 95. It has regular services to Corfu and Igoumenitsa (deck class L60,000; airline-type chair L75,000; shared cabin L105,000) and to Patras (deck class L65,000; airline-type chair L80,000; shared cabin L125,000).

Strintzis Lines (☎ 523 50 20), Stazione Marittima and c/o Barion, Corso A de Tullio 14, runs slightly cheaper services to Corfu and Igoumenitsa from June to September.

Jadrolinija (☎ 521 28 40), c/o P Lorusso & Co at the Stazione Marittima and at Via Piccinni 133. Its services to Croatia were suspended at the time of writing.

Car & Motorbike Bari is on the A14 autostrada, which heads north-west to Foggia and south to Taranto and connects with the A16 to Naples at Canosa di Puglia. Exit at Bari Nord to reach the centre of town. The easiest way to orient yourself is to follow the 'centro' signs to the centre and then the 'stazione' signs for the main train station and Piazza Aldo Moro.

Getting Around

The centre of Bari is reasonably compact – an easy 15-minute walk will take you from Piazza Aldo Moro to the old town. Useful city buses are No 20 from the train station to the Stazione Marittima, and No 1 from Teatro Petruzzelli to the IYHF youth hostel.

There is a guarded car park, the Garage Piccinni, at Via N Piccinni 139, which runs off Corso Cavour, parallel to Corso Vittorio Emanuele II.

THE TRULLI AREA

Trulli are unusual, circular houses made of stone without mortar, with conical roofs. The walls of the trulli are whitewashed, and the roofs, topped with pinnacles, are tiled with concentric rows of grey slate, locally known as *chiancarella*. The origins of the construction, which is typical to the area around Alberobello in central Apulia, are hazy, but it is thought the style was probably adopted to meet primitive building needs. Many trulli have astrological or religious symbols painted on their roofs.

The trulli area, in the Itria Valley, extends from Conversano and Goia del Colle in the west, to Ostuni and Martina Franca in the east, but the greatest number of the houses are in and around Alberobello.

Alberobello

This pretty town exists virtually for tourism these days, but it is well worth visiting to see the trulli, most of which are no longer private dwellings but used as souvenir and wine shops and boutiques.

There is a Pro Loco tourist office just off Piazza del Popolo at Corso Vittorio Emanuele 15 in the town centre, but it has very little information. A private organisation, known as MTG (☎ 080-932 34 62), at Via C Acquaviva 11, can assist with information about accommodation, as well as excursions in the area.

A few km west of the town is the **Barsento Farm**, accessible only if you have a car. Formerly an abbey founded in 591 AD, the small complex features one of the oldest churches in Apulia, built in the 6th century. The church and farm are privately owned, but the owner is proud to show tourists around the property – which he makes available for wedding receptions. To reach the property, take the road from Alberobello to Putignano, and after about six km turn left into the road for Noci. After about two km you will see Barsento Farm to your right.

Places to Stay There is a camping ground just out of town, the *Camping dei Trulli* (☎ 080 932 36 99), Via Castellana Grotte.

Charges are L3500 per person and L6000 for a site. In the town centre, at Piazza Ferdinando IV 31, is *Hotel Lanzillotta* (☎ 080-72 15 11), which has singles/doubles for L40,000/60,000 and triples for L75,000. The town's top hotel is the *Hotel dei Trulli* (☎ 080-932 35 55), Via Cadore 28, which is actually a complex of trulli. Each trullo is self-contained, with its own bathroom and living area, and costs around L200,000 a night.

Trulli are also available for rent through various agencies, with charges ranging from around L100,000 a day to L600,000 a week. Contact Agenzia Immobiliare Fittatrulli (☎ 080-72 27 17), Via Duca d'Aosta 14, Alberobello.

Getting There & Away The easiest way to get to Alberobello is on the FSE private train line (Bari-Taranto). From the station, walk straight ahead along Via Mazzini, which becomes Via Garibaldi, to reach Piazza del Popolo.

Castellana Caves

These spectacular limestone caves (Castellana Grotte in Italian) are among Apulia's prime tourist attractions, and justifiably so. Certainly the best known speleological site in Italy, the series of subterranean caves, with their at times breathtakingly beautiful formations of stalactites and stalagmites, were explored in the 1930s by Italian speleologist Franco Anelli.

Records show that the caves were known as far back as the 17th century and were probably partially explored in the 18th century. Anelli managed to explore about three km of the caves and today tourists can follow his path with a guide. After descending by elevator to a huge cavern known as La Grave, you will be taken on a tour through several caves, culminating in the magnificent White Cave.

The caves are open all year (only in the morning from October to March) and tours leave roughly every hour. You can enter only with a guide, but in the low season they are usually prepared to make the tour even for one person only. There are two tours: a one-km, one-hour trip (L10,000) which does not include the White Cave, and a three-km, two-hour trip (L20,000) which includes the White Cave.

The caves are easily accessible on the FSE train line (Bari-Taranto). The station is about 150 metres from the entrance to the caves.

Martina Franca

Believed to have been founded in the 10th century by refugees fleeing the Arab invasions of Taranto, Martina Franca flourished in the 14th century after it was granted tax exemptions (franchigie, hence the name Franca) by Philip of Anjou.

The town is at the edge of the trulli area and there are not many of the conical constructions here, but it has an interesting historical centre, with a medieval section as well as several examples of Baroque architecture.

Orientation & Information The FSE train station is downhill from the historic centre of town. City buses will take you up to Piazza XX Settembre and the entrance to the old town. Alternatively, you can walk to the right along Viale della Stazione, continuing along Via Alessandro Fighera to Corso Italia; continue to the left along Corso Italia to Piazza XX Settembre. The tourist office (☎ 080-70 57 02) is at Piazza Roma 35, where you can pick up a map of the town and advice on accommodation.

Things to See Next to the tourist office is the 17th century **Ducal Palace**, a vast palace now used as the municipal offices. Several frescoed rooms on the 3rd floor are open to the public (free entry).

From the piazza, follow the narrow Corso Vittorio Emanuele into Piazza Plebiscito and the heart of the historic centre. Of note here is the Baroque façade of the 18th century **Church of San Martino**.

Festival The town stages the annual Festival of the Itria Valley in July and August, a festival of concerts and opera. Information

and tickets are available through the tourist office.

Places to Stay & Eat The cheapest accommodation options are both out of the town. La Cremaillere (☎ 080-70 00 52) is about six km out of town at San Paolo on the road to Taranto. It charges L25,000/48,000 for singles/doubles with bathroom. Da Luigi (☎ 080-90 16 66) is about three km out of town on the road to Taranto and charges L40,000/60,000 for rooms with bathroom. Both places are accessible by FSE bus from Piazza Crispi.

In town all hotels are expensive, including the Park Hotel San Michele (☎ 080-880 70 53), Viale Carella 9, which charges L150,000/200,000.

For a meal, try Trattoria La Tavernetta, Corso Vittorio Emanuele 30, or Trattoria/Pizzeria del Corso, Via Paolo Chiara 5 (follow the signs from Piazza del Plebiscito).

Getting There & Away The easiest way to reach the town is on the FSE train line (Bari-Taranto). FSE buses also connect the town with Taranto, Alberobello, Castellana Grotte and Bari, arriving in Piazza Crispi, off Corso Italia.

Ostuni

This stunning little town of stark, white-washed buildings is set on three hills east of Martina Franca and about 40 km north-west of Brindisi. Its tangle of narrow cobblestone streets, many little more than arched stairways between the white houses, provide a fascinating environment in which to while away a few hours. Its main monuments, including the 15th century, late Gothic cathedral, are in pinkish-brown stone and, from a distance, provide a strong contrast to the whitewashed town.

Ostuni's AAST tourist office (☎ 0831-97 12 68) is in Piazza della Libertà, downhill from the cathedral in the newer part of town. It is open Monday to Friday from 9.30 am to 12.30 pm and 6.30 to 9 pm.

From Piazza della Libertà, walk uphill along Via Cattedrale to the cathedral. From the tiny piazza in front of the cathedral, turn right for a view across to the Adriatic Sea, or turn left to get lost in Ostuni's whitewashed lanes.

Places to Stay & Eat There is no budget accommodation in Ostuni, but its proximity to Brindisi means that you could make it a quick day trip before heading off to Greece. Otherwise, try the *Hotel Orchidea Nera* (☎ 0831-97 13 66), Via Mazzini, which has singles/doubles for L50,000/80,000.

There are some excellent eating places in the old town. The *Osteria del Tempo Perso* is tucked away behind the cathedral. To find it, head up Via Cattedrale and, when you reach the wall of the cathedral, turn right through the archway into Largo Giuseppe Spennati and then follow the signs to the restaurant.

Getting There & Away Società Trasporti Pubblici (STP) buses run between Ostuni and Brindisi about every two hours, arriving in Piazza Italia in the newer part of Ostuni. STP buses also connect the town with Martina Franca. However, the easiest way to reach Ostuni is on the main train line from either Brindisi or Bari. The No 1 city bus will take you from the station into the centre of town.

BRINDISI

Most travellers associate Brindisi with waiting. The major embarkation point for ferries from Italy to Greece, the city swarms with travellers in transit. There is not much to do here, other than wait. Most backpackers gather at the train station, at the port in the Stazione Marittima, or in Piazza Cairoli in between the two. If your budget extends beyond minimum rations, you could while away a few hours in a trattoria.

Orientation

The port and Stazione Marittima are about 10 minutes' walk from the train station along Corso Umberto I, which becomes Corso Garibaldi. There are numerous takeaway food outlets along the route, as well as the offices of most ferry companies.

Information

Tourist Office The helpful EPT tourist office (☎ 0831-52 19 44) is at Viale Regina Margherita 12, a short walk from the end of Corso Garibaldi and the Stazione Marittima (turn left once you reach the waterfront). It is open Monday to Saturday from 8.30 am to 12.30 pm and 4.30 to 7.30 pm.

Money There are numerous exchange offices along the route between the station and the port. Check the rates and choose the best.

Post & Telecommunications The main post office is in Piazza Mercato Coperto, off Corso Garibaldi. The postal code for central Brindisi is 72100.

There are SIP telephones at Via XX Settembre 6, off Via Cristoforo Colombo, to the left as you leave the train station. The town's telephone code is 0831.

Travel Agency There is a CTS office (☎ 56 01 87) at Via Bastioni Carlo V 3, to the right as you leave the train station.

Emergency For immediate police attendance, call ☎ 113. For medical attention, go to the public hospital, the Ospedale Generale Antonio di Summa (☎ 2 14 10), Piazza Antonio di Summa, west of the train station, off Via Appia.

Dangers & Annoyances As in many southern cities, thieves prey on tourists in Brindisi. Women should not walk through the town alone at night and valuables should be carried in a money belt. Under no circumstances should luggage or valuables be left unattended in your car. Brindisi's port is extremely busy during the summer high season, and, if you arrive by car, you should allow extra time for the eternal traffic jam around the port.

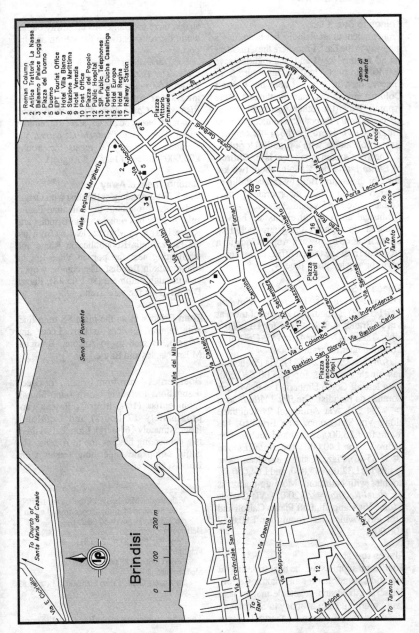

Brindisi

0   100   200 m

1 Roman Column
2 Antica Trattoria La Nassa
3 Balsamo Palace Loggia
4 Piazza del Duomo
5 Duomo
6 EPT Tourist Office
7 Hotel Villa Bianca
8 Stazione Marittima
9 Hotel Venezia
10 Post Office
11 Piazza del Popolo
12 Public Hospital
13 SIP Public Telephones
14 Osteria Cucina Casalinga
15 Hotel Europa
16 Hotel Regina
17 Railway Station

Things to See & Do

From ancient times Brindisi has been Italy's gateway to the East. From here the Crusaders set off for the Holy Land, and tradition says that Roman poet Virgil, on his return from Greece, died in a house near the **Roman Column**, one of two marking the end of the Appian Way (the other was removed to Lecce and only its pedestal remains). In the Piazza del Duomo is the 14th century **Balsamo Palace**, with a beautiful **loggia**.

The town's main monument is the **Church of Santa Maria del Casale**, about two km north of the centre. Built by Prince Philip of Taranto around 1300 it incorporates Gothic, Romanesque and Byzantine styles.

Musical and cultural events are held in Brindisi throughout the year, including Estate Insieme in July and August. Pick up a brochure from the tourist office if you are in town for any length of time.

Places to Stay

The non-IYHF *Ostello per la Gioventù* (☎ 41 31 23) is about two km out of town at Via N Brandi 4. It has beds for L12,000 a night. Take bus No 3 or 4 from Via Cristoforo Colombo near the train station.

Hotel Venezia (☎ 2 54 11), Via Pisanelli 4, has singles/doubles for L25,000/40,000; Turn left off Corso Umberto I onto Via San Lorenzo da Brindisi. The *Hotel Villa Bianca* (☎ 2 54 38), Via Armengol 21 (continue along Via San Lorenzo da Brindisi), has rooms for L25,000/38,000, and doubles with bathroom for L40,000. The *Hotel Europa* (☎ 52 85 46), Piazza Cairoli, has clean, basic rooms for L32,000/45,000, and L64,000 for doubles with bathroom. More up-market is the *Hotel Regina* (☎ 22 20 01), Via Cavour 5 (take Via Cappellini off Piazza Cairoli and turn left), which has rooms for L80,000/100,000.

Places to Eat

To pick up supplies for the boat trip, shop at the Sidis supermarket in Piazza Cairoli. There is a fruit and vegetable market held every morning from Monday to Saturday in Via Battisti, off Corso Umberto I. For a snack, there are numerous takeaway outlets along the route between the station and the port.

For a meal, head for the side streets off this route. The *Osteria Cucina Casalinga*, Via Mazzini 57, near the station, has good-value meals for around L15,000. *Pizzeria/ Ristorante Carlo V* in Piazzetta Ignazio Falconieri has good pizzas, served at outdoor tables. The *Antica Trattoria La Nassa*, Via Colonne 51, has good meals for around L25,000 (closed in July and August).

Getting There & Away

Bus STP buses connect Brindisi with Ostuni and towns throughout the Salentine Peninsula. A daily bus runs between Brindisi and Rome. It is run by Marozzi, leaving from just off Piazza della Repubblica in Rome and terminating near the port in Viale Regina Margherita in Brindisi. The company operates through Pattimare (☎ 2 65 48), Piazza Dionisi 11 on the waterfront.

Train Brindisi is on the main FS train line, with regular services to Bari, Lecce and Taranto, as well as to Ancona, Bologna, Milan, Naples and Rome.

Boat Ferries depart from Brindisi for Greek destinations including Corfu (nine hours), Igoumenitsa (10½ hours), Patras (approximately 17 hours) and Cefalonia (approximately 16 hours). From Patras there is a connecting bus service to Athens. The major companies operating ferries from Brindisi are:

Adriatica
> Viale Regina Margherita 13, and on the 1st floor at the Stazione Marittima, open from 9 am to 1 pm and 4 to 11 pm (☎ 52 38 25)

Hellenic Mediterranean Lines
> Corso Garibaldi 8 (☎ 52 85 31)

Fragline
> Corso Garibaldi 88 (☎ 52 95 61)

Mediterranean Lines
> c/o Angela Gioia, Corso Garibaldi 83 (☎ 52 82 90)

There are numerous other lines, but the companies regularly change hands and names and it is best to arrive in Brindisi and shop around if you are looking for a cheaper fare.

Adriatica and Hellenic are the most expensive, but also the most reliable. They are the only lines that can officially accept Eurail passes and Inter-Rail passes, which means you pay a L25,000 supplement but that's it (deck class). If you want to use your Eurail or Inter-Rail pass, it is important to reserve some weeks in advance, particularly in summer. Holders of an FS Cartaverde (for those aged under 26) are entitled to a 50% discount on Hellenic and Adriatic, while holders of the Italian Tourist Ticket and the Italy Flexi Railcard are entitled to a 30% reduction. Other discounts include a 10% reduction on the cost of a return fare in the off season.

Remember that you must check in at least two hours prior to departure, otherwise you run the risk of losing your reservation (a strong possibility in the high season). There is an embarkation office for Adriatic and Hellenic on the 1st floor of the Stazione Marittima. You will be required to pay a L10,000 port tax.

It should be noted that fares increase by up to 40% in July and August (ferry services also increase during this period). At the time of writing, July/August prices for Adriatica and Hellenic ferries to Patras were L105,000 (deck class), L125,000 (airline-type chair), L195,000 (shared cabin), or L230,000 (2nd class, two-bed cabin). For Fragline ferries to Corfu/Igoumenitsa, prices were L60,000 (deck class), L90,000 (airline-type chair), L125,000 (shared cabin), or L210,000 (2nd class, two-bed cabin).

Remember to bring warm clothing and a sleeping bag if you are planning to travel deck class. Also note that the airline-type chairs are packed into rooms which are generally noisy and smoky. First-class cabins are also available with private services. All boats have snack bars and restaurants, but if you want to save money, buy supplies in Brindisi.

Bicycles can usually be taken free of charge. At the time of writing, the average fares for other vehicles to Corfu/Igoumenitsa were: motorbike L60,000, car L100,000, caravan L190,000.

Car & Motorbike Brindisi is easy to reach by road. Once you approach the city, watch out for the superstrada exit for the 'porto'. Some signs will also point you in the direction of 'Grecia' (Greece). During summer the port area becomes one big traffic jam as cars line up to board ferries. It is a good idea to allow plenty of time to make your way through the traffic.

LECCE

Baroque can be grotesque, but never in Lecce. The style here is so refined and particular to the city that the Italians call it *barocco leccese*, Lecce Baroque. A graceful and intellectual city, close to both the Adriatic and Ionian seas, it can be used as a base from which to explore the main towns of the Salentine Peninsula – Gallipoli and Otranto.

The city has ancient origins, and in the 3rd century BC it was conquered by the Romans, who named it Lupiae. While relatively little is known of this period, Lecce boasts the remains of an imposing Roman amphitheatre, which stand in the city's main square, Piazza Sant'Oronzo. The city passed to the Byzantines, Normans and Swabians, but it was in the 16th to 18th centuries that it really came into its own, when it was embellished with splendid Renaissance and, most notably, Baroque buildings.

It is worth whiling away a few days in Lecce. Certainly there are enough Baroque palaces and churches to keep you busy, and the numerous bars and restaurants are a pleasant surprise for such a small city.

Orientation

The main train station is about one km southwest of Lecce's historic centre. To get to the centre, walk straight ahead from the station and turn right into Viale Gallipoli, then left at Piazza Argento, into Viale Francesco Lo Re. At the end of this street, turn left again to reach Piazza Sant'Oronzo and the city centre. From the bus station in Via Adua, turn left and walk to the Porta Napoli. Turn right

---

■ PLACES TO STAY

9 Hotel Risorgimento
25 Alloggio Faggiano
26 Hotel Cappello
27 Grand Hotel

▼ PLACES TO EAT

2 Perbacco
5 Carlo Quinto
7 Guido e Figlio
13 Caffè Alvino

OTHER

1 Church of SS Nicolò e Cataldo
3 Porta Napoli
4 STP Bus Terminal
6 Basilica of the Holy Cross

8 Church of Sant'Irene
10 AAST/EPT Tourist Information Office
11 Piazza Sant'Oronzo
12 Roman Amphitheatre
14 Castle
15 Piazza Libertini
16 Post Office
17 SIP Public Telephones
18 Rosario Church
19 Church of Santa Teresa
20 Seminary
21 Episcopal Palace
22 Cathedral
23 Piazza del Duomo
24 Church of Santa Chiara
28 Railway Station
29 Provincial Museum
30 Piazza Argento
31 FSE Bus Terminal
32 Public Hospital

---

and follow Via G Palmieri, turn left into Via Vittorio Emanuele and continue until you reach Piazza Sant'Oronzo.

Information

Tourist Office The shared AAST/EPT office (☎ 0832-4 64 58) is in Piazza Sant'Oronzo, in the building known as Il Sedile. It is open Monday to Friday from 9 am to 1 pm and 5.30 to 7.30 pm, Saturday to 1 pm only. It can provide a map of the city, as well as information on accommodation and transport.

Money There are branches of the main banks in Piazza Sant'Oronzo, including the Banca Commerciale Italiana, which will give cash advances on both Visa and MasterCard.

Post & Telecommunications The main post office is in Piazza Libertini, which is reached along Via Salvatore Trinchese from Piazza Sant'Oronzo. The postal code for central Lecce is 73100.

There is an SIP public telephone office at Via Oberdan 13, off Viale Cavallotti. The telephone code for Lecce is 0832.

Emergency For immediate police attendance, call ☎ 113. The public hospital, the

Ospedale Vito Fazzi (☎ 68 51), is in Piazza F Bottazzi, south-east of the centre off Viale XX Settembre.

Things to See & Do

The **Basilica of the Holy Cross** is the most famous example of Lecce Baroque. Artists including Cesare Penna, Francesco Antonio Zimbalo and Giuseppe Zimbalo worked for 150 years to decorate the building, creating an extraordinarily ornate façade, which is divided in two by a large balcony supported by 13 caryatids and fantastic figures.

In Piazza del Duomo are the 12th century **cathedral**, completely restored in the Baroque style, and its 70-metre-high **bell tower**, both designed by Giuseppe Zimbalo. Also in the piazza is the 15th century **Episcopal Palace**, which was reconstructed in 1632. Of note is its beautiful 1st-floor loggia. Opposite the cathedral is the **seminary**, designed by Giuseppe Cino and completed in 1709. Its elegant façade features two levels of windows balanced by a fine portal. Note the well in the seminary's courtyard, also designed by Cino.

On the way to Piazza Sant'Oronzo, in Corso Vittorio Emanuele, is the **Church of Sant'Irene**, completed in 1639. In Piazza Sant'Oronzo are the remains of the 2nd

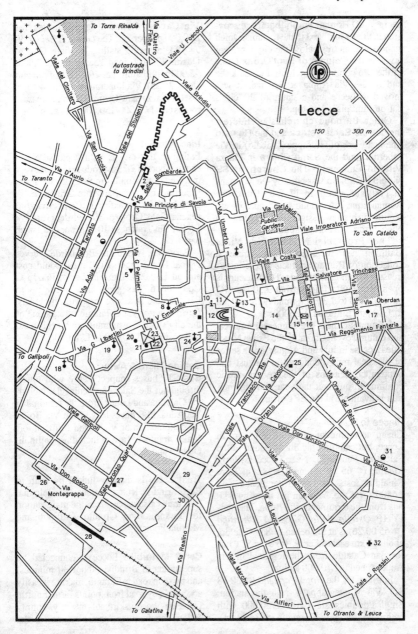

century AD **Roman amphitheatre**, discovered in the 1930s. Next to the remains, which stand some metres below the city's present level, is the **Column of Sant'Oronzo**, one of the two columns which used to mark the end of the Via Appia at Brindisi. It was moved to Lecce and a statue of the city's patron saint placed on top.

Other Baroque churches of interest include the **Santa Teresa** and the **Rosario** (the last work of Giuseppe Zimbalo) in Via Libertini, and the **Santa Chiara** in Piazza Vittorio Emanuele. The **Church of SS Nicolò e Cataldo** was built by the Normans in 1180 and rebuilt in 1716 by Cino. The Romanesque rose window and portal were retained in his new design. It is along Via San Nicola from the Porta Napoli.

The **Provincial Museum** in Viale Gallipoli, near the train station, houses a collection of Roman artefacts and religious treasures from later periods. The museum is open Monday to Friday from 9.30 am to 1 pm and 2.30 to 7.30 pm, Sunday from 9 am to 1.30 pm. Entrance is L5000.

In summer there are numerous musical and cultural events, notably the Estate Musicale Leccese in July and August, and a series of classical music concerts in August and September. Seasons of theatre and music continue throughout the year and information is available at the EPT office.

Places to Stay

Cheap accommodation is not abundant in Lecce, but camping facilities abound in the Salentine Peninsula. Near Lecce is *Torre Rinalda* (☎ 65 21 61), near the sea at Torre Rinalda. Costs are L6000 per person and L6500 for a site. You can get there by STP bus from the terminal in Via Adua. The non-IYHF *Ostello della Gioventù Adriatico* (☎ 65 00 26) is at the beach of San Cataldo, about 12 km east of Lecce. Take the STP bus for San Cataldo from the terminal in Via Adua. A bed is L10,000 a night.

In town, try the *Hotel Cappello* (☎ 30 88 81), Via Montegrappa 4, near the station. Singles/doubles are L40,000/60,000 with bathroom. *Alloggio Faggiano* (☎ 24 28 54),

Via Cavour 4, has singles/doubles for L20,000 per person. The *Grand Hotel* (☎ 30 94 05), near the station at Viale Oronzo Quarta 28, has good rooms for L57,000/95,000 with bathroom. *Hotel Risorgimento* (☎ 24 21 25), Via Imperatore Augusto 19, is just off Piazza Sant'Oronzo. Its very pleasant rooms cost L78,000/150,000 with bathroom.

Places to Eat

Eating in this city is both a pleasure and cheap. There is a fresh produce market every morning from Monday to Saturday in Piazza Libertini, off Via Salvatore Trinchese. A good café for breakfast is *Caffè Alvino* at Piazza Sant'Oronzo 30, while *Guido e Figlio*, Via Trinchese 10, is a popular snack bar.

Perbacco, Via dalle Bombarde, serves typical Lecce food; a full meal could cost around L30,000. *Pizzeria Sonia*, Piazza G Congedo 6, has great pizzas for up to L10,000 and is a favourite with the locals. *Carlo Quinto*, Via G Palmieri 46, is one of the city's better restaurants and a full meal will cost from L50,000 to L70,000.

Getting There & Away

Bus STP buses connect Lecce with towns throughout the Salentine Peninsula, including Galatina and Leuca, from the terminal in Via Adua. FSE buses leave from Via Boito, the continuation of Viale Don Minzoni, off Viale Otranto, for towns including Gallipoli, Otranto and Taranto.

Train Lecce is directly linked by train to Bari, Brindisi, Rome, Naples and Bologna. FSE trains also depart from the main station for Taranto, Bari, Otranto, Gallipoli and Martina Franca.

Car & Motorbike Lecce is connected by superstrada to Brindisi (about 30 minutes) and by state road to Taranto, making it easily accessible by road from points farther north. Once on the outskirts of the city, simply follow the familiar 'centro' signs, or the signs for the 'stazione', to reach the road which rings the historic centre.

Getting Around

The historic centre of Lecce is easily seen on foot. However, useful buses include Nos 1, 3 and 4, which run from the train station to the area around Piazza Sant'Oronzo. Ask the bus driver to let you off near the piazza.

If you have a car, probably the easiest point to enter the historic centre is through the Porta Napoli, a 16th century gate into the old city, just off the ring road. From the gate, follow Via Principe di Savoia and turn right into Corso Umberto I to reach Piazza Sant'Oronzo.

GALATINA

The phenomenon of tarantism, a ritual that had its roots in the mass manias that swept Europe during the Middle Ages, survives in the small town of Galatina, about 30 km south of Lecce. While many will know of the folk dance known as the tarantella, few would be aware that it developed from this dance ritual performed by people known as *tarantolati*, victims of a spider bite. The bite was thought to be that of a tarantula, but in reality it was probably inflicted by one of two smaller spiders found in the region, whose bite can produce pain, fear, vomiting and hallucinations.

Once a person believed they had been bitten, the only way to rid themselves of the poison was to perform a frenzied dance. Victims would literally go into a trance, sometimes dancing for days before collapsing in exhaustion. The phenomenon gave rise to travelling troupes of musicians, who would arrive to provide the accompanying music for the ritual dance. A recognised expert on tarantism, Professor Ernesto de Martino, published the classic *La Terra del Rimorso* (The Land of Remorse) after studying the phenomenon in the Salentine Peninsula in the late 1950s.

Although tarantism survives, occurrences are now extremely rare outside Galatina. Here, once a year, on the feast day of Sts Peter & Paul (29 June), the ritual is performed at the church dedicated to the saints (now deconsecrated).

Galatina is accessible by STP bus from Lecce.

OTRANTO

Without a car it is difficult to tour the picturesque Adriatic Coast of the Salentine Peninsula, which extends to the tip of the heel, at Cape Santa Maria di Leuca. However, it is easy to reach Otranto by bus and on the FSE train line.

Information

The tourist office (☎ 0836-8 14 36) is at Via Basilica 8, next to the cathedral. Just around the corner, in Largo Cavour, is the Cooperativa Iniziativa Otrantina, a private tourism organisation which will organise excursions, provide information on transport and help with accommodation, including through the local agriturismo programme. The staff are generally much more helpful than those at the official tourist office.

Things to See

This port town of whitewashed buildings is unfortunately overrun by tourists in summer, but it is worth a visit if only for the incredible **mosaic** covering the floor of the Romanesque cathedral. The 12th century mosaic, depicting the tree of life, is a masterpiece unrivalled in southern Italy and is stunning in its simplicity. Note the depiction of the legendary King Arthur near the top section of the mosaic – the mounted king is identified by the title 'Rex Arturis'. The mosaic was recently restored, and an earlier mosaic from the 4th century was discovered some 40 cm below the surface. Excavations are planned and the older mosaic will eventually be put on display.

In the chapel to the right of the altar is one of the south's more bizarre sights. The walls are lined with glass cases filled with 800 human skulls, the remains of the victims of the terrible Sack of Otranto in 1480, when Turkish invaders sacked the town and massacred its inhabitants. It is said that the town never really recovered from the event.

The tiny Byzantine **Church of San Pietro** contains some well-preserved Byzantine paintings.

Also of interest is the Aragonese **castle**, at the eastern edge of town beside the port. The castle has been restored.

Places to Stay & Eat

Otranto is not geared for budget tourism and has no one-star hotels. *Il Gabbiano* (☎ 0836-8 12 51), Via Porto Craulo 5, has singles for L45,000 and doubles for L70,000. The *Bellavista* (☎ 0836-8 63 59), Via Vittorio Emanuele 16, has rooms for around the same price.

There are fruit and grocery shops along Corso Garibaldi, on the way from the port to the town centre. For a good meal for under L25,000, try the *Taverna del Leone Marino*, Corso Garibaldi 5.

Getting There & Away

There is a Marozzi bus which runs daily from Rome to Brindisi, Lecce and Otranto, arriving at the port. Enquire at Ellade Viaggi at the port for information.

Otranto is accessible from Lecce by FSE train or bus.

Ferries leave from here for Corfu and Igoumenitsa in Greece. For information and reservations, go to Ellade Viaggi at the port.

TARANTO

Founded around the beginning of the 7th century BC by exiles from Sparta, Taras became the wealthiest and most important colony in Magna Graecia. At the height of its power, the city was home to some 300,000 people. By the 3rd century BC, there was considerable friction between powerful Taras and the growing might of Rome, and the Greek city often gave support to Rome's enemies. Following a long war, it was finally taken by Rome in 272 BC and its name was changed to Tarentum, although Greek customs and laws were maintained in the city.

Sections of the population supported the Carthaginians during the Second Punic War, and the city was occupied by Hannibal.

When Rome retook Tarentum it punished the citizens by pillaging its treasures and sending many people into slavery. Thereafter, the city's history reflects that of southern Italy, which was subject to invasion and domination by the Arabs, Byzantines, Normans, Swabians, Angevins and Aragonese.

One of the city's more interesting claims to fame is that it was allegedly the point where the first cat landed on European shores.

Orientation

As with most Italian cities, Taranto can be divided in two. The new city, its streets based on a grid, houses the hotels, restaurants and commercial district. The dilapidated old city is on an island, between the new city and the port area and train station.

If you arrive at the train station, take bus No 1/2 (that's how it's written) or 8 to the centre of the new town. It is really not advisable to walk through the old city with a backpack or luggage, but if you want to take the risk, walk straight ahead from the station along Viale Duca d'Aosta, cross the bridge and the Piazza Fontana and continue along the waterfront on Via Cariati, which becomes Via Garibaldi. At the end of the street, turn right to reach the bridge to the new city.

Information

Tourist Office Taranto's helpful EPT office (☎ 099-2 12 33) is at Corso Umberto I 113, on the corner of Via Acclavio, in the new city. It is open Monday to Friday from 9 am to 1 pm and 5 to 7 pm, Saturday from 9.30 am to 12.30 pm. You can pick up a map of the city and ask for advice on accommodation.

Post & Telecommunications The main post office is on Lungomare Vittorio Emanuele III, a short distance from the Canale Navigabile which separates the new and old cities. The postal code for central Taranto is 74100.

There is an SIP public telephone office

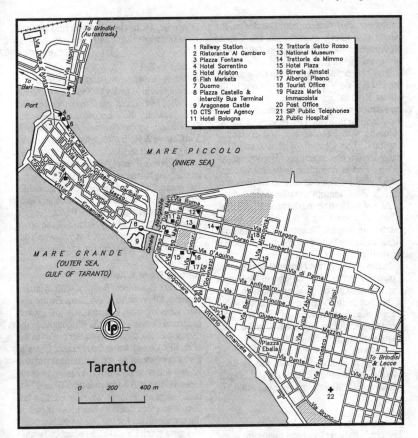

KEY

1 Railway Station	12 Trattoria Gatto Rosso
2 Ristorante Al Gambero	13 National Museum
3 Piazza Fontana	14 Trattoria da Mimmo
4 Hotel Sorrentino	15 Hotel Piaza
5 Hotel Ariston	16 Birreria Amstel
6 Fish Markets	17 Albergo Pisano
7 Duomo	18 Tourist Office
8 Piazza Castello &	19 Piazza Maria
Intercity Bus Terminal	Immacolata
9 Aragonese Castle	20 Post Office
10 CTS Travel Agency	21 SIP Public Telephones
11 Hotel Bologna	22 Public Hospital

MARE PICCOLO
(INNER SEA)

MARE GRANDE
(OUTER SEA,
GULF OF TARANTO)

Taranto

0   200   400 m

slightly farther along the Lungomare. The city's telephone code is 099.

Travel Agency There is a CTS office at Via Matteotti 1, on the corner of the Corso Due Mari, just near the bridge to the old city.

Emergency For immediate police attendance, call ☎ 113. The public hospital, the Ospedale SS Annunziata (☎ 98 51), is on Via Bruno. Follow the Lungomare V Emanuele and turn left at Via de Noto.

Dangers & Annoyances Travellers need to be alert in Taranto, particularly in the old city. Carry all valuables in a money belt. The old city is dangerous at night because of the high risk of theft. Even during the day, women on their own should be wary of where they walk in the old city – keep to the busier streets. Women should also avoid staying out too late even in the new city – try to be indoors before the evening crowds disperse.

Things to See & Do

Taranto's old city is in an extremely dilapidated state, although recent years have seen some efforts to renovate its palaces and churches. The **Aragonese Castle**, at the island's southern extreme on the Canale Navigabile, was completed in 1492. It is occupied by the Italian navy.

The 11th century **Duomo**, in the centre of the old city on Via del Duomo, is one of the oldest Romanesque churches in Apulia. It was remodelled in the 18th century. Its three-nave interior is divided by 16 ancient marble columns with Romanesque and Byzantine capitals. The Chapel of San Cataldo is considered a fine example of Baroque architecture and is decorated with frescoes and inlaid marble. The cathedral is dedicated to San Cataldo, Taranto's patron saint.

Also visit the **fish markets** on Via Cariati, where the morning's remarkably varied catch is on display. Taranto has been famous since antiquity for its seafood, in particular its shellfish.

In the new city, the **National Museum** at Corso Umberto I 41 is one of the most important archaeological museums in Italy. It houses a fascinating collection which traces the development of Greek Taras, including sculpture and pottery, as well as a display of magnificent gold jewellery found in local tombs. It also houses Roman sculpture and mosaics. The museum is open Monday to Saturday from 9 am to 1.30 pm, Sunday to 12.30 pm. Entrance is L6000.

Places to Stay

The city's only really cheap hotels are in the old city, in Piazza Fontana near the bridge leading to the train station. Women on their own should not stay in this area. The *Hotel Sorrentino* (☎ 40 74 56) is reasonable and has singles/doubles for L20,000/30,000. Next door is the *Hotel Ariston* (☎ 40 75 63), with rooms for L22,000/35,000.

In the new city is *Albergo Pisano* (☎ 43 40 87), Via Cavour 43, which is safe and clean and has singles/doubles for L33,000/55,000, or doubles with bathroom for L70,000. *Hotel Bologna* (☎ 452 67 01), Via Regina Margherita 4, has rooms for L40,000/60,000, or L50,000/80,000 with bathroom. The *Hotel Plaza* (☎ 49 07 75), Via

D'Aquino 46, has better rooms for L90,000/130,000; triples are L140,000.

Places to Eat

A fresh-produce market is held every morning from Monday to Saturday in Piazza Castello, just across the Canale Navigabile. For a meal, try the *Trattoria da Mimmo*, Via Giovinazzi, or the *Trattoria Gatto Rosso* at Via Cavour 2. Both offer good food for under L25,000 a full meal.

At *Birreria Amstel*, Via D'Aquino 27, you can choose between self-service, pizza or the full menu, and all prices are very reasonable. *Ristorante Al Gambero* in Piazzale Democrate, across the Ponte Porta Napoli overlooking the old city, is one of the city's better seafood restaurants, but you won't get away for under L50,000 for a full meal.

Getting There & Away

FSE buses connect Taranto with Martina Franca, Alberobello, Castellana Grotte and Bari (leaving from Piazza Castello), as well as Ostuni (leaving from Via Magnaghi, in the east of the new city) and smaller towns in the area. SITA buses leave from Piazza Castello for Matera, stopping at Castellaneta, and also go to Metaponto. Chiruzzi buses also leave Piazza Castello for Metaponto. STP and FSE buses connect Taranto with Lecce. For full details on other intercity bus services, ask at the tourist office for the bus timetable.

Trains (both FS and FSE) connect Taranto with Brindisi, Bari, Martina Franca and Alberobello, as well as Naples and Rome.

Getting Around

Bus Nos 1/2 and 8 will come in useful for the trip from the station to the new city if you want to avoid carrying luggage through the old city.

If you arrive in Taranto by car, particularly from the east, you will find that the drive from the state road into the centre of town is quite a long one. Simply follow the familiar 'centro' signs and aim to reach Lungomare Vittorio Emanuele III, a good point of reference.

CASTELLANETA

Fans of that great Latin lover, Rudolph Valentino, might be interested to know that he was born at Castellaneta, about 40 km west of Taranto. About the only evidence of this is a statue of the actor in the town's main piazza, and only die-hard fans will want to make the pilgrimage. The town is accessible from Taranto by the SITA bus for Matera (from Piazza Castello). It is also on the FSE train line.

Basilicata

This small region stretches across Italy's 'instep', incorporating the provinces of Potenza and Matera and small areas of coastline on both the Tyrrhenian and Ionian seas. While no longer the desolate, malaria-ridden land of poverty-stricken peasants so powerfully described by the Italian writer Carlo Levi in his novel *Christ Stopped at Eboli*, Basilicata retains a strong sense of isolation and is still one of Italy's poorest regions. Levi was exiled to remote Basilicata during the 1930s for his opposition to Fascism, living first in the town of Grassano and then in the tiny hill-top village of Aliano.

Known to the Romans as Lucania (a name revived by Mussolini during the Fascist period), Basilicata is a mountainous region with large tracts of barren and eroded wasteland, the result of systematic deforestation over the centuries. The regional capital is Potenza.

Don't come to Basilicata expecting to find a rich heritage of art, architecture and ancient history. The region's dramatic landscape and its close connection with the peasant culture of which Levi wrote are its main attractions, along with the strange and fascinating city of Matera.

MATERA

This ancient city evokes powerful images of a peasant culture which existed until just over 30 years ago. Its famous *sassi*, stone houses built in two ravines which slice through the city, were home to more than half of Matera's population, about 20,000 people, until the late 1950s when the local government built new residential areas and relocated the entire population. Probably the most striking account of how these people lived is given in *Christ Stopped at Eboli*, when Levi quotes the reactions of his sister to the conditions she observed while passing through Matera on her way to visit him during his detention in nearby Aliano.

Describing the stone dwellings of Sasso Caveoso and Sasso Barisano as 'a schoolboy's idea of Dante's Inferno', she went on to say:

The houses were open on account of the heat, and as I went by I could see into the caves, whose only light came in through the front doors. Some of them had no entrance but a trapdoor and ladder. In these dark holes with walls cut out of the earth I saw a few pieces of miserable furniture, beds, and some ragged clothes hanging up to dry. On the floor lay dogs, sheep, goats, and pigs. Most families have just one cave to live in and there they sleep all together; men, women, children, and animals. This is how twenty thousand people live.

She described children suffering from trachoma and others 'with the wizened faces of old men, their bodies reduced by starvation almost to skeletons, their heads crawling with lice and covered with scabs. Most of them had enormous, dilated stomachs, and faces yellow and worn with malaria.'

This and other accounts in Levi's book of the extreme poverty and appalling conditions suffered by the people of the south came as a shock to the more affluent northerners. More than 50 years and vast amounts of development funds have seen the eradication of malaria and starvation in Basilicata. Today, people are returning to live in Matera's sassi – but now it is trendy, rather than a necessity. Many of the primitive stone dwellings are being renovated and a new population of artists, writers and other 'interesting' types is moving in.

Orientation

The centre of the new city is Piazza Vittorio

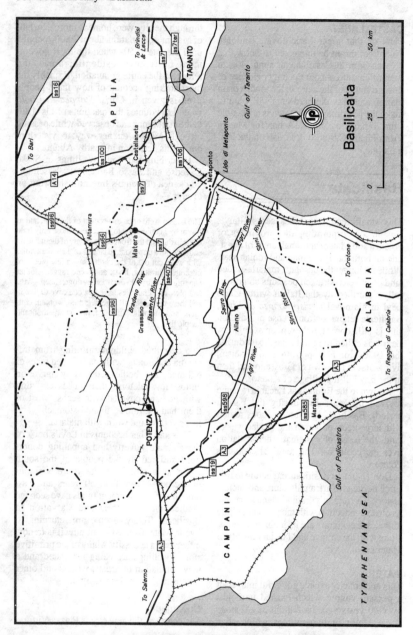

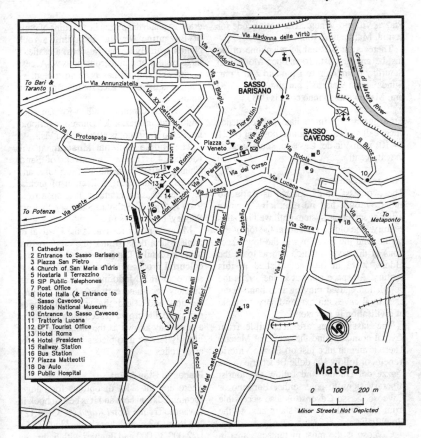

1 Cathedral
2 Entrance to Sasso Barisano
3 Piazza San Pietro
4 Church of San Maria d'Idris
5 Hostaria Il Terrazzino
6 SIP Public Telephones
7 Post Office
8 Hotel Italia (& Entrance to Sasso Caveoso)
9 Ridola National Museum
10 Entrance to Sasso Caveoso
11 Trattoria Lucana
12 EPT Tourist Office
13 Hotel Roma
14 Hotel President
15 Railway Station
16 Bus Station
17 Piazza Matteotti
18 Da Aulo
19 Public Hospital

Matera

0   100   200 m

Minor Streets Not Depicted

Veneto, a short walk down Via Roma from the train station and intercity bus terminal in Piazza Matteotti. The ravine housing the sassi zone opens up to the east of Piazza V Veneto.

Information

Tourist Office The EPT office (☎ 0835-21 24 88) is in Via Viti de Marco 9, off Via Roma. You can pick up a map of the city and information about accommodation and the sights throughout Basilicata. The office can also organise a professional tour guide (about L25,000 an hour). It is open Monday to Friday from 8 am to 2 pm and 4 to 7 pm.

A private organisation, the Coop Amici del Turista, operates an office in Piazza San Pietro in Sasso Caveoso. It will organise guided tours for groups of up to four people for L30,000 an hour and L80,000 for three hours. For groups of five to 10 people the cost is L35,000 an hour.

If you would like to read about the sassi, an excellent book is *Sassi e Secoli* by R Guira Longa. It is available in English from Libreria dell'Arco, Via Ridola 36, near Sasso Caveoso.

Post & Telecommunications The main post office is in Via del Corso, which runs off

Piazza Vittorio Veneto. The postal code for central Matera is 75100.

There is an SIP public telephone office just before the post office, open Monday to Saturday from 9 am to 1 pm and 2 to 7 pm, Sunday from 9 am to 1 pm and 3.30 to 6.30 pm. Matera's telephone code is 0835.

Emergency For immediate police attendance, call ☎ 113. The public hospital (☎ 21 14 10) is in Via del Castello, south-west of the city centre.

Things to See & Do

The two sassi wards, known as **Barisano** and **Caveoso**, had no electricity, running water or sewerage system until well into this century. The oldest sassi are at the top of the ravine, and the dwellings in the lower sections of the ravine, which appear to be the oldest, were in fact established in this century. As space ran out in the 1920s the population started moving into hand-hewn or natural caves, an extraordinary example of civilisation in reverse.

The sassi zones are accessible from several points around the centre of Matera. There is an entrance just off Piazza Vittorio Veneto, or follow Via delle Beccherie to the Piazza del Duomo and follow the tourist itinerary signs to enter either Barisano or Caveoso. Sasso Caveoso is also accessible from Via Ridola, by the stairs next to the Hotel Italia.

Caveoso is the most picturesque area in which to wander, and the most important rock churches are here, including **Santa Maria d'Idris** and **Santa Lucia alla Malve**, both with amazingly well-preserved Byzantine frescoes. As you enter Caveoso, you will probably be approached by young boys wanting to act as tour guides. They generally don't speak any English, but for a few thousand lire will lead you to some of the more interesting sassi. However, if you are interested in formal tours, these are not too expensive (see the earlier Tourist Office section for details).

Recent excavations in Piazza Vittorio Veneto have yielded some amazing discoveries. Beneath the piazza lie the ruins of parts of Byzantine Matera, including a rock church with Byzantine frescoes, a castle, a large cistern and numerous houses. Access to the excavations has been restricted, so enquire at the EPT office for information on guided visits.

The 13th century Apulian-Romanesque **cathedral**, in Piazza del Duomo, overlooking Sasso Barisano, is also worth a visit.

The **Ridola National Museum** at Via Ridola 24 is in the ex-convent of Santa Chiara, dating from the 17th century, and houses an interesting collection of prehistoric and classical artefacts. It is open from 9 am to 2 pm Tuesday to Saturday, to 1 pm Sunday. Entrance is free.

Matera's major festival is the Festival of Santa Maria della Bruna (the city's patron saint) on 2 July. The festival culminates in a colourful procession from the cathedral. A statue of the Madonna is carried in an ornately decorated cart and, when the procession ends (and the statue has been removed), the crowd descends on the cart in a ceremony known as the *assalto al carro*, literally tearing it to pieces in order to take away relics.

Places to Stay & Eat

There are not a lot of options for budget accommodation here and it is best to book in advance. Try the *Hotel Roma* (☎ 33 39 12), Via Roma 62, which has singles/doubles for L22,000/36,000 and doubles with bathroom for L40,000. The *Hotel President* (☎ 33 57 91), Via Roma 13, has rooms for L34,000/60,000, or L62,000/95,000 with bathroom. The very pleasant *Hotel Italia* (☎ 33 35 61), Via Ridola 5, has rooms with bathroom for L80,000/100,000.

The local fare is simple and the focus is on vegetables. There is a Divella supermarket opposite the EPT office, or you can pick up supplies in Piazza Vittorio Veneto at the *Casa del Pane* and the *Casa del Parmigiano* opposite. *Da Aulo*, Via Anza di Lucana, is economical and serves cuisine typical of Basilicata. *Trattoria Lucana*, Via Lucana, has a good selection of vegetables and a full meal will cost around L25,000. *Hostaria Il Terrazzino* is in Vico San Giuseppe, accessible from Piazza Vittorio Veneto down the stairs called Via Lombardi (follow the signs for the restaurant). It has an excellent reputation and the typical local food is excellent. A full meal will cost around L30,000.

Getting There & Away

SITA buses connect Matera with Taranto, Potenza and Metaponto, as well as the many small towns in the province. The city is on the private Ferrovie Apulo-Lucane train line, which connects with Bari, Altamura and Potenza. Both the train station and bus terminal are in Piazza Matteotti. There is also a Marozzi bus from Rome to Matera, which leaves from Piazza della Repubblica in Rome twice a day.

The city is easily accessible by road from Bari (62 km) and from Taranto (77 km). If arriving from Bari or Taranto, follow Via Nazionale, which becomes Via Annunziatella, until you reach Via XX Settembre, which connects with Piazza Vittorio Veneto and the city centre. From Metaponto, follow Via Lucana into the city centre.

ALIANO

Not one of Italy's, or even Basilicata's, great tourist stopovers, this tiny hill-top village south of Matera is nevertheless worth a visit if you have read Carlo Levi's *Christ Stopped at Eboli* and have your own transport. Levi called the town Gagliano, and surprisingly little has changed since he was interned here during the 1930s for his anti-Fascist activities. The landscape is still as he described it, an 'endless sweep of clay, with the white dots of villages, stretching out as far as the invisible sea'.

Wander to the edge of the old village to see the house where he stayed (any local will point it out for you). Although the town's inhabitants are no longer stricken with poverty and malaria, the wheels of progress have still turned rather slowly and you are just as likely to see the locals riding a donkey as driving a car. For the extra keen, Aliano is accessible by SITA bus from Potenza.

METAPONTO

Founded on the Ionian coast between the 8th and 7th centuries BC by Greek colonisers, Metaponto prospered as a grain-producing and commercial centre. One of the city's most famous residents was Pythagoras, who established a school here after being banished from Crotone (in what is now Calabria) towards the end of the 6th century BC.

After the death of Pythagoras, his house and school were incorporated into a Temple of Hera. The remains of the temple – 15 columns and sections of pavement – are known as the **Palatine Tables**, since knights (paladins) were said to have gathered there before heading off to the crusades, and the columns were thought to be the legs of their giant tables. Overtaken by Rome, Metaponto met its end as a result of the Second Punic War. Hannibal had made the city his headquarters after Rome retook Tarentum (Taranto) in 207 BC, and he is said to have relocated the town's entire population to spare it the same fate as the people of Tarentum, who were sold into slavery by the Romans as punishment for supporting the Carthaginians.

The ruins of ancient Metapontum are not overexciting, but are worth a visit if you have the time. If you are without your own transport, the **Archaeological Park** is a few km north-east of the train station. Follow the road north from the station until you reach the Archaeological Park sign pointing to the right. Here you will find the fairly sparse remains of a **Greek Theatre** and the Doric **Temple of Apollo Licius**. Another few km north, across the main road, are the more impressive ruins of the Palatine Tables.

Three km east of the train station is the **Lido di Metaponto**, a relatively modest seaside resort with a pleasant, sandy beach. An EPT information office (☎ 0835-74 19 33) opens in summer in Piazzale Lido, near the beach. It can advise on accommodation, including private rooms. There are several camping grounds, among them *Camping Magna Grecia* (☎ 0835-74 18 55), Via Lido, which is very close to the sea. Hotel options include the *Oasi* (☎ 0835-74 19 30), Via

Olympia 12, which has doubles for L30,000. The *Hotel Kennedy* (☎ 0835-74 19 60), Viale Ionio, has singles/doubles for L28,000/50,000 and doubles with bathroom for L60,000.

Metaponto is accessible from Taranto's Piazza Castello by SITA or Chiruzzi buses, and from Matera by SITA bus. It is on the Taranto-Reggio di Calabria train line. If you arrive by train, remember that the station is three km west of the Lido di Metaponto. If you don't want to walk, you could wait for one of the SITA or Chiruzzi buses to pass by on the way to the beach.

Calabria

Looking at a map of Italy, Calabria is the boot's toe – a fitting location for most northerners, who consider the region to be the end of the earth. For the traveller, Calabria offers much, but its real attractions have to be sought out. The Ionian Sea is to Calabria's east, the Tyrrhenian Sea to the west, and the Strait of Messina separates the region from Sicily. Its vast coastline offers some of Italy's best beaches – indeed some of the only beaches in the country where it is still safe to swim. However, unchecked development, largely the result of 'investment' by the region's brand of Mafia, the 'Ndrangheta, has scarred the virgin territory of 20 years ago with ugly concrete apartment blocks, hideous hotels and tacky tourist resorts.

Calabria's history is one of domination by foreign forces. In the centuries before Christ, the Greeks settled much of the region and it was known as Magna Graecia, literally Greater Greece. Like much of Italy, Calabria was conquered by many peoples including the Byzantines, Arabs, Normans and Aragonese. Its recent history has been one of relentless decline, with hundreds of thousands of Calabrians leaving the region for the north in the postwar years.

Catanzaro is the regional capital, although the city is uninspiring and, apart from its use as a transport hub, offers little to the traveller.

Reggio di Calabria and Cosenza are both vibrant cities – the former was completely rebuilt after an earthquake at the start of the century. Many coastal towns are enchanting and enticing, but if you are seeking the real Calabria, head inland for towns like Aietta in the north and Gerace in the south.

While mostly very tacky, the many tourist villages along the coast can offer excellent package deals and are worth considering. There are plenty of camping grounds along the coast and budget accommodation in the towns, but much of Calabria simply closes from October to April and finding either a room or a place to eat can be difficult. If you are planning to visit during the summer months, book well in advance.

The food is simple peasant fare and relies heavily on what is produced in the region. It would not be surprising to eat in a restaurant where the owners themselves have produced the salami, cheese, vegetables and the grapes for the wine.

Attempting to get around by public transport can be as harsh as the midday sun. There are two competing railways, the locally controlled Calabro-Lucane whose services are always slow, and the national FS railway (often referred to as FFSS in Calabria), which primarily operates fast services between Reggio, Catanzaro and Cosenza to Naples and beyond. Basically, the lines follow the coast, although there are some deviations inland. Buses are irregular and require great patience. See the Getting There & Away section under Reggio di Calabria for information about ferries to/from Sicily.

CATANZARO
Long the administrative hub of Calabria, Catanzaro replaced Reggio di Calabria as the region's capital in the early 1970s. Despite this, the city is still overlooked by tourists – and it is not difficult to see why. The older parts of the city are worth discovering, but apart from its transport connections, there is little to draw you to Catanzaro.

The city is of Byzantine origin, although little evidence remains. Its location, 13 km inland on a rocky peak, was meant to deter

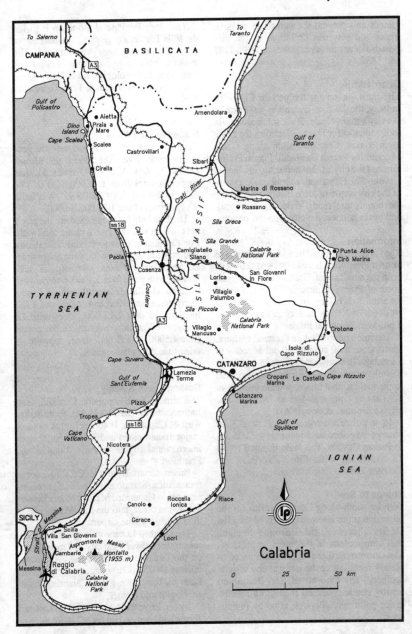

Calabria

0   25   50 km

raiders and prevent the spread of malaria. There are few old buildings in the city because of severe earthquakes in 1688, 1783 and 1832.

Orientation

The train station for the private Calabrian railway, the Calabro-Lucane, is just north of the city's main centre. Walk south along Via Indipendenza for Piazza Matteotti, the city's main square. Continue south along Corso Mazzini for Piazza Garibaldi, Piazza Prefettura and the city's other major square, Piazza Cavour. The FS station is about one km south of the city centre (double that distance along the connecting road, Viale dei Bizantini), and buses connect the city with the station.

Information

The main tourist office, the Catanzaro Tourist Promotion Bureau (☎ 0961-2 98 23), is on the small street, Galleria Mancuso, just north of Piazza Prefettura. There is a small information office in Piazza Prefettura (☎ 0961-74 17 64). Both open from 9 am to 2 pm Monday to Saturday.

The main post office, in Piazza Prefettura, opens from 8.30 am to 1.30 pm Monday to Saturday. The city's postal code is 88100. SIP telephones are in Galleria Mancuso, next to the main tourist office, and are open from 8.30 am to 1 pm and 4.45 to 7.45 pm. The city's telephone code is 0961.

In a police emergency, call ☎ 113, or contact the police headquarters (☎ 72 05 57) in Piazza Cavour. The main hospital (☎ 74 58 51) is on Viale Pio X, north of the Calabro-Lucane train station.

Things to See

Wander south along Corso Mazzini for the older and more interesting parts of the city. Of its churches, the Baroque **Basilica dell'Immacolata** is the most impressive. The **Duomo**, farther south, was almost completely rebuilt after the last war and is quite ordinary. The **Church of San Domenico** nearby contains several interesting Renaissance paintings, although none by famous artists.

The city's **Provincial Museum** is inside the Villa Trieste, a large garden on the eastern edge of the city near Via Jannoni. The museum has a large collection of coins and some local archaeological finds. Entry is free and it opens from 10 am to 1 pm Tuesday to Friday.

Places to Stay & Eat

Catanzaro has few hotels and they are generally expensive. The *Residence Mauro* (☎ 74 37 64), Via V d'Amato 51, has singles/doubles from L45,000/63,000. The *Albergo Belvedere* (☎ 72 05 91), Via Italia 33, has rooms from L38,000/50,000.

The best bets for cheap food are the city's bars, where you can grab a cheap sandwich. *Bar Comunale*, Corso Mazzini near Piazza Matteotti, is popular with younger people. *Lo Stuzzchino*, Piazza Matteotti, is self-service, with pasta from L4000. *Osteria Vini*, in the street called Discesa Poerio, off Piazza Garibaldi, is excellent and cheap, and a full meal could cost L12,000. *Ristorante La Corteccia*, Via Indipendenza 30, has pizzas from L5000, and *Il Ghiottone*, opposite, is one of the city's better cafés.

Getting There & Away

The airport, Sant'Euphemia Lamezia, is at Lamezia Terme (0968-5 15 21), about 30 km west of Catanzaro. It serves flights to most major Italian cities and a small number of international flights to Paris, London and Frankfurt.

Buses depart from the Calabro-Lucane train station. Serratore (☎ 78 28 08) operates services to Catanzaro Marina, other cities on the Ionian coast, into the Sila Massif and to the Lamezia Terme airport.

The Calabro-Lucane railway (☎ 70 13 89) runs trains between the city and most towns on the Ionian coast, while the FS national railway (☎ 75 10 22) connects the city with Lamezia Terme, Reggio di Calabria, Cosenza, Naples and Rome.

By car, leave the A3 autostrada at Lamezia Terme and head east on the ss280 for the city.

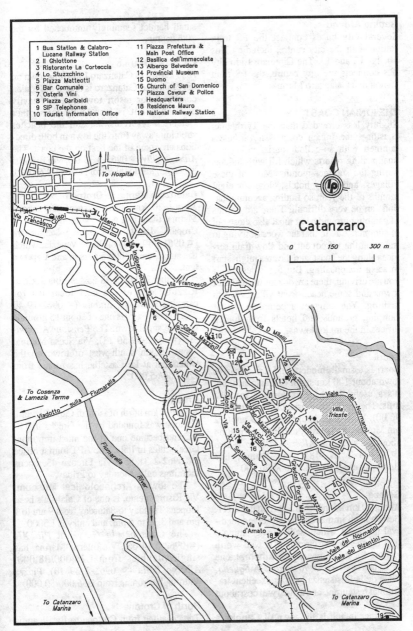

1 Bus Station & Calabro-
  Lucane Railway Station
2 Il Ghiottone
3 Ristorante La Corteccia
4 Lo Stuzzchino
5 Piazza Matteotti
6 Bar Comunale
7 Osteria Vini
8 Piazza Garibaldi
9 SIP Telephones
10 Tourist Information Office
11 Piazza Prefettura &
   Main Post Office
12 Basilica dell'Immacolata
13 Albergo Belvedere
14 Provincial Museum
15 Duomo
16 Church of San Domenico
17 Piazza Cavour & Police
   Headquarters
18 Residence Mauro
19 National Railway Station

Catanzaro

0   150   300 m

To Hospital

Via Francesco

Via L Milano

Via Indipendenza

Via Francesco Acri

Corso Mazzini

Via D Miletti

Via Carlo V

Via Telfa

Viale dei Normanni

Villa Trieste

To Cosenza
& Lamezia Terme

Viadotto sulla Flumarella

Flumarella River

Via Acri Vescovado

Via Mazzini

Via Q Iannoni

Via XX Settembre

Via Carlo V

Corso Porta Marina

Gradoni Porta Marina

Via Carlo V

Via V d'Amato

Viale dei Normanni

Viale dei Bizantini

To Catanzaro
Marina

To Catanzaro
Marina

To Catanzaro
Marina

Getting Around

Several city buses connect the FS train station with the city centre, including Nos 10, 11, 12 and 13. The Circolare Lido city bus connects the city centre, the FS train station and Catanzaro Marina.

THE IONIAN COAST

Slightly less crowded than the Tyrrhenian coastline, the Ionian coast is nevertheless jammed with so-called tourist villages – unappealing resorts which fill with Italians during the summer months. Most of these villages, and many hotels, close for eight months of the year, so finding accommodation can be very difficult. There are dozens of camping grounds, but most also close out of summer. Add to that the woes of trying to travel on the infrequent and slow train services along the coast, and the area might start to seem unappealing. But don't despair. If you are driving, there are dozens of small hill towns and some beach-front villages worth visiting. You can get a complete list of camping grounds and hotels from tourist offices in the major towns.

Locri

Locri is a small, modern and unimpressive town about 100 km south of Catanzaro, but it's a useful base for exploration into the hills. The Pro Loco tourist office (☎ 0964-2 96 00), Via Fiume 1, opens from 9 am to 2 pm Monday to Saturday and has information about the area. The *Albergo Vittorio Veneto* (☎ 0964-2 07 48), Via Roma, has singles/doubles from L20,000/30,000.

Gerace

About 10 km inland from Locri on the ss111, Gerace is an immaculately preserved medieval hill town which, sadly, is becoming a stop on the tourist circuit. It is well worth visiting for its Romanesque **cathedral**, one of Calabria's largest. *Ristorante A Squella*, Viale della Resistenza 8, is an excellent traditional restaurant, and a meal will cost about L25,000.

Farther inland is the town of **Canolo**, a small hamlet seemingly untouched by the 20th century.

Catanzaro Marina

Also known as Catanzaro Lido, this town on the coast near Catanzaro is one of the Ionian coast's major resort towns. It is heavily developed but is less tacky than other Calabrian resort towns, and the beaches stretching away from the town in both directions are some of the best on the coast. The *Albergo Lilly* (☎ 0961-3 36 16), Via Brindisi 8, has singles/doubles from L50,000/65,000.

Catanzaro Marina to Crotone

About 20 km north-east of Catanzaro Marina, there is a good camping ground at Cropani Marina, the *Camping Lungomare* (☎ 0961-96 11 67) on Viale Venezia, which has sites from L8000 a person and L5000 a tent.

Another 20 km north-east is Isola di Capo Rizzuto, one of the best locations for camping. *Camping Stumio* (☎ 0962-79 40 73), Via del Faro, is one of about 15 grounds near the small town. The *Pensione Aragonese* (☎ 0962-79 50 13), Via Scesa Marina, about 10 km south-west of town on the waterfront at Le Castella, has rooms from L45,000/65,000.

Crotone

About 10 km north of Isola di Capo Rizzuto, Crotone was founded by the Greeks in 710 BC and became one of the most important Greek cities in Italy. The APT tourist office (☎ 0962-2 31 85), Via Firenze 43, opens mornings only, Monday to Friday.

The town's **Archaeological Museum**, Via Risorgimento, is one of Calabria's best. It opens Tuesday to Saturday from 9 am to 1 pm and 3.30 to 5 pm, and entry is L5000.

The *Casa per la Gioventù Pio XII* (☎ 0962-2 14 66), Via Interna Marina, has singles/doubles from L28,000/38,000. *Albergo Italia* (☎ 0962-2 39 10), Piazza Vittoria, has rooms from L35,000/50,000.

North of Crotone

The coastline from Crotone to Basilicata is

the region's least developed, and while the coastal road is good, public transport is generally slow and inefficient. Bus services are often too irregular to rely on. Most towns are connected by train.

Cirò Marina About 30 km north of Crotone is Cirò Marina, a reasonably sized town with plenty of hotel rooms and good beaches despite the huge cement-block breakwaters near the town. The *Albergo Santa Lucia* (☎ 0962-3 12 84), Via Lungomare, near the beach, has singles/doubles from L30,000/ 40,000. There is a camping ground, the *Punta Alice* (☎ 0962-3 11 60) at Punta Alice, a couple of km north of the town.

Rossano About 50 km north of Crotone is Rossano, which is really two towns – the glitzy beach resort at Marina di Rossano, also known as Lido Sant'Angelo, and the small hill town itself, about five km inland. The latter is far more interesting, not least for its **cathedral** with its 9th century Byzantine fresco, and the **Diocesan Museum**, an excellent religious museum that opens from 10 am to midday and 4 to 6 pm Monday to Friday (entry is L2000).

The *Albergo Scigliano* (☎ 0983-2 18 46), Viale Margherita, has singles/doubles from L50,000/70,000, and there is a camping ground, the *Camping Torino* (☎ 0983-2 23 94), at Marina di Rossano.

COSENZA

Generally regarded as Calabria's most interesting city, Cosenza has a reasonably well-preserved medieval section worth exploring. It lies at the confluence of two rivers, the Crati and Busento, which add to the city's appeal. Cosenza is surrounded by mountains – the magnificent Sila Massif to the east and the Catena Costiera to the west. As a transportation hub, the city makes a good base for the mountains.

Orientation

Viale Trieste, which runs parallel to Corso Umberto, is one of the main streets and leads through the centre of the city. Piazza della Vittoria, which lies between Corso Umberto and Viale Trieste, is the city's main square. The medieval part of town straddles the Crati River south-east of the confluence with the Busento River. See the following Getting There & Away section for information about Cosenza's three train stations.

Information

The main APT tourist office (☎ 0984-2 78 21) is at Viale Trieste 50 and is open Monday to Friday from 8 am to 2 pm. There is another office on Via Rossi (☎ 0984-3 05 95), at the roundabout north of Viale della Repubblica, which opens similar hours.

The main post office and SIP telephones are on Via Vittorio Veneto on the city centre's western edge, and are open from 8 am to 1.30 pm Monday to Saturday. The postal code for Cosenza is 87100, and the telephone code 0984.

In a police emergency, call ☎ 113, or contact the police headquarters (☎ 3 61 10) on Piazza XV Marzo. There is an office on Via Popilia, north of the Calabro-Lucane train station. The hospital, the Ospedale Civile (☎ 68 11), is on Via Felice Migliori, behind the post office.

Things to See & Do

Although most of the city's nightlife centres around Corso Mazzini, most of the sights are across the Busento River in the medieval city centre. As you cross the river, wander south along Corso Telesio and you will come to the **Duomo**, which dates from the 12th century, although it was rebuilt in the Baroque style in the 18th century. The cathedral features a beautiful 12th century Byzantine cross.

West of Corso Telesio is the 13th century **Church of San Francesco d'Assisi**, with a Gothic cloister. Farther west along Corso Vittorio Emanuele is the **castle**, enlarged in 1222 and now in ruins due to earthquake damage.

At the southern edge of the old city centre is Piazza XV Marzo, the city's most appealing square. The building known as the Accademia Cosentina houses the city's **Archaeological Museum**, containing local

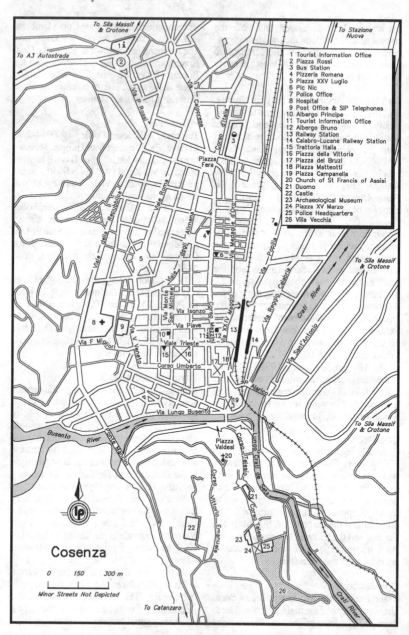

To Sila Massif & Crotone
To Stazione Nuova
To A3 Autostrada
To Sila Massif & Crotone
To Sila Massif & Crotone
To Catanzaro

Piazza Fera

Piazza Valdesi

1 Tourist Information Office
2 Piazza Rossi
3 Bus Station
4 Pizzeria Romana
5 Piazza XXV Luglio
6 Pic Nic
7 Police Office
8 Hospital
9 Post Office & SIP Telephones
10 Albergo Principe
11 Tourist Information Office
12 Albergo Bruno
13 Railway Station
14 Calabro-Lucane Railway Station
15 Trattoria Italia
16 Piazza della Vittoria
17 Piazza del Bruzi
18 Piazza Matteotti
19 Piazza Campanella
20 Church of St Francis of Assisi
21 Duomo
22 Castle
23 Archaeological Museum
24 Piazza XV Marzo
25 Police Headquarters
26 Villa Vecchia

Busento River
Crati River
Crati River

Cosenza

0   150   300 m

Minor Streets Not Depicted

Top Left : One of Palermo's many palace courtyards, Sicily (SC)
Top Right : Greek theatre in Segesta, Sicily (SC)
Bottom Left : The 5th century BC temple of Segesta, Sicily (SC)
Bottom Right : The Palazzo Duca di Santo Stefano, Taormina, Sicily (SC)

Top : Piazza San Marco, Venice (JG)
Bottom Left : Wine cellar, Orvieto, Tuscany (JG)
Bottom Right : Restaurant overlooking the Florence skyline (GI)

archaeological finds. Entry is free and it opens Monday to Saturday from 9 am to 1 pm. South of the piazza is a huge garden, the **Villa Vecchia**.

Places to Stay & Eat

The city has only a few hotels and finding a room can sometimes be difficult. The *Albergo Bruno* (☎ 7 38 89), Corso Mazzini 27, has singles/doubles from L25,000/ 34,000 (prices drop in winter months). The *Albergo Principe* (☎ 2 34 26), Via Monte San Michele 30, has rooms from L38,000/ 52,000.

If you want to eat cheaply, the *Pic Nic*, Corso Mazzini 108, has pasta from L5000. *Pizzeria Romana*, Corso Mazzini 190, is one of the city's best pizzerias, with pizzas from L6000. If you want to sample local dishes, try *Trattoria Italia*, Viale Trieste 93.

Getting There & Away

Bus The city's main bus station (☎ 2 82 76) is just east of Piazza Fera. Bus Parise (☎ 2 14 13) operates services to most major Calabrian towns and to Rome. FCL (☎ 3 68 51) operates services to Catanzaro and into the Sila Massif.

Train The city has three train stations – two serving the national railway and one serving the private regional railway, the Ferrovie Calabro-Lucane. Two of the stations (one national and the other Calabro-Lucane) are close to the city centre, at the eastern end of Corso Umberto; the third station, the Stazione Nuova, is about two km north-east of the city centre, accessible by ATAC city bus No 5.

For information about national trains, call ☎ 2 70 80. Trains for the Sila Massif and Sibari depart from the national train station at the eastern end of Viale Trieste; for Rome and Reggio di Calabria, they depart from the Stazione Nuova. The Calabro-Lucane train station (☎ 2 49 61) serves the Sila Massif and other small towns near Cosenza.

Car & Motorbike Cosenza is on the A3 autostrada. The ss107 road connects the city

with Crotone and the Ionian coast. Maggiore (☎ 7 12 49), Via Alimena 31, is the city's main car rental agency.

Getting Around

Walking is the best way to see the sights, but the local bus company ATAC (☎ 39 04 12) operates buses around the city. Most of the buses outside the Stazione Nuova pass through the city centre. For a taxi, call ☎ 2 88 77.

THE SILA MASSIF

Less spectacular than some of the mountain ranges in the north of Italy, the Sila Massif is still magnificent and offers good walking. With the highest peaks at around 2000 metres, the Sila Massif is more like a vast forest, although there is some winter skiing in the central area, which is known as the Sila Grande. The other main areas are the Sila Greca, north of the Grande, and the Sila Piccola to the south. Sadly, there are few mountain refuges, and camping in the various national parks is forbidden.

The main towns in the Sila Massif are Camigliatello Silano and San Giovanni in Fiore, both accessible by bus along the ss107 which connects Cosenza with Crotone, or by more frequent trains on the train line between Cosenza and San Giovanni. There is accommodation in both towns and at the tourist resorts known as Villagio Palumbo and Villagio Mancuso. The main skiing areas are around these two tourist resorts and Camigliatello Silano.

Information

The tourist infrastructure is hopelessly disorganised, and even discovering such basics as what bus serves what town can be a nightmare. One senior government tourist official tried to tell Lonely Planet it was impossible to hike in the Sila Massif because the vegetation was so dense you would suffocate from a lack of oxygen. It's best to plan your trip in advance, with the help of the tourist offices in Reggio di Calabria, Cosenza or Catanzaro; the small offices in the Sila Massif won't offer much help.

There are several brochures, including *Trekking* and *Conoscere – Comunità Montana Presila Catanzarese*, which are available from some tourist offices and which list accommodation and some itineraries, although both are in Italian only. The Trekking brochure is produced by the Assessorato Regionale al Turismo (☎ 0965-9 82 95) in Reggio di Calabria, Nuove Frontiere, Via Trento 2.

For information about the Sila Grande Calabria National Park, which forms a large chunk of the Sila Grande, contact the office of the park director (☎ 0984-2 65 44), Viale della Repubblica 26, in Cosenza. You might be able to get a copy of the *Itinerari Naturalistici – Sila Grande*, a map detailing 10 walks of varying difficulties in the area (once again, only in Italian).

Camigliatello Silano
There is a branch tourist office here known as the Pro Loco (☎ 0984-57 80 91), Via Forgitelle, a short walk from the train station, although it provides little information.

The skiing here is pretty pathetic by northern Italian standards. Tasso (☎ 57 80 37) operates a couple of lifts on Mt Curcio about three km to the south.

The town has about 20 hotels including the *Miramonti* (☎ 0984-57 83 43), near the tourist office on Via Forgitelle, which has singles/doubles from L25,000/38,000. *Mancuso* (☎ 0984-57 80 82), Via del Turismo, has rooms for about the same price, while the three-star *Aquila & Edelweiss* (☎ 0984-57 80 44), Viale Stazione 11, has rooms from L50,000/80,000. *Ristorante Al Capriolo*, Via Camigliati 8, is an excellent restaurant where a full meal could cost L25,000.

San Giovanni in Fiore
There is a camping ground (☎ 0984-53 70 60) about 15 km west of the town at Lorica, on Lake Arvo. If you are looking for a room in San Giovanni, try the *Albergo Biafora* (☎ 0984-97 00 78), Via Garga 9, which has singles/doubles from L32,000/52,000.

Villagio Palumbo
This is a privately owned town and ski resort, and isn't really worth seeking out unless you are desperate to ski. However, the resort is close to beautiful Lake Ampollino, on the banks of which you could pitch a tent without too much trouble – as long as you do it away from the resort. For further information, call the resort, which is about 15 km south of San Giovanni in Fiore, on ☎ 0962-49 30 17. It offers an excellent package deal including food and accommodation for a weekend at around L140,000.

The management has an interest in Calabria's other main skiing area, which is based abound the **Villagio Mancuso**, about 25 km farther south on the road to Catanzaro. For information, call ☎ 0961-92 20 48.

REGGIO DI CALABRIA
Facing the Strait of Messina and with Mt Etna visible across the water in Sicily, Reggio di Calabria is well worth including on a Calabrian itinerary. It may not be the most interesting Calabrian city, or the most attractive, but it's certainly the region's most worldly metropolis. Southern Italians who have made their fortunes in the north zip between Reggio and Milan in their Lancias and Mercedes, and have brought a level of northern sophistication to this city.

Reggio's main attraction is held in the National Museum: the incredible *Riace Warriors* dating from the 5th century BC, which were discovered about 20 years ago off the coast of the small Ionian town of Riace.

Orientation
The main train station is at the southern edge of town in Piazza Garibaldi. Walk north along Corso G Garibaldi, the city's main street, for the tourist office and other services. The waterfront boulevard, Lungomare Giacomo Matteotti, runs parallel to Corso Garibaldi.

Information
The APT tourist office has branches at the train station (☎ 0965-2 71 20), the airport (☎ 0965-32 02 91), and on the autostrada

near the Rosano Ovest exit (☎ 0965-5 24 02), which all open mornings and afternoons Monday to Saturday. The main APT offices are on Via Roma (☎ 0965-2 11 71) and Via Demetrio Tripepi 72 (☎ 0965-9 84 96), which open Monday to Saturday from 9 am to 2 pm.

The main post office is at Via Miraglia 14 near Piazza Italia, and opens from 8.30 am to 7 pm Monday to Saturday. The city's postal code is 89100. SIP telephones are at Corso Garibaldi 187, and open till late. The telephone code for Reggio di Calabria is 0965.

In a police emergency, call ☎ 113, or head for the police headquarters (☎ 4 71 09), Via Santa Caterina. The city's hospital, the Ospedale Civile (☎ 2 11 04), is at Via Melacrino.

Things to See

The city was completely rebuilt after the 1908 earthquake which devastated southern Calabria. Few historic buildings remain, although those that do were painstakingly rebuilt. Apart from wandering along Lungomare Matteotti, or Corso Garibaldi and through the main piazzas, there is not much to see or do in Reggio.

The city's main attraction is the **National Museum** on Piazza De Nava, at Corso Garibaldi's northern end. Its archaeological collection brings together significant finds from the Magna Graecia period including the magnificent *Riace Warriors*, two bronze statues which were found in shallow water off Riace on the Ionian coast in 1972. Although there was much political pressure for the statues to go to Rome, Calabria won out in the end and was able to keep them. The sculptor remains unknown, but probably lived in the 5th century BC. They are among the world's best examples of ancient Greek sculpture. The museum also houses work by southern Italian artists, a collection recognised as one of southern Italy's best. The museum is open from 9 am to 1 pm and 3 to 6.30 pm Tuesday to Saturday, only mornings on Sunday. Entry is L6000.

The **Duomo** in Piazza del Duomo, just off Corso Garibaldi, is largely unspectacular until you realise it was rebuilt from rubble. Small boards around the cathedral tell the story of the reconstruction. North-east of the Duomo is Piazza Castello and the ruins of a 15th century castle.

Places to Stay

Finding a room is easy, as most visitors to Reggio di Calabria are passing through on their way to Sicily. There are two camping grounds – the *Campeggio degli Ulivi* (no telephone), Via Eremo Botte, in a park of olive trees and eucalypts north-east of the city centre; and the *Paradiso* (☎ 0965-30 24 82), about eight km north of the city at Via Fiumarina in Gallico Marina (follow Via Santa Caterina out of the city).

The *Albergo Saturnia* (☎ 2 10 12), Via Caprera 5, has singles/doubles from L18,000/25,000. *Albergo Noel* (☎ 33 00 44), Via Genoese Zerbi 13, has rooms from L30,000/40,000. *Hotel Diana* (☎ 9 15 22), Via Vitrioli 12, has rooms from L34,000/ 55,000. For a sumptuous stay and a view of Mt Etna, the four-star *Grande Albergo Miramare* (☎ 9 18 81), Via Fata Morgana, near Lungomare Matteotti, has rooms from L90,000/150,000.

Places to Eat

There are plenty of places to buy a snack along Corso Garibaldi, including a bar in the Villa Comunale, a large park off the Corso. The *Pizzeria Rusty*, beside the Duomo on Via Crocefisso, has pizza by the slice from L1500, while *Paninoteca Charlie*, across Corso Garibaldi on Via degli Arconti, on the corner of Via Generale, is a cheap place for a pizza. *Giovanni* on Via Roma has pasta from L6000. *Capignata*, Via Demetrio Tripepi 122, offers some local dishes with pizzas and pasta both starting at L5000, although there's a cover charge of L2000. *Rodrigo*, Via XXIV Maggio 25, specialises in Calabrian cuisine, and a meal could cost about L30,000.

Entertainment

The city hosts an impressive concert series from November to April at the Teatro Margherita, when orchestras from across Europe perform. For information, contact the Associazione Culturale Jonica (☎ 81 11 91), Via Crocefisso 34.

Getting There & Away

Air The city's airport, the Aeroporto Civile Minniti (☎ 64 22 32) at Ravagnese, about four km to the south, serves two flights a day from Rome and one from Milan, as well as charter flights. The Alitalia office (☎ 33 14 44 and 33 14 45) is in the city at Corso Garibaldi 251.

Bus The bus station is in Piazza Garibaldi, in front of the train station. About 10 companies operate buses to towns in Calabria and beyond. For instance, Brosio (☎ 0963-36 10 49) serves Villa San Giovanni; Saja (☎ 81 23 37) and AMA (☎ 62 01 29) serve the Aspromonte Massif; and Lirosi (☎ 0966-93 26 11) has a daily service to Rome.

Train Trains stop at the main train station, Stazione Centrale (☎ 89 81 23), and less frequently at Stazione Lido, near the National Museum. Reggio is a major rail hub and is the terminus of trains (including the fast ETR450 trains) from Milan, Florence, Rome and Naples. The private Ferrovie Calabro-Lucane train company (☎ 0966-5 19 36) also operates from Stazione Centrale, with trains that will take you along the Ionian coast.

Car & Motorbike The A3 autostrada ends at Reggio di Calabria. Maggiore (☎ 9 49 80) operates car-hire agencies at the main train station and the airport.

Boat Several companies operate ferries to Sicily from the port just north of Stazione Lido, although most leave the mainland from Villa San Giovanni, about 15 km to the north. From Reggio, SNAV (☎ 2 95 68) operates hydrofoils and ferries to Messina, Catania,

---

■ PLACES TO STAY

2 Campeggio degli Ulivi
3 Albergo Noel
12 Grande Albergo Miramare
17 Hotel Diana
27 Albergo Saturnia

▼ PLACES TO EAT

5 Giovanni
6 Capignata
11 Rodrigo
21 Paninoteca Charlie
23 Pizzeria Rusty

OTHER

1 Ferry Terminals
4 APT Tourist Office
7 Hospital
8 Stazione Lido
9 National Museum
10 Piazza de Nava
13 SIP Telephones
14 APT Tourist Office
15 Piazza Italia
16 Post Office
18 Piazza Castello & Castle Ruins
19 Police Headquarters
20 Duomo
22 Piazza del Duomo
24 Villa Comunale
25 Main Railway Station
26 Piazza Garibaldi & Bus Station

Syracuse and Malta. Tirrenia (☎ 9 40 03), Via Bozzi 31, serves Sicily and Naples.

If you are catching a train to Sicily from Reggio, it will travel aboard a ferry from Villa San Giovanni. From the Stazione Marittima at Villa San Giovanni (☎ 0965-89 79 57), the national railway (☎ 9 81 23) operates ferries to Messina for L1600 one way, as do SNAV and Tirrenia. SNAV also serves the Lipari Islands from this terminal. An SNAV ferry to Messina from Reggio will also cost L1600; a hydrofoil on the same run will set you back L6000.

Getting Around

City buses, which are generally orange or

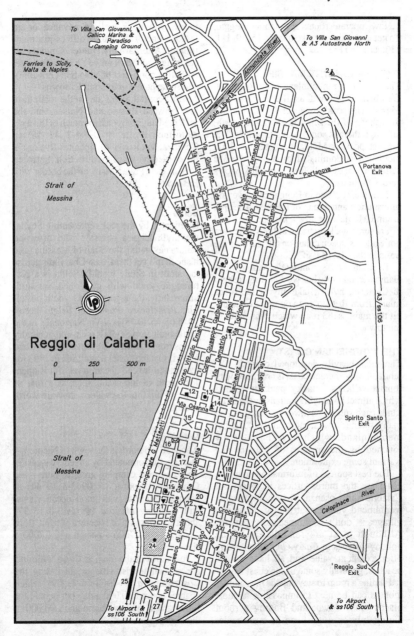

To Villa San Giovanni,
Gallico Marina &
Paradiso
Camping Ground

To Villa San Giovanni
& A3 Autostrada North

Ferries to Sicily,
Malta & Naples

Strait of
Messina

Reggio di Calabria

0   250   500 m

Strait of
Messina

Portanova
Exit

Spirito Santo
Exit

Reggio Sud
Exit

To Airport &
ss106 South

To Airport
& ss106 South

yellow, operate routes throughout Reggio. To get to the airport, take bus No 15, 19, 111, 113, 114 or 115.

THE ASPROMONTE MASSIF

The mountain range inland from Reggio di Calabria is known as the Aspromonte Massif. The peaks are generally much lower than those of the Sila Massif farther north, although there is some skiing in winter. The highest peak is Montalto, at almost 2000 metres. It is dominated by a huge bronze statue of Christ and offers incredible views across to Sicily.

The tourist office in Reggio can give you information and a map of the area. The area around Montalto is now a national park and offers some walking trails, although they are not quite as spectacular, or difficult, as the trails in the Sila Massif.

To reach the Aspromonte's main town of Gambarie, take city bus No 127 from Reggio di Calabria; by car, take any of the roads inland from Reggio and you will eventually hit the main ss183 road which runs north to the town.

THE TYRRHENIAN COAST

The most heavily developed coast in Calabria, the Tyrrhenian coast is crammed with tourist villages – tacky package resorts which attract holidaying Italians by the thousands each summer. However, there are also many smaller towns, most on the coast but many inland, which have been barely touched by the ravages of tourism and warrant some exploration.

The best sources of information about the coast are the tourist offices in Reggio di Calabria and Cosenza. They will probably recommend you stay at one of the tourist villages – don't be immediately put off. Although most are reminiscent of the holiday villages in *Carry On...* films, many offer excellent value and all have private beaches, generally some of the coast's best.

Finding a room to stay outside the summer months can be next to impossible as most places close down; and finding a room during July or August can be even harder unless you book well in advance or go through one of the tourist offices just mentioned. Alternatively, there is plenty of camping, Calabria's only IYHF youth hostel (at Scilla, north-east of Villa San Giovanni), and some hotels in the smaller towns.

Most coastal towns are on the main train line between Reggio and Naples, and the ss18 road hugs the coast for much of the way. Autolinee Preite (☎ 0984-2 49 46) in Cosenza, Via Roma 40, operates five or six buses a day in each direction between Cosenza and Praia a Mare, on the border with Basilicata.

Scilla

Dominated by the rock representing Scylla, the mythical sea monster who drowned sailors navigating the Strait of Messina (and if she didn't get them, then Charybdis across the strait in Sicily would), Scilla is a picturesque town with good beaches and, importantly, the region's only youth hostel. The *Principessa Paola del Belgio* hostel (☎ 0965-75 40 33) is at Via Nazionale, in the castle built atop Scylla's rock, and generally opens from 1 April to 30 September. The bad news is that the hostel was closed in 1993 for restoration, so call ahead to see if it is open. Just north of the castle, there is a row of houses built into the water – they are worth seeing.

Nicotera

About 50 km north is the town of Nicotera – once again, dominated by a medieval castle. There are two camping grounds here – the *Camping Sayonara* (☎ 0963-8 19 44) at Nicotera Marina, with good ocean views, and *Camping Mimosa* (☎ 0963-8 13 97) about six km south of Nicotera Marina. Both charge about L7000 a person and L7000 a site.

Just north of the town at **Cape Vaticano** are several tourist villages, including the *Costa Azzurra* (☎ 0963-66 31 09), which charges about L60,000 a day per person for full board in the low season and L90,000 in the high season.

Tropea

Just north of Cape Vaticano, Tropea is a very pleasant small town where you could easily spend a few days relaxing. It has about 10 hotels, most in the higher price bracket, although *Vulcano* (☎ 0963-6 15 98), Via Campo Superiore, has singles/doubles from L35,000/50,000. The *Stromboli* tourist village (☎ 0963-66 90 93) charges L45,000 in the low season and L105,000 in the high season per person for full board.

The bus line SAV (☎ 0963-6 11 29) operates services in this area, connecting the resorts with Tropea and Pizzo, which both have train stations.

Pizzo

Farther north of Tropea, in the bars of the town of Pizzo, you will find possibly Italy's best *tartufo*, a type of chocolate ice-cream ball.

The town's **Duomo** features the tomb of Joachim Murat, the King of Naples from 1808 to 1815. Just north of the town is the **Piedigrotta Church**, an incredible church carved into the sandstone near the beach. Wander through Pizzo's main square, Piazzetta Garibaldi, a picturesque piazza overlooking the water, before settling in at *Bar Ercole* for an ice-cream fix.

For a typical seafood meal, *La Nave*, in a rusting boat on the waterfront, is a good restaurant, with main courses from L10,000.

Paola

The coast between Pizzo and the next town of interest, Paola, about 80 km to the north, is mostly overdeveloped and ugly. Paola is the main train hub for Cosenza, about 25 km inland, and is a reasonably large centre. Its main attraction is the **Sanctuary of San Francesco di Paola**, a monastery east of the town.

The *Albergo Elena* (☎ 0982-61 24 74), Via San Leonardo, is your best bet for accommodation, with rooms from L25,000/36,000, although the hotels of Cosenza might be more attractive.

Cirella to Praia a Mare

Farther north, the stretch of beach from Cirella to Praia a Mare, close to the border with Basilicata, is one of Calabria's best. That is, of course, if you don't mind pebbles. There are plenty of camping grounds on this stretch too, and less hotel developments than farther south. The *C V Milano Blu* camping ground (☎ 0985-8 60 75) on the ss18 just south of Cirella is close to the beach.

The town of **Scalea** farther north is one of the most picturesque on the Tyrrhenian coast, and is popular because of its five camping grounds. Try the *Camping La Pantera Rosa* (☎ 0985-2 15 46) on Corso Mediterraneo.

Praia a Mare

A couple of km south of the border with Basilicata, Praia a Mare is a modern town built to serve Italian holiday-makers. However, it has a few attractions: an excellent beach (pebbles, not sand); the small **Dino Island** off the coast, with an incredible and easily accessible grotto that is every bit as impressive as Capri's; and the hill town of **Aietta**, a peasant village about 12 km northeast of Praia, which has barely changed over the centuries. Aietta is worth visiting if you have a car, although it can be a bit tricky to get to if you rely on the buses which leave from Praia's train station at irregular intervals.

If you plan to stay in Praia, the *Camping Internazionale* (☎ 0985 7 22 11) is just south of the town at Mantinera. The *Hotel Rex* (☎ 0985-7 21 91), Via C Colombo, a couple of blocks back from Praia's beach, is excellent value with rooms from L45,000/69,000. The hotel also has a very good restaurant.

Sicily

Sicily

Think of Sicily (Sicilia) and two things immediately come to mind: beaches and the Mafia. While many of its beaches are beautiful and the Mafia still manages to assert a powerful influence on the Sicilian lifestyle and economy, Sicily is remarkably diverse. It is a place of contrasts, from the crumbling grandeur of its capital, Palermo, to the up-market glitz of its most famous tourist resort, Taormina; the Greek ruins at Syracuse, Agrigento, Selinunte and Segesta; and the wild beauty of the volcanic Aeolian Islands – and not to forget, spectacular Mt Etna.

The largest island in the Mediterranean, its strategic location made it a prize for successive waves of invaders and colonisers, and, aside from its Greek temples, there are also Roman ruins, Norman churches and castles, Arab and Byzantine domes, and splendid Baroque churches and palaces. It is believed that the first settlers of the island were the Sicanians, Elymians and Siculians, who came from various points around the southern Mediterranean, followed by Phoenicians. Greek colonisation began in the 8th century BC with the foundation of Naxos, followed by the development of important cities such as Syracuse, Catania, Messina and Agrigento. By 210 BC, the island was under Roman domination, with power eventually passing to the Byzantines, who were driven out by the conquest of the Arabs, placing Sicily under Arab rule by 903 AD.

The Norman conquest of the island began in 1060, when Roger I of Hauteville captured Messina, with control passing to the Swabians and eventually to the great king, the Holy Roman emperor Frederick II, known as Stupor Mundi (Wonder of the World). In the 13th century the French Angevins controlled Sicily, a period of misrule which ended with the revolt known as the Sicilian Vespers in 1282. This led to the island being handed to the Spanish Aragon family and, in 1503, the island passed to the Spanish crown. After short periods of Savoy and Austrian rule in the 18th century, Sicily again came under Spanish rule when the Bourbons of Naples took control in 1734, uniting the island with southern Italy in the Kingdom of the Two Sicilies.

On 11 May 1860, Giuseppe Garibaldi landed at Marsala with his One Thousand and began the conquest which would eventually lead to the unification of Italy. Life, however, did not greatly improve for the people, who had for so long been oppressed by foreign domination, and between 1871 and 1914 more than one million Sicilians emigrated, mainly to the USA. During WW II the Allied forces landed on the south coast of Sicily, forming a government of occupation which lasted until early 1944. It became a semi-autonomous region in 1948, and, unlike other such regions in Italy, has its own parliament and powers to legislate. Although industry has developed on the island, its economy still has a largely agricultural base and its people remain strongly connected to the land.

The island's landscape ranges from fertile coast to the mountains of the north and the vast, dry plateau of its interior. Its temperate climate brings mild weather in winter, but its summers are relentlessly hot and the beaches swarm with holidaying Italians and other Europeans. The best times to visit are spring and autumn, when it is hot enough for the beach but not too hot for sightseeing.

Sicilian food is spicier and sweeter than in other parts of Italy. The focus is on seafood along the coast, notably swordfish, and fresh produce. Some say that fruit and vegetables taste better in Sicily. The cakes and pastries can be works of art, but are very sweet. Try the cassata, a rich cake filled with cream of ricotta and candied fruits (you can also buy cassata ice cream); *cannoli*, tubes of pastry filled with cream, ricotta or chocolate; and the many varieties of almond cakes and pastries *(dolci di mandorle)*. Then there is granita, a drink of crushed ice flavoured with lemon, strawberry or coffee, to name a few flavours. Perfect on a hot Sicilian day.

As mentioned, the Mafia remains a powerful force in Sicily and brutal murders have continued to occur with sickening frequency, culminating in the bomb assassinations of two anti-Mafia judges in Palermo in 1992. In early 1993, the arrest of the Sicilian 'godfather', Salvatore ('Toto') Riina, signalled a major blow to the Mafia. But nobody believed that the arrest would destroy an organisation which has become synonymous with the island where it originated. As one politician commented after Riina's arrest, 'The Mafia is interwoven with the fabric of our lives in Sicily. Kill the Mafia and you kill Sicily.' The Italian author Luigi Barzini wrote: 'The phenomenon has deep roots in history, in the character of the Sicilians, in local habits. Its origins disappear down the dim vistas of the centuries.'

While there is no need to fear that you will be caught in the crossfire of a gang war while in Sicily, don't expect to be able to have a long discussion about the Mafia with a local. Sicilian people are, overall, welcoming and friendly, but female tourists might find the local men a little too friendly.

GETTING THERE & AWAY
Air
Flights from all major cities in Italy land at Palermo and Catania. The airports are also serviced by flights from major European cities. Palermo's airport is Punta Raisi, about 32 km out of the city, while Catania's airport is about seven km out. There are bus services from both airports into the centres of the cities (for further details, see the Palermo and Catania Getting There & Away sections). The easiest way to obtain information on flights to/from Sicily is from any CIT or Alitalia office throughout Italy.

Bus
There are direct SAIS bus services between Rome and Sicily, arriving at Messina, Syracuse, Catania and Agrigento, with connections to Palermo. For information in Rome, go to Bar Piccarozzi (☎ 06-488 59 24), Piazza della Repubblica 62. Segesta runs a direct service between Palermo and Rome via Messina. For information, go to its office at Via Paolo Balsamo 26, Palermo. A one-way ticket costs L68,000. In Rome, go to Bar Piccarozzi.

Train
One of the cheapest ways to reach Sicily is to catch a train. The cost of a ticket covers the ferry crossing to Messina, since the train company also runs ferries across the strait, from Villa San Giovanni, just north of Reggio di Calabria. Direct trains run from Milan, Florence, Rome, Naples and Reggio di Calabria to Messina and on to Palermo. Travellers should be prepared for sometimes long delays on intercity trains on this route.

Boat Regular car/passenger ferries crisscross the strait between Villa San Giovanni and Messina. The ferry ride takes about half an hour and costs L1600. SNAV hydrofoils connect Reggio di Calabria and Messina approximately every hour. The trip takes 15 minutes and costs L6000.

Sicily is also accessible by ferry from Genoa, Livorno, Naples and Cagliari, and from Malta and Tunisia. The main company servicing the Mediterranean is Tirrenia and its ferry services to/from Sicily include Palermo-Cagliari, Palermo-Genoa, Palermo-Naples, Trapani-Cagliari, Trapani-Tunisia and Naples-Reggio di Calabria-Catania-Syracuse-Malta.

Grandi Traghetti runs ferries from Livorno and Genoa to Palermo, and Aliscafi SNAV runs hydrofoils from Trapani to Kelibia in Tunisia.

Ferry prices are determined by the season and jump considerably in the summer period (Tirrenia's high season varies according to your destination, but is generally from July through September). Timetables change dramatically each year. Tirrenia publishes an annual booklet listing all routes and prices, which is available at Tirrenia offices and agents throughout the country.

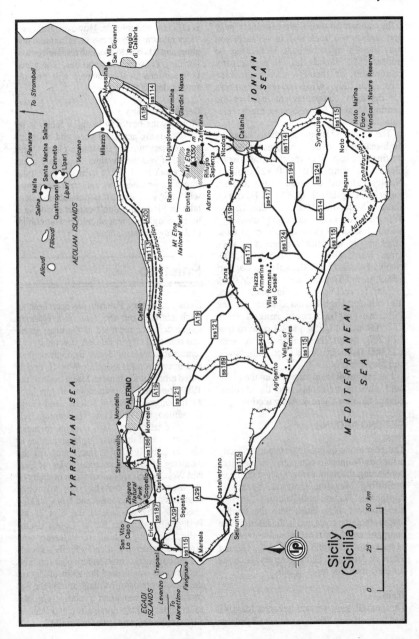

Sicily
(Sicilia)

In summer all routes are extremely busy and, unless you book well in advance, you may literally miss the boat. Tickets can be booked either directly through the company concerned, or through travel agencies throughout Italy. Offices and phone numbers for the ferry companies are listed in the Getting There & Away sections for the relevant cities.

The following is a guide to fares, based on high-season travel on Tirrenia at the time of writing. For an airline-type chair, fares were: Genoa-Palermo L102,200 (22 hours), Naples-Palermo L61,900 (10½ hours), Palermo-Cagliari L44,300 (14 hours), Catania-Malta L81,100 (nine hours), and Trapani-Tunisia L84,700 (eight hours). For a 2nd-class cabin (shared with up to three other people and often segregated by sex), fares were: Genoa-Palermo L115,400, Naples-Palermo L71,700, Palermo-Cagliari L68,200, and Trapani-Tunisia L109,900.

Fares for cars vary according to the size of the vehicle. High-season charges for the Palermo-Cagliari route ranged from L87,700 to L143,200; a small caravan cost L29,200, motorbikes under 200 cc were L23,000 (L37,000 for 200 cc and above), and bicycles cost L9700.

For information on ferries from the mainland directly to Lipari, see the Aeolian Islands Getting There & Away section.

GETTING AROUND
Bus
The best mode of public transport in Sicily is the bus. Numerous companies run services connecting the main towns around the coast including Messina, Catania, Syracuse, Agrigento, Trapani and Palermo. Services also connect these cities with the smaller towns along the coast and in the interior. The companies with the most extensive networks of buses are SAIS and AST. See the Getting There & Away and Getting Around sections for each town for more details.

Train
The coastal train service between Messina and Palermo and Messina down to Syracuse

is efficient and reliable. However, train services into the interior can be infrequent and slow, and it is best to do some research before deciding between train and bus. The transport sections in this chapter will provide further details.

Car & Motorbike
Probably the best way to enjoy Sicily is by car. Roads are generally good and autostradas connect most of the major cities. A car will give you the freedom to explore areas which can be difficult to reach by public transport, or where bus and train timetables will limit your time. It is possible to hitchhike in Sicily, but don't expect a ride in a hurry. Single women should not hitchhike under any circumstances.

Palermo

During its history, Palermo has been both an Arab emirate and the seat of a Norman kingdom. Once regarded as the most grand and beautiful city in Europe, it is today in a remarkable state of decay through neglect and heavy bombing during WW II, and is noted more for the famous Mafia trials of the 1980s and the assassinations of top anti-Mafia judges, Giovanni Falcone and Paolo Borsellino, in 1992. However, enough evidence of its golden days remains to make Palermo one of the most impressive cities to visit in Italy. It is most fascinating for the harmony of the architectural styles of East and West, which are still obvious in many of its monuments, notably the adjacent churches of La Martorana and San Cataldo.

Situated by the sea, at the foot of Mt Pellegrino, with the fertile Conca d'Oro valley opening behind it, Palermo was always considered a prize by Sicily's invaders and colonisers for its superb position. The Phoenicians established the town of Ziz on the site of a prehistoric village around the 8th century BC. It remained a relatively minor town under Roman domination and later as a Byzantine city, and it was not until 831 AD, when it was conquered by the Arabs, that the city's golden years began. Under Arab rule it became an emirate and one of the most important cities in the Islamic world.

Under the Normans from 1072, Palermo became the capital of Sicily and the seat of King Roger's kingdom, and was considered one of the most magnificent and cultured cities of 12th century Europe. For more than half a century after Roger's death the monarchy foundered, eventually passing to the German Hohenstaufens and the Holy Roman emperor Frederick II, who is still considered one of the most enlightened rulers of Sicily. After his death, Palermo and all of Sicily passed to the French Anjou family, who were deposed following the Sicilian Vespers revolt, which started in Palermo. But the city's golden years were over, and its history merged with that of Sicily as a whole.

Orientation

Palermo is a large but easily manageable city. The main streets of the historical centre are Via Roma and Via Maqueda, which extend from the main train station to Piazza Castelnuovo, a vast square in the modern part of town and about a 20-minute walk from the station. The station end of town, where you will find most of the cheaper pensioni and hotels, seems grimy and chaotic, but behind the decaying palaces lining the main streets there is a fascinating maze of narrow lanes and tiny piazzas where you will find markets, trattorias and, unfortunately, get an even better idea of just how decrepit Palermo really is. The area around Piazza Castelnuovo seems a world away, with its malls, outdoor cafés and designer shops. Intersecting both Via Maqueda and Via Roma are Via Vittorio Emanuele and Via Cavour, the main thoroughfares to the port and the Stazione Marittima (about a 10-minute walk from Via Roma).

Information

Tourist Offices The main tourist office, the APT (☎ 091-586 122), is at Piazza Castelnuovo 35. The staff speak English and you can pick up a map of the city and a monthly

calendar of cultural, theatrical and musical events. It is open from 8 am to 12.30 pm and 3 to 8 pm Monday to Saturday, to 2 pm Sunday. The branch office at the train station (open from 8 am to 6.30 pm daily) is much more convenient and has the same information. There are other branch offices at the Stazione Marittima at the port; in Piazza San Sepolcro, off Via Maqueda; and at Punta Raisi Airport. All these offices are open from 8 am to 2 pm Monday to Saturday, although the one at the port opens only in summer.

Money There are exchange offices at the train station, open daily from 7.30 am to 12.30 pm and 2.30 to 8 pm, and at the airport (Banco di Sicilia), open daily from 6.45 am to 1.30 pm and 2.30 to 8 pm. Banks are generally open from 8.30 am to 1.15 pm.

Post & Telecommunications The main post office is at Via Roma 322, about 10 to 15 minutes' walk from the station. It is open from 8.15 am to 7.30 pm, and has fax and telex services. The postal code for central Palermo is 90100.

The main ASST telephone office is opposite the station in Piazza G Cesare and is open 24 hours daily. Other ASST offices are at the port and at the airport (both open from 8 am to 10 pm). There is an SIP office at Via Principe di Belmonte 92, just before Piazza Castelnuovo, between Via Roma and Via Ruggero Settimo. It is open from 8 am to 8 pm daily. The telephone code for Palermo is 091.

Consulates There is a US Consulate (☎ 34 35 32) at Via G Vaccarini 1, off Via della Libertà, past Piazza Castelnuovo. Citizens of most other countries will need to contact their embassies in Rome.

Travel Agencies The CIT office, where you can book train, ferry and air tickets, is at Via della Libertà 12. There is a CTS office at Via Nicolo Garzilli 28 (turn left into Via Carducci, off Via della Libertà). A bit more convenient is Record Viaggi, Via Mariano Stabile 168 (between Via Ruggero Settimo

■ PLACES TO STAY

- 9 Albergo Odeon
- 11 Hotel Principe di Belmonte
- 12 Hotel Petit
- 13 Grand Hotel et des Palmes
- 16 Albergo Villareale
- 18 Albergo Libertà, Hotel Elite & Hotel Boston Madonia
- 19 Hotel Liguria
- 24 Hotel Moderno
- 29 Albergo Columbia
- 30 Centrale Palace Hotel
- 32 Albergo da Luigi
- 33 Grande Albergo Sole
- 35 Hotel La Terrazza
- 48 Albergo Corona
- 53 Albergo Sicilia
- 56 Albergo Rosalia Conca d'Oro
- 58 Albergo Orientale
- 60 Pensione Sud

▼ PLACES TO EAT

- 10 Osteria Lo Bianco
- 25 Vucciria Market & Trattoria Shanghai
- 26 La Cambusa
- 38 Il Crudo e Il Cotto
- 46 Trattoria dei Vespri
- 47 Trattoria Stella

OTHER

- 1 CTS Travel Agency
- 2 CIT Travel Agency
- 3 Roney
- 4 Stazione Marittima
- 5 APT Tourist Information Office
- 6 APT Main Tourist Information Office
- 7 Piazza Castelnuovo
- 8 Piazza Ruggero Settimo
- 14 SIP Public Telephones
- 15 Car Park (Autorimessa Sant'Oliva)
- 17 Record Viaggi Travel Agency
- 20 Teatro Massimo
- 21 Museo Archeologico Regionale
- 22 Post Office
- 23 Church of San Domenico
- 27 Piazza Marina
- 28 Palazzo Chiaramonte
- 31 Quattro Canti
- 34 Church of San Matteo
- 36 Oratory of San Lorenzo
- 37 Church of San Francesco d'Assisi
- 39 Cathedral
- 40 Church of San Giuseppe dei Teatini
- 41 Fountain of Shame
- 42 Church of Santa Caterina
- 43 Palazzo del Municipio
- 44 Church of San Cataldo
- 45 La Martorana
- 49 Porta Nuova
- 50 Piazza della Vittoria
- 51 Police Heaquarters
- 52 Chiesa del Gesù
- 54 Villa Giulia
- 55 Palazzo dei Normanni
- 57 Church of San Giovanni degli Eremiti
- 59 ASST Public Telephones
- 61 Urban Bus Terminal
- 62 Main Train Station
- 63 APT Tourist Information Office
- 64 Intercity Bus Terminal
- 65 Car Park (Trinca Anna)
- 66 Public Hospital

and Via Roma), where you can also book train, ferry and air tickets.

Car rental Europcar (☎ 32 19 49) has an office in the train station.

Emergency Ring the police on ☎ 113, or the carabinieri on ☎ 112. The police headquarters (☎ 21 01 11), where you should go to report thefts and other crimes, are in Piazza della Vittoria, on the corner of Via Vittorio Emanuele, opposite the cathedral. It is open only from 8.30 am to 12.30 pm.

In the event of a medical emergency, phone the Public Hospital, Via Carmelo Lazzaro, on ☎ 606 11 11, or ring an ambulance on ☎ 30 66 44. There is an all-night pharmacy, Lo Cascio, near the train station at Via Roma 1.

Dangers & Annoyances Petty crime is rife in Palermo, and highly adept pickpockets and motorcycle bandits prey on tourists. Avoid wearing jewellery and carrying a bag, and keep all valuables in a money belt. While busy and noisy during the day, the historical centre of Palermo is relatively deserted by 8.30 or 9 pm. Couples and groups should have no problems walking along the streets at night, but single women are advised

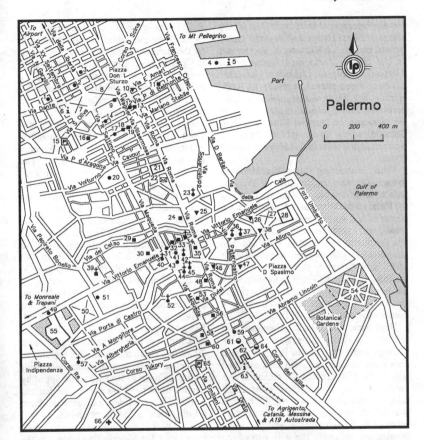

Palermo

Port

Gulf of
Palermo

Cala

Botanical
Gardens

against doing so, even along the busy Via
Roma or Via Maqueda. You will almost certainly be harassed by groups of men,
particularly in kerb-crawling cars.

Car theft is a big problem in Palermo, and
it is best to leave your vehicle in one of the
numerous private car parks in the city centre
(see the following Getting Around section).
The more expensive hotels will generally
have their own parking facilities. Remember
never to leave anything in the car.

Things to See
The busy intersection of Via Vittorio
Emanuele and Via Maqueda marks the

Quattro Canti (the 'Four Corners' of
Palermo), the centre of the oldest part of
town. The four 17th century Spanish
Baroque façades are each decorated with a
fountain and a statue. On the south-west
corner of the intersection is the Baroque
Church of San Giuseppe dei Teatini, its
interior heavily decorated with marble.

Across Via Maqueda is the Piazza Pretoria, with a beautiful fountain created by
Florentine sculptors in the 16th century. At
the time of its unveiling, shocked Palermitans named it the **Fountain of Shame**
because of its nude figures. Also in the piazza
are the Baroque **Church of Santa Caterina**

and the **Palazzo del Municipio**. Just off the piazza is Piazza Bellini and Palermo's most famous church, **La Martorana**, also known as the Santa Maria dell'Ammiraglio. Although the original 12th century structure has been much altered, it retains its Arab-Norman bell tower and its interior is richly decorated with Byzantine mosaics. Also in the piazza is the Norman **Church of San Cataldo**, which also combines Arab and Norman styles, with its battlements and red domes.

While wandering down Via Maqueda towards the train station, note the Baroque palaces in various stages of decay, including the **Palazzo dei Principi di Comitini** on the corner of Via Albergheria. The **Chiesa del Gesù**, also known as the Casa Professa, in Via Ponticello, was built in 1564 and then absorbed into another structure completed in 1633. It was largely destroyed by heavy bombing in 1943, although restoration work has recovered most of the stucco work and frescoes. To the right of the church is a porticoed Baroque courtyard.

Head back to the Quattro Canti and turn left into Via Vittorio Emanuele to reach the Norman **cathedral**, one of Palermo's most important monuments. Built in the second half of the 12th century, the cathedral was modified many times since, most disastrously in the 18th century when the dome was added, spoiling the architectural harmony of the building. In the same period the interior was restored. The only part of the church which has been conserved in pure original Norman style is the apse, although the church overall remains an impressive example of Norman architecture. Inside are royal and imperial tombs, and among those interred in porphyry sarcophagi are King Roger II, Henry VI of Hohenstaufen, Constance de Hauteville and Frederick II of Hohenstaufen. The ashes of St Rosalia, patron saint of Palermo, are contained in a silver urn in one of the church's numerous chapels.

Across the Piazza della Vittoria and the gardens is the **Palazzo dei Normanni**, also known as the Palazzo Reale (Royal Palace).

Built by the Arabs in the 9th century, it was extended by the Normans and restructured by the Hohenstaufens. It is now the seat of the government. Enter from Piazza Indipendenza to see the **Palatine Chapel**, a magnificent example of Arab-Norman architecture, built during the reign of Roger II and decorated with Byzantine mosaics. The chapel was once described as 'the finest religious jewel dreamt of by human thought', and its mosaics are considered rivalled only by those of Ravenna and Istanbul. The chapel is open Monday to Friday from 9 am to midday and 3 to 5 pm, Saturday from 9 am to midday, and Sunday from 9 to 10 am and midday to 1 pm. Entrance is free.

Also worth visiting in the palace is the Sala di Ruggero (King Roger's Room), his former bedroom. It is decorated with 12th century mosaics. It is only possible to visit the room with a guide (free of charge). Go upstairs from the Palatine Chapel.

Next to the palace is the **Porta Nuova**, built in the 16th century to celebrate the arrival of Charles V in Palermo (1535). Behind the palace, in Via dei Benedettini, is the **Church of San Giovanni degli Eremiti** (St John of the Hermits), another fascinating example of Arab-Norman architecture. Built during the reign of Roger II, it is topped by five red domes and has a pretty garden and cloisters. It is now deconsecrated and there is little of interest inside the church.

Head back to the Quattro Canti and continue along Via Vittorio Emanuele. On the left is the Baroque **Church of San Matteo**, with a richly decorated interior. Of note are four statues in the pilasters of the dome representing the Virtues, carved by Giacomo Serpotta in 1728. The **Church of San Domenico** is along Via Roma. The grand 17th century structure houses the tombs of many important Sicilians, as well as a wealth of art works.

The area to the south of the church is occupied by one of Palermo's more down-to-earth attractions, the **Vucciria** markets. With the atmosphere of an eastern bazaar, the markets stretch along the maze of narrow streets heading towards the port.

Continuing along Via Roma, turn left into Via Bara to reach the **Museo Archeologico Regionale** in Piazza Olivella. The museum houses an important collection of Greek metopes from Selinunte, as well as the famous *Bronze Ram of Syracuse*, a Hellenistic work, and finds from other archaeological sites throughout the island. The museum is open Tuesday to Saturday from 9 am to 1.30 pm (also from 3 to 5 pm on Tuesdays and Fridays). Entrance is L2000.

Back on Via Vittorio Emanuele, towards the sea, is the **Oratory of San Lorenzo**, Via dell'Immacolatella, which is decorated with stuccoes by Serpotta, considered to be his greatest work. Caravaggio's last known work, a Nativity, once hung over the altar. It was stolen in 1969 and has never been recovered. Nearby, in Via Paternostro, is the 13th century **Church of San Francesco d'Assisi**. Restored many times, it features a fine rose window and Gothic portal. The 14th century **Palazzo Chiaramonte** in Piazza Marina is a fine medieval building which once served as an architectural model for many buildings in Sicily. On the other side of Via Abramo Lincoln are the **Villa Giulia** and the city's **botanical gardens**, which are worth a visit.

Other sights of interest include the strange **Capuchin Catacombs** in the Capuchin Convent on Piazza Cappuccino, west of the city centre, which contain the mummified bodies and skeletons of some 8000 wealthy Palermitans who died in the 17th to 19th centuries. The bodies are lined along the walls in various attitudes. The catacombs are open daily from 9 am to midday and 3 to 5 pm. Entrance is free.

In the same area is **La Zisa**, a 12th century Arab-Norman castle. The name, which means 'the Splendid', testifies to the magnificence of the palace, which was built for William I and completed by William II. The castle is open Monday to Saturday from 9 am to 1.30 pm, also Tuesday to Friday from 3 to 5.30 pm and on Sunday from 9am to 12.30 pm. Entrance is free.

Back in the city centre in Piazza Verdi, on Via Maqueda, is the 19th century **Teatro Massimo**, one of the largest and most famous theatres in Europe. It has been closed for renovation and is not expected to reopen before the turn of the century.

Places to Stay

There are numerous hotels and pensioni in Palermo and you will have little trouble finding a room, whether you require ultra-budget or top-class accommodation. The tourist office at the station will make recommendations, but will not make bookings.

Head for Via Maqueda or Via Roma for basic, cheap rooms, some in old palaces, but note that rooms facing onto either street will be very noisy. Women on their own should be wary about staying in the area close to the train station, as it is not the safest place at night. The area around Piazza Castelnuovo offers a higher standard of accommodation but has less budget options (catch bus No 7 from the train station to Piazza Sturzo).

Bottom End The best camping ground is *Trinacria* (☎ 53 05 90), Via Barcarello 25, by the sea at Sferracavallo. It costs L9500 per person, with the fee for a tent included. Catch bus No 16 from Piazza Sturzo.

Near the train station, try the *Albergo Orientale* (☎ 616 57 27), Via Maqueda 26, in an old and somewhat decayed palace. Singles/doubles are L25,000/40,000 and triples are L60,000. Just around the corner is *Albergo Rosalia Conca d'Oro* (☎ 616 45 43), Via Santa Rosalia 7, with singles/doubles/triples for L22,000/35,000/ 48,000. The *Pensione Sud* (☎ 617 57 00), Via Maqueda 8, is close to the station and has very basic singles/doubles for L20,000/ 30,000. The *Albergo Corona* (☎ 616 23 40), Via Roma 118, has clean, pleasant rooms for L25,000/40,000; a double with bathroom is L45,000, and triples are L45,000, or L60,000 with bathroom. *Albergo da Luigi* (☎ 58 50 85), Via Vittorio Emanuele 284, is next to the Quattro Canti. It has rooms for L20,000/40,000, and with bathroom for L30,000/50,000 and L36,000/70,000; a triple is L60,000.

Around Piazza Castelnuovo, try the *Albergo Odeon* (☎ 33 27 78), Via Emerico Amari 140. It has clean and spacious rooms, although those facing onto Via Amari are noisy. Singles/doubles are L18,000/32,000 and a double with bathroom is L40,000. The *Albergo Villareale* (☎ 32 16 69), Via Villareale 16, is just off Via Mariano Stabile, near the intersection of Via Ruggero Settimo. It has clean, simple rooms for L22,000/35,000. *Hotel Petit* (☎ 32 36 16), Via Principe di Belmonte 84, has comfortable rooms with bathroom for L33,000/43,000, and singles without bathroom for L25,000. About halfway between the station and Piazza Castelnuovo is the *Albergo Columbia* (☎ 32 06 05), Via del Celso 31, off Via Maqueda near Via Vittorio Emanuele. It has very basic rooms costing L15,000 per person, or L20,000 per person with bathroom.

Middle Near the station, at Via Roma 188, is *Hotel La Terrazza* (☎ 58 63 65). It is a pleasant and clean establishment with great views of the city from its terraces. Rooms are L35,000/52,000 or, with bathroom, L45,000/65,000. Farther along Via Roma at No 276 is the *Hotel Moderno* (☎ 58 86 83), offering a good standard of accommodation. Rooms are L40,000/65,000 and triples are L90,000, all with bathroom. *Albergo Sicilia* (☎ 616 84 60), Via Divisi 99, on the corner of Via Maqueda, has large rooms of a reasonable standard, although they can be quite noisy. Singles/doubles are L38,000/55,000 and triples are L75,000, all with private bathroom.

Near Piazza Castelnuovo is the *Albergo Libertà* (☎ 32 19 11), Via Mariano Stabile 136, which has rooms for L30,000/50,000, or with bathroom for L50,000/75,000; triples are L75,000. There are several other hotels in the same building. The *Hotel Elite* (☎ 32 93 18) has singles/doubles/triples for L50,000/65,000/90,000, all with private bathroom. The *Hotel Boston-Madonia* (☎ 58 02 34) is slightly cheaper, with singles/doubles for L45,000/65,000 and triples for L85,000, all with bathroom. The *Hotel*

Liguria (☎ 58 15 88), Via Mariano Stabile 128, offers a good standard of accommodation. Rooms are L30,000/45,000, and doubles with private bathroom are L58,000. *Hotel Principe di Belmonte* (☎ 33 10 65), Via Principe di Belmonte 25, has rooms for L34,000/59,000, or with bathroom for L45,000/68,000.

Top End The newly renovated *Centrale Palace Hotel* (☎ 33 66 66), Via Vittorio Emanuele 327, has elegantly furnished rooms and full services. All rooms have private bathroom and breakfast is included. Singles are L92,000, doubles L144,000 and triples 190,000. The *Grande Albergo Sole* (☎ 58 18 11), Via Vittorio Emanuele 291, also offers a high standard of accommodation and all rooms are fully serviced. Singles/doubles are L90,000/140,000 and triples are L175,000.

The four-star *Grand Hotel et des Palmes* (☎ 58 39 33), Via Roma 398, at the Piazza Castelnuovo end of town, is one of the best hotels in Palermo. Its beautiful rooms are fully serviced, and singles/doubles cost L150,000/200,000, breakfast included.

Places to Eat

Palermo's cuisine takes advantage of the fresh produce of the sea and the fertile Conca d'Oro valley. One of its most famous dishes is *pasta con le sarde*, with sardines, fennel, peppers, capers and pine nuts. Swordfish is served here sliced into huge steaks. If you can stomach it, head for *Pani Cà Meusa*, at Porta Carbone on the waterfront, to try panini *con milza* (with veal innards). The famous open-air markets, the Vucciria, are held daily (except Sunday) in the narrow streets between Via Roma, Piazza San Domenico and Via Vittorio Emanuele. Here you can buy fresh fruit and vegetables, meat, cheese, seafood and virtually anything else you want. You can watch as huge, freshly caught swordfish and tuna are sliced up and sold within minutes. Numerous stalls sell steaming hot, boiled octopus.

In Via Principe di Belmonte, which is closed to traffic between Via Ruggero

Settimo and Via Roma, there are numerous cafés with outside tables, where you can linger over breakfast or lunch in summer. If you want to spend less, buy a panino in one of the many bars along Via Roma. If you don't take sugar in your coffee, tell the bartender – in Sicily it is common to sweeten coffee as a matter of course. For an expensive afternoon tea, head for *Roney*, Via della Libertà 13, Palermo's most fashionable and best known pasticceria.

For grocery supplies which can't be found at the market, try the Standa supermarket at Via della Libertà 30.

Palermitans are late eaters and restaurants rarely open for dinner before 8 pm.

Bottom End to Mid-Range One of the cheapest options for a full, sit-down meal is *Bar Monte*, a self-service pizzeria/fast-food outlet next to the tourist office in Piazza Castelnuovo. A large slice of focaccia stuffed with spinach and mozzarella costs around L3000. Slices of pizza cost around L2500, and pasta dishes and salads are also available. There is no cover charge to sit down.

Osteria Lo Bianco, Via E Amari 104, off Via Roma at the Castelnuovo end of town, has a menu which changes daily. A full meal will cost under L20,000. *Trattoria Stella*, Via Alloro 104, is in the courtyard of the old Hotel Patria. In summer the entire courtyard is filled with tables. A full meal will come to around L20,000. *Trattoria dei Vespri*, Piazza Santa Croce dei Vespri, off Via Roma, past the church of St Anna, has outside tables and excellent food for under L25,000 for a full meal. Meat and seafood are cooked on an outdoor barbecue in summer.

Trattoria Shanghai, right in the middle of the Vucciria market, is an atmospheric little place if you manage to get a table on the terrace overlooking the market. Despite its Chinese name, the trattoria serves typical Sicilian food, which is reasonably priced but not the best you will eat in Palermo. *La Cambusa* and *il Crudo e il Cotto*, both in Piazza Marina, near the port, are popular trattorias and serve good-quality meals for around L25,000.

Top End Most of the better restaurants are on the outskirts of Palermo or in nearby towns. *I Mandarini* (☎ 671 21 99) is at Pallavicino, near Mondello beach, at Via Rosario da Patanna 18. The food is good and a meal will cost at least L40,000. The locals head for Mondello to eat seafood. Try *La Barcaccia* (☎ 45 40 79), Via Piano di Gallo 4. Again, you will be lucky to eat for under L40,000.

The *Charleston* has long been known as one of Palermo's best restaurants. Its main restaurant is in Palermo at Piazza Ungheria 30, with a branch at Mondello, Viale Regina Elena. Expect to pay around L100,000 a head for a memorable meal.

Getting There & Away

Air The airport is at Punta Raisi, about 30 km west of Palermo, and is a terminal for domestic and European flights. For information about national flights, ring Alitalia on ☎ 601 91 11; for European flights, ring ☎ 59 12 75. Alitalia has an office (☎ 601 93 33) at Via della Libertà 39.

Bus The main (intercity) bus terminal is in the area around Via Paolo Balsamo, to the right as you leave the train station, for destinations throughout Sicily. SAIS and Segesta both run rapid services to Rome, costing L68,000 one way and L100,000 return. SAIS (☎ 616 60 28), which also services Agrigento, Catania, Enna and Ragusa, is at Via Balsamo 16. Segesta (☎ 616 79 19), which also services Trapani, is at Via Balsamo 26. Salemi (☎ 617 54 11), Via Rosario Gregorio 44, runs buses to Marsala. AST runs buses to Syracuse and Ragusa, as well as Cefalù and other towns throughout the province; its office (☎ 625 41 92) is at Piazza Marina 31. Numerous other firms service points throughout Sicily and most have offices in the Via Paolo Balsamo area. Their addresses and phone numbers, as well as destinations, are listed in a booklet of useful information available at the tourist office.

Train Regular trains leave from the central station in Piazza Giulio Cesare for Milazzo,

Messina, Catania and Syracuse, as well as nearby towns such as Cefalù. There are also intercity trains for Reggio di Calabria, Naples and Rome. A one-way ticket from Palermo to Rome costs L63,000, plus a L22,000 supplement for intercity trains. Train timetable information (☎ 616 18 06) is available in English at the station. There is a Transalpino office inside the station, as well as baggage-storage and public bathing facilities.

Car & Motorbike Palermo is accessible by autostrada from Messina (only partially completed) and from Catania (which passes Enna). Trapani and Marsala are also easily accessible by autostrada, while Agrigento and Palermo are linked by a good-quality state road through the interior of the island.

Boat Ferries leave from Molo Vittorio Veneto, off Via Francesco Crispi, for Cagliari (Sardinia), Naples, Livorno and Genoa (see the Getting There & Away section at the beginning of this chapter for further details). The Tirrenia office (☎ 602 11 11) is at the port in Palazzina Stella Maris. Grandi Traghetti (☎ 58 78 32), for Livorno and Genoa, is at Via M Stabile 179. Siremar (☎ 58 24 03) runs ferries and hydrofoils to Ustica and the Aeolian Islands; its office is at Via F Crispi 120. SNAV also runs a service to the Aeolian Islands; it operates through the travel agency Barbaro (☎ 33 33 33), Via Principe di Belmonte 51. There is a baggage-storage service at the Stazione Marittima at the port, open from 7 to 11 am, 12.30 to 5 pm and 7 to 8 pm.

Getting Around

To/From the Airport Taxis to the airport cost upwards of L60,000. The cheaper option is to catch one of the regular blue buses run by Prestia e Comandè, which leave from outside the train station from 5.25 am to 9.45 pm roughly every hour (a timetable is posted at the bus stop, which is to your right as you leave the train station). Buses also stop in Piazza Ruggero Settimo, in front of the Teatro Politeama. The trip takes one hour and costs L4500.

Bus Palermo's city buses (AMAT) are efficient, and most stop at the terminal in front of the train station. Tickets must be purchased before you get on the bus, from a tobacconist or at one of the booths at the terminal. They cost L1000 and are valid for one hour. A day pass costs L3000. Useful routes are:

No 7, from the train station along Via Roma to Piazza Sturzo, near Piazza Castelnuovo
No 39, from the station to the port
No 5, from under the trees diagonally left across the piazza from the train station to the Convento dei Cappuccini
No 9, from the same point to Monreale
No 14 or 77, from Piazza Sturzo to Mondello (No 3 after midnight); the special No 6 runs only in summer from the train station
No 16, from Piazza Sturzo to Sferracavallo
No 14 or 15, from Piazza Sturzo to Pallavicino
No 24, to reach the Zisa Castle

Car & Motorbike Palermo's traffic is nowhere near as chaotic as that in Naples and not as heavy as that in Rome, so you should have no fears driving in the city. The problems begin, however, when you need to park your car, since theft both of and from cars is a major problem in this city. The best advice, particularly if you want to leave luggage in the car, is to leave it in a supervised car park. There are supervised day car parks in Piazza Castelnuovo and Piazza Marina. To leave the car overnight, try Autorimessa Sant'Oliva in Piazza Sant'Oliva, near Piazza Castelnuovo (L15,000 for 24 hours), or Trinca Anna, Via Carlo Pisacane 7, near the train station (up to L18,000 for 24 hours).

Rental Most of the major car-rental firms have offices in Palermo. Europcar (☎ 32 19 49) has an office at the train station. Camper vans are available for rent from Nolocamper (☎ 20 15 29), Via Principe Paternò 119.

AROUND PALERMO

There are beaches north of the city at Mondello and Sferracavallo. **Mondello** is a popular summer gathering place for Palermitans, and Viale Regina Elena, along the beachfront, is the preferred spot for the evening stroll. There are numerous seafood restaurants, as well as stalls along the avenue selling seafood snacks. For bus information, see the Palermo Getting Around section.

Dividing Palermo from Mondello is Mt Pellegrino and the **Sanctuary of Santa Rosalia**, Palermo's patron saint. The saint lived as a hermit in a cave on the mountain, which is now the site of a 17th century shrine. Catch the No 12 bus from Piazza XIII Vittime, at the port end of Via Cavour. The sanctuary is open daily from 7 am to 7 pm.

Monreale

An absolute must is a visit to the cathedral at Monreale, about eight km south-west of Palermo and accessible by frequent city buses (see the Palermo Getting Around section). The magnificent 12th century Norman cathedral was built for King William II. It is said he did not want to be inferior to his grandfather, Roger, who was responsible for the cathedral at Cefalù and the Palatine Chapel at Palermo. Considered the finest example of Norman architecture in Sicily, the cathedral in fact incorporates Norman, Arab, Byzantine and classical elements, and, despite renovations over the centuries, remains substantially intact. The cathedral's central doorway has bronze doors by Bonanno Pisano and its north door is by Barisano di Trani. The interior of the cathedral is almost entirely covered by magnificent gilded mosaics, the work of Byzantine artisans, representing the complete cycle of the Old and New Testaments. Over the altar is a towering mosaic of Jesus Christ.

Outside the cathedral is the entrance to the cloisters, which were part of the Benedictine abbey attached to the church. There are 228 twin columns with polychrome ornamentation. Each of the Romanesque capitals is different, depicting plants, animals and fantastic motifs. The capital of the 19th column on the west aisle depicts King William II offering the cathedral to the Madonna. The cathedral is open daily from 8.30 am to 12.30

pm and 3.30 to 6.30 pm. The cloisters are open Monday to Saturday from 9.30 am to 7 pm, Sunday from 9 am to 12.30 pm. Entrance is L2000.

Cefalù

Just over an hour by train or bus from Palermo, Cefalù has one of the most attractive beaches in Sicily and is fast becoming a major tourist destination, although to date it remains unspoiled by development. The town is easily visited on a day trip from Palermo – you can wander around to see the sights for a few hours, then head for the long, sandy beach.

The AAST tourist information office is at Corso Ruggero 77, the continuation of Via Matteotti. From the train station, turn right into Via Moro to reach Via Matteotti and the old town. If you are heading for the beach, turn left and walk along Via Gramsci, which becomes Via V Martoglio. Cefalù's telephone code is 0921.

Things to See Visit the Norman **cathedral**, built by Roger II in the 12th century to fulfil a vow to God after his fleet was saved during a violent storm off Cefalù. The columns of the cathedral's twin aisles, supporting Arab-style pointed arches, have beautiful capitals. There are Byzantine mosaics on a gilded background, with a towering Christ Pancrator dominating the apse.

Off Piazza del Duomo, in Via Mandralisca, is the private **Museo Mandralisca**. Its collection includes Greek ceramics and Arab pottery, as well as paintings, notably the *Portrait of an Unknown Man* by Antonello da Messina. The museum is open daily from 9 am to 12.30 pm and 3.30 to 7 pm. Entrance is L5000.

From the old town's main street, Via Matteotti, look for the sign pointing uphill to the Temple of Diana and make the one-hour climb to the castle. Both are ruins that can be visited, but the main reason to make the climb is for the view.

Places to Stay & Eat There are several camping grounds in the area, including

Costa Ponente Internazionale (☎ 2 00 85), about three km west of town at Contrada Ogliastrillo. It costs L8500 per person and L7500 for a tent. Catch the bus from the train station heading for Lasari.

In town the only really cheap option is *Locanda Cangelosi* (☎ 2 15 91), Via Umberto 1, with singles/doubles for L24,000/30,000. *La Giara* (☎ 2 15 62), Via Vertani 40, uphill from the beach, off Corso Ruggero, has rooms for L34,000/55,000. *Baia del Capitano* (☎ 2 00 05) is in an olive grove near the beach at Mezzaforno, a few km out of town towards Palermo. Its pleasant rooms are L60,000/100,000.

Trattoria La Botte, Via Veterani 6, just off Corso Ruggero, serves full meals for around L25,000.

Getting There & Away SAIS and AST buses leave Palermo for Cefalù (see the Palermo Getting There & Away section), but both companies run only a couple of buses per day. Trains also link the two towns, but you should double-check timetables at the Palermo train information office to avoid long waits for nonexistent services.

Tindari
Farther along the coast towards Milazzo, at Cape Tindari, are the ruins of ancient Tyndaris, founded in 396 BC as a Greek settlement on a rocky promontory overlooking the sea. It was later occupied by the Romans and was destroyed by Arab invaders. The archaeological site features the remains of the city's ramparts, a Greek theatre and Roman buildings, including a house and public baths. A museum at the site houses a collection of Hellenistic statues as well as Greek and Roman pottery.

Nearby is the **Sanctuary of the Black Madonna**. Built in this century to house a statue of a black Madonna revered since Byzantine times, it is a place of pilgrimage. The archaeological site is open from 9 am to one hour before sunset.

To get to Tindari, catch a train to the town of Patti (on the Palermo-Messina line) and then a bus to the site from outside the station

(three a day, with increased services in summer).

Aeolian Islands

Also known as the Lipari Islands, the seven islands of this archipelago just north of Milazzo are volcanic in origin, and range from the well-developed tourist resort of Lipari and the understated jet-set haunt of Panarea, to the rugged Vulcano, the spectacular scenery of Stromboli and its fiercely active volcano, the fertile vineyards of Salina, and the solitude of Alicudi and Filicudi, which remain relatively undeveloped. The islands have been inhabited since the Neolithic era, when migrants sought the valuable volcanic glass, obsidian.

The Aeolian Islands (Isole Eolie) are so named because the ancient Greeks believed that they were the home of Aeolus, the god of the wind; Homer wrote of the islands in his *Odyssey*. They are noted for their rugged coastlines, violent seas, rich colours and volcanic activity.

The islands have become increasingly popular as a tourist destination in recent years, and, during the summer months, you will need to book accommodation well in advance. Out of season the best time to visit the islands is in May and early June, when it is hot enough to swim, or in September/October. Since ferries and hydrofoils operate throughout the year, it is also possible to visit the islands during the winter months. However, boat services to the outer islands can be cancelled due to heavy seas (this can happen even during summer), making Lipari, Vulcano and Salina the most reliable destinations in this period.

The postal code for the Aeolian Islands is 98055, and the telephone code is 090.

Getting There & Away
Regular boats leave for the islands from Milazzo, the closest and most convenient point of departure. Milazzo is easy to reach by bus or train from Palermo and Messina

(see the Getting There & Away section for Messina). Intercity buses terminate in Piazza della Repubblica, a five-minute walk back along Via Crispi to the port. The train station is some distance from the port and accessible by city bus.

Ferries and hydrofoils depart from the same area, and ticket offices for the companies servicing the route are along Via L Rizzo, at the port. SNAV runs hydrofoils (L16,300 one way to Lipari). Siremar runs ferries for half the price (L8700 one way, cars from L25,000 to L59,000, depending on the size), although they are slower and less regular. Siremar also runs hydrofoils to the islands and prices are the same as for SNAV.

SNAV runs hydrofoils from Palermo twice a day in summer and three times a week in the off season (L55,000 one way to Lipari), as well as from Messina, Reggio di Calabria and Naples. Siremar runs a twice-weekly ferry service from Naples (L53,800 one way), which coincides with a Rome-Naples bus service.

Alimar (associated with SNAV) runs a ferry service from Livorno to Salina and Lipari once a week. One-way tickets range from L105,000 deck class to L130,000 for a bed in a 2nd-class cabin, or L205,000 in a 1st-class cabin.

In Milazzo, the Siremar and SNAV offices are both in Via L Rizzo, opposite the port. Other useful addresses are:

Siremar
    Head office, Via Principe di Belmonte 1C, Palermo (☎ 091-58 26 88)
    c/o Tirrenia Navigazione, Stazione Marittima, Molo Angioino, Naples (☎ 081-720 14 38)
    c/o Tirrenia Navigazione, Via Bissolati 41, Rome (☎ 06-481 47 79)
SNAV
    Aliscafi SNAV, Via Caracciolo 10, Naples (☎ 081-761 23 48)
    Aliscafi SNAV, Via S Raineri 22, Messina (☎ 090-77 75)
    Alimar, Stazione Marittima, Livorno (☎ 0586-88 07 33)

Getting Around

Regular hydrofoil and ferry services operate between the islands, although they can be disrupted to the outer islands by heavy seas. Examples of one-way fares and sailing times from Lipari are:

Alicudi L22,700 and 1½ hours (hydrofoil), or L12,300 and 3¼ hours (ferry)
Panarea L9800 and 30 minutes (hydrofoil), or L5300 and one hour (ferry)
Stromboli L19,500 and 50 minutes (hydrofoil), or L10,500 and 2¾ hours (ferry)

Both Siremar and SNAV have ticket offices in the same building at Marina Corta on Lipari, on the pier where hydrofoils arrive and depart. Full timetable information is available at both offices.

LIPARI

This is the largest and most developed of the islands, and the most popular with tourists. Its main town, also called Lipari, has the typical appearance of a Mediterranean village, with pastel-coloured houses grouped around its two harbours. The town is well equipped for the annual summer invasion of tourists, making it the most convenient and comfortable base for exploring the islands. Once the centre of the obsidian trade, it is now a centre of pumice-stone (another volcanic product) mining.

Orientation

The township of Lipari is the main port and most important town in the archipelago. Its two harbours, Marina Lunga and Marina Corta, are on either side of the cliff-top castle, surrounded by 16th century walls, and the town centre extends between them. Ferries dock at the Marina Lunga on the far side of the castle. The town's main street, Corso Vittorio Emanuele, is to the left of the port. Hydrofoils dock at Marina Corta, and from here, you should walk diagonally to the right across the piazza to Via Garibaldi and follow the 'centro' signs to reach Corso V Emanuele.

Information

Tourist Office The AAST tourist information office (☎ 988 00 95) is at Corso

Vittorio Emanuele 233. It is the main tourist office for the archipelago, although offices open on Stromboli, Vulcano and Salina during summer. The office will assist with finding accommodation, a service which can be particularly useful during the busy summer months. You can also pick up a copy of *Ospitalità in blu*, which contains details of accommodation and services on all of the islands. The office is open Monday to Saturday from 8 am to 2 pm and 4.30 to 7.30 pm.

Money There are several banks in Lipari, including the Banca del Sud in Corso V Emanuele. Using a Visa card to obtain cash advances should present no problems, but there are no facilities for cash advances on MasterCard. Outside banking hours, exchange facilities can be found at the post office.

Post & Telecommunications The post office is at Corso V Emanuele 207, near the tourist office, and is open Monday to Saturday from 8 am to 6 pm. Public telephones can be found throughout the township, or you can use the facilities at the small shop at Via Maurolico 10, off Corso V Emanuele.

Emergency In a medical emergency, contact the hospital (☎ 9 88 51) or Pronto Soccorso (First Aid) on ☎ 988 52 67. The emergency number for police attendance is ☎ 113, or you can call the police station on ☎ 981 13 33.

Things to See & Do
The **castle**, surrounded by massive walls built in the 16th century after Turkish pirates raided Lipari, is an obvious starting point of a historical tour of the island. It stands on the site of an ancient acropolis, which now forms part of an **archaeological park** within the castle complex. Excavations of the area have unearthed buildings dating back to more than 1700 BC. There are several churches in the area, the most interesting being the **cathedral**, between the castle and the **Museo Archeologico Eoliano**. Originally a Norman structure, the cathedral was destroyed

during the pirate raid in 1544 and was rebuilt more than a century later. Its interior is Baroque and its façade was completed in 1861. Excavations have uncovered part of the original 12th century Norman cloisters.

The museum is particularly interesting. Its well-organised exhibits, which include a collection of Neolithic pottery, trace the chronological history of the islands. There is also a section tracing their volcanic history. It is open from 9 am to 2 pm Monday to Friday, to 1 pm Sunday. Entry is free.

It is also worth exploring the island, in particular for views of Salina, Alicudi and Filicudi from the rugged, windy cliffs of Lipari's north-west corner. Sunbathers and swimmers head for **Canneto** and the Spiaggia Bianca (White Beach), a few km north of the Lipari township. In summer there are canoes and small boats for rent along the beach. Farther along the coast are the pumice mines of **Pomiciazzo** and **Porticello**, where there is another beach.

Continuing along the coast you will reach **Quattropani**, a good place to stop and take in the view. Just before the village of Pianoconte you can turn off for **San Calogero** and the thermal baths, famous during Roman times. Back on the main road, stop at Quattrocchi, the island's most famous viewpoint, from where you have a magnificent view of Vulcano and the Faraglioni, strange monoliths of volcanic rock which were formed when lava was thrown from the volcanoes of Lipari into the sea.

The trip around the island is much easier if you have a car or motorbike. Buses service the island, or you can make a few trips on foot. It is also possible to circumnavigate Lipari by boat (see the following Getting Around section for further details).

Scuba diving and sailing are both popular activities. For information on courses, contact the Centro Nautico Eoliano (☎ 981 21 10), Salita San Giuseppe 8, or the tourist office. The tourist office can also advise on interesting walks around the island.

Places to Stay
Lipari provides the best options for a com-

fortable stay in the archipelago. It has numerous hotels, private rooms and apartments, ranging from the budget to the luxurious. Prices go up quite significantly in summer, particularly during the peak period of August, although it should still be possible to find reasonably priced rooms if you book well in advance. The tourist office is usually very willing to assist in finding accommodation, and, during the peak season, staff will billet new arrivals in private homes throughout the island.

When you arrive on Lipari, you are likely to be approached by one of the many people offering rooms. These can be either in a pensione-type establishment or in private homes. They're worth checking because they are usually genuine and provide the best bargains.

To rent an apartment on the island, you will need to contact the tourist office for a list of establishments.

Bottom End The island's camping ground, the *Baia Unci* (☎ 981 19 09), is at Canneto, about two km out of the Lipari township and accessible by bus from the Esso service station at Marina Lunga. Once all the individual charges are added up, it is an expensive option – L8500 per person per night, L3000 for a car, L3000 for electric light and L8500 for your tent or caravan. The IYHF *youth hostel* (☎ 981 15 40), Via Castello 17, is inside the walls of the castle. Bed and breakfast costs L13,000 per person and there are kitchen facilities.

Cassarà Vittorio (☎ 981 15 23), Vico Sparviero 15, off Via Garibaldi near Marina Corta, is excellent value at L15,000 per person in the low season and L30,000 in the high season. There are two terraces with views, and use of the kitchen is L2000. The owner can be found (unless he finds you first) at Via Garibaldi 78, on the way from the port to the city centre. *Locanda Salina* (☎ 981 23 32), Via Garibaldi 18, is also very close to Marina Corta. It has reasonable singles/doubles for L30,000/55,000 and triples with bathroom for L75,000. Ask for a room with a view of the sea. *Enzo il negro*

(☎ 981 31 63) at Via Garibaldi 29 has lovely, newly renovated rooms for L35,000 per person. All rooms have private bathrooms and there is a large terrace.

Middle *Pensione Neri* (☎ 981 14 13), Via G Marconi 43, off Corso V Emanuele, is in a lovely old villa. In the low season, a double costs L75,000 and triples/quads L95,000/115,000; in summer, prices jump to L107,000 a double, L137,000 a triple and L167,000 for a quad. All rooms have private bathrooms and breakfast is included in the price. The owners also have apartments for rent on Salina (see the Salina section).

The *Hotel Oriente* (☎ 981 14 93) is next door at Via Marconi 35. It has a bar and garden, and very comfortable rooms. Prices vary according to the period and range from L45,000 to L75,000 for a single, L60,000 to L120,000 for a double, L80,000 to 160,000 for a triple, and L100,000 to L200,000 for a quad. All rooms have private bathrooms and prices include breakfast. *Hotel Villa Augustus* (☎ 981 12 32) is in Vico Ausonia, off Corso V Emanuele near the Marina Lunga. It has very good rooms, and many open onto a lovely garden (although mosquitoes can be a problem). Again, prices vary according to the period. Singles range from L45,000 to L80,000 and doubles from L80,000 to L150,000. It also offers half pension, ranging from L70,000 per person in the low season to L120,000 in the high season.

Top End Lipari's top hotel is the *Villa Meligunis* (☎ 981 24 26) in Via Marte, on a hill overlooking Marina Corta. It has a terrace restaurant and bar overlooking the sea, and all rooms have full services. According to the season, prices range from L120,000 to L198,000 for a single, L154,000 to L264,000 for a double, and L209,000 to 352,000 for a triple.

Places to Eat

Try a pasta dish prepared with the islands' excellent capers, and be prepared to spend the money to eat freshly caught fish, particularly swordfish. The waters of the archipelago abound in many varieties of fish, including tuna, mullet, cuttlefish and sole, and restaurants include fresh daily catches on their menus. The local wine is the white Malvasia.

People with the good fortune to have access to a kitchen can shop for supplies at the grocery shops along Corso V Emanuele, and at the UPIM supermarket next to the tourist office.

Although prices go up during the peak season, you can still eat surprisingly cheaply on Lipari by sticking to the pizzerias along Corso Emanuele. *Il Galeone*, Corso V Emanuele 222, has good pizzas for around L8000, as well as a full menu. *Zum Willi*, on the corner of Corso Emanuele and Via Umberto I, is basically a bar which serves good pizzas for L6000 to L10,000. For a good meal, eat at *Trattoria D'Oro*, Corso Umberto I 28-32. Nice touches such as complimentary apéritif and hors d'oeuvres make it a pleasant place to dine. A full meal will come to around L25,000, and there is a good-value tourist menu.

Da Bartolo, Via Garibaldi 53, is certainly one of the island's better trattorias and a good choice for seafood. A full meal is more expensive here, at around L30,000 or more, since there are both cover and service charges.

Near Marina Corta, in Via Roma, there are two trattorias which serve good-quality food typical of the islands. *Nenzyna* at No 4 is tiny, so arrive early in summer. You could get away with under L20,000 for a full meal. *A Sfiziusa* at No 31 has similar prices.

Getting There & Away
See the previous Getting There & Away section for the Aeolian Islands.

Getting Around
Urso Guglielmo buses leave from the Esso service station at Marina Lunga for Canneto (10 a day, more frequently in summer), Porticello (seven a day) and Quattroccho (eight a day). There is also a tourist service run by the same company, which makes a round trip of the island. Contact the tourist office for precise details on timetables.

Boats and scooters are available for hire at Foti Roberto (☎ 981 23 52), Via F Crispi, to the right as you leave Marina Lunga. A Vespa costs L25,000 a day and a motorino is L20,000 a day. A motorised rubber dinghy costs L90,000 a day.

SEN (Società Eolie di Navigazione, ☎ 981 23 41), Corso V Emanuele 247, conducts a boat tour around the islands of Lipari and Salina (L30,000 per person), as well as to the other islands. For more information on inter-island connections, see the previous Getting Around section for the Aeolian Islands.

VULCANO
Just south of Lipari, and the first port of call for ferries and hydrofoils, Vulcano is known for its therapeutic mud baths and hot springs. It was known in ancient times as Thermessa, Terasia and Hiera, and was believed to be the workshop of the fire god Vulcan. It was also believed to be the home of the wind god Aeolus.

Vulcano has three volcanoes. The oldest of the three, at the island's southernmost point, was already extinct in ancient times. However, the youngest, Vulcanello, next to the mud baths at the north-east tip of the island, rose from the sea in the 2nd century BC, according to Pliny. The only active volcano is the Gran Cratere, which has a number of fumaroles and whose smoking crater is clearly visible as you arrive at the island.

Despite all of this volcanic activity, Vulcano is a much more relaxed place to stay than Lipari, but people intending to stay on the island should note that it is impossible to escape the all-pervading smell of sulphurous gasses.

Orientation & Information
Boats dock at the Porto di Levante, under the smoking Gran Cratere. To the right as you face the island is the small Vulcanello peninsula. All of the island's facilities are concentrated in the small area between the

Porto di Levante and the Porto di Ponente, where you will find the only smooth, sandy beach on the islands, the Spiaggia Sabbia Nera (Black Sand Beach). It is only a five to 10-minute walk from one port to the other along Via Piano, Via Provinciale and past Vulcanello along Via Porto Ponente.

There is a tourist information office only in summer; ring ☎ 985 20 28 for details. The post office is in Via Piano on the way to Vulcanello. For medical assistance, ring ☎ 985 22 20, and for the police, ☎ 985 21 10.

Activities

There are three activities on Vulcano: climbing the Gran Cratere, lazing in the mud baths, or swimming at the Spiaggia Sabbia Nera. To climb the volcano, turn left from the Porto Levante and follow the road until you reach the cobblestone path which runs off to the left. About halfway up the volcano there is a wire fence and the track forks around it. Bear to the right and follow the path through the bushes. The climb is not demanding and it will take around an hour to reach the crater, but in summer you should avoid making the climb during the hotter part of the day.

The Laghetto di Fanghi (Mud Pool) next to Vulcanello is something of a mecca for people seeking cures for various skin problems. Even if you have no need of a cure, it is very relaxing to lie in the hot, sulphurous mud, but remember to wear an old swimming costume and to remove all jewellery except gold (the sulphur blackens silver). After the mud bath, take a dip in the sea nearby, where underwater volcanic springs create a jacuzzi effect.

Boats and paddle boats are available for rent from the Acquacalda Bar, across from the mud baths. A small boat costs L80,000 a day, while paddle boats are available for L12,000 an hour. SEN offers a boat trip around the island for L15,000 per person. In summer it operates a small information booth on Via Porto Levante, otherwise information is available on Lipari.

Places to Stay & Eat

The island's camping ground is *Eden Park*

(☎ 985 21 20), near the Spiaggia Sabbia Nera (follow the signs from the mud-bath area). It is no great bargain at L15,000 per person, plus L5000 to put up your tent. There are also double rooms for L80,000 (L50,000 if you have sleeping bags and are aged under 26), and apartments ranging in price from L490,000 per week in the low season to L900,000 per week in the high season.

The *Pensione Agostino* (☎ 985 23 42), Via Favaloro 1, is close to the Laghetto di Fanghi and has doubles up to L60,000, depending on the season, with bathroom. *Pensione La Giara* (☎ 985 22 29), Via Provinciale 18, is towards the Gran Cratere. A pleasant establishment, its rooms cost around L80,000 a double, although the management prefers to charge by the week. *Sea Houses Residence* (☎ 985 22 19), very close to the mud baths, is a complex of self-contained three, four and five-bed apartments in a garden setting. For a four-bed apartment, prices range from around L500,000 a week from April to mid-June, to L1,500,000 in August.

For a decent meal, try *Da Maurizio* or *Da Vincenzino*, both in Via Porto di Levante.

Getting There & Away

Ticket offices for Siremar and SNAV are both at the Porto di Levante. See the general Getting There & Away information at the beginning of this Aeolian Islands section for further information.

Getting Around

The best way to make your way around Vulcano is on foot. However, scooters and bicycles are available for rent from Pino Marturano (☎ 985 24 19), Via Comunale Levante, just near the Porto di Levante. A motorino costs L35,000 a day and a Vespa L45,000 a day. The proprietor of Gioelli del Mare (☎ 985 21 70) at Porto di Levante organises bus tours around the island, but for groups of at least 12 people. Just make a booking and hope that a large enough group will form. The tour costs L12,000 per person.

SALINA

Just north-west of Lipari, Salina is the most

fertile of the islands and consists of two volcanoes, Monte dei Porri and Monte Fosse delle Felci, both extinct. The high cliffs of its coastline are topped with vineyards where most of the islands' sweet Malvasia wine is produced.

Orientation & Information

Boats dock at Santa Marina Salina, where you will find most of the island's accommodation, or at Rinella, a small fishing village on the south coast. The other main villages on the island are Malfa, on the north coast, and Leni, slightly inland from Rinella.

The Coop Salina '80 (☎ 984 31 90), Via Risorgimento 152, Santa Marina Salina, provides a tourist information service, or you can contact the tourist office on Lipari. During summer there are AAST information booths at Rinella, Malfa and Santa Marina Salina. For medical assistance, ring ☎ 984 40 05, and for the police, ☎ 984 30 19.

Things to See & Do

If you are feeling energetic, climb the Fosse delle Felci volcano. From Santa Marina Salina, head for Lingua, a small village about three km south, from where paths lead up the mountain.

The **Sanctuary of the Madonna del Terzito** at Valdichiesa, just south of Malfa, is a place of pilgrimage, particularly during the Feast of the Assumption on 15 August.

Rinella is a popular underwater-fishing spot. For information, contact the tourist office or the Centro Nautico Salina (☎ 980 90 33), Via Rotabile 2, at Leni. The Blu Salina Diving Centre (same phone number) at Rinella conducts week-long diving courses from April to September (excluding August) for around L450,000 per person. It also rents motorised rubber dinghies for up to L130,000 a day. Boats are also available for rent from Centro Nautico Levante (☎ 984 31 92), Via E Gerace 13, Santa Marina Salina.

Places to Stay & Eat

The *Camping Tre Pini* (☎ 980 91 55 or 980 90 00) is on the beach at Rinella. It costs L8000 per person, plus L8000 for your tent and L3000 for electric light. *Pensione Mamma Santina* (☎ 984 30 54) is at Via Sanità 26 in Santa Marina Salina. Walk a short distance to the right from the port to reach Via Sanità. Singles/doubles are L35,000/55,000 and a double with bath is L70,000. In summer, half pension is obligatory at L80,000 per person. *Catena De Pasquale* (☎ 984 30 94), Via F Crispi, in Santa Marina Salina, has only six rooms, but all have private bathroom, terrace and facilities for cooking for L30,000 per person.

Hotel Ariana (☎ 980 90 75) is in a turn-of-the-century villa at Via Rotabile 11, overlooking the sea at Rinella. It has terraces and a bar. Half pension ranges from L66,000 in the low season to L102,000 in the high season, and full pension ranges from L87,000 to L119,000.

Apartments are available for rent at Santa Marina Salina at the *Hibiscus Residence Club* (☎ 67 44 68 or 981 17 95). An apartment for four or five people with garden costs L2,500,000 a month in the low season and up to L4,000,000 in August.

Pensione Mamma Santina is also a trattoria, where a full meal will cost around L25,000, and up to L40,000 if you order fish.

Getting There & Away

Both Siremar and SNAV have ticket offices at the port at Santa Marina Salina. For further details, see the general Getting There & Away information for the Aeolian Islands.

Getting Around

Regular buses run from Santa Marina Salina to Malfa and Lingua. Buses also run from Malfa to Leni and Rinella. Motorbikes are available for rent from Bongiorno Antonio (☎ 984 33 08), Via Pozzo d'Agnello, Santa Marina Salina. A Vespa costs L30,000 a day and a motorino L27,000 a day.

PANAREA

Easily the most picturesque of the islands, Panarea is tiny – only three km long and two km wide – and therefore easily explored on foot. It is a haunt of the jet set, which makes it generally overpriced, and there are only a few reasonably priced options at San Pietro, where boats dock.

There is no tourist office on the island, so contact the AAST on Lipari. For medical assistance, ring ☎ 98 30 40. Police are in attendance only during summer and can be contacted on ☎ 98 31 81.

Things to See & Do

After wandering around San Pietro, head south from the village to the Punta Milazzese, about half an hour to 40 minutes' walk (there is a small beach along the way), to see the Bronze-Age village discovered there in 1948. Pottery found at the site is now in the museum at Lipari. Rent a boat at the port to explore the coves and beaches of the island, which are otherwise inaccessible.

Places to Stay & Eat

The *Locanda Rodà* (☎ 98 30 06) in Via San Pietro, uphill from the port and to the left, has rooms for L35,000 per person. Half pension is L100,000 per person in August and L60,000 in the low season. *Hotel Tesoriero* (☎ 98 30 98), Via C Lani, just up from the port, has rooms for L45,000 per person with breakfast, or L30,000 without. Prices jump to L70,000 per person in July/August. *La Sirena* (☎ 98 30 12) is at Via Drautt 4, on the way to the beach and the Bronze-Age village. A lovely little place, it charges L70,000 per person for half pension in the low season and L90,000 per person in July/August. Back at the port, *Lisca Bianca* (☎ 98 30 04), Via Lani 1, has doubles with private bathroom and terrace for L120,000.

The *Locanda Rodà* is also a pizzeria/trattoria which charges average prices. *La Sirena* is also a pleasant trattoria. In the same area is *Trattoria da Nunzio*, with a terrace overlooking the sea. At each of these establishments a full meal should cost between L20,000 and L35,000.

Getting There & Away

Ticket offices for Siremar and SNAV are at the port. For further details, see the general Getting There & Away information for the Aeolian Islands.

Getting Around

The only way to get around Panarea is on foot, but the size of the island means this is hardly a demanding exercise.

STROMBOLI

Without doubt the most spectacular of the Aeolian islands, Stromboli is literally a volcano rising out of the sea. One of the most active volcanoes in Europe, Stromboli erupts almost constantly and these explosions of molten rock are an unforgettable spectacle at night. Lava flow is confined to the Sciara del Fuoco (Trail of Fire) on the volcano's northwestern flank, which means that the villages of San Bartolo, San Vincenzo and Scari (which merge into one town) to the east and Ginostra to the south are quite safe.

While Stromboli is probably the most interesting of the Aeolian Islands, it is not the most convenient as a base. Even by hydrofoil it is about an hour from Lipari and boats can be cancelled due to heavy seas. Spending at least a day or two on the island is, however, highly recommended.

Orientation & Information

Boats arrive at Scari/San Vincenzo, downhill from the township. Accommodation is a short walk up the Scalo Scari to Via Roma, or, if you plan to head straight for the crater, follow the road along the waterfront (see the following section for details).

There is a tourist office open only in summer, otherwise go to the AAST on Lipari. The post office is in Via Roma. The only bank, in Via Nunziante at Ficogrande, is open only from June to September, otherwise exchange facilities are available at the travel agency, Le Isole e Terme d'Italia in Via Roma near the port. For medical attention, ring ☎ 98 60 97, and for the police, ☎ 98 60 21.

Things to See & Do

The main reason to come to Stromboli is to climb up the **volcano** to see the explosive crater and the Sciara del Fuoco. From the port, follow the road along the waterfront, continuing straight ahead past the Centro Mare Stromboli and the beach at Ficogrande. Once past the village the path heads uphill, after about 20 minutes deviating to a bar/pizzeria and observatory. Alternatively, follow it through a slightly confusing section of reeds until it starts to make the ascent to the crater. About halfway up, there is a good view of the Sciara del Fuoco, although during the day it is not possible to see the glow of the molten lava. The path eventually becomes quite steep and rocky. Once you reach the summit, note the warning signs and do not go too close to the edge of the crater.

A round trip to the crater from the village should take about four hours. It is certainly more spectacular to make the climb at night, when the molten lava of the Sciara del Fuoco is visible and the volcanic explosions are something to experience. It is possible to make the climb during the day without a guide, even though the tourist office claims that it is forbidden, but night climbers would be wise to enlist help.

Experienced guides can be contacted through the Club Alpino Italiano office (☎ 98 62 63), just off Piazza San Vincenzo. They take groups of 10 people or more to the crater daily at 6 pm (depending on the weather conditions and whether or not a group of 10 can be formed), returning at 11.30 pm (L20,000 per person). It is necessary to contact the office around midday to make a booking. For the night climb, you will need heavy shoes and clothing for cold, wet weather, a torch (flashlight) and a good supply of water, as well as something to eat. Even during the day, you will need to be equipped with heavy, wet-weather clothing, as weather conditions can be unpredictable.

The Società Navigazione Stromboli (☎ 98 61 35) organises nightly boat trips to view the Sciara del Fuoco from the sea. The boat (named *Pippo*) leaves nightly at 10 pm from Ficogrande. SEN offers a similar boat trip, which originates in Lipari, departing from the Stromboli ferry port for the Sciara del Fuoco at 8.30 pm. The same boat also heads out to **Strombolicchio**, a towering rock rising out of the sea north of San Vincenzo. The rock is a popular spot for underwater fishing.

For those who prefer water sports, the Centro Mare Stromboli (☎ 98 61 56), Via V Nunziante 26 (on the way to the volcano), has canoes, sailboards, catamarans and sailing boats for rent. It also offers windsurfing and sailing courses. Diving Centro Mare (☎ 98 60 18) at the Hotel Villaggio Stromboli, Via Regina Elena, on the waterfront towards Ficogrande, offers diving courses. La Sirenetta Diving Center (☎ 98 60 25) at La Sirenetta Park Hotel, Via Marina 33, offers seven-day diving courses for L350,000. Otherwise it costs L50,000 an hour to rent an oxygen tank, boat and guide. Sailing courses cost L180,000 for seven lessons.

Alternatively, make your way to the beautiful beach of rocks and black volcanic sand at **Ficogrande** to swim and sunbathe.

Places to Stay & Eat

The *Casa del Sole* (☎ 98 60 17) is in Via G Cincotta, off the road leading to the volcano, before reaching the Ficogrande beach. Simple rooms cost L25,000 per person (L30,000 in August) with use of communal bathroom and kitchen facilities. *Locanda Stella* (☎ 98 60 20), Via Fabio Filzi 14, has doubles for L50,000 and charges L77,000 for obligatory half pension in July/August. Down the road at Via Vittorio Emanuele 17 is *Barbablù* (☎ 98 61 18), a very pleasant pensione charging L80,000 to L150,000 a double, depending on the season. *Pensione Roma* (☎ 98 60 88) has simple singles/doubles for up to L35,000/60,000. *Hotel Villaggio Stromboli* (☎ 98 60 18) has rooms for L60,000/100,000 in the high season. It is on the beach front and has a terrace bar/restaurant. More up-market is *La Sirenetta* (☎ 98 60 25), built in the typical Mediterranean style of box-like, whitewashed buildings. It has lovely rooms in a garden setting, starting at L70,000/140,000; in August, obligatory half pension costs L160,000 per person.

Top : Butcher's shop, Cosenza, Calabria (COASIT)
Bottom Left : Vucciria markets, Palermo, Sicily (COASIT)
Bottom Right : Drying peppers, Basilicata (COASIT)

Sardinia

For a reasonably priced meal, try *La Trottola* in Via Roma. The *Punta Lena* on the Lungomare, walking away from the port towards the volcano, is more expensive and has a terrace overlooking the sea. The pizzeria (☎ 98 60 13) at the observatory, about 20 minutes' walk up the volcano (see the previous Things to See & Do section), is open for dinner and will take bookings for lunch.

Getting There & Away
As already mentioned, Stromboli is a fair distance from the other islands, and ferry/hydrofoil connections can be cancelled due to heavy seas. The return trip from Lipari is also reasonably expensive (L21,000 by ferry and L39,000 by hydrofoil). Ticket offices for SNAV and Siremar are at the port. For further information, see the general Getting Around information for the Aeolian Islands.

FILICUDI & ALICUDI
You will really need to have a strong desire to get away from it all if you decide to stay on either of these islands west of Lipari. Apart from the fact that facilities are limited (severely limited on Alicudi), ferries and hydrofoils can be cancelled due to heavy seas, even in summer.

Filicudi is the larger of the two and its attractions include the Grotta del Bue Marino (Grotto of the Monk Seal) and the La Canna rock pinnacle, about one km off the island towards Alicudi. On Cape Graziano, south of the port, are the remains of a prehistoric village, its huts dating back as far as 1800 BC. Boats are available for rent if you want to explore the grotto, and scuba-diving courses are available in summer.

For medical attention, ring ☎ 988 99 61, and for police assistance, ☎ 988 99 42. The island has only two hotels. *La Canna* (☎ 988 99 56), Via Rosa 43, just uphill from the port, has singles/doubles for L45,000/60,000 and half pension for up to L95,000 in the high season. *Phenicusa* (☎ 988 99 46) in Via Porto has rooms for L45,000/70,000 and half pension for up to L122,000.

Alicudi is the island most distant from Lipari and the least developed of the Aeolian group. Facilities on the island are limited. There is only one hotel, the *Ericusa* (☎ 988 99 02) in Via Regina Elena. Doubles cost L60,000 and half pension is L85,000. It is open only during the summer months and bookings are strongly advised. The hotel includes the island's only restaurant. For medical assistance, ring ☎ 988 99 13.

While on the island, make the trek up Mt Filo dell'Arpa to see the crater of the extinct Montagnola volcano and the Timpone delle Femmine, fissures where it is said women took refuge during pirate raids.

Getting There & Away
As already mentioned, boat services to the islands can be cancelled due to heavy seas and this should be taken into account when planning your stay. The return fare to Alicudi, L24,600 on the ferry and L45,400 by hydrofoil, as well as the distance from Lipari, should be taken into consideration if you are thinking about making only a day trip to the island.

The East Coast

MESSINA
The main point of arrival for most tourists in Sicily, Messina does not give the best impression of the island. Devastated and destroyed many times over the centuries, the city is basically modern and has few sights of interest to offer. Known to the ancient Greeks as Zankle (Sickle) for its beautiful curved harbour, it grew into a splendid city as a Greek colony and later thrived under Roman domination, the Byzantines and into the Middle Ages under the Normans. The city was devastated several times during the 18th and 19th centuries, first by plague, then cholera and finally by earthquakes, including the massive 1908 earthquake which almost entirely destroyed the city and killed more than 80,000 people in the region. The city was rebuilt, only to be again destroyed

Greek terracotta Gorgon found on Sicily

by both Allied and Axis bombing during WW II.

If you find it necessary to pass some time in Messina while waiting for transport connections, don't despair. The city centre with its wide avenues is a pleasant place to wander around, and there remain a couple of interesting monuments.

Orientation

Arriving by train or ferry, you will land at the port area, where both the main train station and the maritime station are located in the same complex in Piazza della Repubblica. The main intercity bus terminal is outside the station to the left in the piazza. To get to the city centre, walk either straight across the piazza and directly ahead along Via I Settembre to the Piazza del Duomo, or turn left into Via G Farina and then the first right into Via Cannazzaro to reach Piazza Cairoli.

Information

Tourist Office There is a municipal information office (☎ 090-67 29 44) in Piazza della Repubblica, to the right as you leave the station, and an AAPIT tourist office (☎ 090-67 53 56) a bit farther along at Via Calabria 301. Both have extensive information on Messina, its province and Sicily in general, and the AAPIT's young staff are particularly helpful. Pick up a map, booklet of useful information and list of hotels.

Money There are numerous major banks in the city centre, and an exchange booth at the train-timetable information office at the station.

Post & Telecommunications The main post office is in Piazza Antonello, on Corso Cavour near the cathedral. The postal code for central Messina is 98100.

There is an ASST telephone office to the right as you leave the station (open from 8 am to 10 pm), and in Corso Cavour, near Via Cannazzaro (open 24 hours). The telephone code for Messina is 090.

Emergency For police attendance, call ☎ 113. For medical assistance, go to the public hospital, the Ospedale Piemonte (☎ 22 21) in Viale Europa; at nights, ring ☎ 67 50 48. A booklet is available at the tourist office, which lists pharmacies open at night on a rotation basis.

Dangers & Annoyances Petty crime is a problem in Messina and you should keep your money and other valuables in a money belt. Women on their own are advised against walking along the streets at night.

Things to See & Do

The Norman **cathedral**, built in the 12th century, was almost completely destroyed by the combined effects of the 1908 earthquake and WW II bombing. It has been rebuilt and features a fine 15th century doorway, and a clock tower housing what is believed to be the world's largest astronomical clock, which strikes daily at midday. In the Piazza del Duomo is the **Fontana di Orione**, an elegant 16th century work by Angelo Montorsoli. Nearby, in Piazza Catalani, off Via Garibaldi, is the lovely 12th century **Church of SS Annunziata dei Catalani**.

The **Museo Regionale** is a long walk along Viale della Libertà, or catch bus No 8 from the train station. It houses many inter-

esting works of art, including the *Virgin & Child with Saints* by Antonello da Messina, who was born in Messina in 1430.

Places to Stay & Eat

The *Roma* (☎ 67 55 66), Piazza del Duomo 3, has singles/doubles for L13,000/20,000. *Hotel Monza* (☎ 67 37 55), Viale San Martino 63, has a higher standard of accommodation, with singles/doubles for L55,000/90,000 and triples for L121,000, all with private bathroom. The *Hotel Excelsior* (☎ 293 13 41), Via Maddalena 32, has singles/doubles for L36,000/66,000, or L60,000/98,000 with private bathroom.

La Trappola, Via dei Verdi 39, is near the university area. Its good meals are reasonably priced, but not rock-bottom. *Trattoria del Padrino*, Via Santa Cecilia 54, is another good place to eat.

Getting There & Away

Bus SAIS (☎ 77 19 14) runs a regular service (approximately every hour) to Taormina, Catania and Catania's airport. The company's office and bus terminal are to the left as you leave the station. There is also a direct bus connection to Rome (see the general Getting There & Away information at the beginning of this Sicily chapter). Giuntabus (☎ 67 37 82) runs a service to Milazzo (for the connection with ferries and hydrofoils for the Aeolian Islands) roughly every hour from Via Terranova 8, on the corner of Viale San Martino.

Train Regular trains connect Messina with Catania, Taormina, Syracuse, Palermo and Milazzo, but there are often long delays and it is generally faster to catch a bus. It should also be noted that the train stations for Milazzo and Taormina are inconveniently located some distance from the city centre.

Boat Regular ferries cross the Strait of Messina between Reggio di Calabria on the mainland and Messina, arriving at Messina in the same complex as the main train station. SNAV hydrofoils run between Messina and Reggio di Calabria, as well as to the Aeolian

Islands. The hydrofoil port is on Corso Vittorio Emanuele II, about one km north of the train station. For further information, see the general Getting There & Away and Getting Around information at the beginning of this Sicily chapter.

Car & Motorbike If you arrive in Messina by ferry with a vehicle, it is fairly simple to make your way out of town. If you are heading for Palermo, or to Milazzo to make the crossing to the Aeolian Islands, turn right as you exit the docks and follow the road along the seafront, Viale Garibaldi. Turn left after about one km into Viale Boccetta and follow the green autostrada signs for Palermo. To reach Taormina, Syracuse etc, turn left from the docks into Via Farina and follow the autostrada signs for Catania.

If arriving by car to catch a ferry, there are clear signs around the train/maritime station directing you to the ferry dock.

TAORMINA

Spectacularly located on a terrace of Mt Tauro, overlooking the sea and the fuming Mt Etna, Taormina is easily Sicily's most picturesque town. Since it was founded by the Siculians, Taormina was a favoured settlement of the long line of Sicily's conquerors and colonisers. Under the Greeks, who moved here after Naxos was destroyed during colonial wars in the 5th century BC, Taormina flourished. It later came under Roman dominion and eventually became the capital of Byzantine Sicily, a period of grandeur which ended abruptly in 902 AD when the town was conquered and destroyed by Arab invaders. The town remained an important centre of art and trade throughout the various periods of Norman, Spanish and French rule in Sicily.

Long ago discovered by the European jet set, Taormina is one of the more expensive and heavily touristed towns in Sicily. It is well served by hotels, pensioni and eating places, but unfortunately the town takes its tourism industry a little too seriously and it might be just a bit too glitzy for the tastes of some travellers. However, its magnificent

setting, its Greek Theatre and the nearby beaches remain as seductive now as they were for the likes of Goethe and D H Lawrence.

Orientation

If you arrive by train, you will find yourself at the bottom of Mt Tauro, looking quite a distance up to Taormina. It is too far to walk uphill, but regular SAIS buses carry new arrivals to the bus station (for local and intercity buses) in Via Pirandello. A short walk uphill will bring you to the entrance to the old city and Corso Umberto I, which traverses the town.

Information

Tourist Office The AAST tourist office (☎ 0942-2 32 43) is in the Corvaja Palace, just off the main street, Corso Umberto, near Largo Santa Caterina.

Money There are several banks in Taormina, most of them along Corso Umberto. Out of banking hours, use the exchange facilities at the CIT office, Corso Umberto 101, or Silvestri's, Corso Umberto 145.

Post & Telecommunications The main post office is in Piazza Sant'Antonio, just outside the Porta Catania, at the far end of Corso Umberto from the tourist office. There are public telephone facilities in the Avis Rent-a-Car office, Via San Pancrazio 6, to your right off Via Pirandello at the entrance to the old town. Taormina's postal code is 98039 and the telephone code is 0942.

Emergency There is a free night-time medical service for tourists (☎ 62 54 19) in Piazza San Francesco di Paola. The hospital, the Ospedale San Vincenzo (☎ 57 91), is in Piazza San Vincenzo, just outside the Porta Catania. For emergency first aid, ring ☎ 5 37 45; for the police, ☎ 113, and for the carabinieri, ☎ 112.

Things to See & Do

The **Greek Theatre** at the end of Via Teatro Greco, off Corso Umberto, was built during the Hellenistic period in the 3rd century BC. It was later greatly expanded and remodelled by the Romans, and is thus basically a Roman structure, despite its name. In the final years of the empire, the theatre ceased to be used for performances and instead became an amphitheatre for gladiator fighting. It is the second-largest amphitheatre in Italy, after the Greek Theatre at Syracuse. The structure has been much interfered with, destroyed and restored over the centuries – in fact, the family of the Spanish Costanza d'Aragona built their home in the 12th century over part of the theatre (to the right as you face the stage). However, it remains a most atmospheric place. The view of Mt Etna and the sea through what was once the stage area is quite breathtaking. Concerts are staged here in summer.

From the theatre, wander down to the beautiful **public gardens** on Via Bagnoli Croci. Take a picnic and enjoy the panorama. Back in the town centre is the **Odeon**, a small Roman theatre, badly preserved and partly covered by the adjoining Church of Santa Caterina. It was discovered and excavated in the late 19th century. It is believed that the Odeon was built on the site of a Greek temple of Apollo. Taormina's **cathedral**, in the Piazza del Duomo along Corso Umberto, was built at the beginning of the 15th century.

There are several mansions in Taormina, including the **Corvaja Palace**, which houses the tourist office. Started by the Arabs as a defence tower in the 11th century, the palace was extended several times and includes halls dating from the 14th and 15th centuries. The **Palazzo Duca di Santo Stefano** is an important example of Sicilian Gothic architecture, with a fanciful mix of Arab and Norman styles. The **Badia Vecchia** (Old Abbey) is a 14th century Gothic building, again with a mix of Norman and Arab architecture.

There are beaches at **Isola Bella** and **Mazzarò** directly under Taormina. The cable car which once connected the town and Isola Bella has been closed for reconstruction and regular buses now make the trip, leaving

from the top of Via San Pancrazio near Via Pirandello. Both beaches are almost completely taken up by private operators (a space with deck chairs and umbrella costs about L18,000 a day), but there is still a small space for free sunbathing.

Organised Tours

Excursions from Taormina to Mt Etna can be organised through the CIT (☎ 2 33 01), Corso Umberto 101, or through SAT (☎ 2 46 53), Corso Umberto 73, and cost around L70,000, including the cost of transport to the crater area. For further information about getting to the volcano, see the section on Mt Etna.

Festivals

Festivals, theatre and musical concerts are organised throughout the summer. In late May or early June there is the Raduno del Costume e del Carretto Siciliano, featuring parades of traditional Sicilian carts and folkloric groups.

Places to Stay

Taormina abounds in accommodation, but rooms fill rapidly in summer, particularly during August, and it is advisable to book well in advance. You can camp near the beach at *Campeggio San Leo* (☎ 2 46 58), Via Nazionale, at Capotaormina. The cost is L3800 per person per night and L3300 or L5400 for your tent.

There are numerous private rooms in Taormina and the tourist office has a full list. At *Pensione Ingegneri* (☎ 62 54 80), Via Timeo 8, you will pay L28,000 per person. Cheaper is *Il Leone* (☎ 2 38 78), Via Bagnoli Croci 127, near the gardens, which has singles/doubles for L25,000/40,000, or L55,000 per person for half pension.

Hotel Pensione Corona (☎ 2 30 21), Via Roma 7, overlooking the public gardens, has doubles ranging upwards from L45,000 to L58,000, the more expensive rooms with balconies or terraces. *Pensione Svizzera* (☎ 2 37 90), Via Pirandello 26, on the way from the bus station to the town centre, has simple, pleasant singles/doubles with private bathroom and breakfast for L36,000/65,000; triples are L84,000. *Hotel Villa Gaia* (☎ 2 31 85), Via Fazzello 34, has doubles for L65,000.

Hotel Villa Carlotta (☎ 2 37 32), Via Pirandello 81, is about 10 minutes' walk downhill from the town. A beautifully furnished establishment, it has rooms with terraces and private bathroom for around L100,000 a double, including breakfast; a triple costs L155,000. *Villa Fiorita* (☎ 2 41 22), Via Pirandello 39, is another well-furnished, very comfortable hotel, with a garden, terraces and rooms with full services. Doubles cost between L110,000 and L125,000, and triples are L150,000 to L165,000.

Hotel Villa Belvedere (☎ 2 37 91), Via Bagnoli Croci 79, near the public gardens, is a three-star hotel. Its rooms and terraces all face Mt Etna, and a double with private bathroom costs L158,000; a single costs L87,000.

If you want to stay near the beach at Mazzarò, try the *Villa Caterina* (☎ 2 47 09), Via Nazionale 155, which has pleasant rooms for L53,000 a double, or L70,000 per person for half pension.

Places to Eat

Those on a tight budget will be limited in their choice of eating places. There are several gourmet grocery shops along Corso Umberto, where prices are high. Alternatively, head for the side streets between Via Teatro Greco and the public gardens, where you can buy picnic supplies at the several grocery and pastry shops. There is a Standa supermarket in Via Apollo Arcageta, just up from the post office.

Pizzeria Santa Clara, Via Ibrahim 4, is in a quiet spot up the stairs to your right just before the Porta Catania. For a light meal, head for the *Shelter Pub*, Via Fratelli Bandieri 10, off Corso Umberto, for sandwiches and salads from L4000 to L8000. There is also *Odeon*, Via Ingegnere, off Corso Umberto at the Roman ruins, where you can eat reasonably priced sandwiches with a wide range of fillings.

Trattoria Rosticepi, Via San Pancrazio 10, at the top of Via Pirandello, has good meals for under L25,000 per person. For an excellent meal in lovely surroundings, head for *Ristorante La Piazzetta*, Via Paladini 5, in a tiny piazza downhill from Corso Umberto. A full meal will cost around L30,000 or more. Next door is *Shatulle*, a bar/creperie.

For a quiet drink, head for *Arco Rosso*, Via Naumachia, just off Corso Umberto.

Getting There & Away

Taormina is on the main train line between Messina and Catania, and there are regular trains daily. As previously mentioned, the Taormina train station is on the coast and you will need to wait for an SAIS bus to take you uphill to the town. These buses run roughly every half an hour to 90 minutes and the service is heavily reduced on Sundays.

It is much easier to catch an SAIS bus from either Messina or Catania. Buses leave from the terminal next to the Messina train station roughly every half an hour to an hour (1½-hour trip). They leave Catania from the terminal near the train station every half an hour to an hour (1½-hour trip). See the Getting There & Away sections for these towns for further details.

If arriving by car ferry at Messina, turn left as you exit the ferry and follow Via Farina and the green autostrada signs to reach the autostrada. Alternatively, follow the blue Catania signs to take the coastal road, although this can be very busy in summer. Note that traffic officers are very active at Taormina. Ask if your hotel has car-parking facilities or can recommend a safe place to leave the car.

Getting Around

Taormina is tiny and your only option is to make your way around on foot. Regular buses leave from the top of Via San Pancrazio for the beaches at Isola Bella and Mazzarò.

There are several car-rental agencies in Taormina, including Avis, Hertz and Maggiore. California (☎ 2 37 69), Via Bagnoli Croci 86, rents both cars and motorbikes at reasonable prices. A small car will cost upwards of L300,000 a week. A Vespa costs L27,000 a day or L180,000 a week, while a motorino costs L19,000 a day or L125,000 a week.

AROUND TAORMINA

There is an **archaeological park** at Giardini Naxos, the site of the first Greek settlement in Sicily, Naxos, founded in 735 BC. It was destroyed by Dionysius, the tyrant of Syracuse, in 403 BC. There is not a lot to see, but the park is a pleasant green refuge in what is now a very heavily touristed seaside town. It is open Monday to Saturday from 9 am to one hour before sunset, Sunday to 1 pm, and entrance is free. Regular buses leave from the Taormina bus terminal in Via Pirandello for Giardini Naxos. Giardini's AAST tourist office (☎ 0942-5 10 10) is at Via Tysandros 76E.

Fans of Francis Ford Coppola's *The Godfather* films might be interested to know that the wedding scene in the first film was shot at **Forza d'Agro**, near Taormina.

CATANIA

The crumbling, decrepit appearance of Catania, its chaotic traffic and its reputation as one of Sicily's major crime centres, will make the city seem intimidating to the newly arrived tourist. Certainly it is not one of the island's major tourist attractions, but Catania is well worth a visit for a day or two to take a look at its grand, but in general badly maintained, Baroque palaces and churches. It is well served by hotels and pensioni, as well as good restaurants and trattorias, and is the best base from which to explore Mt Etna by public transport.

A busy industrial and commercial centre and port town, Catania has a somewhat unfortunate history. Situated at the foot of Mt Etna, the city was partially destroyed in a massive eruption in 1669, and, as reconstruction proceeded, the city was almost completely destroyed in 1693 by an earthquake which devastated much of south-eastern Sicily. The 18th century project to rebuild the city in grand Baroque

style was largely overseen by the architect Giovanni Vaccarini.

Orientation

The main train station and intercity bus terminal are near the port at Piazza Giovanni XXIII. From here, Corso Martiri della Libertà heads west towards the city centre, about a 15-minute walk. Follow the road to Piazza della Repubblica and then continue straight ahead along Corso Sicilia to Via Etnea, the main thoroughfare through the city centre, which extends northwards from the Piazza del Duomo. Most of the sights are concentrated to the east and west of the Piazza del Duomo, while the commercial centre of Catania, including shops and the market, are farther north in the area around Via Pacini and Via Umberto I.

Information

Tourist Office The AAPIT tourist office (☎ 095-31 21 24) is at Largo Paisiello 5, just off Via Etnea along Via Pacini. It is open Monday to Friday from 9 am to 1 pm and 4.30 to 6.30 pm, Saturday from 9 am to 1 pm. There are branch offices at the train station on platform No 1, open roughly the same hours, and at the airport, open Monday to Friday from 8 am to 8 pm.

Money Banks are concentrated along Corso Sicilia and there is an exchange office at the train station.

Post & Telecommunications The main post office is at Via Etnea 215, between Via Pacini and Via Umberto I. There is an ASST telephone office opposite the train station, on the corner of Via dei Martiri della Libertà, which is open daily from 8 am to 8 pm, and an SIP office at Corso Sicilia 67, open Monday to Saturday from 9 am to 1 pm and 4 to 8 pm, Sunday from 9 am to 12.30 pm and 4.30 to 8 pm. The postal code for central Catania is 95100, and the city's telephone code is 095.

Emergency For police attention, call ☎ 113. In a medical emergency, go to the Ospedale

Vittorio Emanuele, Via Plebiscito 268, off Via Vittorio Emanuele II. The Crocerossa pharmacy, Via Etnea 274, is open late at night.

Dangers & Annoyances Petty theft is a problem here. If possible, leave your valuables at your hotel, or carry them in a money belt. It is best to avoid carrying a bag. Women are advised not to walk alone in the city at night.

Things to See & Do
Start at the **Piazza del Duomo**, with Vaccarini's **Elephant Fountain** in its centre. The statue, carved from lava, carries an Egyptian obelisk on its back. The architect also redesigned the 11th century **cathedral** after the 1693 earthquake, incorporating the original Norman apses and transept. The **Palazzo del Municipio** (town hall) on the north side of the piazza was also designed by Vaccarini and features an elegant, well-balanced Baroque façade.

West along Via Vittorio Emanuele II, at No 226, is the entrance to the ruins of a **Roman theatre** and **odeon** (a small rehearsal theatre). The ruins are open daily from 9 am to one hour before sunset. From Piazza San Francesco, just before the entrance to the ruins, head north along Via Crociferi, which is lined with Baroque churches. Turn left into Via Gesuiti and follow it to Piazza Dante and the sombre **Church of San Nicolò**. The largest church in Sicily, its façade was never completed. Next to the church is a beautiful 18th century Benedictine monastery, which might still be under renovation when you read this.

The **Castello Ursino**, across Via V Emanuele II, was built in the 13th century by Frederick II of Hohenstaufen. The grim-looking castle, surrounded by a moat, is in an equally grim neighbourhood, where it is best to travel in pairs or groups. Inside the castle is the **Municipal Museum**, which might still be closed for renovations (check with the tourist office).

North along Via Etnea from the Piazza del Duomo are several buildings of interest.

Facing Piazza dell'Università are two buildings designed by Vaccarini, the **Palazzo dell'Università** to the left and, opposite, the **Palazzo San Giuliano**. There are the ruins of a **Roman amphitheatre** in Piazza Stesicoro and, farther along Via Etnea, the lovely **Bellini Gardens**, named for one of Catania's most famous sons, the composer Vincenzo Bellini.

Places to Stay
Camping facilities are available at *Internazionale La Plaja* (☎ 34 08 80), Viale Kennedy 47, on the way out of the city towards Syracuse (take bus No 27 from the station). Budget pensioni are located around the centre, including *Pensione Rubens* (☎ 31 70 73), Via Etnea 196, which has singles/doubles for L28,000/45,000 and triples for L60,000. *Albergo Gresi* (☎ 32 37 09), Via Pacini 28, has singles/doubles for L30,000/50,000 and triples with bath for L70,000. *Pensione Ferrara* (☎ 31 60 00), Via Umberto I 66, has doubles for L50,000, or L60,000 with private bathroom. The *Holland International* (☎ 53 27 79) is closer to the station at Via Vittorio Emanuele II 8, just off Piazza dei Martiri, and has singles/doubles for L20,000/45,000 and doubles with bathroom for L55,000.

Just off the Piazza del Duomo are two hotels which offer a higher standard of accommodation. The *Albergo Savona* (☎ 32 69 82), Via V Emanuele II 210, has singles/doubles for L34,000/53,000, or with bathroom for L51,000/80,000; triples with bathroom are L110,000. *Hotel Centrale Europa* (☎ 31 13 09), Via V Emanuele II 167, has singles/doubles for L30,000/50,000, and doubles with bathroom for L70,000; triples are L90,000 with bathroom and L65,000 without.

The *Villa Dina Hotel* (☎ 44 71 03), Via Caronda 129, is at the other end of Via Etnea, near Piazza Cavour. It has pleasant rooms, a garden and private car park, and singles/doubles/triples are L80,000/120,000/160,000. All rooms have full services. To reach the hotel, take bus No 20 or 36 to the stop at Via Paleo, opposite the

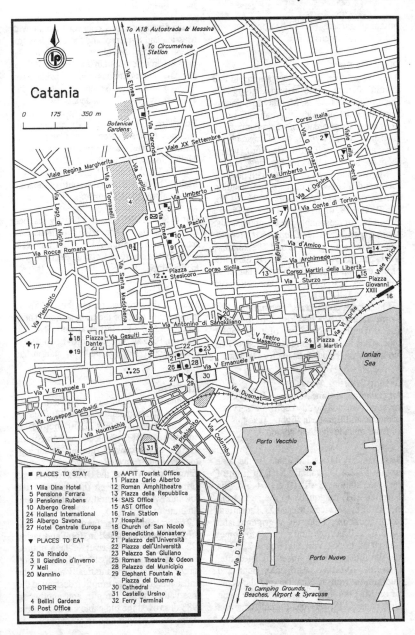

Catania

0   175   350 m

To A18 Autostrada & Messina
To Circumetnea Station
Via Etnea
Botanical Gardens
Corso Italia
Via G. Carnazza
Viale della Libertà
2
3
Viale XX Settembre
Via Caronda
Via Euplio
Viale Regina Margherita
Via Umberto I
Via S. Tomaselli
Via Lago di Nicito
4
Via Umberto I
Via V. Ogrinia
Via Conte di Torino
5
6
Via Etnea
Via Pacini
7
Via Ventimiglia
Via d'Amico
10
11
Via Archimede
14
8
1
9
Via Rocca Romana
Via Santa Maddalena
Corso Martiri della Libertà
Viale Africa
Via Plebiscito
12
Piazza Stesicoro
Corso Sicilia
13
Via L. Sturzo
15
Piazza Giovanni XXIII
16
Via Crociferi
Via Antonino di Sangiuliano
20
Via Aprile
Ionian Sea
17
18
Piazza Dante
Via Gesuiti
V. Teatro Massimo
24
Piazza d. Martiri
19
22
21   23
26   28
Via V Emanuele II
25
30
27
29
Via V Emanuele II
Via Dusmet
Via Giuseppe Garibaldi
Via Naumachia
Porto Vecchio
Via Plebiscito
31
Via Plebiscito
Via Colombo
32
Via D Tempio
Porto Nuovo
To Camping Grounds, Beaches, Airport & Syracuse

■ PLACES TO STAY	8 AAPIT Tourist Office
1 Villa Dina Hotel	11 Piazza Carlo Alberto
5 Pensione Ferrara	12 Roman Amphitheatre
9 Pensione Rubens	13 Piazza della Repubblica
10 Albergo Gresi	14 SAIS Office
24 Holland International	15 AST Office
26 Albergo Savona	16 Train Station
27 Hotel Centrale Europa	17 Hospital
	18 Church of San Nicolò
▼ PLACES TO EAT	19 Benedictine Monastery
	21 Palazzo dell'Università
2 Da Rinaldo	22 Piazza dell'Università
3 Il Giardino d'inverno	23 Palazzo San Giuliano
7 Meli	25 Roman Theatre & Odeon
20 Mannino	28 Palazzo del Municipio
	29 Elephant Fountain &
OTHER	Piazza del Duomo
	30 Cathedral
4 Bellini Gardens	31 Castello Ursino
6 Post Office	32 Ferry Terminal

botanical gardens (not to be confused with the Bellini Gardens).

Places to Eat

There is an open-air produce market in and around Piazza Carlo Alberto, along Via Pacini from Via Etnea, Monday to Saturday until around 1 pm. Here you can pick up all your supplies of bread, cheese, salami, fresh fruit etc. Catania's young people head for the area around Via Teatro Massimo, where there are several sandwich bars and 'pubs'.

Many of the city's trattorias open only for lunch and it is best to check before heading out for dinner. Try *Mannino* (☎ 31 13 39), Via Biondi 19, or *Meli* (☎ 53 69 67), Piazza Bovio 18, for reasonably priced, good meals. More expensive are *Il Giardino d'Inverno*, Via Asilo Sant'Agata 34, and *Da Rinaldo*, Via G Simili 59, both in the area to the north of the train station, to the left off Viale della Libertà. A full meal at either will cost L35,000 to L40,000.

One of the city's better restaurants is the *Costa Azzurra*, Via de Cristoforo 4, by the sea at Ognina, north-east of the city. It specialises in seafood and is expensive. Bus No 22 leaves from Via Etnea for Ognina.

Getting There & Away

Air Catania's airport, Fontanarossa, is seven km south-west of the city centre and services domestic and European flights. Take bus No 24 from outside the train station.

Bus Intercity buses terminate in the area around Piazza Giovanni XXIII, in front of the train station. SAIS (☎ 53 61 68), Via d'Amico 181, diagonally to the right from the station, services Messina, Taormina, Noto, Syracuse, Palermo, Agrigento and Enna, as well as providing a service to Rome. AST (☎ 53 17 56), Via Luigi Sturzo 220, just off the piazza, runs buses to Messina, Taormina, Syracuse, Agrigento, Enna and Palermo, as well as Nicolosi and the cable car on Mt Etna. Etna Trasporti, at the same address as SAIS, services Piazza Armerina and Ragusa.

Train Frequent trains connect Catania with Messina and Syracuse, and there are less frequent services to Palermo and Enna. The private Circumetnea train line circles Mt Etna, stopping at the numerous towns and villages on the volcano's slopes. See the Mt Etna Getting There & Away section for details.

Boat Tirrenia (☎ 31 63 94), Piazza Grenoble 26, runs ferries to Reggio di Calabria and Naples, as well as to Syracuse and on to Malta. Gozo Channel (☎ 31 06 29), Bonanno Fratelli, Via Anzalone 7, also runs ferries to Malta. The ferry terminal is south of the train station along Via VI Aprile.

Car & Motorbike Catania is easily reached from Messina on the A18 autostrada and from Palermo on the A19. From the A18, signs for the centre of Catania will bring you to Via Etnea.

Getting Around

Many of the more useful city buses (AMT) terminate in front of the train station. These include: No 24, station-airport; No 27, station-Piazza del Duomo-Lido Plaja (beach); and Nos 29 and 36, station-Via Etnea.

MT ETNA

Dominating the landscape in eastern Sicily between Taormina and Catania, Mt Etna (at present approximately 3350 metres) is Europe's largest live volcano and one of the world's most active. Eruptions occur frequently, both from the four live craters at the summit (one of these, the Bocca Nuova, was formed in 1968) and on the slopes of the volcano, which is littered with crevices and old craters.

The volcano's most famous and devastating eruption occurred in 1669 and lasted 122 days. A massive river of lava poured down its southern slope, engulfing a good part of Catania and dramatically altering the landscape. In 1971 an eruption destroyed the observatory at the summit, and another in 1983 destroyed the old cable car and tourist centre. Nine people died in an explosion at the south-east crater in 1979, and another two died and 10 were injured in another explosion at the crater in 1987. Its most recent eruption was in 1992, when a stream of lava pouring from a fissure in its south-eastern slope threatened to engulf the town of Zafferana Etnea. The town was saved, but not before one family lost their home and others much of their land.

The unpredictability of the volcano's activity means that people are no longer allowed to make the climb to the craters. Only a rope marks the point where it becomes unsafe to proceed, but it would be extremely foolish to ignore the warning signs and go any farther. See the following Getting There & Away section for different methods of reaching and ascending the volcano.

There is a Pro Loco tourist centre at Linguaglossa (☎ 095-64 30 94), Piazza Annunziata, with information about skiing, trekking and other activities on the volcano. It also has an exhibition of the flora and fauna of the Mt Etna National Park. It is possible to hire a 4WD and guide through the Pro Loco to tour the volcano. The town is accessible from Taormina/Giardini Naxos by CFE bus.

Places to Stay

There is a camping ground at Nicolosi (☎ 095-91 43 09), Via Goethe, as well as at Linguaglossa (095-64 36 11). The *Rifugio Sapienza* (☎ 095-91 10 62) near the cable car has beds for L23,000 a night, and full pension for L50,000 a day.

At Piano Provenzana, a small ski resort, the *Rifugio Nord-Est* (☎ 0337-88 93 77) has beds for L18,000 a night, and the hotel/restaurant *La Provenzana* (☎ 095-64 71 83) has full board for L60,000 to L70,000 per person. Piano Provenzana is accessible from Linguaglossa by FCE (Ferrovia Circumetnea) buses during the ski season and in July.

There are also small hotels in some of the towns along the Circumetnea train line. For full details, contact the tourist office at Catania.

Getting There & Away

Mt Etna can best be reached from Catania in the south, or via Linguaglossa to the north, although the only access from this side is by car.

From Linguaglossa, follow the road to Piano Provenzana past Zafferana to the Rifugio Sapienza (where refreshments are available) and the cable car, which will take you up to 2500 metres (L22,000 return). From there, 4WD minibuses make the trip through a grey lunar landscape of lava to 2920 metres (an extra L15,000 return), just below the craters. The cable-car and minibus service operates from 9 am to 4.30 pm. Many tourists prefer to make the long climb from the refuge to the top (3½ to 4 hours on a track winding up under the cable car and then following the same road used by the minibuses).

By public transport, the only option is to come from Catania by way of Nicolosi. An AST bus leaves from outside the main train station at Catania at 7.30 am, stopping at Nicolosi before heading up to the cable car. It heads back for Catania at 4 pm. The AST office (☎ 095-53 17 56) is at Via L Sturzo 220, near the train station.

Another option, if you are interested in circling rather than ascending Mt Etna, is to take a train on the private Circumetnea line, which extends from Catania to the town of Riposto to the north of the volcano, passing through numerous towns and villages on its slopes, including Linguaglossa. It is possible to reach Riposto (or Giarre, which is in fact joined to Riposto) from Taormina by train or bus, if you want to make the trip from that end. Catania-Riposto is approximately a 3½-hour trip, although it is probably not necessary to go that far. If leaving from Catania, consider finishing the trip at Randazzo (two hours), a small medieval town noted for the fact that it has consistently escaped destruction despite its proximity to the summit. A normal state train line connects Randazzo with Taormina/Giardini Naxos.

The Circumetnea train station at Catania, known as Stazione Borgo, is at Via Caronda

352, off Via Etnea just after Piazza Cavour (also known as Piazza Borgo). Catch bus No 29 or 36 from the central train station to Stazione Borgo, which is one stop after Piazza Borgo.

South-East Sicily

SYRACUSE (SIRACUSA)

Once a powerful Greek city to rival Athens, Syracuse is one of the highlights of a visit to Sicily. The city was founded in 734 BC by colonists from Corinth, who established their settlement on the island of Ortygia. Ruled by a succession of tyrants from the 5th century BC, Syracuse became a dominant sea power in the Mediterranean, prompting Athens to attack the city in 413 BC. In one of the great maritime battles in history, the Athenian fleet was destroyed.

Under the famous tyrant, Dionysius, the city became the most important centre in the Mediterranean. Plato attended the court of Dionysius, but according to legend he bored Dionysius so much that the tyrant ended up trying to sell the philosopher as a slave.

Syracuse was conquered by the Romans in 212 BC, but remained an important and enlightened city. However, in the 5th century AD it was overrun by barbarians. It was later an important Byzantine city, before being taken by the Arabs and then conquered by the Normans in the 11th century.

Syracuse was the birthplace of the Greek mathematician Archimedes, and the apostle Paul stopped here on his way to Rome, converting the city to Christianity.

Orientation

The main sights of Syracuse are in two areas: on the island of Ortygia, which was the site of the original Greek settlement, and two km across the 'new' town in the Neapolis archaeological zone. New arrivals will find themselves halfway between these two points. From the train station, walk to the left along Via Francesco Crispi to Piazzale Marconi, where all of the intercity buses terminate. Heading straight through the piazza to Corso Umberto will bring you to Ortygia after a five-minute walk. Alternatively, turn left from Piazzale Marconi into Via Catania, cross the rail lines and then follow the busy shopping street, Corso Gelone, to Viale Paolo Orsi and the archaeological zone. Most of the city's accommodation is in the newer part of town, while the better eating places are on the island in the old town.

Information

Tourist Offices The APT di Siracusa, which deals with Syracuse and its province (including Noto), has two offices: at the entrance to the archaeological zone in Piazzale Paradiso (☎ 0931-6 05 10), and its head office, which is out of the way at Via San Sebastiano 45 (☎ 0931-6 77 10).

The AAT (☎ 0931-6 52 01), on Ortygia at Via Maestranza 33, deals specifically with Syracuse and is probably the best office to pick up a map, list of hotels and details on the city's monuments. The AAT booth at the train station was closed indefinitely in the early 1990s.

Money There are numerous banks along Corso Gelone and Corso Umberto. At the Banca Commerciale Italiana in Via Savoia, just off Largo XXV Luglio as you cross onto Ortygia, you can exchange travellers' cheques, as well as obtain cash advances on Visa and MasterCard.

Post & Telecommunications The post office is in Piazza della Posta, to your left as you cross the bridge onto Ortygia. It is open Monday to Friday from 8 am to 7 pm, Saturday to 1 pm. There is an SIP telephone office at Via Brenta 35, open from 8 am to 8 pm, and public telephone booths can be found throughout the city. The postal code for Syracuse is 96100 and the telephone code is 0931.

Emergency The public hospital is in Via Testaferrata. For medical emergencies, ring ☎ 6 85 55; for immediate police assistance, call ☎ 113.

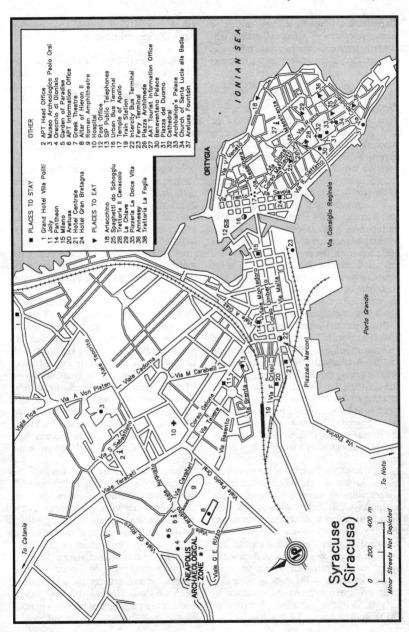

PLACES TO STAY
1 Grand Hotel Villa Politi
11 Jolly
14 Pantheon
15 Milano
20 Aretusa
21 Hotel Centrale
24 Hotel Gran Bretagna

PLACES TO EAT
18 Arlecchino
25 Spaghetti do Schogglu
28 Trattoria Il Cenacolo
29 La Chiave
35 Pizzeria La Dolce Vita
36 Amnessy
38 Trattoria La Foglia

OTHER
2 APT Head Office
3 Museo Archeologico Paolo Orsi
4 Orecchio di Dionisio
5 Garden of Paradise
6 APT Information Office
7 Greek Theatre
8 Altar of Hieron II
9 Roman Amphitheatre
10 Hospital
12 Post Office
13 SIP Public Telephones
16 Urban Bus Terminal
17 Temple of Apollo
19 Train Station
22 Intercity Bus Terminal
23 Ferry Terminal
26 Piazza Archimede
27 AAT Tourist Information Office
30 Beneventano Palace
31 Piazza del Duomo
32 Cathedral
33 Archbishop's Palace
34 Church of Santa Lucia alla Badia
37 Aretusa Fountain

IONIAN SEA

ORTYGIA

Porto Grande

To Catania

To Noto

NEAPOLIS
ARCHAEOLOGICAL
ZONE

Syracuse
(Siracusa)

0   200   400 m

Minor Streets Not Depicted

Dangers & Annoyances Snatch thieves on motorcycles are very active in Syracuse, particularly around the tourist areas on Ortygia. Women carrying shoulder bags are favourite targets.

Things to See & Do

Ortygia The island of Ortygia has always been the spiritual and physical heart of the city. Today its buildings are predominantly medieval, with some Baroque palaces and churches. The 7th century **cathedral** was built on top of a Greek temple of Athena, incorporating most of the original columns of the temple in its three-aisled structure.

The cathedral is a literal melting pot of architectural styles. Rebuilt after various earthquakes, it has a Gothic/Catalan ceiling, a Baroque façade, as well as Baroque chapels and altars. Note the decorative towers on the left side of the church's exterior, built by the Arabs, who used it as a mosque. Also note that some of the columns on the left side of the church have shifted on their bases, the result of an earthquake in 1542.

The Piazza del Duomo, once the site of the Greek acropolis, is lined with Baroque palaces, including the **Beneventano Palace** and the **Archbishop's Palace**, and is considered among the finest Baroque squares in Italy. At the far end of the piazza is the **Church of Santa Lucia alla Badia**, dedicated to St Lucy, the city's patron saint, who was martyred at Syracuse during the reign of the Roman emperor Diocletian. Its Baroque façade is decorated by a wrought-iron balustrade.

Walk down Via Picherali to the waterfront and the **Arethusa Fountain**, a natural freshwater spring only metres from the sea. Greek legend says that the nymph Arethusa, pursued by the river god Alpheus, was turned into a fountain by the goddess Diana in order to escape; Alpheus then turned himself into the river which feeds the spring. Next to the spring is the Foro Vittorio Emanuele II, where locals take in the evening air during their evening stroll. At the entrance to Ortygia, in Piazza Pancali, are the ruins of the **Temple of Apollo**. Little remains of the

6th century BC Doric temple, apart from the bases of a few columns.

Archaeological Zone To get to the archaeological zone, catch bus No 1 from Riva della Posta on Ortygia. The main attraction here is the 5th century BC **Greek Theatre**, its seating area carved out of solid rock. Considered a masterwork and one of the most beautiful structures of its kind in the ancient world, the theatre could seat 16,000 people.

Nearby is the **Garden of Paradise**, a former limestone quarry of the Greek colonisers. It was an early example of a concentration camp, where prisoners worked in subterranean tunnels, cutting blocks of limestone for building projects. Most of the area remained covered by a 'roof' of earth, which collapsed during the massive 1693 earthquake which devastated most of Sicily. After this, the garden of citrus and magnolia trees was created. In the garden is the **Orecchio di Dionisio** (Ear of Dionysius), an artificial grotto, 23 metres high and 65 metres deep, in the shape of an ear. Its extraordinary acoustics led the painter Caravaggio, during a visit in the 17th century, to give the grotto its current name. Caravaggio mused that the tyrant must have taken advantage of the acoustics to overhear the whispered conversations of his prisoners. Next to this grotto is the **Grotta dei Cordari** (Cordmakers' Cave), so named because it was used by cordmakers to practise their craft. The cave has been closed for some years.

Outside the garden area, towards the entrance to the zone, is the 2nd century AD **Roman Amphitheatre**. The structure once had roughly the same proportions as the Arena at Verona, and was used for gladiator fighting and horse races. However, it was largely destroyed by the Spanish in the 16th century, who used it as a quarry to build the city walls on Ortygia. As a point of minor interest, the area between the amphitheatre and Viale Paolo Orsi was used by ancient Romans as a parking area for their chariots. West of the amphitheatre is the 3rd century

BC **Altar of Hieron II**. The monolithic sacrificial altar was the largest in the ancient Greek and Roman worlds and 450 oxen could be killed on it at one time.

The archaeological zone is open daily from 9 am to 6 pm (to 3.30 pm in winter). Admission is L2000.

About 500 metres east of the archaeological zone, off Viale Teocrito, the **Museo Archeologico Paolo Orsi**, in the grounds of the Villa Landolina, was opened in 1988 and contains the best organised and most interesting archaeological collection in Sicily. A visit is highly recommended. The museum is open Tuesday to Sunday from 9 am to 1 pm, and admission is L5000.

Festivals
Since 1914, in every even-numbered year, Syracuse has hosted a festival of Greek classical drama in May and June. Performances are given in the Greek Theatre and prices range from around L15,000 for unreserved seats in the rear, up to L60,000 for reserved seats closest to the stage. Tickets are available from the EPT office or at a booth at the entrance to the theatre.

Places to Stay – bottom end
There are camping facilities at *Agriturist Rinaura* (☎ 72 12 24), about four km west of the city; catch bus No 34 from Corso Umberto. It costs L6500 per person, L7200 for a tent. *Fontane Bianche* (☎ 79 03 33) is about 18 km south-west of Syracuse, at the beach of the same name, and is open from April to October. Catch bus No 21 or 22.

The non-IYHF *Albergo per la Gioventù* (☎ 71 11 18), Viale Epipoli 45, is eight km west of Syracuse; catch bus No 10 or 11 from Corso Umberto. Beds are L18,000.

Close to the train station is *Hotel Centrale* (☎ 52 17 89), Corso Umberto 141. It has small, basic singles/doubles for L18,000/35,000. The *Milano* (☎ 6 69 81), Corso Umberto 10, near Ortygia, has rooms for L23,000/35,000, or L30,000/45,000 with bathroom. In a more quiet position is the *Pantheon* (☎ 2 29 85), Via Foro Siracusano

22. It has clean, pleasant rooms for L36,000 a double and L50,000 a triple.

The two-star *Aretusa* (☎ 2 42 11), Via Francesco Crispi 73-81, is very close to the train station and has comfortable singles/doubles for L35,000/45,000. Triples are L63,000. With private bathroom, singles/doubles are L41,000/58,000. The *Hotel Gran Bretagna* (☎ 6 87 65), Via Savoia 21, is the only hotel on Ortygia (pending the restoration of the more up-market Grand Hotel). A very pleasant little hotel, it has rooms for L30,000/55,000, or L35,000/65,000 with private bathroom.

Places to Stay – middle to top end
Most of the better hotels are on the outskirts of Syracuse. The *Scala Greca* (☎ 75 39 22) is north of the archaeological zone at Via Avola 7. It has singles/doubles with private bathroom for L60,000/80,000. The *Grand Hotel Villa Politi* (41 21 21), Via M Politi 2, has rooms for L80,000/120,000. The city's top hotel, the *Jolly* (☎ 46 11 11), is in the centre at Corso Gelone 45. A single is L155,000 and a double L200,000; all rooms are fully serviced.

Places to Eat
Eating in Syracuse can be expensive. There is an open-air fresh-produce market in the streets behind the Temple of Apollo, daily (except Sunday) until 1 pm. There are several grocery shops and supermarkets along Corso Gelone. Try the excellent takeaway pizza and focaccia at *Casa del Pane*, Corso Gelone 115. Also in Corso Gelone, on the corner of Via della Pace, is an excellent alimentari/rosticceria.

Spaghetti do Schoggiu, Via Scinà 11, is on Ortygia, just off Piazza Archimede. It has pasta dishes from L6000 and mains for around L10,000. *Pizzeria La Dolce Vita*, Via Roma 112, has outside tables in a small courtyard. *Amnessy* is a very pleasant pizzeria/restaurant and bar in a corner of Piazza San Giuseppe, and charges average prices. *I Dammusi*, Via Carceri Vecchie, off the Piazza del Duomo, is a pizzeria which turns into a piano bar on Friday evenings. *Trat-*

toria Il Cenacolo is tucked away in a tiny piazza off Via Consiglio Reginale, near the Piazza del Duomo. It has good food at around L25,000 for a full meal.

At *Trattoria La Foglia*, Via Capodieci 29, off Lago Aretusa, the eccentric owner/chef and her vegetarian husband serve whatever seafood and vegetables are fresh on the day, and cook their own bread. Although the quality of the service and meal can drop dramatically if the restaurant is busy, the food is generally of a high standard. There is no printed menu, but don't be afraid to ask for prices; a full meal could cost around L35,000. *La Chiave*, Via Crocifisso 54, off Via Roma, serves good meals for around L40,000 or more. *Arlecchino* is on the waterfront at Via dei Tolomei 5. It is one of the city's better restaurants and a full meal will come to more than L45,000 a head, more if you order fish.

Getting There & Away

Syracuse is easy to reach by train from Messina and Catania. From other destinations, buses are faster and more convenient. SAIS buses leave from Piazzale Marconi, near the train station, for Catania and its airport, Palermo, Enna and surrounding small towns, including Noto. SAIS also has a direct daily bus service to Rome. Buses leave Syracuse at 8.30 am, connecting with the Rome bus at Catania. A one-way ticket costs L68,000 and the trip takes 12 hours. The SAIS office (☎ 6 67 10) is in Piazzale Marconi. AST buses also leave from Piazzale Marconi, for Palermo, Catania, Piazza Armerina, Avola, Noto and Ragusa. Their office (☎ 6 56 89) is in the Piazza della Posta.

Tirrenia runs ferries to and from Naples once a week, and Reggio di Calabria and Malta three times a week. Its office (☎ 6 69 56) is at Via Mazzini 5.

By car, if arriving from the north, you will enter Syracuse on Via Scala Greca. To reach the centre of the city, turn left at Viale Teracati and follow it around to the right; it eventually becomes Corso Gelone.

Getting Around

Only a few km separate the archaeological zone and Ortygia, about a 20-minute walk. Otherwise, bus Nos 1 and 2 make the trip from the Piazza della Posta to the zone. If you are driving in Syracuse, ask the tourist office to explain the system of one-way streets and to point out where you cannot drive on Ortygia.

NOTO

Completely destroyed by the 1693 earthquake, Noto was rebuilt in grand Baroque style by its many noble families. The warm gold and rose hues of the local stone serve to tone down the heavily embellished palaces and churches, and the town is very picturesque. Although accommodation options are limited, Noto is well worth a visit not only for its sights, but also for its fine culinary traditions. The city is particularly noted for its cakes and pastries.

Orientation & Information

Intercity buses arrive at the public gardens at the main entrance to the town, the Porta Reale, where Corso Vittorio Emanuele, the town's main street, starts. The AAPIT tourist office (☎ 0931-83 67 44) is along the Corso in Piazza XVI Maggio (open in summer from 8 am to 8 pm, and in other months from 8 am to 2 pm and 4 to 6 pm), where you can pick up a map of the town and a guide to its major sights. Noto's telephone code is 0931.

Things to See & Do

Most of the important monuments line Corso Vittorio Emanuele. Overlooking Piazza XVI are the **Church of San Domenico** and the adjacent **Dominican Convent**, both designed by Rosario Gagliardi, an important Sicilian architect who made a major contribution to the reconstruction of the town. Heading back towards the Porta Reale is the **Palazzo Villadorata** (also known as Palazzo Nicolaci), on Via Corrado Nicolaci. On the third Sunday in May the street is transformed into a sea of flowers for the Infiorata, a festival to welcome the spring. The palace is noted for its richly sculpted balconies, each different and featuring centaurs, horses, lions, sirens and tragic masks. Once the home of the princes of Villadorata, it is now partly used as municipal offices, and the more important rooms are open to the public.

The **cathedral** stands at the top of a monumental staircase overlooking Piazza Municipio. The façade is imposing, but less extravagant than most of Noto's other Baroque monuments. Next to the cathedral is the **Palazzo Landolina**, now abandoned, but belonging to the marquises of Sant' Alfano, Noto's oldest noble family. Across the piazza is the **Palazzo Ducrezio**, now the town hall.

Farther along the Corso are the **Church & Monastery of SS Salvatore**. The interior of the church is the most impressive in Noto. The monastery was reserved for the daughters of the town's noble families. Note the fountain suspended on a wall next to the monastery, left there after Noto's streets were lowered in 1840 to facilitate the movement of carriages.

Places to Stay

There is only one hotel in Noto itself, the *Albergo Stella* (☎ 83 56 95), on the corner of Via F Maiore and Via Napoli, near the public gardens. It has singles/doubles for L28,000/48,000.

The rest of the town's tourist accommodation is by the sea at Noto Marina, a 15-minute drive or bus trip (although buses run only in summer). Hotels here include *Residence Korsal* (☎ 81 20 80), which has rooms for L35,000/45,000, and *Hotel Ionio* (☎ 81 20 40) with rooms for L40,000/62,000.

Places to Eat

The people of Noto are very serious about their food and it is well worth enjoying a meal while in the town, followed by a visit to the bar/pasticceria *Corrado Costanzo* at Via Silvio Spaventa 7-9. Signore Costanzo enjoys considerable fame and respect worldwide for his equally considerable skills as a pastry chef. He specialises in dolci di mandorle (almond cakes and sweets) and torrone (nougat). While here, try his heaven-ly gelati and granita made with fragolini (tiny wild strawberries). *Caffè Sicilia*, Corso V Emanuele 125, is also famous for its sweets.

Trattoria del Carmine, Via Ducrezio 9, serves excellent home-style meals for less than L25,000 a head, as does *Trattoria Il Giglio*, Piazza Municipio 8-10. However, here you can also order Spanish paella, due to the fact that the owner's wife is from Spain. *Ristorante Il Barocco*, off Via Cavour in Ronco Sgadari, near Via Nicolaci, is one of Noto's finest restaurants and has a lovely internal courtyard. An excellent meal will come to more than L50,000.

Getting There & Away

Noto is easily accessible by AST and SAIS bus from Catania and Syracuse (see the Getting There & Away sections for those cities). From June to August, buses run frequently between Noto and Noto Marina, but during other months there is no service.

AROUND NOTO

The beach at **Noto Marina** is very pleasant and, as yet, has not been subject to the overdevelopment characteristic of most Italian beach resorts. Nearby, and accessible only by car or by making the 45-minute walk, is the archaeological site of **Eloro**, originally a Greek settlement and later occupied by the Romans. Uncompleted excavations have revealed a city square and sacred area. On either side of the hill where the ruins stand are long, sandy beaches which are not overrun by the usual crowds.

Farther along the coast is the beautiful **Vendicari** nature reserve, a haven for water birds. Bird-watchers are well catered for by special observatories, and there is a superb, long, sandy beach which is popular in summer but never overcrowded. It is possible to reach the park by the AST bus connecting Noto and Pachino.

RAGUSA

This prosperous provincial capital is virtually two towns in one: the old town of Ragusa Ibla, which has a typical medieval and Baroque appearance, and the 18th century 'new' town, simply called Ragusa. This split, which had originally resulted from a need to expand the town past its medieval boundaries, was accentuated after the devastating 17th century earthquake which destroyed much of south-east Sicily. The upper part of the town was rebuilt in the grand style of the day, while the lower town clung to its medieval lines and retained the old name of Ibla.

Orientation

The older, lower town offers most of the sights, while the newer, upper town offers accommodation and transport services. The train station is in Piazza del Popolo, and the intercity bus terminal in the adjacent Piazza Gramsci in the upper town. From the train station, turn left and head along Viale Tenente Lena, across the bridge (Ponte Nuovo) and continue straight ahead along Via Roma to reach Corso Italia, the upper town's main street. Turn right on Corso Italia and follow it to the stairs to Ibla, or follow the road as it makes its winding way to the lower town.

Information

Tourist Office There is an information office with a young, helpful staff in the Piazza del Duomo in Ibla (follow the signs), open from 8.30 am to 1.30 pm and 3 to 8 pm. The AAPIT office (☎ 0932-62 14 21) has an information office close by at Via Duomo 33 on the 1st floor of the Palazzo Rocca.

Post & Telecommunications The main post office is in Piazza Matteotti on Corso Italia. There is an SIP public telephone office on Via Maiorana, on the left as you approach the Ponte dei Cappuccini (the middle bridge) from Corso Italia. Ragusa's telephone code is 0932.

Emergency For police attendance, ring ☎ 113. The public hospital, the Ospedale Civile (☎ 62 27 33 during the day and 62 39 46 at night), is across Piazza del Popolo from the train station.

Things to See & Do

The stairs linking the upper and lower towns are next to the **Church of Santa Maria delle Scale**, rebuilt after the 1693 earthquake, retaining parts of the original 15th century structure including the doorway and bell tower. Take in the panoramic view of Ibla before heading down the stairs.

The **Basilica of San Giorgio**, at the top of a flight of stairs in the Piazza del Duomo, dominates Ibla. Designed by Rosario Gagliardi and built in the late 18th century, it has the boisterous, 'wedding-cake' appearance of high Baroque. Follow Corso XXV Aprile downhill, past the **Church of San Giuseppe**, which bears similarities to San Giorgio, until you reach the **Giardini Iblei**, the town's pleasant public gardens, where you can have a picnic.

In the upper town, visit the early 18th century **cathedral** in Piazza San Giovanni on Corso Italia, and the **Museo Archeologico Ibleo** in Via Natalelli, off Via Roma. The museum is open Tuesday to Saturday from 9 am to 2 pm, Sunday to 1 pm.

Places to Stay

All of Ragusa's accommodation is in the upper town and there are no budget hotels. *Hotel San Giovanni* (☎ 62 10 13), Via Traspontino 3, has singles/doubles with bathroom for L50,000/70,000, and triples for L100,000. To get there from Piazza del Popolo, head down Viale Leonardo da Vinci, turn left at Via I Migliorisi and follow it to the bridge. At Corso Italia 40 is *Hotel Rafael* (☎ 65 40 80), a very pleasant establishment with rooms for L60,000/80,000. Nearby, at Corso Italia 70, is *Hotel Montreal* (☎ 2 11 33), with good singles/doubles for L55,000/85,000, and triples for L110,000. Rooms at both hotels have private bathrooms.

Places to Eat

There is a Standa supermarket at Via Roma 187, near the bridge. Otherwise, if you want to take a picnic to the park, there is a grocery shop on Corso XXV Aprile, between the Piazza del Duomo and Piazza Pola in Ibla, where you can pick up supplies or ask for sandwiches to be made.

Trattoria La Bettola, Largo Camerina, downhill to the left off the Piazza del Duomo, is pleasant, and meals are priced at around L25,000. *La Rusticana*, Via XXV Aprile 68, has a tourist menu for L15,000. *Il Saraceno*, Via del Convento 9, off the Piazza del Duomo, has a slightly more expensive tourist menu, otherwise a full meal will come to around L30,000.

The *Gran Bar Puglisi*, opposite the train station, serves good coffee granitas.

Getting There & Away

Ragusa is accessible by not-so-regular trains from Syracuse, Noto and Agrigento. Buses are probably an easier way to get there. ETNA Trasporti (information and tickets at Gran Bar Puglisi opposite the train station) runs eight buses per day to Catania. AST (☎ 62 12 49) services Catania by way of Syracuse (three buses a day), and has buses to Palermo (three a day) and more regularly to Noto and Syracuse (seven a day). There is an AST timetable posted on the wall of a building at the spot in Piazza Gramsci where AST buses stop.

Getting Around

Walking around Ragusa is not too demanding, and, if you have your own car, you will find it easy to negotiate. City bus Nos 1 and 3 run from Piazza del Popolo in the upper town to Piazza Pola and the gardens in the lower town.

Central Sicily

ENNA

Situated in the sun-scorched centre of Sicily, Enna is somewhat isolated from the main tourist route around the coast. But it is worth the effort to make the journey into the interior to the town, which has been known since Greek times as the 'umbilicus' of Sicily. You can combine the trip with a visit to nearby Piazza Armerina to see the extra-

ordinary mosaics of the Villa Romana (see the Piazza Armerina section).

Enna, which stands at 931 metres above sea level, commands panoramic views of the island's central province, and has always been an important strategic town due to the fact that it was easily defendable. In Byzantine times it became a fortress and one of the main defences against the Arabs, who nonetheless managed to capture the town in 859 AD. Today it is an important agricultural and mining centre.

Orientation

The main road up into the town is Via Pergusa, which eventually links with Via Roma, to the right, the main street of historic Enna. The intercity bus terminal is on Viale Diaz. To get to the town centre, turn right from the terminal and follow Viale Diaz to Corso Sicilia, turn right again and follow it to Via Sant'Agata to the left, which heads down to Via Roma.

Information

The AAPIT tourist office (☎ 0935-50 05 44) is at Via Roma 413. The staff are helpful and you can pick up a map and information in English on the sights at Enna and in the province. There is an office of the AAST, for Enna only, in nearby Piazza Colajanni, next to the Albergo Sicilia.

The main post office is at Via Volta 1, just off Piazza Garibaldi, and the postal code for Enna is 94100. There are SIP public telephones in Piazza Scelfo, just off Via Roma, open from 8 am to 8 pm, and, after hours, at the Albergo Sicilia. The telephone code for Enna is 0935.

In an emergency, contact the police on ☎ 113. For medical assistance, go to the Ospedale Civile Umberto I in Via Trieste, or ring ☎ 4 52 45 or 4 54 89.

Things to See & Do

Enna's most visible monument is the medieval **Castello di Lombardia** at the eastern end of town. Built during the period of Swabian rule in Sicily, the castle was one of the most important defensive structures in

medieval Sicily. It retains six of its original
20 towers. The views of the surrounding
countryside from the castle are spectacular.
The castle is open Tuesday to Sunday from
10 am to 12.30 pm and 3.30 to 7 pm, and
entrance is free.

Back in town, along Via Roma, is the 14th
century **cathedral**. Restructured several
times in the 15th and 16th centuries, the
cathedral retains its Gothic apse and transept.
Behind the cathedral on Via Roma is the
Museo Alessi, which contains the contents
of the cathedral's treasury. It is open Tuesday
to Sunday from 9 am to 1 pm and 4 to 7 pm,
and entrance is free. Across Via Roma in
Piazza Mazzini is the **Museo Archeologico**
(also known as the Museo Varisano), which
is also worth a visit. It is open Monday to
Saturday from 9 am to 1.30 pm and 3.30 to
6.30 pm, Sunday to 12.30 pm, and entrance
is free.

In Piazza Vittorio Emanuele, at the other
end of Via Roma, is the **Church of San
Francesco**, with a 15th century bell tower
featuring fine Gothic windows. The church's
tower once formed part of the city's defence
system. The **Torre di Federico** in the public
gardens in the new part of town was also part
of this system. The octagonal tower, standing
24 metres high, was once linked by a secret
passage to the castle.

For a pleasant evening stroll, head for
Piazza Francesco Crispi and wander along
Viale Marconi to enjoy the view.

During Holy Week at Easter, Enna is the
setting for colourful traditional celebrations,
notably on Good Friday when thousands of
people wearing hoods and capes of different
colours participate in a solemn procession to
the cathedral.

Places to Stay & Eat
Enna has only one hotel, the *Albergo Sicilia*
(☎ 2 46 22), Piazza Colajanni. Singles/
doubles are expensive at L60,000/100,000.
For cheaper accommodation, catch the city
bus No 4 from Piazza V Emanuele to nearby
Lake Pergusa. There are several options
here, including *Hotel La Pergola* (☎ 4 23

33), which has simple rooms for L25,000/
40,000.

There is a market every morning from
Monday to Saturday in Via Mercato
Sant'Antonio, parallel to Via Roma off
Piazza Coppola, where you can find fresh
fruit, bread and cheeses etc. *Knulp*, Via
Restivo 14, is a bar where snacks, including
some creative sandwiches, are served. *Da
Gino* is a pleasant trattoria/pizzeria on Viale
Marconi. It has outdoor tables and a view,
and prices are reasonable. *Ristorante Centrale*, Piazza VI Dicembre 9, is more
expensive. There is a reasonably priced *trat-
toria/pizzeria* set into the hillside just below
the castle. It has tables on an open terrace
with great views of Enna and the surrounding area.

Getting There & Away
SAIS buses (☎ 50 09 02) connect Enna with
towns including Catania (and on to Rome),
Palermo and Syracuse. It is possible to reach
Agrigento via Caltanisetta. Buses terminate
in Viale Diaz. Regular SAIS buses also run
to Piazza Armerina.

PIAZZA ARMERINA
Piazza Armerina is a pleasant town less than
an hour by bus or car south of Enna. The
town has an interesting Baroque cathedral,
but the real reason to visit is to see the
mosaics at the nearby imperial Roman villa,
the Villa Romana del Casale.

The AAST tourist office is at Via Cavour
15 (open from 8 am to 2 pm and 4.30 to 7.30
pm) in the town centre, uphill along Via
Umberto or Via Garibaldi from the intercity
bus stops. It is probably best to pick up a
brochure here about Piazza Armerina, which
contains a plan of the villa and its mosaics,
since it is not always available out at the villa.
SAIS buses connect Enna and Piazza
Armerina (11 a day). There is also a daily
AST bus from Syracuse.

Villa Romana del Casale
The villa, built between the end of the 3rd
century and mid-4th century AD, was probably the home or hunting lodge of an

important Roman dignitary. Buried under mud in a massive 12th century flood, the villa remained hidden for some 700 years before its magnificent and extremely well-preserved floor mosaics were again revealed.

The villa is massive, about 3500 sq metres, and its design was adapted to the lie of the hill on which it stands, creating three main areas. The mosaics cover almost its entire floor space and are considered unique for their narrative style of composition, range of subjects and variety of colours. Their exotic style shows strong African influences.

The villa is well organised to cope with the hordes of tourists who visit annually, and, by following the raised walkways, you will see all of the main areas. The most interesting mosaics include the series of erotic subjects in the area of what were probably private apartments on the north side of the great peristyle. One of the richest mosaics in the villa, the *Little Hunt*, is in the largest room. In this area is the villa's most famous mosaic, illustrating 10 girls clad in what were probably the world's earliest bikinis.

The east side of the peristyle opens onto a long corridor. Its floor is covered with a splendid mosaic of the *Great Hunt*, depicting scenes of hunts for exotic wild animals. On the other side of the corridor is a series of apartments, their floors covered with mosaics depicting scenes from Homer, as well as mythical subjects including Arion playing the lyre on a dolphin's back, and Eros and Pan wrestling. There is also a lively circus scene.

The villa is open daily from 9 am to one hour before sunset, and entrance is L2000. ATAN buses leave for the villa from Piazza Generale Cascino in Piazza Armerina every hour from 9 am to midday and every half hour from 4 to 7 pm.

Places to Stay & Eat

If you want to stay in Piazza Armerina, try the *Hotel Selene* (☎ 0935-68 22 54), Via Generale Gaeta 30, which has singles/doubles for L55,000/85,000. *Hotel Mosaici* (☎ 0935-68 54 53) is three km out of town

on the way to the villa. It has rooms for L35,000/50,000. For a decent meal, try *Del Goloso*, Via Garao 4, just off Piazza Garibaldi near the tourist office.

AGRIGENTO

This pleasant medieval town is situated high on a hill overlooking the sea and the spectacular Valley of the Temples, one of the major Greek archaeological sights in the world. Founded around 582 BC as the Greek town of Akragas by settlers from Gela, who were originally from Rhodes, the town became powerful in the 5th century BC when it was ruled by tyrants, and most of the temples date from this period. The Greek poet, Pindar, described the town as 'the most beautiful of those inhabited by mortals'.

The town was sacked and destroyed by the Carthaginians in 406 BC, but it was rebuilt. Conquered by the Romans in the 3rd century BC, it remained important and was renamed Agrigentum, but it later declined under Byzantine rule and under the Arabs, who called it Girgenti. One of Agrigento's most famous citizens was the Italian playwright Luigi Pirandello (1867-1936), who won the Nobel Prize for literature in 1934.

While the Greek temples are the obvious reason to visit Agrigento, the town itself is well worth exploring.

Orientation

Intercity buses arrive in the area just off Piazza Vittorio Emanuele, and the train station is slightly south in Piazza Marconi. Both are only a short distance across the green oasis of Piazzale Aldo Moro from the main street of the medieval town, Via Atenea. The Valley of the Temples is on a ridge directly below the town (to the south towards the sea) and is easily accessible by frequent city buses (see the following Getting Around section).

Information

Tourist Office The AAST tourist office is at Via Atenea 123, open Monday to Saturday from 8.30 am to 2 pm and 4 to 7 pm. The staff are helpful and you can pick up a map of the town and information about the sights. They will also assist with advice on hotels and restaurants.

Money Banks open from 8.30 am to 2 pm. Out of hours there is an exchange office at the post office.

Post & Telecommunications The post office is in Piazza Vittorio Emanuele and is open Monday to Friday from 8 am to 7 pm, Saturday to 11 am. The postal code for central Agrigento is 92100.

There is an SIP public telephone office at Via Atenea 96, open from 8 am to 7.30 pm. The telephone code is 0922.

Emergency For police attendance, call ☎ 113. In a medical emergency, go to the public hospital, the Ospedale San Giovanni di Dio (☎ 49 21 11), on Via Atenea. There is a late-night pharmacy at Via Atenea 325.

Things to See & Do

Valley of the Temples The five main Doric temples in this 'valley' (actually a ridge) were constructed around the 5th century BC and are in various states of ruin, due to earthquakes and vandalism by early Christians.

The area is divided into two sections. East of the Via dei Templi are the most spectacular temples. The first you will come to is the **Temple of Hercules**, built towards the end of the 6th century BC and believed to be the oldest of the temples. Eight of its 38 columns have been raised and you can wander around the remains of the rest. The **Temple of Concord** is the only one to survive relatively intact. Built around 440 BC, it was transformed into a Christian church in the 6th century AD. Its name is taken from a Roman inscription found nearby. The **Temple of Juno** stands on the edge of the ridge, a five-minute walk uphill to the east. Part of its colonnade remains and there is an impressive sacrificial altar.

This section of the valley is not enclosed and can be visited at any time.

Across the Via dei Templi is the massive **Temple of Jupiter**, which, although never completed, was one of the most imposing constructions of ancient Greece. Now completely in ruins, it once covered an area measuring 112 metres by 56 metres, with columns 20 metres high. Between the columns stood the telamoni, colossal statues of men. One of them was reconstructed and is now housed in the Regional Archaeological Museum of Agrigento. A copy lies on the ground among the ruins of the temple, giving an idea of the immense size of the structure. Work began on the temple around 480 BC and it is believed that it was destroyed during the Carthaginian invasion in 406 BC. Nearby is the **Temple of Castor & Pollux**, which was partly reconstructed in the 19th century.

This area is open daily from 9 am to one hour before sunset. The temples are lit up at night until 11.30 pm.

The **Regional Archaeological Museum** is on Via dei Templi, just before the area of the temples, and it is worth taking a look at its collection before heading down to the valley. It is open Monday to Saturday from 9 am to 6 pm, Sunday to 1 pm. Entrance is free.

Opposite the museum is the **Hellenistic-Roman quarter**, part of the urban area of ancient Agrigento. Some of its structures date back to the 4th century BC, while others were constructed in the 5th century AD.

West of the temples is the house where the writer Pirandello was born, the **Casa Natale di Pirandello**. Now a small museum, it is open daily from 9 am to 1 pm and 3 to 7 pm. Take bus No 8 from the station.

Medieval Agrigento Wandering around the town's narrow, winding streets is relaxing and pleasant after a tiring day among the temples. One of the more interesting monuments is the **Church of Santa Maria dei Greci**, uphill from Piazza Lena, at the end of Via Atenea. This 11th century Norman church was built on the site of a 5th century BC Greek temple. Note the remains of the wooden Norman ceiling and some Byzantine frescoes.

A hard walk farther uphill is the **cathedral**

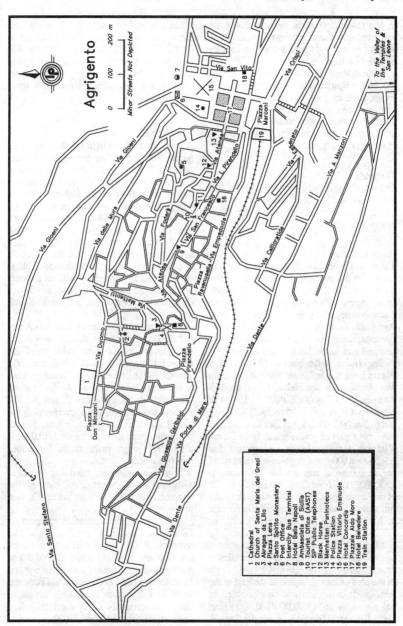

Agrigento

0   100   200 m

Minor Streets Not Depicted

Via San Vito
Via Crispi
To the Valley of the Temples & San Leone
Via Gioeni
Via Gioeni
Via delle Mura
Piazza Marconi
Via L. Pirandello
Via Atenea
Via Foderá
Via San Francesco
Via Empedocle
Via Callicratide
Via L. Agrigento
Via A. Manzoni
Via Dante
Piazza Ravanusella
Via Matteotti
Via Duomo
Via Santo Stefano
Via Porta di Mare
Via Giuseppe Garibaldi
Piazza Pirandello
Piazza Don Minzoni
Via Dante

1 Cathedral
2 Church of Santa Maria dei Greci
3 Akragas da Lillo
4 Piazza Lena
5 Santo Spirito Monastery
6 Post Office
7 Intercity Bus Terminal
8 Hotel Bella Napoli
9 Ambasciata di Sicilia
10 Tourist Office (AAST)
11 SIP Public Telephones
12 Black Horse
13 Manhattan Paninoteca
14 Police Station
15 Piazza Vittorio Emanuele
16 Hotel Concordia
17 Piazzale Aldo Moro
18 Hotel Belvedere
19 Train Station

in Via Duomo. Built in the year 1000, the cathedral was restructured many times. It has a 15th century bell tower and a 17th century panelled ceiling.

Back towards Piazza Vittorio Emanuele, the **Santo Spirito Monastery** was founded by the Cistercian nuns at the end of the 13th century. The chapel features stuccoes by the artist Serpotta. It is also possible to buy cakes and pastries from the nuns (see the following Places to Eat section).

Festivals

The town's main annual event is the Festival of the Almond Blossom, a folk festival held on the first Sunday in February in the Valley of the Temples.

Places to Stay

There are two camping grounds at San Leone, by the sea south of Agrigento. *Internazionale San Leone* (☎ 4 16 12) is open from April to October, while *Camping Nettuno* is open all year. Take bus No 9 from Agrigento, or drive down the Via dei Templi, continue along Viale Emporium towards the sea, and turn left at Lungomare Akragas.

The *Hotel Bella Napoli* (☎ 2 04 35), Piazza Lena 6, is uphill off Via Bac Bac from Via Atenea. It has clean, basic singles/ doubles for L30,000/50,000, or L40,000/ 60,000 with private bathroom. The *Hotel Belvedere* (☎ 2 00 51), Via San Vito 20, is in the newer part of town, uphill from Piazza Vittorio Emanuele. It has rooms for L30,000/50,000, and doubles with bathroom for L60,000; a triple with bathroom is L85,000. The *Hotel Concordia* (☎ 59 42 20) is in Piazza San Francesco, where the daily produce market is held, just off Via Atenea. It has rooms for L20,000/40,000, or L30,000/60,000 with private bathroom.

Most of Agrigento's better hotels are out of town around the Valley of the Temples or near the sea. *Hotel Akrabello* (☎ 60 62 77) is in the area of Parco Angeli, to the east of the temples. It is modern and comfortable and has rooms for up to L90,000/140,000. *Hotel della Valle* (☎ 2 69 66) is in Via dei Templi.

It has lovely rooms with full services, and has a pool and gardens; rooms cost up to L100,000/170,000. *Hotel Kaos* (☎ 59 87 70) is by the sea, about two km from the temples. In a restored villa, it is a large tourist resort complex with all facilities. Rooms cost up to L100,000/150,000.

Places to Eat

A good choice for a light lunch is the *Manhattan Paninoteca*, up the flight of stairs called Salita M Angeli from Via Atenea. *Caffè Amato*, Via Atenea 1, has a good selection of cakes and pastries. However, for the best pastries, and just for the experience, go to the *Santo Spirito Monastery* at the end of Via Foderà (it is marked on the tourist map). The nuns have been making heavenly cakes and pastries to a secret recipe for centuries, and their dolci di mandorle (almond cakes) are particularly special (as well as expensive). Press the door bell and then say *Vorrei comprare qualche dolce*, and see how you go.

Opposite the Hotel Bella Napoli is *Akragas da Lillo*, where the ageing owner/chef will prepare you a memorable meal for around L20,000. The *Black Horse*, Via Atenea, on the corner of Via Celauro, serves good, reasonably priced meals. *Ambasciata di Sicilia*, Via Giambertoni 2, just off Via Atenea, has outside tables overlooking the sea. It serves typical Sicilian fare, and an enjoyable meal will cost under L30,000. It also offers a set-price menu for under L20,000 a head.

If you have a car, head for *Trattoria Kokalos*, Via C Magazzeni, east of the temples, where they serve the area's best pizzas.

One of the best restaurants in Agrigento is *Le Caprice*, between the town and the temples. A full meal will cost between L40,000 and L50,000. Take the No 3 bus from outside the station and get off at the Hotel Colleverde. *Da Gennaro*, Via Petrarca, again downhill from the town, also maintains high standards. A full meal, including seafood, will cost around L70,000.

Getting There & Away

Bus This is the easiest way to get to and from Agrigento. The intercity terminal is in Piazza Roselli, just off Piazza Vittorio Emanuele, and timetables for most services are posted in Bar Sprint in the piazza. Autoservizi Cuffaro and Fratelli Camilleri both run buses to Palermo. SAL services Gela, Syracuse and Porto Empedocle, while Salvatore Lumia services Marsala and Trapani. AST buses service most of the small towns in the province. There is also an AST bus to Ragusa, with a connection at Gela.

Train Trains run to Palermo, Catania and Enna, but bus services are more efficient.

Car Agrigento is easily accessible by road from all of Sicily's main towns. Once you arrive in Agrigento's outskirts, simply follow the 'centro' signs and ask directions for Piazza Vittorio Emanuele, where there is plenty of car-parking space.

Getting Around

City buses (SAIS) run frequent services down to the Valley of the Temples, leaving from in front of the train station. Take bus No 8, 9 or 11 and get off at either the Archaeological Museum or farther downhill at Piazzale dei Templi. Bus No 5 runs from the station to the cathedral at the other end of the medieval town, for those who prefer not to make the uphill walk.

North-West Sicily

MARSALA

Best known for the sweet Marsala wine which is produced here, Marsala is a very pleasant town and well worth a stopover on your travels between Agrigento and Trapani. Founded as Lilybaeon on Cape Lilibeo by Carthaginians, who had fled nearby Mozia (or Motya) after its destruction by Syracuse, the city was eventually conquered by the Arabs, who renamed it Marsah el Allah (Port of God). Giuseppe Garibaldi landed at Marsala in 1860 with his One Thousand to launch his unification campaign.

The Marsala wine was 'discovered' by an Englishman named John Woodhouse who, after landing in the city in 1773 and tasting the local product, decided it should be marketed throughout Europe. His first competitor was Benjamin Ingham, who established his own factory in the town and began exporting the wine to the USA and Australia.

One particularly interesting figure in the Marsala-producing business was Ingham's nephew, Joseph Whitaker, who bought the island of San Pantaleo, the site of ancient Mozia (it is still in his family today), and built his villa there. Whitaker was responsible for renewing interest in the archaeological site of Mozia and for the few excavations which have been carried out. His former villa is now the museum of Mozia, which houses finds from the ancient city, including the statue *il Giovinetto di Mozia*.

Marsala's tourist office, the Pro Loco, is at Via Garibaldi 45, in the centre of town, along Via Mazzini from the train station. The town's telephone code is 0923.

Things to See

Visit the **cathedral** in Piazza della Repubblica, built in the 17th and 18th centuries, and then its small museum, the **Museo degli Arazzi**, at Via Garraffa 57. In the museum are eight 16th century tapestries, woven for the Spanish king Philip II and depicting scenes from the war of Titus against the Jews. The **Museo Nazionale Lilibeo**, in Via Boeo by the sea (follow Via XI Maggio to Piazza Vittoria and then turn left along Via N Sauro), houses a partly reconstructed Carthaginian warship, believed to have been used during the First Punic War. It was found off the coast north of Marsala in 1971. North of the museum, along Viale Vittorio Veneto, is an archaeological zone which has been only partly excavated. The **Insula Romana** at the site was a 3rd century AD Roman house.

Also take the time to visit the island of **San Pantaleo**, the site of ancient Mozia in the lagoon known as the Stagnone. On the island is the museum as well as the excavations of the Carthaginian city, including the ancient port and dry dock. It is about 11 km north along the coast from Marsala, a scenic drive or bus trip, and the island is then accessible by boat. The bus service operates only during the summer months. Ask at the Pro Loco office for bus and boat timetable information.

Places to Stay & Eat

If you want to stay in Marsala, try the *Garden* (☎ 98 23 20) near the train station at Via Gambini 36, which has singles/doubles for L27,000/50,000. The *Villa Favorita* (☎ 98 91 00) at Via Favorita 27 is two km north-east of Marsala. A tourist complex, it has rooms for L42,000/70,000. The *Trattoria Fratelli De Marco*, Via Vaccari 6, just off Piazza della Repubblica, has reasonably priced meals.

Getting There & Away

Marsala is easily reached by bus from Trapani (AST or Lumia), Agrigento (Lumia) and Palermo (Salemi). For further details, see the Getting There & Away sections for these places. Buses arrive at Piazza del Popolo, off Via Mazzini, in the centre of town. Four AST buses per day connect Marsala with Castelvetrano, from where you can catch a bus to Selinunte.

Marsala is accessible from Trapani and Palermo by train, although from Palermo it is necessary to change at Alcamo Diramazione.

From June to September, Sandokan (☎ 71 20 60) runs a boat service to the Egadi Islands.

SELINUNTE

The ancient Greek city of Selinus, founded in the 7th century BC, was a prosperous and powerful city. A great rival of Segesta to the north, Selinunte was eventually destroyed by Segesta's ally, Carthage, in 409 BC. Although the city recovered, first under Syracuse and later under Carthage, it was finally abandoned around 250 BC when the

people of Selinunte destroyed their own city to prevent it passing to the Romans. Its great temples were destroyed by an earthquake in the Middle Ages.

One of the most interesting archaeological sites in Italy, it features the remains of seven temples, known by the letters A to G, and an acropolis. One of the three main temples is **Temple E**, which is nearest the sea and was built in the 5th century BC. It was reconstructed in 1958 in a much-criticised project. **Temple G**, the northernmost, was built in the 6th century BC and, though never completed, was one of the largest in the Greek world. Today it is a massive pile of rubble, but evocative nonetheless.

The **acropolis** is across the depression known as the Gorgo di Cottone. Here are the remains of five temples, including **Temple C**, believed to have been the most magnificent on the acropolis. Some of the more outstanding metopes in Palermo's archaeological museum were taken from this temple.

The archaeological site is close to the village of Marinella di Selinunte, where you can find accommodation if you want to stay overnight. There are camping facilities at *Il Maggiolino* (☎ 0924-4 60 44); charges include L5000 per person, L4000 per tent and L3500 per car. The *Pensione Costa d'Avorio* (☎ 0924-4 60 11), Via Stazione 10, has singles/doubles for L25,000/40,000, or L30,000/50,000 with bathroom. It also has a trattoria, where a full meal will cost around L25,000. *Hotel Alceste* (☎ 0924-4 61 84), Via Alceste 23, has more up-market rooms for L40,000/65,000 with bathroom.

See the Marsala Getting There & Away section for details about transport.

TRAPANI

While not one of Sicily's major tourist towns, Trapani provides a comfortable base from which to explore the surrounding expanse of the island's north-west, which includes the beautiful medieval town of Erice, the Greek archaeological site at Segesta, the beaches of the Golfo di Castellammare, and the Zingaro Natural Park, as well as the Egadi Islands.

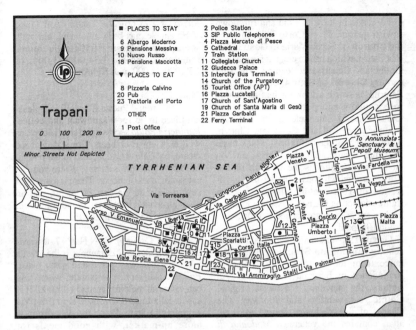

■ PLACES TO STAY	2 Police Station
	3 SIP Public Telephones
6 Albergo Moderno	4 Piazza Mercato di Pesce
9 Pensione Messina	5 Cathedral
10 Nuovo Russo	7 Train Station
18 Pensione Maccotta	11 Collegiate Church
	12 Giudecca Palace
▼ PLACES TO EAT	13 Intercity Bus Terminal
	14 Church of the Purgatory
8 Pizzeria Calvino	15 Tourist Office (APT)
20 Pub	16 Piazza Lucatelli
23 Trattoria del Porto	17 Church of Sant'Agostino
	19 Church of Santa Maria di Gesù
OTHER	21 Piazza Garibaldi
	22 Ferry Terminal
1 Post Office	

Trapani

0   100   200 m

Minor Streets Not Depicted

TYRRHENIAN SEA

A Carthaginian and later Roman city, Trapani became an important trading centre under Arab and Norman rule and, under the Spanish, was western Sicily's most important town. It has been in decline ever since, although its pleasant centre, featuring Baroque churches and piazzas, warrants some exploration. Of particular interest are Trapani's colourful Easter celebrations (see the following Things to See & Do section).

Orientation

By public transport you will arrive close to the centre of town. The main bus terminal is in Piazza Malta, while the train station is around the corner in Piazza Umberto I. From here, follow Via Osorio, turn left into Via XXX Gennaio, then right into Corso Italia to reach Piazza Scarlatti. The old town's main street, Corso Vittorio Emanuele, is to the north, off Via Torreasa.

Information

Tourist Office The APT information office

(☎ 0923-2 90 00) is in Piazzetta Saturno, just off Piazza Scarlatti. It is open Monday to Saturday from 8 am to 8 pm, closing earlier in winter.

Post & Telecommunications The main post office is in Piazza Vittorio Veneto (turn right into Via XXX Gennaio from Via Osorio). There is an SIP public telephone office in Via Scontrino, just off Piazza Umberto near the train station. It is open from 8 am to 9 pm. The postal code for central Trapani is 91100, and the telephone code for the town is 0923.

Emergency For police attention, call ☎ 113. The main police station (☎ 2 23 33) is in Via Virgilio, off Piazza V Veneto. The public hospital, the Ospedale Sant'Antonio Abate (☎ 80 94 50), is in Via Cosenza, some distance from the centre of town.

Things to See & Do

The 16th century **Giudecca Palace** in Via

Giudecca is in the city's old and run-down Jewish quarter. Cross Corso Italia to reach the **Church of Santa Maria di Gesù** in Via San Pietro, which has an elegant façade with Gothic and Renaissance features. The 14th century **Church of Sant'Agostino**, Piazza Saturno, is worth a look for its fine Gothic rose window and portal. Continue along Corso Vittorio Emanuele, noting the 17th century town hall and Collegiate Church, before reaching the **cathedral**, which has a Baroque façade. Off the Corso, on Via Generale D Giglio, is the **Church of the Purgatory**, which houses the *Misteri*, a collection of 18th century life-size wooden figures depicting Christ's Passion. On Good Friday, the *Misteri* are carried in procession around Trapani.

One of Trapani's major sights is the 14th century **Annunziata Sanctuary**, some distance from the centre in Via A Pepoli. Remodelled in Baroque style in the 17th century, the sanctuary retains its original Gothic rose window and doorway. The Chapel of the Madonna, behind the high altar, contains the venerated *Madonna di Trapani*, believed to have been carved by Nino Pisano.

The adjacent **Pepoli Museum** has an interesting archaeological collection, as well as statues and coral carvings. The museum is open Tuesday to Saturday from 9 am to 1.30 pm and also on Tuesday, Thursday and Friday from 3 to 6 pm. On Sunday it is open from 9 am to 12.30 pm. Entrance is L2000.

Places to Stay

The *Pensione Messina* (☎ 2 11 98), Corso V Emanuele 71, is on the 3rd floor of a 17th century palace, but its rooms are very basic; the cost per person is L15,000. *Pensione Maccotta* (☎ 2 84 18), Via degli Argentieri 4, off Piazza Sant'Agostino, has higher standard singles/doubles for L30,000/55,000, or L40,000/70,000 with private bathroom. *Albergo Moderno* (☎ 2 12 47), Via Genovese, which runs parallel to Corso V Emanuele, off Via Roma, is also in an old palace; rooms are L32,000/50,000, or L45,000/55,000 with bathroom. The *Nuovo*

Russo (☎ 2 21 66), Via Tintori 4, off Corso V Emanuele, has been renovated, although some of its classic 1950s-style rooms remain; rooms are L34,000/63,000, or L53,000/81,000 with bathroom.

Places to Eat

The area around Piazza Lucatelli is a pleasant place to go for a sandwich and coffee. *Panineria Poldo* serves good sandwiches, as well as a range of beers. For a decent ice cream, try *Chupa Chupa*, also in the piazza. In Piazza Scarlatti is *Kenny*, where you can eat sandwiches or crêpes. There is a discount supermarket at Via San Pietro 30, and an open-air market is held every morning from Monday to Saturday in the Piazza Mercato di Pesce.

Pizzeria Calvino, Via N Nasi 77, towards the port off Corso V Emanuele, is the town's favourite takeaway pizza and pasta place. *Pub* is a self-service restaurant, where you can eat a full meal for around L15,000. It is at Via della Luce 8. *Trattoria del Porto*, Via Ammiraglio Staiti 45, on the waterfront, is more up-market, with good meals for between L25,000 and L35,000.

Getting There & Away

Trapani has a small airport, 16 km out of town at Birgi. Buses leave from outside Salvo Viaggi, Corso Italia 56, to coincide with flights. Express buses connect Trapani with Palermo (Segesta) and Agrigento (Lumia). These buses terminate in Piazza Garibaldi on the waterfront. All other intercity buses terminate in Piazza Malta. AST buses run from the piazza to Erice (approximately every hour), Castellammare del Golfo (four a day), Castelvetrano (seven a day), Marsala (four a day) and San Vito Lo Capo (nine a day). Autoservizi Tarantola runs a bus service from Trapani to the Greek archaeological site of Segesta and on to Calatafimi.

Trains connect Trapani to Palermo, Castelvetrano and Marsala.

The city is easily reached by autostrada from Palermo. A car makes it much easier to explore the north-west of the island, particularly if you want to spend some time in the Zingaro Natural Park.

Ferries and hydrofoils connect Trapani with the Egadi Islands. Siremar runs both, and its ticket office (☎ 2 77 80) is at Via Ammiraglio Staiti 61. Ferry tickets are also available at Traghetti delle Isole, in the same street at No 23. Aliscafi SNAV runs hydrofoils to the islands, and tickets are available in Via A Staiti, off Piazza Garibaldi.

Tirrenia runs weekly ferries to Tunisia from Trapani. Tickets can be purchased at Salvo Viaggi, Corso Italia 43.

ERICE

This particularly beautiful medieval town, set 750 metres above the sea, is about 40 minutes from Trapani by bus and is a highly recommended day trip or overnight stay. Settled by the Elymians, an ancient mountain people who also founded Segesta, it was an important religious site associated with the cult of the goddess of fertility – first the Carthaginian Astarte, then the Greek Aphrodite and finally the Roman Venus.

Erice's tourist office (☎ 0923-86 93 88) is at Viale Conte Pepoli 11.

The triangular-shaped town is best explored by meandering around its network of narrow streets, peeking through the doorways of palaces to see the courtyards. The main sight in town is the Norman castle, known as the **Castello di Venere** (Castle of Venus). It was built in the 12th to 13th centuries on the site of the ancient temple of Venus. The 14th century main church, known as the **Chiesa Matrice**, in Via V Carvini, has a separate bell tower with mullioned windows. The interior of the church was remodelled in neo-Gothic style in the 19th century, although the 15th century side chapels were conserved.

If you want to stay in Erice, there is an IYHF youth hostel, *G Amodeo* (☎ 0923-55 29 64), which is just out of town and open all year. Bed and breakfast is L17,000 and a meal costs L12,000. Otherwise try the *Edelweiss* (☎ 0923-86 91 58), Cortile P Vincenzo, which has singles/doubles for L50,000/75,000.

Erice is easily accessible by AST buses, which leave from Piazza Malta in Trapani.

SEGESTA

One of three important towns founded by the Elymians (the others were Erice and Entella), Segesta eventually came under Greek influence, and the ruins of its Greek temple and theatre are among the most important archaeological sites in Sicily. The city was in constant conflict with neighbouring Selinunte and this rivalry caused it to seek assistance from its allies of varying periods, including Carthage, Athens, Syracuse and the Romans, eventually leading to the destruction of Selinunte.

Today, little remains of what was once a great city, but the setting of the ruins and the fact that the temple is extraordinarily well preserved make the site well worth a visit. The Doric **temple**, dating from around 430 BC, stands alone on the hillside overlooking the sea in the distance. The Hellenistic **Greek Theatre** is also quite well preserved, the only structure inside the old city walls which has survived. From its terraced seats there is a beautiful panorama of the sea.

In July and August of every odd-numbered year (alternating with Syracuse), performances of Greek plays are staged in the Greek Theatre. For information, contact the tourist office in Trapani.

Segesta is accessible by Autoservizi Tarantola bus from Piazza Malta in Trapani, or from Palermo by buses run by Trepanum (☎ 0923-51 12 32), leaving from Piazza Marina. Otherwise you can catch one of the infrequent trains from Trapani or Palermo to Segesta Tempio; it is then a 20-minute walk from the station to the archaeological zone.

GOLFO DI CASTELLAMMARE

Best explored by car, this area is also accessible by public transport from Trapani, and destinations include the beaches at the tourist resort towns of San Vito Lo Capo and Castellammare del Golfo, and the peaceful **Zingaro Natural Park** on the western side of the gulf. There is also the unspoiled fishing village of Scopello, a few km from the park's southern boundary.

Camping grounds dot the coast, including *Camping Soleado* (☎ 0923-97 21 66) and *Camping La Fata* (☎ 0923-97 21 33) at San Vito Lo Capo; and *Camping Baia di Guidaloca* (☎ 0924-59 60 22) and *Camping Ciauli* (☎ 0924-3 90 49) at Scopello. There are numerous pensioni and hotels at San Vito and Castellammare (the tourist office at Trapani has a full list). *Pensione Tranchina*

(☎ 0924-59 60 63) is at Via Diaz 7, Scopello, and has rooms for L25,000 per person.

San Vito Lo Capo and Castellammare del Golfo are accessible from Trapani's Piazza Malta by AST bus. From Castellammare it is possible to catch a bus to Scopello. There is no public transport to the Zingaro park, so, unless you have your own transport, you could try hitchhiking along the coastal road from either San Vito or Scopello.

Sardinia

Sardinia

The second-largest island in the Mediterranean, Sardinia (Sardegna) was colonised and invaded by the Greeks, Phoenicians and Romans, followed by the Pisans, Genoese and finally the Spanish. But it is often said that the Sardinians, known as Sardi, were never really conquered, they simply retreated into the hills.

The Romans were prompted to call the island's central-eastern mountains Barbagia because of their views on the lifestyle of the locals. This area is still known as the Barbagia. Even today the Sardinians of the interior are a strangely insular people. Some women still wear traditional costume and shepherds still live in almost complete isolation, building enclosures of stone or wood as their ancestors did for their sheep and goats. If you venture into the interior, you will find the people incredibly gracious and hospitable, but easily offended if they sense any lack of respect.

The first inhabitants of the island were the Nuraghic people, thought to have arrived here around 2000 BC. Little is known about them, but the island is dotted with thousands of *nuraghi*, their conical-shaped stone houses and fortresses.

In 1948 Sardinia became a semiautonomous region, and the Italian government's Sardinian Rebirth Plan of 1962 had some influence on the development of tourism, industry and agriculture.

The island's cuisine is as varied as its history. Along the coast most dishes feature seafood and there are many variations of *zuppa di pesce* (fish soup). Inland you will find *porcheddu* (roast suckling pig), kid goat with olives, and even lamb's trotters in garlic sauce. The Sardi eat *pecorino* (sheep's-milk cheese) and you will rarely find Parmesan here. The preferred bread throughout the island is the paper-thin *carta musica*, also called *pane carasau*, often sprinkled with oil and salt.

The landscape of the island ranges from the 'savage, dark-bushed, sky-exposed land' described by D H Lawrence, to the incredibly beautiful gorges and valleys near Dorgali, the rugged isolation of the Gennargentu mountain range, and the unspoiled coastline between Bosa and Alghero. Although hunters have been traditionally active in Sardinia, some wildlife remains, notably albino donkeys on the island of Asinara off the north-west coast, colonies of griffon vultures on the west coast, and miniature horses in the Giara di Gesturi plain, in the south-west. The famous colony of Mediterranean monk seals at the Grotta del Bue Marino, near Cala Gonone, has not been sighted for some years.

Try to avoid the island in August, when the weather is very hot and the beaches are overcrowded. Warm weather generally continues from May to September.

GETTING THERE & AWAY
Air
Airports at Cagliari, Olbia and Alghero link Sardinia with major Italian and European cities. For information, contact the CIT or CTS offices in all major towns, or Alitalia.

Boat
The island is accessible by ferry from Genoa, Civitavecchia, Naples, Palermo, Trapani and Tunis. The departure points in Sardinia are Olbia, Golfo Aranci and Porto Torres in the north, Arbatax on the east coast and Cagliari in the south.

The main ferry company is Tirrenia, although the national railway, Ferrovie dello Stato, runs a slightly cheaper service between Olbia and Civitavecchia. Other companies include Moby Lines, also known as Navarma Lines, which runs ferries between the island and Corsica, as well as from Livorno to Olbia. Note that timetables change dramatically every year and that prices fluctuate according to the season. For

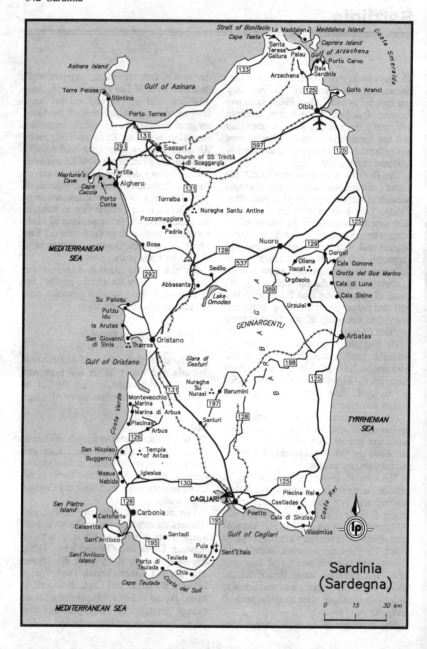

Sardinia
(Sardegna)

0   15   30 km

full information, pick up an annual timetable from any Tirrenia or Moby Lines office.

Addresses and phone numbers for Tirrenia's offices in Sardinia are listed throughout this section. It also has offices throughout Italy, including Rome (☎ 06-474 20 43), Via Bissolati 41; Civitavecchia (☎ 0766-2 88 01); and Genoa (☎ 010-25 80 41). Moby Lines has offices and agents throughout the island. In Livorno it operates through the agency L V Ghianda (☎ 0586-89 03 25), Via Vittorio Veneto 24.

Prices for an airline-type chair on Tirrenia ferries at the time of writing were: Genoa-Porto Torres or Olbia L53,500 (12½ hours); Genoa-Cagliari L77,200 (19 hours); Civitavecchia-Olbia L27,000 (seven hours); Civitavecchia-Cagliari L47,500 (13½ hours); Naples-Cagliari L48,400 (15 hours); and Palermo-Cagliari L44,300 (12½ hours). The cost of taking a small car ranged from L75,000 to L90,000, and L23,000 to L30,000 for a motorbike. Examples of prices per person in a cabin were: Civitavecchia-Olbia L40,000 (2nd class) and L57,700 (1st class); Genoa-Olbia L73,800 (2nd class) and L111,600 (1st class).

GETTING AROUND
Bus
The main bus companies are ARST, which operates extensive services throughout the island, and PANI, which links the main towns. Buses are generally faster than trains.

Train
The main FS train lines link Cagliari with Oristano, Sassari and Olbia and are generally reliable. The private railways which link smaller towns throughout the island can be very slow. However, the little train which runs from Cagliari to Arbatax through the Barbagia is a relaxing way to see part of the interior (for more details, see under Travel Agency in the Cagliari Information section).

Car & Motorbike
The only way to really explore Sardinia is by road. Rental agencies are listed under Cagliari and some other towns around the island.

Hitching
You might find hitchhiking laborious because of the light traffic once you get away from the main towns. Women should not hitchhike alone in Sardinia under any circumstances.

Cagliari

This is a surprisingly pleasant city, notable for its interesting medieval section, its beautiful beach – Poetto – and its population of pink flamingos. The capital of the island, Cagliari warrants a day of sightseeing and is a good base for exploring the southern coast.

Believed to have been founded by Phoenicians, Cagliari became an important Carthaginian port town before coming under Roman control. As with the rest of the island, the city passed through the hands of various conquerors, including the Pisans, Spanish and finally the Piedmontese House of Savoy, before joining the unified Italy. The city was savagely bombed during WW II, suffering significant destruction and loss of life.

Orientation
If you arrive by bus, train or boat you will find yourself at the port area of Cagliari. The main street along the harbour is Via Roma and the old city stretches up the hill behind it to the old fortified area. At the northwestern end of Via Roma, to the left as you leave the port, is Piazza Matteotti and the AAST tourist information office, the ARST intercity bus terminal and the train station. Most of the budget hotels and restaurants are close to the port area.

Information
Tourist Offices The AAST tourist information booth (☎ 070-66 92 55) in Piazza Matteotti is open from 8 am to 8 pm daily during summer, and from 8 am to 2 pm in other months. It has a reasonable amount of

■ **PLACES TO STAY**

20	Locanda Firenze
25	Hotel Quattro Mori
27	Albergo Centrale
28	Albergo La Perla
29	Hotel Italia
33	Pensione Vittoria
34	Locanda Miramare

▼ **PLACES TO EAT**

17	Ristorante Il Corso
21	Trattoria Loddo Umberto
24	Ristorante Flora
30	Trattoria Gennargentu
31	Corsaro
32	Trattoria Congera
35	Trattoria Da Serafino

OTHER

1	Police Headquarters
2	Roman Amphitheatre
3	Piazza Indipendenza
4	St Pancras Tower
5	Piazza Garibaldi
6	National Archaeological Museum
7	Ferrovie Complementari della Sardegna Train Station
8	Piazza della Repubblica
9	Piazza Palazzo
10	Duomo
11	Public Hospital
12	Elephant Tower
13	Church of San Michele
14	Bastione di San Remy
15	Piazza Costituzione
16	Piazza dei Martiri
18	Alitalia Office
19	ESIT Tourist Information
22	Post Office
23	Piazza del Carmine
26	ASST Public Telephones
36	Piazza Amendola
37	Train Station
38	AAST Tourist Information & Piazza Matteotti
39	ARST Bus Terminal
40	Ferry Terminal
41	PANI Bus Terminal
42	Piazza Deffenu

information about the town and will advise on accommodation. There is also a provincial tourist information booth at the airport (the booth at the Stazione Marittima in the port has been closed indefinitely) open from 8.30 am to 1 pm and 3.30 to 9 pm daily in the high season. There is an office of the Ente Sardo Industrie Turistiche (ESIT), which covers all of Sardinia, at Via Goffredo Mameli 97. The office can be useful if you are starting your tour of the island at Cagliari.

Money There are several major banks on Largo Carlo Felice, which runs uphill from Piazza Matteotti, open from 8.30 am to 1.30 pm and 2.30 to 3.30 pm Monday to Friday. Otherwise, there is an exchange office at the train station, open daily from 7 am to 8 pm, and at the airport, open 8 am to 1 pm Monday to Saturday.

Post & Telecommunications The main post office is in Piazza del Carmine, up Via La Maddalena from Via Roma, and open from 8 am to 4.30 pm Monday to Saturday.

The ASST public telephone office is at Via G M Angioj, off Piazza Matteotti, and is open 24 hours a day, seven days a week. The postal code for central Cagliari is 09100 and the telephone code is 070.

Travel Agency There is a CTS office (☎ 48 82 60) at Via Cesare Balbo 4. Karalis Viaggi (☎ 30 69 91), Via della Pineta 199, can provide information on the small train which travels along a scenic route between Cagliari and Arbatax.

Emergency For immediate police attendance, call ☎ 113, or go to the police headquarters (☎ 4 44 44), Via Amat 9. For an ambulance, call ☎ 27 23 45. For medical attention, the closest public hospital to the centre is the Ospedale Civile (☎ 601 82 67), Via Ospedale between the Church of San Michele and the Roman Amphitheatre.

Things to See & Do
There is not a lot to see in Cagliari, but it is pleasant enough to wander through the old

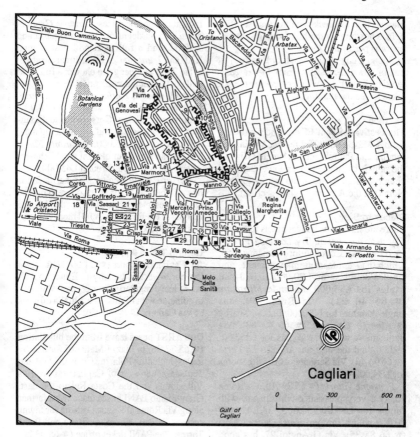

Cagliari

0   300   600 m

Gulf of
Cagliari

quarter around the medieval fortified area. Take a look at the Pisan-Romanesque **Duomo**, originally built in the 13th century, but later remodelled. It has an interesting Romanesque pulpit. From the **Bastione di San Remy** there is a pleasant view of Cagliari and the sea.

The Pisan **St Pancras Tower** in Piazza Indipendenza, and the **Elephant Tower** below in Via Università, both erected in the 14th century, are also worth a look. The latter was used as a prison by the Spanish and Piedmontese.

Also on Piazza Indipendenza is the

National Archaeological Museum, which houses an important collection of Nuraghic statuettes, as well as Phoenician and Roman artefacts. The museum is open from 9 am to 2 pm Monday to Saturday (as well as 3.30 to 6.30 pm on Tuesday and Saturday), and 9 am to 1 pm on Sundays. Entrance is L4000.

The **Roman Amphitheatre**, on Viale Buon Cammino, is considered the most important Roman monument in Sardinia. Hewn out of rock in the 2nd century AD, it was said to be big enough to house up to 20,000 spectators. The amphitheatre has been temporarily closed to visitors and it may be best to check with the tourist office before heading up the hill. During summer, opera is performed there.

Spend a day on the beach of **Poetto**, just out of town (accessible from Piazza Matteotti on bus P), and wander across to the salt lakes to see the flamingos.

Festival
The Festival of Sant'Efisio is held annually from 1 May, a colourful festival mixing the secular and the religious, when an effigy of the saint is carried in procession to the small church of Sant'Efisio in the nearby town of Nora (see the Around Cagliari section).

Places to Stay
There are numerous budget hotels in the old city near the station. Try *Locanda Firenze* (☎ 65 36 78), Corso Vittorio Emanuele 50, which has a pleasant management, and singles/doubles for L20,000/26,000 and triples for L35,000. *Locanda Miramare* (☎ 66 40 21), Via Roma 59, has singles/doubles for L39,000/52,000. Nearby is *Albergo Centrale* (☎ 65 47 83), Via Sardegna 4, which has rooms for L25,000/39,000, and the pleasant *Albergo La Perla* (☎ 66 94 46), Via Sardegna 16B, with rooms for L34,000/44,000.

Pensione Vittoria (☎ 65 79 70), Via Roma 75, is a very pleasant establishment, with rooms for L35,000/54,000, or L41,000/70,000 with bathroom. *Hotel Quattro Mori* (☎ 66 85 35), Via G Angioj 27, has good rooms for L50,000/70,000, or L57,000/90,000 with bathroom. The *Hotel Italia* (☎ 66 04 10), Via Sardegna 31, has more up-market, comfortable rooms for L74,000/100,000.

Places to Eat
There are several reasonably priced trattorias in the area behind Via Roma, particularly around Via Cavour and Via Sardegna. If you want to buy picnic supplies, head for Via Sardegna, where there are several good grocery shops as well as a bakery.

Trattoria Da Serafino, Via Lepanto 6, on the corner of Via Sardegna, has excellent food at reasonable prices. *Trattoria Gennargentu*, Via Sardegna 60, has good pasta and seafood, and a full meal will cost around L20,000. *Trattoria Congera*, down the street at No 37, is another good choice; a full meal will cost about the same price.

A full meal at *Trattoria Loddo Umberto*, Via Sassari 86, will cost around L18,000. *Ristorante Il Corso*, Corso Vittorio Emanuele 78, specialises in seafood and a full meal will cost around L35,000. *Ristorante Flora*, Via Sassari 45, is an elegant establishment where you will spend around L45,000.

Corsaro, Viale Regina Margherita 28, is one of the city's top seafood restaurants. During summer it transfers to the Marina Piccola at Poetto beach. A full meal will cost at least L80,000.

Getting There & Away
Air Cagliari's airport (☎ 24 00 47) is eight km north-west of the city at Elmas. ARST buses leave regularly from Piazza Matteotti to coincide with flights. The Alitalia office is at Via Caprera 14 (☎ 60 10).

Bus ARST buses leave from the bus station (☎ 65 72 36) in Piazza Matteotti for nearby towns, including Pula, the Costa del Sud and Teulada south-west of Cagliari, as well as Villasimius and the Costa Rei to the east. Granturismo PANI buses leave from farther along Via Roma at Piazza Darsena for towns such as Sassari, Nuoro, Oristano and Porto Torres. The PANI ticket office (☎ 65 23 26) is at Piazza Darsena 4.

Train Regular trains leave for Oristano, Sassari, Porto Torres and Olbia. The private Ferrovie Complementari della Sardegna station is in Piazza della Repubblica. For information about the *trenino* (little train), which runs along a scenic route between Cagliari and Arbatax, contact Karalis Viaggi (see Travel Agency in the earlier Information section).

Boat Ferries arrive at the port just off Via Roma. Bookings for Tirrenia can be made at Via Campidano 1 (☎ 66 60 65), at the end of

Via Roma, off Piazza Deffenu. There is also an office at the Stazione Marittima, which opens only before ship departures. Ferries connect Cagliari with Palermo, Trapani, Naples, Civitavecchia and Genoa, as well as Tunisia (via Trapani). See the Getting There & Away section at the beginning of this chapter for further information.

Car & Motorbike If you want to rent a car or motorbike, try Hertz (☎ 66 81 05), Piazza Matteotti 1, or Ruvioli (☎ 65 89 55), Via dei Mille 11.

Getting Around

The only reason you will need to use public transport in Cagliari is if you want to head for the beach at Poetto. Take bus P from Piazza Matteotti.

AROUND CAGLIARI
The Costa Rei

There are good beaches within day-trip distance of Cagliari. To the east is the largely undeveloped Costa Rei, dotted with camping grounds and hotels which are generally expensive.

The town of **Villasimius**, before the Costa Rei, is near reasonable beaches. Try the *Albergo Stella d'Oro* (☎ 070-79 12 55), Via Vittorio Emanuele 21. It has singles/doubles for L30,000/53,000 and half-board is obligatory in August (L84,000 per person). Nearby, at the sea, is *Camping Spiaggia del Riso* (☎ 070-79 71 50); costs are L7500 per person and L12,000 for a site. Other camping grounds include *Cala Sinzias* (☎ 070-99 50 37), on the coast near Castiadas, and, farther north, *Piscina Rei* (☎ 070-99 10 96).

Slightly farther along the coast from Villasimius is the *Hotel Cormoran* (☎ 79 81 01), in the locality of Campus, a lovely resort hotel with a private sandy beach. Prices for full board range from L135,000 up to L220,000 in the high season. Bungalows for up to five people are available for L600,000 to L1,900,000 per week in the high season, and villas for up to seven people can be rented for up to L2,000,000 per week.

For full details on camping and other accommodation along the coast, contact the tourist office at Cagliari. Regular daily ARST buses connect Cagliari with Villasimius and places along the Costa Rei, including camping grounds.

Nora

To the west and south of Cagliari, the main points of interest are the beautiful Costa del Sud and the ruins of the Phoenician city of Nora.

Founded in the 9th century BC by the Phoenicians, Nora was considered important for its strategic position and eventually came under Roman control. The ruins of the city extend into the sea and offer evidence of both civilisations, including temples, houses, and a Roman theatre and baths. The ruins are open daily from 9 am to one hour before sunset in summer, and from 9 am to 12.30 pm and 2 to 5 pm out of season, although it is best to check with Cagliari's tourist office before setting out. To get to the ruins, take an ARST bus from Cagliari to Pula, then a local bus (Autolinee Murgia) to Nora (only three a day).

The Costa del Sud

The small town of Chia marks the start of the beautiful Costa del Sud, which is protected by special ordinances from further development – even private houses can be built only in certain zones. There is one large hotel complex which blights the coastline about halfway between Chia and Teulada, the four-star *Baia delle Ginestre* (☎ 070-927 30 05). Half-board per person per week costs from L700,000 in the low season and up to L1,200,000 in August.

Those happy to settle for something simpler can camp at *Camping Comunale Portu Tramatzu* (☎ 070-927 10 22), just past Porto di Teulada. Situated by the sea, the camping ground has a supermarket, bar, pizzeria and restaurant. Costs are L6000 per person and L9000 for a site. It is open from April to October. To get to the camping ground, take the ARST Cagliari-Teulada bus, get off at Porto di Teulada and then walk the short distance from the port to the camping ground (signs will point you in the right direction).

Your only other option is the *Hotel Sebera* (☎ 070-927 00 20), a pleasant establishment in the town of Teulada, in the central piazza where buses stop. Singles/doubles with full board cost L50,000/85,000.

At Porto di Teulada there is a very pleasant bar/trattoria which specialises in fresh seafood. You can enjoy lunch in a small courtyard for around L25,000 a head.

Regular ARST buses connect Cagliari with Chia, and about eight a day continue on to Teulada.

Travellers can then continue on to the island of Sant'Antioco. If you have a car, make a detour to the **Is Zuddas Caves**, near Santadi, a series of caves with interesting stalagmite and stalactite formations. There is a small, private tourist office at Santadi (☎ 0781-95 59 83), in Piazza Marconi, which organises excursions in the area, including to Is Zuddas and to the nearby **Tombs of the Giants**.

Another deviation would include the remains of the Phoenician/Carthaginian city on **Mt Sirai**, just out of Carbonia. This 7th century BC fort town commanded a view for miles around. Its ruins are still under excavation.

Southern Sardinia

SANT'ANTIOCO & SAN PIETRO ISLANDS

These islands, off the south-west coast of Sardinia, feature sandy beaches and quiet coves, as well as the pleasant towns of Calasetta on Sant'Antioco and Carloforte on San Pietro, both with whitewashed or pastel-coloured houses lining narrow streets. The town of Sant'Antioco is more developed.

Information

The Pro Loco tourist office (☎ 0781-8 20 31) is in the town of Sant'Antioco, at Via Nazionale 175 (it is planning a move farther along Via Nazionale closer to the centre of town). It can provide information and advice on accommodation, including apartments for rent, or you can request information by writing (in English) to the Associazione Turistica Pro Loco, 09017 Sant'Antioco. The telephone code for the islands is 0781.

Places to Stay

Both islands have good camping facilities. Try the *Campeggio Tonnara* (☎ 8 38 03) at Cala Sapone on the island of Sant'Antioco, or *La Caletta* (☎ 85 47 71) on the island of San Pietro. Both grounds are by the sea, away from the towns, and are accessible by the orange FMS buses which service both islands.

In Sant'Antioco, try the *Hotel Moderno* (☎ 8 31 05), Via Nazionale 82, which has singles/doubles for L35,000/60,000. You will need to book well in advance. In Calasetta, the best choice is the *Fiby Hotel* (☎ 8 84 44), Via Solferino 83, a very pleasant establishment with rooms with bathroom for L50,000/65,000.

At Carloforte, on San Pietro, there are few choices and only the camping grounds are cheap. The *Hieracon Hotel* (☎ 85 40 28), Corso Cavour 62, fronting the port, charges L88,000 per person for half-board in the high season and L75,000 a double in other months.

Places to Eat

There is a Coop supermarket in the town of Sant'Antioco on the corner of the Lungomare and Via d'Arborea, while in Carloforte you can pick up supplies at the Mercato Super Crai in Via Diaz.

In Sant'Antioco there are several good trattorias and restaurants, including the pizzeria/restaurant *Il Cartuccio*, Viale Trento, near Piazza Repubblica. In Calasetta, try *L'Anfora*, Via Roma 121, or *Da Pasqualino*, Via Roma 99. A full meal at either will cost around L25,000. At Carloforte, the *Barone Rosso*, Via XX Settembre 26, is the place to go for a sandwich; otherwise, try *Ristorante Da Vanino*, on the waterfront a short walk from the yacht harbour.

Getting There & Away

Sant'Antioco is connected to the mainland by a land bridge. It is accessible by FMS bus from Cagliari and Iglesias. Otherwise, catch a train to Carbonia from Cagliari or Iglesias, and then an FMS bus to the island. Regular ferries connect the two islands, leaving from Calasetta and arriving at Carloforte.

Getting Around

Orange FMS buses link the small towns on Sant'Antioco and the camping grounds and localities on San Pietro. On Sant'Antioco you can rent a scooter (L60,000 a day), motorino or bicycle (L45,000 a day) from in front of the Coop supermarket in the town of Sant'Antioco and make your own tour of the island. At Carloforte, go to SARINAV, Lungomare 6. Here scooters cost L90,000 a day. From both outlets you can also rent motorised rubber dinghies for around L230,000 a day.

IGLESIAS

This mining centre, slightly inland from Sardinia's south-western coast, is left off most tourist itineraries, but is, in fact, well worth a stopover. The town is in a zone rich in minerals, including lead, zinc and some silver and gold, and its mining history extends back to Roman and Carthaginian times. From the 13th century it was occupied by the Pisans, who called it Argentaria (the Place of Silver) after the rich silver mines which were discovered there in that period. However, it was the Spanish Aragons who left a greater mark on the town.

You will have to do without tourism advice while in Iglesias because the town is underprepared for the tourists who do pass through. If you do require any information, ask at the municipal offices (from 8 am to 2 pm Monday to Saturday) in Piazza del Duomo in the centre of town. The town's telephone code is 0781.

Things to See & Do

The **cathedral**, in Piazza del Duomo, opposite the municipal offices, dates from the period of Pisan domination and was built in the Romanesque-Gothic style. Nearby, in Piazza San Francesco, is the Gothic-style **Church of San Francesco**. Above the old town, along Via Campidano, are remains of Pisan towers and parts of the town's fortified walls.

Places to Stay & Eat

The choice is limited to one hotel, the *Artu* (☎ 2 24 92), Piazza Quintino Sella 15, east of the old part of town. It has singles/doubles with bathroom for L60,000/70,000. There are numerous pastry shops, takeaways and grocery shops in the shopping area around Via Martini and Via Azuni, a short walk from Piazza del Duomo. For a meal, try *Stalla* in Via Musio, off Via Azuni.

Getting There & Away

Regular FMS buses link Iglesias with Cagliari, Carbonia, Sant'Antioco and Calasetta. Two FMS buses a day head for Arbus, from where you can pick up connections to the Costa Verde. The bus station is in Via Oristano, off Via XX Settembre, south-east of the old town, and tickets can be purchased at Sulcis Agenzia Viaggi, Via Roma 52 (which is parallel to Via Oristano). The town is also accessible by train from Cagliari, Carbonia and Oristano, and the train station is in Via Garibaldi, a 10 to 15-minute walk along Via Matteotti from the town centre.

AROUND IGLESIAS

About 15 km north of Iglesias towards Fluminimaggiore is the Phoenician-Roman **Temple of Antas**. Set in a wide, picturesque valley, the small temple was dedicated by the Phoenicians to a god of fertility and hunting, while the Romans dedicated it to a local Nuraghic divinity. Six columns remain standing. If you don't have a car, take the FMS bus from Iglesias for Fluminimaggiore and get off just after the village of Sant'Angelo. The temple is then a three-km walk away along a dirt road.

Western Sardinia

THE COSTA VERDE

This magnificent stretch of coastline remains almost entirely unspoiled, despite the fact that much of the area has been extensively mined. Former mining towns such as Buggeru, Masua and Nebida (all three are on the coast, just south of the Costa Verde) are now seeking to make their fortunes as small tourist resorts.

The actual Costa Verde, which starts just north of Buggeru and continues to Montevecchio Marina, features long, white, sandy beaches with little or no development. Laws which protect the area mean that some sections will never be subject to development, and the area remains a paradise for lovers of secluded beaches. Campers and campervanners who remain discreet will find that they can free-camp in the area without any hassle. The isolation of much of the coast makes it difficult, but not impossible, for people to reach without their own transport.

Buggeru, a former mining town turned minor tourist resort, is a good place to make your base. It doesn't have any hotels as yet, but there is space set aside for camping by the waterfront, and you can free-camp along the coast to the south of the town. Many residents rent out rooms and apartments and, by asking at one of the town's bars or supermarkets, you will easily find a bed for the night (although most will be booked out in August).

Between Buggeru and Portixeddu to the north is the long, sandy beach of San Nicolao. Something of a rarity in Italy, this is a clean public beach, where the rows of deck chairs and umbrellas characteristic of the 'privatised' beaches in other parts of Italy have never been heard of.

Buggeru is accessible by FMS bus from Iglesias, which passes the beach of San Nicolao.

In the heart of the Costa Verde is **Piscinas**, at the mouth of the Piscinas River. This magnificent beach is famous for its high sand dunes which give it the appearance of a desert. There is one hotel at the beach, *Le Dune* (☎ 070-97 71 30), located in a reconstructed *colonia* (a former holiday camp for the children of mining families). Full board costs L120,000 per person and half-board is L100,000.

To reach Piscinas from Buggeru, take the road for Ingurtosu and turn off to the left where you see the sign for Le Dune.

Marina di Arbus, also known as Gutturu Flumini, is several km north and is more developed. Accommodation possibilities here include *Camping Costa Verde* (☎ 070-97 70 09), which charges L11,000 per person and L16,000 for a site. There is also an IYHF youth hostel, the *Ostello della Torre* (☎ 070-97 71 55), open all year; bed and breakfast is L18,000 and a meal costs L12,000. Apartments are available for rent at *Residence Piscinas* (☎ 070-97 71 37) for a minimum of one week. A two-person apartment will cost from L510,000, and for four people, over L900,000.

Getting to Marina di Arbus is not simple by public transport. You will need to catch an ARST bus from Oristano, or an FMS bus from Iglesias to Arbus, then a bus from Via della Repubblica to Marina di Arbus – which operates only in summer and only twice a day at 7.30 am and 2.30 pm, returning to Arbus in the evening.

ORISTANO

Like much of interest in Sardinia, the city of Oristano and its province should be approached with the attitude that they are to be 'discovered'. Originally inhabited by the Nuraghic people, the area around what is now Oristano was colonised by the Phoenicians, who established the port town of Tharros, later controlled by Carthaginians and then Romans.

The town of Oristano is believed to have been founded some time in the 7th century AD by the people of Tharros, who abandoned their ancient town, probably to escape raids by Moorish pirates. Oristano grew to prominence in the 14th century, particularly during the rule of Eleonora d'Arborea, who opposed the Spanish occupation of the island and drew up a body of laws known as the *Carta de Logu*, a progressive legal code which was eventually enforced throughout the island. The code is also considered important because it recorded the ancient Sardinian language, in which it was written.

Eleonora began a matriarchal, some would say feminist, tradition which has endured in Oristano. The town has had several women leaders, and recently the Sardinian Women's Cooperative of Sheep-Breeders (Cooperativa Allevatrici Sarde) established a highly successful agriturismo enterprise in the province (see the following Places to Stay section).

Orientation

A good point from which to orient yourself in Oristano is Piazza Roma, where, in summer, there is a tourist information caravan seven days a week from 9 am to 9 pm. The piazza is close to the PANI bus stop, along Via Tirso in Via Lombardia, and is a five-minute walk from the ARST bus terminal in Via Cagliari, just off Piazza Mannu. The train station is a 15 to 20-minute walk away in Piazza Ungheria. To reach Piazza Roma from here, follow Via Vittorio Veneto to Piazza Mariano and then take Via Mazzini.

Information

Tourist Office The mobile tourist office in Piazza Roma has loads of information on the town and the province and will advise on accommodation and transport. Pick up a copy of the booklet *Oristano & its Province*, available in English, which includes a map of the town. There is a Pro Loco office in Via de Castro, off Piazza Roma, open from 9 am to midday and 5 to 8 pm Monday to Friday. There is a provincial tourist office, the EPT, at Via Cagliari 278, open Monday to Friday from 8 am to 2 pm and also in the afternoon on Tuesday and Wednesday, from 4 to 8 pm.

Post & Telecommunications The main post office is at Via Mariano IV d'Arborea 10, and is open Monday to Saturday from

8.15 am to 7.30 pm. There are SIP public telephones in Piazza Eleonora d'Arborea. The postal code for central Oristano is 09170 and the telephone code is 0783.

Emergency For immediate police assistance, call ☎ 113. The police headquarters are in Via Carducci. For an ambulance, call ☎ 7 82 22. There is a public hospital (☎ 7 42 61) at Via Fondazione Rockefeller, along Viale San Martino from Piazza Mannu.

Things to See

In Piazza Roma is the 13th century **Tower of Mariano II**, also known as the Tower of San Cristoforo. From here, walk along Corso Umberto to Piazza Eleonora d'Arborea, where there is a 19th century statue of Oristano's heroine. To the right is the neoclassical **Church of San Francesco**. Of note inside the church is a 15th century polychrome wooden crucifix, a 14th century marble statue of San Basilio by Nino Pisano, and a 16th century polyptych by Pietro Cavaro.

Follow Via Eleonora d'Arborea or Via Duomo to reach the **Duomo**, built in the 13th century but completely remodelled in the 18th century. It has a Baroque bell tower, topped by a multicoloured dome. Also of interest in the town is the 14th century **Convent & Church of Santa Chiara**, between Via Parpaglia and Via Garibaldi.

About three km south of Oristano at Santa Giusta, and easily accessible by local ARST buses, is the **Basilica of Santa Giusta**. Built around 1100, the church is Romanesque, with Pisan and Lombard influences.

Festival

The most important festival in Oristano is the colourful Sa Sartiglia, held on the last Sunday of carnival (late February or early March) and repeated on Shrove Tuesday. Arguably one of the island's most beautiful festive events, the Sartiglia had its origins in a military contest performed by the knights of the Second Crusade. It developed into a festive event during the period of Spanish domination and now involves masked, costumed horsemen who parade through the town before participating in a tournament, whereby they must pierce the centre of a silver star with their swords while riding at full speed.

Places to Stay & Eat

The town is not exactly bursting with hotels and there are no budget options. There is a camping ground, the *Camping Torregrande* (☎ 2 20 08) at Marina di Torre Grande, about seven km west of Oristano (regular ARST buses connect the two towns – see the following Getting There & Away section). It is open from May to October and may be full during August.

In town is the *Piccolo Hotel* (☎ 7 15 00), Via Martignano 19, with singles/doubles for L40,000/60,000. The three-star *Hotel Amiscora* (☎ 7 25 03), Viale San Martino 13, has singles/doubles for L51,000/60,000 and triples/quads for L78,000/94,000, all with private bathroom. *Hotel ISA* (☎ 36 01 01) is close to the station at Piazza Mariano 50 and has doubles for L90,000 with private bathroom.

Agriturismo is very well organised in the province, with bed and breakfast costing around L26,000 a head and half-board around L38,000. It is organised by the Cooperativa Allevatrici Sarde (☎ 41 80 66). For details contact the tourist office or write to the cooperative at Casella Postale 107, 09170 Oristano.

For a quick snack or meal, try *Al Piatto Pronto* at Via Giuseppe Mazzini 21, near Piazza Roma, which has a wide range of pre-prepared dishes. *Trattoria del Teatro*, Via Parpaglia 11, has full meals for around L25,000, while *Il Faro*, Via Bellini 25, is considered one of the town's better and more expensive restaurants.

Getting There & Away

The terminal for ARST buses, which service the province, is on Via Cagliari, opposite the EPT tourist office. Regular buses head for Marina di Torre Grande, Putzu Idu and Su Pallosu, as well as San Giovanni di Sinis and the ruins of Tharros. Four buses a day leave

1	PANI Bus Stop
2	Il Faro
3	Post Office
4	Mobile Tourist Office
5	Tower of Mariano II
6	Al Piatto Pronto
7	Trattoria del Teatro
8	Convent & Church of Santa Chiara
9	Hotel ISA
10	Pro Loco Tourist Office
11	SIP Public Telephones
12	Piazza E d'Arborea
13	Church of San Francesco
14	Duomo
15	Piccolo Hotel
16	EPT Tourist Office
17	ARST Bus Terminal
18	Police Headquarters
19	Hotel Amiscora
20	Public Hospital

for Bosa. The PANI bus stop is in Via Lombardia, outside the Blu Bar at No 30 (where you can check on timetables). There are connections to Cagliari, Sassari and Nuoro.

Oristano is accessible by train from Cagliari, Sassari and Olbia. The train station is in Piazza Ungheria.

Getting Around

Oristano is easy to negotiate on foot, although urban bus No 2 Circolare Destra (clockwise) or Sinistra (anticlockwise) is handy for getting around.

AROUND ORISTANO

Just west of Oristano is the **Sinis Peninsula**, with some lovely sandy beaches (which have been awarded a coveted Blue Flag for cleanliness by the EC), the opportunity to see lots of flamingos, and the ruins of the ancient Phoenician port of Tharros. If you have the time, spend a few days relaxing here. There are only a couple of hotels, but rooms are available for rent and there are several places participating in the local agriturismo programme. Check at the tourist office in Oristano for details.

At the village of **San Giovanni di Sinis**

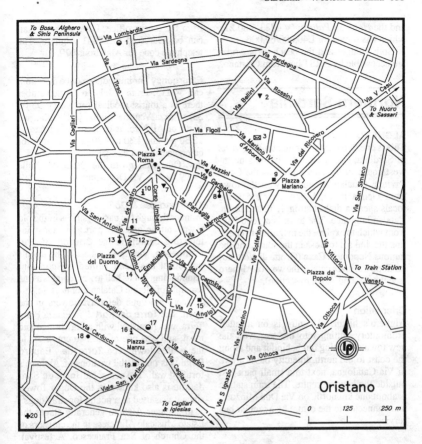

Oristano

is the 5th century Byzantine church of the same name, where Mass is still celebrated. Nearby is the tiny church of San Salvatore, built over a pagan temple in a tiny village of whitewashed houses with pastel-coloured doors.

Tharros, just out of San Giovanni at the southernmost end of the peninsula, was originally a Phoenician and later a Roman port town. These important ruins, discovered in 1851 by an English archaeologist, yielded significant treasures and are well worth a visit. They are open from 9 am to 1 pm and 4 to 7 pm and entrance is free.

San Giovanni and Tharros can be reached from Oristano by regular ARST buses.

At the northern end of the peninsula are the villages of **Putzu Idu** and **Su Pallosu**, both offering peaceful surroundings and lovely beaches. Between the two villages are marshes which are home to hundreds of pink flamingos as well as other water birds. The loveliest beach on the peninsula is nearby at **Is Arutas**.

If you want to stay at Putzu Idu, try *Da Cesare* (☎ 0783-5 20 15), which has singles/doubles for around L35,000/55,000. A short walk away is the quieter Su Pallosu and the *Hotel Su Pallosu* (☎ 0783-5 80 21), which has rooms for L40,000/60,000.

Both villages and the beach of Is Arutas are accessible by ARST bus from Oristano.

Northern Sardinia

ALGHERO

This is one of the most popular tourist resorts in Sardinia, situated on the island's north-west coast, in the area known as the Coral Riviera. Catalan Aragonese won the town from Genoa in 1354, and even today the locals speak a dialect strongly linked to the Catalan language. The town is a good base from which to explore the magnificent coast-line that links it to Bosa in the south, and the famous Neptune's Cave (Grotta di Nettuno) on Cape Caccia, a cape to the west of Alghero (see the Around Alghero section).

Orientation

Alghero's historical centre is on a small promontory, jutting into the sea, with the new town stretching out behind it and along the coast to the north. Intercity buses arrive in Via Catalogna, next to a small park just outside the historic centre. The train station is about one km north, on Via Don Minzoni, and connected to the centre by a regular bus service.

Information

Tourist Office The AAST office (☎ 97 90 54) is at Piazza Porta Terra 9, near the port and just across the gardens from the bus terminal. The staff can be extraordinarily reluctant to give out information, but you can pick up a map of the town and ask for assist-ance in finding a hotel. The old town and most hotels and restaurants are in the area west of the tourist office.

Post & Telecommunications The main post office is at Via XX Settembre 108. There is a row of public telephones on Via Vittorio Emanuele at the opposite end of the gardens from the tourist office. Poste restante mail can be addressed to 07041 Alghero. The telephone code for Alghero is 079.

Emergency For immediate police attention, call ☎ 113. From 1 July to 10 September there is a tourist medical service (☎ 93 05 33), Piazza Venezia Giulia, in Fertilia, just north of Alghero. It is open from 9 am to 12.30 pm and 4.30 to 7.30 pm, although for emergencies you can telephone 24 hours a day. Otherwise go to the Ospedale Civile (☎ 99 62 33), Via Don Minzoni.

Things to See & Do

Wander through the narrow streets of the old town and around the port. The most in-teresting church is the **Church of San Francesco**, Via Carlo Alberto. The town's **cathedral** has been ruined by constant remodelling, but its bell tower remains a fine example of Gothic Catalan architecture.

There are three defensive towers in the town. The **Torre del Portal**, in Piazza Porta Terra, was furnished with a drawbridge and moat, and was one of the two entrances to the walled town. The **Torre de l'Esperó Reial** was one of the bastions of Alghero's fortified wall. The octagonal **Torre de Sant Jaume** is also known as the Dog's Tower, since it was used as a pound for stray dogs.

In summer Alghero generally stages the Estate Musicale Algherese in the cloisters of the Church of San Francesco. A festival, complete with fireworks display, is held annually on 15 August for the Feast of the Assumption.

Places to Stay

It is virtually impossible to find a room in August, unless you book months in advance. At other times of the year you should have little trouble. Camping facilities include the *Calik* (☎ 93 01 11) in Fertilia, about seven km north of town, where charges are L12,000 per person, L4000 for a car and L3000 for electricity. The IYHF *Ostello dei Giuliani* (☎ 93 03 53) is at Via Zara 1, in Fertilia. Take bus AF from Via Catalogna to

Fertilia. Bed and breakfast is L14,000 a night and a meal is L12,000. It is open all year.

In the old town is *Hotel San Francesco* (☎ 97 92 58), Via Ambrogio Machin 2, with singles/doubles for L32,000/55,000, with bathroom. *Pensione Normandie* (☎ 97 53 02), Via Enrico Mattei 6, is out of the centre. Follow Via Cagliari (which becomes Viale Giovanni XXIII). It has slightly shabby, but large, rooms for L20,000/35,000.

The *Miramare* (☎ 97 93 50), Via G Leopardi 9, south along the Lungomare Dante from the old town, has good rooms with bathroom for up to L50,000/80,000. *La Margherita* (☎ 97 90 06), Via Sassari 70, has good rooms with bathroom for up to L81,000/95,000, while the *Gran Catalunia* (☎ 95 31 72), Via Catalogna 24, across the park from the tourist office, has more up-market rooms for L85,000/120,000.

Places to Eat

There are numerous supermarkets around the town, including a Coop in Via Lamarmora. For good sandwiches, head for *Paninoteca al Duomo*, next to the cathedral in Piazza Civica. The best ice cream is at *Paradiso 2*, through the Porta a Mare from Piazza Civica.

Ristorante La Piconia, Via Principe Umberto 29, is also a pizzeria. A full meal will cost around L25,000. *Trattoria Il Vecchio Mulino*, Via Don Deroma 3, is a pleasant establishment, where a full meal will cost about the same. A cheaper option is the *pizzeria* just off Via Roma at Vicolo Adami 17; takeaway pizza by the slice costs about L2000. At Vicolo Adami 25 is *La Posada del Mar*, which serves good pasta for around L9000 and pizzas for around L8000. *La Lepanto*, Via Carlo Alberto 135, overlooks the sea. A good-quality full meal will cost around L40,000.

La Palafitta is a few km north of Alghero, on the way to Fertilia, literally on the beach known as Spiaggia di Maria Pia. Look for the sign and then walk through the small area of pine trees to the restaurant. A full meal will cost around L25,000 and you can follow it up with a moon-lit walk along the beach.

Getting There & Away

The local airport, inland from Fertilia, services domestic flights from major cities throughout Italy. Regular buses leave from Via Catalogna and also from Piazza della Mercedes to coincide with flights.

Intercity buses terminate in Via Catalogna, next to the public park. ARST buses leave for Sassari and Porto Torres; FDS buses service Sassari as well and there is a special service to Olbia to coincide with ferry departures. FDS also runs a service between Alghero and Bosa. Regular buses leave for Cape Caccia and Porto Conte. Timetables are posted in the bar beside the bus stop area.

Trains connect Alghero with Sassari.

Getting Around

Urban bus No AF runs hourly between Alghero and Fertilia from 8 am to 10 pm. The more regular AP goes only as far as the Maria Pia beach. Regular FDS buses run between the port and the train station, a distance of about one km.

If you want to rent a bicycle or motorcycle to explore the coast, try Velosport (☎ 97 71 82), Via Vittorio Veneto 90. A bike will cost about L15,000 a day, a moped L30,000 and a scooter L60,000. *Cicloexpress* (☎ 97 65 92), Via Lamarmora 39, has bikes, mopeds and scooters for the same prices.

AROUND ALGHERO

There are good beaches north of Alghero, including the **Spiaggia di San Giovanni** and the **Spiaggia di Maria Pia**, easily accessible on the Alghero-Fertilia bus.

Near Alghero is **Neptune's Cave**, accessible by regular boats operated by various companies from Alghero's port (L13,000), or by the SFS bus from Via Catalogna. For some services you will need to change at Porto Conte (L1500 one way).

If you have your own means of transport, explore the beautiful Cape Caccia region and visit the **Nuraghe di Palmavera** about 10 km out of Alghero on the road to Porto Conte.

The coastline between Alghero and **Bosa**, to the south, is stunning. Rugged cliffs fall down to isolated beaches, and near Bosa is one of the last habitats of the griffon vulture. It is quite an experience if you are lucky enough to spot one of these huge birds. The only way to explore the coast is by car or motorbike, although you could try hitch-hiking.

SASSARI

The capital of Sardinia's largest province, Sassari is also the island's second-largest city after Cagliari. It is a pleasant town, but there is really not a lot to see and is probably best regarded as a convenient stopover on the way to the northern coast. It is certainly worth visiting in May for the Sardinian Cavalcade, one of Sardinia's most important festivals, generally held on the second last Sunday in May (although the day can change from year to year).

Orientation

Sassari has a compact medieval centre centred around its cathedral. However, most services are in the busy newer part of town, based around the vast 18th century Piazza Italia. Most intercity buses arrive in Emiciclo Garibaldi, a piazza a few minutes' walk downhill from Piazza Italia. Head up Via Brigata Sassari to Piazza Castello and turn right to reach the adjacent Piazza Italia. The train station is about 10 minutes' walk from the centre. From the station, turn left to reach Piazza Sant'Antonio and then right along Corso Vittorio Emanuele to reach Piazza Castello.

Information

Tourist Office The AAST tourist office is at Via Brigata Sassari 19, open Monday to Friday from 8 am to 12.30 pm and 4 to 6 pm, Saturday to midday.

Money There is a branch of the Banca Commerciale Italiana in Piazza Italia, where you exchange travellers' cheques and obtain cash advances on Visa and MasterCard.

Post & Telecommunications The main post office is at Via Brigata Sassari 13, just

off Piazza Castello. There is an SIP public telephone office at Viale Italia 7, across Emiciclo Garibaldi, open Monday to Friday from 9 am to 12.30 pm and 4 to 7.30 pm. Poste restante mail can be addressed to 07100 Sassari. The town's telephone code is 079.

Emergency For immediate police attendance, call ☎ 113. The public hospital, the Ospedale Civile (☎ 22 05 00), is in Via E de Nicola, off Viale Italia.

Things to See

Sassari's **cathedral** is in the old town in Piazza del Duomo. Built in Romanesque style in the 13th century, it was remodelled and given a Baroque façade in the 17th century. Also worth a look is the **Church of Santa Maria di Betlem**, on Viale Coppino near the station, which has a 13th century façade and lovely 14th century cloisters.

The town's **Sanna Museum**, Via Roma 64, is of considerable interest for its Nuraghic collection, as well as its display of traditional costumes.

Festival

The Sardinian Cavalcade (Cavalcata Sarda), on the second-last Sunday in May, attracts participants from all over the island, who dress in traditional costume and participate in a large and colourful parade, followed by equestrian competitions with horsemen in traditional costume. If you can manage it, the town is well worth visiting for the festival.

Places to Stay

Hotels and pensioni are not abundant in Sassari and, if you plan to arrive in high summer, or for the Cavalcade, it is advisable to book a room. The *Pensione Famiglia* (☎ 23 95 43), Viale Umberto 65, is run down, but singles/doubles are cheap at L20,000/25,000. *Hotel Giusy* (☎ 23 33 27), Piazza Sant'Antonio, is close to the station and has singles/doubles with bathroom for L40,000/62,000. At Via Roma 79 is the more up-market *Hotel Leonardo da Vinci* (☎ 28 07 44), which has quality singles/doubles for

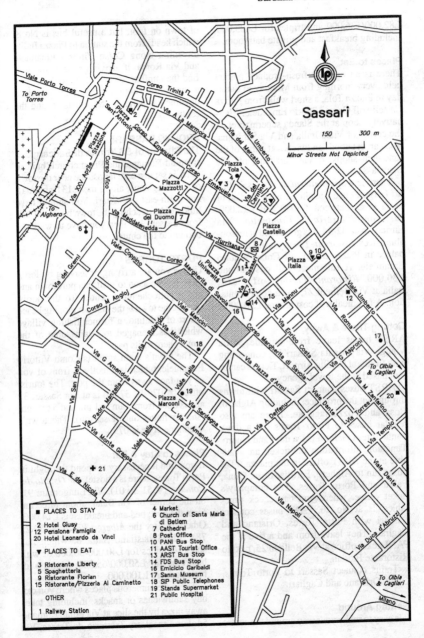

Sassari

0   150   300 m

Minor Streets Not Depicted

PLACES TO STAY

2 Hotel Giusy
12 Pensione Famiglia
20 Hotel Leonardo da Vinci

PLACES TO EAT

3 Ristorante Liberty
5 Spaghetteria
9 Ristorante Florian
15 Ristorante/Pizzeria Al Caminetto

OTHER

1 Railway Station
4 Market
6 Church of Santa Maria di Betlem
7 Cathedral
8 Post Office
10 PANI Bus Stop
11 AAST Tourist Office
13 ARST Bus Stop
14 FDS Bus Stop
16 Emiciclo Garibaldi
17 Sanna Museum
18 SIP Public Telephones
19 Standa Supermarket
21 Public Hospital

L82,000/136,000 and triples for L183,000, including breakfast and private bathroom.

Places to Eat

There is an outdoor fresh-produce market held every morning from Monday to Saturday in Piazza Tola, a short walk from Piazza Castello off Corso Vittorio Emanuele. Alternatively, shop at the Standa supermarket on the corner of Viale Italia and Via Sardegna. You can get good sandwiches at either of the sandwich shops in Via Turritana, off Via Brigata Sassari.

There is a *Spaghetteria* at Via Usai 10A, off Largo Felice Cavallotti, where a dish of pasta costs between L5000 and L12,000. *Ristorante/Pizzeria Al Caminetto*, Via Enrico Costa 32-34, has good food at reasonable prices. *Ristorante Liberty* is in a restored palace in Piazza Sauro, off Corso Vittorio Emanuele. A full meal will cost around L30,000. *Ristorante Florian*, off Piazza Italia at Via Bellieni 27, has a good reputation. A full meal will cost around L30,000.

Getting There & Away

ARST buses leave from outside Sarda Viaggi, Via Brigata Sassari 30, connecting with flights at Fertilia Airport. Tickets can be purchased at the travel agency.

ARST buses connect Sassari with towns throughout the province, including Alghero, Bosa and Pozzomaggiore. There are also regular buses to Porto Torres (28 a day), Santa Teresa Gallura (31 a day) and Nuoro. Timetable information and tickets are available at the ARST office in the piazza. FDS buses run to Alghero, Fertilia, Bosa, Olbia, Palau and Porto Torres. The company's ticket office, where you can check timetables, is at No 26. PANI buses connect Sassari with Porto Torres, Oristano and Cagliari. They leave from and arrive at the PANI ticket office at Via Bellieni 25, next to Ristorante Florian.

Trains connect Sassari to Porto Torres, Olbia, Oristano and Cagliari.

Getting Around

It is easy to make your way around the centre of town on foot, but a useful bus is No 8, which heads from the station to Piazza Italia, travelling along Corso Vittorio Emanuele and Via Roma. If arriving by car, you will find the familiar 'centro' signs to direct you to the centre. There are numerous supervised daytime car parks in the streets around the centre.

AROUND SASSARI

The **Church of SS Trinità di Saccargia**, a splendid Romanesque Pisan church built in 1116, is set in a bare landscape near the town of Codrongianus, along the ss131 about 18 km south-east of Sassari. You should have little trouble reaching the town by ARST bus from Sassari, but then you have to walk the two km to the church.

PORTO TORRES

Unless you are arriving or leaving by ferry, there is no reason to visit this port town and major petrochemical centre. To the north-west of the town is the fast-developing beach resort of Stintino, a former fishing village which has managed to retain some of the atmosphere of its past.

The town's main street is Corso Vittorio Emanuele, which is directly in front of you as you face away from the port. The tourist office (☎ 079-52 37 88) is at Via Sassari 32 and is open from 9 am to 1 pm and 5 to 9 pm (shorter hours out of season). The town's telephone code is 079.

Places to Stay & Eat

If you find it necessary to spend the night in Porto Torres, there is a hostel, the *Ostello del Comune* (☎ 51 30 01), Via Lungomare 91, on the corner of Via Balai, about three km from the port; bed and breakfast is L14,000. Otherwise, try the *Albergo Royal* (☎ 50 22 78), Via Sebastiano Satta 8, which has singles/doubles for L40,000/50,000 or with bathroom for L50,000/65,000; triples with bathroom are L100,000.

There are numerous places where you can buy sandwiches or snacks, including takeaway pizza by the slice at Via Ponte Romano 54. For a meal, try *Trattoria da Teresa*, Via

Giordano Bruno, which has a very cheap set-price menu, or *Sa Cardiga*, Via G Galilei 13, where a full meal will cost around L30,000.

Getting There & Away

Regular ARST buses connect Porto Torres with Sassari, as well as with Stintino. The bus terminal is in Piazzale Colombo at the port and the ticket office is at Acciaro Bar, Corso Vittorio Emanuele 38. Regular trains also connect the town with Sassari. Formerly, trains also stopped at the port, but a new station has been built about two km west.

Tirrenia runs daily ferries to Genoa (three a day in summer). Its office (☎ 51 41 07) is in the Stazione Marittima at the port.

STINTINO

A picturesque fishing village turned tourist resort, Stintino is very crowded in summer. A few km west of the town, facing Asinara Island, is a magnificent sandy beach, the **Spiaggia di Pelosa**, at Torre Pelosa.

If you want to spend a few days in Stintino, try the *Albergo Silvestrino* (☎ 079-52 30 07), Via Sassari 12 in the centre of the village. It has doubles for L60,000 to L70,000, and half-board for L120,000 per person (closed in January and February). The *Hotel Lina* (☎ 079-52 30 71), Via Lepanto 38, facing the village's small port, has doubles for L75,000, breakfast included. Half-board is L120,000 per person and full board is L135,000.

The town is accessible from Porto Torres by ARST bus (five a day in summer).

SANTA TERESA GALLURA

Together with Palau, about 26 km east, this seaside resort has developed into an affordable alternative to the jet-set hang-outs on the Costa Smeralda. It is a very pleasant spot to pass a few relaxing days, particularly if the magnificent coves, rock pools and small beaches of nearby Cape Testa appeal. From the town you can see across the Strait of Bonifacio to Corsica, or even catch one of the regular ferries which make the crossing to Bonifacio on Corsica's southern tip.

Information

Santa Teresa's AAST tourist office (☎ 0789-75 41 27) is in the town centre at Piazza Vittorio Emanuele 24, open Monday to Saturday from 8.30 am to 1 pm and 3.30 to 6.30 pm. The helpful staff can provide loads of information and will assist in finding accommodation. It is possible to ring ahead to request information on hotels, as well as rooms and apartments for rent, or you can write (in English) to: AAST, Piazza V Emanuele 24, 07028 Santa Teresa Gallura.

You can exchange money daily from 8 am to 10 pm at the port, otherwise there is a bank in Piazza V Emanuele. The town's telephone code is 0789.

For medical attention, go to the Guardia Medica in Via Carlo Felice, on the corner of Via Eleonora d'Arborea, a short walk from the town centre.

Things to See & Do

The main reason for a visit to this area is to spend time on the beach. There is the small **Spiaggia Rena Bianca** next to the town, but it is recommended that you head for **Cape Testa**, a small cape connected to the mainland by an isthmus, about five km west of Santa Teresa. There are lovely, small beaches on either side of the cape, as well as a large rock pool. The cape is characterised by granite outcrops, worked and worn smooth by the wind and sea. The road ends just below the cape's lighthouse, from where the path to the right leads to the rock pool and the path to the left leads to a small cove and sandy beach. The area is in fact a military zone, but people move around freely.

Motorised rubber boats for up to six people are available for rent at Santa Teresa's port for L150,000 to L180,000 a day, or L90,000 for half a day. GULP, Via Nazionale 58, also rents boats, as well as bicycles and motorcycles, which are handy for exploring the area. A mountain bike costs L25,000 a day, a motorino L40,000 a day and a Vespa L60,000.

Places to Stay

The town offers extensive accommodation possibilities, including rooms and apartments for rent (contact the tourist office). It is advisable to book if you plan to arrive during late July or August.

Camping facilities are all out of town. Try *La Liccia* (☎ 75 51 90), about six km from Santa Teresa towards Palau, 400 metres from the beach; charges are L10,500 per adult and L2500 for electricity.

In town is *Albergo Da Cecco* (☎ 75 42 20), Via Po 3 (take Via XX Settembre from the tourist office and turn right at Via Po), which has pleasant singles/doubles for L45,000/68,000 with bathroom. *Albergo Riva* (☎ 75 42 83), Via del Porto, on the corner of Via Galliano, has singles/doubles for L40,000/55,000 and triples for L75,000, while the *Hotel al Porto* (☎ 75 41 54), Via del Porto, on the port, has singles/doubles for L35,000/60,000.

At Cape Testa is the *Bocche di Bonifacio* (☎ 75 42 02), which has doubles for L60,000 and full board for L80,000 per person.

Places to Eat

There are plenty of good bars and sandwich shops where you can buy sandwiches, including *Poldo's Pub*, Via Garibaldi 4. For good pizza, try *Pizzeria Azzurra*, close to the port on Via del Porto. *Marinaro*, at the Hotel Marinaro, Via Angioj, has good-quality meals for around L25,000. If visiting Cape Testa, try the trattoria at the Bocche di Bonifacio hotel.

Getting There & Away

Regular ARST buses connect Santa Teresa with Olbia, Golfo Aranci and Palau, arriving in Via Eleonora d'Arborea, off Via Nazionale, a short walk to the centre. There are also two buses a day to Sassari. Tickets can be purchased at the Bar Black & White on Via Nazionale.

Ferry services to Corsica are run by two companies, Navarma Lines (☎ 75 52 60) and Saremar (☎ 75 47 88), which both have small offices at the port. Both companies run several services a day.

PALAU & LA MADDALENA

Close to the Costa Smeralda, Palau is little more than a conglomeration of expensive hotels and private apartment blocks and is much less pleasant than Santa Teresa. Just off the coast are the islands of **La Maddalena**, site of a US navy base, and **Caprera**, which was given to the hero of Italian unification, Giuseppe Garibaldi, by King Victor Emmanuel II. Garibaldi spent his last years there and it is possible to visit his house. Most of the island is a nature reserve, which means that camping is forbidden, although it is the site of a Club Mediterranée (see the following Places to Stay section). La Maddalena has an attractive main town of the same name and several good beaches, and is popular with campers. The two islands are connected by a road bridge.

Information

Palau's tourist office (☎ 0789-70 95 70) is at Via Nazionale 96. It is light-on with tourist information, but can assist with information on accommodation, including apartments and rooms for rent. La Maddalena's tourist office (☎ 0789-73 63 21) is at Via XX Settembre 24, in the town of La Maddalena. The telephone code for the area is 0789.

Places to Stay

Just east of Palau is *Camping Capo d'Orso* (☎ 70 81 82), on the cape of the same name. Located by the sea, its charges are L6500 per person and L13,500 for a site. It also has caravans and bungalows for rent at L110,000 and L160,000 per day respectively.

In the town there are numerous hotels and rooms for rent, but you should book ahead for July and August. The *Hotel La Serra* (☎ 70 95 19), Via Nazionale 17, has doubles for L50,000. *La Roccia* (☎ 70 95 28), Via dei Mille 15, has singles/doubles for L55,000/80,000.

On La Maddalena there is *Villaggio Camping La Maddalena* (☎ 72 80 51) at Moneta, and *Campeggio Abbatoggia* (☎ 73 91 73) on the other side of the island at Lo Strangolato, close to a lovely beach. Both are reasonably cheap and are accessible by local bus from the town of La Maddalena. The *Club Mediterranée* (☎ 72 70 78) on Caprera charges for full board by the week, at around L700,000 per person.

Places to Eat

In Palau, you can buy supplies at the Minimarket da Gemma, Via Nazionale 66. There are several decent places to eat, including *L'Uva Fragola*, Piazza Vittorio Emanuele, just off Via Nazionale near the port, which serves good pizzas, as well as salads for around L10,000. *Da Robertino*, Via Nazionale 22, is a good trattoria, where a full meal will cost around L25,000. At *La Taverna*, Via Rossini, off Via Nazionale, you can eat an excellent meal for around L50,000.

Getting There & Away

Palau is easily accessible by ARST bus from Sassari, Santa Teresa Gallura and Olbia. SFS and Autoservizi Caramelli buses connect Palau with places along the Costa Smeralda, including Baia Sardinia and Porto Cervo. Buses stop at Palau's small port. Timetables are posted inside the small Stazione Marittima at the port.

Ferries make the short crossing between Palau and La Maddalena every 20 minutes during summer, less frequently in the off season. It is not possible to take your car to La Maddalena. There is a car park just outside Palau, where you can leave the car if you want to catch a ferry to La Maddalena, and a bus shuttle service will take you to the port. While it is not obligatory to use the car park, it may be difficult to find a parking spot in town during summer.

Once on the island, catch one of the blue local buses which leave from the port every half an hour and make the round trip of the island. Buses for Caprera leave from the piazza at the end of Via Giovanni Amendola, to the right of the port.

COSTA SMERALDA

For the average tourist, the Costa Smeralda (Emerald Coast) is basically out of reach. There are no hotels of less than three stars, which means that prices for a double room start at around L120,000 a day. The coast was purchased in 1962 by a group of international investors led by Prince Karim Aga Khan, and was basically developed from scratch. Its resorts include Baia Sardinia, Liscia di Vacca and Porto Cervo, all bearing a stronger resemblance to Disneyland than seaside towns. The coastline is certainly beautiful, but it is not the real Sardinia, and unless you have money to burn, or very rich friends with an apartment, it is better to spend the day on one of its beaches and continue your journey.

Those who would like to stay on the Costa Smeralda can obtain information about accommodation from the tourist office at Arzachena (☎ 0789-8 26 24), in Piazza Risorgimento.

The coast is accessible by ARST, SFS and Autoservizi Caramelli buses from Palau and Olbia.

OLBIA

This busy port and industrial centre will very likely be the first glimpse of Sardinia for many tourists. It is a major port for ferries arriving from Civitavecchia, Genoa and Livorno, and while it is not particularly unpleasant, it is not particularly interesting either and is best passed through quickly.

Orientation

If arriving by ferry, you will find yourself at a well-organised port complete with a new Stazione Marittima, and a local bus (No 3) to take you into the centre of town (only about one km). Trains also run from the main station to the port to coincide with ferry departures. Intercity buses terminate at the end of Corso Umberto at Via XX Settembre. Head to the right along Corso Umberto to reach the town centre. The train station is close by in Via Pala, off Piazza Risorgimento.

Information

Tourist Office The AAST office (☎ 0789-2 14 53) is at Via Catello Piro 1, off Corso Umberto, and open from 8 am to 2 pm and 4

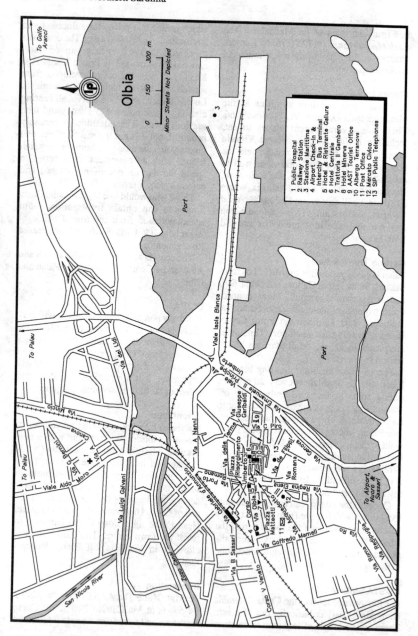

Olbia

Minor Streets Not Depicted

0   150   300 m

To Golfo Aranci

To Palau

To Palau

To Palau

To Airport, Nuoro & Sassari

Port

Port

San Nicola River

1 Public Hospital
2 Railway Station
3 Stazione Marittima
4 Airport Check-In &
   Intercity Bus Terminal
5 Hotel & Ristorante Gallura
6 Hotel Centrale
7 Trattoria Il Gambero
8 Hotel Minerva
9 AAST Tourist Office
10 Albergo Terranova
11 Post Office
12 Mercato Civico
13 SIP Public Telephones

Viale Isola Blanca
Via Emanuele II Principe Umberto
Via A Nanni
Via Giuseppe Garibaldi
Via C Piro
Via delle Terme
Via Regina Elena
Via Romana
Via Ge Filippi
Via Genova
Via Porto Romano
Piazza Risorgimento Umberto
Corso Olbia
Via Acquedotto
Piazza Matteotti
Via Gabriele d'Annunzio
Via B Sassari
Via Goffredo Mameli
Corso V Veneto
Via Regina Elena
Via Ro
Via Luigi Galvani
Viale Aldo Moro
Via del Lidi
Via Mincio
Via Canova
Via G Batteri

to 8 pm. The staff are very keen to help and will advise on places to stay and eat, and can provide information about accommodation and places to visit throughout Sardinia.

Money There are three major banks in Corso Umberto, including the Banca Commerciale Italiana at No 191, where you can obtain cash advances on both Visa and MasterCard.

Post & Telecommunications The main post office is in Via Acquedotto, off Piazza Matteotti, and there is an SIP public telephone office at Via de Filippi 14. Poste restante mail can be addressed to 07026 Olbia. The town's telephone code is 0789.

Emergency For immediate police attendance, call ☎ 113. For medical treatment, the public hospital, the Ospedale Civile (☎ 5 22 01), is in Viale Aldo Moro, about 15 minutes' walk from the centre along Via Porto Romano and Via Gabriele d'Annunzio.

Places to Stay

The *Albergo Terranova* (☎ 2 23 95), Via Giuseppe Garibaldi 3, has singles/doubles for L38,000/50,000. The *Hotel Minerva* (☎ 2 11 90), Via Mazzini 7, has doubles for L50,000, and singles/doubles with bathroom for L38,000/60,000.

The *Hotel Gallura* (☎ 2 46 48), Corso Umberto 145, is a pleasant establishment, with singles/doubles for L48,000/63,000, and with bathroom for L80,000/110,000. The *Hotel Centrale* (☎ 2 30 17), Corso Umberto 85, has more up-market rooms for L90,000/120,000.

Places to Eat

If you want to stock up on food supplies, head for the Mercato Civico in Via Acquedotto. At *Gelateria Il Golosone*, Corso Umberto 41, you can buy good sandwiches, crêpes and ice cream. For an excellent meal, try *Trattoria Il Gambero*, Via Lamarmora 6, off Piazza Matteotti; a full meal will cost over L25,000. One of Olbia's better restaurants is the *Ristorante Gallura* at the

Hotel Gallura, Corso Umberto 145; a full meal here will cost over L50,000.

Getting There & Away

Air Olbia's airport, a few km south-east of the town, services domestic flights to and from Italy's main cities. There is a airport check-in terminal in the town centre on the corner of Corso Umberto and Via XX Settembre. City bus No 2 heads from here to the airport.

Bus ARST buses depart from both the port (coinciding with ferry arrivals) and the bus terminal in the centre for Arzachena and the resorts of the Costa Smeralda, Palau, Santa Teresa Gallura, Sassari and Nuoro.

Train There are train connections to major towns, including Sassari, Cagliari and Oristano.

Boat Tirrenia ferries make the 7½-hour crossing to Civitavecchia five times a day in the high season. The company has an office at the Stazione Marittima and at Corso Umberto 17 (☎ 2 46 91). This is an extremely busy route and it is very important to book at least three weeks in advance during the summer months, particularly if you have a car.

Ferries run by Navarma Lines (also known as Moby Lines) connect Olbia with Livorno twice a day in the high season. The company has an office at the Stazione Marittima and at Corso Umberto 187 (☎ 2 79 27).

If you are taking a car on a ferry, you will find clear signs directing you to the port and to your point of embarkation. From the town centre, head for Viale Principe Umberto and then Viale Isola Bianca to reach the port.

Getting Around

City bus No 3 will take you from the port into the centre of town, while bus No 2 heads for the airport.

GOLFO ARANCI

Ferries run by the FS from Civitavecchia dock here. There is a stazione marittima from where you can catch a train directly to Olbia, or an ARST bus to Olbia, Palau or Santa Teresa Gallura. It is possible, for instance, to buy a ticket in Rome (at Stazione Termini or any CIT office) which covers the cost of the train trip to Civitavecchia, the ferry crossing and the train to Olbia.

Eastern Sardinia

NUORO PROVINCE

This province, about halfway up the east coast of Sardinia, has unspoiled, isolated beaches, spectacular gorges and trekking routes, as well as important Nuraghic sites. It encompasses the area known as the Barbagia, so called by the Romans because of their opinion of the local people. Probably more than in any other part of Sardinia, you will be able to get a sense of the island's traditional culture here. Although tourism in the area is increasing, there remains a strong element of isolation and a connection with traditions which have been swept aside by

Church of San Pietro at Onani, north of Nuoro

tourism in other parts of the island. Shepherds still tend their flocks in remote areas of the province, often living alone in stone or wooden shacks and having little contact with the outside world. It is common to see older women in the traditional black, ankle-length dresses of the area, their heads covered by Spanish-style black, fringed shawls, sometimes with beautiful coloured embroidery.

The locals remain fairly aloof and it is important when visiting the smaller, more remote towns of the area, to behave respectfully. If you manage to befriend a local, you will find them incredibly hospitable and helpful.

Larger towns in the area are accessible by bus, but a car is really a necessity to explore the smaller villages and the mountains. One surprisingly cheap way to explore the area is by trekking with an organised guide.

Nuoro is the capital of the province and the gateway to areas such as: Oliena and the Sopramonte; Dorgali and the beautiful coastline around Cala Gonone; the town of Orgosolo, famous for its tradition of banditry; and the Gennargentu mountain range.

Nuoro

There is not a lot to see and do in the town, but it is a good starting point for an exploration of the Barbagia. The old centre of town is around Piazza delle Grazie, Corso Garibaldi and Via Manzoni. ARST buses terminate in Piazza Vittorio Emanuele, through Piazza G Mameli from Via Manzoni, while PANI buses stop in Via Brigata Sassari, off Piazza Italia near the tourist office, along Via IV Novembre and Via Dante from Piazza delle Grazie. The train station is about 15 minutes' walk from Piazza delle Grazie along Via La Marmora (turn left as you leave the station).

Information The EPT tourist office is at Piazza Italia 9 and is open Monday to Friday from 9 am to 1 pm and 4 to 7 pm. The main post office is in Piazza Crispi, between Corso Garibaldi and Piazza Dante, and there is an SIP public telephone office at Via Brigata

Sassari 6. The town's telephone code is 0784.

Things to See While in town, take a look at the neoclassical **cathedral** in Piazza Santa Maria della Neve, and the monument and square dedicated to the local poet Sebastiano Satta. Well worth a visit is the **Museo della Vita e delle Tradizioni Popolari Sardi** (Museum of the Life & Traditions of the Sardinian People), at Via Antonio Mereu 56, south of the cathedral. Open from 9 am to 1 pm and 3 to 7 pm, the museum houses a collection of traditional costumes and masks.

Places to Stay There are no rock-bottom budget options, but you could try *Il Portico* (☎ 3 75 35) at Via Mannu 1, off Corso Garibaldi, where singles/doubles cost L38,000/50,000. *Mini Hotel* (☎ 3 31 59), Via Brofferio 13, is a pleasant little place which has singles/doubles with bathroom for L50,000/65,000. It is off Via Roma, near Piazza Sebastiano Satta. *Hotel Grillo* (☎ 3 86 78), Via Monsignor Melas 14, is in an ugly building, but its rooms are pleasant. Singles/doubles with bathroom are L60,000/80,000, and triples are L120,000.

Places to Eat To pick up supplies, shop at the Conad supermarket in Via Trieste, just near Piazza Italia, or at the great little grocery shop at Corso Garibaldi 168 and the cheese shop next door. *Pizzeria/Trattoria Da Chicchino*, Via Brofferio 31 (along Via Cattaneo from Piazza S Satta), serves good-quality meals at reasonable prices. Otherwise try *Pizzeria del Diavolo*, Corso Garibaldi 134.

Getting There & Away ARST buses connect Nuoro with Cagliari (two a day), Olbia (six a day) and Sassari (three a day), as well as with towns throughout the province, including Oliena (hourly), Orgosolo (10 a day), Dorgali and Cala Gonone (seven a day). PANI buses head for Cagliari, Sassari and Oristano.

Cala Gonone
This fast-developing seaside resort is an excellent base from which to explore the coves along the coastline, as well as the Nuraghic sites and rugged terrain inland.

There is a Pro Loco tourist information office (☎ 0784-9 33 87) in Viale Bue Marino (where ARST buses terminate), where you can pick up maps, a list of hotels, and information to help you explore the area. There is also a tourist information office in the nearby town of Dorgali, which you will probably need to pass through on your way to Cala Gonone. It is in Via Lamarmora (☎ 0784-9 62 43). The telephone code for Cala Gonone is 0784.

Things to See & Do From Cala Gonone's small port, catch a boat to the **Grotta del Bue Marino** (Cave of the Monk Seal), where a guide will take you on a one-km walk to see vast caves with stalagmites, stalactites and lakes. The caves were one of the last habitats of the rare monk seal, but the colony has not been sighted for some years. The return boat trip plus entrance to the caves costs L12,000.

Boats also leave for the beautiful **Cala di Luna** (L10,000), an isolated beach accessible only by boat or on foot, where you can spend the day by the sea. In August the beach is crowded with day-tripping sunbathers, but at other times it is quite deserted. If the weather is unsuitable for swimming, take a walk along the **Codula di Luna**, a long valley stretching from Cala di Luna almost to Urzulei. Other boats head farther along the coast to the beach at **Cala Sisine** (L21,000). There is a walking track along the coast linking the two beaches (about three hours).

If you want to explore the spectacular **Gorropu Gorge** about 15 km south of Dorgali, inland from Cala di Luna, you may want to seek information from the tourist office about hiring a guide, since it is necessary to use ropes and harnesses to traverse sections of the gorge. The Gruppo Ricerche Ambientali (☎ 9 34 24 at Cala Gonone and ☎ 9 61 78 at Dorgali) organises guided treks in the Gorropu Gorge, the Codula di Luna, as well as in sections of the Grotta del Bue

Marino not open to the public. There are several Nuraghic sites in the area and, once again, the tourist office can provide maps and advice on how to reach them. See also the Oliena section for information about a guided trek that approaches this area from the west.

Boat Marine Charter (☎ 9 69 52), Via Cavour 3, or at the port, runs charter-boat cruises for one day or for longer periods. If you are interested in diving courses, contact the Lupo di Mare Diving Club (☎ 9 32 33) c/o Il Bottegone, Viale Bue Marino (in summer only).

Places to Stay & Eat Try *Camping Cala Gonone* (☎ 9 31 65), Via Collodi 1, which charges up to L17,300 per person. It also has caravans and bungalows for rent. Free camping is strictly forbidden throughout the area.

Hotels include the *Bue Marino* (☎ 9 31 30), Via Vespucci, which has singles/doubles for L45,000/60,000, and the *Gabbiano* (☎ 9 30 21) at the port, with rooms for L35,000/45,000. *Piccolo Hotel* (☎ 9 32 32), Via Cristoforo Colombo, near the port, has very pleasant rooms for L50,000/80,000 with bathroom. *Hotel La Playa* (☎ 9 35 34), Via Collodi, is more up-market; its rooms cost up to L85,000/120,000.

Due Chiacchiere is a trattoria/pizzeria overlooking the sea at Via Acquadolce 13, near the port; a full meal will cost around L25,000. More expensive is the nearby *Ristorante Il Pescatore*, where you will pay around L35,000 or more.

Getting There & Away Catch a PANI bus to Nuoro from Cagliari, Sassari or Oristano and then take an ARST bus to Cala Gonone, via Dorgali. ARST buses also connect Cala Gonone with the town of Oliena. It should be noted that services are drastically reduced to Cala Gonone out of season.

If you are travelling by car, you will need a detailed road map of the area. One of the best is published by the Istituto Geografico de Agostini. The tourist office has maps which detail the locations of the main sights.

Oliena

The value of visiting Oliena, or Orgosolo farther south (see the following section), is to get a better idea of how people live in Sardinia's interior. Neither town offers much in the way of tourist facilities or sights, although both, in their own way, provide an 'alternative' travel experience.

Oliena is about 12 km south-west of Nuoro and easily accessible from there by regular ARST bus. For the more adventurous, it is a place from which to set out on a trekking exploration of the Sopramonte area to the south, and to the isolated Nuraghic site at **Tiscali**, either alone or with a guide. It should be noted, however, that you will need extremely precise directions to find Tiscali without a guide because there are no signs pointing the way.

For information on trekking, contact Viaggi nel Mondo (☎ 06-581 63 65), Via Cino da Pistoia 7, in Rome. Otherwise contact one of the local guides directly by ringing ☎ 0784-28 80 24 in Oliena. Ask for Murena, a local guide who operates a refuge near Tiscali and can take you on a three-day trek from there, through the Gola di Gorropu to the beach at Cala di Luna, where you will camp for several days. He doesn't speak English, but this shouldn't be a problem, particularly if you do all the organising through the Rome office.

Places to Stay Accommodation options are limited. Try *Ci Kappa* (☎ 0784-28 87 33), Via Martin Luther King, which has singles/doubles for L48,000/65,000. It also has a good pizzeria/restaurant. A few km east of town, near the beautiful Lanaittu Valley, is *Su Gologone* (☎ 0784-28 75 12). In a lovely setting, the hotel is a good option for people wanting to explore the area, because it organises guided tours and treks as well as horse-riding expeditions. Singles/doubles cost L76,500/95,000 with bathroom, half-pension costs up to L100,000 and full pension up to L130,000. Its restaurant serves excellent traditional local dishes and is justifiably renowned throughout the island.

Orgosolo

About 18 km farther south, Orgosolo is famous for its tradition of *banditismo* (banditry), although this is not a subject you will find the locals willing to discuss openly. This tradition was immortalised by the 1963 Italian film *The Bandits of Orgosolo*. One of the town's more notorious *banditi* was released from prison in 1992 and acted as an unofficial negotiator in the much-publicised kidnapping of the son of a Costa Smeralda hotelier (and a relative of the Aga Khan). The child was eventually released in the countryside close to the town.

Orgosolo is also interesting for the series of leftist and nationalistic murals which decorate the façades of many of its buildings. The idea of a local art teacher, Francesco del Casino, a native of Siena who has lived in Orgosolo for many years, the murals started appearing in 1973. Generally designed by him, they have been painted by local students as well as other artists. Originally reflecting fairly extreme political views on a range of international issues, such as Vietnam, South Africa and the Palestinian question, the murals now deal mainly with social issues.

Orgosolo is accessible by ARST bus from Nuoro.

Places to Stay & Eat Try the *Petit Hotel* (☎ 0784-40 20 09), Via Mannu, which has singles/doubles for L20,000/32,000, or L25,000/36,000 with bathroom. Just out of town is *Ai Monti del Gennargentu* (☎ 0784-40 23 74), which has singles/doubles for L40,000/55,000 with bathroom.

A local group organises lunches in the country just out of the town, where you can enjoy one of Sardinia's most traditional dishes, porcheddu (roast suckling pig). The travel agency Avitur, (☎ 0789-2 43 27), Corso Vittorio Emanuele 139 in Olbia, organises guided trips by bus to Orgosolo, including the lunch, for L60,000 a head. Otherwise you can arrange to attend a lunch by contacting the organisers in Orgosolo directly (☎ 0784-40 20 71). The cost for lunch only is L25,000 a head.

Central Sardinia

There are innumerable Nuraghic sites on the island, but some of the most interesting are in the interior and are often very difficult to reach without your own transport. The most important is the **Su Nuraxi** fortress, one km west of Barumini, about 60 km north of Cagliari. This vast complex consists of a castle and village. It is open from 8 am to about 6 pm, but on a day trip you will probably spend most of your time travelling if you need to use public transport. There is an ARST bus from Cagliari, but to return you will need to catch an evening bus to Sanluri and then a train to Cagliari. To avoid being stranded, check train and bus timetables at the Cagliari tourist office.

The **Santu Antine** nuraghe, near Torralba, is just off the ss131 between Oristano and Sassari. Said to be the most beautiful nuraghe in Sardinia, it is well worth a visit. By public transport, it can be reached from Sassari by the ARST bus heading for Padria, which stops at Torralba.

An event of particular interest, especially for those who want to experience Sardinia's wilder side, is the Sa Ardia in **Sedilo**, a spectacular festival on 6 and 7 July in honour of St Constantine, which features a dangerous horse race through the town. Thousands of spectators crowd into Sedilo to witness the event and some fire guns into the ground and air to excite the horses further. Needless to say, there are serious injuries every year. The race starts at 6 pm on 6 July and is repeated the following morning at about 7 am. Information about the event is available at the provincial tourist office in Oristano. Sedilo is about 50 km north-east of Oristano, near Abbasanta and Lake Omodeo.

Glossary

AAST – Azienda Autonoma di Soggiorno e Turismo, the local tourist office

ACI – Automobile Club Italiano, the Italian automobile club

aereo – aeroplane

affittacamere – rooms for rent

affresco – fresco; a painting method in which watercolour paint is applied to wet plaster

agriturismo – tourist accommodation on farms

AIG – Associazione Italiana Alberghi per la Gioventù, the Italian youth hostel association

albergo – hotel

albergo diurno – day hotel, with public bathing facilities

aliscafo – hydrofoil

alloggio – lodging

ambulanza – ambulance

appartamento – apartment, flat

apse – domed or arched area at the altar end of a church

APT – Azienda di Promozione Turistica, the provincial tourist office

arco – arch

assicurata/o – insured

autobus – bus

autostazione – bus station/terminal

autostop – hitchhiking

autostrada – freeway, motorway

bagno – bathroom; also toilet, WC

baldacchino – canopy supported by columns over the altar in a church

basilica – in ancient Rome, a building used for public administration, with a rectangular hall flanked by aisles and an apse at the end; later, a Christian church built in the same style

battistero – baptistry

benzina – petrol

bicicletta – bicycle

biglietteria – ticket office

biglietto – ticket

binario – platform

busta – envelope

CAI – Club Alpino Italiano, for information on hiking and mountain refuges

camera – room

campanile – bell tower

cappella – chapel

carabinieri, polizia – police

carta telefonica – telephone card

cartolina – postcard

castello – castle

cattedrale – cathedral

centro – centre

centro storico – (literally, historical centre) old town

chiesa – church

chiostro – cloister; covered walkway, usually enclosed by columns, around a quadrangle

circo – oval or cicular arena

CIT – Compagnia Italiana di Turismo, the Italian national tourist/travel agency

colazione – breakfast

colonna – column

comune – equivalent to a municipality or county; town or city council; historically, a commune (self-governing town or city)

corso – main street, avenue

cortile – courtyard

CTS – Centro Turistico Studentesco e Giovanile, the student/youth travel agency

cupola – dome

deposito bagagli – baggage deposit

distributore di benzina – petrol pump (see *stazione di servizio*)

duomo – cathedral

ENIT – Ente Nazionale Italiano per il Turismo, the Italian state tourist office

EPT – Ente Provinciale per il Turismo, the provincial tourist office

espresso – express mail; express train; short black coffee

festa – festival

fiume – river
fontana – fountain
foro – forum
francobollo – postage stamp
fresco – see *affresco*
FS – Ferrovie dello Stato, the Italian state railway
funicolare – funicular railway
funivia – cable car

gabinetto – toilet, WC
golfo – gulf
grotta – cave

intarsio – inlaid woodwork, especially on wall panels

lago – lake
largo – (small) square
lavasecco – dry-cleaning
lettera – letter
lido – beach
locanda – inn, small hotel
loggia – covered area on the side of a building; porch
lungomare – road along seafront; promenade

mare – sea
mercato – market
monte – mountain, mount
motorino – moped
municipio – town hall

navata centrale – nave; central part of a church
navata laterale – aisle of a church
nave – ship
necropolis – (ancient) cemetery, burial site

ospedale – hospital
ostello – hostel

pacco – package, parcel
palazzo – palace; a large building of any type, including an apartment block
passeggiata – traditional evening stroll
pensione – small hotel, often with board
piazza – square
piazzale – (large) open square

pietà – (literally, pity or compassion) sculpture, drawing or painting of the dead Christ supported by the Madonna
poltrona – (literally, armchair) airline-type chair on a ferry
polyptych – altarpiece consisting of more than three panels (see triptych)
ponte – bridge
portico – portico; covered walkway, usually attached to the outside of buildings
porto – port
posta aerea, via aerea – airmail
pronto soccorso – first aid, casualty ward

questura – police headquarters

raccomandata – registered letter
rifugio – mountain/Alpine refuge
rocca – fortress

sagra – festival
santuario – sanctuary
scalinata – stairway
scavi – excavations
SIP – the Italian state telephone company, pronounced 'sip'
spiaggia – beach
stazione – station
stazione di servizio – service/petrol station
stazione marittima – ferry terminal
strada – street, road
superstrada – expressway; highway with divided lanes

telamoni – large statues of men, used as columns in temples
telegramma – telegram
tempio – temple
terme – (thermal) baths
tesoro – treasury
torre – tower
torrente – stream
traghetto – ferry
travertino – travertine; light-coloured limestone, used extensively as a building material in both ancient and modern Rome because of large deposits in the area
treno – train
triptych – painting or carving on three panels, hinged so that the outer panels fold

over the middle one, often used as altarpiece (see polyptych)

trompe l'oeil – painting or other illustration designed to 'deceive the eye', creating the impression that the image is real

ufficio postale – post office

ufficio stranieri – (police) foreigners' bureau

via – street, road

via aerea – air mail

villa – detached house, country house; also the park surrounding the house

Index

MAPS

Abruzzo 476
Agrigento 631
Airfares Chart 110
Amalfi 527
Ancona 465
Aosta 219
Apulia 535
Arezzo 427
Assisi 445

Bari 548
Basilicata 566
Bergamo 254
Bologna 344
Brescia 252
Brindisi 555

Cagliari 645
Calabria 571
Campania 490
Capri 509
Catania 617
Catanzaro 573
Como 258
Cosenza 576
Cremona 250
Cuneo 214

Emilia-Romagna 342

Ferrara 361
Florence 376
    Duomo to Ponte Vecchio 380
    Around Central Station 389
Friuli-Venezia Guilia 328

Genoa 184

L'Aquila 478
La Spezia 190
Lazio 168

Lecce 559
Liguria 182
Livorno 414
Lombardy 228
Lucca 405

Mantua 247
Marches 463
Matera 567
Milan 230
    Around Stazione Centrale 238
    Around the Duomo 234
    Greater Milan 243
Modena 350
Molise 485

Naples 493
    Around Piazza Dante 497
    Around Piazza Garibaldi 501

Olbia 662
Oristano 653
Orvieto 457

Padua 314
Palermo 593
Parma 356
Pavia 245
Perugia 439
Pescara 482
Piacenza 359
Piedmont 204
Pisa 409
Pistoia 403
Positano 525
Prato 400

Ravenna 365
Reggio di Calabria 581
Reggio Emilia 354
Rimini 369

Rome 122-123
    Around Rome 163
    Pantheon & Trastevere Areas 134
    Stazione Termini Area 146
    St Peter's/Vatican & Spanish
        Steps 136-137

Salerno 530
San Remo 201
Sardinia 642
Sassari 657
Sicily 589
Siena 416
Sorrento 521
Spoleto 453
Syracuse 621

Taranto 563
Terni 460
Trapani 635
Trentino-Alto Adige 266
Trento 271
Trieste 330
Turin 206
Tuscany 372

Udine 335
Umbria 435
Urbino 468

Valle d'Aosta 217
Veneto 283
Venice 285
    Central 288-289
    Railway Station Area 292
    San Marco 297
Verona 324
Vicenza 319
Viterbo 175
Volterra 425

TEXT

Map references are in **bold** type.

Abruzzo 475-483, **476**
Abruzzo National Park 481
Accommodation 89-92
Acquaviva 433
Adria 363

Aeolian Islands 600-609
Agrigento 629-633, **631**
Agropoli 534
Aietta 583
Air travel
    to/from Italy 101-105
    within Italy 110

Alassio 199
Albenga 198-199
Alberobello 552
Alghero 654-655
Aliano 569-570
Alicudi 609
Amalfi 526-528, **527**

Amalfi Coast 523-529
Anacapri 512
Ancona 464-466, **465**
Antagnod 226
Aosta 216-221, **219**
Aprica 257
Apulia 534-565, **535**
l' Aquila, see L'Aquila
Aquileia 333-334
Architecture 38-42
Arezzo 426-428, **427**
Argentario Peninsula 433-434
Armeno 261, 264
Arona 261
Arpuilles 220
Ascoli Piceno 472-474
Aspromonte Massif 582
Assisi 444-449, **445**
Asti 213-215
Ayas, see Val d' Ayas

Baia 507
Barano 514
Bargaining, see Money
Bari 540, 546-551, **548**
Barletta 540, 545-546
Barumini 667
Basilicata 565-570, **566**
Baveno 261
Belluno 322-323
Benevento 508
Bergamo 253-257, **254**
Bitonto 540
Boat Travel 109, 115
Bologna 341-349, **344**
Bolsena 177
Bolzano 279-281
Books 73-74
Bordighera 202
Bormio 257
Borromean Islands 261
Bosa 655
Brenta Group 272-274
Brenta Riviera 313
Brescia 251-253, **252**
Breuil-Cervinia 224-225
Brindisi 554-557, **555**
Brunate 259
Brusson 226
Buggeru 650
Burano 309
Bus travel
    to/from Italy 105-106
    within Italy 110-111
Business Hours 67
Busseto 358

Ca' Vecchia 364
Cagliari 643-648, **645**

Cala Gonone 665-666
Calabria 570-583, **571**
Calasetta 648
Camigliatello Silano 578
Camogli 196-197
Campania 489-534, **490**
Campitello Matese 484
Campo Imperatore 479
Campobasso 484
Campus 647
Canazei 276
Canneto 603
Canoeing, see Water Sports
Cape Caccia 655
Cape Testa 659
Cape Vaticano 582
Capoliveri 433
Caprarola 177
Caprera 661
Caprese Michelangelo 428
Capri 508-513, **509**
Car Travel 107-109, 112-114
    Rental 108, 113
Carabinieri 84
Carbonia 648
Carloforte 648
Carnia 337
Carrara 407
Caserta 507-508
Castellammare del Golfo 638
Castellana Caves 552-553
Castellaneta 564-565
Castelnovo ne' Monti 354
Castiadas 647
Castiglione del Lago 443
Catania 615-618, **617**
Catanzaro 570-574, **573**
Catanzaro Marina 574
Catholics 50
Cefalù 599-600
Cerrentana 474
Cerveteri 172
Cervo 200
Champoluc 226
Chia 647-648
Chianti 421
Chioggia 305-309
Cilento Coast 534
Cinque Terre 193-194
Cirella 583
Cirò Marina 575
Cividale del Friuli 337
Civita 177
Civitavecchia 173
Civitella Alfadena 481
Cles 274
Climate 32-33, 64
Climbing, see Mountaineering
Cocullo 480

Codigoro 363
Cogne 225
Colle della Trinità 441
Colle di Val d'Elsa 423
Comacchio 363-364
Comacina Island 260
Como 259-260, **258**
Comunanza 474
Contrada Ogliastrillo 600
Conversano 540
Corniglia 194
Cortina d' Ampezzo 278-279
Cortona 429-430
Corvara 277-278
Cosenza 575-577, **576**
Costa del Sud 647-648
Costa Rei 647
Costa Smeralda 661
Costa Verde 650
Costacciaro 451
Courmayeur 222-224
Courses 87, 367, 389, 406, 419,
    440-441, 469, 500
Credit Cards, see Money
Cremona 249-251, **250**
Crest 226
Cropani Marina 574
Crotone 574
Culture 48-50
    Avoiding Offence 50
Cumae 507
Cuneo 213, **214**
Currency, see Money
Customs 60
Cycling 86-87, 114, 389

Departure Tax 105
Deruta 443-444
Desenzano del Garda 262
Dino Island 583
Diving, see Water Sports
Dolomites 266-269
Domaso 260
Domodossola 215-216
Dorgali 665
Drinks 97-98
Drugs 84

Education 38
Elba 432-433
Electricity 72
Embassies 57-59
Emilia-Romagna 341-371, **342**
Enna 627-628
Entertainment 98-99
Erice 637
Etruria 167
Etruscan Sites 169-173, 431-432
Euganean Hills 317

Exchange Rates, see Money

Fano 471
Fauna 33-35
Feltre 275
Ferrara 360-363, **361**
Ferries, see Boat Travel
Fertilia 654, 655
Festivals 68-70
Fiames 279
Fiera di Primiero 275
Fiesole 398-399
Filicudi 609
Film 48
Finale Ligure 198
Flora 33-35
Florence 373-398, **376, 380, 389**
    Accademia Gallery 386
    Bargello Museum 385
    Church of Santa Maria Novella
        384-385
    Cycling 389
    Duomo 379-381
    Entertainment 396
    Festivals 390
    Getting Around 397-398
    Getting There & Away 397
    History 374-375
    Information 378-379
    Language Courses 389
    Orientation 375-377
    Places to Eat 393-396
    Places to Stay 390-393
    Pitti Palace 387-388
    Ponte Vecchio 384
    Santa Croce 385-386
    Shopping 396-397
    Things to See 379-389
    Tours, Organised 389-390
    Uffizi Gallery 382-384
Fluminimaggiore 649
Foce 474
Foggia 536-537
Foligno 455
Fonte Cerreto 479
Fontemaggio 448
Food 92-97
Fornace 451
Fosso Sejore 471
Frasassi Caves 466-467
Friuli-Venezia Giulia 327-337,
    328

Galatina 561
Gallico Marina 579
Gallinara Island 199
Gardena, see Val Gardena
Gardone Riviera 262-263
Garfagnana 407

Gargano Promontory 538-543
Genoa 181-189, **184**
Geography 30-32
Gerace 574
Gignese 261
Golfo Aranci 664
Golfo di Castellammare 637-638
Gorizia 333
Government 35-36
    Political Scandals 35-36
Gran Paradiso 225-226
Gran Sasso d'Italia 479
Gressoney, see Val di Gressoney
Gressoney-La Trinité 226, 227
Grosseto 431
Guastalla 354
Gubbio 449-451
Gutturu Flumini, see Marina di
    Arbus

Health 75-81
    Insurance 76
    Medical Kit 76-77
    Medical Problems & Treatment
        77-81
Herculaneum 515-516
Highlights 87-89
Hiking 85-86, 191, 196, 205,
    211-212, 222-227, 256, 259,
    261, 265-266, 269-270, 272-
    273, 279, 281, 316, 322, 331,
    337, 352, 354, 399, 407, 432-
    433, 443, 448, 451, 462, 470,
    474, 484, 527, 531, 578, 582,
    619, 666
History 12-30
Hitching 114-115
Holidays 67-68

Iglesias 649
Imperia 199-200
Introd 221
Ionian Coast 574-575
Is Arutas 653
Ischia 513-514
Iseo 264
Isernia 484
Isola Bella 261
Isola di Capo Rizzuto 574
Isola Giovanni 261
Isola Madre 261
Isola Maggiore 443
Isola Pescatori 261
Isola San Giulio 264
Itria Valley 552

La Ginestrina 279
La Maddalena 660-661
L'Aquila 475-479, **478**

La Salata 542
La Spezia 189-192, **190**
La Trinité 226
Lake Bolsena 177
Lake Bracciano 177
Lake Como 258-260
Lake Corbara 458
Lake Garda 261-264
Lake Iseo 264-265
Lake Maggiore 260-261
Lake Orta 264
Lake Pergusa 628
Lake Scanno 480
Lake Trasimene 442-443
Lake Vico 177
Lakes District 257-265
Lamezia Terme 572
Lanaittu Valley 666
Language 52-56
Laundry 72
Lazio 166-177, **168**
Le Castella 574
Lecce 557-561, **559**
Leghorn, see Livorno
Lerici 192
Lido di Metaponto 569
Lido Sant'Angelo 575
Lignano Sabbiadoro 334
Liguria 181-203, **182**
Linguaglossa 619
Lipari 601-604
Lipari Islands, see Aeolian
    Islands
Literature 46-47
Livigno 257
Livorno 413-415, **414**
Lo Strangolato 660
Locri 574
Lombardy 227-257, **228**
Lonedo di Lugo 322
Lorica 578
Lucca 404-407, **405**
Lucera 537-538
Luni 192

Macerata 472
Madesimo 257
Madonna di Campiglio 273-574
Mafia 50-52
Malé 274
Manarola 194
Manfredonia 538
Mantinera 583
Mantua 246-249, **247**
Maps 74
Maranello 352
Marches 462-474, **463**
Marciana Marina 433
Marina di Arbus 650

Marina di Campo 433
Marina di Rossano, see Lido Sant'Angelo
Marina di Torre Grande 652
Marina Grande 512
Marinella di Selinunte 634
Marsala 633-634
Marsiliana 431
Martina Franca 553
Massa 407
Matera 565-569, **567**
Matese Mountains 484
Mazzarò 614
Media 74-75
Merano 281-282
Messina 609-612
Mestre 305-307, 309
Mezzaforno 600
Milan 227-244, **230, 234, 238, 243**
    Courses 236
    Duomo 233
    Entertainment 241
    Festivals 236
    Galleria Vittorio Emanuele 233
    Getting Around 243-244
    Getting There & Away 242-243
    History 229
    Information 232-233
    La Scala 233-234
    Orientation 229-232
    Places to Eat 239-241
    Places to Stay 236-239
    Shopping 241-242
    Things to See 233-236
    Tours, Organised 236
Miramare 370
Modena 349-353, **350**
Molise 483-486, **485**
Molveno 272-273
Mondello 597, 598
Money 60-64
    Consumer Taxes 63-64
    Costs 62-63
    Credit Cards 61-62
    Currency 60
    Exchange Rates 60
    Receipts 64
    Tipping & Bargaining 63
    Travellers' Cheques 61
Monreale 599
Montagnana 318, 322
Monte Bignone 200
Monte Prata 462
Monte Rosa 226-227
Monte Sant'Angelo 539-540
Montegrotto Terme 316
Montemonaco 474
Montepulciano 430-431

Monterchi 429
Monterosso 194
Monti Sibillini 474-475
Motorbike Travel 107-109, 112-114
Mountaineering 85-86, 198, 212, 218, 223, 270, 277, 462, 531
Mt Etna 618-620
Mt Etna National Park 619
Mt Vesuvius 516
Mugello 399
Murano 309
Music 47-48

Naples 490-506, **493, 497, 501**
    Capodimonte Palace 500
    Courses, Language 500
    Entertainment 503-504
    Festivals 500-501
    Gesù Nuovo 494
    Getting Around 505
    Getting There & Away 504-505
    History 491
    Information 492-494
    National Archaeological Museum 498
    Orientation 491-492
    Places to Eat 502-503
    Places to Stay 501-502
    Shopping 504
    Things to See 494-500
    Tours, Organised 500
Naples, Bay of 508-515
Nervi 189
Nevegal 323
Nicolosi 619
Nicotera 582-583
Noli 197
Non, see Val di Non 274
Nora 647
Norcia 462
Noto 624-625
Nuoro 664-665
Nuoro Province 664-667

Olbia 661-663, **622**
Oliena 666
Opi 481
Orbetello 433-434
Orgosolo 666-667
Oristano 650-652, **653**
Orta San Giulio 264
Ortisei 276
Ortygia 622
Orvieto 456-459, **457**
Ostia Antica 167-169
Ostuni 553-554
Otranto 561-562

Padua 313-317, **314**
Paestum 532-533
Painting 42-46
Palau 660-661
Palermo 590-600, **593**
Palese 550
Pallavicino 597
Palo del Colle 540
Panarea 606-607
Paola 583
Parma 354-358, **356**
Parma Apennines 358
Passignano 443
Passports 59
Pavia 244-246, **245**
Pegli 189
Péio, see Valle di Péio 274
Permits
    Residence (Permesso di Soggiorno) 57-58
    Work 57
Perugia 436-442, **439**
Pesaro 469-471
Pescara 483, **482**
Pescasseroli 481
Peschici 540-542
Petrognano 455
Phlegrean Fields 506-507
Photography 75
Piacenza 358-360, **359**
Piano Provenzana 619
Piazza Armerina 628-629
Piedmont 203-216, **204**
Pietrabbondante 484
Pila 221-222
Pisa 408-412, **409**
Piscinas 650
Pistoia 402-404, **403**
Pitigliano 432
Pizzo 583
Po Delta 363-364
Poetto 646
Police 84
Pompeii 516-521
Port'Ercole 434
Portixeddu 650
Porto Azzurro 433
Porto Conte 655
Porto Maurizio 199
Porto Santo Stefano 434
Porto Torres 658-659
Portoferraio 432-433
Portofino 196
Portovenere 193
Positano 524-526, **525**
Post 70-71
Pozzuoli 507
Praia a Mare 583
Prato 399-402, **400**

Procida 514-515
Punta Alice 575
Putzu Idu 653

Ragusa 625-627
Rapallo 194-195
Ravello 528-529
Ravenna 364-368, **365**
Reggio di Calabria 578-582, **581**
Reggio Emilia 353-354, **354**
Religion 50
Rimini 368-371, **369**
Rinella 606
Riomaggiore 193-194
Riva del Garda 263-264
Riviera di Levante 189-197
Riviera di Ponente 197-203
Romanesque Churches in Apulia
    540-541
Rome 119-166, **122-123, 134,**
    136-137, 146, 163
    Catacombs 145
    Colosseum 129
    Entertainment 160-161
    Getting Around 164-166
    Getting There & Away 162-164
    Information 121-127
    Orientation 120-121
    Palatine Hill 129-131
    Pantheon 133-134
    Piazza Navona 133
    Places to Eat 153-160
    Places to Stay 146-153
    Roman Forum 129-131
    Shopping 161-162
    Spanish Steps 135
    St Peter's Basilica 138-140
    Things to See & Do 127-145
    Tours, Organised 145
    Trajan's Column 128-129
    Vatican City 138-141
Roncole Verdi 358
Rossano 575

Saepinum 484
Sailing, see Water Sports
Salerno 529-532, **530**
Salina 605-606
Salò 262
Saluzzo 213
San Cataldo 560
San Domino 543
San Donato 443, 469
San Fruttuoso 196
San Gimignano 421-423
San Giovanni di Sinis 652
San Giovanni in Fiore 578
San Leone 632
San Marino 371

San Martino di Castrozza 274-
    275
San Maurizio 259
San Nicola 543
San Pantaleo 633
San Paolo 553
San Pietro Islands 648-649
San Remo 200-202, **201**
San Terenzo 192
San Vito Lo Capo 638
Sansepolcro 428-429
Sant' Andrea 433
Sant' Angelo 514
Sant' Antioco 648-649
Santa Cristina 276, 277
Santa Giusta 651
Santa Margherita 195-196
Santa Teresa Gallura 659-660
Santadi 648
Sardinia 641-667, **642**
Sarnico 264
Sarzana 192
Sassari 656-658, **657**
Sassello 198
Savona 197
Scalea 583
Scanno 480-481
Scilla 582
Scopello 638
Sculpture 42-46
Sedilo 667
Segesta 637
Selinunte 634
Sella Group 275-278
Selva 276, 277
Senigallia 471-472
Sestriere 212
Sferracavallo 595
Shopping 99-100
Sicily 587-638, **589**
Siena 415-421, **416**
Sila Massif 577-578
Sinis Peninsula 652
Siponto 538
Sirmione 262
Skiing 86, 198, 212, 215-216,
    218, 221, 224-226, 257, 261-
    262, 269, 270, 273, 278, 322,
    331, 337, 352, 462, 474, 484,
    619
Solfatara Crater 507
Sondrio 257
Sorrento 521-523, **521**
Sovana 432
Spello 449
Spoleto 451-456, **453**
St Jean 226
St Vincent 221, 226
Stelvio National Park 274, 281

Stintino 658, 659
Stresa 261
Stromboli 607-609
Su Pallosu 653
Sulmona 479-480
Susa 212
Susa Valley 212-213
Swimming, see Water Sports
Syracuse 620-624, **621**

Taormina 612-615
Taranto 562-564, **563**
Tarquinia 170-172
Taxis 112
Telephones 71-72
Tellaro 192
Terme di Saturnia 431
Termoli 486
Terni 459-461, **460**
Teulada 647
Tharros 653
Time 72
Tindari 600
Tipping, see Money
Tiscali 666
Tivoli 169
Todi 444
Torcello 307, 309
Torralba 667
Torre Calzolari 451
Torre Pelosa 659
Torre Rinalda 560
Tourist Offices 65-66
Tours 115-116
Train Travel
    to/from Italy 106-107
    within Italy 111-112
Trani 540, 544-545
Trapani 634-637, **635**
Travellers' Cheques, see Money
Trekking, see Hiking
Tremezzo 260
Tremiti Islands 543-544
Trentino-Alto Adige 265-282,
    266
Trento 269-272, **271**
Treviso 318-319
Trieste 328-333, **330**
Troia 538
Tropea 583
Trulli Area 551-554
Turin 205-211, **206**
Tuscany 371-434, **372**
Tyrrhenian Coast 582-583

Udine 334-337, **335**
Umbria 434-462, **435**
Urbino 467-469, **468**

Val Brembana 257
Val d'Ayas 226, 227
Val di Genova 274
Val di Gressoney 226
Val di Non 274
Val Gardena 276-277
Val Seriana 257
Val Veny 223
Valgrisenche 225
Valle Camonica 264, 265
Valle d'Aosta 216-227, **217**
Valle di Péio 274
Valnerina 461-462
Valsavarenche 225, 226
Valtellina 257
Valtournenche 224-225
Varallo 215
Varigotti 198
Vatican City 138-141
Veio 172-173
Velia 534
Veneto 282-327, **283**

Venice 283-313, **285**, **288-289**,
     292, **297**
  Doges' Palace 296-297
  Entertainment 310-311
  Festivals 303
  Galleria dell'Accademia 299
  Getting Around 312-313
  Getting There & Away 311-312
  Grand Canal 292-294
  Guggenheim Collection 300-301
  History 284-286
  Information 287-291
  Language Courses 303
  Orientation 286-287
  Places to Eat 307-313
  Places to Stay 303-307
  Rialto Bridge 298
  Shopping 311
  St Mark's Basilica 294-295
  Things to See 291-303
  Tours, Organised 303
Ventimiglia 202-203

Vernazza 194
Verona 323-327, **324**
Verrès 226-227
Vicenza 319-322, **319**
Vieste 542-543
Villagio Palumbo 578
Villasimius 647
Viterbo 173-176, **175**
Visas 57-59
Volterra 424-426, **425**
Vulcano 604-605

Walking, see Hiking
Water Sports 86, 191, 196-198,
     200, 223, 262-263, 316, 352,
     370, 443, 470, 500, 511, 531,
     606, 608
Windsurfing, see Water Sports
Women Travellers 81
Work 84-85

Facing page 96
People
a. Little boy on the island of Lipari (GI)
b. Fountain at the base of the Spanish Steps, Rome (AL)
c. Family on Panarea, Aeolian Islands (GI)
d. Reflective days in Gerace, Calabria (JG)
e. Brass band for a festival in Trani, Apulia (SC)
f. Farmer in Gerace, Calabria (JG)

Facing page 321
Landscapes
a. Wildflowers in the Monti Sibillini, Marches/Umbria (JG)
b. Mountain goats in Calabria (JG)
c. Sunflowers, near Scorgiano, Tuscany (JG)
d. Mt Etna, Sicily (SC)
e. The isolated hill-top village of Aliano, Basilicata (SC)
f. Sulphurous fumaroles, the Gran Cratere, Vulcano, Sicily (SC)

Facing page 609
Sardinia
a. Weaving (Fotocolor ESIT-Cagliari)
b. Rock pool at Cape Testa (SC)
c. Church of San Giovanni di Sinis, near Oristano (SC)
d. Remains of the Temple of Antas, near Iglesias (SC)
e. Piscinas, the beautiful beach in the heart of the Costa Verde (SC)
f. The Santa Sabina nuraghe, south-east of Alghero (SC)

PLANET TALK
Lonely Planet's FREE quarterly newsletter

We love hearing from you and think you'd like to hear from us.

When...is the right time to see reindeer in Finland?
Where...can you hear the best palm-wine music in Ghana?
How...do you get from Asunción to Areguá by steam train?
What...is the best way to see India?

For the answer to these and many other questions read PLANET TALK.

Every issue is packed with up-to-date travel news and advice including:

- *a letter from Lonely Planet founders Tony and Maureen Wheeler*
- *travel diary from a Lonely Planet author - find out what it's really like out on the road*
- *feature article on an important and topical travel issue*
- *a selection of recent letters from our readers*
- *the latest travel news from all over the world*
- *details on Lonely Planet's new and forthcoming releases*

To join our mailing list contact any Lonely Planet office (address below).

LONELY PLANET PUBLICATIONS
Australia: PO Box 617, Hawthorn 3122, Victoria (tel: 03-819 1877)
USA: Embarcadero West, 155 Filbert St, Suite 251, Oakland, CA 94607 (tel: 510-893 8555)
TOLL FREE: (800) 275-8555
UK: 10 Barley Mow Passage, Chiswick, London W4 4PH (tel: 0181-742 3161)
France: 71 bis rue du Cardinal Lemoine – 75005 Paris (tel: 1-46 34 00 58)

Also available: Lonely Planet T-shirts. 100% heavyweight cotton (S, M, L, XL)

Lonely Planet guides to Europe

Central Europe on a shoestring
From the snow-capped peaks of the Austrian Alps, the medieval castles of Hungary and the vast forests of Poland to the festivals of Germany, the arty scene in Prague and picturesque lakes of Switzerland, this guide is packed with practical travel advice to help you make the most of your visit. This new shoestring guide covers travel in Austria, Czech Republic, Germany, Hungary, Liechtenstein, Poland, Slovakia and Switzerland.

Eastern Europe on a shoestring
This guide has opened up a whole new world for travellers – Albania, Bulgaria, Czechoslovakia, eastern Germany, Hungary, Poland, Romania and the former republics of Yugoslavia.
'...a thorough, well-researched book. Only a fool would go East without it.' – *Great Expeditions*

Mediterranean Europe on a shoestring
Details on hundreds of galleries, museums and architectural masterpieces and information on outdoor activities including hiking, sailing and skiing. Information on travelling in Albania, Andorra, Cyprus, France, Greece, Italy, Malta, Morocco, Portugal, Spain, Tunisia, Turkey and the former republics of Yugoslavia.

Scandinavian & Baltic Europe on a shoestring
A comprehensive guide to travelling in this region including details on galleries, festivals and museums, as well as outdoor activities, national parks and wildlife. Countries featured are Denmark, Estonia, the Faroe Islands, Finland, Iceland, Latvia, Lithuania, Norway and Sweden.

Western Europe on a shoestring
This long-awaited guide covers all of Western Europe's well-loved sights and provides routes for cycling and driving tours, plus details on hiking, climbing and skiing. All the travel facts on Andorra, Austria, Belgium, Britain, France, Germany, Greece, Ireland, Italy, Liechtenstein, Luxembourg, Netherlands, Portugal, Spain and Switzerland.

Baltic States & Kaliningrad – travel survival kit
The Baltic States burst on to the world scene almost from nowhere in the late 1980s. Now that travellers are free to move around the region they will discover nations with a rich and colourful history and culture, and a welcoming attitude to all travellers.

Dublin – city guide
Where to enjoy a pint of Guinness and a plate of Irish stew, where to see spectacular Georgian architecture or experience Irish hospitality – Dublin city guide will ensure you won't miss out on anything.

Finland – travel survival kit
Finland is an intriguing blend of Swedish and Russian influences. With its medieval stone castles, picturesque wooden houses, vast forest and lake district, and interesting wildlife, it is a wonderland to delight any traveller.

France – travel survival kit
Stylish, diverse, celebrated by romantics and revolutionaries alike, France is a destination that's always in fashion. A comprehensive guide packed with invaluable advice.

Greece – travel survival kit
Famous ruins, secluded beaches, sumptuous food, sun-drenched islands, ancient pathways and much more are covered in this comprehensive guide to this ever-popular destination.

Hungary – travel survival kit
Formerly seen as the gateway to eastern Europe, Hungary is a romantic country of music, wine and folklore. This guide contains detailed background information on Hungary's cultural and historical past as well as practical advice on the many activities available to travellers.

Iceland, Greenland & the Faroe Islands – travel survival kit
Iceland, Greenland & the Faroe Islands contain some of the most beautiful wilderness areas in the world.

This practical guidebook will help travellers discover the dramatic beauty of this region, no matter what their budget.

Ireland – travel survival kit
Ireland is one of Europe's least 'spoilt' countries. Green, relaxed and welcoming, it does not take travellers long before they feel at ease. An entertaining and comprehensive guide to this troubled country.

Poland – travel survival kit
With the collapse of communism, Poland has opened up to travellers, revealing a rich cultural heritage. This guide will help you make the most of this safe and friendly country.

Switzerland – travel survival kit
Ski enthusiasts and chocolate addicts know two excellent reasons for heading to Switzerland. This travel survival kit gives travellers many more: jazz, cafés, boating trips...and the Alps of course!

Turkey – a travel survival kit
This acclaimed guide takes you from Istanbul bazaars to Mediterranean beaches, from historic battlegrounds to the stamping grounds of St Paul, Alexander the Great, Emperor Constantine and King Croesus.

USSR – travel survival kit
Invaluable advice on getting around and beating red tape for individual and group travellers alike. This comprehensive guide includes an unsanitised historical background and complete information on art and culture. Over 130 reliable maps, and all place names are given in Cyrillic script. Includes the independent states.

Trekking in Greece
Mountainous landscape, the solitude of ancient pathways and secluded beaches await those who dare to extend their horizons beyond Athens and the antiquities. Covers the main trekking regions and includes contoured maps of trekking routes.

Trekking in Spain
Aimed at both overnight trekkers and day hikers, this guidebook includes useful maps and full details on hikes in some of Spain's most beautiful wilderness areas.

Trekking in Turkey
Few people are aware that Turkey boasts mountains with walks to rival those found in Nepal. This book gives details on treks that are destined to become as popular as those further east.

Also available:
Central Europe phrasebook
Languages in this book cover travel in Austria, the Czech Republic, France, Germany, Hungary, Italy, Liechtenstein, Slovakia and Switzerland.

Eastern Europe phrasebook
Discover the most enjoyable way to get around and make friends in Bulgarian, Czech, Hungarian, Polish, Romanian and Slovak.

Mediterranean Europe phrasebook
Ask for directions to the galleries and museums in Albanian, Greek, Italian, Macedonian, Maltese, Serbian & Croatian and Slovene.

Scandinavian Europe phrasebook
Find your way around the ski trails and enjoy the local festivals in Danish, Finnish, Icelandic, Norwegian and Swedish.

Western Europe phrasebook
Show your appreciation for the great masters in Basque, Catalan, Dutch, French, German, Irish Portuguese and Spanish (Castilian).

Lonely Planet Guidebooks

Lonely Planet guidebooks cover every accessible part of Asia as well as Australia, the Pacific, South America, Africa, the Middle East, Europe and parts of North America. There are five series: *travel survival kits*, covering a country for a range of budgets; *shoestring guides* with compact information for low-budget travel in a major region; *walking guides*; *city guides* and *phrasebooks*.

Australia & the Pacific
Australia
Australian phrasebook
Bushwalking in Australia
Islands of Australia's Great Barrier Reef
Outback Australia
Fiji
Fijian phrasebook
Melbourne city guide
Micronesia
New Caledonia
New South Wales
New Zealand
Tramping in New Zealand
Papua New Guinea
Bushwalking in Papua New Guinea
Papua New Guinea phrasebook
Rarotonga & the Cook Islands
Samoa
Solomon Islands
Sydney city guide
Tahiti & French Polynesia
Tonga
Vanuatu
Victoria

South-East Asia
Bali & Lombok
Bangkok city guide
Cambodia
Indonesia
Indonesia phrasebook
Laos
Malaysia, Singapore & Brunei
Myanmar (Burma)
Burmese phrasebook
Philippines
Pilipino phrasebook
Singapore city guide
South-East Asia on a shoestring
Thailand
Thai phrasebook
Vietnam
Vietnamese phrasebook

North-East Asia
China
Beijing city guide
Cantonese phrasebook
Mandarin Chinese phrasebook
Hong Kong, Macau & Canton
Japan
Japanese phrasebook
Korea
Korean phrasebook
Mongolia
North-East Asia on a shoestring
Seoul city guide
Taiwan
Tibet
Tibet phrasebook
Tokyo city guide

Middle East
Arab Gulf States
Egypt & the Sudan
Arabic (Egyptian) phrasebook
Iran
Israel
Jordan & Syria
Middle East
Turkey
Turkish phrasebook
Trekking in Turkey

Indian Ocean
Madagascar & Comoros
Maldives & Islands of the East Indian Ocean
Mauritius, Réunion & Seychelles

Mail Order

Lonely Planet guidebooks are distributed worldwide. They are also available by mail order from Lonely Planet, so if you have difficulty finding a title please write to us. US and Canadian residents should write to Embarcadero West, 155 Filbert St, Suite 251, Oakland CA 94607, USA ; European residents should write to 10 Barley Mow Passage, Chiswick, London W4 4PH; and residents of other countries to PO Box 617, Hawthorn, Victoria 3122, Australia.

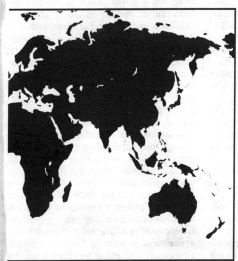

Indian Subcontinent
Bangladesh
India
Hindi/Urdu phrasebook
Trekking in the Indian Himalaya
Karakoram Highway
Kashmir, Ladakh & Zanskar
Nepal
Trekking in the Nepal Himalaya
Nepali phrasebook
Pakistan
Sri Lanka
Sri Lanka phrasebook

Africa
Africa on a shoestring
Central Africa
East Africa
Trekking in East Africa
Kenya
Swahili phrasebook
Morocco, Algeria & Tunisia
Arabic (Moroccan) phrasebook
South Africa, Lesotho & Swaziland
Zimbabwe, Botswana & Namibia
West Africa

Central America & the Caribbean
Baja California
Central America on a shoestring
Costa Rica
Eastern Caribbean
Guatemala, Belize & Yucatán: La Ruta Maya
Mexico

North America
Alaska
Canada
Hawaii

South America
Argentina, Uruguay & Paraguay
Bolivia
Brazil
Brazilian phrasebook
Chile & Easter Island
Colomb
Ecuador & the Galápagos Islan
Latin American Spanish phraseb
P
Quechua phraseb
South America on a shoes
Trekking in the Patagonian A
Vene

Europe
Baltic States & Kaliningrad
Central Europe on a shoestring
Central Europe phrasebook
Dublin city guide
Eastern Europe on a shoestring
Eastern Europe phrasebook
Finland
France
Greece
Hungary
Iceland, Greenland & the Faroe Islands
Ireland
Italy
Mediterranean Europe on a shoestring
Mediterranean Europe phrasebook
Poland
Scandinavian & Baltic Europe on a shoestring
Scandinavian Europe phrasebook
Switzerland
Trekking in Spain
Trekking in Greece
USSR
Russian phrasebook
Western Europe on a shoestring
Western Europe phrasebook

The Lonely Planet Story

Lonely Planet published its first book in 1973 in response to the numerous 'How did you do it?' questions Maureen and Tony Wheeler were asked after driving, bussing, hitching, sailing and railing their way from England to Australia.

Written at a kitchen table and hand collated, trimmed and stapled, *Across Asia on the Cheap* became an instant local bestseller, inspiring thoughts of another book.

Eighteen months in South-East Asia resulted in their second guide, *South-East Asia on a shoestring*, which they put together in a backstreet Chinese hotel in Singapore in 1975. The 'yellow bible' as it quickly became known to backpackers around the world, soon became *the* guide to the region. It has sold well over half a million copies and is now in its 8th edition, still retaining its familiar yellow cover.

Today there are over 140 Lonely Planet titles in print – books that have that same adventurous approach to travel as those early guides; books that 'assume you know how to get your luggage off the carousel' as one reviewer put it.

Although Lonely Planet initially specialised in guides to Asia, they now cover most regions of the world, including the Pacific, South America, Africa, the Middle East and Europe. The list of *walking guides* and *phrasebooks* (for 'unusual' languages such as Quechua, Swahili, Nepali and Egyptian Arabic) is also growing rapidly.

The emphasis continues to be on travel for independent travellers. Tony and Maureen still travel for several months of each year and play an active part in the writing, updating and quality control of Lonely Planet's guides.

They have been joined by over 50 authors, 110 staff – mainly editors, cartographers & designers – at our office in Melbourne, Australia, at our US office in Oakland, California and at our European office in Paris; another five at our office in London handle sales for Britain, Europe and Africa. Travellers themselves also make a valuable contribution to the guides through the feedback we receive in thousands of letters each year.

The people at Lonely Planet strongly believe that travellers can make a positive contribution to the countries they visit, both through their appreciation of the countries' culture, wildlife and natural features, and through the money they spend. In addition, the company makes a direct contribution to the countries and regions it covers. Since 1986 a percentage of the income from each book has been donated to ventures such as famine relief in Africa; aid projects in India; agricultural projects in Central America; Greenpeace's efforts to halt French nuclear testing in the Pacific and Amnesty International. In 1994 over $100,000 was donated to such causes.

Lonely Planet's basic travel philosophy is summed up in Tony Wheeler's comment, 'Don't worry about whether your trip will work out. Just go!'.